PHILIP'S

ATLAS
OF THE
WORLD

PAPERBACK EDITION

The World in Focus
Cartography by Philip's

Picture Acknowledgements
Page 14
Science Photo Library/NOAA

Illustrations
Stefan Chabluk

CONSULTANTS
Philip's are grateful to the following people for acting as specialist geography consultants on 'The World in Focus' front section:

Professor D. Brunsden, Kings College, University of London, UK
Dr C. Clarke, Oxford University, UK
Dr I. S. Evans, Durham University, UK
Professor P. Haggett, University of Bristol, UK
Professor K. McLachlan, University of London, UK
Professor M. Monmonier, Syracuse University, New York, USA
Professor M-L. Hsu, University of Minnesota, Minnesota, USA
Professor M. J. Tooley, University of St Andrews, UK
Dr T. Unwin, Royal Holloway, University of London, UK

Published in Great Britain in 2000
by George Philip Limited,
a division of Octopus Publishing Group Limited,
2–4 Heron Quays, London E14 4JP

Cartography by Philip's

ISBN 0–540–07889–1

A CIP catalogue record for this book is available from the British Library.

Printed in China

Details of other Philip's titles and services can be found on our website at: www.philips-maps.co.uk

Philip's is proud to announce that its World Atlases are now published in association with The Royal Geographical Society (with The Institute of British Geographers).

The Society was founded in 1830 and given a Royal Charter in 1859 for 'the advancement of geographical science'. It holds historical collections of national and international importance, many of which relate to the Society's association with and support for scientific exploration and research from the 19th century onwards. It was pivotal in establishing geography as a teaching and research discipline in British universities close to the turn of the century, and has played a key role in geographical and environmental education ever since.

Today the Society is a leading world centre for geographical learning – supporting education, teaching, research and expeditions, and promoting public understanding of the subject.

The Society welcomes those interested in geography as members. For further information, please visit the website at: www.rgs.org

PHILIP'S

ATLAS
OF THE
WORLD

PAPERBACK EDITION

IN ASSOCIATION WITH
THE ROYAL GEOGRAPHICAL SOCIETY
WITH THE INSTITUTE OF BRITISH GEOGRAPHERS

Contents

v

World Statistics: Countries

This alphabetical list includes all the countries and territories of the world. If a territory is not completely independent, then the country it is associated with is named. The area figures give the total area of land, inland water and ice. The population figures are 2000 estimates. The annual income is the Gross National Product per capita in US dollars. The figures are the latest available, usually 1998.

Country/Territory	Area km² Thousands	Area miles² Thousands	Population Thousands	Capital	Annual Income US $
Afghanistan	652	252	26,511	Kabul	800
Albania	28.8	11.1	3,795	Tirana	810
Algeria	2,382	920	32,904	Algiers	1,550
American Samoa (US)	0.20	0.08	39	Pago Pago	2,600
Andorra	0.45	0.17	49	Andorra La Vella	18,000
Angola	1,247	481	13,295	Luanda	340
Anguilla (UK)	0.1	0.04	8	The Valley	6,800
Antigua & Barbuda	0.44	0.17	79	St John's	8,300
Argentina	2,767	1,068	36,238	Buenos Aires	8,970
Armenia	29.8	11.5	3,968	Yerevan	480
Aruba (Netherlands)	0.19	0.07	58	Oranjestad	22,000
Australia	7,687	2,968	18,855	Canberra	20,300
Austria	83.9	32.4	7,613	Vienna	26,850
Azerbaijan	86.6	33.4	8,324	Baku	490
Azores (Portugal)	2.2	0.87	238	Ponta Delgada	–
Bahamas	13.9	5.4	295	Nassau	20,100
Bahrain	0.68	0.26	683	Manama	7,660
Bangladesh	144	56	150,589	Dhaka	350
Barbados	0.43	0.17	265	Bridgetown	7,890
Belarus	207.6	80.1	10,697	Minsk	2,200
Belgium	30.5	11.8	9,832	Brussels	25,380
Belize	23	8.9	230	Belmopan	2,610
Benin	113	43	6,369	Porto-Novo	380
Bermuda (UK)	0.05	0.02	62	Hamilton	34,000
Bhutan	47	18.1	1,906	Thimphu	1,000
Bolivia	1,099	424	9,724	La Paz/Sucre	1,000
Bosnia-Herzegovina	51	20	4,601	Sarajevo	1,720
Botswana	582	225	1,822	Gaborone	3,600
Brazil	8,512	3,286	179,487	Brasilia	4,570
Brunei	5.8	2.2	333	Bandar Seri Begawan	24,000
Bulgaria	111	43	9,071	Sofia	1,230
Burkina Faso	274	106	12,092	Ouagadougou	240
Burma (= Myanmar)	677	261	51,129	Rangoon	1,200
Burundi	27.8	10.7	7,358	Bujumbura	140
Cambodia	181	70	10,046	Phnom Penh	280
Cameroon	475	184	16,701	Yaoundé	610
Canada	9,976	3,852	28,488	Ottawa	20,020
Canary Is. (Spain)	7.3	2.8	1,494	Las Palmas/Santa Cruz	–
Cape Verde Is.	4	1.6	515	Praia	1,060
Cayman Is. (UK)	0.26	0.10	35	George Town	20,000
Central African Republic	623	241	4,074	Bangui	300
Chad	1,284	496	7,337	Ndjaména	230
Chile	757	292	15,272	Santiago	4,810
China	9,597	3,705	1,299,180	Beijing	750
Colombia	1,139	440	39,397	Bogotá	2,600
Comoros	2.2	0.86	670	Moroni	370
Congo	342	132	3,167	Brazzaville	690
Congo (Dem. Rep. of the)	2,345	905	49,190	Kinshasa	110
Cook Is. (NZ)	0.24	0.09	17	Avarua	900
Costa Rica	51.1	19.7	3,711	San José	2,780
Croatia	56.5	21.8	4,960	Zagreb	4,520
Cuba	111	43	11,504	Havana	1,560
Cyprus	9.3	3.6	762	Nicosia	13,000
Czech Republic	78.9	30.4	10,500	Prague	5,040
Denmark	43.1	16.6	5,153	Copenhagen	33,260
Djibouti	23.2	9	552	Djibouti	1,200
Dominica	0.75	0.29	87	Roseau	3,010
Dominican Republic	48.7	18.8	8,621	Santo Domingo	1,770
Ecuador	284	109	13,319	Quito	1,530
Egypt	1,001	387	64,210	Cairo	1,290
El Salvador	21	8.1	6,739	San Salvador	1,850
Equatorial Guinea	28.1	10.8	455	Malabo	1,500
Eritrea	94	36	4,523	Asmara	200
Estonia	44.7	17.3	1,647	Tallinn	3,390
Ethiopia	1,128	436	61,841	Addis Ababa	100
Faroe Is. (Denmark)	1.4	0.54	49	Tórshavn	16,000
Fiji	18.3	7.1	883	Suva	2,110
Finland	338	131	5,077	Helsinki	24,110
France	552	213	58,145	Paris	24,940
French Guiana (France)	90	34.7	130	Cayenne	6,000
French Polynesia (France)	4	1.5	268	Papeete	10,800
Gabon	268	103	1,612	Libreville	3,950
Gambia, The	11.3	4.4	1,119	Banjul	340
Georgia	69.7	26.9	5,777	Tbilisi	930
Germany	357	138	76,962	Berlin	25,850
Ghana	239	92	20,564	Accra	390
Gibraltar (UK)	0.007	0.003	32	Gibraltar Town	5,000
Greece	132	51	10,193	Athens	11,650
Greenland (Denmark)	2,176	840	60	Nuuk (Godthåb)	16,100
Grenada	0.34	0.13	83	St George's	3,170
Guadeloupe (France)	1.7	0.66	365	Basse-Terre	9,200
Guam (US)	0.55	0.21	128	Agana	19,000
Guatemala	109	42	12,222	Guatemala City	1,640
Guinea	246	95	7,830	Conakry	540
Guinea-Bissau	36.1	13.9	1,197	Bissau	160
Guyana	215	83	891	Georgetown	770
Haiti	27.8	10.7	8,003	Port-au-Prince	410
Honduras	112	43	6,846	Tegucigalpa	730
Hong Kong (China)	1.1	0.40	6,336	–	23,670
Hungary	93	35.9	10,531	Budapest	4,510
Iceland	103	40	274	Reykjavik	28,010
India	3,288	1,269	1,041,543	New Delhi	430
Indonesia	1,905	735	218,661	Jakarta	680
Iran	1,648	636	68,759	Tehran	1,770
Iraq	438	169	26,339	Baghdad	2,400
Ireland	70.3	27.1	4,086	Dublin	18,340
Israel	27	10.3	5,321	Jerusalem	15,940
Italy	301	116	57,195	Rome	20,250
Ivory Coast (Côte d'Ivoire)	322	125	17,600	Yamoussoukro	700
Jamaica	11	4.2	2,735	Kingston	1,680
Japan	378	146	128,470	Tokyo	32,380
Jordan	89.2	34.4	5,558	Amman	1,520
Kazakstan	2,717	1,049	19,006	Astana	1,310
Kenya	580	224	35,060	Nairobi	330
Kiribati	0.72	0.28	72	Tarawa	1,180
Korea, North	121	47	26,117	Pyŏngyang	1,000
Korea, South	99	38.2	46,403	Seoul	7,970
Kuwait	17.8	6.9	2,639	Kuwait City	22,700
Kyrgyzstan	198.5	76.6	5,403	Bishkek	350
Laos	237	91	5,463	Vientiane	330
Latvia	65	25	2,768	Riga	2,430
Lebanon	10.4	4	3,327	Beirut	3,560
Lesotho	30.4	11.7	2,370	Maseru	570
Liberia	111	43	3,575	Monrovia	1,000
Libya	1,760	679	6,500	Tripoli	6,700
Liechtenstein	0.16	0.06	28	Vaduz	50,000
Lithuania	65.2	25.2	3,935	Vilnius	2,440
Luxembourg	2.6	1	377	Luxembourg	43,570
Macau (China)	0.02	0.006	656	Macau	16,000
Macedonia (F.Y.R.O.M.)	25.7	9.9	2,157	Skopje	1,290
Madagascar	587	227	16,627	Antananarivo	260
Madeira (Portugal)	0.81	0.31	253	Funchal	–
Malawi	118	46	12,458	Lilongwe	200
Malaysia	330	127	21,983	Kuala Lumpur	3,600
Maldives	0.30	0.12	283	Malé	1,230
Mali	1,240	479	12,685	Bamako	250
Malta	0.32	0.12	366	Valletta	9,440
Marshall Is.	0.18	0.07	70	Dalap-Uliga-Darrit	1,540
Martinique (France)	1.1	0.42	362	Fort-de-France	10,700
Mauritania	1,030	412	2,702	Nouakchott	410
Mauritius	2.0	0.72	1,201	Port Louis	3,700
Mayotte (France)	0.37	0.14	141	Mamoundzou	1,430
Mexico	1,958	756	107,233	Mexico City	3,970
Micronesia, Fed. States of	0.70	0.27	110	Palikir	1,800
Moldova	33.7	13	4,707	Chişinău	410
Monaco	0.002	0.0001	30	Monaco	25,000
Mongolia	1,567	605	2,847	Ulan Bator	400
Montserrat (UK)	0.10	0.04	13	Plymouth	4,500
Morocco	447	172	31,559	Rabat	1,250
Mozambique	802	309	20,493	Maputo	210
Namibia	825	318	2,437	Windhoek	1,940
Nauru	0.02	0.008	10	Yaren District	10,000
Nepal	141	54	24,084	Katmandu	210
Netherlands	41.5	16	15,829	Amsterdam/The Hague	24,760
Netherlands Antilles (Neths)	0.99	0.38	203	Willemstad	11,500
New Caledonia (France)	18.6	7.2	195	Nouméa	11,400
New Zealand	269	104	3,662	Wellington	14,700
Nicaragua	130	50	5,261	Managua	390
Niger	1,267	489	10,752	Niamey	190
Nigeria	924	357	105,000	Abuja	300
Northern Mariana Is. (US)	0.48	0.18	50	Saipan	9,300
Norway	324	125	4,331	Oslo	34,330
Oman	212	82	2,176	Muscat	7,900
Pakistan	796	307	162,409	Islamabad	480
Palau	0.46	0.18	18	Koror	8,800
Panama	77.1	29.8	2,893	Panama City	3,080
Papua New Guinea	463	179	4,845	Port Moresby	890
Paraguay	407	157	5,538	Asunción	1,760
Peru	1,285	496	26,276	Lima	2,460
Philippines	300	116	77,473	Manila	1,050
Poland	313	121	40,366	Warsaw	3,900
Portugal	92.4	35.7	10,587	Lisbon	10,690
Puerto Rico (US)	9	3.5	3,836	San Juan	9,000
Qatar	11	4.2	499	Doha	17,100
Réunion (France)	2.5	0.97	692	Saint-Denis	4,800
Romania	238	92	24,000	Bucharest	1,390
Russia	17,075	6,592	155,096	Moscow	2,300
Rwanda	26.3	10.2	10,200	Kigali	230
St Kitts & Nevis	0.36	0.14	44	Basseterre	6,130
St Lucia	0.62	0.24	177	Castries	3,410
St Vincent & Grenadines	0.39	0.15	128	Kingstown	2,420
Samoa	2.8	1.1	171	Apia	1,020
San Marino	0.06	0.02	25	San Marino	20,000
São Tomé & Príncipe	0.96	0.37	151	São Tomé	280
Saudi Arabia	2,150	830	20,697	Riyadh	9,000
Senegal	197	76	8,716	Dakar	530
Seychelles	0.46	0.18	75	Victoria	6,450
Sierra Leone	71.7	27.7	5,437	Freetown	140
Singapore	0.62	0.24	3,000	Singapore	30,060
Slovak Republic	49	18.9	5,500	Bratislava	3,700
Slovenia	20.3	7.8	2,055	Ljubljana	9,760
Solomon Is.	28.9	11.2	429	Honiara	750
Somalia	638	246	9,736	Mogadishu	600
South Africa	1,220	471	43,666	C. Town/Pretoria/Bloem.	2,880
Spain	505	195	40,667	Madrid	14,080
Sri Lanka	65.6	25.3	19,416	Colombo	810
Sudan	2,506	967	33,625	Khartoum	290
Surinam	163	63	497	Paramaribo	1,660
Swaziland	17.4	6.7	1,121	Mbabane	1,400
Sweden	450	174	8,560	Stockholm	25,620
Switzerland	41.3	15.9	6,762	Bern	40,080
Syria	185	71	17,826	Damascus	1,020
Taiwan	36	13.9	22,000	Taipei	12,400
Tajikistan	143.1	55.2	7,041	Dushanbe	350
Tanzania	945	365	39,639	Dodoma	210
Thailand	513	198	63,670	Bangkok	2,200
Togo	56.8	21.9	4,861	Lomé	330
Tonga	0.75	0.29	92	Nuku'alofa	1,690
Trinidad & Tobago	5.1	2	1,484	Port of Spain	4,430
Tunisia	164	63	9,924	Tunis	2,050
Turkey	779	301	66,789	Ankara	3,160
Turkmenistan	488.1	188.5	4,585	Ashkhabad	1,630
Turks & Caicos Is. (UK)	0.43	0.17	12	Cockburn Town	5,000
Tuvalu	0.03	0.01	11	Fongafale	600
Uganda	236	91	26,958	Kampala	320
Ukraine	603.7	233.1	52,558	Kiev	850
United Arab Emirates	83.6	32.3	1,951	Abu Dhabi	18,220
United Kingdom	243.3	94	58,393	London	21,400
United States of America	9,373	3,619	266,096	Washington, DC	29,340
Uruguay	177	68	3,274	Montevideo	6,180
Uzbekistan	447.4	172.7	26,044	Tashkent	870
Vanuatu	12.2	4.7	206	Port-Vila	1,270
Venezuela	912	352	24,715	Caracas	350
Vietnam	332	127	82,427	Hanoi	330
Virgin Is. (UK)	0.15	0.06	15	Road Town	–
Virgin Is. (US)	0.34	0.13	135	Charlotte Amalie	12,500
Wallis & Futuna Is. (France)	0.20	0.08	26	Mata-Utu	–
Western Sahara	266	103	228	El Aaiún	300
Yemen	528	204	13,219	Sana	300
Yugoslavia	102.3	39.5	10,761	Belgrade	2,300
Zambia	753	291	12,267	Lusaka	330
Zimbabwe	391	151	13,123	Harare	610

World Statistics: Physical Dimensions

Each topic list is divided into continents and within a continent the items are listed in order of size. The bottom part of many of the lists is selective in order to give examples from as many different countries as possible. The order of the continents is the same as in the atlas, beginning with Europe and ending with South America. The figures are rounded as appropriate.

World, Continents, Oceans

	km²	miles²	%
The World	509,450,000	196,672,000	–
Land	149,450,000	57,688,000	29.3
Water	360,000,000	138,984,000	70.7
Asia	44,500,000	17,177,000	29.8
Africa	30,302,000	11,697,000	20.3
North America	24,241,000	9,357,000	16.2
South America	17,793,000	6,868,000	11.9
Antarctica	14,100,000	5,443,000	9.4
Europe	9,957,000	3,843,000	6.7
Australia & Oceania	8,557,000	3,303,000	5.7
Pacific Ocean	179,679,000	69,356,000	49.9
Atlantic Ocean	92,373,000	35,657,000	25.7
Indian Ocean	73,917,000	28,532,000	20.5
Arctic Ocean	14,090,000	5,439,000	3.9

Ocean Depths

		m	ft
Atlantic Ocean			
Puerto Rico (Milwaukee) Deep		9,220	30,249
Cayman Trench		7,680	25,197
Gulf of Mexico		5,203	17,070
Mediterranean Sea		5,121	16,801
Black Sea		2,211	7,254
North Sea		660	2,165
Indian Ocean		m	ft
Java Trench		7,450	24,442
Red Sea		2,635	8,454
Pacific Ocean		m	ft
Mariana Trench		11,022	36,161
Tonga Trench		10,882	35,702
Japan Trench		10,554	34,626
Kuril Trench		10,542	34,587
Arctic Ocean		m	ft
Molloy Deep		5,608	18,399

Mountains

		m	ft
Europe			
Elbrus	Russia	5,642	18,510
Mont Blanc	France/Italy	4,807	15,771
Monte Rosa	Italy/Switzerland	4,634	15,203
Dom	Switzerland	4,545	14,911
Liskamm	Switzerland	4,527	14,852
Weisshorn	Switzerland	4,505	14,780
Taschorn	Switzerland	4,490	14,730
Matterhorn/Cervino	Italy/Switzerland	4,478	14,691
Mont Maudit	France/Italy	4,465	14,649
Dent Blanche	Switzerland	4,356	14,291
Nadelhorn	Switzerland	4,327	14,196
Grandes Jorasses	France/Italy	4,208	13,806
Jungfrau	Switzerland	4,158	13,642
Grossglockner	Austria	3,797	12,457
Mulhacén	Spain	3,478	11,411
Zugspitze	Germany	2,962	9,718
Olympus	Greece	2,917	9,570
Triglav	Slovenia	2,863	9,393
Gerlachovka	Slovak Republic	2,655	8,711
Galdhöpiggen	Norway	2,468	8,100
Kebnekaise	Sweden	2,117	6,946
Ben Nevis	UK	1,343	4,406
Asia		m	ft
Everest	China/Nepal	8,850	29,035
K2 (Godwin Austen)	China/Kashmir	8,611	28,251
Kanchenjunga	India/Nepal	8,598	28,208
Lhotse	China/Nepal	8,516	27,939
Makalu	China/Nepal	8,481	27,824
Cho Oyu	China/Nepal	8,201	26,906
Dhaulagiri	Nepal	8,172	26,811
Manaslu	Nepal	8,156	26,758
Nanga Parbat	Kashmir	8,126	26,660
Annapurna	Nepal	8,078	26,502
Gasherbrum	China/Kashmir	8,068	26,469
Broad Peak	China/Kashmir	8,051	26,414
Xixabangma	China	8,012	26,286
Kangbachen	India/Nepal	7,902	25,925
Trivor	Pakistan	7,720	25,328
Pik Kommunizma	Tajikistan	7,495	24,590
Demavend	Iran	5,604	18,386
Ararat	Turkey	5,165	16,945
Gunong Kinabalu	Malaysia (Borneo)	4,101	13,455
Fuji-San	Japan	3,776	12,388
Africa		m	ft
Kilimanjaro	Tanzania	5,895	19,340
Mt Kenya	Kenya	5,199	17,057
Ruwenzori (Margherita)	Ug./Congo (D.R.)	5,109	16,762
Ras Dashan	Ethiopia	4,620	15,157
Meru	Tanzania	4,565	14,977
Karisimbi	Rwanda/Congo (D.R.)	4,507	14,787
Mt Elgon	Kenya/Uganda	4,321	14,176
Batu	Ethiopia	4,307	14,130
Toubkal	Morocco	4,165	13,665
Mt Cameroon	Cameroon	4,070	13,353
Oceania		m	ft
Puncak Jaya	Indonesia	5,029	16,499
Puncak Trikora	Indonesia	4,750	15,584

		m	ft
Puncak Mandala	Indonesia	4,702	15,427
Mt Wilhelm	Papua New Guinea	4,508	14,790
Mauna Kea	USA (Hawaii)	4,205	13,796
Mauna Loa	USA (Hawaii)	4,169	13,681
Mt Cook (Aoraki)	New Zealand	3,753	12,313
Mt Kosciuszko	Australia	2,237	7,339
North America		m	ft
Mt McKinley (Denali)	USA (Alaska)	6,194	20,321
Mt Logan	Canada	5,959	19,551
Citlaltepetl	Mexico	5,700	18,701
Mt St Elias	USA/Canada	5,489	18,008
Popocatepetl	Mexico	5,452	17,887
Mt Foraker	USA (Alaska)	5,304	17,401
Ixtaccihuatl	Mexico	5,286	17,342
Lucania	Canada	5,227	17,149
Mt Steele	Canada	5,073	16,644
Mt Bona	USA (Alaska)	5,005	16,420
Mt Whitney	USA	4,418	14,495
Tajumulco	Guatemala	4,220	13,845
Chirripó Grande	Costa Rica	3,837	12,589
Pico Duarte	Dominican Rep.	3,175	10,417
South America		m	ft
Aconcagua	Argentina	6,960	22,834
Bonete	Argentina	6,872	22,546
Ojos del Salado	Argentina/Chile	6,863	22,516
Pissis	Argentina	6,779	22,241
Mercedario	Argentina/Chile	6,770	22,211
Huascaran	Peru	6,768	22,204
Llullaillaco	Argentina/Chile	6,723	22,057
Nudo de Cachi	Argentina	6,720	22,047
Yerupaja	Peru	6,632	21,758
Sajama	Bolivia	6,542	21,463
Chimborazo	Ecuador	6,267	20,561
Pico Colon	Colombia	5,800	19,029
Pico Bolivar	Venezuela	5,007	16,427
Antarctica		m	ft
Vinson Massif		4,897	16,066
Mt Kirkpatrick		4,528	14,855

Rivers

		km	miles
Europe			
Volga	Caspian Sea	3,700	2,300
Danube	Black Sea	2,850	1,770
Ural	Caspian Sea	2,535	1,575
Dnepr (Dnipro)	Black Sea	2,285	1,420
Kama	Volga	2,030	1,260
Don	Black Sea	1,990	1,240
Petchora	Arctic Ocean	1,790	1,110
Oka	Volga	1,480	920
Dnister (Dniester)	Black Sea	1,400	870
Vyatka	Kama	1,370	850
Rhine	North Sea	1,320	820
N. Dvina	Arctic Ocean	1,290	800
Elbe	North Sea	1,145	710
Asia		km	miles
Yangtze	Pacific Ocean	6,380	3,960
Yenisey–Angara	Arctic Ocean	5,550	3,445
Huang He	Pacific Ocean	5,464	3,395
Ob–Irtysh	Arctic Ocean	5,410	3,360
Mekong	Pacific Ocean	4,500	2,795
Amur	Pacific Ocean	4,400	2,730
Lena	Arctic Ocean	4,400	2,730
Irtysh	Ob	4,250	2,640
Yenisey	Arctic Ocean	4,090	2,540
Ob	Arctic Ocean	3,680	2,285
Indus	Indian Ocean	3,100	1,925
Brahmaputra	Indian Ocean	2,900	1,800
Syrdarya	Aral Sea	2,860	1,775
Salween	Indian Ocean	2,800	1,740
Euphrates	Indian Ocean	2,700	1,675
Amudarya	Aral Sea	2,540	1,575
Africa		km	miles
Nile	Mediterranean	6,670	4,140
Congo	Atlantic Ocean	4,670	2,900
Niger	Atlantic Ocean	4,180	2,595
Zambezi	Indian Ocean	3,540	2,200
Oubangi/Uele	Congo (D.R.)	2,250	1,400
Kasai	Congo (D.R.)	1,950	1,210
Shaballe	Indian Ocean	1,930	1,200
Orange	Atlantic Ocean	1,860	1,155
Cubango	Okavango Swamps	1,800	1,120
Limpopo	Indian Ocean	1,600	995
Senegal	Atlantic Ocean	1,600	995
Australia		km	miles
Murray–Darling	Indian Ocean	3,750	2,330
Darling	Murray	3,070	1,905
Murray	Indian Ocean	2,575	1,600
Murrumbidgee	Murray	1,690	1,050
North America		km	miles
Mississippi–Missouri	Gulf of Mexico	6,020	3,740
Mackenzie	Arctic Ocean	4,240	2,630
Mississippi	Gulf of Mexico	3,780	2,350
Missouri	Mississippi	3,780	2,350
Yukon	Pacific Ocean	3,185	1,980
Rio Grande	Gulf of Mexico	3,030	1,880
Arkansas	Mississippi	2,340	1,450
Colorado	Pacific Ocean	2,330	1,445

		m	ft
Red	Mississippi	2,040	1,270
Columbia	Pacific Ocean	1,950	1,210
Saskatchewan	Lake Winnipeg	1,940	1,205
South America		km	miles
Amazon	Atlantic Ocean	6,450	4,010
Paraná–Plate	Atlantic Ocean	4,500	2,800
Purus	Amazon	3,350	2,080
Madeira	Amazon	3,200	1,990
São Francisco	Atlantic Ocean	2,900	1,800
Paraná	Plate	2,800	1,740
Tocantins	Atlantic Ocean	2,750	1,710
Paraguay	Paraná	2,550	1,580
Orinoco	Atlantic Ocean	2,500	1,550
Pilcomayo	Paraná	2,500	1,550
Araguaia	Tocantins	2,250	1,400

Lakes

		km²	miles²
Europe			
Lake Ladoga	Russia	17,700	6,800
Lake Onega	Russia	9,700	3,700
Saimaa system	Finland	8,000	3,100
Vänern	Sweden	5,500	2,100
Asia		km²	miles²
Caspian Sea	Asia	371,800	143,550
Lake Baykal	Russia	30,500	11,780
Aral Sea	Kazakhstan/Uzbekistan	28,687	11,086
Tonlé Sap	Cambodia	20,000	7,700
Lake Balqash	Kazakhstan	18,500	7,100
Africa		km²	miles²
Lake Victoria	East Africa	68,000	26,000
Lake Tanganyika	Central Africa	33,000	13,000
Lake Malawi/Nyasa	East Africa	29,600	11,430
Lake Chad	Central Africa	25,000	9,700
Lake Turkana	Ethiopia/Kenya	8,500	3,300
Lake Volta	Ghana	8,500	3,300
Australia		km²	miles²
Lake Eyre	Australia	8,900	3,400
Lake Torrens	Australia	5,800	2,200
Lake Gairdner	Australia	4,800	1,900
North America		km²	miles²
Lake Superior	Canada/USA	82,350	31,800
Lake Huron	Canada/USA	59,600	23,010
Lake Michigan	USA	58,000	22,400
Great Bear Lake	Canada	31,800	12,280
Great Slave Lake	Canada	28,500	11,000
Lake Erie	Canada/USA	25,700	9,900
Lake Winnipeg	Canada	24,400	9,400
Lake Ontario	Canada/USA	19,500	7,500
Lake Nicaragua	Nicaragua	8,200	3,200
South America		km²	miles²
Lake Titicaca	Bolivia/Peru	8,300	3,200
Lake Poopo	Peru	2,800	1,100

Islands

		km²	miles²
Europe			
Great Britain	UK	229,880	88,700
Iceland	Atlantic Ocean	103,000	39,800
Ireland	Ireland/UK	84,400	32,600
Novaya Zemlya (N.)	Russia	48,200	18,600
Sicily	Italy	25,500	9,800
Corsica	France	8,700	3,400
Asia		km²	miles²
Borneo	Southeast Asia	744,360	287,400
Sumatra	Indonesia	473,600	182,860
Honshu	Japan	230,500	88,980
Sulawesi (Celebes)	Indonesia	189,000	73,000
Java	Indonesia	126,700	48,900
Luzon	Philippines	104,700	40,400
Hokkaido	Japan	78,400	30,300
Africa		km²	miles²
Madagascar	Indian Ocean	587,040	226,660
Socotra	Indian Ocean	3,600	1,400
Réunion	Indian Ocean	2,500	965
Oceania		km²	miles²
New Guinea	Indonesia/Papua NG	821,030	317,000
New Zealand (S.)	Pacific Ocean	150,500	58,100
New Zealand (N.)	Pacific Ocean	114,700	44,300
Tasmania	Australia	67,800	26,200
Hawaii	Pacific Ocean	10,450	4,000
North America		km²	miles²
Greenland	Atlantic Ocean	2,175,600	839,800
Baffin Is.	Canada	508,000	196,100
Victoria Is.	Canada	212,200	81,900
Ellesmere Is.	Canada	212,000	81,800
Cuba	Caribbean Sea	110,860	42,800
Hispaniola	Dominican Rep./Haiti	76,200	29,400
Jamaica	Caribbean Sea	11,400	4,400
Puerto Rico	Atlantic Ocean	8,900	3,400
South America		km²	miles²
Tierra del Fuego	Argentina/Chile	47,000	18,100
Falkland Is. (E.)	Atlantic Ocean	6,800	2,600

Philip's World Maps

The reference maps which form the main body of this atlas have been prepared in accordance with the highest standards of international cartography to provide an accurate and detailed representation of the Earth. The scales and projections used have been carefully chosen to give balanced coverage of the world, while emphasizing the most densely populated and economically significant regions. A hallmark of Philip's mapping is the use of hill shading and relief colouring to create a graphic impression of landforms: this makes the maps exceptionally easy to read. However, knowledge of the key features employed in the construction and presentation of the maps will enable the reader to derive the fullest benefit from the atlas.

Map sequence

The atlas covers the Earth continent by continent: first Europe; then its land neighbour Asia (mapped north before south, in a clockwise sequence), then Africa, Australia and Oceania, North America and South America. This is the classic arrangement adopted by most cartographers since the 16th century. For each continent, there are maps at a variety of scales. First, physical relief and political maps of the whole continent; then a series of larger-scale maps of the regions within the continent, each followed, where required, by still larger-scale maps of the most important or densely populated areas. The governing principle is that by turning the pages of the atlas, the reader moves steadily from north to south through each continent, with each map overlapping its neighbours. A key map showing this sequence, and the area covered by each map, can be found on the endpapers of the atlas.

Map presentation

With very few exceptions (e.g. for the Arctic and Antarctica), the maps are drawn with north at the top, regardless of whether they are presented upright or sideways on the page. In the borders will be found the map title; a locator diagram showing the area covered and the page numbers for maps of adjacent areas; the scale; the projection used; the degrees of latitude and longitude; and the letters and figures used in the index for locating place names and geographical features. Physical relief maps also have a height reference panel identifying the colours used for each layer of contouring.

Map symbols

Each map contains a vast amount of detail which can only be conveyed clearly and accurately by the use of symbols. Points and circles of varying sizes locate and identify the relative importance of towns and cities; different styles of type are employed for administrative, geographical and regional place names. A variety of pictorial symbols denote features such as glaciers and marshes, as well

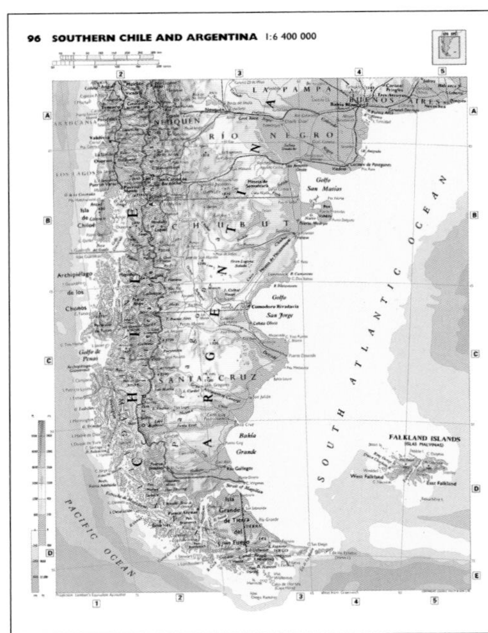

as man-made structures including roads, railways, airports and canals. International borders are shown by red lines. Where neighbouring countries are in dispute, for example in the Middle East, the maps show the *de facto* boundary between nations, regardless of the legal or historical situation. The symbols are explained on the first page of the World Maps section of the atlas.

Map scales

The scale of each map is given in the numerical form known as the 'representative fraction'. The first figure is always one, signifying one unit of distance on the map; the second figure, usually in millions, is the number by which the map unit must be multiplied to give the equivalent distance on the Earth's surface. Calculations can easily be made in centimetres and kilometres, by dividing the Earth units figure by 100 000 (i.e. deleting the last five 0s). Thus 1:1 000 000 means 1 cm = 10 km. The calculation for inches and miles is more laborious, but 1 000 000 divided by 63 360 (the number of inches in a mile) shows that the ratio 1:1 000 000 means approximately 1 inch = 16 miles. The table below provides distance equivalents for scales down to 1:50 000 000.

LARGE SCALE		
1:1 000 000	1 cm = 10 km	1 inch = 16 miles
1:2 500 000	1 cm = 25 km	1 inch = 39.5 miles
1:5 000 000	1 cm = 50 km	1 inch = 79 miles
1:6 000 000	1 cm = 60 km	1 inch = 95 miles
1:8 000 000	1 cm = 80 km	1 inch = 126 miles
1:10 000 000	1 cm = 100 km	1 inch = 158 miles
1:15 000 000	1 cm = 150 km	1 inch = 237 miles
1:20 000 000	1 cm = 200 km	1 inch = 316 miles
1:50 000 000	1 cm = 500 km	1 inch = 790 miles
SMALL SCALE		

Measuring distances

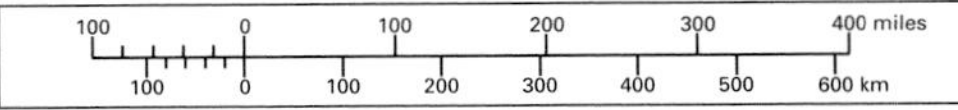

Although each map is accompanied by a scale bar, distances cannot always be measured with confidence because of the distortions involved in portraying the curved surface of the Earth on a flat page. As a general rule, the larger the map scale (i.e. the lower the number of Earth units in the representative fraction), the more accurate and reliable will be the distance measured. On small-scale maps such as those of the world and of entire continents, measurement may only be accurate along the 'standard parallels', or central axes, and should not be attempted without considering the map projection.

Latitude and longitude

Accurate positioning of individual points on the Earth's surface is made possible by reference to the geometrical system of latitude and longitude. Latitude *parallels* are drawn west–east around the Earth and numbered by degrees north and south of the Equator, which is designated 0° of latitude. Longitude *meridians* are drawn north–south and numbered by degrees east and west of the *prime meridian*, 0° of longitude, which passes through Greenwich in England. By referring to these co-ordinates and their subdivisions of minutes ($^1/60$th of a degree) and seconds ($^1/60$th of a minute), any place on Earth can be located to within a few hundred metres. Latitude and longitude are indicated by blue lines on the maps; they are straight or curved according to the projection employed. Reference to these lines is the easiest way of determining the relative positions of places on different maps, and for plotting compass directions.

Name forms

For ease of reference, both English and local name forms appear in the atlas. Oceans, seas and countries are shown in English throughout the atlas; country names may be abbreviated to their commonly accepted form (e.g. Germany, not The Federal Republic of Germany). Conventional English forms are also used for place names on the smaller-scale maps of the continents. However, local name forms are used on all large-scale and regional maps, with the English form given in brackets only for important cities – the large-scale map of Russia and Central Asia thus shows Moskva (Moscow). For countries which do not use a Roman script, place names have been transcribed according to the systems adopted by the British and US Geographic Names Authorities. For China, the Pin Yin system has been used, with some more widely known forms appearing in brackets, as with Beijing (Peking). Both English and local names appear in the index, the English form being cross-referenced to the local form.

The
WORLD IN
FOCUS

Planet Earth

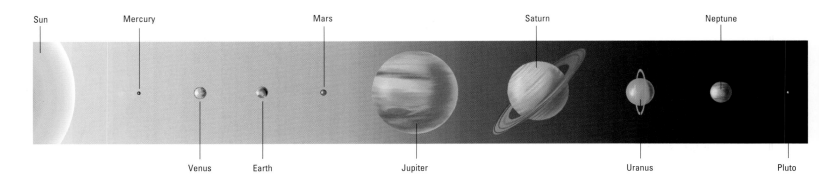

Sun | Mercury | Mars | Saturn | Neptune

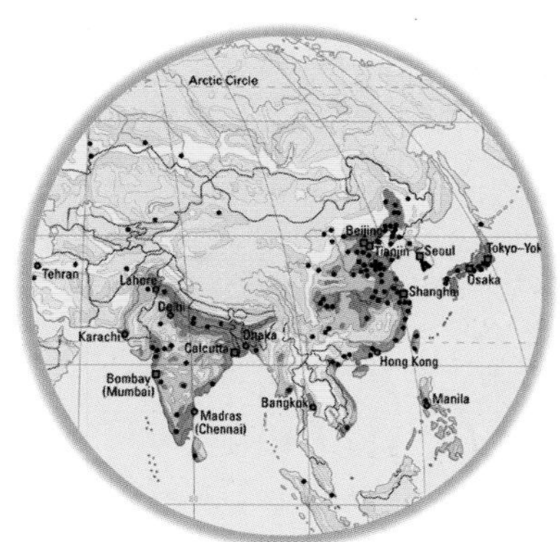

Venus | Earth | Jupiter | Uranus | Pluto

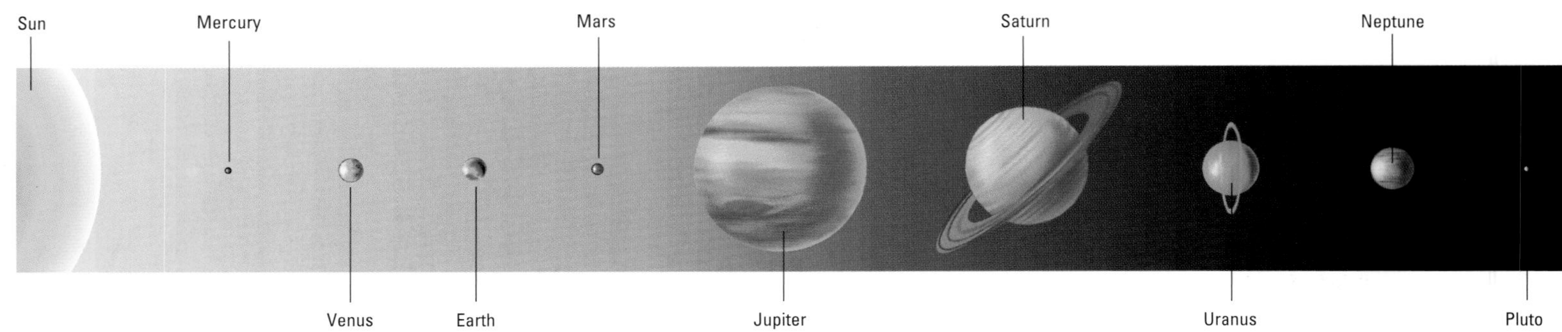

The Solar System

A minute part of one of the billions of galaxies (collections of stars) that comprises the Universe, the Solar System lies some 27,000 light-years from the centre of our own galaxy, the 'Milky Way'. Thought to be over 4,700 million years old, it consists of a central sun with nine planets and their moons revolving around it, attracted by its gravitational pull. The planets orbit the Sun in the same direction – anti-clockwise when viewed from the Northern Heavens – and almost in the same plane. Their orbital paths, however, vary enormously.

The Sun's diameter is 109 times that of Earth, and the temperature at its core – caused by continuous thermonuclear fusions of hydrogen into helium – is estimated to be 15 million degrees Celsius. It is the Solar System's only source of light and heat.

Profile of the Planets

	Mean distance from Sun (million km)	Mass (Earth = 1)	Period of orbit (Earth years)	Period of rotation (Earth days)	Equatorial diameter (km)	Number of known satellites
Mercury	57.9	0.055	0.24 years	58.67	4,878	0
Venus	108.2	0.815	0.62 years	243.00	12,104	0
Earth	149.6	1.0	1.00 years	1.00	12,756	1
Mars	227.9	0.107	1.88 years	1.03	6,787	2
Jupiter	778.3	317.8	11.86 years	0.41	142,800	16
Saturn	1,427	95.2	29.46 years	0.43	120,000	20
Uranus	2,871	14.5	84.01 years	0.75	51,118	15
Neptune	4,497	17.1	164.80 years	0.80	49,528	8
Pluto	5,914	0.002	248.50 years	6.39	2,320	1

All planetary orbits are elliptical in form, but only Pluto and Mercury follow paths that deviate noticeably from a circular one. Near perihelion – its closest approach to the Sun – Pluto actually passes inside the orbit of Neptune, an event that last occurred in 1983. Pluto did not regain its station as outermost planet until February 1999.

The Seasons

Seasons occur because the Earth's axis is tilted at a constant angle of 23½°. When the northern hemisphere is tilted to a maximum extent towards the Sun, on 21 June, the Sun is overhead at the Tropic of Cancer (latitude 23½° North). This is midsummer, or the summer solstice, in the northern hemisphere.

On 22 or 23 September, the Sun is overhead at the Equator, and day and night are of equal length throughout the world. This is the autumn equinox in the northern hemisphere. On 21 or 22 December, the Sun is overhead at the Tropic of Capricorn (23½° South), the winter solstice in the northern hemisphere. The overhead Sun then tracks north until, on 21 March, it is overhead at the Equator. This is the spring (vernal) equinox in the northern hemisphere.

In the southern hemisphere, the seasons are the reverse of those in the north.

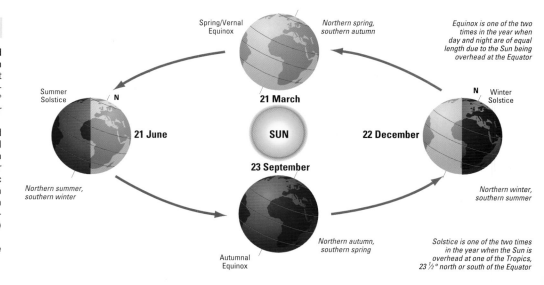

Spring/Vernal Equinox — Northern spring, southern autumn

Equinox is one of the two times in the year when day and night are of equal length due to the Sun being overhead at the Equator

21 March

Summer Solstice — N

21 June — SUN — 22 December — Winter Solstice — N

23 September

Northern summer, southern winter

Northern winter, southern summer

Northern autumn, southern spring

Autumnal Equinox

Solstice is one of the two times in the year when the Sun is overhead at one of the Tropics, 23½° north or south of the Equator

Day and Night

The Sun appears to rise in the east, reach its highest point at noon, and then set in the west, to be followed by night. In reality, it is not the Sun that is moving but the Earth rotating from west to east. The moment when the Sun's upper limb first appears above the horizon is termed sunrise; the moment when the Sun's upper limb disappears below the horizon is sunset.

At the summer solstice in the northern hemisphere (21 June), the Arctic has total daylight and the Antarctic total darkness. The opposite occurs at the winter solstice (21 or 22 December). At the Equator, the length of day and night are almost equal all year.

21 June — N — N. Pole: 6 months daylight

22 December — N. Pole: 6 months darkness Arctic Circle: 24 hours darkness

SHORT NIGHT — 24 hours daylight — 10½ hours daylight — 66½° — 23½° — SHORT DAY — 66½°

12 hours daylight — 0°

LONG DAY — 23½° — 13½ hours daylight — Sun's rays — 23½° — LONG DAY

Equator — 0°

12 hours daylight

SHORT DAY — 0° — 10½ hours daylight — 24 hours daylight — 23½° — Equator

LONG NIGHT — 23½°

Antarctic Circle: 24 hours darkness S. Pole: 6 months darkness — S — Antarctic Circle: 24 hours daylight S. Pole: 6 months daylight

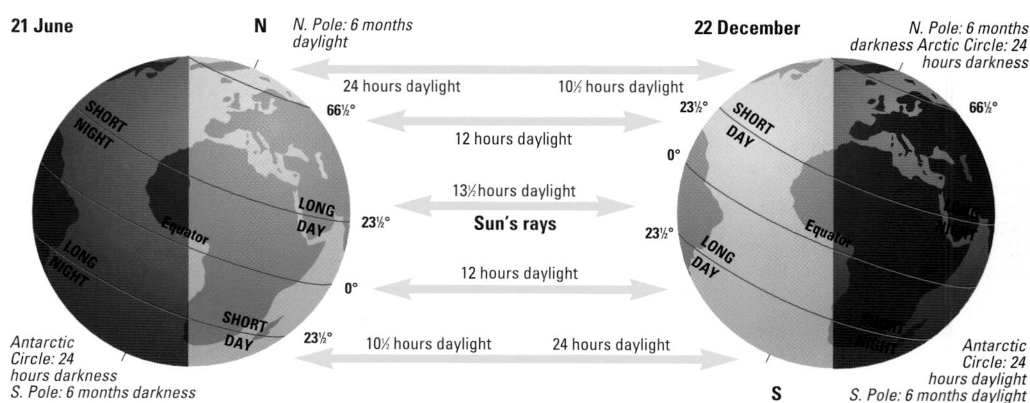

Time

Year: The time taken by the Earth to revolve around the Sun, or 365.24 days.

Leap Year: A calendar year of 366 days, 29 February being the additional day. It offsets the difference between the calendar and the solar year.

Month: The approximate time taken by the Moon to revolve around the Earth. The 12 months of the year in fact vary from 28 (29 in a Leap Year) to 31 days.

Week: An artificial period of 7 days, not based on astronomical time.

Day: The time taken by the Earth to complete one rotation on its axis.

Hour: 24 hours make one day. Usually the day is divided into hours AM (ante meridiem or before noon) and PM (post meridiem or after noon), although most timetables now use the 24-hour system, from midnight to midnight.

Sunrise

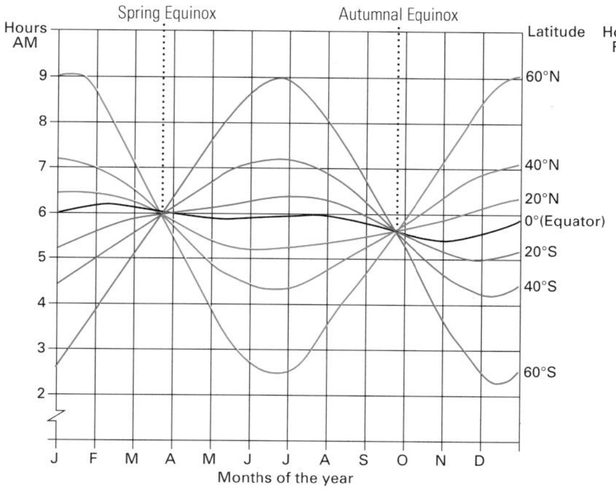

Sunset

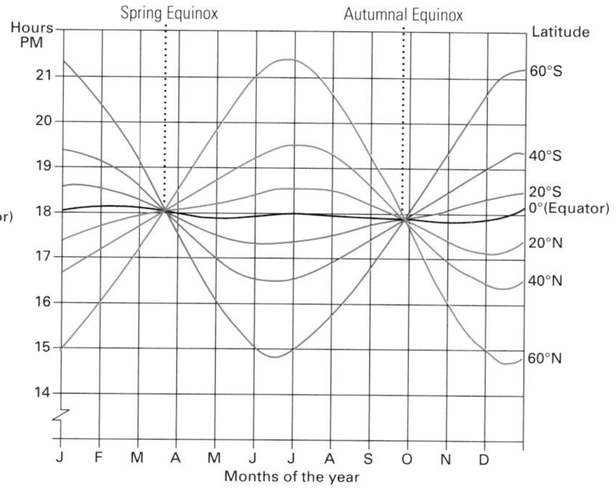

The Moon

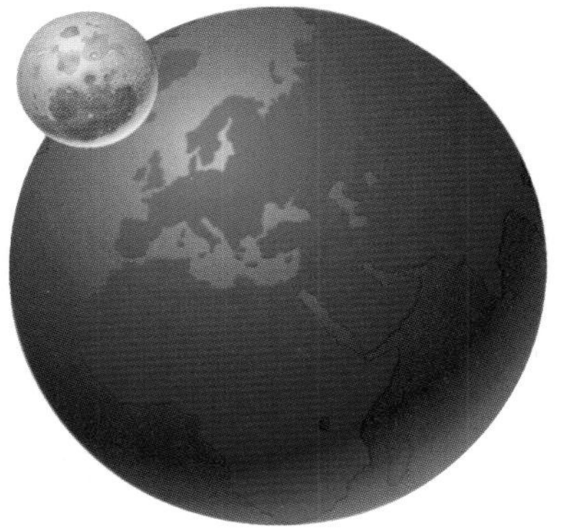

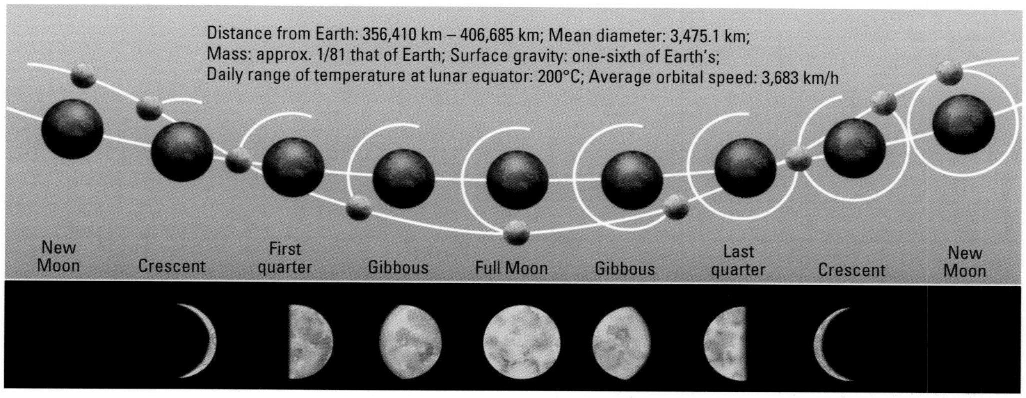

The Moon rotates more slowly than the Earth, making one complete turn on its axis in just over 27 days. Since this corresponds to its period of revolution around the Earth, the Moon always presents the same

Phases of the Moon

Distance from Earth: 356,410 km – 406,685 km; Mean diameter: 3,475.1 km; Mass: approx. 1/81 that of Earth; Surface gravity: one-sixth of Earth's; Daily range of temperature at lunar equator: 200°C; Average orbital speed: 3,683 km/h

New Moon Crescent First quarter Gibbous Full Moon Gibbous Last quarter Crescent New Moon

hemisphere or face to us, and we never see 'the dark side'. The interval between one full Moon and the next (and between new Moons) is about 29½ days – a lunar month. The apparent changes in the shape of the Moon are caused by its changing position in relation to the Earth; like the planets, it produces no light of its own and shines only by reflecting the rays of the Sun.

Eclipses

When the Moon passes between the Sun and the Earth it causes a partial eclipse of the Sun (1) if the Earth passes through the Moon's outer shadow (P), or a total eclipse (2) if the inner cone shadow crosses the Earth's surface. In a lunar eclipse, the Earth's shadow crosses the Moon and, again, provides either a partial or total eclipse.

Eclipses of the Sun and the Moon do not occur every month because of the 5° difference between the plane of the Moon's orbit and the plane in which the Earth moves. In the 1990s only 14 lunar eclipses were possible, for example, seven partial and seven total; each was visible only from certain, and variable, parts of the world. The same period witnessed 13 solar eclipses – six partial (or annular) and seven total.

Partial eclipse (1)

P P P

Solar eclipse

Total eclipse (2)

Lunar eclipse

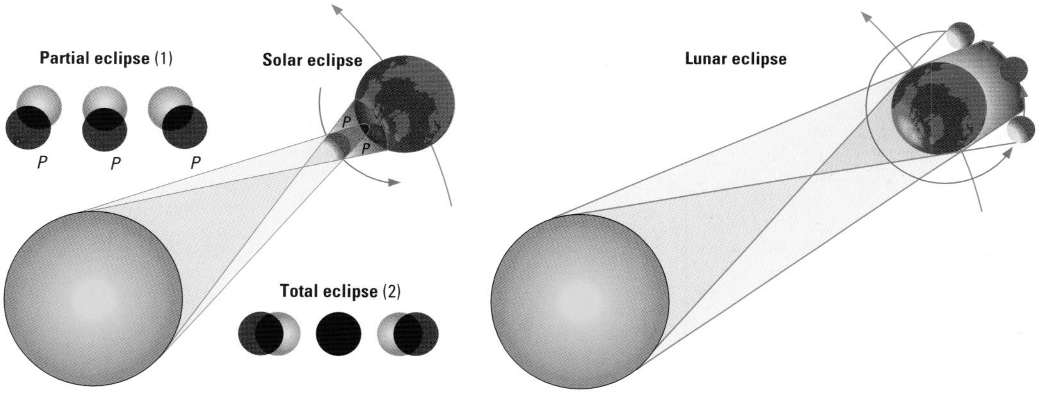

Tides

The daily rise and fall of the ocean's tides are the result of the gravitational pull of the Moon and that of the Sun, though the effect of the latter is only 46.6% as strong as that of the Moon. This effect is greatest on the hemisphere facing the Moon and causes a tidal 'bulge'. When the Sun, Earth and Moon are in line, tide-raising forces are at a maximum and Spring tides occur: high tide reaches the highest values, and low tide falls to low levels. When lunar and solar forces are least coincidental with the Sun and Moon at an angle (near the Moon's first and third quarters), Neap tides occur, which have a small tidal range.

Spring tide

Neap tide

Spring tide

Last quarter

New Moon

Full Moon

Neap tide

Gravitational pull by the Sun

First quarter

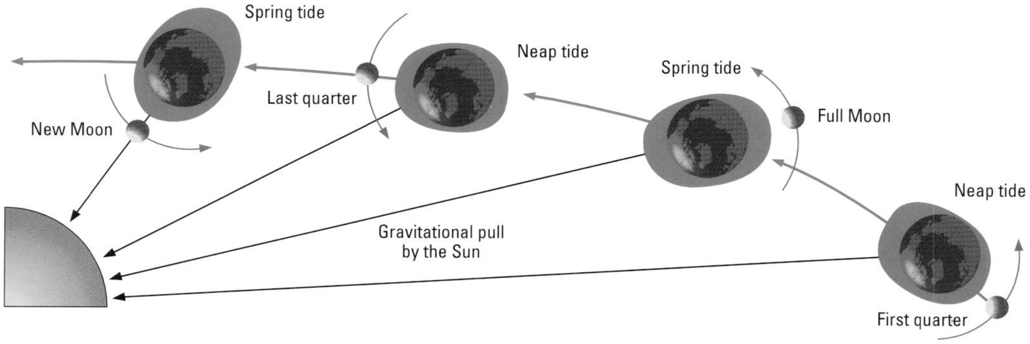

Restless Earth

The Earth's Structure

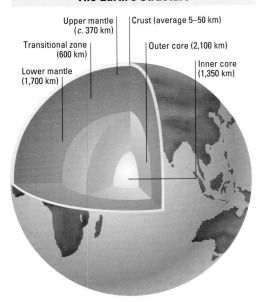

Upper mantle (c. 370 km)
Crust (average 5–50 km)
Transitional zone (600 km)
Outer core (2,100 km)
Lower mantle (1,700 km)
Inner core (1,350 km)

Continental Drift

About 200 million years ago the original Pangaea landmass began to split into two continental groups, which further separated over time to produce the present-day configuration.

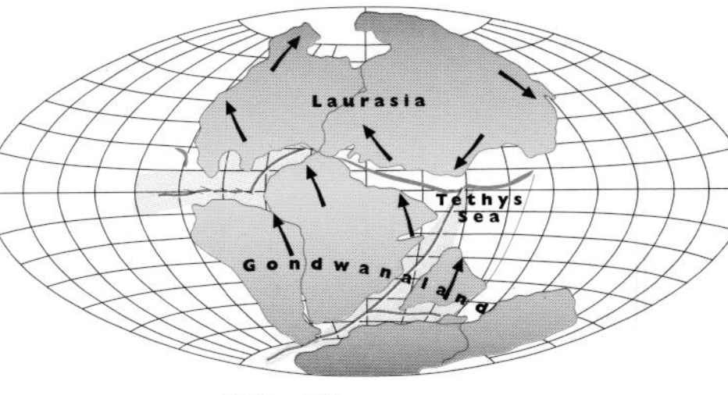

180 million years ago

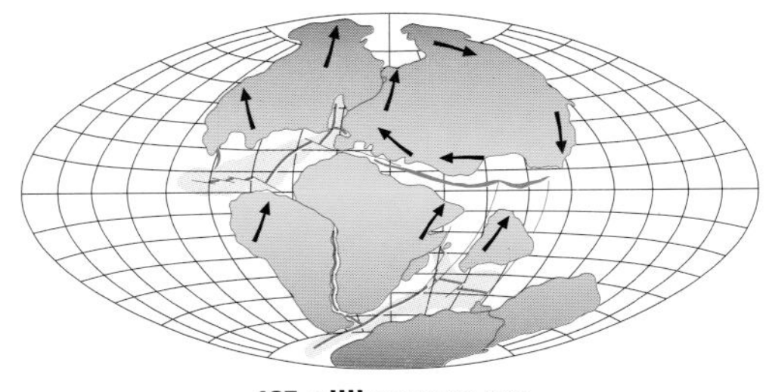

135 million years ago

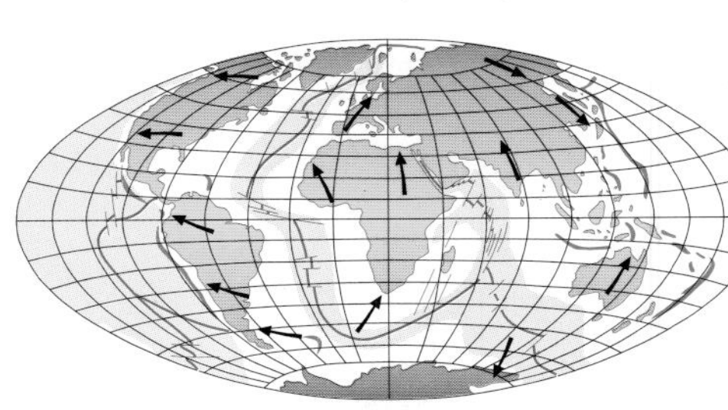

Present day

Trench
Rift
New ocean floor
Zones of slippage

Notable Earthquakes Since 1900

Year	Location	Richter Scale	Deaths
1906	San Francisco, USA	8.3	503
1906	Valparaiso, Chile	8.6	22,000
1908	Messina, Italy	7.5	83,000
1915	Avezzano, Italy	7.5	30,000
1920	Gansu (Kansu), China	8.6	180,000
1923	Yokohama, Japan	8.3	143,000
1927	Nan Shan, China	8.3	200,000
1932	Gansu (Kansu), China	7.6	70,000
1933	Sanriku, Japan	8.9	2,990
1934	Bihar, India/Nepal	8.4	10,700
1935	Quetta, India (now Pakistan)	7.5	60,000
1939	Chillan, Chile	8.3	28,000
1939	Erzincan, Turkey	7.9	30,000
1960	Agadir, Morocco	5.8	12,000
1962	Khorasan, Iran	7.1	12,230
1968	N.E. Iran	7.4	12,000
1970	N. Peru	7.7	66,794
1972	Managua, Nicaragua	6.2	5,000
1974	N. Pakistan	6.3	5,200
1976	Guatemala	7.5	22,778
1976	Tangshan, China	8.2	255,000
1978	Tabas, Iran	7.7	25,000
1980	El Asnam, Algeria	7.3	20,000
1980	S. Italy	7.2	4,800
1985	Mexico City, Mexico	8.1	4,200
1988	N.W. Armenia	6.8	55,000
1990	N. Iran	7.7	36,000
1993	Maharashtra, India	6.4	30,000
1994	Los Angeles, USA	6.6	51
1995	Kobe, Japan	7.2	5,000
1995	Sakhalin Is., Russia	7.5	2,000
1997	N.E. Iran	7.1	2,500
1998	Takhar, Afghanistan	6.1	4,200
1998	Rostaq, Afghanistan	7.0	5,000
1999	Izmit, Turkey	7.4	15,000
1999	Taipei, Taiwan	7.6	1,700

Earthquakes

Earthquake magnitude is usually rated according to either the Richter or the Modified Mercalli scale, both devised by seismologists in the 1930s. The Richter scale measures absolute earthquake power with mathematical precision: each step upwards represents a tenfold increase in shockwave amplitude. Theoretically, there is no upper limit, but the largest earthquakes measured have been rated at between 8.8 and 8.9. The 12–point Mercalli scale, based on observed effects, is often more meaningful, ranging from I (earthquakes noticed only by seismographs) to XII (total destruction); intermediate points include V (people awakened at night; unstable objects overturned), VII (collapse of ordinary buildings; chimneys and monuments fall) and IX (conspicuous cracks in ground; serious damage to reservoirs).

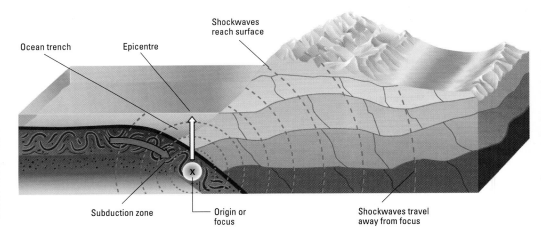

Shockwaves reach surface
Ocean trench
Epicentre
Subduction zone
Origin or focus
Shockwaves travel away from focus

Structure and Earthquakes

- Mobile land areas
- Submarine zones of mobile land areas
- Stable land platforms
- Submarine extensions of stable land platforms
- Mid-oceanic volcanic ridges
- Oceanic platforms

1976○ Principal earthquakes and dates

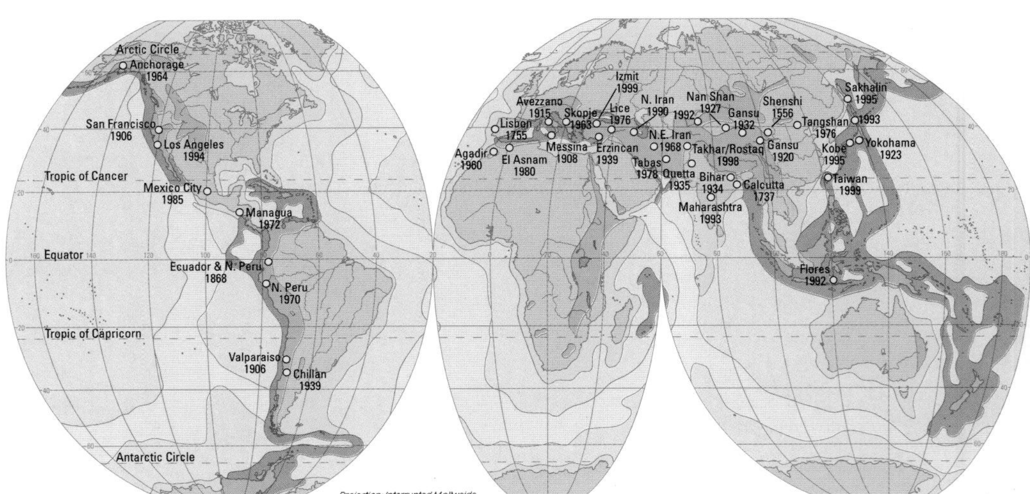

Earthquakes are a series of rapid vibrations originating from the slipping or faulting of parts of the Earth's crust when stresses within build up to breaking point. They usually happen at depths varying from 8 km to 30 km. Severe earthquakes cause extensive damage when they take place in populated areas, destroying structures and severing communications. Most initial loss of life occurs due to secondary causes such as falling masonry, fires and flooding.

Projection: Interrupted Mollweide

Plate Tectonics

The drifting of the continents is a feature that is unique to Planet Earth. The complementary, almost jigsaw-puzzle fit of the coastlines on each side of the Atlantic Ocean inspired Alfred Wegener's theory of continental drift in 1915. The theory suggested that the ancient super-continent, which Wegener named Pangaea, incorporated all of the Earth's landmasses and gradually split up to form today's continents.

The original debate about continental drift was a prelude to a more radical idea: plate tectonics. The basic theory is that the Earth's crust is made up of a series of rigid plates which float on a soft layer of the mantle and are moved about by continental convection currents within the Earth's interior. These plates diverge and converge along margins marked by seismic activity. Plates diverge from mid-ocean ridges where molten lava pushes upwards and forces the plates apart at rates of up to 40 mm [1.6 in] a year.

The three diagrams, left, give some examples of plate boundaries from around the world. Diagram (a) shows sea-floor spreading at the Mid-Atlantic Ridge as the American and African plates slowly diverge. The same thing is happening in (b) where sea-floor spreading at the Mid-Indian Ocean Ridge is forcing the Indian plate to collide into the Eurasian plate. In (c) oceanic crust (sima) is being subducted beneath lighter continental crust (sial).

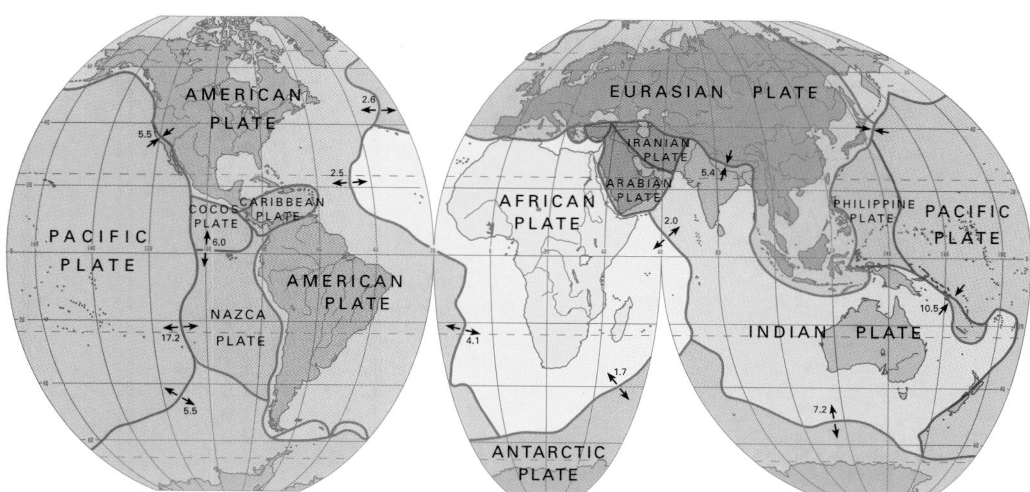

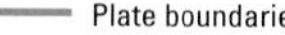

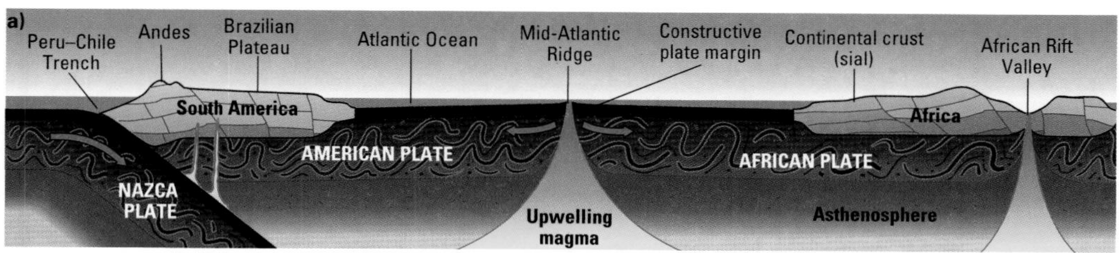

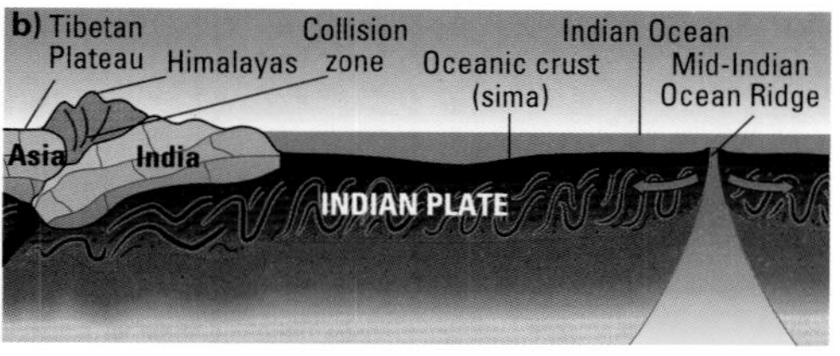

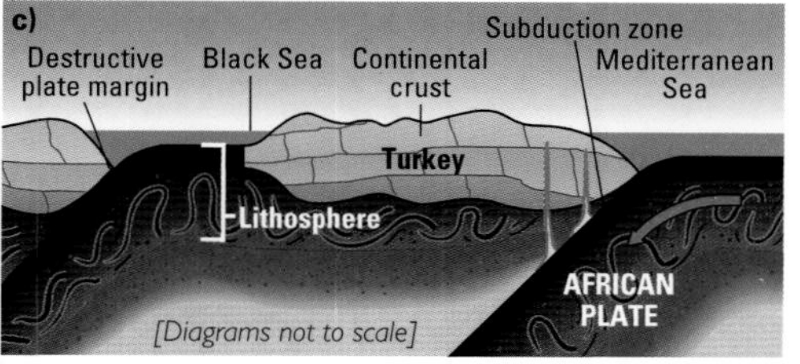

a) Peru–Chile Trench · Andes · Brazilian Plateau · Atlantic Ocean · Mid-Atlantic Ridge · Constructive plate margin · Continental crust (sial) · African Rift Valley · South America · Africa · AMERICAN PLATE · AFRICAN PLATE · NAZCA PLATE · Upwelling magma · Asthenosphere

b) Tibetan Plateau · Himalayas · Collision zone · Oceanic crust (sima) · Indian Ocean · Mid-Indian Ocean Ridge · Asia · India · INDIAN PLATE

c) Destructive plate margin · Black Sea · Continental crust · Subduction zone · Mediterranean Sea · Turkey · Lithosphere · AFRICAN PLATE · [Diagrams not to scale]

Volcanoes

Volcanoes occur when hot liquefied rock beneath the Earth's crust is pushed up by pressure to the surface as molten lava. Some volcanoes erupt in an explosive way, throwing out rocks and ash, whilst others are effusive and lava flows out of the vent. There are volcanoes which are both, such as Mount Fuji. An accumulation of lava and cinders creates cones of variable size and shape. As a result of many eruptions over centuries, Mount Etna in Sicily has a circumference of more than 120 km [75 miles].

Climatologists believe that volcanic ash, if ejected high into the atmosphere, can influence temperature and weather for several years afterwards. The 1991 eruption of Mount Pinatubo in the Philippines ejected more than 20 million tonnes of dust and ash 32 km [20 miles] into the atmosphere and is believed to have accelerated ozone depletion over a large part of the globe.

Ash and gas cloud · Neck or pipe · Volcanic bombs · Eruption at side vent · Layers of cinders and lava from previous eruptions · Lava flow · Main vent

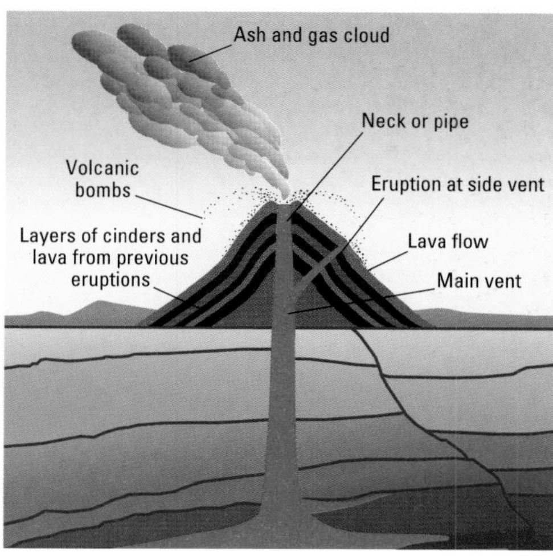

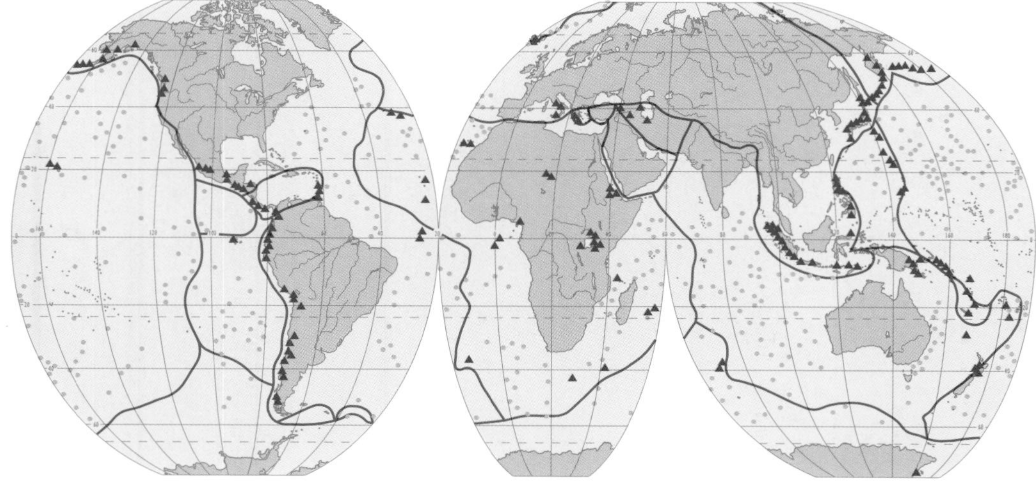

Distribution of Volcanoes

Volcanoes today may be the subject of considerable scientific study but they remain both dramatic and unpredictable: in 1991 Mount Pinatubo, 100 km [62 miles] north of the Philippines capital Manila, suddenly burst into life after lying dormant for more than six centuries. Most of the world's active volcanoes occur in a belt around the Pacific Ocean, on the edge of the Pacific plate, called the 'ring of fire'. Indonesia has the greatest concentration with 90 volcanoes, 12 of which are active. The most famous, Krakatoa, erupted in 1883 with such force that the resulting tidal wave killed 36,000 people and tremors were felt as far away as Australia.

○ Submarine volcanoes

▲ Land volcanoes active since 1700

— Boundaries of tectonic plates

Landforms

The Rock Cycle

James Hutton first proposed the rock cycle in the late 1700s after he observed the slow but steady effects of erosion.

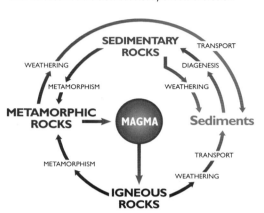

Above and below the surface of the oceans, the features of the Earth's crust are constantly changing. The phenomenal forces generated by convection currents in the molten core of our planet carry the vast segments or 'plates' of the crust across the globe in an endless cycle of creation and destruction. A continent may travel little more than 25 mm [1 in] per year, yet in the vast span of geological time this process throws up giant mountain ranges and creates new land.

Destruction of the landscape, however, begins as soon as it is formed. Wind, water, ice and sea, the main agents of erosion, mount a constant assault that even the most resistant rocks cannot withstand. Mountain peaks may dwindle by as little as a few millimetres each year, but if they are not uplifted by further movements of the crust they will eventually be reduced to rubble and transported away.

Water is the most powerful agent of erosion – it has been estimated that 100 billion tonnes of sediment are washed into the oceans every year. Three

Asian rivers account for 20% of this total, the Huang He, in China, and the Brahmaputra and Ganges in Bangladesh.

Rivers and glaciers, like the sea itself, generate much of their effect through abrasion – pounding the land with the debris they carry with them. But as well as destroying they also create new landforms, many of them spectacular: vast deltas like those of the Mississippi and the Nile, or the deep fjords cut by glaciers in British Columbia, Norway and New Zealand.

Geologists once considered that landscapes evolved from 'young', newly uplifted mountainous areas, through a 'mature' hilly stage, to an 'old age' stage when the land was reduced to an almost flat plain, or peneplain. This theory, called the 'cycle of erosion', fell into disuse when it became evident that so many factors, including the effects of plate tectonics and climatic change, constantly interrupt the cycle, which takes no account of the highly complex interactions that shape the surface of our planet.

Mountain Building

Mountains are formed when pressures on the Earth's crust caused by continental drift become so intense that the surface buckles or cracks. This happens where oceanic crust is subducted by continental crust or, more dramatically, where two tectonic plates collide: the Rockies, Andes, Alps, Urals and Himalayas resulted from such impacts. These are all known as fold mountains because they were formed by the compression of the rocks, forcing the surface to bend and fold like a crumpled rug. The Himalayas are formed from the folded former sediments of the Tethys Sea which was trapped in the collision zone between the Indian and Eurasian plates.

The other main mountain-building process occurs when the crust fractures to create faults, allowing rock to be forced upwards in large blocks; or when the pressure of magma within the crust forces the surface to bulge into a dome, or erupts to form a volcano. Large mountain ranges may reveal a combination of those features; the Alps, for example, have been compressed so violently that the folds are fragmented by numerous faults and intrusions of molten igneous rock.

Over millions of years, even the greatest mountain ranges can be reduced by the agents of erosion (most notably rivers) to a low rugged landscape known as a peneplain.

Types of faults: Faults occur where the crust is being stretched or compressed so violently that the rock strata break in a horizontal or vertical movement. They are classified by the direction in which the blocks of rock have moved. A normal fault results when a vertical movement causes the surface to break apart; compression causes a reverse fault. Horizontal movement causes shearing, known as a strike-slip fault. When the rock breaks in two places, the central block may be pushed up in a horst fault, or sink (creating a rift valley) in a graben fault.

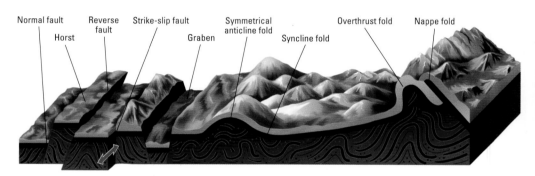

Normal fault Reverse fault Strike-slip fault Symmetrical anticline fold Overthrust fold Nappe fold
Horst Graben Syncline fold

Types of fold: Folds occur when rock strata are squeezed and compressed. They are common therefore at destructive plate margins and where plates have collided, forcing the rocks to buckle into mountain ranges. Geographers give different names to the degrees of fold that result from continuing pressure on the rock. A simple fold may be symmetric, with even slopes on either side, but as the pressure builds up, one slope becomes steeper and the fold becomes asymmetric. Later, the ridge or 'anticline' at the top of the fold may slide over the lower ground or 'syncline' to form a recumbent fold. Eventually, the rock strata may break under the pressure to form an overthrust and finally a nappe fold.

Continental Glaciation

Ice sheets were at their greatest extent about 200,000 years ago. The maximum advance of the last Ice Age was about 18,000 years ago, when ice covered virtually all of Canada and reached as far south as the Bristol Channel in Britain.

200,000 years BP

18,000 years BP

Present day

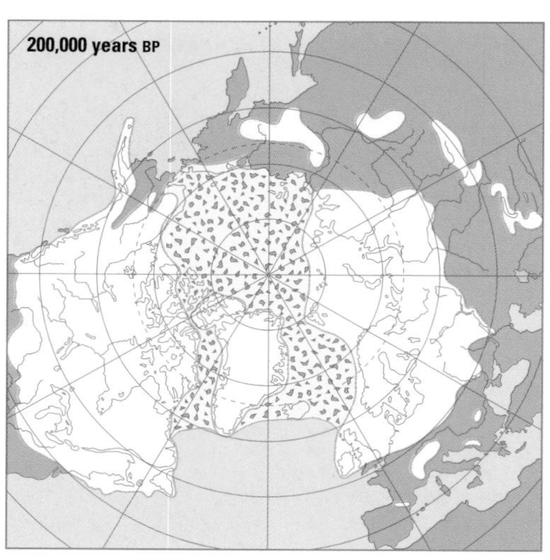

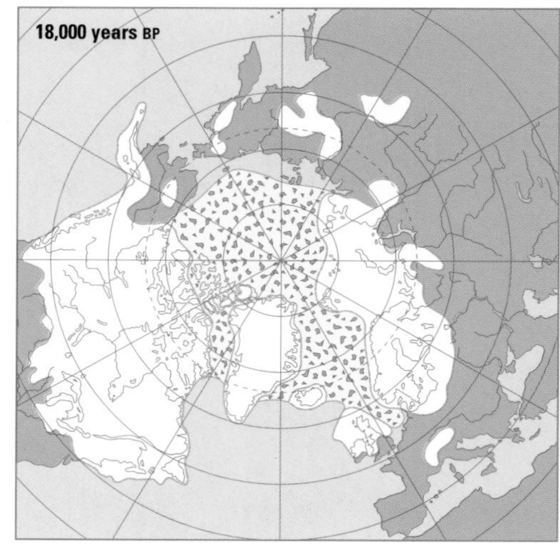

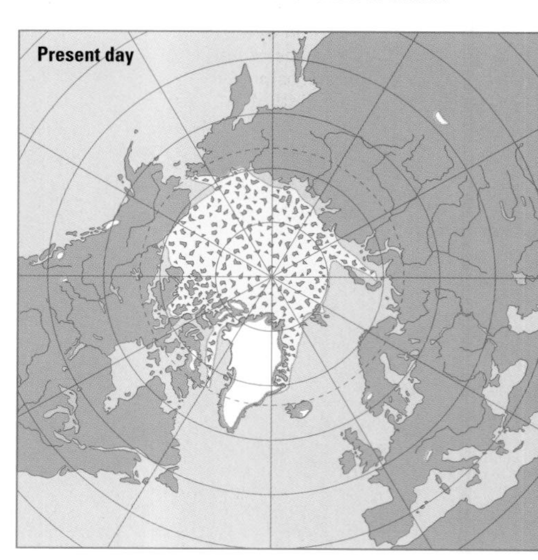

Natural Landforms

A stylized diagram to show a selection of landforms found in the mid-latitudes.

V-shaped valley
Lake
Valley glacier
Arête
Lateral moraine
Medial moraine
Snout
Hanging valley
U-shaped valley
Waterfall
Ice-dammed lake
Drumlin
Cliff
Headland
Stack
Wave-cut platform
Beach

River
Meander
Natural levée
Coastal lowlands
Distributaries
Delta
Ox-bow lake

Continental margin

Deep sea

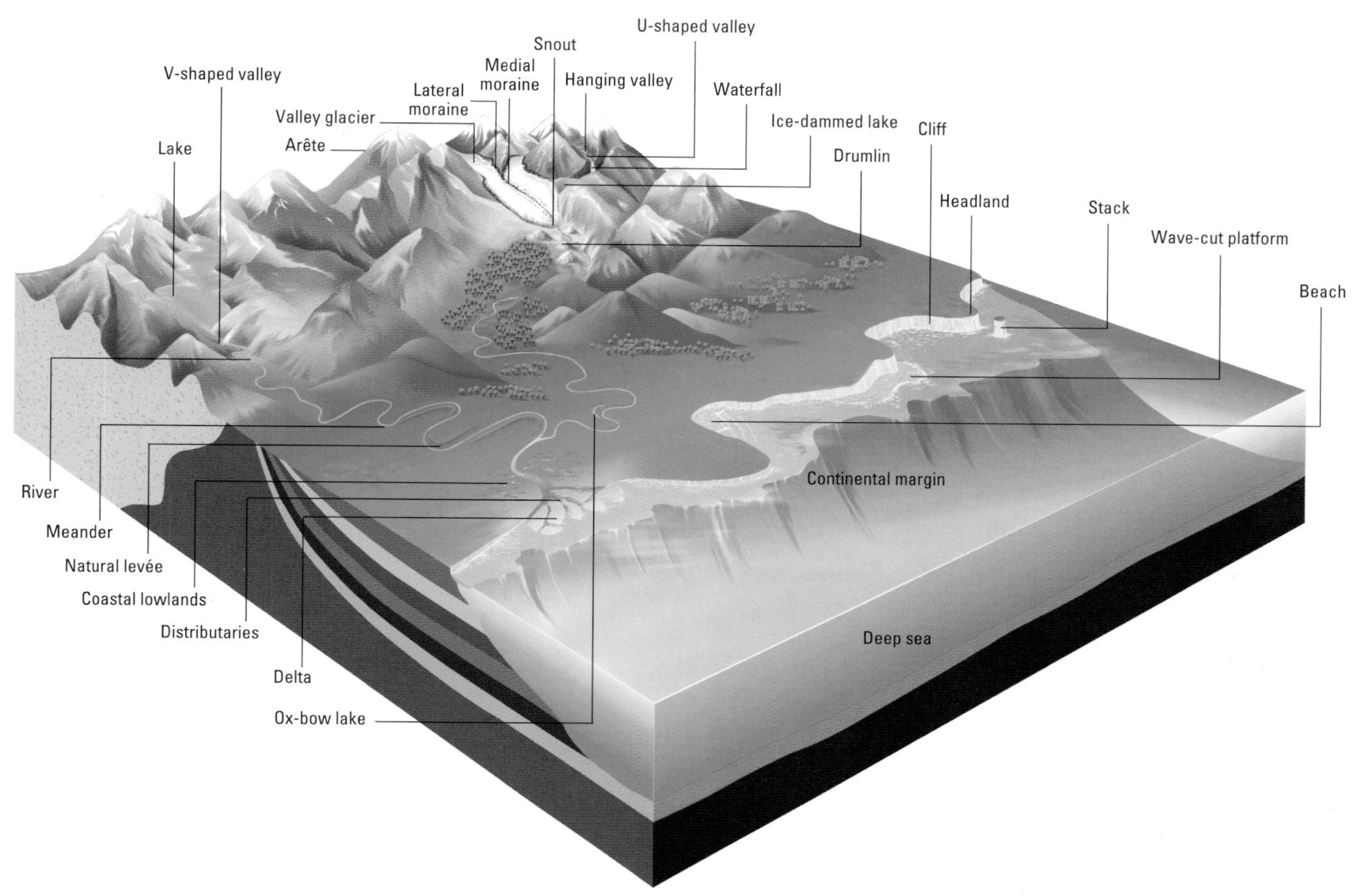

Desert Landscapes

The popular image that deserts are all huge expanses of sand is wrong. Despite harsh conditions, deserts contain some of the most varied and interesting landscapes in the world. They are also one of the most extensive environments – the hot and cold deserts together cover almost 40% of the Earth's surface.

The three types of hot desert are known by their Arabic names: sand desert, called *erg*, covers only about one-fifth of the world's desert; the rest is divided between *hammada* (areas of bare rock) and *reg* (broad plains covered by loose gravel or pebbles).

In areas of *erg*, such as the Namib Desert, the shape of the dunes reflects the character of local winds. Where winds are constant in direction, crescent-shaped *barchan* dunes form. In areas of bare rock, wind-blown sand is a major agent of erosion. The erosion is mainly confined to within 2 m [6.5 ft] of the surface, producing characteristic, mushroom-shaped rocks.

Erg

Hammada

Reg

Surface Processes

Catastrophic changes to natural landforms are periodically caused by such phenomena as avalanches, landslides and volcanic eruptions, but most of the processes that shape the Earth's surface operate extremely slowly in human terms. One estimate, based on a study in the United States, suggested that 1 m [3 ft] of land was removed from the entire surface of the country, on average, every 29,500 years. However, the time-scale varies from 1,300 years to 154,200 years depending on the terrain and climate.

In hot, dry climates, mechanical weathering, a result of rapid temperature changes, causes the outer layers of rock to peel away, while in cold mountainous regions, boulders are prised apart when water freezes in cracks in rocks. Chemical weathering, at its greatest in warm, humid regions, is responsible for hollowing out limestone caves and decomposing granites.

The erosion of soil and rock is greatest on sloping land and the steeper the slope, the greater the tendency for mass wasting – the movement of soil and rock downhill under the influence of gravity. The mechanisms of mass wasting (ranging from very slow to very rapid) vary with the type of material, but the presence of water as a lubricant is usually an important factor.

Running water is the world's leading agent of erosion and transportation. The energy of a river depends on several factors, including its velocity and volume, and its erosive power is at its peak when it is in full flood. Sea waves also exert tremendous erosive power during storms when they hurl pebbles against the shore, undercutting cliffs and hollowing out caves.

Glacier ice forms in mountain hollows and spills out to form valley glaciers, which transport rocks shattered by frost action. As glaciers move, rocks embedded into the ice erode steep-sided, U-shaped valleys. Evidence of glaciation in mountain regions includes cirques, knife-edged ridges, or arêtes, and pyramidal peaks.

Oceans

The Great Oceans

Relative sizes of the world's oceans

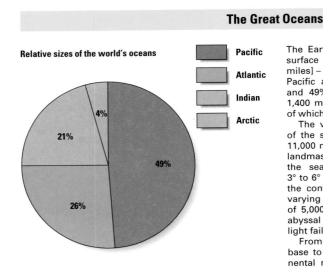

Pacific
Atlantic
Indian
Arctic

4%
21%
49%
26%

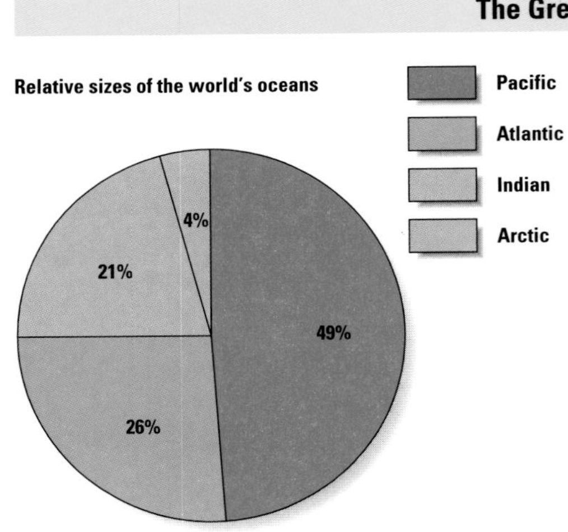

In a strict geographical sense there are only three true oceans – the Atlantic, Indian and Pacific. The legendary 'Seven Seas' would require these to be divided at the Equator and the addition of the Arctic Ocean – which accounts for less than 4% of the total sea area. The International Hydrographic Bureau does not recognize the Antarctic Ocean (even less the 'Southern Ocean') as a separate entity.

The Earth is a watery planet: more than 70% of its surface – over 360,000,000 sq km [140,000,000 sq miles] – is covered by the oceans and seas. The mighty Pacific alone accounts for nearly 36% of the total, and 49% of the sea area. Gravity holds in around 1,400 million cu. km [320 million cu. miles] of water, of which over 97% is saline.

The vast underwater world starts in the shallows of the seaside and plunges to depths of more than 11,000 m [36,000 ft]. The continental shelf, part of the landmass, drops gently to around 200 m [650 ft]; here the seabed falls away suddenly at an angle of 3° to 6° – the continental slope. The third stage, called the continental rise, is more gradual with gradients varying from 1 in 100 to 1 in 700. At an average depth of 5,000 m [16,500 ft] there begins the aptly-named abyssal plain – massive submarine depths where sunlight fails to penetrate and few creatures can survive.

From these plains rise volcanoes which, taken from base to top, rival and even surpass the tallest continental mountains in height. Mount Kea, on Hawaii, reaches a total of 10,203 m [33,400 ft], some 1,355 m [4,500 ft] more than Mount Everest, though scarcely 40% is visible above sea level.

In addition, there are underwater mountain chains up to 1,000 km [600 miles] across, whose peaks sometimes appear above sea level as islands such as Iceland and Tristan da Cunha.

The Ocean Depths

Average and maximum depths of the world's great oceans, in metres

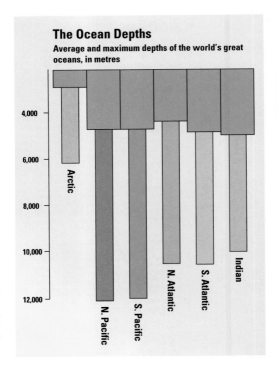

4,000
6,000
8,000
10,000
12,000

Arctic
N. Pacific
S. Pacific
N. Atlantic
S. Atlantic
Indian

Ocean Currents

January temperatures and ocean currents

ACTUAL SURFACE TEMPERATURE

°C
30
20
10
0
−10
−20
−30
−40

OCEAN CURRENTS
Cold Warm Speed (knots)
←-- ←-- Less than 0.5
← ← 0.5 – 1.0
← ← Over 1.0

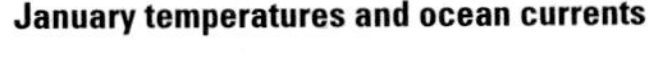

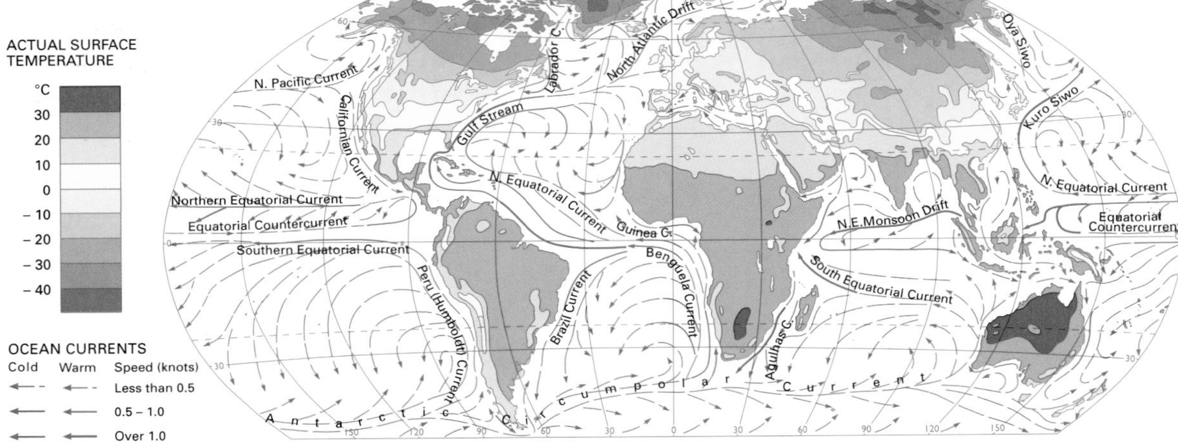

July temperatures and ocean currents

ACTUAL SURFACE TEMPERATURE

°C
30
20
10
0
−10

OCEAN CURRENTS
Cold Warm Speed (knots)
←-- ←-- Less than 0.5
← ← 0.5 – 1.0
← ← Over 1.0

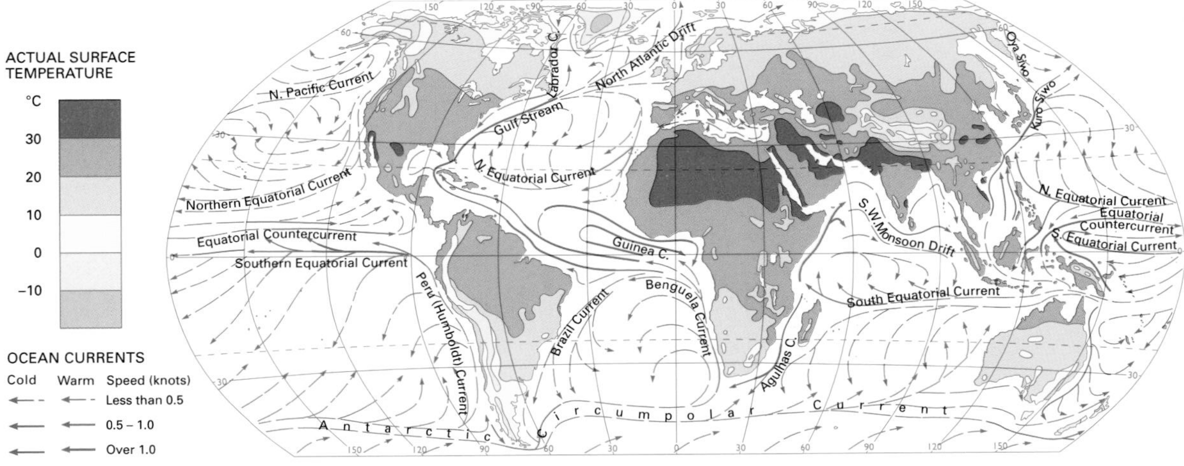

Moving immense quantities of energy as well as billions of tonnes of water every hour, the ocean currents are a vital part of the great heat engine that drives the Earth's climate. They themselves are produced by a twofold mechanism. At the surface, winds push huge masses of water before them; in the deep ocean, below an abrupt temperature gradient that separates the churning surface waters from the still depths, density variations cause slow vertical movements.

The pattern of circulation of the great surface currents is determined by the displacement known as the Coriolis effect. As the Earth turns beneath a moving object – whether it is a tennis ball or a vast mass of water – it appears to be deflected to one side. The deflection is most obvious near the Equator, where the Earth's surface is spinning eastwards at 1,700 km/h [1,050 mph]; currents moving polewards are curved clockwise in the northern hemisphere and anti-clockwise in the southern.

The result is a system of spinning circles known as gyres. The Coriolis effect piles up water on the left of each gyre, creating a narrow, fast-moving stream that is matched by a slower, broader returning current on the right. North and south of the Equator, the fastest currents are located in the west and in the east respectively. In each case, warm water moves from the Equator and cold water returns to it. Cold currents often bring an upwelling of nutrients with them, supporting the world's most economically important fisheries.

Depending on the prevailing winds, some currents on or near the Equator may reverse their direction in the course of the year – a seasonal variation on which Asian monsoon rains depend, and whose occasional failure can bring disaster to millions.

World Fishing Areas

Main commercial fishing areas (numbered FAO regions)

Catch by top marine fishing areas, thousand tonnes (1992)

1. Pacific, NW	[61]	24,199	29.3%
2. Pacific, SE	[87]	13,899	16.8%
3. Atlantic, NE	[27]	11,073	13.4%
4. Pacific, WC	[71]	7,710	9.3%
5. Indian, W	[51]	3,747	4.5%
6. Indian, E	[57]	3,262	4.0%
7. Atlantic, EC	[34]	3,259	3.9%
8. Pacific, NE	[67]	3,149	3.8%

Principal fishing areas

Leading fishing nations

China 17.3% Peru 8.3% Japan 8.0% Chile 5.9% U.S.A. 5.9% Russia 4.4% India 4.3% Indonesia 3.6%

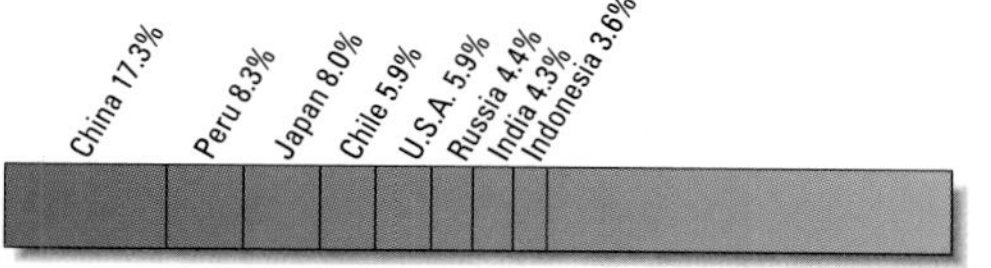

World total (1993): 101,417,500 tonnes
(Marine catch 83.1% Inland catch 16.9%)

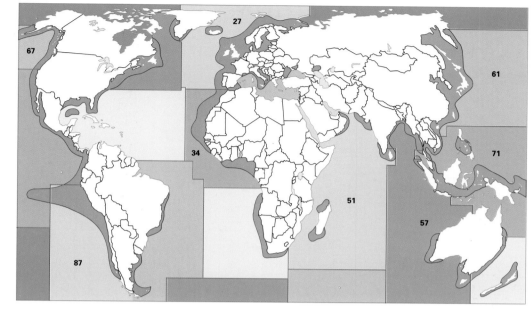

Marine Pollution

Sources of marine oil pollution (latest available year)

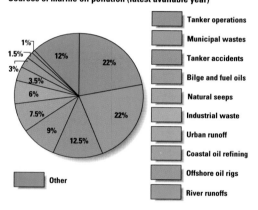

Tanker operations

Municipal wastes

Tanker accidents

Bilge and fuel oils

Natural seeps

Industrial waste

Urban runoff

Coastal oil refining

Offshore oil rigs

River runoffs

Other

Oil Spills

Major oil spills from tankers and combined carriers

Year	Vessel	Location	Spill (barrels)**	Cause
1979	Atlantic Empress	West Indies	1,890,000	collision
1983	Castillo De Bellver	South Africa	1,760,000	fire
1978	Amoco Cadiz	France	1,628,000	grounding
1991	Haven	Italy	1,029,000	explosion
1988	Odyssey	Canada	1,000,000	fire
1967	Torrey Canyon	UK	909,000	grounding
1972	Sea Star	Gulf of Oman	902,250	collision
1977	Hawaiian Patriot	Hawaiian Is.	742,500	fire
1979	Independenta	Turkey	696,350	collision
1993	Braer	UK	625,000	grounding
1996	Sea Empress	UK	515,000	grounding

Other sources of major oil spills

1983	Nowruz oilfield	The Gulf	4,250,000†	war
1979	Ixtoc 1 oilwell	Gulf of Mexico	4,200,000	blow-out
1991	Kuwait	The Gulf	2,500,000†	war

** 1 barrel = 0.136 tonnes/159 lit./35 Imperial gal./42 US gal. † estimated

River Pollution

Sources of river pollution, USA (latest available year)

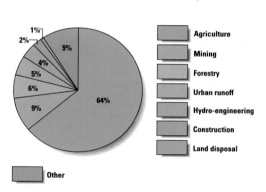

Agriculture

Mining

Forestry

Urban runoff

Hydro-engineering

Construction

Land disposal

Other

Water Pollution

Severely polluted sea areas and lakes

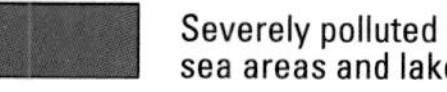

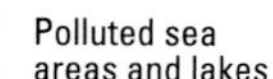

Polluted sea areas and lakes

Areas of frequent oil pollution by shipping

▶ Major oil tanker spills

▲ Major oil rig blow-outs

▼ Offshore dumpsites for industrial and municipal waste

—— Severely polluted rivers and estuaries

The most notorious tanker spillage of the 1980s occurred when the *Exxon Valdez* ran aground in Prince William Sound, Alaska, in 1989, spilling 267,000 barrels of crude oil close to shore in a sensitive ecological area. This rates as the world's 28th worst spill in terms of volume.

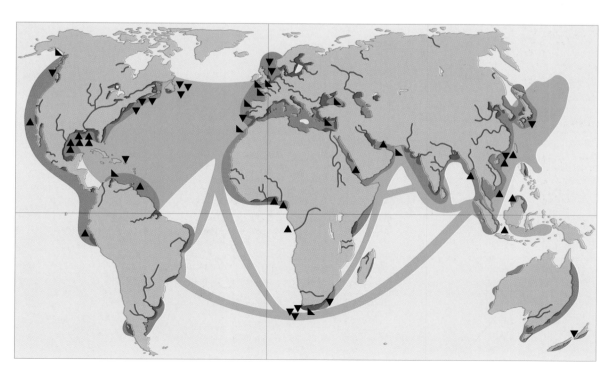

Climate

Climatic Regions

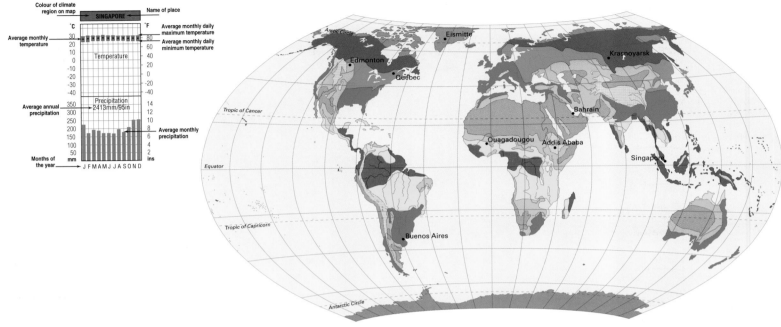

Tropical climate (hot with rain all year)	Steppe climate (warm and dry)	Subarctic climate (very cold winter)
Desert climate (hot and very dry)	Mild climate (warm and wet)	Polar climate (very cold and dry)
Savanna climate (hot with dry season)	Continental climate (wet with cold winter)	Mountainous climate (altitude affects climate)

Climate Records

Temperature

Highest recorded shade temperature: Al Aziziyah, Libya, 58°C [136.4°F], 13 September 1922.

Highest mean annual temperature: Dallol, Ethiopia, 34.4°C [94°F], 1960–66.

Longest heatwave: Marble Bar, W. Australia, 162 days over 38°C [100°F], 23 October 1923 to 7 April 1924.

Lowest recorded temperature (outside poles): Verkhoyansk, Siberia, –68°C [–90°F], 6 February 1933.

Lowest mean annual temperature: Plateau Station, Antarctica, –56.6°C [–72.0°F]

Pressure

Longest drought: Calama, N. Chile, no recorded rainfall in 400 years to 1971.

Wettest place (12 months): Cherrapunji, Meghalaya, N. E. India, 26,470 mm [1,040 in], August 1860 to August 1861. Cherrapunji also holds the record for the most rainfall in one month: 2,930 mm [115 in], July 1861.

Wettest place (average): Mawsynram, India, mean annual rainfall 11,873 mm [467.4 in].

Wettest place (24 hours): Cilaos, Réunion, Indian Ocean, 1,870 mm [73.6 in], 15–16 March 1952.

Heaviest hailstones: Gopalganj, Bangladesh, up to 1.02 kg [2.25 lb], 14 April 1986 (killed 92 people).

Heaviest snowfall (continuous): Bessans, Savoie, France, 1,730 mm [68 in] in 19 hours, 5–6 April 1969.

Heaviest snowfall (season/year): Paradise Ranger Station, Mt Rainier, Washington, USA, 31,102 mm [1,224.5 in], 19 February 1971 to 18 February 1972.

Pressure and winds

Highest barometric pressure: Agata, Siberia (at 262 m [862 ft] altitude), 1,083.8 mb, 31 December 1968.

Lowest barometric pressure: Typhoon Tip, Guam, Pacific Ocean, 870 mb, 12 October 1979.

Highest recorded wind speed: Mt Washington, New Hampshire, USA, 371 km/h [231 mph], 12 April 1934. This is three times as strong as hurricane force on the Beaufort Scale.

Windiest place: Commonwealth Bay, Antarctica, where gales frequently reach over 320 km/h [200 mph].

Climate

Climate is weather in the long term: the seasonal pattern of hot and cold, wet and dry, averaged over time (usually 30 years). At the simplest level, it is caused by the uneven heating of the Earth. Surplus heat at the Equator passes towards the poles, levelling out the energy differential. Its passage is marked by a ceaseless churning of the atmosphere and the oceans, further agitated by the Earth's diurnal spin and the motion it imparts to moving air and water. The heat's means of transport – by winds and ocean currents, by the continual evaporation and recondensation of water molecules – is the weather itself. There are four basic types of climate, each of which can be further subdivided: tropical, desert (dry), temperate and polar.

Composition of Dry Air

Nitrogen	78.09%	Sulphur dioxide	trace
Oxygen	20.95%	Nitrogen oxide	trace
Argon	0.93%	Methane	trace
Water vapour	0.2–4.0%	Dust	trace
Carbon dioxide	0.03%	Helium	trace
Ozone	0.00006%	Neon	trace

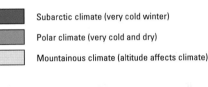

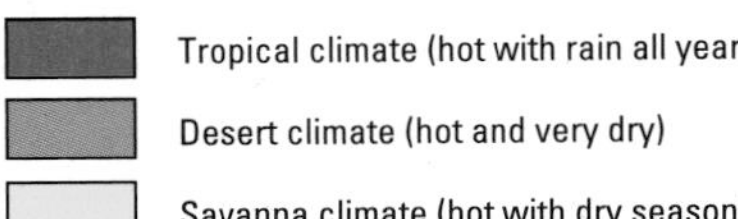

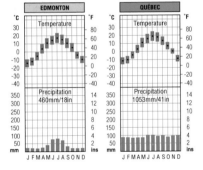

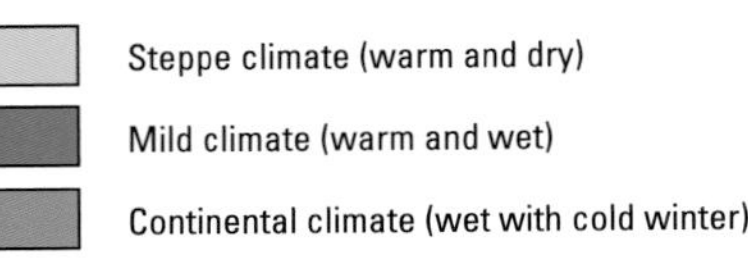

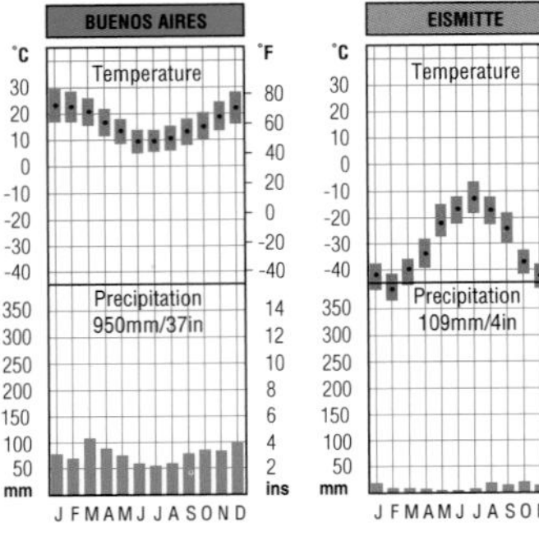

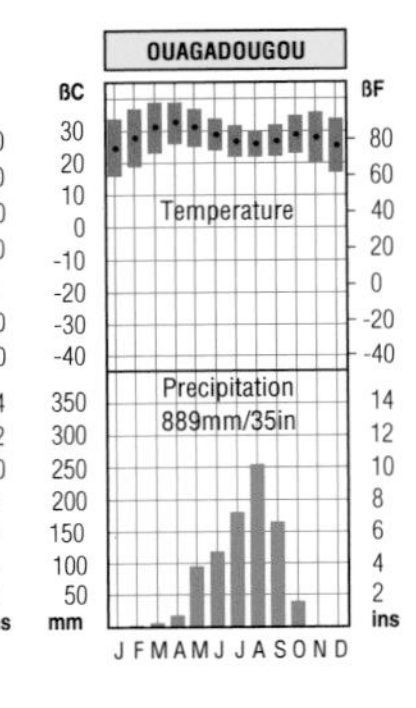

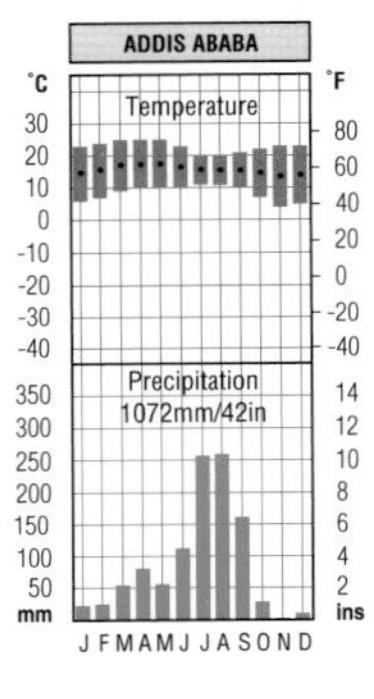

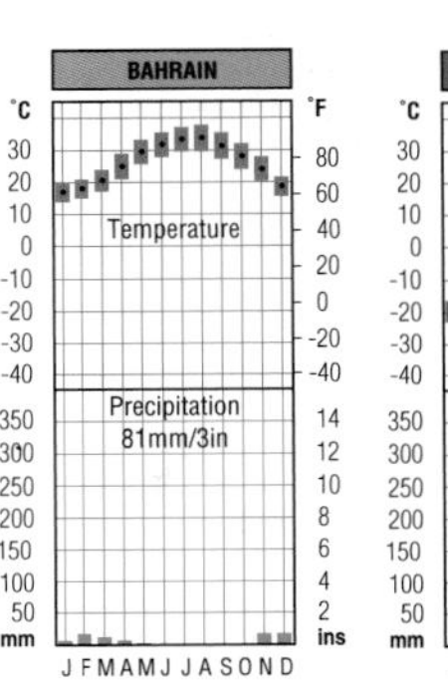

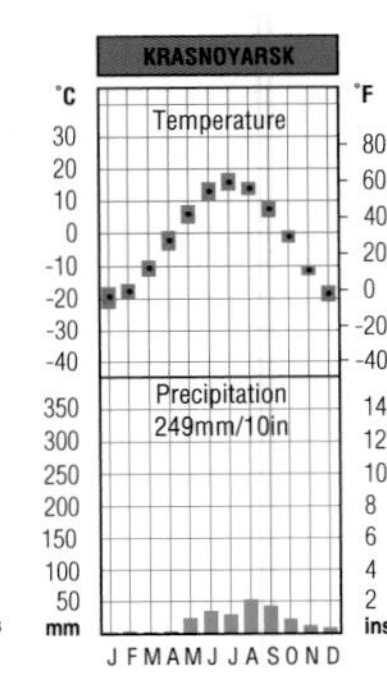

El Niño

In a normal year, south-easterly trade winds drive surface waters westwards off the coast of South America, drawing cold, nutrient-rich water up from below. In an El Niño year (which occurs every 2–7 years), warm water from the west Pacific suppresses up-welling in the east, depriving the region of nutrients. The water is warmed by as much as 7°C [12°F], disturbing the tropical atmospheric circulation. During an intense El Niño, the south-east trade winds change direction and become equatorial westerlies, resulting in climatic extremes in many regions of the world, such as drought in parts of Australia and India, and heavy rainfall in south-eastern USA. An intense El Niño occurred in 1997–8, with resultant freak weather conditions across the entire Pacific region.

Normal year

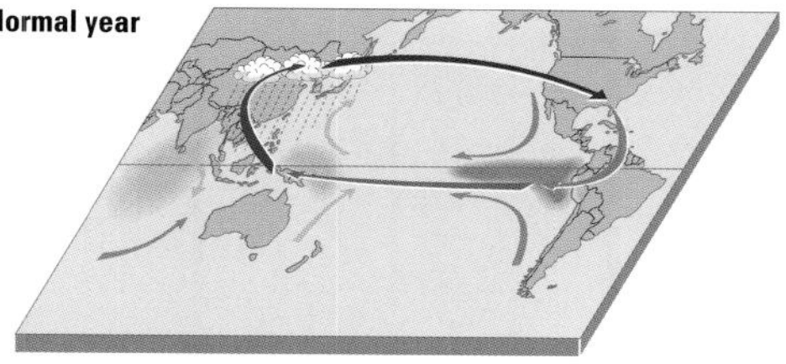

El Niño event

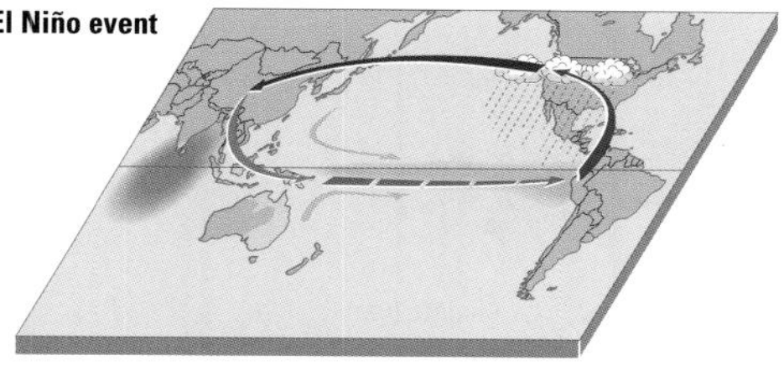

Beaufort Wind Scale

Named after the 19th-century British naval officer who devised it, the Beaufort Scale assesses wind speed according to its effects. It was originally designed as an aid for sailors, but has since been adapted for use on the land.

Scale	Wind speed km/h	mph	Effect
0	0–1	0–1	**Calm** Smoke rises vertically
1	1–5	1–3	**Light air** Wind direction shown only by smoke drift
2	6–11	4–7	**Light breeze** Wind felt on face; leaves rustle; vanes moved by wind
3	12–19	8–12	**Gentle breeze** Leaves and small twigs in constant motion; wind extends small flag
4	20–28	13–18	**Moderate** Raises dust and loose paper; small branches move
5	29–38	19–24	**Fresh** Small trees in leaf sway; wavelets on inland waters
6	39–49	25–31	**Strong** Large branches move; difficult to use umbrellas
7	50–61	32–38	**Near gale** Whole trees in motion; difficult to walk against wind
8	62–74	39–46	**Gale** Twigs break from trees; walking very difficult
9	75–88	47–54	**Strong gale** Slight structural damage
10	89–102	55–63	**Storm** Trees uprooted; serious structural damage
11	103–117	64–72	**Violent storm** Widespread damage
12	118+	73+	**Hurricane**

Conversions

°C = (°F − 32) × 5/9; °F = (°C × 9/5) + 32; 0°C = 32°F
1 in = 25.4 mm; 1 mm = 0.0394 in; 100 mm = 3.94 in

Temperature

Average temperature in January

Temperature
- 30°C
- 20°C
- 10°C
- 0°C
- −10°C
- −20°C
- −30°C
- −40°C

Average temperature in July

Temperature
- 30°C
- 20°C
- 10°C
- 0°C
- −10°C

Precipitation

Average annual precipitation
- 3,000 mm
- 2,000 mm
- 1,000 mm
- 500 mm
- 250 mm

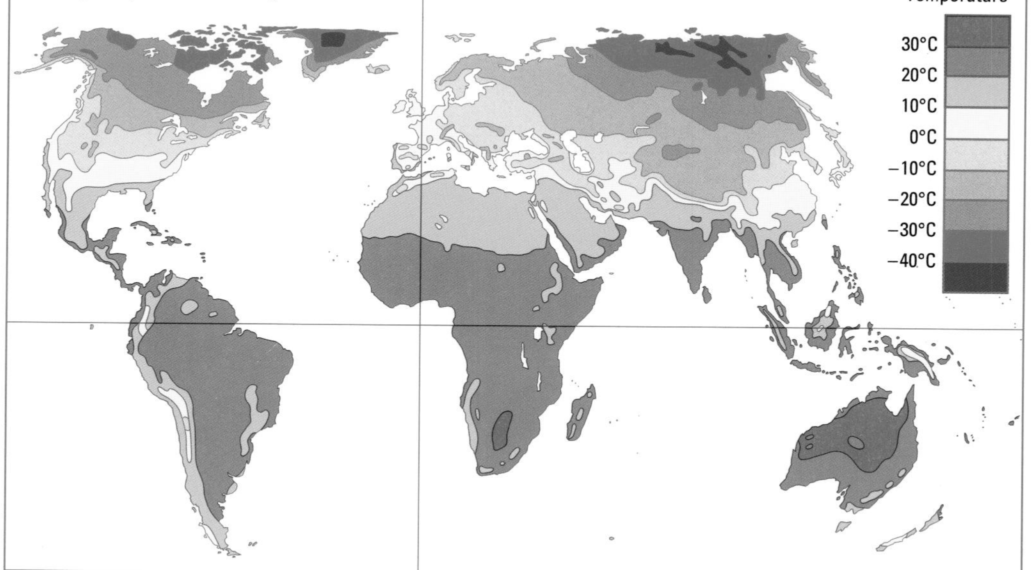

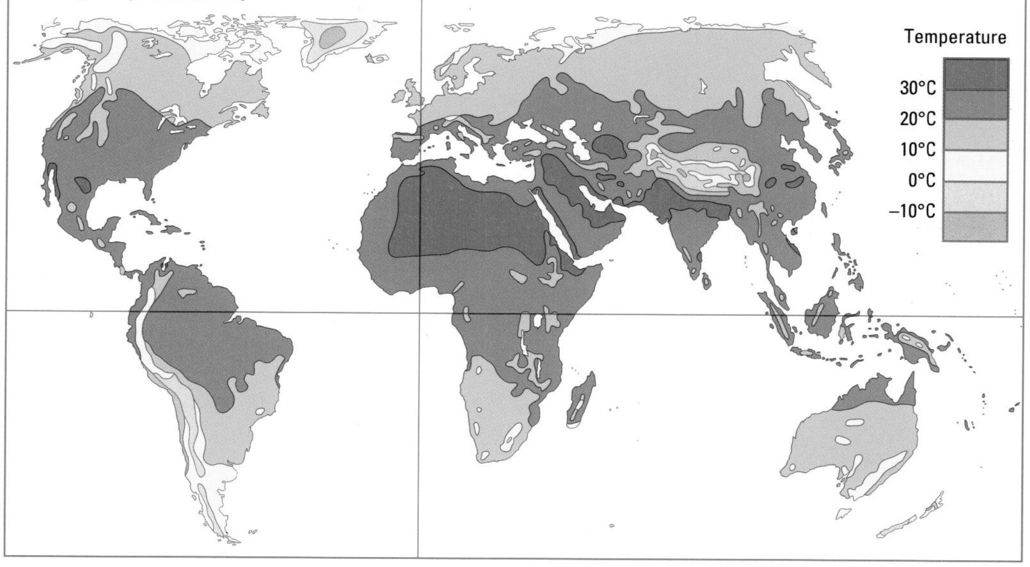

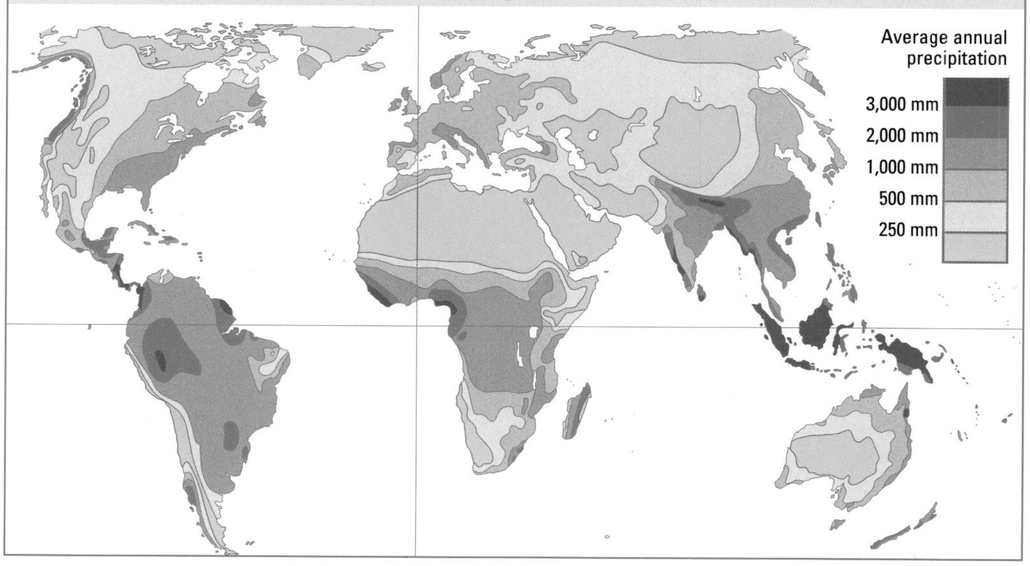

Water and Vegetation

The Hydrological Cycle

The world's water balance is regulated by the constant recycling of water between the oceans, atmosphere and land. The movement of water between these three reservoirs is known as the hydrological cycle. The oceans play a vital role in the hydrological cycle: 74% of the total precipitation falls over the oceans and 84% of the total evaporation comes from the oceans.

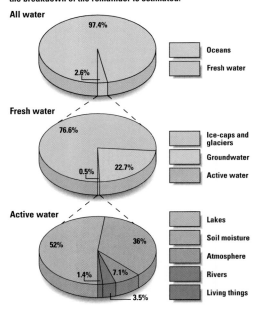

Water Distribution

The distribution of planetary water, by percentage. Oceans and ice-caps together account for more than 99% of the total; the breakdown of the remainder is estimated.

All water
- 97.4% Oceans
- 2.6% Fresh water

Fresh water
- 76.6% Ice-caps and glaciers
- 22.7% Groundwater
- 0.5% Active water

Active water
- 52% Lakes
- 36% Soil moisture
- 7.1% Atmosphere
- 3.5% Rivers
- 1.4% Living things

Water Utilization

Domestic | Industrial | Agriculture

The percentage breakdown of water usage by sector, selected countries (1996)

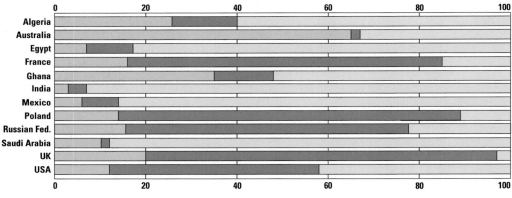

Algeria, Australia, Egypt, France, Ghana, India, Mexico, Poland, Russian Fed., Saudi Arabia, UK, USA

Water Usage

Almost all the world's water is 3,000 million years old, and all of it cycles endlessly through the hydrosphere, though at different rates. Water vapour circulates over days, even hours, deep ocean water circulates over millennia, and ice-cap water remains solid for millions of years.

Fresh water is essential to all terrestrial life. Humans cannot survive more than a few days without it, and even the hardiest desert plants and animals could not exist without some water. Agriculture requires huge quantities of fresh water: without large-scale irrigation most of the world's people would starve. In the USA, agriculture uses 42% and industry 45% of all water withdrawals.

The United States is one of the heaviest users of water in the world. According to the latest figures the average American uses 380 litres a day and the average household uses 415,000 litres a year. This is two to four times more than in Western Europe.

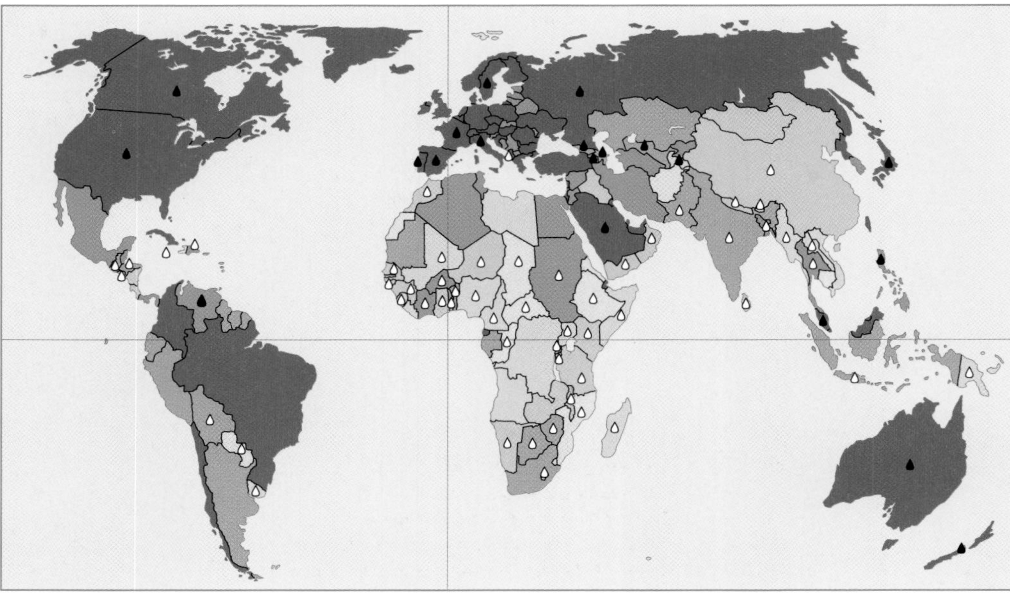

Water Supply

Percentage of total population with access to safe drinking water (1995)

- Over 90% with safe water
- 75 – 90% with safe water
- 60 – 75% with safe water
- 45 – 60% with safe water
- 30 – 45% with safe water
- Under 30% with safe water

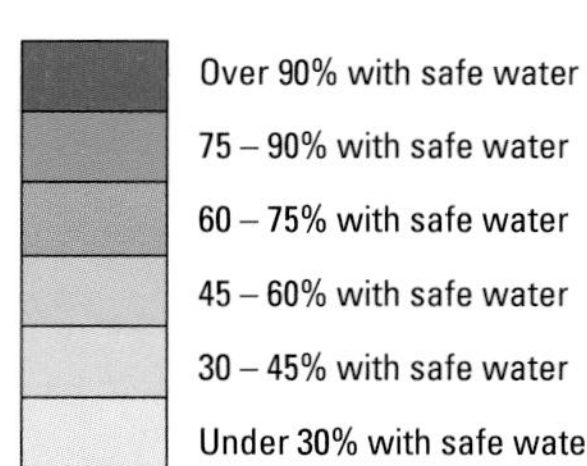

△ Under 80 litres per person per day domestic water consumption

▲ Over 320 litres per person per day domestic water consumption

NB: 80 litres of water a day is considered necessary for a reasonable quality of life.

Least well-provided countries

Paraguay	8%	Central Afr. Rep	18%
Afghanistan	10%	Bhutan	21%
Cambodia	13%	Congo (D. Rep.)	25%

Natural Vegetation

Regional variation in vegetation

- Tundra and mountain vegetation
- Needleleaf evergreen forest
- Mixed needleleaf evergreen & broadleaf deciduous trees
- Broadleaf deciduous woodland
- Mid-latitude grassland
- Evergreen broadleaf and deciduous trees & shrubs
- Semi-desert scrub
- Desert
- Tropical grassland (savanna)
- Tropical broadleaf rainforest and monsoon forest
- Subtropical broadleaf and needleleaf forest

The map shows the natural 'climax vegetation' of regions, as dictated by climate and topography. In most cases, however, agricultural activity has drastically altered the vegetation pattern. Western Europe, for example, lost most of its broadleaf forest many centuries ago, while irrigation has turned some natural semi-desert into productive land.

Land Use by Continent

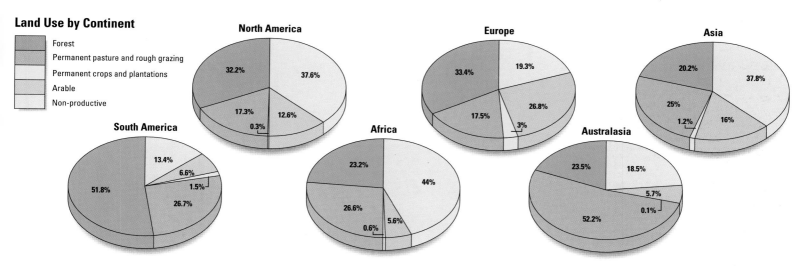

- Forest
- Permanent pasture and rough grazing
- Permanent crops and plantations
- Arable
- Non-productive

North America
37.6% / 32.2% / 17.3% / 12.6% / 0.3%

Europe
19.3% / 33.4% / 17.5% / 26.8% / 3%

Asia
20.2% / 37.8% / 25% / 1.2% / 16%

South America
13.4% / 6.6% / 1.5% / 51.8% / 26.7%

Africa
23.2% / 44% / 26.6% / 0.6% / 5.6%

Australasia
23.5% / 18.5% / 5.7% / 0.1% / 52.2%

Forestry: Production

Forest and woodland (million hectares)	Annual production (1996, million cubic metres) Fuelwood and charcoal	Industrial roundwood*
World **3,987.9**	**1,864.8**	**1,489.5**
S. America 829.3	193.0	129.9
N. & C. America 709.8	155.4	600.4
Africa 684.6	519.9	67.9
Asia 131.8	905.2	280.2
Europe 157.3	82.4	369.7
Australasia 157.2	8.7	41.5

Paper and Board

Top producers (1996)**		Top exporters (1996)**	
USA	85,173	Canada	13,393
China	30,253	USA	9,113
Japan	30,014	Finland	8,529
Canada	18,414	Sweden	7,483
Germany	14,733	Germany	6,319

* roundwood is timber as it is felled
** in thousand tonnes

Forestry: Distribution

- Main areas of coniferous production
- Main areas of non-coniferous production
- 🌲 = 5% of world production of coniferous roundwood
- 🌳 = 5% of world production of non-coniferous roundwood

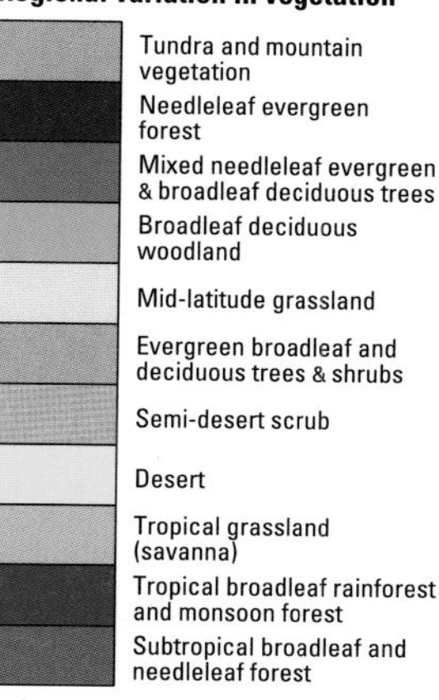

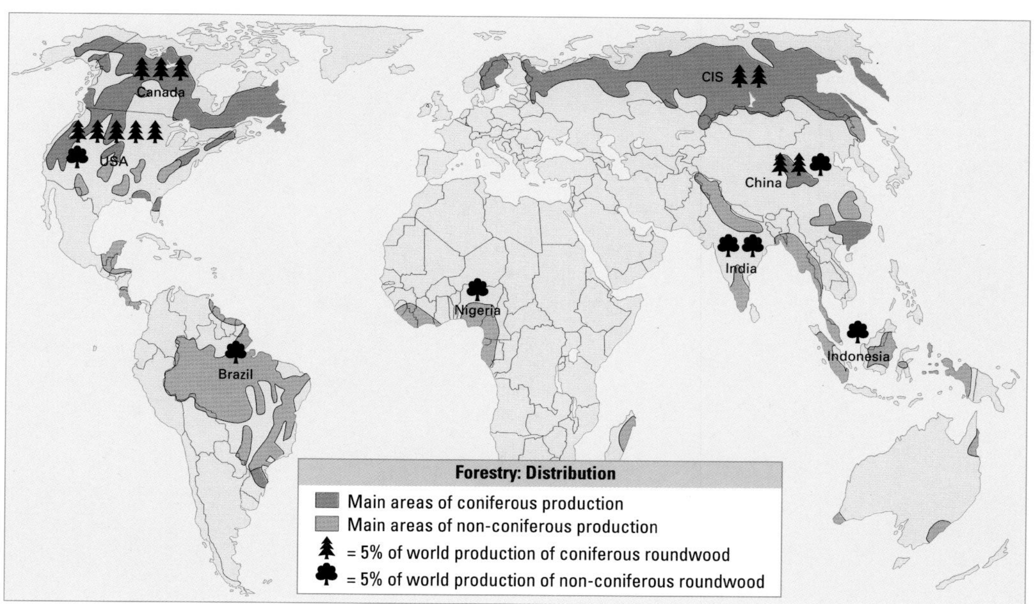

Environment

Humans have always had a dramatic effect on their environment, at least since the development of agriculture almost 10,000 years ago. Generally, the Earth has accepted human interference without obvious ill effects: the complex systems that regulate the global environment have been able to absorb substantial damage while maintaining a stable and comfortable home for the planet's trillions of lifeforms. But advancing human technology and the rapidly-expanding populations it supports are now threatening to overwhelm the Earth's ability to compensate.

Industrial wastes, acid rainfall, desertification and large-scale deforestation all combine to create environmental change at a rate far faster than the great slow cycles of planetary evolution can accommodate. As a result of overcultivation, overgrazing and overcutting of groundcover for firewood, desertification is affecting as much as 60% of the world's croplands. In addition, with fire and chain-saws, humans are destroying more forest in a day than their ancestors could have done in a century, upsetting the balance between plant and animal, carbon dioxide and oxygen, on which all life ultimately depends.

The fossil fuels that power industrial civilization have pumped enough carbon dioxide and other so-called greenhouse gases into the atmosphere to make climatic change a near-certainty. As a result of the combination of these factors, the Earth's average temperature has risen by approximately 0.5°C [1°F] since the beginning of the 20th century, and it is still rising.

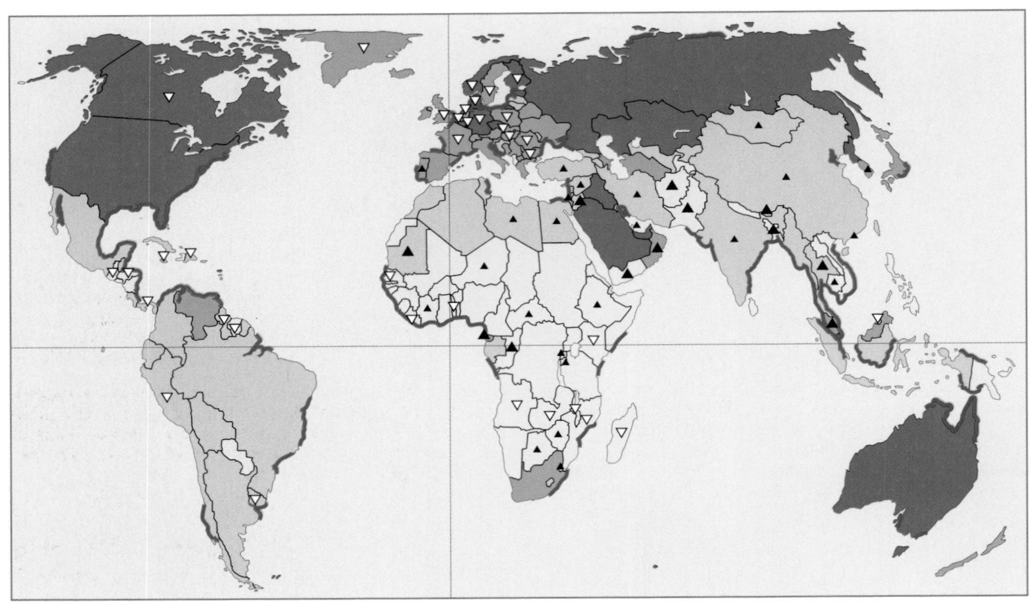

Global Warming

Carbon dioxide emissions in tonnes per person per year (1995)

- Over 10 tonnes of CO_2
- 5 – 10 tonnes of CO_2
- 1 – 5 tonnes of CO_2
- Under 1 tonne of CO_2

Changes in CO_2 emissions 1980–90

- ▲ Over 100% increase in emissions
- ▲ 50–100% increase in emissions
- ▽ Reduction in emissions
- ▬ Coastal areas in danger of flooding from rising sea levels caused by global warming

High atmospheric concentrations of heat-absorbing gases, especially carbon dioxide, appear to be causing a steady rise in average temperatures worldwide – up to 1.5°C [3°F] by the year 2020, according to some estimates. Global warming is likely to bring with it a rise in sea levels that may flood some of the Earth's most densely populated coastal areas.

Greenhouse Power

Relative contributions to the Greenhouse Effect by the major heat-absorbing gases in the atmosphere.

The chart combines greenhouse potency and volume. Carbon dioxide has a greenhouse potential of only 1, but its concentration of 350 parts per million makes it predominate. CFC 12, with 25,000 times the absorption capacity of CO_2, is present only as 0.00044 ppm.

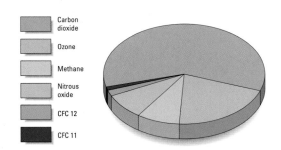

- Carbon dioxide
- Ozone
- Methane
- Nitrous oxide
- CFC 12
- CFC 11

Ozone Layer

The ozone 'hole' over the northern hemisphere on 12 March 1995.

The colours represent Dobson Units (DU). The ozone 'hole' is seen as the dark blue and purple patch in the centre, where ozone values are around 120 DU or lower. Normal levels are around 280 DU. The ozone 'hole' over Antarctica is much larger.

Carbon Dioxide
Carbon dioxide released in millions of tonnes (1992)

The Greenhouse Effect

Carbon dioxide is increased by burning fossil fuels and cutting forests

Carbon Dioxide

Carbon dioxide and other greenhouse gases trap the heat being reflected from the Earth, although some heat is lost

The warming increases water vapour in the air, leading to even greater absorption of heat

Rising temperatures would melt snow and ice causing oceans to rise

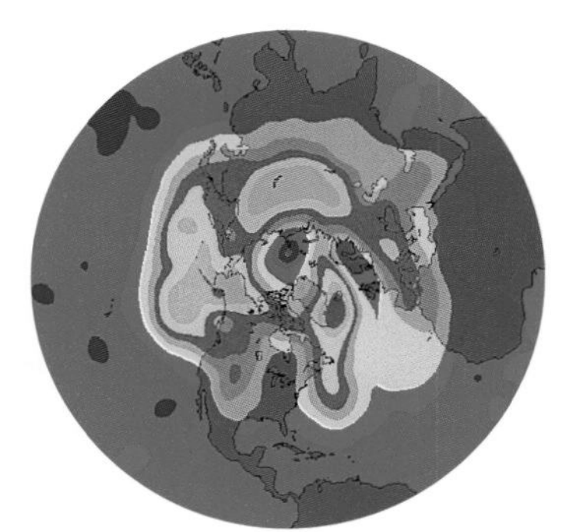

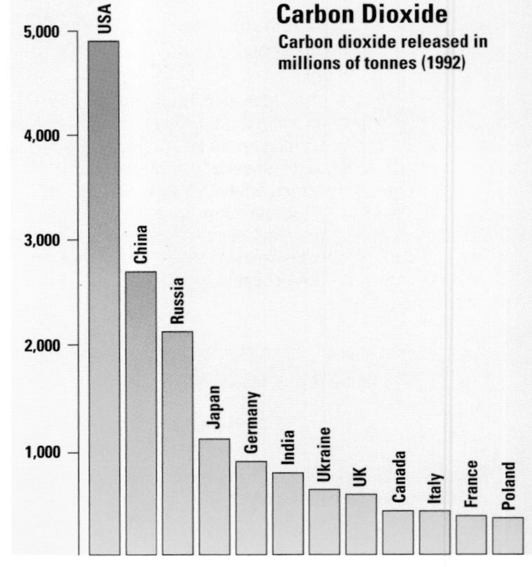

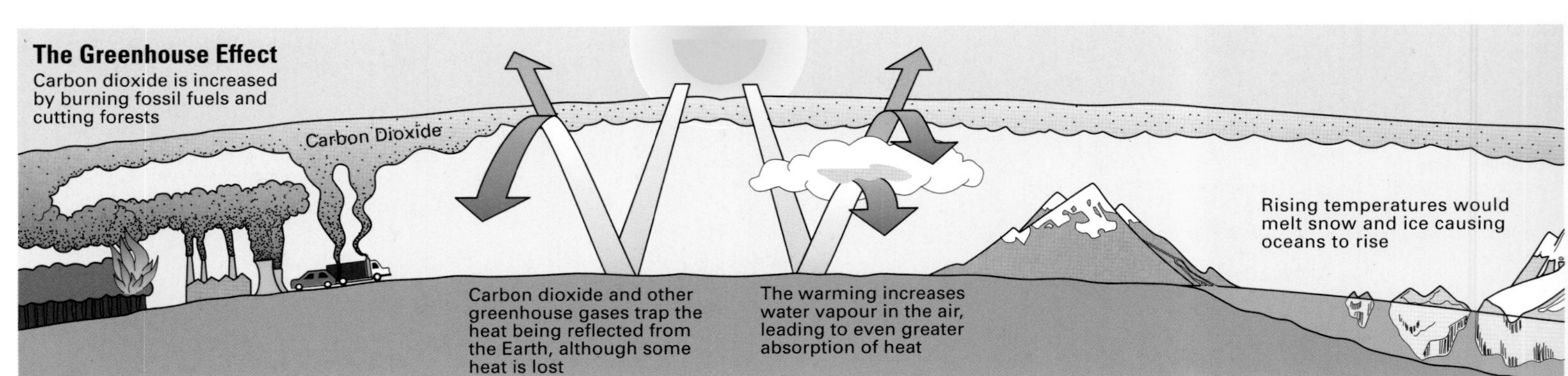

Desertification

- Existing deserts
- Areas with a high risk of desertification
- Areas with a moderate risk of desertification
- Former areas of rainforest
- Existing rainforest

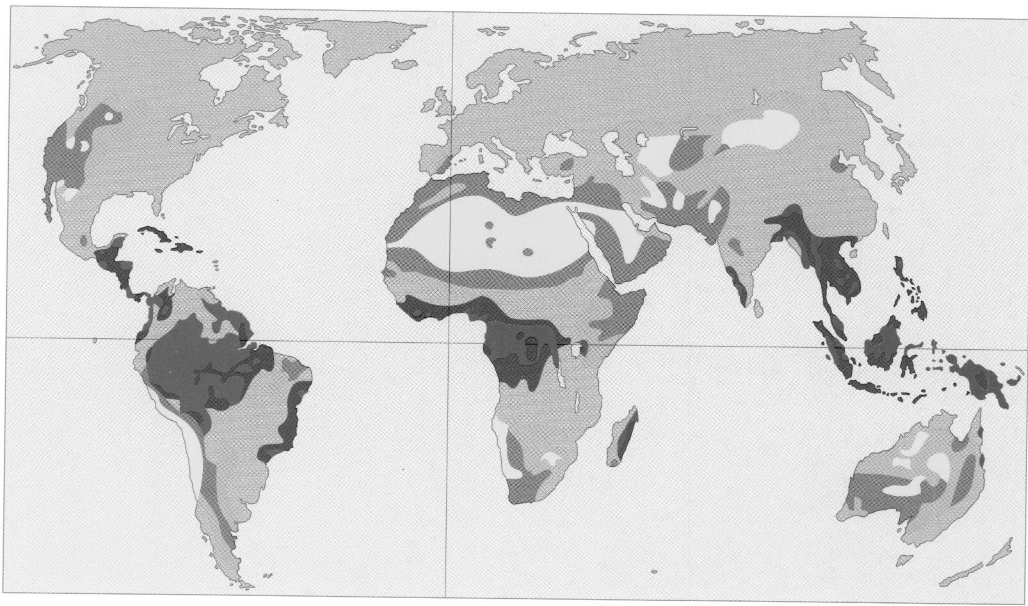

Forest Clearance

Thousands of hectares of forest cleared annually, tropical countries surveyed 1981–85 and 1987–90. Loss as a percentage of remaining stocks is shown in figures on each column.

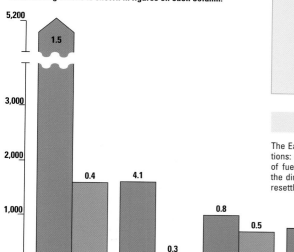

1987–90 **1981–85**

Brazil — 1.5, 0.4
India — 4.1, 0.3
Indonesia — 0.8, 0.5
Burma — 2.1, 0.3
Thailand — 2.5, 2.4
Vietnam — 2.0, 0.7
Philippines — 1.5, 1.0
Costa Rica — 7.6, 4.0
Cameroon — 0.6, 0.4

Deforestation

The Earth's remaining forests are under attack from three directions: expanding agriculture, logging, and growing consumption of fuelwood, often in combination. Sometimes deforestation is the direct result of government policy, as in the efforts made to resettle the urban poor in some parts of Brazil; just as often, it comes about despite state attempts at conservation. Loggers, licensed or unlicensed, blaze a trail into virgin forest, often destroying twice as many trees as they harvest. Landless farmers follow, burning away most of what remains to plant their crops, completing the destruction.

Ozone Depletion

The ozone layer, 25–30 km [15–18 miles] above sea level, acts as a barrier to most of the Sun's harmful ultra-violet radiation, protecting us from the ionizing radiation that can cause skin cancer and cataracts. In recent years, however, two holes in the ozone layer have been observed during winter: one over the Arctic and the other, the size of the USA, over Antarctica. By 1996, ozone had been reduced to around a half of its 1970 amount. The ozone (O_3) is broken down by chlorine released into the atmosphere as CFCs (chlorofluorocarbons) – chemicals used in refrigerators, packaging and aerosols.

Air Pollution

Sulphur dioxide is the main pollutant associated with industrial cities. According to the World Health Organization, at least 600 million people live in urban areas where sulphur dioxide concentrations regularly reach damaging levels. One of the world's most dangerously polluted urban areas is Mexico City, due to a combination of its enclosed valley location, 3 million cars and 60,000 factories. In May 1998, this lethal cocktail was added to by nearby forest fires and the resultant air pollution led to over 20% of the population (3 million people) complaining of respiratory problems.

Acid Rain

Killing trees, poisoning lakes and rivers and eating away buildings, acid rain is mostly produced by sulphur dioxide emissions from industry and volcanic eruptions. By the mid 1990s, acid rain had sterilized 4,000 or more of Sweden's lakes and left 45% of Switzerland's alpine conifers dead or dying, while the monuments of Greece were dissolving in Athens' smog. Prevailing wind patterns mean that the acids often fall many hundred kilometres from where the original pollutants were discharged. In parts of Europe acid deposition has slightly decreased, following reductions in emissions, but not by enough.

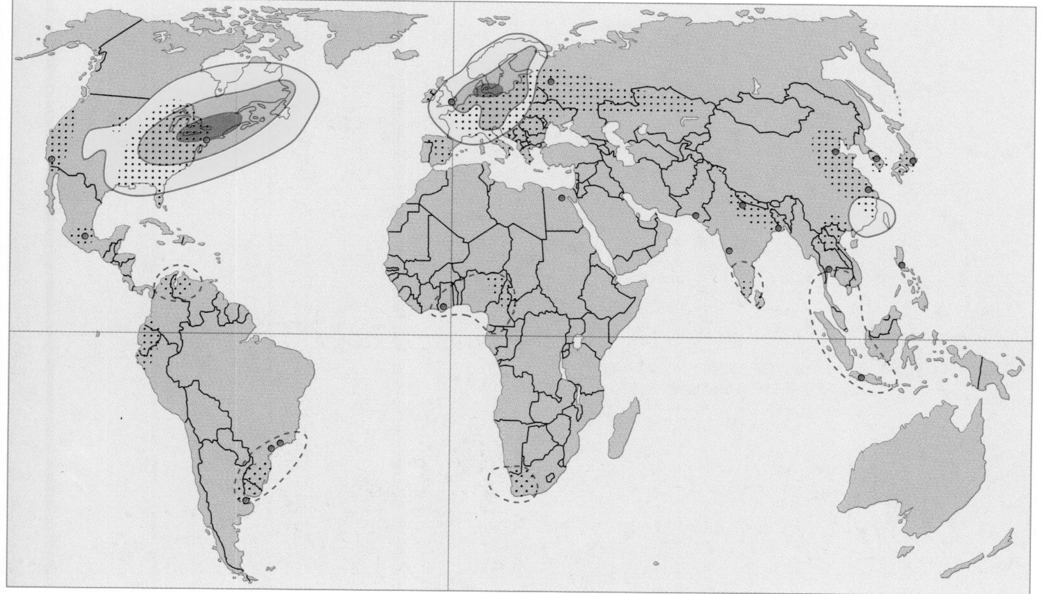

World Pollution

Acid rain and sources of acidic emissions (latest available year)

Acid rain is caused by high levels of sulphur and nitrogen in the atmosphere. They combine with water vapour and oxygen to form acids (H_2SO_4 and HNO_3) which fall as precipitation.

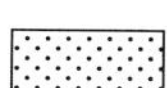

- Regions where sulphur and nitrogen oxides are released in high concentrations, mainly from fossil fuel combustion
- Major cities with high levels of air pollution (including nitrogen and sulphur emissions)

Areas of heavy acid deposition

pH numbers indicate acidity, decreasing from a neutral 7. Normal rain, slightly acid from dissolved carbon dioxide, never exceeds a pH of 5.6.

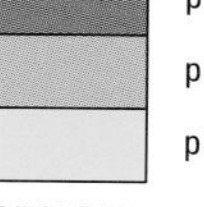

- pH less than 4.0 (most acidic)
- pH 4.0 to 4.5
- pH 4.5 to 5.0
- Areas where acid rain is a potential problem

Population

Demographic Profiles

Developed nations such as the UK have populations evenly spread across the age groups and, usually, a growing proportion of elderly people. The great majority of the people in developing nations, however, are in the younger age groups, about to enter their most fertile years. In time, these population profiles should resemble the world profile (even Kenya has made recent progress with reducing its birth rate), but the transition will come about only after a few more generations of rapid population growth.

World

UK **Kenya**

India **Saudi Arabia**

USA **China**

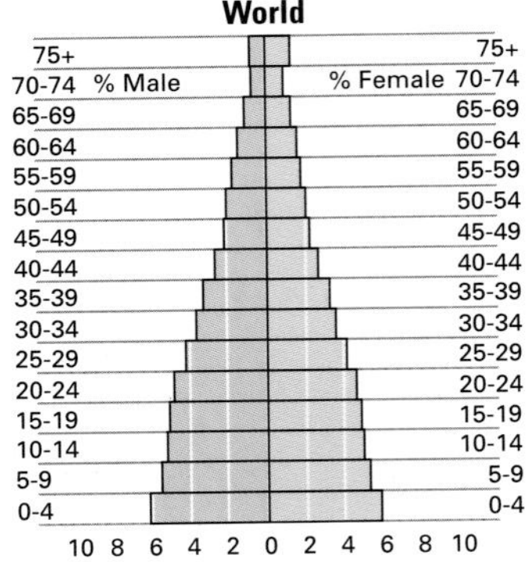

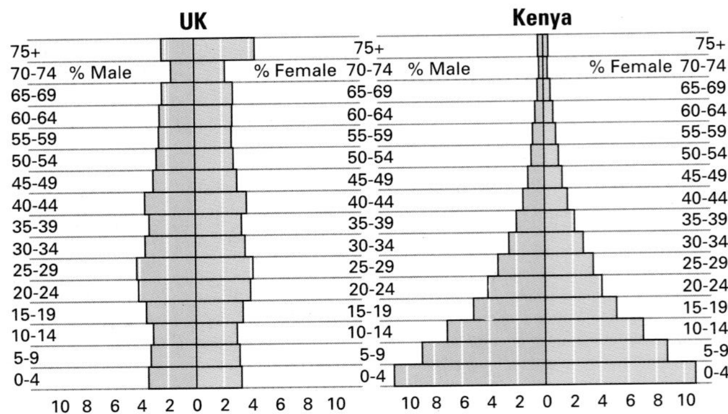

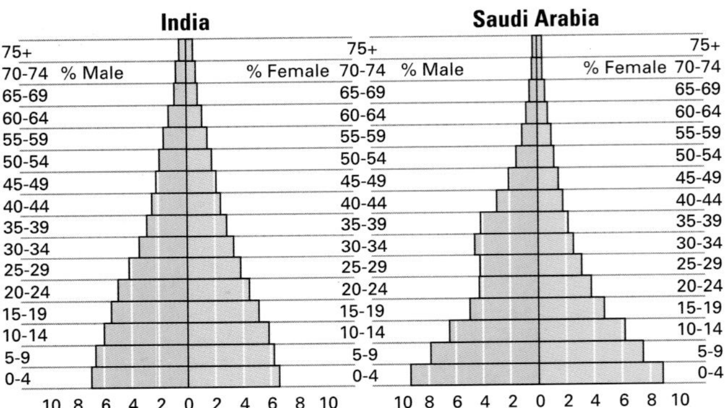

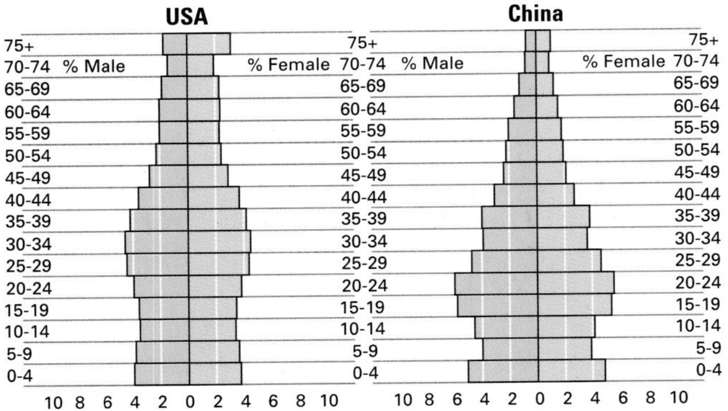

Most Populous Nations [in millions (2000 estimates)]

1.	China	1,299	9. Japan	128	17. Egypt	64
2.	India	1,041	10. Mexico	107	18. Thailand	63
3.	USA	266	11. Nigeria	105	19. Ethiopia	61
4.	Indonesia	218	12. Vietnam	82	20. France	58
5.	Brazil	179	13. Philippines	77	21. UK	58
6.	Pakistan	162	14. Germany	76	22. Italy	57
7.	Russia	155	15. Iran	68	23. Ukraine	52
8.	Bangladesh	150	16. Turkey	66	24. Burma	51

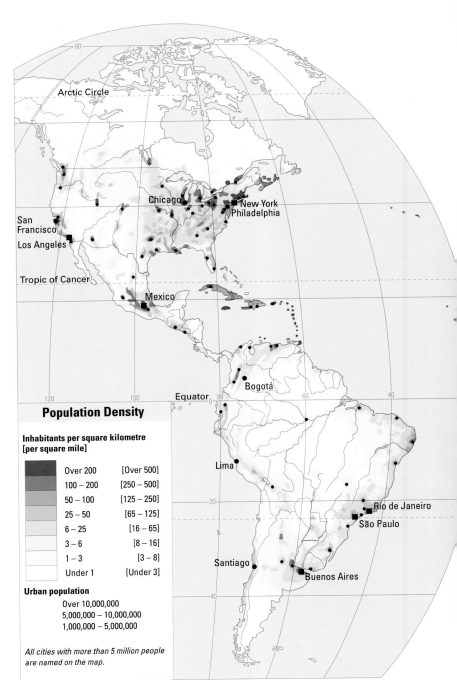

Population Density

Inhabitants per square kilometre [per square mile]

Over 200	[Over 500]
100 – 200	[250 – 500]
50 – 100	[125 – 250]
25 – 50	[65 – 125]
6 – 25	[16 – 65]
3 – 6	[8 – 16]
1 – 3	[3 – 8]
Under 1	[Under 3]

Urban population

Over 10,000,000
5,000,000 – 10,000,000
1,000,000 – 5,000,000

All cities with more than 5 million people are named on the map.

Continental Comparisons

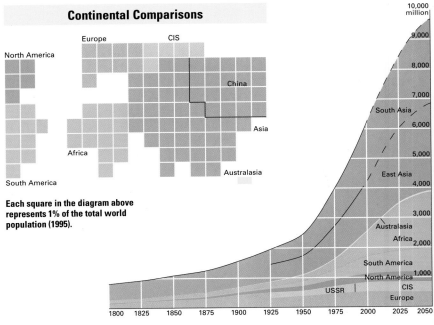

Each square in the diagram above represents 1% of the total world population (1995).

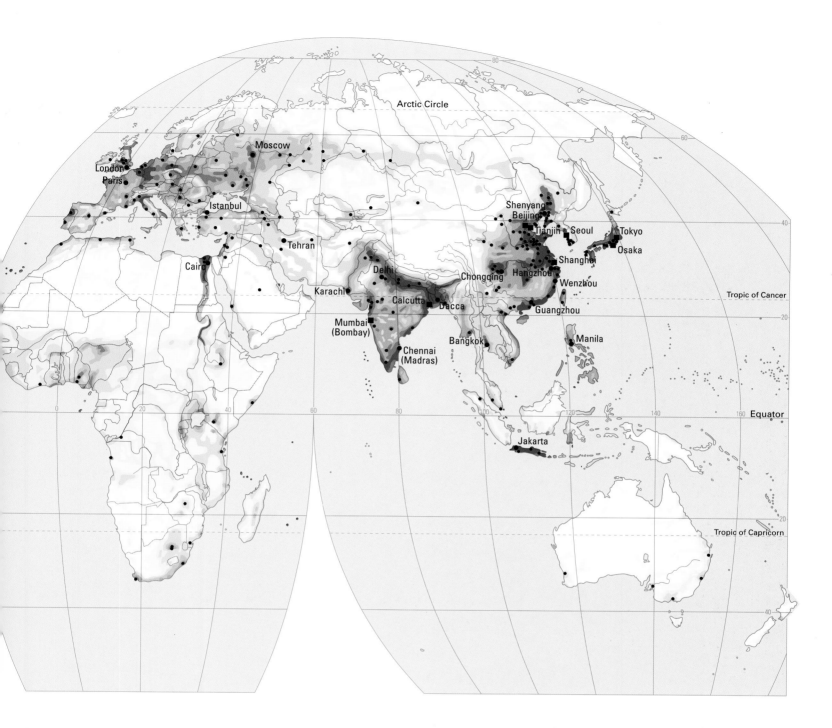

Moscow

London
Paris

Istanbul

Tehran

Cairo

Shenyang
Beijing
Tianjin · Seoul
Tokyo
Osaka
Shanghai

Delhi

Karachi

Calcutta
Dacca

Chongqing
Hangzhou

Wenzhou

Mumbai
(Bombay)

Guangzhou

Chennai
(Madras)

Bangkok

Manila

Jakarta

Arctic Circle

Tropic of Cancer

Equator

Tropic of Capricorn

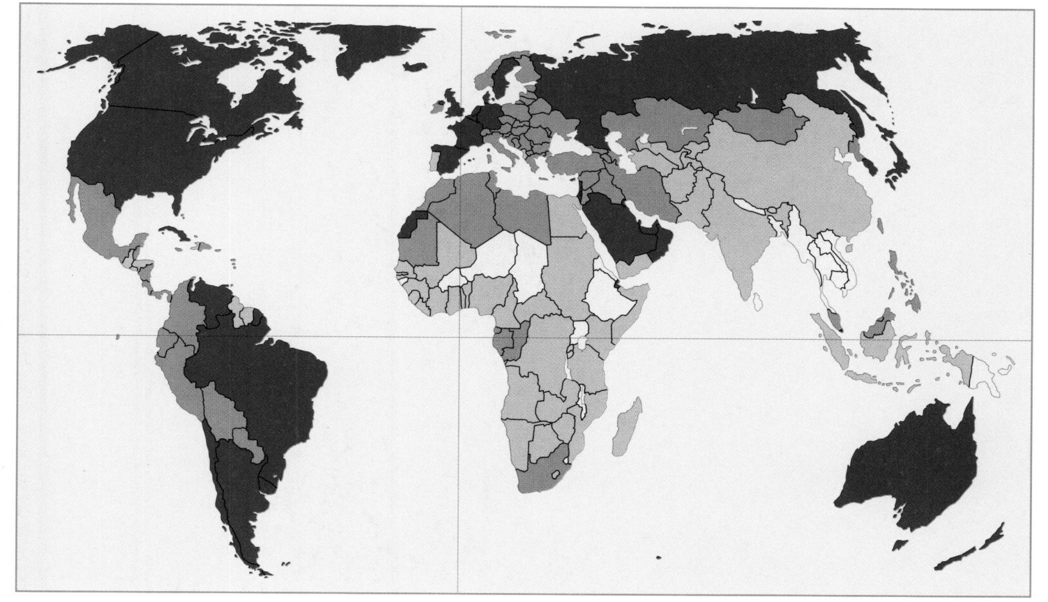

Urban Population

Percentage of total population living in towns and cities (1997)

■	Over 75%
▨	50 – 75%
▨	25 – 50%
□	10 – 25%
▨	Under 10%

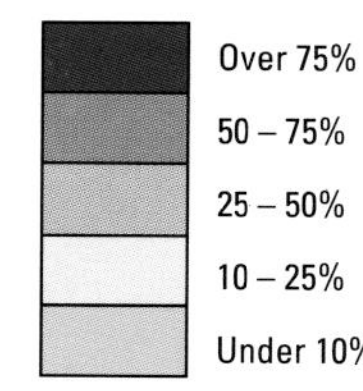

Most urbanized

Singapore	100%
Belgium	97%
Israel	91%
Uruguay	91%
Netherlands	89%

[UK 89%]

Least urbanized

Rwanda	6%
Bhutan	8%
Burundi	8%
Nepal	11%
Swaziland	12%

The Human Family

Predominant Languages

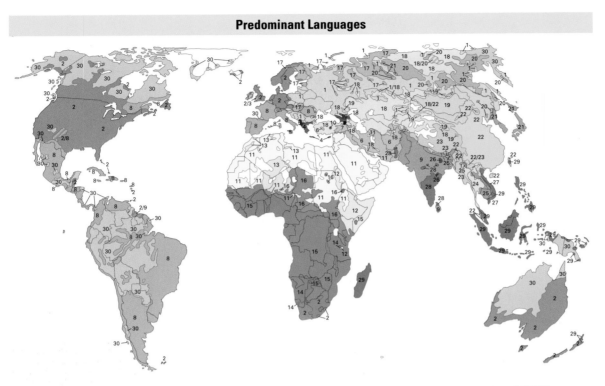

INDO-EUROPEAN FAMILY

1. Balto-Slavic group (incl. Russian, Ukrainian)
2. Germanic group (incl. English, German)
3. Celtic group
4. Greek
5. Albanian
6. Iranian group
7. Armenian
8. Romance group (incl. Spanish, Portuguese, French, Italian)
9. Indo-Aryan group (incl. Hindi, Bengali, Urdu, Punjabi, Marathi)
10. CAUCASIAN FAMILY

AFRO-ASIATIC FAMILY

11. Semitic group (incl. Arabic)
12. Kushitic group
13. Berber group

14. KHOISAN FAMILY

15. NIGER-CONGO FAMILY

16. NILO-SAHARAN FAMILY

17. URALIC FAMILY

ALTAIC FAMILY

18. Turkic group
19. Mongolian group
20. Tungus-Manchu group
21. Japanese and Korean

SINO-TIBETAN FAMILY

22. Sinitic (Chinese) languages
23. Tibetic-Burmic languages

24. TAI FAMILY

AUSTRO-ASIATIC FAMILY

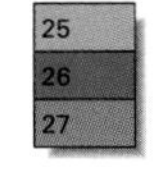

25. Mon-Khmer group
26. Munda group
27. Vietnamese

28. DRAVIDIAN FAMILY (incl. Telugu, Tamil)

29. AUSTRONESIAN FAMILY (incl. Malay-Indonesian)

30. OTHER LANGUAGES

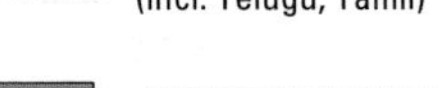

Predominant Religions

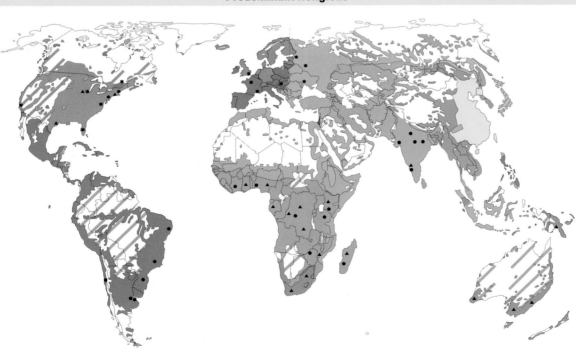

Religious Adherents

Religious adherents in millions:

Christian	1,669	Hindu	663
Roman Catholic	952	Buddhist	312
Protestant	337	Chinese Folk	172
Orthodox	162	Tribal	92
Anglican	70	Jewish	18
Other Christian	148	Sikhs	17
Muslim	966		
Sunni	841		
Shia	125		

- Roman Catholicism
- Orthodox and other Eastern Churches
- Protestantism
- Sunni Islam
- Shia Islam
- Buddhism
- Hinduism
- Confucianism
- Judaism
- Shintoism
- Tribal Religions

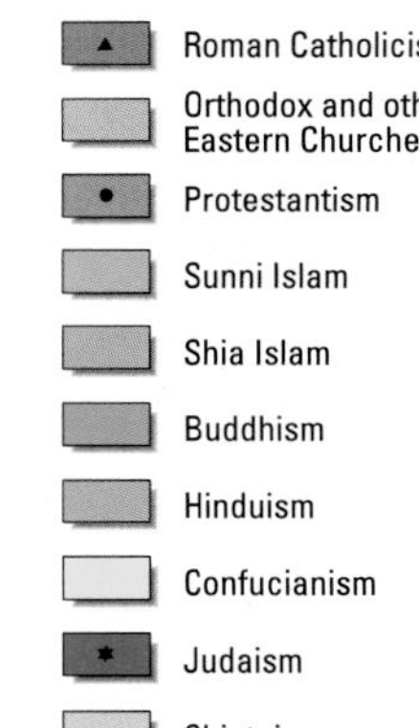

United Nations

Created in 1945 to promote peace and co-operation and based in New York, the United Nations is the world's largest international organization, with 185 members and an annual budget of US $2.6 billion (1996–97). Each member of the General Assembly has one vote, while the permanent members of the 15-nation Security Council – USA, Russia, China, UK and France – hold a veto. The Secretariat is the UN's principal administrative arm. The 54 members of the Economic and Social Council are responsible for economic, social, cultural, educational, health and related matters. The UN has 16 specialized agencies – based in Canada, France, Switzerland and Italy, as well as the USA – which help members in fields such as education (UNESCO), agriculture (FAO), medicine (WHO) and finance (IFC). By the end of 1994, all the original 11 trust territories of the Trusteeship Council had become independent.

Members of UN
Year of joining
- 1940s
- 1950s
- 1960s
- 1970s
- 1980s
- 1990s
- Non-members

★ 1%–10% contribution to funding
☆ Over 10% contribution to funding

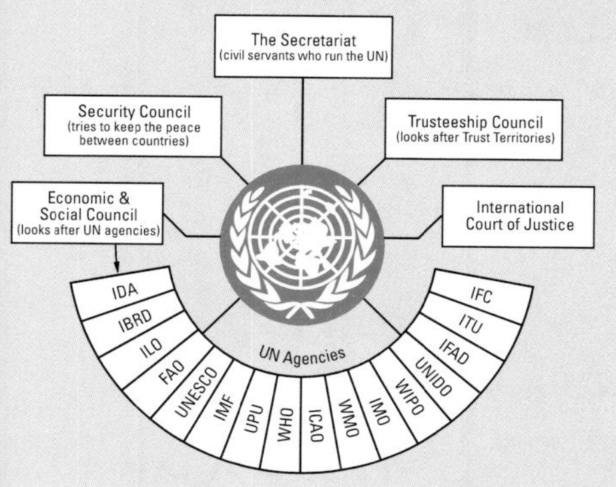

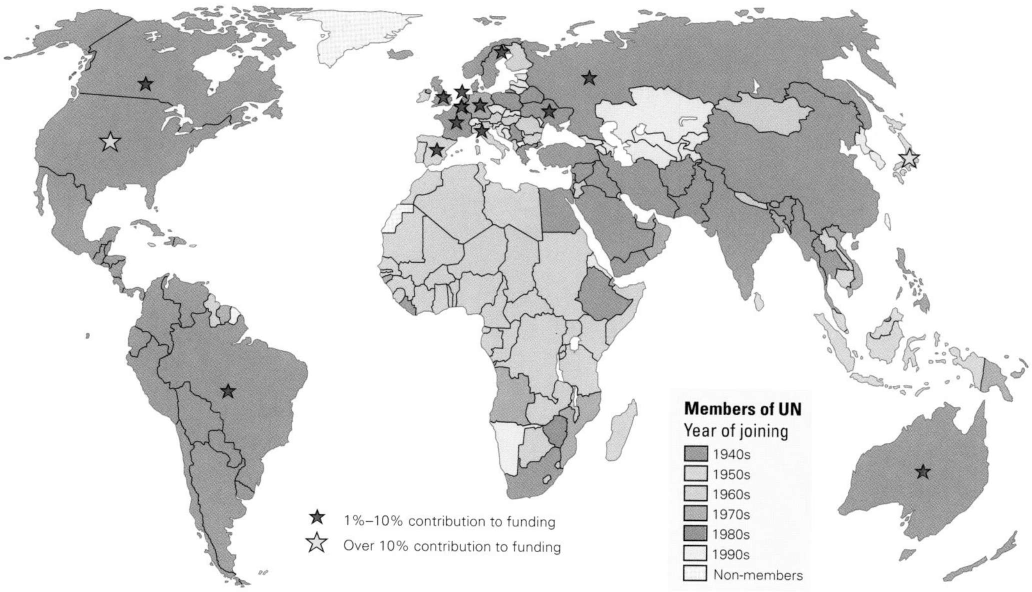

MEMBERSHIP OF THE UN In 1945 there were 51 members; by 2000 membership had increased to 188 following the admission of Kiribati, Nauru and Tonga. There are 4 independent states which are not members of the UN – Switzerland, Taiwan, Tuvalu and the Vatican City. All the successor states of the former USSR had joined by the end of 1992. The official languages of the UN are Chinese, English, French, Russian, Spanish and Arabic.

FUNDING The UN budget for 1996–97 was US $2.6 billion. Contributions are assessed by the members' ability to pay, with the maximum 25% of the total, the minimum 0.01%. Contributions for 1996 were: USA 25.0%, Japan 15.4%, Germany 9.0%, France 6.4%, UK 5.3%, Italy 5.2%, Russia 4.5%, Canada 3.1%, Spain 2.4%, Brazil 1.6%, Netherlands 1.6%, Australia 1.5%, Sweden 1.2%, Ukraine 1.1%, Belgium 1.0%.

International Organizations

EU European Union (evolved from the European Community in 1993). The 15 members – Austria, Belgium, Denmark, Finland, France, Germany, Greece, Ireland, Italy, Luxembourg, Netherlands, Portugal, Spain, Sweden and the UK – aim to integrate economies, co-ordinate social developments and bring about political union. These members of what is now the world's biggest market share agricultural and industrial policies and tariffs on trade. The original body, the European Coal and Steel Community (ECSC), was created in 1951 following the signing of the Treaty of Paris.

EFTA European Free Trade Association (formed in 1960). Portugal left the original 'Seven' in 1989 to join what was then the EC, followed by Austria, Finland and Sweden in 1995. Only 4 members remain: Norway, Iceland, Switzerland and Liechtenstein.

ACP African-Caribbean-Pacific (formed in 1963). Members have economic ties with the EU.

NATO North Atlantic Treaty Organization (formed in 1949). It continues after 1991 despite the winding up of the Warsaw Pact. The Czech Republic, Hungary and Poland were the latest members to join in 1999.

OAS Organization of American States (formed in 1948). It aims to promote social and economic co-operation between developed countries of North America and developing nations of Latin America.

ASEAN Association of South-east Asian Nations (formed in 1967). Cambodia joined in 1999.

OAU Organization of African Unity (formed in 1963). Its 53 members represent over 94% of Africa's population. Arabic, French, Portuguese and English are recognized as working languages.

LAIA Latin American Integration Association (1980). Its aim is to promote freer regional trade.

OECD Organization for Economic Co-operation and Development (formed in 1961). It comprises the 29 major Western free-market economies. Poland, Hungary and South Korea joined in 1996. 'G8' is its 'inner group' comprising Canada, France, Germany, Italy, Japan, Russia, the UK and the USA.

COMMONWEALTH The Commonwealth of Nations evolved from the British Empire; it comprises 16 Queen's realms, 32 republics and 5 indigenous monarchies, giving a total of 53.

OPEC Organization of Petroleum Exporting Countries (formed in 1960). It controls about three-quarters of the world's oil supply. Gabon left the organization in 1996.

OAS　EFTA　EU　OAU　COLOMBO PLAN

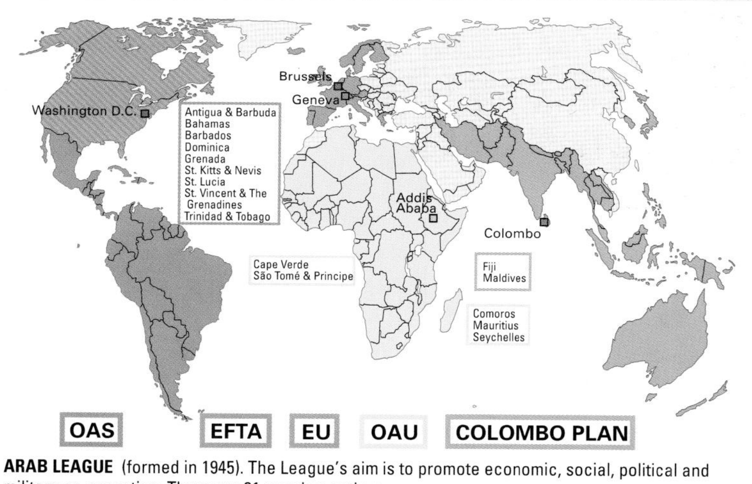

ARAB LEAGUE (formed in 1945). The League's aim is to promote economic, social, political and military co-operation. There are 21 member nations.

COLOMBO PLAN (formed in 1951). Its 26 members aim to promote economic and social development in Asia and the Pacific.

★ G8

OECD　ACP　OPEC　CIS

NATO　LAIA　ARAB LEAGUE　COMMONWEALTH　ASEAN

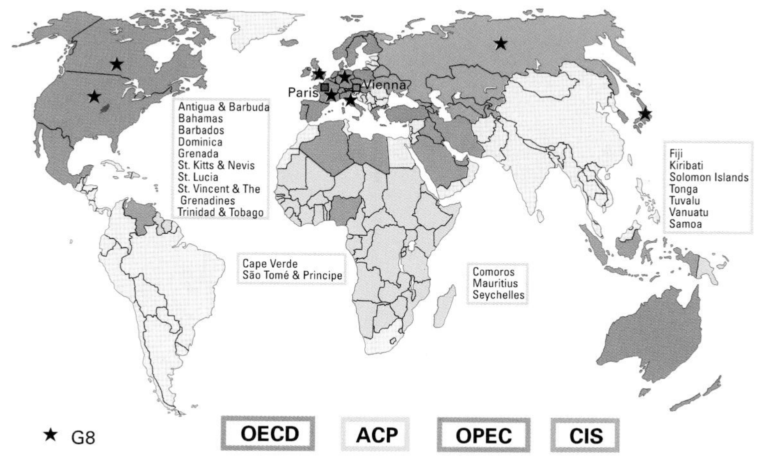

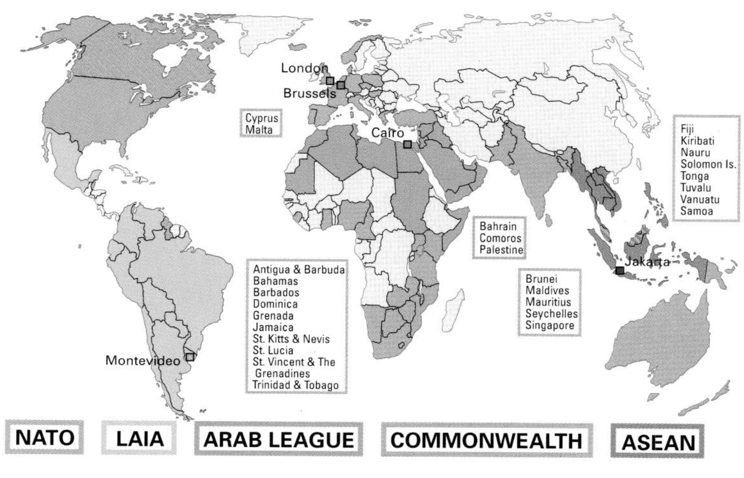

Wealth

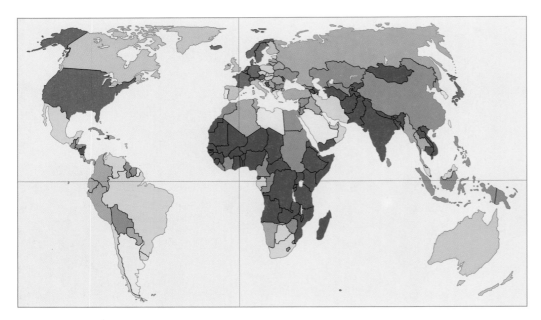

Levels of Income

Gross National Product per capita: the value of total production divided by the population (1997)

- Over 400% of world average
- 200 – 400% of world average
- 100 – 200% of world average

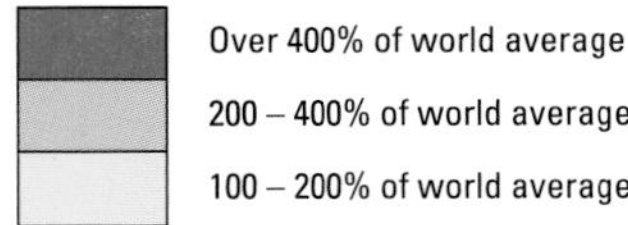

[World average wealth per person US $6,316]

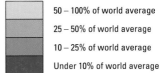

- 50 – 100% of world average
- 25 – 50% of world average
- 10 – 25% of world average
- Under 10% of world average

GNP per capita growth rate (%), selected countries, 1985–94

Thailand	8.2	Brazil	–0.4
Chile	6.9	Zimbabwe	–0.6
Japan	3.2	USA	–1.3
Germany	1.9	UK	–1.4
Australia	1.2	Armenia	–12.9

Wealth Creation

The Gross National Product (GNP) of the world's largest economies, US $ million (1998)

1.	USA	7,922,651	23.	Saudi Arabia	186,000
2.	Japan	4,089,910	24.	Denmark	176,374
3.	Germany	2,122,673	25.	Hong Kong	158,286
4.	Italy	1,666,178	26.	Norway	152,082
5.	France	1,466,014	27.	Poland	150,798
6.	UK	1,263,777	28.	Indonesia	138,501
7.	China	928,950	29.	Thailand	134,433
8.	Botswana	758,043	30.	Finland	124,293
9.	Canada	612,332	31.	Greece	122,880
10.	Spain	553,690	32.	South Africa	119,001
11.	India	421,259	33.	Iran	109,645
12.	Netherlands	388,682	34.	Portugal	106,376
13.	Mexico	380,917	35.	Colombia	106,090
14.	Australia	380,625	36.	Israel	95,179
15.	South Korea	369,890	37.	Singapore	95,095
16.	Russia	337,914	38.	Venezuela	81,347
17.	Argentina	324,084	39.	Malaysia	79,848
18.	Switzerland	284,808	40.	Egypt	79,208
19.	Belgium	259,045	41.	Philippines	78,896
20.	Sweden	226,861	42.	Chile	71,294
21.	Austria	217,163	43.	Ireland	67,491
22.	Turkey	200,505	44.	Pakistan	63,159

The Wealth Gap

The world's richest and poorest countries, by Gross National Product per capita in US $ (1998)

1.	Liechtenstein	50,000	1.	Ethiopia	100
2.	Luxembourg	43,570	2.	Congo (D. Rep.)	110
3.	Switzerland	40,080	3.	Burundi	140
4.	Norway	34,330	4.	Sierra Leone	140
5.	Bermuda	34,000	5.	Guinea-Bissau	160
6.	Denmark	33,260	6.	Niger	190
7.	Japan	32,380	7.	Eritrea	200
8.	Singapore	30,060	8.	Malawi	200
9.	USA	29,340	9.	Mozambique	210
10.	Iceland	28,010	10.	Nepal	210
11.	Austria	26,850	11.	Tanzania	210
12.	Germany	25,850	12.	Chad	230
13.	Sweden	25,620	13.	Rwanda	230
14.	Belgium	25,380	14.	Burkina Faso	240
15.	Monaco	25,000	15.	Mali	250
16.	France	24,940	16.	Madagascar	260
17.	Netherlands	24,760	17.	Cambodia	280
18.	Finland	24,110	18.	São Tomé & Príncipe	280
19.	Brunei	24,000	19.	Sudan	290
20.	Hong Kong	23,670	20.	Central African Rep.	300

GNP per capita is calculated by dividing a country's Gross National Product by its total population.

Continental Shares

Shares of population and of wealth (GNP) by continent

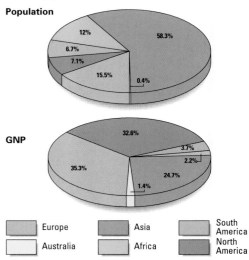

Population

GNP

- Europe
- Asia
- South America
- Australia
- Africa
- North America

Inflation

Average annual rate of inflation (1990–96)

- Over 50%
- 20 – 50%
- 7.5 – 20%
- 1 – 7.5%
- Negative inflation
- No data available

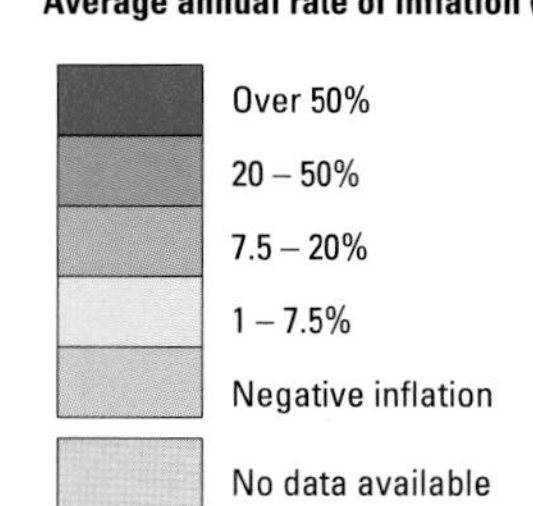

Highest average inflation		Lowest average inflation	
Congo (D. Rep.)	2747%	Oman	–3.0%
Georgia	2279%	Bahrain	–0.5%
Angola	1103%	Brunei	–0.0%
Turkmenistan	1074%	Saudi Araba	1.0%

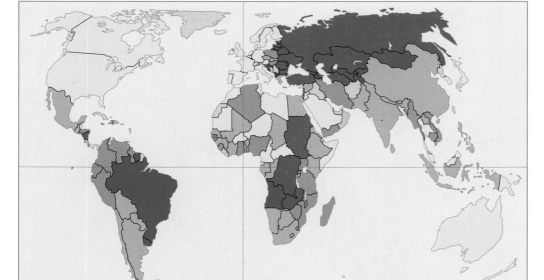

Armenia	897%	Japan	1.0%

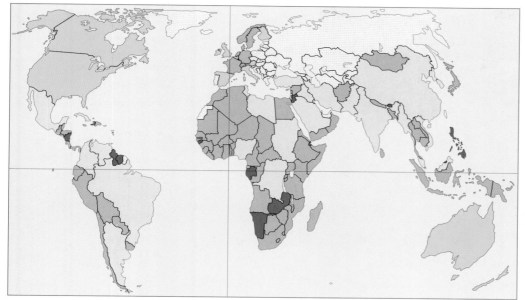

Aid provided or received, divided by the total population, in US $ (1995)

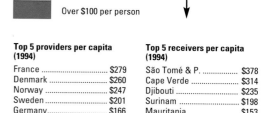

Over $100 per person
$10 – $100 per person
$0 – $10 per person
No aid given or received
$0 – $10 per person
$10 – $100 per person
Over $100 per person

Providers

Receivers

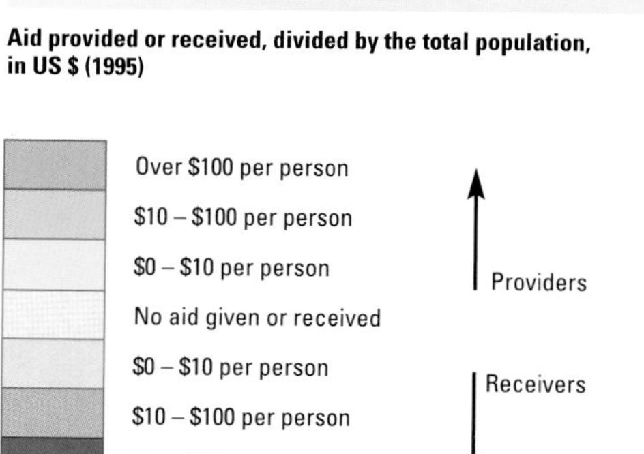

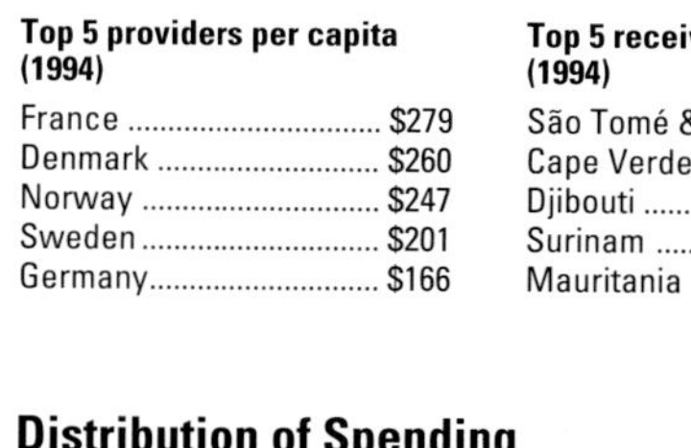

Top 5 providers per capita (1994)

France	$279
Denmark	$260
Norway	$247
Sweden	$201
Germany	$166

Top 5 receivers per capita (1994)

São Tomé & P.	$378
Cape Verde	$314
Djibouti	$235
Surinam	$198
Mauritania	$153

Debt and Aid

International debtors and the aid they receive (1996)

Although aid grants make a vital contribution to many of the world's poorer countries, they are usually dwarfed by the burden of debt that the developing economies are expected to repay. In 1992, they had to pay US $160,000 million in debt service charges alone – more than two and a half times the amount of Official Development Assistance (ODA) the developing countries were receiving, and US $60,000 million more than total private flows of aid in the same year. In 1990, the debts of Mozambique, one of the world's poorest countries, were estimated to be 75 times its entire earnings from exports.

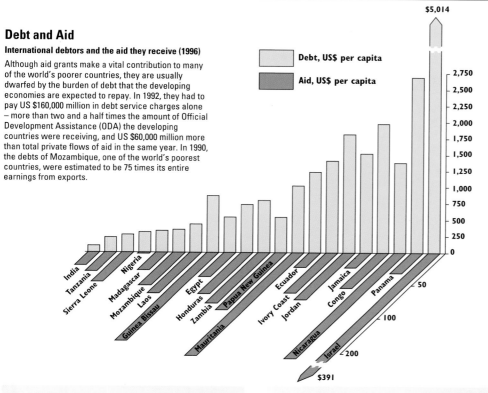

Debt, US$ per capita
Aid, US$ per capita

Distribution of Spending

Percentage share of household spending, selected countries

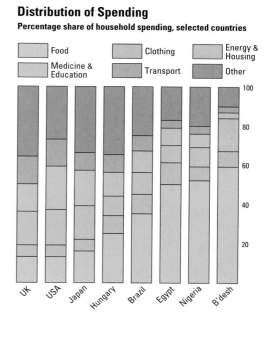

Food
Medicine & Education
Clothing
Transport
Energy & Housing
Other

UK USA Japan Hungary Brazil Egypt Nigeria B'desh

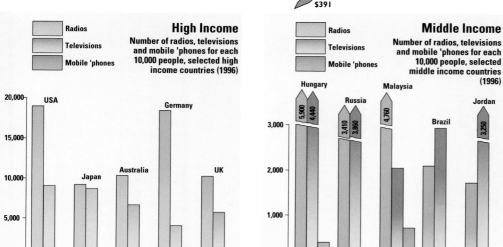

High Income

Radios
Televisions
Mobile 'phones

Number of radios, televisions and mobile 'phones for each 10,000 people, selected high income countries (1996)

Middle Income

Radios
Televisions
Mobile 'phones

Number of radios, televisions and mobile 'phones for each 10,000 people, selected middle income countries (1996)

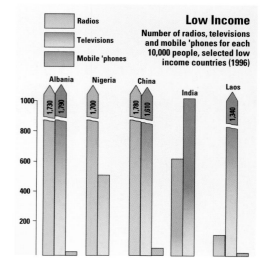

Low Income

Radios
Televisions
Mobile 'phones

Number of radios, televisions and mobile 'phones for each 10,000 people, selected low income countries (1996)

Quality of Life

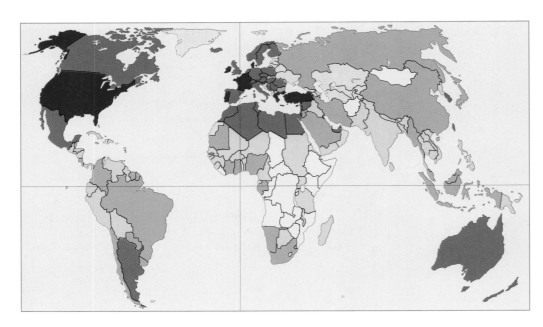

Daily Food Consumption

Average daily food intake in calories per person (1995)

- Over 3,500 calories per person
- 3,000 – 3,500 calories per person
- 2,500 – 3,000 calories per person
- 2,000 – 2,500 calories per person
- Under 2,000 calories per person
- No available data

Top 5 countries

Cyprus	3,708 cal.
Denmark	3,704 cal.
Portugal	3,639 cal.
Ireland	3,638 cal.
USA	3,603 cal.

Bottom 5 countries

Congo (D.Rep.)	1,879 cal.
Djibouti	1,831 cal.
Togo	1,754 cal.
Burundi	1,749 cal.
Mozambique	1,678 cal.

[UK 3,149 calories]

Hospital Capacity

Hospital beds available for each 1,000 people (1996)

Highest capacity		Lowest capacity	
Switzerland	20.8	Benin	0.2
Japan	16.2	Nepal	0.2
Tajikistan	16.0	Afghanistan	0.3
Norway	13.5	Bangladesh	0.3
Belarus	12.4	Ethiopia	0.3
Kazakstan	12.2	Mali	0.4
Moldova	12.2	Burkina Faso	0.5
Ukraine	12.2	Niger	0.5
Latvia	11.9	Guinea	0.6
Russia	11.8	India	0.6

[UK 4.9] [USA 4.2]

Although the ratio of people to hospital beds gives a good approximation of a country's health provision, it is not an absolute indicator. Raw numbers may mask inefficiency and other weaknesses: the high availability of beds in Kazakstan, for example, has not prevented infant mortality rates over three times as high as in the United Kingdom and the United States.

Life Expectancy

Years of life expectancy at birth, selected countries (1997)

The chart shows combined data for both sexes. On average, women live longer than men worldwide, even in developing countries with high maternal mortality rates. Overall, life expectancy is steadily rising, though the difference between rich and poor nations remains dramatic.

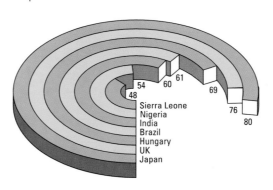

Causes of Death

Causes of death for selected countries by % (1992–94)

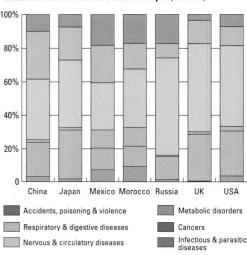

- Accidents, poisoning & violence
- Respiratory & digestive diseases
- Nervous & circulatory diseases
- Metabolic disorders
- Cancers
- Infectious & parasitic diseases

Child Mortality

Number of babies who will die under the age of one, per 1,000 births (average 1990–95)

- Over 150 deaths per 1,000 births
- 100 – 150 deaths per 1,000 births
- 50 – 100 deaths per 1,000 births
- 20 – 50 deaths per 1,000 births
- 10 – 20 deaths per 1,000 births
- Under 10 deaths per 1,000 births

Highest child mortality		Lowest child mortality	
Afghanistan	162	Hong Kong	6
Mali	159	Denmark	6
Sierra Leone	143	Japan	5
Guinea-Bissau	140	Iceland	5
Malawi	138	Finland	5

[UK 8 deaths]

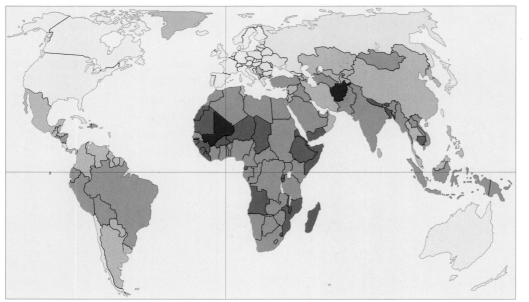

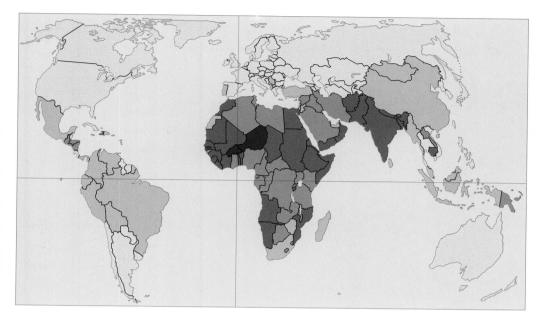

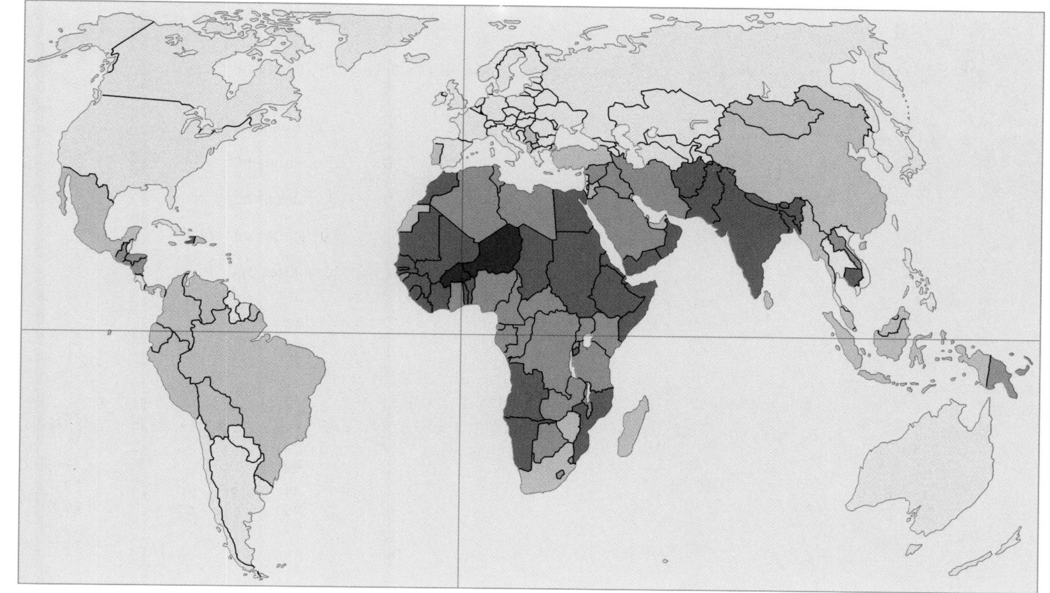

Illiteracy

Percentage of the total population unable to read or write (latest available year)

- Over 75% of population illiterate
- 50 – 75% of population illiterate
- 25 – 50% of population illiterate
- 10 – 25% of population illiterate
- Under 10% of population illiterate

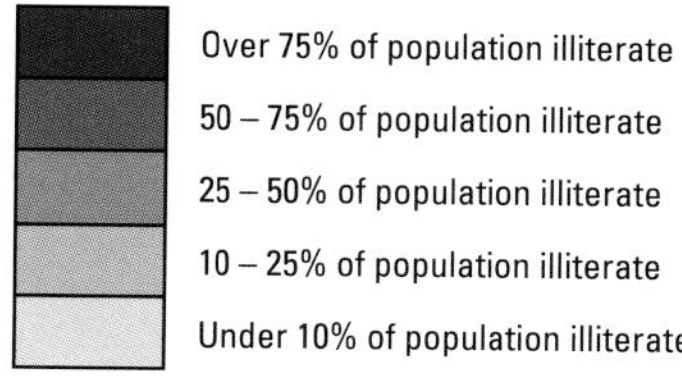

Educational expenditure per person (latest available year)

Top 5 countries		Bottom 5 countries	
Sweden	$997	Chad	$2
Qatar	$989	Bangladesh	$3
Canada	$983	Ethiopia	$3
Norway	$971	Nepal	$4
Switzerland	$796	Somalia	$4

Fertility and Education

Fertility rates compared with female education, selected countries (1992–95)

- Percentage of females aged 12–17 in secondary education
- Fertility rate: average number of children borne per woman

Countries (left to right): Denmark, Austria, France, Canada, Belgium, Switzerland, UK, Poland, Australia, Sri Lanka, Malaysia, Turkey, Saudi Arabia, Thailand, Bolivia, Nigeria, Sierra Leone, Niger

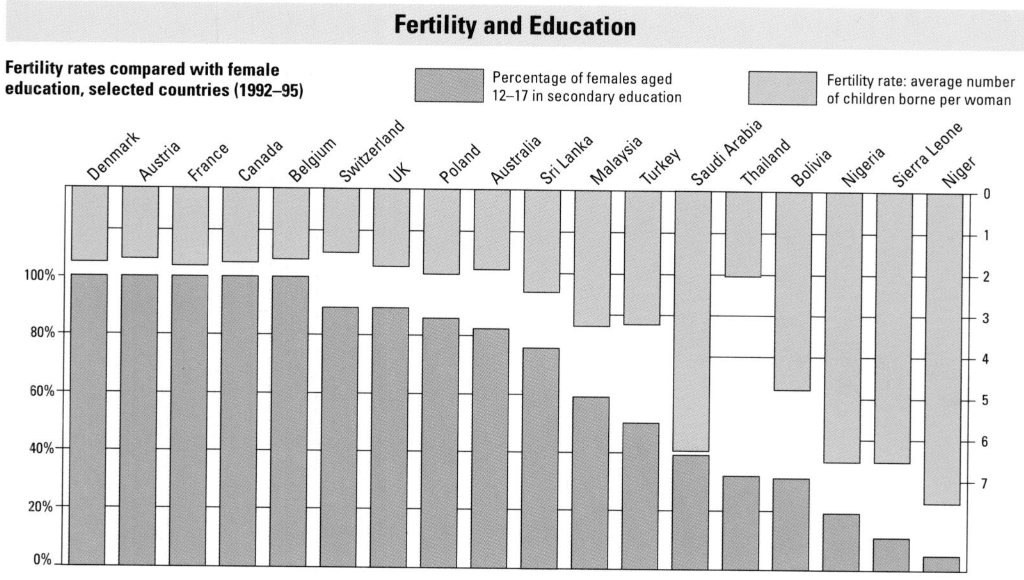

Living Standards

At first sight, most international contrasts in living standards are swamped by differences in wealth. The rich not only have more money, they have more of everything, including years of life. Those with only a little money are obliged to spend most of it on food and clothing, the basic maintenance costs of their existence; air travel and tourism are unlikely to feature on their expenditure lists. However, poverty and wealth are both relative: slum dwellers living on social security payments in an affluent industrial country have far more resources at their disposal than an average African peasant, but feel their own poverty nonetheless. A middle-class Indian lawyer cannot command a fraction of the earnings of a counterpart living in New York, London or Rome; nevertheless, he rightly sees himself as prosperous.

The rich not only live longer, on average, than the poor, they also die from different causes. Infectious and parasitic diseases, all but eliminated in the developed world, remain a scourge in the developing nations. On the other hand, more than two-thirds of the populations of OECD nations eventually succumb to cancer or circulatory disease.

Women in the Workforce

Women in paid employment as a percentage of the total workforce (latest available year)

- Over 50% are women
- 40 – 50% are women
- 30 – 40% are women
- 20 – 30% are women
- 10 – 20% are women
- Under 10% are women

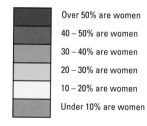

Most women in the workforce		Fewest women in the workforce	
Cambodia	56%	Saudi Arabia	4%
Kazakstan	54%	Oman	6%
Burundi	53%	Afghanistan	8%
Mozambique	53%	Algeria	9%
Turkmenistan	52%	Libya	9%

[USA 45] [UK 44]

CARTOGRAPHY BY PHILIP'S. COPYRIGHT GEORGE PHILIP LTD

Energy

Production

[Each square represents 1% of world energy production]

North America

Europe

CIS

Middle East

Africa

Asia

Japan

South America

Australasia

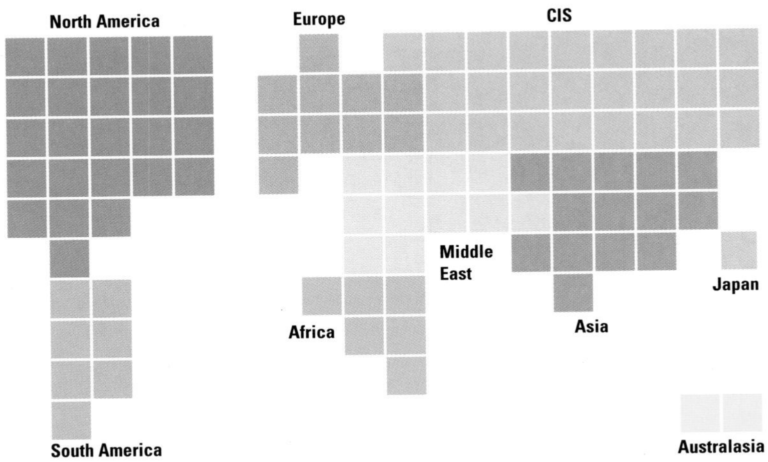

Consumption

[Each square represents 1% of world energy consumption]

North America

Europe

CIS

Middle East

Africa

Asia

Japan

South America

Australasia

Prudhoe Bay
Medicine Hat
California
Texas
Gulf of Mexico
Venezuela
Ecuador
Rio Grande/ Santa Catarina

North Sea
Ruhr
Silesia
Donbas
Yamburg
Algeria
The Gulf
Oman
Nigeria
Transvaal/ Natal

Tangshan
Shanxi
Chongqing
Bihar
Sumatra

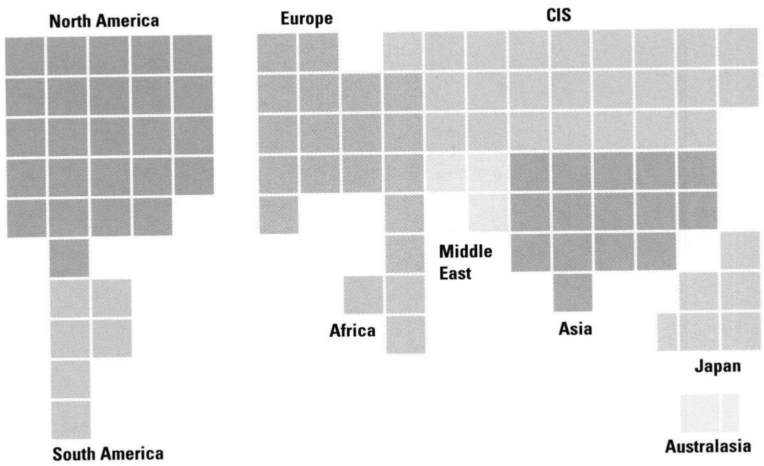

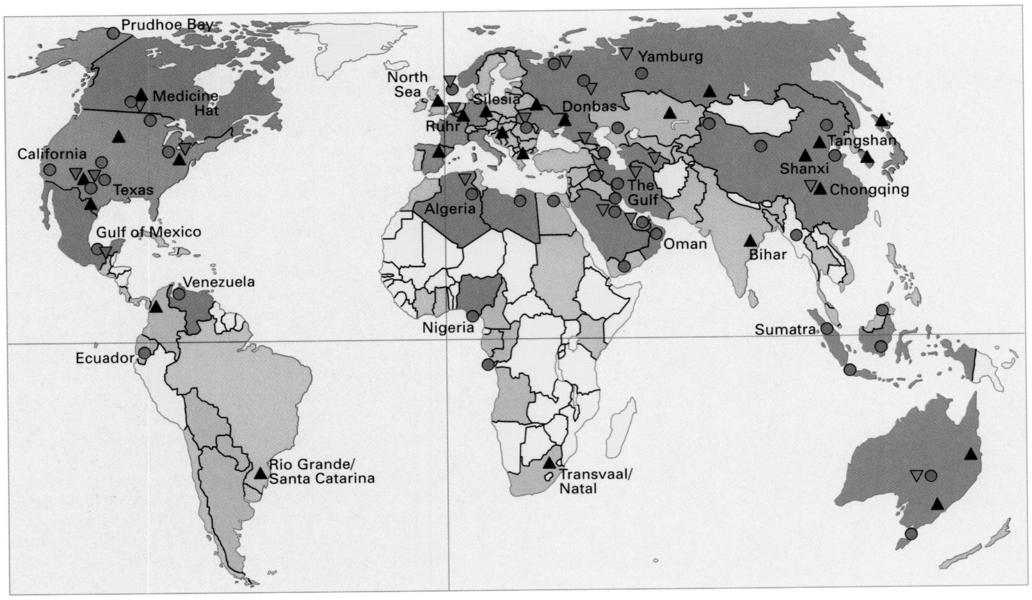

Energy Balance

Difference between energy production and consumption in millions of tonnes of oil equivalent (MtOe) (1993)

Energy deficit ↑

Over 35 MtOe

1 – 35 MtOe

Approx. balance

1 – 35 MtOe

Over 35 MtOe

Energy surplus ↓

⬤ Major oilfields

▽ Major gasfields

▲ Major coalfields

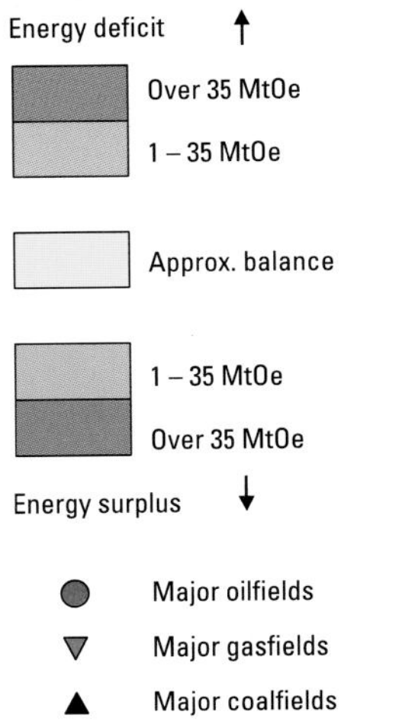

World Energy Consumption

Energy consumed by world regions, measured in million tonnes of oil equivalent in 1997. Total world consumption was 8,509 MtOe. Only energy from oil, gas, coal, nuclear and hydroelectric sources are included. Excluded are fuels such as wood, peat, animal waste, wind, solar and geothermal which, though important in some countries, are unreliably documented in terms of consumption statistics.

Australasia

Africa

Middle East

Latin America

Western Europe

CIS & Eastern Europe

Asia

North America

Oil Gas Coal
Nuclear Hydro

2.7%
7.3%
39.9%
26.9%
23.2%

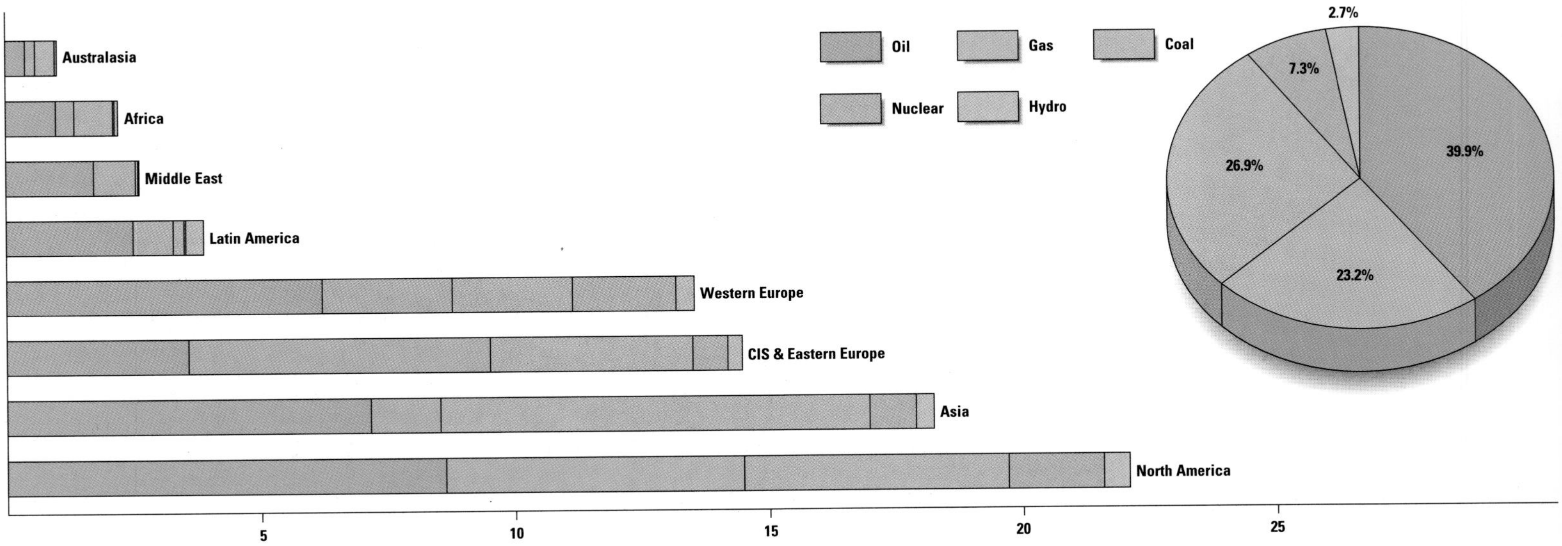

Energy

Energy is used to keep us warm or cool, fuel our industries and our transport systems, and even feed us; high-intensity agriculture, with its use of fertilizers, pesticides and machinery, is heavily energy-dependent. Although we live in a high-energy society, there are vast discrepancies between rich and poor; for example, a North American consumes 13 times as much energy as a Chinese person. But even developing nations have more power at their disposal than was imaginable a century ago.

The distribution of energy supplies, most importantly fossil fuels (coal, oil and natural gas), is very uneven. In addition, the diagrams and map opposite show that the largest producers of energy are not necessarily the largest consumers. The movement of energy supplies around the world is therefore an important component of international trade. In 1995, total world movements in oil amounted to 1,815 million tonnes.

As the finite reserves of fossil fuels are depleted, renewable energy sources, such as solar, hydro-thermal, wind, tidal and biomass, will become increasingly important around the world.

Nuclear Power

Percentage of electricity generated by nuclear power stations, leading nations (1995)

1.	Lithuania	85%	11.	Spain	33%
2.	France	77%	12.	Finland	30%
3.	Belgium	56%	13.	Germany	29%
4.	Slovak Rep.	49%	14.	Japan	29%
5.	Sweden	48%	15.	UK	27%
6.	Bulgaria	41%	16.	Ukraine	27%
7.	Hungary	41%	17.	Czech Rep.	22%
8.	Switzerland	39%	18.	Canada	19%
9.	Slovenia	38%	19.	USA	18%
10.	South Korea	33%	20.	Russia	12%

Although the 1980s were a bad time for the nuclear power industry (major projects ran over budget, and fears of long-term environmental damage were heavily reinforced by the 1986 disaster at Chernobyl), the industry picked up in the early 1990s. However, whilst the number of reactors is still increasing, orders for new plants have shrunk. This is partly due to the increasingly difficult task of disposing of nuclear waste.

Hydroelectricity

Percentage of electricity generated by hydroelectric power stations, leading nations (1995)

1.	Paraguay	99.9%	11.	Rwanda	97.6%
2.	Congo (Zaïre)	99.7%	12.	Malawi	97.6%
3.	Bhutan	99.6%	13.	Cameroon	96.9%
4.	Zambia	99.5%	14.	Nepal	96.7%
5.	Norway	99.4%	15.	Laos	95.3%
6.	Ghana	99.3%	16.	Albania	95.2%
7.	Congo	99.3%	17.	Iceland	94.0%
8.	Uganda	99.1%	17.	Brazil	92.2%
9.	Burundi	98.3%	19.	Honduras	87.6%
10.	Uruguay	98.0%	20.	Tanzania	87.1%

Countries heavily reliant on hydroelectricity are usually small and non-industrial: a high proportion of hydroelectric power more often reflects a modest energy budget than vast hydroelectric resources. The USA, for instance, produces only 9% of power requirements from hydroelectricity; yet that 9% amounts to more than three times the hydropower generated by all of Africa.

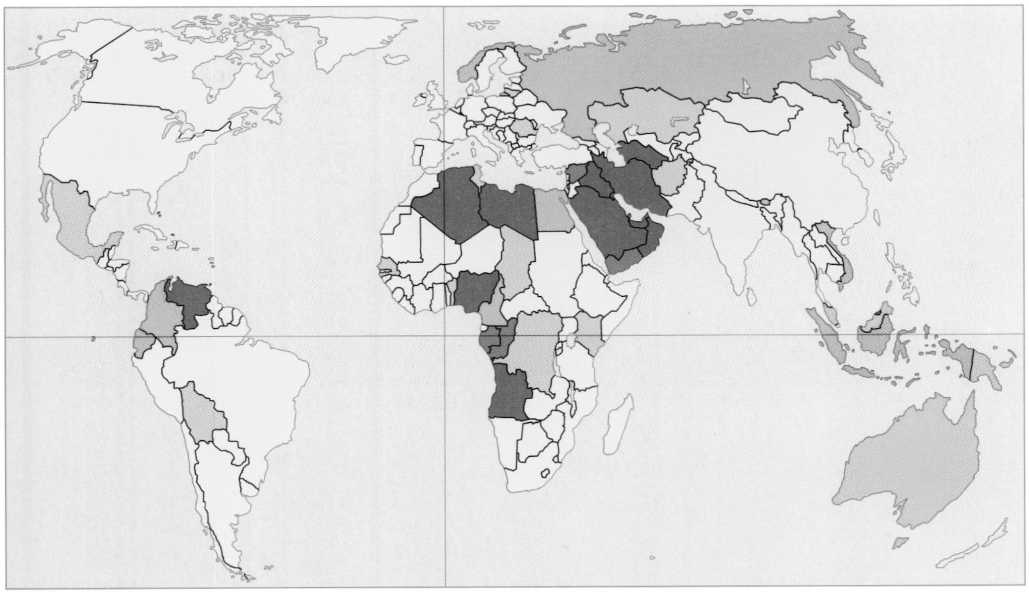

Fuel Exports

Fuels as a percentage of total value of exports (1990–94)

- Over 75%
- 50 – 75%
- 25 – 50%
- 10 – 25%
- Under 10%

Conversion Rates

1 barrel = 0.136 tonnes or 159 litres or 35 Imperial gallons or 42 US gallons

1 tonne = 7.33 barrels or 1,185 litres or 256 Imperial gallons or 261 US gallons

1 tonne oil = 1.5 tonnes hard coal or 3.0 tonnes lignite or 12,000 kWh

1 Imperial gallon = 1.201 US gallons or 4.546 litres or 277.4 cubic inches

Measurements

For historical reasons, oil is traded in 'barrels'. The weight and volume equivalents (shown right) are all based on average-density 'Arabian light' crude oil.

The energy equivalents given for a tonne of oil are also somewhat imprecise: oil and coal of different qualities will have varying energy contents, a fact usually reflected in their price on world markets.

Coal Reserves
World coal reserves by region and country, thousand million tonnes (1995)
Ge: Germany
SAf: South Africa

Gas Reserves
World natural gas reserves by region and country, thousand million tonnes (1995)

Al: Algeria
Ca: Canada
Iq: Iraq
Ka: Kazakstan
Ma: Malaysia
Ni: Nigeria
No: Norway
Qa: Qatar
SA: Saudi Arabia
Tm: Turkmenistan
Uk: Ukraine
UAE: United Arab. Em.

Oil Reserves
World oil reserves by region and country, thousand million tonnes (1995)

Cn: China
Li: Libya
Mx: Mexico
Ru: Russia
UAE: United Arab. Em.
Ve: Venezuela

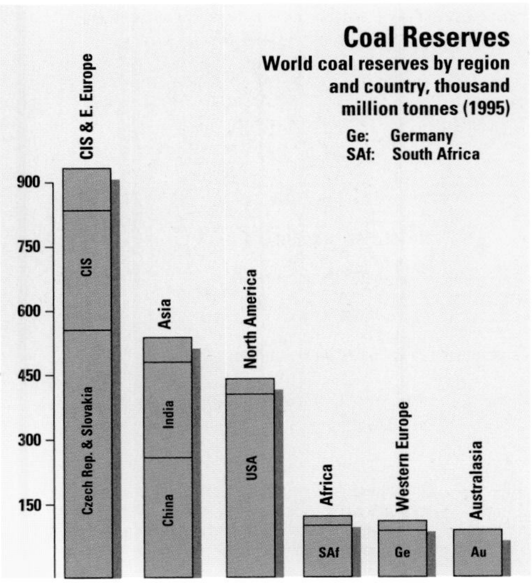

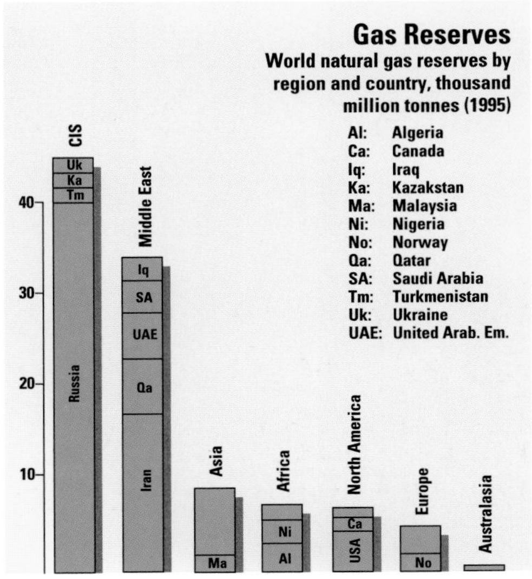

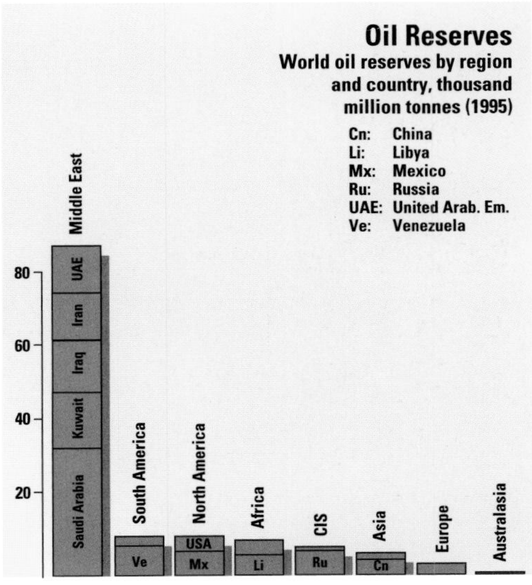

Production

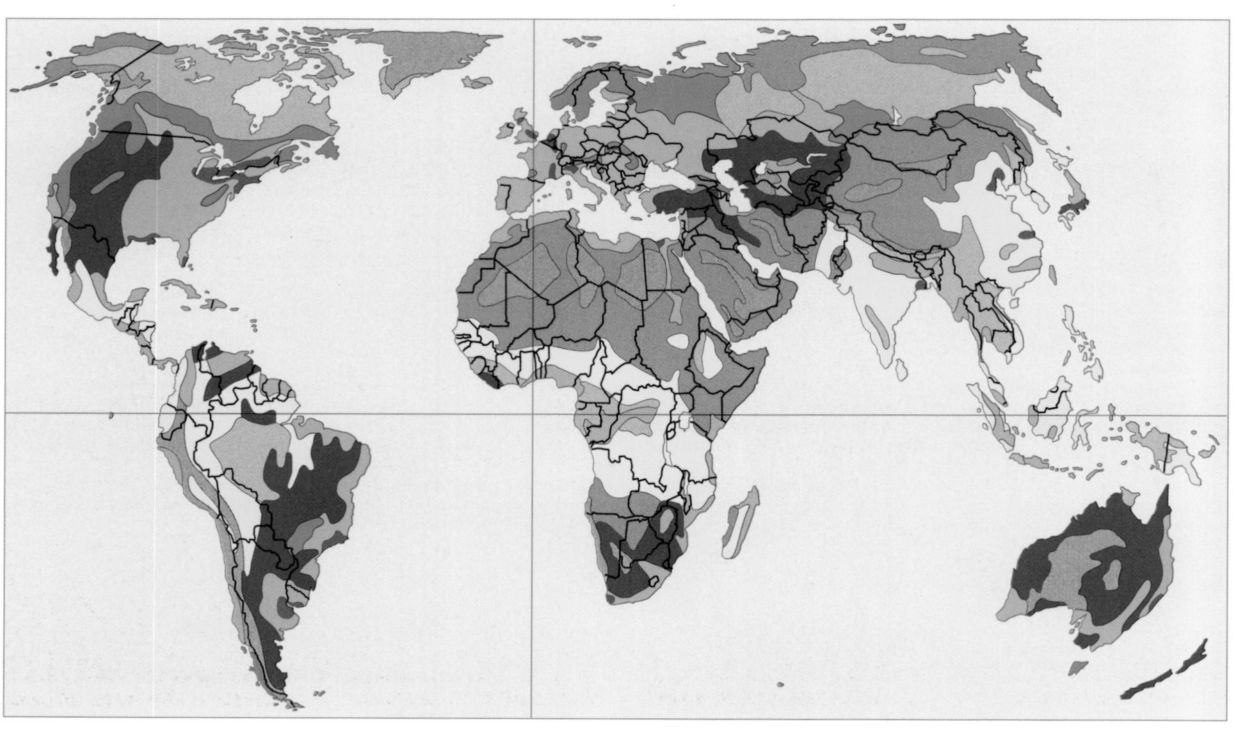

Agriculture

Predominant type of farming or land use.

- Nomadic herding
- Hunting, fishing and gathering
- Subsistence agriculture
- Commercial ranching
- Commercial livestock and grain farming
- Urban areas
- Forestry
- Unproductive land

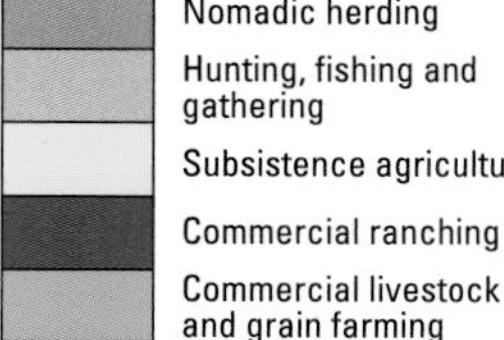

The development of agriculture has transformed human existence more than any other. The whole business of farming is constantly developing: due mainly to the new varieties of rice and wheat, world grain production has increased by over 70% since 1965. New machinery and modern agricultural techniques enable relatively few farmers to produce enough food for the world's 6 billion or so people.

Staple Crops

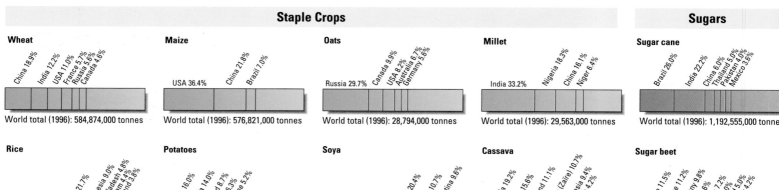

Wheat
China 18.9% · India 12.2% · USA 11.0% · France 5.7% · Russia 5.6% · Canada 4.6%

World total (1996): 584,874,000 tonnes

Maize
USA 36.4% · China 21.8% · Brazil 7.0%

World total (1996): 576,821,000 tonnes

Oats
Russia 29.7% · Canada 9.9% · USA 8.2% · Australia 6.7% · Germany 5.6%

World total (1996): 28,794,000 tonnes

Millet
India 33.2% · Nigeria 18.3% · China 16.1% · Niger 6.4%

World total (1996): 29,563,000 tonnes

Rice
China 34.0% · India 21.7% · Indonesia 9.0% · Bangladesh 4.8% · Vietnam 4.4% · Thailand 3.8%

World total (1996): 562,259,000 tonnes

Potatoes
China 16.0% · Russia 14.0% · Poland 8.7% · India 6.3% · Ukraine 5.2%

World total (1996): 294,834,000 tonnes

Soya
USA 47.1% · Brazil 20.4% · China 10.7% · Argentina 9.6%

World total (1996): 130,302,000 tonnes

Cassava
Nigeria 19.2% · Brazil 15.6% · Thailand 11.1% · Congo (Zaïre) 10.7% · Indonesia 9.4% · Ghana 4.2%

World total (1996): 162,942,000 tonnes

Sugars

Sugar cane
Brazil 26.0% · India 22.2% · China 6.0% · Thailand 5.0% · Pakistan 4.0% · Mexico 3.6%

World total (1996): 1,192,555,000 tonnes

Sugar beet
France 11.5% · Ukraine 11.2% · Germany 9.8% · Russia 9.6% · Italy 7.2% · Poland 5.0% · Turkey 4.2%

World total (1996): 255,500,000 tonnes

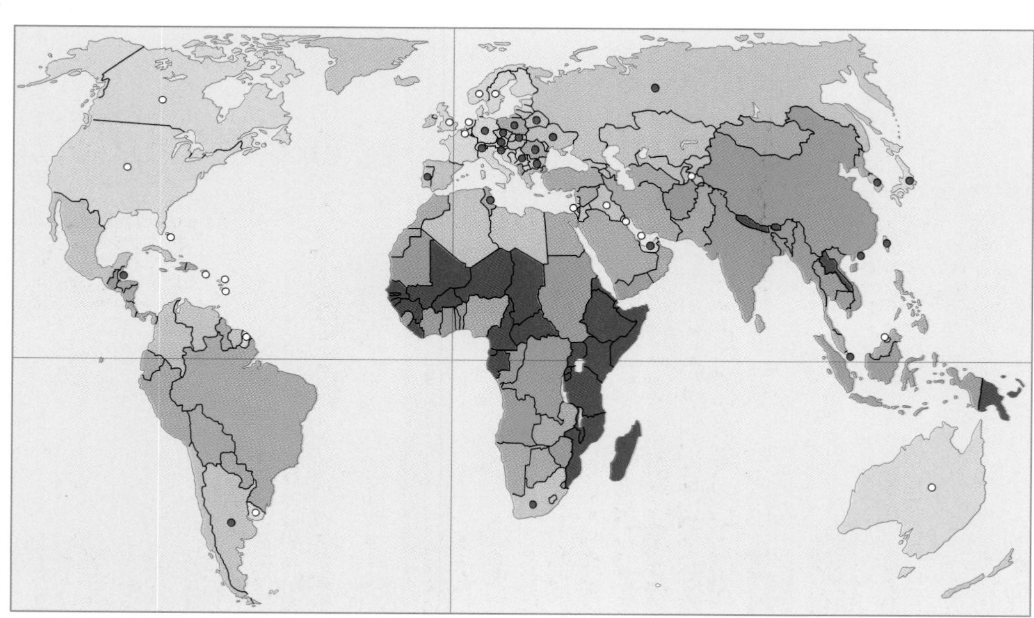

Balance of Employment

Percentage of total workforce employed in agriculture, including forestry and fishing (1990–92)

- Over 75% in agriculture
- 50 – 75% in agriculture
- 25 – 50% in agriculture
- 10 – 25% in agriculture
- Under 10% in agriculture

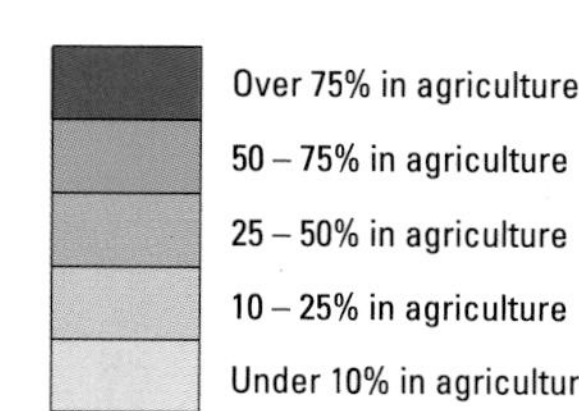

Employment in industry and services

- Over a third of total workforce employed in manufacturing
- Over two-thirds of total workforce employed in service industries (work in offices, shops, tourism, transport, construction and government)

Mineral Production

Copper
Chile 26.9% • USA 19.9% • Canada 7.8% • Indonesia 5.1% • Australia 4.8% • China 4.7% • Poland 4.6% • Zambia 3.7%
World total (1995): 9,311,000 tonnes *

Iron
China 15.0% • Brazil 11.9% • Australia 9.0% • Russia 4.3% • India 4.1% • USA 3.3%
World total (1995): 1,020,000 tonnes*

Chromium
S. Africa 35.9% • Kazakstan 20.2% • India 9.1% • Turkey 7.9% • Finland 5.6% • Zimbabwe 5.2%
World total (1994): 10,000,000 tonnes*

Gold
S. Africa 22.9% • USA 14.5% • Australia 11.2% • Canada 6.6% • Russia 6.2% • China 6.0%
World total (1995): 2,275 tonnes *

Uranium
Canada 31.9% • Australia 11.3% • Niger 8.8% • USA 7.2% • Russia 6.4% • Uzbekistan 6.1% • S. Africa 5.0% • Kazakstan 4.9%
World total (1995): 32,976 tonnes*

Lead
Australia 18.4% • USA 14.3% • Peru 8.5% • Canada 7.7% • Mexico 5.9%
World total (1995): 2,751,000 tonnes*

Tin
China 27.7% • Indonesia 23.6% • Peru 11.4% • Brazil 9.9% • Bolivia 7.4% • Russia 4.6%
World total (1995): 195,000 tonnes*

Manganese
S. Africa 17.3% • China 16.9% • Ukraine 15.0% • Australia 14.0% • Brazil 12.8% • Gabon 9.6%
World total (1994): 7,000,000 tonnes*

Silver
Mexico 18.1% • Peru 13.8% • USA 10.5% • Canada 9.0% • Chile 7.5% • Australia 6.7%
World total (1995): 13,800 tonnes *

Aluminium
USA 28.9% • Canada 9.9% • China 8.2% • Australia 5.9% • Brazil 5.7%
World total (1995): 22,706,000 tonnes *

Mercury
Spain 52.8% • China 19.4% • Algeria 10.3% • Kyrgyzstan 6.0% • Finland 3.2%
World total (1995): 2,837 tonnes *

Zinc
Canada 16.5% • Australia 13.9% • China 11.3% • Peru 10.2% • USA 8.9% • Mexico 5.6%
World total (1995): 6,728,000 tonnes *

Nickel
Russia 24.8% • Canada 18.7% • New Caledonia 13.8% • Australia 10.2% • Indonesia 9.0%
World total (1995): 967,000 tonnes*

Diamonds
Australia 37.8% • Congo (Zaire) 18.5% • Botswana 15.6% • Russia 11.6% • South Africa 8.4%
World total (1995): 107,900,000 carats

Mineral Distribution

The map shows the richest sources of the most important minerals. Major mineral locations are named.

Light metals
● Bauxite

Base metals
□ Copper
▲ Lead
▽ Mercury
▽ Tin
◆ Zinc

Iron and ferro-alloys
● Iron
◗ Chrome
▲ Manganese
■ Nickel

Precious metals
▽ Gold
◠ Silver

Precious stones
◆ Diamonds

The map does not show undersea deposits, most of which are considered inaccessible.

Steel Production
Steel output in thousand tonnes (top ten countries, 1995)

Japan, China, USA, Russia, Germany, South Korea, Canada, Italy, Brazil, Ukraine

Ship Building
Merchant vessels launched by the top ten countries, in thousand gross registered tonnes (1996)

Japan, South Korea, Germany, Taiwan, China, Italy, Spain, Poland, France, Finland

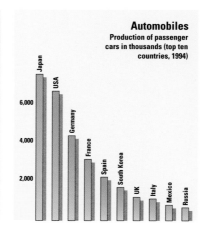

Automobiles
Production of passenger cars in thousands (top ten countries, 1994)

Japan, USA, Germany, France, Spain, South Korea, UK, Italy, Mexico, Russia

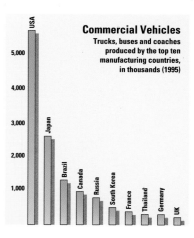

Commercial Vehicles
Trucks, buses and coaches produced by the top ten manufacturing countries, in thousands (1995)

USA, Japan, Brazil, Canada, Russia, South Korea, France, Thailand, Germany, UK

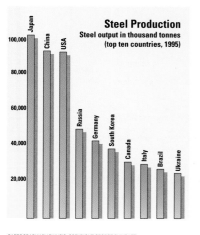

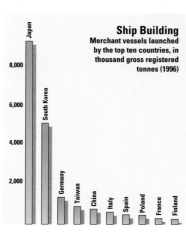

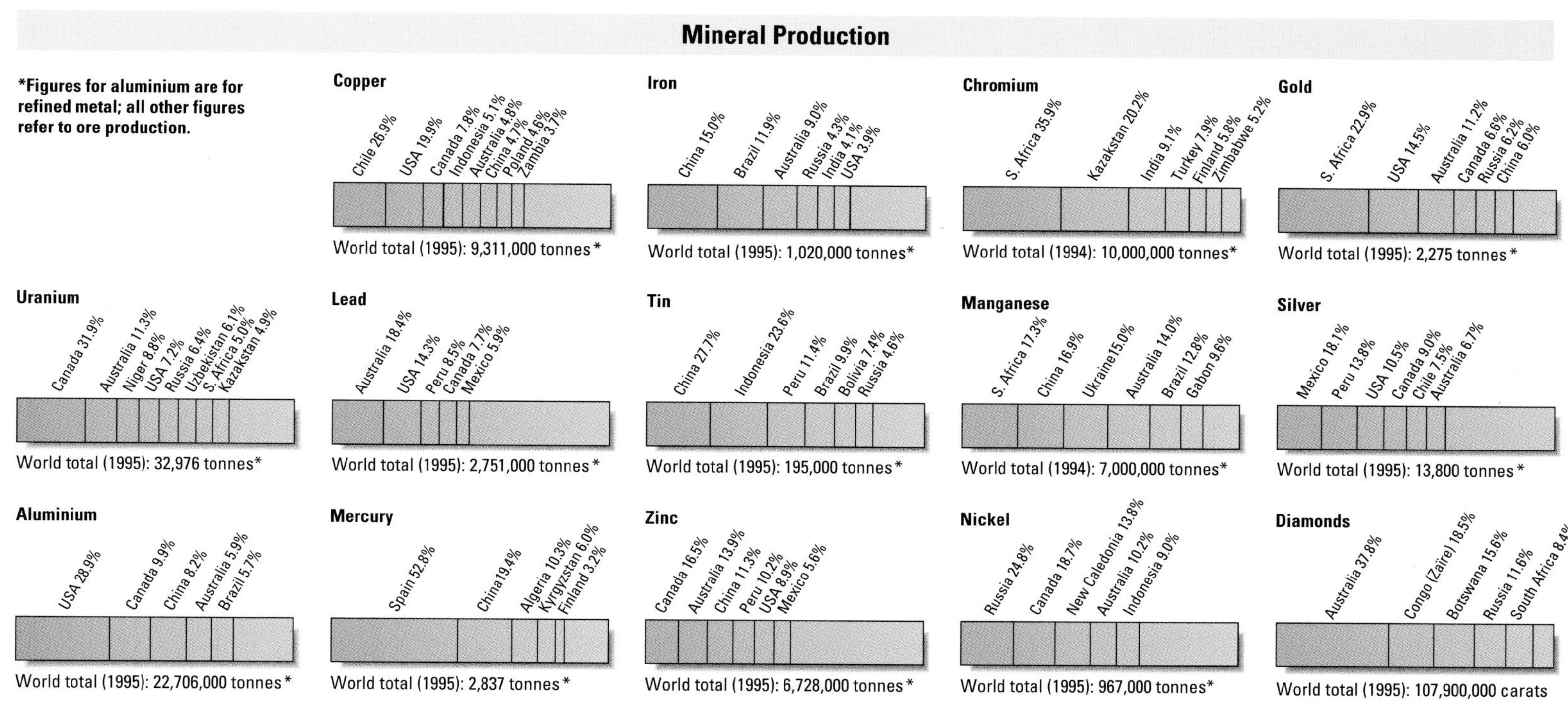

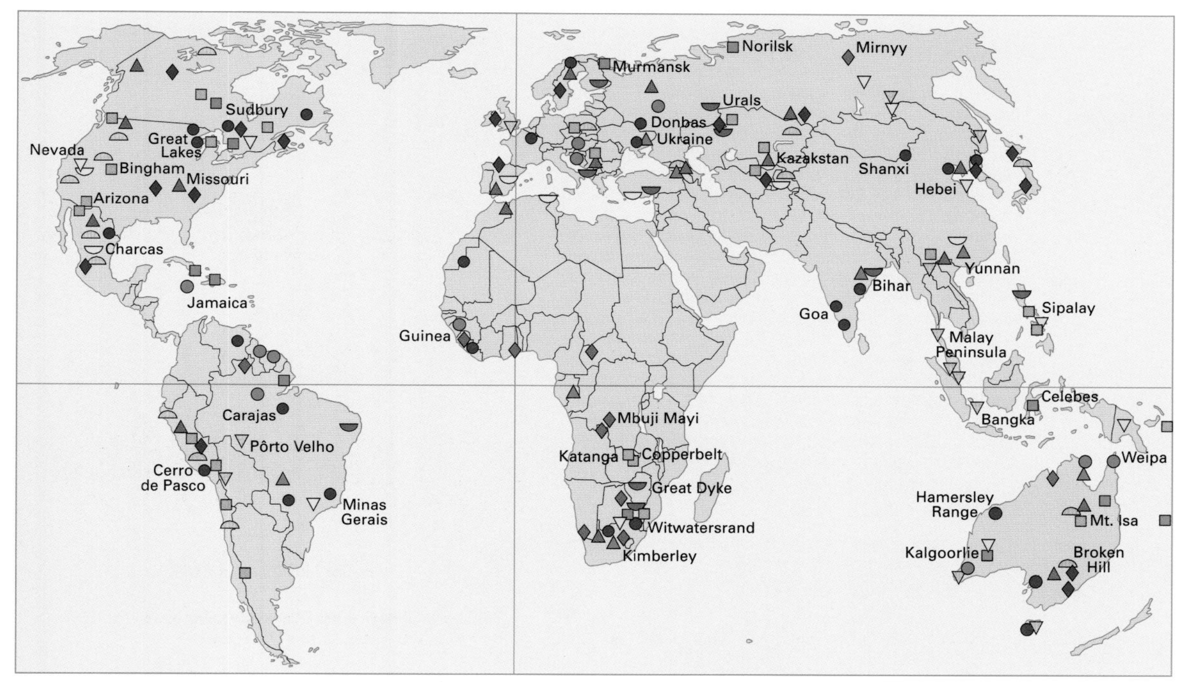

Trade

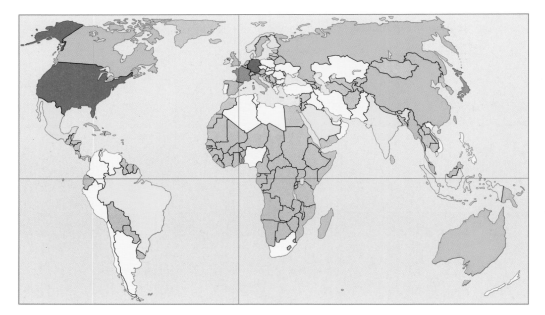

Share of World Trade

Percentage share of total world exports by value (1996)

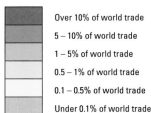

- Over 10% of world trade
- 5 – 10% of world trade
- 1 – 5% of world trade
- 0.5 – 1% of world trade
- 0.1 – 0.5% of world trade
- Under 0.1% of world trade

International trade is dominated by a handful of powerful maritime nations. The members of 'G8', the inner circle of OECD (see page 19), and the top seven countries listed in the diagram below, account for more than half the total. The majority of nations – including all but four in Africa – contribute less than one quarter of 1% to the worldwide total of exports; the EU countries account for 40%, the Pacific Rim nations over 35%.

The Main Trading Nations

The imports and exports of the top ten trading nations as a percentage of world trade (1994). Each country's trade in manufactured goods is shown in dark blue.

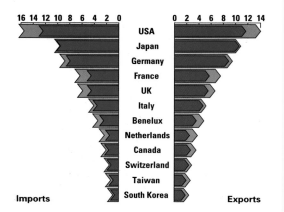

16 14 12 10 8 6 4 2 0 0 2 4 6 8 10 12 14

USA
Japan
Germany
France
UK
Italy
Benelux
Netherlands
Canada
Switzerland
Taiwan
South Korea

Imports **Exports**

Patterns of Trade

Thriving international trade is the outward sign of a healthy world economy, the obvious indicator that some countries have goods to sell and others the means to buy them. Global exports expanded to an estimated US $3.92 trillion in 1994, an increase due partly to economic recovery in industrial nations but also to export-led growth strategies in many developing nations and lowered regional trade barriers. International trade remains dominated, however, by the rich, industrialized countries of the Organization for Economic Development: between them, OECD members account for almost 75% of world imports and exports in most years. However, continued rapid economic growth in some developing countries is altering global trade patterns. The 'tiger economies' of South-east Asia are particularly vibrant, averaging more than 8% growth between 1992 and 1994. The size of the largest trading economies means that imports and exports usually represent only a small percentage of their total wealth. In export-concious Japan, for example, trade in goods and services amounts to less than 18% of GDP. In poorer countries, trade – often in a single commodity – may amount to 50% of GDP.

Traded Products
Top ten manufactures traded, by value in billions of US $ (latest available year)

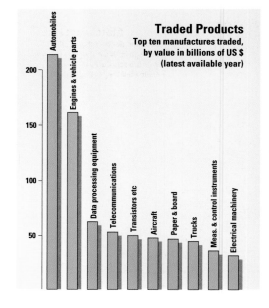

- Automobiles
- Engines & vehicle parts
- Data processing equipment
- Telecommunications
- Transistors etc
- Aircraft
- Paper & board
- Trucks
- Meas. & control instruments
- Electrical machinery

Balance of Trade

Value of exports in proportion to the value of imports (1995)

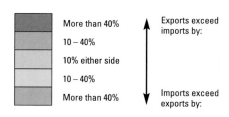

- More than 40%
- 10 – 40%
- 10% either side
- 10 – 40%
- More than 40%

Exports exceed imports by:

Imports exceed exports by:

The total world trade balance should amount to zero, since exports must equal imports on a global scale. In practice, at least $100 billion in exports go unrecorded, leaving the world with an apparent deficit and many countries in a better position than public accounting reveals. However, a favourable trade balance is not necessarily a sign of prosperity: many poorer countries must maintain a high surplus in order to service debts, and do so by restricting imports below the levels needed to sustain successful economies.

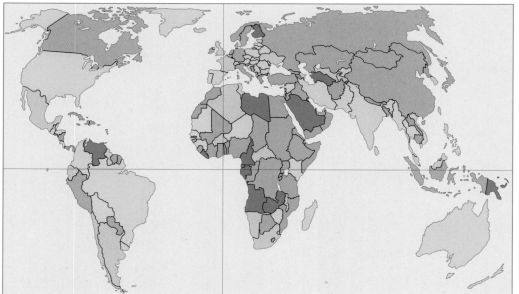

Seaborne Freight

Freight unloaded in millions of tonnes (latest available year)

- Over 100
- 50 – 100
- 10 – 50
- 5 – 10
- Under 5
- Landlocked countries

Major seaports

- ● Over 100 million tonnes per year
- ○ 50–100 million tonnes per year
- — Major shipping routes

Cargoes

Type of seaborne freight

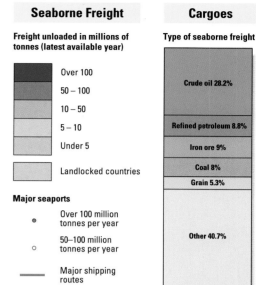

- Crude oil 28.2%
- Refined petroleum 8.8%
- Iron ore 9%
- Coal 8%
- Grain 5.3%
- Other 40.7%

Merchant Fleets

Merchant fleets in thousand gross tonnage (1996). A large number of vessels are registered in Liberia and Panama but they are not part of the national fleet.

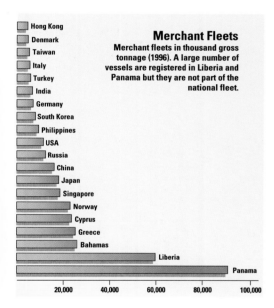

Hong Kong, Denmark, Taiwan, Italy, Turkey, India, Germany, South Korea, Philippines, USA, Russia, China, Japan, Singapore, Norway, Cyprus, Greece, Bahamas, Liberia, Panama

20,000 40,000 60,000 80,000 100,000

The Great Ports

Total Cargo Traffic (1995) '000 tonnes

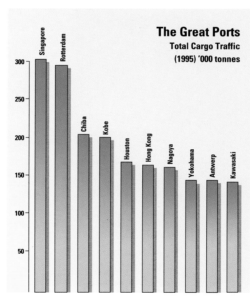

Singapore, Rotterdam, Chiba, Kobe, Houston, Hong Kong, Nagoya, Yokohama, Antwerp, Kawasaki

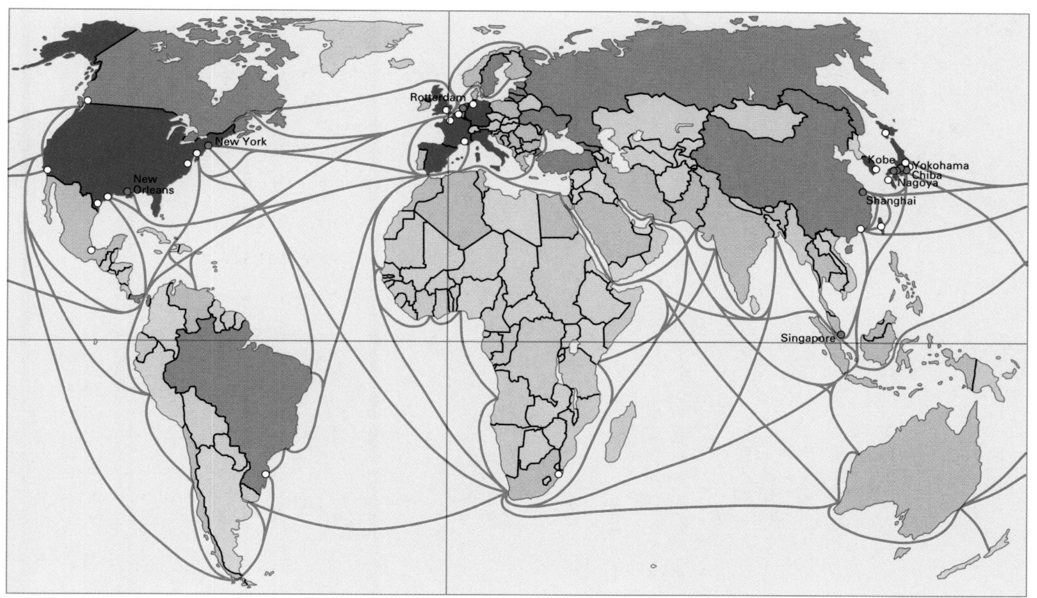

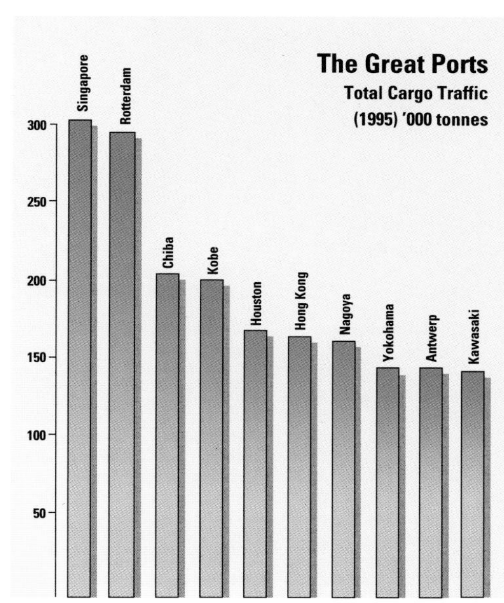

World Shipping

World merchant fleet by type of vessel and deadweight tonnage (latest available year)

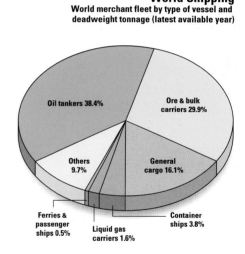

- Oil tankers 38.4%
- Ore & bulk carriers 29.9%
- General cargo 16.1%
- Others 9.7%
- Ferries & passenger ships 0.5%
- Liquid gas carriers 1.6%
- Container ships 3.8%

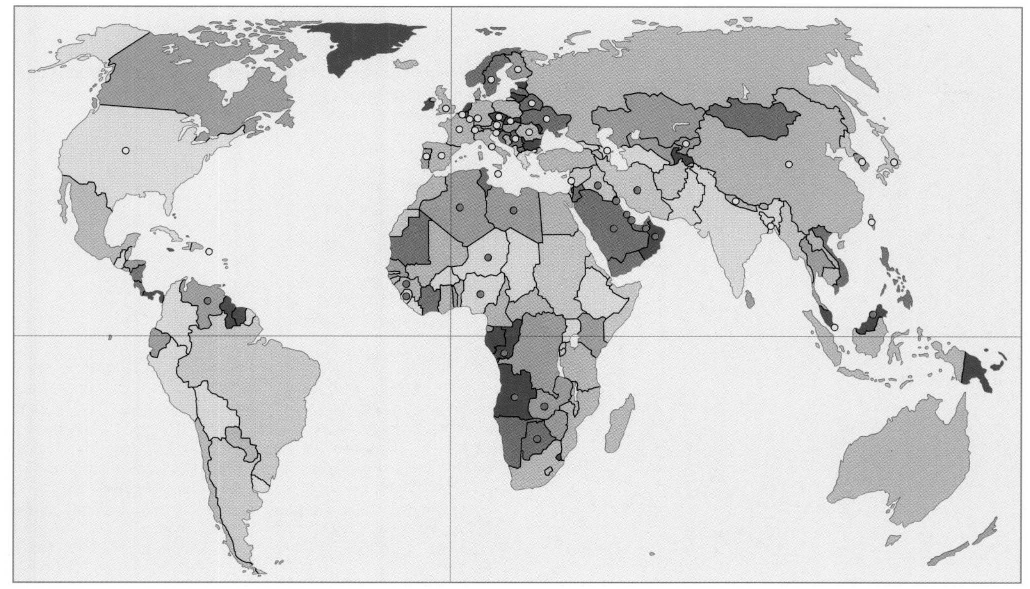

Dependence on Trade

Value of exports as a percentage of Gross Domestic Product (1997)

- Over 50% GDP from exports
- 40 – 50% GDP from exports
- 30 – 40% GDP from exports
- 20 – 30% GDP from exports
- 10 – 20% GDP from exports
- Under 10% GDP from exports

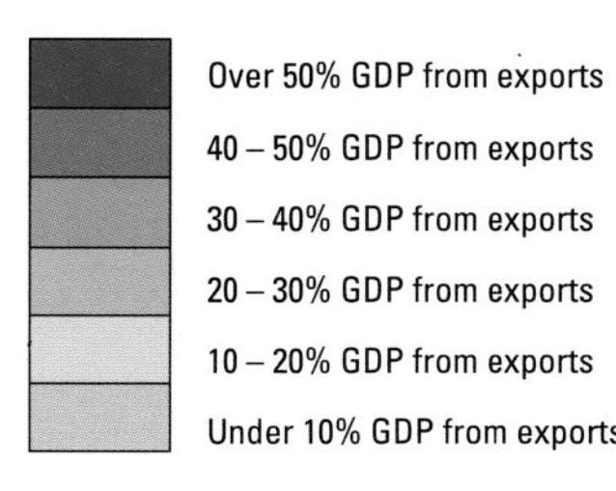

- ○ Most dependent on industrial exports (over 75% of total exports)
- ◑ Most dependent on fuel exports (over 75% of total exports)
- ● Most dependent on mineral and metal exports (over 75% of total exports)

Travel and Tourism

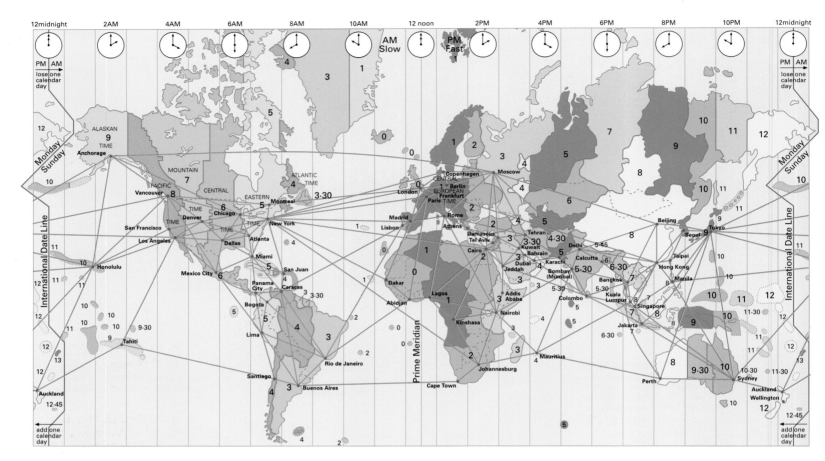

Time Zones

- ▨ Zones using GMT
- ▨ Zones slow of GMT
- ▨ Zones fast of GMT
- ▨ Half-hour zones
- --- International boundaries
- — Time zone boundaries
- — International Date Line
- — Selected air routes
- 10 Hours slow or fast of GMT

Certain time zones are affected by the incidence of 'summer time' in countries where it is adopted.

Actual Solar Time, when it is noon at Greenwich, is shown along the top of the map.

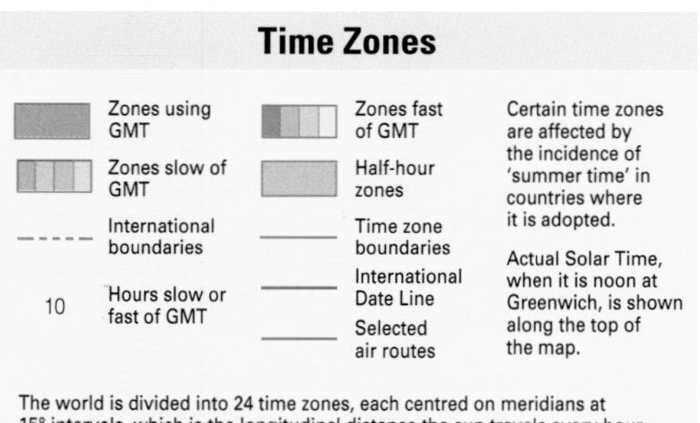

The world is divided into 24 time zones, each centred on meridians at 15° intervals, which is the longitudinal distance the sun travels every hour. The meridian running through Greenwich, London, passes through the middle of the first zone.

Rail and Road: The Leading Nations

Total rail network ('000 km) (1995)	Passenger km per head per year	Total road network ('000 km)	Vehicle km per head per year	Number of vehicles per km of roads
1. USA235.7	Japan2,017	USA6,277.9	USA................12,505	Hong Kong.........284
2. Russia87.4	Belarus1,880	India2,962.5	Luxembourg7,989	Taiwan211
3. India62.7	Russia..............1,826	Brazil1,824.4	Kuwait................7,251	Singapore152
4. China54.6	Switzerland1,769	Japan1,130.9	France7,142	Kuwait140
5. Germany41.7	Ukraine............1,456	China1,041.1	Sweden.............6,991	Brunei...................96
6. Australia............35.8	Austria1,168	Russia884.0	Germany............6,806	Italy.......................91
7. Argentina..........34.2	France1,011	Canada849.4	Denmark6,764	Israel.....................87
8. France................31.9	Netherlands994	France811.6	Austria6,518	Thailand73
9. Mexico...............26.5	Latvia918	Australia810.3	Netherlands5,984	Ukraine.................73
10. South Africa......26.3	Denmark884	Germany636.3	UK5,738	UK67
11. Poland..................24.9	Slovak Rep.862	Romania..............461.9	Canada5,493	Netherlands66
12. Ukraine22.6	Romania851	Turkey.................388.1	Italy....................4,852	Germany62

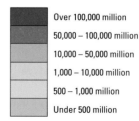

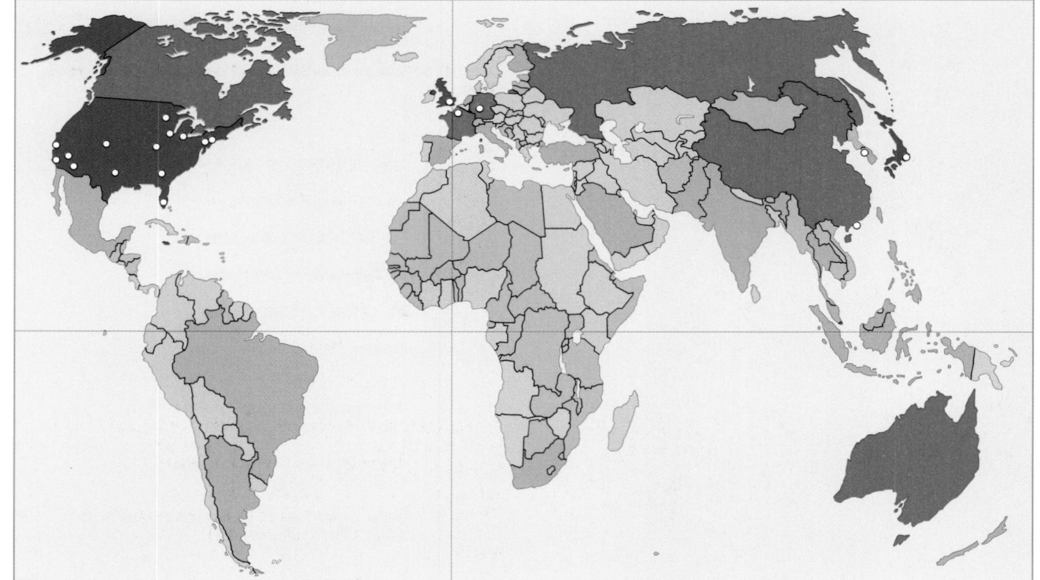

Air Travel

Passenger kilometres (the number of passengers – international and domestic – multiplied by the distance flown by each passenger from the airport of origin) (1996)

- ■ Over 100,000 million
- ■ 50,000 – 100,000 million
- ■ 10,000 – 50,000 million
- ■ 1,000 – 10,000 million
- ■ 500 – 1,000 million
- □ Under 500 million

○ Major airports (handling over 25 million passengers in 1995)

World's busiest airports (total passengers)	World's busiest airports (international passengers)
1. Chicago (O'Hare)	1. London (Heathrow)
2. Atlanta (Hatsfield)	2. London (Gatwick)
3. Dallas (Dallas/Ft Worth)	3. Frankfurt (International)
4. Los Angeles (Intern'l)	4. New York (Kennedy)
5. London (Heathrow)	5. Paris (De Gaulle)

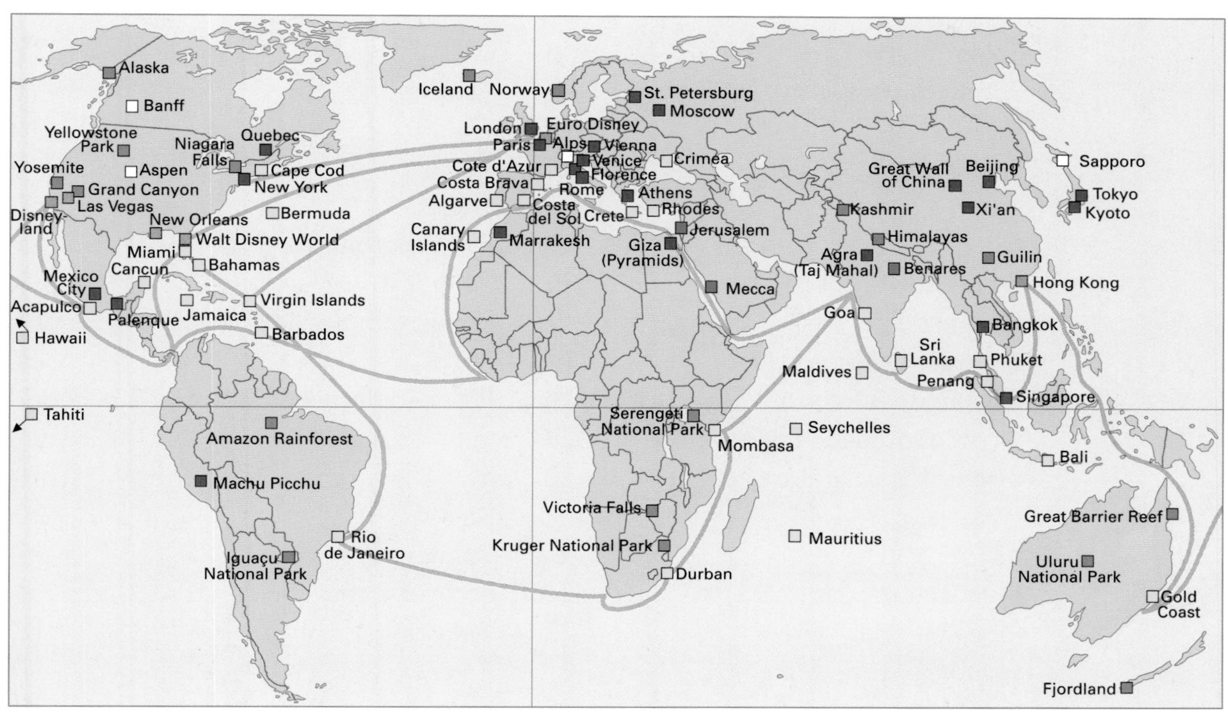

Destinations

- ■ Cultural and historical centres
- □ Coastal resorts
- □ Ski resorts
- ■ Centres of entertainment
- ■ Places of pilgrimage
- ■ Places of great natural beauty
- ── Popular holiday cruise routes

Visitors to the USA

Overseas travellers to the USA, thousands (1997 estimates)

1.	Canada	13,900
2.	Mexico	12,370
3.	Japan	4,640
4.	UK	3,350
5.	Germany	1,990
6.	France	1,030
7.	Taiwan	885
8.	Venezuela	860
9.	South Korea	800
10.	Brazil	785

In 1996, the USA earned the most from tourism, with receipts of more than US $75 billion.

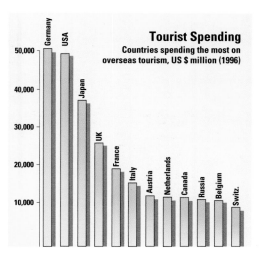

Tourist Spending
Countries spending the most on overseas tourism, US $ million (1996)

Importance of Tourism

		Arrivals from abroad (1996)	% of world total (1996)
1.	France	66,800,000	10.2%
2.	USA	49,038,000	7.5%
3.	Spain	43,403,000	6.6%
4.	Italy	34,087,000	5.2%
5.	UK	25,960,000	3.9%
6.	China	23,770,000	3.6%
7.	Poland	19,514,000	3.0%
8.	Mexico	18,667,000	2.9%
9.	Canada	17,610,000	2.7%
10.	Czech Republic	17,400,000	2.7%
11.	Hungary	17,248,000	2.6%
12.	Austria	16,642,000	2.5%

In 1996, there was a 4.6% rise, to 593 million, in the total number of people travelling abroad. Small economies in attractive areas are often completely dominated by tourism: in some West Indian islands, for example, tourist spending provides over 90% of total income.

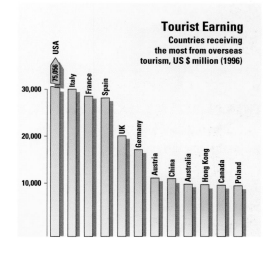

Tourist Earning
Countries receiving the most from overseas tourism, US $ million (1996)

Tourism

Tourism receipts as a percentage of Gross National Product (1994)

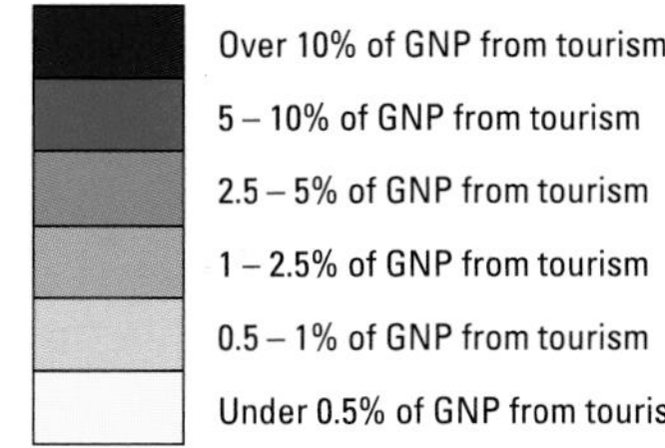

- Over 10% of GNP from tourism
- 5 – 10% of GNP from tourism
- 2.5 – 5% of GNP from tourism
- 1 – 2.5% of GNP from tourism
- 0.5 – 1% of GNP from tourism
- Under 0.5% of GNP from tourism

Countries spending the most on promoting tourism, millions of US $ (1996)

Australia	88
Spain	79
UK	79
France	73
Singapore	54

Fastest growing tourist destinations, % change in receipts (1994–5)

South Korea	49%
Czech Republic	27%
India	21%
Russia	19%
Philippines	18%

The World In Focus: Index

WORLD MAPS

———— SETTLEMENTS ————

■ **PARIS** ■ **Berne** ◉ **Livorno** ◉ Brugge ◎ Algeciras ○ *Frejus* ○ *Oberammergau* ○ *Thira*

Settlement symbols and type styles vary according to the scale of each map and indicate the importance
of towns on the map rather than specific population figures

∴ Ruins or Archæological Sites ˯ Wells in Desert

———— ADMINISTRATION ————

———— International Boundaries

- - - - International Boundaries
(Undefined or Disputed)

··········· Internal Boundaries

National Parks

Country Names
NICARAGUA

Administrative
Area Names

KENT

CALABRIA

International boundaries show the *de facto* situation where there are rival claims to territory

———— COMMUNICATIONS ————

———— Principal Roads

———— Other Roads

+ - - + Road Tunnels

⤬ Passes

⊕ Airfields

———— Principal Railways

- - - Railways
Under Construction

———— Other Railways

+ - - + Railway Tunnels

·········· Principal Canals

———— PHYSICAL FEATURES ————

———— Perennial Streams

- - - Intermittent Streams

⬭ Perennial Lakes

⬭ Intermittent Lakes

Swamps and Marshes

Permanent Ice
and Glaciers

▲ 8848 Elevations in metres

▼ 8500 Sea Depths in metres

1134 Height of Lake Surface
Above Sea Level in metres

Projection: Hammer Equal Area

ARCTIC OCEAN

Severnaya Zemlya
Laptev Sea
New Siberian Is.
East Siberian Sea
Wrangel I.
Barents Sea
Novaya Zemlya
Kara Sea
Murmansk
Norilsk
Verkhoyansk
Arctic Circle
Arkhangelsk
Yakutsk
Magadan
Okhotsk
Bering Sea
Sea of Okhotsk
Petropavlovsk-Kamchatskiy
SWEDEN
FINLAND
Helsinki
St.Petersburg
Perm
Yekaterinburg
Tomsk
Krasnoyarsk
Irkutsk
L. Baikal
Ulan Ude
Sakhalin
Komsomolsk
International Date Line
Stockholm
EST.
LATVIA
LITH.
Kazan
Volga
Omsk
Novosibirsk
Barnaul
Khabarovsk
Amur
MOSCOW
Samara
Astana
Kuril
Vladivostok
Sapporo
Saratov
Chelyabinsk
Harbin
Changchun
BELARUS
Minsk
Qaraghandy
SHENYANG
NORTH KOREA
Warsaw
Kiev
UKRAINE
MONGOLIA
BEIJING
TIANJIN
Pyongyang
JAPAN
Odessa
Volgograd
KAZAKSTAN
Ulan Bator
SEOUL
TOKYO
Budapest
ROMANIA
Astrakhan
L. Balkhash
Almaty
Dalian
SOUTH KOREA
Bucharest
Black Sea
Aral Sea
Bishkek
KYRGYZSTAN
CHINA
Lanzhou
Taiyuan
Osaka
Kitakyushu
BULGARIA
GEORGIA
Tbilisi
UZBEKISTAN
Tashkent
Xi'an
Hwang Ho
ISTANBUL
Ankara
ARM.
AZER.
Baku
Samarkand
TURKMENISTAN
Dushanbe
TAJIKISTAN
TIBET
Chengdu
Wuhan
Nanjing
SHANGHAI
PACIFIC
OCEAN
Izmir
TURKEY
Yerevan
Caspian Sea
Ashkhabad
Lhasa
CHONGQING
East China Sea
TEHRAN
Mashhad
KABUL
Kunming
Fuzhou
Taipei
SYRIA
Beirut
Damascus
Baghdad
Esfahan
AFGHANISTAN
Islamabad
NEPAL
Katmandu
BHU.
GUANGZHOU
TAIWAN
Jerusalem
Amman
IRAQ
IRAN
Shiraz
Lahore
DELHI
Kanpur
BANGLA-
DESH
DACCA
HONG KONG
Hainan
JORDAN
KUWAIT
The Gulf
PAKISTAN
New Delhi
INDIA
KOLKATA
(Calcutta)
BURMA
MYANMAR
Hanoi
BAHRAIN
QATAR
Abu Dhabi
KARACHI
Ahmadabad
Nagpur
Bay of
Bengal
Rangoon
VIET-
NAM
South
China
Sea
MANILA
PHILIPPINES
Riyadh
U.A.E.
Muscat
Arabian
Sea
MUMBAI
(Bombay)
Vientiane
Hyderabad
THAILAND
BANGKOK
CAMBODIA
Sana
YEMEN
Aden
Socotra
(Yemen)
Bangalore
CHENNAI
(Madras)
Andaman Is.
(India)
Phnom
Penh
Ho Chi Minh
City
G. of Aden
DJIBOUTI
Addis Ababa
SOMALI
REP.
Lakshadweep Is.
(India)
SRI LANKA
Nicobar Is.
(India)
MALAYSIA
Medan
SABAH
BRUNEI
ETHIOPIA
Colombo
MALDIVES
Kuala Lumpur
PEN. MALAYSIA
SARAWAK
UGANDA
Kampala
KENYA
Mogadishu
Nairobi
SEYCHELLES
Amirante
Is.
Equator
Palembang
SINGAPORE
Borneo
RWANDA
Dodoma
Mombasa
Aldabra Is.
Diego Garcia
INDONESIA
IRIAN
JAYA
BURUNDI
TANZANIA
Zanzibar
Dar es Salaam
COMOROS
Mayotte
(Fr.)
Chagos Arch.
(U.K.)
JAKARTA
Bandung
Java
Surabaya
PAPUA
NEW
GUINEA
Lubumbashi
Malawi
Ujung Pandang
Port
Moresby
ANGOLA
ZAMBIA
Lilongwe
MALAWI
MADAGASCAR
Cargados Carajos
Timor
Darwin
Lusaka
Harare
Antananarivo
Cairns
Townsville
ZIMBABWE
MOZAMBIQUE
Bulawayo
Rodriguez
MAURITIUS
Tropic of Capricorn
Port Hedland
Alice Springs
Rockhampton
BOTSWANA
REUNION (Fr.)
Gaborone
Pretoria
AUSTRALIA
Brisbane
Johannesburg
Maputo
SWAZILAND
Geraldton
SOUTH
AFRICA
LESOTHO
Durban
Perth
Fremantle
Kalgoorlie-Boulder
Adelaide
Newcastle
Cape Town
C. of Good Hope
Port Elizabeth
Sydney
Canberra
Amsterdam I.
(Fr.)
St.Paul (Fr.)
Great
Australian
Bight
Melbourne
NEW
ZEALAND
Auckland
North I.
Tasman
Sea
Prince Edward Is.
(S.Africa)
Crozet Is.
(Fr.)
Tasmania
Wellington
Kerguelen
(Fr.)
Hobart
Christchurch
South I.
McDonald Is.
(Austral.)
Heard I.
(Austral.)
Stewart I.
Dunedin
SOUTHERN OCEAN
Antarctic Circle
Ross Sea

CARTOGRAPHY BY PHILIP'S

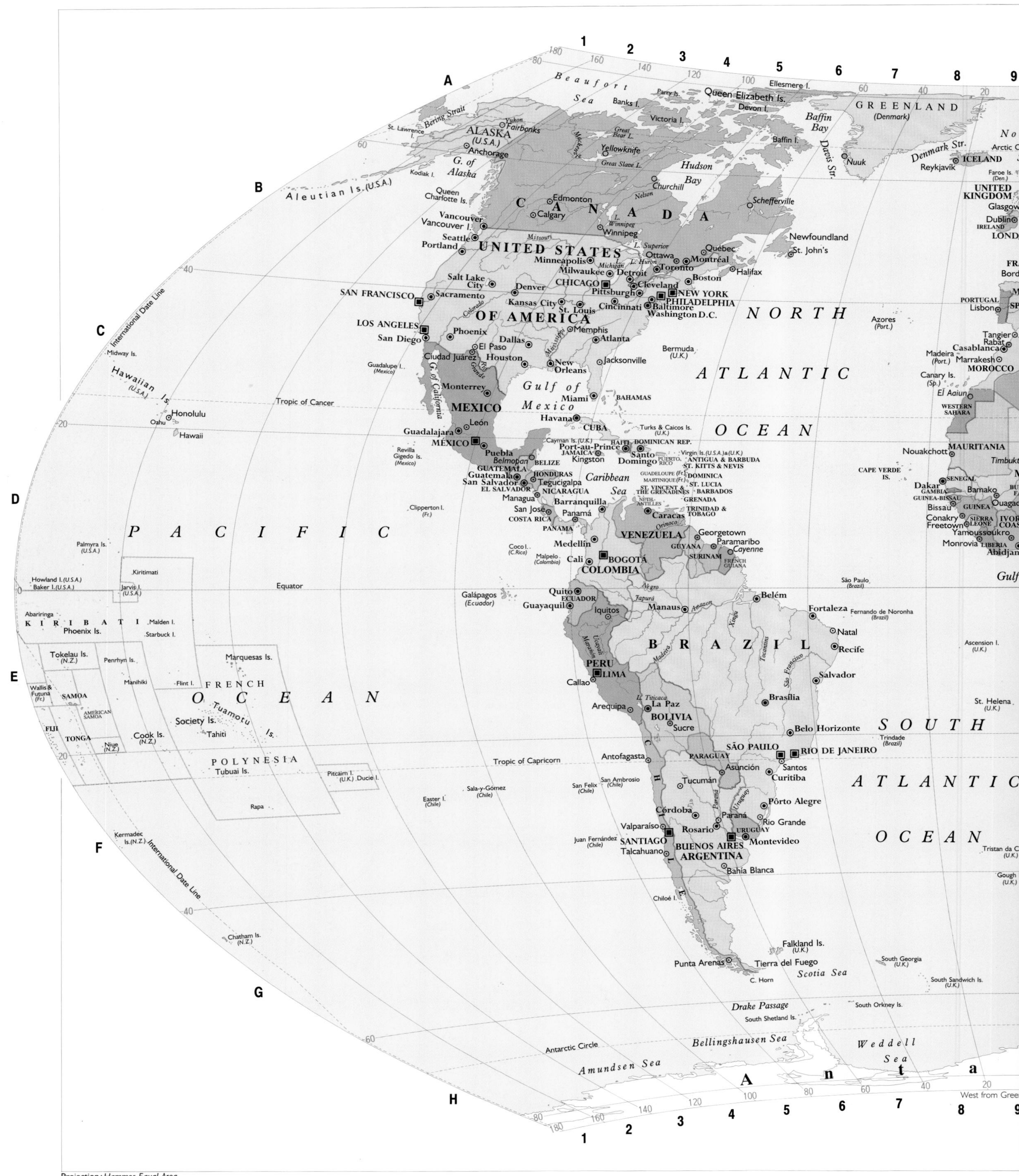

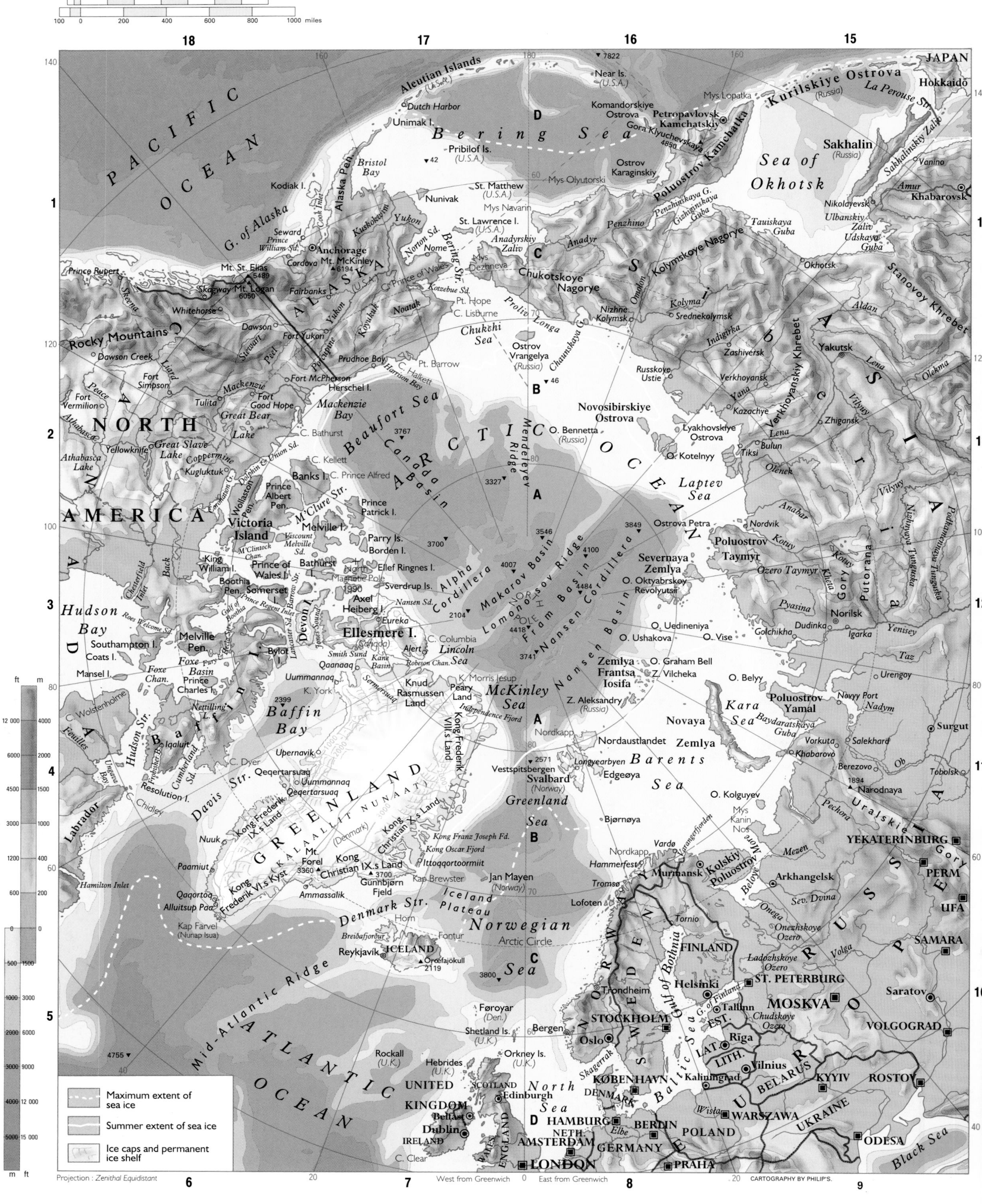

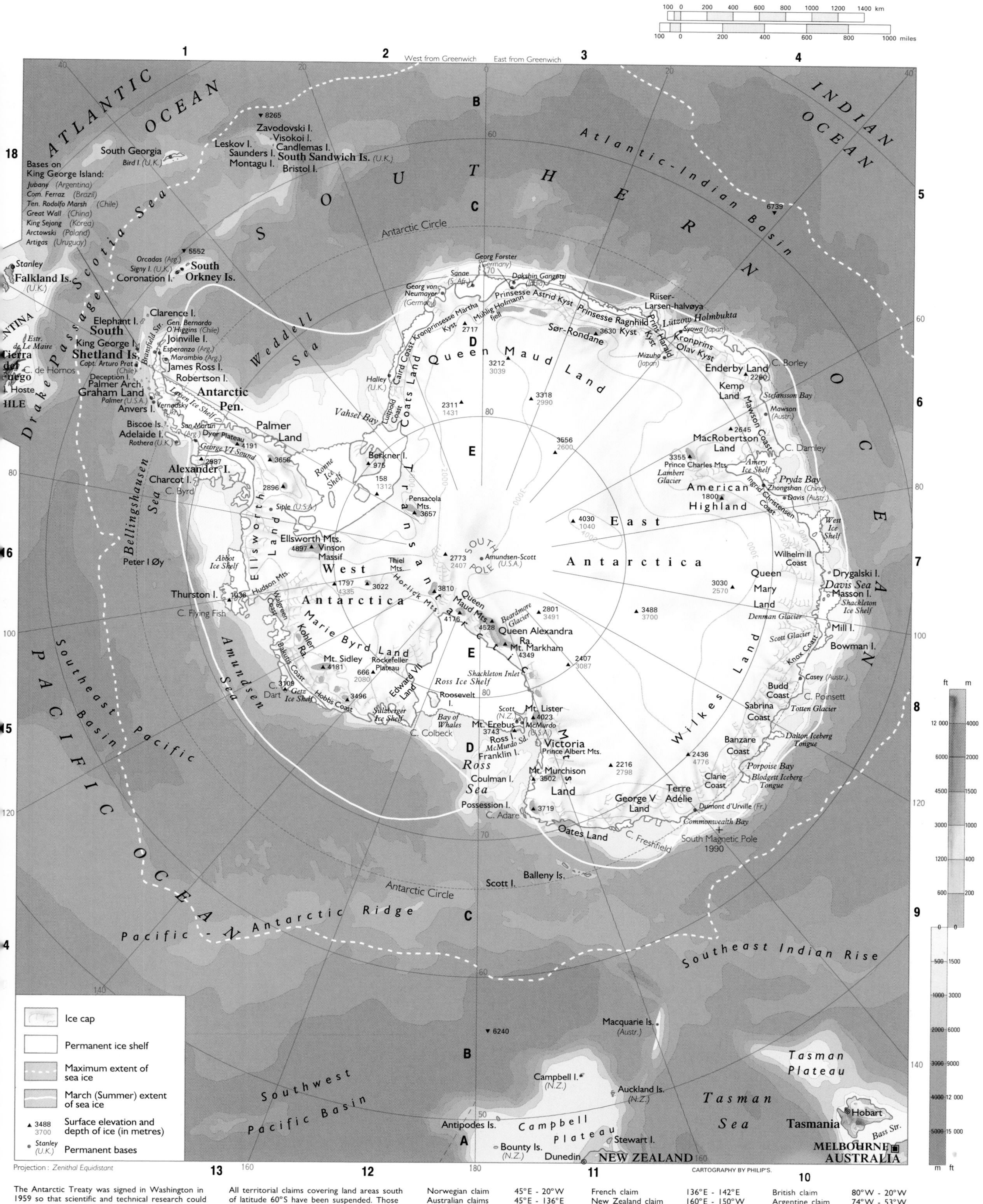

The Antarctic Treaty was signed in Washington in 1959 so that scientific and technical research could continue unhampered by international politics.

All territorial claims covering land areas south of latitude 60°S have been suspended. Those claims were:

Norwegian claim	45°E - 20°W	French claim	136°E - 142°E	British claim	80°W - 20°W
Australian claims	45°E - 136°E	New Zealand claim	160°E - 150°W	Argentine claim	74°W - 53°W
	142°E - 160°E	Chilean claim	90°W - 53°W		

Projection: Zenithal Equidistant

100 0 100 200 300 400 500 600 700 800 km
100 0 100 200 300 400 500 miles

CARTOGRAPHY BY PHILIPS

■ LONDON Capital Cities

Projection: Bonne West from Greenwich 0 East from Greenwich

100 0 100 200 300 400 500 600 700 800 km
100 0 100 200 300 400 500 miles
Norwegian Sea
North Sea
ATLANTIC OCEAN
Bay of Biscay
English Channel
Baltic Sea
G. of Bothnia
White Sea
Black Sea
Caspian Sea
Adriatic Sea
Tyrrhenian Sea
Ionian Sea
Ægean Sea
Mediterranean Sea
Africa
ICELAND
Reykjavik
UNITED KINGDOM
IRELAND
Dublin
LONDON
NORWAY
Oslo
SWEDEN
Stockholm
FINLAND
Helsinki
DENMARK
Copenhagen
ESTONIA
Tallinn
LATVIA
Riga
LITHUANIA
BELARUS
Minsk
RUSSIA
MOSCOW
ST. PETERSBURG
UKRAINE
Kiev
POLAND
Warsaw
GERMANY
Berlin
NETHERLANDS
Amsterdam
BELGIUM
Brussels
LUX.
FRANCE
PARIS
SWITZERLAND
Bern
AUSTRIA
Vienna
CZECH REP.
Prague
SLOVAK REP.
Bratislava
HUNGARY
Budapest
SLOVENIA
Ljubljana
CROATIA
Zagreb
BOSNIA-HERZ.
Sarajevo
YUGOSLAVIA
Belgrade
ROMANIA
Bucharest
MOLDOVA
Kishinev
BULGARIA
Sofia
MACEDONIA
Skopje
ALBANIA
Tirana
GREECE
Athens
ITALY
Rome
SPAIN
Madrid
PORTUGAL
Lisbon
ANDORRA
MONACO
SAN MARINO
MALTA
Valletta
TURKEY
Ankara
ISTANBUL
CYPRUS
Nicosia
SYRIA
IRAQ
IRAN
GEORGIA
Tbilisi
ARMENIA
Yerevan
AZERBAIJAN
Baku
KAZAKSTAN
MOROCCO
ALGERIA
Algiers
TUNISIA
Tunis
LONDON Capital Cities
Projection: Bonne
West from Greenwich
East from Greenwich
CARTOGRAPHY BY PHILIPS.

SCANDINAVIA 1:5 000 000

ICELAND
on same scale

FÆROE
ISLANDS
on same scale

RUSSIA

ESTONIA

LATVIA

LITHUANIA

RUSSIA

BELA

Gulf of Finland

Gulf of Riga

BALTIC SEA

DENMARK

GERMANY

NORWAY

SWEDEN

FINLAND

Helsinki (Helsingfors)

Tallinn

Riga

Kaunas

Vilnius

Kaliningrad (Russia)

STOCKHOLM

Oslo

Göteborg (Gothenburg)

KØBENHAVN (Copenhagen)

Malmö

Gotland

Öland

Bornholm

Rügen

Ålands hav

Skagerrak

Kattegat

Projection: Conical with two standard parallels

East from Greenwich

Key to English unitary authorities on map.

25. HARTLEPOOL
26. DARLINGTON
27. STOCKTON-ON-TEES
28. MIDDLESBROUGH
29. REDCAR AND CLEVELAND
30. BLACKPOOL
31. HALTON
32. BLACKBURN WITH DARWEN
33. WARRINGTON
34. KINGSTON UPON HULL
35. NORTH EAST LINCOLNSHIRE
36. STOKE-ON-TRENT
37. TELFORD AND WREKIN
38. DERBY CITY
39. CITY OF NOTTINGHAM
40. LEICESTER CITY
41. RUTLAND
42. PETERBOROUGH
43. MILTON KEYNES
44. LUTON
45. NORTH SOMERSET
46. CITY OF BRISTOL
47. BATH AND NORTH EAST SOMERSET
48. SWINDON
49. READING
50. WOKINGHAM
51. WINDSOR AND MAIDENHEAD
52. SLOUGH
53. BRACKNELL FOREST
54. THURROCK
55. SOUTHEND-ON-SEA
56. MEDWAY TOWNS
57. PLYMOUTH
58. TORBAY
59. POOLE
60. BOURNEMOUTH
61. SOUTHAMPTON
62. PORTSMOUTH
63. BRIGHTON AND HOVE

Key to Welsh unitary authorities on map.

15. SWANSEA
16. NEATH PORT TALBOT
17. BRIDGEND
18. RHONDDA CYNON TAFF
19. MERTHYR TYDFIL
20. CAERPHILLY
21. BLAENAU GWENT

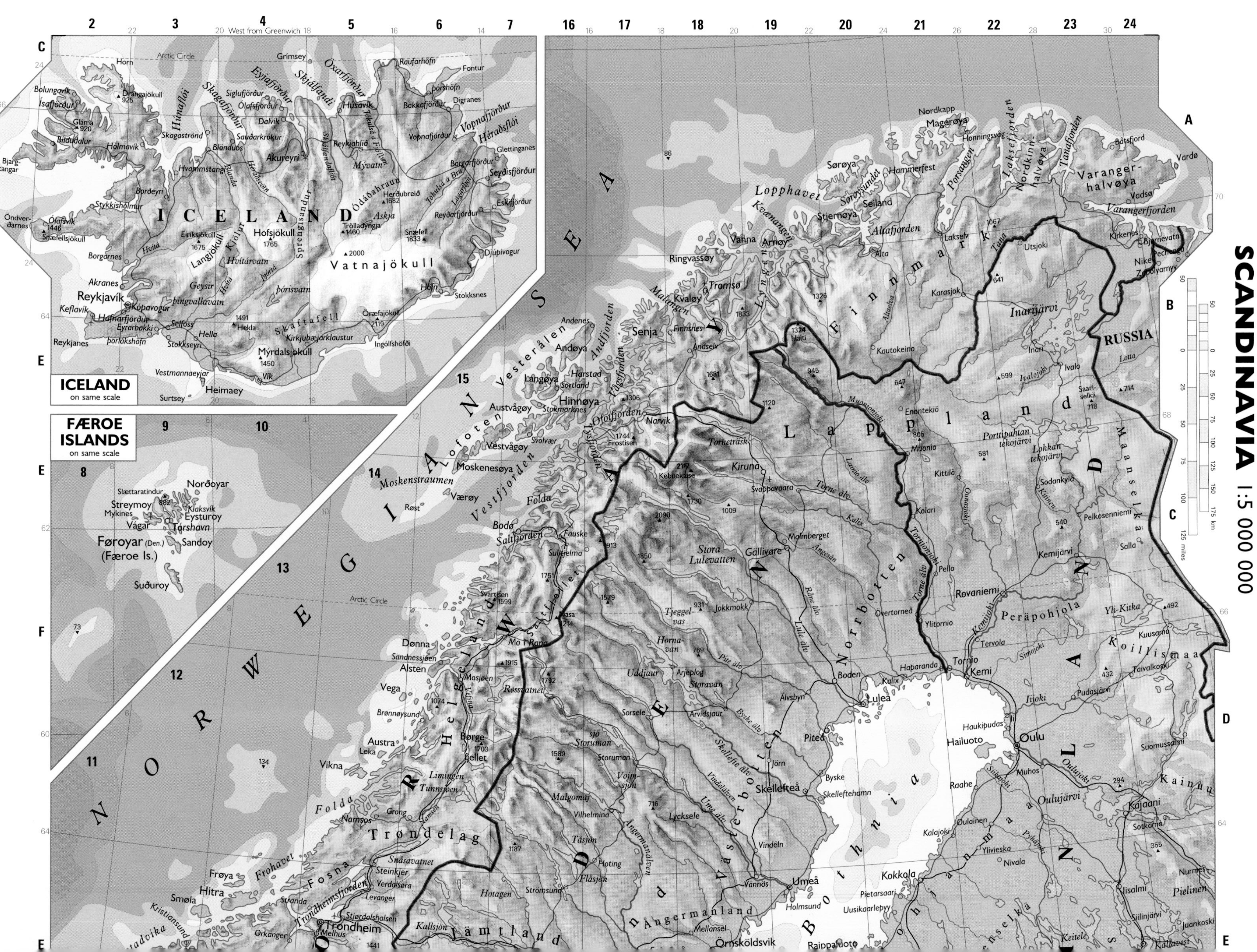

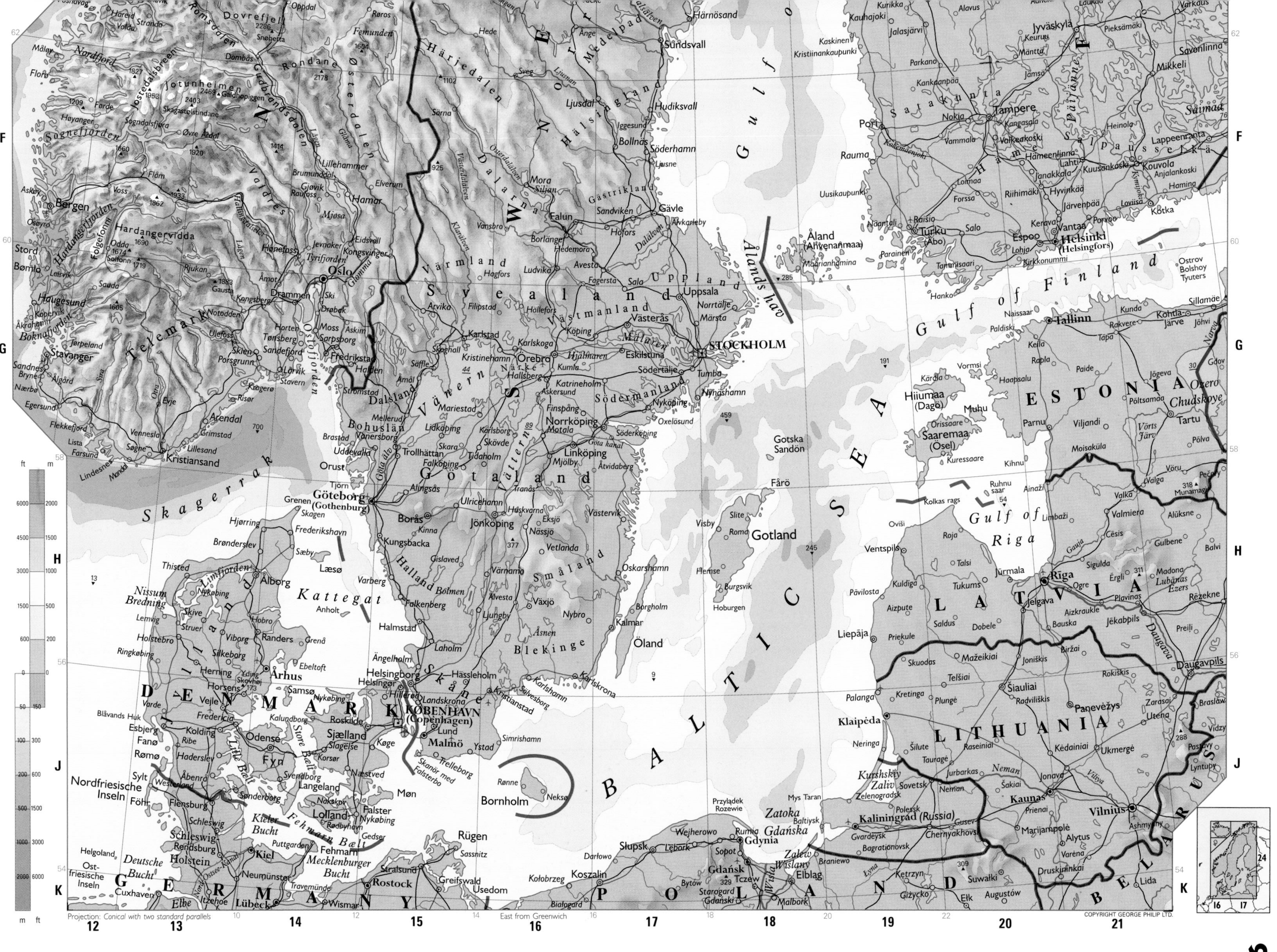

BALTIC SEA
Gulf of Finland
Gulf of Bothnia
Gulf of Riga
Ålands hav
Skagerrak
Kattegat
Store Bælt
Lille Bælt
Fehmarn Bælt
Kieler Bucht
Mecklenburger Bucht
Deutsche Bucht
Zatoka Gdańska
Zalew Wiślany
Kurshskiy Zaliv
Ostfjorden
Sognefjorden
Hardangerfjorden
Nordfjord
Limfjorden
NORWAY
SWEDEN
FINLAND
ESTONIA
LATVIA
LITHUANIA
BELARUS
RUSSIA
POLAND
GERMANY
DENMARK
Oslo
STOCKHOLM
Helsinki (Helsingfors)
Tallinn
Riga
Vilnius
KØBENHAVN (Copenhagen)
Göteborg (Gothenburg)
Bergen
Stavanger
Kristiansand
Malmö
Uppsala
Västerås
Örebro
Norrköping
Linköping
Jönköping
Borås
Gävle
Sundsvall
Härnösand
Hudiksvall
Falun
Tampere
Turku (Åbo)
Pori
Jyväskylä
Lahti
Kouvola
Mikkeli
Savonlinna
Tartu
Pärnu
Kaunas
Klaipėda
Šiauliai
Panevėžys
Liepāja
Ventspils
Daugavpils
Jelgava
Kaliningrad (Russia)
Gdańsk
Gdynia
Elbląg
Słupsk
Koszalin
Rostock
Lübeck
Kiel
Flensburg
Århus
Ålborg
Odense
Esbjerg
Gotland
Öland
Saaremaa (Ösel)
Hiiumaa (Dagö)
Åland (Ahvenanmaa)
Bornholm
Rügen
Sjælland
Fyn
Lolland
Falster
Møn
Fehmarn
Jotunheimen
Hardangervidda
Telemark
Dalarna
Värmland
Svealand
Götaland
Småland
Skåne
Blekinge
Halland
Vänern
Vättern
Mälaren
Nordfriesische Inseln
Projection: Conical with two standard parallels
East from Greenwich
COPYRIGHT GEORGE PHILIP LTD.

22. TORFAEN
23. CARDIFF
24. NEWPORT

II

ENGLAND

WALES

FRANCE

HAUTE-NORMANDIE

ENGLISH CHANNEL

Bristol Channel

Cardigan Bay

CHANNEL ISLANDS (U.K.)

Strait of Dover

Lowestoft, Southwold, Aldeburgh, Orford Ness, Felixstowe, Harwich, Walton-on-the-Naze, Clacton-on-Sea, Ipswich, Woodbridge, Stowmarket, Bury St. Edmunds, Newmarket, Ely, Cambridge, Peterborough, March, Chatteris, Huntingdon, St. Neots, Bedford, Northampton, Kettering, Corby, Wellingborough, Rushden, Milton Keynes, Bletchley, Luton, Dunstable, Hitchin, Stevenage, Letchworth, Welwyn Garden City, Hemel Hempstead, Watford, St. Albans

London, Chelmsford, Brentwood, Basildon, Southend-on-Sea, Canvey I., Rayleigh, Braintree, Halstead, Colchester, Witham, Maldon, Sheerness, Sittingbourne, Gillingham, Chatham, Rochester, Gravesend, Dartford, Maidstone, Royal Tunbridge Wells, Tonbridge, Ashford, Canterbury, Margate, Ramsgate, Deal, Dover, Folkestone, Hythe, New Romney, Dungeness, Rye, Hastings, Bexhill, Eastbourne, Beachy Head

Brighton, Hove, Shoreham by Sea, Worthing, Littlehampton, Bognor Regis, Chichester, Portsmouth, Gosport, Fareham, Southampton, Winchester, Basingstoke, Andover, Salisbury, Bournemouth, Poole, Weymouth, Portland Bill

Bristol, Bath, Gloucester, Cheltenham, Swindon, Oxford, Reading, Newbury, Chippenham, Trowbridge, Yeovil, Taunton, Exeter, Plymouth, Torquay, Paignton, Newton Abbot, Dartmouth, Brixham, Barnstaple, Bideford, Bude, Launceston, Bodmin, Newquay, Truro, Redruth, Camborne, Penzance, Land's End, St. Ives, Falmouth, Helston, Lizard Pt.

Cardiff, Newport, Swansea, Neath, Port Talbot, Bridgend, Merthyr Tydfil, Aberdare, Pontypridd, Caerphilly, Ebbw Vale, Abergavenny, Monmouth, Hereford, Leominster, Worcester, Kidderminster, Birmingham, Wolverhampton, Walsall, Dudley, Coventry, Warwick, Stratford-upon-Avon, Royal Leamington Spa, Rugby, Banbury

Carmarthen, Pembroke, Milford Haven, Fishguard, Aberystwyth, New Quay, Cardigan, Llandovery, Llandrindod Wells, Builth Wells, Brecon, Machynlleth

FRANCE (continental side): Calais, Boulogne-sur-Mer, Le Touquet-Paris-Plage, Berck, Le Tréport, Dieppe, Baie de la Somme, Fécamp, Étretat, Le Havre, Rouen, Mont-St-Aignan, Évreux, Lisieux, Deauville, Trouville-sur-Mer, Caen, Bayeux, Cherbourg, Coutances, St-Lô, Carentan, Valognes, St. Helier, Jersey, Guernsey, St. Peter Port, Alderney, Sark, Herm

Cotentin, Baie de la Seine, MANCHE, CALVADOS, SEINE-MARITIME

Isles of Scilly — On same scale — St. Mary's, Tresco, St. Ives, Camborne, Hayle, Penzance, Newlyn, Land's End

Elevation legend:

m	ft
1000	3000
500	1500
200	600
100	300
0	0

Projection: Lambert's Conformal Conic

COPYRIGHT GEORGE PHILIP LTD.

East from Greenwich · West from Greenwich

Key to Scottish unitary
authorities on map

1. CITY OF ABERDEEN
2. DUNDEE CITY
3. WEST DUNBARTONSHIRE
4. EAST DUNBARTONSHIRE
5. CITY OF GLASGOW
6. INVERCLYDE
7. RENFREWSHIRE
8. EAST RENFREWSHIRE
9. NORTH LANARKSHIRE
10. FALKIRK
11. CLACKMANNANSHIRE
12. WEST LOTHIAN
13. CITY OF EDINBURGH
14. MIDLOTHIAN

ORKNEY IS.
On same scale

SHETLAND IS.
On same scale

Projection : Lambert's Conformal Conic

West from Greenwich

COPYRIGHT GEORGE PHILIP LTD.

10 0 10 20 30 40 50 60 70 80 km
10 0 10 20 30 40 50 miles

ft m
3000 1000
1500 500
600 200
0 0
50 150
100 300
200 600
500 1500
1000 3000
2000 6000
m ft

Projection: Conical with two standard parallels

West from Greenwich

East from Greenwich
COPYRIGHT GEORGE PHILIP LTD.

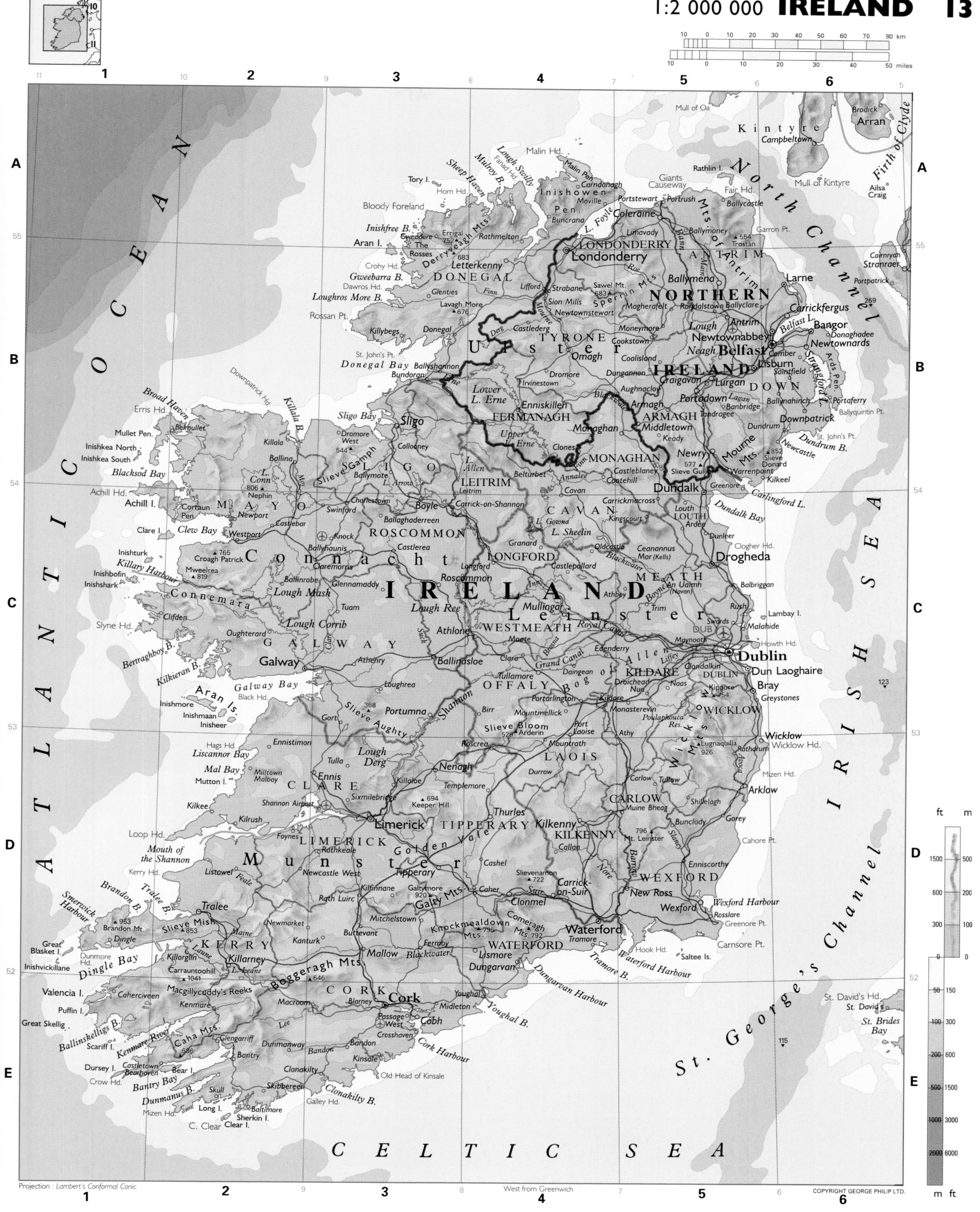

ATLANTIC OCEAN
NORTH SEA
CELTIC SEA
IRISH SEA
English Channel
St. George's Channel
Bristol Channel
North Channel
North Minch
Moray Firth
Pentland Firth
Firth of Clyde
Str. of Dover
The Wash
Cardigan Bay
Galway B.
Shetland Is.
Yell
Unst
Fetlar
Mainland
Lerwick
Foula
Fair Isle
Orkney Is.
Westray
Sanday
Stronsay
Kirkwall
Hoy
South Ronaldsay
C. Wrath
Thurso
Wick
Helmsdale
Outer Hebrides
Inner Hebrides
Lewis
Stornoway
Harris
St. Kilda
North Uist
Benbecula
South Uist
Barra
Skye
Portree
Rhum
Eigg
Coll
Tiree
Mull
Colonsay
Jura
Islay
Arran
North West Highlands
Grampian Mts.
Southern Uplands
SCOTLAND
Lairg
Golspie
Ullapool
Tain
Invergordon
Dingwall
Nairn
Elgin
Buckie
Banff
Fraserburgh
Peterhead
Inverness
L. Ness
Aviemore
Huntly
Inverurie
Aberdeen
Stonehaven
Mallaig
Fort William
Ben Nevis
Tobermory
Oban
Ballater
Montrose
Arbroath
Forfar
Dundee
St. Andrews
Perth
L. Lomond
Stirling
Glenrothes
Kirkcaldy
Dunfermline
Dunbar
Greenock
Paisley
Glasgow
Edinburgh
East Kilbride
Hamilton
Irvine
Kilmarnock
Ayr
Campbeltown
Galashiels
Berwick-upon-Tweed
Jedburgh
Hawick
Cheviot Hills
Alnwick
Girvan
Dumfries
Stranraer
Kirkcudbright
Annan
Mull of Galloway
Malin Hd.
Aran I.
Letterkenny
Buncrana
Coleraine
Londonderry
Ballymena
Larne
Lifford
Ulster
NORTHERN IRELAND
Lough Neagh
Antrim
Bangor
Belfast
Donegal
Bundoran
Omagh
Lower L. Erne
Portadown
Lisburn
Lurgan
Enniskillen
Armagh
Newry
Clones
Sligo
Ballina
Achill I.
L. Conn
Castlebar
Leitrim
Cavan
Castleblayney
Dundalk
Westport
Roscommon
Connacht
Lough Mask
Kells
Ceanannus Mor
Drogheda
Longford
Lough Ree
Connemara
Lough Corrib
Athlone
Mullingar
Boyne
Leinster
Galway
Ballinasloe
Tullamore
Liffey
Dublin
Dun Laoghaire
Bray
IRELAND
Aran Is.
Birr
Lough Derg
Port Laoise
Athy
Wicklow Mts.
Ennis
Nenagh
Carlow
Kilkenny
Arklow
Kilrush
Limerick
Thurles
Shannon
Listowel
Tipperary
Munster
Tralee
Carrick-on-Suir
Wexford
Rosslare
Dingle
Clonmel
Waterford
Carrauntoohill
Killarney
Mallow
Blackwater
Dungarvan
Valencia I.
Macgillycuddy's Reeks
Cork
Youghal
Cobh
Bandon
Kinsale
Bantry
C. Clear
UNITED KINGDOM
I. of Man
Douglas
Whitehaven
Workington
Carlisle
Cumbrian Mts.
Hexham
Gateshead
Newcastle-upon-Tyne
South Shields
Sunderland
Durham
Hartlepool
Redcar
Darlington
Middlesbrough
Stockton-on-Tees
Scarborough
Pennines
Barrow-in-Furness
Lancaster
Harrogate
York
Bridlington
Beverley
Kingston upon Hull
Blackpool
Keighley
Burnley
Leeds
Bradford
Preston
Blackburn
Halifax
Huddersfield
Scunthorpe
Grimsby
Humber
Bolton
Barnsley
Doncaster
Manchester
Oldham
Rotherham
Liverpool
Stockport
Sheffield
Warrington
Lincoln
Louth
Chesterfield
Crewe
Skegness
Mansfield
Anglesey
Holyhead
Bangor
Colwyn Bay
Chester
Wrexham
Snowdon
Stoke on Trent
Derby
Nottingham
Boston
Cromer
Stafford
Grantham
Pwllheli
Shrewsbury
ENGLAND
Telford
King's Lynn
Norwich
Great Yarmouth
Lowestoft
Nuneaton
Leicester
Peterborough
Welshpool
Wolverhampton
BIRMINGHAM
Coventry
Corby
Thetford
Aberystwyth
Cambrian Mts.
Redditch
Rugby
Northampton
Ely
Bury St. Edmunds
Worcester
Royal Leamington Spa
Bedford
Cambridge
Ipswich
WALES
Hereford
Milton Keynes
Felixstowe
Fishguard
Carmarthen
Brecon
Cheltenham
Cotswold Hills
Stevenage
Harwich
Gloucester
Oxford
Hemel Hempstead
Luton
Harlow
Colchester
Haverfordwest
Milford Haven
Pembroke
Merthyr Tydfil
Neath
Cwmbran
Chelmsford
Llanelli
Swansea
Rhondda
Newport
High Wycombe
Watford
Basildon
Southend-on-Sea
Port Talbot
Barry
Cardiff
Bristol
Swindon
Slough
Thames
LONDON
Chatham
Margate
Bath
Newbury
Reading
Canterbury
Weston-super-Mare
Basingstoke
Reigate
Maidstone
Dover
Barnstaple
Exmoor
Guildford
Ashford
Folkestone
Salisbury
Winchester
Crawley
Taunton
Yeovil
Southampton
Fareham
Hastings
Havant
Brighton
Eastbourne
Worthing
Bude
Exeter
Bournemouth
Portsmouth
Poole
Newport
Isle of Wight
Weymouth
Dartmoor
Exmouth
Newquay
Torbay
Truro
St. Austell
Plymouth
Falmouth
Land's End
Penzance
Isles of Scilly
Alderney
C. de la Hague
Pte. de Barfleur
Guernsey
St. Peter Port
Sark
Channel Is. (U.K.)
St. Helier
Jersey
Cherbourg
Valognes
Cotentin
Bayeux
Caen
Le Havre
Trouville-sur-Mer
Lisieux
Fécamp
Bolbec
Pays de Caux
Rouen
Elbeuf
Seine
Dieppe
Le Tréport
Abbeville
Amiens
Somme
Picardie
FRANCE
St-Quentin
Cambrai
Valenciennes
Lens
Béthune
Bruay-la-Buissière
Le Touquet-Paris-Plage
Boulogne-sur-Mer
C. Gris Nez
Calais
St-Omer
Dunkerque
Lille
Tournai
Ostende
Brugge
Gent
Antwerpen
Zeebrugge
Vlissingen
BELGIUM
BRUSSEL (Bruxelles)
NETHERLANDS
's-Gravenhage (Den Haag)
Hoek van Holland
ROTTERDAM
Dordrecht
Haarlem
Alkmaar
Den Helder
NORWAY
Askøy
Bergen
Os
Stord
Bømlo
Haugesund
Kopervik
Åkrahamn
Boknafjorden
Stavanger
Sandnes
Bryne
Nærbø
ft m
3000 1000
1500 500
600 200
0 0
50 150
100 300
200 600
500 1500
1000 3000
2000 6000
m ft
Projection: Conical with two standard parallels
East from Greenwich
West from Greenwich
COPYRIGHT GEORGE PHILIP LTD.

10 0 10 20 30 40 50 60 70 80 90 km
10 0 10 20 30 40 50 60 miles

NORTH SEA

UNITED KINGDOM

Cromer
North Walsham
The Broads
Norwich
Great Yarmouth
Bungay
Beccles
Lowestoft
Southwold
Saxmundham
Aldeburgh
Woodbridge
Orford Ness
Felixstowe

Margate
North Foreland
Ramsgate
Deal
Dover
Calais
Sangatte
Wissant
C. Gris Nez
Marquise
Ardres
Marck
Guines
Boulogne-sur-Mer
Étaples
Berck
Rue
Montreuil

Waddeneilanden

Helgoland Düne
Ostfriesische Inseln
Wangerooge
Langeoog
Spiekeroog
Baltrum
Norderney
Juist
Borkum
Scharhörn
Neuwerk
Alte Mellum
Minsen
Wangerooge

Terschelling
West-Terschelling
Ameland
Schiermonnikoog
Rottumeroog
Vlieland
Texel
Den Burg
Den Helder

Helgoland
Bremerhaven
Nordenham
Wilhelmshaven
Wittmund
Norden
Norddeich
Aurich
Emden
Leer
Oldenburg
Ostfriesland
Wiesmoor
Moormerland
Westerstede
Rastede
Varel
Jade
Bad Zwischenahn
Weener
Papenburg
Friesoythe
Cloppenburg
WESER-EMS

Leeuwarden
Franeker
Harlingen
Dokkum
Kollum
Holwerd
Zoutkamp
Bedum
Delfzijl
Groningen
Winschoten
Zuidhorn
Leek
Hoogezand-Sappemeer
Veendam
Assen
Stadskanaal
Ter Apel
Borger
Emmen
Klazienaveen
Neuenhaus
Emlichheim
Coevorden
Hoogeveen
Haren
Meppen
Lathen
Sögel
Löningen
Quakenbrück
Haselünne
Lohne
Vechta
Damme

FRIESLAND
Sneek
Bolsward
Workum
Staveren
Grouw
Heerenveen
Lemmer
Wolvega
Steenwijk
Oosterwolde
Beilen
DRENTHE

NOORD-HOLLAND
Medemblik
Enkhuizen
Hoorn
Edam
Purmerend
Alkmaar
Bergen
Heerhugowaard
Castricum
IJmuiden
Zaandam
Haarlem
Zandvoort
Hillegom
Noordwijk
Katwijk

Schagen
Urk
Emmeloord
Zwolle
Kampen
Meppel
Dronten
Lelystad
Almere-Stad
FLEVOLAND
IJsselmeer

Amsterdam
Bussum
Hilversum
Leiden
Alphen a/d Rijn
Zeist
Utrecht
UTRECHT
Gouda
Zoetermeer
Delft
's-Gravenhage (Den Haag)
Hoek van Holland
Vlaardingen
Europoort
Schiedam
Rotterdam
ZUID-HOLLAND
Hellevoetsluis
Goeree
Ouddorp
Schouwen
Dordrecht
Zierikzee
Gorinchem

Harderwijk
Heerde
Epe
Nijkerk
Ermelo
Apeldoorn
Deventer
Rijssen
Almelo
Hengelo
Enschede
Haaksbergen
Oldenzaal
Nordhorn
Lochem
Zutphen
Winterswijk
Doetinchem
Aalten
Bocholt
Borken
NORDRHEIN
Münster
Warendorf
Gütersloh
Greven
Rheine
Emsdetten
Steinfurt
Osnabrück
Georgsmarienhütte
Lengerich
Ibbenbüren
Bramsche
Wallenhorst
Lingen
Fürstenau
Bersenbrück

GELDERLAND
Ede
Barneveld
Amersfoort
Soest
Wageningen
Veenendaal
Tiel
Arnhem
Nijmegen
Oss
Cuijk
Kleve
Doesburg
Zevenaar
Emmerich
Kevelaer
Geldern
Xanten
Wesel
Dorsten
Haltern
Recklinghausen
Marl
Dülmen
Coesfeld
Senden
Lüdinghausen
Hamm
Beckum
Lippstadt
Soest
Unna
Kamen
Bergkamen
Werl

's-Hertogenbosch
Boxtel
Uden
Boxmeer
Venray
Venlo
Helmond
Deurne
Weert
Roermond
Maasbracht
Sittard
Heinsberg
Geilenkirchen
Erkelenz
Viersen
Krefeld
Mönchengladbach
München-gladbach
Grevenbroich
Neuss
Düsseldorf
Ratingen
Velbert
Wuppertal
Mülheim
Essen
Bochum
Witten
Hagen
Iserlohn
Menden
Arnsberg
Werdohl
Lüdenscheid
Meinerzhagen
Lennestadt
Gummersbach

Tilburg
Breda
Roosendaal
Bergen op Zoom
Goes
Middelburg
Vlissingen
Terneuzen
ZEELAND
Oosterhout
Essen
Kalmthout
Baarle-Nassau
Brecht
Turnhout
Geldrop
Valkenswaard
Nederweert
LIMBURG
Bree
Leopoldsburg
Maaseik
Geleen
Brunssum
Heerlen
Kerkrade
Jülich
Düren
Kerpen
Köln
Troisdorf
Siegburg
Bonn
Bergisch Gladbach
Wiehl
Overath
Remscheid
Solingen
Leverkusen
Siegen
Dillenburg
Haiger

Knokke-Heist
Zeebrugge
Blankenberge
De Haan
Brugge
Oostende
Nieuwpoort
De Panne
Veurne
Diksmuide
Torhout
Roeselare
Tielt
Deinze
Gent (Gand)
Oudenaarde
Aalst
Wetteren
Dendermonde
Sint-Niklaas
Beveren
Antwerpen
Herentals
Geel
Mol
Lommel
Hamont
Overpelt
Lier
Mechelen
Vilvoorde
Aarschot
Diest
Hasselt
Genk
Sittard
Tongeren
Maastricht
Sittard
Brunssum
Aachen
Stolberg
Eschweiler
Düren
Zülpich
Euskirchen
Schleiden
Prüm
Bitburg

VLAANDEREN
Ieper
Poperinge
Wervik
Menen
Kortrijk
Ronse
Geraardsbergen
Lessines
Ath
Halle
Waterloo
Brussel (Bruxelles)
Leuven
Tienen
Sint-Truiden
Waremme
Liège
Verviers
Eupen
Malmédy
St-Vith

BELGIUM
Nivelles
Gembloux
Wavre
Namur
Charleroi
NAMUR
Andenne
Huy
Seraing
Herstal
Amay
Spa
Stavelot
Vielsalm
Bastogne
Houffalize

NORD
Lille
Roubaix
Tourcoing
Mouscron
Villeneuve-d'Ascq
Seclin
Carvin
Hénin-Beaumont
Lens
Liévin
Béthune
Bully-les-Mines
Bruay-la-Buissière
Douai
Valenciennes
Orchies
St-Amand-les-Eaux
Maubeuge
Le Quesnoy
Avesnes
Fourmies
Hirson
Chimay
Couvin
Philippeville
Beaumont
Thuin
Binche
La Louvière
Courcelles
Mons
HAINAUT
Tournai
Leuze-en-Hainaut

PAS-DE-CALAIS
St-Omer
Cassel
Hazebrouck
Armentières
Aire-sur-la-Lys
St-Pol-sur-Ternoise
Frévent
Hesdin
Auxi-le-Château
Bapaume
Cambrai
Le Cateau-Cambrésis
Caudry
Solesmes
Landrecies

RHEINLAND-PFALZ
Wiesbaden
Mainz
Bingen
Bad Kreuznach
Idar-Oberstein
Kaiserslautern
Neustadt
Koblenz
Lahnstein
Boppard
Simmern
Bernkastel-Kues
Traben-Trarbach
Wittlich
Cochem
Daun
Mayen
Andernach
Neuwied
Bad Neuenahr-Ahrweiler
Remagen
Bad Honnef
Montabaur
Limburg
Hachenburg
Altenkirchen
Linz
Sinzig

LUXEMBOURG
Luxembourg
Diekirch
Vianden
Wiltz
Clervaux
Echternach
Grevenmacher
Mersch
Esch-sur-Alzette
Differdange
Pétange
Arlon
Bastogne
Libramont
Neufchâteau
Bouillon
Florenville
Virton

GERMANY
SAARLAND
Saarbrücken
Saarlouis
Merzig
St. Wendel
Neunkirchen
Homburg
Völklingen
Dillingen
St. Ingbert
Zweibrücken
Blieskastel
Pirmasens
Landau
Trier
Saarburg

FRANCE
Paris
Versailles
St-Denis
Sarcelles
Argenteuil
Nanterre
Créteil
Meaux
Dammartin-en-Goële
Compiègne
Senlis
Creil
Chantilly
Beauvais
Amiens
Albert
Péronne
St-Quentin
Ham
Guise
Vervins
Laon
Soissons
Reims
Château-Thierry
Épernay
Châlons-en-Champagne
Sainte-Menehould
Verdun
Metz
Thionville
Longwy
Longuyon
Montmédy
Sedan
Charleville-Mézières
Rethel
Vouziers
ARDENNES
MEUSE
MOSELLE
MEURTHE-ET-MOSELLE
LORRAINE
St-Mihiel
Commercy
Toul
Nancy
Pont-à-Mousson
Briey
Sarreguemines
Sarralbe
Sarre-Union
Bitche
Niederbronn-les-Bains
Haguenau
Bischwiller
Strasbourg
Kehl

PICARDIE
SOMME
OISE
AISNE
MARNE
SEINE-ET-MARNE
YVELINES
VAL-D'OISE
Gournay-en-Bray
Gisors
Pontoise
Mantes-la-Jolie
Rambouillet

North Sea

Projection: Lambert's Conformal Conic
East from Greenwich
COPYRIGHT GEORGE PHILIP LTD.

ft m
1500 500
600 200
50

m ft

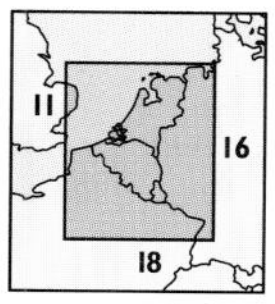

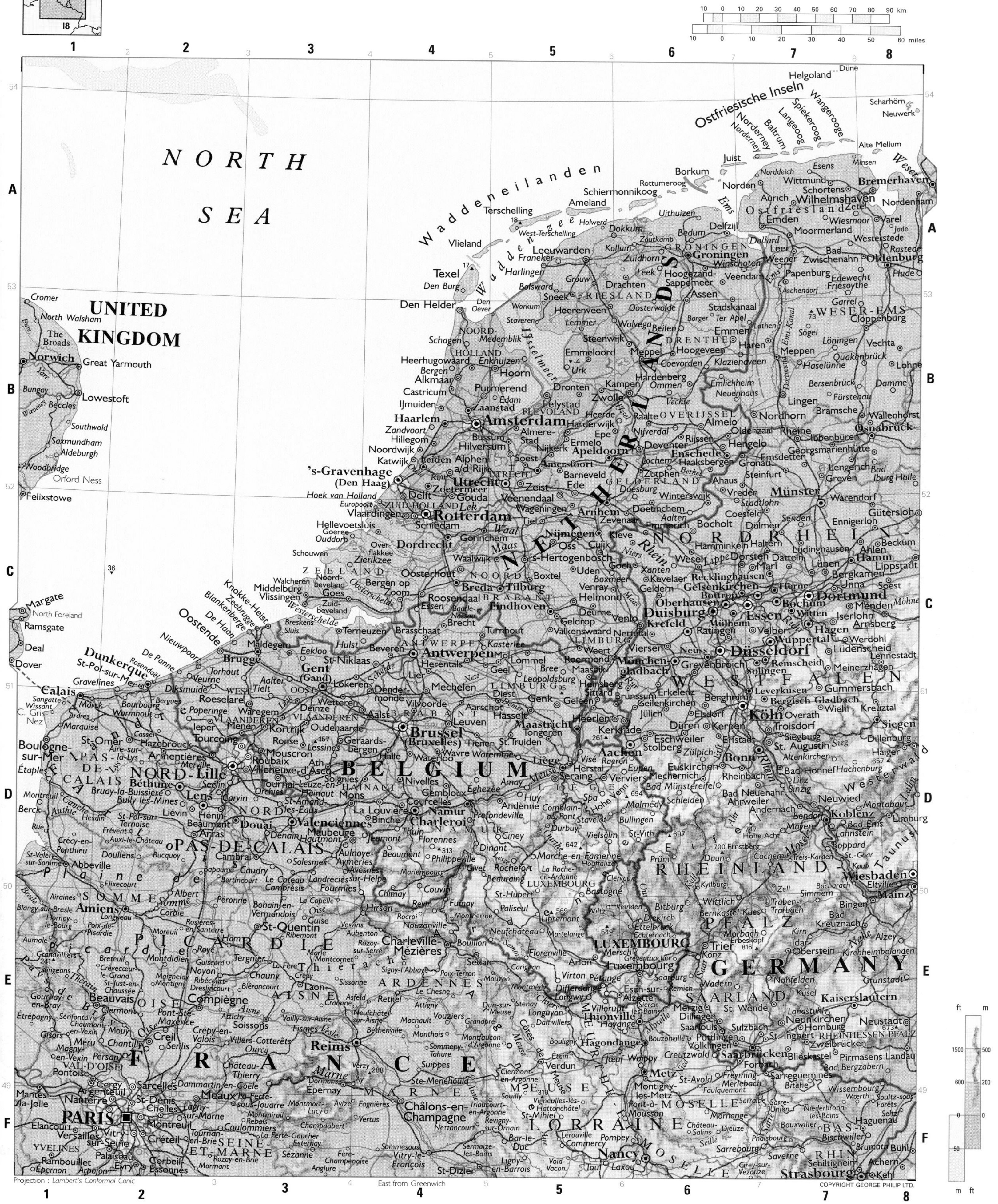

Underlined towns give their name to the administrative area in which they stand.

50 0 25 50 75 100 125 150 175 km
50 0 25 50 75 100 125 miles

Projection: Conical with two standard parallels

COPYRIGHT GEORGE PHILIP LTD

Corse (Corsica)
Ajaccio

C. Corse · Bastia · Calvi · Mte. Cinto 2710 · Corte · Porto-Vecchio · Bonifacio

GERMANY · BELGIUM · LUXEMBOURG · SWITZERLAND · AUSTRIA · ITALY · UNITED KINGDOM · ANDORRA

F R A N C E

English Channel · Bay of Biscay · MEDITERRANEAN SEA · Golfe du Lion · Golfe de Gascogne

PARIS · MARSEILLE · LYON · BORDEAUX · TOULOUSE · MONACO · TORINO (Turin) · MILANO · BRUXELLES Brussel · BRADFORT

West from Greenwich · East from Greenwich

m / ft 4000 3000 2000 1500 1000 500 200 0 · 12000 9000 6000 4500 3000 1500 600 0 · 50 100 200 · 150 300 600 1500 3000 6000 9000 12000

50 0 25 50 75 100 125 150 175 km
50 0 25 50 75 100 125 miles

1 2 3 4 5 6 7

SWITZERLAND
AUSTRIA Steiermark Graz
Kärnten Klagenfurt Wolfsberg
Karnische Alpen Villach
Lienz Bressanone Bolzano Merano
Maribor Nagykanizsa
Domodóssola Matterhorn Mte. Rosa
Sondrio Trento Rovereto Belluno
Vittório Véneto Udine Gorízia
SLOVENIA Ljubljana Celje Varaždin
Como Bérgamo Brescia Verona Vicenza Treviso Pordenone
Koper Trieste Zagreb
CROATIA
Novara **MILANO** Lodi Crema Mántova Pádova Venézia (Venice)
Golfo di Venézia
Karlovac Sisak
TORINO (Turin) Piemonte Pavia Cremona Rovigo Chióggia Istra
Rijeka Velika Kapela
Alessándria Piacenza Parma Módena Ferrara Comácchio Rovinj Pula Krk Senj
Bosanski Gradiška
FRANCE Cúneo Fossano Alba Reggio nell'Emília Bológna Ravenna Losinj Pag Banja Luka
Montélimar Gap Briançon
Savona Génova La Spézia Carrara Massa Lucca Prato Forlì Cesena Rímini Cres Kvarner Bihać
Avignon Digne-les-Bains
Riviera di Ponente Golfo di Génova Viaréggio Pisa **FIRENZE** (Florence) **SAN MARINO** Pésaro Fano Senigállia Ancona Zadar Dugi Otok
Carpentras Orange Aix-en-Provence
Livorno Cáscina Scandicci Arezzo Urbino Fabriano Falconara Maríttima Pasman
MARSEILLE Toulon Hyères
LIGURIAN SEA
Rosignano Maríttimo Volterra Siena Perúgia Assisi Macerata Fermo Šibenik Solta
La Seyne-sur-Mer
C. Corse Capraia Piombino Portoferráio Elba Grosseto L. Trasimeno Mte. Vettore San Benedetto del Tronto Teramo Ascoli Piceno Brač Hvar Vis
Cannes Antibes Monaco Monte-Carlo Menton San Remo Impéria
Calvi Bástia Corte Pianosa Montecristo Orbetello Viterbo Terni Áscoli Gran Sasso d'Itália Pescara Chieti Peljesac Korčula Lastovo
Corse Ajáccio Porto-Vecchio Bonifácio Giglio Mte. Argentario Civitavécchia Viterbo L. di Bolsena Rieti L'Áquila Lanciano Vasto Palagruza
Ólbia Maddalena **Bouches de Bonifácio** Lázio Tívoli Avezzano Térmoli
Asinara Golfo dell'Asinara Porto Torres Sássari **VATICAN CITY** **ROMA** Guidónia-Montecélio Mte. Amaro Sannicandro Gargánico
Alghero Bosa Núoro Pomézia Aprília Frosinone Isérnia Campobasso Manfredónia
Sardegna Mte. del Gennargentu Árbatax Lanusei Latina Cassino Fóggia Barletta Trani
G. di Oristano Oristano Terralba Ánzio Terracina Fórmia Caserta Cerignola Andria Molfetta Bar
Íglesias San Pietro Sant' Antíoco **Quartu Sant' Élena** Íschia Pozzuoli Avellino Altamura Putignano
San Pietro Carbónia **Cágliari** G. di Cágliari Ventoténe **NÁPOLI** Vesúvio Salerno Matera
C. Spartivento Torre del Greco Castellammare di Stábia Capri Sala Consilina Agri Tár
TYRRHENIAN SEA Lauria Cosenza
Ú33tica (Italy) Strómboli Coriglano Cálabro Rossano
Ísole Eólie Salina Lípari Vulcano Cetraro Crotone
Palermo Bagheria Términi Milazzo Messina Nicastro Sambiase Vibo Valéntia Catanzaro
Ísole Égadi Trápani Érice Cefalù Barcellona-Pozzo di Gotto Réggio di Calábria
Favignana Alcamo Segesta Monti Nébrodi Etna Taurianova Palmi
Marsala Castelvetrano Caltanissetta Enna Adrano Giarre Acireale Str. di Messina C. Spartivento
ALGERIA Mazara del Vallo Sciacca Platani Catánia Lentini
Sicília Canicattì Agrigento Gela Ragusa Siracusa Augusta
Collo El-Milia Skikda Bizerte Menzel-Bourguiba Ra's at Tib (C. Bon) Pantelleria (Italy) Licata Módica Avola C. Passero
Azzaba Annaba El Kala Tunis Golfe de Tunis La Marsa Kélibia Porto Empédocle Favara Víttoria Íspica
Guelma Jendouba Tabarka Mateur Ariana Ra's Mustafá Menzel-Temime
Mila Constantine Béja Medjez Korba Nabeul Hammamet Linosa
Souk-Ahras Tébourba Bardo Soliman Ben Arous Golfe de Hammamet
TUNISIA El Kef El Fahs Zaghouan Hamman Sousse **MEDITE**
Oum el Bouaghi Maktar Kalaa-Kebira Sousse Gozo Valletta
Khenchela Thala Moknine Monastir Rabat **MALTA**
Tébessa Makthar Kairouan M'saken Mahdia **Ísole Pelágie** (Italy)
Chéria El Jem Lampione
Aurès Babor Kasserine Sbeitla Sbekhat Sidi el Hani Lampedusa

ft m
12000 4000
9000 3000
6000 2000
4500 1500
3000 1000
1500 500
600 200
0 0
50 150
100 300
200 600
500 1500
1000 3000
2000 6000
3000 9000
4000 12000
m ft

Projection: Conical with two standard parallels

Projection: Conical with two standard parallels

JAPAN 1:5 000 000

50 0 25 50 75 100 125 150 175 km
50 0 25 50 75 100 125 miles

SEA OF OKHOTSK

Sakhalin (Russia)

La Perouse Strait (Sōya-Kaikyō)

HOKKAIDO

SAPPORO

TOHOKU

HONSHU

SEA OF JAPAN

RUSSIA

Lake Khanka

Vladivostok

CHINA

HEILONGJIANG

JILIN

NORTH KOREA

Projection: Conical with two standard parallels

Projection: Mercator

East from Greenwich

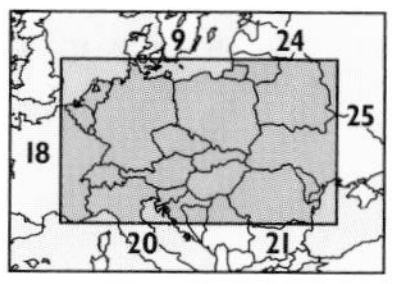

9 10 11 12 13 14 15 16

LITHUANIA
BELARUS
POLAND
UKRAINE
SLOVAK REP.
HUNGARY
ROMANIA
MOLDOVA
YUGOSLAVIA
BOSNIA-HERZEGOVINA
BULGARIA
CROATIA

Zatoka Gdańska
Zalew Wiślany
Kaliningrad (Russia)
Vilnius
MINSK
WARSZAWA (Warsaw)
KYYIV (Kiev)
BUDAPEST
BUCUREŞTI (Bucharest)
BEOGRAD (Belgrade)
Chişinău
Bratislava
Sarajevo

Gdynia
Gdańsk
Elbląg
Olsztyn
Bydgoszcz
Toruń
Grudziądz
Włocławek
Płock
Łódź
Radom
Lublin
Kielce
Częstochowa
Kraków
Katowice
Wrocław
Opole
Rzeszów
Tarnów
Białystok
Hrodna
Brest
Pinsk
Baranavichy
Babruysk
Mahilyow
Homyel
Mazyr
Lviv (Lvov)
Lutsk
Rivne
Ternopil
Zhytomyr
Khmelnytskyy
Vinnytsya
Ivano-Frankivsk
Chernivtsi
Uzhhorod
Košice
Prešov
Miskolc
Debrecen
Nyíregyháza
Szeged
Pécs
Oradea
Cluj-Napoca
Arad
Timişoara
Sibiu
Braşov
Iaşi
Bacău
Galaţi
Brăila
Constanţa
Ploieşti
Craiova
Novi Sad
Subotica
Tiraspol
Tighina
Bălţi
Ruse
Varna
Dobrich

Carpaţi Meridionali
Transilvania
Vojvodina
Podilska Vysochyna
Pripet Marshes
Dunărea (Danube)
Dnister
Dnepr

B
C
D
E
F
G

9 10 11 12 13 14 15

East from Greenwich

FRANCE 1:5 000 000

50 0 25 50 75 100 125 150 175 km

50 0 25 50 75 100 125 miles

Projection: Conical with two standard parallels

West from Greenwich | East from Greenwich

m	ft
4000	12000
3000	9000
2000	6000
1500	4500
1000	3000
500	1500
200	600
0	0
50	150
100	300
200	600
500	1500
1000	3000
2000	6000
3000	9000
4000	12000

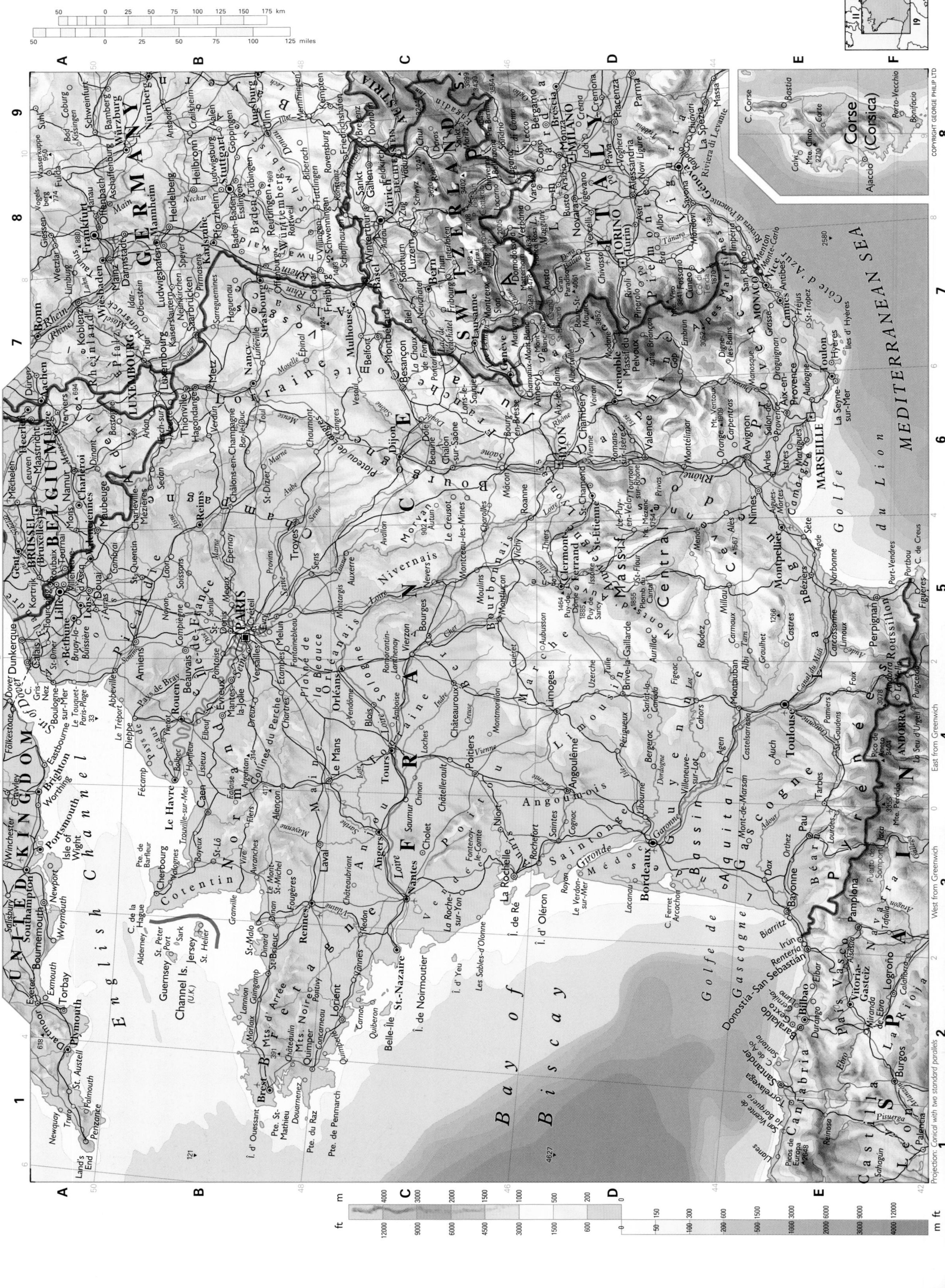

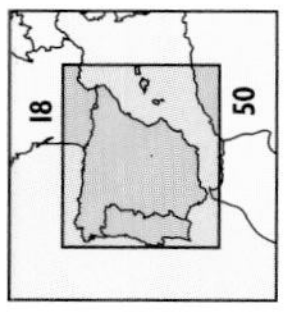

50 0 25 50 75 100 125 150 175 km

50 0 25 50 75 100 125 miles

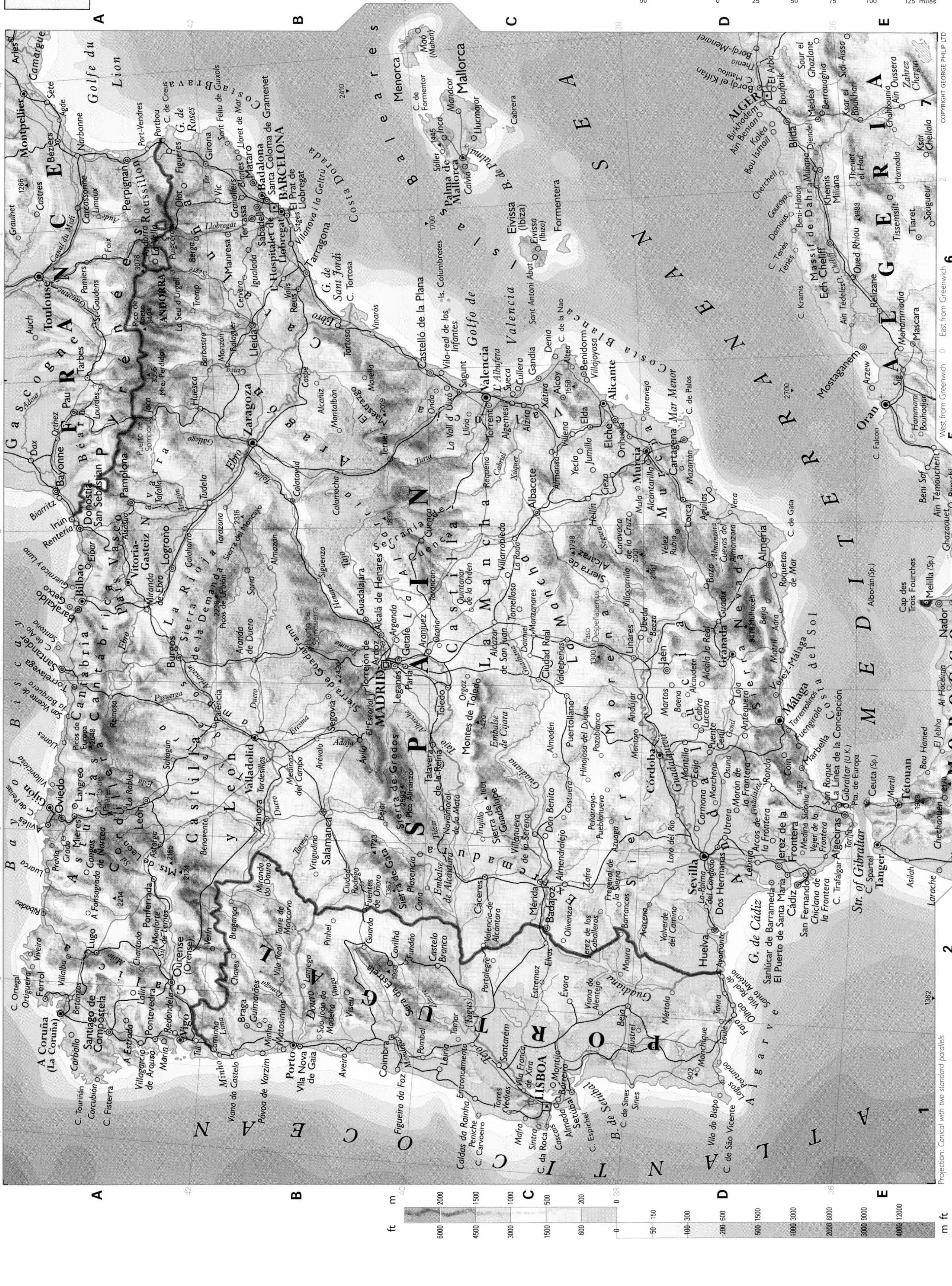

Projection: Conical with two standard parallels

ITALY AND THE BALKAN STATES 1:5 000 000

Projection: Conical with two standard parallels

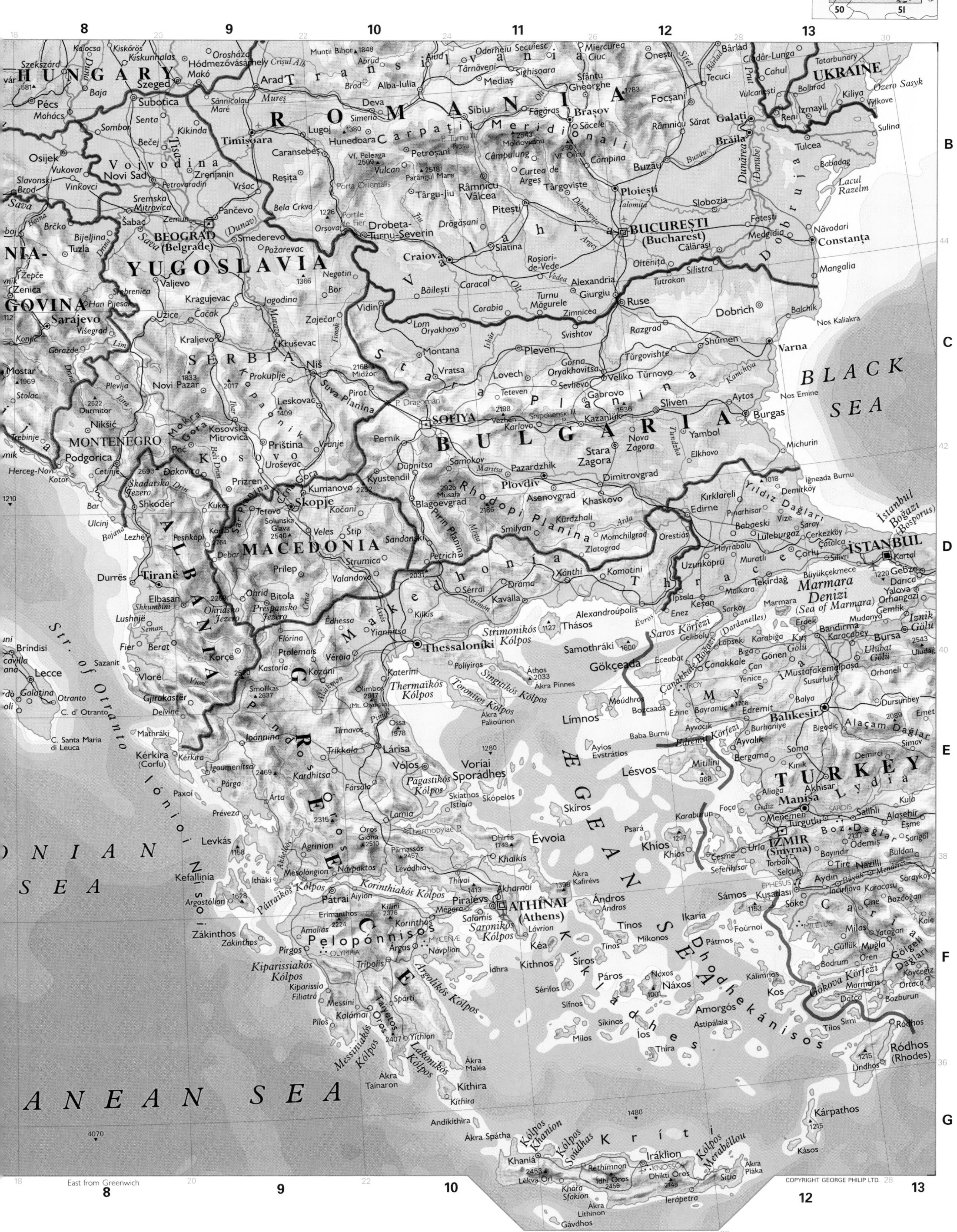
HUNGARY
ROMANIA
UKRAINE
YUGOSLAVIA
SERBIA
MONTENEGRO
Kosovo
MACEDONIA
ALBANIA
BULGARIA
GREECE
TURKEY
Transilvania
Carpații Meridionali
Vojvodina
Walachia
Dobruja
Stara Planina
Rhodopi Planina
Makedhonía
Thrace
Mysia
Lydia
Caria
Pindhos Oros
Pelopónnisos
Kikládhes
Dhodhekánisos
Kríti
BLACK SEA
AEGEAN SEA
IONIAN SEA
MEDITERRANEAN SEA
Marmara Denizi (Sea of Marmara)
Str. of Otranto
Ionioi Nisoi
BUCUREȘTI (Bucharest)
BEOGRAD (Belgrade)
SOFIYA
Skopje
Tiranë
ATHÍNAI (Athens)
İSTANBUL
İZMIR (Smyrna)
Thessaloníki
Sarajevo
Podgorica
Constanța
Varna
Burgas
Plovdiv
Edirne
Bursa
Balıkesir
Manisa
Pátrai
Iráklion
Rodhos (Rhodes)
Kérkira (Corfu)
Lésvos
Khíos
Sámos
Límnos
Thásos
Évvoia
Kefallinía
Zákinthos
Náxos
Kárpathos
Saros Körfezi
Çanakkale Boğazı (Dardanelles)
İstanbul Boğazı (Bosporus)
Thermaïkós Kólpos
Korinthiakós Kólpos
Saronikós Kólpos
Argolikós Kólpos
Lakonikós Kólpos
Messiniakós Kólpos
Kiparissiakós Kólpos
Gökova Körfezi
Dunărea (Danube)
Dunav
East from Greenwich
COPYRIGHT GEORGE PHILIP LTD.

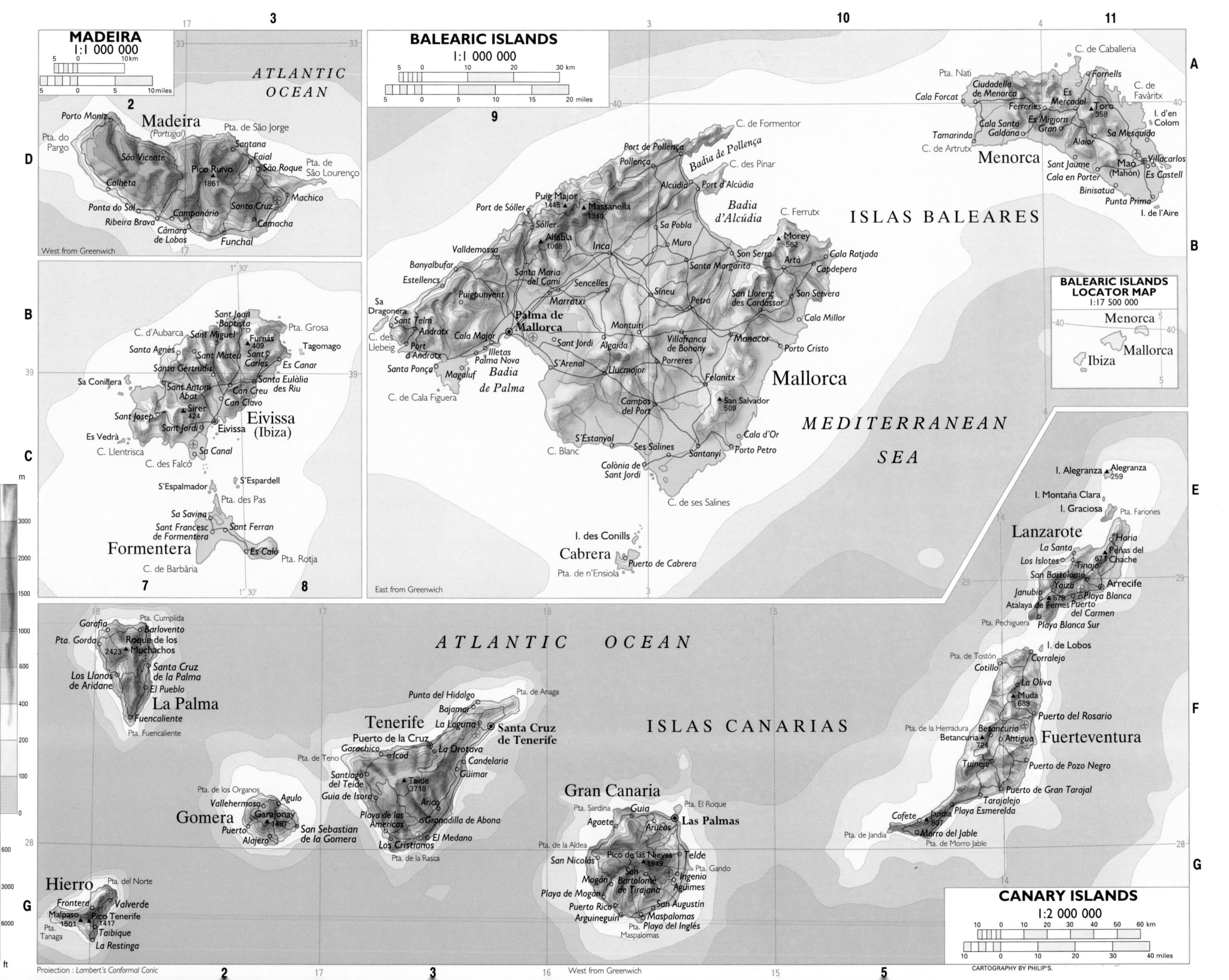
BALEARIC ISLANDS
1:1 000 000
BALEARIC ISLANDS LOCATOR MAP
1:17 500 000
ISLAS BALEARES
MEDITERRANEAN SEA
Menorca
Mallorca
Ibiza
Cabrera
Palma de Mallorca
Badia de Palma
Badia d'Alcúdia
Badia de Pollença
C. de Formentor
C. de Caballeria
Ciudadella de Menorca
Maó (Mahón)
Es Mercadal
Toro 358
Puig Major 1445
Massanella 1348
San Salvador 509
Morey 562
Manacor
Inca
Sóller
Pollença
Alcúdia
Felanitx
Santanyí
Porto Cristo
Cala Ratjada
Andratx
Valldemossa
Sa Dragonera
East from Greenwich
MADEIRA
1:1 000 000
Madeira (Portugal)
ATLANTIC OCEAN
Funchal
Pico Ruivo 1861
Porto Moniz
Santana
Machico
Pta. de São Lourenço
West from Greenwich
Eivissa (Ibiza)
Formentera
Sant Antoni Abat
Santa Eulària des Riu
Sant Joan Baptista
Sa Conillera
Es Vedrà
Sant Francesc de Formentera
C. de Barbària
Pta. de sa Mola
CANARY ISLANDS
1:2 000 000
ISLAS CANARIAS
ATLANTIC OCEAN
Lanzarote
Arrecife
I. Graciosa
I. Alegranza
Fuerteventura
Puerto del Rosario
I. de Lobos
Gran Canaria
Las Palmas
Pico de las Nieves 1949
Maspalomas
Tenerife
Santa Cruz de Tenerife
Teide 3718
Puerto de la Cruz
Los Cristianos
Gomera
San Sebastian de la Gomera
Garajonay 1487
La Palma
Santa Cruz de la Palma
Roque de los Muchachos 2423
Hierro
Valverde
Pico Tenerife 1501
Pta. de Anaga
Pta. de Jandía
Projection : Lambert's Conformal Conic
CARTOGRAPHY BY PHILIP'S.

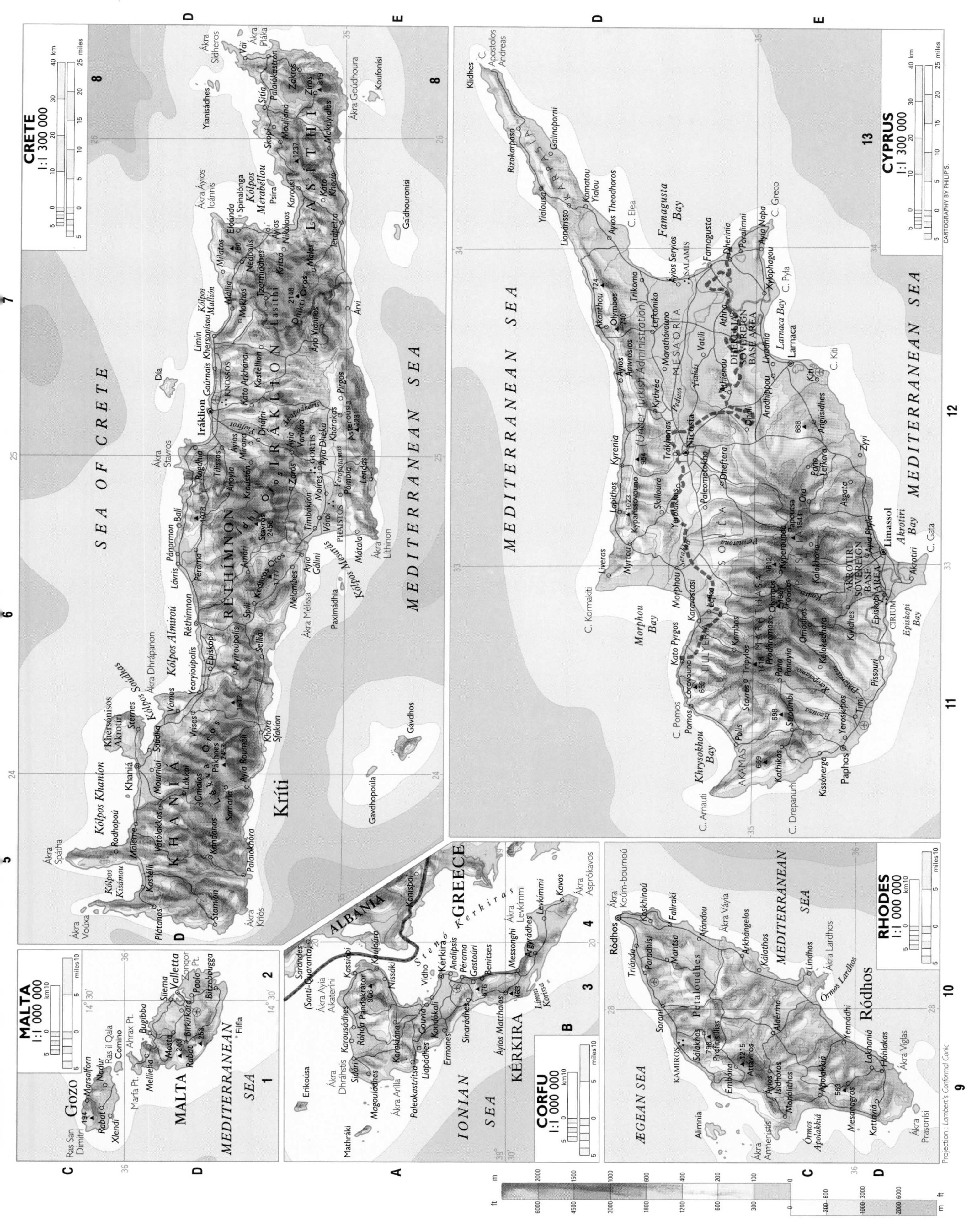
CRETE
1:1 300 000
SEA OF CRETE
MEDITERRANEAN SEA
Kríti
CYPRUS
1:1 300 000
MEDITERRANEAN SEA
Famagusta Bay
Morphou Bay
Larnaca Bay
Akrotiri Bay
Episkopi Bay
MALTA
1:1 000 000
Gozo
MALTA
MEDITERRANEAN SEA
Valletta
CORFU
1:1 000 000
KÉRKIRA
IONIAN SEA
ALBANIA
GREECE
RHODES
1:1 000 000
Ródhos
ÆGEAN SEA
MEDITERRANEAN SEA
Projection : Lambert's Conformal Conic
CARTOGRAPHY BY PHILIP'S.

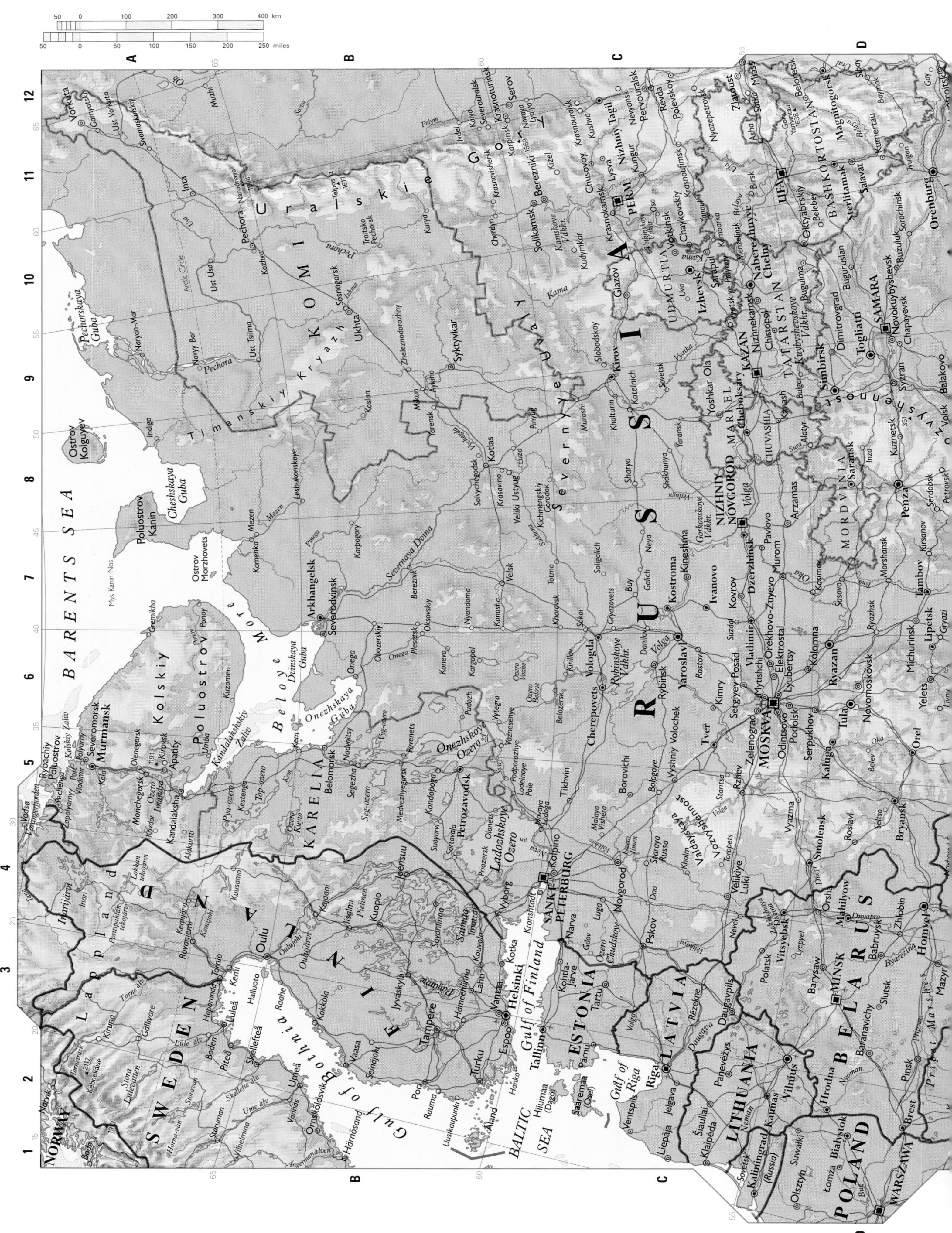

50 0 100 200 300 400 km
50 0 50 100 150 200 250 miles
BARENTS SEA
BALTIC SEA
Gulf of Bothnia
Gulf of Finland
Gulf of Riga
Beloye More
NORWAY
SWEDEN
FINLAND
ESTONIA
LATVIA
LITHUANIA
BELARUS
POLAND
RUSSIA
KARELIA
KOMI
UDMURTIA
TATARSTAN
BASHKORTOSTAN
CHUVASHIA
MORDVINIA
MARI EL
Lappland
Poluostrov Kolskiy
Timanskiy Kryazh
Uralskie Gory
Severnyye Uvaly
Ostrov Kolguyev
Poluostrov Kanin
Cheshskaya Guba
Pechorskaya Guba
MOSKVA
SANKT-PETERBURG
Helsinki
Tallinn
Rīga
Vilnius
MINSK
WARSZAWA
Murmansk
Arkhangelsk
Severodvinsk
Petrozavodsk
Vologda
Yaroslavl
Kostroma
Ivanovo
NIZHNIY NOVGOROD
KAZAN
PERM
UFA
SAMARA
Izhevsk
Kirov
Syktyvkar
Ukhta
Pechora
Inta
Vorkuta
Kotlas
Cherepovets
Novgorod
Pskov
Tver
Smolensk
Bryansk
Kaluga
Tula
Ryazan
Penza
Saransk
Tolyatti
Simbirsk
Orenburg
Oulu
Tampere
Turku
Kuopio
Joensuu
Luleå
Umeå
Kaliningrad
Ladozhskoye Ozero
Onezhskoye Ozero
Volga
Kama
Pechora
Severnaya Dvina
Arctic Circle

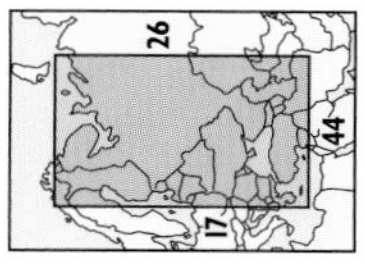

26
17
44

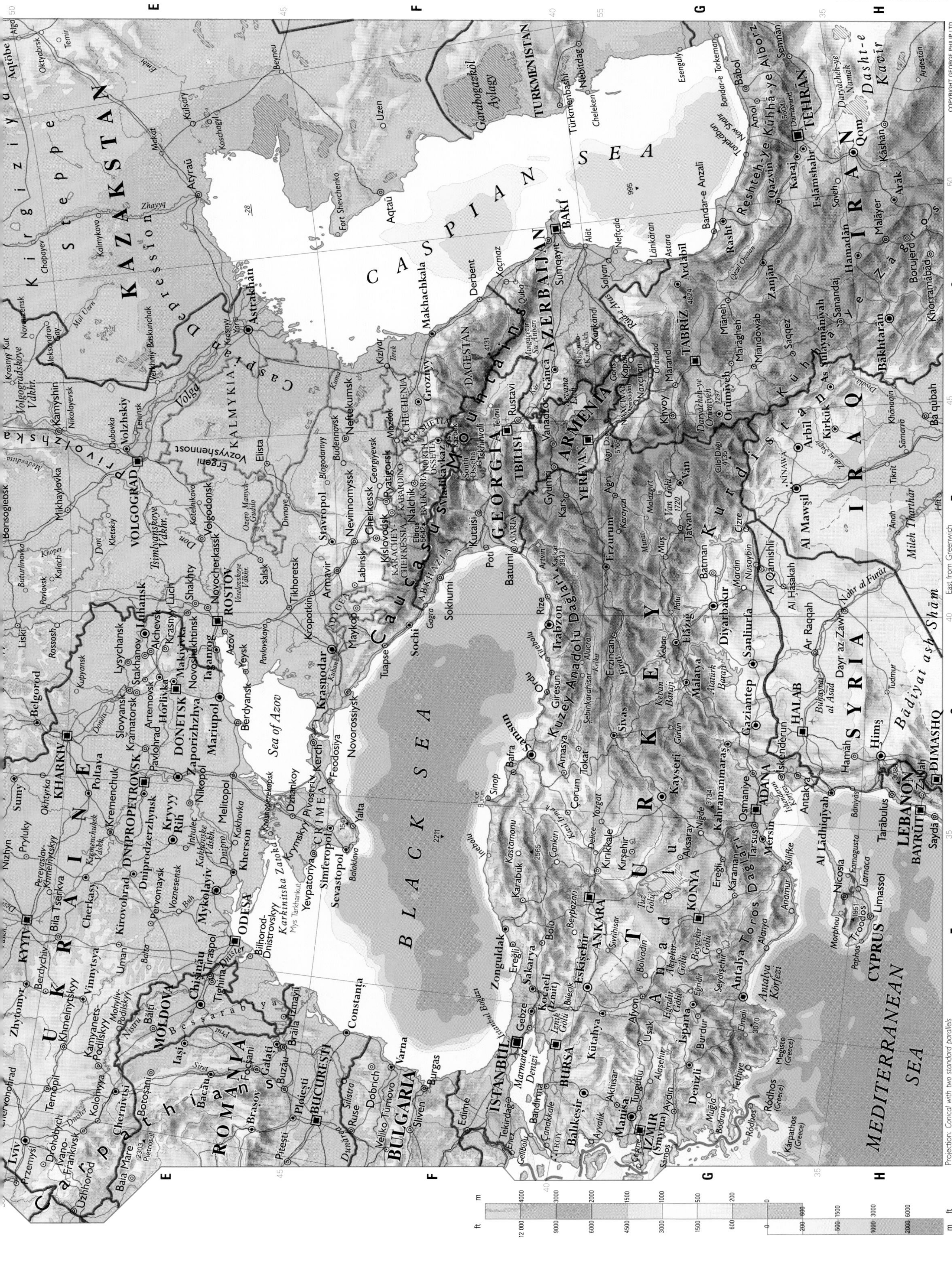

KAZAKSTAN
UKRAINE
ROMANIA
MOLDOVA
BULGARIA
GEORGIA
ARMENIA
AZERBAIJAN
TURKMENISTAN
TURKEY
SYRIA
IRAQ
IRAN
LEBANON
CYPRUS
CASPIAN SEA
BLACK SEA
Sea of Azov
MEDITERRANEAN SEA
Caucasus Mountains
Caspian Depression
KYYIV
KHARKIV
DNIPROPETROVSK
DONETSK
ODESA
VOLGOGRAD
ROSTOV
BUCUREȘTI
ISTANBUL
ANKARA
BURSA
KONYA
ADANA
TBILISI
YEREVAN
BAKI
TEHRĀN
TABRĪZ
HALAB
DIMASHQ
BAYRŪT
Projection: Conical with two standard parallels
East from Greenwich
COPYRIGHT GEORGE PHILIP LTD.
m
ft

A
B
C
D
E
F
9
10
11
12
13
14
15
16
17
18
19
Chukchi Sea
Mys Dezhneva (East C.)
Uelen
St. Lawrence I. (U.S.A.)
Bering Sea
East Siberian Sea
Ostrov Vrangelya
Laptev Sea
OCEAN
Novosibirskiye Ostrova
Ostrov Kotelnyy
Ostrov Faddeyevskiy
Ostrov Novaya Sibir
Ostrov Bennetta
Ostrova Delonga
Ostrov Zhokhova
Ostrov Genriyetty
Ostrov Zhannetty
Ostrov Belkovskiy
Ostrov Stolbovoy
Lyakhovskiye Ostrova
Ostrov Malyy Lyakhovskiy
Ostrov Bolshoy Lyakhovskiy
Proliv Dmitriya Lapteva
Ostrova Medvezhi
Ostrov Ayon
Mys Arkticheskiy
Ostrov Shmidta
Ostrov Komsomolets
Ostrov Pioner
Ostrov Oktyabrskoy Revolyutsii
Ostrov Bolshevik
Severnaya Zemlya
Proliv Vilkitskogo
Mys Chelyuskin
Gory Byrranga
Poluostrov Taymyr
Oz. Taymyr
Ostrov Bolshoy Begichev
Nordvik
Khatanga
Novorybnoye
Volochanka
Kheta
Gory Putorana
Ust Olenek
Saskylakh
Olenek
Tit-Ary
Bulun
Kyusyur
Tiksi
Mys Buorkhaya
Kazachye
Ust Kuyga
Chokurdakh
Indigirka
Nizhne Kolymsk
Srednekolymsk
Cherskiy
Ambarchik
Pevek
Ust Chaun
Bilibino
Chukotskoye Nagorye
Egvekinot
Vankarem
Provideniya
Anadyrskiy Zaliv
Anadyr
Beringovskiy
Khatyrka
Koryakskoye Nagorye
Kamenskoye
Penzhino
Markovo
Yerepol
Omolon
Kolymskoye Nagorye
Kolyma
Zyryanka
Druzhino
Deputatskiy
Verkhoyanskiy Khrebet
Verkhoyansk
Batagai
Khrebet Cherskogo
Gora Chen 2682
Pobeda 3147
Ust-Nera
Oymyakon
Susuman
Yagodnoye
Magadan
Palatka
Atka
Orotukan
Omsukchan
Evensk
Nayakhan
Gizhiga
Paren
Penzhinskaya Guba
Gizhiginskaya Guba
Zaliv Shelikhova
Palana
Tigil
Sredinnyy Khrebet
Poluostrov Kamchatka
Ossora
Ostrov Karaginskiy
Tilichiki
Kavacha
Ust-Kamchatsk
Uka
Kluchevskaya Gora 4750
Petropavlovsk-Kamchatskiy
Ust-Bolsheretsk
Kirovskiy
Ust Khayryuzovo
Komandorskiye Ostrova
Nikolskoye
Sea of Okhotsk
Okhotsk
Ulya
Arka
Okhotskiy Perevoz
Khandyga
Ytyk Kyuyel
Borogontsy
Batamay
Sangar
Lena
Zhigansk
Kystatyam
Arctic Circle
Yakutsk
Mayya
Amga
Pokrovsk
Namtsy
Verkhnevilyuysk
Vilyuysk
Vilyuy
Nyurba
Suntar
Mirnyy
Chernyshevskiy
Yukta
Tura
Noginsk
Nizhnyaya Tunguska
Yessey
Olenek
Zhilinda
SAKHA
RUSSIA
Ust Maya
Ust-Mili
Aim
Maya
Nelkan
Khrebet Dzhugdzur
Ayan
Ostrov Bolshoy Shantar
Sakhalinskiy Zaliv
Okha
Sakhalin
Aleksandrovsk-Sakhalinskiy
Gora Lopatina
Poronaysk
Uglegorsk
Yuzhno-Sakhalinsk
Kholmsk
Korsakov
Kurilskiye Ostrova
Ostrov Paramushir
Severo-Kurilsk
Ostrov Onekotan
Ostrov Simushir
Ostrov Urup
Ostrov Iturup
Kurilsk
Ostrov Kunashir
Nikolayevsk-na-Amur
Chumikan
Tugur
Uda
Amgun
Amur
Khrebet Sikhote Alin
Vanino
Komsomolsk
Amursk
Khabarovsk
Birobidzhan
Smidovich
Obluchye
Bikin
Lesozavodsk
Dalnerechensk
Spassk Dalniy
Ussuriysk
Vladivostok
Artem
Nakhodka
Kraskino
Dalnegorsk
Terney
Olga
Amgu
Sea of Japan
Olekminsk
Aldan
Tommot
Chagda
Uchur
Neryungri
Nagornyy
Stanovoy Khrebet
Tynda
Zeya
Skovorodino
Dzhalinda
Ushumun
Svobodnyy
Blagoveshchensk
Belogorsk
Shimanovsk
Norsk
Bureya
Chegdomyn
Zavitinsk
Raychikhinsk
Poyarkovo
Lensk
Vitim
Mama
Bodaybo
Chara
Kalakan
Karalon
Ust-Nyukzha
Yablonovyy Khrebet
Mogocha
Bagdarin
Barguzin
Ozero Baykal
Chita
Shilka
Nerchinsk
Sretensk
Bukachacha
Argun
Gulian
Kirensk
Korshunovo
Ust-Ilimsk
Makarovo
Ust-Kut
Zheleznogorsk-Ilimskiy
Magistralnyy
Bratsk
Boguchany
Kondratyevo
Angara
Chuna
Yeniseysk
Kezhma
Vanavara
Podkamennaya Tunguska
Kuyumba
Mutoray
Yerbogachen
Severo-Yeniseyskiy
Krasnoyarsk
Kansk
Ilanskiy
Tayshet
Nizhneudinsk
Tulun
Zima
Cheremkhovo
Usolye Sibirskoye
Angarsk
Irkutsk
Ulan Ude
Slyudyanka
Gusinoozersk
Kyakhta
Petrovsk-Zabaykalskiy
Khilok
Aginskoye
Olovyannaya
Borzya
Zabaykalsk
Manzhouli
Hailar
Nenjiang
Da Hinggan Ling
Vostochnyy Sayan
Sayan
Artemovsk
Munku-Sardyk 3491
Turan
Toora-Khem
Kyzyl
Samagaltay
Hovsgol Nuur
Hatgal
Erzin
Zakamensk
Darhan
Hentiyn Nuruu
Ulaanbaatar
Hangayn Nuruu
Hyargas Nuur
Uliastay
Tsetserleg
Lun
Choybalsan
Ondorhaan
Tamsagbulag
Hulun Nur
MONGOLIA
Altay
Gobi
Dalandzadgad
Saynshand
Erenhot
Xilinhot
Linxi
Chifeng
Chengde
Zhangjiakou
Hohhot
Baotou
BEIJING
Hami
Gaxun Nur
CHINA
QIQIHAR
Hegang
Jiamusi
HARBIN
Mudanjiang
JILIN
CHANGCHUN
Siping
FUSHUN
Tonghua
SHENYANG
ANSHAN
Dandong
Yingkou
DALIAN
Dongbei
Ang'angxi
Nen Jiang
Tao'an
Yanji
Ch'ongjin
NORTH KOREA
Wonsan
P'YONGYANG
Nampo
SOUL
Kansong
INCH'ON
SOUTH KOREA
TAEJON
TAEGU
PUSAN
Hokkaido
Wakkanai
Rumoi
Abashiri
Obihiro
Kushiro
SAPPORO
Otaru
Hakodate
Aomori
Hachinohe
Akita
Honshu
Niigata
Kanazawa
Fuji-San 3776
OSAKA
JAPAN
COPYRIGHT GEORGE PHILIP LTD.

ASIA : Physical 1:50 000 000

500 0 250 500 750 1000 1250 1500 1750 km

500 0 250 500 750 1000 1250 miles

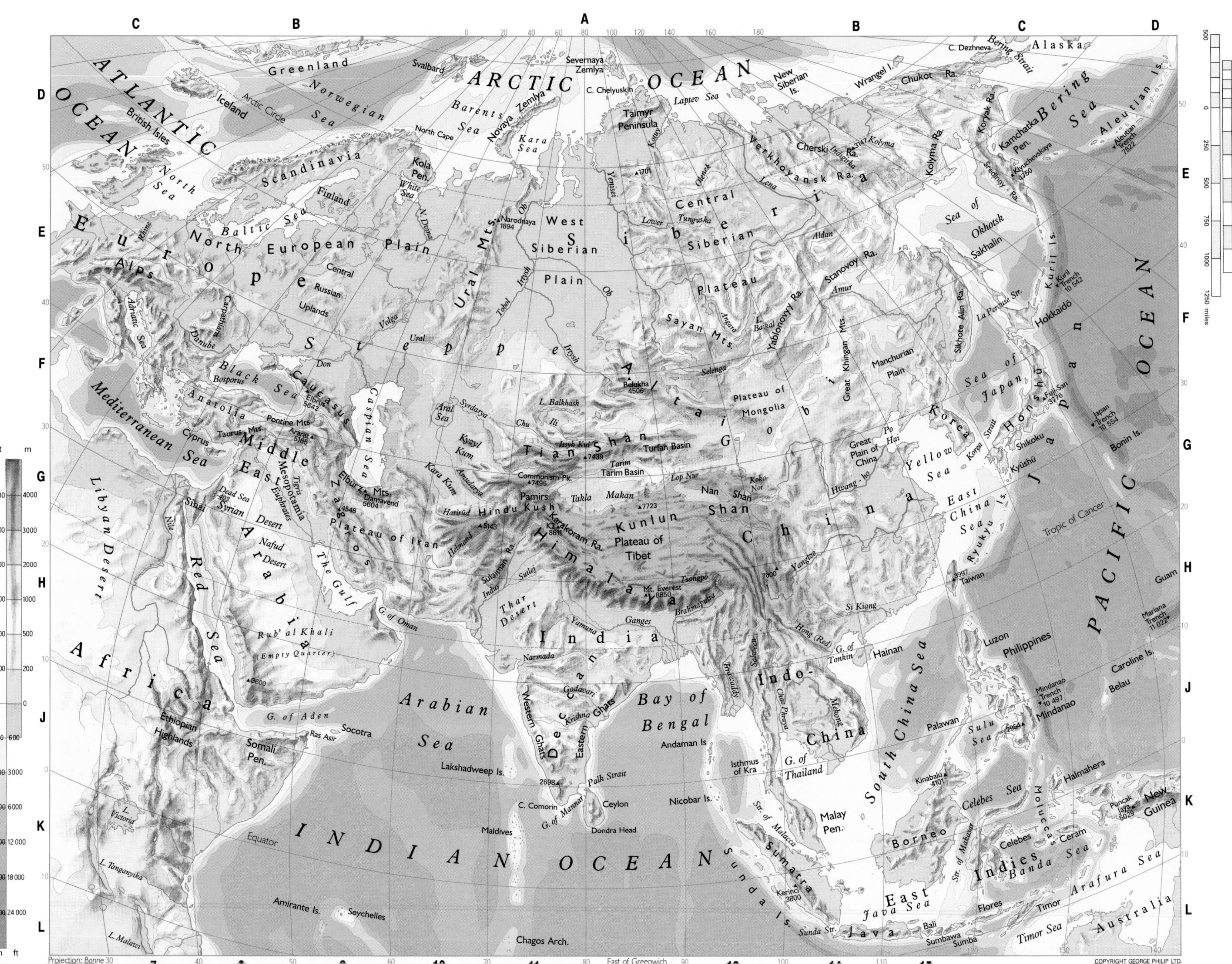

m 4000 3000 2000 1000 500 200 0 200 1000 2000 4000 6000 8000

ft 12 000 9000 6000 3000 1500 600 0 600 3000 6000 12 000 18 000 24 000

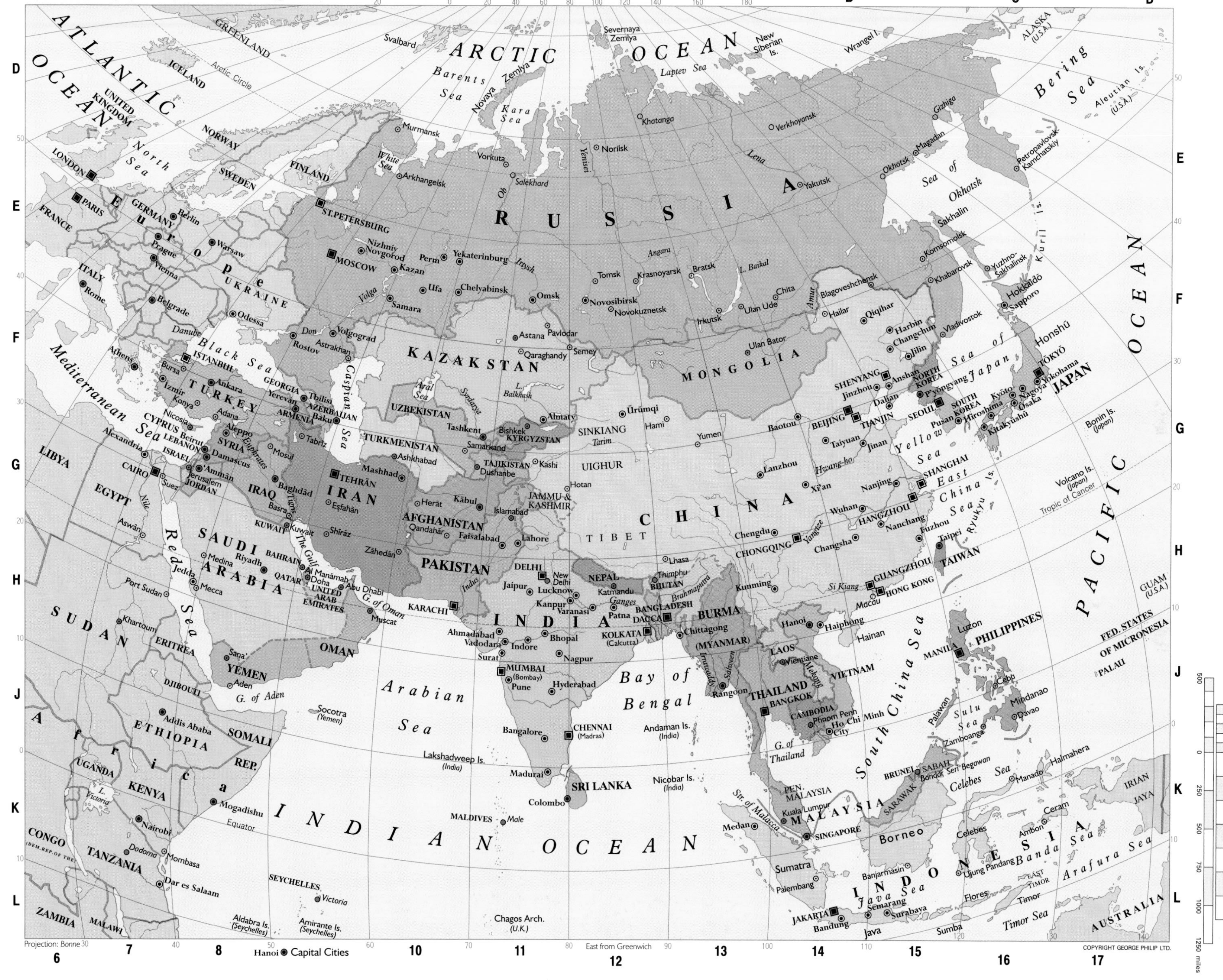
500 0 250 500 750 1000 1250 1500 1750 km
500 0 250 500 750 1000 1250 miles
ARCTIC OCEAN
Barents Sea
Kara Sea
Laptev Sea
Bering Sea
Sea of Okhotsk
Sea of Japan
Yellow Sea
East China Sea
South China Sea
PACIFIC OCEAN
INDIAN OCEAN
ATLANTIC OCEAN
Arabian Sea
Bay of Bengal
Caspian Sea
Black Sea
Mediterranean Sea
Red Sea
R U S S I A
KAZAKSTAN
MONGOLIA
C H I N A
I N D I A
JAPAN
IRAN
AFGHANISTAN
PAKISTAN
SAUDI ARABIA
TURKEY
IRAQ
SYRIA
OMAN
YEMEN
BURMA (MYANMAR)
THAILAND
VIETNAM
PHILIPPINES
MALAYSIA
I N D O N E S I A
SRI LANKA
NEPAL
BANGLADESH
TAIWAN
Africa
Europe
MOSCOW
ST.PETERSBURG
BEIJING
TEHRĀN
TŌKYŌ
Tropic of Cancer
Equator
Arctic Circle
Hanoi ● Capital Cities
Projection: Bonne
East from Greenwich
COPYRIGHT GEORGE PHILIP LTD.

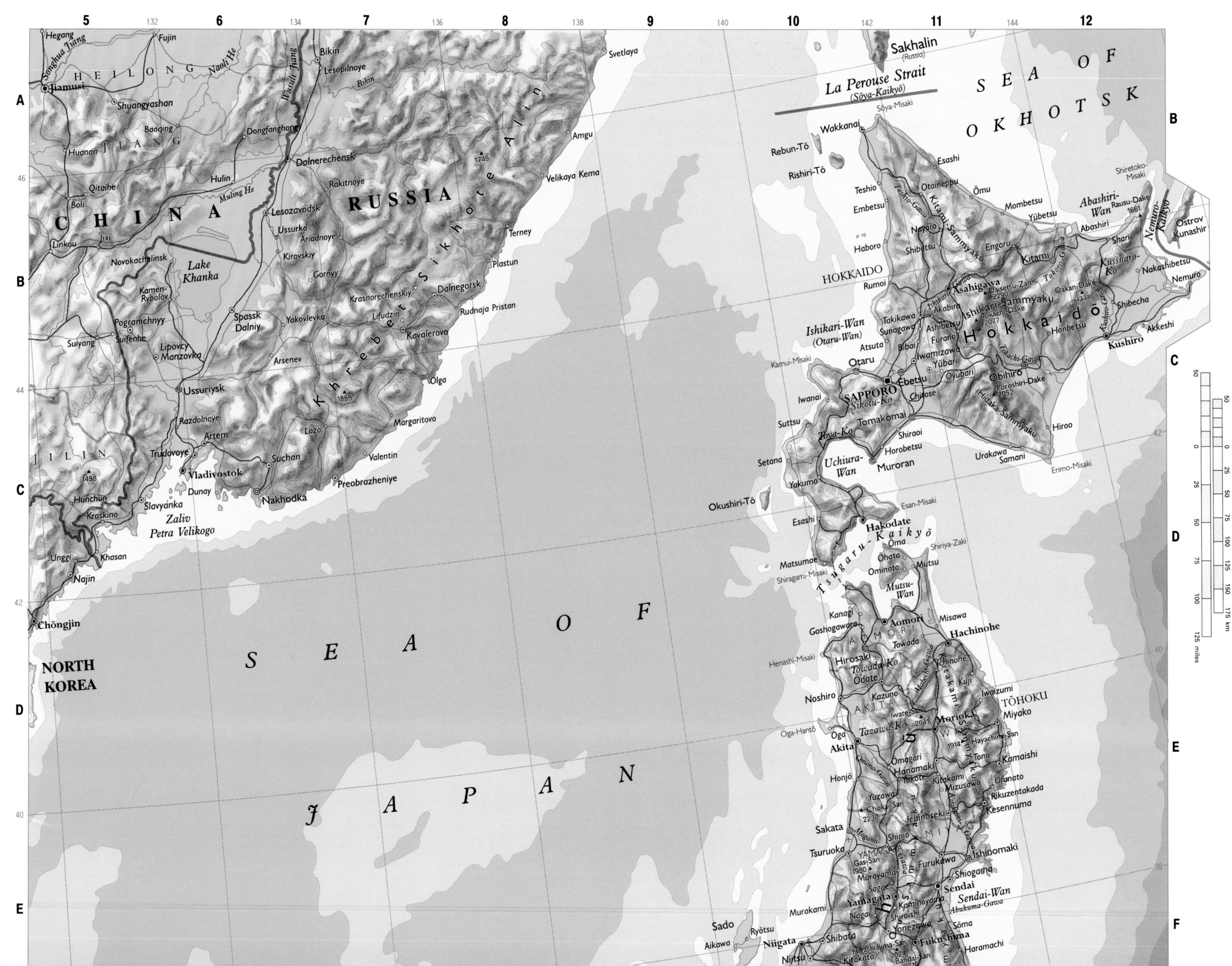

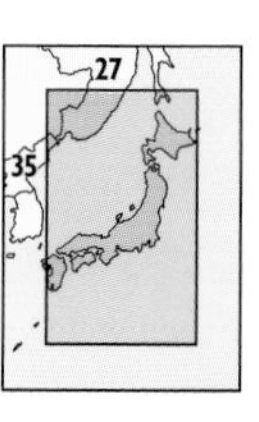
JAPAN
SOUTH KOREA
PACIFIC OCEAN
Korea Strait
RYUKYU ISLANDS
on same scale
EAST CHINA SEA
PACIFIC OCEAN
Nansei-Shotō (Ryukyu Is.)
Senkaku-Shotō
Sakashima-Guntō
Yaeyama-Rettō
Miyako-Rettō
Okinawa-Guntō
Amami-Guntō
Okinawa-Jima
Naha
Koza
Kume-Shima
Amami-Ō-Shima
Tokuno-Shima
KAGOSHIMA
OKINAWA
Ishigaki-Shima
Iriomote-Jima
Miyako-Jima
Yonaguni-Jima
Izu-Shotō
Nanpō-Shotō
Ōsumi-Shotō
Ōsumi-Kaikyō
Tokara-Rettō
Satsunan-Shotō
Kii-Suidō
Bungō-Suidō
Tosa-Wan
Ise-Wan
Suruga-Wan
Wakasa-Wan
Toyama-Wan
Goto-Rettō
Tsushima
Iki
Oki-Shotō
Ullŭng-do
(S. Korea)
Tok-do
Pohang
Yŏngdŏk
Tane-ga-Shima
Yaku-Shima
Miyanoura-Dake
1935
Koshiki-Rettō
Amakusa-Shotō
CHŪGOKU
SHIKOKU
KINKI
KYŪSHŪ
KANTŌ
Honshū
Shikoku
Kyūshū
TŌKYŌ
YOKOHAMA
KAWASAKI
NAGOYA
KYŌTO
ŌSAKA
KŌBE
HIROSHIMA
KITAKYŪSHŪ
FUKUOKA
Nagasaki
Kumamoto
Kagoshima
Miyazaki
Ōita
Okayama
Matsuyama
Kōchi
Takamatsu
Tokushima
Wakayama
Nara
Shizuoka
Hamamatsu
Kanazawa
Toyama
Fukui
Gifu
Tsu
Chiba
Kōfu
Nagano
Maebashi
Utsunomiya
Mito
Hitachi
Chōshi
Kushimoto
Muroto
Shimonoseki
Matsue
Tottori
Izumo
Yonago
8412
9076
6365
7214
Projection: Conical with two standard parallels
East from Greenwich
COPYRIGHT GEORGE PHILIP LTD.
m
ft

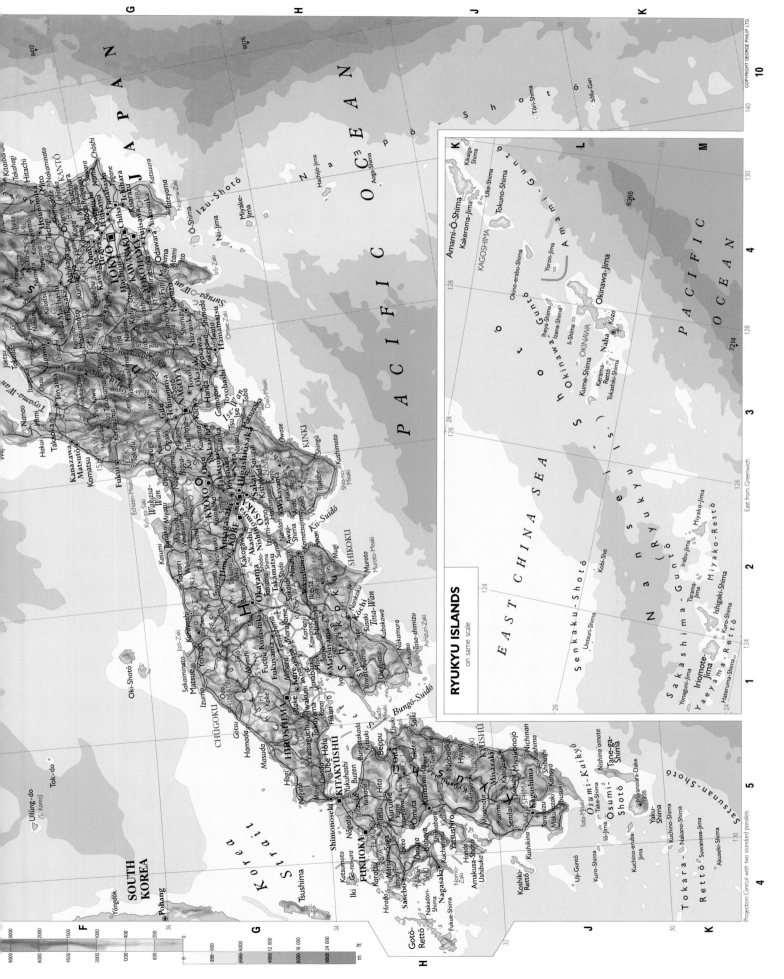

27
40
38
37

6
7
8
9
B
C
D
E
120
130
140
110
50
40
30
20
Bukachacha
Chita
Sretensk
Nerchinsk
Olovyannaya
Borzya
Priargunsk
Manzhouli
Hulun Nur
Hailar
Gulian
Yilehuli Shan
Oroqen Zizhiqi
Nenjiang
Bei'an
Shimanovsk
Svobodnyy
Chegdomyn
Blagoveshchensk
Aihui
Bureya
Amur
Komsomolsk
Aleksandrovsk-Sakhalinskiy
Ozero Bolon
Vanino
Poronaysk
Mys Terpeniya
Sakhalin
Tartarskiy Proliv
Yuzhno-Sakhalinsk
Kholmsk
La Perouse Str.
Wakkanai
Birobidzhan
Obluchye
Khabarovsk
Qianjin
Bikin
Khrebet Sikhote Alin
Hegang
Jiamusi
Shuangyashan
Yichun
Xiao Hinggan Ling
HEILONGJIANG
QIQIHAR
Buir Nur
Choybalsan
Kerulen
Arxan
Solon
Da Hinggan Ling
Butha Qi
Daqing
Anda
Suihua
HARBIN
Hulin
Jixi
Mishan
L. Khanka
Tamsagbulag
Horqin Youyi Qianqi
Baicheng
Shuangcheng
Dongbei (Manchuria)
Tao'an
Fuyu
Mudanjiang
Ussuriysk
Artem
Partizansk
Nakhodka
Vladivostok
Saynshand
Huolin Gol
Xilinhot
1949
Borhoyn Tal
Erenhot
Linxi
NEI MONGOL ZIZHIQU (INNER MONGOLIA)
CHANGCHUN
JILIN
Shuangliao
Dunhua
Songhua Hu
Hunchun
Sonid Youqi
Tongliao
Siping
Liaoyuan
Changbei Shan
Yanji
Baihe
2744
Chŏngjin
Duolun
Chifeng
Tieling
FUSHUN
Fuxin
SHENYANG
Benxi
Tonghua
Chaoyang
Liaoyang
LIAONING
Jinzhou
Yingkou
ANSHAN
Dandong
Yalu Jiang
Kimchaek
SEA OF JAPAN
Hohhot
Jining
Zhangjiakou
Chengde
Qinhuangdao
Xuanhua
Datong
BEIJING (PEKING)
BEIJING SHI
TANGSHAN
Liaodong Wan
Liaodong Bandao
Korea Bay
NORTH KOREA
Hamhung
Hŭngnam
Wŏnsan
P'YŎNGYANG
Namp'o
DALIAN
Baoding
Anci
TIANJIN
TIANJINN SHI
Yuanping
3058
HEBEI
Cangzhou
Bo Hai
Haeju
Kaesŏng
Ch'unch'ŏn
Kangnŭng
SŎUL (SEOUL)
INCH'ŎN
SOUTH KOREA
TAIYUAN
SHIJIAZHUANG
Yangquan
Yuci
Fenyang
Dezhou
Huang He
Ye Xian
Yantai
Weihai
Shandong Bandao
Weifang
YELLOW SEA
JINAN
ZIBO
SHANDONG
QINGDAO
Handan
Anyang
Tai'an
Changzhi
Rizhao
Linfen
Jincheng
Xinxiang
Jining
Zaozhuang
Lianyungang
Tongchuan
Sanmenxia
Luoyang
Kaifeng
ZHENGZHOU
Grand Canal
Shangqiu
Huaibei
Xuzhou
Qingjiang
Yancheng
XI'AN
HENAN
Pingdingshan
Shangshui
Hongze Hu
JIANGSU
Nanyang
Fuyang
Bengbu
Yangzhou
Taizhou
Zhumadian
Huainan
Huai He
Han Shui
Shiyan
Xiangfan
Dabie Shan
Xinyang
HEFEI
NANJING
Changzhou
Wuxi
Nantong
Suzhou
SHANGHAI
SHANGHAI SHI
ANHUI
Ma'anshan
Wuhu
Zhongxiang
HUBEI
Tongling
Wuxing
Jiaxing
Yichang
WUHAN
Anqing
HANGZHOU
Hangzhou Wan
Shashi
Huangshi
Chang Jiang (Yangtze)
Tunxi
Shaoxing
NINGBO
Enshi
Yueyang
Jiujiang
Jingdezhen
ZHEJIANG
Jinhua
EAST CHINA SEA
Changde
Dongting Hu
Poyang Hu
Quzhou
LINHAI
NANCHANG
Shangrao
Yiyang
CHANGSHA
HUNAN
JIANGXI
Wenzhou
Xiangtan
Pingxiang
Fuzhou
Wuyi Shan
2120
Shaoyang
Ji'an
Hengyang
Nanping
Min Jiang
Gan Jiang
Sanming
FUZHOU
Yong'an
Ganzhou
FUJIAN
Xiang Jiang
Ruijin
Putian
Xing'an
Longyan
Quanzhou
Nan Ling
Shaoguan
Zhangzhou
Xiamen
Bei Jiang
Mei Xian
Chaozhou
GUANGDONG
GUANGZHOU (CANTON)
Shantou
Wuzhou
Xun Jiang
Zhaoqing
Foshan
Huizhou
Jiangmen
HONG KONG
Yangjiang
Macau
Xi Jiang
Maoming
Zhanjiang
Haikou
Hainan Dao
1879
HAINAN
SOUTH CHINA SEA
Taiwan Strait
Chilung
T'AIPEI
Hsinchu
T'aichung
Changhua
Chiai
Yu Shan
3997
TAIWAN (FORMOSA)
T'ainan
T'aitung
KAOHSIUNG
P'ingtung
Batan Is.
PHILIPPINES
Babuyan Is.
Taejŏn
TAEGU
PUSAN
Kunsan
Chŏnju
Masan
KWANGJU
1915
Mokp'o
Cheju-do
1950
Korea Strait
Tsushima
Shimonoseki
KITAKYUSHU
FUKUOKA
Sasebo
Nagasaki
Kumamoto
Kyūshū
Miyazaki
Kagoshima
Yaku-Shima
Tane-ga-Shima
HIROSHIMA
Okayama
Kure
Matsuyama
Shikoku
Kōchi
KŌBE
KYŌTO
ŌSAKA
Sakai
Wakayama
Matsue
Komatsu
Kanazawa
Takaoka
Toyama
Wajima
Jōetsu
Niigata
Sado
Yamagata
Sendai
Fukushima
Kōriyama
Utsunomiya
Mito
TŌKYŌ
KAWASAKI
YOKOHAMA
NAGOYA
Fuji-San
3776
Shizuoka
Hamamatsu
Honshū
Akita
Sakata
Ishinomaki
Aomori
Hachinohe
Morioka
Tsugaru-Kaikyō
Hakodate
Muroran
Erimo-misaki
Otaru
SAPPORO
Hokkaidō
Asahigawa
2290
Kitami
Kushiro
Nampō-Shotō
JAPAN
Amami-Ō-Shima
Tokuno-Shima
Ryūkyū-rettō
Okinawa-Jima
Naha
Sakishima-Guntō
Miyako-Jima
Ishigaki-Shima
Iriomote-Jima
Tropic of Cancer
7507
PACIFIC OCEAN
Baykal
Ulan Ude
CHINA
MONGOLIA

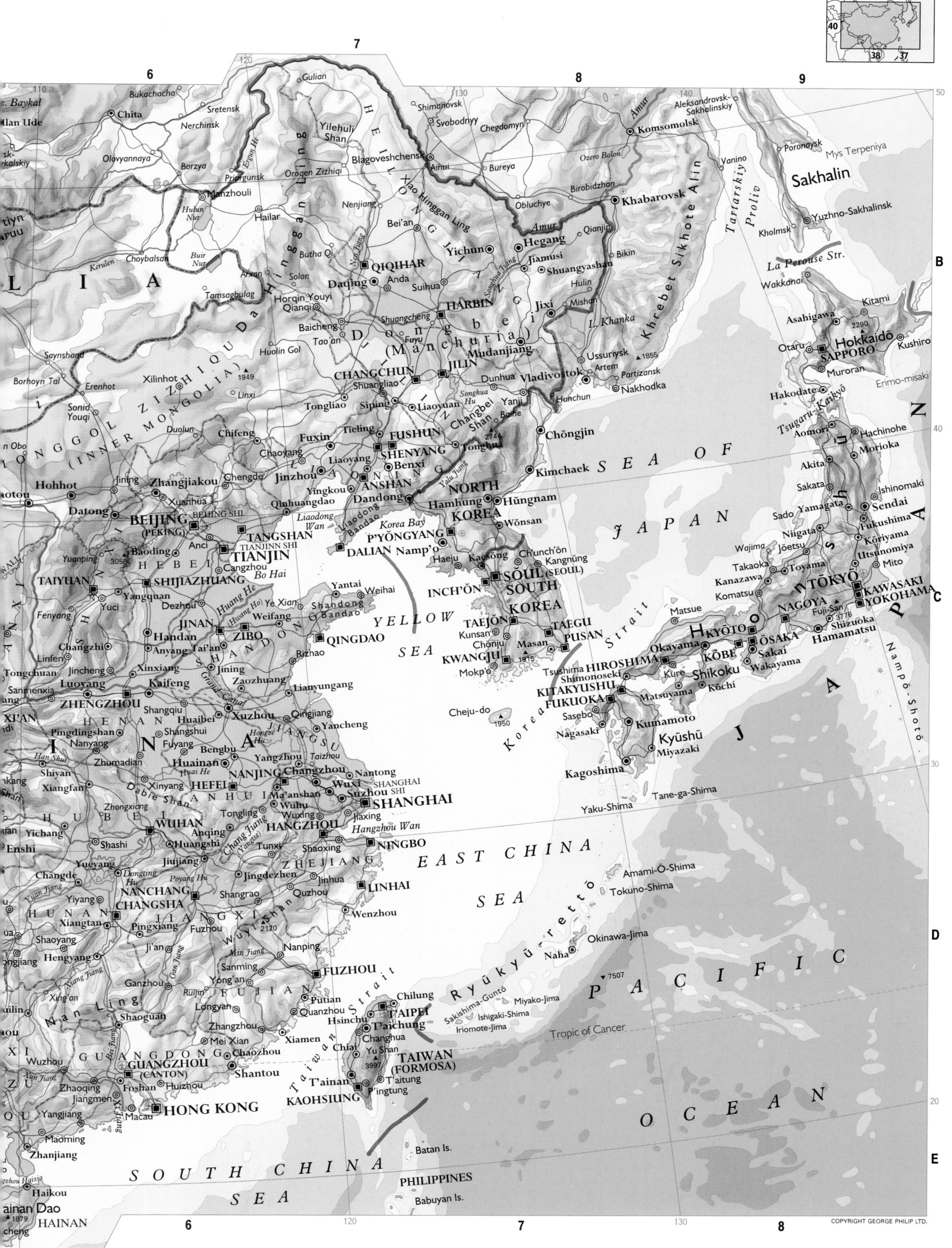

NORTHERN CHINA AND KOREA 1:6 000 000

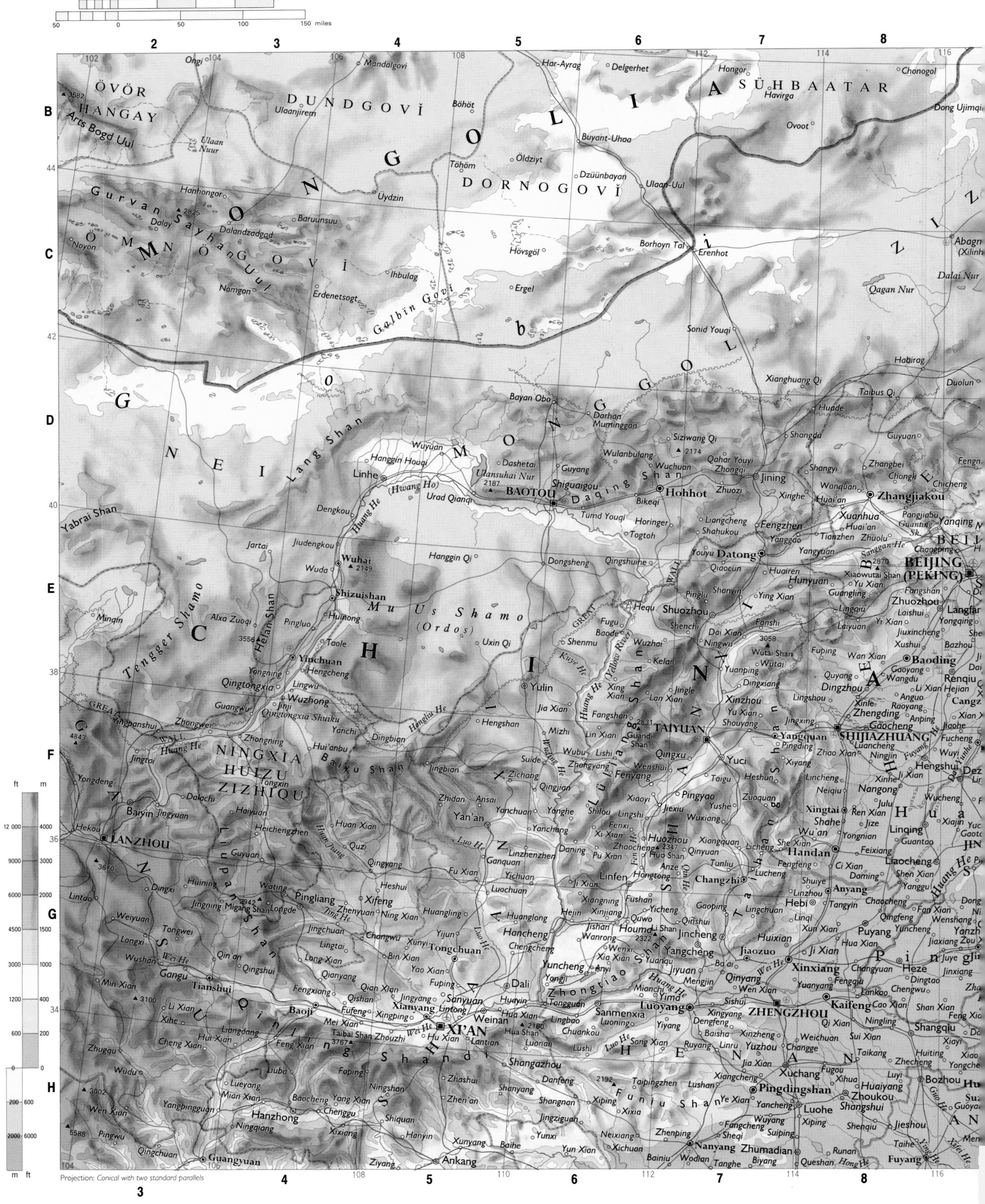

Projection: Conical with two standard parallels

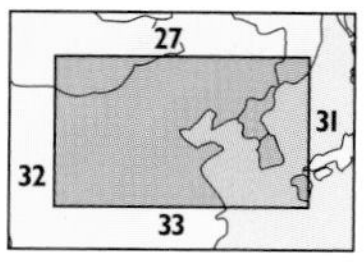

9 10 11 12 13 14 15 16

B C D E F G H

HARBIN
CHANGCHUN
JILIN
SHENYANG
FUSHUN
ANSHAN
DALIAN
TIANJIN
QINGDAO
ZIBO
P'YŎNGYANG
SOUL
INCH'ŎN
TAEJŎN
TAEGU
KWANGJU
PUSAN
Vladivostok
Ussuriysk
Mudanjiang
Jixi
Qiqihar
Daqing
Siping
Jinzhou
Dandong
Yantai
Weihai
Weifang
Linyi
Lianyungang
Huaiyin
Yancheng
Chŏngjin
Hamhung
Wŏnsan
Kaesŏng
Nagasaki

H E I L O N G J I A N G
J I L I N
L I A O N I N G
S H A N D O N G
J I A N G S U
M a n c h u r i a
Dongbei
Changbai Shan
Zhangguangcai Ling
Shandong Bandao
Liaodong Bandao
RUSSIA
NORTH KOREA
SOUTH KOREA
JAPAN

Bo Hai
Liaodong Wan
Laizhou Wan
Korea Bay
HUANG HAI
(Yellow Sea)
SEA OF JAPAN
Tongjosŏn Man
Korea Strait
Cheju-do
Tsushima
Ullŭng-do
Hallasan 1950
Paektu-san 2744

9 10 11 12 13 14 15

118 120 122 124 126 128 130 132
34 36 38 40 42 44

East from Greenwich

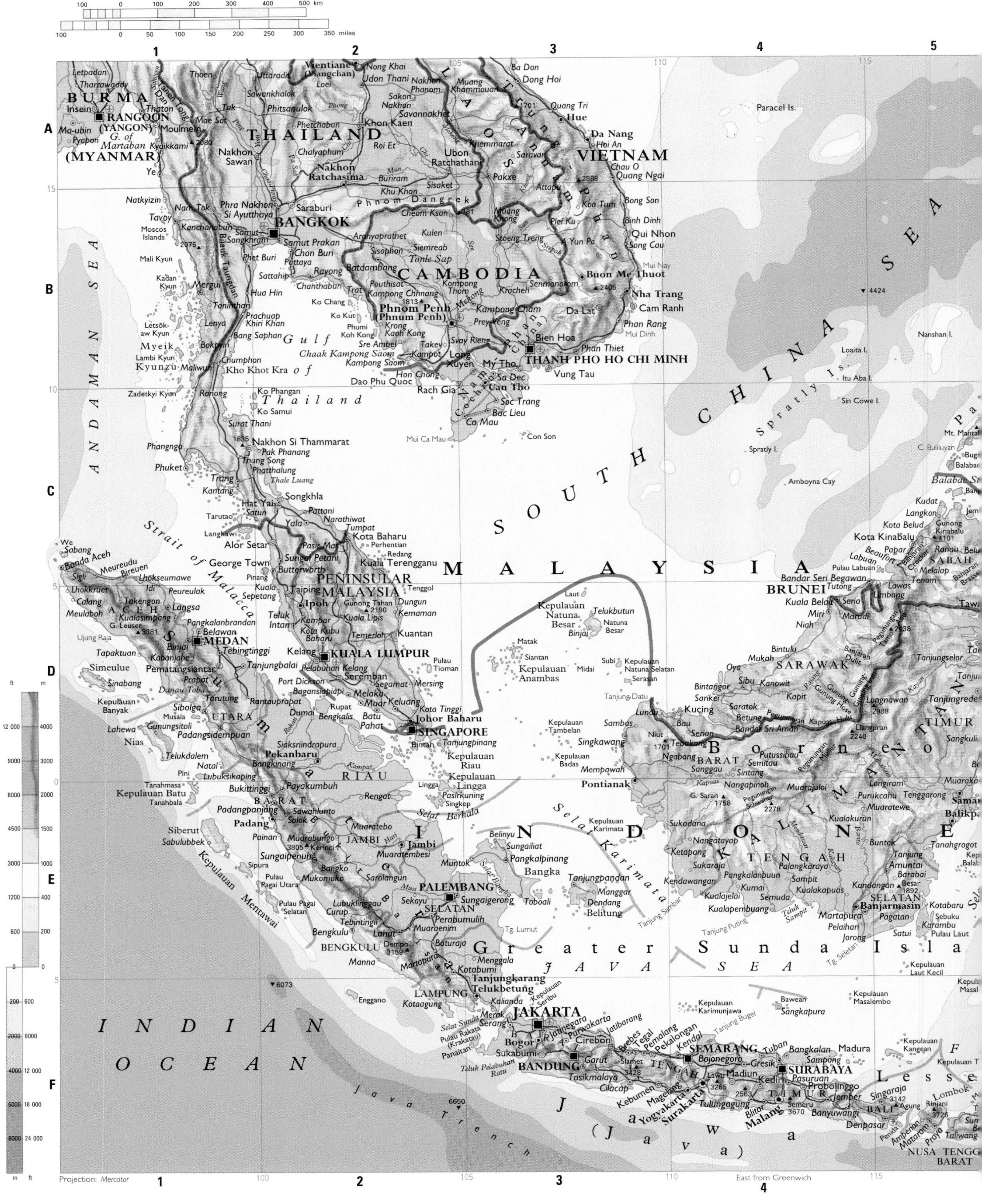

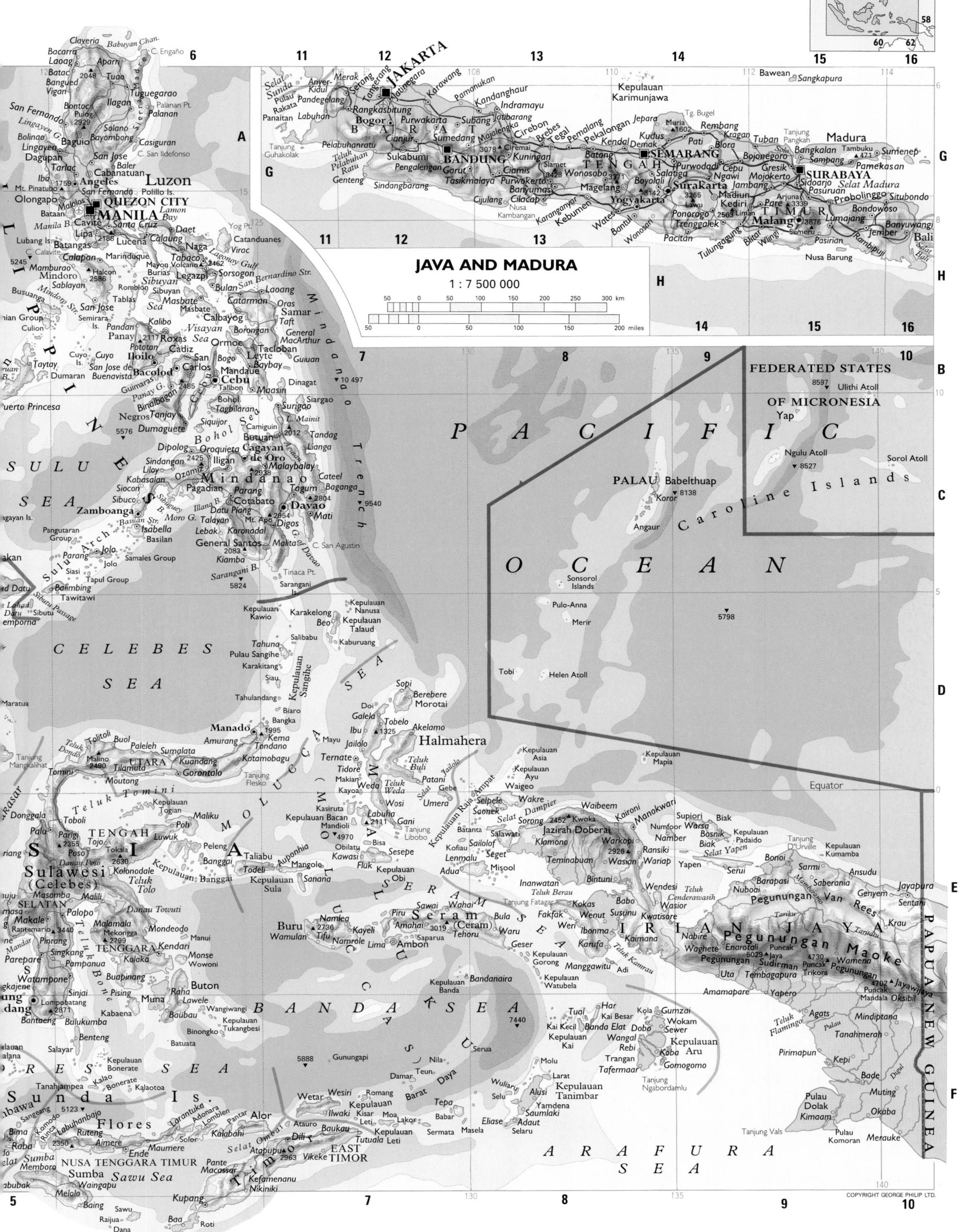

JAVA AND MADURA

1 : 7 500 000

50 0 50 100 150 200 250 300 km
50 0 50 100 150 200 miles

SOUTH CHINA SEA
Gulf of Thailand
MALAYSIA
PENINSULAR MALAYSIA
INDONESIA
Strait of Malacca
Sumatera
SINGAPORE
THANH PHO HO CHI MINH (SAIGON)
Phnom Penh
Kuala Lumpur
Medan
Kepulauan Anambas (Indonesia)
Kepulauan Natuna Besar (Indonesia)
Kepulauan Natuna Selatan (Indonesia)
Borneo
SARAWAK (Malaysia)
Kucing
Pulau Tioman
Con Son
Hon Khoai
Ko Samui
Ko Phangan
Ko Tao
Kho Khot Kra
Pinang
George Town
Ipoh
Kuantan
Kota Baharu
Kuala Terengganu
Johor Baharu
Melaka
Songkhla
Hat Yai
Pattani
Phuket
Surat Thani
Chumphon
Mekong
Chuor Phnum Damrei
Ca Mau
Mui Ca Mau
Tanjung Datu
Projection: Conical with two standard parallels
East from Greenwich
COPYRIGHT GEORGE PHILIP LTD.

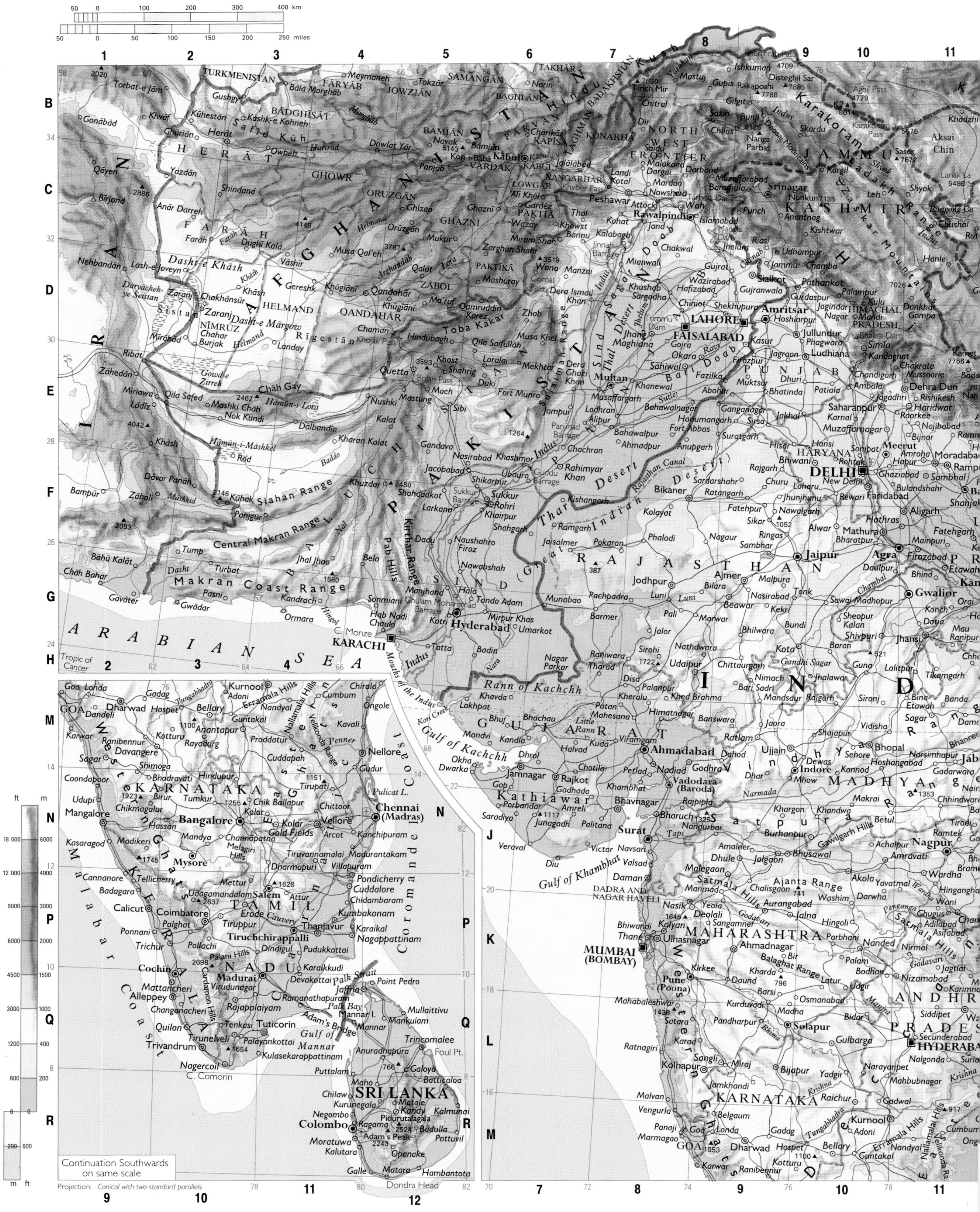

TURKMENISTAN
AFGHANISTAN
PAKISTAN
IRAN
INDIA
SRI LANKA
ARABIAN SEA
KABUL
KARACHI
LAHORE
FAISALABAD
DELHI
MUMBAI (BOMBAY)
HYDERABAD
Hyderabad
Ahmadabad
Chennai (Madras)
Bangalore
Colombo
Jaipur
Agra
Gwalior
Nagpur
Pune (Poona)
Srinagar
Rawalpindi
Peshawar
Islamabad
Multan
Quetta
Amritsar
RAJASTHAN
GUJARAT
MAHARASHTRA
KARNATAKA
TAMIL NADU
KERALA
PUNJAB
HARYANA
HIMACHAL PRADESH
JAMMU & KASHMIR
MADHYA PRADESH
ANDHRA PRADESH
SIND
BALUCHISTAN
NORTH WEST FRONTIER
Thar Desert
Great Indian Desert
Karakoram
Hindu Kush
Makran Coast Range
Central Makran Range
Siahan Range
Kirthar Range
Western Ghats
Eastern Ghats
Satpura Range
Vindhya Range
Ajanta Range
Gulf of Kachchh
Gulf of Khambhat
Rann of Kachchh
Gulf of Mannar
Palk Strait
Coromandel Coast
Malabar Coast
Mouths of the Indus
Tropic of Cancer
C. Comorin
Dondra Head
Continuation Southwards on same scale
Projection: Conical with two standard parallels

32
45
32
38

13
14
15
16
17
18
19
20
21
22
B
C
D
E
F
G
H
J
K
L
M
X I Z A N G
Z I Z H I Q U
(T I B E T)
C H I N A
Q I N G H A I
Huh Xil Shan
Bayan Har Shan
Tanggula (Dangla) Shan
Nyainqentanglha Shan
Kangri
Dogai Coring
Ngoring Hu
Gyaring Hu
Siling Co
Nam Co
Gyaring Co
Tangra Yumco
Mapam Yumco
Yushu
Dainkog
Nangqen
Garzê
Gamtog
Qamdo
Baiyü
Xinlong
Baqên
Dêngqên
Nagqu
Nu Jiang
(Salween)
Lhorong
Zhaxizê
S I C H U A N
Yidun
Litang
Yajiang
Ningjing
(Mekong)
Lancang Jiang
Lhari
Gongbo'gyamda
Goqên
Lhasa
Lhünzhub
Ombu
Coqên
Xainza
Saga
Zhongba
Xigazê
Gyangzê
Lhazê
Maquan He (Tsangpo)
Yarlung Zangbo Jiang
(Brahmaputra)
Nang Xian
Riga
Jido
Muli Zangzu Zizhixian
Mainkung
Zhongdian
Zizhixian
Weixi
Lijiang
Jianchuan
Mustang
Muktinath
Dhaulagiri
Xixabangma Feng
Nyalam
Mt. Everest
Kanchenjunga
Gamba
Dinggyê
Comai
Cona
Lhünzê
Kangto
Subansiri
A R U N A C H A L P R A D E S H
Nizamghat
Minutang
Hkakabo Razi (Thala La)
Putao
Hpungan Pass
Chaukan Pass
Konglu
Kawngtim
Bumhpa Bum
Lawng Pit
N E P A L
Siwalik Range
Nepalganj
Nuwakot
Gurkha
Nawakot
Katmandu
Bhaktapur
Ramechhap
Jarwa
Nautanwa
Bahraich
Balrampur
Gonda
Birganj
Chisapani Garhi
Dhankuta
Darjiling
SIKKIM
Thimphu
Gangtok
Punakha
BHUTAN
Tongsa Dzong
Taga Dzong
Towang
Rupa
North Lakhimpur
Dibrugarh
Tinsukia
Tipongpani
Dum Duma
Sibsagar
Jorhat
Patkai Bum
Hukawng Valley
K A C H I N
Myitkyina
Y U N N A N
Baoshan
Tengchong
Longling
Changning
Sadon
Yunlong
Basti
Gorakhpur
Faizabad
Deoria
Bettiah
Raxaul
Motihari
Darbhanga
Muzaffarpur
Siwan
Chhapra
Patna
Munger
Gaya
Bihar
Bhagalpur
Varanasi
Jaunpur
Mirzapur
Sasaram
Aurangabad
Deoghar
Purnia
Kishanganj
Siliguri
Jalpaiguri
Alipur Duar
Koch Bihar
Goalpara
Barpeta
Gauhati
Shillong
MEGHALAYA
Cherrapunji
Tura
Dhuburi
Brahmaputra
A S S A M
Tezpur
Nowgong
Silghat
Dergaon
Mokokchung
NAGALAND
Kohima
Imphal
MANIPUR
Churachandpur
Silchar
Haflong
Aizawl
MIZORAM
Agartala
TRIPURA
Sylhet
Mymensingh
Jamalpur
Rangpur
Dinajpur
Bogra
Rajshahi
Pabna
DHAKA
B A N G L A D E S H
East Bengal
Narayanganj
Comilla
Chandpur
Jessore
Khulna
Barisal
Chittagong
Cox's Bazar
Maijdi
Hatia
Sundarbans
Mouths of the Ganges
Hugli
Haora
KOLKATA (CALCUTTA)
Port Canning
Diamond Harbour
Haldia
Barddhaman
WEST BENGAL
Durgapur
Asansol
Dhanbad
Giridih
Hazaribag
Ranchi
Jamshedpur
Kharagpur
Medinipur
Contai
Baleshwar
B I H A R
Bharatpur
Chirmiri
Ambikapur
Raurkela
Jharsuguda
Sambalpur
Raigarh
Raipur
Bilaspur
Durg
Kanker
Titlagarh
Bhawanipatna
Keonjhargarh
Bhadrakh
Cuttack
Bhubaneshwar
Puri
Chilka L.
Brahmapur
Chatrapur
Ichchapuram
O R I S S A
Mahanadi
Paradip
Kendrapara
Jeypore
Jagdalpur
Rayagada
Parvatipuram
Bobbili
Tekkali
Srikakulam
Vizianagaram
Anakapalle
Vishakhapatnam
Northern Circars
Pithapuram
Godavari Point
Kakinada
Narasapur
Machilipatnam
Varanasi
Lucknow
Rae Bareli
Sultanpur
Azamgarh
Ghazipur
Faizabad
BAY OF BENGAL
INDIAN OCEAN
B U R M A
(M Y A N M A R)
SAGAING
Mandalay
Monywa
Shwebo
Sagaing
Kalewa
Tamu
Mawlaik
Tiddim
Falam
CHIN
Gangaw
Pakokku
Myingyan
Meiktila
Pauk
Kanpetlet
Paletwa
Sittwe (Akyab)
ARAKAN
Kyaukpyu
Ramree I.
Cheduba I.
Taungup
Sandoway
Arakan Coast
Arakan Yoma
Minbu
Magwe
MAGWE
Taungdwingyi
Thayetmyo
Pyinmana
Toungoo
Prome
Pegu Yoma
Irrawaddy
Gwa
Henzada
Myanaung
Letpadan
Tharrawaddy
Kyongpyaw
Yandoon
Bassein
Insein
PEGU
Pegu
RANGOON
Thaton
Martaban
Moulmein
G. of Martaban
IRRAWADDY
Myaungmya
Ma-ubin
Pyapon
Mouths of the Irrawaddy
Preparis North Channel
Paripari Kyun (Burma)
Preparis South Channel
Koko Kyunzu (Burma)
Moscos Is.
Maungmagan Kyunzu
Launglon Bok
Tavoy
Yebyu
Nam Tok
Sangkhla Buri
Natkyizin
Kalegauk Kyun
Lamaing
Ye
S H A N
KAYAH
Loi-kaw
Taunggyi
Heho
Kalaw
Thazi
Yamethin
Inle L.
Lashio
Hsenwi
Kunlong
Namtu
Mogok
Bawdwin
Mong Yai
Gokteik
Maymyo
Kyaukse
Mong Kung
Mong Hsu
Kengtung
Keng Tawng
Mong Nai
Mong Ton
Mong Pan
Mawk Mai
Mong Hpayak
Pang-Long
Pang-Yang
Kawnro
Mong Pawk
Tropic of Cancer
THAILAND
Chiang Mai
Lamphun
Lampang
Mae Hong Son
Muang Lamphun
Papun
Tak
Kawthule
Salween
Dawna Range
Mai Klong
Tenasserim
Sittang Myit
Bhamo
Katha
Shwegu
Tigyaing
Mogaung
Hkamti
Homalin
Singkaling Hkamti
Chindwin
Maingkwan
Kumon Bum
N'mai
Mali
Mangshi
Ruili
East from Greenwich
COPYRIGHT GEORGE PHILIP LTD.
12
13
14
15
16
17
18
19
20
21

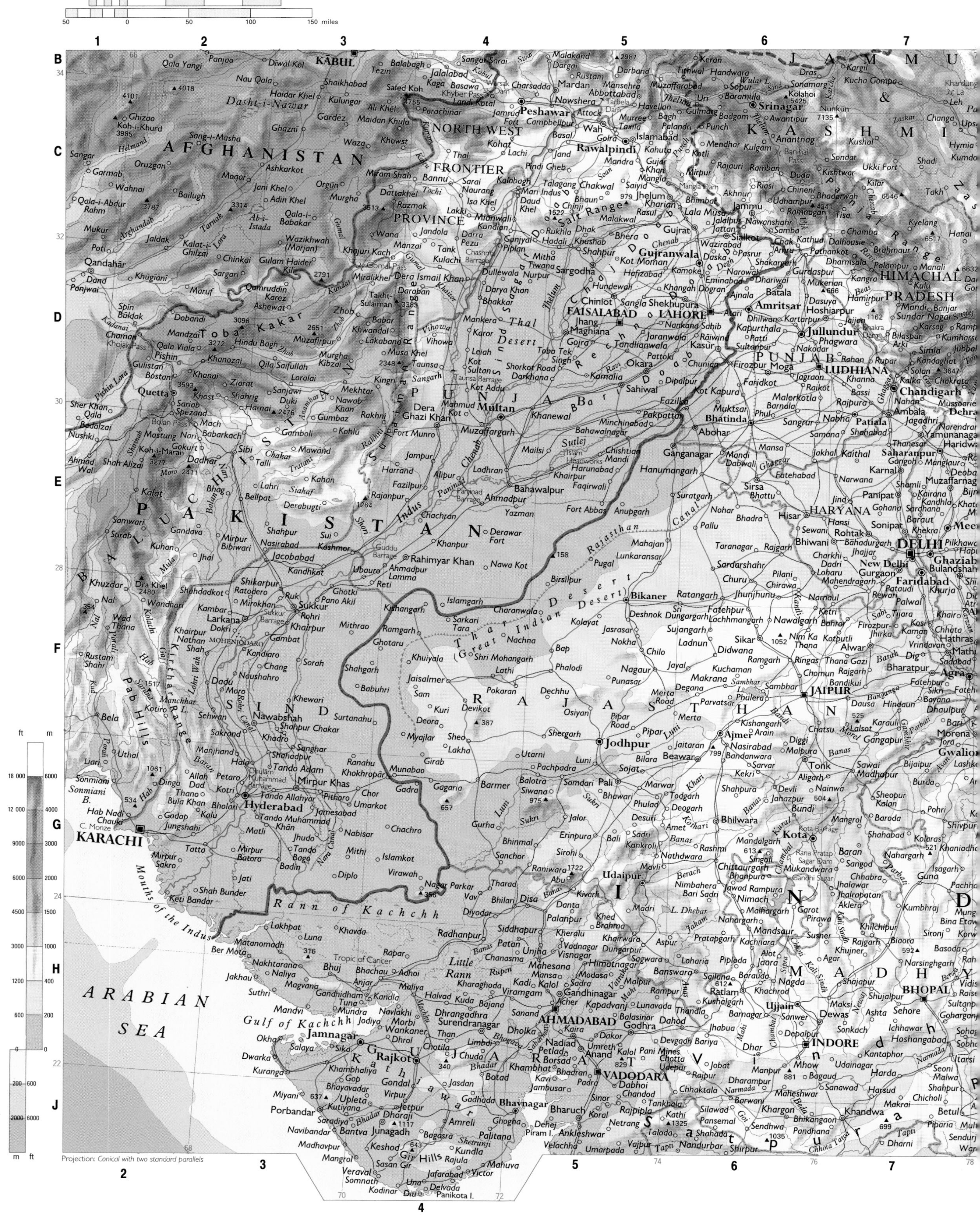

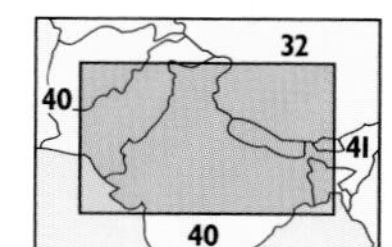

JAMMU AND KASHMIR
On same scale as Main Map

10 0 10 20 30 40 50 60 70 80 100 km

10 0 10 20 30 40 60 miles

1 **2** **3** **4** **5** **6**

Paphos
Episkopi
Akrotiri
Limassol
Episkopi Bay
Akrotiri Bay
C. Gata

CYPRUS

Al Hamidīyah
Tall Kalakh
Ḥimṣ (Homs)
Shinshār
Furqlus

A

ASH SHAMĀL
Al Mīnā'
Tarābulus (Tripoli)
Zgharta
Al Hirmil
Al Quṣayr
HIMŞ
Halbā
Al Qaryatayn

Al Batrūn
Abū 'Alī
Bsharrī
3088 Qurnat as Sawdā'
Al Burayj
2464
Bī'r Ghadīr

Jubayl
Qartabā
Ba'labakk
Al Labwah
An Nabk

Ibrāhīm
2628 Sannīn
Yabrūd

BAYRŪT (Beirut)
Bikfayyā
Sirghāyā
Az Zabadānī
Dumayr
Khān Abū Shāmāt

'Alayh
Zaḥlah
Ḥawsh Mūssā
Al Qutayfah

LEBANON
Ash Shuwayfāt
Ad Dāmūr
1942 J. al Bārūk

B

Saydā (Sidon)
Jazzīn
Dūmā
Dārayyā
DIMASHQ (Damascus)
DIMASHQ

An Nabaṭīyah at Taḥta
2814 J. ash Shaykh (Mt. Hermon)
Qaṭanā
Al Kiswah
A'waj
Al Hājānah

Sūr (Tyre)
Marj 'Uyūn
Golan Heights
Burāq

AL JANŪB
Qiryat Shemona
1197
Al Qunayṭirah
As Sanamayn

Naharīyya
Me'ona
Ar Rafid
DAR'Ā
Izra
Shahbā'

'Akko (Acre)
Zefat
Shaykh Miskin
W. Al Ḥarīr
1800 Sālah

Mifraz Hefa
Hagalil
Qiryat Yam
Karmi'el
Fiq
Saham al Jawlān
As Suwaydā
AS SUWAYDĀ

Hefa (Haifa)
Teverya
Yam -210 (Tiberias)
Dar'ā

Qiryat Ata
Nazerat (Nazareth)
Kinneret
Yarmūk
Ar Ramthā
Salkhad
AD DURŪZ

Dāliyat el Karmel
HAZAFON
Afula
Tayiba
C

TEL MEGIDDO
Umm el Fahm
Bet She'an
Ailūn
Busrā ash Shām
Umm al Qittayn

CAESAREA
Jenin
Ar Ramthā
1247
Al-Mafraq

Hadera
Hanna-Karkur
SHOMRON
Tūbās
Nahr az Zarqā
Jarash
IRBID

ISRAEL
Pardes
Tulkarm
SAMARIA
Umm ad Darai

Netanya
HAMERKAZ
Nāblus
W. al Fari'a
Irbid

Herzliyya
Kefar Sava
SHILO
AL BALQĀ

Benē Beraq

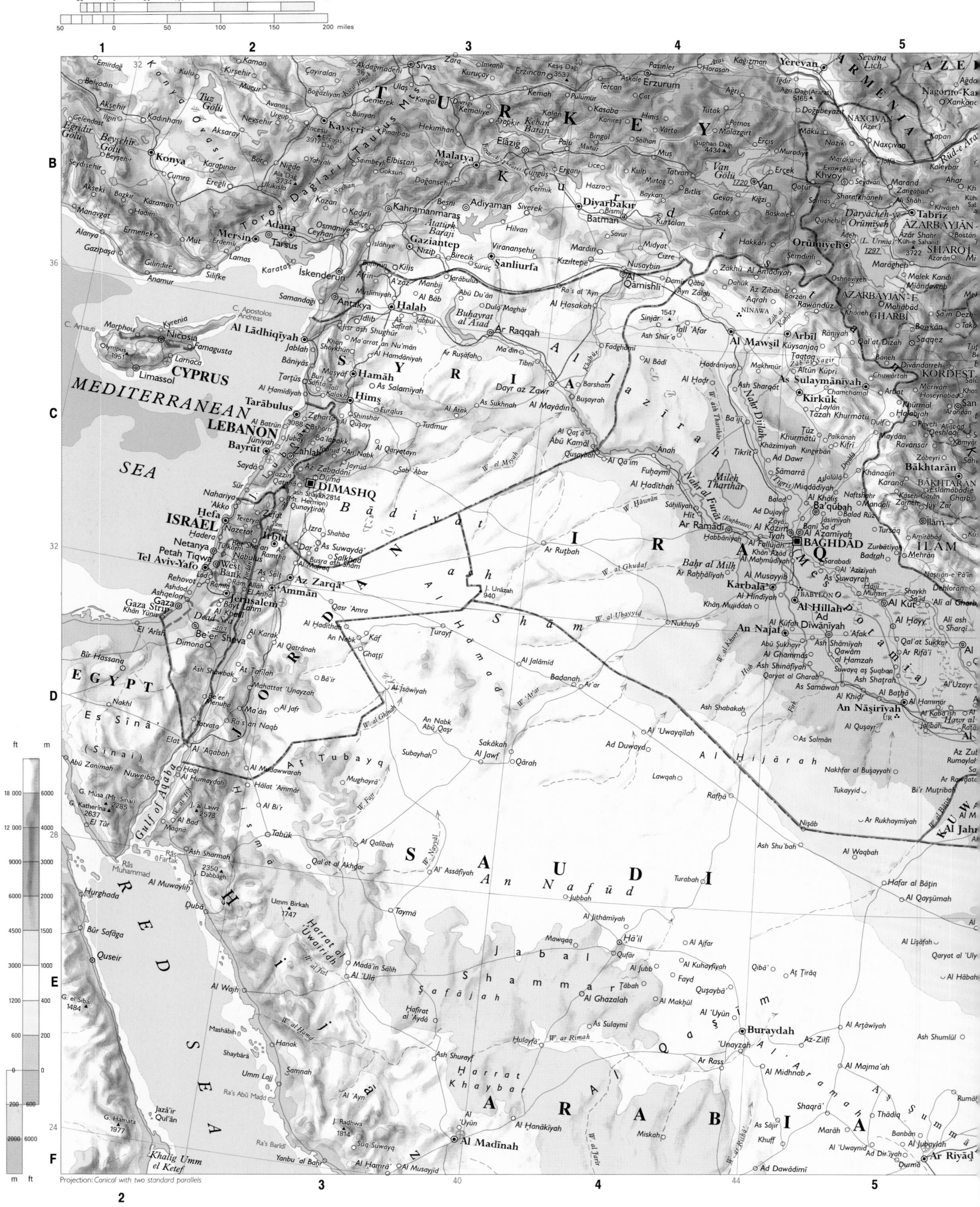

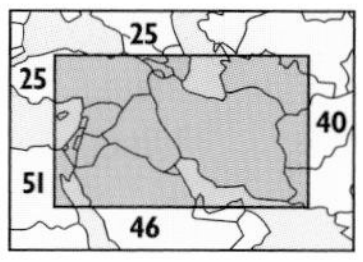

25
25
40
51
46

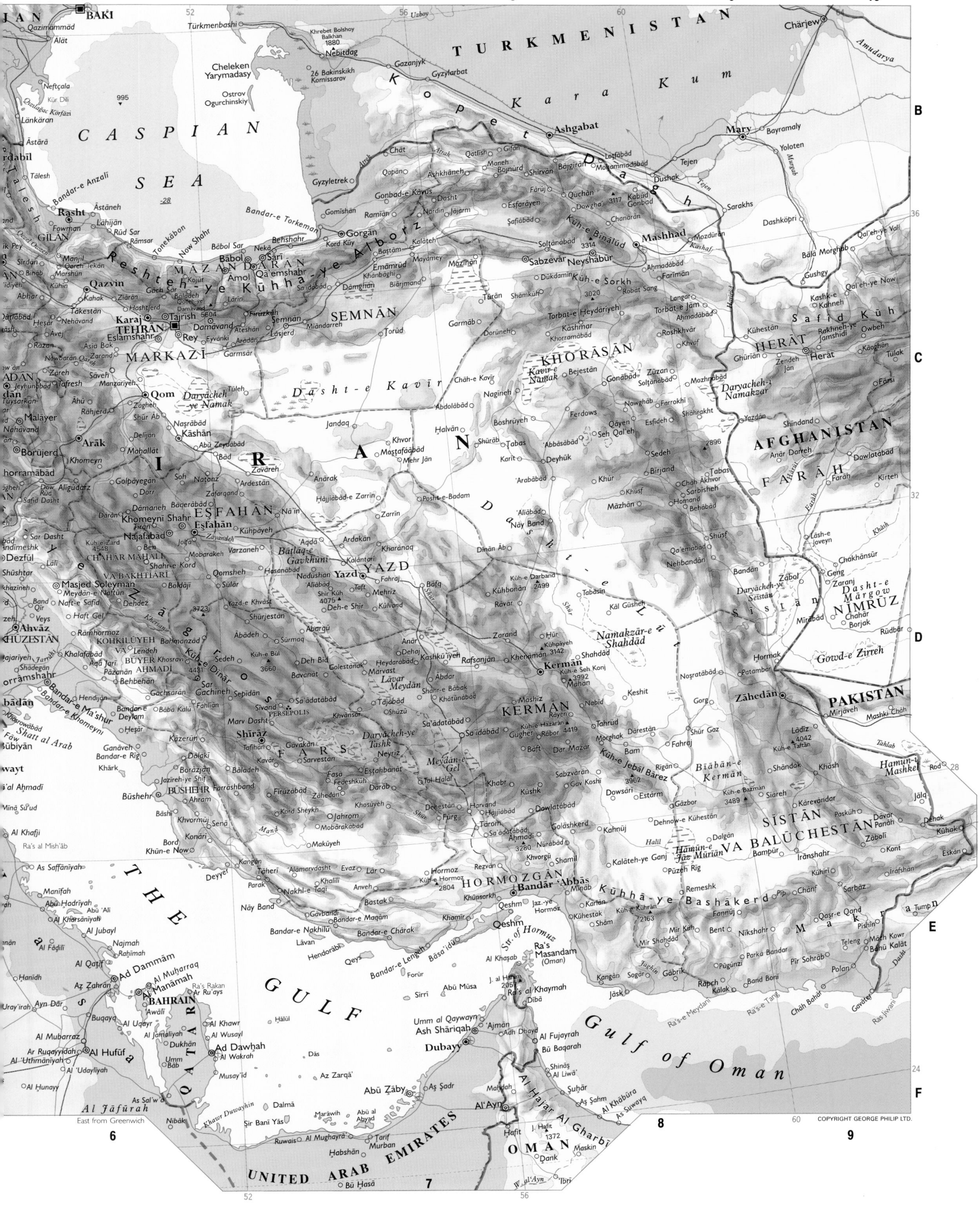

6
7
8
9
10
B
C
D
E
F
TURKMENISTAN
Kara Kum
Kopet Dagh
CASPIAN SEA
Türkmenbashi
Cheleken Yarymadasy
Ostrov Ogurchinskiy
Nebitdag
Gazanjyk
Gyzylarbat
Ashgabat
Mary
Bayramaly
Yoloten
Chärjew
Amudarya
Tejen
Dushak
Sarakhs
Dashköpri
BAKI
Qazimammäd
Älät
Neftçala
Länkäran
Ästärä
Ardabil
Bandar-e Anzali
Rasht
Lähijän
GILAN
Qazvin
Karaj
TEHRAN
Tajrish
Rey
Eslamshahr
Damavand
5604
Reshteh-ye Kuhha-ye Alborz
MAZANDARAN
Babol
Sari
Amol
Qa'emshahr
Gorgan
Gonbad-e Kavus
Bandar-e Torkeman
SEMNAN
Semnan
Damghan
Shahrud
Sabzevar
Neyshabur
Mashhad
Kuh-e Binalud
3314
Quchan
Bojnurd
Esfarayen
Torbat-e Heydariyeh
Kashmar
KHORASAN
Dasht-e Kavir
MARKAZI
Qom
Daryacheh-ye Namak
Kashan
Arak
Malayer
Borujerd
Khomeyn
IRAN
Tabas
Ferdows
Gonabad
Qayen
Birjand
Daryacheh-i Namakzar
HERAT
Herat
Safid Kuh
AFGHANISTAN
FARAH
Farah
Shindand
NIMRUZ
Dasht-e Margow
Zaranj
Zabol
Daryacheh-ye Sistan
Gowd-e Zirreh
PAKISTAN
Zahedan
Mirjaveh
Dasht-e Lut
ESFAHAN
Esfahan
Najafabad
Khomeyni Shahr
Na'in
Ardestan
Natanz
Yazd
YAZD
Mehriz
Bafq
Ardakan
Batlaq-e Gavkhuni
CHAHAR MAHALL VA BAKHTIARI
Shahr-e Kord
Dezful
Shushtar
Masjed Soleyman
Ahvaz
KHUZESTAN
Khorramshahr
Abadan
Shatt al Arab
KOHKILUYEH VA BUYER AHMADI
Kuh-e Dinar
4431
Zagros
FARS
Shiraz
PERSEPOLIS
Marv Dasht
Kazerun
Bushehr
BUSHEHR
Bandar-e Ganaveh
Kharg
Daryacheh-ye Tashk
Neyriz
Estahbanat
Fasa
Darab
Jahrom
Lar
KERMAN
Kerman
Rafsanjan
Sirjan
Bam
Kuh-e Jebal Barez
3962
Kuh-e Hazaran
4419
Namakzar-e Shahdad
Shahdad
Biaban-e Kerman
Jiroft
SISTAN VA BALUCHESTAN
Iranshahr
Hamun-e Jaz Murian
Khash
Hamun-i Mashkel
Saravan
Kuh-e Taftan
4042
HORMOZGAN
Bandar 'Abbas
Minab
Qeshm
Str. of Hormuz
Bandar-e Lengeh
Kuhha-ye Bashakerd
Jask
Chah Bahar
Gavater
Makran
Ra's Jiwani
Ra's Masandam (Oman)
THE GULF
Gulf of Oman
Ad Dammam
Al Manamah
BAHRAIN
QATAR
Ad Dawhah
Al Hufuf
Al Jafurah
Dubayy
Ash Shariqah
Abu Zaby
Al Fujayrah
Al 'Ayn
UNITED ARAB EMIRATES
OMAN
Al Hajar Al Gharbi
Kuwayt
Al Khafji
Ras al Mish'ab
As Saffaniyah
Al Jubayl
Ra's Rakan
Das
Halul
Sirri
Abu Musa
Dalma
East from Greenwich
COPYRIGHT GEORGE PHILIP LTD.

ARABIA AND THE HORN OF AFRICA 1:15 000 000

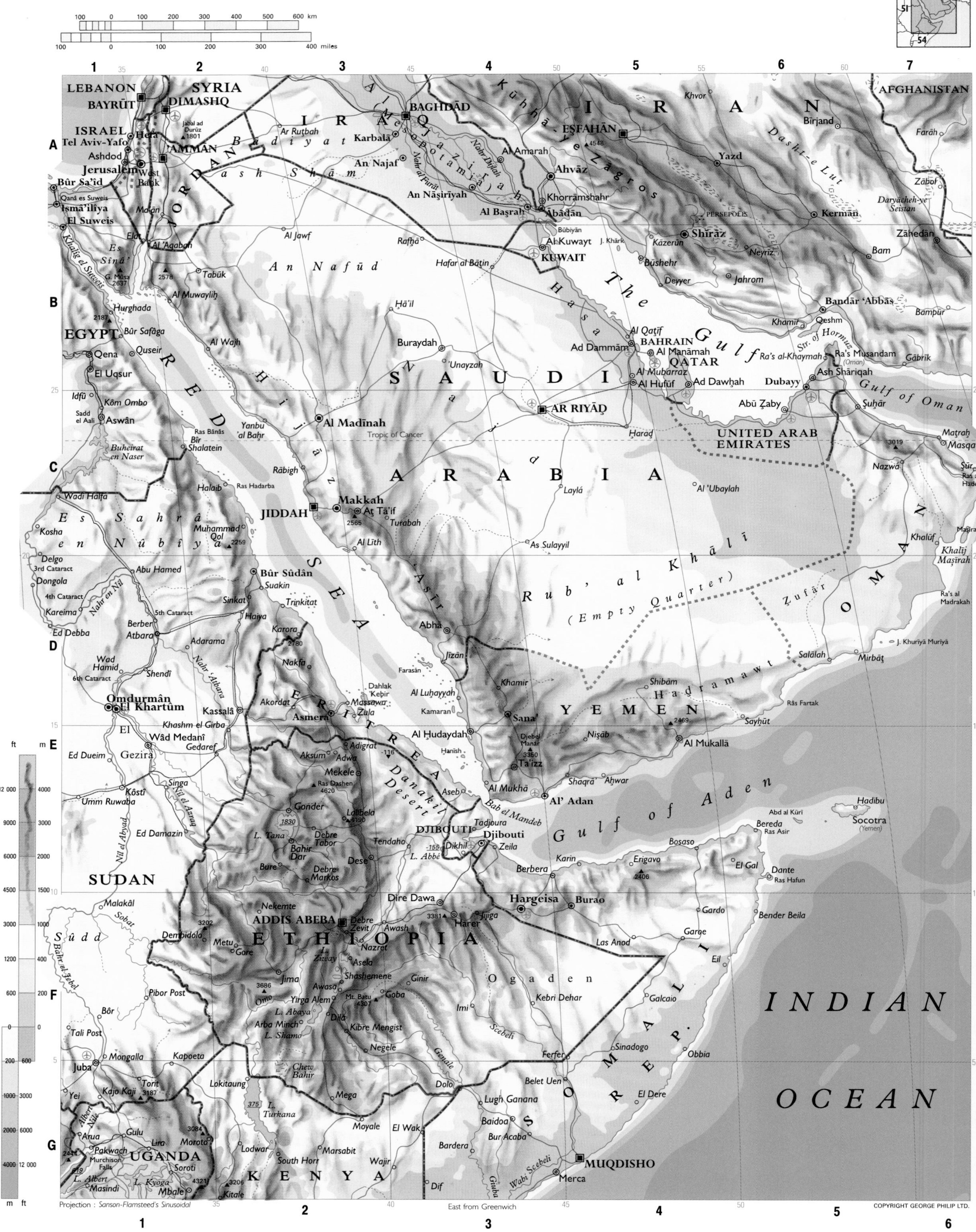

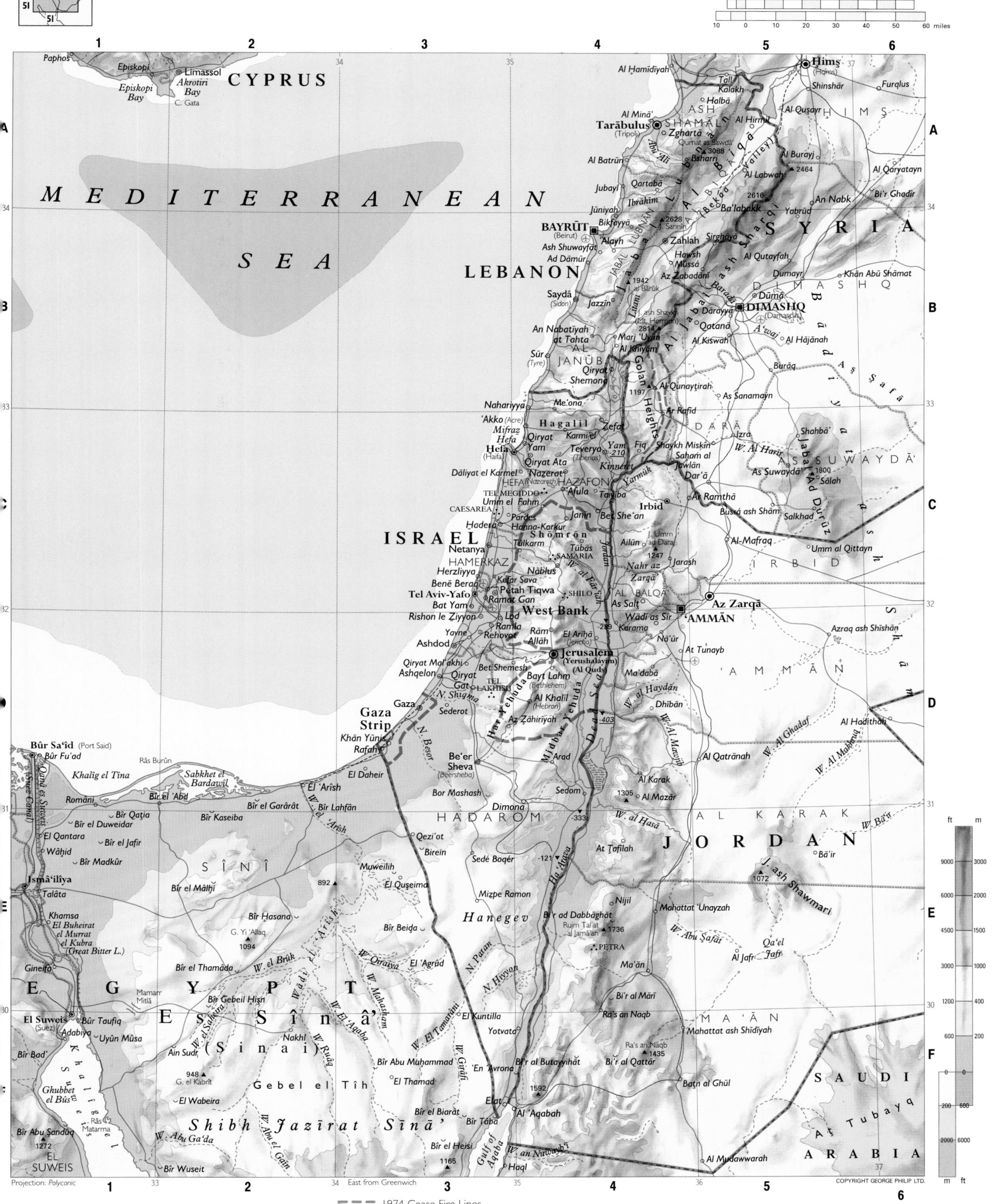

Petah Tiqwa
As Salt
Az Zarqā

Tel Aviv-Yafo
Ramat Gan
289
Wādī as Sīr
AMMĀN

Bat Yam
West Bank
Karama
Na'ūr

Rishon le Ziyyon
Lod
'AMMĀN

Yavne
Ramla
Rām Allāh
At Tunayb

Ashdod
Rehovot
El Arīḥā (Jericho)
Azraq ash Shīshān

Qiryat Mal'akhi
Jerusalem (Yerushalayim) (Al Quds)
Ma'dābā

Ashqelon
Qiryat Gat
Bayt Laḥm (Bethlehem)

TEL LAKHISH
Ma'dābā

Gaza
Sederot
Al Khalīl (Hebron)
Dhībān
Al Hadīthah

D

Gaza Strip
Az Zāhirīyah
-403
W. al Ḥaydān
Al Qaṭrānah
W. Al Ghadaf

Khān Yūnis
Hurat Yehuda
Midbar Yehuda
Arad

Rafah
Be'er Sheva (Beersheba)
Sedom
1305 Al Karak
Al Mazār

Būr Sa'īd (Port Said)
Bīr el 'Abd
Bor Mashash
Al Karak

Būr Fu'ad
Rās Burūn
Dimona
-333
W. al Ḥasā
AL KARAK

Khalīg el Tīna
Sabkhet el Bardawīl
HADAROM
W. Bāīr

El Daheir
Qezi'ot
Bā'ir

Romāni
Bīr el Garārāt
Birein
W. al Maeyib

Bī'r Qaṭia
Bīr Lahfān
Sedé Boqér
-121
At Ṭafīlah
JORDAN
E

El Qantara
Bīr el Jafir
Ha 'Arava
Nijil
Mahaṭṭat 'Unayzah

Wāḥid
Bīr Madkūr
892
Muweilih
Hanegev
Bī'r ad Dabbāghāt
1072 J. ash Shawmari

Ismâ'îlīya
Talâta
El Quṣeima
Rujm Tal'at al Jamāl 1736

Khamsa
S Ī N Ī
G. Yi 'Allaq 1094
Bīr Beiḍa
Mizpe Ramon
PETRA
Qa'el Jafr

El Buheirat el Murrat el Kubra (Great Bitter L.)
Bīr Hasana
Al Jafr

Gineifo
El 'Agrūd
N. Paran
Ma'ān
F

E G Y P T
Bīr el Thamāda
W. el Brūk
W. Quraiya
N. Ḥiyyon
Bī'r al Mārī
M A'Ā N

E S S Ī N Â' (Sinai)
W. Mahashm
Bir Gebeil Hisn
Ra's an Naqb

Mamarr Mitla
W. el Agaba
W. El Tamurāni
En 'Avrona
Ra's an Naqb 1435
Mahaṭṭat ash Shīdīyah

El Suweis (Suez)
Būr Taufiq
Nakhl
Baṭn el Ghūl
S A U D I

Adabiya
Uyūn Mūsa
948 G. el Kabrit
El Thamad
1592
Elat

Bīr Bad'
Bīr Abu Muhammad
Bīr el Biarāt
Al 'Aqabah
A R A B I A

Ghubbet el Būs
Gebel el Tîh
El Wabeira
Bīr Tāba
At Tubayq

Bīr Abu Ṣandūq
Shibh Jazīrat Sinā'
Bīr el Heisi
W. an Nuṭayl

1272
EL SUWEIS
W. Abu el Gan
1165
Haql
Al Mudawwarah

Projection: Polyconic
East from Greenwich
COPYRIGHT GEORGE PHILIP LTD.

1974 Cease Fire Lines

200 0 200 400 600 800 1000 1200 1400 1600 1800 km

200 0 200 400 600 800 1000 1200 miles

1 2 3 4 5 6 7 8 9 10

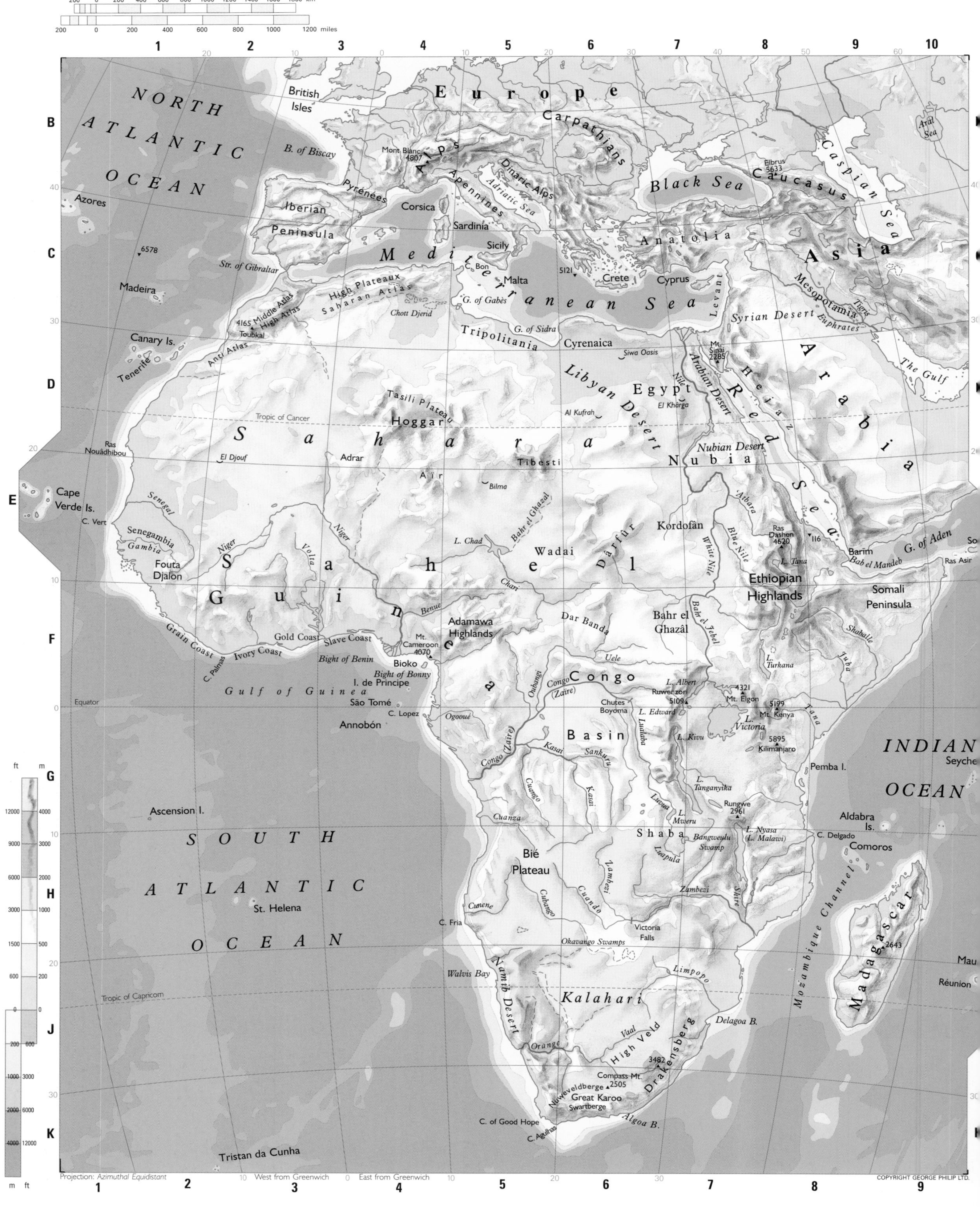

NORTH

ATLANTIC

OCEAN

Azores
(Port.)

Madeira
(Port.)

Canary Is.
(Sp.)

UNITED
KINGDOM
LONDON

PARIS

NETH.
BELG.
FRANCE
SWITZ.

GERMANY
Prague
CZECH REP.
Vienna
AUSTRIA
CROATIA
BOS.
HERZ.
ITALY

POLAND
Warsaw

SLOVAK REP.
HUNGARY
YUG.
N.MAC.
BULGARIA

Kiev
UKRAINE

ROMANIA
Odessa

Black Sea

RUSSIA
Volgograd

KAZAKSTAN

Aral
Sea

B

B. of Biscay

PORTUGAL
Lisbon
SPAIN
Madrid

Corsica
Rome
Sardinia

Sicily

Adriatic Sea

GREECE
Athens
Crete

Ankara
TURKEY
CYPRUS

GEORGIA
ARM.

AZER.
Baku

Caspian Sea

TURKMEN.

C

Rabat
Tetouan
Casablanca
Fès
MOROCCO
Marrakesh

Algiers
Constantine
Annaba
TUNISIA
Tunis
MALTA
Sfax

Mediterranean Sea

Tripoli
Misrātah
Benghazi

Alexandria
Port Said
CAIRO
Suez
El Faiyūm

Tel Aviv-
Jaffa
ISRAEL
JORDAN
Jerusalem

Aleppo
SYRIA
LEB.
Damascus

Euphrates

Syrian Desert

TEHRĀN
Eşfahān

Mosul
Baghdād
IRAQ
Basra
KUWAIT

IRAN

C

Chott Djerid

Ras
Nouâdhibou

El Aaiún
WESTERN SAHARA
Fdérik

ALGERIA
In Salah

Tropic of Cancer

Sahara

LIBYA
Marzūq

Al Jawf

EGYPT

Aswân

Nile

Asyût

Red Sea

Wadi Halfa
Port Sudan

Medina
Mecca
Jedda

SAUDI

ARABIA

BAHRAIN
Riyadh
QATAR

The Gulf

D

Dakhla

VERDE IS.

St-Louis
C. Vert
Dakar
GAMBIA
Banjul
SENEGAL
GUINEA-
BISSAU
Bissau

Nouakchott
MAURITANIA

Tombouctou

Senegal

MALI
Bamako

Agades
Niamey
NIGER

L. Chad
Kano

BURKINA
Ouagadougou
FASO
Bobo-
Dioulasso
BENIN

CHAD
Abéché
Ndjamena

Maiduguri

SUDAN
El Fâsher
El Obeid

Omdurmân
Khartoum
Atbara

Atbara

White Nile
Blue Nile

Wâd Medani

ERITREA
Mesewa
Asmera

L. Tana

YEMEN

G. of Aden

Socotra
(Yemen)

E

GUINEA
Conakry
Freetown
SIERRA
LEONE

IVORY
COAST
Bouaké
Kumasi

Yamoussoukro
Monrovia
LIBERIA
Abidjan
Sekondi-
Takoradi

GHANA
TOGO
Lomé
Accra
Porto
Novo

NIGERIA
Ibadan
Abuja
Enugu
Lagos
Benue

CAMEROON
Douala
Malabo
Yaoundé

CENTRAL
AFRICAN REP.
Bangui

Chari

Wau

Bahr el Jebel

Malakâl

Addis Ababa
ETHIOPIA

Harer

Berbera

DJIBOUTI
Djibouti
Ras Asir

SOMALI REP.

F

Gulf of Guinea
SÃO TOMÉ & PRÍNCIPE

C. Lopez
Annobón

EQUATORIAL
GUINEA
Libreville
GABON

Port
Harcourt
Bight of Benin

Congo
(Zaïre)
Ubangi

Mbandaka
Kisangani

L. Albert
L. Edward
RWANDA
Kigali
L. Kivu
BURUNDI
Bujumbura

UGANDA
Kampala
L. Victoria
Kisumu
Nairobi

L. Turkana

Tana
Juba

KENYA
Mombasa

Mogadishu

Kismayu

INDIAN

OCEAN

SEYCHELLES

G

Ascension I.
(U.K.)

SOUTH

ATLANTIC

Brazzaville
Pointe-Noire
CABINDA
(Angola)

CONGO
CONGO
(DEM. REP. OF THE)
Matadi
Kinshasa

Kasai

Kwango

Kananga

Luanda

Lobito

Cuanza

ANGOLA
Huambo

Namibe

Cubango

Cunene

Likasi
Lubumbashi

Ndola

ZAMBIA
Lusaka

Dodoma
TANZANIA
Zanzibar
Dar es Salaam

L. Tanganyika
L. Mweru

L. Malawi

MALAWI
Lilôngwe
Blantyre

Zambezi

C. Delgado
Moroni
COMOROS

Aldabra
Is.

Mayotte
(Fr.)

Antsiranana

Mahajanga

H

St. Helena
(U.K.)

OCEAN

C. Fria

NAMIBIA

Windhoek

ZIMBABWE
Livingstone
Bulawayo
Harare

MOZAMBIQUE
Moçambique
Beira

Limpopo

Mozambique Channel

Toamasina

MADAGASCAR
Fianarantsoa
Antananarivo

MAURITIUS
Port
Louis
Réunion
(Fr.)

J

Tropic of Capricorn

BOTSWANA
Gaborone

Johannesburg
Kimberley
Vaal
Pretoria
Mbabane
SWAZ.
Maputo

Orange

Maseru
LESOTHO
Durban

SOUTH AFRICA

30

K

Cape Town
C. of Good Hope
C. Agulhas

Port
Elizabeth
East
London

Equator

Projection: Azimuthal Equidistant

Tristan da Cunha
(U.K.)

West from Greenwich

East from Greenwich

Dakar Capital Cities

COPYRIGHT GEORGE PHILIP LTD.

1 2 3 4 5 6 7 8 9

MADAGASCAR

On same scale as
General Map

COPYRIGHT GEORGE PHILIP LTD.

INDIAN

OCEAN

INDIAN

OCEAN

ATLANTIC OCEAN

INDIAN OCEAN

MALAWI

MOZAMBIQUE

ZAMBIA

ZIMBABWE

Mashonaland

Matabeleland

BOTSWANA

Kalahari

NAMIBIA

Damaraland

Ovamboland

Bariotseland

Caprivi Strip

SOUTH AFRICA

Cape Province

Great Karoo

Free State

Transvaal

Natal

LESOTHO

SWAZILAND

Namaland

HARARE

Bulawayo

Lusaka

Lilongwe

Blantyre

Beira

MAPUTO

PRETORIA

JOHANNESBURG

Soweto

Germiston

Vereeniging

DURBAN

CAPE TOWN

Port Elizabeth

East London

Windhoek

Walvis Bay

Namibe

Benguela

Lubango

Projection: Sanson-Flamsteed's Sinusoidal

Tropic of Capricorn

East from Greenwich

Tropic of Capricorn

ft
12 000
9000
6000
4500
3000
1200
600
0

m
4000
3000
2000
1500
1000
400
200
0

200-600
600-1000
1000-2000
2000-3000
3000-4000
4000

m
6000
12 000

ft

Antananarivo

Toamasina

Mahajanga

Fianarantsoa

Toliara

MOZAMBIQUE

CHANNEL

MOZAMBIQUE CHANNEL

INDIAN OCEAN

INDIAN OCEAN

MADAGASCAR

On same scale as General Map

COPYRIGHT GEORGE PHILIP LTD.

East from Greenwich

500 0 250 500 750 1000 1250 1500 1750 km
500 0 250 500 750 1000 1250 miles

Top map (Physical):

INDIAN OCEAN
PACIFIC OCEAN

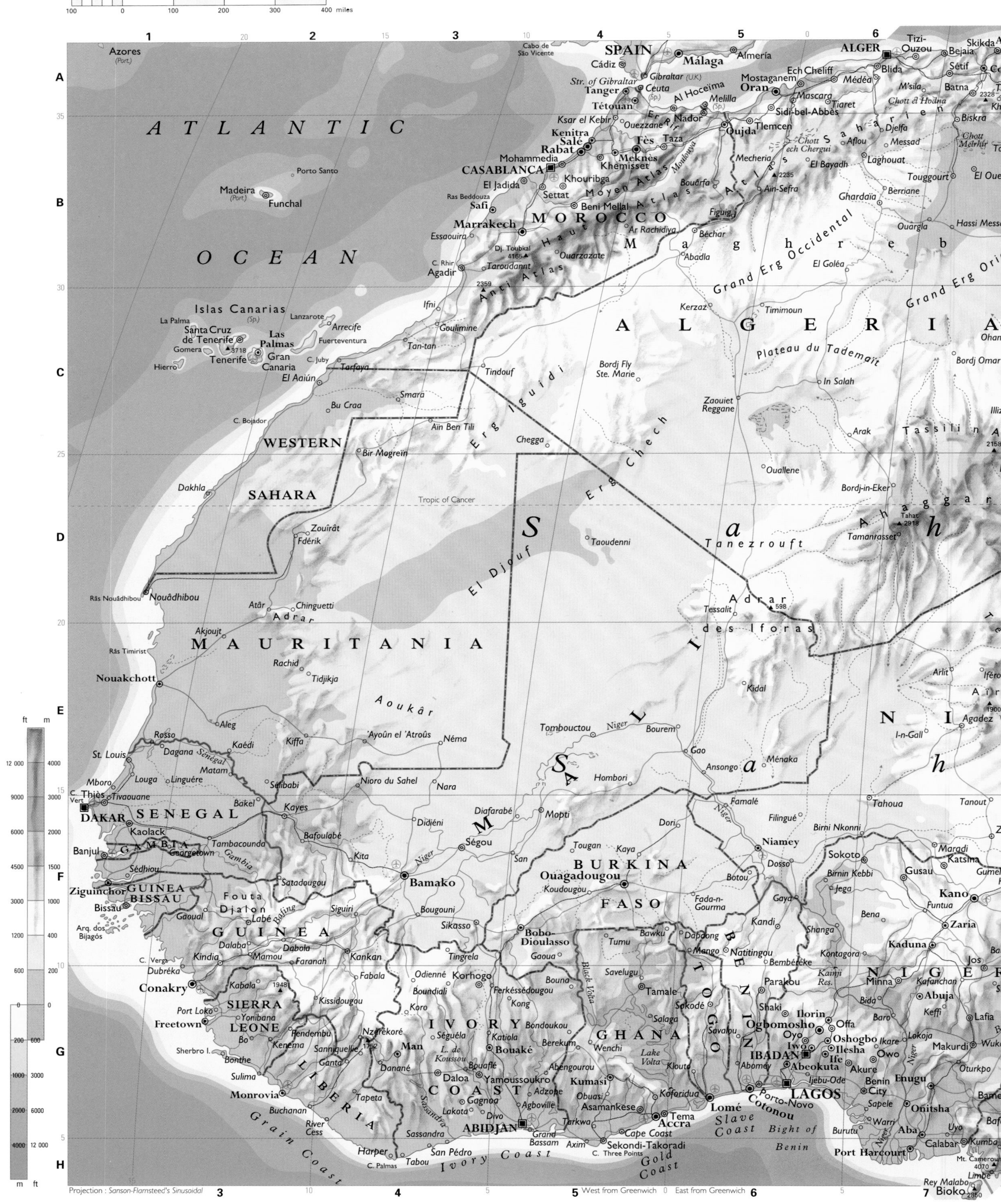

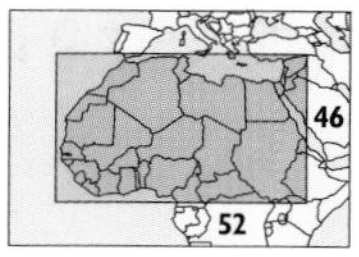

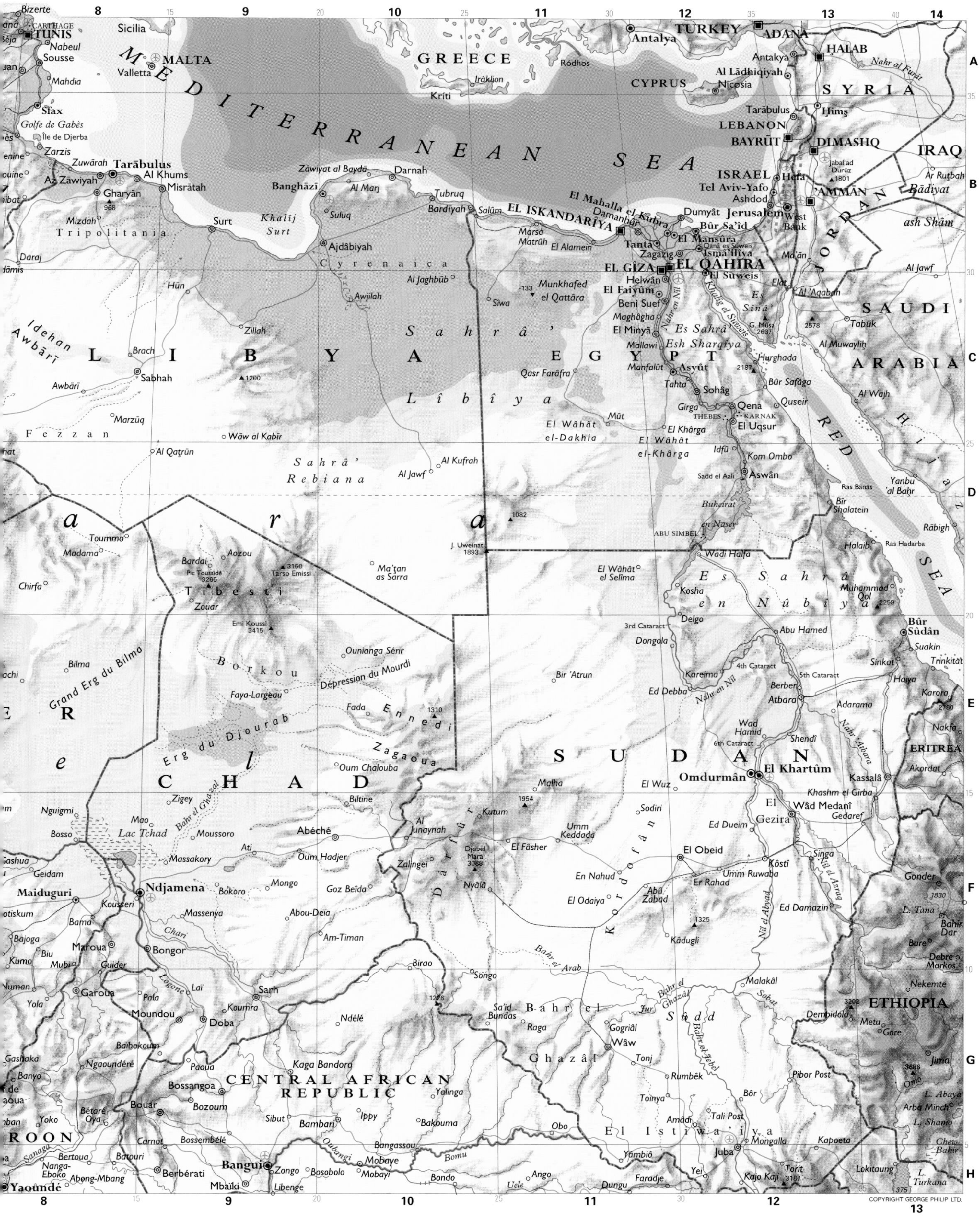

8 9 10 11 12 13 14
15 20 25 30 35 40

Bizerte
CARTHAGE
TUNIS
Nabeul
Sousse
Mahdia
Sfax
Golfe de Gabès
Île de Djerba
Zarzis
Zuwārah
Tarābulus
Az Zāwiyah
Al Khums
Misrātah
Gharyān
968
Mizdah
Tripolitania
Sicilia
MALTA
Valletta
MEDITERRANEAN SEA
GREECE
Iráklion
Kríti
Ródhos
Antalya
TURKEY
ADANA
Antakya
HALAB
Nahr al Furāt
Al Lādhiqiyah
CYPRUS
Nicosia
SYRIA
Tarābulus
Hims
LEBANON
BAYRŪT
DIMASHQ
IRAQ
Jabal ad Durūz
1801
Ar Rutbah
ISRAEL
Tel Aviv-Yafo
Hefa
Ashdod
Jerusalem
West Bank
'AMMĀN
JORDAN
Bādiyat ash Shām
Zāwiyat al Baydā
Darnah
Banghāzī
Al Marj
Suluq
Tubruq
Bardīyah
Salûm
EL ISKANDARÎYA
El Mahalla el Kubra
Damanhûr
Dumyât
Bûr Sa'îd
El Mansûra
Qana es Suweis
Isma'iliya
Tanta
Zagazig
Marsā Matrûh
El Alamein
Khalīj Surt
Surt
Ajdābiyah
Cyrenaica
Daraj
Ghadāmis
Hūn
Al Jaghbūb
Awjilah
EL GIZA
EL QAHIRA
El Suweis
Helwân
El Faiyûm
Beni Suef
Maghâgha
El Minyâ
Mallawi
Manfalût
Asyût
Tahta
Sohâg
Girga
THEBES
KARNAK
Qena
El Uqsur
Nahr en Nîl
Khalîg el Suweis
Es Sînâ'
G. Mûsa 2637
Elat
Al 'Aqabah
Ma'ān
Al Jawf
Tabūk
2578
SAUDI ARABIA
Al Muwaylih
Al Wajh
Hijaz
-133
Munkhafed el Qattâra
Sîwa
Zillah
Idehan Awbārī
LIBYA
Brach
Sabhah
Awbārī
Marzūq
Fezzan
1200
Sahrâ' Lîbîya
EGYPT
Es Sahrâ Esh Sharqîya
Hurghada
2187
Bûr Safâga
Quseir
Qasr Farâfra
Mût
El Wâhât el-Dakhla
El Khârga
El Wâhât el-Khârga
Idfû
Kom Ombo
Aswân
Sadd el Aali
RED SEA
Wāw al Kabīr
Al Qaţrūn
Sahrâ' Rebiana
Al Kufrah
Al Jawf
Ras Bānās
Bîr Shalatein
Yanbu 'al Bahr
Rābigh
Buheirat en Naser
ABU SIMBEL
Sahara
Toummo
Madama
1082
J. Uweinat 1893
Halaib
Ras Hadarba
Wadi Halfa
El Wâhât el Selîma
Es Sahrâ en Nûbîya
Kosha
Muhammad Qol
2259
Bardai
Aozou
Pic Toussidé 3265
3160 Tarso Emissi
Tibesti
Zouar
Chirfa
Ma'tan as Sarra
Emi Koussi 3415
Delgo
3rd Cataract
Abu Hamed
Bûr Sûdân
Suakin
Trinkitat
Dongola
Ounianga Sérir
Borkou
Bilma
Grand Erg du Bilma
Dépression du Mourdi
Bir 'Atrun
Kareima
4th Cataract
5th Cataract
Sinkat
Haiya
Faya-Largeau
Fada
1310
Ennedi
Ed Debba
Nahr en Nîl
Berber
Atbara
Adarama
Karora
2780
Nakfa
ERITREA
Erg du Djourab
Zagaoua
Wad Hamid
6th Cataract
Shendî
Nahr Atbara
Akordat
CHAD
Oum Chalouba
SUDAN
Omdurmân
El Khartûm
Kassalā
Malha
El Wuz
Zigey
Biltine
1954
Khashm el Girba
Nguigmi
Mao
Lac Tchad
Bahr el Ghazal
Moussoro
Abéché
Al Junaynah
Dârfûr
Kutum
Umm Keddada
Sodiri
El Gezira
Wad Medanî
Gedaref
Bosso
Massakory
Ati
Oum Hadjer
Zalingei
Djebel Mara 3088
El Fâsher
Ed Dueim
Gashua
Geidam
Nyâlâ
En Nahud
El Obeid
Kordofân
Umm Ruwaba
Kôstî
Singa
Nîl el Azraq
Gonder
1830
Maiduguri
Ndjamena
Bokoro
Mongo
Goz Beïda
Er Rahad
Abû Zabad
El Odaiya
Ed Damazin
L. Tana
Bahir Dar
Potiskum
Kousseri
Bama
Massenya
Abou-Deïa
Chari
Am-Timan
1325
Kâdugli
Nîl el Abyad
Bure
Debre Markos
Bajoga
Maroua
Biu
Mubi
Guider
Bongor
Bahr el Arab
Birao
Songo
Kumo
Numan
Yola
Garoua
Logone
Laï
Pala
Sarh
1226
Malakâl
Sobat
Nekemte
Moundou
Doba
Koumra
Ndélé
Sa'id Bundas
Bahr el Ghazâl
Jur
Bahr el Ghazâl
Sudd
Bahr el Jebel
3202
Dembidolo
ETHIOPIA
Metu
Gore
Raga
Gogriâl
Wâw
Tonj
Rumbêk
Jima
Gashaka
Ngaoundéré
Baïbokoum
Kaga Bandoro
Paoua
Banyo
CENTRAL AFRICAN REPUBLIC
Pibor Post
3686
Omo
Bossangoa
Yalinga
Bôr
L. Abaya
Arba Minch
Bozoum
Bouar
Bétaré Oya
Yoko
Sibut
Bambari
Ippy
Bakouma
Toinya
Amâdi
Tali Post
L. Shamo
El Istiwâ'iya
Obo
CAMEROON
Carnot
Bossembélé
Bangassou
Mongalla
Kapoeta
Chew Bahir
Sanaga
Bertoua
Batouri
Berbérati
Oubangui
Bomu
Yambio
Juba
Bangui
Zongo
Mobaye
Nanga-Eboko
Abong-Mbang
Bosobolo
Mobayi
Bondo
Yei
Torit
3187
Kajo Kaji
Lokitaung
375
L. Turkana
Yaoundé
Mbaïki
Libenge
Uele
Ango
Dungu
Faradje
A B C D E F G H

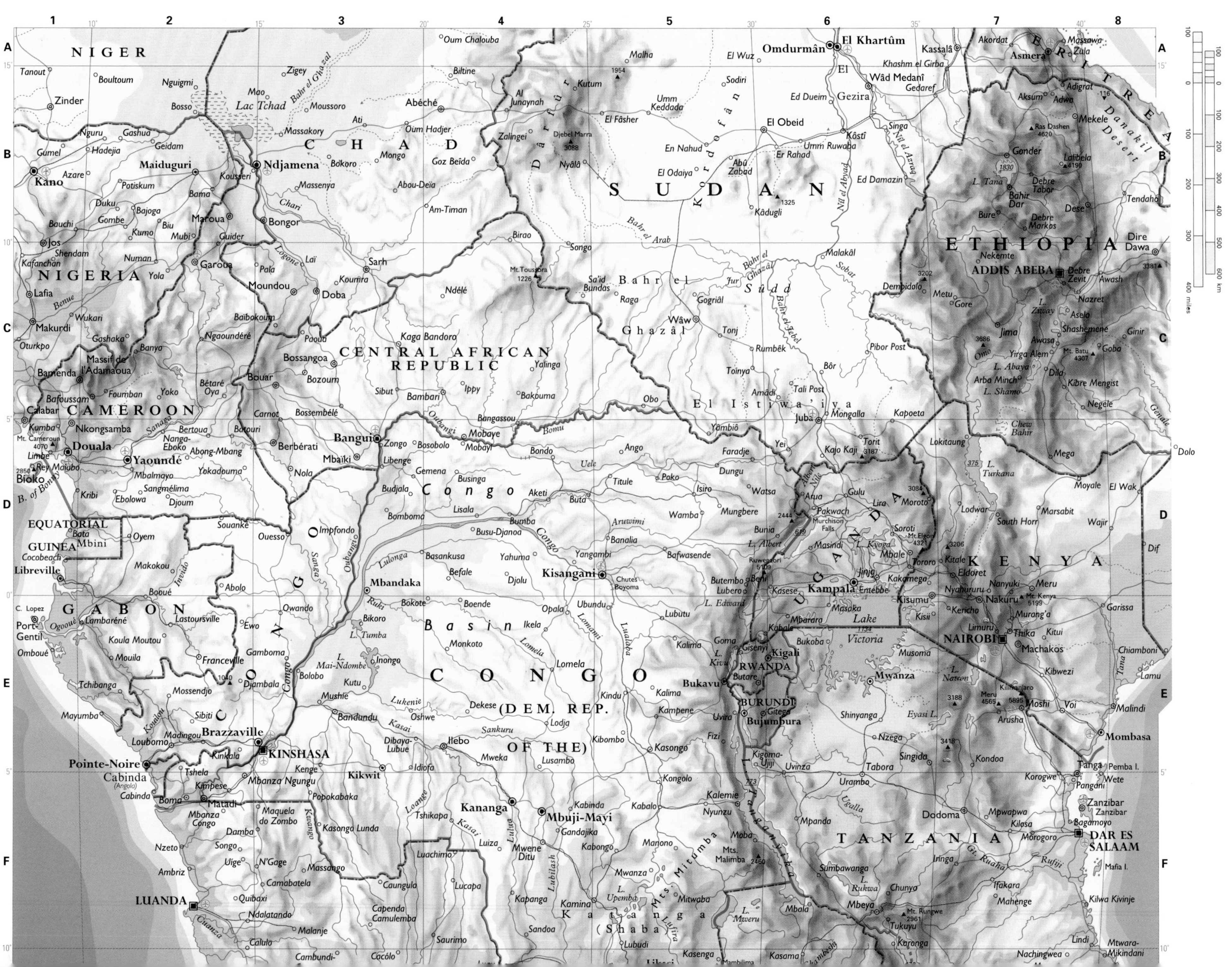
100 0 100 200 300 400 500 600 km
100 0 100 200 300 400 miles
NIGER
NIGERIA
CHAD
SUDAN
ERITREA
ETHIOPIA
CENTRAL AFRICAN REPUBLIC
CAMEROON
EQUATORIAL GUINEA
GABON
CONGO
CONGO (DEM. REP. OF THE)
UGANDA
KENYA
RWANDA
BURUNDI
TANZANIA
El Khartûm
Omdurmân
Asmera
ADDIS ABEBA
Ndjamena
Bangui
Yaoundé
Libreville
Brazzaville
KINSHASA
LUANDA
Kampala
NAIROBI
Kigali
Bujumbura
DAR ES SALAAM
Mombasa
Kisangani
Mbuji-Mayi
Kananga
Pointe-Noire
Douala
Kano
Lac Tchad
Lake Victoria
Congo Basin
Dârfûr
Kordofân
Bahr el Ghazâl
Sûdd
Danakil Desert

ATLANTIC OCEAN
INDIAN OCEAN
MADAGASCAR
On same scale as General Map
COPYRIGHT GEORGE PHILIP LTD.
ANGOLA
NAMIBIA
BOTSWANA
ZAMBIA
ZIMBABWE
MOZAMBIQUE
MALAWI
SOUTH AFRICA
LESOTHO
SWAZILAND
Kalahari
Namib
Namaland
Damaraland
Ovamboland
Barotseland
Matabeleland
Mashonaland
Transvaal
Natal
Orange Free State
Cape Province
Great Karoo
Caprivi Strip
Okavango Swamps
Makgadikgadi Salt Pans
Etosha Pan
Lake Kariba
Tropic of Capricorn
East from Greenwich
Projection : Sanson-Flamsteed's Sinusoidal
CAPE TOWN
Table Mt. 1087
Cape of Good Hope
Cape Agulhas
PRETORIA
JOHANNESBURG
Soweto
DURBAN
Port Elizabeth
East London
Bloemfontein
Kimberley
Pietermaritzburg
Maseru
MAPUTO
HARARE
Bulawayo
Lusaka
Windhoek
Walvis Bay
Swakopmund
Lüderitz
Gaborone
Francistown
Maun
Livingstone
Victoria Falls
Beira
Blantyre
Quelimane
Nampula
Antananarivo
Toamasina
Mahajanga
Fianarantsoa
Toliara
Antsiranana
Taolanaro
Lubango
Namibe
Benguela
Huambo
Menongue
ft
m
12 000
9000
6000
4500
3000
1200
600
0
4000
3000
2000
1500
1000
400
200
0
200
600
1000
2000
4000
3000
6000
12 000

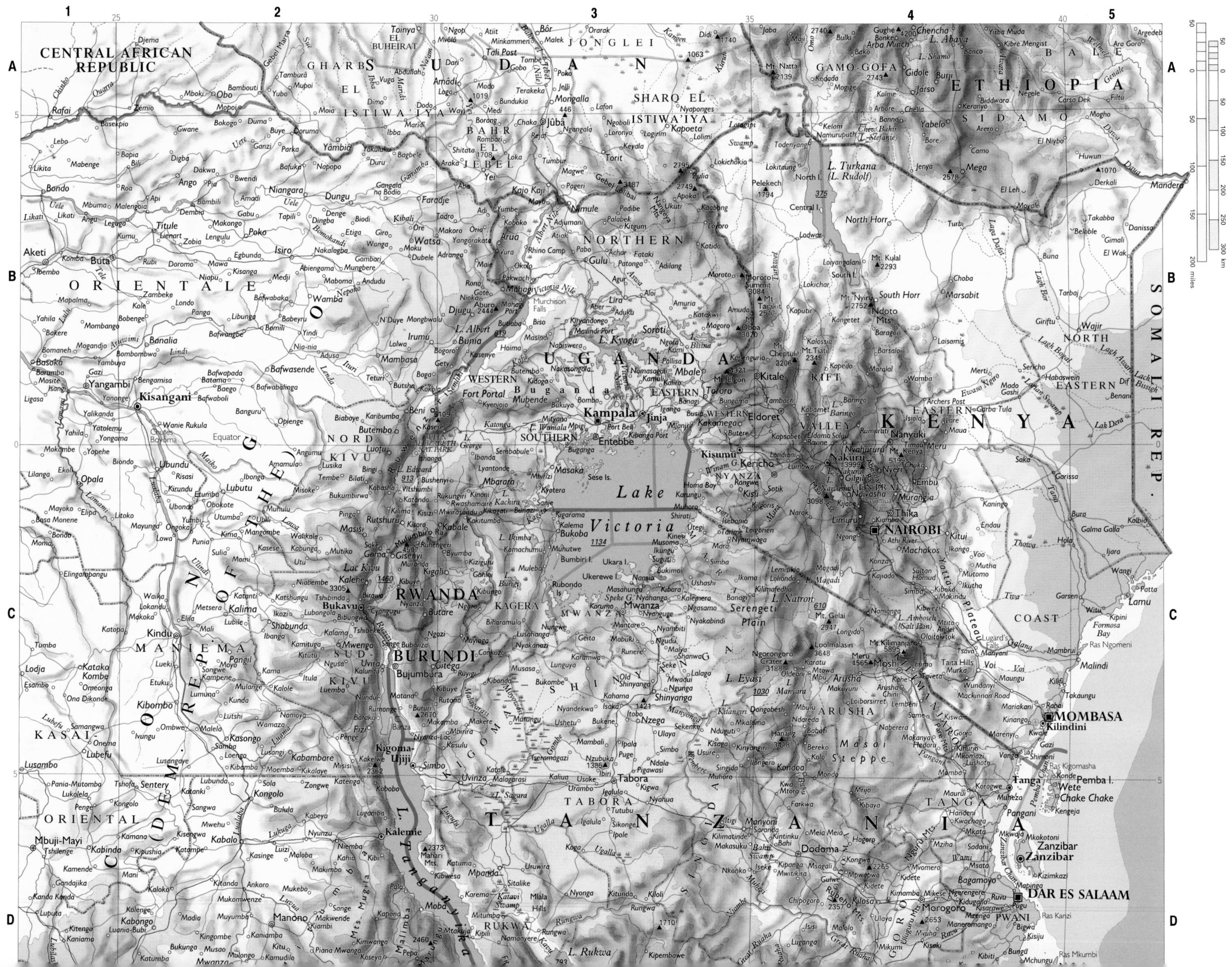
0 50 100 150 200 250 300 km
0 50 100 150 200 miles
1
2
3
4
5
A
B
C
D
CENTRAL AFRICAN REPUBLIC
SUDAN
ETHIOPIA
SOMALI REP.
KENYA
UGANDA
RWANDA
BURUNDI
TANZANIA
NAIROBI
MOMBASA
Kilindini
DAR ES SALAAM
Zanzibar
Kampala
Entebbe
Kisangani
Bujumbura
Kigoma-Ujiji
Lake Victoria
L. Turkana (L. Rudolf)
L. Tanganyika
L. Albert
L. Edward
Lac Kivu
L. Kyoga
L. Natron
L. Eyasi
L. Rukwa
Tanga
Pemba I.
Dodoma
Morogoro
Tabora
Mwanza
Arusha
Moshi
Kisumu
Eldoret
Nakuru
Marsabit
Jûbâ
Yei
Gulu
Lira
Soroti
Mbale
Jinja
Masaka
Bukavu
Kindu
Kalemie
Mbuji-Mayi
Kabalo
Kongolo
Kasongo
Kibombo
Buta
Isiro
Bunia
Butembo
Beni
Lamu
Malindi
Serengeti Plain
Masai Steppe
Yatta Plateau
Equator

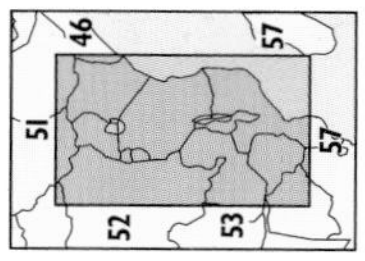

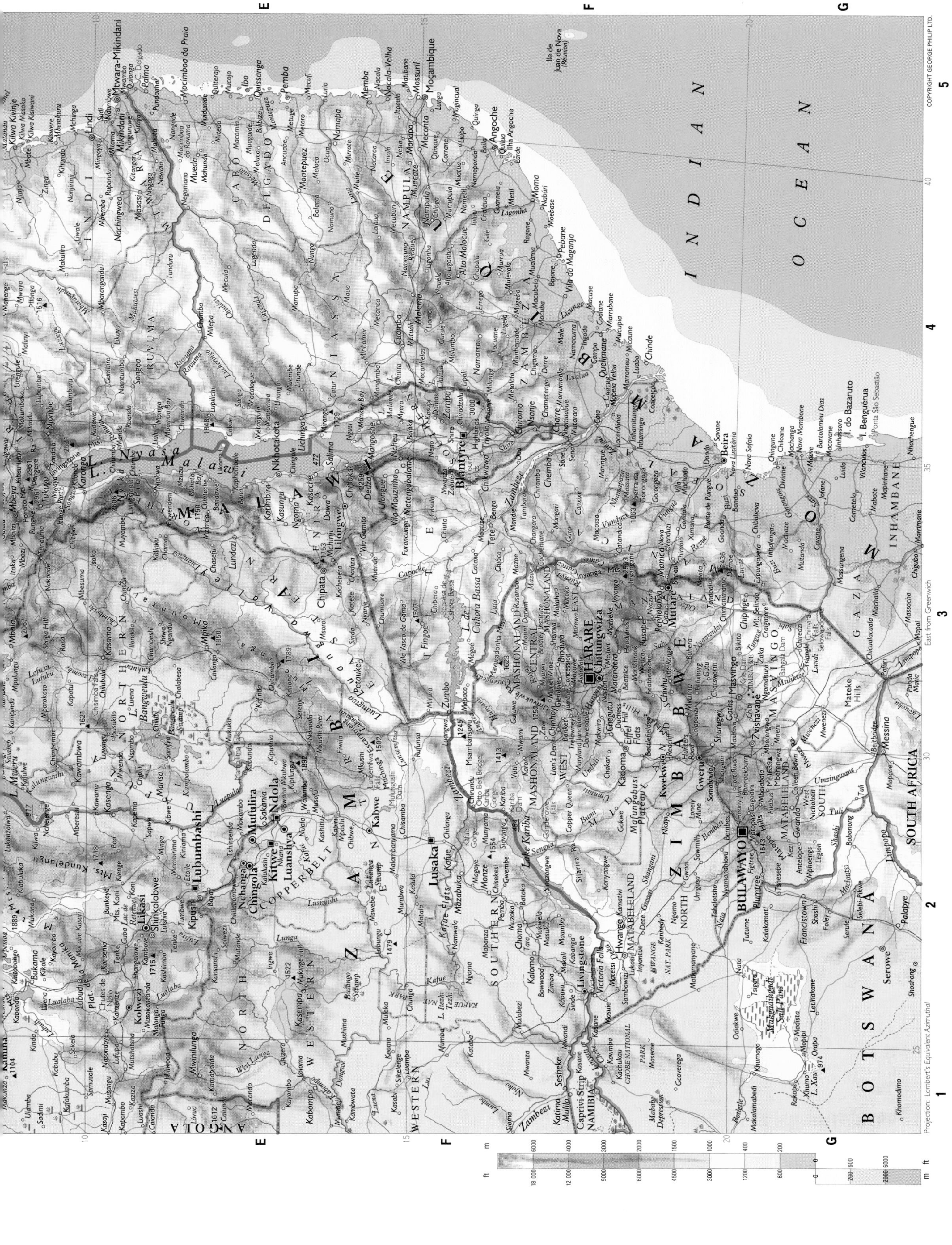

INDIAN OCEAN

MOÇAMBIQUE

MALAWI

ZAMBIA

ZIMBABWE

BOTSWANA

SOUTH AFRICA

NAMIBIA

ANGOLA

Projection: Lambert's Equivalent Azimuthal

East from Greenwich

m	ft
6000	18 000
4000	12 000
3000	9000
2000	6000
1500	4500
1000	3000
400	1200
200	600
0	0
200	600
2000	6000

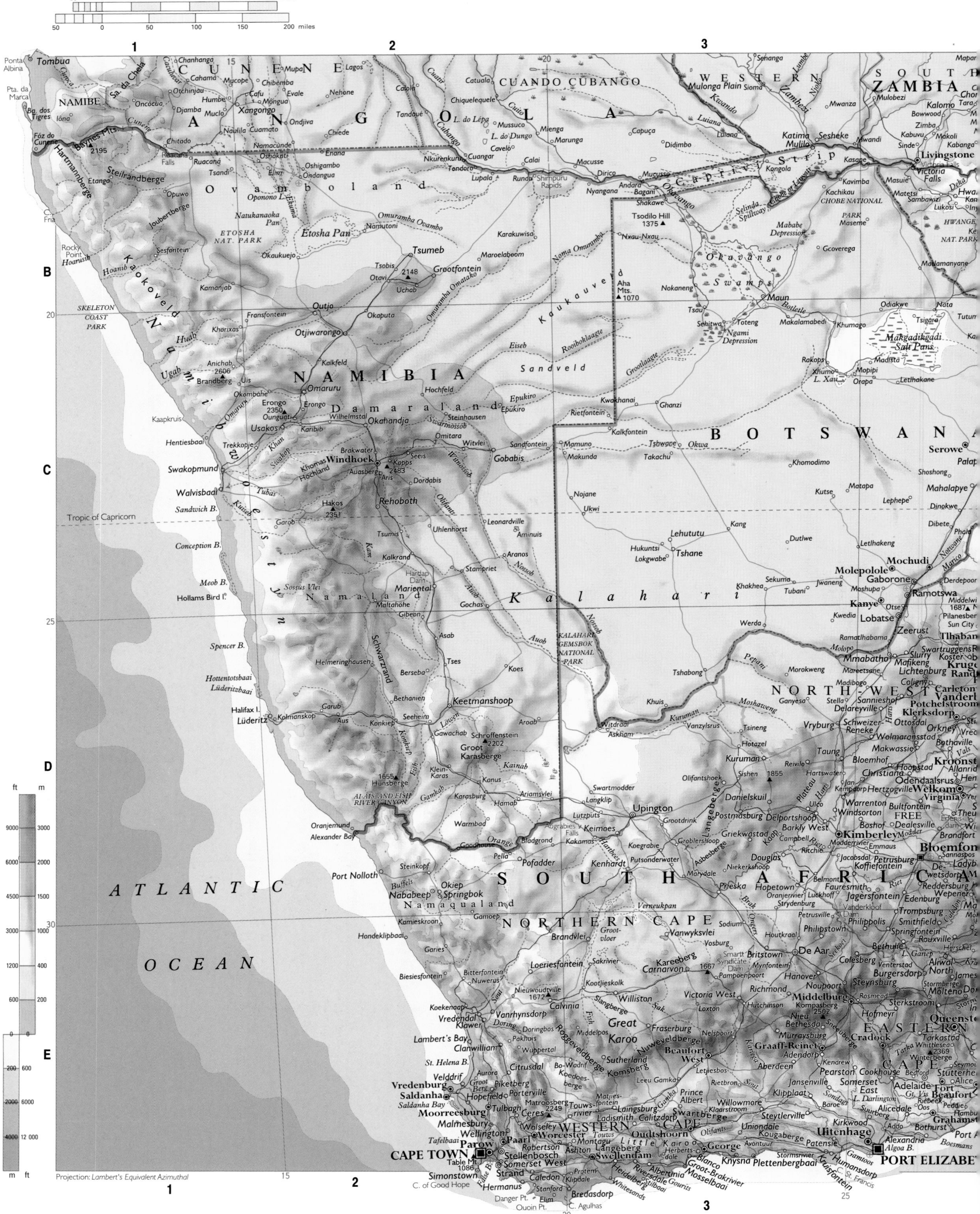

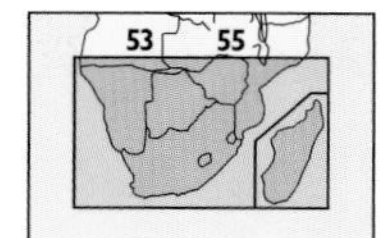
53
55
5
6
7
8
9
A
B
C
D
E
MALAWI
Z A M B E Z I A
T E T E
MOZAMBIQUE CHANNEL
Ile de Júan de Nova (Fr.)
Angoche
I. Angoche
Moma
Pebane
Vila da Maganja
Quelimane
Chinde
Tete
Chiromo
Nsanje
Chemba
Mutare
HARARE
Chitungwiza
MASHONALAND CENTRAL
MASHONALAND WEST
MASHONALAND EAST
Z I M B A B W E
Kadoma
Gweru
Masvingo
M A S V I N G O
Zvishavane
Chipinge
Beira
Nova Sofala
Nova Mambone
I. do Bazaruto
I. Benguérua
Vilanculos
Inhambane
Maxixe
Inharrime
Xai-Xai
Manjacaze
Chibuto
Guijá
Maputo
B. de Maputo
Inhaca
MAPUTO
G A Z A
I N H A M B A N E
M A N I C A
S O F A L A
Z A M B É Z I A
Manica
Chimoio
Messina
Louis Trichardt
Pietersburg
Tzaneen
Phalaborwa
Mateke Hills
Limpopo
Shashi
NORTHERN
PRETORIA
JOHANNESBURG
Benoni
Springs
Germiston
Vereeniging
MPUMALANGA
Middelburg
Witbank
Nelspruit
Barberton
SWAZILAND
Mbabane
Manzini
Standerton
Ermelo
Newcastle
Dundee
Vryheid
Ladysmith
Harrismith
Kestell
K W A Z U L U
N A T A L
Empangeni
Richards Bay
L. St. Lucia
L. Sibayi
Pietermaritzburg
KwaMashu
DURBAN
Umlazi
Mpumalanga
Pinetown
Kokstad
Port Shepstone
Margate
Umtata
Umzimvubu
East London
EASTERN CAPE
I N D I A N
O C E A N
Antsiranana
ANTSIRANANA
Nosy Be
Iharana
Ambanja
Antalaha
Mahajanga
MAHAJANGA
Marovoay
Maevatanana
Tsaratanana
Toamasina
TOAMASINA
ANTANANARIVO
Antsirabe
Mahanoro
Morondava
Miandrivazo
Fianarantsoa
FIANARANTSOA
Mananjary
Manakara
Farafangana
Vangaindrano
Toliara
TOLIARA
Ambovombe
Taolanaro
Tsihombe
Tanjon' i Vohimena
Mt. de Tsaratanana
Is. Glorieuses (Fr.)
Tanjon' i Bobraomby
Nosy Boraha
Nosy Varika
Tropic of Capricorn
M O Z A M B I Q U E
C H A N N E L
M A D A G A S C A R
I N D I A N
O C E A N
MADAGASCAR
On same scale as General Map
East from Greenwich
30
35
40
45
50
15
20
25
COPYRIGHT GEORGE PHILIP LTD.

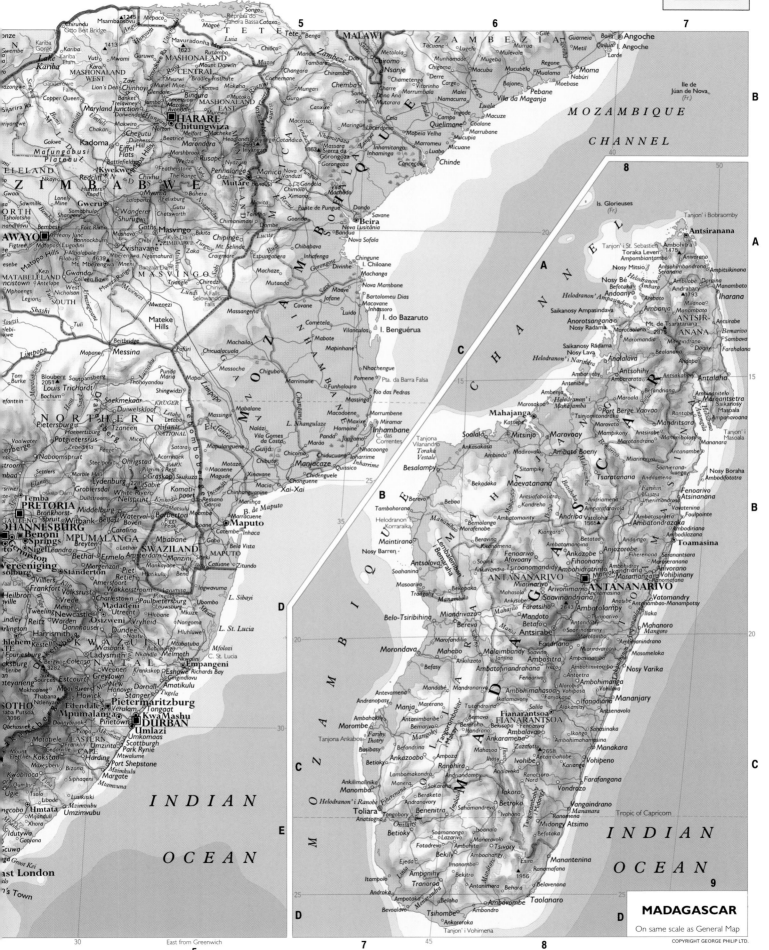

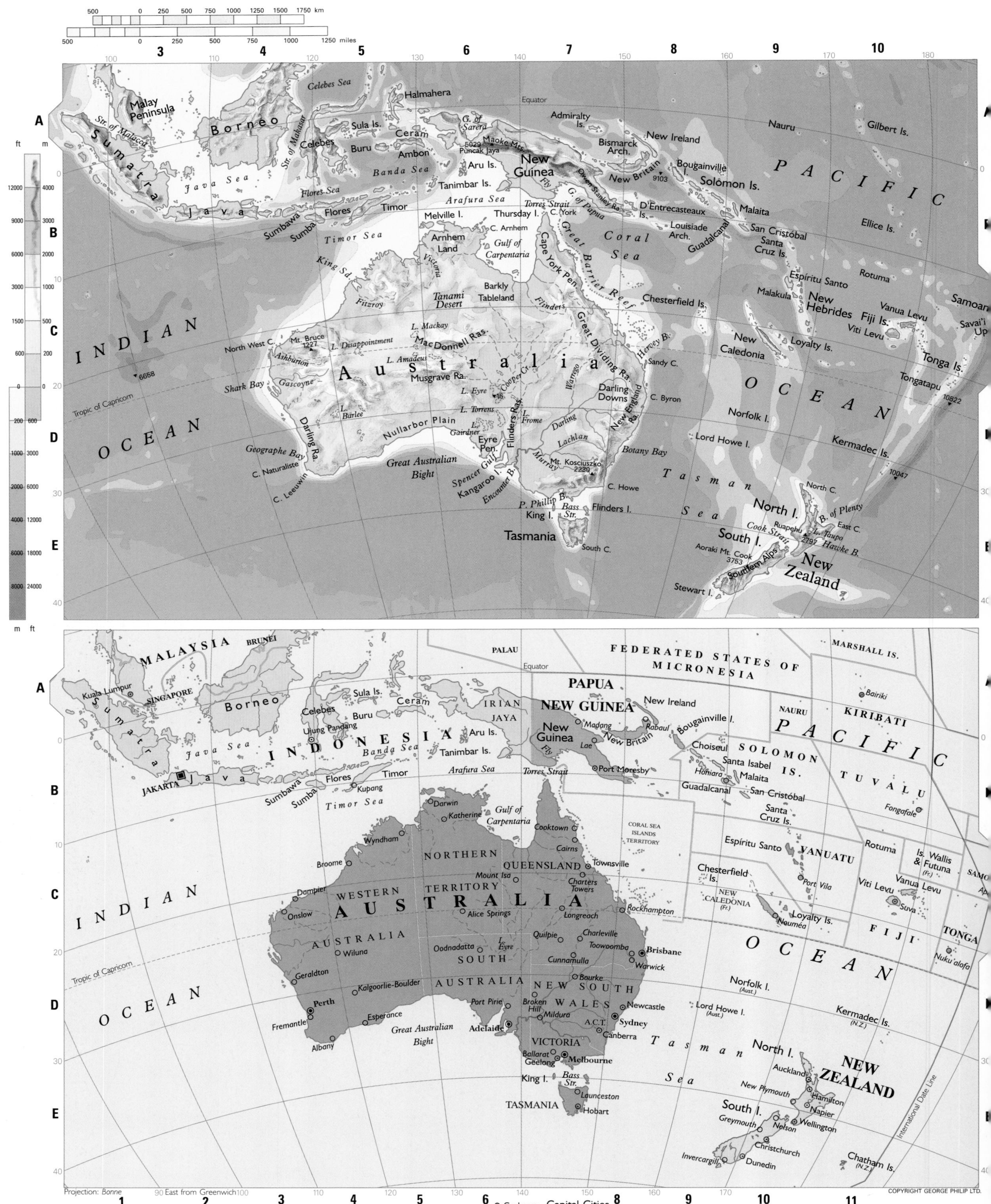

Malay Peninsula
Str. of Malacca
Sumatra
Borneo
Celebes Sea
Halmahera
Celebes
Sula Is.
Buru
Ceram
Ambon
Java Sea
Str. of Makasar
Banda Sea
Flores Sea
Tanimbar Is.
Java
Sumbawa
Flores
Timor
Sumba
Timor Sea
Equator
G. of Sarera
5029 Maoke Mts.
Puncak Jaya
New Guinea
Aru Is.
Arafura Sea
Admiralty Is.
Bismarck Arch.
New Ireland
New Britain 9103
Owen Stanley Ra.
G. of Papua
Torres Strait
Thursday I.
C. York
Bougainville I.
Solomon Is.
D'Entrecasteaux Is.
Malaita
San Cristóbal
Santa Cruz Is.
Guadalcanal
Louisiade Arch.
Nauru
Gilbert Is.
PACIFIC
Ellice Is.
Espíritu Santo
Rotuma
Malakula
New Hebrides
Fiji Is.
Vanua Levu
Viti Levu
Samoa
Savai'i Up
Melville I.
C. Arnhem
Arnhem Land
Gulf of Carpentaria
Cape York Pen.
Great Barrier Reef
Coral Sea
Chesterfield Is.
Loyalty Is.
New Caledonia
OCEAN
Tonga Is.
Tongatapu 10822
King Sd.
Victoria
Barkly Tableland
Flinders
Fitzroy
Tanami Desert
L. Mackay
MacDonnell Ras.
Hervey B.
Sandy C.
Norfolk I.
Kermadec Is.
North West C.
Mt. Bruce 1227
Ashburton
L. Disappointment
L. Amadeus
Musgrave Ra.
Australia
Copper Ck.
Warrego
Darling Downs
C. Byron
New England Ra.
6658
Tropic of Capricorn
Shark Bay
Gascoyne
L. Eyre
L. Torrens
Darling
Lord Howe I.
10047
L. Barlee
Geographe Bay
C. Naturaliste
Darling Ra.
Nullarbor Plain
L. Gairdner
Eyre Pen.
Flinders Ras.
L. Frome
Lachlan
Murray
Mt. Kosciuszko 2230
Botany Bay
Tasman Sea
North C.
Great Australian Bight
Spencer Gulf
Kangaroo I.
Encounter B.
C. Howe
North I.
B. of Plenty
East C.
C. Leeuwin
P. Phillip B.
King I.
Bass Str.
Flinders I.
South C.
Ruapehu 2797
L. Taupo
Hawke B.
Tasmania
Aoraki Mt. Cook 3753
Southern Alps
South I.
New Zealand
Stewart I.

ft m
12000 4000
9000 3000
6000 2000
3000 1000
1500 500
600 200
0 0
200 600
1000 3000
2000 6000
4000 12000
6000 18000
8000 24000
m ft

Bottom map (Political):

MALAYSIA
BRUNEI
PALAU
FEDERATED STATES OF MICRONESIA
MARSHALL IS.
Kuala Lumpur
SINGAPORE
Sumatra
Borneo
Celebes
Buru
Ceram
Sula Is.
IRIAN JAYA
PAPUA NEW GUINEA
New Ireland
NAURU
Bairiki
KIRIBATI
Ujung Pandang
INDONESIA
Aru Is.
Madang
Rabaul
New Britain
Bougainville I.
PACIFIC
Equator
Java Sea
Banda Sea
Tanimbar Is.
New Guinea
Lae
Choiseul
Santa Isabel
SOLOMON IS.
JAKARTA
Java
Flores
Timor
Arafura Sea
Torres Strait
Port Moresby
Honiara
Malaita
San Cristóbal
TUVALU
Sumbawa
Sumba
Kupang
Timor Sea
Guadalcanal
Santa Cruz Is.
Fongafale
INDIAN
Darwin
Katherine
Gulf of Carpentaria
Cooktown
CORAL SEA ISLANDS TERRITORY
Espíritu Santo
Rotuma
Is. Wallis & Futuna (Fr.)
SAMO
Wyndham
NORTHERN
Cairns
VANUATU
Broome
Mount Isa
Townsville
Chesterfield Is.
Port Vila
Viti Levu
Vanua Levu
Dampier
WESTERN
TERRITORY
Charters Towers
NEW CALEDONIA (Fr.)
Suva
Onslow
AUSTRALIA
Alice Springs
Longreach
Rockhampton
Loyalty Is.
FIJI
OCEAN
AUSTRALIA
AUSTRALIA
Quilpie
Charleville
Nouméa
TONGA
Wiluna
Oodnadatta
L. Eyre
SOUTH
Cunnamulla
Toowoomba
Brisbane
Norfolk I. (Aust.)
Nuku'alofa
Geraldton
AUSTRALIA
Warwick
Kalgoorlie-Boulder
Bourke
NEW SOUTH WALES
Lord Howe I. (Aust.)
Kermadec Is. (N.Z.)
Perth
Port Pirie
Broken Hill
Newcastle
Fremantle
Esperance
Mildura
A.C.T.
Sydney
Tropic of Capricorn
Great Australian Bight
Adelaide
Canberra
Tasman Sea
North I.
NEW ZEALAND
VICTORIA
Auckland
Ballarat
Geelong
Melbourne
New Plymouth
Hamilton
King I.
Bass Str.
Napier
OCEAN
Launceston
South I.
Wellington
TASMANIA
Hobart
Greymouth
Nelson
Christchurch
Invercargill
Dunedin
Chatham Is. (N.Z.)

Projection: Bonne
90 East from Greenwich 100
International Date Line
⊚ Canberra Capital Cities
COPYRIGHT GEORGE PHILIP LTD.

64 64 64 64 64
1

50 0 50 100 150 200 km
50 0 50 100 150 miles

34 168 170 172 174 176 178 34

F

C. Reinga
C. Maria
van Diemen
North C.
Rangaunu B.
Houhora Heads
Doubtless B.
Mangonui
Whangaroa Harb.
Ahipara B.
Kaitaia
Tauroa Pt.
Okaihau
B. of Islands
C. Brett
Rawene
Opua
Kaikohe
Hikurangi
Hokianga Harbour
Whangarei
Donnelly's Crossing
Whangarei Harb.
Bream Hd.
Dargaville
Waipu
Bream B.
Little
Barrier I.

PACIFIC
OCEAN

F

G

Kaipara Harbour
Warkworth
C. Rodney
Great Barrier I.
C. Colville
Cuvier I.
Helensville
Coromandel
Hauraki
Gulf
Whitianga
Takapuna
Devonport
AUCKLAND
Manukau
Papakura
Thames
Waiuku
Pukekohe
Mercer
Waihi
Mayor I.
Waikato
Paeroa
Waihi
Tauranga Harb.
Huntly
Te Aroha
Mount
Maunganui
White I. C. Runaway
Hamilton
Morrinsville
Tauranga
Bay of Plenty
Raglan
Te Awamutu
Cambridge
Whakatane
East C.
Kawhia Harbour
Putaruru
Kawerau
Opotiki
Otorohanga
Rotorua
Rotorua
Taneatua
Raukumara Ra.
Mt. Hikurangi
1753
Waipiro

G

North
Island

H

Te Kuiti
Kinleith
Kaingaroa
Murupara
Matu
Te Kaha
Mokau
Taratera L.
Mokai
Wairakei
Taupo
Rangitaiki
Tolaga Bay
North Taranaki
Bight
Ongarue
Taupo
Waikaremoana
L.
Waitara
Taumarunui
Turangi
Kaimanawa Mts.
Ormond
Gisborne
New Plymouth
Whangamomona
Poverty Bay
Inglewood
Mt. Taranaki
(Mt. Egmont)
Ruapehu
2797
Nuhaka
Waikokopu
C. Egmont
2518
Stratford
Ohakune
Waiouru
Mahia Pen.
Opunake
Eltham
Raetihi
Bay
Kapuni
Wairoa
Hawera
Taihape
View
Hawke Bay
South Taranaki
Bight
Waverley
Mangaweka
Ruahine
Ra.
Napier
Patea
Hunterville
Waipawa
Hastings
Wanganui
Marton
Halcombe
Dannevirke
Waipukurau
Bulls
Feilding
Woodville
C. Turnagain

H

J

Palmerston
North
Foxton
Shannon
Levin
Pahiatua
Eketahuna
C. Farewell
Otaki
Tararua Ra.
Masterton
Collingwood
Golden
B.
Paraparaumu
Carterton
Greytown
Takaka
D'Urville I.
Kapiti I.
Featherston
Martinborough
Tasman
Mts.
Tasman
B.
Motueka
Pelorus Sd.
Upper Hutt
Wairarapa
Karamea
Nelson
Havelock
Petone
WELLINGTON
Karamea
Bight
Richmond
Picton
Lower Hutt
Seddonville
Wakefield
Eastbourne
Cook Strait
Granity
Tadmor
Blenheim
Seddon
Westport
Lyell
Wairau
Ward

J

6 **7**

SAMOA ISLANDS
1:12 000 000

Murchison
Inangahua Jc.
Rotoroa
L.
Travers 2338
2885 Mt. Tapuaenuku
Kaikoura
Reefton
Spenser
Mts.
Clarence
Kaikoura
Blackball Grey
Runanga
Hanmer
Springs
SAMOA
AMERICAN
SAMOA
Greymouth
Stillwater
Amuri
Pass
Waiau
Savai'i
Apia
Kumara
L. Brunner
Jacksons
Waiau
Upolu
Pago Pago
Hokitika
Arthur's
Pass
Waikari
Hurunui
Tutuila
West from
Greenwich
Ross
Culverden
Waipara
12 **13** **14**

A

14

B

K

South
Island
Abut Hd.
Coleridge
Rangiora
Oxford
Pegasus Bay
Springfield
Kaiapoi
Whitecliffs
New Brighton
Aoraki Mt. Cook
Methven
Christchurch
3753
Staveley
Riccarton
Lyttelton
Jackson B.
Okuru
Lincoln
Banks Pen.
Tekapo
Southbridge
Akaroa
Rakaia
Little River

8 **9** Futuna **10** **11**
Wallis & Futuna (Fr.)
14

B

L

Mt.
Aspiring
3027
Fairlie
Pukaki
L.
Ashburton Bight
Earnslaw
Wanaka L.
Ohau
Canterbury
Timaru
2818
Milford Sd.
Wanaka
St.
Andrews
Bligh Sound
George Sound
Arrowtown
Cromwell
Kurow
Waimate
Niuafo'ou
(Tonga)
Thikombia
Queenstown
Dunstan Mts.
Tokarahi
Ngapara
Lambasa
Vanua Levu
Secretary I.
Te Anau Kingston
Naseby
Oamaru
FIJI
Doubtful Sd.
L.
Clyde
Maheno
Yasawa Group
Taveuni
Koro
Manapouri
Alexandra
Hampden
Lautoka
1323
Vanua Mbalavu
L.
Roxburgh
Dunback
Levuka
Breaksea Sd.
Lumsden
Palmerston
Nandi
Viti Levu
Ovalau
Lau
Resolution I.
Mossburn
Edievale
Waikouaiti
Suva
Gau
Lakemba
Dusky Sd.
Ohai
Kelso
Port Chalmers
Koro Sea
Group
Nightcaps
Tapanui
Mosgiel
Otago Harbour
Moala
TONGA
(Friendly Is.)
Fairfield
Saunders C.
Milton
Winton
Clinton
Dunedin
Kandavu
Vava'u

L

18

C

D

M

Clifden
Tuatapere
Hedgehope
Balclutha
Orepuki
Gore
Kaitangata
Riverton
Mataura
Wyndham
Vatoa
Tofua
Invercargill
Owaka
Tokanui
Nugget Pt.
Tahakopa
Foveaux Str.
South Invercargill
Bluff
Ruapuke I.
Halfmoon Bay
Stewart I.
Southwest C.
Port Pegasus
Tongatapu
Nuku'alofa

M

20

E

**FIJI AND TONGA
ISLANDS**
1:12 000 000

50 0 50 100 150 200 km
50 0 50 100 150 miles

Projection : Conical with two standard parallels
166 168 East from Greenwich 170 172

22

ft m
9000 3000
6000 2000
3000 1000
1200 400
600 200
0 0
200 600
2000 6000
4000 12 000
6000 18 000
m ft

TASMAN
SEA

Westland Bight
Southern Alps
Gawn Mts.
Otago
Southland

East from Greenwich
West from Greenwich

COPYRIGHT GEORGE PHILIP LTD.

50 0 50 100 150 200 250 300 km
50 0 50 100 150 200 miles

INDONESIA

TIMOR SEA

INDIAN OCEAN

NORTHERN TERRITORY

Tanami Desert

Great Sandy Desert

Gibson Desert

King Leopold Ranges

Kimberley

Hamersley Range

Bali
Lombok
Sumbawa
Sumba
Waingapu
Timor
Kupang
Roti
Sawu

Darwin
Melville I.
Bathurst I.
Cobourg Pen.
KAKADU NAT. PARK
Katherine
Wyndham
Kununurra
Broome
Derby
Fitzroy Crossing
Halls Creek
Port Hedland
Karratha
Onslow
Exmouth

Tropic of Capricorn

Exmouth Gulf

WESTERN

Mt. Olga 1069 ▲
Petermann Ranges
Ayers Rock 868
ULURU NAT. PARK
The Officer
Everard Ranges
Mt. Musgrave Ranges
Morris 1387 ▲ Mann Ras. Amata Mt. Woodroffe 1440

L. Meramangye

SOUTH

Serpentine Lakes

Nurrari Lakes
L. Dey-Dey
L. Wilson

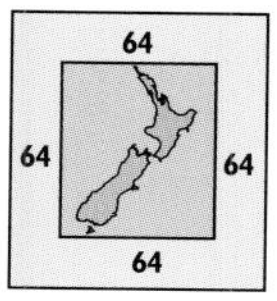

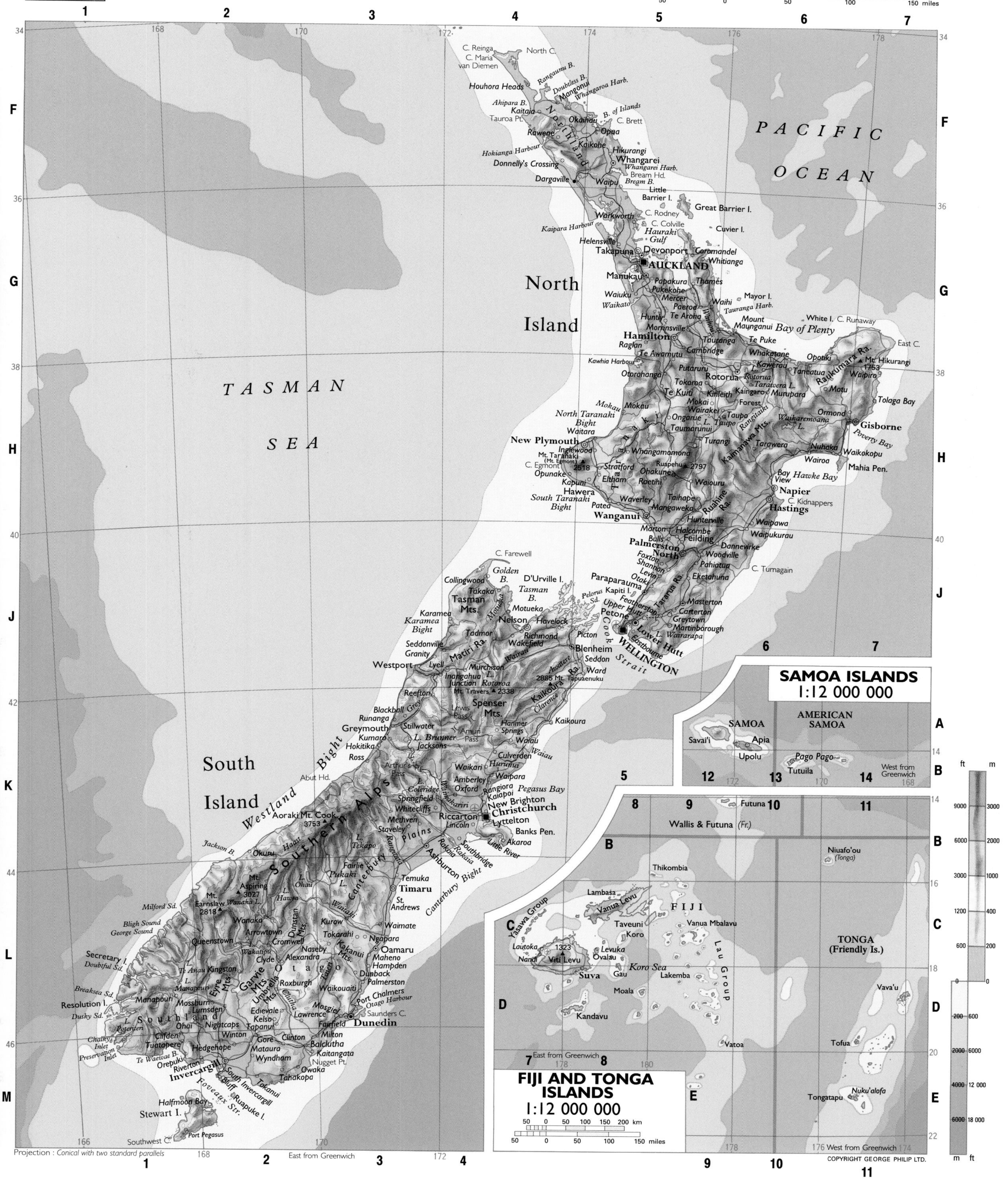

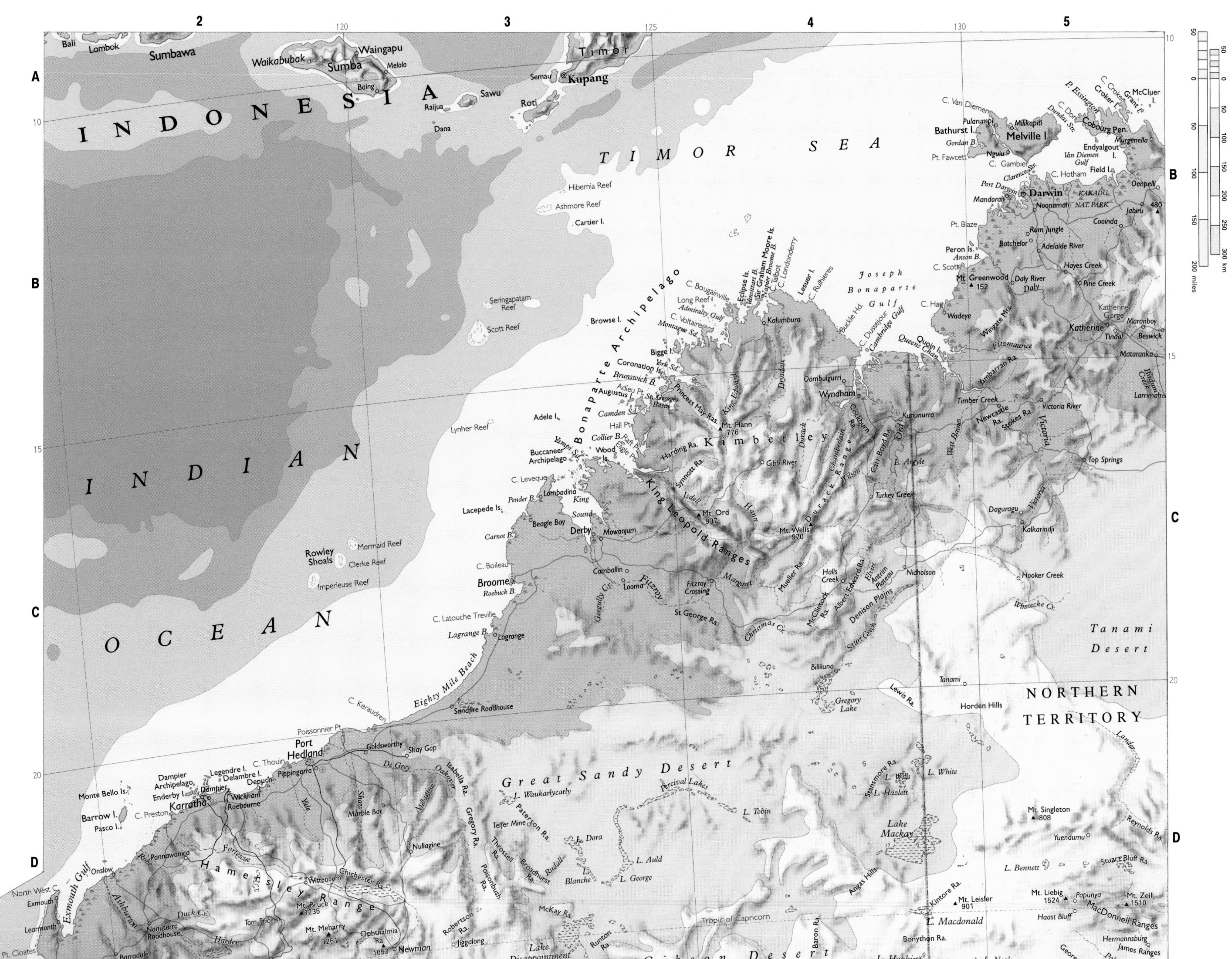

L. Maurice

AUSTRALIA

Great Victoria Desert

Oldea
Watson
Fisher
Marloinga
Cook
Hughes
Forrest
Loongana
Reid
Nullarbor Plain
Hampton Tableland
Mundrabilla
Eucla
Wilson Bluff
Low Pt.

Great Australian Bight

▼5632

SOUTHERN

OCEAN

INDIAN

OCEAN

PERTH
Fremantle
Kwinana
Rockingham
Mandurah
Bunbury
Busselton
Albany

Projection: Bonne

East from Greenwich

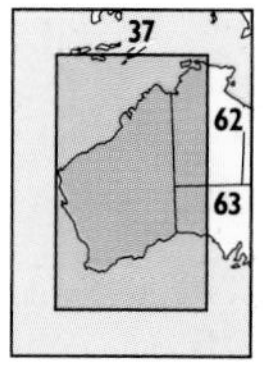

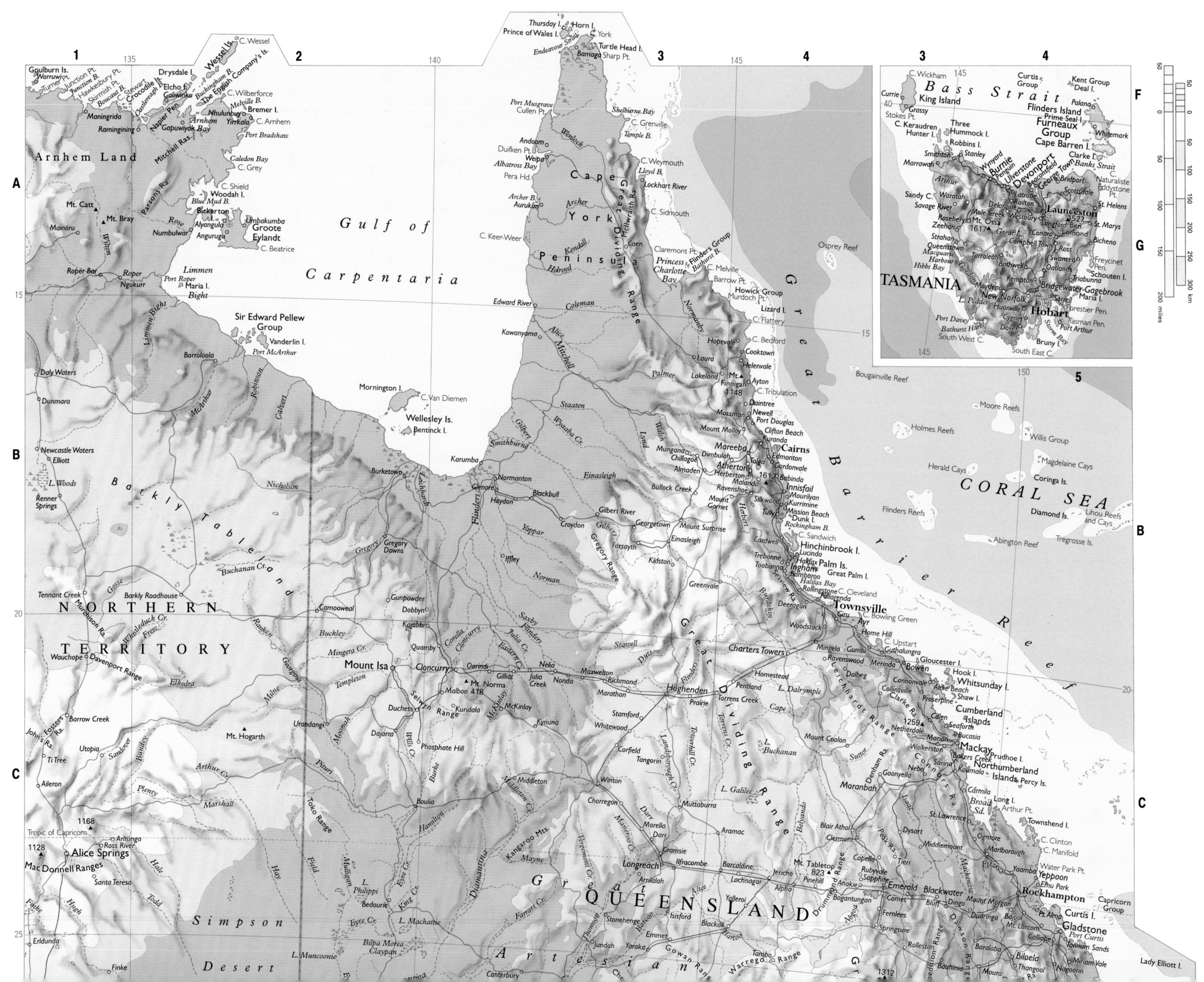

SOUTH AUSTRALIA

NEW SOUTH WALES

VICTORIA

TASMAN SEA

SOUTHERN OCEAN

BRISBANE

SYDNEY

CANBERRA
(AUSTRALIAN CAPITAL TERRITORY)

MELBOURNE

ADELAIDE

Gold Coast

Tweed Heads

Newcastle

Wollongong

Bass Strait

King Island

Flinders Island

Furneaux Group

Cape Barren I.

Great Dividing Range

Darling Downs

Lake Eyre

Lake Torrens

Lake Gairdner

Lake Frome

Spencer Gulf

Gulf St. Vincent

Kangaroo I.

Eyre Peninsula

Yorke Peninsula

East from Greenwich

Projection: Bonne

COPYRIGHT: GEORGE PHILIP LTD.

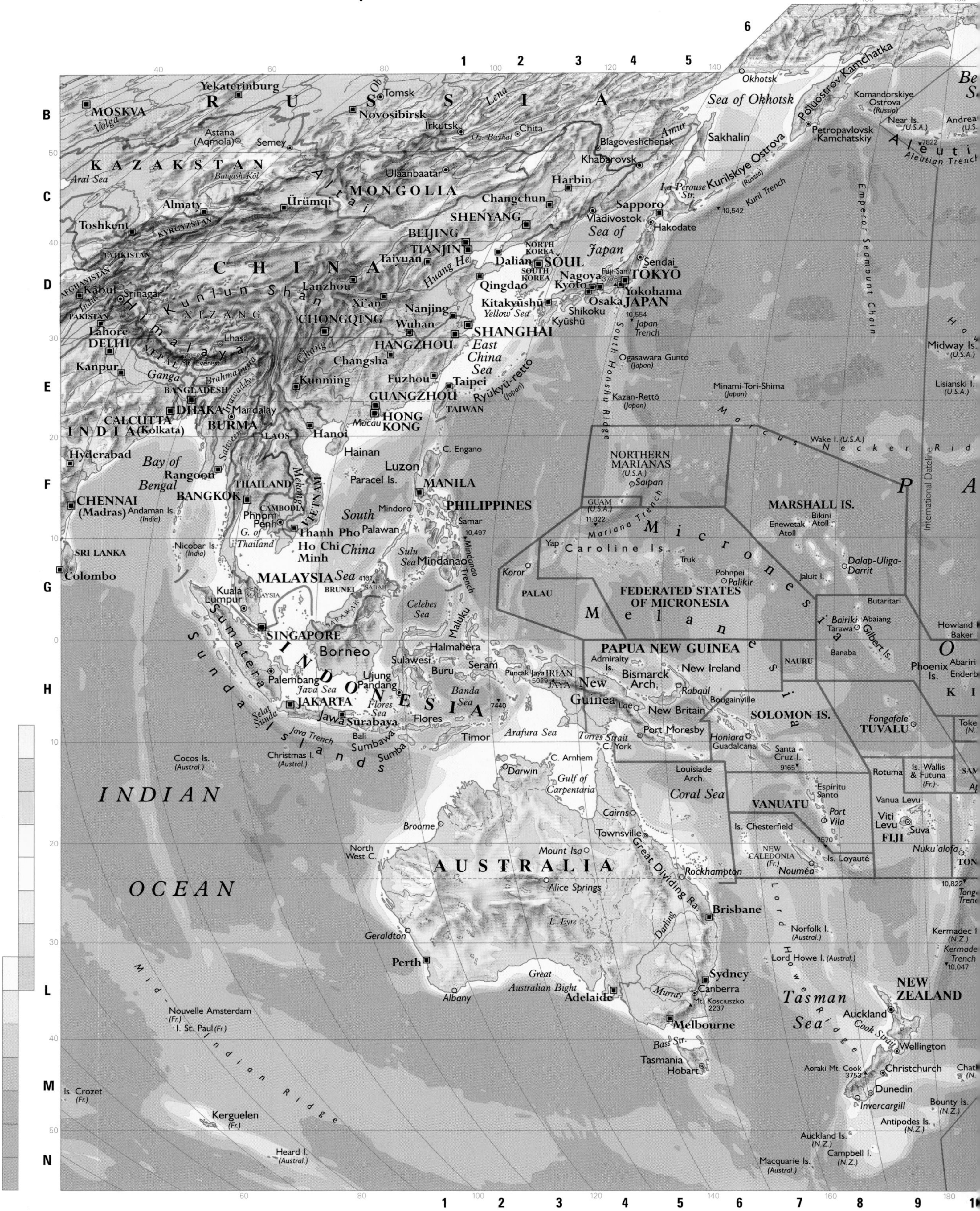

R U S S I A

MOSKVA
Volga
Yekaterinburg
Tomsk
Novosibirsk
Astana
(Aqmola)
Semey
KAZAKSTAN
Irkutsk
Oz. Baykal
Chita
Amur
Blagoveshchensk
Khabarovsk
Sea of Okhotsk
Okhotsk
Poluostrov Kamchatka
Komandorskiye
Ostrova
(Russia)
Near Is.
(U.S.A.)
Petropavlovsk
-Kamchatskiy
Be
Se

MONGOLIA
Ulaanbaatar
Sakhalin
Kurilskiye Ostrova
(Russia)
La Pérouse Str.
7822
Aleuti
Aleutian Trench

Almaty
Ürümqi
Altai
Kuril Trench
10,542
Emperor Seamount Chain

Toshkent
KYRGYZSTAN
Changchun
SHENYANG
Harbin
Sapporo
Hakodate
Vladivostok
Sea of Japan

TAJIKISTAN
C H I N A
BEIJING
TIANJIN
Taiyuan
Dalian
NORTH KOREA
SOUL
Sendai
Midway Is.
(U.S.A.)

AFGHANISTAN
Kabul
Srinagar
Kunlun Shan
Lanzhou
Xi'an
Qingdao
SOUTH KOREA
Nagoya
Kyoto
Fuji-San
3776
TOKYO
Yokohama
JAPAN
Lisianski I.
(U.S.A.)

PAKISTAN
Lahore
DELHI
Kanpur
XIZANG
Lhasa
Himalaya
8850
Everest
CHONGQING
Nanjing
Wuhan
SHANGHAI
HANGZHOU
Kitakyushu
Osaka
Shikoku
Kyūshū
Yellow Sea
Japan Trench
South Honshu Ridge
Ogasawara Gunto
(Japan)
Minami-Tori-Shima
(Japan)

Ganga
Brahmaputra
NEPAL
Changsha
Kunming
Fuzhou
Taipei
Ryukyu-rettó
(Japan)
East China Sea
Kazan-Rettō
(Japan)
Wake I. (U.S.A.)
Necker
Rid
International Dateline

BANGLADESH
DHAKA
CALCUTTA
(Kolkata)
Mandalay
BURMA
Salween
Hanoi
Macau
HONG KONG
GUANGZHOU
TAIWAN
Hainan
C. Engano
Luzon
Paracel Is.
NORTHERN MARIANAS
(U.S.A.)
Saipan
MARSHALL IS.
Bikini
Enewetak
Atoll
P
A

I N D I A
Hyderabad
Bay of
Bengal
Rangoon
THAILAND
BANGKOK
Mekong
VIETNAM
MANILA
PHILIPPINES
Mindoro
Samar
10,497
GUAM
(U.S.A.)
11,022
Mariana Trench
M i c r o n e s i a
Marcus

CHENNAI
(Madras)
Andaman Is.
(India)
CAMBODIA
Phnom
Penh
G. of
Thailand
South
China
Sea
Palawan
Sulu Sea
Mindanao
4101
SABAH
Mindanao Trench
Yap
Caroline Is.
Truk
Koror
PALAU
Pohnpei
Palikir
Dalap-Uliga-Darrit
Jaluit I.

SRI LANKA
Nicobar Is.
(India)
Ho Chi Minh
Thanh Pho
MALAYSIA
BRUNEI
Celebes
Sea
FEDERATED STATES
OF MICRONESIA
M e l
Butaritari
Bairiki
Tarawa
Abaiang
Gilbert Is.
Howland
Baker

Colombo
Kuala
Lumpur
PEN.
MALAYSIA
SARAWAK
Halmahera
Sulawesi
Buru
Seram
NAURU
Banaba
Phoenix
Is.
Abariri
Enderbu
Howard

SINGAPORE
Borneo
Ujung
Pandang
Banda
Sea
Puncak Jaya
5029
IRIAN
JAYA
Admiralty
Is.
New Ireland
PAPUA NEW GUINEA
M e l a n
e
s i
a
K I

Sumatera
Palembang
Java Sea
I N D O N E S I A
7440
Bismarck
Arch.
Rabaul
New Britain
Bougainville
New
Guinea
Lae
SOLOMON IS.
Fongafale
TUVALU
Toke
(N.

JAKARTA
Jawa
Surabaya
Bali
Flores
Sea
Flores
Timor
Arafura Sea
Torres Strait
C. York
Port Moresby
Honiara
Guadalcanal
Santa
Cruz I.
9165
Rotuma
Is. Wallis
& Futuna
(Fr.)
SAM

Selat Sunda
Sunda Islands
Sumbawa
Sumba
Cocos Is.
(Austral.)
Christmas I.
(Austral.)
C. Arnhem
Darwin
Gulf of
Carpentaria
Louisiade
Arch.
Coral Sea
Espíritu
Santo
Is. Chesterfield
VANUATU
Port
Vila
Vanua Levu
Viti
Levu
Suva
FIJI
Nuku'alofa
TON

I N D I A N
North
West C.
Broome
Cairns
Townsville
Mount Isa
Great Dividing Ra.
NEW
CALEDONIA
(Fr.)
Nouméa
Is. Loyauté
7570
10,822
Tonga
Trene

O C E A N
Geraldton
AUSTRALIA
Alice Springs
L. Eyre
Darling
Murray
Rockhampton
Brisbane
Norfolk I.
(Austral.)
Kermadec I.
(N.Z.)
Kermadec
Trench
10,047

Nouvelle Amsterdam
(Fr.)
I. St. Paul (Fr.)
Perth
Great
Australian Bight
Albany
Adelaide
Sydney
Canberra
Mt. Kosciuszko
2237
Lord Howe I. (Austral.)
Tasman
Sea
NEW
ZEALAND
Auckland
Cook Strait
Wellington
Chath
(N.

Mid-Indian Ridge
Melbourne
Bass Str.
Tasmania
Hobart
Aoraki Mt. Cook
3753
Christchurch
Dunedin
Invercargill
Bounty Is.
(N.Z.)

Is. Crozet
(Fr.)
Antipodes Is.
(N.Z.)

Kerguelen
(Fr.)
Auckland Is.
(N.Z.)
Campbell I.
(N.Z.)
Macquarie Is.
(Austral.)

Heard I.
(Austral.)

11 **12** **13** **14** **15** **16** **17** **18** **19** **20**

160 140 120 100 80 60 40 20

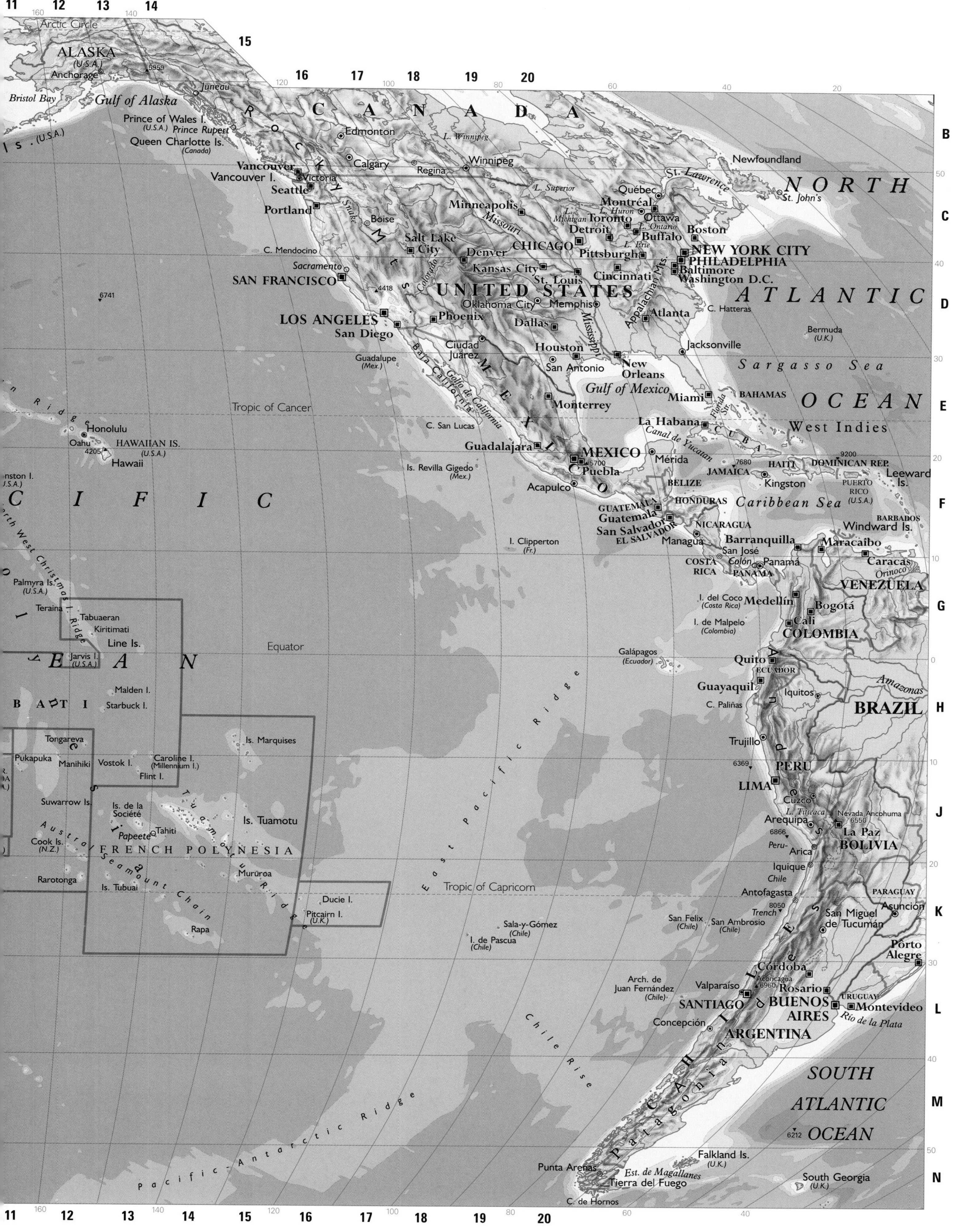

Arctic Circle

ALASKA
(U.S.A.)
Anchorage
5959

Bristol Bay

Gulf of Alaska

Juneau

Prince of Wales I.
(U.S.A.) Prince Rupert
Queen Charlotte Is.
(Canada)

Is. *(U.S.A.)*

C A N A D A

Newfoundland

Edmonton

Calgary

Regina

Winnipeg

L. Winnipeg

St. Lawrence

Vancouver
Vancouver I.
Victoria
Seattle
Portland

Boise

Snake

Minneapolis

Québec
Montréal
Ottawa
Toronto
L. Huron
L. Ontario
L. Erie
Detroit
Buffalo
Boston

St. John's

N O R T H

50

C

Missouri

L. Superior
L. Michigan

C. Mendocino

Salt Lake City
Denver

Kansas City
St. Louis

CHICAGO
Pittsburgh
Cincinnati

NEW YORK CITY
PHILADELPHIA
Baltimore
Washington D.C.

A T L A N T I C

40

D

Sacramento

SAN FRANCISCO

4418

U N I T E D S T A T E S

Oklahoma City
Memphis

Appalachian Mts.

6741

LOS ANGELES
San Diego

Phoenix

Dallas

Atlanta

C. Hatteras

Bermuda
(U.K.)

Ciudad
Juárez

Houston
San Antonio

Mississippi

New
Orleans

Jacksonville

Sargasso Sea

30

E

Guadalupe
(Mex.)

Baja California

M E

Gulf of Mexico

Miami

Florida

BAHAMAS

O C E A N

Tropic of Cancer

HAWAIIAN IS.
(U.S.A.)
Honolulu
Oahu
4205
Hawaii

Gulfo de California

Monterrey

La Habana
Canal de Yucatán

CUBA

West Indies

20

nston I.
U.S.A.)

C. San Lucas

Guadalajara

MEXICO
Puebla

Mérida

7680
5700

9200

HAITI
DOMINICAN REP.

Leeward
Is.

Is. Revilla Gigedo
(Mex.)

Acapulco

I C O

JAMAICA

Kingston

PUERTO
RICO
(U.S.A.)

F

Palmyra Is.
(U.S.A.)

Teraina

I C

BELIZE
GUATEMALA
Guatemala

HONDURAS

Caribbean Sea

BARBADOS

BARBADOS
Windward Is.

10

Tabuaeran
Kiritimati
Line Is.

I. Clipperton
(Fr.)

San Salvador
EL SALVADOR
Managua

NICARAGUA

Barranquilla

Maracaibo

Jarvis I.
(U.S.A.)

E A N

San José
COSTA
RICA
Colón
PANAMA
Panamá

Caracas

VENEZUELA

G

Malden I.
Starbuck I.

I. del Coco
(Costa Rica)

Medellín

Bogotá

B A T I

Equator

I. de Malpelo
(Colombia)

COLOMBIA

0

North West Christmas Ridge

Tongareva

Vostok I.

Caroline I.
(Millennium I.)

Galápagos
(Ecuador)

Quito
ECUADOR

Amazonas

Pukapuka
Manihiki

Flint I.

Guayaquil

Iquitos

BRAZIL

H

Suwarrow Is.

Is. de la
Société

Is. Marquises

C. Paliñas

Trujillo

A.)

Cook Is.
(N.Z.)

Papeete
Tahiti

Is. Tuamotu

6369

PERU

10

J

Australes

FRENCH POLYNESIA

Mururoa

LIMA

Cuzco
L. Titicaca
Nevada Anchuma
6550

Rarotonga

Is. Tubuai

Rapa

East Pacific Ridge

Arequipa

6866

Peru-Chile

La Paz
BOLIVIA

20

Ducie I.

Tropic of Capricorn

Iquique
Chile

Antofagasta

PARAGUAY

K

Pitcairn I.
(U.K.)

San Felix
(Chile)

San Ambrosio
(Chile)

8050
Trench

San Miguel
de Tucumán

Asunción

Sala-y-Gómez
(Chile)

Pôrto
Alegre

30

I. de Pascua
(Chile)

Córdoba

Aconcagua
6960

URUGUAY

L

Arch. de
Juan Fernández
(Chile)

Valparaíso

Rosario

**BUENOS
AIRES**

Montevideo

Chile Rise

SANTIAGO
Concepción

Río de la Plata

ARGENTINA

40

Pacific Antarctic Ridge

Patagonia

S O U T H

M

A T L A N T I C

6212

O C E A N

50

Falkland Is.
(U.K.)

Punta Arenas
Est. de Magallanes
Tierra del Fuego

South Georgia
(U.K.)

N

C. de Hornos

100 0 200 400 600 800 1000 1200 1400 km
100 0 200 400 600 800 1000 miles
ARCTIC OCEAN
Beaufort Sea
Asia
C. Dezhneva
St. Lawrence I.
Bering Strait
Bering Sea
Nunivak I.
C. Prince of Wales
Barrow Pt.
Brooks Ra.
Yukon
Porcupine
Alaska
Mt. McKinley 6194
Alaska Range
Alaska Peninsula
Kodiak I.
Gulf of Alaska
Mt. St. Elias 5489
Mt. Logan 5959
Mackenzie Mts.
Mackenzie
Arctic Circle
Great Bear L.
Great Slave L.
Liard
C. Bathurst
Banks I.
M'Clure Strait
Victoria I.
Viscount Melville Sd.
Melville I.
Parry Is.
Queen Elizabeth Is.
Sverdrup Is.
Axel Heiberg I.
Ellesmere I.
Kane Basin
Nares Str.
Bathurst I.
Devon I.
Lancaster Sd.
Bylot I.
Somerset I.
Prince of Wales I.
Gulf of Boothia
Boothia Pen.
Melville Pen.
Foxe Basin
Foxe Channel
Baffin Island
Baffin Bay
Back
Southampton I.
Hudson Strait
Frobisher B.
Cumberland Sd.
Davis Strait
Disko I.
Greenland
Petermann's Peak 2940
Mt. Forel 3360
Denmark Strait
Iceland
2119
Cape Farewell
C. Chidley
C. Wolstenholme
Ungava Peninsula
Labrador Sea
Hamilton Inlet
Coast of Labrador
Str. of Belle Isle
Newfoundland
C. Race
Hudson Bay
Belcher Is.
C. Henrietta Maria
James Bay
Eastmain
Laurentian Plateau
Gulf of St. Lawrence
St. Lawrence
Pr. Edward I.
Cape Breton I.
Nova Scotia
Sable I.
B. of Fundy
C. Sable
Mt. Washington 1917
C. Cod
Nantucket I.
Hudson
Long I.
Alexander Archipelago
Stikine
Coast Mountains
Queen Charlotte Islands
Skeena
Queen Charlotte Str.
Mt. Waddington 3994
Fraser
Vancouver I.
Juan de Fuca Str.
C. Flattery
Rocky Mountains
Mt. Robson 3954
Selkirk Mts.
Peace
Athabasca
L. Athabasca
Reindeer L.
Churchill
Nelson
Dubawnt
Saskatchewan
L. Winnipeg
Great Plains
Mt. Rainier 4392
Cascade Range
Columbia
C. Blanco
C. Mendocino
Coast Ranges
Mt. Shasta 4317
Sacramento
Sierra Nevada
San Joaquin
Mt. Whitney 4418
Death Valley -86
Snake
Great Salt Lake
Great Basin
Wasatch Ra.
Mt. Elbert 4399
Blanca Peak 4378
Grand Canyon
Colorado Plateau
Colorado
Gila
Missouri
Platte
Arkansas
Red
Ozark Plateau
Mississippi
Great Lakes
L. Superior
L. Michigan
L. Huron
L. Erie
L. Ontario
Niagara Falls
Appalachian Mts.
Allegheny Mts.
Ohio
Cumberland Plateau
Tennessee
Blue Ridge Mts.
Alabama
C. Charles
Chesapeake B.
C. Hatteras
Bermuda
NORTH ATLANTIC OCEAN
Sargasso Sea
Bahamas
Florida
Florida Strait
Mississippi River Delta
Gulf of Mexico
Rio Grande
PACIFIC OCEAN
Guadalupe
Lower California
Gulf of California
Tropic of Cancer
Western Sierra Madre
Mexican Plateau
Eastern Sierra Madre
Santiago
C. San Lucas
C. Corrientes
Clarion Fracture Zone
Revilla Gigedo Is.
Popocatepetl 5452
Citlaltepetl 5700
Balsas
Isthmus of Tehuantepec
G. de Tehuantepec
Guatemala Trench
Central America
Gulf of Campeche
Yucatán Peninsula
Yucatán Channel
Yucatán Basin
Cuba
Greater Antilles
Cayman Trough
Jamaica
Hispaniola
9200
Caribbean Sea
G. of Honduras
C. Gracias a Dios
Coco
Colombian Basin
Sierra Nevada de Santa Marta 5800
G. de Venezuela
L. Maracaibo
G. of Darién
G. of Panamá
Andes
Magdalena
Cord. de Mérida
ft m
9000 3000
6000 2000
3000 1000
1500 500
600 200
0 0
200 600
1000 3000
2000 6000
4000 12000
6000 18000
8000 24000
m ft
Projection: Bonne
West from Greenwich

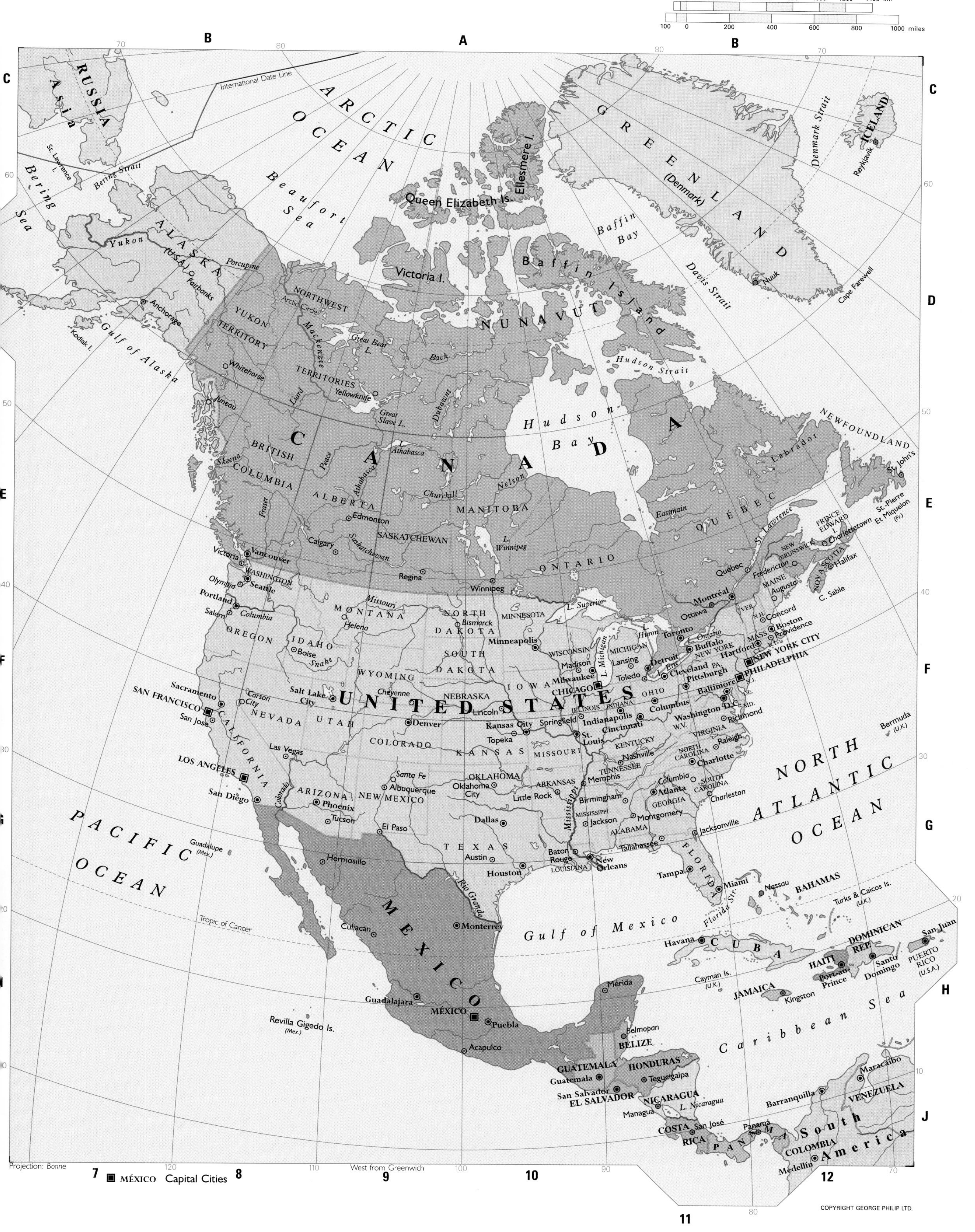

100 0 200 400 600 800 1000 1200 1400 km
100 0 200 400 600 800 1000 miles
ARCTIC OCEAN
Beaufort Sea
RUSSIA
Asia
International Date Line
St. Lawrence I.
Bering Strait
Bering Sea
GREENLAND (Denmark)
Denmark Strait
ICELAND
Reykjavik
Queen Elizabeth Is.
Ellesmere I.
Baffin Bay
Baffin Island
Victoria I.
Davis Strait
Nuuk
Cape Farewell
NUNAVUT
Hudson Strait
Hudson Bay
ALASKA (U.S.A.)
Yukon
Porcupine
Fairbanks
Anchorage
Kodiak I.
Gulf of Alaska
NORTHWEST TERRITORIES
Arctic Circle
YUKON TERRITORY
Mackenzie
Great Bear L.
Back
Whitehorse
Yellowknife
Great Slave L.
Liard
Dubawnt
Juneau
CANADA
BRITISH COLUMBIA
Skeena
Peace
Athabasca
Fraser
ALBERTA
Churchill
Nelson
MANITOBA
Edmonton
SASKATCHEWAN
Saskatchewan
Calgary
L. Winnipeg
Victoria
Vancouver
Regina
ONTARIO
Winnipeg
Eastmain
QUÉBEC
Labrador
NEWFOUNDLAND
St John's
St. Lawrence
PRINCE EDWARD I.
Charlottetown
St.-Pierre Et Miquelon (Fr.)
NEW BRUNSWICK
NOVA SCOTIA
Fredericton
Halifax
C. Sable
Québec
Montréal
Ottawa
MAINE
Augusta
Concord
Boston
Providence
WASHINGTON
Olympia
Seattle
Portland
Salem
Columbia
OREGON
MONTANA
Missouri
Helena
NORTH DAKOTA
Bismarck
MINNESOTA
L. Superior
IDAHO
Boise
Snake
SOUTH DAKOTA
Minneapolis
WISCONSIN
MICHIGAN
L. Huron
Toronto
L. Ontario
Buffalo
NEW YORK
Hartford
NEW YORK CITY
PHILADELPHIA
L. Michigan
Madison
Lansing
Milwaukee
Detroit
L. Erie
Toledo
Cleveland
Pittsburgh
WYOMING
Cheyenne
NEBRASKA
IOWA
CHICAGO
OHIO
Sacramento
SAN FRANCISCO
San Jose
Carson City
Salt Lake City
UNITED STATES
NEVADA
UTAH
Lincoln
ILLINOIS
INDIANA
Indianapolis
Columbus
Baltimore
Washington D.C.
Richmond
Denver
Kansas City
Springfield
Cincinnati
W.V.
VIRGINIA
CALIFORNIA
COLORADO
Topeka
KANSAS
MISSOURI
St. Louis
KENTUCKY
Nashville
NORTH CAROLINA
Raleigh
Charlotte
Las Vegas
LOS ANGELES
Santa Fe
OKLAHOMA
TENNESSEE
Memphis
ARKANSAS
Columbia
SOUTH CAROLINA
Atlanta
Charleston
San Diego
Colorado
ARIZONA
NEW MEXICO
Albuquerque
Oklahoma City
Little Rock
Birmingham
GEORGIA
Phoenix
Tucson
MISSISSIPPI
Jackson
ALABAMA
Montgomery
Mississippi
El Paso
Dallas
Jacksonville
TEXAS
Austin
Houston
Baton Rouge
LOUISIANA
New Orleans
Tallahassee
FLORIDA
Tampa
Miami
Bermuda (U.K.)
NORTH ATLANTIC OCEAN
PACIFIC OCEAN
Guadalupe (Mex.)
Hermosillo
Rio Grande
MEXICO
Culiacan
Monterrey
Tropic of Cancer
Gulf of Mexico
Florida Str.
Nassau
BAHAMAS
Turks & Caicos Is. (U.K.)
Havana
CUBA
DOMINICAN REP.
Santo Domingo
San Juan
PUERTO RICO (U.S.A.)
HAITI
Port-au-Prince
Cayman Is. (U.K.)
JAMAICA
Kingston
Mérida
Guadalajara
MÉXICO
Puebla
Acapulco
Revilla Gigedo Is. (Mex.)
Belmopan
BELIZE
Caribbean Sea
GUATEMALA
Guatemala
HONDURAS
Tegucigalpa
San Salvador
EL SALVADOR
NICARAGUA
Managua
L. Nicaragua
COSTA RICA
San José
PANAMA
Panamá
Maracaibo
Barranquilla
VENEZUELA
South America
COLOMBIA
Medellín
Projection: Bonne
West from Greenwich
MÉXICO Capital Cities
COPYRIGHT GEORGE PHILIP LTD.

100 0 100 200 300 400 500 600 km
100 0 100 200 300 400 miles

4
5
6
7
8
9
10
C
D
PACIFIC OCEAN
YUKON TERRITORY
NORTHWEST TERRITORIES
BRITISH COLUMBIA
ALBERTA
SASKATCHEWAN
MANITOBA
ALASKA
WASHINGTON
MONTANA
NORTH DAKOTA
SOUTH DAKOTA
MINNESOTA
NEBRASKA
IOWA
UNITED STATES
Victoria Island
Banks Island
Prince of Wales I.
Great Bear L.
Great Slave L.
Lake Athabasca
Reindeer Lake
Lake Winnipeg
L. Winnipegosis
L. Manitoba
Rocky Mountains
Mackenzie Mountains
Selwyn Mts.
Cassiar Mountains
Coast Mountains
Selkirk Mts.
Alexander Archipelago
Queen Charlotte Is.
Vancouver I.
Anchorage
Whitehorse
Yellowknife
Edmonton
Calgary
VANCOUVER
Victoria
SEATTLE
Saskatoon
Regina
Winnipeg
MINNEAPOLIS
Omaha
Projection : Bonne
ALASKA
1:30 000 000
100 0 100 200 300 400 500 600 km
100 0 100 200 300 400 miles
CHUKCHI SEA
BERING SEA
GULF OF ALASKA
PACIFIC OCEAN
Brooks Range
Alaska Range
Aleutian Is.
Alaska Peninsula
Kodiak I.
West from Greenwich
1
2
3
4
5
6
9
10

ft
m
9000
3000
6000
2000
4500
1500
3000
1000
1200
400
600
200
0
0
200
600
2000
6000
4000
12 000
m
ft

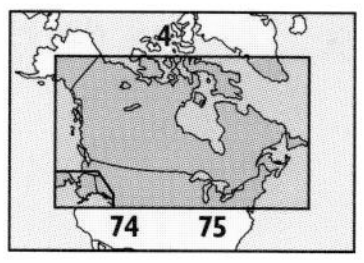

ALASKA
1:30 000 000

B

Devon I.
Lancaster Sound
Arctic Bay
Borden
Pen.
eninsula
1890
Bylot I.
Eclipse Sd.
Pond Inlet
C. Adair
Baffin Bay
2136
Nunavik
Uummannaq
Qeqertarsuaq
Upernavik
Ilulissat
Qasigiannguit
Tasiilak

G R E E N L A N D
(KALAALLIT NUNAAT)
(Denmark)

2850
Kong Frederik VI's Kyst

A T L A N T I C

60

Fury and Hecla Str.
Igloolik
Sanirajak
Clyde River
C. Raper
Home B.
Qikiqtarjuaq
Sisimiut
Kangerlussuaq
Maniitsoq
Nuuk

Melville
Peninsula
Foxe
Prince
Charles
I.
Air
Force
I.
2591
Cumberland
Peninsula
Pangnirtung
Hoare B.
Mercy C.

C

Repulse
Bay
Naujaat
Rae Isthmus
Southampton
I.
Saliq
Bell
Pen.
Foxe
Basin
Netilling L.
C. Dorchester
Amadjuak
L.
Cumberland Sd.

N U N A V U T

Qeqertarsuatsiaat
Paamiut
Arsuk
Qaqortoq
Nanortalik
Uummannarsuaq
Ammittuup Pha

Coats
I.
Mansel
I.
Nottingham
I.
Salisbury
I.
Foxe
Pen.
Cape Dorset
Meta
Incognita
Kimmirut
Iqaluit
Hall
Peninsula
Frobisher Bay
Resolution I.

Foxe Channel
Roes Welcome Sd.

H u d s o n S t r a i t

Hudson
Ivujivik
Salluit
Kangiqsujuaq
Quaqtaq
Akpatok I.
C. Chidley

Labrador

3809

Ottawa Is.
Kangirsuk
Ungava Bay
Kangiqsualujjuaq
1652
Hebron
Nain

S e a

▼257
Bay
Puvirnituq
Péninsule
d'Ungava
L. Payne
Arnaud
Feuilles
Kuujjuaq
Balcine
George
Kangirsuk
Hopedale

Sleeper Is.
King George Is.
Baker's
Dozen
Is.
Inukjuak
L. Minto
Mélès
Caniapiscau
Nakvak
Ripigel
Cartwright

50

Belcher Is.
Kuujjuarapik
L. à l'Eau
Claire
Grande Baleine
L. Bienville
Smallwood
Res.
North West River
Happy Valley-
Goose Bay
Port Hope Simpson
Belle Isle

C. Henrietta
Maria
Pte. Louis
XIV
Kanaaupscow
La Grande
Schefferville
Labrador
Churchill
Falls
Churchill
C. Bauld
St. Anthony

D
Peawanuck
Winisk
Chisasibi
Rés. de
Caniapiscau
Petitsikapau
L.
Esker
Labrador
City
Fermont
Ashuanipi
St-Augustin
Natashquan
Str. of Belle Isle

Big
Trout L.
Attawapiskat
C. Henrietta
Maria
James Bay
Akimiski I.
Wemindji
Eastmain
Kanaaupscow
1135
Gagnon
Rés.
Manicouagan
Havre-
St-Pierre
I. d'Anticosti
814
Deer
Lake
Grand
Falls
Lewisporte
Gander
Bonavista
D

Attawapiskat
Fort Albany
Moosonee
Charlton
I.
Eastmain
Waskaganish
Rupert
Mistassini
L.
Albanel
Chibougamau
Sept-Îles
Port-Cartier
Gulf of
St. Lawrence
Cabot Str.
Stephenville
Corner Brook
Newfoundland
Placentia
C. Race
St. John's
Carbonear

Albany
Missinaibi
Matagami
Rés. Gouin
Dolbeau
St-Jean
Chicoutimi
Baie Comeau
Matane
Pén. de Gaspé
Îs. de la Madeleine
Cape Breton I.
Glace Bay
Sydney

Kenogami
Nakina
Hearst
Cochrane
Amos
Val-d'Or
Roberval
Jonquière
Rimouski
Rivière-du-Loup
Campbellton
Bathurst
Miramichi
Charlottetown
PR. EDWARD I.
Port Hawkesbury
Antigonish

pigon
Geraldton
Kapuskasing
Timmins
Kirkland
Lake
Rouyn-
Noranda
La Tuque
Québec
Lévis
Edmundston
1190
Grand Falls
Woodstock
Fredericton
Moncton
New
Glasgow

Marathon
Oba
Chapleau
New
Liskeard
Rés.
Cabonga
Mont-
Laurier
Shawinigan
Trois-Rivières
Thetford
Mines
**NEW
BRUNSWICK**
Amherst
Kentville
NOVA SCOTIA
Truro
Dartmouth

Thunder Bay
Wawa
Sault Ste.
Marie
Elliot
Lake
Sudbury
L. Nipissing
North
Bay
Outaouais
Hull
MONTRÉAL
Granby
Sherbrooke
Saint
John
B. of Fundy
Digby
Halifax
Bridgewater

E
Lake Superior

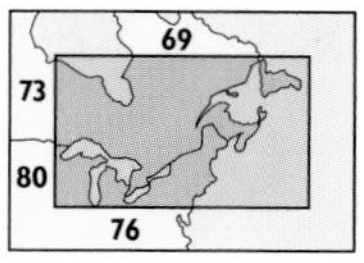

6 7 8 9

A B C D

LABRADOR SEA

NEWFOUNDLAND

Labrador

QUÉBEC

Newfoundland

GULF OF ST. LAWRENCE

Î. d'Anticosti

Pén. de Gaspé

NEW BRUNSWICK

NOVA SCOTIA

PRINCE EDWARD ISLAND

Cape Breton Island

Cabot Strait

Bay of Fundy

MAINE

UNITED STATES

ATLANTIC OCEAN

ST.-PIERRE ET MIQUELON (France)

Smallwood Reservoir

Rés. Manicouagan

St. Lawrence

Sable I. (Nova Scotia)

Nain

Hopedale

Makkovik

Cartwright

Happy Valley-Goose Bay

Churchill Falls

Labrador City

Schefferville

Sept-Îles

Baie Comeau

Rimouski

Chicoutimi

Jonquière

Gaspé

Campbellton

Bathurst

Edmundston

Fredericton

Moncton

Saint John

Charlottetown

Summerside

Sydney

Halifax

Dartmouth

Truro

Yarmouth

Corner Brook

Grand Falls Windsor

Gander

St. John's

Stephenville

Channel-Port aux Basques

Bangor

Augusta

Portland

Manchester

BOSTON

Sherbrooke

70 65 60 55 50

West from Greenwich

6 7 8

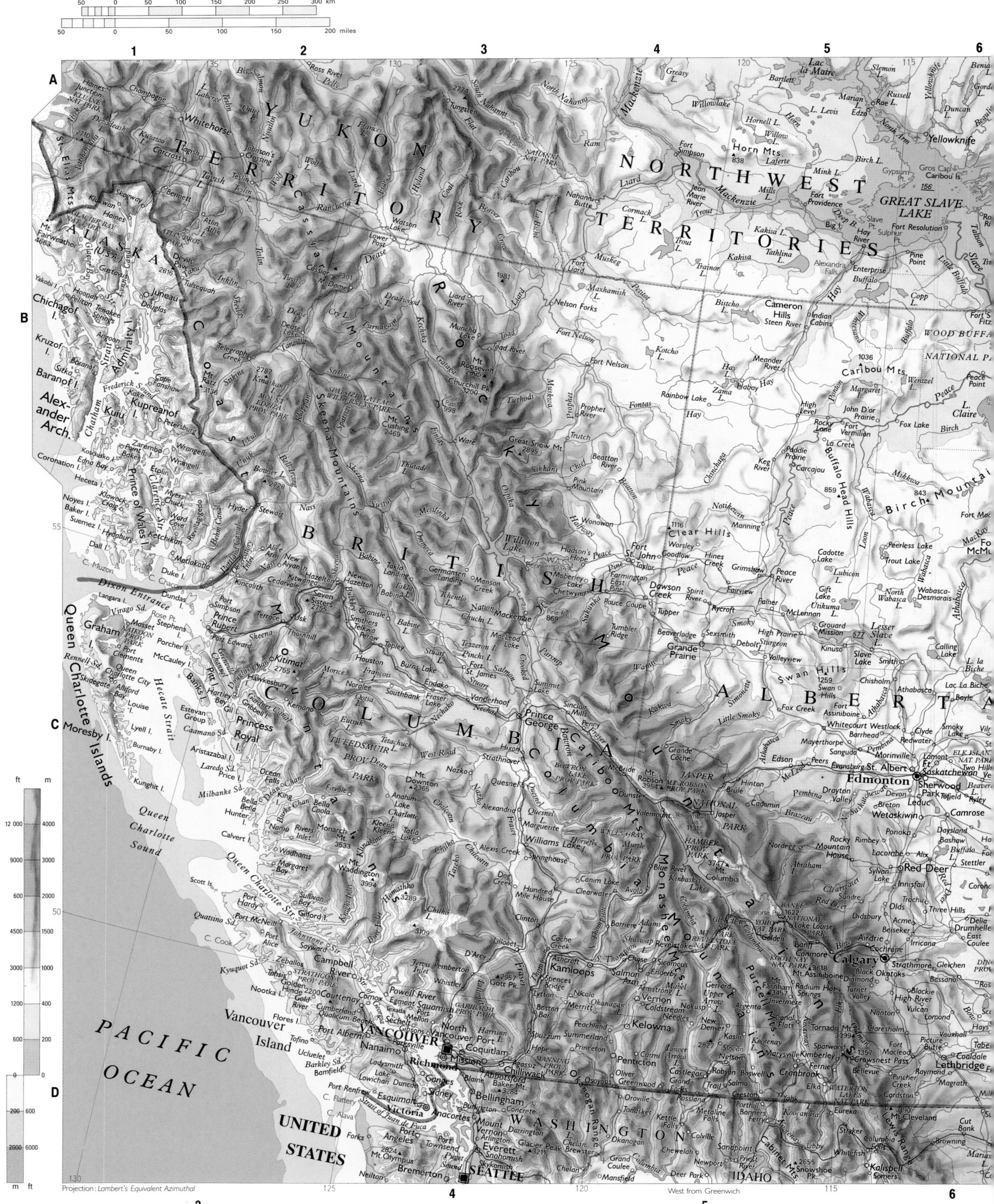

7 8 9 10 11

A B C D

NUNAVUT

HUDSON BAY

MANITOBA

SASKATCHEWAN

ONTARIO

LAKE WINNIPEG

MINNESOTA

NORTH DAKOTA

MONTANA

7 8 9 10

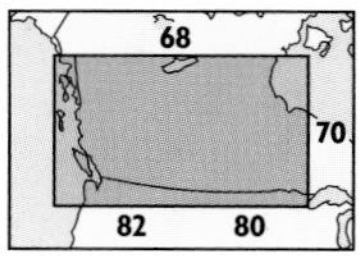

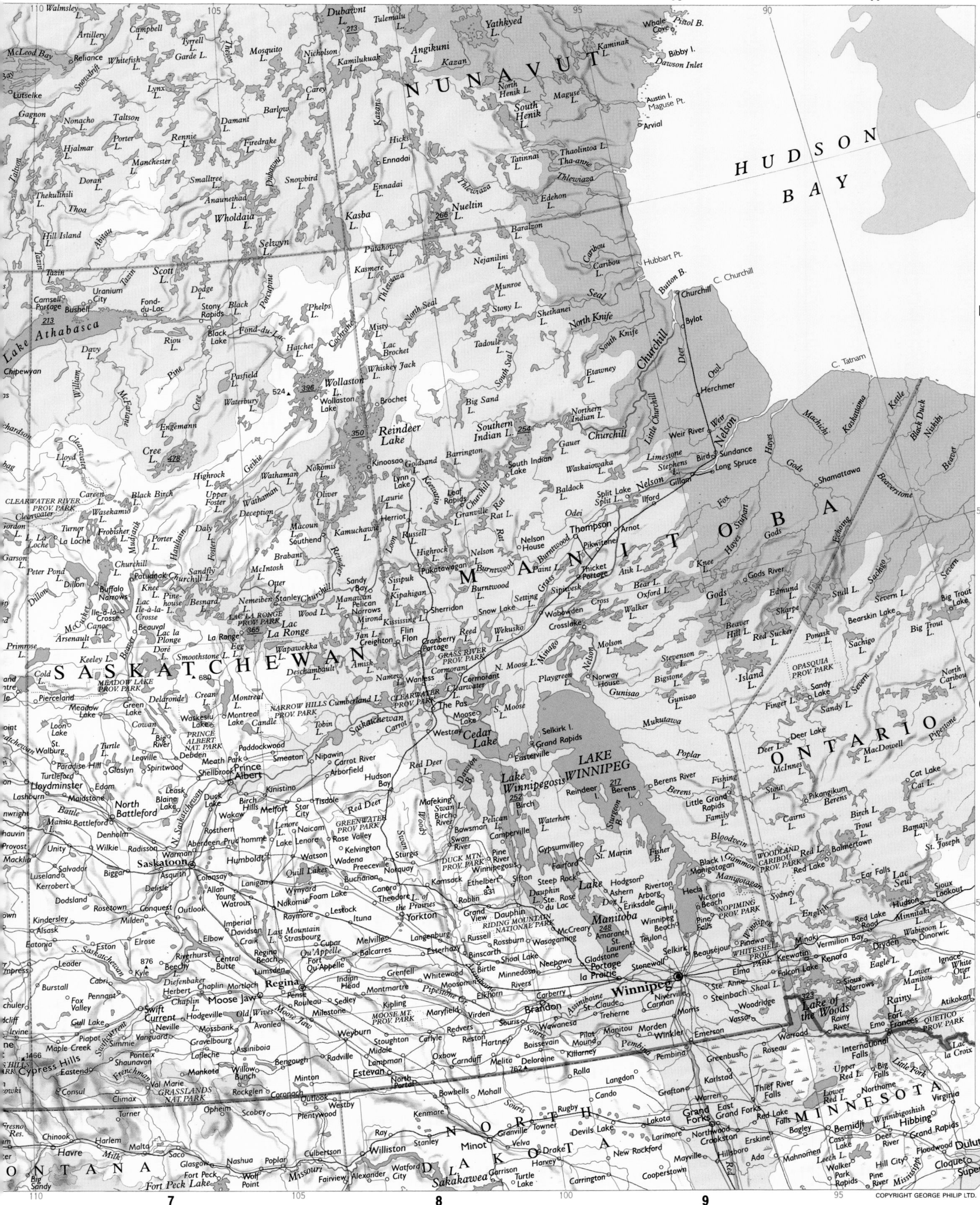

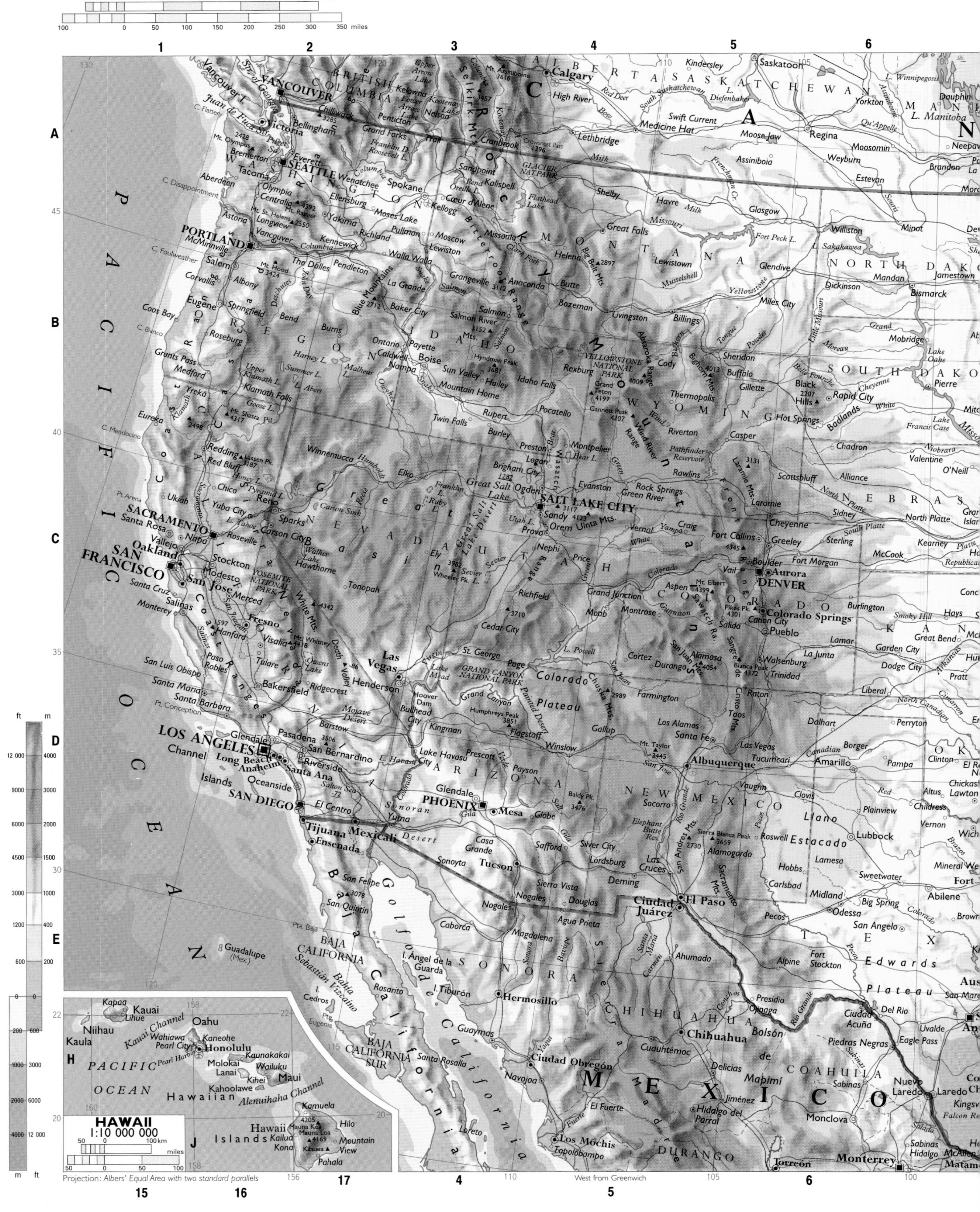

100 0 100 200 300 400 500 km
100 0 50 100 150 200 250 300 350 miles
1 2 3 4 5 6
A B C D E
PACIFIC OCEAN
BRITISH COLUMBIA
ALBERTA
SASKATCHEWAN
MANITOBA
WASHINGTON
OREGON
IDAHO
MONTANA
WYOMING
NORTH DAKOTA
SOUTH DAKOTA
NEBRASKA
KANSAS
COLORADO
UTAH
NEVADA
CALIFORNIA
ARIZONA
NEW MEXICO
TEXAS
OKLAHOMA
MEXICO
BAJA CALIFORNIA
BAJA CALIFORNIA SUR
SONORA
CHIHUAHUA
COAHUILA
DURANGO
Rocky Mts.
Great Basin
Coast Ranges
Sierra Nevada
Cascade Range
Colorado Plateau
Golfo de California
Llano Estacado
Edwards Plateau
Bolsón de Mapimí
Sierra Madre
VANCOUVER
Victoria
SEATTLE
Tacoma
Spokane
PORTLAND
Salem
Eugene
Boise
Calgary
Lethbridge
Medicine Hat
Regina
Saskatoon
Great Falls
Helena
Billings
Bismarck
Pierre
Rapid City
Cheyenne
Casper
Laramie
SALT LAKE CITY
Ogden
Provo
Reno
Carson City
SACRAMENTO
SAN FRANCISCO
Oakland
San Jose
Fresno
Bakersfield
Las Vegas
LOS ANGELES
Long Beach
Anaheim
SAN DIEGO
Tijuana
Mexicali
PHOENIX
Mesa
Tucson
Flagstaff
Albuquerque
Santa Fe
El Paso
Ciudad Juárez
DENVER
Aurora
Colorado Springs
Pueblo
Amarillo
Lubbock
Odessa
San Angelo
Hermosillo
Chihuahua
Ciudad Obregón
Monterrey
Nuevo Laredo
Laredo
Torreón
YELLOWSTONE NATIONAL PARK
GLACIER NAT. PARK
YOSEMITE NATIONAL PARK
GRAND CANYON NATIONAL PARK
Mt. Rainier 4392
Mt. Hood 3424
Mt. Shasta 4317
Mt. Whitney 4418
Mt. Elbert 4399
Death Valley -86
Great Salt Lake
Salton Sea -72
ft m
12 000 4000
9000 3000
6000 2000
4500 1500
3000 1000
1200 400
600 200
0 0
200 600
1000 3000
2000 6000
4000 12 000
m ft
HAWAII
1:10 000 000
Kauai
Niihau
Oahu
Honolulu
Molokai
Lanai
Maui
Kahoolawe
Hawaii
Hilo
Mauna Kea 4205
Mauna Loa 4169
PACIFIC OCEAN
Hawaiian Islands
Projection: Albers' Equal Area with two standard parallels
West from Greenwich
15 16 17 4 5 6

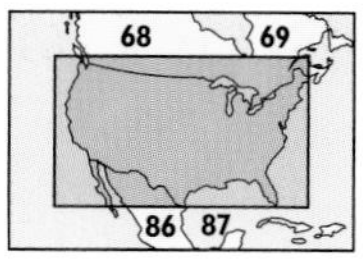

68
69
86
87

8
9
10
11
12
13
A
B
C
D
E
F
C A N A D A
O N T A R I O
Q U E B E C
Lake Winnipeg
Lake of the Woods
Lake Nipigon
Lake Superior
Lake Michigan
Lake Huron
Lake Erie
Lake Ontario
Georgian Bay
North Channel
Moosonee
Chibougamau
Baie-Comeau
Matane
St. Lawrence
Chicoutimi
Alma
Jonquière
Rimouski
Rivière-du-Loup
Edmundston
NEW BRUNSWICK
Fort Kent
Caribou
Presque Isle
Houlton
Millinocket
Saint John
Calais
Roberval
La Tuque
Québec
Shawinigan
Trois-Rivières
Drummondville
Sherbrooke
MONTRÉAL
Ottawa
Hull
Pembroke
Sudbury
North Bay
Huntsville
Orillia
Peterborough
Kingston
TORONTO
Kitchener
Hamilton
London
Oshawa
Barrie
Owen Sound
Parry Sound
Manitoulin I.
Sault Ste. Marie
Wawa
Thunder Bay
Nipigon
Marathon
Geraldton
Nakina
Hearst
Cochrane
Timmins
Kirkland Lake
Rouyn-Noranda
Amos
Kenora
Dryden
Sioux Lookout
Fort Frances
International Falls
Thief River Falls
Grand Forks
Bemidji
Hibbing
Virginia
Duluth
Superior
MINNESOTA
MINNEAPOLIS
ST. PAUL
Rochester
Mankato
WISCONSIN
MILWAUKEE
Madison
Green Bay
Oshkosh
Sheboygan
Racine
Kenosha
Eau Claire
La Crosse
Wausau
Marquette
Houghton
Escanaba
MICHIGAN
DETROIT
Windsor
Lansing
Flint
Saginaw
Bay City
Grand Rapids
Kalamazoo
Battle Creek
Ann Arbor
Jackson
Toledo
CHICAGO
Rockford
Joliet
Aurora
Gary
South Bend
Elkhart
Fort Wayne
Midwest
IOWA
Des Moines
Cedar Rapids
Dubuque
Davenport
Waterloo
Council Bluffs
Sioux City
ILLINOIS
Peoria
Springfield
Champaign
Decatur
Bloomington
INDIANA
INDIANAPOLIS
Muncie
Terre Haute
Evansville
OHIO
CLEVELAND
COLUMBUS
CINCINNATI
Dayton
Akron
Youngstown
Canton
Mansfield
Lima
PENNSYLVANIA
PITTSBURGH
PHILADELPHIA
Harrisburg
Allentown
Scranton
Wilkes-Barre
Erie
Johnstown
Altoona
Reading
Lancaster
NEW YORK
BUFFALO
Rochester
Syracuse
Utica
Albany
Binghamton
Ithaca
Schenectady
Troy
Poughkeepsie
Yonkers
Long I.
NEW JERSEY
Newark
Jersey City
Paterson
Trenton
Atlantic City
CONNECTICUT
HARTFORD
New Haven
Bridgeport
MASSACHUSETTS
BOSTON
Springfield
Worcester
Providence
Fall River
New Bedford
Lowell
Lawrence
C. Cod
Nantucket I.
Martha's Vineyard
VERMONT
Burlington
Montpelier
NEW HAMPSHIRE
Concord
Manchester
Nashua
White Mts.
MAINE
Portland
Bangor
Augusta
Lewiston
Penobscot Bay
Adirondack Mts.
Catskill Mts.
BALTIMORE
WASHINGTON D.C.
Annapolis
Wilmington
Dover
Delaware B.
Chesapeake Bay
MARYLAND
DELAWARE
Salisbury
VIRGINIA
WEST VIRGINIA
Charleston
Huntington
Parkersburg
Wheeling
Morgantown
Clarksburg
Richmond
Norfolk
Virginia Beach
Newport News
Roanoke
Lynchburg
Charlottesville
Harrisonburg
Danville
KENTUCKY
Louisville
Lexington
Frankfort
Bowling Green
Owensboro
Paducah
TENNESSEE
Nashville
Memphis
Knoxville
Chattanooga
Jackson
Murfreesboro
Kingsport
Johnson City
NORTH CAROLINA
CHARLOTTE
Greensboro
Winston-Salem
Raleigh
Durham
Fayetteville
Wilmington
Asheville
SOUTH CAROLINA
Columbia
Greenville
Spartanburg
Charleston
Myrtle Beach
C. Hatteras
C. Fear
Albemarle Sd.
Pamlico Sd.
GEORGIA
ATLANTA
Augusta
Macon
Columbus
Savannah
Albany
Valdosta
Brunswick
ALABAMA
Birmingham
Montgomery
Mobile
Huntsville
Tuscaloosa
Dothan
MISSISSIPPI
Jackson
Vicksburg
Meridian
Hattiesburg
Biloxi
Gulfport
Tupelo
LOUISIANA
NEW ORLEANS
Baton Rouge
Lafayette
Lake Charles
Shreveport
Monroe
Alexandria
Lake Pontchartrain
Mississippi River Delta
ARKANSAS
Little Rock
Fort Smith
Hot Springs
Pine Bluff
Texarkana
Ozark Plateau
Ouachita Mts.
MISSOURI
KANSAS CITY
ST. LOUIS
Springfield
Columbia
Jefferson City
Joplin
Tulsa
Oklahoma City
DALLAS
HOUSTON
Galveston
Beaumont
Port Arthur
Pasadena
Topeka
FLORIDA
Jacksonville
Tallahassee
Pensacola
Panama City
Gainesville
Ocala
Orlando
Daytona Beach
St. Augustine
TAMPA
Clearwater
St. Petersburg
Sarasota
Lakeland
Melbourne
C. Canaveral
Fort Pierce
West Palm Beach
Fort Lauderdale
MIAMI
Fort Myers
Cape Coral
Naples
Key West
Florida Keys
Florida Bay
C. Sable
L. Okeechobee
The Everglades
Straits of Florida
BAHAMAS
Grand Bahama I.
Freeport
Great Abaco I.
Eleuthera I.
Nassau
New Providence I.
Andros I.
Cat I.
Exuma Sound
Great Exuma I.
Long I.
N.E. Providence Channel
N.W. Providence Channel
Apalachee B.
Apalachicola
C. San Blas
Atchafalaya B.
GULF OF MEXICO
ATLANTIC OCEAN
APPALACHIAN MOUNTAINS
Cumberland Plateau
Piedmont
95
90
85
80
75
65
45
40
35
30
25

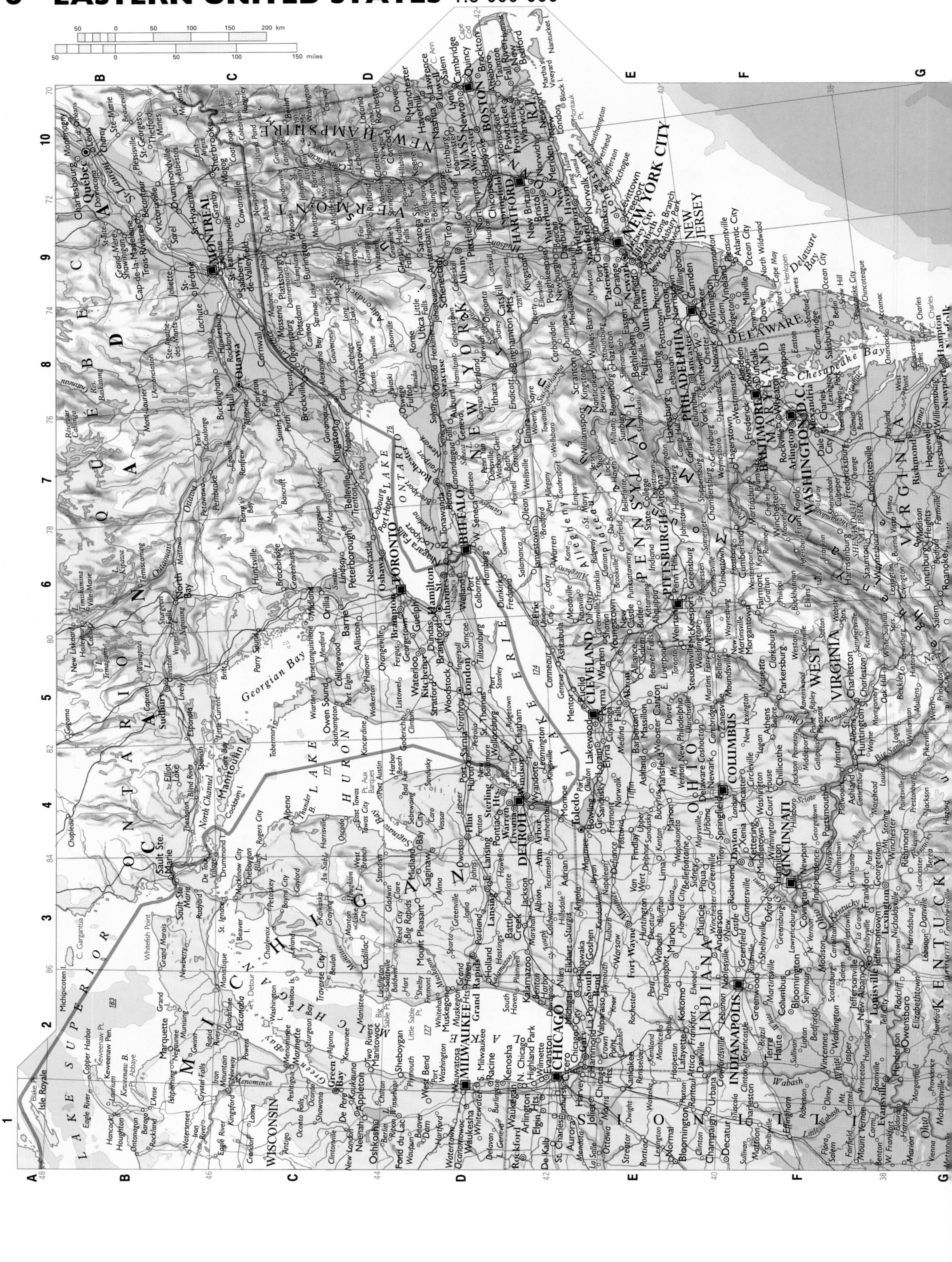

70
80
81
87

ATLANTIC OCEAN
GULF OF MEXICO
BAHAMAS
TENNESSEE
NORTH CAROLINA
SOUTH CAROLINA
GEORGIA
ALABAMA
FLORIDA
MISSISSIPPI
MAINE
NEW HAMPSHIRE
CANADA
APPALACHIAN MTS.
Nashville
Knoxville
Chattanooga
Atlanta
Birmingham
Montgomery
Mobile
Pensacola
Tallahassee
Jacksonville
Savannah
Charleston
Columbia
Charlotte
Raleigh
Wilmington
Orlando
Tampa
St. Petersburg
Miami
Macon
Augusta
Portland
Bangor
Augusta
Continuation Eastwards On same scale.
Projection: Albers' Equal Area with two standard parallels
West from Greenwich
COPYRIGHT GEORGE PHILIP LTD.

Georgian Bay
Bruce Peninsula
LAKE HURON
LAKE ONTARIO
LAKE ERIE
MICHIGAN
ONTARIO
OHIO
PENNSYLVANIA
NEW YORK
CANADA
TORONTO
DETROIT
CLEVELAND
PITTSBURGH
BUFFALO
Hamilton
Mississauga
London
Windsor
Rochester
Erie
Akron
Youngstown
Kitchener
Guelph
Brampton
Oshawa
Peterborough
Barrie
L. Simcoe
L. St. Clair
Allegheny Plateau
Allegheny Mountains
Tuscarora Mts.
Projection: Bonne

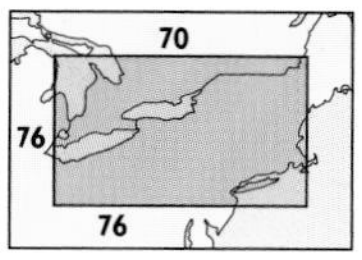

Houghton 183
Marquette
Sault Ste.
Marie
Manitoulin
L. Huron
Parry
Sound
Huntsville
Ottawa
Cornwall
L. Champlain
MAINE
Bangor
Yarmouth
Liverpool
Sable I.
(Nova Scotia)
6309▼

40

ESI·C· M·I
Escanaba
Menominee
Manistique
Georgian
Bay
Barrie
Peterborough
Belleville
Kingston
Burlington
Montpelier
VERMONT
Augusta
Lewiston
Portland
C. Sable
C. Cod

SIN
Green
Bay
Petoskey
Traverse City
Cadillac
Owen Sound
Oshawa
**NEW
HAMPSHIRE**
Concord
Manchester

leton
Wausau
TORONTO
Syracuse
Albany
Springfield
BOSTON
MASS.
E

WAUKEE
Grand
Rapids
Saginaw
Flint
Kitchener
London
Hamilton
Niagara
Falls
Rochester
NEW YORK
HARTFORD
CONN.
R.I.
Providence

on
Racine
Kenosha
Lansing
Sarnia
L. Erie
174
Erie
Jamestown
Binghamton
Scranton
Bridgeport
New Haven

CHICAGO DETROIT
Windsor
Toledo
CLEVELAND
Elmira
PENNSYLVANIA
Newark
N.J.
NEW YORK

NOIS
Gary
South Bend
INDIANA
OHIO
Allentown
Trenton

Projection: Albers' Equal Area with two standard parallels

50 0 50 100 150 200 km
50 0 50 100 150 miles

Grid references across the top and bottom: 8, 9, 10, 11, 12, 13, 14
Grid references down the sides: A, B, C, D, E, F, G
Latitude lines: 45, 44, 43, 42, 41, 40

QUÉBEC

MONTREAL, Longueuil, Greenfield Park, St-Pie, Granby, Sherbrooke, Cookshire, Snow Mt. ▲1203, Longueuil, Pointe-Claire, Lachine, Chambly, Marieville, Waterloo, Eastman, Sherbrooke, Lennoxville, Notre-Dame-des-Bois

Ottawa, Hull, Gatineau, Quyon, Arnprior, Pakenham, Almonte

VERMONT

Burlington, Montpelier, St. Albans, Rutland, Brattleboro, Bennington

NEW HAMPSHIRE

Concord, Manchester, Nashua, Mt. Washington 1917, Hanover, Lebanon, Keene

MAINE

Flagstaff L., Rangeley, Rumford, Berlin, Gilead, Bethel

MASSACHUSETTS

BOSTON, Worcester, Springfield, Cambridge, Quincy, Lowell, Lawrence, Framingham

CONNECTICUT

HARTFORD, New Haven, Bridgeport, Waterbury, Stamford, New London

RHODE ISLAND

Providence, Cranston, Pawtucket, Newport

NEW YORK

NEW YORK, Albany, Syracuse, Utica, Rome, Schenectady, Troy, Watertown, Binghamton, Kingston, Poughkeepsie, Yonkers, Newark

NEW JERSEY

Newark, Jersey City, Elizabeth, Paterson, Trenton, New Brunswick, Camden

PENNSYLVANIA

PHILADELPHIA, Reading, Allentown, Bethlehem, Easton, Scranton, Wilkes-Barre, Lancaster

ATLANTIC OCEAN

Long Island, Long Beach, Martha's Vineyard, Block I., Buzzards Bay

from Greenwich 76 74 73 72 71 COPYRIGHT GEORGE PHILIP LTD.

Projection: Albers' Equal Area with two standard parallels

West from Greenwich

WESTERN WASHINGTON REGION
On same scale

REFERENCE TO NUMBERS

1 Distrito Federal 5 México
2 Aguascalientes 6 Morelos
3 Guanajuato 7 Querétaro
4 Hidalgo 8 Tlaxcala

Projection: Bi-polar oblique Conical Orthomorphic

West from Greenwich

5　　　　6　　　　7　　　　8

A

B

C

D

E

ichita Falls
Denison
Sherman
Paris
Hope
Camden
ARKANSAS
Greenville
Tuscaloosa
Opelika
McRae
ossum kingdom Res.
Denton
Greenville
Texarkana
El Dorado
MISSISSIPPI
ALABAMA
Phenix City
Columbus
Cordele
Brazos
FORT WORTH
DALLAS
Marshall
Monroe
Vicksburg
Meridian
Selma
Montgomery
Troy
Americus
Tifton
GEORGIA
Albany
Waycross
Valdosta
Ranger
ene
Cleburne
Tyler
Longview
Shreveport
LOUISIANA
Natchez
Jackson
Laurel
Hattiesburg
Flomaton
Dothan
Jim Woodruff Res.
Chattahoochee
Tallahassee
Lake City
FLORIDA

D
Hillsboro
Corsicana
Palestine
Nacogdoches
Pearl
McComb
Bogalusa
Pensacola
Panama City
Brownwood
Waco
Lufkin
Sam Rayburn Reservoir
Alexandria
Baton Rouge
Hammond
Biloxi
MOBILE
Gulfport
Temple
Huntsville
Beaumont
Lafayette
L. Pontchartrain
NEW ORLEANS
Breton Sd.
C. San Blas
Apalachee Bay
Suwannee

Austin
Bryan
HOUSTON
Port Arthur
Atchafalaya Bay
Terrebonne Bay
Mississippi River Delta
Clearwater

SAN ANTONIO
Victoria
Galveston

Dilley
Rosenberg

Alice
Corpus Christi
GULF　　　　**OF**

Laredo
Kingsville
MEXICO

evo Laredo
Zapata
Laguna Madre

Camargo
McAllen
Harlingen
Brownsville

Presa M.R. Gomez China
Reynosa
Matamoros
Valle Hermoso
Santa Teresa
Laguna Madre
Tropic of Cancer
La Esperanza

Villagran
Hidalgo
San Fernando
CUBA
Guane
agoza
Santander Jiménez
La Esperanza
Soto la Marina
La Pesca
Guane
La Fé

iudad ictoria
Llera
Aldama
Pta. Jerez
I. Desterrada
í. Pérez (Mexico)
Canal de Yucatán
C. San Antonio
C. Corrientes

ampo
Ciudad Mante
Calles
Pta. Yalkubul
Rio Lagartos
C. Catoche

Altamira
Ciudad Madero
Tampico
Dzilam de Bravo
El Cuyo
Cancún
Puerto Juárez
ardenas de Valles
Pánuco
Progreso
DZIBILCHALTUN
Temax
Tizimín
OS Í
Ozuluama
L. de Tamiahua
Motul
Izamal
Espita
Puerto Morelos
Tempoal
Magozal
C. Rojo
Mérida
MAYAPAN
CHICHEN ITZA
Valladolid
Isla Cozumel
uma
Tantoyuca
Tamazunchale
Maxcanú
YUCATÁN
Sotuta
Ticul
Peto
Cozumel
Chicontepec
Tuxpan
AXMAL
Tekax

Zimapán
Zacualtipán
Poza Rica
Papantla
Tenabo
Tenabo
Vigía Chico
B. de la Ascensión

uan del Río
Huauchinango
Nautla
Golfo
BECAL
Hopelchén
B. del Espíritu Santo
Pachuca
Tulancingo
Teziutlán
Campeche
EDZNA
Felipe Carrillo
QUINTANA
Zumpango
Misantla
de
Champotón
Puerto
ula
Jalapa Enríquez
ZEMPOALA
Chenkán
ROO
Banco Chinchorro
MÉXICO
Apizaco
Coatepec
Veracruz
Campeche
Bacalar
Chetumal
B. de Chetumal
Tlaxcala
Citlaltépetl
Alvarado
Ciudad del Carmen
Matamoros
Corozal
Tenango
Amecameca
PUEBLA
Tlacotalpan
San Andrés
L. de Términos
Orange Walk
Ambergris Cay

Popocatépetl
Córdoba
Tuxtla
Frontera
Concepción
nrnavaca
PUEBLA
Orizaba
San Andrés
Paraíso
CAMPECHE
Hondo
Izúcar de
Cosamaloapan
Comalcalco
Palizada
Belize City
Matamoros
Tehuacán
Tres Valles
Balancán
Turneffe Is.
Iguala
Ajalpan
Acatlán
Presa Miguel Alemán
Coatzacoalcos
TABASCO
Villahermosa
LA VENTA
Macuspana
Uaxactún
Dangriga
Chiautla
Huajuapan de León
Acayucan
Minatitlán
Cárdenas
Tenosique
TIKAL
San Ignacio
Belmopan
BELIZE
Is. de la Bahía

ERO
Chilapa
Asunción Nochixtlán
Istmo
Raudales de Teapa
PALENQUE
Benque Viejo
Roatán
Puerto Castilla
Iriona
Silacayoapan
Jesús Carranza
Simojovel
Ocosingo
L. Petén Itzá
Maya Mts.
Golfo de Honduras
Chilpancingo
Tlaxiaco
Oaxaca
de
Presa Malpaso
La Libertad
Flores
Monkey River
Tierra Colorada
Tlacolula
Netzahualcoyotl
Copainalá
Chiapa de
Usumacinta
Tela
Ayutla
MONTE ALBAN
OAXACA
Tuxtla
Corzo
San Cristóbal de
San Luis
Punta Gorda
Puerto Barrios
Balfate
Ometepec
Ocotlán
Matías Romero
Ixtepec
Gutiérrez
las Casas
Comitán
Santa Rosa L. de Yojoa
HONDURAS
Jamiltepec
Taviche
Tehuantepec
Juchitán
Arriaga
Tonalá
La Concordia
Sierra
de Izabal
Motagua
San Pedro Sula
El Progreso
Olanchito
Pinotepa Nacional
Ejutla
San Jerónimo
Miahuatlán
Salina Cruz
La Concordia
Cuilco
Huehuetenango
Cobán
Gualán
Zacapa
Chiquimula de Copán
Santa Bárbara
Yoro
Juticalpa
Catacamas
Punta Maldonado
Pochutla
Puerto Ángel
San Pedro Mixtepec
Puerto Arista
Pijijiapan
Motozintla
GUATEMALA
Cuchumatanes
Totonicapán
Sololá
Jalapa
La Esperanza
La Paz
Tegucigalpa
Danli
Yuscarán
Comayagua
Pachuca

Golfo de
Tehuantepec
Huixtla
Tapachula
San Marcos
Coatepeque
GUATEMALA
Amatitlán
Chimaltenango
Antigua
Retalhuleu

Projection: Conical with two standard parallels

87

92 93

5 6 7 8

A T L A N T I C

O C E A N

Tropic of Cancer

ft m

12 000 4000

9000 3000

6000 2000

4500 1500

3000 1000

1200 400

600 200

0 0

200 600

2000 6000

4000 12 000

6000 18 000

8000 24 000

m m
ft

A

B

C

D

E

MAS

r's Town

The Bight
Cat I.

Conception I.

Long I.
Clarence Town
Crooked I. Passage
Samana Cay

Albert Town
Snug Corner
Mayaguana I.
Crooked I.

ay Verde
Mira por vos Cay
Acklins I.
Caicos Passage

Hogsty Reef

Little Inagua I.
Turks & Caicos
Caicos Is. (U.K.)

santa
ingo

Lake Rosa
Great Inagua I.
Matthew Town
Turks Island Passage
Turks Is.

ari

Moa

Baracoa
Pta. de Maisi
Î. de la Tortue

Maisí
Î. de la Tortue

ntánamo
Paso de los Vientos (Windward Passage)
Cap-Haïtien
Monte Cristi
LA ISABELA
Puerto Rico Trench

Jean Rabel
Port-de-Paix
Fort Liberté
Puerto Plata
Santiago de los Cabelleros
San Francisco de Macorís
Milwaukee Deep 9200

Cap-à-Foux
G. de la Gonâve
Gonaïves
Cord. Central
La Vega
3175
Nagua
Samana
B. de Samana

St-Marc
Hinche
Sabana de la Mar
Sánchez

HAITI
DOMINICAN
Hato Mayor
Bayamón
SAN JUAN
Carolina

Jérémie
Î. de la Gonâve
PORT-
San Juan
REP.
Higüey
C. Engaño
Aguadilla
Arecibo
Virgin Is.
(U.K.)
Anegada
Virgin Gorda
Sombrero (U.K.)

sa I.
Dame Marie
AU-PRINCE
San Pedro de Macorís
La Romana
Ponce
Carolina
Caguas
Charlotte Amalie
Virgin Is.
(U.S.A.)
St. Thomas
Road Town
Tortola
Anguilla (U.K.)
St.-Martin
St.-Barthélemy (Fr.)

Carcasse
Massif de la Hotte
2680
SANTO
DOMINGO
Azua de Compostela
Baní
San Cristóbal
Isla
Mayagüez
Guayama
Frederiksted
St. Croix
Christiansted
St. Maarten (Neth.)
Saba (Neth.)
Barbuda

Les Cayes
Aquin
Goâve
Jacmel
Barahona
L. Enriquillo
I. Saona
B. de Yuma
Mona
(U.S.A.)
ST. KITTS
& NEVIS
Basseterre
St. Eustatius
(Neth.)
ANTIGUA
& BARBUDA
St. John's
Antigua

Pointe-à-Gravois
Petit
Pedernales
I. Beata
C. Beata
PUERTO
RICO
(U.S.A.)
Redonda
(U.K.)
Montserrat
Soufrière
Nevis
Hills

Hispaniola
Antilles
Ste.-Rose
GUADELOUPE
La Désirade
Le Moule
Pointe-à-Pitre
Marie-Galante (Fr.)
Grand-Bourg

Î. à Vache

Antilles
Leeward Islands
Guadeloupe Passage
Basse-Terre
I. des Saintes (Fr.)
Dominica Passage

I. de Aves
(Venezuela)
Portsmouth
Roseau
DOMINICA

B E A N
S E A
Martinique Passage
Mt. Pelée 1397
Ste.-Marie
Le François

Lesser Antilles
Fort-de-France
Rivière-Pilote
MARTINIQUE (Fr.)

St. Lucia Channel
Castries
Soufrière
ST. LUCIA

St. Vincent Passage
La Soufrière 1234
ST. VINCENT
Speightstown
Bridgetown
BARBADOS

Windward Islands
Kingstown
& THE
Hillsborough
Grenadines
GRENADINES

St. George's
GRENADA

Lesser Antilles

Pta. Gallinas
Aruba (Neth.)
Oranjestad
Curaçao
Bonaire
NETH. ANTILLES
I. Blanquilla (Ven.)
Is. Los Hermanos (Ven.)
Is. Los Testigos (Ven.)
Tobago
Scarborough
Galera Point

C. San Román
Pen. de Paraguaná
Willemstad
Is. Las Aves (Ven.)
I. Orchila (Ven.)
Port of Spain
Trinidad

SANTA MARTA
RAN-
ILLA
Ríohacha
Uribia
GUAJIRA
Pen. de la Guajira
Pta. Espada
Punta Cardón
Puerto Cumarebo
Coro
La Vela de Coro
Is. Los Roques (Ven.)
I. de Margarita
La Asunción
NUEVA ESPARTA
Porlamar
Pen. de Paria
Arima
Río Claro
TRINIDAD & TOBAGO

ranoa
THICO
Ciénaga
Soledad
Sierra Nevada de Santa Marta 5800
San Rafael
Altagracia
Mene de Mauroa
FALCÓN
Tucuyo
Tucacas
Puerto Cabello
Maracay
Maiquetía
La Guaira
CARACAS
DISTRITO FEDERAL
La Tortuga (Ven.)
Cumaná
Carúpano
Car: b:
G. de Paria
San Fernando
Serpent's Mouth

SUCRE

Sabanalarga
Fundación
Calamar
MAGDALENA
Plato
Valledupar
Agustín Codazzi
La Concepción
Villa del Rosario
Cabimas
Carora
San Felipe
YARACUY
Barquisimeto
Valencia
CARABOBO
ARAGUA
Maracay
MIRANDA
Los Teques
Río Chico
Ocumare del Tuy
Higuerote
Puerto La Cruz
Barcelona
Caripito
Caicara
Maturín
MONAGAS
DELTA
Tucupita
AMACURO

Zambrano
CÉSAR
Machiques
Lago de Maracaibo
Mene Grande
LARA
El Tocuyo
Carpano
Villa
de Cura
San Carlos
COJEDES
San Juan
de los Morros
Aragua de Barcelona
Anaco
Cantaura
El Tigre
Los Barrancos

Corozal
Mompós
El Banco
ZULIA
TRUJILLO
Acarigua
Valle de la Pasqua
Santa María de Ipire
Ciudad Guayana
Sierra Imataca

Magangué
NORTE
DE
SANTANDER
Encontrados
San Carlos del Zulia
PORTUGUESA
El Baúl
GUÁRICO
ANZOÁTEGUI
Soledad
El Pao

Ayapel
Simití
Cúcuta
TÁCHIRA
MÉRIDA
Barinas
Guanare
Portuguesa
Calabozo
Ciudad Bolívar
Upata

Caucasia
Cord. de Mérida
Ciudad Bolivia
BARINAS
San Fernando de Apure
Mapire
Ciudad Bolívar
El Callao
Tumeremo

BOLÍVAR
Santa Bárbara
V E N E Z U E L A
Bruzual
Puerto de Nutrias
Achaguas
Apure
Caicara
Orinoco
Embalse de Guri
Guasipati

50 0 50 100 150 200 250 300 km
50 0 50 100 150 200 miles

West from Greenwich
COPYRIGHT GEORGE PHILIP LTD

75 70 5 65 7 60

Tropic of Cancer

NORTH

ATLANTIC

OCEAN

Yucatán Channel
Gulf of Campeche

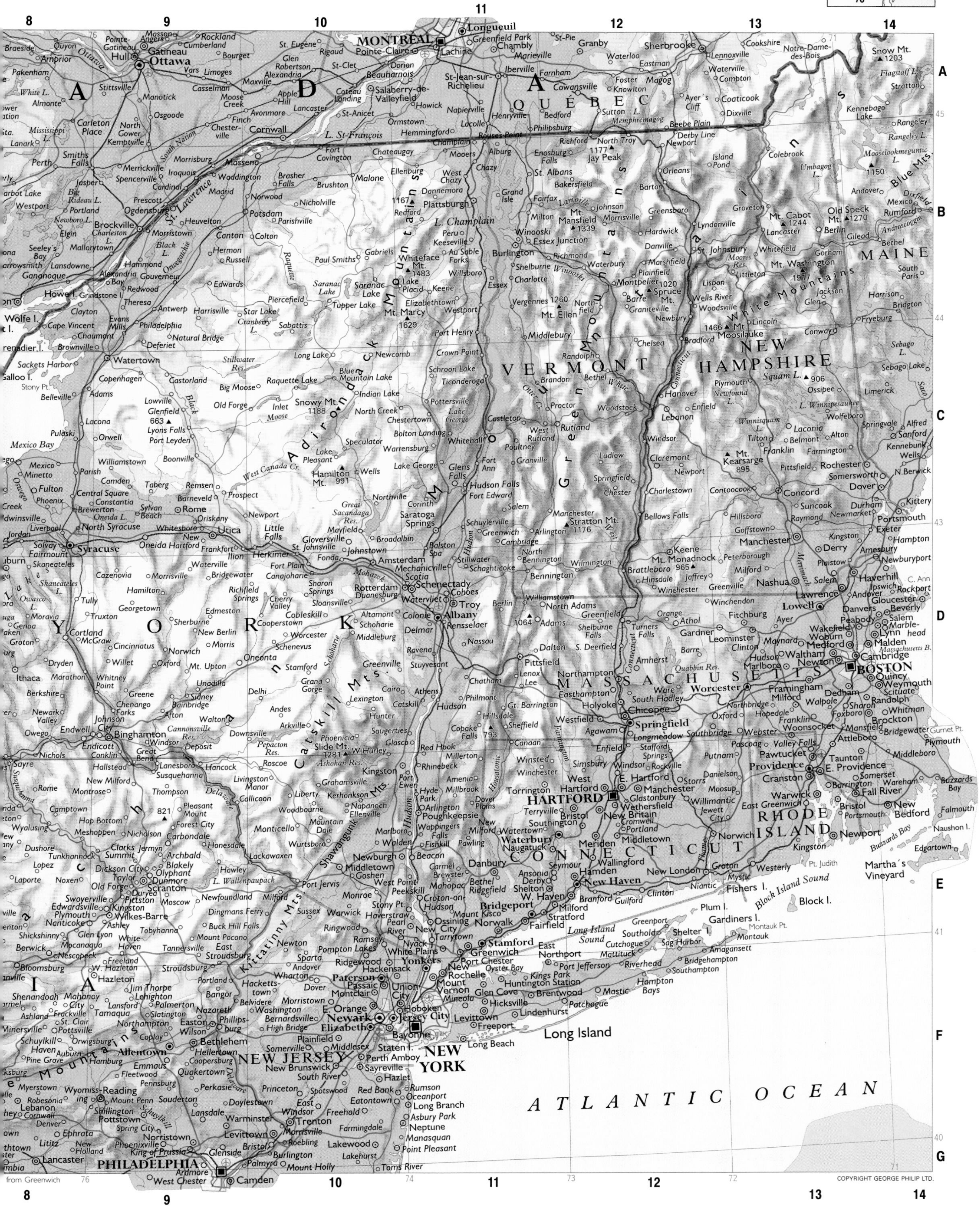

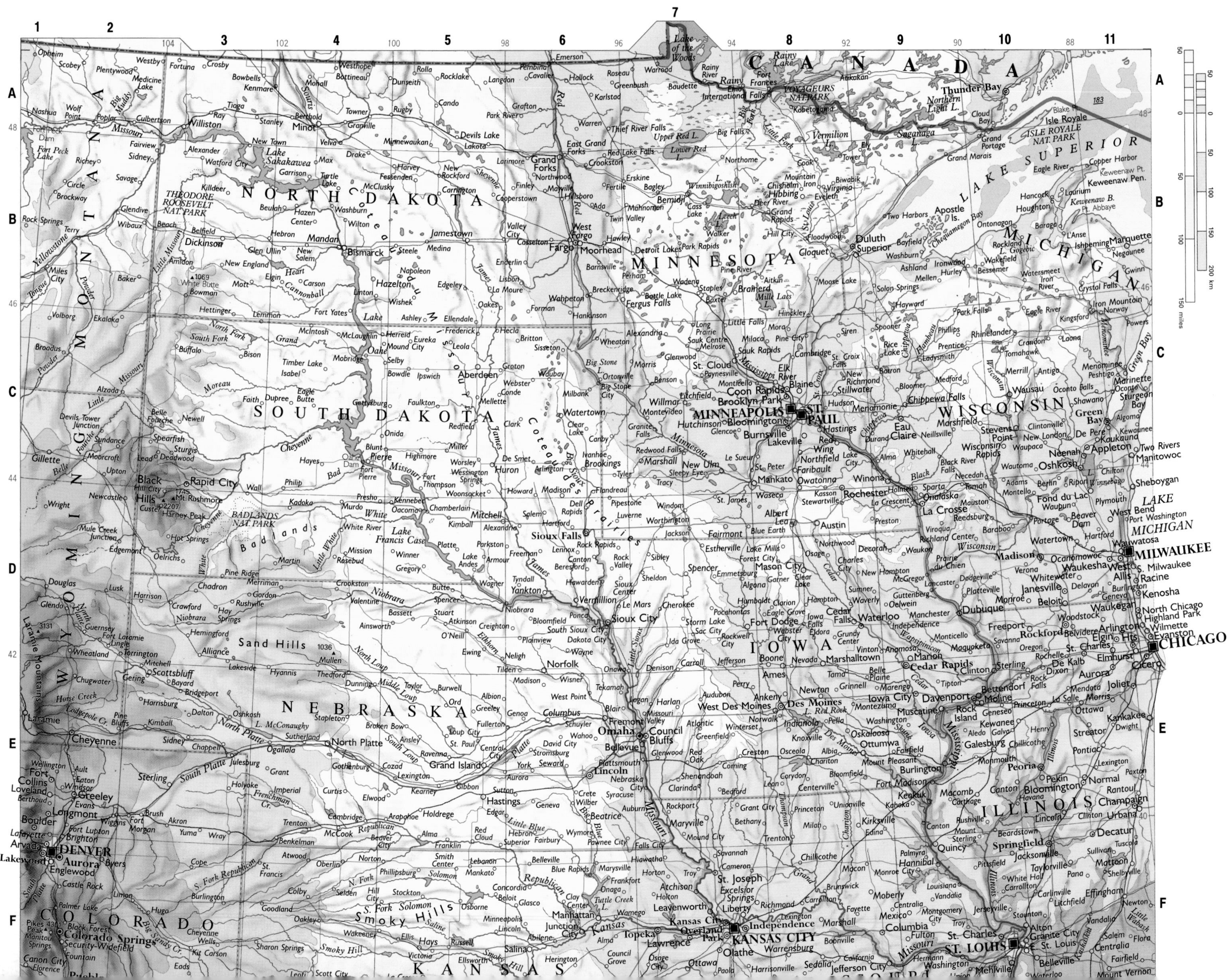

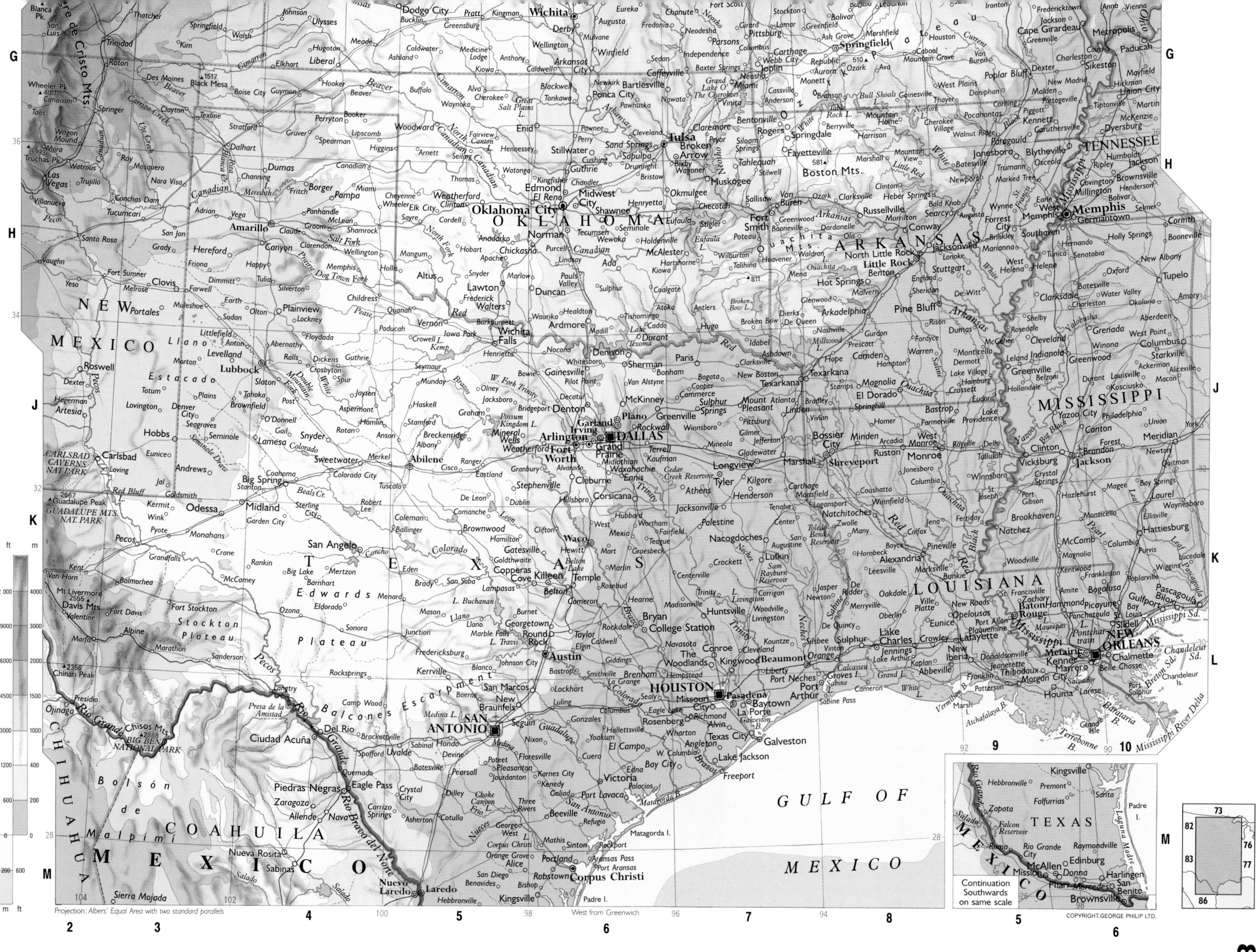
OKLAHOMA
ARKANSAS
TEXAS
LOUISIANA
MISSISSIPPI
TENNESSEE
NEW MEXICO
MEXICO
COAHUILA
CHIHUAHUA
GULF OF MEXICO
Oklahoma City
Tulsa
Wichita
Springfield
Memphis
Little Rock
North Little Rock
Fort Smith
Hot Springs
Pine Bluff
Texarkana
Shreveport
Monroe
Alexandria
Lake Charles
Lafayette
Baton Rouge
NEW ORLEANS
Jackson
Vicksburg
Hattiesburg
Biloxi
Gulfport
Meridian
Tupelo
Columbus
Greenville
DALLAS
Fort Worth
Arlington
Irving
Garland
Plano
Denton
Waco
Austin
SAN ANTONIO
HOUSTON
Pasadena
Galveston
Beaumont
Port Arthur
Corpus Christi
Laredo
Nuevo Laredo
Brownsville
Harlingen
McAllen
Edinburg
Kingsville
Victoria
Bryan
College Station
Tyler
Longview
Lubbock
Amarillo
Abilene
San Angelo
Midland
Odessa
Big Spring
Wichita Falls
Lawton
Norman
Enid
Roswell
Clovis
Carlsbad
Hobbs
Del Rio
Eagle Pass
Piedras Negras
Ciudad Acuña
Ozark Plateau
Boston Mts.
Ouachita Mts.
Llano Estacado
Edwards Plateau
Stockton Plateau
Balcones Escarpment
Bolsón de Mapimí
CARLSBAD CAVERNS NAT. PARK
GUADALUPE MTS. NAT. PARK
BIG BEND NATIONAL PARK
Sangre de Cristo Mts.
Mississippi
Red
Arkansas
Canadian
Brazos
Colorado
Pecos
Rio Grande
Río Bravo del Norte
Sabine
Neches
Trinity
Ouachita
Continuation Southwards on same scale
Projection: Albers' Equal Area with two standard parallels
West from Greenwich
COPYRIGHT.GEORGE PHILIP LTD.

COLORADO
NEW MEXICO
ARIZONA
TEXAS
MEXICO
SONORA
CHIHUAHUA
BAJA CALIFORNIA
PACIFIC OCEAN
Golfo de California
Desierto de Altar
Colorado Plateau
Painted Desert
Sonoran Desert
Mojave Desert
Death Valley
Grand Canyon
Sangre de Cristo Mts.
San Juan Mts.
Sacramento Mts.
Chuska Mts.
Mogollon Rim
Chocolate Mts.
Sierra de Juárez
Sierra de San Pedro Mártir
Santa Lucia Range
Channel Is.
LOS ANGELES
SAN DIEGO
PHOENIX
Tijuana
Mexicali
Ensenada
Tucson
Albuquerque
Santa Fe
El Paso
Ciudad Juárez
Chihuahua
Hermosillo
Las Vegas
Fresno
Bakersfield
Flagstaff
Yuma
Nogales
Rio Grande
Río Bravo del Norte
Isla Guadalupe (Mexico)
I. Tiburón
I. Ángel de la Guarda
Projection: Albers' Equal Area with two standard parallels
West from Greenwich
COPYRIGHT GEORGE PHILIP LTD.
ft m
12 000 4000
9000 3000
6000 2000
4500 1500
3000 1000
1200 400
600 200
0 0
200 600
2000 6000
4000 12 000

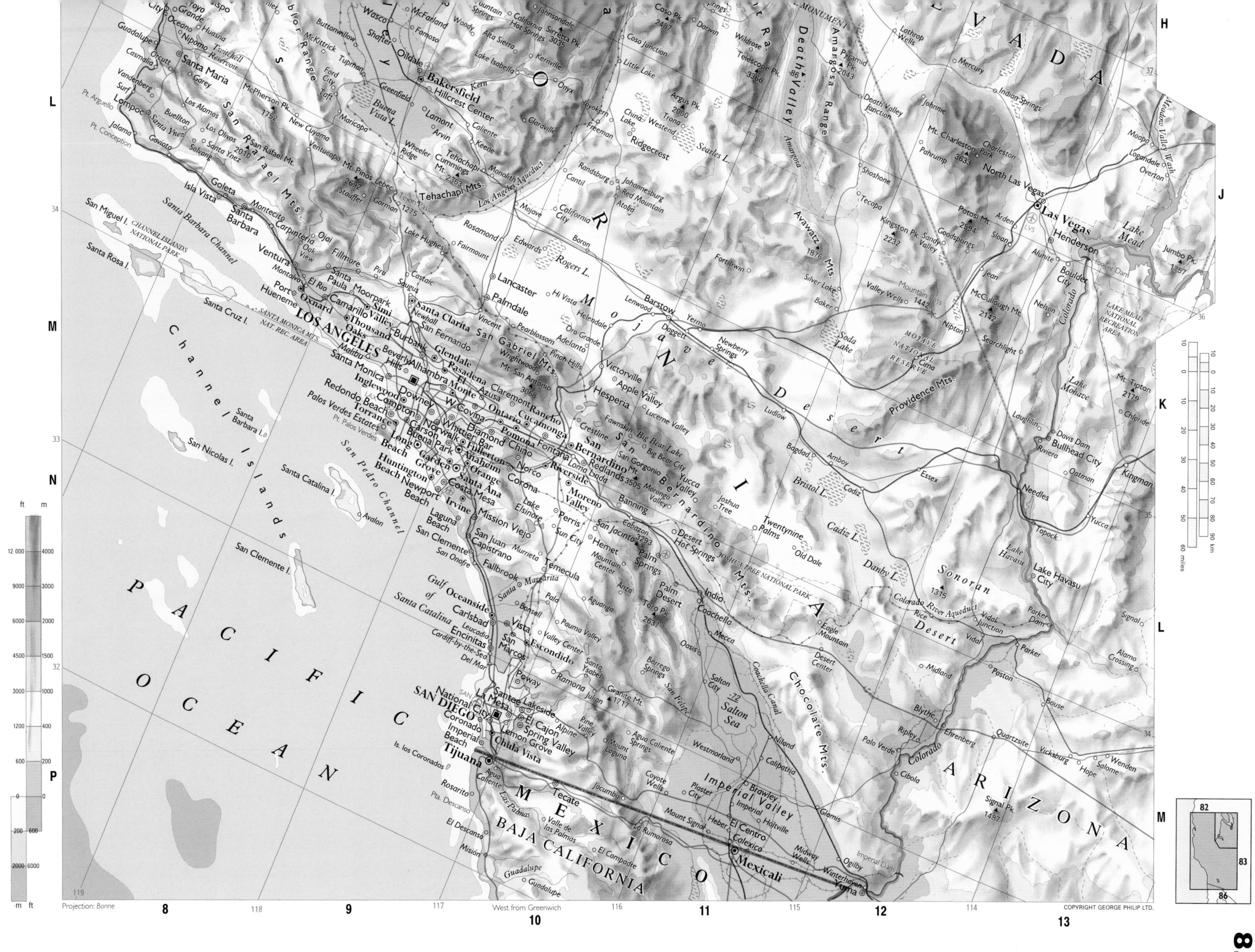

N E V A D A
A R I Z O N A
C A L I F O R N I A
M E X I C O
BAJA CALIFORNIA
P A C I F I C   O C E A N
Mojave Desert
Sonoran Desert
Death Valley
Amargosa Range
Chocolate Mts.
San Bernardino Mts.
San Gabriel Mts.
Tehachapi Mts.
San Rafael Mts.
Providence Mts.
Channel Islands
Santa Barbara Channel
San Pedro Channel
Gulf of Santa Catalina
Santa Catalina I.
San Clemente I.
San Nicolas I.
Santa Barbara I.
Santa Cruz I.
Santa Rosa I.
San Miguel I.
Salton Sea
Imperial Valley
Lake Mead
Lake Mohave
Lake Havasu
Colorado
Las Vegas
Henderson
North Las Vegas
Boulder City
Bullhead City
Kingman
Needles
Lake Havasu City
Parker
Blythe
Yuma
Mexicali
Calexico
El Centro
Brawley
Indio
Palm Springs
Palm Desert
Twentynine Palms
Barstow
Victorville
Hesperia
Apple Valley
Lancaster
Palmdale
Bakersfield
Ridgecrest
LOS ANGELES
Long Beach
Santa Ana
Anaheim
Riverside
San Bernardino
Oxnard
Ventura
Santa Barbara
Santa Maria
Lompoc
Oceanside
Escondido
SAN DIEGO
Chula Vista
Tijuana
Tecate
Pt. Conception
Pt. Arguello
West from Greenwich
Projection: Bonne
COPYRIGHT GEORGE PHILIP LTD.
km
miles
m
ft

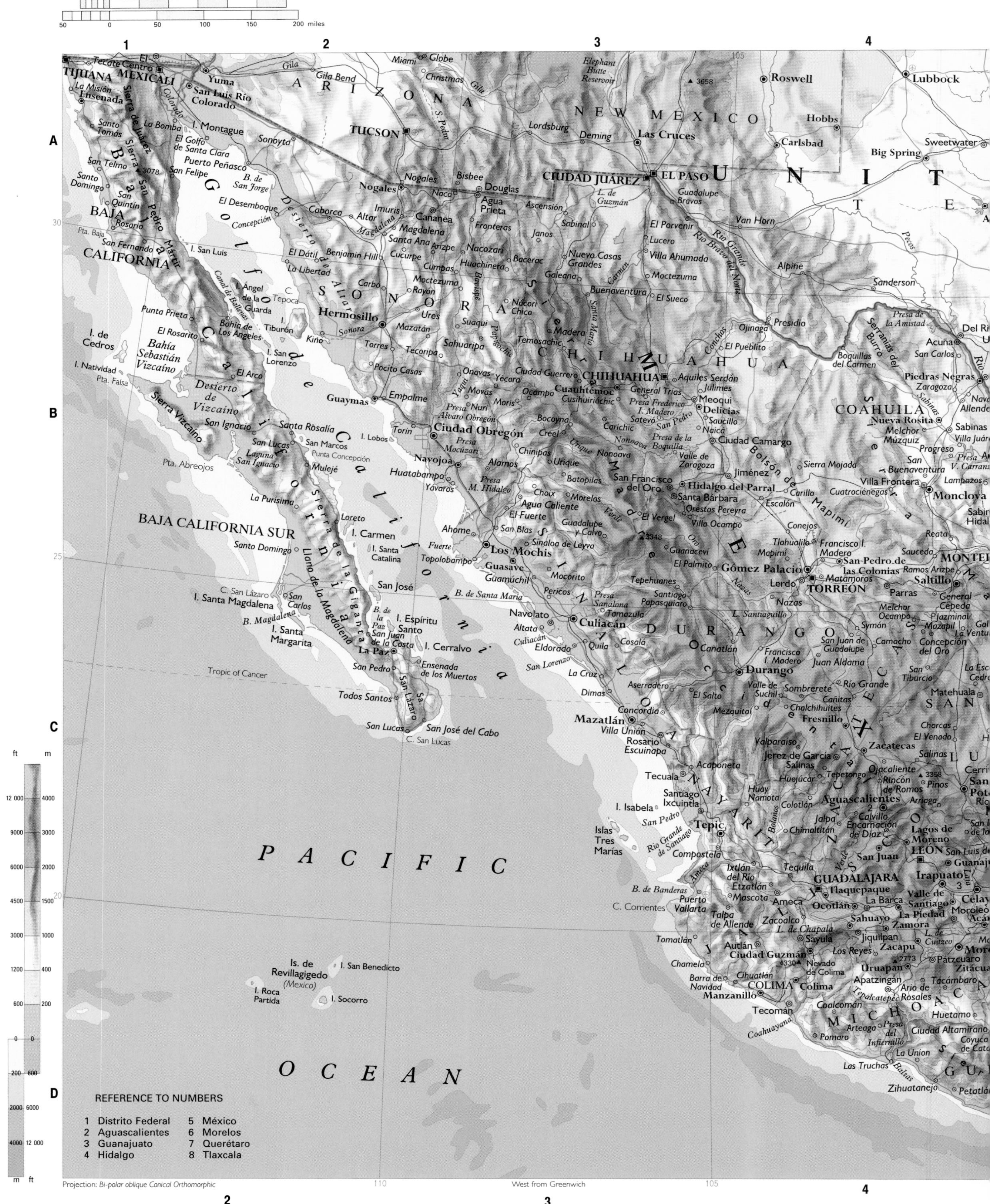

50 0 50 100 150 200 250 300 km
50 0 50 100 150 200 miles
1 2 3 4
A B C D
TIJUANA
MEXICALI
Tecate
Ensenada
Yuma
San Luis Río Colorado
TUCSON
Nogales
Douglas
Agua Prieta
CIUDAD JUÁREZ
EL PASO
Las Cruces
Roswell
Lubbock
Carlsbad
Hobbs
Big Spring
Sweetwater
N E W M E X I C O
A R I Z O N A
U N I T E
Deming
Lordsburg
Van Horn
Alpine
Sanderson
Presidio
Ojinaga
BAJA CALIFORNIA
Golfo de California
I. Ángel de la Guarda
I. Tiburón
Hermosillo
Guaymas
Empalme
Ciudad Obregón
Navojoa
Huatabampo
Los Mochis
Culiacán
Mazatlán
Durango
Gómez Palacio
TORREÓN
Saltillo
Monclova
Piedras Negras
Sabinas
Nueva Rosita
COAHUILA
CHIHUAHUA
Cuauhtémoc
Delicias
Hidalgo del Parral
Ciudad Camargo
Jiménez
SONORA
SINALOA
DURANGO
NAYARIT
ZACATECAS
Zacatecas
Aguascalientes
Fresnillo
Tepic
GUADALAJARA
Tlaquepaque
LEÓN
Irapuato
Ciudad Guzmán
COLIMA
Colima
Manzanillo
Uruapan
Zamora
Puerto Vallarta
B. de Banderas
C. Corrientes
I. de Cedros
I. Natividad
Bahía Sebastián Vizcaíno
Desierto de Vizcaíno
Santa Rosalía
Mulegé
Loreto
I. Carmen
BAJA CALIFORNIA SUR
Santo Domingo
I. Santa Magdalena
B. Magdalena
I. Santa Margarita
Llano de la Magdalena
Sierra de la Giganta
La Paz
I. Espíritu Santo
I. Cerralvo
Todos Santos
San Lucas
San José del Cabo
C. San Lucas
Tropic of Cancer
Islas Tres Marías
I. Isabela
Is. de Revillagigedo (Mexico)
I. San Benedicto
I. Roca Partida
I. Socorro
P A C I F I C
O C E A N
Sierra Madre Occidental
Bolsón de Mapimí
Río Bravo del Norte
Río Grande
REFERENCE TO NUMBERS
1 Distrito Federal
2 Aguascalientes
3 Guanajuato
4 Hidalgo
5 México
6 Morelos
7 Querétaro
8 Tlaxcala
ft m
12 000 4000
9000 3000
6000 2000
4500 1500
3000 1000
1200 400
600 200
0 0
200 600
2000 6000
4000 12 000
m ft
Projection: Bi-polar oblique Conical Orthomorphic
110
West from Greenwich
105

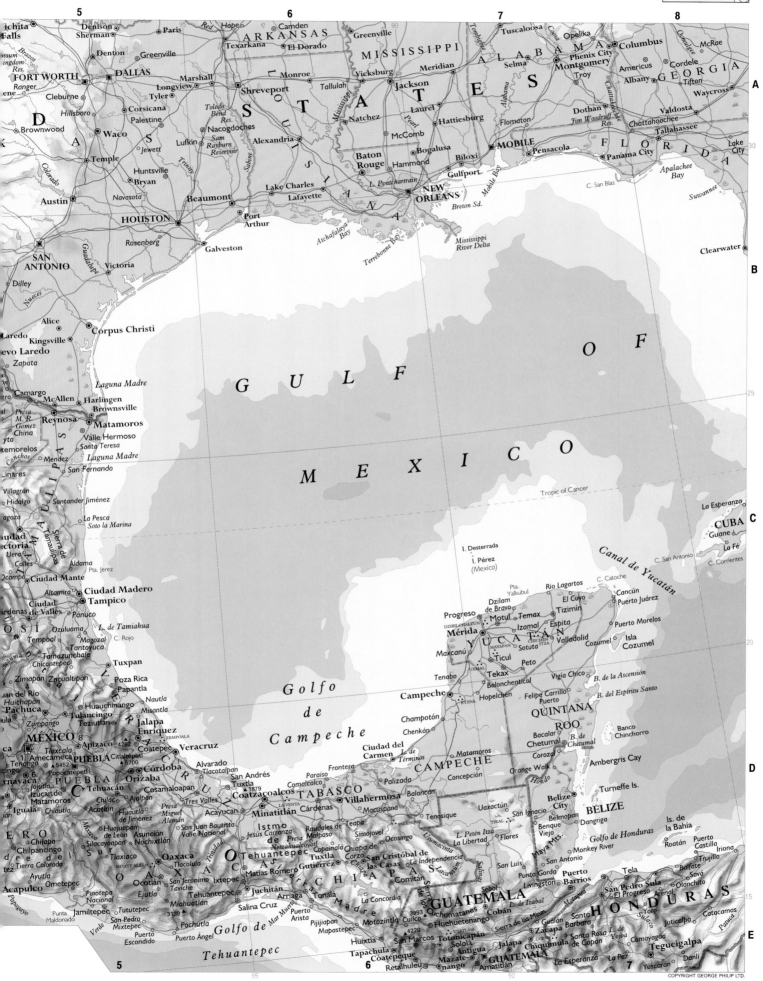

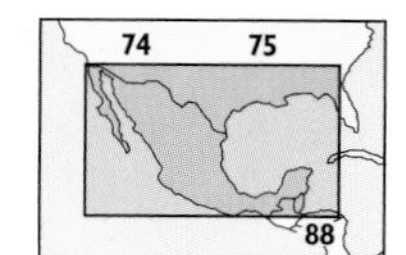
GULF OF MEXICO
Golfo de Campeche
Golfo de Tehuantepec
Golfo de Honduras
Canal de Yucatán
UNITED STATES
ARKANSAS
MISSISSIPPI
ALABAMA
GEORGIA
LOUISIANA
TEXAS
FLORIDA
CUBA
YUCATÁN
QUINTANA ROO
CAMPECHE
TABASCO
CHIAPAS
OAXACA
VERACRUZ
PUEBLA
TAMAULIPAS
BELIZE
GUATEMALA
HONDURAS
FORT WORTH
DALLAS
HOUSTON
SAN ANTONIO
NEW ORLEANS
MOBILE
Shreveport
Jackson
Montgomery
Baton Rouge
Tallahassee
Corpus Christi
Galveston
Beaumont
Tampico
Veracruz
Mérida
Campeche
Villahermosa
Coatzacoalcos
Oaxaca
MÉXICO
Acapulco
Belize City
GUATEMALA
Tegucigalpa
San Pedro Sula
Tropic of Cancer
Mississippi River Delta
I. Desterrada
I. Pérez (Mexico)
Istmo de Tehuantepec
Sierra Madre
Cancún
Cozumel
Chetumal
Brownsville
Matamoros
Reynosa
Laguna Madre
Tuxpan
Jalapa Enríquez
Puebla
Orizaba
Córdoba
Tuxtla Gutiérrez
Salina Cruz
Tapachula
Quetzaltenango
Ambergris Cay
Turneffe Is.
Is. de la Bahía
Roatán
Clearwater
Pensacola
Panama City
Biloxi
Gulfport
Lake Charles
Lafayette
Port Arthur
Laredo
Austin
Waco
Victoria

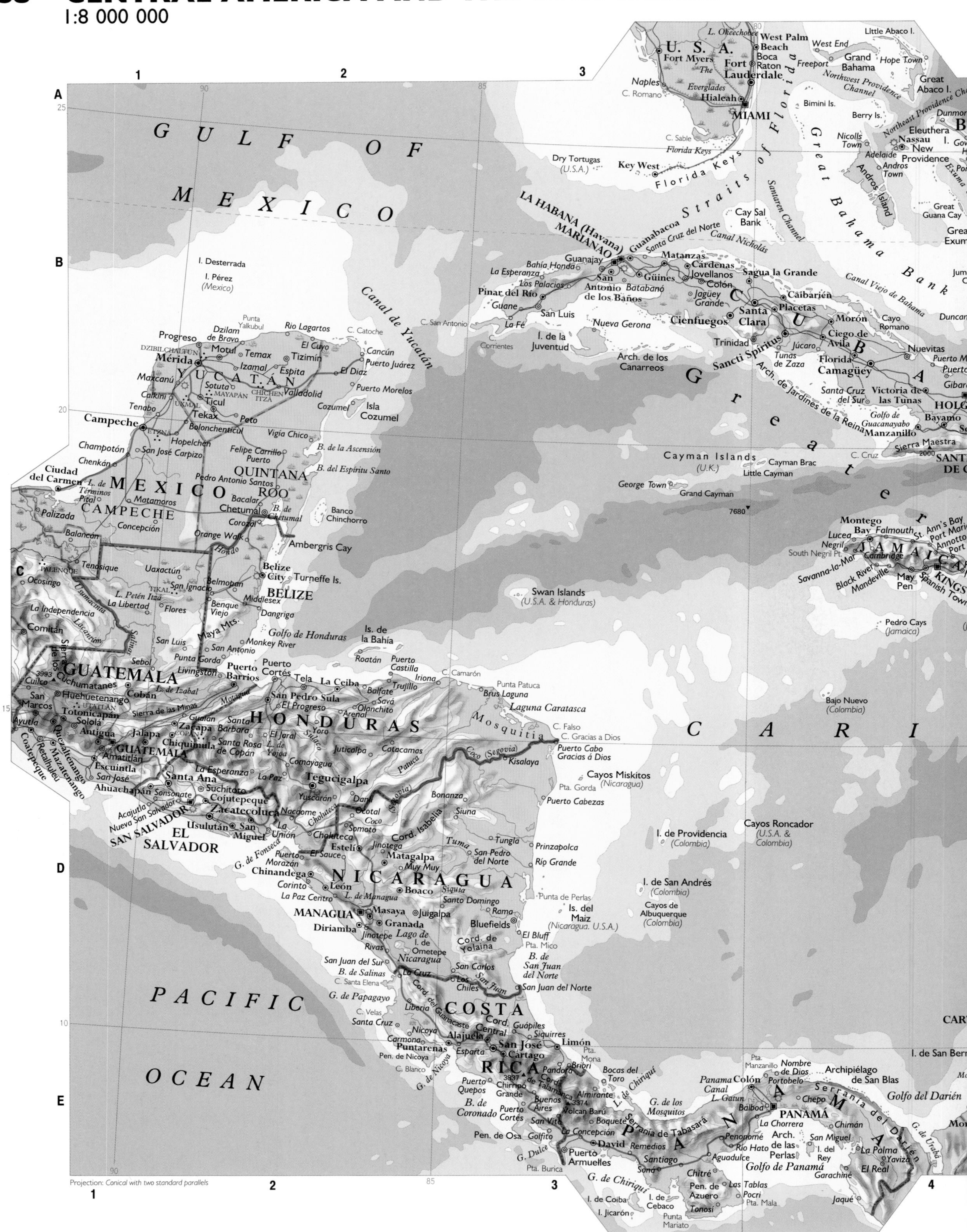

ATLANTIC OCEAN
Tropic of Cancer
Puerto Rico Trench
Milwaukee Deep 9200
Turks & Caicos (U.K.)
Caicos Is.
Turks Is.
Turks Island Passage
Caicos Passage
San Salvador I.
Conception I.
Rum Cay
Long I.
Clarence Town
Crooked I. Passage
Samana Cay
Crooked I.
Plana Cays
Albert Town
Snug Corner
Mayaguana I.
Acklins I.
Mira por vos Cay
Hogsty Reef
Little Inagua I.
Lake Rosa
Great Inagua I.
Matthew Town
Baracoa
Maisí
Paso de los Vientos (Windward Passage)
Î. de la Tortue
Cap-Haïtien
Monte Cristi
LA ISABELA
Santiago de los Caballeros
San Francisco de Macorís
Puerto Plata
Port-de-Paix
Fort Liberté
Gonaïves
Hinche
St-Marc
HAITI
PORT-AU-PRINCE
Jérémie
Î. de la Gonâve
Massif de la Hotte
Les Cayes
Aquin
Petit Goâve
Jacmel
Î. à Vache
Pointe-à-Gravois
DOMINICAN REP.
La Vega
Cord. Central
3175
San Juan
L. Enriquillo
Barahona
Pedernales
Azua de Compostela
Bani
San Cristóbal
SANTO DOMINGO
San Pedro de Macorís
Nagua
Samana
Sánchez
Sabana de la Mar
Hato Mayor
Higüey
La Romana
C. Engaño
B. de Yuma
I. Saona
Canal de la Mona
Isla Mona (U.S.A.)
I. Beata
C. Beata
Hispaniola
Aguadilla
Arecibo
Bayamón
SAN JUAN
Carolina
Mayagüez
Ponce
1338
Guayama
Fajardo
Caguas
PUERTO RICO (U.S.A.)
St. Thomas
Tortola
Virgin Gorda
Road Town
Charlotte Amalie
Virgin Is. (U.S.A.)
Anegada
Virgin Is. (U.K.)
Anegada Passage
Sombrero (U.K.)
Christiansted
Frederiksted
St. Croix
Anguilla (U.K.)
St.-Martin (Fr.)
St.-Barthélemy (Fr.)
St. Maarten (Neth.)
Saba (Neth.)
St. Eustatius (Neth.)
Basseterre
Nevis
ST. KITTS & NEVIS
Barbuda
ANTIGUA & BARBUDA
St. John's
Antigua
Redonda
Montserrat (U.K.)
Soufrière Hills
Guadeloupe Passage
Leeward Islands
Lesser Antilles
Ste.-Rose
Le Moule
La Désirade
GUADELOUPE (Fr.)
Pointe-à-Pitre
Marie-Galante (Fr.)
Grand-Bourg
Basse-Terre
I. des Saintes (Fr.)
Dominica Passage
Portsmouth
DOMINICA
Roseau
I. de Aves (Venezuela)
Martinique Passage
Mt. Pelée 1397
Ste.-Marie
Le François
Fort-de-France
Rivière-Pilote
MARTINIQUE (Fr.)
St. Lucia Channel
Castries
Soufrière
ST. LUCIA
St. Vincent Passage
La Soufrière 1234
ST. VINCENT
Speightstown
Bridgetown
BARBADOS
Kingstown
& THE GRENADINES
Grenadines
Hillsborough
St. George's
GRENADA
Windward Islands
Antilles
CARIBBEAN SEA
Lesser Antilles
Aruba (Neth.)
Oranjestad
Curaçao
Willemstad
Bonaire
NETH. ANTILLES
Pta. Gallinas
C. San Román
Pen. de la Guajira
Pta. Espada
Pen. de Paraguaná
Punto Fijo
Puerto Cumarebo
Punta Cardón
Is. Las Aves (Ven.)
Is. Los Roques (Ven.)
I. Orchila (Ven.)
I. Blanquilla (Ven.)
Is. Los Hermanos (Ven.)
Is. Los Testigos (Ven.)
Tobago
Scarborough
Dragon's Mouth
Port of Spain
Galera Point
Trinidad
Arima
Rio Claro
G. de Paria
San Fernando
TRINIDAD & TOBAGO
Serpent's Mouth
SANTA MARTA
Riohacha
Uribia
GUAJIRA
Golfo de Venezuela
Ciénaga
Sierra Nevada de Santa Marta 5800
Soledad
Sabanalarga
Fundación
Valledupar
Calamar
MAGDALENA
Plato
Zambrano
Agustín Codazzi
CÉSAR
Corozal
Mompós
Magangué
Sahagún
El Banco
Majagual
Ayapel
BOLÍVAR
Simití
Caucasia
San Rafael
MARACAIBO
Altagracia
La Concepción
Santa Rita
Cabimas
Villa del Rosario
Ciudad Ojeda
Machiques
Lago de Maracaibo
ZULIA
Sierra de Perijá
Mene Grande
TRUJILLO
Betijoque
Valera
Trujillo
San Carlos del Zulia
Encontrados
NORTE DE SANTANDER
Ocaña
Cúcuta
TÁCHIRA
MÉRIDA
Mérida
Cord. de Mérida
Santa Bárbara
FALCÓN
Coro
La Vela de Coro
Mene de Mauroa
Baragua
Carora
LARA
BARQUISIMETO
Tocuyo
El Tocuyo
Acarigua
PORTUGUESA
Guanare
Barinas
BARINAS
Ciudad Bolivia
Libertad
Bruzual
Puerto de Nutrias
Tucacas
Puerto Cabello
San Felipe
YARACUY
CARABOBO
Valencia
Yaritagua
Los Morros
San Carlos
COJEDES
El Baúl
Maracay
Maiquetía
La Guaira
CARACAS
DISTRITO FEDERAL
Guatire
ARAGUA
MIRANDA
Los Teques
Villa de Cura
San Juan de los Morros
El Sombrero
Calabozo
GUÁRICO
Valle de la Pascua
Santa María de Ipire
San Fernando de Apure
Apure
Achaguas
Caicara
Orinoco
C. Codera
Higuerote
Río Chico
Ocumare del Tuy
Altagracia de Orituco
I. La Tortuga (Ven.)
I. de Margarita
La Asunción
Porlamar
NUEVA ESPARTA
Cumaná
Carúpano
Río Caribe
Pen. de Paria
Güiria
Cariaco
SUCRE
Puerto La Cruz
Barcelona
Caripito
Caicara
Maturín
MONAGAS
Aragua de Barcelona
Anaco
Cantaura
Unare
El Tigre
Tigre
Pariaguán
ANZOÁTEGUI
Soledad
Manapire
DELTA AMACURO
Tucupita
Los Barrancos
Ciudad Guayana
Sierra Imataca
El Pao
Upata
Ciudad Bolívar
Embalse de Guri
Caroní
Guasipati
El Callao
Tumeremo
Mapire
VENEZUELA
West from Greenwich
COPYRIGHT GEORGE PHILIP LTD

Yucatán Peninsula
Isthmus of Tehuantepec
Guatemala Trench
G. de Honduras
Coco
L. Nicaragua
C. Gracias a Dios

C u b a

G r e a t e r A n t i l l e s

Turks & Caicos Is.
Hispaniola
9200
Puerto Rico
Jamaica

L e s s e r A n t i l l e s

Guadeloupe
Dominica
Martinique
St. Lucia
St. Vincent
Barbados
Grenada
Tobago
Trinidad

C a r i b b e a n S e a

I. Margarita

Panama Canal
G. of Darién
C. de la Aguja
Sierra Nevada de Santa Marta
5800
L. Maracaibo
Cord. de Mérida
Cordillera Occidental
Cordillera Central
Cordillera Oriental
C. de San Francisco

L l a n o s
Orinoco
Meta

G u i a n a H i g h l a n d s
Mt. Roraima 2810
Sierra Pacaraima
Serra Tumucumaque
Canaima
Serra

C. Orange

Gulf of Panamá
Gulf of Guayaquil
Cotopaxi 5897
Chimborazo 6267
Galapagos Is.

Guaviare
Caquetá
Negro
Branco
Essequibo

Equator

Pta. Pariñas
Pta. Negra
Marañón
Napo
Putumayo
Japurá
Amazon
Amazon
Marajó I.

S e l v a s

Huascarán 6768
Ucayali
Juruá
Purus
Madeira
Tapajós
Xingu
Tocantins
Parnaíba
C. de São Roque

Plat. of Borborema

Madre de Dios
Javari
Purus
Rooseveld
Aripuanã
Tapajós
Teles Pires
Araguaia
São Francisco

Chincha Alta
L. Titicaca
Nevada Ancohuma 6580
Bolivian Plateau
Guaporé
Mamoré
Plateau of Mato Grosso

B r a z i l i a n H i g h l a n d s

PACIFIC

L. de Poopó

Abrolhos Bank

Tropic of Capricorn
San Félix
San Ambrosio

8050
Atacama Desert
Cerro Ojos del Salado 6863
Gran Chaco
Paraguay
Pilcomayo
Paraná
Iguaçu Falls
Serra da Mantiqueira 2890
Pico da Bandeira
C. Frio
Serra do Mar

OCEAN

Salinas Grandes
Salado
Entre Ríos
Uruguay
L. dos Patos

Arch. de Juan Fernández

Mt. Aconcagua 6960
Sierra de Córdoba
L. Mar Chiquita
Paraná
Río de la Plata

P a m p a s

SOUTH

ATLANTIC

OCEAN

Colorado
Bahía Blanca
Negro
G. San Matías
Valdés Peninsula
40

A n d e s

Chile Rise
Chiloé I.
Chonos Archipelago
Taitao Peninsula
Gulf of Penas
Wellington I.
Madre de Dios I.

P a t a g o n i a

Mte. San Valentín 4058
Chubut
G. San Jorge

Argentine Basin

6212

Magellan's Str.
Santa Inés I.
Canal Cockburn
Canal Beagle
C. Horn
Tierra del Fuego
Staten I.

Falkland Is.
West Falkland
East Falkland

South Georgia

West from Greenwich

ft m
12000 4000
9000 3000
6000 2000
3000 1000
1500 500
600 200
0 0
200 600
1000 3000
2000 6000
4000 12000
6000 18000
8000 24000
m ft

Projection: Lambert's Azimuthal Equal Area

100 0 200 400 600 800 1000 1200 1400 km
100 0 200 400 600 800 1000 miles

100 0 200 400 600 800 1000 1200 1400 km
100 0 200 400 600 800 1000 miles

A

Havana BAHAMAS
C U B A
Turks & Caicos Is. (U.K.)

NORTH

Tropic of Cancer

A

Virgin Is. (U.K.)

HAITI DOMINICAN REP.
San Juan
ATLANTIC
JAMAICA Kingston
Port-au-Prince
PUERTO RICO (U.S.A.)
ST. KITTS & NEVIS
Basse-Terre
DOMINICA
Fort-de-France
ANTIGUA & BARBUDA
GUADELOUPE (Fr.)
MARTINIQUE (Fr.)
Castries ST. LUCIA
ST. VINCENT
Kingstown
BARBADOS
Bridgetown
GRENADA St. George's

B

MEXICO
BELIZE
GUATEMALA HONDURAS
Guatemala Tegucigalpa
San Salvador
EL SALVADOR NICARAGUA
Managua
COSTA San José
RICA
Panamá
Caribbean Sea
Barranquilla
Aruba Curaçao
Maracaibo
Cartagena
G. of Darién
Caracas
Barquisimeto Valencia
Port of Spain TRINIDAD & TOBAGO

OCEAN

B

C

Medellín
Cúcuta San Cristóbal
Bucaramanga
Bogotá
Cali
Magdalena
Orinoco
Ciudad Guayana
VENEZUELA
GUYANA
Georgetown
Paramaribo
SURINAM
Cayenne
C. Orange
FRENCH GUIANA
COLOMBIA
RORAIMA
Esequibo
Branco
AMAPÁ

C

Galapagos Is. (Ecuador)
Quito
ECUADOR
Guayaquil
G. of Guayaquil
Napo
Putumayo
Japurá
Equator
Amazon
Marajó I.
Belém

0

0

D

Iquitos
Marañón
Ucayali
AMAZONAS
Juruá
Purus
Madeira
Manaus
Santarém
Tapajós
PARÁ
Xingu
Tocantins
São Luís
MARANHÃO
Teresina
Fortaleza
C. de São Roque
CEARÁ
RIO G. DO NORTE
Natal

D

Chiclayo
Trujillo
Chimbote
ACRE
Purus
Pôrto Velho
RONDÔNIA
Madre de Dios
B R A Z I L
PIAUÍ
Parnaíba
Campina Grande
PARAÍBA
PERNAMBUCO
Recife
ALAGOAS
Maceió

PERU
Callao LIMA
Cuzco
Mamoré
MATO GROSSO
TOCANTINS
GOIÁS
Brasília
BAHÍA
SERGIPE
Aracaju
Salvador

E

PACIFIC
L. Titicaca
Arequipa
La Paz
BOLIVIA
Cochabamba
Santa Cruz
Sucre
Cuiabá
DIS. FED.
Goiânia
São Francisco
MINAS GERAIS

E

Iquique
MATO GROSSO DO SUL
PARAGUAY
Paraguay
Pilcomayo
Asunción
Paraná
SÃO PAULO
Ribeirão Prêto
Belo Horizonte
Juiz de Fora
ESPÍRITO SANTO
Vitória
R. DE J.
Campos

Antofagasta
Salta
San Miguel de Tucumán
Salado
Resistencia
Corrientes
PARANÁ
SÃO PAULO
Campinas
Niterói
RIO DE JANEIRO

Tropic of Capricorn

F

San Félix (Chile)
San Ambrosio (Chile)
A R G E N T I N A
Córdoba
San Juan
Santa Fe
Paraná
Rosario
URUGUAY
SANTA CATARINA
Uruguay
RIO GRANDE DO SUL
Pôrto Alegre
Curitiba

F

OCEAN

G

Arch. de Juan Fernández (Chile)
Viña del Mar
Valparaíso
SANTIAGO
Talca
C H I L E
Mendoza
BUENOS AIRES
Montevideo
La Plata
Rio de la Plata
Mar del Plata
Concepción
Bahía Blanca
Colorado
SOUTH

G

Valdivia
Negro
Viedma

ATLANTIC

H

Puerto Montt
Chubut
Comodoro Rivadavia
Gulf of San Jorge
OCEAN

H

Gulf of Penas
West Falkland
FALKLAND IS. (U.K.)
Stanley
East Falkland
Magellan's Str.
Punta Arenas
Tierra del Fuego
South Georgia (U.K.)

Projection: Lambert's Azimuthal Equal Area
C. Horn
West from Greenwich
CARTOGRAPHY BY PHILIP'S.

LIMA Capital Cities

A

B

C

D

E

F

G

H

8　　9　　10　　11　　12　　13

A T L A N T I C

O C E A N

São Paulo
(Braz.)

Equator

Fernando de Noronha
(Braz.)

Rocas

FRENCH
GUIANA

AMAPÁ

Macapá

BELÉM

São Luís

FORTALEZA

Natal

João Pessoa
Olinda
RECIFE
Jaboatão

Maceió

Aracaju

SALVADOR

BRASÍLIA

Goiânia

BELO HORIZONTE

Vitória
Vila Velha

Trindade
(Braz.)

RIO DE JANEIRO

6059 ▾

COPYRIGHT GEORGE PHILIP LTD.

55　　8　　50　　9　　45　　10　　40　　11　　35　　12　　30　　13

100 0 200 400 600 800 1000 1200 1400 km
100 0 200 400 600 800 1000 miles
Tropic of Cancer
Havana
CUBA
BAHAMAS
Turks & Caicos Is. (U.K.)
MEXICO
BELIZE
GUATEMALA
Guatemala
HONDURAS
Tegucigalpa
San Salvador
EL SALVADOR
NICARAGUA
Managua
COSTA RICA
San José
Panamá
PANAMA
JAMAICA
Kingston
HAITI
Port-au-Prince
DOMINICAN REP.
San Juan
PUERTO RICO (U.S.A.)
Virgin Is. (U.K.)
ST. KITTS & NEVIS
Basse-Terre
ANTIGUA & BARBUDA
GUADELOUPE (Fr.)
DOMINICA
Fort-de-France
MARTINIQUE (Fr.)
Castries
ST. LUCIA
ST. VINCENT
Kingstown
BARBADOS
Bridgetown
GRENADA
St. George's
Port of Spain
TRINIDAD & TOBAGO
Caribbean Sea
Aruba
Curaçao
C. de la Aguja
Barranquilla
Cartagena
Maracaibo
Barquisimeto
Caracas
Valencia
G. of Darién
Cúcuta
San Cristóbal
Orinoco
Ciudad Guayana
VENEZUELA
Bucaramanga
Medellín
Magdalena
Bogotá
Cali
Gulf of Panamá
COLOMBIA
Georgetown
GUYANA
Paramaribo
SURINAM
Cayenne
C. Orange
FRENCH GUIANA
Essequibo
RORAIMA
Branco
AMAPÁ
NORTH ATLANTIC OCEAN
Equator
Galapagos Is. (Ecuador)
Quito
ECUADOR
Guayaquil
G. of Guayaquil
Putumayo
Napo
Japurá
Marajó I.
Belém
Amazon
Manaus
Santarém
São Luís
Iquitos
Marañón
AMAZONAS
PARÁ
Tapajós
Xingu
Tocantins
Fortaleza
MARANHÃO
Teresina
C. de São Roque
CEARÁ
RIO G. DO NORTE
Natal
Juruá
Purus
Madeira
Parnaíba
PIAUÍ
PARAÍBA
Campina Grande
Chiclayo
Ucayali
Trujillo
ACRE
Pôrto Velho
Araguaia
PERNAMBUCO
Recife
Chimbote
ALAGOAS
Maceió
PERU
RONDÔNIA
TOCANTINS
SERGIPE
Aracaju
Callao
LIMA
Madre de Dios
BRAZIL
Cuzco
Mamoré
MATO GROSSO
BAHÍA
Salvador
L. Titicaca
GOIÁS
São Francisco
Cuiabá
Arequipa
La Paz
BOLIVIA
DIS. FED.
Brasília
Goiânia
PACIFIC OCEAN
Cochabamba
Santa Cruz
MINAS GERAIS
Paraguay
Sucre
MATO GROSSO DO SUL
Belo Horizonte
ESPÍRITO SANTO
Iquique
Ribeirão Prêto
Juiz de Fora
Vitória
Paraná
SÃO PAULO
Campos
PARAGUAY
Campinas
R. DE J.
Antofagasta
Pilcomayo
SÃO PAULO
Niterói
RIO DE JANEIRO
Salta
Asunción
PARANÁ
Tropic of Capricorn
Curitiba
San Félix (Chile)
San Ambrosio (Chile)
San Miguel de Tucumán
Resistencia
Corrientes
SANTA CATARINA
Uruguay
Salado
RIO GRANDE DO SUL
Pôrto Alegre
Córdoba
Santa Fe
Paraná
San Juan
Pelotas
Viña del Mar
Valparaíso
SANTIAGO
Mendoza
Rosario
URUGUAY
Arch. de Juan Fernández (Chile)
BUENOS AIRES
Montevideo
La Plata
Río de la Plata
Talca
CHILE
ARGENTINA
Concepción
Bahía Blanca
Mar del Plata
Colorado
SOUTH ATLANTIC OCEAN
Valdivia
Negro
Viedma
Puerto Montt
Chubut
Comodoro Rivadavia
Gulf of San Jorge
Gulf of Penas
West Falkland
FALKLAND IS. (U.K.)
Stanley
East Falkland
Magellan's Str.
Punta Arenas
Tierra del Fuego
C. Horn
South Georgia (U.K.)
Projection: Lambert's Azimuthal Equal Area
LIMA Capital Cities
West from Greenwich
CARTOGRAPHY BY PHILIP'S.

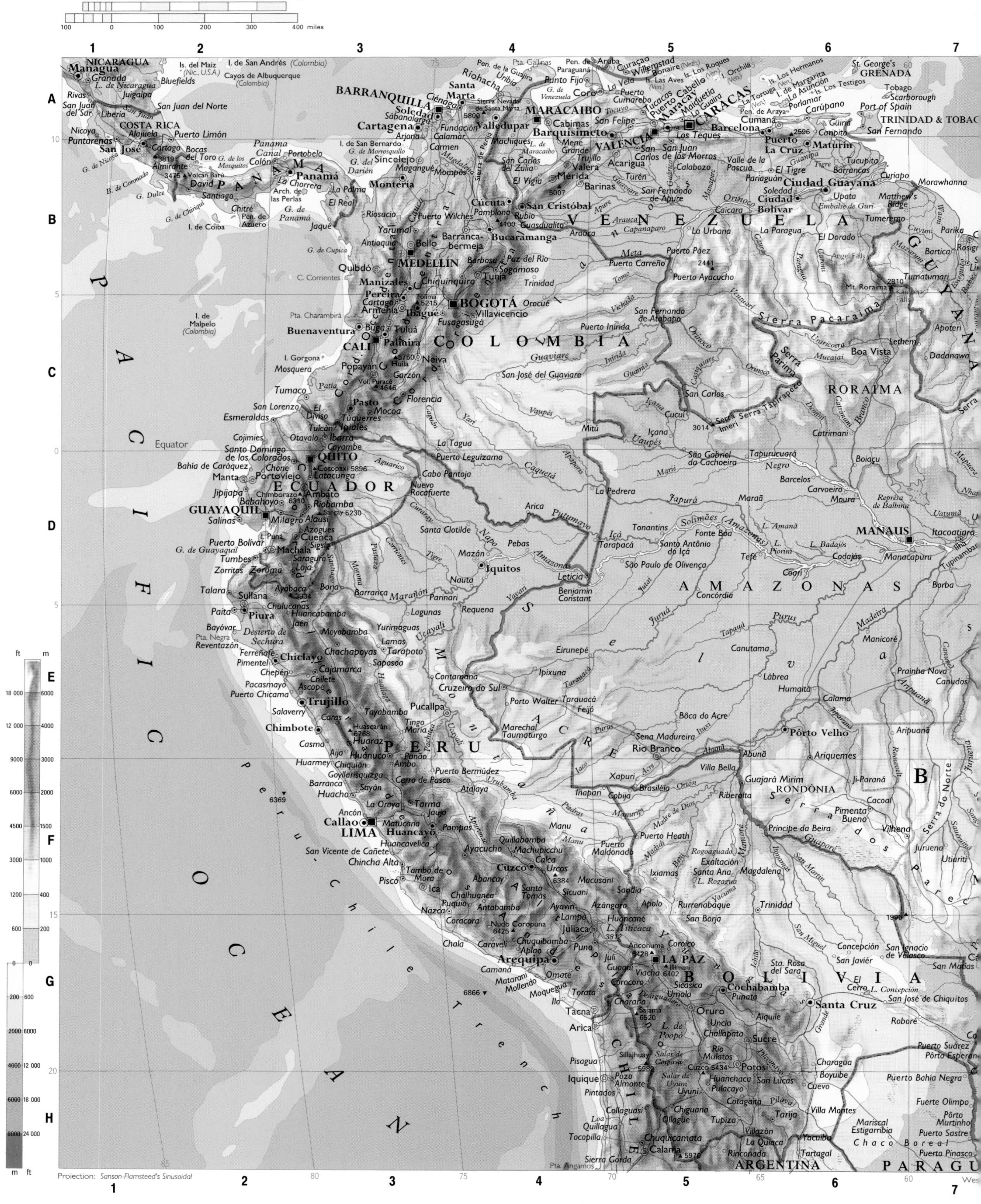

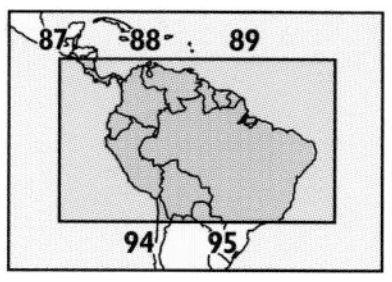

8 9 10 11 12 13

A B C D E F G H

ATLANTIC

OCEAN

FRENCH GUIANA
AMAPÁ
PARÁ
MARANHÃO
PIAUÍ
CEARÁ
RIO GRANDE DO NORTE
PARAÍBA
PERNAMBUCO
ALAGOAS
SERGIPE
BAHIA
TOCANTINS
GOIÁS
DIST. FED.
MINAS GERAIS
SÃO PAULO
RIO DE JANEIRO
ESPÍRITO SANTO
BRAZIL
MATO GROSSO
MATO GROSSO DO SUL

Equator

Paramaribo
Nieuw Amsterdam
Moengo
St-Laurent
Albina
Iracoubo
Sinnamary
Kourou
Cayenne
Kaw
C. Orange
St-Georges
Oiapoque
Camopi
Amapá
I. de Maracá
Serra do Navio
Macapá
Mazagão
I. Caviana
I. Mexiana
C. Maguarinho
Chaves
Soure
I. de Marajó
Afuá
Curuçá
Salinópolis
Vigia
Bragança
BELÉM
Castanhal
Abaetetuba
Cametá
Breves
Gurupá
Almeirim
Prainha
Monte Alegre
Óbidos
Alenquer
Santarém
Belterra
Aveiro
Altamira
Brasília Legal
Itaituba
Tucuruí
Baião
Viseu
Turiaçu
Gurupi
Gurupu
B. de São Marcos
Alcântara
São Luís
Pinheiro
Rosário
Itapecuru-Mirim
Barreirinhas
Tutóia
Luís Correia
Camocim
Parnaíba
Granja
Itapipoca
Caucaia
FORTALEZA
Cascavel
Maranguape
Sobral
Baturité
Aracati
Russas
Quixadá
Ipu
Crateús
Senador Pompeu
Iguatu
Mossoró
Macau
Areia Branca
Ceará Mirim
C. de São Roque
Natal
Caraúbas
Caicó
Currais Novos
Canguaretama
Mamanguape
Cabedelo
João Pessoa
Campina Grande
Patos
Sousa
Cajàzeiras
Crato
Juàzeiro do Norte
Salgueiro
Caruaru
Olinda
RECIFE
Jaboatão
Vitória de Santo Antão
Palmares
Garanhuns
Arapiraca
Maceió
Penedo
Propriá
Aracaju
São Cristóvão
Estância
Santa Inês
Bacabal
Codó
Caxias
Pedreiras
Coroatá
Brejo
Piripiri
Campo Maior
Teresina
Açailândia
Imperatriz
Marabá
Carajás
São João do Araguaia
Tocantinópolis
Pôrto Franco
Estreito
Carolina
Barra do Corda
Grajaú
Colinas
Floriano
Amarante
Valença do Piauí
Oeiras
Picos
Nova Iorque
Uruçuí
Loreto
Riachão
Araguaína
Conceição do Araguaia
Araguacema
Pedro Afonso
Santa Filomena
São João do Piauí
Petrolina
Juàzeiro
Paulo Afonso
Represa de Sobradinho
Senhor-do-Bonfim
Jacobina
Xique-Xique
Barra
Parnaguá
Palmas
Pôrto Nacional
Peixe
Gurupi
Paranã
Barreiras
Ibotirama
Bom Jesus da Lapa
Santa Maria da Vitória
Feira de Santana
Alagoinhas
Cachoeira
Santo Amaro
SALVADOR
Valença
Jequié
Vitória da Conquista
Itabuna
Ilhéus
Canavieiras
Belmonte
Pôrto Seguro
Itamaraju
Caravelas
Teófilo Otoni
Governador Valadares
Montes Claros
Januária
Formosa
BRASÍLIA
Taguatinga
Luziânia
Anápolis
Goiânia
Goiás
Barra do Garças
Rondonópolis
Campo Grande
Uberlândia
Uberaba
Araguari
Patos de Minas
Diamantina
Ipatinga
Colatina
Linhares
São Mateus
BELO HORIZONTE
Divinópolis
Sete Lagoas
Vitória
Vila Velha
Cariacica
Cachoeiro de Itapemirim
Campos
Juiz de Fora
Barbacena
Petrópolis
Nova Friburgo
Niterói
Volta Redonda
RIO DE JANEIRO
Cabo Frio
Ribeirão Prêto
Franca
São José do Rio Prêto
Araçatuba
Presidente Prudente
Marília
Bauru
Araraquara
São Carlos
Piracicaba
Limeira
Campinas
Poços de Caldas
Dourados
Ponta Porã
Rocas
Fernando de Noronha (Braz.)
São Paulo (Braz.)
Trindade (Braz.)

92 93
96

BELO HORIZONTE

Nova Lima
Itabirito

Vitória
Itaquari
Vila Velha
Guarapari

O GROSSO
DO SUL
Três Lagoas
Andradina
Mirassol
São
do Rio Prêto
Olímpia
Batatais
Passos
Oliveira
Conselheiro
Lafaiete
Ouro
Prêto
Ponte Nova
Carangola
Castelo
Cachoeiro
de Itapemirim

Sidrolândia
Nioaque
Xavantina
Mirandópolis
Araçatuba
Catanduva
Bebedouro
Ribeirão
São Sebastião
do Paraíso
Campo Belo
Lavras
Barbacena
Cataguases
Itaperuna

Lopes
Iguna
Maracaju
Nova Alvorada
do Sul
Panorama
Birigui
Taquaritinga
Jaboticabal Prêto
Mococa
Guaxupé
Três
Pontas
São João
del Rei
Ubá
Muriaé
Alegre

Dourados
Nova
Andradina
Adamantina
S Ã O
P A U L O
Penápolis
Novo
Horizonte
Casa
Branca
Alfenas
Varginha
Santos
Dumont
Leopoldina
Cambuí
Guarus

Ponta Porã
Presidente
Epitácio
Santo
Anastácio
Tupã
Lins
Araraquara
São João
da Boa Vista
Poços de
Caldas
Pouso
Alegre
Juiz de Fora
Três
Rios
Paraíba do Sul
CAMPOS
Cabo de
São Tomé

Pedro Juan Caballero
Euclides da
Cunha Paulista
Presidente
Prudente
Martinópolis
Marília
Garça
Bauru
Bariri
Jaú
São
Carlos
Araras
Pinhal
Ouro Fino
Itajubá
Volta
Barra do Pirai
Nova Friburgo
Macaé

Naviraí
Rosana
Paraguaçu
Paulista
Rancharia
Assis
Santa Cruz
do Rio Pardo
Rio Claro
Limeira
Americana
Mogi-Mirim
Serra
Cruzeiro
Redonda
Barra
Mansa
Petrópolis
RIO DE JANEIRO

Centenário do Sul
Paranavaí
Nova
Esperança
Rolândia
Cambará
Ourinhos
Piracicaba
CAMPINAS
Bragança
Paulista
Guaratinguetá
Angra dos
Reis
NOVA IGUAÇU
DUQUE DE CAXIAS
SÃO GONÇALO
Cabo Frio

Amambaí
Ivaí
Maringá
Apucarana
Arapongas
Cornélio
Procópio
Avaré
Botucatu
Tatui
Itu
Jundiaí
Taubaté
Ilha Grande
Bahia da Ilha Grande
NITERÓI
La. de Araruama

Mundo Novo
Salto do Guairá
Umuarama
Cianorte
Mandaguari
Joaquim
Távora
Itapetininga
SÃO PAULO
Sorocaba
São Bernardo
do Campo
Jacareí
Moji das Cruzes
Pta. de Juatinga
RIO DE JANEIRO
Tropic of Capricorn

CANINDEY
Curuguaty
Ido
Guaíra
Goio-Erê
Campo
Mourão
P A R A N Á
Ibaití
Itaporanga
Itararé
Itapeva
Paranapiacaba
SANTO ANDRÉ
São Vicente
Guarujá
Ilha de São Sebastião

ALTO
Hernandarias
Oviedo
Ciudad
del Este
Foz do Iguaçu
Cat. del
Iguaçu
Cruzeiro
do Oeste
Cascavel
Sa. das Araras
Cândido de Abreu
Pitanga
B R A Z I L
Tibagi
Castro
Jaguariaíva
Apiaí
Juquiá
Registro
Itanhaém
Pta. de Boi
Ilha de São Sebastião

PARANÁ
Irala
Medianeira
Guarapuava
Prudentópolis
1889
Ponta
Grossa
Palmeira
CURITIBA
Iguape
Ilha Comprida

PUA
ná
Arrigos
ncarnación
Eldorado
Represa de Toledo
Itaipú
Bernardo
de Irigoyen
Francisco
Beltrão
Laranjeiras
do Sul
União da
Vitória
São Mateus
do Sul
Irati
Lapa
Antonina
Paranaguá
Matinhos
Guaratuba
Ilha do Cardoso

San
Pedro
Pato Branco
Sa. da Fartura
Palmas
Pôrto União
Rio Negro
Mafra
São Francisco do Sul
Joinville

MISIONES
Leandro N. Alem
Uruguai
Corpus
Cleveländia
Pelotas
Xanxerê
Caçador
1340
Blumenau
Itajaí

Obera
Candelaria
Monteagudo
Frederico
Westphalen
Chapecó
Joaçaba
SANTA CATARINA
Santa Cecília
Brusque

Apóstoles
Liui
Erechim
Campos
Novos
Curitibanos
Rio do Sul
São
José
Ilha de Santa Catarina
Florianópolis

Santo Angelo
São Luís
Gonzaga
Palmeira
das Missões
Carazinho
Passo
Fundo
Lajes
1808

Cruz Alta
Ijuí
Lagoa
Vermelha
São
Joaquim
Tubarão
Laguna
Cabo Santa Marta Grande

Borja
Santa Rosa
Guaporé
Vacaria
Criciúma
Araranguá

Santiago
RIO GRANDE
Bento Gonçalves
Caxias do Sul
Torres

Santa Maria
Santa Cruz
do Sul
Montenegro
Nôvo Hamburgo
Taquara

alegrete
o do Sul
Cachoeira do Sul
Rio Pardo
Canoas
Leopoldo
Osorio

D O S U L
Santana do
Livramento
São
Gabriel
Caçapava
do Sul
Sa.
Encantadas
Viamão
PÔRTO ALEGRE

Rivera
Santana
Dom Pedrito
Camaquã
Tapes

JAY
uarembó
Bagé
Sa. do Canguçu
Camaquã
Patos
Mostardas

Fraile
Muerto
Pinheiro
Machado
Pelotas
São Lourenço
do Sul
Canguçu

Melo
Rio Branco
Jaguarão
Lagoa dos
Rio Grande
São José
do Norte

Gregorio
Blanquillo
Cerro
Chato
Vergara
Lagoa
Mirim

Sarandi del Yi
Treinta y Tres
Santa Vitória do Palmar

José Batlle
y Ordóñez
Lascano
Chuy
Lagoa Mangueira

Aigua
Castillos

nes
dras
Minas
Rocha

San Carlos

TEVIDEO
Maldonado

A T L A N T I C

O C E A N

5304
▼

25

A

B

30

C

35

D

West from Greenwich
55
50
6
45
7
40
COPYRIGHT GEORGE PHILIP LTD

5
6
7

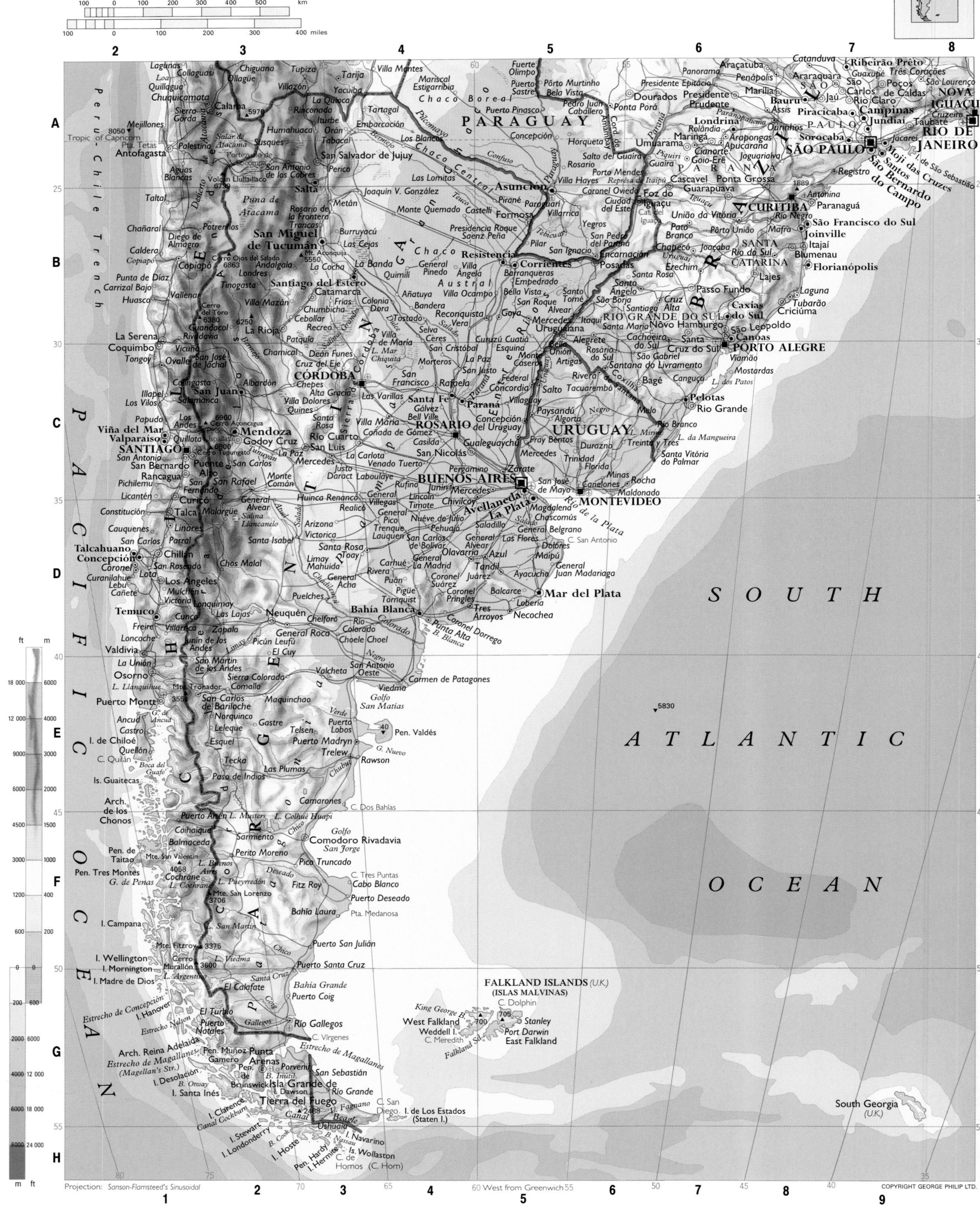

INDEX

The index contains the names of all the principal places and features shown on the World Maps. Each name is followed by an additional entry in italics giving the country or region within which it is located. The alphabetical order of names composed of two or more words is governed primarily by the first word and then by the second. This is an example of the rule:

Mīr Kūh, *Iran* **45 E8** 26 22N 58 55 E
Mīr Shahdād, *Iran* **45 E8** 26 15N 58 29 E
Mira, *Italy* **20 B5** 45 26N 12 8 E
Mira por vos Cay, *Bahamas* . **89 B5** 22 9N 74 30 W
Miraj, *India* **40 L9** 16 50N 74 45 E

Physical features composed of a proper name (Erie) and a description (Lake) are positioned alphabetically by the proper name. The description is positioned after the proper name and is usually abbreviated:

Erie, L., *N. Amer.* **78 D4** 42 15N 81 0 W

Where a description forms part of a settlement or administrative name however, it is always written in full and put in its true alphabetic position:

Mount Morris, *U.S.A.* **78 D7** 42 44N 77 52 W

Names beginning with M' and Mc are indexed as if they were spelled Mac. Names beginning St. are alphabetised under Saint, but Sankt, Sint, Sant', Santa and San are all spelt in full and are alphabetised accordingly. If the same place name occurs two or more times in the index and all are in the same country, each is followed by the name of the administrative subdivision in which it is located. The names are placed in the alphabetical order of the subdivisions. For example:

Jackson, *Ky., U.S.A.* **76 G4** 37 33N 83 23 W
Jackson, *Mich., U.S.A.* **76 D3** 42 15N 84 24 W
Jackson, *Minn., U.S.A.* **80 D7** 43 37N 95 1 W

The number in bold type which follows each name in the index refers to the number of the map page where that feature or place will be found. This is usually the largest scale at which the place or feature appears.

The letter and figure which are in bold type immediately after the page number give the grid square on the map page, within which the feature is situated. The letter represents the latitude and the figure the longitude.

In some cases the feature itself may fall within the specified square, while the name is outside. This is usually the case only with features which are larger than a grid square.

For a more precise location the geographical coordinates which follow the letter/figure references give the latitude and the longitude of each place. The first set of figures represent the latitude which is the distance north or south of the Equator measured as an angle at the centre of the earth. The Equator is latitude 0°, the North Pole is 90°N, and the South Pole 90°S.

The second set of figures represent the longitude, which is the distance East or West of the prime meridian, which runs through Greenwich, England. Longitude is also measured as an angle at the centre of the earth and is given East or West of the prime meridian, from 0° to 180° in either direction.

The unit of measurement for latitude and longitude is the degree, which is subdivided into 60 minutes. Each index entry states the position of a place in degrees and minutes, a space being left between the degrees and the minutes.

The latitude is followed by N(orth) or S(outh) and the longitude by E(ast) or W(est).

Rivers are indexed to their mouths or confluences, and carry the symbol ➤ after their names. A solid square ■ follows the name of a country, while an open square □ refers to a first order administrative area.

Abbreviations used in the index

A.C.T. – Australian Capital Territory
Afghan. – Afghanistan
Ala. – Alabama
Alta. – Alberta
Amer. – America(n)
Arch. – Archipelago
Ariz. – Arizona
Ark. – Arkansas
Atl. Oc. – Atlantic Ocean
B. – Baie, Bahía, Bay, Bucht, Bugt
B.C. – British Columbia
Bangla. – Bangladesh
Barr. – Barrage
Bos.-H. – Bosnia-Herzegovina
C. – Cabo, Cap, Cape, Coast
C.A.R. – Central African Republic
C. Prov. – Cape Province
Calif. – California
Cent. – Central
Chan. – Channel
Colo. – Colorado
Conn. – Connecticut
Cord. – Cordillera
Cr. – Creek
Czech. – Czech Republic
D.C. – District of Columbia
Del. – Delaware
Dep. – Dependency
Des. – Desert
Dist. – District
Dj. – Djebel
Domin. – Dominica
Dom. Rep. – Dominican Republic
E. – East

E. Salv. – El Salvador
Eq. Guin. – Equatorial Guinea
Fla. – Florida
Falk. Is. – Falkland Is.
G. – Golfe, Golfo, Gulf, Guba, Gebel
Ga. – Georgia
Gt. – Great, Greater
Guinea-Biss. – Guinea-Bissau
H.K. – Hong Kong
H.P. – Himachal Pradesh
Hants. – Hampshire
Harb. – Harbor, Harbour
Hd. – Head
Hts. – Heights
I.(s). – Île, Ilha, Insel, Isla, Island, Isle
Ill. – Illinois
Ind. – Indiana
Ind. Oc. – Indian Ocean
Ivory C. – Ivory Coast
J. – Jabal, Jebel, Jazira
Junc. – Junction
K. – Kap, Kapp
Kans. – Kansas
Kep. – Kepulauan
Ky. – Kentucky
L. – Lac, Lacul, Lago, Lagoa, Lake, Limni, Loch, Lough
La. – Louisiana
Liech. – Liechtenstein
Lux. – Luxembourg
Mad. P. – Madhya Pradesh
Madag. – Madagascar
Man. – Manitoba
Mass. – Massachusetts

Md. – Maryland
Me. – Maine
Medit. S. – Mediterranean Sea
Mich. – Michigan
Minn. – Minnesota
Miss. – Mississippi
Mo. – Missouri
Mont. – Montana
Mozam. – Mozambique
Mt.(e) – Mont, Monte, Monti, Montaña, Mountain
N. – Nord, Norte, North, Northern, Nouveau
N.B. – New Brunswick
N.C. – North Carolina
N. Cal. – New Caledonia
N. Dak. – North Dakota
N.H. – New Hampshire
N.I. – North Island
N.J. – New Jersey
N. Mex. – New Mexico
N.S. – Nova Scotia
N.S.W. – New South Wales
N.W.T. – North West Territory
N.Y. – New York
N.Z. – New Zealand
Nebr. – Nebraska
Neths. – Netherlands
Nev. – Nevada
Nfld. – Newfoundland
Nic. – Nicaragua
O. – Oued, Ouadi
Occ. – Occidentale
Okla. – Oklahoma
Ont. – Ontario
Or. – Orientale

Oreg. – Oregon
Os. – Ostrov
Oz. – Ozero
P. – Pass, Passo, Pasul, Pulau
P.E.I. – Prince Edward Island
Pa. – Pennsylvania
Pac. Oc. – Pacific Ocean
Papua N.G. – Papua New Guinea
Pass. – Passage
Pen. – Peninsula, Péninsule
Phil. – Philippines
Pk. – Park, Peak
Plat. – Plateau
Prov. – Province, Provincial
Pt. – Point
Pta. – Ponta, Punta
Pte. – Pointe
Qué. – Québec
Queens. – Queensland
R. – Rio, River
R.I. – Rhode Island
Ra.(s). – Range(s)
Raj. – Rajasthan
Reg. – Region
Rep. – Republic
Res. – Reserve, Reservoir
S. – San, South, Sea
Si. Arabia – Saudi Arabia
S.C. – South Carolina
S. Dak. – South Dakota
S.I. – South Island
S. Leone – Sierra Leone
Sa. – Serra, Sierra
Sask. – Saskatchewan
Scot. – Scotland
Sd. – Sound

Sev. – Severnaya
Sib. – Siberia
Sprs. – Springs
St. – Saint
Sta. – Santa, Station
Ste. – Sainte
Sto. – Santo
Str. – Strait, Stretto
Switz. – Switzerland
Tas. – Tasmania
Tenn. – Tennessee
Tex. – Texas
Tg. – Tanjung
Trin. & Tob. – Trinidad & Tobago
U.A.E. – United Arab Emirates
U.K. – United Kingdom
U.S.A. – United States of America
Ut. P. – Uttar Pradesh
Va. – Virginia
Vdkhr. – Vodokhranilishche
Vf. – Vírful
Vic. – Victoria
Vol. – Volcano
Vt. – Vermont
W. – Wadi, West
W. Va. – West Virginia
Wash. – Washington
Wis. – Wisconsin
Wlkp. – Wielkopolski
Wyo. – Wyoming
Yorks. – Yorkshire
Yug. – Yugoslavia

A

A Coruña, Spain	19 A1	43 20N	8 25W
A Estrada, Spain	19 A1	42 43N	8 27W
A Fonsagrada, Spain	19 A2	43 8N	7 4W
Aachen, Germany	16 C4	50 45N	6 6 E
Aalborg = Ålborg, Denmark	9 H13	57 2N	9 54 E
Aalen, Germany	16 D6	48 51N	10 6 E
Aalst, Belgium	15 D4	50 56N	4 2 E
Aalten, Neths.	15 C6	51 56N	6 35 E
Aalter, Belgium	15 C3	51 5N	3 28 E
Äänekoski, Finland	9 E21	62 36N	25 44 E
Aarau, Switz.	18 C8	47 23N	8 4 E
Aare →, Switz.	18 C8	47 33N	8 14 E
Aarhus = Århus, Denmark	9 H14	56 8N	10 11 E
Aarschot, Belgium	15 D4	50 59N	4 49 E
Aba, Dem. Rep. of the Congo	54 B3	3 58N	30 17 E
Aba, Nigeria	50 G7	5 10N	7 19 E
Ābādān, Iran	45 D6	30 22N	48 20 E
Ābādeh, Iran	45 D7	31 8N	52 40 E
Abadla, Algeria	50 B5	31 2N	2 45W
Abaetetuba, Brazil	93 D9	1 40S	48 50W
Abagnar Qi, China	34 C9	43 52N 116	2 E
Abai, Paraguay	95 B4	25 58S	55 54W
Abakan, Russia	27 D10	53 40N	91 10 E
Abancay, Peru	92 F4	13 35S	72 55W
Abariringa, Kiribati	64 H10	2 50S 171 40W	
Abarqū, Iran	45 D7	31 10N	53 20 E
Abashiri, Japan	30 C12	44 0N 144 15 E	
Abashiri-Wan, Japan	30 C12	44 0N 144 30 E	
Abay, Kazakstan	26 E8	49 38N	72 53 E
Abaya, L., Ethiopia	46 F2	6 30N	37 50 E
Abaza, Russia	26 D10	52 39N	90 6 E
'Abbāsābād, Iran	45 C8	33 34N	58 23 E
Abbay = Nîl el Azraq →, Sudan	51 E12	15 38N	32 31 E
Abbaye, Pt., U.S.A.	76 B1	46 58N	88 8W
Abbé, L., Ethiopia	46 E3	11 8N	41 47 E
Abbeville, France	18 A4	50 6N	1 49 E
Abbeville, Ala., U.S.A.	77 K3	31 34N	85 15W
Abbeville, La., U.S.A.	81 L8	29 58N	92 8W
Abbeville, S.C., U.S.A.	77 H4	34 11N	82 23W
Abbot Ice Shelf, Antarctica	5 D16	73 0S	92 0W
Abbottabad, Pakistan	42 B5	34 10N	73 15 E
Abd al Kūrī, Ind. Oc.	46 E5	12 5N	52 20 E
Ābdar, Iran	45 D7	30 16N	55 19 E
'Abdolābād, Iran	45 C8	34 12N	56 30 E
Abdulpur, Bangla.	43 G13	24 15N	88 59 E
Abéché, Chad	51 F10	13 50N	20 35 E
Abengourou, Ivory C.	50 G5	6 42N	3 27W
Åbenrå, Denmark	9 J13	55 3N	9 25 E
Abeokuta, Nigeria	50 G6	7 3N	3 19 E
Aber, Uganda	54 B3	2 12N	32 25 E
Aberaeron, U.K.	11 E3	52 15N	4 15W
Aberayron = Aberaeron, U.K.	11 E3	52 15N	4 15W
Aberchirder, U.K.	12 D6	57 34N	2 37W
Abercorn = Mbala, Zambia	55 D3	8 46S	31 24 E
Abercorn, Australia	63 D5	25 12S 151 5 E	
Aberdare, U.K.	11 F4	51 43N	3 27W
Aberdare Ra., Kenya	54 C4	0 15S	36 50 E
Aberdeen, Australia	63 E5	32 9S 150 56 E	
Aberdeen, Canada	73 C7	52 20N 106	8W
Aberdeen, S. Africa	56 E3	32 28S	24 2 E
Aberdeen, U.K.	12 D6	57 9N	2 5W
Aberdeen, Ala., U.S.A.	77 J1	33 49N	88 33W
Aberdeen, Idaho, U.S.A.	82 E7	42 57N 112 50W	
Aberdeen, Md., U.S.A.	76 F7	39 31N	76 10W
Aberdeen, S. Dak., U.S.A.	80 C5	45 28N	98 29W
Aberdeen, Wash., U.S.A.	84 D3	46 59N 123 50W	
Aberdeen, City of □, U.K.	12 D6	57 10N	2 10W
Aberdeenshire □, U.K.	12 D6	57 17N	2 36W
Aberdovey = Aberdyfi, U.K.	11 E3	52 33N	4 3W
Aberdyfi, U.K.	11 E3	52 33N	4 3W
Aberfeldy, U.K.	12 E5	56 37N	3 51W
Abergavenny, U.K.	11 F4	51 49N	3 1W
Abergele, U.K.	10 D4	53 17N	3 35W
Abernathy, U.S.A.	81 J4	33 50N 101 51W	
Abert, L., U.S.A.	82 E3	42 38N 120 14W	
Aberystwyth, U.K.	11 E3	52 25N	4 5W
Abhā, Si. Arabia	46 D3	18 0N	42 34 E
Abhar, Iran	45 B6	36 9N	49 13 E
Abhayapuri, India	43 F14	26 24N	90 38 E
Abidjan, Ivory C.	50 G5	5 26N	3 58W
Abilene, Kans., U.S.A.	80 F6	38 55N	97 13W
Abilene, Tex., U.S.A.	81 J5	32 28N	99 43W
Abingdon, U.K.	11 F6	51 40N	1 17W
Abingdon, U.S.A.	77 G5	36 43N	81 59W
Abington Reef, Australia	62 B4	18 0S 149 35 E	
Abitau →, Canada	73 B7	59 53N 109	3W
Abitibi →, Canada	70 B3	51 3N	80 55W
Abitibi, L., Canada	70 C4	48 40N	79 40W
Abkhaz Republic = Abkhazia □, Georgia	25 F7	43 12N	41 5 E
Abkhazia □, Georgia	25 F7	43 12N	41 5 E
Abminga, Australia	63 D1	26 8S 134 51 E	
Åbo = Turku, Finland	9 F20	60 30N	22 19 E
Abohar, India	42 D6	30 10N	74 10 E
Abolo, Congo	52 D2	0 8N	14 16 E
Abomey, Benin	50 G6	7 10N	2 5 E
Abong-Mbang, Cameroon	52 D2	4 0N	13 8 E
Abou-Deïa, Chad	51 F9	11 20N	19 20 E
Aboyne, U.K.	12 D6	57 4N	2 47W
Abra Pampa, Argentina	94 A2	22 43S	65 42W
Abraham L., Canada	72 C5	52 15N 116 35W	
Abreojos, Pta., Mexico	86 B2	26 50N 113 40W	
Abrud, Romania	17 E12	46 19N	23 5 E
Absaroka Range, U.S.A.	82 D9	44 45N 109 50W	
Abu, India	42 G5	24 41N	72 50 E
Abu al Abyad, U.A.E.	45 E7	24 11N	53 50 E
Abū al Khaşīb, Iraq	45 D6	30 25N	48 0 E
Abū 'Alī, Si. Arabia	45 E6	27 20N	49 27 E
Abū 'Alī →, Lebanon	47 A4	34 25N	35 50 E
Abu Dhabi = Abū Ẓāby, U.A.E.	45 E7	24 28N	54 22 E
Abū Du'ān, Syria	44 B3	36 25N	38 15 E
Abū el Gairi, W. →, Egypt	47 F2	29 35N	33 30 E
Abu Ga'da, W. →, Egypt	47 F1	29 15N	32 53 E
Abū Ḥadrīyah, Si. Arabia	45 E6	27 20N	48 58 E
Abu Hamed, Sudan	51 E12	19 32N	33 13 E
Abū Kamāl, Syria	44 C4	34 30N	41 0 E
Abū Madd, Ra's, Si. Arabia	44 E3	24 50N	37 7 E
Abū Mūsā, U.A.E.	45 E7	25 52N	55 3 E
Abu Şafāt, W. →, Jordan	47 E5	30 24N	36 7 E

Abu Simbel, Egypt	51 D12	22 18N	31 40 E
Abū Şukhayr, Iraq	44 D5	31 54N	44 30 E
Abū Zabad, Sudan	51 F11	12 25N	29 10 E
Abū Ẓāby, U.A.E.	45 E7	24 28N	54 22 E
Abū Zeydābād, Iran	45 C6	33 54N	51 45 E
Abuja, Nigeria	50 G7	9 16N	7 2 E
Abukuma-Gawa →, Japan	30 E10	38 6N 140 52 E	
Abukuma-Sammyaku, Japan	30 F10	37 30N 140 45 E	
Abunã, Brazil	92 E5	9 40S	65 20W
Abunã →, Brazil	92 E5	9 41S	65 20W
Aburo, Dem. Rep. of the Congo	54 B3	2 4N	30 53 E
Abut Hd., N.Z.	59 K3	43 7S 170 15 E	
Acadia National Park, U.S.A.	77 C11	44 20N	68 13W
Açailândia, Brazil	93 D9	4 57S	47 0W
Acajutla, El Salv.	88 D2	13 36N	89 50W
Acámbaro, Mexico	86 D4	20 0N 100 40W	
Acaponeta, Mexico	86 C3	22 30N 105 20W	
Acapulco, Mexico	87 D5	16 51N	99 56W
Acarai, Serra, Brazil	92 C7	1 50N	57 50W
Acarigua, Venezuela	92 B5	9 33N	69 12W
Acatlán, Mexico	87 D5	18 10N	98 3W
Acayucan, Mexico	87 D6	17 59N	94 58W
Accomac, U.S.A.	76 G8	37 43N	75 40W
Accra, Ghana	50 G5	5 35N	0 6W
Accrington, U.K.	10 D5	53 45N	2 22W
Acebal, Argentina	94 C3	33 20S	60 50W
Aceh □, Indonesia	36 D1	4 15N	97 30 E
Achalpur, India	40 J10	21 22N	77 32 E
Acheng, China	35 B14	45 30N 126 58 E	
Acher, India	42 H5	23 10N	72 32 E
Achill Hd., Ireland	13 C1	53 58N	10 15W
Achill I., Ireland	13 C1	53 58N	10 1W
Achinsk, Russia	27 D10	56 20N	90 20 E
Acireale, Italy	20 F6	37 37N	15 10 E
Ackerman, U.S.A.	81 J10	33 19N	89 11W
Acklins I., Bahamas	89 B5	22 30N	74 0W
Acme, Canada	72 C6	51 33N 113 30W	
Acme, U.S.A.	78 F5	40 8N	79 26W
Aconcagua, Cerro, Argentina	94 C2	32 39S	70 0W
Aconquija, Mt., Argentina	94 B2	27 0S	66 0W
Açores, Is. dos = Azores, Atl. Oc.	50 A1	38 44N	29 0W
Acraman, L., Australia	63 E2	32 2S 135 23 E	
Acre = 'Akko, Israel	47 C4	32 55N	35 4 E
Acre □, Brazil	92 E4	9 1S	71 0W
Acre →, Brazil	92 E5	8 45S	67 22W
Acton, Canada	78 C4	43 38N	80 3W
Acuña, Mexico	86 B4	29 18N 100 55W	
Ad Dammām, Si. Arabia	45 E6	26 20N	50 5 E
Ad Dāmūr, Lebanon	47 B4	33 44N	35 27 E
Ad Dawādimī, Si. Arabia	44 E5	24 35N	44 15 E
Ad Dawḥah, Qatar	45 E6	25 15N	51 35 E
Ad Dawr, Iraq	44 C4	34 27N	43 47 E
Ad Dir'īyah, Si. Arabia	44 E5	24 44N	46 35 E
Ad Dīwānīyah, Iraq	44 D5	32 0N	45 0 E
Ad Dujayl, Iraq	44 C5	33 51N	44 14 E
Ad Duwayd, Si. Arabia	44 D4	30 15N	42 17 E
Ada, Minn., U.S.A.	80 B6	47 18N	96 31W
Ada, Okla., U.S.A.	81 H6	34 46N	96 41W
Adabiya, Egypt	47 F1	29 53N	32 28 E
Adair, C., Canada	69 A12	71 31N	71 24W
Adaja →, Spain	19 B3	41 32N	4 52W
Adak I., U.S.A.	68 C2	51 45N 176 45W	
Adamaoua, Massif de l', Cameroon	52 C2	7 20N	12 20 E
Adamawa Highlands = Adamaoua, Massif de l', Cameroon	52 C2	7 20N	12 20 E
Adamello, Mte., Italy	18 C9	46 9N	10 30 E
Adaminaby, Australia	63 F4	36 0S 148 45 E	
Adams, Mass., U.S.A.	79 D11	42 38N	73 7W
Adams, N.Y., U.S.A.	79 C8	43 49N	76 1W
Adams, Wis., U.S.A.	80 D10	43 57N	89 49W
Adam's Bridge, Sri Lanka	40 Q11	9 15N	79 40 E
Adams L., Canada	72 C5	51 10N 119 40W	
Adams Mt., U.S.A.	84 D5	46 12N 121 30W	
Adam's Peak, Sri Lanka	40 R12	6 48N	80 30 E
Adana, Turkey	25 G6	37 0N	35 16 E
Adapazan = Sakarya, Turkey	25 F5	40 48N	30 25 E
Adarama, Sudan	51 E12	17 10N	34 52 E
Adare, C., Antarctica	5 D11	71 0S 171 0 E	
Adaut, Indonesia	37 F8	8 8S 131 7 E	
Adavale, Australia	63 D3	25 52S 144 32 E	
Adda →, Italy	18 D8	45 8N	9 53 E
Addis Ababa = Addis Abeba, Ethiopia	46 F2	9 2N	38 42 E
Addis Abeba, Ethiopia	46 F2	9 2N	38 42 E
Addison, U.S.A.	78 D7	42 1N	77 14W
Addo, S. Africa	56 E4	33 32S	25 45 E
Ādeh, Iran	44 B5	37 42N	45 11 E
Adel, U.S.A.	77 K4	31 8N	83 25W
Adelaide, Australia	63 E2	34 52S 138 30 E	
Adelaide, Bahamas	88 A4	25 4N	77 31W
Adelaide, S. Africa	56 E4	32 42S	26 20 E
Adelaide I., Antarctica	5 C17	67 15S	68 30W
Adelaide Pen., Canada	68 B10	68 15N	97 30W
Adelaide River, Australia	60 B5	13 15S 131 7 E	
Adelanto, U.S.A.	85 L9	34 35N 117 22W	
Adele I., Australia	60 C3	15 32S 123 9 E	
Adélie, Terre, Antarctica	5 C10	68 0S 140 0 E	
Adélie Land = Adélie, Terre, Antarctica	5 C10	68 0S 140 0 E	
Aden = Al 'Adan, Yemen	46 E4	12 45N	45 0 E
Aden, G. of, Asia	46 E4	12 30N	47 30 E
Adendorp, S. Africa	56 E3	32 15S	24 30 E
Adh Dhayd, U.A.E.	45 E7	25 17N	55 53 E
Adhoi, India	42 H4	23 26N	70 32 E
Adi, Indonesia	37 E8	4 15S 133 30 E	
Adieu, C., Australia	61 F5	32 0S 132 10 E	
Adieu Pt., Australia	60 C3	15 14S 124 35 E	
Adige →, Italy	20 B5	45 9N	12 20 E
Adigrat, Ethiopia	46 E2	14 20N	39 26 E
Adilabad, India	40 K11	19 33N	78 20 E
Adin Khel, Afghan.	40 C6	32 45N	68 5 E
Adjumani, Uganda	54 B3	3 20N	31 50 E
Adlavik Is., Canada	71 A8	55 2N	57 45W
Admiralty G., Australia	60 B4	14 20S 125 55 E	
Admiralty I., U.S.A.	72 B2	57 30N 134 30W	
Admiralty Is., Papua N. G.	64 H6	2 0S 147 0 E	
Adonara, Indonesia	37 F6	8 15S 123 5 E	
Adoni, India	40 M10	15 33N	77 18 E
Adour →, France	18 E3	43 32N	1 32W
Adra, India	43 H12	23 30N	86 42 E

Adra, Spain	19 D4	36 43N	3 3W
Adrano, Italy	20 F6	37 40N	14 50 E
Adrar, Algeria	48 D4	27 51N	0 11 E
Adrar, Mauritania	50 D3	20 30N	7 30 E
Adrian, Mich., U.S.A.	76 E3	41 54N	84 2W
Adrian, Tex., U.S.A.	81 H3	35 16N 102 40W	
Adriatic Sea, Medit. S.	20 C6	43 0N	16 0 E
Adua, Indonesia	37 E7	1 45S 129 50 E	
Adwa, Ethiopia	46 E2	14 15N	38 52 E
Adygea □, Russia	25 F7	45 0N	40 0 E
Adzhar Republic = Ajaria □, Georgia	25 F7	41 30N	42 0 E
Adzopé, Ivory C.	50 G5	6 7N	3 49W
Ægean Sea, Medit. S.	21 E11	38 30N	25 0 E
Aerhtai Shan, Mongolia	32 B4	46 40N	92 45 E
'Afak, Iraq	44 C5	32 4N	45 15 E
Afándou, Greece	23 C10	36 18N	28 12 E
Afghanistan ■, Asia	40 C4	33 0N	65 0 E
Aflou, Algeria	50 B6	34 7N	2 3 E
Africa	48 E6	10 0N	20 0 E
'Afrīn, Syria	44 B3	36 32N	36 50 E
Afton, N.Y., U.S.A.	79 D9	42 14N	75 32W
Afton, Wyo., U.S.A.	82 E8	42 44N 110 56W	
Afuá, Brazil	93 D8	0 15S	50 20W
'Afula, Israel	47 C4	32 37N	35 17 E
Afyon, Turkey	25 G5	38 45N	30 33 E
Afyonkarahisar = Afyon, Turkey	25 G5	38 45N	30 33 E
Agadès = Agadez, Niger	50 E7	16 58N	7 59 E
Agadez, Niger	50 E7	16 58N	7 59 E
Agadir, Morocco	50 B4	30 28N	9 55W
Agaete, Canary Is.	22 F4	28 6N	15 43W
Agar, India	42 H7	23 40N	76 2 E
Agartala, India	41 H17	23 50N	91 23 E
Agassiz, Canada	72 D4	49 14N	121 46W
Agats, Indonesia	37 F9	5 33S 138 0 E	
Agawam, U.S.A.	79 D12	42 5N	72 37W
Agboville, Ivory C.	50 G5	5 55N	4 15W
Ağdam, Azerbaijan	44 B5	40 0N	46 58 E
Agde, France	18 E5	43 19N	3 28 E
Agen, France	18 D4	44 12N	0 38 E
Āgh Kand, Iran	45 B6	37 15N	48 4 E
Aginskoye, Russia	27 D12	51 6N 114 32 E	
Agnew, Australia	61 E3	28 1S 120 31 E	
Agori, India	43 G10	24 33N	82 57 E
Agra, India	42 F7	27 17N	77 58 E
Ağri, Turkey	25 G7	39 44N	43 3 E
Agri →, Italy	20 D7	40 13N	16 44 E
Ağri Daği, Turkey	25 G7	39 50N	44 15 E
Ağri Karakose = Ağri, Turkey	25 G7	39 44N	43 3 E
Agrigento, Italy	20 F5	37 19N	13 34 E
Agrínion, Greece	21 E9	38 37N	21 27 E
Agua Caliente, Baja Calif., Mexico	85 N10	32 29N 116 59W	
Agua Caliente, Sinaloa, Mexico	86 B3	26 30N 108 20W	
Agua Caliente Springs, U.S.A.	85 N10	32 56N 116 19W	
Água Clara, Brazil	93 H8	20 25S	52 45W
Agua Hechicero, Mexico	85 N10	32 26N 116 14W	
Agua Prieta, Mexico	86 A3	31 20N 109 32W	
Aguadilla, Puerto Rico	89 C6	18 26N	67 10W
Aguadulce, Panama	88 E3	8 15N	80 20W
Aguanga, U.S.A.	85 M10	33 27N 116 51W	
Aguanish, Canada	71 B7	50 14N	62 2W
Aguanus →, Canada	71 B7	50 13N	62 5W
Aguapey →, Argentina	94 B4	29 7S	56 36W
Aguaray Guazú →, Paraguay	94 A4	24 47S	57 19W
Aguarico →, Ecuador	92 D3	0 59S	75 11W
Aguas Blancas, Chile	94 A2	24 15S	69 55W
Aguas Calientes, Sierra de, Argentina	94 B2	25 26S	66 40W
Aguascalientes, Mexico	86 C4	21 53N 102 12W	
Aguascalientes □, Mexico	86 C4	22 0N 102 20W	
Aguilares, Argentina	94 B2	27 26S	65 35W
Aguilas, Spain	19 D5	37 23N	1 35W
Agüimes, Canary Is.	22 G4	27 58N	15 27W
Aguja, C. de la, Colombia	90 B3	11 18N	74 12W
Agulhas, C., S. Africa	56 E3	34 52S	20 0 E
Agulo, Canary Is.	22 F2	28 11N	17 12W
Agung, Indonesia	36 F5	8 20S 115 28 E	
Agur, Uganda	54 B3	2 28N	32 55 E
Agusan →, Phil.	37 C7	9 0N 125 30 E	
Aha Mts., Botswana	56 B3	19 45S	21 0 E
Ahaggar, Algeria	50 D7	23 0N	6 30 E
Ahar, Iran	44 B5	38 35N	47 0 E
Ahipara B., N.Z.	59 F4	35 5S 173 5 E	
Ahiri, India	40 K12	19 30N	80 0 E
Ahmad Wal, Pakistan	42 E4	29 18N	65 58 E
Ahmadabad, India	42 H5	23 0N	72 40 E
Aḥmadābād, Khorāsān, Iran	45 C9	35 3N	60 50 E
Aḥmadābād, Khorāsān, Iran	45 C8	35 49N	59 42 E
Aḥmadī, Iran	45 E8	27 56N	56 42 E
Ahmadnagar, India	40 K9	19 7N	74 46 E
Ahmadpur, Pakistan	42 E4	29 12N	71 10 E
Ahmadpur Lamma, Pakistan	42 E4	28 19N	70 3 E
Ahmedabad = Ahmadabad, India	42 H5	23 0N	72 40 E
Ahmednagar = Ahmadnagar, India	40 K9	19 7N	74 46 E
Ahome, Mexico	86 B3	25 55N 109 11W	
Ahoskie, U.S.A.	77 G7	36 17N	76 59W
Ahram, Iran	45 D6	28 52N	51 16 E
Ahrax Pt., Malta	23 D1	35 59N	14 22 E
Āhū, Iran	45 C6	34 33N	50 2 E
Ahuachapán, El Salv.	88 D2	13 54N	89 52W
Ahvāz, Iran	45 D6	31 20N	48 40 E
Ahvenanmaa = Åland, Finland	9 F19	60 15N	20 0 E
Aḥwar, Yemen	46 E4	13 30N	46 40 E
Ai →, India	43 F14	26 26N	90 44 E
Aichi □, Japan	31 G8	35 0N 137 15 E	
Aigua, Uruguay	95 C5	34 13S	54 46W
Aigues-Mortes, France	18 E6	43 35N	4 12 E
Aihui, China	33 A7	50 10N 127 30 E	
Aija, Peru	92 E3	9 50S	77 45W
Aikawa, Japan	30 E9	38 2N 138 15 E	
Aiken, U.S.A.	77 J5	33 34N	81 43W
Aileron, Australia	62 C1	22 39S 133 20 E	
Aillik, Canada	71 A8	55 11N	59 18W
Ailsa Craig, U.K.	12 F3	55 15N	5 6W
Aïm, Russia	27 D14	59 0N 133 55 E	
Aimere, Indonesia	37 F6	8 45S 121 3 E	
Aimogasta, Argentina	94 B2	28 33S	66 50W

Aïn Ben Tili, Mauritania	50 C4	25 59N	9 27W
Aïn-Sefra, Algeria	50 B5	32 47N	0 37W
'Ain Sudr, Egypt	47 F2	29 50N	33 6 E
Ainaži, Latvia	9 H21	57 50N	24 24 E
Ainsworth, U.S.A.	80 D5	42 33N	99 52W
Aiquile, Bolivia	92 G5	18 10S	65 10W
Aïr, Niger	50 E7	18 30N	8 0 E
Air Force I., Canada	69 B12	67 58N	74 5W
Air Hitam, Malaysia	39 M4	1 55N 103 11 E	
Airdrie, Canada	72 C6	51 18N 114	2W
Airdrie, U.K.	12 F5	55 52N	3 57W
Aire →, U.K.	10 D7	53 43N	0 55W
Aire, I. de l', Spain	22 B11	39 48N	4 16 E
Airlie Beach, Australia	62 C4	20 16S 148 43 E	
Aisne →, France	18 B5	49 26N	2 50 E
Ait, India	43 G8	25 54N	79 14 E
Aitkin, U.S.A.	80 B8	46 32N	93 42W
Aiud, Romania	17 E12	46 19N	23 44 E
Aix-en-Provence, France	18 E6	43 32N	5 27 E
Aix-la-Chapelle = Aachen, Germany	16 C4	50 45N	6 6 E
Aix-les-Bains, France	18 D6	45 41N	5 53 E
Aiyion, Greece	21 E10	38 15N	22 5 E
Aizawl, India	41 H18	23 40N	92 44 E
Aizkraukle, Latvia	9 H21	56 36N	25 11 E
Aizpute, Latvia	9 H19	56 43N	21 40 E
Aizuwakamatsu, Japan	30 F9	37 30N 139 56 E	
Ajaccio, France	18 F8	41 55N	8 40 E
Ajaigarh, India	43 G9	24 52N	80 16 E
Ajalpan, Mexico	87 D5	18 22N	97 15W
Ajanta Ra., India	40 J9	20 28N	75 50 E
Ajari Rep. = Ajaria □, Georgia	25 F7	41 30N	42 0 E
Ajaria □, Georgia	25 F7	41 30N	42 0 E
Ajax, Canada	78 C5	43 50N	79 1W
Ajdâbiyâ, Libya	51 B10	30 54N	20 4 E
Ajka, Hungary	17 E9	47 4N	17 31 E
'Ajmān, U.A.E.	45 E7	25 25N	55 30 E
Ajmer, India	42 F6	26 28N	74 37 E
Ajnala, India	42 D6	31 50N	74 48 E
Ajo, U.S.A.	83 K7	32 22N 112 52W	
Ajo, C. de, Spain	19 A4	43 31N	3 35W
Akabira, Japan	30 C11	43 33N 142 5 E	
Akamas □, Cyprus	23 D11	35 3N	32 18 E
Akanthou, Cyprus	23 D12	35 22N	33 45 E
Akaroa, N.Z.	59 K4	43 49S 172 59 E	
Akashi, Japan	31 G7	34 45N 134 58 E	
Akbarpur, Bihar, India	43 G10	24 39N	83 58 E
Akbarpur, Ut. P., India	43 F10	26 25N	82 32 E
Akelamo, Indonesia	37 D7	1 35N 129 40 E	
Aketi, Dem. Rep. of the Congo	52 D4	2 38N	23 47 E
Akharnaí, Greece	21 E10	38 5N	23 44 E
Akhelóös →, Greece	21 E9	38 19N	21 7 E
Akhisar, Turkey	21 E12	38 56N	27 48 E
Akhnur, India	43 C6	32 52N	74 45 E
Akhtyrka = Okhtyrka, Ukraine	25 D5	50 25N	35 0 E
Aki, Japan	31 H6	33 30N 133 54 E	
Akimiski I., Canada	70 B3	52 50N	81 30W
Akita, Japan	30 E10	39 45N 140 7 E	
Akita □, Japan	30 E10	39 40N 140 30 E	
Akjoujt, Mauritania	50 E3	19 45N	14 15W
Akkeshi, Japan	30 C12	43 2N 144 51 E	
'Akko, Israel	47 C4	32 55N	35 4 E
Aklavik, Canada	68 B6	68 12N 135 0W	
Aklera, India	42 G7	24 26N	76 32 E
Akmolinsk = Astana, Kazakstan	26 D8	51 10N	71 30 E
Akô, Japan	31 G7	34 45N 134 24 E	
Akola, India	40 J10	20 42N	77 2 E
Akordat, Eritrea	46 D2	15 30N	37 40 E
Akpatok I., Canada	69 B13	60 25N	68 8W
Åkrahamn, Norway	9 G11	59 15N	5 10 E
Akranes, Iceland	8 D2	64 19N	22 5W
Akron, Colo., U.S.A.	80 E3	40 10N 103 13W	
Akron, Ohio, U.S.A.	78 E3	41 5N	81 31W
Akrotiri, Cyprus	23 E11	34 36N	32 57 E
Akrotiri Bay, Cyprus	23 E12	34 35N	33 10 E
Aksai Chin, India	43 B8	35 15N	79 55 E
Aksaray, Turkey	25 G5	38 25N	34 2 E
Aksay, Kazakstan	25 D9	51 11N	53 0 E
Akşehir, Turkey	25 G5	38 18N	31 30 E
Akşehir Gölü, Turkey	25 G5	38 30N	31 25 E
Aksu, China	32 B3	41 5N	80 10 E
Aksum, Ethiopia	46 E2	14 5N	38 40 E
Aktogay, Kazakstan	26 E8	46 57N	79 40 E
Aktsyabrski, Belarus	17 B15	52 38N	28 53 E
Aktyubinsk = Aqtöbe, Kazakstan	25 D10	50 17N	57 10 E
Akure, Nigeria	50 G7	7 15N	5 5 E
Akureyri, Iceland	8 D4	65 40N	18 6W
Akuseki-Shima, Japan	31 K4	29 27N 129 37 E	
Akyab = Sittwe, Burma	41 J18	20 18N	92 45 E
Al 'Adan, Yemen	46 E4	12 45N	45 0 E
Al Aḥsā = Hasa □, Si. Arabia	45 E6	25 50N	49 0 E
Al Ajfar, Si. Arabia	44 E4	27 26N	41 53 E
Al Amādīyah, Iraq	44 B4	37 5N	43 30 E
Al 'Amārah, Iraq	44 D5	31 55N	47 15 E
Al 'Aqabah, Jordan	47 F4	29 31N	35 0 E
Al 'Aramah, Si. Arabia	44 E5	25 30N	46 0 E
Al Arṭāwīyah, Si. Arabia	44 E5	26 31N	45 20 E
Al 'Āṣimah = 'Ammān □, Jordan	47 D5	31 40N	36 30 E
Al 'Assāfīyah, Si. Arabia	44 D3	28 17N	38 59 E
Al 'Ayn, Oman	45 E7	24 15N	55 45 E
Al 'Ayn, Si. Arabia	44 E3	25 4N	38 6 E
Al 'Azīzīyah, Iraq	44 C5	32 54N	45 4 E
Al Bāb, Syria	44 B3	36 23N	37 29 E
Al Bad', Si. Arabia	44 D2	28 28N	35 1 E
Al Bādī, Iraq	44 C4	35 56N	41 32 E
Al Baḥrah, Kuwait	44 D5	29 40N	47 52 E
Al Baḥral Mayyit = Dead Sea, Asia	47 D4	31 30N	35 30 E
Al Balqā' □, Jordan	47 C4	32 5N	35 45 E
Al Bārūk, J., Lebanon	47 B4	33 39N	35 40 E
Al Başrah, Iraq	44 D5	30 30N	47 50 E
Al Baṭḥā, Iraq	44 D5	31 6N	45 53 E
Al Baṭrūn, Lebanon	47 A4	34 15N	35 40 E
Al Bayḍā, Libya	51 B10	32 50N	21 44 E
Al Bi'r, Si. Arabia	44 E3	28 51N	36 16 E
Al Biqā, Lebanon	47 A5	34 10N	36 10 E
Al Burayj, Syria	47 A5	34 15N	36 46 E
Al Faḍilī, Si. Arabia	45 E6	26 58N	49 10 E

Amadi,
Dem. Rep. of the Congo . 54 B2 3 40N 26 40 E
Amâdi, Sudan 51 G12 5 29N 30 25 E
Amadjuak L., Canada . . . 69 B12 65 0N 71 8W
Amagansett, U.S.A. 79 F12 40 59N 72 9W
Amagasaki, Japan 31 G7 34 42N 135 20 E
Amahai, Indonesia 37 E7 3 20S 128 55 E
Amakusa-Shotō, Japan . . 31 H5 32 15N 130 10 E
Åmål, Sweden 9 G15 59 3N 12 42 E
Amaliás, Greece 21 F9 37 47N 21 22 E
Amalner, India 40 J9 21 5N 75 5 E
Amamapare, Indonesia . . 37 E9 4 53S 136 38 E
Amambaí, Brazil 95 A4 23 5S 55 13W
Amambaí →, Brazil 95 A5 23 22S 53 56W
Amambay □, Paraguay . . 95 A4 23 0S 56 0W
Amambay, Cordillera de,
 S. Amer. 95 A4 23 0S 55 45W
Amami-Guntō, Japan . . . 31 L4 27 16N 129 21 E
Amami-Ō-Shima, Japan . 31 L4 28 0N 129 0 E
Amaná, L., Brazil 92 D6 2 35S 64 40W
Amanat →, India 43 G11 24 7N 84 4 E
Amanda Park, U.S.A. . . . 84 C3 47 28N 123 55W
Amangeldy, Kazakstan . . 26 D7 50 10N 65 10 E
Amapá, Brazil 93 C8 2 5N 50 50W
Amapá □, Brazil 93 C8 1 40N 52 0W
Amarante, Brazil 93 E10 6 14S 42 50W
Amaranth, Canada 73 C9 50 36N 98 43W
Amargosa →, U.S.A. 85 J10 36 14N 116 51W
Amargosa Range, U.S.A. . 85 J10 36 20N 116 45W
Amári, Greece 23 D6 35 13N 24 40 E
Amarillo, U.S.A. 81 H4 35 13N 101 50W
Amarkantak, India 43 H9 22 40N 81 45 E
Amaro, Mte., Italy 20 C6 42 5N 14 5 E
Amarpur, India 43 G12 25 5N 87 0 E
Amarwara, India 43 H8 22 18N 79 10 E
Amasya □, Turkey 25 F6 40 40N 35 50 E
Amata, Australia 61 E5 26 9S 131 9 E
Amatikulu, S. Africa 57 D5 29 3S 31 33 E
Amatitlán, Guatemala . . 88 D1 14 29N 90 38W
Amay, Belgium 15 D5 50 33N 5 19 E
Amazon = Amazonas →,
 S. Amer. 93 D9 0 5S 50 0W
Amazonas □, Brazil 92 E6 5 0S 65 0W
Amazonas →, S. Amer. . . 93 D9 0 5S 50 0W
Ambah, India 42 F8 26 43N 78 13 E
Ambahakily, Madag. 57 C7 21 36S 43 41 E
Ambala, India 42 D7 30 23N 76 56 E
Ambalavao, Madag. 57 C8 21 50S 46 56 E
Ambanja, Madag. 57 A8 13 40S 48 27 E
Ambarchik, Russia 27 C17 69 40N 162 20 E
Ambarijeby, Madag. 57 A8 14 56S 47 41 E
Ambaro, Helodranon',
 Madag. 57 A8 13 23S 48 38 E
Ambato, Ecuador 92 D3 1 5S 78 42W
Ambato, Sierra de,
 Argentina 94 B2 28 25S 66 10W
Ambato Boeny, Madag. . . 57 B8 16 28S 46 43 E
Ambatofinandrahana,
 Madag. 57 C8 20 33S 46 48 E
Ambatolampy, Madag. . . 57 B8 19 20S 47 35 E
Ambatondrazaka, Madag. 57 B8 17 55S 48 28 E
Ambatosoratra, Madag. . 57 B8 17 37S 48 31 E
Ambenja, Madag. 57 B8 15 17S 46 58 E
Amberg, Germany 16 D6 49 26N 11 52 E
Ambergris Cay, Belize . . 87 D7 18 0N 88 0W
Amberley, N.Z. 59 K4 43 9S 172 44 E
Ambikapur, India 43 H10 23 15N 83 15 E
Ambilobé, Madag. 57 A8 13 10S 49 3 E
Ambinanindrano, Madag. . 57 C8 20 5S 48 23 E
Amble, U.K. 10 B6 55 20N 1 36W
Ambleside, U.K. 10 C5 54 26N 2 58W
Ambo, Peru 92 F3 10 5S 76 10W
Ambodifototra, Madag. . . 57 B8 16 59S 49 52 E
Ambodilazana, Madag. . . 57 B8 18 6S 49 10 E
Ambohimahasoa, Madag. 57 C8 21 7S 47 13 E
Ambohimanga, Madag. . . 57 C8 20 52S 47 36 E
Ambohitra, Madag. 57 A8 12 30S 49 10 E
Amboise, France 18 C4 47 24N 1 2 E
Ambon, Indonesia 37 E7 3 35S 128 20 E
Amboseli, L., Kenya 54 C4 2 40S 37 10 E
Ambositra, Madag. 57 C8 20 31S 47 25 E
Ambovombe, Madag. 57 D8 25 11S 46 5 E
Amboy, U.S.A. 85 L11 34 33N 115 45W
Amboyna Cay, S. China Sea 36 C4 7 50N 112 50 E
Ambridge, U.S.A. 78 F4 40 36N 80 14W
Ambriz, Angola 52 F2 7 48S 13 8 E
Amchitka I., U.S.A. 68 C1 51 32N 179 0 E
Amderma, Russia 26 C7 69 45N 61 30 E
Amdhi, India 43 H9 23 51N 81 27 E
Ameca, Mexico 86 C4 20 30N 104 0W
Ameca →, Mexico 86 C3 20 40N 105 15W
Amecameca, Mexico 87 D5 19 7N 98 46W
Ameland, Neths. 15 A5 53 27N 5 45 E
Amenia, U.S.A. 79 E11 41 51N 73 33W
American Falls, U.S.A. . . 82 E7 42 47N 112 51W
American Falls Reservoir,
 U.S.A. 82 E7 42 47N 112 52W
American Fork, U.S.A. . . . 82 F8 40 23N 111 48W
American Highland,
 Antarctica 5 D6 73 0S 75 0 E
American Samoa ■,
 Pac. Oc. 59 B13 14 20S 170 40W
Americana, Brazil 95 A6 22 45S 47 20W
Americus, U.S.A. 77 K3 32 4N 84 14W
Amersfoort, Neths. 15 B5 52 9N 5 23 E
Amersfoort, S. Africa . . . 57 D4 26 59S 29 53 E
Amery Ice Shelf, Antarctica 5 C6 69 30S 72 0 E
Ames, U.S.A. 80 E8 42 2N 93 37W
Amesbury, U.S.A. 79 D14 42 51N 70 56W
Amet, India 42 G5 25 18N 73 56 E
Amga, Russia 27 C14 60 50N 132 0 E
Amga →, Russia 27 C14 62 38N 134 32 E
Amgu, Russia 27 E14 45 45N 137 15 E
Amgun →, Russia 27 D14 52 56N 139 38 E
Amherst, Burma 41 L20 16 2N 97 20 E
Amherst, Canada 71 C7 45 48N 64 8W
Amherst, Mass., U.S.A. . . 79 D12 42 23N 72 31W
Amherst, N.Y., U.S.A. . . . 78 D6 42 59N 78 48W
Amherst, Ohio, U.S.A. . . . 78 E2 41 24N 82 14W
Amherst I., Canada 79 B8 44 8N 76 43W
Amherstburg, Canada . . . 70 D3 42 6N 83 6W
Amiata, Mte., Italy 20 C4 42 53N 11 37 E
Amidon, U.S.A. 80 B3 46 29N 103 19W
Amiens, France 18 B5 49 54N 2 16 E
Amīrābād, Iran 44 C5 33 20N 46 16 E
Amirante Is., Seychelles . 28 K9 6 0S 53 0 E
Amisk L., Canada 73 C8 54 35N 102 15W

Amistad, Presa de la,
 Mexico 86 B4 29 24N 101 0W
Amite, U.S.A. 81 K9 30 44N 90 30W
Amla, India 42 J8 21 56N 78 7 E
Amlia I., U.S.A. 68 C2 52 4N 173 30W
Amlwch, U.K. 10 D3 53 24N 4 20W
'Ammān, Jordan 47 D4 31 57N 35 52 E
'Ammān □, Jordan 47 D5 31 40N 36 30 E
Ammanford, U.K. 11 F4 51 48N 3 59W
Ammassalik =
 Angmagssalik, Greenland 4 C6 65 40N 37 20W
Ammon, U.S.A. 82 E8 43 28N 111 58W
Amnat Charoen, Thailand 38 E5 15 51N 104 38 E
Amnura, Bangla. 43 G13 24 37N 88 25 E
Åmol, Iran 45 B7 36 23N 52 20 E
Amorgós, Greece 21 F11 36 50N 25 57 E
Amory, U.S.A. 77 J1 33 59N 88 29W
Amos, Canada 70 C4 48 35N 78 5W
Amoy = Xiamen, China . . 33 D6 24 25N 118 4 E
Ampang, Malaysia 39 L3 3 8N 101 45 E
Ampanihy, Madag. 57 C7 24 40S 44 45 E
Ampasinadava, Helodranon',
 Madag. 57 A8 13 40S 48 15 E
Ampasindava, Saikanosy,
 Madag. 57 A8 13 42S 47 55 E
Ampenan, Indonesia 36 F5 8 35S 116 13 E
Amper →, Germany 16 D6 48 29N 11 55 E
Ampotaka, Madag. 57 D7 25 3S 44 41 E
Ampoza, Madag. 57 C7 22 20S 44 44 E
Amqui, Canada 71 C6 48 28N 67 27W
Amravati, India 40 J10 20 55N 77 45 E
Amreli, India 42 J4 21 35N 71 17 E
Amritsar, India 42 D6 31 35N 74 57 E
Amroha, India 43 E8 28 53N 78 30 E
Amsterdam, Neths. 15 B4 52 23N 4 54 E
Amsterdam, U.S.A. 79 D10 42 56N 74 11W
Amsterdam, I., Ind. Oc. . . 3 F13 38 30S 77 30 E
Amstetten, Austria 16 D8 48 7N 14 51 E
Amudarya →, Uzbekistan . 26 E6 43 58N 59 34 E
Amundsen Gulf, Canada . 68 A7 71 0N 124 0W
Amundsen Sea, Antarctica 5 D15 72 0S 115 0W
Amuntai, Indonesia 36 E5 2 28S 115 25 E
Amur →, Russia 27 D15 52 56N 141 10 E
Amurang, Indonesia 37 D6 1 5N 124 0 E
Amuri Pass, N.Z. 59 K4 42 31S 172 11 E
Amursk, Russia 27 D14 50 14N 136 54 E
Amyderya = Amudarya →,
 Uzbekistan 26 E6 43 58N 59 34 E
An Bien, Vietnam 39 H5 9 45N 105 0 E
An Hoa, Vietnam 38 E7 15 40N 108 5 E
An Nabatīyah at Tahta,
 Lebanon 47 B4 33 23N 35 27 E
An Nabk, Si. Arabia 44 D3 31 20N 37 20 E
An Nabk, Syria 47 A5 34 2N 36 44 E
An Nabk Abū Qaşr,
 Si. Arabia 44 D3 30 21N 38 34 E
An Nafūd, Si. Arabia 44 D4 28 15N 41 0 E
An Najaf, Iraq 44 C5 32 3N 44 15 E
An Nāşirīyah, Iraq 44 D5 31 0N 46 15 E
An Nhon, Vietnam 38 F7 13 55N 109 7 E
An Nu'ayrīyah, Si. Arabia . 45 E6 27 30N 48 30 E
An Nuwayb'ī, W. →,
 Si. Arabia 47 F3 29 18N 34 57 E
An Thoi, Dao, Vietnam . . . 39 H5 9 58N 104 0 E
An Uaimh, Ireland 13 C5 53 39N 6 41W
Anabar →, Russia 27 B12 73 8N 113 36 E
'Anabtā, West Bank 47 C4 32 19N 35 7 E
Anaconda, U.S.A. 82 C7 46 8N 112 57W
Anacortes, U.S.A. 84 B4 48 30N 122 37W
Anadarko, U.S.A. 81 H5 35 4N 98 15W
Anadolu, Turkey 25 G5 39 0N 30 0 E
Anadyr, Russia 27 C18 64 35N 177 20 E
Anadyr →, Russia 27 C18 64 55N 176 5 E
Anadyrskiy Zaliv, Russia . 27 C19 64 0N 180 0 E
Anaga, Pta. de, Canary Is. 22 F3 28 34N 16 9W
'Ānah, Iraq 44 C4 34 25N 42 0 E
Anaheim, U.S.A. 85 M9 33 50N 117 55W
Anahim Lake, Canada . . . 72 C3 52 28N 125 18W
Anáhuac, Mexico 86 B4 27 14N 100 9W
Anakapalle, India 41 L13 17 42N 83 6 E
Anakie, Australia 62 C4 23 32S 147 45 E
Analalava, Madag. 57 A8 14 35S 48 0 E
Análipsis, Greece 23 A3 39 36N 19 55 E
Anambar →, Pakistan . . . 42 D3 30 15N 68 50 E
Anambas, Kepulauan,
 Indonesia 39 L6 3 20N 106 30 E
Anambas Is. = Anambas,
 Kepulauan, Indonesia . . 39 L6 3 20N 106 30 E
Anamosa, U.S.A. 80 D9 42 7N 91 17W
Anamur, Turkey 25 G5 36 8N 32 58 E
Anan, Japan 31 H7 33 54N 134 40 E
Anand, India 42 H5 22 32N 72 59 E
Anantnag, India 43 C6 33 45N 75 10 E
Ananyiv, Ukraine 17 E15 47 44N 29 58 E
Anapodháris →, Greece . . 23 E7 34 59N 25 20 E
Anápolis, Brazil 93 G9 16 15S 48 50W
Anapu →, Brazil 93 D8 1 53S 50 53W
Anār, Iran 45 D7 30 55N 55 13 E
Anārak, Iran 45 C7 33 25N 53 40 E
Anas →, India 42 H5 23 26N 74 0 E
Anatolia = Anadolu, Turkey 25 G5 39 0N 30 0 E
Anatsogno, Madag. 57 C7 23 33S 43 46 E
Añatuya, Argentina 94 B3 28 20S 62 50W
Anaunethad L., Canada . . 73 A8 60 55N 104 25W
Anbyŏn, N. Korea 35 E14 39 1N 127 35 E
Ancaster, Canada 78 C5 43 13N 79 59W
Anchor Bay, U.S.A. 84 G3 38 48N 123 34W
Anchorage, U.S.A. 68 B5 61 13N 149 54W
Anci, China 34 E9 39 20N 116 40 E
Ancohuma, Nevada, Bolivia 92 G5 16 0S 68 50W
Ancón, Peru 92 F3 11 50S 77 10W
Ancona, Italy 20 C5 43 38N 13 30 E
Ancud, Chile 96 E2 42 0S 73 0W
Ancud, G. de, Chile 96 E2 42 0S 73 0W
Anda, China 33 B7 46 24N 125 19 E
Andacollo, Argentina . . . 94 D1 37 10S 70 42W
Andacollo, Chile 94 C1 30 14S 71 6W
Andalgalá, Argentina . . . 94 B2 27 40S 66 30W
Åndalsnes, Norway 9 E12 62 35N 7 43 E
Andalucía □, Spain 19 D3 37 35N 5 0W
Andalusia = Andalucía □,
 Spain 19 D3 37 35N 5 0W
Andalusia, U.S.A. 77 K2 31 18N 86 29W
Andaman Is., Ind. Oc. . . . 28 H13 12 30N 92 30 E
Andaman Sea, Ind. Oc. . . 36 B1 13 0N 96 0 E

Andamooka Opal Fields,
 Australia 63 E2 30 27S 137 9 E
Andapa, Madag. 53 G9 14 30S 49 30 E
Andara, Namibia 56 B3 18 2S 21 9 E
Andenes, Norway 8 B17 69 19N 16 18 E
Andenne, Belgium 15 D5 50 28N 5 5 E
Anderson, Alaska, U.S.A. . 68 B5 64 25N 149 15W
Anderson, Calif., U.S.A. . . 82 F2 40 27N 122 18W
Anderson, Ind., U.S.A. . . . 76 E3 40 10N 85 41W
Anderson, Mo., U.S.A. . . . 81 G7 36 39N 94 27W
Anderson, S.C., U.S.A. . . . 77 H4 34 31N 82 39W
Anderson →, Canada . . . 68 B7 69 42N 129 0W
Andes, U.S.A. 79 D10 42 12N 74 47W
Andes, Cord. de los,
 S. Amer. 92 H5 20 0S 68 0W
Andfjorden, Norway 8 B17 69 10N 16 20 E
Andhra Pradesh □, India . 40 L11 18 0N 79 0 E
Andijon, Uzbekistan 26 E8 41 10N 72 15 E
Andikíthira, Greece 21 G10 35 52N 23 15 E
Andīmeshk, Iran 45 C6 32 27N 48 21 E
Andizhan = Andijon,
 Uzbekistan 26 E8 41 10N 72 15 E
Andoany, Madag. 57 A8 13 25S 48 16 E
Andong, S. Korea 35 F15 36 40N 128 43 E
Andongwei, China 35 G10 35 6N 119 20 E
Andoom, Australia 62 A3 12 25S 141 53 E
Andorra ■, Europe 18 E4 42 30N 1 30 E
Andorra La Vella, Andorra 18 E4 42 31N 1 32 E
Andover, U.K. 11 F6 51 12N 1 29W
Andover, Maine, U.S.A. . . 79 B14 44 38N 70 45W
Andover, Mass., U.S.A. . . 79 D13 42 40N 71 8W
Andover, N.J., U.S.A. 79 F10 40 59N 74 45W
Andover, N.Y., U.S.A. 78 D7 42 9N 77 48W
Andover, Ohio, U.S.A. . . . 78 E4 41 36N 80 34W
Andøya, Norway 8 B16 69 10N 15 50 E
Andradina, Brazil 93 H8 20 54S 51 23W
Andrahary, Mt., Madag. . . 57 A8 13 37S 49 17 E
Andramasina, Madag. . . . 57 B8 19 11S 47 35 E
Andranopasy, Madag. . . . 57 C7 21 17S 43 44 E
Andratx, Spain 22 B9 39 39N 2 25 E
Andreanof Is., U.S.A. 68 C2 51 30N 176 0W
Andrews, S.C., U.S.A. . . . 77 J6 33 27N 79 34W
Andrews, Tex., U.S.A. . . . 81 J3 32 19N 102 33W
Ándria, Italy 20 D7 41 13N 16 17 E
Andriba, Madag. 57 B8 17 30S 46 58 E
Androka, Madag. 57 C7 24 58S 44 2 E
Andropov = Rybinsk, Russia 24 C6 58 5N 38 50 E
Ándros, Greece 21 F11 37 50N 24 57 E
Andros I., Bahamas 88 B4 24 30N 78 0W
Andros Town, Bahamas . . 88 B4 24 43N 77 47W
Androscoggin →, U.S.A. . . 79 C14 43 58N 70 0W
Andselv, Norway 8 B18 69 4N 18 34 E
Andújar, Spain 19 C3 38 3N 4 5W
Andulo, Angola 52 G3 11 25S 16 45 E
Anegada, I., Virgin Is. . . . 89 C7 18 45N 64 20W
Anegada Passage, W. Indies 89 C7 18 15N 63 45W
Aneto, Pico de, Spain . . . 19 A6 42 37N 0 40 E
Ang Thong, Thailand 38 E3 14 35N 100 31 E
Angamos, Punta, Chile . . 94 A1 23 1S 70 32W
Angara →, Russia 27 D10 58 5N 94 20 E
Angarsk, Russia 27 D11 52 30N 104 0 E
Angas Hills, Australia . . . 60 D4 23 0S 127 50 E
Angaston, Australia 63 E2 34 30S 139 8 E
Angaur I., Pac. Oc. 37 C8 6 54N 134 9 E
Ånge, Sweden 9 E16 62 31N 15 35 E
Ángel, Salto = Angel Falls,
 Venezuela 92 B6 5 57N 62 30W
Ángel de la Guarda, I.,
 Mexico 86 B2 29 30N 113 30W
Angel Falls, Venezuela . . 92 B6 5 57N 62 30W
Angeles, Phil. 37 A6 15 9N 120 33 E
Ängelholm, Sweden 9 H15 56 15N 12 58 E
Angels Camp, U.S.A. 84 G6 38 4N 120 32W
Ångermanälven →,
 Sweden 8 E17 62 40N 18 0 E
Ångermanland, Sweden . . 8 E18 63 36N 17 45 E
Angers, Canada 79 A9 45 31N 75 29W
Angers, France 18 C3 47 30N 0 35W
Ängesån →, Sweden 8 C20 66 16N 22 47 E
Angikuni L., Canada 73 A9 62 0N 100 0W
Angkor, Cambodia 38 F4 13 22N 103 50 E
Anglesey, U.K. 10 D3 53 17N 4 20W
Anglesey, Isle of □, U.K. . 10 D3 53 16N 4 18W
Angleton, U.S.A. 81 L7 29 10N 95 26W
Anglisidhes, Cyprus 23 E12 34 51N 33 27 E
Angmagssalik, Greenland 4 C6 65 40N 37 20W
Ango,
 Dem. Rep. of the Congo . 54 B2 4 10N 26 5 E
Angoche, Mozam. 55 F4 16 8S 39 55 E
Angoche, I., Mozam. 55 F4 16 20S 39 50 E
Angol, Chile 94 D1 37 56S 72 45W
Angola, Ind., U.S.A. 76 E3 41 38N 85 0W
Angola, N.Y., U.S.A. 78 D5 42 38N 79 2W
Angola ■, Africa 53 G3 12 0S 18 0 E
Angoulême, France 18 D4 45 39N 0 10 E
Angoumois, France 18 D3 45 50N 0 25 E
Angra dos Reis, Brazil . . 95 A7 23 0S 44 10W
Angren, Uzbekistan 26 E8 41 1N 70 12 E
Angtassom, Cambodia . . 39 G5 11 1N 104 41 E
Angu,
 Dem. Rep. of the Congo . 54 B1 3 25N 24 28 E
Anguang, China 35 B12 45 15N 123 45 E
Anguilla ■, W. Indies . . . 89 C7 18 14N 63 5W
Anguo, China 34 E8 38 28N 115 15 E
Angurugu, Australia 62 A2 14 0S 136 25 E
Angus □, U.K. 12 E6 56 46N 2 56W
Anhanduí →, Brazil 95 A5 21 46S 52 9W
Anholt, Denmark 9 H14 56 42N 11 33 E
Anhui □, China 33 C6 32 0N 117 0 E
Anhwei = Anhui □, China . 33 C6 32 0N 117 0 E
Anichab, Namibia 56 C1 21 0S 14 46 E
Animas →, U.S.A. 83 H9 36 43N 108 13W
Anivorano, Madag. 57 B8 18 44S 48 58 E
Anjar, India 42 H4 23 6N 70 10 E
Anjidiv I., India 40 M9 14 40N 74 10 E
Anjou, France 18 C3 47 20N 0 15W
Anjozorobe, Madag. 57 B8 18 22S 47 52 E
Anju, N. Korea 35 E13 39 36N 125 40 E
Ankaboa, Tanjon, Madag. . 57 C7 21 58S 43 20 E
Ankang, China 34 H5 32 40N 109 1 E
Ankara, Turkey 25 G5 39 57N 32 54 E
Ankaramena, Madag. . . . 57 C8 21 57S 46 39 E
Ankazoabo, Madag. 57 C7 22 18S 44 31 E
Ankazobe, Madag. 57 B8 18 20S 47 10 E
Ankeny, U.S.A. 80 E8 41 44N 93 36W

Ankisabe, Madag. 57 B8 19 17S 46 29 E
Ankoro,
 Dem. Rep. of the Congo . 54 D2 6 45S 26 55 E
Anmyŏn-do, S. Korea . . . 35 F14 36 25N 126 25 E
Ann, C., U.S.A. 79 D14 42 38N 70 35W
Ann Arbor, U.S.A. 76 D4 42 17N 83 45W
Anna, U.S.A. 81 G10 37 28N 89 15W
Annaba, Algeria 50 A7 36 50N 7 46 E
Annalee →, Ireland 13 B4 54 2N 7 24W
Annam, Vietnam 38 E7 16 0N 108 0 E
Annamitique, Chaîne, Asia 38 D6 17 0N 106 0 E
Annan, U.K. 12 G5 54 59N 3 16W
Annan →, U.K. 12 G5 54 58N 3 16W
Annapolis, U.S.A. 76 F7 38 59N 76 30W
Annapolis Royal, Canada . 71 D6 44 44N 65 32W
Annapurna, Nepal 43 E10 28 34N 83 50 E
Annean, L., Australia 61 E2 26 54S 118 14 E
Annecy, France 18 D7 45 55N 6 8 E
Anning, China 32 D5 24 55N 102 26 E
Anniston, U.S.A. 77 J3 33 39N 85 50W
Annobón, Atl. Oc. 49 G4 1 25S 5 36 E
Annotto Bay, Jamaica . . . 88 C4 18 17N 76 45W
Annville, U.S.A. 79 F8 40 20N 76 31W
Áno Viánnos, Greece . . . 23 D7 35 2N 25 21 E
Anorotsangana, Madag. . 57 A8 13 56S 47 55 E
Anóyia, Greece 23 D6 35 16N 24 52 E
Anping, Hebei, China 34 E8 38 15N 115 30 E
Anping, Liaoning, China . . 35 D12 41 5N 123 30 E
Anqing, China 33 C6 30 30N 117 3 E
Anqiu, China 35 F10 36 25N 119 10 E
Ansai, China 34 F5 36 50N 109 20 E
Ansbach, Germany 16 D6 49 28N 10 34 E
Anshan, China 35 D12 41 5N 122 58 E
Anshun, China 32 D5 26 18N 105 57 E
Ansley, U.S.A. 80 E5 41 18N 99 23W
Anson, U.S.A. 81 J5 32 45N 99 54W
Anson B., Australia 60 B5 13 20S 130 6 E
Ansongo, Mali 50 E6 15 25N 0 35 E
Ansonia, U.S.A. 79 E11 41 21N 73 5W
Anstruther, U.K. 12 E6 56 14N 2 41W
Ansudu, Indonesia 37 E9 2 11S 139 22 E
Antabamba, Peru 92 F4 14 40S 73 0W
Antakya, Turkey 25 G6 36 14N 36 10 E
Antalaha, Madag. 57 A9 14 57S 50 20 E
Antalya, Turkey 25 G5 36 52N 30 45 E
Antalya Körfezi, Turkey . . 25 G5 36 15N 31 30 E
Antananarivo, Madag. . . . 57 B8 18 55S 47 31 E
Antananarivo □, Madag. . 57 B8 19 0S 47 0 E
Antanimbaka, Madag. . . . 57 C7 21 30S 44 48 E
Antarctic Pen., Antarctica 5 C18 67 0S 60 0W
Antarctica 5 E3 90 0S 0 0 E
Antelope, Zimbabwe 55 G2 21 2S 28 31 E
Antequera, Paraguay . . . 94 A4 24 8S 57 7W
Antequera, Spain 19 D3 37 5N 4 33W
Antero, Mt., U.S.A. 83 G10 38 41N 106 15W
Anthony, Kans., U.S.A. . . 81 G5 37 9N 98 2W
Anthony, N. Mex., U.S.A. . 83 K10 32 0N 106 36W
Anti Atlas, Morocco 50 C4 30 0N 8 30W
Anti-Lebanon = Ash Sharqi,
 Al Jabal, Lebanon 47 B5 33 40N 36 10 E
Antibes, France 18 E7 43 34N 7 6 E
Anticosti, Î. d', Canada . . 71 C7 49 30N 63 0W
Antigo, U.S.A. 80 C10 45 9N 89 9W
Antigonish, Canada 71 C7 45 38N 61 58W
Antigua, Canary Is. 22 F5 28 24N 14 1W
Antigua, W. Indies 89 C7 17 0N 61 50W
Antigua & Barbuda ■,
 W. Indies 89 C7 17 20N 61 48W
Antigua Guatemala,
 Guatemala 88 D1 14 34N 90 41W
Antilla, Cuba 88 B4 20 40N 75 50W
Antilles = West Indies,
 Cent. Amer. 89 D7 15 0N 65 0W
Antioch, U.S.A. 84 G5 38 1N 121 48W
Antioquia, Colombia 92 B3 6 40N 75 55W
Antipodes Is., Pac. Oc. . . 64 M9 49 45S 178 40 E
Antlers, U.S.A. 81 H7 34 14N 95 37W
Antofagasta, Chile 94 A1 23 50S 70 30W
Antofagasta □, Chile 94 A2 24 0S 69 0W
Antofagasta de la Sierra,
 Argentina 94 B2 26 5S 67 20W
Antofalla, Argentina 94 B2 25 30S 68 5W
Antofalla, Salar de,
 Argentina 94 B2 25 40S 67 45W
Anton, U.S.A. 81 J3 33 49N 102 10W
Antongila, Helodrano,
 Madag. 57 B8 15 30S 49 50 E
Antonibé, Madag. 57 B8 15 7S 47 24 E
Antonibé, Presqu'île d',
 Madag. 57 A8 14 55S 47 20 E
Antonina, Brazil 95 B6 25 26S 48 42W
Antrim, U.K. 13 B5 54 43N 6 14W
Antrim, U.S.A. 78 F3 40 31N 80 21W
Antrim □, U.K. 13 B5 54 56N 6 25W
Antrim, Mts. of, U.K. 13 A5 55 3N 6 4W
Antrim Plateau, Australia 60 C4 18 8S 128 20 E
Antsalova, Madag. 57 B7 18 40S 44 37 E
Antsiranana, Madag. 57 A8 12 25S 49 20 E
Antsohimbondrona
 Seranana, Madag. 57 A8 13 7S 48 48 E
Antu, China 35 C15 42 30N 128 20 E
Antwerp = Antwerpen,
 Belgium 15 C4 51 13N 4 25 E
Antwerp, U.S.A. 79 B9 44 12N 75 37W
Antwerpen, Belgium 15 C4 51 13N 4 25 E
Antwerpen □, Belgium . . 15 C4 51 15N 4 40 E
Anupgarh, India 42 E5 29 10N 73 10 E
Anuppur, India 43 H9 23 6N 81 41 E
Anuradhapura, Sri Lanka . 40 Q12 8 22N 80 28 E
Anveh, Iran 45 E7 27 23N 54 11 E
Anvers = Antwerpen,
 Belgium 15 C4 51 13N 4 25 E
Anvers I., Antarctica 5 C17 64 30S 63 40W
Anxi, China 32 B4 40 30N 95 43 E
Anxious B., Australia 63 E1 33 24S 134 45 E
Anyang, China 34 F8 36 5N 114 21 E
Anyer-Kidul, Indonesia . . 37 G11 6 4S 105 52 E
Anyi, China 34 G6 35 2N 111 2 E
Anza, U.S.A. 85 M10 33 35N 116 39W
Anze, China 34 F7 36 10N 112 12 E
Anzhero-Sudzhensk, Russia 26 D9 56 10N 86 0 E
Ánzio, Italy 20 D5 41 27N 12 37 E
Aoga-Shima, Japan 31 H9 32 28N 139 46 E
Aomen = Macau, China . . 33 D6 22 16N 113 35 E
Aomori, Japan 30 D10 40 45N 140 45 E

102

Bahir Dar, *Ethiopia* **46 E2** 11 37N 37 10 E
Bahmanzād, *Iran* **45 D6** 31 15N 51 47 E
Bahr el Ghazâl □, *Sudan* . **51 G11** 7 0N 28 0 E
Bahraich, *India* **43 F9** 27 38N 81 37 E
Bahrain ■, *Asia* **45 E6** 26 0N 50 35 E
Bahror, *India* **42 F7** 27 51N 76 20 E
Bāhū Kalāt, *Iran* **45 E9** 25 43N 61 25 E
Bai Bung, Mui = Ca Mau,
 Mui, *Vietnam* **39 H5** 8 38N 104 44 E
Bai Duc, *Vietnam* **38 C5** 18 3N 105 49 E
Bai Thuong, *Vietnam* **38 C5** 19 54N 105 23 E
Baia Mare, *Romania* ... **17 E12** 47 40N 23 35 E
Baião, *Brazil* **93 D9** 2 40S 49 40W
Baïbokoum, *Chad* **51 G9** 7 46N 15 43 E
Baicheng, *China* **35 B12** 45 38N 122 42 E
Baidoa, *Somali Rep.* **46 G3** 3 8N 43 30 E
Baie Comeau, *Canada* .. **71 C6** 49 12N 68 10W
Baie-St-Paul, *Canada* .. **71 C5** 47 28N 70 32W
Baie Trinité, *Canada* ... **71 C6** 49 25N 67 20W
Baie Verte, *Canada* **71 C8** 49 55N 56 12W
Baihar, *India* **43 H9** 22 6N 80 33 E
Baihe, *China* **34 H6** 32 50N 110 5 E
Ba'ijī, *Iraq* **44 C4** 35 0N 43 30 E
Baijnath, *India* **43 E8** 29 55N 79 37 E
Baikal, L. = Baykal, Oz.,
 Russia **27 D11** 53 0N 108 0 E
Baikunthpur, *India* **43 H10** 23 15N 82 33 E
Baile Atha Cliath = Dublin,
 Ireland **13 C5** 53 21N 6 15W
Băilești, *Romania* **17 F12** 44 1N 23 20 E
Bainbridge, Ga., *U.S.A.* . **77 K3** 30 55N 84 35W
Bainbridge, N.Y., *U.S.A.* . **79 D9** 42 18N 75 29W
Baing, *Indonesia* **37 F6** 10 14S 120 34 E
Bainiu, *China* **34 H7** 32 50N 112 15 E
Bā'ir, *Jordan* **47 E5** 30 45N 36 55 E
Bairiki, *Kiribati* **64 G9** 1 30N 173 0 E
Bairin Youqi, *China* ... **35 C10** 43 30N 118 15 E
Bairin Zuoqi, *China* ... **35 C10** 43 58N 119 15 E
Bairnsdale, *Australia* .. **63 F4** 37 48S 147 36 E
Baisha, *China* **34 G7** 34 20N 112 32 E
Baitadi, *Nepal* **43 E9** 29 35N 80 25 E
Baiyin, *China* **34 F3** 36 45N 104 14 E
Baiyu Shan, *China* **34 F4** 37 15N 107 30 E
Baj Baj, *India* **43 H13** 22 30N 88 5 E
Baja, *Hungary* **17 E10** 46 12N 18 59 E
Baja, Pta., *Mexico* **86 B1** 29 50N 116 0W
Baja California, *Mexico* . **86 A1** 31 10N 115 12W
Baja California □, *Mexico* . **86 B2** 30 0N 115 0W
Baja California Sur □,
 Mexico **86 B2** 25 50N 111 50W
Bajag, *India* **43 H9** 22 40N 81 21 E
Bajamar, *Canary Is.* **22 F3** 28 33N 16 20W
Bajana, *India* **42 H4** 23 7N 71 49 E
Bājgīrān, *Iran* **45 B8** 37 36N 58 24 E
Bajimba, Mt., *Australia* . **63 D5** 29 17S 152 6 E
Bajo Nuevo, *Caribbean* .. **88 C4** 15 40N 78 50W
Bajoga, *Nigeria* **51 F8** 10 57N 11 20 E
Bajool, *Australia* **62 C5** 23 40S 150 35 E
Bakel, *Senegal* **50 F3** 14 56N 12 20W
Baker, Calif., *U.S.A.* ... **85 K10** 35 16N 116 4W
Baker, Mont., *U.S.A.* ... **80 B2** 46 22N 104 17W
Baker, L., *Canada* **68 B10** 64 0N 96 0W
Baker City, *U.S.A.* **82 D5** 44 47N 117 50W
Baker I., *Pac. Oc.* **64 G10** 0 10N 176 35W
Baker I., *U.S.A.* **72 B2** 55 20N 133 40W
Baker L., *Australia* **61 E4** 26 54S 126 5 E
Baker Lake, *Canada* **68 B10** 64 20N 96 3W
Baker Mt., *U.S.A.* **82 B3** 48 50N 121 49W
Bakers Creek, *Australia* . **62 C4** 21 13S 149 7 E
Baker's Dozen Is., *Canada* . **70 A4** 56 45N 78 45W
Bakersfield, Calif., *U.S.A.* . **85 K8** 35 23N 119 1W
Bakersfield, Vt., *U.S.A.* . **79 B12** 44 45N 72 48W
Bākhtarān, *Iran* **44 C5** 34 23N 47 0 E
Bākhtarān □, *Iran* **44 C5** 34 0N 46 30 E
Bakı, *Azerbaijan* **25 F8** 40 29N 49 56 E
Bakkafjörður, *Iceland* ... **8 C6** 66 2N 14 48W
Bakony, *Hungary* **17 E9** 47 10N 17 30 E
Bakony Forest = Bakony,
 Hungary **17 E9** 47 10N 17 30 E
Bakouma, *C.A.R.* **52 C4** 5 40N 22 56 E
Bakswaho, *India* **43 G8** 24 15N 79 18 E
Bakutis Coast, *Antarctica* . **5 D15** 74 0S 120 0W
Baku = Bakı, *Azerbaijan* . **25 F8** 40 29N 49 56 E
Bala, *Canada* **78 A5** 45 1N 79 37W
Bala, *U.K.* **10 E4** 52 54N 3 36W
Bala, L., *U.K.* **10 E4** 52 53N 3 37W
Balabac I., *Phil.* **36 C5** 8 0N 117 0 E
Balabac Str., *E. Indies* .. **36 C5** 7 53N 117 5 E
Balabagh, *Afghan.* **42 B4** 34 25N 70 12 E
Ba'labakk, *Lebanon* **47 B5** 34 0N 36 10 E
Balabalangan, Kepulauan,
 Indonesia **36 E5** 2 20S 117 30 E
Balad, *Iraq* **44 C5** 34 1N 44 9 E
Balad Rūz, *Iraq* **44 C5** 33 42N 45 5 E
Bālādeh, *Fārs, Iran* **45 D6** 29 17N 51 56 E
Bālādeh, *Māzandarān, Iran* . **45 B6** 36 12N 51 48 E
Balaghat, *India* **40 J12** 21 49N 80 12 E
Balaghat Ra., *India* **40 K10** 18 50N 76 30 E
Balaguer, *Spain* **19 B6** 41 50N 0 50 E
Balaklava, *Ukraine* **25 F5** 44 30N 33 30 E
Balakovo, *Russia* **24 D8** 52 4N 47 55 E
Balamau, *India* **43 F9** 27 10N 80 21 E
Balancán, *Mexico* **87 D6** 17 48N 91 32W
Balashov, *Russia* **25 D7** 51 30N 43 10 E
Balasinor, *India* **42 H5** 22 57N 73 23 E
Balasore = Baleshwar, *India* **41 J15** 21 35N 87 3 E
Balaton, *Hungary* **17 E9** 46 50N 17 40 E
Balbina, Reprêsa de, *Brazil* **92 D7** 2 0S 59 30W
Balboa, *Panama* **88 E4** 8 57N 79 34W
Balbriggan, *Ireland* **13 C5** 53 37N 6 11W
Balcarce, *Argentina* ... **94 D4** 38 0S 58 10W
Balcarres, *Canada* **73 C8** 50 50N 103 35W
Balchik, *Bulgaria* **21 C13** 43 28N 28 11 E
Balclutha, *N.Z.* **59 M2** 46 15S 169 45 E
Balcones Escarpment,
 U.S.A. **81 L5** 29 30N 99 15W
Bald Hd., *Australia* **61 G2** 35 6S 118 1 E
Bald I., *Australia* **61 F2** 34 57S 118 27 E
Bald Knob, *U.S.A.* **81 H9** 35 19N 91 34W
Baldock L., *Canada* **73 B9** 56 33N 97 57W
Baldwin, Mich., *U.S.A.* . **76 D3** 43 54N 85 51W
Baldwin, Pa., *U.S.A.* ... **78 F5** 40 23N 79 59W
Baldwinsville, *U.S.A.* ... **79 C8** 43 10N 76 20W
Baldy Mt., *U.S.A.* **82 B9** 48 9N 109 39W
Baldy Peak, *U.S.A.* **83 K9** 33 54N 109 34W
Baleares, Is., *Spain* ... **22 B10** 39 30N 3 0 E

Balearic Is. = Baleares, Is.,
 Spain **22 B10** 39 30N 3 0 E
Baleine = Whale →,
 Canada **71 A6** 58 15N 67 40W
Baler, *Phil.* **37 A6** 15 46N 121 34 E
Baleshare, *U.K.* **12 D1** 57 31N 7 22W
Baleshwar, *India* **41 J15** 21 35N 87 3 E
Balfate, *Honduras* **88 C2** 15 48N 86 25W
Bali, *Greece* **23 D6** 35 25N 24 47 E
Bali, *India* **42 G5** 25 11N 73 17 E
Bali □, *Indonesia* **36 F5** 8 20S 115 0 E
Bali, Selat, *Indonesia* .. **37 H16** 8 18S 114 25 E
Baliapal, *India* **43 J12** 21 40N 87 17 E
Balikeşir, *Turkey* **21 E12** 39 39N 27 53 E
Balikpapan, *Indonesia* .. **36 E5** 1 10S 116 55 E
Balimbing, *Phil.* **37 C5** 5 10N 119 58 E
Baling, *Malaysia* **39 K3** 5 41N 100 55 E
Balipara, *India* **41 F18** 26 50N 92 45 E
Balkan Mts. = Stara Planina,
 Bulgaria **21 C10** 43 15N 23 0 E
Balkhash = Balqash,
 Kazakhstan **26 E8** 46 50N 74 50 E
Balkhash, Ozero = Balqash
 Köl, *Kazakhstan* **26 E8** 46 0N 74 50 E
Balla, *Bangla.* **41 G17** 24 10N 91 35 E
Ballachulish, *U.K.* **12 E3** 56 41N 5 8W
Balladonia, *Australia* .. **61 F3** 32 27S 123 51 E
Ballaghaderreen, *Ireland* . **13 C3** 53 55N 8 34W
Ballarat, *Australia* **63 F3** 37 33S 143 50 E
Ballard, L., *Australia* .. **61 E3** 29 20S 120 40 E
Ballater, *U.K.* **12 D5** 57 3N 3 3W
Ballenas, Canal de, *Mexico* **86 B2** 29 10N 113 45W
Balleny Is., *Antarctica* . **5 C11** 66 30S 163 0 E
Ballia, *India* **43 G11** 25 46N 84 12 E
Ballina, *Australia* **63 D5** 28 50S 153 31 E
Ballina, *Ireland* **13 B2** 54 7N 9 9W
Ballinasloe, *Ireland* ... **13 C3** 53 20N 8 13W
Ballinger, *U.S.A.* **81 K5** 31 45N 99 57W
Ballinrobe, *Ireland* **13 C2** 53 38N 9 13W
Ballinskelligs B., *Ireland* . **13 E1** 51 48N 10 13W
Ballston Spa, *U.S.A.* ... **79 D11** 43 0N 73 51W
Ballycastle, *U.K.* **13 A5** 55 12N 6 15W
Ballyclare, *U.K.* **13 B5** 54 46N 6 0W
Ballyhaunis, *Ireland* ... **13 C3** 53 46N 8 46W
Ballymena, *U.K.* **13 B5** 54 52N 6 17W
Ballymoney, *U.K.* **13 A5** 55 5N 6 31W
Ballymote, *Ireland* **13 B3** 54 5N 8 31W
Ballynahinch, *U.K.* **13 B6** 54 24N 5 54W
Ballyquintin Pt., *U.K.* .. **13 B6** 54 20N 5 30W
Ballyshannon, *Ireland* .. **13 B3** 54 30N 8 11W
Balmaceda, *Chile* **96 F2** 46 0S 71 50W
Balmertown, *Canada* ... **73 C10** 51 4N 93 41W
Balmoral, *Australia* **63 F3** 37 15S 141 48 E
Balmorhea, *U.S.A.* **81 K3** 30 59N 103 45W
Balonne →, *Australia* .. **63 D4** 28 47S 147 56 E
Balotra, *India* **42 G5** 25 50N 72 14 E
Balqash, *Kazakhstan* ... **26 E8** 46 50N 74 50 E
Balqash Köl, *Kazakhstan* . **26 E8** 46 0N 74 50 E
Balrampur, *India* **43 F10** 27 30N 82 20 E
Balranald, *Australia* ... **63 E3** 34 38S 143 33 E
Balsas, *Mexico* **87 D5** 18 0N 99 40W
Balsas →, *Brazil* **93 E9** 7 15S 44 35W
Balsas →, *Mexico* **86 D4** 17 55N 102 10W
Balston Spa, *U.S.A.* ... **79 D11** 43 0N 73 52W
Balta, *Ukraine* **17 D15** 48 2N 29 45 E
Bălți, *Moldova* **17 E14** 47 48N 27 58 E
Baltic Sea, *Europe* **9 H18** 57 0N 19 0 E
Baltimore, *Ireland* **13 E2** 51 29N 9 22W
Baltimore, Md., *U.S.A.* . **76 F7** 39 17N 76 37W
Baltimore, Ohio, *U.S.A.* . **78 G2** 39 51N 82 36W
Baltit, *Pakistan* **43 A6** 36 15N 74 40 E
Baltiysk, *Russia* **9 J18** 54 41N 19 58 E
Balurghat, *India* **43 G13** 25 15N 88 44 E
Balvi, *Latvia* **9 H22** 57 8N 27 15 E
Balya, *Turkey* **21 E12** 39 44N 27 35 E
Bam, *Iran* **45 D8** 29 7N 58 14 E
Bama, *Nigeria* **51 F8** 11 33N 13 41 E
Bamaga, *Australia* **62 A3** 10 50S 142 25 E
Bamaji L., *Canada* **70 B1** 51 9N 91 25W
Bamako, *Mali* **50 F4** 12 34N 7 55W
Bambari, *C.A.R.* **52 C4** 5 40N 20 35 E
Bambaroo, *Australia* ... **62 B4** 18 50S 146 10 E
Bamberg, *Germany* **16 D6** 49 54N 10 54 E
Bamberg, *U.S.A.* **77 J5** 33 18N 81 2W
Bambili, Dem. Rep. of
 the Congo **54 B2** 3 40N 26 0 E
Bamenda, *Cameroon* ... **52 C1** 5 57N 10 11 E
Bamfield, *Canada* **72 D3** 48 45N 125 10W
Bāmīān □, *Afghan.* **40 B5** 35 0N 67 0 E
Bamiancheng, *China* ... **35 C13** 43 15N 124 2 E
Bampūr, *Iran* **45 E9** 27 15N 60 21 E
Ban Ban, *Laos* **38 C4** 19 31N 103 30 E
Ban Bang Hin, *Thailand* . **39 H2** 9 32N 98 35 E
Ban Chiang Klang, *Thailand* **38 C3** 19 25N 100 55 E
Ban Chik, *Laos* **38 D4** 17 15N 102 22 E
Ban Choho, *Thailand* ... **38 E4** 15 2N 102 9 E
Ban Dan Lan Hoi, *Thailand* **38 D2** 17 0N 99 35 E
Ban Don = Surat Thani,
 Thailand **39 H2** 9 6N 99 20 E
Ban Don, *Vietnam* **38 F6** 12 53N 107 48 E
Ban Don, Ao →, *Thailand* **39 H2** 9 20N 99 25 E
Ban Dong, *Thailand* ... **38 C3** 19 30N 100 59 E
Ban Hong, *Thailand* ... **38 C2** 18 18N 98 50 E
Ban Kaeng, *Thailand* .. **38 D3** 17 29N 100 7 E
Ban Kantang, *Thailand* . **39 J2** 7 25N 99 31 E
Ban Keun, *Laos* **38 C4** 18 22N 102 35 E
Ban Khai, *Thailand* **38 F3** 12 46N 101 18 E
Ban Kheun, *Laos* **38 B3** 20 13N 101 7 E
Ban Khlong Kua, *Thailand* **39 J3** 6 57N 100 8 E
Ban Khuan Mao, *Thailand* **39 J2** 7 50N 99 37 E
Ban Ko Yai Chim, *Thailand* **39 J2** 11 17N 99 26 E
Ban Kok, *Thailand* **38 D4** 16 40N 103 40 E
Ban Laem, *Thailand* ... **38 F2** 13 13N 99 59 E
Ban Lao Ngam, *Laos* ... **38 E6** 15 28N 106 10 E
Ban Le Thanh, *Thailand* . **38 C2** 19 11N 99 31 E
Ban Mae Chedi, *Thailand* **38 C2** 19 11N 99 33 E
Ban Mae Laeng, *Thailand* **38 B2** 20 1N 99 17 E
Ban Mae Sariang, *Thailand* **38 C1** 18 10N 97 56 E
Ban Mê Thuôt = Buon Ma
 Thuot, *Vietnam* **38 F7** 12 40N 108 3 E
Ban Mi, *Thailand* **38 E3** 15 3N 100 32 E
Ban Muong Mo, *Laos* .. **38 C4** 19 4N 103 58 E
Ban Na Mo, *Laos* **38 D5** 17 7N 105 40 E
Ban Na Tong, *Laos* **38 B3** 20 56N 101 47 E
Ban Nam Bac, *Laos* ... **38 B4** 20 38N 102 20 E
Ban Nam Ma, *Laos* **38 A3** 22 2N 101 37 E

Ban Ngang, *Laos* **38 E6** 15 59N 106 11 E
Ban Nong Bok, *Laos* ... **38 D5** 17 5N 104 48 E
Ban Nong Boua, *Laos* .. **38 E5** 15 40N 106 33 E
Ban Nong Pling, *Thailand* **38 E3** 15 40N 100 10 E
Ban Pak Chan, *Thailand* . **39 G2** 10 32N 98 51 E
Ban Phai, *Thailand* **38 D4** 16 4N 102 44 E
Ban Pong, *Thailand* ... **38 F2** 13 50N 99 55 E
Ban Ron Phibun, *Thailand* **39 H2** 8 9N 99 51 E
Ban Sanam Chai, *Thailand* **39 J3** 7 33N 100 25 E
Ban Sangkha, *Thailand* . **38 E4** 14 37N 103 52 E
Ban Tak, *Thailand* **38 D2** 17 2N 99 4 E
Ban Tako, *Thailand* **38 E4** 14 5N 102 40 E
Ban Tha Dua, *Thailand* . **38 D2** 17 59N 98 39 E
Ban Tha Li, *Thailand* ... **38 D3** 17 37N 101 25 E
Ban Tha Nun, *Thailand* . **39 H2** 8 12N 98 18 E
Ban Thahine, *Laos* **38 E5** 14 12N 105 33 E
Ban Xien Kok, *Laos* **38 B3** 20 54N 100 39 E
Ban Yen Nhan, *Vietnam* . **38 B6** 20 57N 106 2 E
Banaba, *Kiribati* **64 H8** 0 45S 169 50 E
Banalia, Dem. Rep. of
 the Congo **54 B2** 1 32N 25 5 E
Banam, *Cambodia* **39 G5** 11 20N 105 17 E
Bananal, I. do, *Brazil* .. **93 F8** 11 30S 50 30W
Banaras = Varanasi, *India* **43 G10** 25 22N 83 0 E
Banas →, *Gujarat, India* **42 H4** 23 45N 71 25 E
Banas →, *Mad. P., India* **43 G9** 24 15N 81 30 E
Bânâs, Ras, *Egypt* **51 D13** 23 57N 35 59 E
Banbān, *Si. Arabia* **44 E5** 25 1N 46 35 E
Banbridge, *U.K.* **13 B5** 54 22N 6 16W
Banbury, *U.K.* **11 E6** 52 4N 1 20W
Banchory, *U.K.* **12 D6** 57 3N 2 29W
Bancroft, *Canada* **78 A7** 45 3N 77 51W
Band Boni, *Iran* **45 E8** 25 30N 59 33 E
Band Qīr, *Iran* **45 D6** 31 39N 48 53 E
Banda, *India* **43 G9** 25 30N 80 26 E
Banda, Mad. P., *India* .. **43 G8** 24 3N 78 57 E
Banda, Kepulauan,
 Indonesia **37 E7** 4 37S 129 50 E
Banda Aceh, *Indonesia* . **36 C1** 5 35N 95 20 E
Banda Banda, Mt., *Australia* **63 E5** 31 10S 152 28 E
Banda Elat, *Indonesia* .. **37 F8** 5 40S 133 5 E
Banda Is. = Banda,
 Kepulauan, *Indonesia* . **37 E7** 4 37S 129 50 E
Banda Sea, *Indonesia* .. **37 F8** 6 0S 130 0 E
Bandai-San, *Japan* **30 F10** 37 36N 140 4 E
Bandān, *Iran* **45 D9** 31 23N 60 44 E
Bandanaira, *Indonesia* . **37 E7** 4 32S 129 54 E
Bandanwara, *India* **42 F6** 26 9N 74 38 E
Bandar = Machilipatnam,
 India **41 L12** 16 12N 81 8 E
Bandar 'Abbās, *Iran* ... **45 E8** 27 15N 56 15 E
Bandar-e Anzalī, *Iran* .. **45 B6** 37 30N 49 30 E
Bandar-e Bushehr =
 Büshehr, *Iran* **45 D6** 28 55N 50 55 E
Bandar-e Chārak, *Iran* . **45 E7** 26 45N 54 20 E
Bandar-e Deylam, *Iran* . **45 D6** 30 5N 50 10 E
Bandar-e Khomeynī, *Iran* **45 D6** 30 30N 49 5 E
Bandar-e Lengeh, *Iran* . **45 E7** 26 35N 54 58 E
Bandar-e Maqām, *Iran* . **45 E7** 26 56N 53 29 E
Bandar-e Ma'shur, *Iran* . **45 D6** 30 35N 49 10 E
Bandar-e Nakhīlū, *Iran* . **45 E7** 26 58N 53 30 E
Bandar-e Rīg, *Iran* **45 D6** 29 29N 50 38 E
Bandar-e Torkeman, *Iran* **45 B7** 37 0N 54 10 E
Bandar Maharani = Muar,
 Malaysia **39 L4** 2 3N 102 34 E
Bandar Penggaram = Batu
 Pahat, *Malaysia* **39 M4** 1 50N 102 56 E
Bandar Seri Begawan,
 Brunei **36 D5** 4 52N 115 0 E
Bandar Sri Aman, *Malaysia* **36 D4** 1 15N 111 32 E
Bandawe, *Malawi* **55 E3** 11 58S 34 5 E
Bandeira, Pico da, *Brazil* **95 A7** 20 26S 41 47W
Bandera, *Argentina* **94 B3** 28 55S 62 20W
Banderas, B. de, *Mexico* **86 C3** 20 40N 105 30W
Bandhogarh, *India* **43 H9** 23 40N 81 2 E
Bandi →, *India* **42 F6** 26 12N 75 47 E
Bandikui, *India* **42 F7** 27 3N 76 34 E
Bandırma, *Turkey* **21 D13** 40 20N 28 0 E
Bandon, *Ireland* **13 E3** 51 44N 8 44W
Bandon →, *Ireland* **13 E3** 51 43N 8 37W
Bandula, *Mozam.* **55 F3** 19 0S 33 7 E
Bandundu, Dem. Rep. of
 the Congo **52 E3** 3 15S 17 22 E
Bandung, *Indonesia* ... **37 G12** 6 54S 107 36 E
Bāneh, *Iran* **44 C5** 35 59N 45 53 E
Banes, *Cuba* **89 B4** 21 0N 75 42W
Banff, *Canada* **72 C5** 51 10N 115 34W
Banff, *U.K.* **12 D6** 57 40N 2 33W
Banff Nat. Park, *Canada* . **72 C5** 51 30N 116 15W
Bang Fai →, *Laos* **38 D5** 16 57N 104 45 E
Bang Hieng →, *Laos* ... **38 D5** 16 10N 105 10 E
Bang Krathum, *Thailand* **38 D3** 16 34N 100 18 E
Bang Lamung, *Thailand* . **38 F3** 13 3N 100 56 E
Bang Mun Nak, *Thailand* **38 D3** 16 2N 100 23 E
Bang Pa In, *Thailand* ... **38 E3** 14 14N 100 35 E
Bang Rakam, *Thailand* . **38 D3** 16 45N 100 7 E
Bang Saphan, *Thailand* . **39 G2** 11 14N 99 28 E
Bangaduni I., *India* **43 J13** 21 34N 88 52 E
Bangala Dam, *Zimbabwe* **55 G3** 21 7S 31 25 E
Bangalore, *India* **40 N10** 12 59N 77 40 E
Banganga →, *India* **42 F6** 26 7N 76 49 E
Bangaon, *India* **43 H13** 23 0N 88 47 E
Bangassou, *C.A.R.* **52 D4** 4 55N 23 7 E
Banggai, *Indonesia* **37 E6** 1 34S 123 30 E
Banggai, Kepulauan,
 Indonesia **37 E6** 1 40S 123 30 E
Banggai Arch. = Banggai,
 Kepulauan, *Indonesia* . **37 E6** 1 40S 123 30 E
Banggi, *Malaysia* **36 C5** 7 17N 117 12 E
Banghāzī, *Libya* **51 B10** 32 11N 20 3 E
Bangka, Sulawesi,
 Indonesia **37 D7** 1 50N 125 5 E
Bangka, Sumatera,
 Indonesia **36 E3** 2 0S 105 50 E
Bangka, Selat, *Indonesia* **36 E3** 2 30S 105 30 E
Bangkalan, *Indonesia* .. **37 G15** 7 2S 112 46 E
Bangkinang, *Indonesia* . **36 D2** 0 18N 101 5 E
Bangko, *Indonesia* **36 E2** 2 5S 102 9 E
Bangkok, *Thailand* **38 F3** 13 45N 100 35 E
Bangladesh ■, *Asia* ... **41 H17** 24 0N 90 0 E
Bangong Co, *India* **43 B8** 35 50N 79 20 E
Bangor, Down, *U.K.* ... **13 B6** 54 40N 5 40W
Bangor, Gwynedd, *U.K.* . **10 D3** 53 14N 4 8W
Bangor, Maine, *U.S.A.* . **69 D13** 44 48N 68 46W
Bangor, Pa., *U.S.A.* ... **79 F9** 40 52N 75 13W
Bangued, *Phil.* **37 A6** 17 40N 120 37 E
Bangui, *C.A.R.* **52 D3** 4 23N 18 35 E

Banguru, Dem. Rep. of
 the Congo **54 B2** 0 30N 27 10 E
Bangweulu, L., *Zambia* . **55 E3** 11 0S 30 0 E
Bangweulu Swamp,
 Zambia **55 E3** 11 20S 30 15 E
Bani, *Dom. Rep.* **89 C5** 18 16N 70 22W
Bani Sa'd, *Iraq* **44 C5** 33 34N 44 32 E
Banihal Pass, *India* **43 C6** 33 30N 75 12 E
Bāniyās, *Syria* **44 C3** 35 10N 36 0 E
Banja Luka, *Bos.-H.* ... **20 B7** 44 49N 17 11 E
Banjar, *India* **42 D7** 31 38N 77 21 E
Banjar →, *India* **43 H9** 22 36N 80 22 E
Banjarmasin, *Indonesia* . **36 E4** 3 20S 114 35 E
Banjul, *Gambia* **50 F2** 13 28N 16 40W
Banka, *India* **43 G12** 24 53N 86 55 E
Banket, *Zimbabwe* **55 F3** 17 27S 30 19 E
Bankipore, *India* **41 G14** 25 35N 85 10 E
Banks I., B.C., *Canada* . **72 C3** 53 20N 130 0W
Banks I., N.W.T., *Canada* **4 B1** 73 15N 121 30W
Banks Pen., *N.Z.* **59 K4** 43 45S 173 15 E
Banks Str., *Australia* ... **62 G4** 40 40S 148 10 E
Bankura, *India* **43 H12** 23 11N 87 18 E
Banmankhi, *India* **43 G12** 25 53N 87 11 E
Bann →, Arm., *U.K.* ... **13 B5** 54 30N 6 31W
Bann →, L'derry., *U.K.* . **13 A5** 55 8N 6 41W
Bannang Sata, *Thailand* . **39 J3** 6 16N 101 16 E
Banning, *U.S.A.* **85 M10** 33 56N 116 53W
Banningville = Bandundu,
 Dem. Rep. of the Congo **52 E3** 3 15S 17 22 E
Bannockburn, *Canada* .. **78 B7** 44 39N 77 33W
Bannockburn, *U.K.* **12 E5** 56 5N 3 55W
Bannockburn, *Zimbabwe* **55 G2** 20 17S 29 48 E
Bannu, *Pakistan* **40 C7** 33 0N 70 18 E
Bano, *India* **43 H11** 22 40N 84 55 E
Bansgaon, *India* **43 F10** 26 33N 83 21 E
Banská Bystrica,
 Slovak Rep. **17 D10** 48 46N 19 14 E
Banswara, *India* **42 H6** 23 32N 74 24 E
Bantaeng, *Indonesia* ... **37 F5** 5 32S 119 56 E
Bantry, *Ireland* **13 E2** 51 41N 9 27W
Bantry B., *Ireland* **13 E2** 51 37N 9 44W
Bantul, *Indonesia* **37 G14** 7 55S 110 19 E
Bantva, *India* **42 J4** 21 29N 70 12 E
Banu, *Afghan.* **40 B6** 35 35N 69 5 E
Banyak, Kepulauan,
 Indonesia **36 D1** 2 10N 97 10 E
Banyalbufar, *Spain* **22 B9** 39 42N 2 31 E
Banyo, *Cameroon* **52 C2** 6 52N 11 45 E
Banyumas, *Indonesia* .. **37 G13** 7 32S 109 18 E
Banyuwangi, *Indonesia* . **37 H16** 8 13S 114 21 E
Banzare Coast, *Antarctica* **5 C9** 68 0S 125 0 E
Banzyville = Mobayi,
 Dem. Rep. of the Congo **52 D4** 4 15N 21 8 E
Bao Lac, *Vietnam* **38 A5** 22 57N 105 40 E
Bao Loc, *Vietnam* **39 G6** 11 32N 107 48 E
Baocheng, *China* **34 H4** 33 12N 106 56 E
Baode, *China* **34 E6** 39 1N 111 5 E
Baodi, *China* **35 E9** 39 38N 117 20 E
Baoding, *China* **34 E8** 38 50N 115 28 E
Baoji, *China* **34 G4** 34 20N 107 5 E
Baoshan, *China* **32 D4** 25 10N 99 5 E
Baoying, *China* **35 H10** 33 17N 119 20 E
Bap, *India* **42 F5** 27 23N 72 18 E
Bapatla, *India* **41 M12** 15 55N 80 30 E
Bāqerābād, *Iran* **45 C6** 33 2N 51 58 E
Ba'qūbah, *Iraq* **44 C5** 33 45N 44 50 E
Baquedano, *Chile* **94 A2** 23 20S 69 52W
Bar, *Montenegro, Yug.* . **21 C8** 42 8N 19 6 E
Bar, *Ukraine* **17 D14** 49 4N 27 40 E
Bar Bigha, *India* **43 G11** 25 21N 85 47 E
Bar Harbor, *U.S.A.* **77 C11** 44 23N 68 13W
Bar-le-Duc, *France* **18 B6** 48 47N 5 10 E
Bara, *India* **43 F9** 26 55N 81 12 E
Bara Banki, *India* **43 F9** 26 55N 81 12 E
Barabai, *Indonesia* **36 E5** 2 32S 115 34 E
Baraboo, *U.S.A.* **80 D10** 43 28N 89 45W
Baracoa, *Cuba* **89 B5** 20 20N 74 30W
Baradá →, *Syria* **47 B5** 33 20N 36 49 E
Baradero, *Argentina* ... **94 C4** 33 52S 59 29W
Baradine, *Australia* **63 E4** 30 56S 149 4 E
Baraga, *U.S.A.* **80 B10** 46 47N 88 30W
Barah →, *India* **42 F7** 27 42N 77 5 E
Barahona, *Dom. Rep.* .. **89 C5** 18 13N 71 7W
Barail Range, *India* **41 G18** 25 15N 93 20 E
Barakaldo, *Spain* **19 A4** 43 18N 2 59W
Barakar →, *India* **43 G12** 24 7N 86 14 E
Barakhola, *India* **41 G18** 25 0N 92 45 E
Barakpur, *India* **43 H13** 22 44N 88 30 E
Baralaba, *Australia* **62 C4** 24 13S 149 50 E
Baramula, *India* **43 B6** 34 15N 74 20 E
Baran, *India* **42 G7** 25 9N 76 40 E
Baran →, *Pakistan* **42 G3** 25 13N 68 17 E
Baranavichy, *Belarus* ... **17 B14** 53 10N 26 0 E
Baranof, *U.S.A.* **72 B2** 57 5N 134 50W
Baranof I., *U.S.A.* **68 C6** 57 0N 135 0W
Barapasi, *Indonesia* ... **37 E9** 2 15S 137 5 E
Barasat, *India* **43 H13** 22 46N 88 31 E
Barat Daya, Kepulauan,
 Indonesia **37 F7** 7 30S 128 0 E
Barataria B., *U.S.A.* ... **81 L10** 29 20N 89 55W
Barauda, *India* **42 H6** 23 33N 75 15 E
Baraut, *India* **42 E7** 29 13N 77 7 E
Barbacena, *Brazil* **95 A7** 21 15S 43 56W
Barbados ■, W. Indies .. **89 D8** 13 10N 59 30W
Bárbara, C. de, *Spain* .. **22 C7** 38 39N 1 24 E
Barbastro, *Spain* **19 A6** 42 2N 0 5 E
Barberton, S. Africa **57 D5** 25 42S 31 2 E
Barberton, *U.S.A.* **78 E3** 41 0N 81 39W
Barbosa, *Colombia* **92 B4** 5 57N 73 37W
Barbourville, *U.S.A.* ... **77 G4** 36 52N 83 53W
Barbuda, W. Indies **89 C7** 17 30N 61 40W
Barcaldine, *Australia* .. **62 C4** 23 43S 145 6 E
Barcellona Pozzo di Gotto,
 Italy **20 E6** 38 9N 15 13 E
Barcelona, *Spain* **19 B7** 41 21N 2 10 E
Barcelona, *Venezuela* .. **92 A6** 10 10N 64 40W
Barcelos, *Brazil* **92 D6** 1 0S 63 0W
Barcoo →, *Australia* ... **62 D3** 25 30S 142 50 E
Bardaï, *Chad* **51 D9** 21 25N 17 0 E
Bardas Blancas, *Argentina* **94 D2** 35 49S 69 45W
Barddhaman, *India* **43 H12** 23 14N 87 39 E
Bardejov, Slovak Rep. .. **17 D11** 49 18N 21 15 E
Bardera, *Somali Rep.* .. **46 G3** 2 20N 42 27 E
Bardīyah, *Libya* **51 B10** 31 45N 25 5 E
Bardsey I., *U.K.* **10 E3** 52 45N 4 47W
Bardstown, *U.S.A.* **76 G3** 37 49N 85 28W

Bareilly

Bareilly, India 43 E8 28 22N 79 27 E
Barela, India 43 H9 23 6N 80 3 E
Barents Sea, Arctic 4 B9 73 0N 39 0 E
Barfleur, Pte. de, France .. 18 B3 49 42N 1 16W
Bargara, Australia 62 C5 24 50S 152 25 E
Barguzin, Russia 27 D11 53 37N 109 37 E
Barh, India 43 G11 25 29N 85 46 E
Barhaj, India 43 F10 26 18N 83 44 E
Barham, Australia 63 F3 35 36S 144 8 E
Barharwa, India 43 G12 24 52N 87 47 E
Barhi, India 43 G11 24 15N 85 25 E
Bari, India 42 F7 26 39N 77 39 E
Bari, Italy 20 D7 41 8N 16 51 E
Bari Doab, Pakistan 42 D5 30 20N 73 0 E
Bari Sadri, India 42 G6 24 28N 74 30 E
Barīdī, Ra's, Si. Arabia ... 44 E3 24 17N 37 31 E
Barīm, Yemen 48 E8 12 39N 43 25 E
Barinas, Venezuela 92 B4 8 36N 70 15W
Baring, C., Canada 68 B8 70 0N 117 30W
Baringo, Kenya 54 B4 0 47N 36 16 E
Baringo, L., Kenya 54 B4 0 47N 36 16 E
Barisal, Bangla. 41 H17 22 45N 90 20 E
Barisan, Bukit, Indonesia . 36 E2 3 30S 102 15 E
Barito →, Indonesia 36 E4 4 0S 114 50 E
Bark L., Canada 78 A7 45 27N 77 51W
Barkakana, India 43 H11 23 37N 85 29 E
Barker, U.S.A. 78 C6 43 20N 78 33W
Barkley, L., U.S.A. 77 G2 37 1N 88 14W
Barkley Sound, Canada ... 72 D3 48 50N 125 10W
Barkly East, S. Africa 56 E4 30 58S 27 33 E
Barkly Roadhouse, Australia 62 B2 19 52S 135 50 E
Barkly Tableland, Australia 62 B2 17 50S 136 40 E
Barkly West, S. Africa 56 D3 28 5S 24 31 E
Barkol Kazak Zizhixian, China 32 B4 43 37N 93 2 E
Bârlad, Romania 17 E14 46 15N 27 38 E
Bârlad →, Romania 17 F14 45 38N 27 32 E
Barlee, L., Australia 61 E2 29 15S 119 30 E
Barlee, Mt., Australia 61 D4 24 38S 128 13 E
Barletta, Italy 20 D7 41 19N 16 17 E
Barlovento, Canary Is. 22 F2 28 48N 17 48W
Barlow L., Canada 73 A8 62 0N 103 0W
Barmedman, Australia 63 E4 34 9S 147 21 E
Barmer, India 42 G4 25 45N 71 20 E
Barmera, Australia 63 E3 34 15S 140 28 E
Barmouth, U.K. 10 E3 52 44N 4 4W
Barna →, India 43 G10 25 21N 83 3 E
Barnagar, India 42 H6 23 7N 75 19 E
Barnala, India 42 D6 30 23N 75 33 E
Barnard Castle, U.K. 10 C6 54 33N 1 55W
Barnaul, Russia 26 D9 53 20N 83 40 E
Barnesville, U.S.A. 77 J3 33 3N 84 9W
Barnet, U.K. 11 F7 51 38N 0 9W
Barneveld, Neths. 15 B5 52 7N 5 36 E
Barneveld, U.S.A. 79 C9 43 16N 75 14W
Barnhart, U.S.A. 81 K4 31 8N 101 10W
Barnsley, U.K. 10 D6 53 34N 1 27W
Barnstaple, U.K. 11 F3 51 5N 4 4W
Barnstaple Bay = Bideford Bay, U.K. 11 F3 51 5N 4 20W
Barnsville, U.S.A. 80 B6 46 43N 96 28W
Barnwell, U.S.A. 77 J5 33 15N 81 23W
Baro, Nigeria 50 G7 8 35N 6 18 E
Baroda = Vadodara, India . 42 H5 22 20N 73 10 E
Baroda, India 42 G7 25 29N 76 35 E
Baroe, S. Africa 56 E3 33 13S 24 33 E
Baron Ra., Australia 60 D4 23 30S 127 45 E
Barotseland, Zambia 53 H4 15 0S 24 0 E
Barpeta, India 41 F17 26 20N 91 10 E
Barques, Pt. Aux, U.S.A. .. 78 B2 44 4N 82 58W
Barquísimeto, Venezuela . 92 A5 10 4N 69 19W
Barr Smith Range, Australia 61 E3 27 4S 120 20 E
Barra, Brazil 93 F10 11 5S 43 10W
Barra, U.K. 12 E1 57 0N 7 29W
Barra, Sd. of, U.K. 12 D1 57 4N 7 25W
Barra de Navidad, Mexico . 86 D4 19 12N 104 41W
Barra do Corda, Brazil 93 E9 5 30S 45 10W
Barra do Piraí, Brazil 95 A7 22 30S 43 50W
Barra Falsa, Pta. da, Mozam. 57 C6 22 58S 35 37 E
Barra Hd., U.K. 12 E1 56 47N 7 40W
Barra Mansa, Brazil 95 A7 22 35S 44 12W
Barraba, Australia 63 E5 30 21S 150 35 E
Barrackpur = Barakpur, India 43 H13 22 44N 88 30 E
Barradale Roadhouse, Australia 60 D1 22 42S 114 58 E
Barraigh = Barra, U.K. 12 E1 57 0N 7 29W
Barranca, Lima, Peru 92 F3 10 45S 77 50W
Barranca, Loreto, Peru 92 D3 4 50S 76 50W
Barrancabermeja, Colombia 92 B4 7 0N 73 50W
Barrancas, Venezuela 92 B6 8 55N 62 5W
Barrancos, Portugal 19 C2 38 10N 6 58W
Barranqueras, Argentina .. 94 B4 27 30S 59 0W
Barranquilla, Colombia ... 92 A4 11 0N 74 50W
Barraute, Canada 70 C4 48 26N 77 38W
Barre, Mass., U.S.A. 79 D12 42 25N 72 6W
Barre, Vt., U.S.A. 79 B12 44 12N 72 30W
Barreal, Argentina 94 C2 31 33S 69 28W
Barreiras, Brazil 93 F10 12 8S 45 0W
Barreirinhas, Brazil 93 D10 2 30S 42 50W
Barreiro, Portugal 19 C1 38 40N 9 6W
Barren, Nosy, Madag. 57 B7 18 25S 43 40 E
Barretos, Brazil 93 H9 20 30S 48 35W
Barrhead, Canada 72 C6 54 10N 114 24W
Barrie, Canada 78 B5 44 24N 79 40W
Barrier Ra., Australia 63 E3 31 0S 141 30 E
Barrière, Canada 72 C4 51 12N 120 7W
Barrington, U.S.A. 79 E13 41 44N 71 18W
Barrington L., Canada 73 B8 56 55N 100 15W
Barrington Tops, Australia . 63 E5 32 6S 151 28 E
Barringun, Australia 63 D4 29 1S 145 41 E
Barro do Garças, Brazil ... 93 G8 15 54S 52 16W
Barron, U.S.A. 80 C9 45 24N 91 51W
Barrow, U.S.A. 68 A4 71 18N 156 47W
Barrow →, Ireland 13 D5 52 25N 6 58W
Barrow Creek, Australia .. 62 C1 21 30S 133 55 E
Barrow I., Australia 60 D2 20 45S 115 20 E
Barrow-in-Furness, U.K. .. 10 C4 54 7N 3 14W
Barrow Pt., Australia 62 A3 14 20S 144 40 E
Barrow Pt., U.S.A. 66 B4 71 24N 156 29W
Barrow Ra., Australia 61 E4 26 0S 127 40 E
Barrow Str., Canada 4 B3 74 20N 95 0W
Barry, U.K. 11 F4 51 24N 3 16W
Barry's Bay, Canada 78 A7 45 29N 77 41W
Barsat, Pakistan 43 A5 36 10N 72 45 E
Barsham, Syria 44 C4 35 21N 40 33 E
Barsi, India 40 K9 18 10N 75 50 E

Barsoi, India 41 G15 25 48N 87 57 E
Barstow, U.S.A. 85 L9 34 54N 117 1W
Barthélemy, Col, Vietnam . 38 C5 19 26N 104 6 E
Bartica, Guyana 92 B7 6 25N 58 40W
Bartlesville, U.S.A. 81 G7 36 45N 95 59W
Bartlett, U.S.A. 84 J8 36 29N 118 2W
Bartlett, L., Canada 72 A5 63 5N 118 20W
Bartolomeu Dias, Mozam. . 55 G4 21 10S 35 8 E
Barton, U.S.A. 79 B12 44 45N 72 11W
Barton upon Humber, U.K. . 10 D7 53 41N 0 25W
Bartow, U.S.A. 77 M5 27 54N 81 50W
Barú, Volcan, Panama 88 E3 8 55N 82 35W
Barumba,
 Dem. Rep. of the Congo . 54 B1 1 3N 23 37 E
Baruunsuu, Mongolia ... 34 C3 43 43N 105 35 E
Barwani, India 42 H6 22 2N 74 57 E
Barysaw, Belarus 17 A15 54 17N 28 28 E
Barzân, Iraq 44 B5 36 55N 44 3 E
Bāsa'idū, Iran 45 E7 26 35N 55 20 E
Basal, Pakistan 42 C5 33 33N 72 13 E
Basankusa,
 Dem. Rep. of the Congo . 52 D3 1 5N 19 50 E
Basarabeasca, Moldova .. 17 E15 46 21N 28 58 E
Basawa, Afghan. 42 B4 34 15N 70 50 E
Bascuñán, C., Chile 94 B1 28 52S 71 35W
Basel, Switz. 18 C7 47 35N 7 35 E
Bashākerd, Kūhhā-ye, Iran . 45 E8 26 42N 58 35 E
Bashaw, Canada 72 C6 52 35N 112 58W
Bāshī, Iran 45 D6 28 41N 51 4 E
Bashkir Republic =
 Bashkortostan □, Russia . 24 D10 54 0N 57 0 E
Bashkortostan □, Russia .. 24 D10 54 0N 57 0 E
Basilan, Phil. 37 C6 6 35N 122 0 E
Basilan Str., Phil. 37 C6 6 50N 122 0 E
Basildon, U.K. 11 F8 51 34N 0 28 E
Basim = Washim, India .. 40 J10 20 3N 77 0 E
Basin, U.S.A. 82 D9 44 23N 108 2W
Basingstoke, U.K. 11 F6 51 15N 1 5W
Baskatong, Rés., Canada .. 70 C4 46 46N 75 50W
Basle = Basel, Switz. 18 C7 47 35N 7 35 E
Basoda, India 42 H7 23 52N 77 54 E
Basoka,
 Dem. Rep. of the Congo . 54 B1 1 16N 23 40 E
Basque Provinces = País
 Vasco □, Spain 19 A4 42 50N 2 45W
Basra = Al Başrah, Iraq ... 44 D5 30 30N 47 50 E
Bass Str., Australia 62 F4 39 15S 146 30 E
Bassano, Canada 72 C6 50 48N 112 20W
Bassano del Grappa, Italy . 20 B4 45 46N 11 44 E
Bassas da India, Ind. Oc. .. 53 J7 22 0S 39 0 E
Basse-Terre, Guadeloupe . 89 C7 16 0N 61 44W
Bassein, Burma 41 L19 16 45N 94 30 E
Basseterre, St. Kitts & Nevis 89 C7 17 17N 62 43W
Bassett, U.S.A. 80 D5 42 35N 99 32W
Bassi, India 42 D7 30 44N 76 21 E
Bastak, Iran 45 E7 27 15N 54 25 E
Baştām, Iran 45 B7 36 29N 55 4 E
Bastar, India 41 K12 19 15N 81 40 E
Basti, India 43 F10 26 52N 82 55 E
Bastia, France 18 E8 42 40N 9 30 E
Bastogne, Belgium 15 D5 50 1N 5 43 E
Bastrop, La., U.S.A. 81 J9 32 47N 91 55W
Bastrop, Tex., U.S.A. 81 K6 30 7N 97 19W
Bat Yam, Israel 47 C3 32 2N 34 44 E
Bata, Eq. Guin. 52 D1 1 57N 9 50 E
Bataan, Phil. 37 B6 14 40N 120 25 E
Batabanó, Cuba 88 B3 22 40N 82 20W
Batabanó, G. de, Cuba ... 88 B3 22 30N 82 30W
Batac, Phil. 37 A6 18 3N 120 34 E
Batagai, Russia 27 C14 67 38N 134 38 E
Batala, India 42 D6 31 48N 75 12 E
Batama,
 Dem. Rep. of the Congo . 54 B2 0 58N 26 33 E
Batamay, Russia 27 C13 63 30N 129 15 E
Batang, Indonesia 37 G13 6 55S 109 45 E
Batangas, Phil. 37 B6 13 35N 121 10 E
Batanta, Indonesia 37 E8 0 55S 130 40 E
Batatais, Brazil 95 A6 20 54S 47 37W
Batavia, U.S.A. 78 D6 43 0N 78 11W
Batchelor, Australia 60 B5 13 4S 131 1 E
Batdambang, Cambodia .. 38 F4 13 7N 103 12 E
Bateman's B., Australia ... 63 F5 35 40S 150 12 E
Batemans Bay, Australia .. 63 F5 35 44S 150 11 E
Bates Ra., Australia 61 E3 27 27S 121 5 E
Batesburg, U.S.A. 77 J5 33 54N 81 33W
Batesville, Ark., U.S.A. ... 81 H9 35 46N 91 39W
Batesville, Miss., U.S.A. .. 81 H10 34 19N 89 57W
Batesville, Tex., U.S.A. ... 81 L5 28 58N 99 37W
Bath, Canada 79 B8 44 11N 76 47W
Bath, U.K. 11 F5 51 23N 2 22W
Bath, Maine, U.S.A. 77 D11 43 55N 69 49W
Bath, N.Y., U.S.A. 78 D7 42 20N 77 19W
Bath & North East
 Somerset □, U.K. 11 F5 51 21N 2 27W
Batheay, Cambodia 39 G5 11 59N 104 57 E
Bathurst = Banjul, Gambia 50 F2 13 28N 16 40W
Bathurst, Australia 63 E4 33 25S 149 31 E
Bathurst, Canada 71 C6 47 37N 65 43W
Bathurst, S. Africa 56 E4 33 30S 26 50 E
Bathurst, C., Canada 68 A7 70 34N 128 0W
Bathurst B., Australia 62 A3 14 16S 144 25 E
Bathurst Harb., Australia . 62 G4 43 15S 146 10 E
Bathurst I., Australia 60 B5 11 30S 130 10 E
Bathurst I., Canada 4 B2 76 0N 100 30W
Bathurst Inlet, Canada ... 68 B9 66 50N 108 1W
Batlow, Australia 63 F4 35 31S 148 9 E
Batman, Turkey 25 G7 37 55N 41 5 E
Baţn al Ghūl, Jordan 47 F4 29 36N 35 56 E
Batna, Algeria 50 A7 35 34N 6 15 E
Batoka, Zambia 55 F2 16 45S 27 15 E
Baton Rouge, U.S.A. 81 K9 30 27N 91 11W
Batong, Ko, Thailand 39 J2 6 32N 99 12 E
Batopilas, Mexico 86 B3 27 0N 107 45W
Batouri, Cameroon 52 D2 4 30N 14 25 E
Båtsfjord, Norway 8 A23 70 38N 29 39 E
Battambang = Batdambang,
 Cambodia 38 F4 13 7N 103 12 E
Batticaloa, Sri Lanka 40 R12 7 43N 81 45 E
Battipáglia, Italy 20 D6 40 37N 14 58 E
Battle, U.K. 11 G8 50 55N 0 30 E
Battle →, Canada 73 C7 52 43N 108 15W
Battle Creek, U.S.A. 76 D3 42 19N 85 11W
Battle Ground, U.S.A. ... 84 E4 45 47N 122 32W
Battle Harbour, Canada .. 71 B8 52 16N 55 35W
Battle Lake, U.S.A. 80 B7 46 17N 95 43W
Battle Mountain, U.S.A. .. 82 F5 40 38N 116 56W
Battlefields, Zimbabwe .. 55 F2 18 37S 29 47 E

Battleford, Canada 73 C7 52 45N 108 15W
Batu, Kepulauan, Indonesia 36 E1 0 30S 98 25 E
Batu, Mt., Ethiopia 46 F2 6 55N 39 45 E
Batu Caves, Malaysia 39 L3 3 15N 101 40 E
Batu Gajah, Malaysia 39 K3 4 28N 101 3 E
Batu Is. = Batu, Kepulauan,
 Indonesia 36 E1 0 30S 98 25 E
Batu Pahat, Malaysia 39 M4 1 50N 102 56 E
Batuata, Indonesia 37 F6 6 12S 122 42 E
Baturaja, Indonesia 36 E2 4 11S 104 15 E
Baturité, Brazil 93 D11 4 28S 38 45W
Bau, Malaysia 36 D4 1 25N 110 9 E
Baubau, Indonesia 37 F6 5 25S 122 38 E
Bauchi, Nigeria 50 F7 10 22N 9 48 E
Baudette, U.S.A. 80 A7 48 43N 94 36W
Bauer, C., Australia 63 E1 32 44S 134 4 E
Bauhinia, Australia 62 C4 24 35S 149 18 E
Baukau, Indonesia 37 F7 8 27S 126 27 E
Bauld, C., Canada 69 C14 51 38N 55 26W
Bauru, Brazil 95 A6 22 10S 49 0W
Bausi, India 43 G12 24 48N 87 1 E
Bauska, Latvia 9 H21 56 24N 24 15 E
Bautzen, Germany 16 C8 51 10N 14 26 E
Bavānāt, Iran 45 D7 30 28N 53 27 E
Bavaria = Bayern □,
 Germany 16 D6 48 50N 12 0 E
Bavispe →, Mexico 86 B3 29 30N 109 11W
Bawdwin, Burma 41 H20 23 5N 97 20 E
Bawean, Indonesia 36 F4 5 46S 112 35 E
Bawku, Ghana 50 F5 11 3N 0 19W
Bawlake, Burma 41 K20 19 11N 97 21 E
Baxley, U.S.A. 77 K4 31 47N 82 21W
Baxter, U.S.A. 80 B7 46 21N 94 17W
Baxter Springs, U.S.A. ... 81 G7 37 2N 94 44W
Bay City, Mich., U.S.A. ... 76 D4 43 36N 83 54W
Bay City, Tex., U.S.A. 81 L7 28 59N 95 58W
Bay Minette, U.S.A. 77 K2 30 53N 87 46W
Bay Roberts, Canada 71 C9 47 36N 53 16W
Bay St. Louis, U.S.A. 81 K10 30 19N 89 20W
Bay Springs, U.S.A. 81 K10 31 59N 89 17W
Bay View, N.Z. 59 H6 39 25S 176 50 E
Baya,
 Dem. Rep. of the Congo . 55 E2 11 53S 27 25 E
Bayamo, Cuba 88 B4 20 20N 76 40W
Bayamón, Puerto Rico ... 89 C6 18 24N 66 10W
Bayan Har Shan, China ... 32 C4 34 0N 98 0 E
Bayan Hot = Alxa Zuoqi,
 China 34 E3 38 50N 105 40 E
Bayan Obo, China 34 D5 41 52N 109 59 E
Bayan-Ovoo = Erdenetsogt,
 Mongolia 34 C4 42 55N 106 5 E
Bayana, India 42 F7 26 55N 77 18 E
Bayanaūyl, Kazakstan ... 26 D8 50 45N 75 45 E
Bayandalay, Mongolia ... 34 C2 43 30N 103 29 E
Bayanhongor, Mongolia . 32 B5 46 8N 102 43 E
Bayard, N. Mex., U.S.A. .. 83 K9 32 46N 108 8W
Bayard, Nebr., U.S.A. ... 80 E3 41 45N 103 20W
Baybay, Phil. 37 B6 10 40N 124 55 E
Bayern □, Germany 16 D6 48 50N 12 0 E
Bayeux, France 18 B3 49 17N 0 42W
Bayfield, Canada 78 C3 43 34N 81 42W
Bayfield, U.S.A. 80 B9 46 49N 90 49W
Bayındır, Turkey 21 E12 38 13N 27 39 E
Baykal, Oz., Russia 27 D11 53 0N 108 0 E
Baykan, Turkey 44 B4 38 7N 41 44 E
Baykonur = Bayqongyr,
 Kazakstan 26 E7 47 48N 65 50 E
Baymak, Russia 24 D10 52 36N 58 19 E
Baynes Mts., Namibia ... 56 B1 17 15S 13 0 E
Bayombong, Phil. 37 A6 16 30N 121 10 E
Bayonne, France 18 E3 43 30N 1 28W
Bayonne, U.S.A. 79 F10 40 40N 74 7W
Bayovar, Peru 92 E2 5 50S 81 0W
Bayqongyr, Kazakstan ... 26 E7 47 48N 65 50 E
Bayram-Ali = Bayramaly,
 Turkmenistan 26 F7 37 37N 62 10 E
Bayramaly, Turkmenistan 26 F7 37 37N 62 10 E
Bayramiç, Turkey 21 E12 39 48N 26 36 E
Bayreuth, Germany 16 D6 49 56N 11 35 E
Bayrūt, Lebanon 47 B4 33 53N 35 31 E
Bays, L. of, Canada 78 A5 45 15N 79 4W
Baysville, Canada 78 A5 45 9N 79 7W
Bayt Lahm, West Bank ... 47 D4 31 43N 35 12 E
Baytown, U.S.A. 81 L7 29 43N 94 59W
Baza, Spain 19 D4 37 30N 2 47W
Bazaruto, I. do, Mozam. .. 57 C6 21 40S 35 28 E
Bazhou, China 34 E9 39 8N 116 22 E
Bazmān, Kūh-e, Iran 45 D9 28 4N 60 1 E
Beach, U.S.A. 80 B3 46 58N 104 0W
Beach City, U.S.A. 78 F3 40 39N 81 35W
Beachport, Australia 63 F3 37 29S 140 0 E
Beachy Hd., U.K. 11 G8 50 44N 0 15 E
Beacon, Australia 61 F2 30 26S 117 52 E
Beacon, U.S.A. 79 E11 41 30N 73 58W
Beaconsfield, Australia .. 62 G4 41 11S 146 48 E
Beagle, Canal, S. Amer. .. 96 H3 55 0S 68 30W
Beagle Bay, Australia ... 60 C3 16 58S 122 40 E
Bealanana, Madag. 57 A8 14 33S 48 44 E
Beals Cr. →, U.S.A. 81 J4 32 10N 100 51W
Beamsville, Canada 78 C5 43 12N 79 28W
Bear →, Calif., U.S.A. .. 84 G5 38 56N 121 36W
Bear →, Utah, U.S.A. ... 74 B4 41 30N 112 8W
Bear I., Ireland 13 E2 51 38N 9 50W
Bear L., Canada 73 B9 55 8N 96 0W
Bear L., U.S.A. 82 F8 41 59N 111 21W
Beardmore, Canada 70 C2 49 36N 87 57W
Beardmore Glacier,
 Antarctica 5 E11 84 30S 170 0 E
Beardstown, U.S.A. 80 F9 40 1N 90 26W
Bearma →, India 43 G8 24 20N 79 51 E
Béarn, France 18 E3 43 20N 0 30W
Bearpaw Mts., U.S.A. ... 82 B9 48 12N 109 30W
Bearskin Lake, Canada .. 70 B1 53 58N 91 2W
Beas →, India 42 D6 31 10N 74 59 E
Beata, C., Dom. Rep. 89 C5 17 40N 71 30W
Beata, I., Dom. Rep. 89 C5 17 34N 71 31W
Beatrice, U.S.A. 80 E6 40 16N 96 45W
Beatrice, Zimbabwe 55 F3 18 15S 30 55 E
Beatrice, C., Australia ... 62 A2 14 20S 136 55 E
Beatton →, Canada 72 B4 56 15N 120 45W
Beatton River, Canada .. 72 B4 57 26N 121 20W
Beatty, U.S.A. 84 J10 36 54N 116 46W
Beauce, Plaine de la, France 18 B4 48 10N 1 45 E
Beauceville, Canada 71 C5 46 13N 70 46W
Beaudesert, Australia ... 63 D5 27 59S 153 0 E
Beaufort, Malaysia 36 C5 5 30N 115 40 E

Beaufort, N.C., U.S.A. ... 77 H7 34 43N 76 40W
Beaufort, S.C., U.S.A. ... 77 J5 32 26N 80 40W
Beaufort Sea, Arctic 4 B1 72 0N 140 0W
Beaufort West, S. Africa .. 56 E3 32 18S 22 36 E
Beauharnois, Canada ... 79 A11 45 20N 73 52W
Beaulieu →, Canada 72 A6 62 3N 113 11W
Beauly, U.K. 12 D4 57 30N 4 28W
Beauly →, U.K. 12 D4 57 29N 4 27W
Beaumaris, U.K. 10 D3 53 16N 4 6W
Beaumont, Belgium ... 15 D4 50 15N 4 14 E
Beaumont, U.S.A. 81 K7 30 5N 94 6W
Beaune, France 18 C6 47 2N 4 50 E
Beaupré, Canada 71 C5 47 3N 70 54W
Beauraing, Belgium 15 D4 50 7N 4 57 E
Beauséjour, Canada 73 C9 50 5N 96 35W
Beauvais, France 18 B5 49 25N 2 8 E
Beauval, Canada 73 B7 55 9N 107 37W
Beaver, Okla., U.S.A. ... 81 G4 36 49N 100 31W
Beaver, Pa., U.S.A. 78 F4 40 42N 80 19W
Beaver, Utah, U.S.A. ... 83 G7 38 17N 112 38W
Beaver →, B.C., Canada . 72 B4 59 52N 124 20W
Beaver →, Ont., Canada . 70 A2 55 55N 87 48W
Beaver →, Sask., Canada 73 B7 55 26N 107 45W
Beaver City, U.S.A. 80 E5 40 8N 99 50W
Beaver Creek, Canada .. 68 B5 63 0N 141 0W
Beaver Dam, U.S.A. 80 D10 43 28N 88 50W
Beaver Falls, U.S.A. 78 F4 40 46N 80 20W
Beaver Hill L., Canada .. 73 C10 54 5N 94 50W
Beaver I., U.S.A. 76 C3 45 40N 85 33W
Beaverhill L., Canada ... 72 C6 53 27N 112 32W
Beaverlodge, Canada ... 72 B5 55 11N 119 29W
Beaverstone →, Canada . 70 B2 54 59N 89 25W
Beaverton, Canada 78 B5 44 26N 79 9W
Beaverton, U.S.A. 84 E4 45 29N 122 48W
Beawar, India 42 F6 26 3N 74 18 E
Bebedouro, Brazil 95 A6 21 0S 48 25W
Beboa, Madag. 57 B7 17 22S 44 33 E
Beccles, U.K. 11 E9 52 27N 1 35 E
Bečej, Serbia, Yug. 21 B9 45 36N 20 3 E
Béchar, Algeria 50 B5 31 38N 2 18W
Beckley, U.S.A. 76 G5 37 47N 81 11W
Beddouza, Ras, Morocco . 50 B4 32 33N 9 9W
Bedford, Canada 79 A12 45 7N 72 59W
Bedford, S. Africa 56 E4 32 40S 26 10 E
Bedford, U.K. 11 E7 52 8N 0 28W
Bedford, Ind., U.S.A. ... 76 F2 38 52N 86 29W
Bedford, Iowa, U.S.A. ... 80 E7 40 40N 94 44W
Bedford, Ohio, U.S.A. .. 78 E3 41 23N 81 32W
Bedford, Va., U.S.A. ... 76 G6 37 20N 79 31W
Bedford, C., Australia ... 62 B4 15 14S 145 21 E
Bedfordshire □, U.K. ... 11 E7 52 4N 0 28W
Bedourie, Australia 62 C2 24 30S 139 30 E
Bedum, Neths. 15 A6 53 18N 6 36 E
Beebe Plain, Canada ... 79 A12 45 1N 72 9W
Beech Creek, U.S.A. ... 78 E7 41 5N 77 36W
Beenleigh, Australia ... 63 D5 27 43S 153 10 E
Be'er Menuha, Israel ... 44 D2 30 19N 35 8 E
Be'er Sheva, Israel 47 D3 31 15N 34 48 E
Beersheba = Be'er Sheva,
 Israel 47 D3 31 15N 34 48 E
Beeston, U.K. 10 E6 52 56N 1 14W
Beeville, U.S.A. 81 L6 28 24N 97 45W
Befale,
 Dem. Rep. of the Congo . 52 D4 0 25N 20 45 E
Befandriana, Madag. ... 57 C8 21 55S 44 0 E
Befotaka, Madag. 57 C8 23 49S 47 0 E
Bega, Australia 63 F4 36 41S 149 51 E
Begusarai, India 43 G12 25 24N 86 9 E
Behābād, Iran 45 C8 32 24N 59 47 E
Behala, India 43 H13 22 30N 88 20 E
Behara, Madag. 57 C8 24 55S 46 20 E
Behbehān, Iran 45 D6 30 30N 50 15 E
Behm Canal, U.S.A. ... 72 B2 55 10N 131 0W
Behshahr, Iran 45 B7 36 45N 53 35 E
Bei Jiang →, China 33 D6 23 2N 112 58 E
Bei'an, China 33 B7 48 10N 126 20 E
Beihai, China 33 D5 21 28N 109 6 E
Beijing, China 34 E9 39 55N 116 20 E
Beijing □, China 34 E9 39 55N 116 20 E
Beilen, Neths. 15 B6 52 52N 6 27 E
Beilpajah, Australia 63 E3 32 54S 143 52 E
Beinn na Faoghla =
 Benbecula, U.K. 12 D1 57 26N 7 21W
Beipiao, China 35 D11 41 52N 120 32 E
Beira, Mozam. 55 F3 19 50S 34 52 E
Beirut = Bayrūt, Lebanon . 47 B4 33 53N 35 31 E
Beiseker, Canada 72 C6 51 23N 113 32W
Beitaolaizhao, China ... 35 B13 44 58N 125 58 E
Beitbridge, Zimbabwe .. 55 G3 22 12S 30 0 E
Beizhen = Binzhou, China . 35 F10 37 20N 118 2 E
Beizhen, China 35 D11 41 38N 121 54 E
Beizhengzhen, China ... 35 B12 44 31N 123 30 E
Beja, Portugal 19 C2 38 2N 7 53W
Béja, Tunisia 51 A7 36 43N 9 12 E
Bejaia, Algeria 50 A7 36 42N 5 2 E
Béjar, Spain 19 B3 40 23N 5 46W
Bejestān, Iran 45 C8 34 30N 58 5 E
Békéscsaba, Hungary ... 17 E11 46 40N 21 5 E
Bekily, Madag. 57 C8 24 13S 45 19 E
Bekok, Malaysia 39 L4 2 20N 103 7 E
Bela, India 43 G10 25 50N 82 0 E
Bela, Pakistan 42 F2 26 12N 66 20 E
Bela Crkva, Serbia, Yug. . 21 B9 44 55N 21 27 E
Bela Vista, Brazil 94 A4 22 12S 56 20W
Bela Vista, Mozam. 57 D5 26 10S 32 44 E
Belan →, India 43 G9 24 2N 81 45 E
Belarus ■, Europe 17 B14 53 30N 27 0 E
Belau = Palau ■, Pac. Oc. . 28 J17 7 30N 134 30 E
Belavenona, Madag. ... 57 C8 24 50S 47 4 E
Belawan, Indonesia 36 D1 3 33N 98 32 E
Belaya →, Russia 24 C9 54 40N 56 0 E
Belaya Tserkov = Bila
 Tserkva, Ukraine 17 D16 49 45N 30 10 E
Belcher Is., Canada 70 A3 56 15N 78 45W
Belden, U.S.A. 84 E5 40 2N 121 17W
Belebey, Russia 24 D9 54 7N 54 7 E
Belém, Brazil 93 D9 1 20S 48 30W
Belén, Paraguay 94 A4 23 30S 57 6W
Belen, U.S.A. 83 J10 34 40N 106 46W
Belet Uen, Somali Rep. .. 46 G4 4 30N 45 5 E
Belev, Russia 24 D6 53 50N 36 5 E
Belfair, U.S.A. 84 C4 47 27N 122 50W
Belfast, S. Africa 57 D5 25 42S 30 2 E
Belfast, U.K. 13 B6 54 37N 5 56W

Belfast, *Maine, U.S.A.* **77 C11** 44 26N 69 1W
Belfast, *N.Y., U.S.A.* **78 D6** 42 21N 78 7W
Belfield, *U.S.A.* **80 B3** 46 53N 103 12W
Belfort, *France* **18 C7** 47 38N 6 50 E
Belfry, *U.S.A.* **82 D9** 45 9N 109 1W
Belgaum, *India* **40 M9** 15 55N 74 35 E
Belgium ■, *Europe* **15 D4** 50 30N 5 0 E
Belgorod, *Russia* **25 D6** 50 35N 36 35 E
Belgorod-Dnistrovskiy =
 Bilhorod-Dnistrovskyy,
 Ukraine **25 E5** 46 11N 30 23 E
Belgrade = Beograd,
 Serbia, Yug. **21 B9** 44 50N 20 37 E
Belgrade, *U.S.A.* **82 D8** 45 47N 111 11W
Belhaven, *U.S.A.* **77 H7** 35 33N 76 37W
Beli Drim →, *Europe* **21 C9** 42 6N 20 25 E
Belinyu, *Indonesia* **36 E3** 1 35S 105 50 E
Beliton Is. = Belitung,
 Indonesia **36 E3** 3 10S 107 50 E
Belitung, *Indonesia* **36 E3** 3 10S 107 50 E
Belize ■, *Cent. Amer.* **87 D7** 17 0N 88 30W
Belize City, *Belize* **87 D7** 17 25N 88 0W
Belkovskiy, Ostrov, *Russia* .. **27 B14** 75 32N 135 44 E
Bell →, *Canada* **70 C4** 49 48N 77 38W
Bell I., *Canada* **71 B8** 50 46N 55 35W
Bell-Irving →, *Canada* **72 B3** 56 12N 129 5W
Bell Peninsula, *Canada* ... **69 B11** 63 50N 82 0W
Bell Ville, *Argentina* **94 C3** 32 40S 62 40W
Bella Bella, *Canada* **72 C3** 52 10N 128 10W
Bella Coola, *Canada* **72 C3** 52 25N 126 40W
Bella Unión, *Uruguay* **94 C4** 30 15S 57 40W
Bella Vista, *Corrientes,
 Argentina* **94 B4** 28 33S 59 0W
Bella Vista, *Tucuman,
 Argentina* **94 B2** 27 10S 65 25W
Bellaire, *U.S.A.* **78 F4** 40 1N 80 45W
Bellary, *India* **40 M10** 15 10N 76 56 E
Bellata, *Australia* **63 D4** 29 53S 149 46 E
Belle-Chasse, *U.S.A.* **81 L10** 29 51N 89 59W
Belle Fourche, *U.S.A.* **80 C3** 44 40N 103 51W
Belle Fourche →, *U.S.A.* .. **80 C3** 44 26N 102 18W
Belle Glade, *U.S.A.* **77 M5** 26 41N 80 40W
Belle-Île, *France* **18 C2** 47 20N 3 10W
Belle Isle, *Canada* **71 B8** 51 57N 55 25W
Belle Isle, Str. of, *Canada* . **71 B8** 51 30N 56 30W
Belle Plaine, *U.S.A.* **80 E8** 41 54N 92 17W
Bellefontaine, *U.S.A.* **76 E4** 40 22N 83 46W
Bellefonte, *U.S.A.* **78 F7** 40 55N 77 47W
Belleoram, *Canada* **71 C8** 47 31N 55 25W
Belleville, *Canada* **78 B7** 44 10N 77 23W
Belleville, *Ill., U.S.A.* **80 F10** 38 31N 89 59W
Belleville, *Kans., U.S.A.* .. **80 F6** 39 50N 97 38W
Belleville, *N.Y., U.S.A.* ... **79 C8** 43 46N 76 10W
Bellevue, *Canada* **72 D6** 49 35N 114 22W
Bellevue, *Idaho, U.S.A.* .. **82 E6** 43 28N 114 16W
Bellevue, *Nebr., U.S.A.* .. **80 E7** 41 8N 95 53W
Bellevue, *Ohio, U.S.A.* ... **78 E2** 41 17N 82 51W
Bellevue, *Wash., U.S.A.* .. **84 C4** 47 37N 122 12W
Bellin = Kangirsuk, *Canada* . **69 C13** 60 0N 70 0W
Bellingen, *Australia* **63 E5** 30 25S 152 50 E
Bellingham, *U.S.A.* **68 D7** 48 46N 122 29W
Bellingshausen Sea,
 Antarctica **5 C17** 66 0S 80 0W
Bellinzona, *Switz.* **18 C8** 46 11N 9 1 E
Bello, *Colombia* **92 B3** 6 20N 75 33W
Bellows Falls, *U.S.A.* **79 C12** 43 8N 72 27W
Bellpat, *Pakistan* **42 E3** 29 0N 68 5 E
Belluno, *Italy* **20 A5** 46 9N 12 13 E
Bellwood, *U.S.A.* **78 F6** 40 36N 78 20W
Belmont, *Canada* **78 D3** 42 53N 81 5W
Belmont, *S. Africa* **56 D3** 29 28S 24 22 E
Belmont, *U.S.A.* **78 D6** 42 14N 78 2W
Belmonte, *Brazil* **93 G11** 16 0S 39 0W
Belmopan, *Belize* **87 D7** 17 18N 88 30W
Belmullet, *Ireland* **13 B2** 54 14N 9 58W
Belo Horizonte, *Brazil* ... **93 G10** 19 55S 43 56W
Belo-sur-Mer, *Madag.* **57 C7** 20 42S 44 0 E
Belo-Tsiribihina, *Madag.* .. **57 B7** 19 40S 44 30 E
Belogorsk, *Russia* **27 D13** 51 0N 128 20 E
Beloha, *Madag.* **57 D8** 25 10S 45 3 E
Belogorsk, *Kans., U.S.A.* .. **80 F5** 39 28N 98 6W
Beloit, *Wis., U.S.A.* **80 D10** 42 31N 89 2W
Belokorovichi, *Ukraine* ... **17 C15** 51 7N 28 2 E
Belomorsk, *Russia* **24 B5** 64 35N 34 54 E
Belonia, *India* **41 H17** 23 15N 91 30 E
Belorussia = Belarus ■,
 Europe **17 B14** 53 30N 27 0 E
Belovo, *Russia* **26 D9** 54 30N 86 0 E
Beloye, Ozero, *Russia* **24 B6** 60 10N 37 35 E
Beloye More, *Russia* **24 A6** 66 30N 38 0 E
Belozersk, *Russia* **24 B6** 60 1N 37 45 E
Belpre, *U.S.A.* **76 F5** 39 17N 81 34W
Belrain, *India* **43 E9** 28 23N 80 55 E
Belt, *U.S.A.* **82 C8** 47 23N 110 55W
Beltana, *Australia* **63 E2** 30 48S 138 25 E
Belterra, *Brazil* **93 D8** 2 45S 55 0W
Belton, *U.S.A.* **81 K6** 31 3N 97 28W
Belton L., *U.S.A.* **81 K6** 31 8N 97 32W
Beltsy = Bălţi, *Moldova* .. **17 E14** 47 48N 27 58 E
Belturbet, *Ireland* **13 B4** 54 6N 7 26W
Belukha, *Russia* **26 E9** 49 50N 86 50 E
Beluran, *Malaysia* **36 C5** 5 48N 117 35 E
Belvidere, *Ill., U.S.A.* **80 D10** 42 15N 88 50W
Belvidere, *N.J., U.S.A.* ... **79 F9** 40 50N 75 5W
Belyando →, *Australia* ... **62 C4** 21 38S 146 50 E
Belyy, Ostrov, *Russia* **26 B8** 73 30N 71 0 E
Belyy Yar, *Russia* **26 D9** 58 26N 84 39 E
Belzoni, *U.S.A.* **81 J9** 33 11N 90 29W
Bemarivo, Lembaleman' i,
 Madag. **57 B7** 18 40S 44 45 E
Bemarivo, *Madag.* **57 B7** 21 45S 44 45 E
Bemarivo →, *Madag.* **57 B8** 15 27S 47 40 E
Bemavo, *Madag.* **57 C8** 21 33S 45 25 E
Bembéréke, *Benin* **50 F6** 10 11N 2 43 E
Bembesi, *Zimbabwe* **55 G2** 20 0S 28 58 E
Bembesi →, *Zimbabwe* ... **55 F2** 18 57S 27 47 E
Bemetara, *India* **43 J9** 21 42N 81 32 E
Bemidji, *U.S.A.* **80 B7** 47 28N 94 53W
Ben, *Iran* **45 C6** 32 32N 50 45 E
Ben Cruachan, *U.K.* **12 E3** 56 26N 5 8W
Ben Dearg, *U.K.* **12 D4** 57 47N 4 56W
Ben Hope, *U.K.* **12 C4** 58 25N 4 36W
Ben Lawers, *U.K.* **12 E4** 56 32N 4 14W
Ben Lomond, *N.S.W.,
 Australia* **63 E5** 30 1S 151 43 E

Ben Lomond, *Tas., Australia* **62 G4** 41 38S 147 42 E
Ben Lomond, *U.K.* **12 E4** 56 11N 4 38W
Ben Luc, *Vietnam* **39 G6** 10 39N 106 29 E
Ben Macdhui, *U.K.* **12 D5** 57 4N 3 40W
Ben Mhor, *U.K.* **12 D1** 57 15N 7 18W
Ben More, *Arg. & Bute, U.K.* **12 E2** 56 26N 6 1W
Ben More, *Stirl., U.K.* **12 E4** 56 23N 4 32W
Ben More Assynt, *U.K.* ... **12 C4** 58 8N 4 52W
Ben Nevis, *U.K.* **12 E3** 56 48N 5 1W
Ben Quang, *Vietnam* **38 D6** 17 3N 106 55 E
Ben Vorlich, *U.K.* **12 E4** 56 21N 4 14W
Ben Wyvis, *U.K.* **12 D4** 57 40N 4 35W
Bena, *Nigeria* **50 F7** 11 20N 5 50 E
Benalla, *Australia* **63 F4** 36 30S 146 0 E
Benares = Varanasi, *India* . **43 G10** 25 22N 83 0 E
Benavente, *Spain* **19 A3** 42 2N 5 43W
Benavides, *U.S.A.* **81 M5** 27 36N 98 25W
Benbecula, *U.K.* **12 D1** 57 26N 7 21W
Benbonyathe, *Australia* .. **63 E2** 30 25S 139 11 E
Bend, *U.S.A.* **82 D3** 44 4N 121 19W
Bendemeer, *Australia* **63 E5** 30 53S 151 8 E
Bender Beila, *Somali Rep.* . **46 F5** 9 30N 50 48 E
Bendery = Tighina,
 Moldova **17 E15** 46 50N 29 30 E
Bendigo, *Australia* **63 F3** 36 40S 144 15 E
Bene Beraq, *Israel* **47 C3** 32 6N 34 51 E
Benenitra, *Madag.* **57 C8** 23 27S 45 5 E
Benevento, *Italy* **20 D6** 41 8N 14 45 E
Benga, *Mozam.* **55 F3** 16 11S 33 40 E
Bengal, Bay of, *Ind. Oc.* .. **41 M17** 15 0N 90 0 E
Benghazi = Banghāzī, *Libya* **51 B10** 32 11N 20 3 E
Bengkalis, *Indonesia* **36 D2** 1 30N 102 10 E
Bengkulu, *Indonesia* **36 E2** 3 50S 102 12 E
Bengkulu □, *Indonesia* ... **36 E2** 3 48S 102 16 E
Bengough, *Canada* **73 D7** 49 25N 105 10W
Benguela, *Angola* **53 G2** 12 37S 13 25 E
Benguérua, I., *Mozam.* ... **57 C6** 21 58S 35 28 E
Beni,
 Dem. Rep. of the Congo . **54 B2** 0 30N 29 27 E
Beni →, *Bolivia* **92 F5** 10 23S 65 24W
Beni Mellal, *Morocco* **50 B4** 32 21N 6 21W
Beni Suef, *Egypt* **51 C12** 29 5N 31 6 E
Beniah L., *Canada* **72 A6** 63 23N 112 17W
Benicia, *U.S.A.* **84 G4** 38 3N 122 9W
Benidorm, *Spain* **19 C5** 38 33N 0 9W
Benin ■, *Africa* **50 G6** 10 0N 2 0 E
Benin, Bight of, *W. Afr.* .. **50 H6** 5 0N 3 0 E
Benin City, *Nigeria* **50 G7** 6 20N 5 31 E
Benitses, *Greece* **23 A3** 39 32N 19 55 E
Benjamin Aceval, *Paraguay* **94 A4** 24 58S 57 34W
Benjamin Constant, *Brazil* . **92 D4** 4 40S 70 15W
Benjamin Hill, *Mexico* **86 A2** 30 10N 111 10W
Benkelman, *U.S.A.* **80 E4** 40 3N 101 32W
Bennett, *Canada* **72 B2** 59 56N 134 53W
Bennett, L., *Australia* **60 D5** 22 50S 131 2 E
Bennetta, Ostrov, *Russia* . **27 B15** 76 21N 148 56 E
Bennettsville, *U.S.A.* **77 H6** 34 37N 79 41W
Bennington, *N.H., U.S.A.* . **79 D11** 43 0N 71 55W
Bennington, *Vt., U.S.A.* ... **79 D11** 42 53N 73 12W
Benoni, *S. Africa* **57 D4** 26 11S 28 18 E
Benque Viejo, *Belize* **87 D7** 17 5N 89 8W
Benson, *Ariz., U.S.A.* **83 L8** 31 58N 110 18W
Benson, *Minn., U.S.A.* **80 C7** 45 19N 95 36W
Bent, *Iran* **45 E8** 26 20N 59 31 E
Benteng, *Indonesia* **37 F6** 6 10S 120 30 E
Bentinck I., *Australia* **62 B2** 17 3S 139 35 E
Bento Gonçalves, *Brazil* .. **95 B5** 29 10S 51 31W
Benton, *Calif., U.S.A.* **84 H8** 37 48N 118 32W
Benton, *Ill., U.S.A.* **80 G10** 38 0N 88 55W
Benton, *Pa., U.S.A.* **79 E8** 41 12N 76 23W
Benton Harbor, *U.S.A.* ... **76 D2** 42 6N 86 27W
Bentonville, *U.S.A.* **81 G7** 36 22N 94 13W
Bentung, *Malaysia* **39 L3** 3 31N 101 55 E
Benue →, *Nigeria* **50 G7** 7 48N 6 46 E
Benxi, *China* **35 D12** 41 20N 123 48 E
Beo, *Indonesia* **37 D7** 4 25N 126 50 E
Beograd, *Serbia, Yug.* **21 B9** 44 50N 20 37 E
Beppu, *Japan* **31 H5** 33 15N 131 30 E
Beqaa Valley = Al Biqā,
 Lebanon **47 A5** 34 10N 36 10 E
Ber Mota, *India* **42 H3** 23 27N 68 34 E
Berach →, *India* **42 G6** 25 15N 75 2 E
Berati, *Albania* **21 D8** 40 43N 19 59 E
Berau, Teluk, *Indonesia* .. **37 E8** 2 30S 132 30 E
Berber, *Sudan* **51 E12** 18 0N 34 0 E
Berbera, *Somali Rep.* **46 E4** 10 30N 45 2 E
Berbérati, *C.A.R.* **52 D3** 4 15N 15 40 E
Berbice →, *Guyana* **92 B7** 6 20N 57 32W
Berdichev = Berdychiv,
 Ukraine **17 D15** 49 57N 28 30 E
Berdsk, *Russia* **26 D9** 54 47N 83 2 E
Berdyansk, *Ukraine* **25 E6** 46 45N 36 50 E
Berdychiv, *Ukraine* **17 D15** 49 57N 28 30 E
Berea, *U.S.A.* **76 G3** 37 34N 84 17W
Berebere, *Indonesia* **37 D7** 2 25N 128 45 E
Bereda, *Somali Rep.* **46 E5** 11 45N 51 0 E
Berehove, *Ukraine* **17 D12** 48 15N 22 35 E
Berekum, *Ghana* **50 G5** 7 29N 2 34W
Berens →, *Canada* **73 C9** 52 25N 97 2W
Berens I., *Canada* **73 C9** 52 18N 97 18W
Berens River, *Canada* **73 C9** 52 25N 97 0W
Beresford, *U.S.A.* **80 D6** 43 5N 96 47W
Berestechko, *Ukraine* **17 C13** 50 22N 25 5 E
Berevo, Mahajanga, *Madag.* **57 B7** 17 14S 44 17 E
Berevo, Toliara, *Madag.* .. **57 B7** 19 44S 44 58 E
Bereza, *Belarus* **17 B13** 52 31N 24 51 E
Berezhany, *Ukraine* **17 D13** 49 26N 24 58 E
Berezina = Byarezina →,
 Belarus **17 B16** 52 33N 30 14 E
Bereznik, *Russia* **24 B7** 62 51N 42 40 E
Berezniki, *Russia* **24 C10** 59 24N 56 46 E
Berezovo, *Russia* **26 C7** 64 0N 65 0 E
Berga, *Spain* **19 A6** 42 6N 1 48 E
Bergama, *Turkey* **21 E12** 39 8N 27 11 E
Bérgamo, *Italy* **18 D8** 45 41N 9 43 E
Bergen, *Neths.* **15 B4** 52 40N 4 43 E
Bergen, *Norway* **9 F11** 60 20N 5 20 E
Bergen op Zoom, *Neths.* .. **15 C4** 51 28N 4 18 E
Bergerac, *France* **18 D4** 44 51N 0 30 E
Bergholz, *U.S.A.* **78 F4** 40 31N 80 53W
Bergisch Gladbach,
 Germany **15 D7** 50 59N 7 8 E
Bergville, *S. Africa* **57 D4** 28 52S 29 18 E
Berhala, Selat, *Indonesia* . **36 E2** 1 0S 104 15 E

Berhampore = Baharampur,
 India **43 G13** 24 2N 88 27 E
Berhampur = Brahmapur,
 India **41 K14** 19 15N 84 54 E
Bering Sea, *Pac. Oc.* **68 C1** 58 0N 171 0 E
Bering Strait, *Pac. Oc.* ... **68 B3** 65 30N 169 0W
Beringovskiy, *Russia* **27 C18** 63 3N 179 19 E
Berisso, *Argentina* **94 C4** 34 56S 57 50W
Berja, *Spain* **19 D4** 36 50N 2 56W
Berkeley, *U.S.A.* **84 H4** 37 52N 122 16W
Berkner I., *Antarctica* **5 D18** 79 30S 50 0W
Berkshire □, *U.K.* **11 F6** 51 33N 1 29W
Berkshire Downs, *U.K.* ... **11 F6** 51 33N 1 29W
Berlin, *Germany* **16 B7** 52 30N 13 25 E
Berlin, *Md., U.S.A.* **76 F8** 38 20N 75 13W
Berlin, *N.H., U.S.A.* **79 B13** 44 28N 71 11W
Berlin, *N.Y., U.S.A.* **79 D11** 42 42N 73 23W
Berlin, *Wis., U.S.A.* **76 D1** 43 58N 88 57W
Berlin L., *U.S.A.* **78 E4** 41 3N 81 0W
Bermejo →, *Formosa,
 Argentina* **94 B4** 26 51S 58 23W
Bermejo →, *San Juan,
 Argentina* **94 C2** 32 30S 67 30W
Bermen, L., *Canada* **71 B6** 53 35N 68 55W
Bermuda ■, *Atl. Oc.* **66 F13** 32 45N 65 0W
Bern, *Switz.* **18 C7** 46 57N 7 28 E
Bernalillo, *U.S.A.* **83 J10** 35 18N 106 33W
Bernardo de Irigoyen,
 Argentina **95 B5** 26 15S 53 40W
Bernardo O'Higgins □, *Chile* **94 C1** 34 15S 70 45W
Bernardsville, *U.S.A.* **79 F10** 40 43N 74 34W
Bernasconi, *Argentina* **94 D3** 37 55S 63 44W
Bernburg, *Germany* **16 C6** 51 47N 11 44 E
Berne = Bern, *Switz.* **18 C7** 46 57N 7 28 E
Berneray, *U.K.* **12 D1** 57 43N 7 11W
Bernier I., *Australia* **61 D1** 24 50S 113 12 E
Bernina, Piz, *Switz.* **18 C8** 46 20N 9 54 E
Beroroha, *Madag.* **57 C8** 21 40S 45 10 E
Beroun, *Czech Rep.* **16 D8** 49 57N 14 5 E
Berri, *Australia* **63 E3** 34 14S 140 35 E
Berriane, *Algeria* **50 B6** 32 50N 3 46 E
Berrigan, *Australia* **63 F4** 35 38S 145 49 E
Berry, *Australia* **63 E5** 34 46S 150 43 E
Berry, *France* **18 C5** 46 50N 2 0 E
Berry Is., *Bahamas* **88 A4** 25 40N 77 50W
Berryville, *U.S.A.* **81 G8** 36 22N 93 34W
Berryessa L., *U.S.A.* **84 G4** 38 31N 122 6W
Bershad, *Ukraine* **17 D15** 48 22N 29 31 E
Berthold, *U.S.A.* **80 A4** 48 19N 101 44W
Berthoud, *U.S.A.* **80 E2** 40 19N 105 5W
Bertoua, *Cameroon* **52 D2** 4 30N 13 45 E
Bertraghboy B., *Ireland* ... **13 C2** 53 22N 9 54W
Berwick, *U.S.A.* **79 E8** 41 3N 76 14W
Berwick-upon-Tweed, *U.K.* **10 B6** 55 46N 2 0W
Berwyn Mts., *U.K.* **10 E4** 52 54N 3 26W
Besal, *Pakistan* **43 B5** 35 4N 73 56 E
Besalampy, *Madag.* **57 B7** 16 43S 44 29 E
Besançon, *France* **18 C7** 47 15N 6 2 E
Besar, *Indonesia* **36 E5** 2 40S 116 0 E
Besnard L., *Canada* **73 B7** 55 25N 106 0W
Besni, *Turkey* **44 B3** 37 41N 37 52 E
Besor, N. →, *Egypt* **47 D3** 31 28N 34 22 E
Bessarabiya, *Moldova* **17 E15** 47 0N 28 10 E
Bessarabka = Basarabeasca,
 Moldova **17 E15** 46 21N 28 58 E
Bessemer, *Ala., U.S.A.* ... **77 J2** 33 24N 86 58W
Bessemer, *Mich., U.S.A.* . **80 B9** 46 29N 90 3W
Bessemer, *Pa., U.S.A.* **78 F4** 40 59N 80 30W
Beswick, *Australia* **60 B5** 14 34S 132 53 E
Bet She'an, *Israel* **47 C4** 32 30N 35 30 E
Bet Shemesh, *Israel* **47 D4** 31 44N 35 0 E
Betafo, *Madag.* **57 B8** 19 50S 46 51 E
Betancuria, *Canary Is.* **22 F5** 28 25N 14 3W
Betanzos, *Spain* **19 A1** 43 15N 8 12W
Bétaré Oya, *Cameroon* ... **52 C2** 5 40N 14 5 E
Bethal, *S. Africa* **57 D4** 26 27S 29 28 E
Bethanien, *Namibia* **56 D2** 26 31S 17 8 E
Bethany, *Canada* **78 B6** 44 11N 78 34W
Bethany, *U.S.A.* **80 E7** 40 16N 94 2W
Bethel, *Alaska, U.S.A.* **68 B3** 60 48N 161 45W
Bethel, *Conn., U.S.A.* **79 E11** 41 22N 73 25W
Bethel, *Maine, U.S.A.* **79 B14** 44 25N 70 47W
Bethel, *Vt., U.S.A.* **79 C12** 43 50N 72 38W
Bethel Park, *U.S.A.* **78 F4** 40 20N 80 1W
Bethlehem = Bayt Lahm,
 West Bank **47 D4** 31 43N 35 12 E
Bethlehem, *S. Africa* **57 D4** 28 14S 28 18 E
Bethlehem, *U.S.A.* **79 F9** 40 37N 75 23W
Bethulie, *S. Africa* **56 E4** 30 30S 25 59 E
Béthune, *France* **18 A5** 50 30N 2 38 E
Betioky, *Madag.* **57 C7** 23 48S 44 20 E
Betong, *Thailand* **39 K3** 5 45N 101 5 E
Betoota, *Australia* **62 D3** 25 45S 140 42 E
Betroka, *Madag.* **57 C8** 23 16S 46 0 E
Betsiamites, *Canada* **71 C6** 48 56N 68 40W
Betsiamites →, *Canada* ... **71 C6** 48 56N 68 38W
Betsiboka →, *Madag.* **57 B8** 16 3S 46 36 E
Bettendorf, *U.S.A.* **80 E9** 41 32N 90 30W
Bettiah, *India* **43 F11** 26 48N 84 33 E
Betul, *India* **40 J10** 21 58N 77 59 E
Betung, *Malaysia* **36 D4** 1 24N 111 31 E
Beulah, *Mich., U.S.A.* **76 C2** 44 38N 86 6W
Beulah, *N. Dak., U.S.A.* ... **80 B4** 47 16N 101 47W
Beveren, *Belgium* **15 C4** 51 12N 4 16 E
Beverley, *Australia* **61 F2** 32 9S 116 56 E
Beverley, *U.K.* **10 D7** 53 51N 0 26W
Beverly Hills, *U.S.A.* **77 L4** 28 56N 82 28W
Beverly, *U.S.A.* **79 D14** 42 33N 70 53W
Beverly Hills, *U.S.A.* **85 L8** 34 4N 118 25W
Bewas →, *India* **43 H8** 23 59N 79 21 E
Bexhill, *U.K.* **11 G8** 50 51N 0 29 E
Beyānlū, *Iran* **44 C5** 36 0N 47 51 E
Beyneu, *Kazakstan* **25 E10** 45 18N 55 9 E
Beypazarı, *Turkey* **25 F5** 40 10N 31 56 E
Beyşehir Gölü, *Turkey* **25 G5** 37 41N 31 33 E
Béziers, *France* **18 E5** 43 20N 3 12 E
Bezwada = Vijayawada,
 India **41 L12** 16 31N 80 39 E
Bhabua, *India* **43 G10** 25 3N 83 37 E
Bhachau, *India* **40 H7** 23 20N 70 16 E
Bhadar →, *Gujarat, India* . **42 H5** 21 57N 73 15 E
Bhadar →, *Gujarat, India* . **42 J3** 21 27N 69 47 E
Bhadarwah, *India* **43 C6** 32 58N 75 46 E
Bhadohi, *India* **43 G10** 25 25N 82 34 E
Bhadra, *India* **42 E6** 29 8N 75 14 E
Bhadrakh, *India* **41 J15** 21 10N 86 30 E

Bhadran, *India* **42 H5** 22 19N 72 6 E
Bhadravati, *India* **40 N9** 13 49N 75 40 E
Bhag, *Pakistan* **42 E2** 29 2N 67 49 E
Bhagalpur, *India* **43 G12** 25 10N 87 0 E
Bhagirathi →, *Ut. P., India* **43 D8** 30 8N 78 35 E
Bhagirathi →, *W. Bengal,
 India* **43 H13** 23 25N 88 23 E
Bhakkar, *Pakistan* **42 D4** 31 40N 71 5 E
Bhakra Dam, *India* **42 D7** 31 30N 76 45 E
Bhamo, *Burma* **41 G20** 24 15N 97 15 E
Bhandara, *India* **40 J11** 21 5N 79 42 E
Bhanpura, *India* **42 G6** 24 31N 75 44 E
Bhanrer Ra., *India* **43 H8** 23 40N 79 45 E
Bhaptiahi, *India* **43 F12** 26 19N 86 44 E
Bharat = India ■, *Asia* ... **40 K11** 20 0N 78 0 E
Bharatpur, *Mad. P., India* . **43 H9** 23 44N 81 46 E
Bharatpur, *Raj., India* **42 F7** 27 15N 77 30 E
Bharno, *India* **43 H11** 23 14N 84 53 E
Bhatinda, *India* **42 D6** 30 15N 74 57 E
Bhatpara, *India* **43 H13** 22 50N 88 25 E
Bhattu, *India* **42 E6** 29 36N 75 19 E
Bhaun, *Pakistan* **42 C5** 32 55N 72 40 E
Bhaunagar = Bhavnagar,
 India **40 J8** 21 45N 72 10 E
Bhavnagar, *India* **40 J8** 21 45N 72 10 E
Bhawanipatna, *India* **41 K12** 19 55N 80 10 E
Bhawari, *India* **42 G5** 25 42N 73 4 E
Bhayavadar, *India* **42 J4** 21 51N 70 15 E
Bhera, *Pakistan* **42 C5** 32 29N 72 57 E
Bhikangaon, *India* **42 J6** 21 52N 75 57 E
Bhilai = Bhilainagar-Durg,
 India **42 H7** 23 28N 77 53 E
Bhilwara, *India* **42 G6** 25 25N 74 38 E
Bhima →, *India* **40 L10** 16 25N 77 17 E
Bhimbar, *Pakistan* **43 C6** 32 59N 74 3 E
Bhind, *India* **43 F8** 26 30N 78 46 E
Bhinga, *India* **43 F9** 27 43N 81 56 E
Bhinmal, *India* **42 G5** 25 0N 72 15 E
Bhiwandi, *India* **40 K8** 19 20N 73 0 E
Bhiwani, *India* **42 E7** 28 50N 76 9 E
Bhogava →, *India* **42 G6** 22 26N 72 20 E
Bhola, *Bangla.* **41 H17** 22 45N 90 35 E
Bholari, *Pakistan* **42 G3** 25 19N 68 13 E
Bhopal, *India* **42 H7** 23 20N 77 30 E
Bhubaneshwar, *India* **41 J14** 20 15N 85 50 E
Bhuj, *India* **42 H3** 23 15N 69 49 E
Bhusaval, *India* **40 J9** 21 3N 75 46 E
Bhutan ■, *Asia* **41 F17** 27 25N 90 30 E
Biafra, B. of = Bonny, Bight
 of, *Africa* **52 D1** 3 30N 9 20 E
Biak, *Indonesia* **37 E9** 1 10S 136 6 E
Biała Podlaska, *Poland* ... **17 B12** 52 4N 23 6 E
Białogard, *Poland* **16 A8** 54 2N 15 58 E
Białystok, *Poland* **17 B12** 53 10N 23 10 E
Biaora, *India* **42 H7** 23 56N 76 56 E
Bīārjmand, *Iran* **45 B7** 36 6N 55 53 E
Biaro, *Indonesia* **37 D7** 2 5N 125 26 E
Biarritz, *France* **18 E3** 43 29N 1 33W
Bibai, *Japan* **30 C10** 43 19N 141 52 E
Bibby I., *Canada* **73 A10** 61 55N 93 0W
Biberach, *Germany* **16 D5** 48 5N 9 47 E
Bibungwa,
 Dem. Rep. of the Congo . **54 C2** 2 40S 28 15 E
Bic, *Canada* **71 C6** 48 20N 68 41W
Bicester, *U.K.* **11 F6** 51 54N 1 9W
Bicheno, *Australia* **62 G4** 41 52S 148 18 E
Bichia, *India* **43 H9** 22 27N 80 42 E
Bickerton I., *Australia* **62 A2** 13 45S 136 10 E
Bida, *Nigeria* **50 G7** 9 3N 5 58 E
Bidar, *India* **40 L10** 17 55N 77 35 E
Biddeford, *U.S.A.* **77 D10** 43 30N 70 28W
Bideford, *U.K.* **11 F3** 51 1N 4 13W
Bideford Bay, *U.K.* **11 F3** 51 5N 4 20W
Bidhuna, *India* **43 F8** 26 49N 79 31 E
Bidor, *Malaysia* **39 K3** 4 6N 101 15 E
Bié, Planalto de, *Angola* .. **53 G3** 12 0S 16 0 E
Bieber, *U.S.A.* **82 F3** 41 7N 121 8W
Biel, *Switz.* **18 C7** 47 8N 7 14 E
Bielefeld, *Germany* **16 B5** 52 1N 8 33 E
Biella, *Italy* **18 D8** 45 34N 8 3 E
Bielsk Podlaski, *Poland* ... **17 B12** 52 47N 23 12 E
Bielsko-Biała, *Poland* **17 D10** 49 50N 19 2 E
Bien Hoa, *Vietnam* **39 G6** 10 57N 106 49 E
Bienne = Biel, *Switz.* **18 C7** 47 8N 7 14 E
Bienville, L., *Canada* **70 A5** 55 5N 72 40W
Biesiesfontein, *S. Africa* .. **56 E2** 30 57S 17 58 E
Big →, *Canada* **71 B8** 54 50N 58 55W
Big B., *Canada* **71 A7** 55 43N 60 35W
Big Bear City, *U.S.A.* **85 L10** 34 16N 116 51W
Big Bear Lake, *U.S.A.* **85 L10** 34 15N 116 56W
Big Belt Mts., *U.S.A.* **82 C8** 46 30N 111 25W
Big Bend, *Swaziland* **57 D5** 26 50S 31 58 E
Big Bend National Park,
 U.S.A. **81 L3** 29 20N 103 5W
Big Black →, *U.S.A.* **81 K9** 32 3N 91 4W
Big Blue →, *U.S.A.* **80 F6** 39 35N 96 34W
Big Creek, *U.S.A.* **84 H7** 37 11N 119 14W
Big Cypress National
 Preserve, *U.S.A.* **77 M5** 26 0N 81 10W
Big Cypress Swamp, *U.S.A.* **77 M5** 26 12N 81 10W
Big Falls, *U.S.A.* **80 A8** 48 12N 93 48W
Big Fork →, *U.S.A.* **80 A8** 48 31N 93 43W
Big Horn Mts. = Bighorn
 Mts., *U.S.A.* **82 D10** 44 30N 107 30W
Big I., *Canada* **72 A5** 61 7N 116 45W
Big Lake, *U.S.A.* **81 K4** 31 12N 101 28W
Big Moose, *U.S.A.* **79 C10** 43 49N 74 58W
Big Muddy Cr. →, *U.S.A.* . **80 A2** 48 8N 104 36W
Big Pine, *U.S.A.* **84 H8** 37 10N 118 17W
Big Piney, *U.S.A.* **82 E8** 42 32N 110 7W
Big Rapids, *U.S.A.* **76 D3** 43 42N 85 29W
Big Rideau L., *Canada* **79 B8** 44 40N 76 15W
Big River, *Canada* **73 C7** 53 50N 107 0W
Big Run, *U.S.A.* **78 F6** 40 57N 78 55W
Big Sable Pt., *U.S.A.* **76 C2** 44 3N 86 1W
Big Salmon →, *Canada* ... **72 A2** 61 52N 134 55W
Big Sand L., *Canada* **73 B9** 57 45N 99 45W
Big Sandy, *U.S.A.* **82 B8** 48 11N 110 7W
Big Sandy →, *U.S.A.* **76 F4** 38 25N 82 36W
Big Sandy Cr. →, *U.S.A.* .. **80 F3** 38 7N 102 29W
Big Sioux →, *U.S.A.* **80 D6** 42 29N 96 27W
Big Spring, *U.S.A.* **81 J4** 32 15N 101 28W
Big Stone City, *U.S.A.* **80 C6** 45 18N 96 28W
Big Stone Gap, *U.S.A.* **77 G4** 36 52N 82 47W
Big Stone L., *U.S.A.* **80 C6** 45 30N 96 35W
Big Sur, *U.S.A.* **84 J5** 36 15N 121 48W
Big Timber, *U.S.A.* **82 D9** 45 50N 109 57W

Big Trout L.

Bolton, U.K. 10 D5 53 35N 2 26W
Bolton Landing, U.S.A. . 79 C11 43 32N 73 35W
Bolu, Turkey 25 F5 40 45N 31 35 E
Bolungavík, Iceland 8 C2 66 9N 23 15W
Bolvadin, Turkey 25 G5 38 45N 31 4 E
Bolzano, Italy 20 A4 46 31N 11 22 E
Bom Jesus da Lapa, Brazil . 93 F10 13 15S 43 25W
Boma,
 Dem. Rep. of the Congo . 52 F2 5 50S 13 4 E
Bombala, Australia 63 F4 36 56S 149 15 E
Bombay = Mumbai, India . 40 K8 18 55N 72 50 E
Bomboma,
 Dem. Rep. of the Congo . 52 D3 2 25N 18 55 E
Bombombwa,
 Dem. Rep. of the Congo . 54 B2 1 40N 25 40 E
Bomili,
 Dem. Rep. of the Congo . 54 B2 1 45N 27 5 E
Bømlo, Norway 9 G11 59 37N 5 13 E
Bomokandi →,
 Dem. Rep. of the Congo . 54 B2 3 39N 26 8 E
Bomu →, C.A.R. 52 D4 4 40N 22 30 E
Bon, C., Tunisia 48 C5 37 1N 11 2 E
Bon Sar Pa, Vietnam 38 F6 12 24N 107 35 E
Bonaigarh, India 43 J11 21 50N 84 57 E
Bonaire, Neth. Ant. 89 D6 12 10N 68 15W
Bonang, Australia 63 F4 37 11S 148 41 E
Bonanza, Nic. 88 D3 13 54N 84 35W
Bonaparte Arch., Australia . 60 B3 14 0S 124 30 E
Bonaventure, Canada 71 C6 48 5N 65 32W
Bonavista, Canada 71 C9 48 40N 53 5W
Bonavista, C., Canada 71 C9 48 42N 53 5W
Bonavista B., Canada 71 C9 48 45N 53 25W
Bondo,
 Dem. Rep. of the Congo . 54 B1 3 55N 23 53 E
Bondoukou, Ivory C. 50 G5 8 2N 2 47W
Bondowoso, Indonesia 37 G15 7 55S 113 49 E
Bone, Teluk, Indonesia 37 E6 4 10S 120 50 E
Bonerate, Indonesia 37 F6 7 25S 121 5 E
Bonerate, Kepulauan,
 Indonesia 37 F6 6 30S 121 10 E
Bo'ness, U.K. 12 E5 56 1N 3 37W
Bonete, Cerro, Argentina .. 94 B2 27 55S 68 40W
Bong Son = Hoai Nhon,
 Vietnam 38 E7 14 28N 109 1 E
Bongor, Chad 51 F9 10 35N 15 20 E
Bonham, U.S.A. 81 J6 33 35N 96 11W
Bonifacio, France 18 F8 41 24N 9 10 E
Bonifacio, Bouches de,
 Medit. S. 20 D3 41 12N 9 15 E
Bonin Is. = Ogasawara
 Gunto, Pac. Oc. 28 G18 27 0N 142 0 E
Bonn, Germany 16 C4 50 46N 7 6 E
Bonne Terre, U.S.A. 81 G9 37 55N 90 33W
Bonners Ferry, U.S.A. 82 B5 48 42N 116 19W
Bonney, L., Australia 63 F3 37 50S 140 20 E
Bonnie Rock, Australia .. 61 F2 30 29S 118 22 E
Bonny, Bight of, Africa .. 52 D1 3 30N 9 20 E
Bonnyrigg, U.K. 12 F5 55 53N 3 6W
Bonnyville, Canada 73 C6 54 20N 110 45W
Bonoi, Indonesia 37 E9 1 45S 137 41 E
Bonsall, U.S.A. 85 M9 33 16N 117 14W
Bontang, Indonesia 36 D5 0 10N 117 30 E
Bonthe, S. Leone 50 G3 7 30N 12 33W
Bontoc, Phil. 37 A6 17 7N 120 58 E
Bonython Ra., Australia .. 60 D4 23 40S 128 45 E
Bookabie, Australia 61 F5 31 50S 132 41 E
Booker, U.S.A. 81 G4 36 27N 100 32W
Booligal, Australia 63 E3 33 58S 144 53 E
Boonah, Australia 63 D5 27 58S 152 41 E
Boone, Iowa, U.S.A. 80 D8 42 4N 93 53W
Boone, N.C., U.S.A. 77 G5 36 13N 81 41W
Booneville, Ark., U.S.A. .. 81 H8 35 8N 93 55W
Booneville, Miss., U.S.A. .. 77 H1 34 39N 88 34W
Boonville, Calif., U.S.A. .. 84 F3 39 1N 123 22W
Boonville, Ind., U.S.A. .. 76 F2 38 3N 87 16W
Boonville, Mo., U.S.A. .. 80 F8 38 58N 92 44W
Boonville, N.Y., U.S.A. .. 79 C9 43 29N 75 20W
Boorindal, Australia 63 E4 30 22S 146 11 E
Boorowa, Australia 63 E4 34 28S 148 44 E
Boothia, Gulf of, Canada . 69 A11 71 0N 90 0W
Boothia Pen., Canada .. 68 A10 71 0N 94 0W
Bootle, U.K. 10 D4 53 28N 3 1W
Booué, Gabon 52 E2 0 5S 11 55 E
Boquete, Panama 88 E3 8 46N 82 27W
Boquilla, Presa de la,
 Mexico 86 B3 27 40N 105 30W
Boquillas del Carmen,
 Mexico 86 B4 29 17N 102 53W
Bor, Serbia, Yug. 21 B10 44 5N 22 7 E
Bôr, Sudan 51 G12 6 10N 31 40 E
Bor Mashash, Israel 47 D3 31 7N 34 50 E
Borah Peak, U.S.A. 82 D7 44 8N 113 47W
Borås, Sweden 9 H15 57 43N 12 56 E
Borāzjān, Iran 45 D6 29 22N 51 10 E
Borba, Brazil 92 D7 4 12S 59 34W
Borborema, Planalto da,
 Brazil 90 D7 7 0S 37 0W
Bord Khūn-e Now, Iran .. 45 D6 28 3N 51 28 E
Borda, C., Australia 63 F2 35 45S 136 34 E
Bordeaux, France 18 D3 44 50N 0 36W
Borden, Australia 61 F2 34 3S 118 12 E
Borden, Canada 71 C7 46 18N 63 47W
Borden I., Canada 4 B2 78 30N 111 30W
Borden Pen., Canada .. 69 A11 73 0N 83 0W
Borders = Scottish
 Borders □, U.K. 12 F6 55 35N 2 50W
Bordertown, Australia .. 63 F3 36 19S 140 45 E
Borðeyri, Iceland 8 D3 65 12N 21 6W
Bordj-in-Eker, Algeria .. 50 D7 24 9N 5 3 E
Bordj Omar Driss, Algeria . 50 C7 28 10N 6 40 E
Borehamwood, U.K. 11 F7 51 40N 0 15W
Borgå = Porvoo, Finland . 9 F21 60 24N 25 40 E
Borgarfjörður, Iceland .. 8 D7 65 31N 13 49W
Borgarnes, Iceland 8 D3 64 32N 21 55W
Borgefjellet, Norway 8 D15 65 20N 13 45 E
Borger, Neths. 15 B6 52 54N 6 44 E
Borger, U.S.A. 81 H4 35 39N 101 24W
Borgholm, Sweden 9 H17 56 52N 16 39 E
Borhoyn Tal, Mongolia .. 34 C6 43 50N 111 58 E
Borikhane, Laos 38 C4 18 33N 103 43 E
Borisoglebsk, Russia 25 D7 51 27N 42 5 E
Borisov = Barysaw, Belarus 17 A15 54 17N 28 28 E
Borja, Peru 92 D3 4 20S 77 40W
Borkou, Chad 51 E9 18 15N 18 50 E
Borkum, Germany 16 B4 53 34N 6 40 E
Borlänge, Sweden 9 F16 60 29N 15 26 E

Borley, C., Antarctica 5 C5 66 15S 52 30 E
Borneo, E. Indies 36 D5 1 0N 115 0 E
Bornholm, Denmark 9 J16 55 10N 15 0 E
Borogontsy, Russia 27 C14 62 42N 131 8 E
Boron, U.S.A. 85 L9 35 0N 117 39W
Borongan, Phil. 37 B7 11 37N 125 26 E
Borovichi, Russia 24 C5 58 25N 33 55 E
Borrego Springs, U.S.A. .. 85 M10 33 15N 116 23W
Borroloola, Australia 62 B2 16 4S 136 17 E
Borşa, Romania 17 E13 47 41N 24 50 E
Borsad, India 42 H5 22 25N 72 54 E
Borth, U.K. 11 E3 52 29N 4 2W
Borüjerd, Iran 45 C6 33 55N 48 50 E
Boryslav, Ukraine 17 D12 49 18N 23 28 E
Borzya, Russia 27 D12 50 24N 116 31 E
Bosa, Italy 20 D3 40 18N 8 30 E
Bosanska Gradiška, Bos.-H. 20 B7 45 10N 17 15 E
Bosaso, Somali Rep. 46 E4 11 12N 49 18 E
Boscastle, U.K. 11 G3 50 41N 4 42W
Boshan, China 35 F9 36 28N 117 49 E
Boshof, S. Africa 56 D4 28 31S 25 13 E
Boshrüyeh, Iran 45 C8 33 50N 57 30 E
Bosna →, Bos.-H. 21 B8 45 4N 18 29 E
Bosna i Hercegovina =
 Bosnia-Herzegovina ■,
 Europe 20 B7 44 0N 18 0 E
Bosnia-Herzegovina ■,
 Europe 20 B7 44 0N 18 0 E
Bosnik, Indonesia 37 E9 1 5S 136 10 E
Bosobolo,
 Dem. Rep. of the Congo . 52 D3 4 15N 19 50 E
Bosporus = İstanbul Boğazı,
 Turkey 21 D13 41 10N 29 10 E
Bosque Farms, U.S.A. 83 J10 34 53N 106 40W
Bossangoa, C.A.R. 52 C3 6 35N 17 30 E
Bossier City, U.S.A. 81 J8 32 31N 93 44W
Bosso, Niger 51 F8 13 43N 13 19 E
Bostan, Pakistan 42 D2 30 26N 67 2 E
Bostānābād, Iran 44 B5 37 50N 46 50 E
Bosten Hu, China 32 B3 41 55N 87 40 E
Boston, U.K. 10 E7 52 59N 0 2W
Boston, U.S.A. 79 D13 42 22N 71 4W
Boston Bar, Canada 72 D4 49 52N 121 30W
Boston Mts., U.S.A. 81 H8 35 42N 93 15W
Boswell, Canada 72 D5 49 28N 116 45W
Boswell, U.S.A. 78 F5 40 10N 79 2W
Botad, India 42 H4 22 15N 71 40 E
Botene, Laos 38 D3 17 35N 101 12 E
Bothaville, S. Africa 56 D4 27 23S 26 34 E
Bothnia, G. of, Europe .. 8 E19 63 0N 20 15 E
Bothwell, Australia 62 G4 42 20S 147 1 E
Bothwell, Canada 78 D3 42 38N 81 52W
Botletle →, Botswana .. 56 C3 20 10S 23 15 E
Botoşani, Romania 17 E14 47 42N 26 41 E
Botou, Burkina Faso 50 F6 12 40N 2 3 E
Botswana ■, Africa 56 C3 22 0S 24 0 E
Bottineau, U.S.A. 80 A4 48 50N 100 27W
Bottrop, Germany 15 C6 51 31N 6 58 E
Botucatu, Brazil 95 A6 22 55S 48 30W
Botwood, Canada 71 C8 49 6N 55 23W
Bouaflé, Ivory C. 50 G4 7 1N 5 47W
Bouaké, Ivory C. 50 G4 7 40N 5 2W
Bouar, C.A.R. 52 C3 6 0N 15 40 E
Bouârfa, Morocco 50 B5 32 32N 1 58W
Boucaut B., Australia 62 A1 12 0S 134 25 E
Bougainville, Canada 80 B4 13 57S 126 4 E
Bougainville I., Papua N. G. 64 H7 6 0S 155 0 E
Bougainville Reef, Australia 62 B4 15 30S 147 5 E
Bougie = Bejaia, Algeria .. 50 A7 36 42N 5 2 E
Bougouni, Mali 50 F4 11 30N 7 20W
Bouillon, Belgium 15 E5 49 44N 5 3 E
Boulder, Colo., U.S.A. .. 80 E2 40 1N 105 17W
Boulder, Mont., U.S.A. .. 82 C7 46 14N 112 7W
Boulder City, U.S.A. 85 K12 35 59N 114 50W
Boulder Creek, U.S.A. .. 84 H4 37 7N 122 7W
Boulder Dam = Hoover
 Dam, U.S.A. 85 K12 36 1N 114 44W
Boulia, Australia 62 C2 22 52S 139 51 E
Boulogne-sur-Mer, France . 18 A4 50 42N 1 36 E
Boultoum, Niger 51 F8 14 45N 10 25 E
Boun Neua, Laos 38 B3 21 38N 101 54 E
Boun Tai, Laos 38 B3 21 23N 101 58 E
Bouna, Ivory C. 50 G5 9 10N 3 0W
Boundary Peak, U.S.A. .. 84 H8 37 51N 118 21W
Boundiali, Ivory C. 50 G4 9 30N 6 20W
Bountiful, U.S.A. 82 F8 40 53N 111 53W
Bounty Is., Pac. Oc. 64 M9 48 0S 178 30 E
Bourbonnais, France 18 C5 46 28N 3 0 E
Bourdel L., Canada 70 A5 56 43N 74 10W
Bourem, Mali 50 E5 17 0N 0 24W
Bourg-en-Bresse, France .. 18 C6 46 13N 5 12 E
Bourg-St-Maurice, France . 18 D7 45 35N 6 46 E
Bourges, France 18 C5 47 9N 2 25 E
Bourget, Canada 79 A9 45 26N 75 9W
Bourgogne, France 18 C6 47 0N 4 50 E
Bourke, Australia 63 E4 30 8S 145 55 E
Bourne, U.K. 10 E7 52 47N 0 22W
Bournemouth, U.K. 11 G6 50 43N 1 52W
Bournemouth □, U.K. .. 11 G6 50 43N 1 52W
Bouse, U.S.A. 85 M13 33 56N 114 0W
Bouvet I. = Bouvetøya,
 Antarctica 3 G10 54 26S 3 24 E
Bouvetøya, Antarctica .. 3 G10 54 26S 3 24 E
Bovill, U.S.A. 82 C5 46 51N 116 24W
Bovril, Argentina 94 C4 31 21S 59 26W
Bow →, Canada 72 C6 49 57N 111 41W
Bow Island, Canada 72 D6 49 50N 111 23W
Bowbells, U.S.A. 80 A3 48 48N 102 15W
Bowdle, U.S.A. 80 C5 45 27N 99 39W
Bowelling, Australia 61 F2 33 25S 116 30 E
Bowen, Argentina 94 D2 35 0S 67 31W
Bowen, Australia 62 C4 20 0S 148 16 E
Bowen Mts., Australia .. 63 F4 37 0S 147 50 E
Bowie, Ariz., U.S.A. 83 K9 32 19N 109 29W
Bowie, Tex., U.S.A. 81 J6 33 34N 97 51W
Bowkän, Iran 44 B5 36 31N 46 12 E
Bowland, Forest of, U.K. . 10 D5 54 0N 2 30W
Bowling Green, Ky., U.S.A. 76 G2 36 59N 86 27W
Bowling Green, Ohio, U.S.A. 76 E4 41 23N 83 39W
Bowling Green, C., Australia 62 B4 19 19S 147 25 E
Bowman, U.S.A. 80 B3 46 11N 103 24W
Bowman I., Antarctica .. 5 C8 65 0S 104 0 E
Bowmanville, Canada .. 78 C6 43 55N 78 41W
Bowmore, U.K. 12 F2 55 45N 6 17W
Bowral, Australia 63 E5 34 26S 150 27 E
Bowraville, Australia 63 E5 30 37S 152 52 E
Bowron →, Canada 72 C4 54 3N 121 50W

Bowron Lake Prov. Park,
 Canada 72 C4 53 10N 121 5W
Bowser L., Canada 72 B3 56 30N 129 30W
Bowsman, Canada 73 C8 52 14N 101 12W
Bowwood, Zambia 55 F2 17 5S 26 20 E
Box Cr. →, Australia .. 63 E3 34 10S 143 50 E
Boxmeer, Neths. 15 C5 51 38N 5 56 E
Boxtel, Neths. 15 C5 51 36N 5 20 E
Boyce, U.S.A. 81 K8 31 23N 92 40W
Boyd L., Canada 70 B4 52 46N 76 42W
Boyle, Canada 72 C6 54 35N 112 49W
Boyle, Ireland 13 C3 53 59N 8 18W
Boyne →, Ireland 13 C5 53 43N 6 15W
Boyne City, U.S.A. 76 C3 45 13N 85 1W
Boynton Beach, U.S.A. .. 77 M5 26 32N 80 4W
Boyolali, Indonesia 37 G14 7 32S 110 35 E
Boyoma, Chutes,
 Dem. Rep. of the Congo . 54 B2 0 35N 25 23 E
Boysen Reservoir, U.S.A. . 82 E9 43 25N 108 11W
Boyuibe, Bolivia 92 G6 20 25S 63 17W
Boyup Brook, Australia .. 61 F2 33 50S 116 23 E
Boz Dağları, Turkey 21 E13 38 20N 28 0 E
Bozcaada, Turkey 21 E12 39 49N 26 3 E
Bozdoğan, Turkey 21 F13 37 40N 28 17 E
Bozeman, U.S.A. 82 D8 45 41N 111 2W
Bozen = Bolzano, Italy .. 20 A4 46 31N 11 22 E
Bozhou, China 34 H8 33 55N 115 41 E
Bozoum, C.A.R. 52 C3 6 25N 16 35 E
Bra, Italy 18 D7 44 42N 7 51 E
Brabant □, Belgium 15 D4 50 46N 4 30 E
Brabant L., Canada 73 B8 55 58N 103 43W
Brač, Croatia 20 C7 43 20N 16 40 E
Bracadale, L., U.K. 12 D2 57 20N 6 30W
Bracciano, L. di, Italy .. 20 C5 42 7N 12 14 E
Bracebridge, Canada .. 78 A5 45 2N 79 19W
Brach, Libya 51 C8 27 31N 14 20 E
Bräcke, Sweden 9 E16 62 45N 15 26 E
Brackettville, U.S.A. 81 L4 29 19N 100 25W
Bracknell, U.K. 11 F7 51 25N 0 43W
Bracknell Forest □, U.K. . 11 F7 51 25N 0 44W
Brad, Romania 17 E12 46 10N 22 50 E
Bradenton, U.S.A. 77 M4 27 30N 82 34W
Bradford, Canada 78 B5 44 7N 79 34W
Bradford, U.K. 10 D6 53 47N 1 45W
Bradford, Pa., U.S.A. .. 78 E6 41 58N 78 38W
Bradford, Vt., U.S.A. .. 79 C12 43 59N 72 9W
Bradley, Ark., U.S.A. .. 81 J8 33 6N 93 39W
Bradley, Calif., U.S.A. .. 84 K6 35 52N 120 48W
Bradley Institute, Zimbabwe 55 F3 17 7S 31 25 E
Brady, U.S.A. 81 K5 31 9N 99 20W
Braemar, U.K. 12 D5 57 0N 3 23W
Braeside, Canada 79 A8 45 28N 76 24W
Braga, Portugal 19 B1 41 35N 8 25W
Bragado, Argentina 94 D3 35 2S 60 27W
Braganca, Brazil 93 D9 1 0S 47 2W
Bragança, Portugal 19 B2 41 48N 6 50W
Bragança Paulista, Brazil .. 95 A6 22 55S 46 32W
Brahmanbaria, Bangla. .. 41 H17 23 58N 91 15 E
Brahmani →, India 41 J15 20 39N 86 46 E
Brahmapur, India 41 K14 19 15N 84 54 E
Brahmaputra →, India .. 43 H13 23 58N 89 50 E
Braich-y-pwll, U.K. 10 E3 52 47N 4 46W
Braidwood, Australia .. 63 F4 35 27S 149 49 E
Brăila, Romania 17 F14 45 19N 27 59 E
Brainerd, U.S.A. 80 B7 46 22N 94 12W
Braintree, U.K. 11 F8 51 53N 0 34 E
Braintree, U.S.A. 79 D14 42 13N 71 0W
Brak →, S. Africa 56 D3 29 35S 22 55 E
Brakwater, Namibia 56 C2 22 28S 17 3 E
Brampton, Canada 78 C5 43 45N 79 45W
Brampton, U.K. 10 C5 54 57N 2 44W
Branco →, Brazil 92 D6 1 20S 61 50W
Brandenburg =
 Neubrandenburg,
 Germany 16 B7 53 33N 13 15 E
Brandenburg, Germany . 16 B7 52 25N 12 33 E
Brandenburg □, Germany . 16 B6 52 50N 13 0 E
Brandfort, S. Africa 56 D4 28 40S 26 30 E
Brandon, Canada 73 D9 49 50N 99 57W
Brandon, U.S.A. 79 C11 43 48N 73 4W
Brandon B., Ireland 13 D1 52 17N 10 8W
Brandon Mt., Ireland .. 13 D1 52 15N 10 15W
Brandsen, Argentina .. 94 D4 35 10S 58 15W
Brandvlei, S. Africa 56 E3 30 25S 20 30 E
Branford, U.S.A. 79 E12 41 17N 72 49W
Braniewo, Poland 17 A10 54 25N 19 50 E
Bransfield Str., Antarctica . 5 C18 63 0S 59 0W
Branson, U.S.A. 81 G8 36 39N 93 13W
Brantford, Canada 78 C4 43 10N 80 15W
Bras d'Or L., Canada .. 71 C7 45 50N 60 50W
Brasher Falls, U.S.A. .. 79 B10 44 49N 74 47W
Brasil, Planalto, Brazil .. 90 E6 18 0S 46 30W
Brasiléia, Brazil 92 F5 11 0S 68 45W
Brasília, Brazil 93 G9 15 47S 47 55W
Brasília Legal, Brazil .. 93 D7 3 49S 55 36W
Braslaw, Belarus 9 J22 55 38N 27 0 E
Braşov, Romania 17 F13 45 38N 25 35 E
Brasschaat, Belgium .. 15 C4 51 19N 4 27 E
Brassey, Banjaran, Malaysia 36 D5 5 0N 117 15 E
Brassey Ra., Australia .. 61 E3 25 8S 122 15 E
Brasstown Bald, U.S.A. .. 77 H4 34 53N 83 49W
Brastad, Sweden 9 G14 58 23N 11 30 E
Bratislava, Slovak Rep. .. 17 D9 48 10N 17 7 E
Bratsk, Russia 27 D11 56 10N 101 30 E
Brattleboro, U.S.A. 79 D12 42 51N 72 34W
Braunau, Austria 16 D7 48 15N 13 3 E
Braunschweig, Germany . 16 B6 52 15N 10 31 E
Braunton, U.K. 11 F3 51 7N 4 10W
Bravo del Norte, Rio =
 Grande, Rio →, U.S.A. . 81 N6 25 58N 97 9W
Brawley, U.S.A. 85 N11 32 59N 115 31W
Bray, Ireland 13 C5 53 13N 6 7W
Bray, Mt., Australia 62 A1 14 0S 134 30 E
Bray, Pays de, France .. 18 B4 49 46N 1 26 E
Brazeau →, Canada .. 72 C5 52 55N 115 14W
Brazil, U.S.A. 76 F2 39 32N 87 8W
Brazil ■, S. Amer. 93 F9 12 0S 50 0W
Brazilian Highlands = Brasil,
 Planalto, Brazil 90 E6 18 0S 46 30W
Brazo Sur →, S. Amer. . 94 B4 25 21S 57 42W
Brazos →, U.S.A. 81 L7 28 53N 95 23W
Brazzaville, Congo 52 E3 4 9S 15 12 E
Brčko, Bos.-H. 21 B8 44 54N 18 46 E
Breaden, L., Australia .. 61 E4 25 51S 125 28 E
Breaksea Sd., N.Z. 59 L1 45 35S 166 35 E
Bream B., N.Z. 59 F5 35 56S 174 28 E

Bream Hd., N.Z. 59 F5 35 51S 174 36 E
Breas, Chile 94 B1 25 29S 70 24W
Brebes, Indonesia 37 G13 6 52S 109 3 E
Brechin, Canada 78 B5 44 32N 79 10W
Brechin, U.K. 12 E6 56 44N 2 39W
Brecht, Belgium 15 C4 51 21N 4 38 E
Breckenridge, Colo., U.S.A. 82 G10 39 29N 106 3W
Breckenridge, Minn., U.S.A. 80 B6 46 16N 96 35W
Breckenridge, Tex., U.S.A. 81 J5 32 45N 98 54W
Breckland, U.K. 11 E8 52 30N 0 40 E
Brecon, U.K. 11 F4 51 57N 3 23W
Brecon Beacons, U.K. .. 11 F4 51 53N 3 26W
Breda, Neths. 15 C4 51 35N 4 45 E
Bredasdorp, S. Africa .. 56 E3 34 33S 20 2 E
Bree, Belgium 15 C5 51 8N 5 35 E
Bregenz, Austria 16 E5 47 30N 9 45 E
Breiðafjörður, Iceland .. 8 D2 65 15N 23 15W
Brejo, Brazil 93 D10 3 41S 42 47W
Bremen, Germany 16 B5 53 4N 8 47 E
Bremer Bay, Australia .. 61 F2 34 21S 119 20 E
Bremer I., Australia 62 A2 12 5S 136 45 E
Bremerhaven, Germany . 16 B5 53 33N 8 36 E
Bremerton, U.S.A. 84 C4 47 34N 122 38W
Brenham, U.S.A. 81 K6 30 10N 96 24W
Brennerpass, Austria .. 16 E6 47 2N 11 30 E
Brent, U.S.A. 77 J2 32 56N 87 10W
Brentwood, U.K. 11 F8 51 37N 0 19 E
Brentwood, Calif., U.S.A. 84 H5 37 56N 121 42W
Brentwood, N.Y., U.S.A. 79 F11 40 47N 73 15W
Bréscia, Italy 18 D9 45 33N 10 15 E
Breskens, Neths. 15 C3 51 33N 3 33 E
Breslau = Wrocław, Poland 17 C9 51 5N 17 5 E
Bressanone, Italy 20 A4 46 43N 11 39 E
Bressay, U.K. 12 A7 60 9N 1 6W
Brest, Belarus 17 B12 52 10N 23 40 E
Brest, France 18 B1 48 24N 4 31W
Brest-Litovsk = Brest,
 Belarus 17 B12 52 10N 23 40 E
Bretagne, France 18 B2 48 10N 3 0W
Breton, Canada 72 C6 53 7N 114 28W
Breton Sd., U.S.A. 81 L10 29 35N 89 15W
Brett, C., N.Z. 59 F5 35 10S 174 20 E
Brevard, U.S.A. 77 H4 35 14N 82 44W
Breves, Brazil 93 D8 1 40S 50 29W
Brewarrina, Australia .. 63 E4 30 0S 146 51 E
Brewer, U.S.A. 77 C11 44 48N 68 46W
Brewer, Mt., U.S.A. .. 84 J8 36 44N 118 28W
Brewster, N.Y., U.S.A. .. 79 E11 41 23N 73 37W
Brewster, Ohio, U.S.A. .. 78 F3 40 43N 81 36W
Brewster, Wash., U.S.A. . 82 B4 48 6N 119 47W
Brewster, Kap, Greenland . 4 B6 70 7N 22 0W
Brewton, U.S.A. 77 K2 31 7N 87 4W
Breyten, S. Africa 57 D5 26 16S 30 0 E
Brezhnev = Naberezhnyye
 Chelny, Russia 24 C9 55 42N 52 19 E
Briançon, France 18 D7 44 54N 6 39 E
Bribie I., Australia 63 D5 27 0S 153 10 E
Bribri, Costa Rica 88 E3 9 38N 82 50W
Bridgehampton, U.S.A. .. 79 F12 40 56N 72 19W
Bridgend, U.K. 11 F4 51 30N 3 34W
Bridgend □, U.K. 11 F4 51 36N 3 36W
Bridgeport, Calif., U.S.A. . 84 G7 38 15N 119 14W
Bridgeport, Conn., U.S.A. 79 E11 41 11N 73 12W
Bridgeport, Nebr., U.S.A. 80 E3 41 40N 103 6W
Bridgeport, Tex., U.S.A. . 81 J6 33 13N 97 45W
Bridger, U.S.A. 82 D9 45 18N 108 55W
Bridgeton, U.S.A. 76 F8 39 26N 75 14W
Bridgetown, Australia .. 61 F2 33 58S 116 7 E
Bridgetown, Barbados .. 89 D8 13 5N 59 30W
Bridgetown, Canada .. 71 D6 44 55N 65 18W
Bridgewater, Canada .. 71 D7 44 25N 64 31W
Bridgewater, Mass., U.S.A. 79 E14 41 59N 70 58W
Bridgewater, N.Y., U.S.A. 79 D9 42 53N 75 15W
Bridgewater, C., Australia . 63 F3 38 23S 141 23 E
Bridgewater-Gagebrook,
 Australia 62 G4 42 44S 147 14 E
Bridgnorth, U.K. 11 E5 52 32N 2 25W
Bridgton, U.S.A. 79 B14 44 3N 70 42W
Bridgwater, U.K. 11 F5 51 8N 2 59W
Bridgwater B., U.K. 11 F4 51 15N 3 15W
Bridlington, U.K. 10 C7 54 5N 0 12W
Bridlington B., U.K. 10 C7 54 4N 0 10W
Bridport, Australia 62 G4 40 59S 147 23 E
Bridport, U.K. 11 G5 50 44N 2 45W
Brig, Switz. 18 C7 46 18N 7 59 E
Brigg, U.K. 10 D7 53 34N 0 28W
Brigham City, U.S.A. .. 82 F7 41 31N 112 1W
Bright, Australia 63 F4 36 42S 146 56 E
Brighton, Australia 63 F2 35 5S 138 30 E
Brighton, Canada 78 B7 44 2N 77 44W
Brighton, U.K. 11 G7 50 49N 0 7W
Brighton, Colo., U.S.A. .. 80 F2 39 59N 104 49W
Brighton, N.Y., U.S.A. .. 78 C7 43 8N 77 34W
Brilliant, U.S.A. 78 F4 40 15N 80 39W
Bríndisi, Italy 21 D7 40 39N 17 55 E
Brinkley, U.S.A. 81 H9 34 53N 91 12W
Brinnon, U.S.A. 84 C4 47 41N 122 54W
Brion, I., Canada 71 C7 47 46N 61 26W
Brisbane, Australia 63 D5 27 24S 153 9 E
Brisbane →, Australia .. 63 D5 27 25S 153 9 E
Bristol, U.K. 11 F5 51 26N 2 35W
Bristol, Conn., U.S.A. .. 79 E12 41 40N 72 57W
Bristol, Pa., U.S.A. 79 F10 40 6N 74 51W
Bristol, R.I., U.S.A. 79 E13 41 40N 71 16W
Bristol, Tenn., U.S.A. .. 77 G4 36 36N 82 11W
Bristol, City of □, U.K. . 11 F5 51 27N 2 36W
Bristol B., U.S.A. 68 C4 58 0N 160 0W
Bristol Channel, U.K. .. 11 F3 51 18N 4 30W
Bristol I., Antarctica .. 5 B1 58 45S 28 0W
Bristol L., U.S.A. 83 J5 34 23N 116 50W
Bristow, U.S.A. 81 H6 35 50N 96 23W
Britain = Great Britain,
 Europe 6 E5 54 0N 2 15W
British Columbia □, Canada 72 C3 55 0N 125 15W
British Indian Ocean Terr. =
 Chagos Arch., Ind. Oc. . 29 K11 6 0S 72 0 E
British Isles, Europe 6 E5 54 0N 4 0W
Brits, S. Africa 57 D4 25 37S 27 48 E
Britstown, S. Africa 56 E3 30 37S 23 30 E
Britt, Canada 78 A4 45 46N 80 34W
Brittany = Bretagne, France 18 B2 48 10N 3 0W
Brive-la-Gaillarde, France . 18 D4 45 10N 1 32 E
Brixen = Bressanone, Italy 20 A4 46 43N 11 39 E
Brixham, U.K. 11 G4 50 23N 3 31W
Brno, Czech Rep. 17 D9 49 10N 16 35 E
Broad →, U.S.A. 77 J5 34 1N 81 4W

Cabora Bassa Dam = Cahora Bassa, Reprêsa de, Mozam. ... 55 F3 15 20S 32 50 E
Caborca, Mexico ... 86 A2 30 40N 112 10W
Cabot, Mt., U.S.A. ... 79 B13 44 30N 71 25W
Cabot Hd., Canada ... 78 A3 45 14N 81 17W
Cabot Str., Canada ... 71 C8 47 15N 59 40W
Cabra, Spain ... 19 D3 37 30N 4 28W
Cabrera, Spain ... 22 B9 39 8N 2 57 E
Cabri, Canada ... 73 C7 50 35N 108 25W
Cabriel →, Spain ... 19 C5 39 14N 1 3W
Caçador, Brazil ... 95 B5 26 47S 51 0W
Čačak, Serbia, Yug. ... 21 C9 43 54N 20 20 E
Caçapava do Sul, Brazil ... 95 C5 30 30S 53 30W
Cáceres, Brazil ... 92 G7 16 5S 57 40W
Cáceres, Spain ... 19 C2 39 26N 6 23W
Cache Bay, Canada ... 70 C4 46 22N 80 0W
Cache Cr. →, U.S.A. ... 84 G5 38 42N 121 42W
Cache Creek, Canada ... 72 C4 50 48N 121 19W
Cachi, Argentina ... 94 B2 25 5S 66 10W
Cachimbo, Serra do, Brazil ... 93 E7 9 30S 55 30W
Cachinal de la Sierra, Chile ... 94 A2 24 58S 69 32W
Cachoeira, Brazil ... 93 F11 12 30S 39 0W
Cachoeira do Sul, Brazil ... 95 C5 30 3S 52 53W
Cachoeiro de Itapemirim, Brazil ... 95 A7 20 51S 41 7W
Cacoal, Brazil ... 92 F6 11 32S 61 18W
Cacólo, Angola ... 52 G3 10 9S 19 21 E
Caconda, Angola ... 53 G3 13 48S 15 8 E
Caddo, U.S.A. ... 81 H6 34 7N 96 16W
Cader Idris, U.K. ... 11 E4 52 42N 3 53W
Cadereyta, Mexico ... 86 B5 25 36N 100 0W
Cadibarrawirracanna, L., Australia ... 63 D2 28 52S 135 27 E
Cadillac, U.S.A. ... 76 C3 44 15N 85 24W
Cádiz, Spain ... 19 D2 36 30N 6 20W
Cadiz, Calif., U.S.A. ... 85 L11 34 30N 115 28W
Cadiz, Ohio, U.S.A. ... 78 F4 40 22N 81 0W
Cádiz, G. de, Spain ... 19 D2 36 40N 7 0W
Cadiz L., U.S.A. ... 83 J6 34 18N 115 24W
Cadney Park, Australia ... 63 D1 27 55S 134 3 E
Cadomin, Canada ... 72 C5 53 2N 117 20W
Cadotte Lake, Canada ... 72 B5 56 26N 116 23W
Cadoux, Australia ... 61 F2 30 46S 117 7 E
Caen, France ... 18 B3 49 10N 0 22W
Caernarfon, U.K. ... 10 D3 53 8N 4 16W
Caernarfon B., U.K. ... 10 D3 53 4N 4 40W
Caernarvon = Caernarfon, U.K. ... 10 D3 53 8N 4 16W
Caerphilly, U.K. ... 11 F4 51 35N 3 13W
Caerphilly □, U.K. ... 11 F4 51 37N 3 12W
Caesarea, Israel ... 47 C3 32 30N 34 53 E
Caetité, Brazil ... 93 F10 13 50S 42 32W
Cafayate, Argentina ... 94 B2 26 2S 66 0W
Cafu, Angola ... 56 B2 16 30S 15 8 E
Cagayan de Oro, Phil. ... 37 C6 8 30N 124 40 E
Cagayan Is., Phil. ... 37 C5 9 40N 121 16 E
Cágliari, Italy ... 20 E3 39 13N 9 7 E
Cágliari, G. di, Italy ... 20 E3 39 8N 9 11 E
Cagúan →, Colombia ... 92 D4 0 8S 74 18W
Caguas, Puerto Rico ... 89 C6 18 14N 66 2W
Caha Mts., Ireland ... 13 E2 51 45N 9 40W
Cahama, Angola ... 56 B1 16 17S 14 19 E
Caher, Ireland ... 13 D4 52 22N 7 56W
Caherciveen, Ireland ... 13 E1 51 56N 10 14W
Cahora Bassa, Reprêsa de, Mozam. ... 55 F3 15 20S 32 50 E
Cahore Pt., Ireland ... 13 D5 52 33N 6 12W
Cahors, France ... 18 D4 44 27N 1 27 E
Cahul, Moldova ... 17 F15 45 50N 28 15 E
Cai Nuoc, Vietnam ... 39 H5 8 56N 105 1 E
Caia, Mozam. ... 55 F4 17 51S 35 24 E
Caianda, Angola ... 55 E1 11 2S 23 31 E
Caibarién, Cuba ... 88 B4 22 30N 79 30W
Caicara, Venezuela ... 92 B5 7 38N 66 10W
Caicó, Brazil ... 93 E11 6 20S 37 0W
Caicos Is., W. Indies ... 89 B5 21 40N 71 40W
Caicos Passage, W. Indies ... 89 B5 22 45N 72 45W
Caird Coast, Antarctica ... 5 D1 75 0S 25 0W
Cairn Gorm, U.K. ... 12 D5 57 7N 3 39W
Cairngorm Mts., U.K. ... 12 D5 57 6N 3 42W
Cairnryan, U.K. ... 12 G3 54 59N 5 1W
Cairns, Australia ... 62 B4 16 57S 145 45 E
Cairns L., Canada ... 73 C10 51 42N 94 30W
Cairo = El Qâhira, Egypt ... 51 B12 30 1N 31 14 E
Cairo, Ga., U.S.A. ... 77 K3 30 52N 84 13W
Cairo, Ill., U.S.A. ... 81 G10 37 0N 89 11W
Cairo, N.Y., U.S.A. ... 79 D11 42 18N 74 0W
Caithness, Ord of, U.K. ... 12 C5 58 8N 3 36W
Cajamarca, Peru ... 92 E3 7 5S 78 28W
Cajàzeiras, Brazil ... 93 E11 6 52S 38 30W
Cala d'Or, Spain ... 22 B10 39 23N 3 14 E
Cala en Porter, Spain ... 22 B11 39 52N 4 8 E
Cala Figuera, C. de, Spain ... 22 B10 39 27N 2 31 E
Cala Forcat, Spain ... 22 B10 40 0N 3 47 E
Cala Major, Spain ... 22 B9 39 33N 2 37 E
Cala Mezquida = Sa Mesquida, Spain ... 22 B11 39 55N 4 16 E
Cala Millor, Spain ... 22 B10 39 35N 3 22 E
Cala Ratjada, Spain ... 22 B10 39 43N 3 27 E
Cala Santa Galdana, Spain ... 22 B10 39 56N 3 58 E
Calabar, Nigeria ... 50 H7 4 57N 8 20 E
Calabogie, Canada ... 79 A8 45 18N 76 43W
Calabozo, Venezuela ... 92 B5 9 0N 67 28W
Calábria □, Italy ... 20 E7 39 0N 16 30 E
Calafate, Argentina ... 96 G2 50 19S 72 15W
Calahorra, Spain ... 19 A5 42 18N 1 59W
Calais, France ... 18 A4 50 57N 1 56 E
Calais, U.S.A. ... 77 C12 45 11N 67 17W
Calalaste, Cord. de, Argentina ... 94 B2 25 0S 67 0W
Calama, Brazil ... 92 E6 8 0S 62 50W
Calama, Chile ... 94 A2 22 30S 68 55W
Calamar, Colombia ... 92 A4 10 15N 74 55W
Calamian Group, Phil. ... 37 B5 11 50N 119 55 E
Calamocha, Spain ... 19 B5 40 50N 1 17W
Calang, Indonesia ... 36 D1 4 37N 95 37 E
Calápan, Phil. ... 37 B6 13 25N 121 7 E
Calárași, Romania ... 17 F14 44 12N 27 20 E
Calatayud, Spain ... 19 B5 41 20N 1 40W
Calauag, Phil. ... 37 B6 13 55N 122 15 E
Calavite, C., Phil. ... 37 B6 13 26N 120 20 E
Calbayog, Phil. ... 37 B6 12 4N 124 38 E
Calca, Peru ... 92 F4 13 22S 72 0W
Calcasieu L., U.S.A. ... 81 L8 29 55N 93 18W
Calcutta = Kolkata, India ... 43 H13 22 36N 88 24 E
Calcutta, U.S.A. ... 78 F4 40 40N 80 34W

Caldas da Rainha, Portugal ... 19 C1 39 24N 9 8W
Calder →, U.K. ... 10 D6 53 44N 1 22W
Caldera, Chile ... 94 B1 27 5S 70 55W
Caldwell, Idaho, U.S.A. ... 82 E5 43 40N 116 41W
Caldwell, Kans., U.S.A. ... 81 G6 37 2N 97 37W
Caldwell, Tex., U.S.A. ... 81 K6 30 32N 96 42W
Caledon, S. Africa ... 56 E2 34 14S 19 26 E
Caledon →, S. Africa ... 56 E4 30 31S 26 5 E
Caledon B., Australia ... 62 A2 12 45S 137 0 E
Caledonia, Canada ... 78 C5 43 7N 79 58W
Caledonia, U.S.A. ... 78 D7 42 58N 77 51W
Calemba, Angola ... 56 B2 16 0S 15 44 E
Calen, Australia ... 62 C4 20 56S 148 48 E
Caletones, Chile ... 94 C1 34 6S 70 27W
Calexico, U.S.A. ... 85 N11 32 40N 115 30W
Calf of Man, U.K. ... 10 C3 54 3N 4 48W
Calgary, Canada ... 72 C6 51 0N 114 10W
Calheta, Madeira ... 22 D2 32 44N 17 11W
Calhoun, U.S.A. ... 77 H3 34 30N 84 57W
Cali, Colombia ... 92 C3 3 25N 76 35W
Calicut, India ... 40 P9 11 15N 75 43 E
Caliente, U.S.A. ... 83 H6 37 37N 114 31W
California, Mo., U.S.A. ... 80 F8 38 38N 92 34W
California, Pa., U.S.A. ... 78 F5 40 4N 79 54W
California □, U.S.A. ... 84 H7 37 30N 119 30W
California, Baja, Mexico ... 86 A1 32 10N 115 12W
California □, Mexico ... 86 B2 30 0N 115 0W
California, Baja, T.S. = Baja California Sur □, Mexico ... 86 B2 25 50N 111 50W
California, G. de, Mexico ... 86 B2 27 0N 111 0W
California City, U.S.A. ... 85 K9 35 10N 117 55W
California Hot Springs, U.S.A. ... 85 K8 35 51N 118 41W
Calingasta, Argentina ... 94 C2 31 15S 69 30W
Calipatria, U.S.A. ... 85 M11 33 8N 115 31W
Calistoga, U.S.A. ... 84 G4 38 35N 122 35W
Calitzdorp, S. Africa ... 56 E3 33 33S 21 42 E
Callabonna, L., Australia ... 63 D3 29 40S 140 5 E
Callan, Ireland ... 13 D4 52 32N 7 24W
Callander, U.K. ... 12 E4 56 15N 4 13W
Callao, Peru ... 92 F3 12 0S 77 0W
Calles, Mexico ... 87 C5 23 2N 98 42W
Callicoon, U.S.A. ... 79 E9 41 46N 75 3W
Calling Lake, Canada ... 72 B6 55 15N 113 12W
Calliope, Australia ... 62 C5 24 0S 151 16 E
Calne, U.K. ... 11 F6 51 26N 2 0W
Calola, Angola ... 56 B2 16 25S 17 48 E
Caloundra, Australia ... 63 D5 26 45S 153 10 E
Calpella, U.S.A. ... 84 F3 39 14N 123 12W
Calpine, U.S.A. ... 84 F6 39 40N 120 27W
Calstock, Canada ... 70 C3 49 47N 84 9W
Caltagirone, Italy ... 20 F6 37 14N 14 31 E
Caltanissetta, Italy ... 20 F6 37 29N 14 4 E
Calulo, Angola ... 52 G2 10 1S 14 56 E
Caluquembe, Angola ... 53 G2 13 47S 14 44 E
Calvert →, Australia ... 62 B2 16 17S 137 44 E
Calvert I., Canada ... 72 C3 51 30N 128 0W
Calvert Ra., Australia ... 60 D3 24 0S 122 30 E
Calvi, France ... 18 E8 42 34N 8 45 E
Calvià, Spain ... 19 C7 39 34N 2 31 E
Calvillo, Mexico ... 86 C4 21 51N 102 43W
Calvinia, S. Africa ... 56 E2 31 28S 19 45 E
Calwa, U.S.A. ... 84 J7 36 42N 119 46W
Cam →, U.K. ... 11 E8 52 21N 0 16 E
Cam Lam, Vietnam ... 39 G7 11 54N 109 10 E
Cam Ranh, Vietnam ... 39 G7 11 54N 109 12 E
Cam Xuyen, Vietnam ... 38 C6 18 15N 106 0 E
Camabatela, Angola ... 52 F3 8 20S 15 26 E
Camacha, Madeira ... 22 D3 32 41N 16 49 E
Camacho, Mexico ... 86 C4 24 25N 102 18W
Camacupa, Angola ... 53 G3 11 58S 17 22 E
Camaná, Peru ... 92 G4 16 30S 72 50W
Camanche Reservoir, U.S.A. ... 84 G6 38 14N 121 1W
Camaquã, Brazil ... 95 C5 30 51S 51 49W
Camaquã →, Brazil ... 95 C5 31 17S 51 47W
Câmara de Lobos, Madeira ... 22 D3 32 39N 16 59W
Camargo, Mexico ... 87 B5 26 19N 98 50W
Camargue, France ... 18 E6 43 34N 4 34 E
Camarillo, U.S.A. ... 85 L7 34 13N 119 2W
Camarón, C., Honduras ... 88 C2 16 0N 85 5W
Camarones, Argentina ... 96 E3 44 50S 65 40W
Camas, U.S.A. ... 84 E4 45 35N 122 24W
Camas Valley, U.S.A. ... 82 E2 43 2N 123 40W
Camballin, Australia ... 60 C3 17 59S 124 12 E
Cambará, Brazil ... 95 A5 23 2S 50 5W
Cambay = Khambhat, G. of, India ... 40 J8 20 45N 72 30 E
Cambodia ■, Asia ... 38 F5 12 15N 105 0 E
Camborne, U.K. ... 11 G2 50 12N 5 19W
Cambrai, France ... 18 A5 50 11N 3 14 E
Cambria, U.S.A. ... 84 K5 35 34N 121 5W
Cambrian Mts., U.K. ... 11 E4 52 3N 3 57W
Cambridge, Canada ... 78 C4 43 23N 80 15W
Cambridge, Jamaica ... 88 C4 18 18N 77 54W
Cambridge, N.Z. ... 59 G5 37 54S 175 29 E
Cambridge, U.K. ... 11 E8 52 12N 0 8 E
Cambridge, Mass., U.S.A. ... 79 D13 42 22N 71 6W
Cambridge, Md., U.S.A. ... 75 C11 38 34N 76 5W
Cambridge, Minn., U.S.A. ... 80 C8 45 34N 93 13W
Cambridge, N.Y., U.S.A. ... 79 C11 43 2N 73 22W
Cambridge, Nebr., U.S.A. ... 80 E4 40 17N 100 10W
Cambridge, Ohio, U.S.A. ... 78 F3 40 2N 81 35W
Cambridge Bay = Ikaluktutiak, Canada ... 68 B9 69 10N 105 0W
Cambridge G., Australia ... 60 B4 14 55S 128 15 E
Cambridge Springs, U.S.A. ... 78 E4 41 48N 80 4W
Cambridgeshire □, U.K. ... 11 E7 52 25N 0 7W
Cambuci, Brazil ... 95 A7 21 35S 41 55W
Cambundi-Catembo, Angola ... 52 G3 10 10S 17 35 E
Camden, Australia ... 63 E5 34 1S 150 43 E
Camden, Ala., U.S.A. ... 77 K2 31 59N 87 17W
Camden, Ark., U.S.A. ... 81 J8 33 35N 92 50W
Camden, Maine, U.S.A. ... 77 C11 44 13N 69 4W
Camden, N.J., U.S.A. ... 79 G9 39 56N 75 7W
Camden, S.C., U.S.A. ... 77 H5 34 16N 80 36W
Camden Sd., Australia ... 60 C3 15 27S 124 25 E
Camdenton, U.S.A. ... 81 F8 38 1N 92 45W
Cameron, Ariz., U.S.A. ... 83 J8 35 53N 111 25W
Cameron, La., U.S.A. ... 81 L8 29 48N 93 20W
Cameron, Mo., U.S.A. ... 80 F7 39 44N 94 14W
Cameron, Tex., U.S.A. ... 81 K6 30 51N 96 59W
Cameron Highlands, Malaysia ... 39 K3 4 27N 101 22 E

Cameron Hills, Canada ... 72 B5 59 48N 118 0W
Cameroon ■, Africa ... 52 C2 6 0N 12 30 E
Cameroun, Mt., Cameroon ... 52 D1 4 13N 9 10 E
Cametá, Brazil ... 93 D9 2 12S 49 30W
Camiguin I., Phil. ... 37 C6 18 56N 121 55 E
Camilla, U.S.A. ... 77 K3 31 14N 84 12W
Caminha, Portugal ... 19 B1 41 50N 8 50W
Camino, U.S.A. ... 84 G6 38 44N 120 41W
Camira Creek, Australia ... 63 D5 29 15S 152 58 E
Cammal, U.S.A. ... 78 E7 41 24N 77 28W
Camocim, Brazil ... 93 D10 2 55S 40 50W
Camooweal, Australia ... 62 B2 19 56S 138 7 E
Camopi, Fr. Guiana ... 93 C8 3 12N 52 17W
Camp Borden, Canada ... 78 B5 44 18N 79 56W
Camp Hill, U.S.A. ... 78 F8 40 14N 76 55W
Camp Nelson, U.S.A. ... 85 J8 36 8N 118 39W
Camp Pendleton, U.S.A. ... 85 M9 33 16N 117 23W
Camp Verde, U.S.A. ... 83 J8 34 34N 111 51W
Camp Wood, U.S.A. ... 81 L5 29 40N 100 1W
Campana, Argentina ... 94 C4 34 10S 58 55W
Campana, I., Chile ... 96 F1 48 20S 75 20W
Campanário, Madeira ... 22 D2 32 39N 17 2W
Campánia □, Italy ... 20 D6 41 0N 14 30 E
Campbell, S. Africa ... 56 D3 28 48S 23 44 E
Campbell, Calif., U.S.A. ... 84 H5 37 17N 121 57W
Campbell, Ohio, U.S.A. ... 78 E4 41 5N 80 37W
Campbell I., Pac. Oc. ... 64 N8 52 30S 169 0 E
Campbell L., Canada ... 73 A7 63 14N 106 55W
Campbell River, Canada ... 72 C3 50 5N 125 20W
Campbell Town, Australia ... 62 G4 41 52S 147 30 E
Campbellford, Canada ... 78 B7 44 18N 77 48W
Campbellpur, Pakistan ... 42 C5 33 46N 72 26 E
Campbellsville, U.S.A. ... 76 G3 37 21N 85 20W
Campbellton, Canada ... 71 C6 47 57N 66 43W
Campbelltown, Australia ... 63 E5 34 4S 150 49 E
Campbeltown, U.K. ... 12 F3 55 26N 5 36W
Campeche, Mexico ... 87 D6 19 50N 90 32W
Campeche □, Mexico ... 87 D6 19 50N 90 32W
Campeche, Golfo de, Mexico ... 87 D6 19 30N 93 0W
Camperdown, Australia ... 63 F3 38 14S 143 9 E
Camperville, Canada ... 73 C8 51 59N 100 9W
Câmpina, Romania ... 17 F13 45 10N 25 45 E
Campina Grande, Brazil ... 93 E11 7 20S 35 47W
Campinas, Brazil ... 95 A6 22 50S 47 0W
Campo Grande, Brazil ... 93 H8 20 25S 54 40W
Campo Maior, Brazil ... 93 D10 4 50S 42 12W
Campo Mourão, Brazil ... 95 A5 24 3S 52 22W
Campobasso, Italy ... 20 D6 41 34N 14 39 E
Campos, Brazil ... 95 A7 21 50S 41 20W
Campos Belos, Brazil ... 93 F9 13 10S 47 3W
Campos del Puerto, Spain ... 22 B10 39 26N 3 1 E
Campos Novos, Brazil ... 95 B5 27 21S 51 50W
Camptonville, U.S.A. ... 84 F5 39 27N 121 3W
Camptown, U.S.A. ... 79 E8 41 44N 76 14W
Câmpulung, Romania ... 17 F13 45 17N 25 3 E
Camrose, Canada ... 72 C6 53 0N 112 50W
Camsell Portage, Canada ... 73 B7 59 37N 109 15W
Çan, Turkey ... 21 D12 40 2N 27 3 E
Can Clavo, Spain ... 22 C7 38 57N 1 27 E
Can Creu, Spain ... 22 C7 38 58N 1 28 E
Can Gio, Vietnam ... 39 G6 10 25N 106 58 E
Can Tho, Vietnam ... 39 G5 10 2N 105 46 E
Canaan, U.S.A. ... 79 D11 42 2N 73 20W
Canada ■, N. Amer. ... 68 C10 60 0N 100 0W
Cañada de Gómez, Argentina ... 94 C3 32 40S 61 30W
Canadian, U.S.A. ... 81 H4 35 55N 100 23W
Canadian →, U.S.A. ... 81 H7 35 28N 95 3W
Canajoharie, U.S.A. ... 79 D10 42 54N 74 35W
Çanakkale, Turkey ... 21 D12 40 17N 26 24 E
Çanakkale Boğazı, Turkey ... 21 D12 40 17N 26 32 E
Canal Flats, Canada ... 72 C5 50 10N 115 48W
Canalejas, Argentina ... 94 D2 35 15S 66 34W
Canals, Argentina ... 94 C3 33 35S 62 53W
Canandaigua, U.S.A. ... 78 D7 42 54N 77 17W
Canandaigua L., U.S.A. ... 78 D7 42 47N 77 19W
Cananea, Mexico ... 86 A2 31 0N 110 20W
Canarias, Is., Atl. Oc. ... 22 F4 28 30N 16 0W
Canarreos, Arch. de los, Cuba ... 88 B3 21 35N 81 40W
Canary Is. = Canarias, Is., Atl. Oc. ... 22 F4 28 30N 16 0W
Canaseraga, U.S.A. ... 78 D7 42 27N 77 45W
Canatlán, Mexico ... 86 C4 24 31N 104 47W
Canaveral, C., U.S.A. ... 77 L5 28 27N 80 32W
Canavieiras, Brazil ... 93 G11 15 39S 39 0W
Canberra, Australia ... 63 F4 35 15S 149 8 E
Canby, Calif., U.S.A. ... 82 F3 41 27N 120 52W
Canby, Minn., U.S.A. ... 80 C6 44 43N 96 16W
Canby, Oreg., U.S.A. ... 84 E4 45 16N 122 42W
Cancún, Mexico ... 87 C7 21 8N 86 44W
Candela, Argentina ... 95 B4 27 29S 55 44W
Candelaria, Canary Is. ... 22 F3 28 22N 16 22W
Candelo, Australia ... 63 F4 36 47S 149 43 E
Candia = Iráklion, Greece ... 23 D7 35 20N 25 12 E
Candle L., Canada ... 73 C7 53 50N 105 18W
Candlemas I., Antarctica ... 5 B1 57 3S 26 40W
Cando, U.S.A. ... 80 A5 48 32N 99 12W
Canea = Khaniá, Greece ... 23 D6 35 30N 24 4 E
Canelones, Uruguay ... 95 C4 34 32S 56 17W
Cañete, Chile ... 94 D1 37 50S 73 30W
Cañete, Peru ... 92 F3 13 8S 76 30W
Cangas de Narcea, Spain ... 19 A2 43 10N 6 32W
Canguaretama, Brazil ... 93 E11 6 20S 35 5W
Canguçu, Brazil ... 95 C5 31 22S 52 43W
Canguçu, Serra do, Brazil ... 95 C5 31 20S 52 40W
Cangzhou, China ... 34 E9 38 19N 116 52 E
Caniapiscau →, Canada ... 71 A6 56 40N 69 30W
Caniapiscau Rés. de, Canada ... 71 B6 54 10N 69 55W
Canicattì, Italy ... 20 F5 37 21N 13 51 E
Canim Lake, Canada ... 72 C4 51 15N 120 54W
Canindeyu □, Paraguay ... 95 A5 24 10S 55 0W
Canisteo, U.S.A. ... 78 D7 42 16N 77 36W
Canisteo →, U.S.A. ... 78 D7 42 7N 77 8W
Cañitas, Mexico ... 86 C4 23 36N 102 43W
Çankırı, Turkey ... 25 F5 40 40N 33 37 E
Cankuzo, Burundi ... 54 C3 3 10S 30 31 E
Canmore, Canada ... 72 C5 51 7N 115 18W
Cann River, Australia ... 63 F4 37 35S 149 7 E
Canna, U.K. ... 12 D2 57 3N 6 33W
Cannanore, India ... 40 P9 11 53N 75 27 E
Cannes, France ... 18 E7 43 32N 7 1 E
Canning Town = Port Canning, India ... 43 H13 22 23N 88 40 E
Cannington, Canada ... 78 B5 44 20N 79 2W
Cannock, U.K. ... 11 E5 52 41N 2 1W

Cannon Ball →, U.S.A. ... 80 B4 46 20N 100 38W
Cannondale Mt., Australia ... 62 D4 25 13S 148 57 E
Cannonsville Reservoir, U.S.A. ... 79 D9 42 4N 75 22W
Cannonvale, Australia ... 62 C4 20 17S 148 43 E
Canoas, Brazil ... 95 B5 29 56S 51 11W
Canoe L., Canada ... 73 B7 55 10N 108 15W
Canon City, U.S.A. ... 80 F2 38 27N 105 14W
Canora, Canada ... 73 C8 51 40N 102 30W
Canowindra, Australia ... 63 E4 33 35S 148 38 E
Canso, Canada ... 71 C7 45 20N 61 0W
Cantabria □, Spain ... 19 A4 43 10N 4 0W
Cantabrian Mts. = Cantábrica, Cordillera, Spain ... 19 A3 43 0N 5 10W
Cantábrica, Cordillera, Spain ... 19 A3 43 0N 5 10W
Cantal, Plomb du, France ... 18 D5 45 3N 2 45 E
Canterbury, Australia ... 62 D3 25 23S 141 53 E
Canterbury, U.K. ... 11 F9 51 16N 1 6 E
Canterbury □, N.Z. ... 59 K3 43 45S 171 19 E
Canterbury Bight, N.Z. ... 59 L3 44 16S 171 55 E
Canterbury Plains, N.Z. ... 59 K3 43 55S 171 22 E
Cantil, U.S.A. ... 85 K9 35 18N 117 58W
Canton = Guangzhou, China ... 33 D6 23 5N 113 10 E
Canton, Ga., U.S.A. ... 77 H3 34 14N 84 29W
Canton, Ill., U.S.A. ... 80 E9 40 33N 90 2W
Canton, Miss., U.S.A. ... 81 J9 32 37N 90 2W
Canton, Mo., U.S.A. ... 80 E9 40 8N 91 32W
Canton, N.Y., U.S.A. ... 79 B9 44 36N 75 10W
Canton, Ohio, U.S.A. ... 78 F3 40 48N 81 23W
Canton, Pa., U.S.A. ... 78 E8 41 39N 76 51W
Canton, S. Dak., U.S.A. ... 80 D6 43 18N 96 35W
Canton L., U.S.A. ... 81 G5 36 6N 98 35W
Canudos, Brazil ... 92 E7 7 13S 58 5W
Canumã →, Brazil ... 92 D7 3 55S 59 10W
Canutama, Brazil ... 92 E6 6 30S 64 20W
Canutillo, U.S.A. ... 83 L10 31 55N 106 36W
Canvey, U.K. ... 11 F8 51 31N 0 37 E
Canyon, U.S.A. ... 81 H4 34 59N 101 55W
Canyonlands National Park, U.S.A. ... 83 G9 38 15N 110 0W
Canyonville, U.S.A. ... 82 E2 42 56N 123 17W
Cao He →, China ... 35 D13 40 10N 124 32 E
Cao Lanh, Vietnam ... 39 G5 10 27N 105 38 E
Cao Xian, China ... 34 G8 34 50N 115 35 E
Cap-aux-Meules, Canada ... 71 C7 47 23N 61 52W
Cap-Chat, Canada ... 71 C6 49 6N 66 40W
Cap-de-la-Madeleine, Canada ... 70 C5 46 22N 72 31W
Cap-Haïtien, Haiti ... 89 C5 19 40N 72 20W
Capac, U.S.A. ... 78 C2 43 1N 82 56W
Capanaparo →, Venezuela ... 92 B5 7 1N 67 7W
Cape →, Australia ... 62 C4 20 59S 146 51 E
Cape Barren I., Australia ... 62 G4 40 25S 148 15 E
Cape Breton Highlands Nat. Park, Canada ... 71 C7 46 50N 60 40W
Cape Breton I., Canada ... 71 C7 46 0N 60 30W
Cape Charles, U.S.A. ... 76 G8 37 16N 76 1W
Cape Coast, Ghana ... 50 G5 5 5N 1 15W
Cape Coral, U.S.A. ... 77 M5 26 33N 81 57W
Cape Dorset, Canada ... 69 B12 64 14N 76 32W
Cape Fear →, U.S.A. ... 77 H6 33 53N 78 1W
Cape Girardeau, U.S.A. ... 81 G10 37 19N 89 32W
Cape May, U.S.A. ... 76 F8 38 56N 74 56W
Cape May Point, U.S.A. ... 75 C12 38 56N 74 58W
Cape Province □, S. Africa ... 53 L3 32 0S 23 0 E
Cape Tormentine, Canada ... 71 C7 46 8N 63 47W
Cape Town, S. Africa ... 56 E2 33 55S 18 22 E
Cape Verde Is. ■, Atl. Oc. ... 49 E1 17 10N 25 20W
Cape Vincent, U.S.A. ... 79 B8 44 8N 76 20W
Cape York Peninsula, Australia ... 62 A3 12 0S 142 30 E
Capela, Brazil ... 93 F11 10 30S 37 0W
Capella, Australia ... 62 C4 23 2S 148 1 E
Capenda Camulemba, Angola ... 52 F3 9 24S 18 27 E
Capim →, Brazil ... 93 D9 1 40S 47 47W
Capitan, U.S.A. ... 83 K11 33 35N 105 35W
Capitol Reef National Park, U.S.A. ... 83 G8 38 15N 111 10W
Capitola, U.S.A. ... 84 J5 36 59N 121 57W
Capoche →, Mozam. ... 55 F3 15 35S 33 0 E
Capraia, Italy ... 18 E8 43 2N 9 50 E
Capreol, Canada ... 70 C3 46 43N 80 56W
Capri, Italy ... 20 D6 40 33N 14 14 E
Capricorn Group, Australia ... 62 C5 23 30S 151 55 E
Capricorn Ra., Australia ... 60 D2 23 20S 116 50 E
Caprivi Strip, Namibia ... 56 B3 18 0S 23 0 E
Captain's Flat, Australia ... 63 F4 35 35S 149 27 E
Caquetá →, Colombia ... 92 D5 1 15S 69 15W
Caracal, Romania ... 17 F13 44 8N 24 22 E
Caracas, Venezuela ... 92 A5 10 30N 66 55W
Caracol, Brazil ... 94 A4 22 18S 57 1W
Caracol, Piauí, Brazil ... 93 E10 9 15S 43 22W
Carajás, Brazil ... 93 E8 6 5S 50 23W
Carajás, Serra dos, Brazil ... 93 E8 6 0S 51 30W
Carangola, Brazil ... 95 A7 20 44S 42 5W
Caransebeş, Romania ... 17 F12 45 28N 22 18 E
Caraquet, Canada ... 71 C6 47 48N 64 57W
Caras, Peru ... 92 E3 9 3S 77 47W
Caratasca, L., Honduras ... 88 C3 15 20N 83 40W
Caratinga, Brazil ... 93 G10 19 50S 42 10W
Caraúbas, Brazil ... 93 E11 5 43S 37 33W
Caravaca = Caravaca de la Cruz, Spain ... 19 C5 38 8N 1 52W
Caravaca de la Cruz, Spain ... 19 C5 38 8N 1 52W
Caravelas, Brazil ... 93 G11 17 45S 39 15W
Caraveli, Peru ... 92 G4 15 45S 73 25W
Carázinho, Brazil ... 95 B5 28 16S 52 46W
Carballo, Spain ... 19 A1 43 13N 8 41W
Carberry, Canada ... 73 D9 49 50N 99 25W
Carbó, Mexico ... 86 B2 29 42N 110 58W
Carbonara, C., Italy ... 20 E3 39 6N 9 31 E
Carbondale, Colo., U.S.A. ... 82 G10 39 24N 107 13W
Carbondale, Ill., U.S.A. ... 81 G10 37 44N 89 13W
Carbondale, Pa., U.S.A. ... 79 E9 41 35N 75 30W
Carbónia, Italy ... 20 E3 39 10N 8 31 E
Carcajou, Canada ... 72 B5 57 47N 117 6W
Carcarana →, Argentina ... 94 C3 32 27S 60 48W
Carcasse, C., Haiti ... 89 C5 18 30N 74 28W
Carcassonne, France ... 18 E5 43 13N 2 20 E
Carcross, Canada ... 72 A2 60 13N 134 45W
Cardamon Hills, India ... 40 Q10 9 30N 77 15 E
Cárdenas, Cuba ... 88 B3 23 0N 81 30W
Cárdenas, Mexico ... 87 C5 22 0N 99 41W

Cárdenas

Cárdenas, Tabasco, Mexico 87 D6 17 59N 93 21W
Cardiff, U.K. 11 F4 51 29N 3 10W
Cardiff □, U.K. 11 F4 51 31N 3 12W
Cardiff-by-the-Sea, U.S.A. 85 M9 33 1N 117 17W
Cardigan, U.K. 11 E3 52 5N 4 40W
Cardigan B., U.K. 11 E3 52 30N 4 30W
Cardinal, Canada 79 B9 44 47N 75 23W
Cardona, Uruguay 94 C4 33 53S 57 18W
Cardoso, Ilha do, Brazil 95 B5 25 8S 47 58W
Cardston, Canada 72 D6 49 15N 113 20W
Cardwell, Australia 62 B4 18 14S 146 2 E
Careen L., Canada 73 B7 57 0N 108 11W
Carei, Romania 17 E12 47 40N 22 29 E
Careme = Ciremai, Indonesia 37 G13 6 55S 108 27 E
Carey, U.S.A. 82 E7 43 19N 113 57W
Carey, L., Australia 61 E3 29 0S 122 15 E
Carey, L., Canada 73 A8 62 12N 102 55W
Carhué, Argentina 94 D3 37 10S 62 50W
Caria, Turkey 21 F13 37 20N 28 10 E
Cariacica, Brazil 93 H10 20 16S 40 25W
Caribbean Sea, W. Indies 89 D5 15 0N 75 0W
Cariboo Mts., Canada 72 C4 53 0N 121 0W
Caribou, U.S.A. 77 B12 46 52N 68 1W
Caribou →, Man., Canada 73 B10 59 20N 94 44W
Caribou →, N.W.T., Canada 72 A3 61 27N 125 45W
Caribou I., Canada 70 C2 47 22N 85 49W
Caribou Is., Canada 72 A6 61 55N 113 15W
Caribou L., Man., Canada 73 B9 59 21N 96 10W
Caribou L., Ont., Canada 70 B2 50 25N 89 5W
Caribou Mts., Canada 72 B5 59 12N 115 40W
Carichic, Mexico 86 B3 27 56N 107 3W
Carinda, Australia 63 E4 30 28S 147 41 E
Carinhanha, Brazil 93 F10 14 15S 44 46W
Carinhanha →, Brazil 93 F10 14 20S 43 47W
Carinthia = Kärnten □, Austria 16 E8 46 52N 13 30 E
Caripito, Venezuela 92 A6 10 8N 63 6W
Carleton, Mt., Canada 71 C6 47 23N 66 53W
Carleton Place, Canada 79 A8 45 8N 76 9W
Carletonville, S. Africa 56 D4 26 23S 27 22 E
Carlin, U.S.A. 82 F5 40 43N 116 7W
Carlingford L., U.K. 13 B5 54 3N 6 9W
Carlinville, U.S.A. 80 F10 39 17N 89 53W
Carlisle, U.K. 10 C5 54 54N 2 56W
Carlisle, U.S.A. 78 F7 40 12N 77 12W
Carlos Casares, Argentina 94 D3 35 32S 61 20W
Carlos Tejedor, Argentina 94 D3 35 25S 62 25W
Carlow, Ireland 13 D5 52 50N 6 56W
Carlow □, Ireland 13 D5 52 43N 6 50W
Carlsbad, Calif., U.S.A. 85 M9 33 10N 117 21W
Carlsbad, N. Mex., U.S.A. 81 J2 32 25N 104 14W
Carlsbad Caverns National Park, U.S.A. 81 J2 32 10N 104 35W
Carluke, U.K. 12 F5 55 45N 3 50W
Carlyle, Canada 73 D8 49 40N 102 20W
Carmacks, Canada 68 B6 62 5N 136 16W
Carman, Canada 73 D9 49 30N 98 0W
Carmarthen, U.K. 11 F3 51 52N 4 19W
Carmarthen B., U.K. 11 F3 51 40N 4 30W
Carmarthenshire □, U.K. 11 F3 51 55N 4 13W
Carmaux, France 18 D5 44 3N 2 10 E
Carmel, U.S.A. 79 E11 41 26N 73 41W
Carmel-by-the-Sea, U.S.A. 84 J5 36 33N 121 55W
Carmel Valley, U.S.A. 84 J5 36 29N 121 43W
Carmelo, Uruguay 94 C4 34 0S 58 20W
Carmen, Colombia 92 B3 9 43N 75 8W
Carmen, Paraguay 95 B4 27 13S 56 12W
Carmen →, Mexico 86 A3 30 42N 106 29W
Carmen, I., Mexico 86 B2 26 0N 111 20W
Carmen de Patagones, Argentina 96 E4 40 50S 63 0W
Carmensa, Argentina 94 D2 35 15S 67 40W
Carmi, Canada 72 D5 49 36N 119 8W
Carmi, U.S.A. 76 F1 38 5N 88 10W
Carmichael, U.S.A. 84 G5 38 38N 121 19W
Carmila, Australia 62 C4 21 55S 149 24 E
Carmona, Costa Rica 88 E2 10 0N 85 15W
Carmona, Spain 19 D3 37 28N 5 42W
Carn Ban, U.K. 12 D4 57 7N 4 15W
Carn Eige, U.K. 12 D3 57 17N 5 8W
Carnac, France 18 C2 47 35N 3 6W
Carnamah, Australia 61 E2 29 41S 115 53 E
Carnarvon, Australia 61 D1 24 51S 113 42 E
Carnarvon, S. Africa 56 E3 30 56S 22 8 E
Carnarvon Ra., Queens., Australia 62 D4 25 15S 148 30 E
Carnarvon Ra., W. Austral., Australia 61 E3 25 20S 120 45 E
Carndonagh, Ireland 13 A4 55 16N 7 15W
Carnduff, Canada 73 D8 49 10N 101 50W
Carnegie, U.S.A. 78 F4 40 24N 80 5W
Carnegie, L., Australia 61 E3 26 5S 122 30 E
Carnic Alps = Karnische Alpen, Europe 16 E7 46 36N 13 0 E
Carniche Alpi = Karnische Alpen, Europe 16 E7 46 36N 13 0 E
Carnot, C.A.R. 52 D3 4 59N 15 56 E
Carnot, C., Australia 63 E2 34 57S 135 38 E
Carnot B., Australia 60 C3 17 20S 122 15 E
Carnoustie, U.K. 12 E6 56 30N 2 42W
Carnsore Pt., Ireland 13 D5 52 10N 6 22W
Caro, U.S.A. 76 D4 43 29N 83 24W
Carol City, U.S.A. 77 N5 25 56N 80 16W
Carolina, Brazil 93 E9 7 10S 47 30W
Carolina, Puerto Rico 89 C6 18 23N 65 58W
Carolina, S. Africa 57 D5 26 5S 30 6 E
Caroline I., Kiribati 65 H12 9 15S 150 3W
Caroline Is., Micronesia 28 J17 8 0N 150 0 E
Caroni →, Venezuela 92 B6 8 21N 62 43W
Caroníe = Nébrodi, Monti, Italy 20 F6 37 54N 14 35 E
Caroona, Australia 63 E5 31 24S 150 26 E
Carpathians, Europe 17 D11 49 30N 21 0 E
Carpații Meridionali, Romania 17 F13 45 30N 25 0 E
Carpentaria, G. of, Australia 62 A2 14 0S 139 0 E
Carpentras, France 18 D6 44 3N 5 2 E
Carpi, Italy 20 B4 44 47N 10 53 E
Carpinteria, U.S.A. 85 L7 34 24N 119 31W
Carr Boyd Ra., Australia 60 C4 16 15S 128 35 E
Carrabelle, U.S.A. 77 L3 29 51N 84 40W
Carranza, Presa V., Mexico 86 B4 27 20N 100 50W
Carrara, Italy 18 D9 44 5N 10 6 E

Carrauntoohill, Ireland 13 D2 52 0N 9 45W
Carrick-on-Shannon, Ireland 13 C3 53 57N 8 5W
Carrick-on-Suir, Ireland 13 D4 52 21N 7 24W
Carrickfergus, U.K. 13 B6 54 43N 5 49W
Carrickmacross, Ireland 13 C5 53 59N 6 43W
Carrieton, Australia 63 E2 32 25S 138 31 E
Carrington, U.S.A. 80 B5 47 27N 99 8W
Carrizal Bajo, Chile 94 B1 28 5S 71 20W
Carrizalillo, Chile 94 B1 29 5S 71 30W
Carrizo Cr. →, U.S.A. 81 G3 36 55N 103 55W
Carrizo Springs, U.S.A. 81 L5 28 31N 99 52W
Carrizozo, U.S.A. 83 K11 33 38N 105 53W
Carroll, U.S.A. 80 D7 42 4N 94 52W
Carrollton, Ga., U.S.A. 77 J3 33 35N 85 5W
Carrollton, Ill., U.S.A. 80 F9 39 18N 90 24W
Carrollton, Ky., U.S.A. 76 F3 38 41N 85 11W
Carrollton, Mo., U.S.A. 80 F8 39 22N 93 30W
Carrollton, Ohio, U.S.A. 78 F3 40 34N 81 5W
Carron →, U.K. 12 D4 57 53N 4 22W
Carron, L., U.K. 12 D3 57 22N 5 35W
Carrot →, Canada 73 C8 53 50N 101 17W
Carrot River, Canada 73 C8 53 17N 103 35W
Carruthers, Canada 73 C7 52 52N 109 16W
Carson, Calif., U.S.A. 85 M8 33 48N 118 17W
Carson, N. Dak., U.S.A. 80 B4 46 25N 101 34W
Carson →, U.S.A. 84 F8 39 45N 118 40W
Carson City, U.S.A. 84 F7 39 10N 119 46W
Carson Sink, U.S.A. 82 G4 39 50N 118 25W
Cartagena, Colombia 92 A3 10 25N 75 33W
Cartagena, Spain 19 D5 37 38N 0 59W
Cartago, Colombia 92 C3 4 45N 75 55W
Cartago, Costa Rica 88 E3 9 50N 83 55W
Cartersville, U.S.A. 77 H3 34 10N 84 48W
Carterton, N.Z. 59 J5 41 2S 175 31 E
Carthage, Tunisia 51 A8 36 50N 10 21 E
Carthage, Ill., U.S.A. 80 E9 40 25N 91 8W
Carthage, Mo., U.S.A. 81 G7 37 11N 94 19W
Carthage, N.Y., U.S.A. 76 D8 43 59N 75 37W
Carthage, Tex., U.S.A. 81 J7 32 9N 94 20W
Cartier I., Australia 60 B3 12 31S 123 29 E
Cartwright, Canada 71 B8 53 41N 56 58W
Caruaru, Brazil 93 E11 8 15S 35 55W
Carúpano, Venezuela 92 A6 10 39N 63 15W
Caruthersville, U.S.A. 81 G10 36 11N 89 39W
Carvoeiro, Brazil 92 D6 1 30S 61 59W
Carvoeiro, C., Portugal 19 C1 39 21N 9 24W
Cary, U.S.A. 77 H6 35 47N 78 46W
Casa Grande, U.S.A. 83 K8 32 53N 111 45W
Casablanca, Chile 94 C1 33 20S 71 25W
Casablanca, Morocco 50 B4 33 36N 7 36W
Cascade, Idaho, U.S.A. 82 D5 44 31N 116 2W
Cascade, Mont., U.S.A. 82 C8 47 16N 111 42W
Cascade Locks, U.S.A. 84 E5 45 40N 121 54W
Cascade Ra., U.S.A. 84 D5 47 0N 121 30W
Cascade Reservoir, U.S.A. 82 D5 44 32N 116 3W
Cascais, Portugal 19 C1 38 41N 9 25W
Cascavel, Brazil 95 A5 24 57S 53 28W
Cáscina, Italy 20 C4 43 41N 10 33 E
Casco B., U.S.A. 77 D10 43 45N 70 0W
Caserta, Italy 20 D6 41 4N 14 20 E
Cashel, Ireland 13 D4 52 30N 7 53W
Casiguran, Phil. 37 A6 16 22N 122 7 E
Casilda, Argentina 94 C3 33 10S 61 10W
Casino, Australia 63 D5 28 52S 153 3 E
Casiquiare →, Venezuela 92 C5 2 1N 67 7W
Casma, Peru 92 E3 9 30S 78 20W
Casmalia, U.S.A. 85 L6 34 50N 120 32W
Caspe, Spain 19 B5 41 14N 0 1W
Casper, U.S.A. 82 E10 42 51N 106 19W
Caspian Depression, Eurasia 25 E8 47 0N 48 0 E
Caspian Sea, Eurasia 25 F9 43 0N 50 0 E
Cass Lake, U.S.A. 80 B7 47 23N 94 37W
Cassadaga, U.S.A. 78 D5 42 20N 79 19W
Casselman, Canada 79 A9 45 19N 75 5W
Casselton, U.S.A. 80 B6 46 54N 97 13W
Cassiar, Canada 72 B3 59 16N 129 40W
Cassiar Mts., Canada 72 B2 59 30N 130 30W
Cassino, Italy 20 D5 41 30N 13 49 E
Cassville, U.S.A. 81 G8 36 41N 93 52W
Castaic, U.S.A. 85 L8 34 30N 118 38W
Castalia, U.S.A. 78 E2 41 24N 82 49W
Castanhal, Brazil 93 D9 1 18S 47 55W
Castellammare di Stábia, Italy 20 D6 40 42N 14 29 E
Castelli, Argentina 94 D4 36 7S 57 47W
Castelló de la Plana, Spain 19 C5 39 58N 0 3W
Castelo, Brazil 95 A7 20 33S 41 14W
Castelo Branco, Portugal 19 C2 39 50N 7 31W
Castelsarrasin, France 18 E4 44 2N 1 7 E
Castelvetrano, Italy 20 F5 37 41N 12 47 E
Casterton, Australia 63 F3 37 30S 141 30 E
Castilla-La Mancha □, Spain 19 C4 39 30N 3 30W
Castilla y Leon □, Spain 19 B3 42 0N 5 0W
Castillos, Uruguay 95 C5 34 12S 53 52W
Castle Dale, U.S.A. 82 G8 39 13N 111 1W
Castle Douglas, U.K. 12 G5 54 56N 3 56W
Castle Rock, Colo., U.S.A. 80 F2 39 22N 104 51W
Castle Rock, Wash., U.S.A. 84 D4 46 17N 122 54W
Castlebar, Ireland 13 C2 53 52N 9 18W
Castleblaney, Ireland 13 B5 54 7N 6 44W
Castlederg, U.K. 13 B4 54 42N 7 35W
Castleford, U.K. 10 D6 53 43N 1 21W
Castlegar, Canada 72 D5 49 20N 117 40W
Castlemaine, Australia 63 F3 37 2S 144 12 E
Castlepollard, Ireland 13 C4 53 41N 7 19W
Castlerea, Ireland 13 C3 53 46N 8 29W
Castlereagh →, Australia 63 E4 30 12S 147 32 E
Castlereagh B., Australia 62 A2 12 10S 135 10 E
Castleton, U.S.A. 79 C11 43 37N 73 11W
Castletown, U.K. 10 C3 54 5N 4 38W
Castletown Bearhaven, Ireland 13 E2 51 39N 9 55W
Castor, Canada 72 C6 52 15N 111 50W
Castor →, Canada 70 B4 53 24N 78 58W
Castres, France 18 E5 43 37N 2 13 E
Castricum, Neths. 15 B4 52 33N 4 40 E
Castries, St. Lucia 89 D7 14 2N 60 58W
Castro, Brazil 95 A6 24 45S 50 0W
Castro, Chile 96 E2 42 30S 73 50W
Castro Alves, Brazil 93 F11 12 46S 39 33W
Castroville, U.S.A. 84 J5 36 46N 121 45W
Castuera, Spain 19 C3 38 43N 5 37W
Cat I., Bahamas 89 B4 24 30N 75 30W
Cat L., Canada 70 B1 51 40N 91 50W

Cat Lake, Canada 70 B1 51 40N 91 50W
Catacamas, Honduras 88 D2 14 54N 85 56W
Cataguases, Brazil 95 A7 21 23S 42 39W
Catalão, Brazil 93 G9 18 10S 47 57W
Çatalca, Turkey 21 D13 41 8N 28 27 E
Catalina, Canada 71 C9 48 31N 53 4W
Catalina, Chile 94 B2 25 13S 69 43W
Catalina, U.S.A. 83 K8 32 30N 110 50W
Catalonia = Cataluña □, Spain 19 B6 41 40N 1 15 E
Cataluña □, Spain 19 B6 41 40N 1 15 E
Catamarca, Argentina 94 B2 28 30S 65 50W
Catamarca □, Argentina 94 B2 27 0S 65 50W
Catanduanes, Phil. 37 B6 13 50N 124 20 E
Catanduva, Brazil 95 A6 21 5S 48 58W
Catánia, Italy 20 F6 37 30N 15 6 E
Catanzaro, Italy 20 E7 38 54N 16 35 E
Cataman, Phil. 37 B6 12 28N 124 35 E
Cateel, Phil. 37 C7 7 47N 126 24 E
Caterham, U.K. 11 F7 51 15N 0 4W
Cathcart, S. Africa 56 E4 32 18S 27 10 E
Cathlamet, U.S.A. 84 D3 46 12N 123 23W
Catlettsburg, U.S.A. 76 F4 38 25N 82 36W
Catoche, C., Mexico 87 C7 21 40N 87 8W
Catril, Argentina 94 D3 36 26S 63 24W
Catrimani, Brazil 92 C6 0 27N 61 41W
Catrimani →, Brazil 92 C6 0 28N 61 44W
Catskill, U.S.A. 79 D11 42 14N 73 52W
Catskill Mts., U.S.A. 79 D10 42 10N 74 25W
Catt, Mt., Australia 62 A1 13 49S 134 23 E
Cattaraugus, U.S.A. 78 D6 42 22N 78 52W
Catuala, Angola 56 B2 16 25S 19 2 E
Catur, Mozam. 55 E4 13 45S 35 30 E
Catwick Is., Vietnam 39 H7 10 0N 109 0 E
Cauca →, Colombia 92 B4 8 54N 74 28W
Caucaia, Brazil 93 D11 3 40S 38 35W
Caucasus Mountains, Eurasia 25 F7 42 50N 44 0 E
Caungula, Angola 52 F3 8 26S 18 38 E
Cauquenes, Chile 94 D1 35 58S 72 22W
Caura →, Venezuela 92 B6 7 38N 64 53W
Cauresi →, Mozam. 55 F3 18 8S 33 0 E
Causapscal, Canada 71 C6 48 19N 67 12W
Cauvery →, India 40 P11 11 9N 78 52 E
Caux, Pays de, France 18 B4 49 38N 0 35 E
Cavalier, U.S.A. 80 A6 48 48N 97 37W
Cavalleria, C. de, Spain 22 A11 40 5N 4 5 E
Cavan, Ireland 13 B4 54 0N 7 22W
Cavan □, Ireland 13 C4 54 1N 7 16W
Cave Creek, U.S.A. 83 K7 33 50N 111 57W
Cavenagh Ra., Australia 61 E4 26 12S 127 55 E
Cavendish, Australia 63 F3 37 31S 142 2 E
Caviana, I., Brazil 93 C8 0 10N 50 10W
Cavite, Phil. 37 B6 14 29N 120 55 E
Cawndilla L., Australia 63 E3 32 30S 142 15 E
Cawnpore = Kanpur, India 43 F9 26 28N 80 20 E
Caxias, Brazil 93 D10 4 55S 43 20W
Caxias do Sul, Brazil 95 B5 29 10S 51 10W
Cay Sal Bank, Bahamas 88 B4 23 45N 80 0W
Cayambe, Ecuador 92 C3 0 3N 78 8W
Cayenne, Fr. Guiana 93 B8 5 5N 52 18W
Cayman Brac, Cayman Is. 88 C4 19 43N 79 49W
Cayman Is. ■, W. Indies 88 C3 19 40N 80 30W
Cayo Romano, Cuba 88 B4 22 0N 78 0W
Cayuga, Canada 78 D5 42 59N 79 50W
Cayuga, U.S.A. 79 D8 42 54N 76 44W
Cayuga L., U.S.A. 79 D8 42 41N 76 41W
Cazenovia, U.S.A. 79 D9 42 56N 75 51W
Cazombo, Angola 53 G4 11 54S 22 56 E
Ceanannus Mor, Ireland 13 C5 53 44N 6 53W
Ceará = Fortaleza, Brazil 93 D11 3 45S 38 35W
Ceará □, Brazil 93 E11 5 0S 40 0W
Ceará Mirim, Brazil 93 E11 5 38S 35 25W
Cebaco, I. de, Panama 88 E3 7 33N 81 9W
Cebollar, Argentina 94 B2 29 10S 66 35W
Cebu, Phil. 37 B6 10 18N 123 54 E
Cecil Plains, Australia 63 D5 27 30S 151 11 E
Cedar →, U.S.A. 80 E9 41 17N 91 21W
Cedar City, U.S.A. 83 H7 37 41N 113 4W
Cedar Creek Reservoir, U.S.A. 81 J6 32 11N 96 4W
Cedar Falls, Iowa, U.S.A. 80 D8 42 32N 92 27W
Cedar Falls, Wash., U.S.A. 84 C5 47 25N 121 45W
Cedar L., Canada 73 C9 53 10N 100 0W
Cedar Rapids, U.S.A. 80 E9 41 59N 91 40W
Cedartown, U.S.A. 77 H3 34 1N 85 15W
Cedarvale, Canada 72 B3 55 1N 128 22W
Cedarville, S. Africa 57 E4 30 23S 29 3 E
Cedral, Mexico 86 C4 23 50N 100 42W
Cedro, Brazil 93 E11 6 34S 39 3W
Cedros, I. de, Mexico 86 B1 28 10N 115 20W
Ceduna, Australia 63 E1 32 7S 133 46 E
Cefalù, Italy 20 E6 38 2N 14 1 E
Cegléd, Hungary 17 E10 47 11N 19 47 E
Celaya, Mexico 86 C4 20 31N 100 37W
Celebes = Sulawesi □, Indonesia 37 E6 2 0S 120 0 E
Celebes Sea, Indonesia 37 D6 3 0N 123 0 E
Celina, U.S.A. 76 E3 40 33N 84 35W
Celje, Slovenia 16 E8 46 16N 15 18 E
Celle, Germany 16 B6 52 37N 10 4 E
Cenderwasih, Teluk, Indonesia 37 E9 3 0S 135 20 E
Center, N. Dak., U.S.A. 80 B4 47 7N 101 18W
Center, Tex., U.S.A. 81 K7 31 48N 94 11W
Centerburg, U.S.A. 78 F2 40 18N 82 42W
Centerville, Calif., U.S.A. 84 J7 36 44N 119 30W
Centerville, Iowa, U.S.A. 80 E8 40 44N 92 52W
Centerville, Pa., U.S.A. 78 F5 40 3N 79 59W
Centerville, Tenn., U.S.A. 77 H2 35 47N 87 28W
Centerville, Tex., U.S.A. 81 K7 31 16N 95 59W
Central □, Kenya 54 C4 0 30S 37 30 E
Central □, Zambia 55 E2 14 25S 28 50 E
Central, Cordillera, Colombia 92 C4 5 0N 75 0W
Central, Cordillera, Costa Rica 88 D3 10 10N 84 5W
Central, Cordillera, Dom. Rep. 89 C5 19 15N 71 0W
Central African Rep. ■, Africa 52 C4 7 0N 20 0 E
Central America, America 66 H11 12 0N 85 0W
Central Butte, Canada 73 C7 50 48N 106 31W
Central City, Colo., U.S.A. 82 G11 39 48N 105 31W
Central City, Ky., U.S.A. 76 G2 37 18N 87 7W
Central City, Nebr., U.S.A. 80 E6 41 7N 98 0W

Central I., Kenya 54 B4 3 30N 36 0 E
Central Makran Range, Pakistan 40 F4 26 30N 64 15 E
Central Patricia, Canada 70 B1 51 30N 90 9W
Central Point, U.S.A. 82 E2 42 23N 122 55W
Central Russian Uplands, Europe 6 E13 54 0N 36 0 E
Central Siberian Plateau, Russia 28 C14 65 0N 105 0 E
Central Square, U.S.A. 79 C8 43 17N 76 9W
Centralia, Ill., U.S.A. 80 F10 38 32N 89 8W
Centralia, Mo., U.S.A. 80 F8 39 13N 92 8W
Centralia, Wash., U.S.A. 84 D4 46 43N 122 58W
Cephalonia = Kefallinía, Greece 21 E9 38 20N 20 30 E
Cepu, Indonesia 37 G14 7 9S 111 35 E
Ceram = Seram, Indonesia 37 E7 3 10S 129 0 E
Ceram Sea = Seram Sea, Indonesia 37 E7 2 30S 128 30 E
Ceredigion □, U.K. 11 E3 52 16N 4 15W
Ceres, Argentina 94 B3 29 55S 61 55W
Ceres, S. Africa 56 E2 33 21S 19 18 E
Ceres, U.S.A. 84 H6 37 35N 120 57W
Cerignola, Italy 20 D6 41 17N 15 53 E
Cerigo = Kíthira, Greece 21 F10 36 8N 23 0 E
Çerkezköy, Turkey 21 D12 41 17N 28 0 E
Cerralvo, I., Mexico 86 C3 24 20N 109 45W
Cerritos, Mexico 86 C4 22 27N 100 20W
Cerro Chato, Uruguay 95 C4 33 6S 55 8W
Cerventes, Australia 61 F2 30 31S 115 3 E
Cervera, Spain 19 B6 41 40N 1 16 E
Cesena, Italy 20 B5 44 8N 12 15 E
Cēsis, Latvia 9 H21 57 18N 25 15 E
České Budějovice, Czech Rep. 16 D8 48 55N 14 25 E
Českomoravská Vrchovina, Czech Rep. 16 D8 49 30N 15 40 E
Çeşme, Turkey 21 E12 38 20N 26 23 E
Cessnock, Australia 63 E5 32 50S 151 21 E
Cetinje, Montenegro, Yug. 21 C8 42 23N 18 59 E
Cetraro, Italy 20 E6 39 31N 15 55 E
Ceuta, N. Afr. 19 E3 35 52N 5 18W
Cévennes, France 18 D5 44 10N 3 50 E
Ceyhan, Turkey 44 B2 37 4N 35 47 E
Ceylon = Sri Lanka ■, Asia 40 R12 7 30N 80 50 E
Cha-am, Thailand 38 F2 12 48N 99 58 E
Cha Pa, Vietnam 38 A4 22 20N 103 47 E
Chacabuco, Argentina 94 C3 34 40S 60 27W
Chachapoyas, Peru 92 E3 6 15S 77 50W
Chachoengsao, Thailand 38 F3 13 42N 101 5 E
Chachran, Pakistan 40 E7 28 55N 70 30 E
Chachro, Pakistan 42 G4 25 5N 70 15 E
Chaco □, Argentina 94 B3 26 30S 61 0W
Chaco □, Paraguay 94 B4 26 0S 60 0W
Chaco →, U.S.A. 83 H9 36 46N 108 39W
Chaco Austral, S. Amer. 96 B4 27 0S 61 30W
Chaco Boreal, S. Amer. 92 H6 22 0S 60 0W
Chaco Central, S. Amer. 96 A4 24 0S 61 0W
Chacon, C., U.S.A. 72 C2 54 42N 132 0W
Chad ■, Africa 51 F8 15 0N 17 15 E
Chad, L. = Tchad, L., Chad 51 F8 13 30N 14 30 E
Chadan, Russia 27 D10 51 17N 91 35 E
Chadileuvú →, Argentina 94 D2 37 46S 66 0W
Chadiza, Zambia 55 E3 14 45S 32 27 E
Chadron, U.S.A. 80 D3 42 50N 103 0W
Chadyr-Lunga = Ciadâr-Lunga, Moldova 17 E15 46 3N 28 51 E
Chae Hom, Thailand 38 C2 18 43N 99 35 E
Chaem →, Thailand 38 C2 18 11N 98 38 E
Chaeryŏng, N. Korea 35 E13 38 24N 125 36 E
Chagai Hills, Afghan. 40 E3 29 30N 63 0 E
Chagda, Russia 27 D14 58 45N 130 38 E
Chagos Arch., Ind. Oc. 29 K11 6 0S 72 0 E
Chagrin Falls, U.S.A. 78 E3 41 26N 81 24W
Chāh Ākhvor, Iran 45 C8 32 41N 59 40 E
Chāh Bahār, Iran 45 E9 25 20N 60 40 E
Chāh-e Kavīr, Iran 45 C8 34 29N 56 52 E
Chahar Burjak, Afghan. 40 D3 30 15N 62 0 E
Chahār Mahāll va Bakhtiārī □, Iran 45 C6 32 0N 49 0 E
Chaibasa, India 41 H14 22 42N 85 49 E
Chainat, Thailand 38 E3 15 11N 100 8 E
Chaiya, Thailand 39 H2 9 23N 99 14 E
Chajari, Argentina 94 C4 30 42S 58 0W
Chak Amru, Pakistan 42 C6 32 22N 75 11 E
Chakar →, Pakistan 42 E3 29 29N 68 2 E
Chake Chake, Tanzania 54 D4 5 15S 39 45 E
Chakhānsūr, Afghan. 40 D3 31 10N 62 0 E
Chakonipau, L., Canada 71 A6 56 18N 68 30W
Chakradharpur, India 43 H11 22 45N 85 40 E
Chakrata, India 42 D7 30 42N 77 51 E
Chakwal, Pakistan 42 C5 32 56N 72 53 E
Chala, Peru 92 G4 15 48S 74 20W
Chalchihuites, Mexico 86 C4 23 29N 103 53W
Chalcis = Khalkís, Greece 21 E10 38 27N 23 42 E
Chalfant, U.S.A. 84 H8 37 32N 118 21W
Chalhuanca, Peru 92 F4 14 15S 73 15W
Chalisgaon, India 40 J9 20 30N 75 10 E
Chalk River, Canada 70 C4 46 1N 77 27W
Chalky Inlet, N.Z. 59 M1 46 3S 166 31 E
Challapata, Bolivia 92 G5 18 53S 66 50W
Challis, U.S.A. 82 D6 44 30N 114 14W
Chalmette, U.S.A. 81 L10 29 56N 89 58W
Chalon-sur-Saône, France 18 C6 46 48N 4 50 E
Châlons-en-Champagne, France 18 B6 48 58N 4 20 E
Chalyaphum, Thailand 38 E4 15 48N 102 2 E
Cham, Cu Lao, Vietnam 38 E7 15 57N 108 30 E
Chama, U.S.A. 83 H10 36 54N 106 35W
Chamaicó, Argentina 94 D3 35 3S 64 58W
Chaman, Pakistan 40 D5 30 58N 66 25 E
Chamba, India 42 C7 32 35N 76 10 E
Chamba, Tanzania 55 E4 11 37S 37 0 E
Chambal →, India 43 F8 26 29N 79 15 E
Chamberlain, U.S.A. 80 D5 43 49N 99 20W
Chamberlain →, Australia 60 C4 15 30S 127 54 E
Chamberlain L., U.S.A. 77 B11 46 14N 69 19W
Chambers, U.S.A. 83 J9 35 11N 109 26W
Chambersburg, U.S.A. 76 F7 39 56N 77 40W
Chambeshi →, Zambia 52 G6 11 53S 29 48 E
Chambly, Canada 79 A11 45 27N 73 17W
Chambord, Canada 71 C5 48 25N 72 6W
Chamchamal, Iraq 44 C5 35 32N 44 50 E
Chamela, Mexico 86 D3 19 32N 105 5W

Chamical, *Argentina* **94 C2** 30 22S 66 27W
Chamkar Luong, *Cambodia* **39 G4** 11 0N 103 45 E
Chamoli, *India* **43 D8** 30 24N 79 21 E
Chamonix-Mont Blanc,
France **18 D7** 45 55N 6 51 E
Chamouchouane ➤,
Canada **70 C5** 48 37N 72 20W
Champa, *India* **43 H10** 22 2N 82 43 E
Champagne, *Canada* **72 A1** 60 49N 136 30W
Champagne, *France* **18 B6** 48 40N 4 20 E
Champaign, *U.S.A.* **76 E1** 40 7N 88 15W
Champassak, *Laos* **38 E5** 14 53N 105 52 E
Champawat, *India* **43 E9** 29 20N 80 6 E
Champdoré, L., *Canada* **71 A6** 55 55N 65 49W
Champion, *U.S.A.* **78 E4** 41 19N 80 51W
Champlain, *U.S.A.* **79 B11** 44 59N 73 27W
Champlain, L., *U.S.A.* **79 B11** 44 40N 73 20W
Champotón, *Mexico* **87 D6** 19 20N 90 50W
Champua, *India* **43 H11** 22 5N 85 40 E
Chana, *Thailand* **39 J3** 6 55N 100 44 E
Chañaral, *Chile* **94 B1** 26 23S 70 40W
Chanārān, *Iran* **45 B8** 36 39N 59 6 E
Chanasma, *India* **42 H5** 23 44N 72 5 E
Chanco, *Chile* **94 D1** 35 44S 72 32W
Chand, *India* **43 J8** 21 57N 79 7 E
Chandan, *India* **43 G12** 24 38N 86 40 E
Chandan Chauki, *India* **43 E9** 28 33N 80 47 E
Chandausi, *India* **43 E8** 28 27N 78 49 E
Chandeleur Is., *U.S.A.* **81 L10** 29 55N 88 57W
Chandeleur Sd., *U.S.A.* **81 L10** 29 55N 89 0W
Chandigarh, *India* **42 D7** 30 43N 76 47 E
Chandil, *India* **43 H12** 22 58N 86 3 E
Chandler, *Australia* **63 D1** 27 0S 133 19 E
Chandler, *Canada* **71 C7** 48 18N 64 46W
Chandler, *Ariz., U.S.A.* **83 K8** 33 18N 111 50W
Chandler, *Okla., U.S.A.* **81 H6** 35 42N 96 53W
Chandod, *India* **42 J5** 21 59N 73 28 E
Chandpur, *Bangla.* **41 H17** 23 8N 90 45 E
Chandrapur, *India.* **40 K11** 19 57N 79 25 E
Chānf, *Iran* **45 E9** 26 38N 60 29 E
Chang, *Pakistan* **42 F3** 26 59N 68 30 E
Chang, Ko, *Thailand* **39 G4** 12 0N 102 23 E
Ch'ang Chiang = Chang
Jiang ➤, *China* **33 C7** 31 48N 121 10 E
Chang Jiang ➤, *China* **33 C7** 31 48N 121 10 E
Changa, *India* **43 C7** 33 53N 77 35 E
Changanacheri, *India* **40 Q10** 9 25N 76 31 E
Changane ➤, *Mozam.* **57 C5** 24 30S 33 30 E
Changbai, *China* **35 D15** 41 25N 128 5 E
Changbai Shan, *China* **35 C15** 42 20N 129 0 E
Changchiak'ou =
Zhangjiakou, *China* **34 D8** 40 48N 114 55 E
Ch'angchou = Changzhou,
China **33 C6** 31 47N 119 58 E
Changchun, *China* **35 C13** 43 57N 125 17 E
Changchunling, *China* **35 B13** 45 18N 125 27 E
Changde, *China* **33 D6** 29 4N 111 35 E
Changdo-ri, *N. Korea* **35 E14** 38 30N 127 40 E
Changhai = Shanghai,
China **33 C7** 31 15N 121 26 E
Changhua, *Taiwan* **33 D7** 24 2N 120 30 E
Changhŭng, *S. Korea* **35 G14** 34 41N 126 52 E
Changhŭngni, *N. Korea* **35 D15** 40 24N 128 19 E
Changjiang, *China* **38 C7** 19 20N 108 55 E
Changjin, *N. Korea* **35 D14** 40 23N 127 15 E
Changjin-chŏsuji, *N. Korea* . . **35 D14** 40 30N 127 15 E
Changli, *China* **35 E10** 39 40N 119 13 E
Changling, *China* **35 B12** 44 20N 123 58 E
Changlun, *Malaysia* **39 J3** 6 25N 100 26 E
Changping, *China* **34 D9** 40 14N 116 12 E
Changsha, *China* **33 D6** 28 12N 113 0 E
Changwu, *China* **34 G4** 35 10N 107 45 E
Changyi, *China* **35 F10** 36 40N 119 30 E
Changyŏn, *N. Korea* **35 E13** 38 15N 125 6 E
Changyuan, *China* **34 G8** 35 15N 114 42 E
Changzhi, *China* **34 F7** 36 10N 113 6 E
Changzhou, *China* **33 C6** 31 47N 119 58 E
Chanhanga, *Angola* **56 B1** 16 0S 14 8 E
Channapatna, *India* **40 N10** 12 40N 77 15 E
Channel Is., *U.K.* **11 H5** 49 19N 2 24W
Channel Is., *U.S.A.* **85 M7** 33 40N 119 15W
Channel Islands National
Park, *U.S.A.* **85 M8** 33 30N 119 0W
Channel-Port aux Basques,
Canada **71 C8** 47 30N 59 9W
Channel Tunnel, *Europe* **11 F9** 51 0N 1 30 E
Channing, *U.S.A.* **81 H3** 35 41N 102 20W
Chantada, *Spain* **19 A2** 42 36N 7 46W
Chanthaburi, *Thailand* **38 F4** 12 38N 102 12 E
Chantrey Inlet, *Canada* **68 B10** 67 48N 96 20W
Chanute, *U.S.A.* **81 G7** 37 41N 95 27W
Chao Phraya ➤, *Thailand* . . **38 F3** 13 32N 100 36 E
Chao Phraya Lowlands,
Thailand **38 E3** 15 30N 100 0 E
Chaocheng, *China* **34 F8** 36 4N 115 37 E
Chaoyang, *China* **35 D11** 41 35N 120 22 E
Chaozhou, *China* **33 D6** 23 42N 116 32 E
Chapais, *Canada* **70 C5** 49 47N 74 51W
Chapala, *U.S.A.* **55 F4** 15 50S 37 35 E
Chapala, L. de, *Mexico* **86 C4** 20 10N 103 20W
Chapayev, *Kazakstan* **25 D9** 50 25N 51 10 E
Chapayevsk, *Russia* **24 D8** 53 0N 49 40 E
Chapecó, *Brazil* **95 B5** 27 14S 52 41W
Chapel Hill, *U.S.A.* **77 H6** 35 55N 79 4W
Chapleau, *Canada* **70 C3** 47 50N 83 24W
Chaplin, *Canada* **73 C7** 50 28N 106 40W
Chaplin L., *Canada* **73 C7** 50 22N 106 36W
Chappell, *U.S.A.* **80 E3** 41 6N 102 28W
Chapra = Chhapra, *India* . . . **43 G11** 25 48N 84 44 E
Chara, *Russia* **27 D12** 56 54N 118 20 E
Charadai, *Argentina* **94 B4** 27 35S 59 55W
Charagua, *Bolivia* **92 G6** 19 45S 63 10W
Charambirá, Punta,
Colombia **92 C3** 4 16N 77 32W
Charaña, *Bolivia* **92 G5** 17 30S 69 25W
Charanwala, *India* **42 F5** 27 51N 72 10 E
Charata, *Argentina* **94 B3** 27 13S 61 14W
Charcas, *Mexico* **86 C4** 23 10N 101 20W
Chard, *U.K.* **11 G5** 50 52N 2 58W
Chardon, *U.S.A.* **78 E3** 41 35N 81 12W
Chardzhou = Chärjew,
Turkmenistan **26 F7** 39 6N 63 34 E
Charente ➤, *France* **18 D3** 45 57N 1 5W
Chārī, *Chad* **51 F8** 12 58N 14 31 E
Chārīkār, *Afghan.* **40 B6** 35 0N 69 10 E
Chariton ➤, *U.S.A.* **80 F8** 39 19N 92 58W

Chärjew, *Turkmenistan* **26 F7** 39 6N 63 34 E
Charkhari, *India* **43 G8** 25 24N 79 45 E
Charkhi Dadri, *India* **42 E7** 28 37N 76 17 E
Charleroi, *Belgium* **15 D4** 50 24N 4 27 E
Charleroi, *U.S.A.* **78 F5** 40 9N 79 57W
Charles, C., *U.S.A.* **76 G8** 37 7N 75 58W
Charles City, *U.S.A.* **80 D8** 43 4N 92 41W
Charles L., *Canada* **73 B6** 59 50N 110 33W
Charles Town, *U.S.A.* **76 F7** 39 17N 77 52W
Charleston, *Ill., U.S.A.* **76 F1** 39 30N 88 10W
Charleston, *Miss., U.S.A.* . . . **81 H9** 34 1N 90 4W
Charleston, *Mo., U.S.A.* **81 G10** 36 55N 89 21W
Charleston, *S.C., U.S.A.* **77 J6** 32 46N 79 56W
Charleston, *W. Va., U.S.A.* . . **76 F5** 38 21N 81 38W
Charleston L., *Canada* **79 B9** 44 32N 76 0W
Charleston Peak, *U.S.A.* **85 J11** 36 16N 115 42W
Charlestown, *Ireland* **13 C3** 53 58N 8 48W
Charlestown, *S. Africa* **57 D4** 27 26S 29 53 E
Charlestown, *Ind., U.S.A.* . . . **76 F3** 38 27N 85 40W
Charlestown, *N.H., U.S.A.* . . **79 C12** 43 14N 72 25W
Charleville = Rath Luirc,
Ireland **13 D3** 52 21N 8 40W
Charleville, *Australia* **63 D4** 26 24S 146 15 E
Charleville-Mézières, *France* **18 B6** 49 44N 4 40 E
Charlevoix, *U.S.A.* **76 C3** 45 19N 85 16W
Charlotte, *Mich., U.S.A.* **76 D3** 42 34N 84 50W
Charlotte, *N.C., U.S.A.* **77 H5** 35 13N 80 51W
Charlotte, *Vt., U.S.A.* **79 B11** 44 19N 73 14W
Charlotte Amalie, *Virgin Is.* . **89 C7** 18 21N 64 56W
Charlotte Harbor, *U.S.A.* **77 M4** 26 50N 82 10W
Charlotte L., *Canada* **72 C3** 52 12N 125 19W
Charlottesville, *U.S.A.* **76 F6** 38 2N 78 30W
Charlottetown, *Nfld.,
Canada* **71 B8** 52 46N 56 7W
Charlottetown, *P.E.I.,
Canada* **71 C7** 46 14N 63 8W
Charlton, *Australia* **63 F3** 36 16S 143 24 E
Charlton, *U.S.A.* **80 E8** 40 59N 93 20W
Charlton I., *Canada* **70 B4** 52 0N 79 20W
Charny, *Canada* **71 C5** 46 43N 71 15W
Charolles, *France* **18 C6** 46 27N 4 16 E
Charre, *Mozam.* **55 F4** 17 13S 35 10 E
Charsadda, *Pakistan* **42 B4** 34 7N 71 45 E
Charters Towers, *Australia* . . **62 C4** 20 5S 146 13 E
Chartres, *France* **18 B4** 48 29N 1 30 E
Chascomús, *Argentina* **94 D4** 35 30S 58 0W
Chasefu, *Zambia* **55 E3** 11 55S 33 8 E
Chashma Barrage, *Pakistan* . **42 C4** 32 27N 71 20 E
Chāt, *Iran* **45 B7** 37 59N 55 16 E
Châteaubriant, *France* **18 C3** 47 43N 1 23W
Chateauguay, L., *Canada* . . . **79 B10** 54 56N 74 5W
Châteauguay, L., *Canada* . . . **71 A5** 56 26N 70 3W
Châteaulin, *France* **18 B1** 48 11N 4 8W
Châteauroux, *France* **18 C4** 46 50N 1 40 E
Châtellerault, *France* **18 C4** 46 50N 0 30 E
Chatham = Miramichi,
Canada **71 C6** 47 2N 65 28W
Chatham, *U.K.* **11 F8** 51 22N 0 32 E
Chatham, *U.S.A.* **79 D11** 42 21N 73 36W
Chatham Is., *Pac. Oc.* **64 M10** 44 0S 176 40W
Chatmohar, *Bangla.* **43 G13** 24 15N 89 15 E
Chatra, *India* **43 G11** 24 12N 84 56 E
Chatrapur, *India* **41 K14** 19 22N 85 2 E
Chats, L. des, *Canada* **79 A8** 45 30N 76 20W
Chatsu, *India* **42 F6** 26 36N 75 57 E
Chatsworth, *Canada* **78 B4** 44 27N 80 54W
Chatsworth, *Zimbabwe* **55 F3** 19 38S 31 13 E
Chattahoochee, *U.S.A.* **77 K3** 30 42N 84 51W
Chattahoochee ➤, *U.S.A.* . . **77 K3** 30 54N 84 57W
Chattanooga, *U.S.A.* **77 H3** 35 3N 85 19W
Chatteris, *U.K.* **11 E8** 52 28N 0 2 E
Chaturat, *Thailand* **38 E3** 15 40N 101 51 E
Chau Doc, *Vietnam* **39 G5** 10 42N 105 7 E
Chauk, *Burma* **41 J19** 20 53N 94 49 E
Chaukan La, *Burma* **41 F20** 27 0N 97 15 E
Chaumont, *France* **18 B6** 48 7N 5 8 E
Chaumont, *U.S.A.* **79 B8** 44 4N 76 8W
Chautauqua L., *U.S.A.* **78 D5** 42 10N 79 24W
Chauvin, *Canada* **73 C6** 52 45N 110 10W
Chaves, *Brazil* **93 D9** 0 15S 49 55W
Chaves, *Portugal* **19 B2** 41 45N 7 32W
Chawang, *Thailand* **39 H2** 8 25N 99 30 E
Chazy, *U.S.A.* **79 B11** 44 53N 73 26W
Cheb, *Czech Rep.* **16 C7** 50 9N 12 28 E
Cheboksary, *Russia* **24 C8** 56 8N 47 12 E
Cheboygan, *U.S.A.* **76 C3** 45 39N 84 29W
Chech, Erg, *Africa* **50 D5** 25 0N 2 15W
Chechenia □, *Russia* **25 F8** 43 30N 45 29 E
Checheno-Ingush Republic
= Chechenia □, *Russia* . . **25 F8** 43 30N 45 29 E
Chechnya = Chechenia □,
Russia **25 F8** 43 30N 45 29 E
Chech'ŏn, *S. Korea* **35 F15** 37 8N 128 12 E
Checotah, *U.S.A.* **81 H7** 35 28N 95 31W
Chedabucto B., *Canada* **71 C7** 45 25N 61 8W
Cheduba I., *Burma* **41 K18** 18 45N 93 40 E
Cheepie, *Australia* **63 D4** 26 33S 145 1 E
Chegdomyn, *Russia* **27 D14** 51 7N 133 1 E
Chegga, *Mauritania* **50 C4** 25 27N 5 40W
Chegutu, *Zimbabwe* **55 F3** 18 10S 30 14 E
Chehalis, *U.S.A.* **84 D4** 46 40N 122 58W
Chehalis ➤, *U.S.A.* **84 D3** 46 57N 123 50W
Cheju do, *S. Korea* **35 H14** 33 29N 126 34 E
Chekiang = Zhejiang □,
China **33 D7** 29 0N 120 0 E
Chela, Sa. da, *Angola* **56 B1** 16 20S 13 20 E
Chelan, *U.S.A.* **82 C4** 47 51N 120 1W
Chelan, L., *U.S.A.* **82 B3** 48 11N 120 30W
Cheleken, *Turkmenistan* **25 G9** 39 34N 53 16 E
Cheleken Yarymadasy,
Turkmenistan **45 B7** 39 30N 53 15 E
Chelforó, *Argentina* **96 D3** 39 0S 66 33W
Chelkar = Shalqar,
Kazakstan **26 E6** 47 48N 59 39 E
Chelkar Tengiz, Solonchak,
Kazakstan **26 E7** 48 5N 63 7 E
Chelm, *Poland* **17 C12** 51 8N 23 30 E
Chelmno, *Poland* **17 B10** 53 20N 18 30 E
Chelmsford, *U.K.* **11 F8** 51 44N 0 29 E
Chelsea, *U.S.A.* **79 C12** 43 59N 72 27W
Cheltenham, *U.K.* **11 F5** 51 54N 2 4W
Chelyabinsk, *Russia* **26 D7** 55 10N 61 24 E
Chelyuskin, C., *Russia* **28 B14** 77 30N 103 0 E
Chemainus, *Canada* **84 B3** 48 55N 123 42W
Chemba, *Mozam.* **53 H6** 17 9S 34 53 E

Chemnitz, *Germany* **16 C7** 50 51N 12 54 E
Chemult, *U.S.A.* **82 E3** 43 14N 121 47W
Chenab ➤, *Pakistan* **42 D4** 30 23N 71 2 E
Chenango Forks, *U.S.A.* **79 D9** 42 15N 75 51W
Cheney, *U.S.A.* **82 C5** 47 30N 117 35W
Cheng Xian, *China* **34 H3** 33 43N 105 42 E
Chengcheng, *China* **34 G5** 35 8N 109 56 E
Chengchou = Zhengzhou,
China **34 G7** 34 45N 113 34 E
Chengde, *China* **35 D9** 40 59N 117 58 E
Chengdu, *China* **32 C5** 30 38N 104 2 E
Chenggu, *China* **34 H4** 33 10N 107 21 E
Chengjiang, *China* **32 D5** 24 39N 103 0 E
Ch'engmai, *China* **38 C7** 19 50N 109 58 E
Chengwu, *China* **34 G8** 34 58N 115 50 E
Chengyang, *China* **35 F11** 36 18N 120 21 E
Chenjiagang, *China* **35 G10** 34 23N 119 47 E
Chenkán, *Mexico* **87 D6** 19 8N 90 58W
Chennai, *India* **40 N12** 13 8N 80 19 E
Cheo Reo, *Vietnam* **36 B3** 13 25N 108 28 E
Cheom Ksan, *Cambodia* **38 E5** 14 13N 104 56 E
Chepén, *Peru* **92 E3** 7 15S 79 23W
Chepes, *Argentina* **94 C2** 31 20S 66 35W
Chepo, *Panama* **88 E4** 9 10N 79 6W
Chepstow, *U.K.* **11 F5** 51 38N 2 41W
Cheptulil, Mt., *Kenya* **54 B4** 1 25N 35 35 E
Chequamegon B., *U.S.A.* . . . **80 B9** 46 40N 90 30W
Cher ➤, *France* **18 C4** 47 21N 0 29 E
Cheraw, *U.S.A.* **77 H6** 34 42N 79 53W
Cherbourg, *France* **18 B3** 49 39N 1 40W
Cherdyn, *Russia* **24 B10** 60 24N 56 29 E
Cheremkhovo, *Russia* **27 D11** 53 8N 103 1 E
Cherepanovo, *Russia* **26 D9** 54 15N 83 30 E
Cherepovets, *Russia* **24 C6** 59 5N 37 55 E
Chergui, Chott ech, *Algeria* . **50 B6** 34 21N 0 25 E
Cherikov = Cherykaw,
Belarus **17 B16** 53 32N 31 20 E
Cherkasy, *Ukraine* **25 E5** 49 27N 32 4 E
Cherkessk, *Russia* **25 F7** 44 15N 42 5 E
Cherlak, *Russia* **26 D8** 54 15N 74 55 E
Chernaya, *Russia* **27 B9** 70 30N 89 10 E
Chernigov = Chernihiv,
Ukraine **24 D5** 51 28N 31 20 E
Chernihiv, *Ukraine* **24 D5** 51 28N 31 20 E
Chernivtsi, *Ukraine* **17 D13** 48 15N 25 52 E
Chernobyl = Chornobyl,
Ukraine **17 C16** 51 20N 30 15 E
Chernogorsk, *Russia* **27 D10** 53 49N 91 18 E
Chernovtsy = Chernivtsi,
Ukraine **17 D13** 48 15N 25 52 E
Chernyakhovsk, *Russia* **9 J19** 54 36N 21 48 E
Chernysheyskiy, *Russia* **27 C12** 63 0N 112 30 E
Cherokee, *Iowa, U.S.A.* **80 D7** 42 45N 95 33W
Cherokee, *Okla., U.S.A.* **81 G5** 36 45N 98 21W
Cherokee Village, *U.S.A.* **81 G9** 36 17N 91 30W
Cherokees, Grand Lake O'
The, *U.S.A.* **81 G7** 36 28N 95 2W
Cherrapunji, *India* **41 G17** 25 17N 91 47 E
Cherry Valley, *Calif., U.S.A.* . **85 M10** 33 59N 116 57W
Cherry Valley, *N.Y., U.S.A.* . . **79 D10** 42 48N 74 45W
Cherskiy, *Russia* **27 C17** 68 45N 161 18 E
Cherskogo Khrebet, *Russia* . **27 C15** 65 0N 143 0 E
Cherven, *Belarus* **17 B15** 53 45N 28 28 E
Chervonohrad, *Ukraine* **17 C13** 50 25N 24 10 E
Cherwell ➤, *U.K.* **11 F6** 51 44N 1 14W
Cherykaw, *Belarus* **17 B16** 53 32N 31 20 E
Chesapeake, *U.S.A.* **76 G7** 36 50N 76 17W
Chesapeake B., *U.S.A.* **76 G7** 38 0N 76 10W
Cheshire □, *U.K.* **10 D5** 53 14N 2 30W
Cheshskaya Guba, *Russia* . . **24 A8** 67 20N 47 0 E
Cheshunt, *U.K.* **11 F7** 51 43N 0 1W
Chesil Beach, *U.K.* **11 G5** 50 37N 2 33W
Chesley, *Canada* **78 B3** 44 17N 81 5W
Chester, *U.K.* **10 D5** 53 12N 2 53W
Chester, *Calif., U.S.A.* **82 F3** 40 19N 121 14W
Chester, *Ill., U.S.A.* **81 G10** 37 55N 89 49W
Chester, *Mont., U.S.A.* **82 B8** 48 31N 110 58W
Chester, *Pa., U.S.A.* **76 F8** 39 51N 75 22W
Chester, *S.C., U.S.A.* **77 H5** 34 43N 81 12W
Chester, *Vt., U.S.A.* **79 C12** 43 16N 72 36W
Chester, *W. Va., U.S.A.* **78 F4** 40 37N 80 34W
Chester-le-Street, *U.K.* **10 C6** 54 51N 1 34W
Chesterfield, *U.K.* **10 D6** 53 15N 1 25W
Chesterfield, Is., *N. Cal.* **64 J7** 19 52S 158 15 E
Chesterfield Inlet, *Canada* . . **68 B10** 63 30N 90 45W
Chesterton Ra., *Australia* . . . **63 D4** 25 30S 147 27 E
Chestertown, *U.S.A.* **79 C11** 43 40N 73 48W
Chesterville, *Canada* **79 A9** 45 6N 75 14W
Chestnut Ridge, *U.S.A.* **78 F5** 40 20N 79 10W
Chesuncook L., *U.S.A.* **77 C11** 46 0N 69 21W
Chetumal, *Mexico* **87 D7** 18 30N 88 20W
Chetumal, B. de, *Mexico* **87 D7** 18 40N 88 10W
Chetwynd, *Canada* **72 B4** 55 45N 121 36W
Cheviot, The, *U.K.* **10 B5** 55 29N 2 9W
Cheviot Hills, *U.K.* **10 B5** 55 29N 2 9W
Cheviot Ra., *Australia* **62 D3** 25 20S 143 45 E
Chew Bahir, *Ethiopia* **46 G2** 4 40N 36 50 E
Chewelah, *U.S.A.* **82 B5** 48 17N 117 43W
Cheyenne, *Okla., U.S.A.* **81 H5** 35 37N 99 40W
Cheyenne, *Wyo., U.S.A.* **80 E2** 41 8N 104 49W
Cheyenne ➤, *U.S.A.* **80 C4** 44 41N 101 18W
Cheyenne Wells, *U.S.A.* **80 F3** 38 49N 102 21W
Cheyne B., *Australia* **61 F2** 34 35S 118 50 E
Chhabra, *India* **42 G7** 24 40N 76 54 E
Chhaktala, *India* **42 H6** 22 6N 74 11 E
Chhapra, *India* **43 G11** 25 48N 84 44 E
Chhata, *India* **42 F7** 27 42N 77 30 E
Chhatarpur, *Bihar, India* **43 G11** 24 23N 84 11 E
Chhatarpur, *Mad. P., India* . . **43 G8** 24 55N 79 35 E
Chhep, *Cambodia* **38 F5** 13 45N 105 24 E
Chhindwara, *Mad. P., India* . . **43 H8** 23 3N 79 29 E
Chhindwara, *Mad. P., India* . . **43 H8** 22 2N 78 59 E
Chhlong, *Cambodia* **39 F5** 12 15N 105 58 E
Chhota Tawa ➤, *India* **42 H7** 22 14N 76 36 E
Chhoti Kali Sindh ➤, *India* . . **42 G6** 24 2N 75 31 E
Chhuikhadan, *India* **43 J9** 21 32N 80 59 E
Chhuk, *Cambodia* **39 G5** 10 46N 104 28 E
Chi ➤, *Thailand* **38 E5** 15 11N 104 43 E
Chiai, *Taiwan* **33 D7** 23 29N 120 25 E
Chiamboni, *Somali Rep.* **52 E8** 1 39S 41 35 E
Chiamussu = Jiamusi,
China **33 B8** 46 40N 130 26 E
Chiang Dao, *Thailand* **38 C2** 19 22N 98 58 E
Chiang Kham, *Thailand* **38 C3** 19 32N 100 18 E

Chiang Khan, *Thailand* **38 D3** 17 52N 101 36 E
Chiang Mai, *Thailand* **38 C2** 18 47N 98 59 E
Chiang Rai, *Thailand* **38 C2** 19 52N 99 50 E
Chiapa ➤, *Mexico* **87 D6** 16 42N 93 0W
Chiapa de Corzo, *Mexico* . . . **87 D6** 16 42N 93 0W
Chiapas □, *Mexico* **87 D6** 17 0N 92 45W
Chiautla, *Mexico* **87 D5** 18 18N 98 34W
Chiávari, *Italy* **18 D8** 44 19N 9 19 E
Chiavenna, *Italy* **18 C8** 46 19N 9 24 E
Chiba, *Japan* **31 G10** 35 30N 140 7 E
Chiba □, *Japan* **31 G10** 35 30N 140 20 E
Chibabava, *Mozam.* **57 C5** 20 17S 33 35 E
Chibemba, *Cunene, Angola* . **53 H2** 15 48S 14 8 E
Chibemba, *Huila, Angola* . . . **56 B2** 16 20S 15 20 E
Chibia, *Angola* **53 H2** 15 10S 13 42 E
Chibougamau, *Canada* **70 C5** 49 56N 74 24W
Chibougamau, L., *Canada* . . . **70 C5** 49 50N 74 20W
Chic-Chocs, Mts., *Canada* . . **71 C6** 48 55N 66 0W
Chicacole = Srikakulam,
India **41 K13** 18 14N 83 58 E
Chicago, *U.S.A.* **76 E2** 41 53N 87 38W
Chicago Heights, *U.S.A.* **76 E2** 41 30N 87 38W
Chichagof I., *U.S.A.* **68 C6** 57 30N 135 30W
Chichén-Itzá, *Mexico* **87 C7** 20 40N 88 36W
Chicheng, *China* **34 D8** 40 55N 115 55 E
Chichester, *U.K.* **11 G7** 50 50N 0 47W
Chichester Ra., *Australia* **60 D2** 22 12S 119 15 E
Chichibu, *Japan* **31 F9** 36 5N 139 10 E
Ch'ich'ihaerh = Qiqihar,
China **27 E13** 47 26N 124 0 E
Chicholi, *India* **42 H8** 22 1N 77 40 E
Chickasha, *U.S.A.* **81 H6** 35 3N 97 58W
Chiclana de la Frontera,
Spain **19 D2** 36 26N 6 9W
Chiclayo, *Peru* **92 E3** 6 42S 79 50W
Chico, *U.S.A.* **84 F5** 39 44N 121 50W
Chico ➤, *Chubut,
Argentina* **96 E3** 44 0S 67 0W
Chico ➤, *Santa Cruz,
Argentina* **96 G3** 50 0S 68 30W
Chicomo, *Mozam.* **57 C5** 24 31S 34 6 E
Chicontepec, *Mexico* **87 C5** 20 58N 98 10W
Chicopee, *U.S.A.* **79 D12** 42 9N 72 37W
Chicoutimi, *Canada* **71 C5** 48 28N 71 5W
Chicualacuala, *Mozam.* **57 C5** 22 6S 31 42 E
Chidambaram, *India* **40 P11** 11 20N 79 45 E
Chidenguele, *Mozam.* **57 C5** 24 55S 34 11 E
Chidley, C., *Canada* **69 B13** 60 23N 64 26W
Chiede, *Angola* **56 B2** 17 15S 16 22 E
Chiefs Pt., *Canada* **78 B3** 44 41N 81 18W
Chiem Hoa, *Vietnam* **38 A5** 22 12N 105 17 E
Chiemsee, *Germany* **16 E7** 47 53N 12 28 E
Chiengi, *Zambia* **55 D2** 8 45S 29 10 E
Chiengmai = Chiang Mai,
Thailand **38 C2** 18 47N 98 59 E
Chiese ➤, *Italy* **18 D9** 45 8N 10 25 E
Chieti, *Italy* **20 C6** 42 21N 14 10 E
Chifeng, *China* **35 C10** 42 18N 118 58 E
Chignecto B., *Canada* **71 C7** 45 30N 64 40W
Chiguana, *Bolivia* **94 A2** 21 0S 67 58W
Chigwell, *U.K.* **11 F8** 51 37N 0 5 E
Chiha-ri, *N. Korea* **35 E14** 38 40N 126 30 E
Chihli, G. of = Bo Hai, *China* **35 E10** 39 0N 119 0 E
Chihuahua, *Mexico* **86 B3** 28 40N 106 3W
Chihuahua □, *Mexico* **86 B3** 28 40N 106 3W
Chiili, *Kazakstan* **26 E7** 44 20N 66 15 E
Chik Bollapur, *India* **40 N10** 13 25N 77 45 E
Chikmagalur, *India* **40 N9** 13 15N 75 45 E
Chikwawa, *Malawi* **55 F3** 16 2S 34 50 E
Chilac, *Mexico* **87 D5** 18 20N 97 24W
Chilam Chavki, *Pakistan* **43 B6** 35 5N 75 5 E
Chilanga, *Zambia* **55 F2** 15 33S 28 16 E
Chilapa, *Mexico* **87 D5** 17 40N 99 11W
Chilas, *Pakistan* **43 B6** 35 25N 74 5 E
Chilaw, *Sri Lanka* **40 R11** 7 30N 79 50 E
Chilcotin ➤, *Canada* **72 C4** 51 44N 122 23W
Childers, *Australia* **63 D5** 25 15S 152 17 E
Childress, *U.S.A.* **81 H4** 34 25N 100 13W
Chile ■, *S. Amer.* **96 D2** 35 0S 72 0W
Chile Rise, *Pac. Oc.* **65 L18** 38 0S 92 0W
Chilecito, *Argentina* **94 B2** 29 10S 67 30W
Chilete, *Peru* **92 E3** 7 10S 78 50W
Chililabombwe, *Zambia* **55 E2** 12 18S 27 43 E
Chilin = Jilin, *China* **35 C14** 43 44N 126 30 E
Chilka L., *India* **41 K14** 19 40N 85 25 E
Chilko ➤, *Canada* **72 C4** 52 0N 123 40W
Chilko, L., *Canada* **72 C4** 51 20N 124 10W
Chillagoe, *Australia* **62 B3** 17 7S 144 33 E
Chillán, *Chile* **94 D1** 36 40S 72 10W
Chillicothe, *Ill., U.S.A.* **80 E10** 40 55N 89 29W
Chillicothe, *Mo., U.S.A.* **80 F8** 39 48N 93 33W
Chillicothe, *Ohio, U.S.A.* **76 F4** 39 20N 82 59W
Chilliwack, *Canada* **72 D4** 49 10N 121 54W
Chilo, *India* **42 F5** 27 25N 73 32 E
Chiloane, I., *Mozam.* **57 C5** 20 40S 34 55 E
Chiloé, I. de, *Chile* **96 E2** 42 30S 73 50W
Chilpancingo, *Mexico* **87 D5** 17 30N 99 30W
Chiltern Hills, *U.K.* **11 F7** 51 40N 0 53W
Chilton, *U.S.A.* **76 C1** 44 2N 88 10W
Chilubi, *Zambia* **55 E2** 11 5S 29 58 E
Chilubula, *Zambia* **55 E3** 10 14S 30 51 E
Chilumba, *Malawi* **55 E3** 10 28S 34 12 E
Chilung, *Taiwan* **33 D7** 25 3N 121 45 E
Chilwa, L., *Malawi* **55 F4** 15 15S 35 40 E
Chimaltitán, *Mexico* **86 C4** 21 46N 103 50W
Chimán, *Panama* **88 E4** 8 45N 78 40W
Chimay, *Belgium* **15 D4** 50 3N 4 20 E
Chimayo, *U.S.A.* **83 H11** 36 0N 105 56W
Chimbay, *Uzbekistan* **26 E6** 42 57N 59 47 E
Chimborazo, *Ecuador* **92 D3** 1 29S 78 55W
Chimbote, *Peru* **92 E3** 9 0S 78 35W
Chimkent = Shymkent,
Kazakstan **26 E7** 42 18N 69 36 E
Chimoio, *Mozam.* **55 F3** 19 4S 33 30 E
Chimpembe, *Zambia* **55 D2** 9 31S 29 33 E
Chin □, *Burma* **41 J18** 22 0N 93 0 E
Chin Ling Shan = Qinling
Shandi, *China* **34 H5** 33 50N 108 10 E
China, *Mexico* **87 B5** 25 40N 99 20W
China ■, *Asia* **33 D6** 30 0N 110 0 E
China Lake, *U.S.A.* **85 K9** 35 44N 117 37W
Chinan = Jinan, *China* **34 F9** 36 38N 117 1 E
Chinandega, *Nic.* **88 D2** 12 35N 87 12W
Chinati Peak, *U.S.A.* **81 L2** 29 57N 104 29W
Chincha Alta, *Peru* **92 F3** 13 25S 76 7W
Chinchaga ➤, *Canada* **72 B5** 58 53N 118 20W
Chinchilla, *Australia* **63 D5** 26 45S 150 38 E

Cobán, *Guatemala* **88 C1** 15 30N 90 21W
Cobar, *Australia* **63 E4** 31 27S 145 48 E
Cobargo, *Australia* **63 F4** 36 20S 149 55 E
Cóbh, *Ireland* **13 E3** 51 51N 8 17W
Cobija, *Bolivia* **92 F5** 11 0S 68 50W
Cobleskill, *U.S.A.* **79 D10** 42 41N 74 29W
Coboconk, *Canada* **78 B6** 44 39N 78 48W
Cobourg, *Canada* **78 C6** 43 58N 78 10W
Cobourg Pen., *Australia* .. **60 B5** 11 20S 132 15 E
Cobram, *Australia* **63 F4** 35 54S 145 40 E
Cóbué, *Mozam.* **55 E3** 12 0S 34 58 E
Coburg, *Germany* **16 C6** 50 15N 10 58 E
Cocanada = Kakinada, *India* **41 L13** 16 57N 82 11 E
Cochabamba, *Bolivia* **92 G5** 17 26S 66 10W
Cochemane, *Mozam.* **55 F3** 17 0S 32 54 E
Cochin, *India* **40 Q10** 9 59N 76 22 E
Cochin China, *Vietnam* ... **39 G6** 10 30N 106 0 E
Cochran, *U.S.A.* **77 J4** 32 23N 83 21W
Cochrane, *Alta., Canada* .. **72 C6** 51 11N 114 30W
Cochrane, *Ont., Canada* .. **70 C3** 49 0N 81 0W
Cochrane, *Chile* **96 F2** 47 15S 72 33W
Cochrane →, *Canada* **73 B8** 59 0N 103 40W
Cochrane, L., *Chile* **96 F2** 47 10S 72 0W
Cochranton, *U.S.A.* **78 E4** 41 31N 80 3W
Cockburn, *Australia* **63 E3** 32 5S 141 0 E
Cockburn, Canal, *Chile* ... **96 G2** 54 30S 72 0W
Cockburn I., *Canada* **70 C3** 45 55N 83 22W
Cockburn Ra., *Australia* .. **60 C4** 15 46S 128 0 E
Cockermouth, *U.K.* **10 C4** 54 40N 3 22W
Cocklebiddy, *Australia* ... **61 F4** 32 0S 126 3 E
Coco →, *Cent. Amer.* **88 D3** 15 0N 83 8W
Coco, I. del, *Pac. Oc.* **65 G19** 5 25N 87 55W
Cocoa, *U.S.A.* **77 L5** 28 21N 80 44W
Cocobeach, *Gabon* **52 D1** 0 59N 9 34 E
Cocos Is., *Ind. Oc.* **64 J1** 12 10S 96 55 E
Cod, C., *U.S.A.* **76 D10** 42 5N 70 10W
Codajás, *Brazil* **92 D6** 3 55S 62 0W
Codó, *Brazil* **93 D10** 4 30S 43 55W
Cody, *U.S.A.* **82 D9** 44 32N 109 3W
Coe Hill, *Canada* **78 B7** 44 52N 77 50W
Coelemu, *Chile* **94 D1** 36 30S 72 48W
Coen, *Australia* **62 A3** 13 52S 143 12 E
Cœur d'Alene, *U.S.A.* **82 C5** 47 45N 116 51W
Cœur d'Alene L., *U.S.A.* .. **82 C5** 47 32N 116 48W
Coevorden, *Neths.* **15 B6** 52 40N 6 44 E
Cofete, *Canary Is.* **22 F5** 28 6N 14 23W
Coffeyville, *U.S.A.* **81 G7** 37 2N 95 37W
Coffin B., *Australia* **63 E2** 34 38S 135 28 E
Coffin Bay, *Australia* **63 E2** 34 37S 135 29 E
Coffin Bay Peninsula, *Australia* **63 E2** 34 32S 135 15 E
Coffs Harbour, *Australia* .. **63 E5** 30 16S 153 5 E
Cognac, *France* **18 D3** 45 41N 0 20W
Cohocton, *U.S.A.* **78 D7** 42 30N 77 30W
Cohocton →, *U.S.A.* **78 D7** 42 9N 77 6W
Cohoes, *U.S.A.* **79 D11** 42 46N 73 42W
Cohuna, *Australia* **63 F3** 35 45S 144 15 E
Coiba, I., *Panama* **88 E3** 7 30N 81 40W
Coig →, *Argentina* **96 G3** 51 0S 69 10W
Coigeach, Rubha, *U.K.* ... **12 C3** 58 6N 5 26W
Coihaique, *Chile* **96 F2** 45 30S 71 45W
Coimbatore, *India* **40 P10** 11 2N 76 59 E
Coimbra, *Brazil* **92 G7** 19 55S 57 48W
Coimbra, *Portugal* **19 B1** 40 15N 8 27W
Coín, *Spain* **19 D3** 36 40N 4 48W
Coipasa, Salar de, *Bolivia* . **92 G5** 19 26S 68 9W
Cojimies, *Ecuador* **92 C3** 0 20N 80 0W
Cojutepequé, *El Salv.* **88 D2** 13 41N 88 54W
Cokeville, *U.S.A.* **82 E8** 42 5N 110 57W
Colac, *Australia* **63 F3** 38 21S 143 35 E
Colatina, *Brazil* **93 G10** 19 32S 40 37W
Colbeck, C., *Antarctica* ... **5 D13** 77 6S 157 48W
Colborne, *Canada* **78 C7** 44 0N 77 53W
Colby, *U.S.A.* **80 F4** 39 24N 101 3W
Colchester, *U.K.* **11 F8** 51 54N 0 55 E
Cold L., *Canada* **73 C7** 54 33N 110 5W
Coldstream, *Canada* **72 C5** 50 13N 119 11W
Coldstream, *U.K.* **12 F6** 55 39N 2 15W
Coldwater, *Canada* **78 B5** 44 42N 79 40W
Coldwater, *Kans., U.S.A.* . **81 G5** 37 16N 99 20W
Coldwater, *Mich., U.S.A.* . **76 E3** 41 57N 85 0W
Coleambally, *Australia* ... **63 E4** 34 49S 145 52 E
Colebrook, *U.S.A.* **79 B13** 44 54N 71 30W
Coleman, *U.S.A.* **81 K5** 31 50N 99 26W
Coleman →, *Australia* ... **62 B3** 15 6S 141 38 E
Colenso, *S. Africa* **57 D4** 28 44S 29 50 E
Coleraine, *Australia* **63 F3** 37 36S 141 40 E
Coleraine, *U.K.* **13 A5** 55 8N 6 41W
Coleridge, L., *N.Z.* **59 K3** 43 17S 171 30 E
Colesberg, *S. Africa* **56 E4** 30 45S 25 5 E
Coleville, *U.S.A.* **84 G7** 38 34N 119 30W
Colfax, *Calif., U.S.A.* **84 F6** 39 6N 120 57W
Colfax, *La., U.S.A.* **81 K8** 31 31N 92 42W
Colfax, *Wash., U.S.A.* **82 C5** 46 53N 117 22W
Colhué Huapi, L., *Argentina* **96 F3** 45 30S 69 0W
Coligny, *S. Africa* **57 D4** 26 17S 26 15 E
Colima, *Mexico* **86 D4** 19 14N 103 43W
Colima □, *Mexico* **86 D4** 19 10N 103 40W
Colima, Nevado de, *Mexico* **86 D4** 19 30N 103 40W
Colina, *Chile* **94 C1** 33 13S 70 45W
Colinas, *Brazil* **93 E10** 6 0S 44 10W
Coll, *U.K.* **12 E2** 56 39N 6 34W
Collaguasi, *Chile* **94 A2** 21 5S 68 45W
Collarenebri, *Australia* ... **63 D4** 29 33S 148 34 E
Colleen Bawn, *Zimbabwe* . **55 G2** 21 0S 29 12 E
College Park, *U.S.A.* **77 J3** 33 40N 84 27W
College Station, *U.S.A.* ... **81 K6** 30 37N 96 21W
Collie, *Australia* **61 F2** 33 22S 116 8 E
Collier B., *Australia* **60 C3** 16 10S 124 15 E
Collier Ra., *Australia* **61 D2** 24 45S 119 10 E
Collina, Passo di, *Italy* **20 B4** 44 2N 10 56 E
Collingwood, *Canada* **78 B4** 44 29N 80 13W
Collingwood, *N.Z.* **59 J4** 40 41S 172 40 E
Collins, *Canada* **70 B2** 50 17N 89 27W
Collinsville, *Australia* **62 C4** 20 30S 147 56 E
Collipulli, *Chile* **94 D1** 37 55S 72 30W
Collooney, *Ireland* **13 B3** 54 11N 8 29W
Colmar, *France* **18 B7** 48 5N 7 20 E
Colo →, *Australia* **63 E5** 33 25S 150 52 E
Cologne = Köln, *Germany* . **16 C4** 50 56N 6 57 E
Colom, I. d'en, *Spain* **22 B11** 39 58N 4 16 E
Coloma, *U.S.A.* **84 G6** 38 48N 120 53W
Colomb-Béchar = Béchar, *Algeria* **50 B5** 31 38N 2 18W
Colombia ■, *S. Amer.* **92 C4** 3 45N 73 0W
Colombian Basin, *S. Amer.* **66 H12** 14 0N 76 0W
Colombo, *Sri Lanka* **40 R11** 6 56N 79 58 E

Colón, *Buenos Aires, Argentina* **94 C3** 33 53S 61 7W
Colón, *Entre Ríos, Argentina* **94 C4** 32 12S 58 10W
Colón, *Cuba* **88 B3** 22 42N 80 54W
Colón, *Panama* **88 E4** 9 20N 79 54W
Colonia de Sant Jordi, *Spain* **22 B9** 39 19N 2 59 E
Colonia del Sacramento, *Uruguay* **94 C4** 34 25S 57 50W
Colonia Dora, *Argentina* .. **94 B3** 28 34S 62 59W
Colonial Beach, *U.S.A.* ... **76 F7** 38 15N 76 58W
Colonie, *U.S.A.* **79 D11** 42 43N 73 50W
Colonsay, *Canada* **73 C7** 51 59N 105 52W
Colonsay, *U.K.* **12 E2** 56 5N 6 12W
Colorado □, *U.S.A.* **83 G10** 39 30N 105 30W
Colorado →, *Argentina* .. **96 D4** 39 50S 62 8W
Colorado →, *N. Amer.* ... **83 L6** 31 45N 114 40W
Colorado →, *U.S.A.* **81 L7** 28 36N 95 59W
Colorado City, *U.S.A.* **81 J4** 32 24N 100 52W
Colorado Desert, *U.S.A.* .. **74 D3** 34 20N 116 0W
Colorado Plateau, *U.S.A.* . **83 H8** 37 0N 111 0W
Colorado River Aqueduct, *U.S.A.* **85 L12** 34 17N 114 10W
Colorado Springs, *U.S.A.* . **80 F2** 38 50N 104 49W
Colotlán, *Mexico* **86 C4** 22 6N 103 16W
Colstrip, *U.S.A.* **82 D10** 45 53N 106 38W
Colton, *U.S.A.* **79 B10** 44 33N 74 56W
Columbia, *Ky., U.S.A.* **76 G3** 37 6N 85 18W
Columbia, *La., U.S.A.* **81 J8** 32 6N 92 5W
Columbia, *Miss., U.S.A.* .. **81 K10** 31 15N 89 50W
Columbia, *Mo., U.S.A.* ... **80 F8** 38 57N 92 20W
Columbia, *Pa., U.S.A.* ... **79 F8** 40 2N 76 30W
Columbia, *S.C., U.S.A.* ... **77 J5** 34 0N 81 2W
Columbia, *Tenn., U.S.A.* . **77 H2** 35 37N 87 2W
Columbia →, *N. Amer.* .. **84 D2** 46 15N 124 5W
Columbia, C., *Canada* **4 A4** 83 0N 70 0W
Columbia, District of □, *U.S.A.* **76 F7** 38 55N 77 0W
Columbia, Mt., *Canada* .. **72 C5** 52 8N 117 20W
Columbia Basin, *U.S.A.* .. **82 C4** 46 45N 119 5W
Columbia Falls, *U.S.A.* ... **82 B6** 48 23N 114 11W
Columbia Mts., *Canada* .. **72 C5** 52 0N 119 0W
Columbia Plateau, *U.S.A.* . **82 D5** 44 0N 117 30W
Columbiana, *U.S.A.* **78 F4** 40 53N 80 42W
Columbretes, Is., *Spain* .. **19 C6** 39 50N 0 50 E
Columbus, *Ga., U.S.A.* ... **77 J3** 32 28N 84 59W
Columbus, *Ind., U.S.A.* .. **76 F3** 39 13N 85 55W
Columbus, *Kans., U.S.A.* . **81 G7** 37 10N 94 50W
Columbus, *Miss., U.S.A.* . **77 J1** 33 30N 88 25W
Columbus, *Mont., U.S.A.* **82 D9** 45 38N 109 15W
Columbus, *N. Mex., U.S.A.* **83 L10** 31 50N 107 38W
Columbus, *Nebr., U.S.A.* . **80 E6** 41 26N 97 22W
Columbus, *Ohio, U.S.A.* . **76 F4** 39 58N 83 0W
Columbus, *Tex., U.S.A.* .. **81 L6** 29 42N 96 33W
Colusa, *U.S.A.* **84 F4** 39 13N 122 1W
Colville, *U.S.A.* **82 B5** 48 33N 117 54W
Colville →, *U.S.A.* **68 A4** 70 25N 150 30W
Colville, C., *N.Z.* **59 G5** 36 29S 175 21 E
Colwood, *Canada* **84 B3** 48 26N 123 29W
Colwyn Bay, *U.K.* **10 D4** 53 18N 3 44W
Comácchio, *Italy* **20 B5** 44 42N 12 11 E
Comalcalco, *Mexico* **87 D6** 18 16N 93 13W
Comallo, *Argentina* **96 E2** 41 0S 70 5W
Comanche, *U.S.A.* **81 K5** 31 54N 98 36W
Comayagua, *Honduras* ... **88 D2** 14 25N 87 37W
Combahee →, *U.S.A.* ... **77 J5** 32 30N 80 31W
Combarbalá, *Chile* **94 C1** 31 11S 71 2W
Comber, *Canada* **78 D2** 42 14N 82 33W
Comber, *U.K.* **13 B6** 54 33N 5 45W
Combermere, *Canada* ... **78 A7** 45 22N 77 37W
Comblain-au-Pont, *Belgium* **15 D5** 50 29N 5 35 E
Comeragh Mts., *Ireland* .. **13 D4** 52 18N 7 34W
Comet, *Australia* **62 C4** 23 36S 148 38 E
Comilla, *Bangla.* **41 H17** 23 28N 91 10 E
Comino, *Malta* **23 C1** 36 2N 14 20 E
Comino, C., *Italy* **20 D3** 40 32N 9 49 E
Comitán, *Mexico* **87 D6** 16 18N 92 9W
Commerce, *Ga., U.S.A.* .. **77 H4** 34 12N 83 28W
Commerce, *Tex., U.S.A.* . **81 J7** 33 15N 95 54W
Committee B., *Canada* ... **69 B11** 68 30N 86 30W
Commonwealth B., *Antarctica* **5 C10** 67 0S 144 0 E
Commoron Cr. →, *Australia* **63 D5** 28 22S 150 8 E
Communism Pk. = Kommunizma, Pik, *Tajikistan* **26 F8** 39 0N 72 2 E
Como, *Italy* **18 D8** 45 47N 9 5 E
Como, Lago di, *Italy* **18 D8** 46 0N 9 11 E
Comodoro Rivadavia, *Argentina* **96 F3** 45 50S 67 40W
Comorin, C., *India* **40 Q10** 8 3N 77 40 E
Comoro Is. = Comoros ■, *Ind. Oc.* **49 H8** 12 10S 44 15 E
Comoros ■, *Ind. Oc.* **49 H8** 12 10S 44 15 E
Comox, *Canada* **72 D4** 49 42N 124 55W
Compiègne, *France* **18 B5** 49 24N 2 50 E
Compostela, *Mexico* **86 C4** 21 15N 104 53W
Comprida, I., *Brazil* **95 A6** 24 50S 47 42W
Compton, *Canada* **79 A13** 45 14N 71 49W
Compton, *U.S.A.* **85 M8** 33 54N 118 13W
Comrat, *Moldova* **17 E15** 46 18N 28 40 E
Con Cuong, *Vietnam* **38 C5** 19 2N 104 54 E
Con Son, *Vietnam* **39 H6** 8 41N 106 37 E
Conakry, *Guinea* **50 G3** 9 29N 13 49W
Conara, *Australia* **62 G4** 41 50S 147 26 E
Concarneau, *France* **18 C2** 47 52N 3 56W
Conceição, *Mozam.* **55 F4** 18 47S 36 7 E
Conceição da Barra, *Brazil* **93 G11** 18 35S 39 45W
Conceição do Araguaia, *Brazil* **93 E9** 8 0S 49 2W
Concepción, *Argentina* ... **94 B2** 27 20S 65 35W
Concepción, *Bolivia* **92 G6** 16 15S 62 8W
Concepción, *Chile* **94 D1** 36 50S 73 0W
Concepción, *Mexico* **87 D6** 18 15N 90 5W
Concepción, *Paraguay* ... **94 A4** 23 22S 57 26W
Concepción □, *Chile* **94 D1** 37 0S 72 30W
Concepción →, *Mexico* .. **86 A2** 30 32N 113 2W
Concepción, Est. de, *Chile* **96 G2** 50 30S 74 55W
Concepción, L., *Bolivia* ... **92 G6** 17 20S 61 20W
Concepción, Punta, *Mexico* **86 B2** 26 55N 111 59W
Concepción del Oro, *Mexico* **86 C4** 24 40N 101 30W
Concepción del Uruguay, *Argentina* **94 C4** 32 35S 58 20W
Conception, Pt., *U.S.A.* ... **85 L6** 34 27N 120 28W
Conception B., *Canada* ... **71 C9** 47 45N 53 0W

Conception B., *Namibia* .. **56 C1** 23 55S 14 22 E
Conception I., *Bahamas* .. **89 B4** 23 52N 75 9W
Concession, *Zimbabwe* .. **55 F3** 17 27S 30 56 E
Conchas Dam, *U.S.A.* ... **81 H2** 35 22N 104 11W
Concho, *U.S.A.* **83 J9** 34 28N 109 36W
Concho →, *U.S.A.* **81 K5** 31 34N 99 43W
Conchos →, *Chihuahua, Mexico* **86 B4** 29 32N 105 0W
Conchos →, *Tamaulipas, Mexico* **87 B5** 25 9N 98 35W
Concord, *Calif., U.S.A.* ... **84 H4** 37 59N 122 2W
Concord, *N.C., U.S.A.* **77 H5** 35 25N 80 35W
Concord, *N.H., U.S.A.* **79 C13** 43 12N 71 32W
Concordia, *Argentina* **94 C4** 31 20S 58 2W
Concórdia, *Brazil* **92 D5** 4 36S 66 36W
Concordia, *Mexico* **86 C3** 23 18N 106 2W
Concordia, *U.S.A.* **80 F6** 39 34N 97 40W
Concrete, *U.S.A.* **82 B3** 48 32N 121 45W
Condamine, *Australia* **63 D5** 26 56S 150 9 E
Conde, *U.S.A.* **80 C5** 45 9N 98 6W
Condeúba, *Brazil* **93 F10** 14 52S 42 0W
Condobolin, *Australia* **63 E4** 33 4S 147 6 E
Condon, *U.S.A.* **82 D3** 45 14N 120 11W
Conegliano, *Italy* **20 B5** 45 53N 12 18 E
Conejera, I. = Conills, I. des, *Spain* **22 B9** 39 11N 2 58 E
Conejos, *Mexico* **86 B4** 26 14N 103 53W
Confuso →, *Paraguay* ... **94 B4** 25 9S 57 34W
Congleton, *U.K.* **10 D5** 53 10N 2 13W
Congo (Kinshasa) = Congo, Dem. Rep. of the ■, *Africa* **52 E4** 3 0S 23 0 E
Congo ■, *Africa* **52 E3** 1 0S 16 0 E
Congo →, *Africa* **52 F2** 6 4S 12 24 E
Congo, Dem. Rep. of the ■, *Africa* **52 E4** 3 0S 23 0 E
Congo Basin, *Africa* **52 E4** 0 10S 24 30 E
Congonhas, *Brazil* **95 A7** 20 30S 43 52W
Congress, *U.S.A.* **83 J7** 34 9N 112 51W
Conills, I. des, *Spain* **22 B9** 39 11N 2 58 E
Coniston, *Canada* **70 C3** 46 29N 80 51W
Conjeeveram = Kanchipuram, *India* **40 N11** 12 52N 79 45 E
Conklin, *Canada* **73 B6** 55 38N 111 5W
Conklin, *U.S.A.* **79 D9** 42 2N 75 49W
Conn, L., *Ireland* **13 B2** 54 3N 9 15W
Connacht □, *Ireland* **13 C2** 53 43N 9 12W
Conneaut, *U.S.A.* **78 E4** 41 57N 80 34W
Connecticut □, *U.S.A.* ... **79 E12** 41 30N 72 45W
Connecticut →, *U.S.A.* .. **79 E12** 41 16N 72 20W
Connell, *U.S.A.* **82 C4** 46 40N 118 52W
Connellsville, *U.S.A.* **78 F5** 40 1N 79 35W
Connemara □, *Ireland* ... **13 C2** 53 29N 9 45W
Connemaugh →, *U.S.A.* **78 F5** 40 28N 79 19W
Connersville, *U.S.A.* **76 F3** 39 39N 85 8W
Connors Ra., *Australia* ... **62 C4** 21 40S 149 10 E
Conquest, *Canada* **73 C7** 51 32N 107 14W
Conrad, *U.S.A.* **82 B8** 48 10N 111 57W
Conran, C., *Australia* **63 F4** 37 49S 148 44 E
Conroe, *U.S.A.* **81 K7** 30 19N 95 27W
Consecon, *Canada* **78 C7** 44 0N 77 31W
Conselheiro Lafaiete, *Brazil* **95 A7** 20 40S 43 48W
Consett, *U.K.* **10 C6** 54 51N 1 50W
Consort, *Canada* **73 C6** 52 1N 110 46W
Constance = Konstanz, *Germany* **16 E5** 47 40N 9 10 E
Constance, L. = Bodensee, *Europe* **18 C8** 47 35N 9 25 E
Constanța, *Romania* **17 F15** 44 14N 28 38 E
Constantia, *U.S.A.* **79 C8** 43 15N 76 1W
Constantine, *Algeria* **50 A7** 36 25N 6 42 E
Constitución, *Chile* **94 D1** 35 20S 72 30W
Constitución, *Uruguay* ... **94 C4** 31 0S 57 50W
Consul, *Canada* **73 D7** 49 20N 109 30W
Contact, *U.S.A.* **82 F6** 41 46N 114 45W
Contai, *India* **43 J12** 21 54N 87 46 E
Contamana, *Peru* **92 E4** 7 19S 74 55W
Contas →, *Brazil* **93 F11** 14 17S 39 1W
Contoocook, *U.S.A.* **79 C13** 43 13N 71 45W
Contra Costa, *Mozam.* ... **57 D5** 25 9S 33 30 E
Contwoyto L., *Canada* ... **68 B8** 65 42N 110 50W
Conway = Conwy, *U.K.* .. **10 D4** 53 17N 3 50W
Conway = Conwy →, *U.K.* **10 D4** 53 17N 3 50W
Conway, *Ark., U.S.A.* **81 H8** 35 5N 92 26W
Conway, *N.H., U.S.A.* **79 C13** 43 59N 71 7W
Conway, *S.C., U.S.A.* **77 J6** 33 51N 79 3W
Conway, L., *Australia* **63 D2** 28 17S 135 35 E
Conwy, *U.K.* **10 D4** 53 17N 3 50W
Conwy □, *U.K.* **10 D4** 53 10N 3 44W
Conwy →, *U.K.* **10 D4** 53 17N 3 50W
Coober Pedy, *Australia* ... **63 D1** 29 1S 134 43 E
Cooch Behar = Koch Bihar, *India* **41 F16** 26 22N 89 29 E
Cooinda, *Australia* **60 B5** 13 15S 130 5 E
Cook, *Australia* **61 F5** 30 37S 130 25 E
Cook, *U.S.A.* **80 B8** 47 49N 92 39W
Cook, Aoraki Mt., *N.Z.* ... **59 K3** 43 36S 170 9 E
Cook, B., *Chile* **96 H3** 55 10S 70 0W
Cook, C., *Canada* **72 C3** 50 8N 127 55W
Cook Inlet, *U.S.A.* **68 C4** 60 0N 152 0W
Cook Is., *Pac. Oc.* **65 J12** 17 0S 160 0W
Cook Strait, *N.Z.* **59 J5** 41 15S 174 29 E
Cookeville, *U.S.A.* **77 G3** 36 10N 85 30W
Cookhouse, *S. Africa* **56 E4** 32 44S 25 47 E
Cookshire, *Canada* **79 A13** 45 25N 71 38W
Cookstown, *U.K.* **13 B5** 54 39N 6 45W
Cooksville, *Canada* **78 C5** 43 36N 79 35W
Cooktown, *Australia* **62 B4** 15 30S 145 16 E
Coolabah, *Australia* **63 E4** 31 1S 146 43 E
Cooladdi, *Australia* **63 D4** 26 37S 145 23 E
Coolah, *Australia* **63 E4** 31 48S 149 41 E
Coolamon, *Australia* **63 E4** 34 46S 147 8 E
Coolgardie, *Australia* **61 F3** 30 55S 121 8 E
Coolidge, *U.S.A.* **83 K8** 32 59N 111 31W
Coolidge Dam, *U.S.A.* ... **83 K8** 33 0N 110 20W
Cooma, *Australia* **63 F4** 36 12S 149 8 E
Coon Rapids, *U.S.A.* **80 C8** 45 9N 93 19W
Coonabarabran, *Australia* **63 E4** 31 14S 149 18 E
Coonalpyn, *Australia* **63 F2** 35 43S 139 52 E
Coonamble, *Australia* **63 E4** 30 56S 148 27 E
Coonana, *Australia* **61 F3** 31 0S 123 0 E
Coondapoor, *India* **40 N9** 13 42N 74 40 E
Cooninie, L., *Australia* **63 D2** 26 4S 139 59 E
Cooper, *U.S.A.* **81 J7** 33 23N 95 42W
Cooper Cr. →, *Australia* . **63 D2** 28 29S 137 46 E
Cooperstown, *N. Dak., U.S.A.* **80 B5** 47 27N 98 8W
Cooperstown, *N.Y., U.S.A.* **79 D10** 42 42N 74 56W
Coorabie, *Australia* **61 F5** 31 54S 132 18 E

Coorow, *Australia* **61 E2** 29 53S 116 2 E
Cooroy, *Australia* **63 D5** 26 22S 152 54 E
Coos Bay, *U.S.A.* **82 E1** 43 22N 124 13W
Coosa →, *U.S.A.* **77 J2** 32 30N 86 16W
Cootamundra, *Australia* .. **63 E4** 34 36S 148 1 E
Cootehill, *Ireland* **13 B4** 54 4N 7 5W
Copahue Paso, *Argentina* . **94 D1** 37 49S 71 8W
Copainalá, *Mexico* **87 D6** 17 8N 93 11W
Copake Falls, *U.S.A.* **79 D11** 42 7N 73 31W
Copán, *Honduras* **88 D2** 14 50N 89 9W
Cope, *U.S.A.* **80 F3** 39 40N 102 51W
Copenhagen = København, *Denmark* **9 J15** 55 41N 12 34 E
Copenhagen, *U.S.A.* **79 C9** 43 54N 75 41W
Copiapó, *Chile* **94 B1** 27 30S 70 20W
Copiapó →, *Chile* **94 B1** 27 19S 70 56W
Coplay, *U.S.A.* **79 F9** 40 44N 75 29W
Copp L., *Canada* **72 A6** 60 14N 114 40W
Coppename →, *Surinam* . **93 B7** 5 48N 55 55W
Copper Harbor, *U.S.A.* ... **76 B2** 47 28N 87 53W
Copper Queen, *Zimbabwe* **55 F2** 17 29S 29 18 E
Copperas Cove, *U.S.A.* .. **81 K6** 31 8N 97 54W
Copperbelt □, *Zambia* ... **55 E2** 13 15S 27 30 E
Coppermine = Kugluktuk, *Canada* **68 B8** 67 50N 115 5W
Coppermine →, *Canada* . **68 B8** 67 49N 116 4W
Copperopolis, *U.S.A.* **84 H6** 37 58N 120 38W
Coquet →, *U.K.* **10 B6** 55 20N 1 32W
Coquilhatville = Mbandaka, *Dem. Rep. of the Congo* **52 D3** 0 1N 18 18 E
Coquille, *U.S.A.* **82 E1** 43 11N 124 11W
Coquimbo, *Chile* **94 C1** 30 0S 71 20W
Coquimbo □, *Chile* **94 C1** 31 0S 71 0W
Corabia, *Romania* **17 G13** 43 48N 24 30 E
Coracora, *Peru* **92 G4** 15 5S 73 45W
Coraki, *Australia* **63 D5** 28 59S 153 17 E
Coral, *U.S.A.* **78 F5** 40 29N 79 10W
Coral Gables, *U.S.A.* **77 N5** 25 45N 80 16W
Coral Harbour = Salliq, *Canada* **69 B11** 64 8N 83 10W
Coral Sea, *Pac. Oc.* **64 J7** 15 0S 150 0 E
Coral Springs, *U.S.A.* **77 M5** 26 16N 80 13W
Coraopolis, *U.S.A.* **78 F4** 40 31N 80 10W
Corato, *Italy* **20 D7** 41 9N 16 25 E
Corbin, *U.S.A.* **76 G3** 36 57N 84 6W
Corby, *U.K.* **11 E7** 52 30N 0 41W
Corcaigh = Cork, *Ireland* . **13 E3** 51 54N 8 29W
Corcoran, *U.S.A.* **84 J7** 36 6N 119 33W
Corcubión, *Spain* **19 A1** 42 56N 9 12W
Cordele, *U.S.A.* **77 K4** 31 58N 83 47W
Cordell, *U.S.A.* **81 H5** 35 17N 98 59W
Córdoba, *Argentina* **94 C3** 31 20S 64 10W
Córdoba, *Mexico* **87 D5** 18 50N 97 0W
Córdoba, *Spain* **19 D3** 37 50N 4 50W
Córdoba □, *Argentina* **94 C3** 31 22S 64 15W
Córdoba, Sierra de, *Argentina* **94 C3** 31 10S 64 25W
Cordova, *U.S.A.* **68 B5** 60 33N 145 45W
Corella →, *Australia* **62 B3** 19 34S 140 47 E
Corfield, *Australia* **62 C3** 21 40S 143 21 E
Corfu = Kérkira, *Greece* .. **23 A3** 39 38N 19 50 E
Corfu, Str. of, *Greece* **23 A4** 39 34N 20 0 E
Coria, *Spain* **19 C2** 39 58N 6 33W
Corigliano Cálabro, *Italy* .. **20 E7** 39 36N 16 31 E
Coringa Is., *Australia* **62 B4** 16 58S 149 58 E
Corinth = Kórinthos, *Greece* **21 F10** 37 56N 22 55 E
Corinth, *Miss., U.S.A.* **77 H1** 34 56N 88 31W
Corinth, *N.Y., U.S.A.* **79 C11** 43 14N 73 49W
Corinth, *N.Y., U.S.A.* **79 C11** 43 15N 73 49W
Corinth, G. of = Korinthiakós Kólpos, *Greece* **21 E10** 38 16N 22 30 E
Corinto, *Brazil* **93 G10** 18 20S 44 30W
Corinto, *Nic.* **88 D2** 12 30N 87 10W
Cork, *Ireland* **13 E3** 51 54N 8 29W
Cork □, *Ireland* **13 E3** 51 57N 8 40W
Cork Harbour, *Ireland* ... **13 E3** 51 47N 8 16W
Çorlu, *Turkey* **21 D12** 41 11N 27 49 E
Cormack L., *Canada* **72 A4** 60 56N 121 37W
Cormorant, *Canada* **73 C8** 54 14N 100 35W
Cormorant L., *Canada* ... **73 C8** 54 15N 100 50W
Corn Is. = Maiz, Is. del, *Nic.* **88 D3** 12 15N 83 4W
Cornélio Procópio, *Brazil* . **95 A5** 23 7S 50 40W
Corner Brook, *Canada* ... **71 C8** 48 57N 57 58W
Corneşti, *Moldova* **17 E15** 47 21N 28 1 E
Corning, *Ark., U.S.A.* **81 G9** 36 25N 90 35W
Corning, *Calif., U.S.A.* **82 G2** 39 56N 122 11W
Corning, *Iowa, U.S.A.* **80 E7** 40 59N 94 44W
Corning, *N.Y., U.S.A.* **78 D7** 42 9N 77 3W
Cornwall, *Canada* **79 A10** 45 2N 74 44W
Cornwall, *U.S.A.* **79 F8** 40 17N 76 25W
Cornwall □, *U.K.* **11 G3** 50 26N 4 40W
Corny Pt., *Australia* **63 E2** 34 55S 137 0 E
Coro, *Venezuela* **92 A5** 11 25N 69 41W
Coroatá, *Brazil* **93 D10** 4 8S 44 0W
Corocoro, *Bolivia* **92 G5** 17 15S 68 28W
Coroico, *Bolivia* **92 G5** 16 0S 67 50W
Coromandel, *N.Z.* **59 G5** 36 45S 175 31 E
Coromandel Coast, *India* . **40 N12** 12 30N 81 0 E
Corona, *Calif., U.S.A.* **85 M9** 33 53N 117 34W
Corona, *N. Mex., U.S.A.* . **83 J11** 34 15N 105 36W
Coronach, *Canada* **73 D7** 49 7N 105 31W
Coronado, *U.S.A.* **85 N9** 32 41N 117 11W
Coronado, B. de, *Costa Rica* **88 E3** 9 0N 83 40W
Coronation, *Canada* **72 C6** 52 5N 111 27W
Coronation I., *Antarctica* . **5 C18** 60 45S 46 0W
Coronda, *Argentina* **94 C3** 31 58S 60 56W
Coronel, *Chile* **94 D1** 37 0S 73 10W
Coronel Bogado, *Paraguay* **94 B4** 27 11S 56 18W
Coronel Dorrego, *Argentina* **94 D3** 38 40S 61 10W
Coronel Oviedo, *Paraguay* **94 B4** 25 24S 56 30W
Coronel Pringles, *Argentina* **94 D3** 38 0S 61 30W
Coronel Suárez, *Argentina* **94 D3** 37 30S 61 52W
Coronel Vidal, *Argentina* . **94 D4** 37 28S 57 45W
Corowa, *Australia* **63 F4** 35 58S 146 21 E
Corozal, *Belize* **87 D7** 18 23N 88 23W
Corpus, *Argentina* **95 B4** 27 10S 55 30W
Corpus Christi, *U.S.A.* ... **81 M6** 27 47N 97 24W
Corpus Christi, L., *U.S.A.* . **81 L6** 28 2N 97 52W
Corralejo, *Canary Is.* **22 F6** 28 43N 13 53W
Corrán Pen., *U.K.* **13 C3** 54 55S 8 25W
Corrente →, *Brazil* **93 F10** 13 8S 43 28W
Correntes, C. das, *Mozam.* **57 C6** 24 6S 35 34 E
Corrib, L., *Ireland* **13 C2** 53 27N 9 16W
Corrientes, *Argentina* **94 B4** 27 30S 58 45W

Corrientes

Despeñaperros, Paso, Spain 19 C4 38 24N 3 30W
Dessau, Germany 16 C7 51 51N 12 14 E
Dessye = Dese, Ethiopia 46 E2 11 5N 39 40 E
D'Estrees B., Australia 63 F2 35 55 S 137 45 E
Desuri, India 42 G5 25 18N 73 35 E
Det Udom, Thailand 38 E5 14 54N 105 5 E
Dete, Zimbabwe 55 F2 18 38 S 26 50 E
Detmold, Germany 16 C5 51 56N 8 52 E
Detour, Pt., U.S.A. 76 C2 45 40N 86 40W
Detroit, U.S.A. 78 D1 42 20N 83 3W
Detroit Lakes, U.S.A. 80 B7 46 49N 95 51W
Deurne, Neths. 15 C5 51 27N 5 49 E
Deutsche Bucht, Germany 16 A5 54 15N 8 0 E
Deva, Romania 17 F12 45 53N 22 55 E
Devakottai, India 40 Q11 9 55N 78 45 E
Devaprayag, India 43 D8 30 13N 78 35 E
Deventer, Neths. 15 B6 52 15N 6 10 E
Deveron →, U.K. 12 D6 57 41N 2 32W
Devgadh Bariya, India 42 H5 22 40N 73 55 E
Devikot, India 42 F4 26 42N 71 12 E
Devils Den, U.S.A. 84 K7 35 46N 119 58W
Devils Lake, U.S.A. 80 A5 48 7N 98 52W
Devils Paw, Canada 72 B2 58 47N 134 0W
Devils Tower Junction,
U.S.A. 80 C2 44 31N 104 57W
Devine, U.S.A. 81 L5 29 8N 98 54W
Devizes, U.K. 11 F6 51 22N 1 58W
Devli, India 42 G6 25 50N 75 20 E
Devon, India 72 C6 53 24N 113 44W
Devon □, U.K. 11 G4 50 50N 3 40W
Devon I., Canada 4 B3 75 10N 85 0W
Devonport, Australia 62 G4 41 10 S 146 22 E
Devonport, N.Z. 59 G5 36 49 S 174 49 E
Dewas, India 42 H7 22 59N 76 3 E
Dewetsdorp, S. Africa 56 D4 29 33 S 26 39 E
Dexter, Maine, U.S.A. 77 C11 45 1N 69 18W
Dexter, Mo., U.S.A. 81 G10 36 48N 89 57W
Dexter, N. Mex., U.S.A. 81 J2 33 12N 104 22W
Dey-Dey, L., Australia 61 E5 29 12 S 131 4 E
Deyyer, Iran 45 E6 27 55N 51 55 E
Dezadeash L., Canada 72 A1 60 28N 136 58W
Dezfûl, Iran 45 C6 32 20N 48 30 E
Dezhneva, Mys, Russia 27 C19 66 5N 169 40W
Dezhou, China 34 F9 37 26N 116 18 E
Dhadhar →, India 43 G11 24 56N 85 24 E
Dháfni, Greece 23 D7 35 13N 25 3 E
Dhahiriya = Aẓ Ẓāhirīyah,
West Bank 47 D3 31 25N 34 58 E
Dhahran = Aẓ Ẓahrān,
Si. Arabia 45 E6 26 10N 50 7 E
Dhak, Pakistan 42 C5 32 25N 72 33 E
Dhaka, Bangla. 43 H14 23 43N 90 26 E
Dhaka □, Bangla. 43 G14 24 25N 90 25 E
Dhali, Cyprus 23 D12 35 1N 33 25 E
Dhampur, India 43 E8 29 19N 78 33 E
Dhamtari, India 41 J12 20 42N 81 35 E
Dhanbad, India 43 H12 23 50N 86 30 E
Dhangarhi, Nepal 41 E12 28 55N 80 40 E
Dhankuta, Nepal 43 F12 26 55N 87 40 E
Dhar, India 42 H6 22 35N 75 26 E
Dharampur, India 42 H6 22 13N 75 18 E
Dharamsala = Dharmsala,
India 42 C7 32 16N 76 23 E
Dhariwal, India 42 D6 31 57N 75 19 E
Dharla →, Bangla. 43 G13 25 46N 89 42 E
Dharmapuri, India 40 N11 12 10N 78 10 E
Dharmjaygarh, India 43 H10 22 28N 83 13 E
Dharmsala, India 42 C7 32 16N 76 23 E
Dharni, India 42 J7 21 33N 76 53 E
Dhasan →, India 43 G8 25 48N 79 24 E
Dhaulagiri, Nepal 43 E10 28 39N 83 28 E
Dhebar, L., India 42 G6 24 10N 74 0 E
Dheftera, Cyprus 23 D12 35 5N 33 16 E
Dhenkanal, India 41 J14 20 45N 85 35 E
Dherinia, Cyprus 23 D12 35 3N 33 57 E
Dhiarrizos →, Cyprus 23 E11 34 41N 32 34 E
Dhībān, Jordan 47 D4 31 30N 35 46 E
Dhikti Óros, Greece 23 D7 35 8N 25 30 E
Dhilwan, India 42 D6 31 31N 75 21 E
Dhimarkhera, India 43 H9 23 28N 80 22 E
Dhírfis = Dhírfis Óros,
Greece 21 E10 38 40N 23 54 E
Dhírfis Óros, Greece 21 E10 38 40N 23 54 E
Dhodhekánisos, Greece 21 F12 36 35N 27 0 E
Dholka, India 42 H5 22 44N 72 29 E
Dhoraji, India 42 J4 21 45N 70 37 E
Dhrángadhra, India 23 A3 39 48N 19 40 E
Dhrol, India 42 H4 22 59N 71 31 E
Dhubri, India 41 F16 26 2N 89 59 E
Dhule, India 40 J9 20 58N 74 50 E
Di Linh, Vietnam 39 G7 11 35N 108 4 E
Di Linh, Cao Nguyen,
Vietnam 39 G7 11 30N 108 0 E
Día, Greece 23 D7 35 26N 25 14 E
Diablo, Mt., U.S.A. 84 H5 37 53N 121 56W
Diablo Range, U.S.A. 84 J5 37 20N 121 25W
Diafarabé, Mali 50 F5 14 9N 4 57W
Diamante, Argentina 94 C3 32 5S 60 40W
Diamante →, Argentina 94 C2 34 30 S 66 46W
Diamantina, Brazil 93 G10 18 17 S 43 40W
Diamantina →, Australia 63 D2 26 45 S 139 10 E
Diamantino, Brazil 93 F7 14 30 S 56 30W
Diamond Bar, U.S.A. 85 L9 34 1N 117 48W
Diamond Harbour, India 43 H13 22 11N 88 14 E
Diamond Is., Australia 62 B5 17 25 S 151 5 E
Diamond Mts., U.S.A. 82 G6 39 50N 115 30W
Diamond Springs, U.S.A. 84 G6 38 42N 120 49W
Dibā, Oman 45 E8 25 45N 56 16 E
Dibai, India 42 E8 28 13N 78 15 E
Dibaya-Lubue,
Dem. Rep. of the Congo 52 E3 4 12 S 19 54 E
Dibete, Botswana 56 C4 23 45 S 26 32 E
Dibrugarh, India 41 F19 27 29N 94 55 E
Dickens, U.S.A. 81 J4 33 37N 100 50W
Dickinson, U.S.A. 80 B3 46 53N 102 47W
Dickson = Dikson, Russia 26 B9 73 40N 80 5 E
Dickson, U.S.A. 77 G2 36 5N 87 23W
Dickson City, U.S.A. 79 E9 41 29N 75 40W
Didiéni, Mali 50 F4 13 53N 8 6W
Didsbury, Canada 72 C6 51 35N 114 10W
Didwana, India 42 F6 27 23N 74 36 E
Diefenbaker, L., Canada 73 C7 51 0N 106 55W
Diego de Almagro, Chile 94 B1 26 22 S 70 3W
Diego Garcia, Ind. Oc. 3 E13 7 50 S 72 50 E

Diekirch, Lux. 15 E6 49 52N 6 10 E
Dien Ban, Vietnam 38 E7 15 53N 108 16 E
Dien Khanh, Vietnam 39 F7 12 15N 109 6 E
Dieppe, France 18 B4 49 54N 1 4 E
Dierks, U.S.A. 81 H8 34 7N 94 1W
Diest, Belgium 15 D5 50 58N 5 4 E
Dif, Somali Rep. 46 G3 0 59N 0 56 E
Differdange, Lux. 15 E5 49 31N 5 54 E
Dig, India 42 F7 27 28N 77 20 E
Digba,
Dem. Rep. of the Congo 54 B2 4 25N 25 48 E
Digby, Canada 71 D6 44 38N 65 50W
Diggi, India 42 F6 26 22N 75 26 E
Dighinala, Bangla. 41 H18 23 15N 92 5 E
Dighton, U.S.A. 80 F4 38 29N 100 28W
Digne-les-Bains, France 18 D7 44 5N 6 12 E
Digos, Phil. 37 C7 6 45N 125 20 E
Digranes, Iceland 8 C6 66 4N 14 44W
Digul →, Indonesia 37 F9 7 7 S 138 42 E
Dihang →, India 41 F19 27 48N 95 30 E
Dijlah, Nahr →, Asia 44 D5 31 0N 47 25 E
Dijon, France 18 C6 47 20N 5 3 E
Dikkil, Djibouti 46 E3 11 8N 42 20 E
Dikomu di Kai, Botswana 56 C3 24 58 S 24 36 E
Diksmuide, Belgium 15 C2 51 2N 2 52 E
Dikson, Russia 26 B9 73 40N 80 5 E
Dila, Ethiopia 46 F2 6 21N 38 22 E
Dili, Indonesia 37 F7 8 39 S 125 34 E
Dilley, U.S.A. 81 L5 28 40N 99 10W
Dillingham, U.S.A. 68 C4 59 3N 158 28W
Dillon, Canada 73 B7 55 56N 108 35W
Dillon, Mont., U.S.A. 82 D7 45 13N 112 38W
Dillon, S.C., U.S.A. 77 H6 34 25N 79 22W
Dillon →, Canada 73 B7 55 56N 108 56W
Dillsburg, U.S.A. 78 F7 40 7N 77 2W
Dilolo,
Dem. Rep. of the Congo 52 G4 10 28 S 22 18 E
Dimas, Mexico 86 C3 23 43N 106 47W
Dimashq, Syria 47 B5 33 30N 36 18 E
Dimashq □, Syria 47 B5 33 30N 36 30 E
Dimbaza, S. Africa 57 E4 32 50 S 27 14 E
Dimboola, Australia 63 F3 36 28 S 142 7 E
Dîmboviţa =
Dâmboviţa →, Romania 17 F14 44 12N 26 26 E
Dimbulah, Australia 62 B4 17 8 S 145 4 E
Dimitrovgrad, Bulgaria 21 C11 42 5N 25 35 E
Dimitrovgrad, Russia 24 D8 54 14N 49 39 E
Dimitrovo = Pernik, Bulgaria 21 C10 42 35N 23 2 E
Dimmitt, U.S.A. 81 H3 34 33N 102 19W
Dimona, Israel 47 D4 31 2N 35 1 E
Dinagat, Phil. 37 B7 10 10N 125 40 E
Dinajpur, Bangla. 41 G16 25 33N 88 43 E
Dinan, France 18 B2 48 28N 2 2W
Dīnān Āb, Iran 45 C8 32 4N 56 49 E
Dinant, Belgium 15 D4 50 16N 4 55 E
Dinapur, India 43 G11 25 38N 85 5 E
Dinâr, Küh-e, Iran 45 D6 30 42N 51 46 E
Dinara Planina, Croatia 20 C7 44 0N 16 30 E
Dinard, France 18 B2 48 38N 2 6W
Dinaric Alps = Dinara
Planina, Croatia 20 C7 44 0N 16 30 E
Dindigul, India 40 P11 10 25N 78 0 E
Dindori, India 43 H9 22 57N 81 5 E
Ding Xian = Dingzhou,
China 34 E8 38 30N 114 59 E
Dinga, Pakistan 42 G2 25 26N 67 10 E
Dingbian, China 34 F4 37 35N 107 32 E
Dingle, Ireland 13 D1 52 9N 10 17W
Dingle B., Ireland 13 D1 52 3N 10 20W
Dingmans Ferry, U.S.A. 79 E10 41 13N 74 55W
Dingo, Australia 62 C4 23 38 S 149 19 E
Dingtao, China 34 G8 35 5N 115 35 E
Dingwall, U.K. 12 D4 57 36N 4 26W
Dingxi, China 34 G3 35 30N 104 33 E
Dingxiang, China 34 E7 38 30N 112 58 E
Dingzhou, China 34 E8 38 30N 114 59 E
Dinh, Mui, Vietnam 39 G7 11 22N 109 1 E
Dinokwe, Botswana 56 C4 23 29 S 26 37 E
Dinorwic, Canada 73 D10 49 41N 92 30W
Dinosaur National
Monument, U.S.A. 82 F9 40 30N 108 45W
Dinosaur Prov. Park, Canada 72 C6 50 47N 111 30W
Dinuba, U.S.A. 84 J7 36 32N 119 23W
Dipalpur, Pakistan 42 D5 30 40N 73 39 E
Dipolog, Phil. 37 C6 8 36N 123 20 E
Dir, Pakistan 40 B7 35 8N 71 59 E
Dire Dawa, Ethiopia 46 F3 9 35N 41 45 E
Diriamba, Nic. 88 D2 11 51N 86 19W
Dirk Hartog I., Australia 61 E1 25 50 S 113 5 E
Dirranbandi, Australia 63 D4 28 33 S 148 17 E
Disa, India 42 G5 24 18N 72 10 E
Disappointment, C., U.S.A. 82 C2 46 18N 124 5W
Disappointment, L.,
Australia 60 D3 23 20 S 122 40 E
Disaster B., Australia 63 F4 37 15 S 149 58 E
Discovery B., Australia 63 F3 38 10 S 140 40 E
Disko, Greenland 4 C5 69 45N 53 30W
Disko Bugt, Greenland 4 C5 69 10N 52 0W
Diss, U.K. 11 E9 52 23N 1 7 E
Disteghil Sar, Pakistan 43 A6 36 20N 75 12 E
Distrito Federal □, Brazil 93 G9 15 45 S 47 45W
Distrito Federal □, Mexico 87 D5 19 15N 99 10W
Diu, India 42 J4 20 45N 70 58 E
Dīvāndarreh, Iran 44 C5 35 55N 47 2 E
Divide, U.S.A. 82 D7 45 45N 112 45W
Dividing Ra., Australia 61 E2 27 45 S 116 0 E
Divinópolis, Brazil 93 H10 20 10 S 44 54W
Divnoye, Russia 25 E7 45 55N 43 21 E
Divo, Ivory C. 50 G4 5 48N 5 15W
Diwāl Kol, Afghan. 42 B2 34 23N 67 52 E
Dixie, U.S.A. 82 D6 45 33N 115 28W
Dixon, Calif., U.S.A. 84 G5 38 27N 121 49W
Dixon, Ill., U.S.A. 80 E10 41 50N 89 29W
Dixon Entrance, U.S.A. 68 C6 54 30N 132 0W
Dixville, Canada 79 A13 45 4N 71 46W
Diyālā →, Iraq 44 C5 33 14N 44 31 E
Diyarbakır, Turkey 25 G7 37 55N 40 18 E
Diyodar, India 42 G4 24 8N 71 50 E
Djakarta = Jakarta,
Indonesia 37 G12 6 9 S 106 49 E
Djamba, Angola 56 B1 16 45 S 13 58 E
Djambala, Congo 52 E2 2 32 S 14 30 E
Djanet, Algeria 50 D7 24 35N 9 32 E
Djawa = Jawa, Indonesia 37 G14 7 0 S 110 0 E
Djelfa, Algeria 50 B6 34 40N 3 15 E
Djema, C.A.R. 54 A2 6 3N 25 15 E

Djerba, I. de, Tunisia 51 B8 33 50N 10 48 E
Djerid, Chott, Tunisia 50 B7 33 42N 8 30 E
Djibouti, Djibouti 46 E3 11 30N 43 5 E
Djibouti ■, Africa 46 E3 12 0N 43 0 E
Djolu,
Dem. Rep. of the Congo 52 D4 0 35N 22 5 E
Djoum, Cameroon 52 D2 2 41N 12 35 E
Djourab, Erg du, Chad 51 E9 16 40N 18 50 E
Djugu,
Dem. Rep. of the Congo 54 B3 1 55N 30 35 E
Djúpivogur, Iceland 8 D6 64 39N 14 17W
Dmitriya Lapteva, Proliv,
Russia 27 B15 73 0N 140 0 E
Dnepr = Dnipro →,
Ukraine 25 E5 46 30N 32 18 E
Dneprodzerzhinsk =
Dniprodzerzhynsk, Ukraine 25 E5 48 32N 34 37 E
Dnepropetrovsk =
Dnipropetrovsk, Ukraine 25 E6 48 30N 35 0 E
Dnestr = Dnister →,
Europe 17 E16 46 18N 30 17 E
Dnestrovski = Belgorod,
Russia 25 D6 50 35N 36 35 E
Dnieper = Dnipro →,
Ukraine 25 E5 46 30N 32 18 E
Dniester = Dnister →,
Europe 17 E16 46 18N 30 17 E
Dnipro →, Ukraine 25 E5 46 30N 32 18 E
Dniprodzerzhynsk, Ukraine 25 E5 48 32N 34 37 E
Dnipropetrovsk, Ukraine 25 E6 48 30N 35 0 E
Dnister →, Europe 17 E16 46 18N 30 17 E
Dnistrovskyy Lyman,
Ukraine 17 E16 46 15N 30 17 E
Dno, Russia 24 C4 57 50N 29 58 E
Dnyapro = Dnipro →,
Ukraine 25 E5 46 30N 32 18 E
Doaktown, Canada 71 C6 46 33N 66 8W
Doba, Chad 51 G9 8 40N 16 50 E
Dobandi, Pakistan 42 D2 31 13N 66 50 E
Dobbyn, Australia 62 B3 19 44 S 140 2 E
Dobele, Latvia 9 H20 56 37N 23 16 E
Doberai, Jazirah, Indonesia 37 E8 1 25 S 133 0 E
Doblas, Argentina 94 D3 37 5 S 64 0W
Dobo, Indonesia 37 F8 5 45 S 134 15 E
Doboj, Bos.-H. 21 B8 44 46N 18 4 E
Dobreta-Turnu Severin,
Romania 17 F12 44 39N 22 41 E
Dobrich, Bulgaria 21 C12 43 37N 27 49 E
Dobruja, Europe 17 F15 44 30N 28 15 E
Dobrush, Belarus 17 B16 52 25N 31 22 E
Doc, Mui, Vietnam 38 D6 17 58N 106 30 E
Docker River, Australia 61 D4 24 52 S 129 5 E
Doctor Arroyo, Mexico 86 C4 23 40N 100 11W
Doda, India 43 C6 33 10N 75 34 E
Doda, L., Canada 70 C4 49 25N 75 13W
Dodecanese =
Dhodhekánisos, Greece 21 F12 36 35N 27 0 E
Dodge City, U.S.A. 81 G5 37 45N 100 1W
Dodge L., Canada 73 B7 59 50N 105 36W
Dodgeville, U.S.A. 80 D9 42 58N 90 8W
Dodoma, Tanzania 54 D4 6 8 S 35 45 E
Dodoma □, Tanzania 54 D4 6 0 S 36 0 E
Dodsland, Canada 73 C7 51 50N 108 45W
Dodson, U.S.A. 82 B9 48 24N 108 15W
Doesburg, Neths. 15 B6 52 1N 6 9 E
Doetinchem, Neths. 15 C6 51 59N 6 18 E
Dog Creek, Canada 72 C4 51 35N 122 14W
Dog L., Man., Canada 73 C9 51 2N 98 31W
Dog L., Ont., Canada 70 C2 48 48N 89 30W
Dogi, Afghan. 40 C3 32 20N 62 50 E
Dogran, Pakistan 42 D5 31 48N 73 35 E
Doğubayazıt, Turkey 44 B5 39 31N 44 5 E
Doha = Ad Dawḥah, Qatar 45 E6 25 15N 51 35 E
Dohazari, Bangla. 41 H18 22 10N 92 5 E
Dohrighat, India 43 F10 26 16N 83 31 E
Doi, Indonesia 37 D7 2 14N 127 49 E
Doi Luang, Thailand 38 C3 18 30N 101 0 E
Doi Saket, Thailand 38 C2 18 52N 99 9 E
Dois Irmãos, Sa., Brazil 93 E10 9 0 S 42 30W
Dokkum, Neths. 15 A5 53 20N 5 59 E
Dokri, Pakistan 42 F3 27 25N 68 7 E
Dolak, Pulau, Indonesia 37 F9 8 0 S 138 30 E
Dolbeau, Canada 71 C5 48 53N 72 18W
Dole, France 18 C6 47 7N 5 31 E
Dolgellau, U.K. 10 E4 52 45N 3 53W
Dolgelley = Dolgellau, U.K. 10 E4 52 45N 3 53W
Dollard, Neths. 15 A7 53 20N 7 10 E
Dolo, Ethiopia 46 G3 4 11N 42 3 E
Dolomites = Dolomiti, Italy 20 A4 46 23N 11 51 E
Dolomiti, Italy 20 A4 46 23N 11 51 E
Dolores, Argentina 94 D4 36 20 S 57 40W
Dolores, Uruguay 94 C4 33 34 S 58 15W
Dolores, U.S.A. 83 H9 37 28N 108 30W
Dolores →, U.S.A. 83 G9 38 49N 109 17W
Dolphin, C., Falk. Is. 96 G5 51 10 S 59 0W
Dolphin and Union Str.,
Canada 68 B8 69 5N 114 45W
Dom Pedrito, Brazil 95 C5 31 0 S 54 40W
Domariaganj →, India 43 F10 26 17N 83 44 E
Domasi, Malawi 55 F4 15 15 S 35 22 E
Dombarovskiy, Russia 26 D6 50 46N 59 32 E
Dombås, Norway 9 E13 62 4N 9 8 E
Domel I. = Letsôk-aw Kyun,
Burma 39 G2 11 30N 98 25 E
Domeyko, Chile 94 B1 29 0 S 71 0W
Domeyko, Cordillera, Chile 94 A2 24 30 S 69 0W
Dominador, Chile 94 A2 24 21 S 69 20W
Dominica ■, W. Indies 89 C7 15 20N 61 20W
Dominica Passage,
W. Indies 89 C7 15 10N 61 20W
Dominican Rep. ■,
W. Indies 89 C5 19 0N 70 30W
Domodóssola, Italy 18 C8 46 7N 8 17 E
Domville, Mt., Australia 63 D5 28 1 S 151 15 E
Don →, Russia 25 E6 47 4N 39 18 E
Don →, Aberds., U.K. 12 D6 57 11N 2 5W
Don →, S. Yorks., U.K. 10 D7 53 41N 0 52W
Don, C., Australia 60 B5 11 18 S 131 46 E
Don Benito, Spain 19 C3 38 53N 5 51W
Dona Ana = Nhamaabué,
Mozam. 55 F4 17 25 S 35 5 E
Donaghadee, U.K. 13 B6 54 39N 5 33W
Donald, Australia 63 F3 36 23 S 143 0 E
Donalda, Canada 72 C6 52 35N 112 34W
Donaldsonville, U.S.A. 81 K9 30 6N 90 59W
Donalsonville, U.S.A. 77 K3 31 3N 84 53W
Donau = Dunărea →,
Europe 17 F15 45 20N 29 40 E

Donau →, Austria 15 D3 48 10N 17 0
Donauwörth, Germany 16 D6 48 43N 10 47
Doncaster, U.K. 10 D6 53 32N 1 6V
Dondo, Mozam. 55 F3 19 33 S 34 46
Dondo, Teluk, Indonesia 37 D6 0 50N 120 30
Dondra Head, Sri Lanka 40 S12 5 55N 80 40
Donegal, Ireland 13 B3 54 39N 8 5W
Donegal □, Ireland 13 B4 54 53N 8 0W
Donegal B., Ireland 13 B3 54 31N 8 5W
Donets →, Russia 25 E7 47 33N 40 55
Donetsk, Ukraine 25 E6 48 0N 37 45
Dong Ba Thin, Vietnam 39 F7 12 8N 109 13
Dong Giam, Vietnam 38 C5 19 25N 105 31
Dong Ha, Vietnam 38 D6 16 55N 107 8
Dong Hene, Laos 38 D5 16 40N 105 18
Dong Hoi, Vietnam 38 D6 17 29N 106 36
Dong Khe, Vietnam 38 A6 22 26N 106 27
Dong Ujimqin Qi, China 34 B9 45 32N 116 55
Dong Van, Vietnam 38 A5 23 16N 105 22
Dong Xoai, Vietnam 39 G6 11 32N 106 55
Dongara, Australia 61 E1 29 14 S 114 57
Dongbei, China 35 D13 42 0N 125 0
Dongchuan, China 32 D5 26 8N 103 1
Dongfang, China 38 C7 18 50N 108 33
Dongfeng, China 35 C13 42 40N 125 34
Donggala, Indonesia 37 E5 0 30 S 119 40
Donggou, China 35 E13 39 52N 124 10
Dongguang, China 34 F9 37 50N 116 30
Dongjingcheng, China 35 B15 44 5N 129 10
Dongning, China 35 B16 44 2N 131 5
Dongola, Sudan 51 E12 19 9N 30 22
Dongping, China 34 G9 35 55N 116 20
Dongsheng, China 34 E6 39 50N 110 0
Dongtai, China 35 H11 32 51N 120 21
Dongting Hu, China 33 D6 29 18N 112 45
Donington, C., Australia 63 E2 34 45 S 136 0
Doniphan, U.S.A. 81 G9 36 37N 90 50W
Dønna, Norway 8 C15 66 6N 12 30
Donna, U.S.A. 81 M5 26 9N 98 4W
Donnaconna, Canada 71 C5 46 41N 71 41
Donnelly's Crossing, N.Z. 59 F4 35 42 S 173 38
Donnybrook, Australia 61 F2 33 34 S 115 48
Donnybrook, S. Africa 57 D4 29 59 S 29 48
Donora, U.S.A. 78 F5 40 11N 79 52
Donostia = Donostia-San
Sebastián, Spain 19 A5 43 17N 1 58
Donostia-San Sebastián,
Spain 19 A5 43 17N 1 58
Doon →, U.K. 12 F4 55 27N 4 39
Dora, L., Australia 60 D3 22 0 S 123 0
Dora Báltea →, Italy 18 D8 45 11N 8 3
Doran L., Canada 73 A7 61 13N 108 6
Dorchester, U.K. 11 G5 50 42N 2 27
Dorchester, C., Canada 69 B12 65 27N 77 27
Dordogne →, France 18 D3 45 2N 0 36
Dordrecht, Neths. 15 C4 51 48N 4 39
Dordrecht, S. Africa 56 E4 31 20 S 27 3
Doré L., Canada 73 C7 54 46N 107 17
Doré Lake, Canada 73 C7 54 38N 107 36
Dori, Burkina Faso 50 F5 14 3N 0 2
Doring →, S. Africa 56 E2 31 54 S 18 39
Doringbos, S. Africa 56 E2 31 59 S 19 16
Dorion, Canada 79 A10 45 23N 74 3
Dornbirn, Austria 16 E5 47 25N 9 45
Dornie, U.K. 12 D3 57 17N 5 31
Dornoch, U.K. 12 D4 57 53N 4 2
Dornoch Firth, U.K. 12 D4 57 51N 4 4
Dornogovi □, Mongolia 34 C6 44 0N 110 0
Dorohoi, Romania 17 E14 47 56N 26 23
Döröö Nuur, Mongolia 32 B4 48 0N 93 0
Dorr, Iran 45 C6 33 17N 50 38
Dorre I., Australia 61 E1 25 13 S 113 12
Dorrigo, Australia 63 E5 30 20 S 152 44
Dorris, U.S.A. 82 F3 41 58N 121 55
Dorset, Canada 78 A6 45 14N 78 54
Dorset □, U.K. 11 G5 50 45N 2 26
Dorset, C., Canada 69 B12 64 2N 76 54
Dortmund, Germany 16 C4 51 30N 7 28
Doruma,
Dem. Rep. of the Congo 54 B2 4 42N 27 33
Dorūneh, Iran 45 C8 35 10N 57 18
Dos Bahías, C., Argentina 96 E3 44 58 S 65 32
Dos Hermanas, Spain 19 D3 37 16N 5 55
Dos Palos, U.S.A. 84 J6 36 59N 120 37
Dosso, Niger 50 F6 13 0N 3 13
Dothan, U.S.A. 77 K3 31 13N 85 24
Doty, U.S.A. 84 D3 46 38N 123 17
Douai, France 18 A5 50 21N 3 4
Douala, Cameroon 52 D1 4 0N 9 45
Douarnenez, France 18 B1 48 6N 4 21
Double Island Pt., Australia 63 D5 25 56 S 153 11
Double Mountain Fork →,
U.S.A. 81 J4 33 16N 100 0
Doubs →, France 18 C6 46 53N 5 1
Doubtful Sd., N.Z. 59 L1 45 20 S 166 49
Doubtless B., N.Z. 59 F4 34 55 S 173 26
Douglas, S. Africa 56 D3 29 4 S 23 46
Douglas, U.K. 10 C3 54 10N 4 28
Douglas, Ariz., U.S.A. 83 L9 31 21N 109 33
Douglas, Ga., U.S.A. 77 K4 31 31N 82 51
Douglas, Wyo., U.S.A. 80 D2 42 45N 105 24
Douglas Chan., Canada 72 C3 53 40N 129 20
Douglas Pt., Canada 78 B3 44 19N 81 37
Douglasville, U.S.A. 77 J3 33 45N 84 45
Dounreay, U.K. 12 C5 58 35N 3 44
Dourada, Serra, Brazil 93 F9 13 10 S 48 45
Dourados, Brazil 95 A5 22 9 S 54 50
Dourados →, Brazil 95 A5 21 58 S 54 18
Dourados, Serra dos, Brazil 95 A5 23 30 S 53 30
Douro →, Europe 19 B1 41 8N 8 40
Dove →, U.K. 10 E6 52 51N 1 36
Dove Creek, U.S.A. 83 H9 37 46N 108 54
Dover, Australia 62 G4 43 18 S 147 2
Dover, U.K. 11 F9 51 7N 1 19
Dover, Del., U.S.A. 76 F8 39 10N 75 32
Dover, N.H., U.S.A. 79 C14 43 12N 70 56
Dover, N.J., U.S.A. 79 F10 40 53N 74 34
Dover, Ohio, U.S.A. 78 F3 40 32N 81 29
Dover, Pt., Australia 61 F4 32 32 S 125 32
Dover, Str. of, Europe 11 G9 51 0N 1 30
Dover-Foxcroft, U.S.A. 77 C11 45 11N 69 13
Dover Plains, U.S.A. 79 E11 41 43N 73 35
Dovey = Dyfi →, U.K. 11 E3 52 32N 4 3
Dovrefjell, Norway 9 E13 62 15N 9 33
Dowa, Malawi 55 E3 13 38 S 33 58
Dowagiac, U.S.A. 76 E2 41 59N 86 6

Ede, Neths. 15 B5 52 4N 5 40 E
Edehon L., Canada 73 A9 60 25N 97 15W
Eden, Australia 63 F4 37 3S 149 55 E
Eden, N.C., U.S.A. 77 G6 36 29N 79 53W
Eden, N.Y., U.S.A. 78 D6 42 39N 78 55W
Eden, Tex., U.S.A. 81 K5 31 13N 99 51W
Eden →, U.K. 10 C4 54 57N 3 1W
Edenburg, S. Africa 56 D4 29 43S 25 58 E
Edendale, S. Africa 57 D5 29 39S 30 18 E
Edenderry, Ireland 13 C4 53 21N 7 4W
Edenhope, Australia 63 F3 37 4S 141 19 E
Edenton, U.S.A. 77 G7 36 4N 76 39W
Edenville, S. Africa 57 D4 27 37S 27 34 E
Eder →, Germany 16 C5 51 12N 9 28 E
Edgar, U.S.A. 80 E6 40 22N 97 58W
Edgartown, U.S.A. 79 E14 41 23N 70 31W
Edge Hill, U.K. 11 E6 52 8N 1 26W
Edgefield, U.S.A. 77 J5 33 47N 81 56W
Edgeley, U.S.A. 80 B5 46 22N 98 43W
Edgemont, U.S.A. 80 D3 43 18N 103 50W
Edgeøya, Svalbard 4 B9 77 45N 22 30 E
Édhessa, Greece 21 D10 40 48N 22 5 E
Edievale, N.Z. 59 L2 45 49S 169 22 E
Edina, U.S.A. 80 E8 40 10N 92 11W
Edinboro, U.S.A. 78 E4 41 52N 80 8W
Edinburg, U.S.A. 81 M5 26 18N 98 10W
Edinburgh, U.K. 12 F5 55 57N 3 13W
Edineț, Moldova 17 D14 48 9N 27 18 E
Edirne, Turkey 21 D12 41 40N 26 34 E
Edison, U.S.A. 84 B4 48 33N 122 27W
Edithburgh, Australia 63 F2 35 5S 137 43 E
Edmeston, U.S.A. 79 D9 42 42N 75 15W
Edmond, U.S.A. 81 H6 35 39N 97 29W
Edmonds, U.S.A. 84 C4 47 49N 122 23W
Edmonton, Australia 62 B4 17 2S 145 46 E
Edmonton, Canada 72 C6 53 30N 113 30W
Edmund L., Canada 70 B1 54 45N 93 17W
Edmundston, Canada 71 C6 47 23N 68 20W
Edna, U.S.A. 81 L6 28 59N 96 39W
Edremit, Turkey 21 E12 39 34N 27 0 E
Edremit Körfezi, Turkey 21 E12 39 30N 26 45 E
Edson, Canada 72 C5 53 35N 116 28W
Eduardo Castex, Argentina 94 D3 35 50S 64 18W
Edward →, Australia 63 F3 35 5S 143 30 E
Edward, L., Africa 54 C2 0 25S 29 40 E
Edward River, Australia 62 A3 14 59S 141 26 E
Edward VII Land, Antarctica 5 E13 80 0S 150 0W
Edwards, Calif., U.S.A. 85 L9 34 55N 117 51W
Edwards, N.Y., U.S.A. 79 B9 44 20N 75 15W
Edwards Air Force Base, U.S.A. 85 L9 34 50N 117 40W
Edwards Plateau, U.S.A. 81 K4 30 45N 101 20W
Edwardsville, U.S.A. 79 E9 41 15N 75 56W
Edzo, Canada 72 A5 62 49N 116 4W
Eeklo, Belgium 15 C3 51 11N 3 33 E
Effingham, U.S.A. 76 F1 39 7N 88 33W
Égadi, Ísole, Italy 20 F5 37 55N 12 16 E
Egan Range, U.S.A. 82 G6 39 35N 114 55W
Eganville, Canada 78 A7 45 32N 77 5W
Eger = Cheb, Czech Rep. 16 C7 50 9N 12 28 E
Eger, Hungary 17 E11 47 53N 20 27 E
Egersund, Norway 9 G12 58 26N 6 1 E
Egg L., Canada 73 B7 55 5N 105 30W
Éghezée, Belgium 15 D4 50 35N 4 55 E
Egmont, Canada 72 D4 49 45N 123 56W
Egmont, C., N.Z. 59 H4 39 16S 173 45 E
Egmont, Mt., N.Z. 59 H5 39 17S 174 5 E
Egra, India 43 J12 21 54N 87 32 E
Eğridir, Turkey 25 G5 37 52N 30 51 E
Eğridir Gölü, Turkey 25 G5 37 53N 30 50 E
Egvekinot, Russia 27 C19 66 19N 179 50W
Egypt ■, Africa 51 C12 28 0N 31 0 E
Ehime □, Japan 31 H6 33 30N 132 40 E
Ehrenberg, U.S.A. 85 M12 33 36N 114 31W
Eibar, Spain 19 A4 43 11N 2 28W
Eidsvold, Australia 63 D5 25 25S 151 12 E
Eidsvoll, Norway 9 F14 60 19N 11 14 E
Eifel, Germany 16 C4 50 15N 6 50 E
Eiffel Flats, Zimbabwe 55 F3 18 20S 30 0 E
Eigg, U.K. 12 E2 56 54N 6 10W
Eighty Mile Beach, Australia 60 C3 19 30S 120 40 E
Eil, Somali Rep. 46 F4 8 0N 49 50 E
Eil, L., U.K. 12 E3 56 51N 5 16W
Eildon, Australia 63 F4 37 14S 145 55 E
Eildon, L., Australia 63 F4 37 10S 146 0 E
Einasleigh, Australia 62 B3 18 32S 144 5 E
Einasleigh →, Australia 62 B3 17 30S 142 17 E
Eindhoven, Neths. 15 C5 51 26N 5 28 E
Eire = Ireland ■, Europe 13 C4 53 50N 7 52W
Eiríksjökull, Iceland 8 D3 64 46N 20 24W
Eirunepé, Brazil 92 E5 6 35S 69 53W
Eisenach, Germany 16 C6 50 58N 10 19 E
Eisenerz, Austria 16 E8 47 32N 14 54 E
Eivissa, Spain 22 C7 38 54N 1 26 E
Ejutla, Mexico 87 D5 16 34N 96 44W
Ekalaka, U.S.A. 80 C2 45 53N 104 33W
Eketahuna, N.Z. 59 J5 40 38S 175 43 E
Ekibastuz, Kazakstan 26 D8 51 50N 75 10 E
Ekoli, Dem. Rep. of the Congo 54 C1 0 23S 24 13 E
Eksjö, Sweden 9 H16 57 40N 14 58 E
Ekwan →, Canada 70 B3 53 12N 82 15W
Ekwan Pt., Canada 70 B3 53 16N 82 7W
El Aaiún, W. Sahara 50 C3 27 9N 13 12W
El Abanico, Chile 94 D1 37 20S 71 31W
El 'Agrūd, Egypt 47 E3 30 14N 34 24 E
El Alamein, Egypt 51 B11 30 48N 28 58 E
El 'Aqaba, W. →, Egypt 47 E2 30 7N 33 54 E
El Arīḥā, West Bank 47 D4 31 52N 35 27 E
El 'Arîsh, Egypt 47 D2 31 8N 33 50 E
El 'Arîsh, W. →, Egypt 47 D2 31 8N 33 47 E
El Asnam = Ech Cheliff, Algeria 50 A6 36 10N 1 20 E
El Bayadh, Algeria 50 B6 33 40N 1 1 E
El Bluff, Nic. 88 D3 11 59N 83 40W
El Brûk, W. →, Egypt 47 E2 30 15N 33 50 E
El Cajon, U.S.A. 85 N10 32 48N 116 58W
El Campo, U.S.A. 81 L6 29 12N 96 16W
El Centro, U.S.A. 85 N11 32 48N 115 34W
El Cerro, Bolivia 92 G6 17 30S 61 40W
El Compadre, Mexico 85 N10 32 20N 116 14W
El Cuy, Argentina 96 D3 39 55S 68 25W
El Cuyo, Mexico 87 C7 21 30N 87 40W
El Daheir, Egypt 47 D3 31 13N 34 10 E
El Dátil, Mexico 86 B2 30 7N 112 15W
El Dere, Somali Rep. 46 G4 3 50N 47 8 E

El Descanso, Mexico 85 N10 32 12N 116 58W
El Desemboque, Mexico 86 A2 30 30N 112 57W
El Diviso, Colombia 92 C3 1 22N 78 14W
El Djouf, Mauritania 50 D4 20 0N 9 0W
El Dorado, Ark., U.S.A. 81 J8 33 12N 92 40W
El Dorado, Kans., U.S.A. 81 G6 37 49N 96 52W
El Dorado, Venezuela 92 B6 6 55N 61 37W
El Escorial, Spain 19 B3 40 35N 4 7W
El Faiyûm, Egypt 51 C12 29 19N 30 50 E
El Fâsher, Sudan 51 F11 13 33N 25 26 E
El Ferrol = Ferrol, Spain 19 A1 43 29N 8 15W
El Fuerte, Mexico 86 B3 26 30N 108 40W
El Gal, Somali Rep. 46 E5 10 58N 50 20 E
El Geneina = Al Junaynah, Sudan 51 F10 13 27N 22 45 E
El Gîza, Egypt 51 C12 30 0N 31 10 E
El Goléa, Algeria 50 B6 30 30N 2 50 E
El Iskandarîya, Egypt 51 B11 31 13N 29 58 E
El Istiwa'îya, Sudan 51 G11 5 0N 28 0 E
El Jadida, Morocco 50 B4 33 11N 8 17W
El Jardal, Honduras 88 D2 14 54N 88 50W
El Kabrît, G., Egypt 47 F2 29 42N 33 16 E
El Khârga, Egypt 51 C12 25 30N 30 33 E
El Khartûm, Sudan 51 E12 15 31N 32 35 E
El Kuntilla, Egypt 47 E3 30 1N 34 45 E
El Maestrazgo, Spain 19 B5 40 30N 0 25W
El Mahalla el Kubra, Egypt 51 B12 31 0N 31 0 E
El Mansûra, Egypt 51 B12 31 0N 31 19 E
El Medano, Canary Is. 22 F3 28 3N 16 32W
El Milagro, Argentina 94 C2 30 59S 65 59W
El Minyâ, Egypt 51 C12 28 7N 30 33 E
El Monte, U.S.A. 85 L8 34 4N 118 1W
El Obeid, Sudan 51 F12 13 8N 30 10 E
El Odaiya, Sudan 51 F11 12 8N 28 12 E
El Oro, Mexico 87 D4 19 48N 100 8W
El Oued, Algeria 50 B7 33 20N 6 58 E
El Palmito, Presa, Mexico 86 B3 25 40N 105 30W
El Paso, U.S.A. 83 L10 31 45N 106 29W
El Paso Robles, U.S.A. 84 K6 35 38N 120 41W
El Portal, U.S.A. 84 H7 37 41N 119 47W
El Porvenir, Mexico 86 A3 31 15N 105 51W
El Prat de Llobregat, Spain 19 B7 41 18N 2 3 E
El Progreso, Honduras 88 C2 15 26N 87 51W
El Pueblito, Mexico 86 B3 29 3N 105 4W
El Pueblo, Canary Is. 22 F2 28 36N 17 47W
El Puerto de Santa María, Spain 19 D2 36 36N 6 13W
El Qâhira, Egypt 51 B12 30 1N 31 14 E
El Qantara, Egypt 47 E1 30 51N 32 20 E
El Quseima, Egypt 47 E3 30 40N 34 15 E
El Real, Panama 92 B3 8 0N 77 40W
El Reno, U.S.A. 81 H6 35 32N 97 57W
El Rio, U.S.A. 85 L7 34 14N 119 10W
El Roque, Pta., Canary Is. 22 F4 28 10N 15 25W
El Rosarito, Mexico 86 B2 28 38N 114 4W
El Saheira, W. →, Egypt 47 E2 30 5N 33 25 E
El Salto, Mexico 86 C3 23 47N 105 22W
El Salvador ■, Cent. Amer. 88 D2 13 50N 89 0W
El Sauce, Nic. 88 D2 13 0N 86 40W
El Sueco, Mexico 86 B3 29 54N 106 24W
El Suweis, Egypt 51 C12 29 58N 32 31 E
El Tamarâni, W. →, Egypt 47 E3 30 7N 34 43 E
El Thamad, Egypt 47 F3 29 40N 34 28 E
El Tigre, Venezuela 92 B6 8 44N 64 15W
El Tîh, Gebal, Egypt 47 F2 29 40N 33 50 E
El Tina, Khalig, Egypt 47 D1 31 10N 32 40 E
El Tofo, Chile 94 B1 29 22S 71 18W
El Tránsito, Chile 94 B1 28 52S 70 17W
El Tûr, Egypt 44 D2 28 14N 33 36 E
El Turbio, Argentina 96 G2 51 45S 72 5W
El Uqsur, Egypt 51 C12 25 41N 32 38 E
El Venado, Mexico 86 C4 22 56N 101 10W
El Vergel, Mexico 86 B3 26 28N 106 22W
El Vigía, Venezuela 92 B4 8 38N 71 39W
El Wabeira, Egypt 47 F2 29 34N 33 6 E
El Wak, Kenya 54 B5 2 49N 40 56 E
El Wuz, Sudan 51 E12 15 5N 30 7 E
Elat, Israel 47 F3 29 30N 34 56 E
Elâzığ, Turkey 25 G6 38 37N 39 14 E
Elba, Italy 20 C4 42 46N 10 17 E
Elba, U.S.A. 77 K2 31 25N 86 4W
Elbasani, Albania 21 D9 41 9N 20 9 E
Elbe →, Europe 16 B5 53 50N 9 0 E
Elbert, Mt., U.S.A. 83 G10 39 7N 106 27W
Elberton, U.S.A. 77 H4 34 7N 82 52W
Elbeuf, France 18 B4 49 17N 1 2 E
Elbidtan, Turkey 44 B3 38 13N 37 12 E
Elbing = Elbląg, Poland 17 A10 54 10N 19 25 E
Elbląg, Poland 17 A10 54 10N 19 25 E
Elbow, Canada 73 C7 51 7N 106 35W
Elbrus, Asia 25 F7 43 21N 42 30 E
Elburz Mts. = Alborz, Reshteh-ye Kūhhā-ye, Iran 45 C7 36 0N 52 0 E
Elche, Spain 19 C5 38 15N 0 42W
Elcho I., Australia 62 A2 11 55S 135 45 E
Elda, Spain 19 C5 38 29N 0 47W
Elde →, Germany 16 B6 53 7N 11 15 E
Eldon, Mo., U.S.A. 80 F8 38 21N 92 35W
Eldon, Wash., U.S.A. 84 C3 47 33N 123 3W
Eldora, U.S.A. 80 D8 42 22N 93 5W
Eldorado, Argentina 95 B5 26 28S 54 43W
Eldorado, Canada 73 B7 44 35N 77 31W
Eldorado, Mexico 86 C3 24 20N 107 22W
Eldorado, Ill., U.S.A. 76 G1 37 49N 88 26W
Eldorado, Tex., U.S.A. 81 K4 30 52N 100 36W
Eldorado Springs, U.S.A. 81 G8 37 52N 94 1W
Eldoret, Kenya 54 B4 0 30N 35 17 E
Eldred, U.S.A. 78 E6 41 58N 78 23W
Eleanora, Pk., Australia 61 F3 32 57S 121 9 E
Electra, U.S.A. 74 D7 34 2N 98 55W
Elefantes →, Mozam. 57 C5 24 10S 32 40 E
Elektrostal, Russia 24 C6 55 41N 38 32 E
Elephant Butte Reservoir, U.S.A. 83 K10 33 9N 107 11W
Elephant I., Antarctica 5 C18 61 0S 55 0W
Eleuthera, Bahamas 88 B4 25 0N 76 20W
Elgin, Canada 79 B8 44 36N 76 13W
Elgin, U.K. 12 D5 57 39N 3 19W
Elgin, Ill., U.S.A. 76 D1 42 2N 88 17W
Elgin, N. Dak., U.S.A. 80 B4 46 24N 101 51W
Elgin, Oreg., U.S.A. 82 D5 45 34N 117 55W
Elgin, Tex., U.S.A. 81 K6 30 21N 97 22W
Elgon, Mt., Africa 54 B3 1 10N 34 30 E
Eliase, Indonesia 37 F8 8 21S 130 48 E
Elim, S. Africa 56 E2 34 35S 19 45 E

Elisabethville = Lubumbashi, Dem. Rep. of the Congo 55 E2 11 40S 27 28 E
Elista, Russia 25 E7 46 16N 44 14 E
Elizabeth, Australia 63 E2 34 42S 138 41 E
Elizabeth, N.J., U.S.A. 79 F10 40 39N 74 13W
Elizabeth, N.J., U.S.A. 79 F10 40 40N 74 13W
Elizabeth City, U.S.A. 77 G7 36 18N 76 14W
Elizabethton, U.S.A. 77 G4 36 21N 82 13W
Elizabethtown, Ky., U.S.A. 76 G3 37 42N 85 52W
Elizabethtown, N.Y., U.S.A. 79 B11 44 13N 73 36W
Elizabethtown, Pa., U.S.A. 79 F8 40 9N 76 36W
Elk, Poland 17 B12 53 50N 22 21 E
Elk →, Canada 72 C5 49 11N 115 14W
Elk →, U.S.A. 77 H2 34 46N 87 16W
Elk City, U.S.A. 81 H5 35 25N 99 25W
Elk Creek, U.S.A. 84 F4 39 36N 122 32W
Elk Grove, U.S.A. 84 G5 38 25N 121 22W
Elk Island Nat. Park, Canada 72 C6 53 35N 112 59W
Elk Lake, Canada 70 C3 47 40N 80 25W
Elk Point, Canada 73 C6 53 54N 110 55W
Elk River, Idaho, U.S.A. 82 C5 46 47N 116 11W
Elk River, Minn., U.S.A. 80 C8 45 18N 93 35W
Elkedra →, Australia 62 C2 21 8S 136 22 E
Elkhart, Ind., U.S.A. 76 E3 41 41N 85 58W
Elkhart, Kans., U.S.A. 81 G4 37 0N 101 54W
Elkhorn, Canada 73 D8 49 59N 101 14W
Elkhorn →, U.S.A. 80 E6 41 8N 96 19W
Elkhovo, Bulgaria 21 C12 42 10N 26 35 E
Elkin, U.S.A. 77 G5 36 15N 80 51W
Elkins, U.S.A. 76 F6 38 55N 79 51W
Elkland, U.S.A. 78 E7 41 59N 77 19W
Elko, Canada 72 D5 49 20N 115 10W
Elko, U.S.A. 82 F6 40 50N 115 46W
Elkton, U.S.A. 78 C1 43 49N 83 11W
Ell, L., Australia 61 E4 29 13S 127 46 E
Ellef Ringnes I., Canada 4 B2 78 30N 102 2W
Ellen, Mt., U.S.A. 79 B12 44 9N 72 56W
Ellenburg, U.S.A. 79 B11 44 54N 73 48W
Ellendale, U.S.A. 80 B5 46 0N 98 32W
Ellensburg, U.S.A. 82 C3 46 59N 120 34W
Ellenville, U.S.A. 79 E10 41 43N 74 24W
Ellery, Mt., Australia 63 F4 37 28S 148 47 E
Ellesmere, L., N.Z. 59 M4 47 47S 172 28 E
Ellesmere I., Canada 4 B4 79 30N 80 0W
Ellesmere Port, U.K. 10 D5 53 17N 2 54W
Ellice Is. = Tuvalu ■, Pac. Oc. 64 H9 8 0S 178 0 E
Ellicottville, U.S.A. 78 D6 42 17N 78 40W
Elliot, Australia 62 B1 17 33S 133 32 E
Elliot, S. Africa 57 E4 31 22S 27 48 E
Elliot Lake, Canada 70 C3 46 25N 82 35W
Elliotdale = Xhora, S. Africa 57 E4 31 55S 28 38 E
Elliston, Australia 63 E1 33 39S 134 53 E
Ellisville, U.S.A. 81 K10 31 36N 89 12W
Ellon, U.K. 12 D6 57 22N 2 4W
Ellore = Eluru, India 41 L12 16 48N 81 8 E
Ellsworth, Kans., U.S.A. 80 F5 38 44N 98 14W
Ellsworth, Maine, U.S.A. 77 C11 44 33N 68 25W
Ellsworth Land, Antarctica 5 D16 76 0S 89 0W
Ellsworth Mts., Antarctica 5 D16 78 30S 85 0W
Ellwood City, U.S.A. 78 F4 40 52N 80 17W
Elma, Canada 73 D9 49 52N 95 55W
Elma, U.S.A. 84 D3 47 0N 123 25W
Elmalı, Turkey 25 G4 36 44N 29 56 E
Elmhurst, U.S.A. 76 E2 41 53N 87 56W
Elmira, Canada 78 C4 43 36N 80 33W
Elmira, U.S.A. 78 D8 42 6N 76 48W
Elmira Heights, U.S.A. 78 D8 42 8N 76 50W
Elmore, Australia 63 F3 36 30S 144 37 E
Elmore, U.S.A. 85 M11 33 7N 115 49W
Elmshorn, Germany 16 B5 53 43N 9 40 E
Elmvale, Canada 78 B5 44 35N 79 52W
Elora, Canada 78 C4 43 41N 80 26W
Eloúnda, Greece 23 D7 35 16N 25 42 E
Eloy, U.S.A. 83 K8 32 45N 111 33W
Elrose, Canada 73 C7 51 12N 108 0W
Elsie, U.S.A. 84 E3 45 52N 123 36W
Elsinore = Helsingør, Denmark 9 H15 56 2N 12 35 E
Eltham, N.Z. 59 H5 39 26S 174 19 E
Eluru, India 41 L12 16 48N 81 8 E
Elvas, Portugal 19 C2 38 50N 7 10W
Elverum, Norway 9 F14 60 53N 11 34 E
Elvire, Mt., Australia 61 E2 29 22S 119 36 E
Elwell, L., U.S.A. 82 B8 48 22N 111 17W
Elwood, Ind., U.S.A. 76 E3 40 17N 85 50W
Elwood, Nebr., U.S.A. 80 E5 40 36N 99 52W
Elx = Elche, Spain 19 C5 38 15N 0 42W
Ely, U.K. 11 E8 52 24N 0 16 E
Ely, Minn., U.S.A. 80 B9 47 55N 91 51W
Ely, Nev., U.S.A. 82 G6 39 15N 114 54W
Elyria, U.S.A. 78 E2 41 22N 82 7W
Emāmrūd, Iran 45 B7 36 30N 55 0 E
Emba, Kazakstan 26 E6 48 50N 58 8 E
Emba →, Kazakstan 26 E6 46 55N 53 28 E
Embarcación, Argentina 94 A3 23 10S 64 0W
Embarras Portage, Canada 73 B6 58 27N 111 28W
Embetsu, Japan 30 B10 44 44N 141 47 E
Embi = Emba, Kazakstan 26 E6 48 50N 58 8 E
Embi →, = Emba →, Kazakstan 26 E9 46 55N 53 28 E
Embóna, Greece 23 C9 36 13N 27 51 E
Embrun, France 18 D7 44 34N 6 30 E
Embu, Kenya 54 C4 0 32S 37 38 E
Emden, Germany 16 B4 53 21N 7 12 E
Emerald, Australia 62 C4 23 32S 148 10 E
Emerson, Canada 73 D9 49 0N 97 10W
Emet, Turkey 21 E13 39 20N 29 15 E
Emi Koussi, Chad 51 E9 19 45N 18 55 E
Eminabad, Pakistan 42 C6 32 2N 74 8 E
Emine, Nos, Bulgaria 21 C12 42 40N 27 56 E
Emlenton, U.S.A. 78 E5 41 11N 79 43W
Emmaus, U.S.A. 79 F9 40 32N 75 30W
Emmeloord, Neths. 15 B5 52 44N 5 46 E
Emmen, Neths. 15 B6 52 48N 6 57 E
Emmet, Australia 62 C3 24 45S 144 30 E
Emmetsburg, U.S.A. 80 D7 43 7N 94 41W
Emmett, Idaho, U.S.A. 82 E5 43 52N 116 30W
Emmett, Mich., U.S.A. 78 D2 42 59N 82 46W
Emmonak, U.S.A. 68 B3 62 46N 164 30W
Emo, Canada 73 D10 48 38N 93 50W
Empalme, Mexico 86 B2 28 1N 110 49W
Empangeni, S. Africa 57 D5 28 50S 31 52 E
Empedrado, Argentina 94 B4 28 0S 58 46W

Emperor Seamount Chain, Pac. Oc. 64 D9 40 0N 170 0 E
Emporia, Kans., U.S.A. 80 F6 38 25N 96 11W
Emporia, Va., U.S.A. 77 G7 36 42N 77 32W
Emporium, U.S.A. 78 E6 41 31N 78 14W
Empress, Canada 73 C7 50 57N 110 0W
Empty Quarter = Rub' al Khālī, Si. Arabia 46 D4 18 0N 48 0 E
Ems →, Germany 16 B4 53 20N 7 12 E
Emsdale, Canada 78 A5 45 32N 79 19W
Emu, China 35 C15 43 40N 128 6 E
Emu Park, Australia 62 C5 23 13S 150 50 E
'En 'Avrona, Israel 47 F4 29 43N 35 0 E
En Nahud, Sudan 51 F11 12 45N 28 25 E
Ena, Japan 31 G8 35 25N 137 25 E
Enana, Namibia 56 B2 17 30S 16 23 E
Enaratoli, Indonesia 37 E9 3 55S 136 21 E
Enard B., U.K. 12 C3 58 5N 5 20W
Enare = Inarijärvi, Finland 8 B22 69 0N 28 0 E
Encampment, U.S.A. 82 F10 41 12N 106 47W
Encantadas, Serra, Brazil 95 C5 30 40S 53 0W
Encarnación, Paraguay 95 B4 27 15S 55 50W
Encarnación de Díaz, Mexico 86 C4 21 30N 102 13W
Encinitas, U.S.A. 85 M9 33 3N 117 17W
Encino, U.S.A. 83 J11 34 39N 105 28W
Encounter B., Australia 63 F2 35 45S 138 45 E
Endako, Canada 72 C3 54 6N 125 2W
Ende, Indonesia 37 F6 8 45S 121 40 E
Endeavour Str., Australia 62 A3 10 45S 142 0 E
Enderbury I., Kiribati 64 H10 3 8S 171 5W
Enderby, Canada 72 C5 50 35N 119 10W
Enderby I., Australia 60 D2 20 35S 116 30 E
Enderby Land, Antarctica 5 C5 66 0S 53 0 E
Enderlin, U.S.A. 80 B6 46 38N 97 36W
Endicott, U.S.A. 79 D8 42 6N 76 4W
Endwell, U.S.A. 79 D8 42 6N 76 2W
Endyalgout I., Australia 60 B5 11 40S 132 35 E
Eneabba, Australia 61 E2 29 49S 115 16 E
Enewetak Atoll, Marshall Is. 64 F8 11 30N 162 15 E
Enez, Turkey 21 D12 40 45N 26 5 E
Enfield, Canada 71 D7 44 56N 63 32W
Enfield, Conn., U.S.A. 79 E12 41 58N 72 36W
Enfield, N.H., U.S.A. 79 C12 43 39N 72 9W
Engadin, Switz. 18 C9 46 45N 10 10 E
Engaño, C., Dom. Rep. 89 C6 18 30N 68 20W
Engaño, C., Phil. 37 A6 18 35N 122 23 E
Engaru, Japan 30 B11 44 3N 143 31 E
Engcobo, S. Africa 57 E4 31 37S 28 0 E
Engels, Russia 25 D8 51 28N 46 6 E
Engemann L., Canada 73 B7 58 0N 106 55W
Enggano, Indonesia 36 F2 5 20S 102 40 E
England, U.S.A. 81 H9 34 33N 91 58W
Englee, Canada 71 B8 50 45N 56 5W
Englehart, Canada 70 C4 47 49N 79 52W
Englewood, U.S.A. 80 F2 39 39N 104 59W
English →, Canada 73 C10 50 35N 93 30W
English Bazar = Ingraj Bazar, India 43 G13 24 58N 88 10 E
English Channel, Europe 11 G6 50 0N 2 0W
English River, Canada 70 C1 49 14N 91 0W
Enid, U.S.A. 81 G6 36 24N 97 53W
Enkhuizen, Neths. 15 B5 52 42N 5 17 E
Enna, Italy 20 F6 37 34N 14 16 E
Ennadai, Canada 73 A8 61 8N 100 53W
Ennadai L., Canada 73 A8 61 0N 101 0W
Ennedi, Chad 51 E10 17 15N 22 0 E
Enngonia, Australia 63 D4 29 21S 145 50 E
Ennis, Ireland 13 D3 52 51N 8 59W
Ennis, Mont., U.S.A. 82 D8 45 21N 111 44W
Ennis, Tex., U.S.A. 81 J6 32 20N 96 38W
Enniscorthy, Ireland 13 D5 52 30N 6 34W
Enniskillen, U.K. 13 B4 54 21N 7 39W
Ennistimon, Ireland 13 D2 52 57N 9 17W
Enns →, Austria 16 D8 48 14N 14 32 E
Enontekiö, Finland 8 B20 68 23N 23 37 E
Enosburg Falls, U.S.A. 79 B12 44 55N 72 48W
Enriquillo, Dom. Rep. 89 C5 17 55N 71 20W
Ensenada, Neths. 15 B6 52 13N 6 53 E
Ensenada, Argentina 94 C4 34 55S 57 55W
Ensenada, Mexico 86 A1 31 50N 116 50W
Ensenada de los Muertos, Mexico 86 C2 23 59N 109 50W
Ensiola, Pta. de n', Spain 22 B9 39 7N 2 55 E
Entebbe, Uganda 54 B3 0 4N 32 28 E
Enterprise, Canada 72 A5 60 47N 115 45W
Enterprise, Ala., U.S.A. 77 K3 31 19N 85 51W
Enterprise, Oreg., U.S.A. 82 D5 45 25N 117 17W
Entre Ríos, Bolivia 94 A3 21 30S 64 25W
Entre Ríos □, Argentina 94 C4 30 30S 58 30W
Entroncamento, Portugal 19 C1 39 28N 8 28W
Enugu, Nigeria 50 G7 6 20N 7 30 E
Enumclaw, U.S.A. 84 C5 47 12N 121 59W
Eólie, Ís., Italy 20 E6 38 30N 14 57 E
Epe, Neths. 15 B5 52 21N 5 59 E
Épernay, France 18 B5 49 3N 3 56 E
Ephesus, Turkey 21 F12 37 55N 27 22 E
Ephraim, U.S.A. 82 G8 39 22N 111 35W
Ephrata, Pa., U.S.A. 79 F8 40 11N 76 11W
Ephrata, Wash., U.S.A. 82 C4 47 19N 119 33W
Épinal, France 18 B7 48 10N 6 27 E
Episkopi, Cyprus 23 E11 34 40N 32 54 E
Episkopi, Greece 23 D6 35 20N 24 20 E
Episkopi Bay, Cyprus 23 E11 34 35N 32 50 E
Epsom, U.K. 11 F7 51 19N 0 16W
Epukiro, Namibia 56 C2 21 40S 19 9 E
Equatorial Guinea ■, Africa 52 D1 2 0N 8 0 E
Er Rahad, Sudan 51 F12 12 45N 30 32 E
Er Rif, Morocco 50 A5 35 1N 4 1W
Erāwadi Myit = Irrawaddy →, Burma 41 M19 15 50N 95 6 E
Erbil = Arbīl, Iraq 44 B5 36 15N 44 5 E
Ercıyaş Dağı, Turkey 25 G6 38 30N 35 30 E
Érd, Hungary 17 E10 47 22N 18 56 E
Erdao Jiang →, China 35 C14 43 0N 127 0 E
Erdek, Turkey 21 D12 40 23N 27 47 E
Erdene = Ulaan-Uul, Mongolia 34 B6 44 13N 111 10 E
Erdenetsogt, Mongolia 34 C4 42 55N 106 5 E
Erechim, Brazil 95 B5 27 35S 52 15W
Ereğli, Konya, Turkey 25 G5 37 31N 34 4 E
Ereğli, Zonguldak, Turkey 25 F5 41 15N 31 24 E
Erenhot, China 34 C7 43 48N 112 2 E
Eresma →, Spain 19 B3 41 26N 4 45W
Erewadi Myitwanya, Burma 41 M19 15 30N 95 6 E

Erfenisdam, S. Africa	56 D4	28 30S	26 50 E
Erfurt, Germany	16 C6	50 58N	11 2 E
Erg Iguidi, Africa	50 C4	27 0N	7 0 E
Ergani, Turkey	44 B3	38 17N	39 49 E
Ergel, Mongolia	34 C5	43 8N	109 5 E
Ergeni Vozvyshennost, Russia	25 E7	47 0N	44 0 E
Ērgļi, Latvia	9 H21	56 54N	25 38 E
Eriboll, L., U.K.	12 C4	58 30N	4 42W
Érice, Italy	20 E5	38 2N	12 35 E
Erie, U.S.A.	78 D4	42 8N	80 5W
Erie, L., N. Amer.	78 D4	42 15N	81 0W
Erie Canal, U.S.A.	78 C7	43 5N	78 43W
Erieau, Canada	78 D3	42 16N	81 57W
Erigavo, Somali Rep.	46 E4	10 35N	47 20 E
Erikoúsa, Greece	23 A3	39 53N	19 34 E
Eriksdale, Canada	73 C9	50 52N	98 7W
Erímanthos, Greece	21 F9	37 57N	21 50 E
Erinpura, India	42 G5	25 9N	73 3 E
Eriskay, U.K.	12 D1	57 4N	7 18W
Eritrea ■, Africa	46 D2	14 0N	38 30 E
Erlangen, Germany	16 D6	49 36N	11 0 E
Erldunda, Australia	62 D1	25 14S	133 12 E
Ermelo, Neths.	15 B5	52 18N	5 35 E
Ermelo, S. Africa	57 D4	26 31S	29 59 E
Ermenek, Turkey	44 B2	36 38N	33 0 E
Ermones, Greece	23 A3	39 37N	19 46 E
Ermoúpolis = Síros, Greece	21 F11	37 28N	24 57 E
Ernakulam = Cochin, India	40 Q10	9 59N	76 22 E
Erne →, Ireland	13 B3	54 30N	8 16W
Erne, Lower L., U.K.	13 B4	54 28N	7 47W
Erne, Upper L., U.K.	13 B4	54 14N	7 32W
Ernest Giles Ra., Australia	61 E3	27 0S	123 45 E
Erode, India	40 P10	11 24N	77 45 E
Eromanga, Australia	63 D3	26 40S	143 11 E
Erongo, Namibia	56 C2	21 39S	15 58 E
Erramala Hills, India	40 M11	15 30N	78 15 E
Errigal, Ireland	13 A3	55 2N	8 6W
Erris Hd., Ireland	13 B1	54 19N	10 0W
Erskine, U.S.A.	80 B7	47 40N	96 0W
Ertis = Irtysh →, Russia	26 C7	61 4N	68 52 E
Erwin, U.S.A.	77 G4	36 9N	82 25W
Erzgebirge, Germany	16 C7	50 27N	12 55 E
Erzin, Russia	27 D10	50 15N	95 10 E
Erzincan, Turkey	25 G6	39 46N	39 30 E
Erzurum, Turkey	25 G7	39 57N	41 15 E
Es Caló, Spain	22 C8	38 40N	1 30 E
Es Canar, Spain	22 B8	39 2N	1 36 E
Es Mercadal, Spain	22 B11	39 59N	4 5 E
Es Migjorn Gran, Spain	22 B11	39 57N	4 3 E
Es Sahrâ' Esh Sharqîya, Egypt	51 C12	27 30N	32 30 E
Es Sînâ', Egypt	47 F3	29 0N	34 0 E
Es Vedrà, Spain	22 C7	38 52N	1 12 E
Esambo, Dem. Rep. of the Congo	54 C1	3 48S	23 30 E
Esan-Misaki, Japan	30 D10	41 40N	141 10 E
Esashi, Hokkaidō, Japan	30 B11	44 56N	142 35 E
Esashi, Hokkaidō, Japan	30 D10	41 52N	140 7 E
Esbjerg, Denmark	9 J13	55 29N	8 29 E
Escalante, U.S.A.	83 H8	37 47N	111 36W
Escalante →, U.S.A.	83 H8	37 24N	110 57W
Escalón, Mexico	86 B4	26 46N	104 20W
Escambia →, U.S.A.	77 K2	30 32N	87 11W
Escanaba, U.S.A.	76 C2	45 45N	87 4W
Esch-sur-Alzette, Lux.	18 B6	49 32N	6 0 E
Escondido, U.S.A.	85 M9	33 7N	117 5W
Escuinapa, Mexico	86 C3	22 50N	105 50W
Escuintla, Guatemala	88 D1	14 20N	90 48W
Esenguly, Turkmenistan	26 F6	37 37N	53 59 E
Eşfahān, Iran	45 C6	32 39N	51 43 E
Eşfahān □, Iran	45 C6	32 50N	51 50 E
Esfarāyen, Iran	45 B8	37 4N	57 30 E
Esfideh, Iran	45 C8	33 39N	59 46 E
Esh Sham = Dimashq, Syria	47 B5	33 30N	36 18 E
Esha Ness, U.K.	12 A7	60 29N	1 38W
Esher, U.K.	11 F7	51 21N	0 20W
Eshowe, S. Africa	57 D5	28 50S	31 30 E
Esil = Ishim →, Russia	26 D8	57 45N	71 10 E
Esk →, Cumb., U.K.	12 G5	54 58N	3 2W
Esk →, N. Yorks., U.K.	10 C7	54 30N	0 37W
Eskān, Iran	45 E9	26 48N	63 9 E
Esker, Canada	71 B6	53 53N	66 25W
Eskifjörður, Iceland	8 D7	65 3N	13 55W
Eskilstuna, Sweden	9 G17	59 22N	16 32 E
Eskimo Pt., Canada	68 B10	61 10N	94 15W
Eskişehir, Turkey	25 G5	39 50N	30 30 E
Esla →, Spain	19 B2	41 29N	6 3W
Eslāmābād-e Gharb, Iran	44 C5	34 10N	46 30 E
Eslāmshahr, Iran	45 C6	35 40N	51 10 E
Eşme, Turkey	21 E13	38 23N	28 58 E
Esmeraldas, Ecuador	92 C3	1 0N	79 40W
Esnagi L., Canada	70 C3	48 36N	84 33W
Espanola, Canada	70 C3	46 15N	81 46W
Espanola, U.S.A.	83 H10	35 59N	106 5W
Esparta, Costa Rica	88 E3	9 59N	84 40W
Esperance, Australia	61 F3	33 45S	121 55 E
Esperance B., Australia	61 F3	33 48S	121 55 E
Esperanza, Argentina	94 C3	31 29S	61 3W
Espichel, C., Portugal	19 C1	38 22N	9 16W
Espigão, Serra do, Brazil	95 B5	26 35S	50 30W
Espinazo, Sierra del = Espinhaço, Serra do, Brazil	93 G10	17 30S	43 30W
Espinhaço, Serra do, Brazil	93 G10	17 30S	43 30W
Espinilho, Serra do, Brazil	95 B5	28 30S	55 0W
Espírito Santo □, Brazil	93 H10	20 0S	40 45W
Espíritu Santo, Vanuatu	64 J8	15 15S	166 50 E
Espíritu Santo, B. del, Mexico	87 D7	19 15N	87 0W
Espíritu Santo, I., Mexico	86 C2	24 30N	110 23W
Espita, Mexico	87 C7	21 1N	88 19W
Espoo, Finland	9 F21	60 12N	24 40 E
Espungabera, Mozam.	57 C5	20 29S	32 45 E
Esquel, Argentina	96 E2	42 55S	71 20W
Esquimalt, Canada	72 D4	48 26N	123 25W
Esquina, Argentina	94 C4	30 0S	59 30W
Essaouira, Morocco	50 B4	31 32N	9 42W
Essebie, Dem. Rep. of the Congo	54 B3	2 58N	30 40 E
Essen, Belgium	15 C4	51 28N	4 28 E
Essen, Germany	16 C4	51 28N	7 2 E
Essendon, Mt., Australia	61 E3	25 0S	120 29 E
Essequibo →, Guyana	92 B7	6 50N	58 30W
Essex, Canada	78 D2	42 10N	82 49W
Essex, Calif., U.S.A.	85 L11	34 44N	115 15W

Essex, N.Y., U.S.A.	79 B11	44 19N	73 21W
Essex □, U.K.	11 F8	51 54N	0 27 E
Essex Junction, U.S.A.	79 B11	44 29N	73 7W
Esslingen, Germany	16 D5	48 44N	9 18 E
Estados, I. de Los, Argentina	96 G4	54 40S	64 30W
Eşţahbānāt, Iran	45 D7	29 8N	54 4 E
Estância, Brazil	93 F11	11 16S	37 26W
Estancia, U.S.A.	83 J10	34 46N	106 4W
Estārm, Iran	45 D8	28 21N	58 21 E
Estcourt, S. Africa	57 D4	29 0S	29 53 E
Estellencs, Spain	22 B9	39 39N	2 29 E
Estelí, Nic.	88 D2	13 9N	86 22W
Esterhazy, Canada	73 C8	50 37N	102 5W
Estevan, Canada	73 D8	49 10N	102 59W
Estevan Group, Canada	72 C3	53 3N	129 38W
Estherville, U.S.A.	80 D7	43 24N	94 50W
Eston, Canada	73 C7	51 8N	108 40W
Estonia ■, Europe	9 G21	58 30N	25 30 E
Estreito, Brazil	93 E9	6 32S	47 25W
Estrela, Serra da, Portugal	19 B2	40 10N	7 45W
Estremoz, Portugal	19 C2	38 51N	7 39W
Estrondo, Serra do, Brazil	93 E9	7 20S	48 0W
Esztergom, Hungary	17 E10	47 47N	18 44 E
Etah, India	43 F8	27 35N	78 40 E
Étampes, France	18 B5	48 26N	2 10 E
Etanga, Namibia	56 B1	17 55S	13 0 E
Etawah, India	43 F8	26 48N	79 6 E
Etawney L., Canada	73 B9	57 50N	96 50W
Ethel, U.S.A.	84 D4	46 32N	122 46W
Ethelbert, Canada	73 C8	51 32N	100 25W
Ethiopia ■, Africa	46 F3	8 0N	40 0 E
Ethiopian Highlands, Ethiopia	28 J7	10 0N	37 0 E
Etive, L., U.K.	12 E3	56 29N	5 10W
Etna, Italy	20 F6	37 50N	14 55 E
Etoile, Dem. Rep. of the Congo	55 E2	11 33S	27 30 E
Etosha Pan, Namibia	56 B2	18 40S	16 30 E
Etowah, U.S.A.	77 H3	35 20N	84 32W
Ettelbruck, Lux.	15 E6	49 51N	6 5 E
Ettrick Water →, U.K.	12 F6	55 31N	2 55W
Etuku, Dem. Rep. of the Congo	54 C2	3 42S	25 45 E
Etzatlán, Mexico	86 C4	20 48N	104 5W
Etzná, Mexico	87 D6	19 35N	90 15W
Euboea = Évvoia, Greece	21 E11	38 30N	24 0 E
Eucla, Australia	61 F4	31 41S	128 52 E
Euclid, U.S.A.	78 E3	41 34N	81 32W
Eucumbene, L., Australia	63 F4	36 2S	148 40 E
Eudora, U.S.A.	81 J9	33 7N	91 16W
Eufaula, Okla., U.S.A.	81 H7	35 17N	95 35W
Eufaula L., U.S.A.	81 H7	35 18N	95 21W
Eugene, U.S.A.	82 E2	44 5N	123 4W
Eugowra, Australia	63 E4	33 22S	148 24 E
Eulo, Australia	63 D4	28 10S	145 3 E
Eunice, La., U.S.A.	81 K8	30 30N	92 25W
Eunice, N. Mex., U.S.A.	81 J3	32 26N	103 10W
Eupen, Belgium	15 D6	50 37N	6 3 E
Euphrates = Furāt, Nahr al →, Asia	44 D5	31 0N	47 25 E
Eureka, Canada	4 B3	80 0N	85 56W
Eureka, Calif., U.S.A.	82 F1	40 47N	124 9W
Eureka, Kans., U.S.A.	81 G6	37 49N	96 17W
Eureka, Mont., U.S.A.	82 B6	48 53N	115 3W
Eureka, Nev., U.S.A.	82 G5	39 31N	115 58W
Eureka, S. Dak., U.S.A.	80 C5	45 46N	99 38W
Eureka, Mt., Australia	61 E3	26 35S	121 35 E
Euroa, Australia	63 F4	36 44S	145 35 E
Europa, Île, Ind. Oc.	53 J8	22 20S	40 22 E
Europa, Picos de, Spain	19 A3	43 10N	4 49W
Europa, Pta. de, Gib.	19 D3	36 3N	5 21W
Europe	6 E10	50 0N	20 0 E
Europoort, Neths.	15 C4	51 57N	4 10 E
Eustis, U.S.A.	77 L5	28 51N	81 41W
Euston, Australia	63 E3	34 30S	142 46 E
Eutsuk L., Canada	72 C3	53 20N	126 45W
Evale, Angola	56 B2	16 33S	15 44 E
Evans, Canada	70 B4	50 50N	77 0W
Evans, L., Canada	70 B4	50 50N	77 0W
Evans City, U.S.A.	78 F4	40 46N	80 4W
Evans Head, Australia	63 D5	29 7S	153 27 E
Evans Mills, U.S.A.	79 B9	44 6N	75 48W
Evansburg, Canada	72 C5	53 36N	114 59W
Evanston, Ill., U.S.A.	76 E2	42 3N	87 41W
Evanston, Wyo., U.S.A.	82 F8	41 16N	110 58W
Evansville, U.S.A.	76 G2	37 58N	87 35W
Evaz, Iran	45 E7	27 46N	53 59 E
Eveleth, U.S.A.	80 B8	47 28N	92 32W
Evensk, Russia	27 C16	62 12N	159 30 E
Everard, L., Australia	63 E2	31 30S	135 0 E
Everard Ranges, Australia	61 E5	27 5S	132 28 E
Everest, Mt., Nepal	43 E12	28 5N	86 58 E
Everett, Pa., U.S.A.	78 F6	40 1N	78 23W
Everett, Wash., U.S.A.	84 C4	47 59N	122 12W
Everglades, U.S.A.	77 N5	25 50N	81 0W
Everglades National Park, U.S.A.	77 N5	25 30N	81 0W
Evergreen, Ala., U.S.A.	77 K2	31 26N	86 57W
Evergreen, Mont., U.S.A.	82 B6	48 9N	114 13W
Evesham, U.K.	11 E6	52 6N	1 56W
Evje, Norway	9 G12	58 36N	7 51 E
Évora, Portugal	19 C2	38 33N	7 57W
Evowghlī, Iran	44 B5	38 43N	45 13 E
Évreux, France	18 B4	49 3N	1 8 E
Évros →, Bulgaria	21 D12	41 40N	26 34 E
Évry, France	18 B5	48 38N	2 27 E
Évvoia, Greece	21 E11	38 30N	24 0 E
Ewe, L., U.K.	12 D3	57 49N	5 38W
Ewing, U.S.A.	80 D5	42 16N	98 21W
Ewo, Congo	52 E2	0 48S	14 45 E
Exaltación, Bolivia	92 F5	13 10S	65 20W
Excelsior Springs, U.S.A.	80 F7	39 20N	94 13W
Exe →, U.K.	11 G4	50 41N	3 29W
Exeter, Canada	78 C3	43 21N	81 29W
Exeter, U.K.	11 G4	50 43N	3 31W
Exeter, Calif., U.S.A.	84 J7	36 18N	119 9W
Exeter, N.H., U.S.A.	79 D14	42 59N	70 57W
Exmoor, U.K.	11 F4	51 12N	3 45W
Exmouth, Australia	60 D1	21 54S	114 10 E
Exmouth, U.K.	11 G4	50 37N	3 25W
Exmouth G., Australia	60 D1	22 15S	114 15 E
Expedition Ra., Australia	62 C4	24 30S	149 12 E
Extremadura □, Spain	19 C2	39 30N	6 5W
Exuma Sound, Bahamas	88 B4	24 30N	76 20W
Eyasi, L., Tanzania	54 C4	3 30S	35 0 E
Eye Pen., U.K.	12 C2	58 13N	6 10W

Eyemouth, U.K.	12 F6	55 52N	2 5W
Eyjafjörður, Iceland	8 C4	66 15N	18 30W
Eyre (North), L., Australia	63 D2	28 30S	137 20 E
Eyre (South), L., Australia	63 D2	29 18S	137 25 E
Eyre Mts., N.Z.	59 L2	45 25S	168 25 E
Eyre Pen., Australia	63 E2	33 30S	136 17 E
Eysturoy, Færoe Is.	8 E9	62 13N	6 54W
Eyvānki, Iran	45 C6	35 24N	51 56 E
Ezine, Turkey	21 E12	39 48N	26 20 E
Ezouza →, Cyprus	23 E11	34 44N	32 27 E

F

F.Y.R.O.M. = Macedonia ■, Europe	21 D9	41 53N	21 40 E
Fabala, Guinea	50 G4	9 44N	9 5W
Fabens, U.S.A.	83 L10	31 30N	106 10W
Fabriano, Italy	20 C5	43 20N	12 54 E
Fachi, Niger	51 E8	18 6N	11 34 E
Fada, Chad	51 E10	17 13N	21 34 E
Fada-n-Gourma, Burkina Faso	50 F6	12 10N	0 30 E
Faddeyevskiy, Ostrov, Russia	27 B15	76 0N	144 0 E
Fadghāmī, Syria	44 C4	35 53N	40 52 E
Faenza, Italy	20 B4	44 17N	11 53 E
Færoe Is. = Føroyar, Atl. Oc.	8 F9	62 0N	7 0W
Făgăraş, Romania	17 F13	45 48N	24 58 E
Fagersta, Sweden	9 F16	60 1N	15 46 E
Fagnano, L., Argentina	96 G3	54 30S	68 0W
Fahlīān, Iran	45 D6	30 11N	51 28 E
Fahraj, Kermān, Iran	45 D8	29 0N	59 0 E
Fahraj, Yazd, Iran	45 D7	31 46N	54 36 E
Faial, Madeira	22 D3	32 47N	16 53W
Fair Haven, U.S.A.	79 B11	43 36N	73 16W
Fair Hd., U.K.	13 A5	55 14N	6 9W
Fair Oaks, U.S.A.	84 G5	38 39N	121 16W
Fairbanks, U.S.A.	68 B5	64 51N	147 43W
Fairbury, U.S.A.	80 E6	40 8N	97 11W
Fairfax, U.S.A.	79 B11	44 40N	73 1W
Fairfield, Ala., U.S.A.	77 J2	33 29N	86 55W
Fairfield, Calif., U.S.A.	84 G4	38 15N	122 3W
Fairfield, Conn., U.S.A.	79 E11	41 9N	73 16W
Fairfield, Idaho, U.S.A.	82 E6	43 21N	114 44W
Fairfield, Ill., U.S.A.	76 F1	38 23N	88 22W
Fairfield, Iowa, U.S.A.	80 E9	40 56N	91 57W
Fairfield, Tex., U.S.A.	81 K7	31 44N	96 10W
Fairford, Canada	73 C9	51 37N	98 38W
Fairhope, U.S.A.	77 K2	30 31N	87 54W
Fairlie, N.Z.	59 L3	44 5S	170 49 E
Fairmead, U.S.A.	84 H6	37 5N	120 10W
Fairmont, Minn., U.S.A.	80 D7	43 39N	94 28W
Fairmont, W. Va., U.S.A.	76 F5	39 29N	80 9W
Fairmount, Calif., U.S.A.	85 L8	34 45N	118 26W
Fairmount, N.Y., U.S.A.	79 C8	43 5N	76 12W
Fairplay, U.S.A.	83 G11	39 15N	106 2W
Fairport, U.S.A.	78 C7	43 6N	77 27W
Fairport Harbor, U.S.A.	78 E3	41 45N	81 17W
Fairview, Canada	72 B5	56 5N	118 25W
Fairview, Mont., U.S.A.	80 B2	47 51N	104 3W
Fairview, Okla., U.S.A.	81 G5	36 16N	98 29W
Fairweather, Mt., U.S.A.	72 B1	58 55N	137 32W
Faisalabad, Pakistan	42 D5	31 30N	73 5 E
Faith, U.S.A.	80 C3	45 2N	102 2W
Faizabad, India	43 F10	26 45N	82 10 E
Fajardo, Puerto Rico	89 C6	18 20N	65 39W
Fajr, Wādī, Si. Arabia	44 D3	29 10N	38 10 E
Fakenham, U.K.	10 E8	52 51N	0 51 E
Fakfak, Indonesia	37 E8	3 0S	132 15 E
Faku, China	35 C12	42 32N	123 21 E
Falaise, France	18 B3	48 54N	0 12W
Falaise, Mui, Vietnam	38 C5	19 6N	105 45 E
Falam, Burma	41 H18	23 0N	93 45 E
Falcó, C. des, Spain	22 C7	38 50N	1 23 E
Falcón, Presa, Mexico	87 B5	26 35N	99 10W
Falcon Lake, Canada	73 D9	49 42N	95 15W
Falcon Reservoir, U.S.A.	81 M5	26 34N	99 10W
Falconara Maríttima, Italy	20 C5	43 37N	13 24 E
Falcone, C. del, Italy	20 D3	40 58N	8 12 E
Falconer, U.S.A.	78 D5	42 7N	79 13W
Faleshty = Făleşti, Moldova	17 E14	47 32N	27 44 E
Făleşti, Moldova	17 E14	47 32N	27 44 E
Falfurrias, U.S.A.	81 M5	27 14N	98 9W
Falher, Canada	72 B5	55 44N	117 15W
Falirakí, Greece	23 C10	36 22N	28 12 E
Falkenberg, Sweden	9 H15	56 54N	12 30 E
Falkirk, U.K.	12 F5	56 0N	3 47W
Falkirk □, U.K.	12 F5	55 58N	3 49W
Falkland □, U.K.	12 E5	56 16N	3 12W
Falkland Is. □, Atl. Oc.	96 G5	51 30S	59 0W
Falkland Sd., Falk. Is.	96 G5	52 0S	60 0W
Falköping, Sweden	9 G15	58 12N	13 33 E
Fall River, U.S.A.	79 E13	41 43N	71 9W
Fallbrook, U.S.A.	85 M9	33 23N	117 15W
Fallon, U.S.A.	82 G4	39 28N	118 47W
Falls City, U.S.A.	80 E7	40 3N	95 36W
Falls Creek, U.S.A.	78 E6	41 9N	78 48W
Falmouth, Jamaica	88 C4	18 30N	77 40W
Falmouth, U.K.	11 G2	50 9N	5 5W
Falmouth, U.S.A.	79 E14	41 33N	70 37W
Falsa, Pta., Mexico	86 B1	27 51N	115 3W
False B., S. Africa	56 E2	34 15S	18 40 E
Falso, C., Honduras	88 C3	15 12N	83 21W
Falster, Denmark	9 J14	54 45N	11 55 E
Falsterbo, Sweden	9 J15	55 23N	12 50 E
Fălticeni, Romania	17 E14	47 21N	26 20 E
Falun, Sweden	9 F16	60 37N	15 37 E
Famagusta, Cyprus	23 D12	35 8N	33 55 E
Famagusta Bay, Cyprus	23 D13	35 15N	34 0 E
Famalé, Niger	50 F6	14 33N	1 5 E
Famatina, Sierra de, Argentina	94 B2	27 30S	68 0W
Family L., Canada	73 C9	51 54N	95 27W
Famoso, U.S.A.	85 K7	35 37N	119 12W
Fan Xian, China	34 G8	35 55N	115 38 E
Fanad Hd., Ireland	13 A4	55 17N	7 38W
Fandriana, Madag.	57 C8	20 14S	47 21 E
Fangcheng, China	34 H7	33 18N	112 59 E
Fangzi, China	35 F10	36 33N	119 10 E
Fannich, L., U.K.	12 D4	57 38N	4 59W
Fannūj, Iran	45 E8	26 35N	59 38 E
Fanø, Denmark	9 J13	55 25N	8 25 E

Fano, Italy	20 C5	43 50N	13 1 E
Fanshi, China	34 E7	39 12N	113 20 E
Fao = Al Fāw, Iraq	45 D6	30 0N	48 30 E
Faqirwali, Pakistan	42 E5	29 27N	73 0 E
Faradje, Dem. Rep. of the Congo	54 B2	3 50N	29 45 E
Farafangana, Madag.	57 C8	22 49S	47 50 E
Farāh, Afghan.	40 C3	32 20N	62 7 E
Farāh □, Afghan.	40 C3	32 25N	62 10 E
Farahalana, Madag.	57 A9	14 26S	50 10 E
Faranah, Guinea	50 F3	10 3N	10 45W
Farasān, Jazā'ir, Si. Arabia	46 D3	16 45N	41 55 E
Farasan Is. = Farasān, Jazā'ir, Si. Arabia	46 D3	16 45N	41 55 E
Faratsiho, Madag.	57 B8	19 24S	46 57 E
Fareham, U.K.	11 G6	50 51N	1 11W
Farewell, U.S.A.	59 J4	40 29S	172 43 E
Farewell C. = Farvel, Kap, Greenland	4 D5	59 48N	43 55W
Farghona, Uzbekistan	26 E8	40 23N	71 19 E
Fargo, U.S.A.	80 B6	46 53N	96 48W
Fār'iah, W. al →, West Bank	47 C4	32 12N	35 27 E
Faribault, U.S.A.	80 C8	44 18N	93 16W
Faridabad, India	42 E6	28 26N	77 19 E
Faridkot, India	42 D6	30 44N	74 45 E
Faridpur, Bangla.	43 H13	23 15N	89 55 E
Faridpur, India	43 E8	28 13N	79 33 E
Farīmān, Iran	45 C8	35 40N	59 49 E
Farina, Australia	63 E2	30 3S	138 15 E
Fariones, Pta., Canary Is.	22 E6	29 13N	13 28W
Farmerville, U.S.A.	81 J8	32 47N	92 24W
Farmingdale, U.S.A.	79 F10	40 12N	74 10W
Farmington, Canada	72 B4	55 54N	120 30W
Farmington, Calif., U.S.A.	84 H6	37 55N	120 59W
Farmington, Maine, U.S.A.	77 C10	44 40N	70 9W
Farmington, Mo., U.S.A.	81 G9	37 47N	90 25W
Farmington, N.H., U.S.A.	79 C13	43 24N	71 4W
Farmington, N. Mex., U.S.A.	83 H9	36 44N	108 12W
Farmington, Utah, U.S.A.	82 F8	41 0N	111 12W
Farmington →, U.S.A.	79 E12	41 51N	72 38W
Farmville, U.S.A.	76 G6	37 18N	78 24W
Farne Is., U.K.	10 B6	55 38N	1 37W
Farnham, Canada	79 A12	45 17N	72 59W
Farnham, Mt., Canada	72 C5	50 29N	116 30W
Faro, Brazil	93 D7	2 10S	56 39W
Faro, Canada	68 B6	62 11N	133 22W
Faro, Portugal	19 D2	37 2N	7 55W
Fårö, Sweden	9 H18	57 55N	19 5 E
Farquhar, C., Australia	61 D1	23 50S	113 36 E
Farrars Cr. →, Australia	62 D3	25 35S	140 43 E
Farrāshband, Iran	45 D7	28 57N	52 5 E
Farrell, U.S.A.	78 E4	41 13N	80 30W
Farrokhī, Iran	45 C8	33 50N	59 31 E
Farruch, C. = Ferrutx, C., Spain	22 B10	39 47N	3 21 E
Farrukhabad-cum-Fatehgarh, India	40 F11	27 30N	79 32 E
Fārs □, Iran	45 D7	29 30N	55 0 E
Fársala, Greece	21 E10	39 17N	22 23 E
Farson, U.S.A.	82 E9	42 6N	109 27W
Farsund, Norway	9 G12	58 5N	6 55 E
Fartak, Râs, Si. Arabia	44 D2	28 5N	34 34 E
Fartak, Ra's, Yemen	46 D5	15 38N	52 15 E
Fartura, Serra da, Brazil	95 B5	26 21S	52 52W
Fārūj, Iran	45 B8	37 14N	58 14 E
Farvel, Kap, Greenland	4 D5	59 48N	43 55W
Farwell, U.S.A.	81 H3	34 23N	103 2W
Fasā, Iran	45 D7	29 0N	53 39 E
Fasano, Italy	20 D7	40 50N	17 22 E
Fastiv, Ukraine	17 C15	50 7N	29 57 E
Fastov = Fastiv, Ukraine	17 C15	50 7N	29 57 E
Fatagar, Tanjung, Indonesia	37 E8	2 46S	131 57 E
Fatehabad, Haryana, India	42 E6	29 31N	75 27 E
Fatehabad, Ut. P., India	42 F8	27 1N	78 19 E
Fatehgarh, India	43 F8	27 25N	79 35 E
Fatehpur, Bihar, India	43 G11	24 38N	85 14 E
Fatehpur, Raj., India	42 F6	28 0N	74 40 E
Fatehpur, Ut. P., India	43 G9	25 56N	81 13 E
Fatehpur, Ut. P., India	43 F9	27 10N	81 13 E
Fatehpur Sikri, India	42 F6	27 6N	77 40 E
Fatima, Canada	71 C7	47 24N	61 53W
Faulkton, U.S.A.	80 C5	45 2N	99 8W
Faure I., Australia	61 E1	25 52S	113 50 E
Fauresmith, S. Africa	56 D4	29 44S	25 17 E
Fauske, Norway	8 C16	67 17N	15 25 E
Favara, Italy	20 F5	37 19N	13 39 E
Favàritx, C. de, Spain	22 B11	40 0N	4 15 E
Favignana, Italy	20 F5	37 56N	12 20 E
Fawcett, Pt., Australia	60 B5	11 46S	130 2 E
Fawn →, Canada	70 A2	55 20N	87 35W
Fawnskin, U.S.A.	85 L10	34 16N	116 56W
Faxaflói, Iceland	8 D2	64 29N	23 0W
Faya-Largeau, Chad	51 E9	17 58N	19 6 E
Fayd, Si. Arabia	44 E4	27 1N	42 52 E
Fayette, Ala., U.S.A.	77 J2	33 41N	87 50W
Fayette, Mo., U.S.A.	80 F8	39 9N	92 41W
Fayetteville, Ark., U.S.A.	81 G7	36 4N	94 10W
Fayetteville, N.C., U.S.A.	77 H6	35 3N	78 53W
Fayetteville, Tenn., U.S.A.	77 H2	35 9N	86 34W
Fazilka, India	42 D6	30 27N	74 2 E
Fazilpur, Pakistan	42 E4	29 18N	70 29 E
Fdérik, Mauritania	50 D3	22 40N	12 45W
Feale →, Ireland	13 D2	52 27N	9 37W
Fear, C., U.S.A.	77 J7	33 50N	77 58W
Feather →, U.S.A.	82 G3	38 47N	121 36W
Feather Falls, U.S.A.	84 F5	39 36N	121 16W
Featherston, N.Z.	59 J5	41 6S	175 20 E
Featherstone, Zimbabwe	55 F3	18 42S	30 55 E
Fécamp, France	18 B4	49 45N	0 22 E
Fedala = Mohammedia, Morocco	50 B4	33 44N	7 21W
Federación, Argentina	94 C4	31 0S	57 55W
Federal, Argentina	96 C5	30 57S	58 48W
Federal Way, U.S.A.	84 C4	47 18N	122 19W
Fedeshküh, Iran	45 D7	28 49N	53 50 E
Fehmarn, Germany	16 A6	54 27N	11 7 E
Fehmarn Bælt, Europe	9 J14	54 35N	11 20 E
Fehmarn Belt = Fehmarn Bælt, Europe	9 J14	54 35N	11 20 E
Fei Xian, China	35 G9	35 18N	117 59 E
Feijó, Brazil	92 E4	8 9S	70 21W
Feilding, N.Z.	59 J5	40 13S	175 35 E
Feira de Santana, Brazil	93 F11	12 15S	38 57W
Feixiang, China	34 F8	36 30N	114 45 E
Felanitx, Spain	22 B10	39 28N	3 9 E
Feldkirch, Austria	16 E5	47 15N	9 37 E

rankfurt, Brandenburg, Germany . 16 B8 52 20N 14 32 E
rankfurt, Hessen, Germany . 16 C5 50 7N 8 41 E
ränkische Alb, Germany . 16 D6 49 10N 11 23 E
rankland →, Australia . 61 G2 35 0S 116 48 E
ranklin, Ky., U.S.A. . 77 G2 36 43N 86 35W
ranklin, La., U.S.A. . 81 L9 29 48N 91 30W
ranklin, Mass., U.S.A. . 79 D13 42 5N 71 24W
ranklin, N.H., U.S.A. . 79 C13 43 27N 71 39W
ranklin, Nebr., U.S.A. . 80 E5 40 6N 98 57W
ranklin, Pa., U.S.A. . 78 E5 41 24N 79 50W
ranklin, Va., U.S.A. . 77 G7 36 41N 76 56W
ranklin, W. Va., U.S.A. . 76 F6 38 39N 79 20W
ranklin B., Canada . 68 B7 69 45N 126 0 E
ranklin D. Roosevelt L., U.S.A. . 82 B4 48 18N 118 9W
ranklin I., Antarctica . 5 D11 76 10S 168 30 E
ranklin L., U.S.A. . 82 F6 40 25N 115 22W
ranklin Mts., Canada . 68 B7 65 0N 125 0W
ranklin Str., Canada . 68 A10 72 0N 96 0W
ranklinton, U.S.A. . 81 K9 30 51N 90 9W
ranklinville, U.S.A. . 78 D6 42 20N 78 27W
ranks Pk., U.S.A. . 82 E9 43 58N 109 18W
rankston, Australia . 63 F4 38 8S 145 8 E
rantsa Iosifa, Zemlya, Russia . 26 A6 82 0N 55 0 E
ranz, Canada . 70 C3 48 25N 84 30W
ranz Josef Land = Frantsa Iosifa, Zemlya, Russia . 26 A6 82 0N 55 0 E
raser, U.S.A. . 78 D2 42 32N 82 57W
raser →, B.C., Canada . 72 D4 49 7N 123 11W
raser →, Nfld., Canada . 71 A7 56 39N 62 10W
raser, Mt., Australia . 61 E2 25 35S 118 20 E
raser I., Australia . 63 D5 25 15S 153 10 E
raser Lake, Canada . 72 C4 54 0N 124 50W
raserburg, S. Africa . 56 E3 31 55S 21 30 E
raserburgh, U.K. . 12 D6 57 42N 2 1W
raserdale, Canada . 70 C3 49 55N 81 37W
ray Bentos, Uruguay . 94 C4 33 10S 58 15W
rederica, Denmark . 9 J13 55 34N 9 45 E
rederick, Md., U.S.A. . 76 F7 39 25N 77 25W
rederick, Okla., U.S.A. . 81 H5 34 23N 99 1W
rederick, S. Dak., U.S.A. . 80 C5 45 50N 98 31W
redericksburg, Pa., U.S.A. . 79 F8 40 27N 76 26W
redericksburg, Tex., U.S.A. . 81 K5 30 16N 98 52W
redericksburg, Va., U.S.A. . 76 F7 38 18N 77 28W
redericktown, Mo., U.S.A. . 81 G9 37 34N 90 18W
redericktown, Ohio, U.S.A. . 78 F2 40 29N 82 33W
rederico I. Madero, Presa, Mexico . 86 B3 28 7N 105 40W
rederico Westphalen, Brazil . 95 B5 27 22S 53 24W
redericton, Canada . 71 C6 45 57N 66 40W
redericton Junction, Canada . 71 C6 45 41N 66 40W
rederikshåb, Greenland . 4 C5 62 0N 49 43W
rederikshavn, Denmark . 9 H14 57 28N 10 31 E
rederiksted, Virgin Is. . 89 C7 17 43N 64 53W
redonia, Ariz., U.S.A. . 83 H7 36 57N 112 32W
redonia, Kans., U.S.A. . 81 G7 37 32N 95 49W
redonia, N.Y., U.S.A. . 78 D5 42 26N 79 20W
redrikstad, Norway . 9 G14 59 13N 10 57 E
ree State □, S. Africa . 56 D4 28 30S 27 0 E
reehold, U.S.A. . 79 F10 40 16N 74 17W
reel Peak, U.S.A. . 84 G7 38 52N 119 54W
reeland, U.S.A. . 79 E9 41 1N 75 54W
reels, C., Canada . 71 C9 49 15N 53 30W
reeman, Calif., U.S.A. . 85 K9 35 35N 117 53W
reeman, S. Dak., U.S.A. . 80 D6 43 21N 97 26W
reeport, Bahamas . 88 A4 26 30N 78 47W
reeport, Ill., U.S.A. . 80 D10 42 17N 89 36W
reeport, N.Y., U.S.A. . 79 F11 40 39N 73 35W
reeport, Ohio, U.S.A. . 78 F3 40 12N 81 15W
reeport, Pa., U.S.A. . 78 F5 40 41N 79 41W
reeport, Tex., U.S.A. . 81 L7 28 57N 95 21W
reetown, S. Leone . 50 G3 8 30N 13 17W
régate, L., Canada . 70 B5 53 15N 74 45W
regenal de la Sierra, Spain . 19 C2 38 10N 6 30W
reiburg = Fribourg, Switz. . 18 C7 46 49N 7 9 E
reiburg, Germany . 16 E4 47 59N 7 51 E
reire, Chile . 96 D2 38 54S 72 38W
reirina, Chile . 94 B1 30 5S 71 10W
reising, Germany . 16 D6 48 24N 11 45 E
reistadt, Austria . 16 D8 48 30N 14 30 E
réjus, France . 18 E7 43 25N 6 44 E
remantle, Australia . 61 F2 32 7S 115 47 E
remont, Calif., U.S.A. . 84 H4 37 32N 121 57W
remont, Mich., U.S.A. . 76 D3 43 28N 85 57W
remont, Nebr., U.S.A. . 80 E6 41 26N 96 30W
remont, Ohio, U.S.A. . 76 E4 41 21N 83 7W
remont →, U.S.A. . 83 G8 38 24N 110 42W
rench Camp, U.S.A. . 84 H5 37 53N 121 16W
rench Creek →, U.S.A. . 78 E5 41 24N 79 50W
rench Guiana ■, S. Amer. . 93 C8 4 0N 53 0W
rench Pass, N.Z. . 59 J4 40 55S 173 55 E
rench Polynesia ■, Pac. Oc. . 65 K13 20 0S 145 0W
renchman Cr. →, N. Amer. . 82 B10 48 31N 107 10W
renchman Cr. →, U.S.A. . 80 E4 40 14N 100 50W
resco →, Brazil . 93 E8 7 15S 51 30W
reshfield, C., Antarctica . 5 C10 68 25S 151 10 E
resnillo, Mexico . 86 C4 23 10N 103 0W
resno, U.S.A. . 84 J7 36 44N 119 47W
resno Reservoir, U.S.A. . 82 B9 48 36N 109 57W
rew →, Australia . 62 C2 20 0S 135 38 E
rewsburg, U.S.A. . 78 D5 42 3N 79 10W
reycinet Pen., Australia . 62 G4 42 10S 148 25 E
ria, C., Namibia . 56 B1 18 0S 12 0 E
riant, U.S.A. . 84 J7 36 59N 119 43W
rias, Argentina . 94 B2 28 40S 65 5W
ribourg, Switz. . 18 C7 46 49N 7 9 E
riday Harbor, U.S.A. . 84 B3 48 32N 123 1W
riedens, U.S.A. . 78 F6 40 3N 78 59W
riedrichshafen, Germany . 16 E5 47 39N 9 30 E
riendly Is. = Tonga ■, Pac. Oc. . 59 D11 19 50S 174 30W
riendship, U.S.A. . 78 D6 42 12N 78 8W
riesland □, Neths. . 15 A5 53 5N 5 50 E
rio, U.S.A. . 81 L5 28 26N 98 11W
rio, C., Brazil . 90 F6 22 50S 41 50W
ritch, U.S.A. . 81 H3 35 38N 101 36W
ritch, U.S.A. . 81 H4 35 38N 101 36W
robisher B., Canada . 69 B13 62 30N 66 0W
robisher Bay = Iqaluit, Canada . 69 B13 63 44N 68 31W
robisher L., Canada . 73 B7 56 20N 108 15W
rohavet, Norway . 8 E13 64 0N 9 30 E
rome, U.K. . 11 F5 51 14N 2 19W

Frome →, U.K. . 11 G5 50 41N 2 6W
Frome, L., Australia . 63 E2 30 45S 139 45 E
Front Range, U.S.A. . 74 C5 40 25N 105 45W
Front Royal, U.S.A. . 76 F6 38 55N 78 12W
Frontera, Canary Is. . 22 G2 27 47N 17 59W
Frontera, Mexico . 87 D6 18 30N 92 40W
Fronteras, Mexico . 86 A3 30 56N 109 31W
Frosinone, Italy . 20 D5 41 38N 13 19 E
Frostburg, U.S.A. . 76 F6 39 39N 78 56W
Frostisen, Norway . 8 B17 68 14N 17 10 E
Frøya, Norway . 8 E13 63 43N 8 40 E
Frunze = Bishkek, Kyrgyzstan . 26 E8 42 54N 74 46 E
Frutal, Brazil . 93 H9 20 0S 49 0W
Frýdek-Místek, Czech Rep. . 17 D10 49 40N 18 20 E
Fryeburg, U.S.A. . 79 B14 44 1N 70 59W
Fu Xian = Wafangdian, China . 35 E11 39 38N 121 58 E
Fu Xian, China . 34 G5 36 0N 109 20 E
Fucheng, China . 34 F9 37 50N 116 10 E
Fuchou = Fuzhou, China . 33 D6 26 5N 119 16 E
Fuchū, Japan . 31 G6 34 34N 133 14 E
Fuencaliente, Canary Is. . 22 F2 28 28N 17 50W
Fuencaliente, Pta., Canary Is. . 22 F2 28 27N 17 51W
Fuengirola, Spain . 19 D3 36 32N 4 41W
Fuentes de Oñoro, Spain . 19 B2 40 33N 6 52W
Fuerte →, Mexico . 86 B3 25 50N 109 25W
Fuerte Olimpo, Paraguay . 94 A4 21 0S 57 51W
Fuerteventura, Canary Is. . 22 F6 28 30N 14 0W
Fufeng, China . 34 G5 34 22N 108 0 E
Fugou, China . 34 G8 34 3N 114 25 E
Fugu, China . 34 E6 39 2N 111 3 E
Fuhai, China . 32 B3 47 2N 87 25 E
Fuḥaymī, Iraq . 44 C4 34 16N 42 10 E
Fuji, Japan . 31 G9 35 9N 138 39 E
Fuji-San, Japan . 31 G9 35 22N 138 44 E
Fuji-yoshida, Japan . 31 G9 35 30N 138 46 E
Fujian □, China . 33 D6 26 0N 118 0 E
Fujinomiya, Japan . 31 G9 35 10N 138 40 E
Fujisawa, Japan . 31 G9 35 22N 139 29 E
Fujiyama, Mt. = Fuji-San, Japan . 31 G9 35 22N 138 44 E
Fukien = Fujian □, China . 33 D6 26 0N 118 0 E
Fukuchiyama, Japan . 31 G7 35 19N 135 9 E
Fukue-Shima, Japan . 31 H4 32 40N 128 45 E
Fukui, Japan . 31 F8 36 5N 136 10 E
Fukui □, Japan . 31 G8 36 0N 136 12 E
Fukuoka, Japan . 31 H5 33 39N 130 21 E
Fukuoka □, Japan . 31 H5 33 30N 131 0 E
Fukushima, Japan . 30 F10 37 44N 140 28 E
Fukushima □, Japan . 30 F10 37 30N 140 15 E
Fukuyama, Japan . 31 G6 34 35N 133 20 E
Fulda, Germany . 16 C5 50 32N 9 40 E
Fulda →, Germany . 16 C5 51 25N 9 39 E
Fulford Harbour, Canada . 84 B3 48 47N 123 27W
Fullerton, Calif., U.S.A. . 85 M9 33 53N 117 56W
Fullerton, Nebr., U.S.A. . 80 E6 41 22N 97 58W
Fulongquan, China . 35 B13 44 20N 124 42 E
Fulton, Mo., U.S.A. . 80 F9 38 52N 91 57W
Fulton, N.Y., U.S.A. . 79 C8 43 19N 76 25W
Funabashi, Japan . 31 G10 35 45N 140 0 E
Funchal, Madeira . 22 D3 32 38N 16 54W
Fundación, Colombia . 92 A4 10 31N 74 11W
Fundão, Portugal . 19 B2 40 8N 7 30W
Fundy, B. of, Canada . 71 D6 45 0N 66 0W
Funing, Hebei, China . 35 E10 39 53N 119 12 E
Funing, Jiangsu, China . 35 H10 33 45N 119 50 E
Funiu Shan, China . 34 H7 33 30N 112 20 E
Funtua, Nigeria . 50 F7 11 30N 7 18 E
Fuping, Hebei, China . 34 E8 38 48N 114 12 E
Fuping, Shaanxi, China . 34 G5 34 42N 109 10 E
Furano, Japan . 30 C11 43 21N 142 23 E
Furāt, Nahr al →, Asia . 44 D5 31 0N 47 25 E
Fürg, Iran . 45 D7 28 18N 55 13 E
Furnás, Spain . 22 B8 39 3N 1 32 E
Furnas, Reprêsa de, Brazil . 95 A6 20 50S 45 30W
Furneaux Group, Australia . 62 G4 40 10S 147 50 E
Furqlus, Syria . 47 A6 34 36N 37 8 E
Fürstenwalde, Germany . 16 B8 52 22N 14 3 E
Fürth, Germany . 16 D6 49 28N 10 59 E
Furukawa, Japan . 30 E10 38 34N 140 58 E
Fury and Hecla Str., Canada . 69 B11 69 56N 84 0W
Fusagasugá, Colombia . 92 C4 4 21N 74 22W
Fushan, Shandong, China . 35 F11 37 30N 121 15 E
Fushan, Shanxi, China . 34 G6 35 58N 111 51 E
Fushun, China . 35 D12 41 50N 123 56 E
Fusong, China . 35 C14 42 20N 127 15 E
Fuxin, China . 35 C11 42 5N 121 48 E
Fuyang, China . 34 H8 33 0N 115 48 E
Fuyang He →, China . 34 E9 38 12N 117 0 E
Fuyu, China . 35 B13 45 12N 124 43 E
Fuzhou, China . 33 D6 26 5N 119 16 E
Fylde, U.K. . 10 D5 53 50N 2 58W
Fyn, Denmark . 9 J14 55 20N 10 30 E
Fyne, L., U.K. . 12 F3 55 59N 5 23W

G

Gabela, Angola . 52 G2 11 0S 14 24 E
Gabès, Tunisia . 51 B8 33 53N 10 2 E
Gabès, G. de, Tunisia . 51 B8 34 0N 10 30 E
Gabon ■, Africa . 52 E2 0 10S 10 0 E
Gaborone, Botswana . 56 C4 24 45S 25 57 E
Gabriels, U.S.A. . 79 B10 44 26N 74 12W
Gäbrik, Iran . 45 E8 25 44N 58 28 E
Gabrovo, Bulgaria . 21 C11 42 52N 25 19 E
Gāch Sār, Iran . 45 B6 36 7N 51 19 E
Gachsārān, Iran . 45 D6 30 15N 50 45 E
Gadag, India . 40 M9 15 30N 75 45 E
Gadap, Pakistan . 42 G2 25 5N 67 28 E
Gadarwara, India . 43 H8 22 50N 78 50 E
Gadhada, India . 42 J4 22 0N 71 35 E
Gadra, Pakistan . 42 G4 25 40N 70 38 E
Gadsden, U.S.A. . 77 H3 34 1N 86 1W
Gadwal, India . 40 L10 16 10N 77 50 E
Gaffney, U.S.A. . 77 H5 35 5N 81 39W
Gafsa, Tunisia . 50 B7 34 24N 8 43 E
Gagaria, India . 42 G4 25 43N 70 46 E
Gagnoa, Ivory C. . 50 G4 6 56N 5 16W
Gagnon, Canada . 71 B6 51 50N 68 5W
Gagnon, L., Canada . 73 A6 62 3N 110 27W
Gahini, Rwanda . 54 C3 1 50S 30 30 E
Gahmar, India . 43 G10 25 27N 83 49 E

Gai Xian = Gaizhou, China . 35 D12 40 22N 122 20 E
Gaïdhouronísi, Greece . 23 E7 34 53N 25 41 E
Gail, U.S.A. . 81 J4 32 46N 101 27W
Gaillimh = Galway, Ireland . 13 C2 53 17N 9 3W
Gaines, U.S.A. . 78 E7 41 46N 77 35W
Gainesville, Fla., U.S.A. . 77 L4 29 40N 82 20W
Gainesville, Ga., U.S.A. . 77 H4 34 18N 83 50W
Gainesville, Mo., U.S.A. . 81 G8 36 36N 92 26W
Gainesville, Tex., U.S.A. . 81 J6 33 38N 97 8W
Gainsborough, U.K. . 10 D7 53 24N 0 46W
Gairdner, L., Australia . 63 E2 31 30S 136 0 E
Gairloch, L., U.K. . 12 D3 57 43N 5 45W
Gaj →, Pakistan . 42 F2 26 26N 67 21 E
Gakuch, Pakistan . 43 A5 36 7N 73 45 E
Galán, Cerro, Argentina . 94 B2 25 55S 66 52W
Galana →, Kenya . 54 C5 3 9S 40 8 E
Galápagos, Pac. Oc. . 90 D1 0 0 91 0W
Galashiels, U.K. . 12 F6 55 37N 2 49W
Galați, Romania . 17 F15 45 27N 28 2 E
Galatina, Italy . 21 D8 40 10N 18 10 E
Galax, U.S.A. . 77 G5 36 40N 80 56W
Galcaio, Somali Rep. . 46 F4 6 30N 47 30 E
Galdhøpiggen, Norway . 9 F12 61 38N 8 18 E
Galeana, Mexico . 86 C4 24 50N 100 4W
Galeana, Nuevo León, Mexico . 86 A3 24 50N 100 4W
Galela, Indonesia . 37 D7 1 50N 127 49 E
Galena, U.S.A. . 68 B4 64 44N 156 56W
Galera Point, Trin. & Tob. . 89 D7 10 8N 61 0W
Galesburg, U.S.A. . 80 E9 40 57N 90 22W
Galeton, U.S.A. . 78 E7 41 44N 77 39W
Galich, Russia . 24 C7 58 22N 42 24 E
Galicia □, Spain . 19 A2 42 43N 7 45W
Galilee = Hagalil, Israel . 47 C4 32 53N 35 18 E
Galilee, L., Australia . 62 C4 22 20S 145 50 E
Galilee, Sea of = Yam Kinneret, Israel . 47 C4 32 45N 35 35 E
Galinoporni, Cyprus . 23 D13 35 31N 34 18 E
Galion, U.S.A. . 78 F2 40 44N 82 47W
Galiuro Mts., U.S.A. . 83 K8 32 30N 110 20W
Galiwinku, Australia . 62 A2 12 2S 135 34 E
Gallan Hd., U.K. . 12 C1 58 15N 7 2W
Gallatin, U.S.A. . 77 G2 36 24N 86 27W
Galle, Sri Lanka . 40 R12 6 5N 80 10 E
Gállego →, Spain . 19 B5 41 39N 0 51W
Gallegos →, Argentina . 96 G3 51 35S 69 0W
Galley Hd., Ireland . 13 E3 51 32N 8 55W
Gallinas, Pta., Colombia . 92 A4 12 28N 71 40W
Gallipoli = Gelibolu, Turkey . 21 D12 40 28N 26 43 E
Gallipoli, Italy . 21 D8 40 3N 17 58 E
Gallipolis, U.S.A. . 76 F4 38 49N 82 12W
Gällivare, Sweden . 8 C19 67 9N 20 40 E
Galloo I., U.S.A. . 79 C8 43 55N 76 25W
Galloway, U.K. . 12 F4 55 1N 4 29W
Galloway, Mull of, U.K. . 12 G4 54 39N 4 52W
Gallup, U.S.A. . 83 J9 35 32N 108 45W
Galoya, Sri Lanka . 40 Q12 8 10N 80 55 E
Galt, U.S.A. . 84 G5 38 15N 121 18W
Galty Mts., Ireland . 13 D3 52 22N 8 10W
Galtymore, Ireland . 13 D3 52 21N 8 11W
Galva, U.S.A. . 80 E9 41 10N 90 3W
Galveston, U.S.A. . 81 L7 29 18N 94 48W
Galveston B., U.S.A. . 81 L7 29 36N 94 50W
Gálvez, Argentina . 94 C3 32 0S 61 14W
Galway, Ireland . 13 C2 53 17N 9 3W
Galway □, Ireland . 13 C2 53 22N 9 1W
Galway B., Ireland . 13 C2 53 13N 9 10W
Gam →, Vietnam . 38 B5 21 55N 105 12 E
Gamagōri, Japan . 31 G8 34 50N 137 14 E
Gambat, Pakistan . 42 F3 27 17N 68 26 E
Gambhir →, India . 42 F6 26 58N 77 27 E
Gambia ■, W. Afr. . 50 F2 13 25N 16 0W
Gambia →, W. Afr. . 50 F2 13 28N 16 34W
Gambier, U.S.A. . 78 F2 40 22N 82 23W
Gambier, C., Australia . 60 B5 11 56S 130 57 E
Gambier Is., Australia . 63 F2 35 3S 136 30 E
Gambo, Canada . 71 C9 48 47N 54 13W
Gamboli, Pakistan . 42 E3 29 53N 68 24 E
Gamboma, Congo . 52 E3 1 55S 15 52 E
Gamlakarleby = Kokkola, Finland . 8 E20 63 50N 23 8 E
Gammon →, Canada . 73 C9 51 24N 95 44W
Gan Jiang →, China . 33 D6 29 15N 116 0 E
Ganado, U.S.A. . 83 J9 35 43N 109 33W
Gananoque, Canada . 79 B8 44 20N 76 10W
Ganāveh, Iran . 45 D6 29 35N 50 35 E
Gäncä, Azerbaijan . 25 F8 40 45N 46 20 E
Gancheng, China . 38 C7 18 51N 108 37 E
Gand = Gent, Belgium . 15 C3 51 2N 3 42 E
Ganda, Angola . 53 G2 13 3S 14 35 E
Gandajika, Dem. Rep. of the Congo . 52 F4 6 45S 23 57 E
Gandak →, India . 43 G11 25 39N 85 13 E
Gandava, Pakistan . 42 E2 28 32N 67 32 E
Gander, Canada . 71 C9 48 58N 54 35W
Gander L., Canada . 71 C9 48 58N 54 35W
Ganderowe Falls, Zimbabwe . 55 F2 17 20S 29 10 E
Gandhi Sagar, India . 42 G6 24 40N 75 40 E
Gandhinagar, India . 42 H5 23 15N 72 45 E
Gandía, Spain . 19 C5 38 58N 0 9W
Gando, Pta., Canary Is. . 22 G4 27 55N 15 22W
Ganedidalem = Gani, Indonesia . 37 E7 0 48S 128 14 E
Ganga →, India . 43 H14 23 20N 90 30 E
Ganga Sagar, India . 43 J13 21 38N 88 5 E
Gangan →, India . 43 E8 28 38N 78 58 E
Ganganagar, India . 42 E5 29 56N 73 56 E
Gangapur, India . 42 F7 26 32N 76 49 E
Gangaw, Burma . 41 H19 22 5N 94 5 E
Gangdisê Shan, China . 41 D12 31 20N 81 0 E
Ganges = Ganga →, India . 43 H14 23 20N 90 30 E
Ganges, Canada . 72 D4 48 51N 123 31W
Ganges, Mouths of the, India . 43 J14 21 30N 90 0 E
Gangoh, India . 42 E7 29 46N 77 18 E
Gangroti, India . 43 D8 30 50N 79 10 E
Gangtok, India . 41 F16 27 20N 88 37 E
Gangu, China . 34 G3 34 40N 105 15 E
Gangyao, China . 35 B14 44 12N 126 37 E
Gani, Indonesia . 37 E7 0 48S 128 14 E
Ganj, India . 43 F8 27 45N 78 57 E
Gannett Peak, U.S.A. . 82 E9 43 11N 109 39W
Ganquan, China . 34 F5 36 20N 109 20 E
Gansu □, China . 34 G3 36 0N 104 0 E
Ganta, Liberia . 50 G4 7 15N 8 59W
Gantheaume, C., Australia . 63 F2 36 4S 137 32 E

Gantheaume B., Australia . 61 E1 27 40S 114 10 E
Gantsevichi = Hantsavichy, Belarus . 17 B14 52 49N 26 30 E
Ganyem = Genyem, Indonesia . 37 E10 2 46S 140 12 E
Ganyu, China . 35 G10 34 50N 119 8 E
Ganzhou, China . 33 D6 25 51N 114 56 E
Gao, Mali . 50 E5 16 15N 0 5W
Gaomi, China . 35 F10 36 20N 119 42 E
Gaoping, China . 34 G7 35 45N 112 55 E
Gaotang, China . 34 F9 36 50N 116 15 E
Gaoua, Burkina Faso . 50 F5 10 20N 3 8W
Gaoual, Guinea . 50 F3 11 45N 13 25W
Gaoxiong = Kaohsiung, Taiwan . 33 D7 22 35N 120 16 E
Gaoyang, China . 34 E8 38 40N 115 45 E
Gaoyou Hu, China . 35 H10 32 45N 119 20 E
Gaoyuan, China . 35 F9 37 8N 117 58 E
Gap, France . 18 D7 44 33N 6 5 E
Gapat →, India . 43 G10 24 30N 82 28 E
Gapuwiyak, Australia . 62 A2 12 25S 135 43 E
Gar, China . 32 C2 32 10N 79 58 E
Garabogazköl Aylagy, Turkmenistan . 25 F9 41 0N 53 30 E
Garachico, Canary Is. . 22 F3 28 22N 16 46W
Garachiné, Panama . 88 E4 8 0N 78 12W
Garafia, Canary Is. . 22 F2 28 48N 17 57W
Garah, Australia . 63 D4 29 5S 149 38 E
Garajonay, Canary Is. . 22 F2 28 7N 17 14W
Garanhuns, Brazil . 93 E11 8 50S 36 30W
Garautha, India . 43 G8 25 34N 79 18 E
Garba Tula, Kenya . 54 B4 0 30N 38 32 E
Garberville, U.S.A. . 82 F2 40 6N 123 48W
Garbiyang, India . 43 D9 30 8N 80 54 E
Garda, L. di, Italy . 20 B4 45 40N 10 41 E
Garde L., Canada . 73 A7 62 50N 106 13W
Garden City, Ga., U.S.A. . 77 J5 32 6N 81 9W
Garden City, Kans., U.S.A. . 81 G4 37 58N 100 53W
Garden City, Tex., U.S.A. . 81 K4 31 52N 101 29W
Garden Grove, U.S.A. . 85 M9 33 47N 117 55W
Gardēz, Afghan. . 42 C3 33 37N 69 9 E
Gardiner, Maine, U.S.A. . 77 C11 44 14N 69 47W
Gardiner, Mont., U.S.A. . 82 D8 45 2N 110 22W
Gardiners I., U.S.A. . 79 E12 41 6N 72 6W
Gardner, U.S.A. . 79 D13 42 34N 71 59W
Gardner Canal, Canada . 72 C3 53 27N 128 8W
Gardnerville, U.S.A. . 84 G7 38 56N 119 45W
Gardo, Somali Rep. . 46 F4 9 30N 49 6 E
Garey, U.S.A. . 85 L6 34 53N 120 19W
Garfield, U.S.A. . 82 C5 47 1N 117 9W
Garforth, U.K. . 10 D6 53 47N 1 24W
Gargano, Mte., Italy . 20 D6 41 43N 15 43 E
Garibaldi Prov. Park, Canada . 72 D4 49 50N 122 40W
Garies, S. Africa . 56 E2 30 32S 17 59 E
Garigliano →, Italy . 20 D5 41 13N 13 45 E
Garissa, Kenya . 54 C4 0 25S 39 40 E
Garland, Tex., U.S.A. . 81 J6 32 55N 96 38W
Garland, Utah, U.S.A. . 82 F7 41 47N 112 10W
Garm, Tajikistan . 26 F8 39 0N 70 20 E
Garmāb, Iran . 45 C8 35 25N 56 45 E
Garmisch-Partenkirchen, Germany . 16 E6 47 30N 11 6 E
Garmsār, Iran . 45 C7 35 20N 52 25 E
Garner, U.S.A. . 80 D8 43 6N 93 36W
Garnett, U.S.A. . 80 F7 38 17N 95 14W
Garo Hills, India . 43 G14 25 30N 90 30 E
Garoe, Somali Rep. . 46 F4 8 25N 48 33 E
Garonne →, France . 18 D3 45 2N 0 36W
Garot, India . 42 G6 24 19N 75 41 E
Garoua, Cameroon . 51 G8 9 19N 13 21 E
Garrauli, India . 43 G8 25 5N 79 22 E
Garrison, Mont., U.S.A. . 82 C7 46 31N 112 49W
Garrison, N. Dak., U.S.A. . 80 B4 47 40N 101 25W
Garrison Res. = Sakakawea, L., U.S.A. . 80 B4 47 30N 101 25W
Garron Pt., U.K. . 13 A6 55 3N 5 59W
Garry →, U.K. . 12 E5 56 44N 3 47W
Garry, L., Canada . 68 B9 65 58N 100 18W
Garsen, Kenya . 54 C5 2 20S 40 5 E
Garson L., Canada . 73 B6 56 19N 110 2W
Garu, India . 43 H11 23 40N 84 14 E
Garub, Namibia . 56 D2 26 37S 16 0 E
Garut, Indonesia . 37 G12 7 14S 107 53 E
Garvie Mts., N.Z. . 59 L2 45 30S 168 50 E
Garwa = Garoua, Cameroon . 51 G8 9 19N 13 21 E
Garwa, India . 43 G10 24 11N 83 47 E
Gary, U.S.A. . 76 E2 41 36N 87 20W
Garzê, China . 32 C5 31 38N 100 1 E
Garzón, Colombia . 92 C3 2 10N 75 40W
Gas-San, Japan . 30 E10 38 32N 140 1 E
Gasan Kuli = Esenguly, Turkmenistan . 26 F6 37 37N 53 59 E
Gascogne, France . 18 E4 43 45N 0 20 E
Gascogne, G. de, Europe . 18 D2 44 0N 2 0W
Gascony = Gascogne, France . 18 E4 43 45N 0 20 E
Gascoyne →, Australia . 61 D1 24 52S 113 37 E
Gascoyne Junction, Australia . 61 E2 25 2S 115 17 E
Gashaka, Nigeria . 51 G8 7 20N 11 29 E
Gasherbrum, Pakistan . 43 B7 35 40N 76 40 E
Gashua, Nigeria . 51 F8 12 54N 11 0 E
Gaspé, Canada . 71 C7 48 52N 64 30W
Gaspé, C. de, Canada . 71 C7 48 48N 64 7W
Gaspé, Pén. de, Canada . 71 C6 48 45N 65 40W
Gaspésie, Parc de Conservation de la, Canada . 71 C6 48 55N 65 50W
Gasteiz = Vitoria-Gasteiz, Spain . 19 A4 42 50N 2 41W
Gastonia, U.S.A. . 77 H5 35 16N 81 11W
Gastre, Argentina . 96 E3 42 20S 69 15W
Gata, C., Cyprus . 23 E12 34 34N 33 2 E
Gata, C. de, Spain . 19 D4 36 41N 2 13W
Gata, Sierra de, Spain . 19 B2 40 20N 6 45W
Gataga →, Canada . 72 B3 58 35N 126 59W
Gatehouse of Fleet, U.K. . 12 G4 54 53N 4 12W
Gates, U.S.A. . 78 C7 43 9N 77 42W
Gateshead, U.K. . 10 C6 54 57N 1 35W
Gatesville, U.S.A. . 81 K6 31 26N 97 45W
Gaths, Zimbabwe . 55 G3 20 2S 30 32 E
Gatico, Chile . 94 A1 22 29S 70 20W
Gatineau, Canada . 79 A9 45 29N 75 42W
Gatineau →, Canada . 70 C4 45 27N 75 42W
Gatineau, Parc Nat. de la, Canada . 70 C4 45 40N 76 0W
Gatton, Australia . 63 D5 27 32S 152 17 E

Goldsworthy, *Australia*	**60 D2**	20 21S 119 30 E	
Goldthwaite, *U.S.A.*	**81 K5**	31 27N 98 34W	
Goleniów, *Poland*	**16 B8**	53 35N 14 50 E	
Golestának, *Iran*	**45 D7**	30 36N 54 14 E	
Goleta, *U.S.A.*	**85 L7**	34 27N 119 50W	
Golfito, *Costa Rica*	**88 E3**	8 41N 83 5W	
Golfo Aranci, *Italy*	**20 D3**	40 59N 9 38 E	
Goliad, *U.S.A.*	**81 L6**	28 40N 97 23W	
Golpâyegân, *Iran*	**45 C6**	33 27N 50 18 E	
Golra, *Pakistan*	**42 C5**	33 37N 72 56 E	
Golspie, *U.K.*	**12 D5**	57 58N 3 59W	
Goma, *Dem. Rep. of the Congo*	**54 C2**	1 37S 29 10 E	
Gomal Pass, *Pakistan*	**42 D3**	31 56N 69 20 E	
Gomati →, *India*	**43 G10**	25 32N 83 11 E	
Gombari, *Dem. Rep. of the Congo*	**54 B2**	2 45N 29 3 E	
Gombe, *Nigeria*	**51 F8**	10 19N 11 2 E	
Gombe →, *Tanzania*	**54 C3**	4 38S 31 40 E	
Gomera, *Canary Is.*	**22 F2**	28 7N 17 14W	
Gómez Palacio, *Mexico*	**86 B4**	25 40N 104 0W	
Gomishân, *Iran*	**45 B7**	37 4N 54 6 E	
Gomogomo, *Indonesia*	**37 F8**	6 39S 134 43 E	
Gomoh, *India*	**41 H15**	23 52N 86 10 E	
Gompa = Ganta, *Liberia*	**50 G4**	7 15N 8 59W	
Gonâbâd, *Iran*	**45 C8**	34 15N 58 45 E	
Gonaïves, *Haiti*	**89 C5**	19 20N 72 42W	
Gonâve, G. de la, *Haiti*	**89 C5**	19 29N 72 42W	
Gonâve, I. de la, *Haiti*	**89 C5**	18 45N 73 0W	
Gonbad-e Kâvûs, *Iran*	**45 B7**	37 20N 55 25 E	
Gonda, *India*	**43 F9**	27 9N 81 58 E	
Gondal, *India*	**42 J4**	21 58N 70 52 E	
Gonder, *Ethiopia*	**46 E2**	12 39N 37 30 E	
Gondia, *India*	**40 J12**	21 23N 80 10 E	
Gondola, *Mozam.*	**55 F3**	19 10S 33 37 E	
Gönen, *Turkey*	**21 D12**	40 6N 27 39 E	
Gonghe, *China*	**32 C5**	36 18N 100 32 E	
Gongolgon, *Australia*	**63 E4**	30 21S 146 54 E	
Gongzhuling, *China*	**35 C13**	43 30N 124 40 E	
Gonzales, *Calif., U.S.A.*	**84 J5**	36 30N 121 26W	
Gonzales, *Tex., U.S.A.*	**81 L6**	29 30N 97 27W	
González Chaves, *Argentina*	**94 D3**	38 2S 60 5W	
Good Hope, C. of, *S. Africa*	**56 E2**	34 24S 18 30 E	
Gooderham, *Canada*	**78 B6**	44 54N 78 21W	
Gooding, *U.S.A.*	**82 E6**	42 56N 114 43W	
Goodland, *U.S.A.*	**80 F4**	39 21N 101 43W	
Goodlow, *Canada*	**72 B4**	56 20N 120 8W	
Goodooga, *Australia*	**63 D4**	29 3S 147 28 E	
Goodsprings, *U.S.A.*	**85 K11**	35 49N 115 27W	
Goole, *U.K.*	**10 D7**	53 42N 0 53W	
Goolgowi, *Australia*	**63 E4**	33 58S 145 41 E	
Goolwa, *Australia*	**63 F2**	35 30S 138 47 E	
Goomalling, *Australia*	**61 F2**	31 15S 116 49 E	
Goomeri, *Australia*	**63 D5**	26 12S 152 6 E	
Goonda, *Mozam.*	**55 F3**	19 48S 33 57 E	
Goondiwindi, *Australia*	**63 D5**	28 30S 150 21 E	
Goongarrie, L., *Australia*	**61 F3**	30 3S 121 9 E	
Goonyella, *Australia*	**62 C4**	21 47S 147 58 E	
Goose →, *Canada*	**71 B7**	53 20N 60 35W	
Goose Creek, *U.S.A.*	**77 J5**	32 59N 80 2W	
Goose L., *U.S.A.*	**82 F3**	41 56N 120 26W	
Gop, *India*	**40 H6**	22 5N 69 50 E	
Gopalganj, *India*	**43 F11**	26 28N 84 30 E	
Göppingen, *Germany*	**16 D5**	48 42N 9 39 E	
Gorakhpur, *India*	**43 F10**	26 47N 83 23 E	
Gorda, *U.S.A.*	**84 K5**	35 53N 121 26W	
Gorda, Pta., *Canary Is.*	**22 F2**	28 45N 18 0W	
Gorda, Pta., *Nic.*	**88 D3**	14 20N 83 10W	
Gordan B., *Australia*	**60 B5**	11 35S 130 10 E	
Gordon, *U.S.A.*	**80 D3**	42 48N 102 12W	
Gordon →, *Australia*	**62 G4**	42 27S 145 30 E	
Gordon L., *Alta., Canada*	**73 B6**	56 30N 110 25W	
Gordon L., *N.W.T., Canada*	**72 A6**	63 5N 113 11W	
Gordonvale, *Australia*	**62 B4**	17 5S 145 50 E	
Gore, *Ethiopia*	**46 F2**	8 12N 35 32 E	
Gore, *N.Z.*	**59 M2**	46 5S 168 58 E	
Gore Bay, *Canada*	**70 C3**	45 57N 82 28W	
Gorey, *Ireland*	**13 D5**	52 41N 6 18W	
Gorg, *Iran*	**45 D8**	29 29N 59 43 E	
Gorgân, *Iran*	**45 B7**	36 50N 54 29 E	
Gorgona, I., *Colombia*	**92 C3**	3 0N 78 10W	
Gorham, *U.S.A.*	**79 B13**	44 23N 71 10W	
Goriganga →, *India*	**43 E9**	29 45N 80 23 E	
Gorinchem, *Neths.*	**15 C4**	51 50N 4 59 E	
Goris, *Armenia*	**25 G8**	39 31N 46 22 E	
Gorizia, *Italy*	**20 B5**	45 56N 13 37 E	
Gorki = Nizhniy Novgorod, *Russia*	**24 C7**	56 20N 44 0 E	
Gorkiy = Nizhniy Novgorod, *Russia*	**24 C7**	56 20N 44 0 E	
Gorkovskoye Vdkhr., *Russia*	**24 C7**	57 2N 43 4 E	
Görlitz, *Germany*	**16 C8**	51 9N 14 58 E	
Gorlovka = Horlivka, *Ukraine*	**25 E6**	48 19N 38 5 E	
Gorman, *U.S.A.*	**85 L8**	34 47N 118 51W	
Gorna Dzhumayo = Blagoevgrad, *Bulgaria*	**21 C10**	42 2N 23 5 E	
Gorna Oryakhovitsa, *Bulgaria*	**21 C11**	43 7N 25 40 E	
Gorno-Altay □, *Russia*	**26 D9**	51 0N 86 0 E	
Gorno-Altaysk, *Russia*	**26 D9**	51 50N 86 5 E	
Gornyatski, *Russia*	**24 A11**	67 32N 64 3 E	
Gornyy, *Russia*	**30 B6**	44 57N 133 59 E	
Gorodenka = Horodenka, *Ukraine*	**17 D13**	48 41N 25 29 E	
Gorodok = Horodok, *Ukraine*	**17 D12**	49 46N 23 32 E	
Gorokhov = Horokhiv, *Ukraine*	**17 C13**	50 30N 24 45 E	
Goromonzi, *Zimbabwe*	**55 F3**	17 52S 31 22 E	
Gorong, Kepulauan, *Indonesia*	**37 E8**	3 59S 131 25 E	
Gorongose →, *Mozam.*	**57 C5**	20 30S 34 40 E	
Gorongoza, *Mozam.*	**55 F3**	18 44S 34 2 E	
Gorongoza, Sa. da, *Mozam.*	**55 F3**	18 27S 34 2 E	
Gorontalo, *Indonesia*	**37 D6**	0 35N 123 5 E	
Gort, *Ireland*	**13 C3**	53 3N 8 49W	
Gortis, *Greece*	**23 D6**	35 4N 24 58 E	
Gorzów Wielkopolski, *Poland*	**16 B8**	52 43N 15 15 E	
Gosford, *Australia*	**63 E5**	33 23S 151 18 E	
Goshen, *Calif., U.S.A.*	**84 J7**	36 21N 119 25W	
Goshen, *Ind., U.S.A.*	**76 E3**	41 35N 85 50W	
Goshen, *N.Y., U.S.A.*	**79 E10**	41 24N 74 20W	
Goshogawara, *Japan*	**30 D10**	40 48N 140 27 E	

Goslar, *Germany*	**16 C6**	51 54N 10 25 E	
Gospič, *Croatia*	**16 F8**	44 35N 15 23 E	
Gosport, *U.K.*	**11 G6**	50 48N 1 9W	
Gosse →, *Australia*	**62 B1**	19 32S 134 37 E	
Göta älv →, *Sweden*	**9 H14**	57 42N 11 54 E	
Göta kanal, *Sweden*	**9 G16**	58 30N 15 58 E	
Götaland, *Sweden*	**9 G15**	57 30N 14 30 E	
Göteborg, *Sweden*	**9 H14**	57 43N 11 59 E	
Gotha, *Germany*	**16 C6**	50 56N 10 42 E	
Gothenburg = Göteborg, *Sweden*	**9 H14**	57 43N 11 59 E	
Gothenburg, *U.S.A.*	**80 E4**	40 56N 100 10W	
Gotland, *Sweden*	**9 H18**	57 30N 18 33 E	
Gotō-Rettō, *Japan*	**31 H4**	32 55N 129 5 E	
Gotska Sandön, *Sweden*	**9 G18**	58 24N 19 15 E	
Götsu, *Japan*	**31 G6**	35 0N 132 14 E	
Gott Pk., *Canada*	**72 C4**	50 18N 122 16W	
Göttingen, *Germany*	**16 C5**	51 31N 9 55 E	
Gottwaldov = Zlín, *Czech Rep.*	**17 D9**	49 14N 17 40 E	
Goubangzi, *China*	**35 D11**	41 20N 121 52 E	
Gouda, *Neths.*	**15 B4**	52 1N 4 42 E	
Goúdhoura, Ákra, *Greece*	**23 E8**	34 59N 26 6 E	
Gough I., *Atl. Oc.*	**2 G9**	40 10S 9 45W	
Gouin, Rés., *Canada*	**70 C5**	48 35N 74 40W	
Goulburn, *Australia*	**63 E4**	34 44S 149 44 E	
Goulburn Is., *Australia*	**62 A1**	11 40S 133 20 E	
Goulimine, *Morocco*	**50 C3**	28 56N 10 0W	
Gourits →, *S. Africa*	**56 E3**	34 21S 21 52 E	
Goúrnais, *Greece*	**23 D7**	35 19N 25 16 E	
Gouverneur, *U.S.A.*	**79 B9**	44 20N 75 28W	
Gouviá, *Greece*	**23 A3**	39 39N 19 50 E	
Governador Valadares, *Brazil*	**93 G10**	18 15S 41 57W	
Governor's Harbour, *Bahamas*	**88 A4**	25 10N 76 14W	
Govindgarh, *India*	**43 G9**	24 23N 81 18 E	
Gowan Ra., *Australia*	**62 D4**	25 0S 145 0 E	
Gowanda, *U.S.A.*	**78 D6**	42 28N 78 56W	
Gowd-e Zirreh, *Afghan.*	**40 E3**	29 45N 62 0 E	
Gower, *U.K.*	**11 F3**	51 35N 4 10W	
Gowna, L., *Ireland*	**13 C4**	53 51N 7 34W	
Goya, *Argentina*	**94 B4**	29 10S 59 10W	
Goyder Lagoon, *Australia*	**63 D2**	27 3S 138 58 E	
Goyllarisquisga, *Peru*	**92 F3**	10 31S 76 24W	
Goz Beïda, *Chad*	**51 F10**	12 10N 21 20 E	
Gozo, *Malta*	**23 C1**	36 3N 14 13 E	
Graaff-Reinet, *S. Africa*	**56 E3**	32 13S 24 32 E	
Gračac, *Croatia*	**16 F8**	44 18N 15 57 E	
Gracias a Dios, C., *Honduras*	**88 D3**	15 0N 83 10W	
Graciosa, I., *Canary Is.*	**22 E6**	29 15N 13 32W	
Grado, *Spain*	**19 A2**	43 23N 6 4W	
Grady, *U.S.A.*	**81 H3**	34 49N 103 19W	
Grafham Water, *U.K.*	**11 E7**	52 19N 0 18W	
Grafton, *Australia*	**63 D5**	29 38S 152 58 E	
Grafton, *N. Dak., U.S.A.*	**80 A6**	48 25N 97 25W	
Grafton, *W. Va., U.S.A.*	**76 F5**	39 21N 80 2W	
Graham, *Canada*	**70 C1**	49 20N 90 30W	
Graham, *U.S.A.*	**81 J5**	33 6N 98 35W	
Graham Bell, Ostrov = Greem-Bell, Ostrov, *Russia*	**26 A7**	81 0N 62 0 E	
Graham I., *B.C., Canada*	**72 C2**	53 40N 132 30W	
Graham I., *N.W.T., Canada*	**68 C6**	77 25N 90 30W	
Graham Land, *Antarctica*	**5 C17**	65 0S 64 0W	
Grahamstown, *S. Africa*	**56 E4**	33 19S 26 31 E	
Grahamsville, *U.S.A.*	**79 E10**	41 51N 74 33W	
Grain Coast, *W. Afr.*	**50 H3**	4 20N 10 0W	
Grajaú, *Brazil*	**93 E9**	5 50S 46 4W	
Grajaú →, *Brazil*	**93 D10**	3 41S 44 48W	
Grampian, *U.S.A.*	**78 F6**	40 58N 78 37W	
Grampian Highlands = Grampian Mts., *U.K.*	**12 E5**	56 50N 4 0W	
Grampian Mts., *U.K.*	**12 E5**	56 50N 4 0W	
Grampians, The, *Australia*	**63 F3**	37 0S 142 20 E	
Gran Canaria, *Canary Is.*	**22 G4**	27 55N 15 35W	
Gran Chaco, *S. Amer.*	**94 B3**	25 0S 61 0W	
Gran Paradiso, *Italy*	**18 D7**	45 33N 7 17 E	
Gran Sasso d'Itália, *Italy*	**20 C5**	42 27N 13 42 E	
Granada, *Nic.*	**88 D2**	11 58N 86 0W	
Granada, *Spain*	**19 D4**	37 10N 3 35W	
Granada, *U.S.A.*	**81 F3**	38 4N 102 19W	
Granadilla de Abona, *Canary Is.*	**22 F3**	28 7N 16 33W	
Granard, *Ireland*	**13 C4**	53 47N 7 30W	
Granbury, *U.S.A.*	**81 J6**	32 27N 97 47W	
Granby, *Canada*	**79 A12**	45 25N 72 45W	
Granby, *U.S.A.*	**82 F11**	40 5N 105 56W	
Grand →, *Canada*	**78 D5**	42 51N 79 34W	
Grand →, *Mo., U.S.A.*	**80 F8**	39 23N 93 7W	
Grand →, *S. Dak., U.S.A.*	**80 C4**	45 40N 100 45W	
Grand Bahama, *Bahamas*	**88 A4**	26 40N 78 30W	
Grand Bank, *Canada*	**71 C8**	47 6N 55 48W	
Grand Bassam, *Ivory C.*	**50 G5**	5 10N 3 49W	
Grand-Bourg, *Guadeloupe*	**89 C7**	15 53N 61 19W	
Grand Canal = Yun Ho →, *China*	**35 E9**	39 10N 117 10 E	
Grand Canyon, *U.S.A.*	**83 H7**	36 3N 112 9W	
Grand Canyon National Park, *U.S.A.*	**83 H7**	36 15N 112 30W	
Grand Cayman, *Cayman Is.*	**88 C3**	19 20N 81 20W	
Grand Centre, *Canada*	**73 C6**	54 25N 110 13W	
Grand Coulee, *U.S.A.*	**82 C4**	47 57N 119 0W	
Grand Coulee Dam, *U.S.A.*	**82 C4**	47 57N 118 59W	
Grand Erg du Bilma, *Niger*	**51 E8**	18 30N 14 0 E	
Grand Erg Occidental, *Algeria*	**50 B6**	30 20N 1 0 E	
Grand Erg Oriental, *Algeria*	**50 B7**	30 0N 6 30 E	
Grand Falls, *Canada*	**71 C6**	47 3N 67 44W	
Grand Falls-Windsor, *Canada*	**71 C8**	48 56N 55 40W	
Grand Forks, *Canada*	**72 D5**	49 0N 118 30W	
Grand Forks, *U.S.A.*	**80 B6**	47 55N 97 3W	
Grand Gorge, *U.S.A.*	**79 D10**	42 21N 74 29W	
Grand Haven, *U.S.A.*	**76 D2**	43 4N 86 13W	
Grand I., *Mich., U.S.A.*	**76 B2**	46 31N 86 40W	
Grand I., *N.Y., U.S.A.*	**78 D6**	43 0N 78 58W	
Grand Island, *U.S.A.*	**80 E5**	40 55N 98 21W	
Grand Isle, *La., U.S.A.*	**81 L9**	29 14N 90 0W	
Grand Isle, *Vt., U.S.A.*	**79 B11**	44 43N 73 18W	
Grand Junction, *U.S.A.*	**83 G9**	39 4N 108 33W	
Grand L., *N.B., Canada*	**71 C6**	45 57N 66 7W	
Grand L., *Nfld., Canada*	**71 C8**	49 0N 57 30W	
Grand L., *Nfld., Canada*	**71 B7**	53 40N 60 30W	
Grand L., *U.S.A.*	**81 L8**	29 55N 92 47W	
Grand Lake, *U.S.A.*	**82 F11**	40 15N 105 49W	

Grand Manan I., *Canada*	**71 D6**	44 45N 66 52W	
Grand Marais, *Canada*	**80 B9**	47 45N 90 25W	
Grand Marais, *U.S.A.*	**76 B3**	46 40N 85 59W	
Grand-Mère, *Canada*	**70 C5**	46 36N 72 40W	
Grand Prairie, *U.S.A.*	**81 J6**	32 47N 97 0W	
Grand Rapids, *Canada*	**73 C9**	53 12N 99 19W	
Grand Rapids, *Mich., U.S.A.*	**76 D2**	42 58N 85 40W	
Grand Rapids, *Minn., U.S.A.*	**80 B8**	47 14N 93 31W	
Grand St-Bernard, Col du, *Europe*	**18 D7**	45 50N 7 10 E	
Grand Teton, *U.S.A.*	**82 E8**	43 54N 111 50W	
Grand Teton National Park, *U.S.A.*	**82 D8**	43 50N 110 50W	
Grand Union Canal, *U.K.*	**11 E7**	52 7N 0 53W	
Grand View, *Canada*	**73 C8**	51 10N 100 42W	
Grande →, *Jujuy, Argentina*	**94 A2**	24 20S 65 2W	
Grande →, *Mendoza, Argentina*	**94 D2**	36 52S 69 45W	
Grande →, *Bahia, Brazil*	**93 F10**	11 30S 44 30W	
Grande →, *Minas Gerais, Brazil*	**93 H8**	20 6S 51 4W	
Grande, B., *Argentina*	**96 G3**	50 30S 68 20W	
Grande, Rio →, *U.S.A.*	**81 N6**	25 58N 97 9W	
Grande Baleine, R. de la →, *Canada*	**70 A4**	55 16N 77 47W	
Grande Cache, *Canada*	**72 C5**	53 53N 119 8W	
Grande-Entrée, *Canada*	**71 C7**	47 30N 61 40W	
Grande Prairie, *Canada*	**72 B5**	55 10N 118 50W	
Grande-Rivière, *Canada*	**71 C7**	48 26N 64 30W	
Grande-Vallée, *Canada*	**71 C6**	49 14N 65 8W	
Grandfalls, *U.S.A.*	**81 K3**	31 20N 102 51W	
Grandview, *U.S.A.*	**82 C4**	46 15N 119 54W	
Graneros, *Chile*	**94 C1**	34 5S 70 45W	
Grangemouth, *U.K.*	**12 E5**	56 1N 3 42W	
Granger, *U.S.A.*	**82 F9**	41 35N 109 58W	
Grangeville, *U.S.A.*	**82 D5**	45 56N 116 7W	
Granisle, *Canada*	**72 C3**	54 53N 126 13W	
Granite City, *U.S.A.*	**80 F9**	38 42N 90 9W	
Granite Falls, *U.S.A.*	**80 C7**	44 49N 95 33W	
Granite L., *Canada*	**71 C8**	48 8N 57 5W	
Granite Mt., *U.S.A.*	**85 M10**	33 5N 116 28W	
Granite Pk., *U.S.A.*	**82 D9**	45 10N 109 48W	
Graniteville, *U.S.A.*	**79 B12**	44 8N 72 29W	
Granity, *N.Z.*	**59 J3**	41 39S 171 51 E	
Granja, *Brazil*	**93 D10**	3 7S 40 50W	
Granollers, *Spain*	**19 B7**	41 39N 2 18 E	
Grant, *U.S.A.*	**80 E4**	40 53N 101 42W	
Grant, Mt., *U.S.A.*	**82 G4**	38 34N 118 48W	
Grant City, *U.S.A.*	**80 E7**	40 29N 94 25W	
Grant I., *Australia*	**60 B5**	11 10S 132 52 E	
Grant Range, *U.S.A.*	**83 G6**	38 30N 115 25W	
Grantham, *U.K.*	**10 E7**	52 55N 0 38W	
Grantown-on-Spey, *U.K.*	**12 D5**	57 20N 3 36W	
Grants, *U.S.A.*	**83 J10**	35 9N 107 52W	
Grants Pass, *U.S.A.*	**82 E2**	42 26N 123 19W	
Grantsville, *U.S.A.*	**82 F7**	40 36N 112 28W	
Granville, *France*	**18 B3**	48 50N 1 35W	
Granville, *N. Dak., U.S.A.*	**80 A4**	48 16N 100 47W	
Granville, *N.Y., U.S.A.*	**79 C11**	43 24N 73 16W	
Granville, *Ohio, U.S.A.*	**78 F2**	40 4N 82 31W	
Granville L., *Canada*	**73 B8**	56 18N 100 30W	
Graskop, *S. Africa*	**57 C5**	24 56S 30 49 E	
Grass →, *Canada*	**73 B9**	56 3N 96 33W	
Grass Range, *U.S.A.*	**82 C9**	47 0N 109 0W	
Grass River Prov. Park, *Canada*	**73 C8**	54 40N 100 50W	
Grass Valley, *Calif., U.S.A.*	**84 F6**	39 13N 121 4W	
Grass Valley, *Oreg., U.S.A.*	**82 D3**	45 22N 120 47W	
Grasse, *France*	**18 E7**	43 38N 6 56 E	
Grassflat, *U.S.A.*	**78 F6**	41 0N 78 6W	
Grasslands Nat. Park, *Canada*	**73 D7**	49 11N 107 38W	
Grassy, *Australia*	**62 G3**	40 3S 144 5 E	
Graulhet, *France*	**18 E4**	43 45N 1 59 E	
Gravelbourg, *Canada*	**73 D7**	49 50N 106 35W	
's-Gravenhage, *Neths.*	**15 B4**	52 7N 4 17 E	
Gravenhurst, *Canada*	**78 B5**	44 52N 79 20W	
Gravesend, *Australia*	**63 D5**	29 35S 150 20 E	
Gravesend, *U.K.*	**11 F8**	51 26N 0 22 E	
Gravois, Pointe-à-, *Haiti*	**89 C5**	18 15N 73 56W	
Grayling, *U.S.A.*	**76 C3**	44 40N 84 43W	
Grays Harbor, *U.S.A.*	**82 C1**	46 59N 124 1W	
Grays L., *U.S.A.*	**82 E8**	43 4N 111 26W	
Grays River, *U.S.A.*	**84 D3**	46 21N 123 37W	
Graz, *Austria*	**16 E8**	47 4N 15 27 E	
Greasy L., *Canada*	**72 A4**	62 55N 122 12W	
Great Abaco I., *Bahamas*	**88 A4**	26 25N 77 10W	
Great Artesian Basin, *Australia*	**62 C3**	23 0S 144 0 E	
Great Australian Bight, *Australia*	**61 F5**	33 30S 130 0 E	
Great Bahama Bank, *Bahamas*	**88 B4**	23 15N 78 0W	
Great Barrier I., *N.Z.*	**59 G5**	36 11S 175 25 E	
Great Barrier Reef, *Australia*	**62 B4**	18 0S 146 50 E	
Great Barrington, *U.S.A.*	**79 D11**	42 12N 73 22W	
Great Basin, *U.S.A.*	**82 G5**	40 0N 117 0W	
Great Basin Nat. Park, *U.S.A.*	**82 G6**	38 55N 114 14W	
Great Bear →, *Canada*	**68 B7**	65 0N 124 0W	
Great Bear L., *Canada*	**68 B8**	65 30N 120 0W	
Great Belt = Store Bælt, *Denmark*	**9 J14**	55 20N 11 0 E	
Great Bend, *Kans., U.S.A.*	**80 F5**	38 22N 98 46W	
Great Bend, *Pa., U.S.A.*	**79 E9**	41 58N 75 45W	
Great Blasket I., *Ireland*	**13 D1**	52 6N 10 32W	
Great Britain, *Europe*	**6 E5**	54 0N 2 15W	
Great Codroy, *Canada*	**71 C8**	47 51N 59 16W	
Great Dividing Ra., *Australia*	**62 C4**	23 0S 146 0 E	
Great Driffield = Driffield, *U.K.*	**10 C7**	54 0N 0 26W	
Great Exuma I., *Bahamas*	**88 B4**	23 30N 75 50W	
Great Falls, *U.S.A.*	**82 C8**	47 30N 111 17W	
Great Fish = Groot Vis →, *S. Africa*	**56 E4**	33 28S 27 5 E	
Great Guana Cay, *Bahamas*	**88 B4**	24 0N 76 20W	
Great Inagua I., *Bahamas*	**89 B5**	21 0N 73 20W	
Great Indian Desert = Thar Desert, *India*	**42 F5**	28 0N 72 0 E	
Great Karoo, *S. Africa*	**56 E3**	31 55S 21 0 E	
Great Lake, *Australia*	**62 G4**	41 50S 146 40 E	
Great Lakes, *N. Amer.*	**66 E11**	46 0N 84 0W	
Great Malvern, *U.K.*	**11 E5**	52 7N 2 18W	
Great Miami →, *U.S.A.*	**76 F3**	39 20N 84 40W	
Great Ormes Head, *U.K.*	**10 D4**	53 20N 3 52W	

Great Ouse →, *U.K.*	**10 E8**	52 48N 0 21 E	
Great Palm I., *Australia*	**62 B4**	18 45S 146 40 E	
Great Plains, *N. Amer.*	**74 A6**	47 0N 105 0W	
Great Ruaha →, *Tanzania*	**54 D4**	7 56S 37 52 E	
Great Sacandaga Res., *U.S.A.*	**79 C10**	43 6N 74 16W	
Great Saint Bernard Pass = Grand St-Bernard, Col du, *Europe*	**18 D7**	45 50N 7 10 E	
Great Salt L., *U.S.A.*	**82 F7**	41 15N 112 40W	
Great Salt Lake Desert, *U.S.A.*	**82 F7**	40 50N 113 30W	
Great Salt Plains L., *U.S.A.*	**81 G5**	36 45N 98 8W	
Great Sandy Desert, *Australia*	**60 D3**	21 0S 124 0 E	
Great Sangi = Sangihe, Pulau, *Indonesia*	**37 D7**	3 45N 125 30 E	
Great Skellig, *Ireland*	**13 E1**	51 47N 10 33W	
Great Slave L., *Canada*	**72 A5**	61 23N 115 38W	
Great Smoky Mts. Nat. Park, *U.S.A.*	**77 H4**	35 40N 83 40W	
Great Snow Mt., *Canada*	**72 B4**	57 26N 124 0W	
Great Stour = Stour →, *U.K.*	**11 F9**	51 18N 1 22 E	
Great Victoria Desert, *Australia*	**61 E4**	29 30S 126 30 E	
Great Wall, *China*	**34 E5**	38 30N 109 30 E	
Great Whernside, *U.K.*	**10 C6**	54 10N 1 58W	
Great Yarmouth, *U.K.*	**11 E9**	52 37N 1 44 E	
Greater Antilles, *W. Indies*	**89 C5**	17 40N 74 0W	
Greater London □, *U.K.*	**11 F7**	51 31N 0 6W	
Greater Manchester □, *U.K.*	**10 D5**	53 30N 2 15W	
Greater Sunda Is., *Indonesia*	**36 F4**	7 0S 112 0 E	
Greco, C., *Cyprus*	**23 E13**	34 57N 34 5 E	
Gredos, Sierra de, *Spain*	**19 B3**	40 20N 5 0W	
Greece, *U.S.A.*	**78 C7**	43 13N 77 41W	
Greece ■, *Europe*	**21 E9**	40 0N 23 0 E	
Greeley, *Colo., U.S.A.*	**80 E2**	40 25N 104 42W	
Greeley, *Nebr., U.S.A.*	**80 E5**	41 33N 98 32W	
Greem-Bell, Ostrov, *Russia*	**26 A7**	81 0N 62 0 E	
Green, *U.S.A.*	**82 E2**	43 9N 123 22W	
Green →, *Ky., U.S.A.*	**76 G2**	37 54N 87 30W	
Green →, *Utah, U.S.A.*	**83 G9**	38 11N 109 53W	
Green B., *U.S.A.*	**76 C2**	45 0N 87 30W	
Green Bay, *U.S.A.*	**76 C2**	44 31N 88 0W	
Green C., *Australia*	**63 F5**	37 13S 150 1 E	
Green Cove Springs, *U.S.A.*	**77 L5**	29 59N 81 42W	
Green Lake, *Canada*	**73 C7**	54 17N 107 47W	
Green Mts., *U.S.A.*	**79 C12**	43 45N 72 45W	
Green River, *Utah, U.S.A.*	**83 G8**	38 59N 110 10W	
Green River, *Wyo., U.S.A.*	**82 F9**	41 32N 109 28W	
Green Valley, *U.S.A.*	**83 L8**	31 52N 110 56W	
Greenbank, *U.S.A.*	**84 B4**	48 6N 122 34W	
Greenbush, *Mich., U.S.A.*	**78 B1**	44 35N 83 19W	
Greenbush, *Minn., U.S.A.*	**80 A6**	48 42N 96 11W	
Greencastle, *U.S.A.*	**76 F2**	39 38N 86 52W	
Greene, *U.S.A.*	**79 D9**	42 20N 75 46W	
Greenfield, *Calif., U.S.A.*	**84 J5**	36 19N 121 15W	
Greenfield, *Calif., U.S.A.*	**85 K8**	35 15N 119 0W	
Greenfield, *Ind., U.S.A.*	**76 F3**	39 47N 85 46W	
Greenfield, *Iowa, U.S.A.*	**80 E7**	41 18N 94 28W	
Greenfield, *Mass., U.S.A.*	**79 D12**	42 35N 72 36W	
Greenfield, *Mo., U.S.A.*	**81 G8**	37 25N 93 51W	
Greenfield Park, *Canada*	**79 A11**	45 29N 73 29W	
Greenland ■, *N. Amer.*	**4 C5**	66 0N 45 0W	
Greenland Sea, *Arctic*	**4 B7**	73 0N 10 0W	
Greenock, *U.K.*	**12 F4**	55 57N 4 46W	
Greenore, *Ireland*	**13 B5**	54 2N 6 8W	
Greenore Pt., *Ireland*	**13 D5**	52 14N 6 19W	
Greenough, *Australia*	**61 E1**	28 58S 114 43 E	
Greenough →, *Australia*	**61 E1**	28 51S 114 38 E	
Greenport, *U.S.A.*	**79 E12**	41 6N 72 22W	
Greensboro, *Ga., U.S.A.*	**77 J4**	33 35N 83 11W	
Greensboro, *N.C., U.S.A.*	**77 G6**	36 4N 79 48W	
Greensburg, *Ind., U.S.A.*	**76 F3**	39 20N 85 29W	
Greensburg, *Kans., U.S.A.*	**81 G5**	37 36N 99 18W	
Greensburg, *Pa., U.S.A.*	**78 F5**	40 18N 79 33W	
Greenstone Pt., *U.K.*	**12 D3**	57 55N 5 37W	
Greenvale, *Australia*	**62 B4**	18 59S 145 7 E	
Greenville, *Ala., U.S.A.*	**77 K2**	31 50N 86 38W	
Greenville, *Calif., U.S.A.*	**84 E6**	40 8N 120 57W	
Greenville, *Maine, U.S.A.*	**77 C11**	45 28N 69 35W	
Greenville, *Mich., U.S.A.*	**76 D3**	43 11N 85 15W	
Greenville, *Miss., U.S.A.*	**81 J9**	33 24N 91 4W	
Greenville, *Mo., U.S.A.*	**81 G9**	37 8N 90 27W	
Greenville, *N.C., U.S.A.*	**77 H7**	35 37N 77 23W	
Greenville, *N.H., U.S.A.*	**79 D13**	42 46N 71 49W	
Greenville, *N.Y., U.S.A.*	**79 D10**	42 25N 74 1W	
Greenville, *Ohio, U.S.A.*	**76 E3**	40 6N 84 38W	
Greenville, *Pa., U.S.A.*	**78 E4**	41 24N 80 23W	
Greenville, *S.C., U.S.A.*	**77 H4**	34 51N 82 24W	
Greenville, *Tenn., U.S.A.*	**77 G4**	36 13N 82 51W	
Greenville, *Tex., U.S.A.*	**81 J6**	33 8N 96 7W	
Greenwater Lake Prov. Park, *Canada*	**73 C8**	52 32N 103 30W	
Greenwich, *U.K.*	**11 F8**	51 29N 0 1 E	
Greenwich, *Conn., U.S.A.*	**79 E11**	41 2N 73 38W	
Greenwich, *N.Y., U.S.A.*	**79 C11**	43 5N 73 30W	
Greenwich, *Ohio, U.S.A.*	**78 E2**	41 2N 82 31W	
Greenwood, *Canada*	**72 D5**	49 10N 118 40W	
Greenwood, *Ark., U.S.A.*	**81 H7**	35 13N 94 16W	
Greenwood, *Miss., U.S.A.*	**81 J9**	33 31N 90 11W	
Greenwood, *S.C., U.S.A.*	**77 H4**	34 12N 82 10W	
Greenwood, Mt., *Australia*	**60 B5**	13 48S 130 4 E	
Gregory, *U.S.A.*	**80 D5**	43 14N 99 20W	
Gregory →, *Australia*	**62 B2**	17 53S 139 17 E	
Gregory, L., *S. Austral., Australia*	**63 D2**	28 55S 139 0 E	
Gregory, L., *W. Austral., Australia*	**61 E2**	25 38S 119 58 E	
Gregory Downs, *Australia*	**62 B2**	18 35S 138 45 E	
Gregory L., *Australia*	**60 D4**	20 0S 127 40 E	
Gregory Ra., *Queens., Australia*	**62 B3**	19 30S 143 40 E	
Gregory Ra., *W. Austral., Australia*	**60 D3**	21 20S 121 12 E	
Greifswald, *Germany*	**16 A7**	54 5N 13 23 E	
Greiz, *Germany*	**16 C7**	50 39N 12 10 E	
Gremikha, *Russia*	**24 A6**	67 59N 39 47 E	
Grená, *Denmark*	**9 H14**	56 25N 10 53 E	
Grenada, *U.S.A.*	**81 J10**	33 47N 89 49W	
Grenada ■, *W. Indies*	**89 D7**	12 10N 61 40W	
Grenadier I., *U.S.A.*	**79 B8**	44 3N 76 22W	
Grenadines, *W. Indies*	**89 D7**	12 40N 61 20W	

123

Hamadān □, *Iran* **45 C6** 35 0N 49 0 E
Hamāh, *Syria* **44 C3** 35 5N 36 40 E
Hamamatsu, *Japan* **31 G8** 34 45N 137 45 E
Hamar, *Norway* **9 F14** 60 48N 11 7 E
Hamāta, Gebel, *Egypt* **44 E2** 24 17N 35 0 E
Hambantota, *Sri Lanka* . . **40 R12** 6 10N 81 10 E
Hamber Prov. Park, *Canada* **72 C5** 52 20N 118 0W
Hamburg, *Germany* **16 B5** 53 33N 9 59 E
Hamburg, *Ark., U.S.A.* . . . **81 J9** 33 14N 91 48W
Hamburg, *N.Y., U.S.A.* . . . **78 D6** 42 43N 78 50W
Hamburg, *Pa., U.S.A.* **79 F9** 40 33N 75 59W
Ḥamḍ, W. al ←, *Si. Arabia* **44 E3** 24 55N 36 20 E
Hamden, *U.S.A.* **79 E12** 41 23N 72 54W
Häme, *Finland* **9 F20** 61 38N 25 10 E
Hämeenlinna, *Finland* **9 F21** 61 0N 24 28 E
Hamelin Pool, *Australia* . . **61 E1** 26 22S 114 20 E
Hameln, *Germany* **16 B5** 52 6N 9 21 E
Hamerkaz □, *Israel* **47 C3** 32 15N 34 55 E
Hamersley Ra., *Australia* . . **60 D2** 22 0S 117 45 E
Hamhung, *N. Korea* **35 E14** 39 54N 127 30 E
Hami, *China* **32 B4** 42 55N 93 25 E
Hamilton, *Australia* **63 F3** 37 45S 142 2 E
Hamilton, *Canada* **78 C5** 43 15N 79 50W
Hamilton, *N.Z.* **59 G5** 37 47S 175 19 E
Hamilton, *U.K.* **12 F4** 55 46N 4 2W
Hamilton, *Ala., U.S.A.* . . . **77 H1** 34 9N 87 59W
Hamilton, *Mont., U.S.A.* . . **82 C6** 46 15N 114 10W
Hamilton, *N.Y., U.S.A.* . . . **79 D9** 42 50N 75 33W
Hamilton, *Ohio, U.S.A.* . . . **76 F3** 39 24N 84 34W
Hamilton, *Tex., U.S.A.* . . . **81 K5** 31 42N 98 7W
Hamilton ←, *Australia* . . . **62 C2** 23 30S 139 47 E
Hamilton City, *U.S.A.* **84 F4** 39 45N 122 1W
Hamilton Inlet, *Canada* . . . **71 B8** 54 0N 57 30W
Hamilton Mt., *U.S.A.* . . . **79 C10** 43 25N 74 22W
Hamina, *Finland* **9 F22** 60 34N 27 12 E
Hamirpur, *H.P., India* . . . **42 D7** 31 41N 76 31 E
Hamirpur, *Ut. P., India* . . **43 G9** 25 57N 80 9 E
Hamlet, *U.S.A.* **77 H6** 34 53N 79 42W
Hamley Bridge, *Australia* . . **63 E2** 34 17S 138 35 E
Hamlin = Hameln, *Germany* **16 B5** 52 6N 9 21 E
Hamlin, *N.Y., U.S.A.* **78 C7** 43 17N 77 55W
Hamlin, *Tex., U.S.A.* **81 J4** 32 53N 100 8W
Hamm, *Germany* **16 C4** 51 40N 7 50 E
Ḩammār, Hawr al, *Iraq* . . **44 D5** 30 50N 47 10 E
Hammerfest, *Norway* **8 A20** 70 39N 23 41 E
Hammond, *Ind., U.S.A.* . . . **76 E2** 41 38N 87 30W
Hammond, *La., U.S.A.* . . . **81 K9** 30 30N 90 28W
Hammond, *N.Y., U.S.A.* . . **79 B9** 44 27N 75 42W
Hammondsport, *U.S.A.* . . . **78 D7** 42 25N 77 13W
Hammonton, *U.S.A.* **76 F8** 39 39N 74 48W
Hampden, *N.Z.* **59 L3** 45 18S 170 50 E
Hampshire □, *U.K.* **11 F6** 51 7N 1 23W
Hampshire Downs, *U.K.* . . **11 F6** 51 15N 1 10W
Hampton, *N.B., Canada* . . . **71 C6** 45 32N 65 51W
Hampton, *Ont., Canada* . . . **78 C6** 43 58N 78 45W
Hampton, *Ark., U.S.A.* . . . **81 J8** 33 32N 92 28W
Hampton, *Iowa, U.S.A.* . . . **80 D8** 42 45N 93 13W
Hampton, *N.H., U.S.A.* . . **79 D14** 42 57N 70 50W
Hampton, *S.C., U.S.A.* . . . **77 J5** 32 52N 81 7W
Hampton, *Va., U.S.A.* **76 G7** 37 2N 76 21W
Hampton Bays, *U.S.A.* . . . **79 F12** 40 53N 72 30W
Hampton Tableland,
 Australia **61 F4** 32 0S 127 0 E
Hamyang, *S. Korea* **35 G14** 35 32N 127 42 E
Han Pijesak, *Bos.-H.* **21 B8** 44 5N 18 57 E
Hanak, *Si. Arabia* **44 E3** 25 32N 37 0 E
Hanamaki, *Japan* **30 E10** 39 23N 141 7 E
Hanang, *Tanzania* **54 C4** 4 30S 35 25 E
Hanau, *Germany* **16 C5** 50 7N 8 56 E
Hanbogd = Ihbulag,
 Mongolia **34 C4** 43 11N 107 10 E
Hancheng, *China* **34 G6** 35 31N 110 25 E
Hancock, *Mich., U.S.A.* . . **80 B10** 47 8N 88 35W
Hancock, *N.Y., U.S.A.* . . . **79 E9** 41 57N 75 17W
Handa, *Japan* **31 G8** 34 53N 136 55 E
Handan, *China* **34 F8** 36 35N 114 28 E
Handeni, *Tanzania* **54 D4** 5 25S 38 2 E
Handwara, *India* **43 B6** 34 21N 74 20 E
Hanegev, *Israel* **47 E4** 30 50N 35 0 E
Hanford, *U.S.A.* **84 J7** 36 20N 119 39W
Hang Chat, *Thailand* **38 C2** 18 20N 99 21 E
Hang Dong, *Thailand* **38 C2** 18 41N 98 55 E
Hangang ←, *S. Korea* . . . **35 F14** 37 50N 126 30 E
Hangayn Nuruu, *Mongolia* . **32 B4** 47 30N 99 0 E
Hangchou = Hangzhou,
 China **33 C7** 30 18N 120 11 E
Hanggin Houqi, *China* **34 D4** 40 58N 107 4 E
Hanggin Qi, *China* **34 E5** 39 52N 108 50 E
Hangu, *China* **35 E9** 39 18N 117 53 E
Hangzhou, *China* **33 C7** 30 18N 120 11 E
Hangzhou Wan, *China* . . . **33 C7** 30 15N 120 45 E
Hanhongor, *Mongolia* **34 C3** 43 55N 104 28 E
Ḩanīdh, *Si. Arabia* **45 E6** 26 35N 48 38 E
Ḩanīsh, *Yemen* **46 E3** 13 45N 42 46 E
Hankinson, *U.S.A.* **80 B6** 46 4N 96 54W
Hanko, *Finland* **9 G20** 59 50N 22 57 E
Hanksville, *U.S.A.* **83 G8** 38 22N 110 43W
Hanle, *India* **43 C8** 32 42N 79 4 E
Hanmer Springs, *N.Z.* . . . **59 K4** 42 32S 172 50 E
Hann ←, *Australia* **60 C4** 17 26S 126 17 E
Hann, Mt., *Australia* **60 C4** 15 45S 126 0 E
Hanna, *Canada* **72 C6** 51 40N 111 54W
Hanna, *U.S.A.* **82 F10** 41 52N 106 34W
Hannah B., *Canada* **70 B4** 51 40N 80 0W
Hannibal, *Mo., U.S.A.* . . . **80 F9** 39 42N 91 22W
Hannibal, *N.Y., U.S.A.* . . . **79 C8** 43 19N 76 35W
Hannover, *Germany* **16 B5** 52 22N 9 46 E
Hanoi, *Vietnam* **32 D5** 21 5N 105 55 E
Hanover = Hannover,
 Germany **16 B5** 52 22N 9 46 E
Hanover, *Canada* **78 B3** 44 9N 81 2W
Hanover, *S. Africa* **56 E3** 31 4S 24 29 E
Hanover, *N.H., U.S.A.* . . **79 C12** 43 42N 72 17W
Hanover, *Ohio, U.S.A.* . . . **78 F2** 40 4N 82 16W
Hanover, *Pa., U.S.A.* **76 F7** 39 48N 76 59W
Hanover, I., *Chile* **96 G2** 51 0S 74 50W
Hansdiha, *India* **43 G12** 24 36N 87 5 E
Hansi, *India* **42 E6** 29 10N 75 57 E
Hanson, L., *Australia* **63 E2** 31 0S 136 15 E
Hantsavichy, *Belarus* **17 B14** 52 49N 26 30 E
Hanumangarh, *India* **42 E6** 29 35N 74 19 E
Hanzhong, *China* **34 H4** 33 10N 107 1 E
Haora, *India* **43 H13** 22 37N 88 20 E
Haparanda, *Sweden* **8 D21** 65 52N 24 8 E
Happy, *U.S.A.* **81 H4** 34 45N 101 52W

Happy Camp, *U.S.A.* **82 F2** 41 48N 123 23W
Happy Valley-Goose Bay,
 Canada **71 B7** 53 15N 60 20W
Hapsu, *N. Korea* **35 D15** 41 13N 128 51 E
Hapur, *India* **42 E7** 28 45N 77 45 E
Ḥaql, *Si. Arabia* **47 F3** 29 10N 34 58 E
Har, *Indonesia* **37 F8** 5 16S 133 14 E
Har-Ayrag, *Mongolia* **34 B5** 45 47N 109 16 E
Har Hu, *China* **32 C4** 38 20N 97 38 E
Har Us Nuur, *Mongolia* . . . **32 B4** 48 0N 92 0 E
Har Yehuda, *Israel* **47 D3** 31 35N 34 57 E
Ḩaraḍ, *Si. Arabia* **46 C4** 24 22N 49 0 E
Haranomachi, *Japan* **30 F10** 37 38N 140 58 E
Harare, *Zimbabwe* **55 F3** 17 43S 31 2 E
Harbin, *China* **35 B14** 45 48N 126 40 E
Harbor Beach, *U.S.A.* **78 C2** 43 51N 82 39W
Harbour Breton, *Canada* . . **71 C8** 47 29N 55 50W
Harbour Deep, *Canada* . . . **71 B8** 50 25N 56 32W
Harda, *India* **42 H7** 22 27N 77 5 E
Hardangerfjorden, *Norway* . **9 F12** 60 5N 6 0 E
Hardangervidda, *Norway* . . **9 F12** 60 7N 7 20 E
Hardap Dam, *Namibia* . . . **56 C2** 24 32S 17 50 E
Hardenberg, *Neths.* **15 B6** 52 34N 6 37 E
Harderwijk, *Neths.* **15 B5** 52 21N 5 38 E
Hardey ←, *Australia* **60 D2** 22 45S 116 8 E
Hardin, *U.S.A.* **82 D10** 45 44N 107 37W
Harding, *S. Africa* **57 E4** 30 35S 29 55 E
Harding Ra., *Australia* **60 C3** 16 17S 124 55 E
Hardisty, *Canada* **72 C6** 52 40N 111 18W
Hardoi, *India* **43 F9** 27 26N 80 6 E
Hardwar = Haridwar, *India* **42 E8** 29 58N 78 9 E
Hardwick, *U.S.A.* **79 B12** 44 30N 72 22W
Hardy, Pen., *Chile* **96 H3** 55 30S 68 20W
Hare B., *Canada* **71 B8** 51 15N 55 45W
Hareid, *Norway* **9 E12** 62 22N 6 1 E
Harer, *Ethiopia* **46 F3** 9 20N 42 8 E
Hargeisa, *Somali Rep.* **46 F3** 9 30N 44 2 E
Hari ←, *Indonesia* **36 E2** 1 16S 104 5 E
Haria, *Canary Is.* **22 E6** 29 8N 13 32W
Haridwar, *India* **42 E8** 29 58N 78 9 E
Harim, Jabal al, *Oman* . . . **45 E8** 25 58N 56 14 E
Haringhata ←, *Bangla.* . . . **41 J16** 22 0N 89 58 E
Härjedalen, *Sweden* **9 E15** 62 22N 13 5 E
Harlan, *Iowa, U.S.A.* **80 E7** 41 39N 95 19W
Harlan, *Ky., U.S.A.* **77 G4** 36 51N 83 19W
Harlech, *U.K.* **10 E3** 52 52N 4 6W
Harlem, *U.S.A.* **82 B9** 48 32N 108 47W
Harlingen, *Neths.* **15 A5** 53 11N 5 25 E
Harlingen, *U.S.A.* **81 M6** 26 12N 97 42W
Harlow, *U.K.* **11 F8** 51 46N 0 8 E
Harlowton, *U.S.A.* **82 C9** 46 26N 109 50W
Harnai, *Pakistan* **42 D2** 30 6N 67 56 E
Harney Basin, *U.S.A.* **82 E4** 43 30N 119 0W
Harney L., *U.S.A.* **82 E4** 43 14N 119 8W
Harney Peak, *U.S.A.* **80 D3** 43 52N 103 32W
Härnösand, *Sweden* **9 E17** 62 38N 17 55 E
Haroldswick, *U.K.* **12 A8** 60 48N 0 50W
Harp L., *Canada* **71 A7** 55 5N 61 50W
Harper, *Liberia* **50 H4** 4 25N 7 43W
Harrai, *India* **43 H8** 22 37N 79 13 E
Harrand, *Pakistan* **42 E4** 29 28N 70 3 E
Harricana ←, *Canada* . . . **70 B4** 50 56N 79 32W
Harriman, *U.S.A.* **77 H3** 35 56N 84 33W
Harrington Harbour, *Canada* **71 B8** 50 31N 59 30W
Harris, *U.K.* **12 D2** 57 50N 6 55W
Harris, L., *Australia* **63 E2** 31 10S 135 10 E
Harris Pt., *Canada* **78 C2** 43 6N 82 9W
Harrisburg, *Ill., U.S.A.* . . **81 G10** 37 44N 88 32W
Harrisburg, *Nebr., U.S.A.* . . **80 E3** 41 33N 103 44W
Harrisburg, *Pa., U.S.A.* . . . **78 F8** 40 16N 76 53W
Harrismith, *S. Africa* **57 D4** 28 15S 29 8 E
Harrison, *Ark., U.S.A.* . . . **81 G8** 36 14N 93 7W
Harrison, *Maine, U.S.A.* . . **79 B14** 44 7N 70 39W
Harrison, *Nebr., U.S.A.* . . . **80 D3** 42 41N 103 53W
Harrison, C., *Canada* **71 B8** 54 55N 57 55W
Harrison L., *Canada* **72 D4** 49 33N 121 50W
Harrisonburg, *U.S.A.* **76 F6** 38 27N 78 52W
Harriston, *Canada* **78 C4** 43 57N 80 53W
Harrisville, *Mich., U.S.A.* . . **78 B1** 44 39N 83 17W
Harrisville, *N.Y., U.S.A.* . . **79 B9** 44 9N 75 19W
Harrisville, *Pa., U.S.A.* . . . **78 E5** 41 8N 80 0W
Harrodsburg, *U.S.A.* **76 G3** 37 46N 84 51W
Harrogate, *U.K.* **10 C6** 54 0N 1 33W
Harrow, *U.K.* **11 F7** 51 35N 0 21W
Harrowsmith, *Canada* **79 B8** 44 24N 76 40W
Harry S. Truman Reservoir,
 U.S.A. **80 F7** 38 16N 93 24W
Harsin, *Iran* **44 C5** 34 18N 47 33 E
Harstad, *Norway* **8 B17** 68 48N 16 30 E
Harsud, *India* **42 H7** 22 6N 76 44 E
Hart, *U.S.A.* **76 D2** 43 42N 86 22W
Hart, L., *Australia* **63 E2** 31 10S 136 25 E
Hartbees ←, *S. Africa* **56 D3** 28 45S 20 32 E
Hartford, *Conn., U.S.A.* . . **79 E12** 41 46N 72 41W
Hartford, *Ky., U.S.A.* **76 G2** 37 27N 86 55W
Hartford, *S. Dak., U.S.A.* . . **80 D6** 43 38N 96 57W
Hartford, *Wis., U.S.A.* . . **80 D10** 43 19N 88 22W
Hartford City, *U.S.A.* **76 E3** 40 27N 85 22W
Hartland, *Canada* **71 C6** 46 20N 67 32W
Hartland Pt., *U.K.* **11 F3** 51 1N 4 32W
Hartlepool, *U.K.* **10 C6** 54 42N 1 13W
Hartlepool □, *U.K.* **10 C6** 54 42N 1 17W
Hartley Bay, *Canada* **72 C3** 53 25N 129 15W
Hartmannberge, *Namibia* . . **56 B1** 17 0S 13 0 E
Hartney, *Canada* **73 D8** 49 30N 100 35W
Harts ←, *S. Africa* **56 D3** 28 24S 24 17 E
Hartselle, *U.S.A.* **77 H2** 34 27N 86 56W
Hartshorne, *U.S.A.* **81 H7** 34 51N 95 34W
Hartstown, *U.S.A.* **78 E4** 41 33N 80 23W
Hartsville, *U.S.A.* **77 H5** 34 23N 80 4W
Hartwell, *U.S.A.* **77 H4** 34 21N 82 56W
Harunabad, *Pakistan* **42 E5** 29 35N 73 8 E
Harvand, *Iran* **45 D7** 28 25N 55 43 E
Harvey, *Australia* **61 F2** 33 5S 115 54 E
Harvey, *Ill., U.S.A.* **76 E2** 41 36N 87 50W
Harvey, *N. Dak., U.S.A.* . . **80 B5** 47 47N 99 56W
Harwich, *U.K.* **11 F9** 51 56N 1 17 E
Haryana □, *India* **42 E7** 29 0N 76 10 E
Haryn ←, *Belarus* **17 B14** 52 7N 27 17 E
Harz, *Germany* **16 C6** 51 38N 10 44 E
Hasa □, *Si. Arabia* **45 E6** 25 50N 49 0 E
Ḥasanābād, *Iran* **45 C7** 32 8N 52 44 E
Hasdo ←, *India* **43 J10** 21 44N 82 44 E
Hashimoto, *Japan* **31 G7** 34 19N 135 37 E

Hashtjerd, *Iran* **45 C6** 35 52N 50 40 E
Haskell, *U.S.A.* **81 J5** 33 10N 99 44W
Haslemere, *U.K.* **11 F7** 51 5N 0 43W
Hasselt, *Belgium* **15 D5** 50 56N 5 21 E
Hassi Messaoud, *Algeria* . . **50 B7** 31 51N 6 1 E
Hässleholm, *Sweden* **9 H15** 56 10N 13 46 E
Hastings, *N.Z.* **59 H6** 39 39S 176 52 E
Hastings, *U.K.* **11 G8** 50 51N 0 35 E
Hastings, *Mich., U.S.A.* . . **76 D3** 42 39N 85 17W
Hastings, *Minn., U.S.A.* . . **80 C8** 44 44N 92 51W
Hastings, *Nebr., U.S.A.* . . **80 E5** 40 35N 98 23W
Hastings Ra., *Australia* . . . **63 E5** 31 15S 152 14 E
Hat Yai, *Thailand* **39 J3** 7 1N 100 27 E
Hatanbulag = Ergel,
 Mongolia **34 C5** 43 8N 109 5 E
Hatay = Antalya, *Turkey* . . **25 G5** 36 52N 30 45 E
Hatch, *U.S.A.* **83 K10** 32 40N 107 9W
Hatchet L., *Canada* **73 B8** 58 36N 103 40W
Hateruma-Shima, *Japan* . . **31 M1** 24 3N 123 47 E
Hatfield P.O., *Australia* . . . **63 E3** 33 54S 143 49 E
Hatgal, *Mongolia* **32 A5** 50 26N 100 9 E
Hathras, *India* **42 F8** 27 36N 78 6 E
Hatia, *Bangla.* **41 H17** 22 30N 91 5 E
Hato Mayor, *Dom. Rep.* . . **89 C6** 18 46N 69 15W
Hatta, *India* **43 G8** 24 7N 79 36 E
Hattah, *Australia* **63 E3** 34 48S 142 17 E
Hatteras, C., *U.S.A.* **77 H8** 35 14N 75 32W
Hattiesburg, *U.S.A.* **81 K10** 31 20N 89 17W
Hatvan, *Hungary* **17 E10** 47 40N 19 45 E
Hau Bon = Cheo Reo,
 Vietnam **36 B3** 13 25N 108 28 E
Hau Duc, *Vietnam* **38 E7** 15 20N 108 13 E
Haugesund, *Norway* **9 G11** 59 23N 5 13 E
Haukipudas, *Finland* **8 D21** 65 12N 25 20 E
Haultain ←, *Canada* **73 B7** 55 51N 106 46W
Hauraki G., *N.Z.* **59 G5** 36 35S 175 5 E
Haut Atlas, *Morocco* **50 B4** 32 30N 5 0W
Haut-Zaïre = Orientale □,
 Dem. Rep. of the Congo . **54 B2** 2 20N 26 0 E
Hautes Fagnes = Hohe
 Venn, *Belgium* **15 D6** 50 30N 6 5 E
Hauts Plateaux, *Algeria* . . **48 C4** 35 0N 1 0 E
Havana = La Habana, *Cuba* **88 B3** 23 8N 82 22W
Havana, *U.S.A.* **80 E9** 40 18N 90 4W
Havant, *U.K.* **11 G7** 50 51N 0 58W
Havasu, L., *U.S.A.* **85 L12** 34 18N 114 28W
Havel ←, *Germany* **16 B7** 52 50N 12 3 E
Havelian, *Pakistan* **42 B5** 34 2N 73 10 E
Havelock, *Canada* **78 B7** 44 26N 77 53W
Havelock, *N.Z.* **59 J4** 41 17S 173 48 E
Havelock, *U.S.A.* **77 H7** 34 53N 76 54W
Haverford West, *U.K.* **11 F3** 51 48N 4 58W
Haverhill, *U.S.A.* **79 D13** 42 47N 71 5W
Haverstraw, *U.S.A.* **79 E11** 41 12N 73 58W
Havirga, *Mongolia* **34 B7** 45 41N 113 5 E
Havířov, *Czech.* **17 D10** 49 46N 18 20 E
Havlíčkův Brod, *Czech Rep.* **16 D8** 49 36N 15 33 E
Havre, *U.S.A.* **82 B9** 48 33N 109 41W
Havre-Aubert, *Canada* . . . **71 C7** 47 12N 61 56W
Havre-St.-Pierre, *Canada* . . **71 B7** 50 18N 63 33W
Haw ←, *U.S.A.* **77 H6** 35 36N 79 3W
Hawaii □, *U.S.A.* **74 H16** 19 30N 156 30W
Hawaii I., *Pac. Oc.* **74 J17** 20 0N 155 0W
Hawaiian Is., *Pac. Oc.* . . **74 H17** 20 30N 156 0W
Hawaiian Ridge, *Pac. Oc.* . **65 E11** 24 0N 165 0W
Hawarden, *U.S.A.* **80 D6** 43 0N 96 29W
Hawea, L., *N.Z.* **59 L2** 44 28S 169 19 E
Hawera, *N.Z.* **59 H5** 39 35S 174 19 E
Hawick, *U.K.* **12 F6** 55 26N 2 47W
Hawk Junction, *Canada* . . **70 C3** 48 5N 84 38W
Hawke, B., *N.Z.* **59 H6** 39 25S 177 20 E
Hawker, *Australia* **63 E2** 31 59S 138 22 E
Hawkesbury, *Canada* **70 C5** 45 37N 74 37W
Hawkesbury I., *Canada* . . . **72 C3** 53 37N 129 3W
Hawkesbury Pt., *Australia* . **62 A1** 11 55S 134 5 E
Hawkinsville, *U.S.A.* **77 J4** 32 17N 83 28W
Hawley, *Minn., U.S.A.* . . . **80 B6** 46 53N 96 19W
Hawley, *Pa., U.S.A.* **79 E9** 41 28N 75 11W
Ḩawrān, W. ←, *Iraq* **44 C4** 33 58N 42 34 E
Hawsh Mūssá, *Lebanon* . . **47 B4** 33 45N 35 55 E
Hawthorne, *U.S.A.* **82 G4** 38 32N 118 38W
Hay, *Australia* **63 E3** 34 30S 144 51 E
Hay ←, *Australia* **62 C2** 24 50S 138 0 E
Hay ←, *Canada* **72 A5** 60 50N 116 26W
Hay, C., *Australia* **60 B4** 14 5S 129 29 E
Hay I., *Canada* **78 B4** 44 53N 80 58W
Hay L., *Canada* **72 B5** 58 50N 118 50W
Hay-on-Wye, *U.K.* **11 E4** 52 5N 3 8W
Hay River, *Canada* **72 A5** 60 51N 115 44W
Hay Springs, *U.S.A.* **80 D3** 42 41N 102 41W
Haya = Tehoru, *Indonesia* . **37 E7** 3 19S 129 37 E
Hayachine-San, *Japan* . . **30 E10** 39 34N 141 29 E
Hayden, *U.S.A.* **82 F10** 40 30N 107 16W
Haydon, *Australia* **62 B3** 18 0S 141 30 E
Hayes, *U.S.A.* **80 C4** 44 23N 101 1W
Hayes ←, *Canada* **70 A1** 57 3N 92 12W
Hayes Creek, *Australia* . . . **60 B5** 13 43S 131 22 E
Hayle, *U.K.* **11 G2** 50 11N 5 26W
Hayling I., *U.K.* **11 G7** 50 48N 0 59W
Hayrabolu, *Turkey* **21 D12** 41 12N 27 5 E
Hays, *Canada* **72 C6** 50 6N 111 48W
Hays, *U.S.A.* **80 F5** 38 53N 99 20W
Haysyn, *Ukraine* **17 D15** 48 57N 29 25 E
Hayvoron, *Ukraine* **17 D15** 48 22N 29 52 E
Hayward, *Calif., U.S.A.* . . **84 H4** 37 40N 122 5W
Hayward, *Wis., U.S.A.* . . . **80 B9** 46 1N 91 29W
Haywards Heath, *U.K.* . . . **11 G7** 51 0N 0 5W
Hazafon □, *Israel* **47 C4** 32 40N 35 20 E
Hazārān, Kūh-e, *Iran* **45 D8** 29 35N 57 2 E
Hazard, *U.S.A.* **76 G4** 37 15N 83 12W
Hazaribag, *India* **43 H11** 23 58N 85 26 E
Hazaribag Road, *India* . . **43 G11** 24 12N 85 57 E
Hazelton, *Canada* **72 B3** 55 20N 127 42W
Hazelton, *U.S.A.* **80 B4** 46 29N 100 17W
Hazen, *U.S.A.* **80 B4** 47 18N 101 38W
Hazlehurst, *Ga., U.S.A.* . . **77 K4** 31 52N 82 36W
Hazlehurst, *Miss., U.S.A.* . **81 K9** 31 52N 90 24W
Hazlet, *U.S.A.* **79 F10** 40 25N 74 12W
Hazleton, *U.S.A.* **79 F9** 40 57N 75 59W
Hazlett, L., *Australia* **60 D4** 21 30S 128 48 E
Hazro, *Turkey* **44 B4** 38 15N 40 47 E
Head of Bight, *Australia* . . **61 F5** 31 30S 131 5 E
Headlands, *Zimbabwe* . . . **55 F3** 18 15S 32 2 E
Healdsburg, *U.S.A.* **84 G4** 38 37N 122 52W
Healdton, *U.S.A.* **81 H6** 34 14N 97 29W
Healesville, *Australia* **63 F4** 37 35S 145 30 E
Heard I., *Ind. Oc.* **3 G13** 53 0S 74 0 E

Hearne, *U.S.A.* **81 K6** 30 53N 96 36W
Hearst, *Canada* **70 C3** 49 40N 83 41W
Heart ←, *U.S.A.* **80 B4** 46 46N 100 50W
Heart's Content, *Canada* . . **71 C9** 47 54N 53 27W
Heath Pt., *Canada* **71 C7** 49 8N 61 40W
Heavener, *U.S.A.* **81 H7** 34 53N 94 36W
Hebbronville, *U.S.A.* **81 M5** 27 18N 98 41W
Hebei □, *China* **34 E9** 39 0N 116 0 E
Hebel, *Australia* **63 D4** 28 58S 147 47 E
Heber, *U.S.A.* **85 N11** 32 44N 115 32W
Heber City, *U.S.A.* **82 F8** 40 31N 111 25W
Heber Springs, *U.S.A.* . . . **81 H9** 35 30N 92 2W
Hebert, *Canada* **73 C7** 50 30N 107 10W
Hebgen L., *U.S.A.* **82 D8** 44 52N 111 20W
Hebi, *China* **34 G8** 35 57N 114 7 E
Hebrides, *U.K.* **6 D4** 57 30N 7 0W
Hebron = Al Khalīl,
 West Bank **47 D4** 31 32N 35 6 E
Hebron, *Canada* **69 C13** 58 5N 62 30W
Hebron, *N. Dak., U.S.A.* . . **80 B3** 46 54N 102 3W
Hebron, *Nebr., U.S.A.* . . . **80 E6** 40 10N 97 35W
Hecate Str., *Canada* **72 C2** 53 10N 130 30W
Heceta I., *U.S.A.* **72 B2** 55 46N 133 40W
Hechi, *China* **32 D5** 24 40N 108 2 E
Hechuan, *China* **32 C5** 30 2N 106 12 E
Hecla, *U.S.A.* **80 C5** 45 53N 98 9W
Hecla I., *Canada* **73 C9** 51 10N 96 43W
Hede, *Sweden* **9 E16** 62 23N 13 30 E
Hedemora, *Sweden* **9 F16** 60 18N 15 58 E
Heerde, *Neths.* **15 B6** 52 24N 6 2 E
Heerenveen, *Neths.* **15 B5** 52 57N 5 55 E
Heerhugowaard, *Neths.* . . **15 B4** 52 40N 4 51 E
Heerlen, *Neths.* **18 A6** 50 55N 5 58 E
Ḥefa, *Israel* **47 C4** 32 46N 35 0 E
Ḥefa □, *Israel* **47 C4** 32 40N 35 0 E
Hefei, *China* **33 C6** 31 52N 117 18 E
Hegang, *China* **35 B16** 47 20N 130 19 E
Heichengzhen, *China* **34 F4** 36 24N 106 3 E
Heidelberg, *Germany* **16 D5** 49 24N 8 42 E
Heidelberg, *S. Africa* **56 E3** 34 6S 20 59 E
Heilbron, *S. Africa* **57 D4** 27 16S 27 59 E
Heilbronn, *Germany* **16 D5** 49 9N 9 13 E
Heilongjiang □, *China* . . . **33 B7** 48 0N 126 0 E
Heilunkiang =
 Heilongjiang □, *China* . . **33 B7** 48 0N 126 0 E
Heimaey, *Iceland* **8 E3** 63 26N 20 17W
Heinola, *Finland* **9 F22** 61 13N 26 2 E
Heinze Is., *Burma* **41 M20** 14 25N 97 45 E
Heishan, *China* **35 D12** 41 40N 122 5 E
Heishui, *China* **35 C10** 42 8N 119 30 E
Hejaz = Ḥijāz □, *Si. Arabia* **46 C3** 24 0N 40 0 E
Hejian, *China* **34 E9** 38 25N 116 5 E
Hejin, *China* **34 G6** 35 35N 110 42 E
Hekimhan, *Turkey* **44 B3** 38 50N 37 55 E
Hekla, *Iceland* **8 E4** 63 56N 19 35W
Hekou, *China* **32 D5** 22 30N 103 59 E
Helan Shan, *China* **34 E3** 38 30N 105 55 E
Helen Atoll, *Pac. Oc.* **37 D8** 2 40N 132 0 E
Helena, *Ark., U.S.A.* **81 H9** 34 32N 90 36W
Helena, *Mont., U.S.A.* . . . **82 C7** 46 36N 112 2W
Helendale, *U.S.A.* **85 L9** 34 44N 117 19W
Helensburgh, *U.K.* **12 E4** 56 1N 4 43W
Helensville, *N.Z.* **59 G5** 36 41S 174 29 E
Helenvale, *Australia* **62 B4** 15 43S 145 14 E
Helgeland, *Norway* **8 C15** 66 7N 13 29 E
Helgoland, *Germany* **16 A4** 54 10N 7 53 E
Heligoland = Helgoland,
 Germany **16 A4** 54 10N 7 53 E
Heligoland B. = Deutsche
 Bucht, *Germany* **16 A5** 54 15N 8 0 E
Hella, *Iceland* **8 E3** 63 50N 20 24W
Hellertown, *U.S.A.* **79 F9** 40 35N 75 21W
Hellespont = Çanakkale
 Boğazı, *Turkey* **21 D12** 40 17N 26 32 E
Hellevoetsluis, *Neths.* **15 C4** 51 50N 4 8 E
Hellín, *Spain* **19 C5** 38 31N 1 40W
Helmand □, *Afghan.* **40 D4** 31 20N 64 0 E
Helmand ←, *Afghan.* **40 D2** 31 12N 61 34 E
Helmond, *Neths.* **15 C5** 51 29N 5 41 E
Helmsdale, *U.K.* **12 C5** 58 7N 3 39W
Helmsdale ←, *U.K.* **12 C5** 58 8N 3 40W
Helong, *China* **35 C15** 42 40N 129 0 E
Helper, *U.S.A.* **82 G8** 39 41N 110 51W
Helsingborg, *Sweden* . . . **9 H15** 56 3N 12 42 E
Helsingfors = Helsinki,
 Finland **9 F21** 60 15N 25 3 E
Helsingør, *Denmark* **9 H15** 56 2N 12 35 E
Helsinki, *Finland* **9 F21** 60 15N 25 3 E
Helston, *U.K.* **11 G2** 50 6N 5 17W
Helvellyn, *U.K.* **10 C4** 54 32N 3 1W
Helwân, *Egypt* **51 C12** 29 50N 31 20 E
Hemel Hempstead, *U.K.* . . **11 F7** 51 44N 0 28W
Hemet, *U.S.A.* **85 M10** 33 45N 116 58W
Hemingford, *U.S.A.* **80 D3** 42 19N 103 4W
Hemmingford, *Canada* . . **79 A11** 45 3N 73 35W
Hempstead, *U.S.A.* **81 K6** 30 6N 96 5W
Hemse, *Sweden* **9 H18** 57 15N 18 22 E
Henan □, *China* **34 H8** 34 0N 114 0 E
Henares ←, *Spain* **19 B4** 40 24N 3 30W
Henashi-Misaki, *Japan* . . **30 D9** 40 37N 139 51 E
Henderson, *Argentina* . . . **94 D3** 36 18S 61 43W
Henderson, *Ky., U.S.A.* . . **76 G2** 37 50N 87 35W
Henderson, *N.C., U.S.A.* . . **77 G6** 36 20N 78 25W
Henderson, *Nev., U.S.A.* . **85 J12** 36 2N 114 59W
Henderson, *Tenn., U.S.A.* . **77 H1** 35 26N 88 38W
Henderson, *Tex., U.S.A.* . . **81 J7** 32 9N 94 48W
Hendersonville, *N.C., U.S.A.* **77 H4** 35 19N 82 28W
Hendersonville, *Tenn.,
 U.S.A.* **77 G2** 36 18N 86 37W
Hendijān, *Iran* **45 D6** 30 14N 49 43 E
Hendorābī, *Iran* **45 E7** 26 40N 53 37 E
Hengcheng, *China* **34 E4** 38 18N 106 28 E
Hengdaohezi, *China* **35 B15** 44 52N 129 0 E
Hengelo, *Neths.* **15 B6** 52 16N 6 48 E
Hengshan, *China* **34 F5** 37 58N 109 5 E
Hengshui, *China* **34 F8** 37 41N 115 40 E
Hengyang, *China* **33 D6** 26 52N 112 33 E
Henlopen, C., *U.S.A.* **76 F8** 38 48N 75 6W
Hennenman, *S. Africa* . . . **56 D4** 27 59S 27 1 E
Hennessey, *U.S.A.* **81 G6** 36 6N 97 54W
Henrietta, *U.S.A.* **81 J5** 33 49N 98 12W
Henrietta, Ostrov =
 Genriyetty, Ostrov, *Russia* **27 B16** 77 6N 156 30 E
Henrietta Maria, C., *Canada* **80 E10** 41 7N 89 22W
Henry, *U.S.A.* **80 E10** 41 7N 89 22W
Henryetta, *U.S.A.* **81 H7** 35 27N 95 59W
Henryville, *Canada* **79 A11** 45 8N 73 11W

Hensall, *Canada* **78 C3** 43 26N 81 30W
Hentiyn Nuruu, *Mongolia* . **33 B5** 48 30N 108 30 E
Henty, *Australia* **63 F4** 35 30S 147 0 E
Henzada, *Burma* **41 L19** 17 38N 95 26 E
Heppner, *U.S.A.* **82 D4** 45 21N 119 33W
Hepworth, *Canada* **78 B3** 44 37N 81 9W
Hequ, *China* **34 E6** 39 20N 111 15 E
Héraðsflói, *Iceland* **8 D6** 65 42N 14 12W
Héraðsvötn →, *Iceland* .. **8 D4** 65 45N 19 25W
Herald Cays, *Australia* ... **62 B4** 16 58S 149 9 E
Herāt, *Afghan.* **40 B3** 34 20N 62 7 E
Herāt □, *Afghan.* **40 B3** 35 0N 62 0 E
Herbert →, *Australia* **62 B4** 18 31S 146 17 E
Herberton, *Australia* **62 B4** 17 20S 145 25 E
Herceg-Novi,
 Montenegro, Yug. **21 C8** 42 30N 18 33 E
Herchmer, *Canada* **73 B10** 57 22N 94 10W
Herðubreið, *Iceland* **8 D5** 65 11N 16 21W
Hereford, *U.K.* **11 E5** 52 4N 2 43W
Hereford, *U.S.A.* **81 H3** 34 49N 102 24W
Herefordshire □, *U.K.* ... **11 E5** 52 8N 2 40W
Herentals, *Belgium* **15 C4** 51 12N 4 51 E
Herford, *Germany* **16 B5** 52 7N 8 39 E
Herington, *U.S.A.* **80 F6** 38 40N 96 57W
Herkimer, *U.S.A.* **79 D10** 43 0N 74 59W
Herlong, *U.S.A.* **84 E6** 40 8N 120 8W
Herm, *U.K.* **11 H5** 49 30N 2 28W
Hermann, *U.S.A.* **80 F9** 38 42N 91 27W
Hermannsburg, *Australia* . **60 D5** 23 57S 132 45 E
Hermanus, *S. Africa* **56 E2** 34 27S 19 12 E
Hermidale, *Australia* **63 E4** 31 30S 146 42 E
Hermiston, *U.S.A.* **82 D4** 45 51N 119 17W
Hermitage, *N.Z.* **59 K3** 43 44S 170 5 E
Hermite, I., *Chile* **96 H3** 55 50S 68 0W
Hermon, *U.S.A.* **79 B9** 44 28N 75 14W
Hermon, Mt. = Shaykh, J.
 ash, *Lebanon* **47 B4** 33 25N 35 50 E
Hermosillo, *Mexico* **86 B2** 29 10N 111 0W
Hernád →, *Hungary* **17 D11** 47 56N 21 8 E
Hernandarias, *Paraguay* .. **95 B5** 25 20S 54 40W
Hernandez, *U.S.A.* **84 J6** 36 24N 120 46W
Hernando, *Argentina* **94 C3** 32 28S 63 40W
Hernando, *U.S.A.* **81 H10** 34 50N 90 0W
Herndon, *U.S.A.* **78 F8** 40 43N 76 51W
Herne, *Germany* **15 C7** 51 32N 7 14 E
Herne Bay, *U.K.* **11 F9** 51 21N 1 8 E
Herning, *Denmark* **9 H13** 56 8N 8 58 E
Heroica = Caborca, *Mexico* **86 A2** 30 40N 112 10W
Heroica Nogales = Nogales,
 Mexico **86 A2** 31 20N 110 56W
Heron Bay, *Canada* **70 C2** 48 40N 86 25W
Herradura, Pta. de la,
 Canary Is. **22 F5** 28 26N 14 8W
Herreid, *U.S.A.* **80 C4** 45 50N 100 4W
Herrin, *U.S.A.* **81 G10** 37 48N 89 2W
Herriot, *Canada* **73 B8** 56 22N 101 16W
Hershey, *U.S.A.* **79 F8** 40 17N 76 39W
Hersonissos, *Greece* **23 D7** 35 18N 25 22 E
Herstal, *Belgium* **15 D5** 50 40N 5 38 E
Hertford, *U.K.* **11 F7** 51 48N 0 4W
Hertfordshire □, *U.K.* ... **11 F7** 51 51N 0 5W
's-Hertogenbosch, *Neths.* . **15 C5** 51 42N 5 17 E
Hertzogville, *S. Africa* ... **56 D4** 28 9S 25 30 E
Hervey B., *Australia* **62 C5** 25 0S 152 52 E
Herzliyya, *Israel* **47 C3** 32 10N 34 50 E
Heşār, *Fārs, Iran* **45 D6** 29 52N 50 16 E
Heşār, *Markazī, Iran* **45 C6** 35 50N 49 12 E
Heshui, *China* **34 G5** 35 48N 108 0 E
Heshun, *China* **34 F7** 37 22N 113 32 E
Hesperia, *U.S.A.* **85 L9** 34 25N 117 18W
Hesse = Hessen □,
 Germany **16 C5** 50 30N 9 0 E
Hessen □, *Germany* **16 C5** 50 30N 9 0 E
Hetch Hetchy Aqueduct,
 U.S.A. **84 H5** 37 29N 122 19W
Hettinger, *U.S.A.* **80 C3** 46 0N 102 42W
Heuvelton, *U.S.A.* **79 B9** 44 37N 75 25W
Hewitt, *U.S.A.* **81 K6** 31 27N 97 11W
Hexham, *U.K.* **10 C5** 54 58N 2 4W
Hexigten Qi, *China* **35 C9** 43 18N 117 30 E
Ḥeydarābād, *Iran* **45 D7** 30 33N 55 38 E
Heysham, *U.K.* **10 C5** 54 3N 2 53W
Heywood, *Australia* **63 F3** 38 8S 141 37 E
Heze, *China* **85 L9** 34 45N 117 46W
Hi Vista, *U.S.A.* **85 L9** 34 45N 117 46W
Hialeah, *U.S.A.* **77 N5** 25 50N 80 17W
Hiawatha, *U.S.A.* **80 F7** 39 51N 95 32W
Hibbing, *U.S.A.* **80 B8** 47 25N 92 56W
Hibbs B., *Australia* **62 G4** 42 35S 145 15 E
Hibernia Reef, *Australia* .. **60 B3** 12 0S 123 23 E
Hickman, *U.S.A.* **81 G10** 36 34N 89 11W
Hickory, *U.S.A.* **77 H5** 35 44N 81 21W
Hicks, Pt., *Australia* **63 F4** 37 49S 149 17 E
Hicks L., *Canada* **73 A9** 61 25N 100 0W
Hicksville, *U.S.A.* **79 F11** 40 46N 73 32W
Hida-Gawa →, *Japan* **31 G8** 35 26N 137 3 E
Hida-Sammyaku, *Japan* ... **31 F8** 36 30N 137 40 E
Hidaka-Sammyaku, *Japan* . **30 C11** 42 35N 142 45 E
Hidalgo, *Mexico* **87 C5** 24 15N 99 26W
Hidalgo □, *Mexico* **87 C5** 20 30N 99 10W
Hidalgo, Presa M., *Mexico* **86 B3** 26 30N 108 35W
Hidalgo, Pta. del, *Canary Is.* **22 F3** 28 33N 16 19W
Hidalgo del Parral, *Mexico* **86 B3** 26 58N 105 40W
Hierro, *Canary Is.* **22 G1** 27 44N 18 0W
Higashiajima-San, *Japan* .. **30 F10** 37 40N 140 10 E
Higashiōsaka, *Japan* **31 G7** 34 40N 135 37 E
Higgins, *U.S.A.* **81 G4** 36 7N 100 2W
Higgins Corner, *U.S.A.* ... **84 F5** 39 2N 121 5W
High Atlas = Haut Atlas,
 Morocco **50 B4** 32 30N 5 0W
High Bridge, *U.S.A.* **79 F10** 40 40N 74 54W
High Level, *Canada* **72 B5** 58 31N 117 8W
High Point, *U.S.A.* **77 H6** 35 57N 80 0W
High Prairie, *Canada* **72 B5** 55 30N 116 30W
High River, *Canada* **72 C6** 50 30N 113 50W
High Tatra = Tatry,
 Slovak Rep. **17 D11** 49 20N 20 0 E
High Veld, *Africa* **48 J6** 27 0S 27 0 E
High Wycombe, *U.K.* **11 F7** 51 37N 0 45W
Highland □, *U.K.* **12 D4** 57 17N 4 21W
Highland Park, *U.S.A.* **76 D2** 42 11N 87 48W
Highmore, *U.S.A.* **80 C5** 44 31N 99 27W
Highrock L., *Canada* **73 B8** 55 45N 100 30W
Highrock L., *Sask., Canada* **73 B7** 57 5N 105 32W
Higüey, *Dom. Rep.* **89 C6** 18 37N 68 42W
Hiiumaa, *Estonia* **9 G20** 58 50N 22 45 E
Ḥijāz □, *Si. Arabia* **46 C3** 24 0N 40 0 E

Hijo = Tagum, *Phil.* **37 C7** 7 33N 125 53 E
Hikari, *Japan* **31 H5** 33 58N 131 58 E
Hiko, *U.S.A.* **84 H11** 37 32N 115 14W
Hikone, *Japan* **31 G8** 35 15N 136 10 E
Hikurangi, *N.Z.* **59 F5** 35 36S 174 17 E
Hikurangi, Mt., *N.Z.* **59 H6** 38 21S 176 52 E
Hildesheim, *Germany* **16 B5** 52 9N 9 56 E
Hill →, *Australia* **61 F2** 30 23S 115 3 E
Hill City, *Idaho, U.S.A.* ... **82 E6** 43 18N 115 3W
Hill City, *Kans., U.S.A.* ... **80 F5** 39 22N 99 51W
Hill City, *S. Dak., U.S.A.* . **80 D3** 43 56N 103 35W
Hill Island L., *Canada* **73 A7** 60 30N 109 50W
Hillcrest Center, *U.S.A.* ... **85 K8** 35 23N 118 57W
Hillegom, *Neths.* **15 B4** 52 18N 4 35 E
Hillerød, *Denmark* **9 J15** 55 56N 12 19 E
Hillsboro, *Kans., U.S.A.* .. **80 F6** 38 21N 97 12W
Hillsboro, *N. Dak., U.S.A.* **80 B6** 47 26N 97 3W
Hillsboro, *N.H., U.S.A.* ... **79 C13** 43 7N 71 54W
Hillsboro, *Ohio, U.S.A.* ... **76 F4** 39 12N 83 37W
Hillsboro, *Oreg., U.S.A.* .. **84 E4** 45 31N 122 59W
Hillsboro, *Tex., U.S.A.* ... **81 J6** 32 1N 97 8W
Hillsborough, *Grenada* ... **89 D7** 12 28N 61 28W
Hillsdale, *Mich., U.S.A.* ... **76 E3** 41 56N 84 38W
Hillsdale, *N.Y., U.S.A.* ... **79 D11** 42 11N 73 30W
Hillsport, *Canada* **70 C2** 49 27N 85 34W
Hillston, *Australia* **63 E4** 33 30S 145 31 E
Hilo, *U.S.A.* **74 J17** 19 44N 155 5W
Hilton, *U.S.A.* **78 C7** 43 17N 77 48W
Hilton Head Island, *U.S.A.* **77 J5** 32 13N 80 45W
Hilversum, *Neths.* **15 B5** 52 14N 5 10 E
Himachal Pradesh □, *India* **42 D7** 31 30N 77 0 E
Himalaya, *Asia* **43 E11** 29 0N 84 0 E
Himatnagar, *India* **40 H8** 23 37N 72 57 E
Himeji, *Japan* **31 G7** 34 50N 134 40 E
Himi, *Japan* **31 F8** 36 50N 136 55 E
Ḥimş, *Syria* **47 A5** 34 40N 36 45 E
Ḥimş □, *Syria* **47 A6** 34 30N 37 0 E
Hinche, *Haiti* **89 C5** 19 9N 72 1W
Hinchinbrook I., *Australia* . **62 B4** 18 20S 146 15 E
Hinckley, *U.K.* **11 E6** 52 33N 1 22W
Hinckley, *U.S.A.* **80 B8** 46 1N 92 56W
Hindaun, *India* **42 F7** 26 44N 77 5 E
Hindmarsh, L., *Australia* .. **63 F3** 36 5S 141 55 E
Hindu Bagh, *Pakistan* **42 D2** 30 56N 67 50 E
Hindu Kush, *Asia* **40 B7** 36 0N 71 0 E
Hindubagh, *Pakistan* **40 D5** 30 56N 67 57 E
Hindupur, *India* **40 N10** 13 49N 77 32 E
Hines Creek, *Canada* **72 B5** 56 20N 118 40W
Hinesville, *U.S.A.* **77 K5** 31 51N 81 36W
Hinganghat, *India* **40 J11** 20 30N 78 52 E
Hingham, *U.S.A.* **82 B8** 48 33N 110 25W
Hingir, *India* **43 J10** 21 57N 83 41 E
Hingoli, *India* **40 K10** 19 41N 77 15 E
Hinna = Imi, *Ethiopia* **8 B16** 68 35N 15 50 E
Hinojosa del Duque, *Spain* **79 D12** 42 47N 72 29W
Hinsdale, *U.S.A.* **72 C5** 53 26N 117 34W
Hinton, *Canada* **76 G5** 37 40N 80 54W
Hinton, *U.S.A.* **31 H4** 33 22N 129 33 E
Hirado, *Japan* **41 J13** 21 32N 83 45 E
Hirakud Dam, *India* **43 H8** 22 56N 79 41 E
Hiran →, *India* **43 G8** 24 22N 79 13 E
Hirapur, *India* **30 C11** 42 17N 143 19 E
Hiratsuka, *Japan* **30 C11** 42 17N 143 19 E
Hiroo, *Japan* **30 D10** 40 34N 140 28 E
Hirosaki, *Japan* **31 G6** 34 24N 132 30 E
Hiroshima, *Japan* **31 G6** 34 50N 133 0 E
Hiroshima □, *Japan* **42 E6** 29 12N 75 45 E
Hisar, *India* **44 D5** 31 45N 44 17 E
Hisb →, *Iraq* **44 D3** 28 30N 36 0 E
Ḥismā, *Si. Arabia* **89 C5** 19 0N 71 0W
Hispaniola, *W. Indies* **44 C4** 33 38N 42 49 E
Ḥīt, *Iraq* **31 H5** 33 20N 130 58 E
Hita, *Japan* **31 F10** 36 36N 140 39 E
Hitachi, *Japan* **11 F7** 51 58N 0 16W
Hitchin, *U.K.* **31 H5** 32 13N 130 45 E
Hitoyoshi, *Japan* **8 E13** 63 30N 8 45 E
Hitra, *Norway* **72 C4** 53 25N 122 35W
Hixon, *Canada* **47 E4** 31 20N 34 42 E
Ḥiyyon, N. →, *Israel* **73 A7** 61 33N 109 25W
Hjalmar L., *Canada* **9 G16** 59 18N 15 40 E
Hjälmaren, *Sweden* **9 H13** 57 29N 9 59 E
Hjørring, *Denmark* **57 D5** 28 1S 32 15 E
Hluhluwe, *S. Africa* **17 D13** 48 5N 25 56 E
Hlyboka, *Ukraine*
Ho Chi Minh City = Thanh
 Pho Ho Chi Minh,
 Vietnam **39 G6** 10 58N 106 40 E
Ho Thuong, *Vietnam* **38 C5** 19 32N 105 48 E
Hoa Da, *Vietnam* **39 G7** 11 16N 108 40 E
Hoa Hiep, *Vietnam* **39 G5** 11 34N 105 51 E
Hoai Nhon, *Vietnam* **38 E7** 14 28N 109 1 E
Hoang Lien Son, *Vietnam* . **38 A4** 22 0N 104 0 E
Hoare B., *Canada* **69 B13** 65 17N 62 30W
Hobart, *Australia* **62 G4** 42 50S 147 21 E
Hobart, *U.S.A.* **81 H5** 35 1N 99 6W
Hobbs, *U.S.A.* **81 J3** 32 42N 103 8W
Hobbs Coast, *Antarctica* .. **5 D14** 74 50S 131 0W
Hobe Sound, *U.S.A.* **77 M5** 27 4N 80 8W
Hoboken, *U.S.A.* **79 F10** 40 45N 74 4W
Hobro, *Denmark* **9 H13** 56 39N 9 46 E
Hoburgen, *Sweden* **9 H18** 56 55N 18 7 E
Hodaka-Dake, *Japan* **31 F8** 36 17N 137 39 E
Hodgeville, *Canada* **73 C7** 50 7N 106 58W
Hodgson, *Canada* **73 C9** 51 13N 97 36W
Hódmezővásárhely,
 Hungary **17 E11** 46 28N 20 22 E
Hodna, Chott el, *Algeria* .. **50 A6** 35 26N 4 43 E
Hodonín, *Czech Rep.* **17 D9** 48 50N 17 0 E
Hoeamdong, *N. Korea* ... **35 C16** 42 30N 130 16 E
Hoek van Holland, *Neths.* . **15 C4** 52 0N 4 7 E
Hoengsŏng, *S. Korea* **35 F14** 37 29N 127 59 E
Hoeryong, *N. Korea* **35 C15** 42 30N 129 45 E
Hoeyang, *N. Korea* **35 E14** 38 43N 127 36 E
Hof, *Germany* **16 C6** 50 19N 11 55 E
Hofmeyr, *S. Africa* **56 E4** 31 39S 25 50 E
Höfn, *Iceland* **8 D6** 64 15N 15 13W
Hofors, *Sweden* **9 F17** 60 31N 16 15 E
Hofsjökull, *Iceland* **8 D4** 64 49N 18 48W
Hōfu, *Japan* **31 G5** 34 3N 131 34 E
Hogan Group, *Australia* .. **63 F4** 39 13S 147 1 E
Hogarth, Mt., *Australia* ... **62 C2** 21 48S 136 58 E
Hoggar = Ahaggar, *Algeria* **50 D7** 23 0N 6 30 E
Hogsty Reef, *Bahamas* ... **89 B5** 21 41N 73 48W
Hoh →, *U.S.A.* **84 C2** 47 45N 124 29W
Hohe Venn, *Belgium* **15 D6** 50 30N 6 5 E
Hohenwald, *U.S.A.* **77 H2** 35 33N 87 33W

Hohhot, *China* **34 D6** 40 52N 111 40 E
Hóhlakas, *Greece* **23 D9** 35 57N 27 53 E
Hoi An, *Vietnam* **38 E7** 15 30N 108 19 E
Hoisington, *U.S.A.* **80 F5** 38 31N 98 47W
Hōjō, *Japan* **31 H6** 33 58N 132 46 E
Hokianga Harbour, *N.Z.* .. **59 F4** 35 31S 173 22 E
Hokitika, *N.Z.* **59 K3** 42 42S 171 0 E
Hokkaidō □, *Japan* **30 C11** 43 30N 143 0 E
Holbrook, *Australia* **63 F4** 35 42S 147 18 E
Holbrook, *U.S.A.* **83 J8** 34 54N 110 10W
Holden, *U.S.A.* **82 G7** 39 6N 112 16W
Holdenville, *U.S.A.* **81 H6** 35 5N 96 24W
Holdrege, *U.S.A.* **80 E5** 40 26N 99 23W
Holguín, *Cuba* **88 B4** 20 50N 76 20W
Hollams Bird I., *Namibia* .. **56 C1** 24 40S 14 30 E
Holland, *Mich., U.S.A.* ... **76 D2** 42 47N 86 7W
Holland, *N.Y., U.S.A.* **78 D6** 42 38N 78 32W
Hollandale, *U.S.A.* **81 J9** 33 10N 90 51W
Hollandia = Jayapura,
 Indonesia **37 E10** 2 28S 140 38 E
Holley, *U.S.A.* **78 C6** 43 14N 78 2W
Hollidaysburg, *U.S.A.* **78 F6** 40 26N 78 24W
Hollis, *U.S.A.* **81 H5** 34 41N 99 55W
Hollister, *Calif., U.S.A.* ... **84 J5** 36 51N 121 24W
Hollister, *Idaho, U.S.A.* ... **82 E6** 42 21N 114 35W
Holly Hill, *U.S.A.* **77 L5** 29 16N 81 3W
Holly Springs, *U.S.A.* **81 H10** 34 46N 89 27W
Hollywood, *Calif., U.S.A.* . **74 D3** 34 7N 118 25W
Hollywood, *Fla., U.S.A.* .. **77 N5** 26 1N 80 9W
Holman, *U.S.A.* **68 A8** 70 42N 117 41W
Holman, *N.W.T., Canada* . **68 A8** 70 44N 117 44W
Hólmavík, *Iceland* **8 D3** 65 42N 21 40W
Holmen, *U.S.A.* **80 D9** 43 58N 91 15W
Holmes Reefs, *Australia* .. **62 B4** 16 27S 148 0 E
Holmsund, *Sweden* **8 E19** 63 41N 20 20 E
Holroyd →, *Australia* **62 A3** 14 10S 141 36 E
Holstebro, *Denmark* **9 H13** 56 22N 8 37 E
Holsworthy, *U.K.* **11 G3** 50 48N 4 22W
Holton, *Canada* **71 B8** 54 31N 57 12W
Holton, *U.S.A.* **80 F7** 39 28N 95 44W
Holtville, *U.S.A.* **85 N11** 32 49N 115 23W
Holwerd, *Neths.* **15 A5** 53 22N 5 54 E
Holy I., *Angl., U.K.* **10 D3** 53 17N 4 37W
Holy I., *Northumb., U.K.* .. **10 B6** 55 40N 1 47W
Holyhead, *U.K.* **10 D3** 53 18N 4 38W
Holyoke, *Colo., U.S.A.* ... **80 E3** 40 35N 102 18W
Holyoke, *Mass., U.S.A.* .. **79 D12** 42 12N 72 37W
Holyrood, *Canada* **71 C9** 47 27N 53 8W
Homa Bay, *Kenya* **54 C3** 0 36S 34 30 E
Homalin, *Burma* **41 G19** 24 55N 95 0 E
Homand, *Iran* **45 C8** 32 28N 59 37 E
Homathko →, *Canada* ... **72 C4** 51 0N 124 56W
Hombori, *Mali* **50 E5** 15 20N 1 38W
Home B., *Canada* **69 B13** 68 40N 67 10W
Home Hill, *Australia* **62 B4** 19 43S 147 25 E
Homedale, *U.S.A.* **82 E5** 43 37N 116 56W
Homer, *Alaska, U.S.A.* ... **68 C4** 59 39N 151 33W
Homer, *La., U.S.A.* **81 J8** 32 48N 93 4W
Homer City, *U.S.A.* **78 F5** 40 32N 79 10W
Homestead, *Australia* **62 C4** 20 20S 145 40 E
Homestead, *U.S.A.* **77 N5** 25 28N 80 29W
Homewood, *U.S.A.* **84 F6** 39 4N 120 8W
Homoine, *Mozam.* **57 C6** 23 55S 35 8 E
Homs = Ḥimş, *Syria* **47 A5** 34 40N 36 45 E
Homyel, *Belarus* **17 B16** 52 28N 31 0 E
Hon Chong, *Vietnam* **39 G5** 10 25N 104 30 E
Hon Me, *Vietnam* **38 C5** 19 23N 105 56 E
Honan = Henan □, *China* . **34 H8** 34 0N 114 0 E
Honbetsu, *Japan* **30 C11** 43 7N 143 37 E
Honcut, *U.S.A.* **84 F5** 39 20N 121 32W
Hondeklipbaai, *S. Africa* .. **56 E2** 30 19S 17 17 E
Hondo, *Japan* **31 H5** 32 27N 130 12 E
Hondo, *U.S.A.* **81 L5** 29 21N 99 9W
Hondo →, *Belize* **87 D7** 18 25N 88 21W
Honduras ■, *Cent. Amer.* . **88 D2** 14 40N 86 30W
Honduras, G. de, *Caribbean* **88 C2** 16 50N 87 0W
Hønefoss, *Norway* **9 F14** 60 10N 10 18 E
Honesdale, *U.S.A.* **79 E9** 41 34N 75 16W
Honey L., *U.S.A.* **84 E6** 40 15N 120 19W
Honfleur, *France* **18 B4** 49 25N 0 13 E
Hong →, *Vietnam* **32 D5** 20 0N 104 0 E
Hong He →, *China* **34 H8** 32 25N 115 35 E
Hong Kong □, *China* **33 D6** 22 11N 114 14 E
Hongch'ŏn, *S. Korea* **35 F14** 37 44N 127 53 E
Hongjiang, *China* **33 D5** 27 7N 109 59 E
Hongliu He →, *China* **34 F5** 38 0N 109 50 E
Hongor, *Mongolia* **34 B7** 45 45N 112 50 E
Hongsa, *Laos* **38 C3** 19 43N 101 20 E
Hongshui He →, *China* ... **33 D5** 23 48N 109 30 E
Hongsŏng, *S. Korea* **35 F14** 36 37N 126 38 E
Hongtong, *China* **34 F6** 36 16N 111 40 E
Honguedo, Détroit d',
 Canada **71 C7** 49 15N 64 0W
Hongwon, *N. Korea* **35 E14** 40 0N 127 56 E
Hongze Hu, *China* **35 H10** 33 15N 118 35 E
Honiara, *Solomon Is.* **64 H7** 9 27S 159 57 E
Honiton, *U.K.* **11 G4** 50 47N 3 11W
Honjō, *Japan* **30 E10** 39 23N 140 3 E
Honningsvåg, *Norway* **8 A21** 70 59N 25 59 E
Honolulu, *U.S.A.* **74 H16** 21 19N 157 52W
Honshū, *Japan* **31 G9** 36 0N 138 0 E
Hood, Mt., *U.S.A.* **82 D3** 45 23N 121 42W
Hood, Pt., *Australia* **61 F2** 34 23S 119 34 E
Hood River, *U.S.A.* **82 D3** 45 43N 121 31W
Hoodsport, *U.S.A.* **84 C3** 47 24N 123 9W
Hoogeveen, *Neths.* **15 B6** 52 44N 6 28 E
Hoogezand-Sappemeer,
 Neths. **15 A6** 53 9N 6 45 E
Hooghly →, *India* **43 J13** 21 56N 88 4 E
Hooghly-Chinsura =
 Chunchura, *India* **43 H13** 22 53N 88 27 E
Hook Hd., *Ireland* **13 D5** 52 7N 6 56W
Hook I., *Australia* **62 C4** 20 4S 149 0 E
Hook of Holland = Hoek van
 Holland, *Neths.* **15 C4** 52 0N 4 7 E
Hooker, *U.S.A.* **81 G4** 36 52N 101 13W
Hooker Creek, *Australia* .. **60 C5** 18 23S 130 38 E
Hoonah, *U.S.A.* **72 B1** 58 7N 135 27W
Hooper Bay, *U.S.A.* **68 B3** 61 32N 166 6W
Hoopeston, *U.S.A.* **76 E2** 40 28N 87 40W
Hoopstad, *S. Africa* **56 D4** 27 50S 25 55 E
Hoorn, *Neths.* **15 B5** 52 38N 5 4 E
Hoover, *U.S.A.* **77 J2** 33 20N 86 49W
Hoover Dam, *U.S.A.* **85 K12** 36 1N 114 44W
Hooversville, *U.S.A.* **78 F6** 40 9N 78 46W
Hop Bottom, *U.S.A.* **79 E9** 41 42N 75 46W
Hope, *Canada* **72 D4** 49 25N 121 25W

Hope, *Ariz., U.S.A.* **85 M13** 33 43N 113 42W
Hope, *Ark., U.S.A.* **81 J8** 33 40N 93 36W
Hope, L., *S. Austral.,*
 Australia **63 D2** 28 24S 139 18 E
Hope, L., *W. Austral.,*
 Australia **61 F3** 32 35S 120 15 E
Hope I., *Canada* **78 B4** 44 55N 80 11W
Hope Town, *Bahamas* **88 A4** 26 35N 76 57W
Hopedale, *Canada* **71 A7** 55 28N 60 13W
Hopedale, *U.S.A.* **79 D13** 42 8N 71 33W
Hopefield, *S. Africa* **56 E2** 33 3S 18 22 E
Hopei = Hebei □, *China* .. **34 E9** 39 0N 116 0 E
Hopelchén, *Mexico* **87 D7** 19 46N 89 50W
Hopetoun, *Vic., Australia* . **63 F3** 35 42S 142 22 E
Hopetoun, *W. Austral.,*
 Australia **61 F3** 33 57S 120 7 E
Hopetown, *S. Africa* **56 D3** 29 34S 24 3 E
Hopevale, *Australia* **62 B4** 15 16S 145 20 E
Hopewell, *U.S.A.* **76 G7** 37 18N 77 17W
Hopkins, L., *Australia* **60 D4** 24 15S 128 35 E
Hopkinsville, *U.S.A.* **77 G2** 36 52N 87 29W
Hopland, *U.S.A.* **84 G3** 38 58N 123 7W
Hoquiam, *U.S.A.* **84 D3** 46 59N 123 53W
Horden Hills, *Australia* ... **60 D5** 20 15S 130 0 E
Horinger, *China* **34 D6** 40 28N 111 48 E
Horlick Mts., *Antarctica* .. **5 E15** 84 0S 102 0W
Horlivka, *Ukraine* **25 E6** 48 19N 38 5 E
Hormak, *Iran* **45 D9** 29 58N 60 51 E
Hormoz, *Iran* **45 E7** 27 35N 55 0 E
Hormoz, Jaz.-ye, *Iran* **45 E8** 27 8N 56 28 E
Hormozgān □, *Iran* **45 E8** 27 30N 56 0 E
Hormuz, Küh-e, *Iran* **45 E7** 27 27N 55 10 E
Hormuz, Str. of, *The Gulf* . **45 E8** 26 30N 56 30 E
Horn, *Austria* **16 D8** 48 39N 15 40 E
Horn, *Iceland* **8 C2** 66 28N 22 28W
Horn →, *Canada* **72 A5** 61 30N 118 1W
Horn, Cape = Hornos, C. de,
 Chile **96 H3** 55 50S 67 30W
Horn Head, *Ireland* **13 A3** 55 14N 8 0W
Horn I., *Australia* **62 A3** 10 37S 142 17 E
Horn Mts., *Canada* **72 A5** 62 15N 119 15W
Hornavan, *Sweden* **8 C17** 66 15N 17 30 E
Hornbeck, *U.S.A.* **81 K8** 31 20N 93 24W
Hornbrook, *U.S.A.* **82 F2** 41 55N 122 33W
Horncastle, *U.K.* **10 D7** 53 13N 0 7W
Hornell, *U.S.A.* **78 D7** 42 20N 77 40W
Hornell L., *Canada* **72 A5** 62 20N 119 25W
Hornepayne, *Canada* **70 C3** 49 14N 84 48W
Hornings Mills, *Canada* ... **78 B4** 44 9N 80 12W
Hornitos, *U.S.A.* **84 H6** 37 30N 120 14W
Hornos, C. de, *Chile* **96 H3** 55 50S 67 30W
Hornsea, *U.K.* **10 D7** 53 55N 0 11W
Horobetsu, *Japan* **30 C10** 42 24N 141 6 E
Horodenka, *Ukraine* **17 D13** 48 41N 25 29 E
Horodok, *Khmelnytskyy,*
 Ukraine **17 D14** 49 10N 26 34 E
Horodok, *Lviv, Ukraine* ... **17 D12** 49 46N 23 32 E
Horokhiv, *Ukraine* **17 C13** 50 30N 24 45 E
Horqin Youyi Qianqi, *China* **35 A12** 46 5N 122 3 E
Horqueta, *Paraguay* **94 A4** 23 15S 56 55W
Horse Creek, *U.S.A.* **80 E3** 41 57N 105 10W
Horse Is., *Canada* **71 B8** 50 15N 55 50W
Horsefly L., *Canada* **72 C4** 52 25N 121 0W
Horseheads, *U.S.A.* **78 D8** 42 10N 76 49W
Horsens, *Denmark* **9 J13** 55 52N 9 51 E
Horsham, *Australia* **63 F3** 36 44S 142 13 E
Horsham, *U.K.* **11 F7** 51 4N 0 20W
Horten, *Norway* **9 G14** 59 25N 10 32 E
Horton, *U.S.A.* **80 F7** 39 40N 95 32W
Horton →, *Canada* **68 B7** 69 56N 126 52W
Horwood L., *Canada* **70 C3** 48 5N 82 20W
Hose, Gunung-Gunung,
 Malaysia **36 D4** 2 5N 114 6 E
Ḥoseynābād, *Khuzestān,*
 Iran **45 C6** 32 45N 48 20 E
Ḥoseynābād, *Kordestān,*
 Iran **44 C5** 35 33N 47 8 E
Hoshangabad, *India* **42 H7** 22 45N 77 45 E
Hoshiarpur, *India* **42 D6** 31 30N 75 58 E
Hospet, *India* **40 M10** 15 15N 76 20 E
Hoste, I., *Chile* **96 H3** 55 0S 69 0W
Hot, *Thailand* **38 C2** 18 8N 98 29 E
Hot Creek Range, *U.S.A.* . **82 G6** 38 40N 116 20W
Hot Springs, *Ark., U.S.A.* . **81 H8** 34 31N 93 3W
Hot Springs, *S. Dak., U.S.A.* **80 D3** 43 26N 103 29W
Hotagen, *Sweden* **8 E16** 63 50N 14 30 E
Hotan, *China* **32 C2** 37 25N 79 55 E
Hotazel, *S. Africa* **56 D3** 27 17S 22 58 E
Hotchkiss, *U.S.A.* **83 G10** 38 48N 107 43W
Hotham, C., *Australia* **60 B5** 12 2S 131 18 E
Hoting, *Sweden* **8 D17** 64 8N 16 15 E
Hotte, Massif de la, *Haiti* . **89 C5** 18 30N 73 45W
Hottentotsbaai, *Namibia* . **56 D1** 26 8S 14 59 E
Houffalize, *Belgium* **15 D5** 50 8N 5 48 E
Houghton, *Mich., U.S.A.* . **80 B10** 47 7N 88 34W
Houghton, *N.Y., U.S.A.* .. **78 D6** 42 25N 78 10W
Houghton L., *U.S.A.* **76 C3** 44 21N 84 44W
Houhora Heads, *N.Z.* **59 F4** 34 49S 173 9 E
Houlton, *U.S.A.* **77 B12** 46 8N 67 51W
Houma, *U.S.A.* **81 L9** 29 36N 90 43W
Housatonic →, *U.S.A.* ... **79 E11** 41 10N 73 7W
Houston, *Canada* **72 C3** 54 25N 126 39W
Houston, *Mo., U.S.A.* **81 G9** 37 22N 91 58W
Houston, *Tex., U.S.A.* **81 L7** 29 46N 95 22W
Houtman Abrolhos,
 Australia **61 E1** 28 43S 113 48 E
Hovd, *Mongolia* **32 B4** 48 2N 91 37 E
Hove, *U.K.* **11 G7** 50 50N 0 10W
Hoveyzeh, *Iran* **45 D6** 31 27N 48 4 E
Hövsgöl, *Mongolia* **34 C5** 43 37N 109 39 E
Hövsgöl Nuur, *Mongolia* . **32 A5** 51 0N 100 30 E
Howard, *Australia* **63 D5** 25 16S 152 32 E
Howard, *Pa., U.S.A.* **78 F7** 41 1N 77 40W
Howard, *S. Dak., U.S.A.* .. **80 C6** 44 1N 97 32W
Howe, *U.S.A.* **82 E7** 43 48N 113 0W
Howe, C., *Australia* **63 F5** 37 30S 150 0 E
Howe I., *Canada* **79 B8** 44 16N 76 17W
Howell, *U.S.A.* **76 D4** 42 36N 83 56W
Howick, *Canada* **79 A11** 45 11N 73 51W
Howick, *S. Africa* **57 D5** 29 28S 30 14 E
Howick Group, *Australia* . **62 A4** 14 20S 145 30 E
Howitt, L., *Australia* **63 D2** 27 40S 138 40 E
Howland I., *Pac. Oc.* **64 G10** 0 48N 176 38W
Howrah = Haora, *India* ... **43 H13** 22 37N 88 20 E
Howth Hd., *Ireland* **13 C5** 53 22N 6 4W
Höxter, *Germany* **16 C5** 51 46N 9 22 E
Hoy, *U.K.* **12 C5** 58 50N 3 15W
Høyanger, *Norway* **9 F12** 61 13N 6 4 E

oyerswerda, Germany	16 C8	51 26N	14 14 E
oylake, U.K.	10 D4	53 24N	3 10W
pungan Pass, Burma	41 F20	27 30N	96 55 E
radec Králové, Czech Rep.	16 C8	50 15N	15 50 E
rodna, Belarus	17 B12	53 42N	23 52 E
rodzyanka, Belarus	17 B15	53 31N	28 42 E
ron →, Slovak Rep.	17 E10	47 49N	18 45 E
rvatska = Croatia ■, Europe	16 F9	45 20N	16 0 E
rymayliv, Ukraine	17 D14	49 20N	26 5 E
senwi, Burma	41 H20	23 22N	97 55 E
siamen = Xiamen, China	33 D6	24 25N	118 4 E
sian = Xi'an, China	34 G5	34 15N	109 0 E
sinchu, Taiwan	33 D7	24 48N	120 58 E
sinhailien = Lianyungang, China	35 G10	34 40N	119 11 E
süchou = Xuzhou, China	35 G9	34 18N	117 10 E
ua Xian, China	34 G5	38 8N	108 42 E
ua Hin, Thailand	38 F2	12 34N	99 58 E
ua Xian, Henan, China	34 G8	35 30N	114 30 E
ua Xian, Shaanxi, China	34 G5	34 30N	109 48 E
uachinera, Mexico	86 A3	30 9N	108 55W
uacho, Peru	92 F3	11 10S	77 35W
uade, China	34 D7	41 55N	113 59 E
uadian, China	35 C14	43 0N	126 40 E
uai He →, China	33 C6	33 0N	118 30 E
uai Yot, Thailand	39 J2	7 45N	99 37 E
uai'an, Hebei, China	34 D8	40 30N	114 20 E
uai'an, Jiangsu, China	35 H10	33 30N	119 10 E
uaibei, China	34 G9	34 0N	116 48 E
uaide = Gongzhuling, China	35 C13	43 30N	124 40 E
uaidezhen, China	35 C13	43 48N	124 50 E
uainan, China	33 C6	32 38N	116 58 E
uairen, China	34 E7	39 48N	113 20 E
uairou, China	34 D9	40 20N	116 35 E
uaiyang, China	34 H8	33 40N	114 52 E
uaiyin, China	35 H10	33 30N	119 2 E
uaiyuan, China	35 H9	32 55N	117 10 E
uajianzi, China	35 D13	41 23N	125 20 E
uajuapan de Leon, Mexico	87 D5	17 50N	97 48W
ualapai Peak, U.S.A.	83 J7	35 5N	113 54W
uallaga →, Peru	92 E3	5 15S	75 30W
uambo, Angola	53 G3	12 42S	15 54 E
uan Jiang →, China	34 G5	34 28N	109 0 E
uan Xian, China	34 F4	36 33N	107 7 E
uancabamba, Peru	92 E3	5 10S	79 15W
uancane, Peru	92 G5	15 10S	69 44W
uancavelica, Peru	92 F3	12 50S	75 5W
uancayo, Peru	92 F3	12 5S	75 12W
uanchaca, Bolivia	92 H5	20 15S	66 40W
uang Hai = Yellow Sea, China	35 G12	35 0N	123 0 E
uang He →, China	35 F10	37 55N	118 50 E
uang Xian, China	35 F11	37 38N	120 30 E
uanglong, China	34 G5	35 30N	109 59 E
uangshan, China	33 D6	29 42N	118 25 E
uangshi, China	33 C6	30 10N	115 3 E
uangsongdian, China	35 C14	43 45N	127 25 E
uangtai, China	35 F9	36 58N	117 56 E
uánuco, Peru	92 E3	9 55S	76 15W
uarmey, Peru	92 F3	10 5S	78 5W
uascarán, Peru	92 E3	9 8S	77 36W
uasco, Chile	94 B1	28 30S	71 15W
uasco →, Chile	94 B1	28 27S	71 13W
uasna, U.S.A.	85 K6	35 6N	120 24W
uatabampo, Mexico	86 B3	26 50N	109 50W
uauchinango, Mexico	87 C5	20 11N	98 3W
uautla de Jiménez, Mexico	87 D5	18 8N	96 51W
uay Namota, Mexico	86 C4	21 56N	104 30W
uayin, China	34 G6	34 35N	110 5 E
ubbard, Ohio, U.S.A.	78 E4	41 9N	80 34W
ubbard, Tex., U.S.A.	81 K6	31 51N	96 48W
ubbart Pt., Canada	73 B10	59 21N	94 41W
ubei □, China	33 C6	31 0N	112 0 E
ubli, India	40 M9	15 22N	75 15 E
uch'ang, N. Korea	35 D14	41 25N	127 2 E
ucknall, U.K.	10 D6	53 3N	1 13W
uddersfield, U.K.	10 D6	53 39N	1 47W
udiksvall, Sweden	9 F17	61 43N	17 10 E
udson, Canada	70 B1	50 6N	92 9W
udson, Mass., U.S.A.	79 D13	42 23N	71 34W
udson, N.Y., U.S.A.	79 D11	42 15N	73 46W
udson, Wis., U.S.A.	80 C8	44 58N	92 45W
udson, Wyo., U.S.A.	82 E9	42 54N	108 35W
udson →, U.S.A.	79 F10	40 42N	74 2W
udson Bay, N.W.T., Canada	69 C11	60 0N	86 0W
udson Bay, Sask., Canada	73 C8	52 51N	102 23W
udson Falls, U.S.A.	79 C11	43 18N	73 35W
udson Mts., Antarctica	5 D16	74 32S	99 20W
udson Str., Canada	69 B13	62 0N	70 0W
udson's Hope, Canada	72 B4	56 0N	121 54W
ue, Vietnam	38 D6	16 30N	107 35 E
uehuetenango, Guatemala	88 C1	15 20N	91 28W
uejúcar, Mexico	86 C4	22 21N	103 13W
uelva, Spain	19 D2	37 18N	6 57W
uentelauquén, Chile	94 C1	31 38S	71 33W
uerta, Sa. de la, Argentina	94 C2	31 10S	67 30W
uesca, Spain	19 A5	42 8N	0 25W
uetamo, Mexico	86 D4	18 36N	100 54W
ugh →, Australia	62 D1	25 1S	134 1 E
ughenden, Australia	62 C3	20 52S	144 10 E
ughes, Australia	61 F4	30 42S	129 31 E
ughesville, U.S.A.	79 E8	41 14N	76 44W
ugli →, India	43 J13	21 56N	88 4 E
ugo, Colo., U.S.A.	80 F3	39 8N	103 28W
ugo, Okla., U.S.A.	81 H7	34 1N	95 31W
ugoton, U.S.A.	81 G4	37 11N	101 21W
ui Xian = Huixian, China	34 G7	35 27N	113 12 E
ui'anbu, China	34 F4	37 28N	106 38 E
uichapán, Mexico	87 C5	20 24N	99 40W
uifa He →, China	35 C14	43 0N	127 50 E
uila, Nevado del, Colombia	92 C3	3 0N	76 0W
uimin, China	35 F9	37 30N	117 28 E
uinan, China	35 C14	42 40N	126 2 E
uinca Renancó, Argentina	94 C3	34 51S	64 22W
uining, China	34 G3	35 5N	105 5 E
uinong, China	34 E4	39 5N	106 35 E
uisache, Mexico	86 C4	22 30N	100 25W
uiting, China	34 G9	34 5N	116 5 E
uixian, China	34 G7	35 27N	113 12 E

Huixtla, Mexico	87 D6	15 9N	92 28W
Huize, China	32 D5	26 24N	103 15 E
Hukawng Valley, Burma	41 F20	26 30N	96 30 E
Hukuntsi, Botswana	56 C3	23 58S	21 45 E
Ḩulayfā', Si. Arabia	44 E4	25 58N	40 45 E
Huld = Ulaanjirem, Mongolia	34 B3	45 5N	105 30 E
Hulin He →, China	35 B12	45 0N	122 10 E
Hull = Kingston upon Hull, U.K.	10 D7	53 45N	0 21W
Hull, Canada	79 A9	45 25N	75 44W
Hull →, U.K.	10 D7	53 44N	0 20W
Hulst, Neths.	15 C4	51 17N	4 2 E
Hulun Nur, China	33 B6	49 0N	117 30 E
Humahuaca, Argentina	94 A2	23 10S	65 25W
Humaitá, Brazil	92 E6	7 35S	63 1W
Humaitá, Paraguay	94 B4	27 2S	58 31W
Humansdorp, S. Africa	56 E3	34 2S	24 46 E
Humbe, Angola	56 B1	16 40S	14 55 E
Humber →, U.K.	10 D7	53 42N	0 27W
Humboldt, Canada	73 C7	52 15N	105 9W
Humboldt, Iowa, U.S.A.	80 D7	42 44N	94 13W
Humboldt, Tenn., U.S.A.	81 H10	35 50N	88 55W
Humboldt →, U.S.A.	82 F4	39 59N	118 36W
Humboldt Gletscher, Greenland	4 B4	79 30N	62 0W
Hume, U.S.A.	84 J8	36 48N	118 54W
Hume, L., Australia	63 F4	36 0S	147 5 E
Humenné, Slovak Rep.	17 D11	48 55N	21 50 E
Humphreys, Mt., U.S.A.	84 H8	37 17N	118 40W
Humphreys Peak, U.S.A.	83 J8	35 21N	111 41W
Humptulips, U.S.A.	84 C3	47 14N	123 57W
Hūn, Libya	51 C9	29 2N	16 0 E
Hun Jiang →, China	35 D13	40 50N	125 38 E
Húnaflói, Iceland	8 D3	65 50N	20 50W
Hunan □, China	33 D6	27 30N	112 0 E
Hunchun, China	35 C16	42 52N	130 28 E
Hundewali, Pakistan	42 D5	31 55N	72 38 E
Hundred Mile House, Canada	72 C4	51 38N	121 18W
Hunedoara, Romania	17 F12	45 40N	22 50 E
Hungary ■, Europe	17 E10	47 20N	19 20 E
Hungary, Plain of, Europe	6 F10	47 0N	20 0 E
Hungerford, Australia	63 D3	28 58S	144 24 E
Hŭngnam, N. Korea	35 E14	39 49N	127 45 E
Hunsberge, Namibia	56 D2	27 45S	17 12 E
Hunsrück, Germany	16 D4	49 56N	7 27 E
Hunstanton, U.K.	10 E8	52 56N	0 29 E
Hunter I., Australia	62 G3	40 30S	144 45 E
Hunter I., Canada	72 C3	51 55N	128 0W
Hunter Ra., Australia	63 E5	32 45S	150 15 E
Hunters Road, Zimbabwe	55 F2	19 9S	29 49 E
Hunterville, N.Z.	59 H5	39 56S	175 35 E
Huntingburg, U.S.A.	76 F2	38 18N	86 57W
Huntingdon, Canada	70 C5	45 6N	74 10W
Huntingdon, U.K.	11 E7	52 20N	0 11W
Huntingdon, U.S.A.	78 F6	40 30N	78 1W
Huntington, Ind., U.S.A.	76 E3	40 53N	85 30W
Huntington, Oreg., U.S.A.	82 D5	44 21N	117 16W
Huntington, Utah, U.S.A.	82 G8	39 20N	110 58W
Huntington, W. Va., U.S.A.	76 F4	38 25N	82 27W
Huntington Beach, U.S.A.	85 M9	33 40N	118 5W
Huntington Station, U.S.A.	79 F11	40 52N	73 26W
Huntly, N.Z.	59 G5	37 34S	175 11 E
Huntly, U.K.	12 D6	57 27N	2 47W
Huntsville, Canada	78 A5	45 20N	79 14W
Huntsville, Ala., U.S.A.	77 H2	34 44N	86 35W
Huntsville, Tex., U.S.A.	81 K7	30 43N	95 33W
Hunyani →, Zimbabwe	55 F3	15 57S	30 39 E
Hunyuan, China	34 E7	39 42N	113 42 E
Hunza →, India	43 B6	35 54N	74 20 E
Huo Xian = Huozhou, China	34 F6	36 36N	111 42 E
Huong Hoa, Vietnam	38 D6	16 37N	106 45 E
Huong Khe, Vietnam	38 C5	18 13N	105 41 E
Huonville, Australia	62 G4	43 0S	147 5 E
Huozhou, China	34 F6	36 36N	111 42 E
Hupeh = Hubei □, China	33 C6	31 0N	112 0 E
Ḩūr, Iran	45 D8	30 50N	57 7 E
Hurd, C., Canada	78 A3	45 13N	81 44W
Hure Qi, China	35 C11	42 45N	121 45 E
Hurghada, Egypt	51 C12	27 15N	33 50 E
Hurley, N. Mex., U.S.A.	83 K9	32 42N	108 8W
Hurley, Wis., U.S.A.	80 B9	46 27N	90 11W
Huron, Calif., U.S.A.	84 J6	36 12N	120 6W
Huron, Ohio, U.S.A.	78 E2	41 24N	82 33W
Huron, S. Dak., U.S.A.	80 C5	44 22N	98 13W
Huron, L., U.S.A.	78 B2	44 30N	82 40W
Hurricane, U.S.A.	83 H7	37 11N	113 17W
Hurunui →, N.Z.	59 K4	42 54S	173 18 E
Húsavík, Iceland	8 C5	66 3N	17 21W
Huşi, Romania	17 E15	46 41N	28 7 E
Huskvarna, Sweden	9 H16	57 47N	14 15 E
Hustadvika, Norway	8 E12	63 0N	7 0 E
Hustontown, U.S.A.	78 F6	40 3N	78 2W
Hutchinson, Kans., U.S.A.	81 F6	38 5N	97 56W
Hutchinson, Minn., U.S.A.	80 C7	44 54N	94 22W
Hutte Sauvage, L. de la, Canada	71 A7	56 15N	64 45W
Hutton, Mt., Australia	63 D4	25 51S	148 20 E
Huy, Belgium	15 D5	50 31N	5 15 E
Huzhou, China	33 C7	30 51N	120 8 E
Hvammstangi, Iceland	8 D3	65 24N	20 57W
Hvar, Croatia	20 C7	43 11N	16 28 E
Hvítá →, Iceland	8 D3	64 30N	21 58W
Hwachŏn-chŏsuji, S. Korea	35 E14	38 5N	127 50 E
Hwang Ho = Huang He →, China	35 F10	37 55N	118 50 E
Hwange, Zimbabwe	55 F2	18 18S	26 30 E
Hwange Nat. Park, Zimbabwe	56 B4	19 0S	26 30 E
Hyannis, Mass., U.S.A.	76 E10	41 39N	70 17W
Hyannis, Nebr., U.S.A.	80 E4	42 0N	101 46W
Hyargas Nuur, Mongolia	32 B4	49 0N	93 0 E
Hydaburg, U.S.A.	72 B2	55 15N	132 50W
Hyde Park, U.S.A.	79 E11	41 47N	73 56W
Hyden, Australia	61 F2	32 24S	118 53 E
Hyderabad, India	40 L11	17 22N	78 29 E
Hyderabad, Pakistan	42 G3	25 23N	68 24 E
Hyères, France	18 E7	43 8N	6 9 E
Hyères, Îs. d', France	18 E7	43 0N	6 20 E
Hyesan, N. Korea	35 D15	41 20N	128 10 E
Hyland →, Canada	72 B3	59 52N	128 12W
Hymia, India	43 C8	33 40N	78 2 E
Hyndman Peak, U.S.A.	82 E6	43 45N	114 8W
Hyōgo □, Japan	31 G7	35 15N	134 50 E

Hyrum, U.S.A.	82 F8	41 38N	111 51W
Hysham, U.S.A.	82 C10	46 18N	107 14W
Hythe, U.K.	11 F9	51 4N	1 5 E
Hyūga, Japan	31 H5	32 25N	131 35 E
Hyvinge = Hyvinkää, Finland	9 F21	60 38N	24 50 E
Hyvinkää, Finland	9 F21	60 38N	24 50 E

I

I-n-Gall, Niger	50 E7	16 51N	7 1 E
Iaco →, Brazil	92 E5	9 3S	68 34W
Iakora, Madag.	57 C8	23 6S	46 40 E
Ialomiţa →, Romania	17 F14	44 42N	27 51 E
Iaşi, Romania	17 E14	47 10N	27 40 E
Ib →, India	43 J10	21 34N	83 48 E
Ibadan, Nigeria	50 G6	7 22N	3 58 E
Ibagué, Colombia	92 C3	4 20N	75 20W
Ibar →, Serbia, Yug.	21 C9	43 43N	20 45 E
Ibaraki □, Japan	31 F10	36 10N	140 10 E
Ibarra, Ecuador	92 C3	0 21N	78 7W
Ibembo, Dem. Rep. of the Congo	54 B1	2 35N	23 35 E
Ibera, L., Argentina	94 B4	28 30S	57 9W
Iberian Peninsula, Europe	6 H5	40 0N	5 0W
Iberville, Canada	79 A11	45 19N	73 17W
Iberville, Lac d', Canada	70 A5	55 55N	73 15W
Ibiá, Brazil	93 G9	19 30S	46 30W
Ibiapaba, Sa. da, Brazil	93 D10	4 0S	41 30W
Ibicuí →, Brazil	95 B4	29 25S	56 47W
Ibicuy, Argentina	94 C4	33 55S	59 10W
Ibiza = Eivissa, Spain	22 C7	38 54N	1 26 E
Ibo, Mozam.	55 E5	12 22S	40 40 E
Ibonma, Indonesia	37 E8	3 29S	133 31 E
Ibotirama, Brazil	93 F10	12 13S	43 12W
Ibrāhīm →, Lebanon	47 A4	34 4N	35 38 E
'Ibri, Oman	45 F8	23 14N	56 30 E
Ibu, Indonesia	37 D7	1 35N	127 33 E
Ibusuki, Japan	31 J5	31 12N	130 40 E
Ica, Peru	92 F3	14 0S	75 48W
Iça →, Brazil	92 D5	2 55S	67 58W
Içana, Brazil	92 C5	0 21N	67 19W
Içana →, Brazil	92 C5	0 26N	67 19W
İçel = Mersin, Turkey	25 G5	36 51N	34 36 E
Iceland ■, Europe	8 D4	64 45N	19 0W
Ich'ang = Yichang, China	33 C6	30 40N	111 20 E
Ichchapuram, India	41 K14	19 10N	84 40 E
Ichhawar, India	42 H7	23 1N	77 1 E
Ichihara, Japan	31 G10	35 28N	140 5 E
Ichikawa, Japan	31 G9	35 44N	139 55 E
Ichilo →, Bolivia	92 G6	15 57S	64 50W
Ichinohe, Japan	30 D10	40 13N	141 17 E
Ichinomiya, Japan	31 G8	35 18N	136 48 E
Ichinoseki, Japan	30 E10	38 55N	141 8 E
Ichŏn, S. Korea	35 F14	37 17N	127 27 E
Icod, Canary Is.	22 F3	28 22N	16 43W
Ida Grove, U.S.A.	80 D7	42 21N	95 28W
Idabel, U.S.A.	81 J7	33 54N	94 50W
Idaho □, U.S.A.	82 D7	45 0N	115 0W
Idaho City, U.S.A.	82 E6	43 50N	115 50W
Idaho Falls, U.S.A.	82 E7	43 30N	112 2W
Idar-Oberstein, Germany	16 D4	49 43N	7 16 E
Idfû, Egypt	51 D12	24 55N	32 49 E
Ídhi Óros, Greece	23 D6	35 15N	24 45 E
Ídhra, Greece	21 F10	37 20N	23 28 E
Idi, Indonesia	36 C1	5 2N	97 37 E
Idiofa, Dem. Rep. of the Congo	52 E3	4 55S	19 42 E
Idlib, Syria	44 C3	35 55N	36 36 E
Idria, U.S.A.	84 J6	36 25N	120 41W
Idutywa, S. Africa	57 E4	32 8S	28 18 E
Ieper, Belgium	15 D2	50 51N	2 53 E
Ierápetra, Greece	23 E7	35 1N	25 44 E
Iesi, Italy	20 C5	43 31N	13 14 E
Ifakara, Tanzania	52 F7	8 8S	36 41 E
'Ifāl, W. al →, Si. Arabia	44 D2	28 7N	35 3 E
Ifanadiana, Madag.	57 C8	21 19S	47 39 E
Ife, Nigeria	50 G6	7 30N	4 31 E
Iférouâne, Niger	50 E7	19 5N	8 24 E
Iffley, Australia	62 B3	18 53S	141 12 E
Ifni, Morocco	50 C3	29 29N	10 12W
Iforas, Adrar des, Mali	50 E6	19 40N	1 40 E
Ifould, L., Australia	61 F5	30 52S	132 6 E
Iganga, Uganda	54 B3	0 37N	33 28 E
Igarapava, Brazil	93 H9	20 3S	47 47W
Igarka, Russia	26 C9	67 30N	86 33 E
Igatimi, Paraguay	95 A4	24 5S	55 40W
Iggesund, Sweden	9 F17	61 39N	17 10 E
Iglésias, Italy	20 E3	39 19N	8 32 E
Igloolik, Canada	69 B11	69 20N	81 49W
Igluligaarjuk, Canada	69 B10	63 21N	90 42W
Ignace, Canada	70 C1	49 30N	91 40W
Iğneada Burnu, Turkey	21 D13	41 53N	28 2 E
Igoumenitsa, Greece	21 E9	39 32N	20 18 E
Iguaçu →, Brazil	95 B5	25 36S	54 36W
Iguaçu, Cat. del, Brazil	95 B5	25 41S	54 26W
Iguaçu Falls = Iguaçu, Cat. del, Brazil	95 B5	25 41S	54 26W
Iguala, Mexico	87 D5	18 21N	99 32W
Igualada, Spain	19 B6	41 37N	1 37 E
Iguassu = Iguaçu →, Brazil	95 B5	25 36S	54 36W
Iguatu, Brazil	93 E11	6 20S	39 18W
Iharana, Madag.	57 A9	13 25S	50 0 E
Ihbulag, Mongolia	34 C4	43 11N	107 10 E
Iheya-Shima, Japan	31 L3	27 4N	127 58 E
Ihosy, Madag.	57 C8	22 24S	46 8 E
Ihotry, L., Madag.	57 C7	21 56S	43 41 E
Ii, Finland	8 D21	65 19N	25 22 E
Ii-Shima, Japan	31 L3	26 43N	127 47 E
Iida, Japan	31 G8	35 35N	137 50 E
Iijoki →, Finland	8 D21	65 20N	25 20 E
Iisalmi, Finland	8 E22	63 32N	27 10 E
Iiyama, Japan	31 F9	36 51N	138 22 E
Iizuka, Japan	31 H5	33 38N	130 42 E
Ijebu-Ode, Nigeria	50 G6	6 47N	3 58 E
IJmuiden, Neths.	15 B4	52 28N	4 35 E
IJssel →, Neths.	15 B5	52 35N	5 50 E
IJsselmeer, Neths.	15 B5	52 45N	5 20 E
Ijuí, Brazil	95 B5	28 23S	53 55W
Ijuí →, Brazil	95 B4	27 58S	55 20W
Ikaluktutiak, Canada	68 B9	69 10N	105 0W
Ikare, Nigeria	50 G7	7 32N	5 40 E
Ikaría, Greece	21 F12	37 35N	26 10 E
Ikeda, Japan	31 G6	34 1N	133 48 E

Ikela, Dem. Rep. of the Congo	52 E4	1 6S	23 6 E
Iki, Japan	31 H4	33 45N	129 42 E
Ikimba L., Tanzania	54 C3	1 30S	31 20 E
Ikopa →, Madag.	57 B8	16 45S	46 40 E
Ikungu, Tanzania	54 C3	1 33S	33 42 E
Ilagan, Phil.	37 A6	17 7N	121 53 E
Ilām, Iran	44 C5	33 36N	46 36 E
Ilam, Nepal	43 F12	26 58N	87 58 E
Ilām □, Iran	44 C5	33 0N	47 0 E
Ilanskiy, Russia	27 D10	56 14N	96 3 E
Iława, Poland	17 B10	53 36N	19 34 E
Île-à-la-Crosse, Canada	73 B7	55 27N	107 53W
Île-à-la-Crosse, Lac, Canada	73 B7	55 40N	107 45W
Île-de-France □, France	18 B5	49 0N	2 20 E
Ilebo, Dem. Rep. of the Congo	52 E4	4 17S	20 55 E
Ilek, Russia	26 D6	51 32N	53 21 E
Ilek →, Russia	24 D9	51 30N	53 22 E
Ilesha, Nigeria	50 G6	7 37N	4 40 E
Ilford, Canada	73 B9	56 4N	95 35W
Ilfracombe, Australia	62 C3	23 30S	144 30 E
Ilfracombe, U.K.	11 F3	51 12N	4 8W
Ilhéus, Brazil	93 F11	14 49S	39 2W
Ili →, Kazakstan	26 E8	45 53N	77 10 E
Iliamna L., U.S.A.	68 C4	59 30N	155 0W
Iligan, Phil.	37 C6	8 12N	124 13 E
Ilion, U.S.A.	79 D9	43 1N	75 2W
Ilkeston, U.K.	10 E6	52 58N	1 19W
Ilkley, U.K.	10 D6	53 56N	1 48W
Illampu = Ancohuma, Nevada, Bolivia	92 G5	16 0S	68 50W
Illana B., Phil.	37 C6	7 35S	123 45 E
Illapel, Chile	94 C1	32 0S	71 10W
Iller →, Germany	16 D6	48 23N	9 58 E
Illetas, Spain	22 B9	39 32N	2 35 E
Illimani, Nevado, Bolivia	92 G5	16 30S	67 50W
Illinois □, U.S.A.	80 E10	40 15N	89 30W
Illinois →, U.S.A.	75 C8	38 58N	90 28W
Illium = Troy, Turkey	21 E12	39 57N	26 12 E
Illizi, Algeria	50 C7	26 31N	8 32 E
Ilmajoki, Finland	9 E20	62 44N	22 34 E
Ilmen, Ozero, Russia	24 C5	58 15N	31 10 E
Ilo, Peru	92 G4	17 40S	71 20W
Iloilo, Phil.	37 B6	10 45N	122 33 E
Ilorin, Nigeria	50 G6	8 30N	4 35 E
Ilwaco, U.S.A.	84 D2	46 19N	124 3W
Ilwaki, Indonesia	37 F7	7 55S	126 30 E
Imabari, Japan	31 G6	34 4N	133 0 E
Imaloto →, Madag.	57 C8	23 27S	45 13 E
Imandra, Ozero, Russia	24 A5	67 30N	33 0 E
Imari, Japan	31 H4	33 15N	129 52 E
Imatra, Finland	24 B4	61 12N	28 48 E
Imbil, Australia	63 D5	26 22S	152 32 E
imeni 26 Bakinskikh Komissarov = Neftçala, Azerbaijan	25 G8	39 19N	49 12 E
Imeri, Serra, Brazil	92 C5	0 50N	65 25W
Imerimandroso, Madag.	57 B8	17 26S	48 35 E
Imi, Ethiopia	46 F3	6 28N	42 10 E
Imlay, U.S.A.	82 F4	40 40N	118 9W
Imlay City, U.S.A.	78 D1	43 2N	83 5W
Immingham, U.K.	10 D7	53 37N	0 13W
Immokalee, U.S.A.	77 M5	26 25N	81 25W
Ímola, Italy	20 B4	44 20N	11 42 E
Imperatriz, Brazil	93 E9	5 30S	47 29W
Impéria, Italy	18 E8	43 53N	8 3 E
Imperial, Canada	73 C7	51 21N	105 28W
Imperial, Calif., U.S.A.	85 N11	32 51N	115 34W
Imperial, Nebr., U.S.A.	80 E4	40 31N	101 39W
Imperial Beach, U.S.A.	85 N9	32 35N	117 8W
Imperial Dam, U.S.A.	85 N12	32 55N	114 25W
Imperial Reservoir, U.S.A.	85 N12	32 53N	114 28W
Imperial Valley, U.S.A.	85 N11	33 0N	115 30W
Imperieuse Reef, Australia	60 C2	17 36S	118 50 E
Impfondo, Congo	52 D3	1 40N	18 0 E
Imphal, India	41 G18	24 48N	93 56 E
Imroz = Gökçeada, Turkey	21 D11	40 10N	25 50 E
Imuris, Mexico	86 A2	30 47N	110 52W
Imuruan B., Phil.	37 B5	10 40N	119 10 E
In Salah, Algeria	50 C6	27 10N	2 32 E
Ina, Japan	31 G8	35 50N	137 55 E
Inangahua Junction, N.Z.	59 J3	41 52S	171 59 E
Inanwatan, Indonesia	37 E8	2 10S	132 14 E
Iñapari, Peru	92 F5	11 0S	69 40W
Inari, Finland	8 B22	68 54N	27 5 E
Inarijärvi, Finland	8 B22	69 0N	28 0 E
Inawashiro-Ko, Japan	30 F10	37 29N	140 6 E
Inca, Spain	22 B9	39 43N	2 54 E
Inca de Oro, Chile	94 B2	26 45S	69 54W
Incaguasi, Chile	94 B1	29 12S	71 5W
Ince Burun, Turkey	25 F5	42 7N	34 56 E
Incesu, Turkey	44 B2	38 38N	35 11 E
Inch'ŏn, S. Korea	35 F14	37 27N	126 40 E
Incirliova, Turkey	21 F12	37 50N	27 41 E
Incline Village, U.S.A.	82 G4	39 10N	119 58W
Incomáti →, Mozam.	57 D5	25 46S	32 43 E
Indalsälven →, Sweden	9 E17	62 36N	17 30 E
Indaw, Burma	41 G20	24 15N	96 5 E
Independence, Calif., U.S.A.	84 J8	36 48N	118 12W
Independence, Iowa, U.S.A.	80 D9	42 28N	91 54W
Independence, Kans., U.S.A.	81 G7	37 14N	95 42W
Independence, Ky., U.S.A.	76 F3	38 57N	84 33W
Independence, Mo., U.S.A.	80 F7	39 6N	94 25W
Independence Fjord, Greenland	4 A6	82 10N	29 0W
Independence Mts., U.S.A.	82 F5	41 20N	116 0W
Index, U.S.A.	84 C5	47 50N	121 33W
India ■, Asia	40 K11	20 0N	78 0 E
Indian →, U.S.A.	77 M5	27 59N	80 34W
Indian Cabins, Canada	72 B5	59 52N	117 40W
Indian Harbour, Canada	71 B8	54 27N	57 13W
Indian Head, Canada	73 C8	50 30N	103 41W
Indian Lake, U.S.A.	79 C10	43 47N	74 16W
Indian Ocean	28 K11	5 0S	75 0 E
Indian Springs, U.S.A.	85 J11	36 35N	115 40W
Indiana, U.S.A.	78 F3	40 37N	79 9W
Indiana □, U.S.A.	76 F3	40 0N	86 0W
Indianapolis, U.S.A.	76 F2	39 46N	86 9W
Indianola, Iowa, U.S.A.	80 E8	41 22N	93 34W
Indianola, Miss., U.S.A.	81 J9	33 27N	90 39W
Indiga, Russia	24 A8	67 38N	49 9 E
Indigirka →, Russia	27 B15	70 48N	148 54 E
Indio, U.S.A.	85 M10	33 43N	116 13W
Indo-China, Asia	28 H14	15 0N	102 0 E
Indonesia ■, Asia	36 F5	5 0S	115 0 E

127

Indore

Jalūlā, *Iraq* **44 C5** 34 16N 45 10 E
Jamaica ■, *W. Indies* **88 C4** 18 10N 77 30W
Jamalpur, *Bangla.* **41 G16** 24 52N 89 56 E
Jamalpur, *India* **43 G12** 25 18N 86 28 E
Jamalpurganj, *India* **43 H13** 23 2N 87 59 E
Jamanxim →, *Brazil* **93 D7** 4 43S 56 18W
Jambi, *Indonesia* **36 E2** 1 38S 103 30 E
Jambi □, *Indonesia* **36 E2** 1 30S 102 30 E
Jambusar, *India* **42 H5** 22 3N 72 51 E
James →, *S. Dak., U.S.A.* . **80 D6** 42 52N 97 18W
James →, *Va., U.S.A.* **76 G7** 36 56N 76 27W
James B., *Canada* **70 B3** 54 0N 80 0W
James Ranges, *Australia* ... **60 D5** 24 10S 132 30 E
James Ross I., *Antarctica* .. **5 C18** 63 58S 57 50W
Jamesabad, *Pakistan* **42 G3** 25 17N 69 15 E
Jamestown, *Australia* **63 E2** 33 10S 138 32 E
Jamestown, *S. Africa* **56 E4** 31 6S 26 45 E
Jamestown, *N. Dak., U.S.A.* **80 B5** 46 54N 98 42W
Jamestown, *N.Y., U.S.A.* .. **78 D5** 42 6N 79 14W
Jamestown, *Pa., U.S.A.* ... **78 E4** 41 29N 80 27W
Jamilābād, *Iran* **45 C6** 34 24N 48 28 E
Jamiltepec, *Mexico* **87 D5** 16 17N 97 49W
Jamira →, *India* **43 J13** 21 35N 88 28 E
Jamkhandi, *India* **40 L9** 16 30N 75 15 E
Jammu, *India* **42 C6** 32 43N 74 54 E
Jammu & Kashmir □, *India* **43 B7** 34 25N 77 0 E
Jamnagar, *India* **42 H4** 22 30N 70 6 E
Jamni →, *India* **43 G8** 25 13N 78 35 E
Jampur, *Pakistan* **42 E4** 29 39N 70 40 E
Jamrud, *Pakistan* **42 C4** 33 59N 71 24 E
Jämsä, *Finland* **9 F21** 61 53N 25 10 E
Jamshedpur, *India* **43 H12** 22 44N 86 12 E
Jamtara, *India* **43 H12** 23 59N 86 49 E
Jämtland, *Sweden* **8 E15** 63 31N 14 0 E
Jan L., *Canada* **73 C8** 54 56N 102 55W
Jan Mayen, *Arctic* **4 B7** 71 0N 9 0W
Janaúba, *Brazil* **93 G10** 15 48S 43 19W
Jand, *Pakistan* **42 C5** 33 30N 72 6 E
Jandaq, *Iran* **45 C7** 34 3N 54 22 E
Jandia, *Canary Is.* **22 F5** 28 6N 14 21W
Jandia, Pta. de, *Canary Is.* **22 F5** 28 3N 14 31W
Jandola, *Pakistan* **42 C4** 32 20N 70 9 E
Jandowae, *Australia* **63 D5** 26 45S 151 7 E
Janesville, *U.S.A.* **80 D10** 42 41N 89 1W
Janghai, *India* **43 G10** 25 33N 82 19 E
Janin, *West Bank* **47 C4** 32 28N 35 18 E
Janjgir, *India* **43 J10** 22 1N 82 34 E
Janos, *Mexico* **86 A3** 30 45N 108 10W
Januária, *Brazil* **93 G10** 15 25S 44 25W
Janubio, *Canary Is.* **22 F6** 28 56N 13 50W
Jaora, *India* **42 H6** 23 40N 75 10 E
Japan ■, *Asia* **31 G8** 36 0N 136 0 E
Japan, Sea of, *Asia* **30 E7** 40 0N 135 0 E
Japan Trench, *Pac. Oc.* ... **28 F18** 32 0N 142 0 E
Japen = Yapen, *Indonesia* **37 E9** 1 50S 136 0 E
Japla, *India* **43 G11** 24 33N 84 1 E
Japurá →, *Brazil* **92 D5** 3 8S 65 46W
Jaquarão, *Brazil* **95 C5** 32 34S 53 23W
Jaqué, *Panama* **88 E4** 7 27N 78 8W
Jarābulus, *Syria* **44 B3** 36 49N 38 1 E
Jarama →, *Spain* **19 B4** 40 24N 3 32W
Jaranwala, *Pakistan* **42 D5** 31 15N 73 26 E
Jarash, *Jordan* **47 C4** 32 17N 35 54 E
Jardim, *Brazil* **94 A4** 21 28S 56 2W
Jardines de la Reina, Arch.
 de los, *Cuba* **88 B4** 20 50N 78 50W
Jargalang, *China* **35 C12** 43 5N 122 55 E
Jargalant = Hovd, *Mongolia* **32 B4** 48 2N 91 37 E
Jari →, *Brazil* **93 D8** 1 9S 51 54W
Jarīr, W. al →, *Si. Arabia* . **44 E4** 25 38N 42 30 E
Jarosław, *Poland* **17 C12** 50 2N 22 42 E
Jarrahdale, *Australia* **61 F2** 32 24S 116 5 E
Jarrahi →, *Iran* **45 D6** 30 49N 48 48 E
Jarres, Plaine des, *Laos* ... **38 C4** 19 27N 103 10 E
Jartai, *China* **34 E3** 39 45N 105 48 E
Jarud Qi, *China* **35 B11** 44 28N 120 50 E
Järvenpää, *Finland* **9 F21** 60 29N 25 5 E
Jarvis, *Canada* **78 D4** 42 53N 80 6W
Jarvis I., *Pac. Oc.* **65 H12** 0 15S 159 55W
Jarwa, *India* **43 F10** 27 38N 82 30 E
Jasdan, *India* **42 H4** 22 2N 71 12 E
Jashpurnagar, *India* **43 H11** 22 54N 84 9 E
Jasidih, *India* **43 G12** 24 31N 86 39 E
Jāsimīyah, *Iraq* **44 C5** 33 45N 44 41 E
Jasin, *Malaysia* **39 L4** 2 20N 102 26 E
Jāsk, *Iran* **45 E8** 25 38N 57 45 E
Jasło, *Poland* **17 D11** 49 45N 21 30 E
Jaso, *India* **43 G9** 24 30N 80 29 E
Jasper, *Alta., Canada* **72 C5** 52 55N 118 5W
Jasper, *Ont., Canada* **79 B9** 44 52N 75 57W
Jasper, *Ala., U.S.A.* **77 J2** 33 50N 87 17W
Jasper, *Fla., U.S.A.* **77 K4** 30 31N 82 57W
Jasper, *Ind., U.S.A.* **76 F2** 38 24N 86 56W
Jasper, *Tex., U.S.A.* **81 K8** 30 56N 94 1W
Jasper Nat. Park, *Canada* . **72 C5** 52 50N 118 8W
Jasrasar, *India* **42 F5** 27 43N 73 49 E
Jászberény, *Hungary* **17 E10** 47 30N 19 55 E
Jataí, *Brazil* **93 G8** 17 58S 51 48W
Jati, *Pakistan* **42 G3** 24 20N 68 19 E
Jatibarang, *Indonesia* **37 G13** 6 28S 108 18 E
Jatinegara, *Indonesia* **37 G12** 6 13S 106 52 E
Játiva = Xàtiva, *Spain* **19 C5** 38 59N 0 32W
Jaú, *Brazil* **95 A6** 22 10S 48 30W
Jauja, *Peru* **92 F3** 11 45S 75 15W
Jaunpur, *India* **43 G10** 25 46N 82 44 E
Java = Jawa, *Indonesia* ... **37 G14** 7 0S 110 0 E
Java Barat □, *Indonesia* .. **37 G12** 7 0S 107 0 E
Java Sea, *Indonesia* **36 E3** 4 35S 107 15 E
Java Timur □, *Indonesia* .. **37 G15** 8 0S 113 0 E
Java Trench, *Ind. Oc.* **36 F3** 9 0S 105 0 E
Javhlant = Uliastay,
 Mongolia **32 B4** 47 56N 97 28 E
Jawa, *Indonesia* **37 G14** 7 0S 110 0 E
Jawad, *India* **42 G6** 24 36N 74 51 E
Jay Peak, *U.S.A.* **79 B12** 44 55N 72 32W
Jaya, Puncak, *Indonesia* .. **37 E9** 3 57S 137 17 E
Jayanti, *India* **41 F16** 26 45N 89 40 E
Jayapura, *Indonesia* **37 E10** 2 28S 140 38 E
Jayawijaya, Pegunungan,
 Indonesia **37 F9** 5 0S 139 0 E
Jaynagar, *India* **41 F15** 26 43N 86 9 E
Jaypur, *India* **37 G14** 7 0S 110 0 E
Jayrūd, *Syria* **44 C3** 33 49N 36 44 E
Jayton, *U.S.A.* **81 J4** 33 15N 100 34W
Jāz Mūrīān, Hāmūn-e, *Iran* **45 E8** 27 20N 58 55 E
Jazīreh-ye Shīf, *Iran* **45 D6** 29 4N 50 54 E

Jazminal, *Mexico* **86 C4** 24 56N 101 25W
Jazzīn, *Lebanon* **47 B4** 33 31N 35 35 E
Jean, *U.S.A.* **85 K11** 35 47N 115 20W
Jean Marie River, *Canada* . **72 A4** 61 32N 120 38W
Jean Rabel, *Haiti* **89 C5** 19 50N 73 5W
Jeanerette, *U.S.A.* **81 L9** 29 55N 91 40W
Jeannette, Ostrov =
 Zhannetty, Ostrov, *Russia* **27 B16** 76 43N 158 0 E
Jeannette, *U.S.A.* **78 F5** 40 20N 79 36W
Jebāl Bārez, Kūh-e, *Iran* .. **45 D8** 28 30N 58 20 E
Jebel, Bahr el →, *Sudan* .. **51 G12** 9 30N 30 25 E
Jedburgh, *U.K.* **12 F6** 55 29N 2 33W
Jedda = Jiddah, *Si. Arabia* **46 C2** 21 29N 39 10 E
Jeddore L., *Canada* **71 C8** 48 3N 55 55W
Jędrzejów, *Poland* **17 C11** 50 35N 20 15 E
Jefferson, *Iowa, U.S.A.* ... **80 D7** 42 1N 94 23W
Jefferson, *Ohio, U.S.A.* ... **78 E4** 41 44N 80 46W
Jefferson, *Tex., U.S.A.* ... **81 J7** 32 46N 94 21W
Jefferson, Mt., *Nev., U.S.A.* **82 G5** 38 51N 117 0W
Jefferson, Mt., *Oreg., U.S.A.* **82 D3** 44 41N 121 48W
Jefferson City, *Mo., U.S.A.* **80 F8** 38 34N 92 10W
Jefferson City, *Tenn., U.S.A.* **77 G4** 36 7N 83 30W
Jeffersontown, *U.S.A.* **76 F3** 38 12N 85 35W
Jeffersonville, *U.S.A.* **76 F3** 38 17N 85 44W
Jeffrey City, *U.S.A.* **82 E10** 42 30N 107 49W
Jega, *Nigeria* **50 F6** 12 15N 4 23 E
Jēkabpils, *Latvia* **9 H21** 56 29N 25 57 E
Jekyll I., *U.S.A.* **77 K5** 31 4N 81 25W
Jelenia Góra, *Poland* **16 C8** 50 50N 15 45 E
Jelgava, *Latvia* **9 H20** 56 41N 23 49 E
Jemaja, *Indonesia* **39 L5** 3 5N 105 45 E
Jemaluang, *Malaysia* **39 L4** 2 16N 103 52 E
Jember, *Indonesia* **37 H15** 8 11S 113 41 E
Jembongan, *Malaysia* **36 C5** 6 45N 117 20 E
Jena, *Germany* **16 C6** 50 54N 11 35 E
Jena, *U.S.A.* **81 K8** 31 41N 92 8W
Jenkins, *U.S.A.* **76 G4** 37 10N 82 38W
Jenner, *U.S.A.* **84 G3** 38 27N 123 7W
Jennings, *U.S.A.* **81 K8** 30 13N 92 40W
Jepara, *Indonesia* **37 G14** 7 40S 109 14 E
Jeparit, *Australia* **63 F3** 36 8S 142 1 E
Jequié, *Brazil* **93 F10** 13 51S 40 5W
Jequitinhonha, *Brazil* **93 G10** 16 30S 41 0W
Jequitinhonha →, *Brazil* . **93 G11** 15 51S 38 53W
Jerantut, *Malaysia* **39 L4** 3 56N 102 22 E
Jérémie, *Haiti* **89 C5** 18 40N 74 10W
Jerez, Punta, *Mexico* **87 C5** 22 58N 97 40W
Jerez de García Salinas,
 Mexico **86 C4** 22 39N 103 0W
Jerez de la Frontera, *Spain* **19 D2** 36 41N 6 7W
Jerez de los Caballeros,
 Spain **19 C2** 38 20N 6 45W
Jericho = El Arīḥā,
 West Bank **47 D4** 31 52N 35 27 E
Jericho, *Australia* **62 C4** 23 38S 146 6 E
Jerilderie, *Australia* **63 F4** 35 20S 145 41 E
Jermyn, *U.S.A.* **79 E9** 41 31N 75 31W
Jerome, *U.S.A.* **82 E6** 42 44N 114 31W
Jerramungup, *Australia* .. **61 F2** 33 55S 118 55 E
Jersey, *U.K.* **11 H5** 49 11N 2 7W
Jersey City, *U.S.A.* **79 F10** 40 44N 74 4W
Jersey Shore, *U.S.A.* **78 E7** 41 12N 77 15W
Jerseyville, *U.S.A.* **80 F9** 39 7N 90 20W
Jerusalem, *Israel* **47 D4** 31 47N 35 10 E
Jervis B., *Australia* **63 F5** 35 8S 150 46 E
Jervis Inlet, *Canada* **72 C4** 50 0N 123 57W
Jesselton = Kota Kinabalu,
 Malaysia **36 C5** 6 0N 116 4 E
Jessore, *Bangla.* **41 H16** 23 10N 89 10 E
Jesup, *U.S.A.* **77 K5** 31 36N 81 53W
Jesús Carranza, *Mexico* .. **87 D5** 17 28N 95 1W
Jesús María, *Argentina* ... **94 C3** 30 59S 64 5W
Jetmore, *U.S.A.* **81 F5** 38 4N 99 54W
Jetpur, *India* **42 J4** 21 45N 70 10 E
Jevnaker, *Norway* **9 F14** 60 15N 10 26 E
Jewett, *U.S.A.* **78 F3** 40 22N 81 2W
Jewett City, *U.S.A.* **79 E13** 41 36N 72 0W
Jeyḥūnābād, *Iran* **45 C6** 34 58N 48 59 E
Jeypore, *India* **41 K13** 18 50N 82 38 E
Jha Jha, *India* **43 G12** 24 46N 86 22 E
Jhabua, *India* **42 H6** 22 46N 74 36 E
Jhajjar, *India* **42 E7** 28 37N 76 42 E
Jhal, *Pakistan* **40 F4** 26 20N 65 35 E
Jhal Jhao, *Pakistan* **40 F4** 26 20N 65 35 E
Jhalawar, *India* **42 G7** 24 40N 76 10 E
Jhalida, *India* **43 H11** 23 22N 85 58 E
Jhalrapatan, *India* **42 G7** 24 33N 76 10 E
Jhang Maghiana, *Pakistan* **42 D5** 31 15N 72 22 E
Jhansi, *India* **43 G8** 25 30N 78 36 E
Jhargram, *India* **43 H12** 22 27N 86 59 E
Jharia, *India* **43 H12** 23 45N 86 26 E
Jharsuguda, *India* **41 J14** 21 56N 84 5 E
Jhelum, *Pakistan* **42 C5** 33 0N 73 45 E
Jhelum →, *Pakistan* **42 D5** 31 20N 72 10 E
Jhilmilli, *India* **43 H10** 23 24N 82 51 E
Jhudo, *Pakistan* **42 G3** 24 58N 69 18 E
Jhunjhunu, *India* **42 E6** 28 10N 75 30 E
Ji-Paraná, *Brazil* **92 F6** 10 52S 62 57W
Ji Xian, *Hebei, China* **34 F8** 37 35N 115 30 E
Ji Xian, *Henan, China* **34 G8** 35 22N 114 5 E
Ji Xian, *Shanxi, China* **34 F6** 36 7N 110 40 E
Jia Xian, *Henan, China* ... **34 H7** 33 59N 113 12 E
Jia Xian, *Shaanxi, China* .. **34 E6** 38 12N 110 28 E
Jiamusi, *China* **33 B8** 46 40N 130 26 E
Ji'an, *Jiangxi, China* **33 D6** 27 6N 114 59 E
Ji'an, *Jilin, China* **35 D14** 41 5N 126 10 E
Jianchang, *China* **35 D11** 40 55N 120 35 E
Jianchangying, *China* **35 D10** 40 10N 118 50 E
Jiangcheng, *China* **32 D5** 22 36N 101 52 E
Jiangmen, *China* **33 D6** 22 32N 113 0 E
Jiangsu □, *China* **35 H11** 33 0N 120 0 E
Jiangxi □, *China* **33 D6** 27 30N 116 0 E
Jiao Xian = Jiaozhou, *China* **35 F11** 36 18N 120 1 E
Jiaohe, *Hebei, China* **34 E9** 38 2N 116 20 E
Jiaohe, *Jilin, China* **35 C14** 43 40N 127 22 E
Jiaozhou, *China* **35 F11** 36 18N 120 1 E
Jiaozhou Wan, *China* **35 F11** 36 5N 120 10 E
Jiaozuo, *China* **34 G7** 35 16N 113 12 E
Jiawang, *China* **35 G9** 34 28N 117 26 E
Jiaxiang, *China* **34 G9** 35 25N 116 20 E
Jiaxing, *China* **33 C7** 30 49N 120 45 E
Jiayi = Chiai, *Taiwan* **33 D7** 23 29N 120 25 E
Jibuti = Djibouti ■, *Africa* **46 E3** 12 0N 43 0 E
Jicarón, I., *Panama* **88 E3** 7 10N 81 50W
Jiddah, *Si. Arabia* **46 C2** 21 29N 39 10 E
Jido, *India* **41 E19** 29 2N 94 58 E
Jieshou, *China* **34 H8** 33 18N 115 22 E

Jiexiu, *China* **34 F6** 37 2N 111 55 E
Jiggalong, *Australia* **60 D3** 23 21S 120 47 E
Jigni, *India* **43 G8** 25 45N 79 25 E
Jihlava, *Czech Rep.* **16 D8** 49 28N 15 35 E
Jihlava →, *Czech Rep.* ... **17 D9** 48 55N 16 36 E
Jijiga, *Ethiopia* **46 F3** 9 20N 42 50 E
Jilin, *China* **35 C14** 43 44N 126 30 E
Jilin □, *China* **35 C14** 44 0N 127 0 E
Jilong = Chilung, *Taiwan* . **33 D7** 25 3N 121 45 E
Jim Thorpe, *U.S.A.* **79 F9** 40 52N 75 44W
Jima, *Ethiopia* **46 F2** 7 40N 36 47 E
Jiménez, *Mexico* **86 B4** 27 10N 104 54W
Jimo, *China* **35 F11** 36 23N 120 30 E
Jin Xian = Jinzhou, *China* . **34 E8** 38 2N 115 2 E
Jin Xian, *China* **35 E11** 38 55N 121 42 E
Jinan, *China* **34 F9** 36 38N 117 1 E
Jincheng, *China* **34 G7** 35 29N 112 50 E
Jind, *India* **42 E7** 29 19N 76 22 E
Jindabyne, *Australia* **63 F4** 36 25S 148 35 E
Jindřichův Hradec,
 Czech Rep. **16 D8** 49 10N 15 2 E
Jing He →, *China* **34 G5** 34 27N 109 4 E
Jingbian, *China* **34 F5** 37 20N 108 30 E
Jingchuan, *China* **34 G4** 35 20N 107 20 E
Jingdezhen, *China* **33 D6** 29 20N 117 11 E
Jinggu, *China* **32 D5** 23 35N 100 41 E
Jinghai, *China* **34 E9** 38 55N 116 55 E
Jingle, *China* **34 E6** 38 20N 111 55 E
Jingning, *China* **34 G3** 35 30N 105 43 E
Jingpo Hu, *China* **35 C15** 43 55N 128 55 E
Jingtai, *China* **34 F3** 37 10N 104 6 E
Jingxing, *China* **34 E8** 38 2N 114 8 E
Jingyang, *China* **34 G5** 34 30N 108 50 E
Jingyu, *China* **35 C14** 42 25N 126 45 E
Jingyuan, *China* **34 F3** 36 30N 104 40 E
Jingziguan, *China* **34 H6** 33 15N 111 0 E
Jinhua, *China* **33 D6** 29 8N 119 38 E
Jining, *Nei Mongol Zizhiqu,
 China* **34 D7** 41 5N 113 0 E
Jining, *Shandong, China* .. **34 G9** 35 22N 116 34 E
Jinja, *Uganda* **54 B3** 0 25N 33 12 E
Jinjang, *Malaysia* **39 L3** 3 13N 101 39 E
Jinji, *China* **34 F4** 37 58N 106 8 E
Jinnah Barrage, *Pakistan* . **40 C7** 32 58N 71 33 E
Jinotega, *Nic.* **88 D2** 13 6N 85 59W
Jinotepe, *Nic.* **88 D2** 11 50N 86 10W
Jinsha Jiang →, *China* ... **32 D5** 28 50N 104 36 E
Jinxi, *China* **35 D11** 40 52N 120 50 E
Jinxiang, *China* **34 G9** 35 5N 116 22 E
Jinzhou, *Hebei, China* **34 E8** 38 2N 115 2 E
Jinzhou, *Liaoning, China* .. **35 D11** 41 5N 121 3 E
Jiparaná →, *Brazil* **92 E6** 8 3S 62 52W
Jipijapa, *Ecuador* **92 D2** 1 0S 80 40W
Jiquilpan, *Mexico* **86 D4** 19 57N 102 42W
Jishan, *China* **34 G6** 35 34N 110 58 E
Jisr ash Shughūr, *Syria* ... **44 C3** 35 49N 36 18 E
Jitarning, *Australia* **61 F2** 32 48S 117 57 E
Jitra, *Malaysia* **39 J3** 6 16N 100 25 E
Jiu →, *Romania* **17 F12** 43 47N 23 48 E
Jiudengkou, *China* **34 E4** 39 56N 106 40 E
Jiujiang, *China* **33 D6** 29 42N 115 58 E
Jiutai, *China* **35 B13** 44 10N 125 50 E
Jiuxiangcheng, *China* **34 H8** 33 12N 114 50 E
Jiuxincheng, *China* **34 E8** 39 17N 115 59 E
Jixi, *China* **35 B16** 45 20N 130 50 E
Jiyang, *China* **35 F9** 37 0N 117 12 E
Jiyuan, *China* **34 G7** 35 7N 112 57 E
Jīzān, *Si. Arabia* **46 D3** 17 0N 42 20 E
Jize, *China* **34 F8** 36 54N 114 56 E
Jīzl, Wādī al, *Si. Arabia* .. **44 E3** 25 39N 38 25 E
Jīzō-Zaki, *Japan* **31 G6** 35 34N 133 20 E
Jizzakh, *Uzbekistan* **26 E7** 40 6N 67 50 E
Joaçaba, *Brazil* **95 B5** 27 5S 51 31W
João Pessoa, *Brazil* **93 E12** 7 10S 34 52W
Joaquín V. González,
 Argentina **94 B3** 25 10S 64 0W
Jobat, *India* **42 H6** 22 25N 74 34 E
Jodhpur, *India* **42 F5** 26 23N 73 8 E
Jodiya, *India* **42 H4** 22 42N 70 18 E
Joensuu, *Finland* **8 E23** 62 37N 29 49 E
Jōetsu, *Japan* **31 F9** 37 12N 138 10 E
Jofane, *Mozam.* **57 C5** 21 15S 34 18 E
Jogbani, *India* **43 F12** 26 25N 87 15 E
Jõgeva, *Estonia* **9 G22** 58 45N 26 24 E
Jogjakarta = Yogyakarta,
 Indonesia **37 G14** 7 49S 110 22 E
Johannesburg, *S. Africa* ... **57 D4** 26 10S 28 2 E
Johannesburg, *U.S.A.* **85 K9** 35 22N 117 38W
Johilla →, *India* **43 H9** 23 37N 81 14 E
John Day, *U.S.A.* **82 D4** 44 25N 118 57W
John Day →, *U.S.A.* **82 D3** 45 44N 120 39W
John D'Or Prairie, *Canada* **72 B5** 58 30N 115 8W
John H. Kerr Reservoir,
 U.S.A. **77 G6** 36 36N 78 18W
John o' Groats, *U.K.* **12 C5** 58 38N 3 4W
Johnnie, *U.S.A.* **85 J10** 36 25N 116 5W
John's Ra., *Australia* **62 C1** 21 55S 133 23 E
Johnson, *Kans., U.S.A.* ... **81 G4** 37 34N 101 45W
Johnson, *Vt., U.S.A.* **79 B12** 44 38N 72 41W
Johnson City, *N.Y., U.S.A.* **79 D9** 42 7N 75 58W
Johnson City, *Tenn., U.S.A.* **77 G4** 36 19N 82 21W
Johnson City, *Tex., U.S.A.* **81 K5** 30 17N 98 25W
Johnsonburg, *U.S.A.* **78 E6** 41 29N 78 41W
Johnsondale, *U.S.A.* **85 K8** 35 58N 118 32W
Johnson's Crossing, *Canada* **72 A2** 60 29N 133 18W
Johnston, L., *Australia* ... **61 F3** 32 25S 120 30 E
Johnston Falls =
 Mambilima Falls, *Zambia* **55 E2** 10 31S 28 45 E
Johnston I., *Pac. Oc.* **65 F11** 17 10N 169 8W
Johnstone Str., *Canada* ... **72 C3** 50 28N 126 0W
Johnstown, *N.Y., U.S.A.* .. **79 C10** 43 0N 74 22W
Johnstown, *Ohio, U.S.A.* . **78 F2** 40 9N 82 41W
Johnstown, *Pa., U.S.A.* .. **78 F6** 40 20N 78 55W
Johor Baharu, *Malaysia* .. **39 M4** 1 28N 103 46 E
Joinville, *Brazil* **95 B6** 26 15S 48 55W
Joinville I., *Antarctica* **5 C18** 65 0S 55 30W
Jojutla, *Mexico* **87 D5** 18 37N 99 11W
Jokkmokk, *Sweden* **8 C18** 66 35N 19 50 E
Jökulsá á Bru →, *Iceland* . **8 D6** 65 40N 14 16W
Jökulsá á Fjöllum →,
 Iceland **8 C5** 66 10N 16 30W
Jolfā, *Āzarbājān-e Sharqī,
 Iran* **44 B5** 38 57N 45 38 E
Jolfā, *Eṣfahan, Iran* **45 C6** 32 58N 51 37 E
Joliet, *U.S.A.* **76 E1** 41 32N 88 5W
Joliette, *Canada* **70 C5** 46 3N 73 24W

Jolo, *Phil.* **37 C6** 6 0N 121 0 E
Jolon, *U.S.A.* **84 K5** 35 58N 121 9W
Jombang, *Indonesia* **37 G15** 7 33S 112 14 E
Jonava, *Lithuania* **9 J21** 55 8N 24 12 E
Jones Sound, *Canada* **4 B3** 76 0N 85 0W
Jonesboro, *Ark., U.S.A.* .. **81 H9** 35 50N 90 42W
Jonesboro, *La., U.S.A.* ... **81 J8** 32 15N 92 43W
Joniškis, *Lithuania* **9 H20** 56 13N 23 35 E
Jönköping, *Sweden* **9 H16** 57 45N 14 10 E
Jonquière, *Canada* **71 C5** 48 27N 71 14W
Joplin, *U.S.A.* **81 G7** 37 6N 94 31W
Jora, *India* **42 F6** 26 20N 77 49 E
Jordan, *Mont., U.S.A.* **82 C10** 47 19N 106 55W
Jordan, *N.Y., U.S.A.* **79 C8** 43 4N 76 29W
Jordan ■, *Asia* **47 E5** 31 0N 36 0 E
Jordan →, *Asia* **47 D4** 31 48N 35 32 E
Jordan Valley, *U.S.A.* **82 E5** 42 59N 117 3W
Jorhat, *India* **41 F19** 26 45N 94 12 E
Jörn, *Sweden* **8 D19** 65 4N 20 1 E
Jorong, *Indonesia* **36 E4** 3 58S 114 56 E
Jørpeland, *Norway* **9 G11** 59 3N 6 1 E
Jorquera →, *Chile* **94 B2** 28 3S 69 58W
Jos, *Nigeria* **50 G7** 9 53N 8 51 E
José Batlle y Ordóñez,
 Uruguay **95 C4** 33 20S 55 10W
Joseph, L., *Nfld., Canada* . **71 B6** 52 45N 65 18W
Joseph, L., *Ont., Canada* . **78 A5** 45 10N 79 44W
Joseph Bonaparte G.,
 Australia **60 B4** 14 35S 128 50 E
Joshinath, *India* **43 D8** 30 34N 79 34 E
Joshua Tree, *U.S.A.* **85 L10** 34 8N 116 19W
Joshua Tree National Park,
 U.S.A. **85 M10** 33 55N 116 0W
Jostedalsbreen, *Norway* . **9 F12** 61 40N 6 59 E
Jotunheimen, *Norway* ... **9 F13** 61 35N 8 25 E
Jourdanton, *U.S.A.* **81 L5** 28 55N 98 33W
Jovellanos, *Cuba* **88 B3** 22 40N 81 10W
Ju Xian, *China* **35 F10** 36 35N 118 20 E
Juan Aldama, *Mexico* **86 C4** 24 20N 103 23W
Juan Bautista Alberdi,
 Argentina **94 C3** 34 26S 61 48W
Juan de Fuca Str., *Canada* **84 B3** 48 15N 124 0W
Juan de Nova, *Ind. Oc.* .. **57 B7** 17 3S 43 45 E
Juan Fernández, Arch. de,
 Pac. Oc. **90 G2** 33 50S 80 0W
Juan José Castelli,
 Argentina **94 B3** 25 27S 60 57W
Juan L. Lacaze, *Uruguay* . **94 C4** 34 26S 57 25W
Juankoski, *Finland* **8 E23** 63 3N 28 19 E
Juárez, *Argentina* **94 D4** 37 40S 59 43W
Juárez, *Mexico* **85 N11** 32 20N 115 57W
Juárez, Sierra de, *Mexico* . **86 A1** 32 0N 116 0W
Juàzeiro, *Brazil* **93 E10** 9 30S 40 30W
Juàzeiro do Norte, *Brazil* . **93 E11** 7 10S 39 18W
Juba, *Sudan* **51 H12** 4 50N 31 35 E
Jubayl, *Lebanon* **47 A4** 34 5N 35 39 E
Jubbah, *Si. Arabia* **44 D4** 28 2N 40 56 E
Jubbal, *India* **42 D7** 31 5N 77 40 E
Jubbulpore = Jabalpur,
 India **43 H8** 23 9N 79 58 E
Jubilee L., *Australia* **61 E4** 29 0S 126 50 E
Juby, C., *Morocco* **50 C3** 28 0N 12 59W
Júcar = Xúquer →, *Spain* **19 C5** 39 5N 0 10W
Júcaro, *Cuba* **88 B4** 21 37N 78 51W
Juchitán, *Mexico* **87 D5** 16 27N 95 5W
Judaea = Har Yehuda, *Israel* **47 D3** 31 35N 34 57 E
Judith →, *U.S.A.* **82 C9** 47 44N 109 39W
Judith, Pt., *U.S.A.* **79 E13** 41 22N 71 29W
Judith Gap, *U.S.A.* **82 C9** 46 41N 109 45W
Jugoslavia = Yugoslavia ■,
 Europe **21 B9** 43 20N 20 0 E
Juigalpa, *Nic.* **88 D2** 12 6N 85 26W
Juiz de Fora, *Brazil* **95 A7** 21 43S 43 19W
Jujuy □, *Argentina* **94 A2** 23 20S 65 40W
Juli, *Peru* **92 G5** 16 10S 69 25W
Julia Cr. →, *Australia* **62 C3** 20 0S 141 11 E
Julia Creek, *Australia* **62 C3** 20 39S 141 44 E
Juliaca, *Peru* **92 G4** 15 25S 70 10W
Julian, *U.S.A.* **85 M10** 33 4N 116 38W
Julian L., *Canada* **70 B4** 54 25N 77 57W
Julianatop, *Surinam* **93 C7** 3 40N 56 30W
Julianehåb, *Greenland* ... **4 C5** 60 43N 46 0W
Julimes, *Mexico* **86 B3** 28 25N 105 27W
Jullundur, *India* **42 D6** 31 20N 75 40 E
Julu, *China* **34 F8** 37 15N 115 2 E
Jumbo, *Zimbabwe* **55 F3** 17 30S 30 58 E
Jumbo Pk., *U.S.A.* **85 J12** 36 12N 114 11W
Jumentos Cays, *Bahamas* **89 B4** 23 0N 75 40W
Jumilla, *Spain* **19 C5** 38 28N 1 19W
Jumla, *Nepal* **43 E10** 29 15N 82 13 E
Jumna = Yamuna →,
 India **43 G9** 25 30N 81 53 E
Junagadh, *India* **42 J4** 21 30N 70 30 E
Junction, *Tex., U.S.A.* ... **81 K5** 30 29N 99 46W
Junction, *Utah, U.S.A.* ... **83 G7** 38 14N 112 13W
Junction B., *Australia* **62 A1** 11 52S 133 55 E
Junction City, *Kans., U.S.A.* **80 F6** 39 2N 96 50W
Junction City, *Oreg., U.S.A.* **82 D2** 44 13S 123 12W
Junction Pt., *Australia* ... **62 A1** 11 45S 133 50 E
Jundah, *Australia* **62 C3** 24 46S 143 2 E
Jundiaí, *Brazil* **95 A6** 24 30S 47 0W
Juneau, *U.S.A.* **72 B2** 58 18N 134 25W
Junee, *Australia* **63 E4** 34 53S 147 35 E
Jungfrau, *Switz.* **18 C7** 46 32N 7 58 E
Junggar Pendi, *China* **32 B3** 44 30N 86 0 E
Jungshahi, *Pakistan* **42 G2** 24 52N 67 44 E
Juniata →, *U.S.A.* **78 F7** 40 30N 77 40W
Junín, *Argentina* **94 C3** 34 33S 60 57W
Junín de los Andes,
 Argentina **96 D2** 39 45S 71 0W
Jūniyah, *Lebanon* **47 B4** 33 59N 35 38 E
Juntas, *Chile* **94 B2** 28 24S 69 58W
Juntura, *U.S.A.* **82 E4** 43 45N 118 5W
Jur, Nahr el →, *Sudan* ... **51 G11** 8 45N 29 15 E
Jura = Jura, Mts. du,
 Europe **18 C7** 46 40N 6 5 E
Jura = Schwäbische Alb,
 Germany **16 D5** 48 20N 9 30 E
Jura, *U.K.* **12 F3** 56 0N 5 50W
Jura, Mts. du, *Europe* **18 C7** 46 40N 6 5 E
Jura, Sd. of, *U.K.* **12 F3** 55 57N 5 45W
Jurbarkas, *Lithuania* **9 J20** 55 4N 22 46 E
Jurien, *Australia* **61 F2** 30 18S 115 2 E
Jūrmala, *Latvia* **9 H20** 56 58N 23 34 E
Juruá →, *Brazil* **92 D5** 2 37S 65 44W
Juruena, *Brazil* **92 F7** 13 0S 58 10W

Juruena

Juruena →, Brazil	92 E7	7 20S	58 3W
Juruti, Brazil	93 D7	2 9S	56 4W
Justo Daract, Argentina	94 C2	33 52S	65 12W
Jutaí →, Brazil	92 D5	2 43S	66 57W
Juticalpa, Honduras	88 D2	14 40N	86 12W
Jutland = Jylland, Denmark	9 H13	56 25N	9 30 E
Juventud, I. de la, Cuba	88 B3	21 40N	82 40W
Juwain, Afghan.	40 D2	31 45N	61 30 E
Jüy Zar, Iran	44 C5	33 50N	46 18 E
Juye, China	34 G9	35 22N	116 5 E
Jwaneng, Botswana	53 J4	24 45S	24 50 E
Jylland, Denmark	9 H13	56 25N	9 30 E
Jyväskylä, Finland	9 E21	62 14N	25 50 E

K

K2, Pakistan	43 B7	35 58N	76 32 E
Kaap Plateau, S. Africa	56 D3	28 30S	24 0 E
Kaapkruis, Namibia	56 C1	21 55S	13 57 E
Kaapstad = Cape Town, S. Africa	56 E2	33 55S	18 22 E
Kabaena, Indonesia	37 F6	5 15S	122 0 E
Kabala, S. Leone	50 G3	9 38N	11 37W
Kabale, Uganda	54 C3	1 15S	30 0 E
Kabalo, Dem. Rep. of the Congo	54 D2	6 0S	27 0 E
Kabambare, Dem. Rep. of the Congo	54 C2	4 41S	27 39 E
Kabango, Dem. Rep. of the Congo	55 D2	8 35S	28 30 E
Kabanjahe, Indonesia	36 D1	3 6N	98 30 E
Kabardino-Balkar Republic = Kabardino-Balkaria □, Russia	25 F7	43 30N	43 30 E
Kabardino-Balkaria □, Russia	25 F7	43 30N	43 30 E
Kabarega Falls = Murchison Falls, Uganda	54 B3	2 15N	31 30 E
Kabasalan, Phil.	37 C6	7 47N	122 44 E
Kabetogama, U.S.A.	80 A8	48 28N	92 59W
Kabin Buri, Thailand	38 F3	13 57N	101 43 E
Kabinakagami L., Canada	70 C3	48 54N	84 25W
Kabinda, Dem. Rep. of the Congo	52 F4	6 19S	24 20 E
Kabompo, Zambia	55 E1	13 36S	24 14 E
Kabompo →, Zambia	53 G4	14 10S	23 11 E
Kabondo, Dem. Rep. of the Congo	55 D2	8 58S	25 40 E
Kabongo, Dem. Rep. of the Congo	54 D2	7 22S	25 33 E
Kabüd Gonbad, Iran	45 B8	37 5N	59 45 E
Kābul, Afghan.	42 B3	34 28N	69 11 E
Kābul □, Afghan.	40 B6	34 30N	69 0 E
Kabul →, Pakistan	42 C5	33 55N	72 14 E
Kabunga, Dem. Rep. of the Congo	54 C2	1 38S	28 3 E
Kaburuang, Indonesia	37 D7	3 50N	126 30 E
Kabwe, Zambia	55 E2	14 30S	28 29 E
Kachchh, Gulf of, India	42 H3	22 50N	69 15 E
Kachchh, Rann of, India	42 H4	24 0N	70 0 E
Kachchhidhana, India	43 J8	21 44N	78 46 E
Kachebera, Zambia	55 E3	13 50S	32 50 E
Kachin □, Burma	41 G20	26 0N	97 30 E
Kachira, L., Uganda	54 C3	0 40S	31 7 E
Kachiry, Kazakstan	26 D8	53 10N	75 50 E
Kachnara, India	42 H6	23 50N	75 6 E
Kachot, Cambodia	39 G4	11 30N	103 3 E
Kaçkar, Turkey	25 F7	40 45N	41 10 E
Kadan Kyun, Burma	38 F2	12 30N	98 20 E
Kadanai →, Afghan.	42 D1	31 22N	65 45 E
Kadi, India	42 H5	23 18N	72 23 E
Kadina, Australia	63 E2	33 55S	137 43 E
Kadipur, India	43 F10	26 10N	82 23 E
Kadirli, Turkey	44 B3	37 23N	36 5 E
Kadiyevka = Stakhanov, Ukraine	25 E6	48 35N	38 40 E
Kadoka, U.S.A.	80 D4	43 50N	101 31W
Kadoma, Zimbabwe	55 F2	18 20S	29 52 E
Kâdugli, Sudan	51 F11	11 0N	29 45 E
Kaduna, Nigeria	50 F7	10 30N	7 21 E
Kaédi, Mauritania	50 E3	16 9N	13 28W
Kaeng Khoï, Thailand	38 E3	14 35N	101 0 E
Kaesŏng, N. Korea	35 F14	37 58N	126 35 E
Kāf, Si. Arabia	44 D3	31 25N	37 29 E
Kafan = Kapan, Armenia	25 G8	39 18N	46 27 E
Kafanchan, Nigeria	50 G7	9 40N	8 20 E
Kafinda, Zambia	55 E3	12 32S	30 20 E
Kafirévs, Ákra, Greece	21 E11	38 9N	24 38 E
Kafue, Zambia	55 F2	15 46S	28 9 E
Kafue →, Zambia	53 H5	15 30S	29 0 E
Kafue Flats, Zambia	55 F2	15 40S	27 25 E
Kafue Nat. Park, Zambia	55 F2	15 0S	25 30 E
Kafulwe, Zambia	55 D2	9 0S	29 1 E
Kaga, Afghan.	42 B4	34 14N	70 10 E
Kaga Bandoro, C.A.R.	52 C3	7 0N	19 10 E
Kagan, Uzbekistan	26 F7	39 43N	64 33 E
Kagawa □, Japan	31 G7	34 15N	134 0 E
Kagera □, Tanzania	54 C3	2 0S	31 30 E
Kagera →, Uganda	54 C3	0 57S	31 47 E
Kağızman, Turkey	44 A4	40 5N	43 10 E
Kagoshima, Japan	31 J5	31 35N	130 33 E
Kagoshima □, Japan	31 J5	31 30N	130 30 E
Kagul = Cahul, Moldova	17 F15	45 50N	28 15 E
Kahak, Iran	45 B6	36 6N	49 46 E
Kahama, Tanzania	54 C3	4 8S	32 30 E
Kahan, Pakistan	42 E3	29 18N	68 54 E
Kahang, Malaysia	39 L4	2 12N	103 32 E
Kahayan →, Indonesia	36 E4	3 40S	114 0 E
Kahe, Tanzania	54 C4	3 30S	37 25 E
Kahnūj, Iran	45 E8	27 55N	57 40 E
Kahoka, U.S.A.	80 E9	40 25N	91 44W
Kahoolawe, U.S.A.	74 H16	20 33N	156 37W
Kahramanmaraş, Turkey	25 G6	37 37N	36 53 E
Kahuta, Pakistan	42 C5	33 35N	73 24 E
Kai, Kepulauan, Indonesia	37 F8	5 55S	132 45 E
Kai Besar, Indonesia	37 F8	5 35S	133 0 E
Kai Is. = Kai, Kepulauan, Indonesia	37 F8	5 55S	132 45 E
Kai Kecil, Indonesia	37 F8	5 45S	132 40 E
Kaiapoi, N.Z.	59 K4	43 24S	172 40 E
Kaieteur Falls, Guyana	92 B7	5 1N	59 10W
Kaifeng, China	34 G8	34 48N	114 21 E
Kaikohe, N.Z.	59 F4	35 25S	173 49 E
Kaikoura, N.Z.	59 K4	42 25S	173 43 E

Kaikoura Ra., N.Z.	59 J4	41 59S	173 41 E
Kailu, China	35 C11	43 38N	121 18 E
Kailua Kona, U.S.A.	74 J17	19 39N	155 59W
Kaimana, Indonesia	37 E8	3 39S	133 45 E
Kaimanawa Mts., N.Z.	59 H5	39 15S	175 56 E
Kaimganj, India	43 F8	27 33N	79 24 E
Kaimur Hills, India	43 G10	24 30N	82 0 E
Kaingaroa Forest, N.Z.	59 H6	38 24S	176 30 E
Kainji Res., Nigeria	50 F6	10 1N	4 40 E
Kaipara Harbour, N.Z.	59 G5	36 25S	174 14 E
Kaipokok B., Canada	71 B8	54 54N	59 47W
Kaira, India	42 H5	22 45N	72 50 E
Kairana, India	42 E7	29 24N	77 15 E
Kaironi, Indonesia	37 E8	0 47S	133 40 E
Kairouan, Tunisia	51 A8	35 45N	10 5 E
Kaitaia, N.Z.	59 F4	35 8S	173 17 E
Kaitangata, N.Z.	59 M2	46 17S	169 51 E
Kaithal, India	42 E7	29 48N	76 26 E
Kaitu →, Pakistan	42 C4	33 10N	70 30 E
Kaiwi Channel, U.S.A.	74 H16	21 15N	157 30W
Kaiyuan, China	35 C13	42 28N	124 1 E
Kajaani, Finland	8 D22	64 17N	27 46 E
Kajabbi, Australia	62 C3	20 0S	140 1 E
Kajana = Kajaani, Finland	8 D22	64 17N	27 46 E
Kajang, Malaysia	39 L3	2 59N	101 48 E
Kajiado, Kenya	54 C4	1 53S	36 48 E
Kajo Kaji, Sudan	51 H12	3 58N	31 40 E
Kakabeka Falls, Canada	70 C2	48 24N	89 37W
Kakadu Nat. Park, Australia	60 B5	12 30S	132 5 E
Kakamas, S. Africa	56 D3	28 45S	20 33 E
Kakamega, Kenya	54 B3	0 20N	34 46 E
Kakanui Mts., N.Z.	59 L3	45 10S	170 30 E
Kakdwip, India	43 J13	21 53N	88 11 E
Kake, Japan	31 G6	34 36N	132 19 E
Kake, U.S.A.	72 B2	56 59N	133 57W
Kakegawa, Japan	31 G9	34 45N	138 1 E
Kakeroma-Jima, Japan	31 K4	28 8N	129 14 E
Kakhovka, Ukraine	25 E5	46 45N	33 30 E
Kakhovske Vdskh., Ukraine	25 E5	47 5N	34 0 E
Kakinada, India	41 L13	16 57N	82 11 E
Kakisa →, Canada	72 A5	61 3N	118 10W
Kakisa L., Canada	72 A5	60 56N	117 43W
Kakogawa, Japan	31 G7	34 46N	134 51 E
Kakwa →, Canada	72 C5	54 37N	118 28W
Kāl Güsheh, Iran	45 D8	30 59N	58 12 E
Kal Safid, Iran	44 C5	34 52N	47 23 E
Kalabagh, Pakistan	42 C4	33 0N	71 28 E
Kalabahi, Indonesia	37 F6	8 13S	124 31 E
Kalach, Russia	25 D7	50 22N	41 0 E
Kaladan →, Burma	41 J18	20 20N	93 5 E
Kaladar, Canada	78 B7	44 37N	77 5W
Kalahari, Africa	56 C3	24 0S	21 30 E
Kalahari Gemsbok Nat. Park, S. Africa	56 D3	25 30S	20 30 E
Kalajoki, Finland	8 D20	64 12N	24 10 E
Kālak, Iran	45 E8	25 29N	59 22 E
Kalakamati, Botswana	57 C4	20 40S	27 25 E
Kalakan, Russia	27 D12	55 15N	116 45 E
K'alak'unlun Shank'ou, Pakistan	43 B7	35 33N	77 46 E
Kalam, Pakistan	43 B5	35 34N	72 30 E
Kalama, Dem. Rep. of the Congo	54 C2	2 52S	28 35 E
Kalama, U.S.A.	84 E4	46 1N	122 51W
Kalámai, Greece	21 F10	37 3N	22 10 E
Kalamata = Kalámai, Greece	21 F10	37 3N	22 10 E
Kalamazoo, U.S.A.	76 D3	42 17N	85 35W
Kalamazoo →, U.S.A.	76 D2	42 40N	86 10W
Kalambo Falls, Tanzania	55 D3	8 37S	31 35 E
Kalan, Turkey	44 B3	39 7N	39 32 E
Kalannie, Australia	61 F2	30 22S	117 5 E
Kalāntari, Iran	45 C7	32 10N	54 8 E
Kalao, Indonesia	37 F6	7 21S	121 0 E
Kalaotoa, Indonesia	37 F6	7 20S	121 50 E
Kalasin, Thailand	38 D4	16 26N	103 30 E
Kalat, Pakistan	40 E5	29 8N	66 31 E
Kalāteh, Iran	45 B7	36 33N	55 41 E
Kalāteh-ye Ganj, Iran	45 E8	27 31N	57 55 E
Kalbarri, Australia	61 E1	27 40S	114 10 E
Kalce, Slovenia	16 F8	45 54N	14 13 E
Kale, Turkey	21 F13	37 27N	28 49 E
Kalegauk Kyun, Burma	41 M20	15 33N	97 35 E
Kalehe, Dem. Rep. of the Congo	54 C2	2 6S	28 50 E
Kalema, Tanzania	54 C3	1 12S	31 55 E
Kalewa, Burma	41 H19	23 10N	94 15 E
Kaleybar, Iran	44 B5	38 47N	47 2 E
Kalgan = Zhangjiakou, China	34 D8	40 48N	114 55 E
Kalgoorlie-Boulder, Australia	61 F3	30 40S	121 22 E
Kali →, India	43 F8	27 6N	79 55 E
Kali Sindh →, India	42 G6	25 32N	76 17 E
Kalianda, Indonesia	36 F3	5 50S	105 45 E
Kalibo, Phil.	37 B6	11 43N	122 22 E
Kalima, Dem. Rep. of the Congo	54 C2	2 33S	26 32 E
Kalimantan □, Indonesia	36 E4	0 0	114 0 E
Kalimantan Barat □, Indonesia	36 E4	0 0	110 30 E
Kalimantan Selatan □, Indonesia	36 E5	2 30S	115 30 E
Kalimantan Tengah □, Indonesia	36 E4	2 0S	113 30 E
Kalimantan Timur □, Indonesia	36 D5	1 30N	116 30 E
Kálimnos, Greece	21 F12	37 0N	27 0 E
Kalimpong, India	43 F13	27 4N	88 35 E
Kalinin = Tver, Russia	24 C6	56 55N	35 55 E
Kaliningrad, Russia	9 J19	54 42N	20 32 E
Kalinkavichy, Belarus	17 B15	52 12N	29 20 E
Kalinkovichi = Kalinkavichy, Belarus	17 B15	52 12N	29 20 E
Kaliro, Uganda	54 B3	0 56N	33 30 E
Kalispell, U.S.A.	82 B6	48 12N	114 19W
Kalisz, Poland	17 C10	51 45N	18 8 E
Kaliua, Tanzania	54 D3	5 5S	31 48 E
Kalix, Sweden	8 D20	65 53N	23 12 E
Kalix →, Sweden	8 D20	65 50N	23 11 E
Kalka, India	42 D7	30 46N	76 57 E
Kalkarindji, Australia	60 C5	17 30S	130 47 E
Kalkaska, U.S.A.	76 C3	44 44N	85 11W
Kalkfeld, Namibia	56 C2	20 57S	16 14 E

Kalkfontein, Botswana	56 C3	22 4S	20 57 E
Kalkrand, Namibia	56 C2	24 1S	17 35 E
Kallavesi, Finland	8 E22	62 58N	27 30 E
Kallsjön, Sweden	8 E15	63 38N	13 0 E
Kalmar, Sweden	9 H17	56 40N	16 20 E
Kalmyk Republic = Kalmykia □, Russia	25 E8	46 5N	46 1 E
Kalmykia □, Russia	25 E8	46 5N	46 1 E
Kalmykovo, Kazakstan	25 E9	49 0N	51 47 E
Kalna, India	43 H13	23 13N	88 25 E
Kalnai, India	43 H10	22 46N	83 30 E
Kalocsa, Hungary	17 E10	46 32N	19 0 E
Kalokhorio, Cyprus	23 E12	34 51N	33 2 E
Kaloko, Dem. Rep. of the Congo	54 D2	6 47S	25 48 E
Kalol, Gujarat, India	42 H5	22 37N	73 31 E
Kalol, Gujarat, India	42 H5	23 15N	72 33 E
Kalomo, Zambia	55 F2	17 0S	26 30 E
Kalpi, India	43 F8	26 8N	79 47 E
Kalu, Pakistan	42 G2	25 5N	67 39 E
Kaluga, Russia	24 D6	54 35N	36 10 E
Kalulushi, Zambia	55 E2	12 50S	28 3 E
Kalundborg, Denmark	9 J14	55 41N	11 5 E
Kalush, Ukraine	17 D13	49 3N	24 23 E
Kalutara, Sri Lanka	40 R12	6 35N	80 0 E
Kalya, Russia	24 B10	60 15N	59 59 E
Kama, Dem. Rep. of the Congo	54 C2	3 30S	27 5 E
Kama →, Russia	24 C9	55 45N	52 0 E
Kamachumu, Tanzania	54 C3	1 37S	31 37 E
Kamaishi, Japan	30 E10	39 16N	141 53 E
Kamalia, Pakistan	42 D5	30 44N	72 42 E
Kaman, India	42 F6	27 39N	77 16 E
Kamapanda, Zambia	55 E1	12 5S	24 0 E
Kamaran, Yemen	46 D3	15 21N	42 35 E
Kamativi, Zimbabwe	55 F2	18 15S	27 27 E
Kambalda, Australia	61 F3	31 10S	121 37 E
Kambar, Pakistan	42 F3	27 37N	68 1 E
Kambarka, Russia	24 C9	56 15N	54 11 E
Kambolé, Zambia	55 D3	8 47S	30 48 E
Kambos, Cyprus	23 D11	35 2N	32 44 E
Kambove, Dem. Rep. of the Congo	55 E2	10 51S	26 33 E
Kamchatka, Poluostrov, Russia	27 D17	57 0N	160 0 E
Kamchatka Pen. = Kamchatka, Poluostrov, Russia	27 D17	57 0N	160 0 E
Kamchiya →, Bulgaria	21 C12	43 4N	27 44 E
Kamen, Russia	26 D9	53 50N	81 30 E
Kamen-Rybolov, Russia	30 B6	44 46N	132 2 E
Kamenjak, Rt., Croatia	16 F7	44 47N	13 55 E
Kamenka, Russia	24 A7	65 58N	44 0 E
Kamenka Bugskaya = Kamyanka-Buzka, Ukraine	17 C13	50 8N	24 16 E
Kamensk Uralskiy, Russia	26 D7	56 25N	62 2 E
Kamenskoye, Russia	27 C17	62 45N	165 30 E
Kameoka, Japan	31 G7	35 0N	135 35 E
Kami, Japan	30 E10	38 9N	140 17 E
Kamieskroon, S. Africa	56 E2	30 9S	17 56 E
Kamilukuak, L., Canada	73 A8	62 22N	101 40W
Kamin-Kashyrskyy, Ukraine	17 C13	51 39N	24 56 E
Kamina, Dem. Rep. of the Congo	55 D2	8 45S	25 0 E
Kaminak L., Canada	73 A10	62 10N	95 0W
Kaministiquia, Canada	70 C1	48 32N	89 35W
Kaminoyama, Japan	30 E10	38 9N	140 17 E
Kamiros, Greece	23 C9	36 20N	27 56 E
Kamituga, Dem. Rep. of the Congo	54 C2	3 2S	28 10 E
Kamla →, India	43 G12	25 35N	86 36 E
Kamloops, Canada	72 C4	50 40N	120 20W
Kamo, Japan	30 F9	37 39N	139 3 E
Kamoke, Pakistan	42 C6	32 4N	74 4 E
Kampala, Uganda	54 B3	0 20N	32 30 E
Kampang Chhnang, Cambodia	39 F5	12 20N	104 35 E
Kampar, Malaysia	39 K3	4 18N	101 9 E
Kampar →, Indonesia	36 D2	0 30N	103 8 E
Kampen, Neths.	15 B5	52 33N	5 53 E
Kampene, Dem. Rep. of the Congo	54 C2	3 36S	26 40 E
Kamphaeng Phet, Thailand	38 D2	16 28N	99 30 E
Kampolombo, L., Zambia	55 E2	11 37S	29 42 E
Kampong Saom, Cambodia	39 G4	10 38N	103 30 E
Kampong Saom, Chaak, Cambodia	36 B2	10 50N	103 30 E
Kampong To, Thailand	39 J3	6 3N	101 13 E
Kampot, Cambodia	39 G5	10 36N	104 10 E
Kampuchea = Cambodia ■, Asia	38 F5	12 15N	105 0 E
Kampung Air Putih, Malaysia	39 K4	4 15N	103 10 E
Kampung Jerangau, Malaysia	39 K4	4 50N	103 10 E
Kampung Raja, Malaysia	39 K4	5 45N	102 35 E
Kampungbaru = Tolitoli, Indonesia	37 D6	1 5N	120 50 E
Kamrau, Teluk, Indonesia	37 E8	3 30S	133 36 E
Kamsack, Canada	73 C8	51 34N	101 54W
Kamskoye Vdkhr., Russia	24 C10	58 41N	56 7 E
Kamuchawie, L., Canada	73 B8	56 18N	101 59W
Kamuela, U.S.A.	74 H17	20 1N	155 41W
Kamui-Misaki, Japan	30 C10	43 20N	140 21 E
Kamyanets-Podilskyy, Ukraine	17 D14	48 45N	26 40 E
Kamyanka-Buzka, Ukraine	17 C13	50 8N	24 16 E
Kāmyārān, Iran	44 C5	34 47N	46 56 E
Kamyshin, Russia	25 D8	50 10N	45 24 E
Kanaaupscow, Canada	70 B4	54 2N	76 30W
Kanaaupscow →, Canada	69 C12	53 39N	77 9W
Kanab, U.S.A.	83 H7	37 3N	112 32W
Kanab →, U.S.A.	83 H7	36 24N	112 38W
Kanagi, Japan	30 D10	40 54N	140 27 E
Kanairiktok →, Canada	71 A7	55 2N	60 18W
Kananga, Dem. Rep. of the Congo	52 F4	5 55S	22 18 E
Kanash, Russia	24 C8	55 30N	47 32 E
Kanaskat, U.S.A.	84 C5	47 19N	121 54W
Kanawha →, U.S.A.	76 F4	38 50N	82 9W
Kanazawa, Japan	31 F8	36 30N	136 38 E
Kanchanaburi, Thailand	38 E2	14 2N	99 31 E
Kanchenjunga, Nepal	43 F13	27 50N	88 10 E

Kanchipuram, India	40 N11	12 52N	79 45 E
Kandaghat, India	42 D7	30 59N	77 7 E
Kandahar = Qandahār, Afghan.	40 D4	31 32N	65 30 E
Kandalaksha, Russia	24 A5	67 9N	32 30 E
Kandalakshkiy Zaliv, Russia	24 A6	66 0N	35 0 E
Kandalu, Afghan.	40 E3	29 55N	63 20 E
Kandangan, Indonesia	36 E5	2 50S	115 20 E
Kandanghaur, Indonesia	37 G13	6 21S	108 6 E
Kandhkot, Pakistan	42 E3	28 16N	69 8 E
Kandhla, India	42 E7	29 18N	77 19 E
Kandi, Benin	50 F6	11 7N	2 55 E
Kandiaro, Pakistan	43 H13	23 58N	88 5 E
Kandla, India	42 H4	23 0N	70 10 E
Kandos, Australia	63 E4	32 45S	149 58 E
Kandy, Sri Lanka	40 R12	7 18N	80 43 E
Kane, U.S.A.	78 E6	41 40N	78 49W
Kane Basin, Greenland	4 B4	79 1N	70 0W
Kangân, Fārs, Iran	45 E7	27 50N	52 3 E
Kangān, Hormozgān, Iran	45 E8	25 48N	57 28 E
Kangar, Malaysia	39 J3	6 27N	100 12 E
Kangaroo I., Australia	63 F2	35 45S	137 0 E
Kangaroo Mts., Australia	62 C3	23 29S	141 51 E
Kangasala, Finland	9 F21	61 28N	24 4 E
Kangāvar, Iran	45 C6	34 40N	48 0 E
Kangdong, N. Korea	35 E14	39 9N	126 5 E
Kangean, Kepulauan, Indonesia	36 F5	6 55S	115 23 E
Kangean Is. = Kangean, Kepulauan, Indonesia	36 F5	6 55S	115 23 E
Kanggye, N. Korea	35 D14	41 0N	126 35 E
Kanggyŏng, S. Korea	35 F14	36 10N	127 0 E
Kanghwa, S. Korea	35 F14	37 45N	126 30 E
Kangiqsualujjuaq, Canada	69 C13	58 30N	65 59W
Kangiqsujuaq, Canada	69 B12	61 30N	72 0W
Kangirsuk, Canada	69 C13	60 0N	70 0W
Kangnŭng, S. Korea	35 F15	37 45N	128 54 E
Kangping, China	35 C12	42 43N	123 18 E
Kangra, India	42 C7	32 6N	76 16 E
Kangto, India	41 F18	27 50N	92 35 E
Kanhar →, India	43 G10	24 28N	83 8 E
Kaniama, Dem. Rep. of the Congo	54 D1	7 30S	24 12 E
Kaniapiskau = Caniapiscau →, Canada	71 A6	56 40N	69 30W
Kaniapiskau, Res. = Caniapiscau Rés. de, Canada	71 B6	54 10N	69 55W
Kanin, Poluostrov, Russia	24 A8	68 0N	45 0 E
Kanin Nos, Mys, Russia	24 A7	68 39N	43 32 E
Kanin Pen. = Kanin, Poluostrov, Russia	24 A8	68 0N	45 0 E
Kaniva, Australia	63 F3	36 22S	141 18 E
Kanjut Sar, Pakistan	43 A6	36 7N	75 25 E
Kankaanpää, Finland	9 F20	61 44N	22 50 E
Kankakee, U.S.A.	76 E2	41 7N	87 52W
Kankakee →, U.S.A.	76 E1	41 23N	88 15W
Kankan, Guinea	50 F4	10 23N	9 15W
Kankendy = Xankändi, Azerbaijan	25 G8	39 52N	46 49 E
Kanker, India	41 J12	20 10N	81 40 E
Kankroli, India	42 G5	25 4N	73 53 E
Kannapolis, U.S.A.	77 H5	35 30N	80 37W
Kannauj, India	43 F8	27 3N	79 56 E
Kannod, India	40 H10	22 45N	76 40 E
Kano, Nigeria	50 F7	12 2N	8 30 E
Kan'onji, Japan	31 G6	34 7N	133 39 E
Kanowit, Malaysia	36 D4	2 14N	112 20 E
Kanoya, Japan	31 J5	31 25N	130 50 E
Kanpetlet, Burma	41 J18	21 10N	93 59 E
Kanpur, India	43 F9	26 28N	80 20 E
Kansas □, U.S.A.	80 F6	38 30N	99 0W
Kansas →, U.S.A.	80 F7	39 7N	94 37W
Kansas City, Kans., U.S.A.	80 F7	39 7N	94 38W
Kansas City, Mo., U.S.A.	80 F7	39 6N	94 35W
Kansenia, Dem. Rep. of the Congo	55 E2	10 20S	26 0 E
Kansk, Russia	27 D10	56 20N	95 37 E
Kansŏng, S. Korea	35 E15	38 24N	128 30 E
Kansu = Gansu □, China	34 G3	36 0N	104 0 E
Kantaphor, India	42 H7	22 35N	76 34 E
Kantharalak, Thailand	38 E5	14 39N	104 39 E
Kantō □, Japan	31 F9	36 15N	139 30 E
Kantō-Sanchi, Japan	31 G9	35 59N	138 50 E
Kanturk, Ireland	13 D3	52 11N	8 54W
Kanuma, Japan	31 F9	36 34N	139 42 E
Kanus, Namibia	56 D2	27 50S	18 39 E
Kanye, Botswana	56 C4	24 55S	25 28 E
Kanzenze, Dem. Rep. of the Congo	55 E2	10 30S	25 12 E
Kanzi, Ras, Tanzania	54 D4	7 1S	39 33 E
Kaohsiung, Taiwan	33 D7	22 35N	120 16 E
Kaokoveld, Namibia	56 B1	19 15S	14 30 E
Kaolack, Senegal	50 F2	14 5N	16 8W
Kaoshan, China	35 B13	44 38N	124 50 E
Kapaa, U.S.A.	74 G15	22 5N	159 19W
Kapadvanj, India	42 H5	23 5N	73 0 E
Kapan, Armenia	25 G8	39 18N	46 27 E
Kapanga, Dem. Rep. of the Congo	52 F4	8 30S	22 40 E
Kapchagai = Qapshaghay, Kazakstan	26 E8	43 51N	77 14 E
Kapela = Velika Kapela, Croatia	16 F8	45 10N	15 5 E
Kapema, Dem. Rep. of the Congo	55 E2	10 45S	28 22 E
Kapfenberg, Austria	16 E8	47 26N	15 18 E
Kapiri Mposhi, Zambia	55 E2	13 59S	28 43 E
Kapiskau →, Canada	70 B3	52 47N	81 55W
Kapit, Malaysia	36 D4	2 0N	112 55 E
Kapiti I., N.Z.	59 J5	40 50S	174 56 E
Kaplan, U.S.A.	81 K8	30 0N	92 17W
Kapoe, Thailand	39 H2	9 34N	98 32 E
Kapoeta, Sudan	51 H12	4 50N	33 35 E
Kaposvár, Hungary	17 E9	46 25N	17 47 E
Kapps, Namibia	56 C2	22 32S	17 18 E
Kapsan, N. Korea	35 D15	41 4N	128 19 E
Kapsukas = Marijampole, Lithuania	9 J20	54 33N	23 19 E
Kapuas →, Indonesia	36 E3	0 25S	109 20 E
Kapuas Hulu, Pegunungan, Malaysia	36 D4	1 30N	113 30 E

130

Kapuas Hulu Ra. = Kapuas Hulu, Pegunungan, Malaysia 36 D4 1 30N 113 30 E
Kapulo, Dem. Rep. of the Congo . 55 D2 8 18S 29 15 E
Kapunda, Australia 63 E2 34 20S 138 56 E
Kapuni, N.Z. 59 H5 39 29S 174 8 E
Kapurthala, India 42 D6 31 23N 75 25 E
Kapuskasing, Canada 70 C3 49 25N 82 30W
Kapuskasing →, Canada ... 70 C3 49 49N 82 0W
Kaputar, Australia 63 E5 30 15S 150 10 E
Kaputir, Kenya 54 B4 2 5N 35 28 E
Kara, Russia 26 C7 69 10N 65 0 E
Kara Bogaz Gol, Zaliv = Garabogazköl Aylagy, Turkmenistan 25 F9 41 0N 53 30 E
Kara Kalpak Republic = Karakalpakstan □, Uzbekistan 26 E6 43 0N 58 0 E
Kara Kum, Turkmenistan . 26 F7 39 30N 60 0 E
Kara Sea, Russia 26 B8 75 0N 70 0 E
Karabiğa, Turkey 21 D12 40 23N 27 17 E
Karabük, Turkey 25 F5 41 12N 32 37 E
Karaburun, Turkey 21 E12 38 41N 26 28 E
Karabutak = Qarabutaq, Kazakstan 26 E7 49 59N 60 14 E
Karacabey, Turkey 21 D13 40 12N 28 21 E
Karacasu, Turkey 21 F13 37 43N 28 35 E
Karachey-Cherkessia □, Russia 25 F7 43 40N 41 30 E
Karachi, Pakistan 42 G2 24 53N 67 0 E
Karad, India 40 L9 17 15N 74 10 E
Karaganda = Qaraghandy, Kazakstan 26 E8 49 50N 73 10 E
Karagayly, Kazakstan 26 E8 49 26N 76 0 E
Karaginskiy, Ostrov, Russia 27 D17 58 45N 164 0 E
Karagiye, Vpadina, Kazakstan 25 F9 43 27N 51 45 E
Karagiye Depression = Karagiye, Vpadina, Kazakstan 25 F9 43 27N 51 45 E
Karagola Road, India 43 G12 25 29N 87 23 E
Karaikal, India 40 P11 10 59N 79 50 E
Karaikkudi, India 40 P11 10 5N 78 45 E
Karaj, India 45 C6 35 48N 51 0 E
Karak, Malaysia 39 L4 3 25N 102 2 E
Karakalpakstan □, Uzbekistan 26 E6 43 0N 58 0 E
Karakelong, Indonesia 37 D7 4 35N 126 50 E
Karakitang, Indonesia 37 D7 3 14N 125 28 E
Karaklis = Vanadzor, Armenia 25 F7 40 48N 44 30 E
Karakoram Pass, Pakistan . 43 B7 35 33N 77 50 E
Karakoram Ra., Pakistan . 43 B7 35 30N 77 0 E
Karalon, Russia 27 D12 57 5N 115 50 E
Karama, Jordan 47 D4 31 57N 35 35 E
Karaman, Turkey 25 G5 37 14N 33 13 E
Karamay, China 32 B3 45 30N 84 58 E
Karambu, Indonesia 36 E5 3 53S 116 6 E
Karamea Bight, N.Z. 59 J3 41 22S 171 40 E
Karamnasa →, India 43 G10 25 31N 83 52 E
Karand, Iran 44 C5 34 16N 46 15 E
Karanganyar, Indonesia . 37 G13 7 38S 109 37 E
Karanjia, India 43 J11 21 47N 85 58 E
Karasburg, Namibia 56 D2 28 0S 18 44 E
Karasino, Russia 26 C9 66 50N 86 50 E
Karasjok, Norway 8 B21 69 27N 25 30 E
Karasuk, Russia 26 D8 53 44N 78 2 E
Karasuyama, Japan 31 F10 36 39N 140 9 E
Karatau = Qarataū, Kazakstan 26 E8 43 10N 70 28 E
Karatau, Khrebet, Kazakstan 26 E7 43 30N 69 30 E
Karatsu, Japan 31 H5 33 26N 129 58 E
Karaul, Russia 26 B9 70 6N 82 15 E
Karauli, India 42 F7 26 30N 77 4 E
Karavostasi, Cyprus 23 D11 35 8N 32 50 E
Karawang, Indonesia 37 G12 6 30S 107 15 E
Karawanken, Europe 16 E8 46 30N 14 40 E
Karayazı, Turkey 25 G7 39 41N 42 9 E
Karazhal, Kazakstan 26 E8 48 2N 70 49 E
Karbalā', Iraq 44 C5 32 36N 44 3 E
Karcag, Hungary 17 E11 47 19N 20 57 E
Karcha →, Pakistan 43 B7 34 45N 76 10 E
Karchana, India 43 G9 25 17N 81 56 E
Kardhitsa, Greece 21 E9 39 23N 21 54 E
Kärdla, Estonia 9 G20 58 50N 22 40 E
Kareeberge, S. Africa 56 E3 30 59S 21 50 E
Kareha →, India 43 G12 25 44N 86 21 E
Kareima, Sudan 51 E12 18 30N 31 49 E
Karelia □, Russia 24 A5 65 30N 32 30 E
Karelian Republic = Karelia □, Russia 24 A5 65 30N 32 30 E
Karera, India 42 G8 25 32N 78 9 E
Kārevāndar, Iran 45 E9 27 53N 60 44 E
Kargasok, Russia 26 D9 59 3N 80 53 E
Kargat, Russia 26 D9 55 10N 80 15 E
Kargil, India 43 B7 34 32N 76 12 E
Kargopol, Russia 24 B6 61 30N 38 58 E
Karhal, India 43 F8 27 1N 78 57 E
Kariān, Iran 45 E8 26 57N 57 14 E
Kariba, Zimbabwe 55 F2 16 28S 28 50 E
Kariba, L., Zimbabwe 55 F2 16 40S 28 25 E
Kariba Dam, Zimbabwe ... 55 F2 16 30S 28 35 E
Kariba Gorge, Zambia 55 F2 16 30S 28 50 E
Karibib, Namibia 56 C2 22 0S 15 56 E
Karimata, Kepulauan, Indonesia 36 E3 1 25S 109 0 E
Karimata, Selat, Indonesia . 36 E3 2 0S 108 40 E
Karimata Is. = Karimata, Kepulauan, Indonesia . 36 E3 1 25S 109 0 E
Karimnagar, India 40 K11 18 26N 79 10 E
Karimunjawa, Kepulauan, Indonesia 36 F4 5 50S 110 30 E
Karin, Somali Rep. 46 E4 10 50N 45 52 E
Karīt, Iran 45 C8 33 29N 56 55 E
Kariya, Japan 31 G8 34 58N 137 1 E
Karkaralinsk = Qarqaraly, Kazakstan
Karkheh →, Iran 44 D5 31 2N 47 29 E
Karkinitska Zatoka, Ukraine 25 E5 45 56N 33 0 E
Karkinitskiy Zaliv = Karkinitska Zatoka, Ukraine 25 E5 45 56N 33 0 E
Karl-Marx-Stadt = Chemnitz, Germany 16 C7 50 51N 12 54 E
Karlovac, Croatia 16 F8 45 31N 15 36 E
Karlovo, Bulgaria 21 C11 42 38N 24 47 E

Karlovy Vary, Czech Rep. .. 16 C7 50 13N 12 51 E
Karlsbad = Karlovy Vary, Czech Rep. 16 C7 50 13N 12 51 E
Karlsborg, Sweden 9 G16 58 33N 14 33 E
Karlshamn, Sweden 9 H16 56 10N 14 51 E
Karlskoga, Sweden 9 G16 59 28N 14 33 E
Karlskrona, Sweden 9 H16 56 10N 15 35 E
Karlsruhe, Germany 16 D5 49 0N 8 23 E
Karlstad, Sweden 9 G15 59 23N 13 30 E
Karlstad, U.S.A. 80 A6 48 35N 96 31W
Karmi'el, Israel 47 C4 32 55N 35 18 E
Karnak, Egypt 51 C12 25 43N 32 39 E
Karnal, India 42 E7 29 42N 77 2 E
Karnali →, Nepal 43 E9 28 45N 81 16 E
Karnaphuli Res., Bangla. . 41 H18 22 40N 92 20 E
Karnaprayag, India 43 D8 30 16N 79 15 E
Karnataka □, India 40 N10 13 15N 77 0 E
Karnes City, U.S.A. 81 L6 28 53N 97 54W
Karnische Alpen, Europe . 16 E7 46 36N 13 0 E
Kärnten □, Austria 16 E8 46 52N 13 30 E
Karoi, Zimbabwe 55 F2 16 48S 29 45 E
Karonga, Malawi 55 D3 9 57S 33 55 E
Karoonda, Australia 63 F2 35 1S 139 59 E
Karor, Pakistan 42 D4 31 15N 70 59 E
Karora, Sudan 51 E13 17 44N 38 15 E
Karpasia □, Cyprus 23 D13 35 32N 34 15 E
Kárpathos, Greece 21 G12 35 37N 27 10 E
Karpinsk, Russia 24 C11 59 45N 60 1 E
Karpogory, Russia 24 B7 64 0N 44 27 E
Karpuz Burnu = Apostolos Andreas, C., Cyprus .. 23 D13 35 42N 34 35 E
Karratha, Australia 60 D2 20 53S 116 40 E
Kars, Turkey 25 F7 40 40N 43 5 E
Karsakpay, Kazakstan 26 E7 47 55N 66 40 E
Karshi = Qarshi, Uzbekistan 26 F7 38 53N 65 48 E
Karsiyang, India 43 F13 26 56N 88 18 E
Karsog, India 42 D7 31 23N 77 12 E
Kartala, Russia 26 D7 53 3N 60 40 E
Kartapur, India 42 D6 31 27N 75 32 E
Karthaus, U.S.A. 78 E6 41 8N 78 9W
Karufa, Indonesia 37 E8 3 50S 133 20 E
Karumba, Australia 62 B3 17 31S 140 50 E
Karumo, Tanzania 54 C3 2 25S 32 50 E
Karumwa, Tanzania 54 C3 3 12S 32 38 E
Kārūn →, Iran 45 D6 30 26N 48 10 E
Karungu, Kenya 54 C3 0 50S 34 10 E
Karviná, Czech Rep. 17 D10 49 53N 18 31 E
Karwan →, India 42 F8 27 26N 78 4 E
Karwar, India 40 M9 14 55N 74 13 E
Karwi, India 43 G9 25 12N 80 57 E
Kasache, Malawi 55 E3 13 25S 34 20 E
Kasai →, Dem. Rep. of the Congo . 52 E3 3 30S 16 10 E
Kasaï-Oriental □, Dem. Rep. of the Congo . 54 D1 5 0S 24 30 E
Kasaji, Dem. Rep. of the Congo . 55 E1 10 25S 23 27 E
Kasama, Zambia 55 E3 10 16S 31 9 E
Kasan-dong, N. Korea ... 35 D14 41 18N 126 55 E
Kasane, Namibia 56 B3 17 34S 24 50 E
Kasanga, Tanzania 55 D3 8 30S 31 10 E
Kasaragod, India 40 N9 12 30N 74 58 E
Kasba L., Canada 73 A8 60 20N 102 10W
Käseh Garän, Iran 44 C5 34 5N 46 2 E
Kasempa, Zambia 55 E2 13 30S 25 44 E
Kasenga, Dem. Rep. of the Congo . 55 E2 10 20S 28 45 E
Kasese, Uganda 54 B3 0 13N 30 3 E
Kasewa, Zambia 55 E2 14 28S 28 53 E
Kasganj, India 43 F8 27 48N 78 42 E
Kashabowie, Canada 70 C1 48 40N 90 26W
Kashaf, Iran 45 C9 35 58N 61 7 E
Kashän, Iran 45 C6 34 5N 51 30 E
Kashechewan, Canada 70 B3 52 18N 81 37W
Kashi, China 32 C2 39 30N 76 2 E
Kashimbo, Dem. Rep. of the Congo . 55 E2 11 12S 26 19 E
Kashipur, India 43 E8 29 15N 79 0 E
Kashiwazaki, Japan 31 F9 37 22N 138 33 E
Kashk-e Kohneh, Afghan. . 40 B3 34 55N 62 30 E
Kashkū'īyeh, Iran 45 D7 30 31N 55 40 E
Kashmar, Iran 45 C8 35 16N 58 26 E
Kashmir, Asia 43 C7 34 0N 76 0 E
Kashmor, Pakistan 42 E3 28 28N 69 32 E
Kashun Noerh = Gaxun Nur, China 32 B5 42 22N 100 30 E
Kasiari, India 43 H12 22 8N 87 14 E
Kasimov, Russia 24 D7 54 55N 41 20 E
Kasinge, Dem. Rep. of the Congo . 54 D2 6 15S 26 58 E
Kasiruta, Indonesia 37 E7 0 25S 127 12 E
Kaskaskia →, U.S.A. 80 G10 37 58N 89 57W
Kaskattama →, Canada . 73 B10 57 3N 90 4W
Kaskinen, Finland 9 E19 62 22N 21 15 E
Kaslo, Canada 72 D5 49 55N 116 55W
Kasmere L., Canada 73 B8 59 34N 101 10W
Kasongo, Dem. Rep. of the Congo . 54 C2 4 30S 26 33 E
Kasongo Lunda, Dem. Rep. of the Congo . 52 F3 6 35S 16 49 E
Kásos, Greece 21 G12 35 20N 26 55 E
Kassalâ, Sudan 51 E13 15 30N 36 0 E
Kassel, Germany 16 C5 51 18N 9 26 E
Kassiópi, Greece 23 A3 39 48N 19 53 E
Kasson, U.S.A. 80 C8 44 2N 92 45W
Kastamonu, Turkey 25 F5 41 25N 33 43 E
Kastélli, Greece 23 D5 35 29N 23 38 E
Kastéllion, Greece 23 D7 35 12N 25 20 E
Kasterlee, Belgium 15 C4 51 15N 4 59 E
Kastoria, Greece 21 D9 40 30N 21 19 E
Kasulu, Tanzania 54 C3 4 37S 30 5 E
Kasumi, Japan 31 G7 35 38N 134 38 E
Kasungu, Malawi 55 E3 13 0S 33 29 E
Kasur, Pakistan 42 D6 31 5N 74 25 E
Kataba, Zambia 55 F2 16 5S 25 10 E
Katahdin, Mt., U.S.A. . 77 C11 45 54N 68 56W
Katako Kombe, Dem. Rep. of the Congo . 54 C1 3 25S 24 20 E
Katale, Tanzania 54 C3 4 52S 31 7 E
Katanda, Katanga, Dem. Rep. of the Congo . 54 D1 7 52S 24 13 E
Katanda, Nord-Kivu, Dem. Rep. of the Congo . 54 C2 0 55S 29 21 E
Katanga □, Dem. Rep. of the Congo . 54 D2 8 0S 25 0 E
Katangi, India 40 J11 21 56N 79 50 E

Katanning, Australia 61 F2 33 40S 117 33 E
Katavi Swamp, Tanzania . 54 D3 6 50S 31 10 E
Katerini, Greece 21 D10 40 18N 22 37 E
Katghora, India 43 H10 22 30N 82 33 E
Katha, Burma 41 G20 24 10N 96 30 E
Katherîna, Gebel, Egypt . 44 D2 28 30N 33 57 E
Katherine, Australia 60 B5 14 27S 132 20 E
Katherine Gorge, Australia 60 B5 14 18S 132 28 E
Kathi, India 42 J6 21 47N 74 3 E
Kathiawar, India 42 H4 22 20N 71 0 E
Kathikas, Cyprus 23 E11 34 55N 32 25 E
Kathua, India 42 C6 32 23N 75 34 E
Katihar, India 43 G12 25 34N 87 36 E
Katima Mulilo, Zambia . 56 B3 17 28S 24 13 E
Katimbira, Malawi 55 E3 12 40S 34 0 E
Katingan = Mendawai →, Indonesia 36 E4 3 30S 113 0 E
Katiola, Ivory C. 50 G4 8 10N 5 10W
Katmandu, Nepal 43 F11 27 45N 85 20 E
Katni, India 43 H9 23 51N 80 24 E
Káto Arkhánai, Greece . 23 D7 35 15N 25 10 E
Káto Khorió, Greece 23 D7 35 3N 25 47 E
Kato Pyrgos, Cyprus 23 D11 35 11N 32 41 E
Katompe, Dem. Rep. of the Congo . 54 D2 6 2S 26 23 E
Katonga →, Uganda 54 B3 0 34N 31 50 E
Katoomba, Australia 63 E5 33 41S 150 19 E
Katowice, Poland 17 C10 50 17N 19 5 E
Katrine, L., U.K. 12 E4 56 15N 4 30W
Katrineholm, Sweden 9 G17 59 9N 16 12 E
Katsepe, Madag. 57 B8 15 45S 46 15 E
Katsina, Nigeria 50 F7 13 0N 7 32 E
Katsumoto, Japan 31 H4 33 51N 129 42 E
Katsuura, Japan 31 G10 35 10N 140 20 E
Katsuyama, Japan 31 F8 36 3N 136 30 E
Kattaviá, Greece 23 D9 35 57N 27 46 E
Kattegat, Denmark 9 H14 56 40N 11 20 E
Katumba, Dem. Rep. of the Congo . 54 D2 7 40S 25 17 E
Katungu, Kenya 54 C5 2 55S 40 3 E
Katwa, India 43 H13 23 30N 88 5 E
Katwijk, Neths. 15 B4 52 12N 4 24 E
Kauai, U.S.A. 74 H15 22 3N 159 30W
Kauai Channel, U.S.A. . 74 H15 21 45N 158 50W
Kaufman, U.S.A. 81 J6 32 35N 96 19W
Kauhajoki, Finland 9 E20 62 25N 22 10 E
Kaukauna, U.S.A. 76 C1 44 17N 88 17W
Kaukauveld, Namibia 56 C3 20 0S 20 15 E
Kaunakakai, U.S.A. 74 H16 21 6N 157 1W
Kaunas, Lithuania 9 J20 54 54N 23 54 E
Kaunia, Bangla. 43 G13 25 46N 89 26 E
Kautokeino, Norway 8 B20 69 0N 23 4 E
Kauwapur, India 43 F10 27 31N 82 18 E
Kavacha, Russia 27 C17 60 16N 169 51 E
Kavalerovo, Russia 30 B7 44 15N 135 4 E
Kavali, India 40 M12 14 55N 80 1 E
Kaválla, Greece 21 D11 40 57N 24 28 E
Kavār, Iran 45 D7 29 11N 52 44 E
Kavi, India 42 H5 22 12N 72 38 E
Kavīr, Dasht-e, Iran ... 45 C7 34 30N 55 0 E
Kavos, Greece 23 B4 39 23N 20 3 E
Kaw, Fr. Guiana 93 C8 4 30N 52 15W
Kawagama L., Canada ... 78 A6 45 18N 78 45W
Kawagoe, Japan 31 G9 35 55N 139 29 E
Kawaguchi, Japan 31 G9 35 52N 139 45 E
Kawaihae, U.S.A. 74 H17 20 3N 155 50W
Kawambwa, Zambia 55 D2 9 48S 29 3 E
Kawanoe, Japan 31 G6 34 1N 133 34 E
Kawardha, India 43 J9 22 0N 81 17 E
Kawasaki, Japan 31 G9 35 35N 139 42 E
Kawasi, Indonesia 37 E7 1 38S 127 28 E
Kawerau, N.Z. 59 H6 38 7S 176 42 E
Kawhia Harbour, N.Z. .. 59 H5 38 5S 174 51 E
Kawio, Kepulauan, Indonesia 37 D7 4 30N 125 30 E
Kawnro, Burma 41 H21 22 48N 99 8 E
Kawthaung, Burma 39 H2 10 5N 98 36 E
Kawthoolei = Kawthule □, Burma 41 L20 18 0N 97 30 E
Kawthule □, Burma 41 L20 18 0N 97 30 E
Kaya, Burkina Faso 50 F5 13 4N 1 10W
Kayah □, Burma 41 K20 19 15N 97 15 E
Kayan →, Indonesia 36 D5 2 55N 117 35 E
Kaycee, U.S.A. 82 E10 43 43N 106 38W
Kayeli, Indonesia 37 E7 3 20S 127 10 E
Kayenta, U.S.A. 83 H8 36 44N 110 15W
Kayes, Mali 50 F3 14 25N 11 30W
Kayin = Kawthule □, Burma 41 L20 18 0N 97 30 E
Kayoa, Indonesia 37 D7 0 1N 127 28 E
Kayomba, Zambia 55 E1 13 11S 24 2 E
Kayseri, Turkey 25 G6 38 45N 35 30 E
Kaysville, U.S.A. 82 F8 41 2N 111 56W
Kazachye, Russia 27 B14 70 52N 135 58 E
Kazakstan ■, Asia 26 E8 50 0N 70 0 E
Kazan, Russia 24 C8 55 50N 49 10 E
Kazan →, Canada 73 A9 64 3N 95 35W
Kazan-Rettō, Pac. Oc. . 64 E6 25 0N 141 0 E
Kazanlŭk, Bulgaria 21 C11 42 38N 25 20 E
Kazatin = Kozyatyn, Ukraine 17 D15 49 45N 28 50 E
Kāzerūn, Iran 45 D6 29 38N 51 40 E
Kazi Magomed = Qazimämmäd, Azerbaijan 45 A6 40 3N 49 0 E
Kazuno, Japan 30 D10 40 10N 140 45 E
Kazym →, Russia 26 C7 63 54N 65 50 E
Kéa, Greece 21 F11 37 35N 24 22 E
Keady, U.K. 13 B5 54 15N 6 42W
Kearney, U.S.A. 80 E5 40 42N 99 5W
Kearny, U.S.A. 83 K8 33 3N 110 55W
Kearsarge, Mt., U.S.A. . 79 C13 43 22N 71 50W
Keban, Turkey 25 G6 38 50N 38 50 E
Keban Baraji, Turkey .. 25 G6 38 41N 38 33 E
Kebnekaise, Sweden 8 C18 67 53N 18 33 E
Kebri Dehar, Ethiopia . 46 F3 6 45N 44 17 E
Kebumen, Indonesia 37 G13 7 42S 109 40 E
Kechika →, Canada 72 B3 59 41N 127 12W
Kecskemét, Hungary 17 E10 46 57N 19 42 E
Kedainiai, Lithuania ... 9 J21 55 15N 24 2 E
Kedarnath, India 43 D8 30 44N 79 4 E
Kedgwick, Canada 71 C6 47 40N 67 20W
Kédhros Óros, Greece ... 23 D6 35 11N 24 37 E
Kedia Hill, Botswana .. 56 C3 21 28S 24 37 E
Kediri, Indonesia 37 G15 7 51S 112 1 E
Keeler, U.S.A. 84 J9 36 29N 117 52W
Keeley L., Canada 73 C7 54 54N 108 8W
Keeling Is. = Cocos Is., Ind. Oc. 64 J1 12 10S 96 55 E

Keelung = Chilung, Taiwan 33 D7 25 3N 121 45 E
Keene, Canada 78 B6 44 15N 78 10W
Keene, Calif., U.S.A. .. 85 K8 35 13N 118 33W
Keene, N.H., U.S.A. ... 79 D12 42 56N 72 17W
Keene, N.Y., U.S.A. ... 79 B11 44 16N 73 46W
Keeper Hill, Ireland ... 13 D3 52 45N 8 16W
Keer-Weer, C., Australia 62 A3 14 0S 141 32 E
Keeseville, U.S.A. 79 B11 44 29N 73 30W
Keetmanshoop, Namibia . 56 D2 26 35S 18 8 E
Keewatin, Canada 73 D10 49 46N 94 34W
Keewatin →, Canada ... 73 B8 56 29N 100 46W
Kefallinía, Greece 21 E9 38 20N 20 30 E
Kefamenanu, Indonesia . 37 F6 9 28S 124 29 E
Kefar Sava, Israel 47 C3 32 11N 34 54 E
Keffi, Nigeria 50 G7 8 55N 7 43 E
Keflavík, Iceland 8 D2 64 2N 22 35W
Keg River, Canada 72 B5 57 54N 117 55W
Kegaska, Canada 71 B7 50 9N 61 18W
Keighley, U.K. 10 D6 53 52N 1 54W
Keila, Estonia 9 G21 59 18N 24 25 E
Keimoes, S. Africa 56 D3 28 41S 20 59 E
Keitele, Finland 8 E22 63 10N 26 20 E
Keith, Australia 63 F3 36 6S 140 20 E
Keith, U.K. 12 D6 57 32N 2 57W
Keizer, U.S.A. 82 D2 44 57N 123 1W
Kejimkujik Nat. Park, Canada 71 D6 44 25N 65 25W
Kejser Franz Joseph Fjord = Kong Franz Joseph Fd., Greenland 4 B6 73 30N 24 30W
Kekri, India 42 G6 26 0N 75 10 E
Kelan, China 34 E6 38 43N 111 31 E
Kelang, Malaysia 39 L3 3 2N 101 26 E
Kelantan □, Malaysia .. 39 J4 6 13N 102 14 E
Kelantan →, Malaysia .. 39 J4 6 13N 102 14 E
Kelkit →, Turkey 25 F6 40 45N 36 32 E
Kellerberrin, Australia . 61 F2 31 36S 117 38 E
Kellett, C., Canada 4 B1 72 0N 126 0W
Kelleys I., U.S.A. 78 E2 41 36N 82 42W
Kellogg, U.S.A. 82 C5 47 32N 116 7W
Kells = Ceanannus Mor, Ireland 13 C5 53 44N 6 53W
Kelokedhara, Cyprus 23 E11 34 48N 32 39 E
Kelowna, Canada 72 D5 49 50N 119 25W
Kelseyville, U.S.A. 84 G4 38 59N 122 50W
Kelso, N.Z. 59 L2 45 54S 169 15 E
Kelso, U.K. 12 F6 55 36N 2 26W
Kelso, U.S.A. 84 D4 46 9N 122 54W
Keluang, Malaysia 39 L4 2 3N 103 18 E
Kelvington, Canada 73 C8 52 10N 103 30W
Kem, Russia 24 B5 65 0N 34 38 E
Kem →, Russia 24 B5 65 0N 34 41 E
Kema, Indonesia 37 D7 1 22N 125 8 E
Kemah, Turkey 44 B3 39 32N 39 5 E
Kemaman, Malaysia 36 D2 4 12N 103 18 E
Kemano, Canada 72 C3 53 35N 128 0W
Kemasik, Malaysia 39 K4 4 25N 103 27 E
Kemerovo, Russia 26 D9 55 20N 86 5 E
Kemi, Finland 8 D21 65 44N 24 34 E
Kemi älv = Kemijoki →, Finland 8 D21 65 47N 24 32 E
Kemijärvi, Finland 8 C22 66 43N 27 22 E
Kemijoki →, Finland ... 8 D21 65 47N 24 32 E
Kemmerer, U.S.A. 82 F8 41 48N 110 32W
Kemmuna = Comino, Malta 23 C1 36 2N 14 20 E
Kemp, L., U.S.A. 81 J5 33 46N 99 9W
Kemp Land, Antarctica . 5 C5 69 0S 55 0 E
Kempsey, Australia 63 E5 31 1S 152 50 E
Kempt, L., Canada 70 C5 47 25N 74 22W
Kempten, Germany 16 E6 47 45N 10 17 E
Kempton, Australia 62 G4 42 31S 147 12 E
Kemptville, Canada 79 B9 45 0N 75 38W
Ken →, India 43 G9 25 13N 80 27 E
Kenai, U.S.A. 68 B4 60 33N 151 16W
Kendai, India 43 H10 22 45N 82 37 E
Kendal, Indonesia 37 G14 6 56S 110 14 E
Kendal, U.K. 10 C5 54 20N 2 44W
Kendall, Australia 63 E5 31 35S 152 44 E
Kendall →, Australia .. 62 A3 14 4S 141 35 E
Kendallville, U.S.A. .. 76 E3 41 27N 85 16W
Kendari, Indonesia 37 E6 3 50S 122 30 E
Kendawangan, Indonesia 36 E4 2 32S 110 17 E
Kendrapara, India 41 J15 20 35N 86 30 E
Kendrew, S. Africa 56 E3 32 32S 24 30 E
Kene Thao, Laos 38 D3 17 44N 101 10 E
Kenedy, U.S.A. 81 L6 28 49N 97 51W
Kenema, S. Leone 50 G3 7 50N 11 14W
Keng Kok, Laos 38 D5 16 26N 105 12 E
Keng Tawng, Burma 41 J21 20 45N 98 18 E
Keng Tung, Burma 41 J21 21 0N 99 30 E
Kenge, Dem. Rep. of the Congo . 52 E3 4 50S 17 4 E
Kengeja, Tanzania 54 D4 5 26S 39 45 E
Kenhardt, S. Africa ... 56 D3 29 19S 21 12 E
Kenitra, Morocco 50 B4 34 15N 6 40W
Kenli, China 35 F10 37 30N 118 20 E
Kenmare, Ireland 13 E2 51 53N 9 36W
Kenmare, U.S.A. 80 A3 48 41N 102 5W
Kenmare River, Ireland 13 E2 51 48N 9 51W
Kennebago Lake, U.S.A. 79 A14 45 4N 70 40W
Kennebec, U.S.A. 80 D5 43 54N 99 52W
Kennebec →, U.S.A. ... 77 D11 43 45N 69 46W
Kennebunk, U.S.A. 79 C14 43 23N 70 33W
Kennedy, Zimbabwe 55 F2 18 52S 27 10 E
Kennedy Ra., Australia . 61 D2 24 45S 115 10 E
Kennedy Taungdeik, Burma 41 H18 23 15N 93 45 E
Kenner, U.S.A. 81 L9 29 59N 90 15W
Kennet →, U.K. 11 F7 51 27N 0 57W
Kenneth Ra., Australia 61 D2 23 50S 117 8 E
Kennett, U.S.A. 81 G9 36 14N 90 3W
Kennewick, U.S.A. 82 C4 46 12N 119 7W
Kenogami →, Canada ... 70 B3 51 6N 84 28W
Kenora, Canada 73 D10 49 47N 94 29W
Kenosha, U.S.A. 76 D2 42 35N 87 49W
Kensington, Canada 71 C7 46 28N 63 34W
Kent, Ohio, U.S.A. 78 E3 41 9N 81 22W
Kent, Tex., U.S.A. 81 K2 31 4N 104 13W
Kent □, U.K. 11 F8 51 12N 0 40 E
Kent Group, Australia . 62 F4 39 30S 147 20 E
Kent Pen., Canada 68 B9 68 30N 107 0W
Kentau, Kazakstan 26 E7 43 32N 68 36 E
Kentland, U.S.A. 76 E2 40 46N 87 27W
Kenton, U.S.A. 76 E4 40 39N 83 37W
Kentucky □, U.S.A. 76 G3 37 0N 84 0W
Kentucky →, U.S.A. ... 76 F3 38 41N 85 11W
Kentucky L., U.S.A. ... 77 G2 37 1N 88 16W

Kyustendil, *Bulgaria* **21 C10** 42 16N 22 41 E
Kyusyur, *Russia* **27 B13** 70 19N 127 30 E
Kyyiv, *Ukraine* **17 C16** 50 30N 30 28 E
Kyyivske Vdskh., *Ukraine* . . **17 C16** 51 0N 30 25 E
Kyzyl, *Russia* **27 D10** 51 50N 94 30 E
Kyzyl Kum, *Uzbekistan* . . **26 E7** 42 30N 65 0 E
Kyzyl-Kyya, *Kyrgyzstan* . . **26 E8** 40 16N 72 8 E
Kzyl-Orda = Qyzylorda,
 Kazakstan **26 E7** 44 48N 65 28 E

L

a Alcarria, *Spain* **19 B4** 40 31N 2 45W
a Asunción, *Venezuela* . . **92 A6** 11 2N 63 53W
a Baie, *Canada* **71 C5** 48 19N 70 53W
a Banda, *Argentina* **94 B3** 27 45S 64 10W
a Barca, *Mexico* **86 C4** 20 20N 102 40W
a Barge, *U.S.A.* **82 E8** 42 16N 110 12W
a Belle, *U.S.A.* **77 M5** 26 46N 81 26W
a Biche →, *Canada* **72 B4** 59 57N 123 50W
a Biche, L., *Canada* **72 C6** 54 50N 112 5W
a Bomba, *Mexico* **86 A1** 31 53N 115 2W
a Calera, *Chile* **94 C1** 32 50S 71 10W
a Canal = Sa Canal, *Spain* **22 C7** 38 51N 1 23 E
a Carlota, *Argentina* **94 C3** 33 30S 63 20W
a Ceiba, *Honduras* **88 C2** 15 40N 86 50W
a Chaux-de-Fonds, *Switz.* . **18 C7** 47 7N 6 50 E
a Chorrera, *Panama* **88 E4** 8 53N 79 47W
a Cocha, *Argentina* **94 B2** 27 50S 65 40W
a Concepción, *Panama* . . **88 E3** 8 31N 82 37W
a Concordia, *Mexico* **87 D6** 16 8N 92 38W
a Coruña = A Coruña,
 Spain **19 A1** 43 20N 8 25W
a Crescent, *U.S.A.* **80 D9** 43 50N 91 18W
a Crete, *Canada* **72 B5** 58 11N 116 24W
a Crosse, *Kans., U.S.A.* . . **80 F5** 38 32N 99 18W
a Crosse, *Wis., U.S.A.* . . **80 D9** 43 48N 91 15W
a Cruz, *Costa Rica* **88 D2** 11 4N 85 39W
a Cruz, *Mexico* **86 C3** 23 55N 106 54W
a Désirade, *Guadeloupe* . **89 C7** 16 18N 61 3W
a Escondida, *Mexico* . . . **86 C5** 24 6N 99 55W
a Esmeralda, *Paraguay* . . **94 A3** 22 16S 62 33W
a Esperanza, *Cuba* **88 B3** 22 46N 83 44W
a Esperanza, *Honduras* . . **88 D2** 14 15N 88 10W
a Estrada = A Estrada,
 Spain **19 A1** 42 43N 8 27W
a Fayette, *U.S.A.* **77 H3** 34 42N 85 17W
a Fé, *Cuba* **88 B3** 22 2N 84 15W
a Follette, *U.S.A.* **77 G3** 36 23N 84 7W
a Grande, *U.S.A.* **82 D4** 45 20N 118 5W
a Grande →, *Canada* . . . **70 B5** 53 50N 79 0W
a Grande Deux, Rés.,
 Canada **70 B4** 53 40N 76 55W
a Grande Quatre, Rés.,
 Canada **70 B5** 54 0N 73 15W
a Grande Trois, Rés.,
 Canada **70 B4** 53 40N 75 10W
a Grange, *Calif., U.S.A.* . . **84 H6** 37 42N 120 27W
a Grange, *Ga., U.S.A.* . . **77 J3** 33 2N 85 2W
a Grange, *Ky., U.S.A.* . . **76 F3** 38 25N 85 23W
a Grange, *Tex., U.S.A.* . . **81 L6** 29 54N 96 52W
a Guaira, *Venezuela* **92 A5** 10 36N 66 56W
a Habana, *Cuba* **88 B3** 23 8N 82 22W
a Independencia, *Mexico* . **87 D6** 16 31N 91 47W
a Isabela, *Dom. Rep.* . . **89 C5** 19 58N 71 2W
a Junta, *U.S.A.* **81 F3** 37 59N 103 33W
a Laguna, *Canary Is.* . . . **22 F3** 32 50S 71 10W
a Libertad, *Guatemala* . . **88 C1** 16 47N 90 7W
a Libertad, *Mexico* **86 B2** 29 55N 112 41W
a Ligua, *Chile* **94 C1** 32 30S 71 16W
a Línea de la Concepción,
 Spain **19 D3** 36 15N 5 23W
a Loche, *Canada* **73 B7** 56 29N 109 26W
a Louvière, *Belgium* **15 D4** 50 27N 4 10 E
a Malbaie, *Canada* **71 C5** 47 40N 70 10W
a Mancha, *Spain* **19 C4** 39 10N 2 54W
a Martre, L., *Canada* **72 A5** 63 15N 117 55W
a Mesa, *U.S.A.* **85 N9** 32 46N 117 3W
a Misión, *Mexico* **86 A1** 32 5N 116 50W
a Moure, *Canada* **80 B5** 46 21N 98 18W
a Negra, *Chile* **94 A1** 23 46S 70 18W
a Oliva, *Canary Is.* **22 F6** 28 36N 13 57W
a Orotava, *Canary Is.* . . . **22 F3** 28 22N 16 31W
a Oroya, *Peru* **92** 11 32S 75 54W
a Palma, *Canary Is.* **22 F2** 28 40N 17 50W
a Palma, *Panama* **88 E4** 8 15N 78 0W
a Palma del Condado,
 Spain **19 D2** 37 21N 6 38W
a Paloma, *Chile* **94 C1** 30 35S 71 0W
a Pampa □, *Argentina* . . **94 D2** 36 50S 66 0W
a Paragua, *Venezuela* . . . **92 B6** 6 50N 63 20W
a Paz, *Entre Ríos,*
 Argentina **94 C4** 30 50S 59 45W
a Paz, *San Luis, Argentina* **94 C2** 33 30S 67 20W
a Paz, *Bolivia* **92 G5** 16 20S 68 10W
a Paz, *Honduras* **88 D2** 14 20N 87 47W
a Paz, *Mexico* **86 C2** 24 10N 110 20W
a Paz Centro, *Nic.* **88 D2** 12 20N 86 41W
a Pedrera, *Colombia* **92 D5** 1 18S 69 43W
a Pérade, *Canada* **71 C5** 46 35N 72 12W
a Perouse Str., *Asia* . . . **30 B11** 45 40N 142 0 E
a Pesca, *Mexico* **87 C5** 23 46N 97 47W
a Piedad, *Mexico* **86 C4** 20 20N 102 1W
a Pine, *U.S.A.* **82 E3** 43 40N 121 30W
a Plata, *Argentina* **94 D4** 35 0S 57 55W
a Pocatière, *Canada* **71 C5** 47 22N 70 2W
a Porte, *Ind., U.S.A.* **76 E2** 41 36N 86 43W
a Porte, *Tex., U.S.A.* **81 L7** 29 39N 95 1W
a Purísima, *Mexico* **86 B2** 26 10N 112 4W
a Push, *U.S.A.* **84 C2** 47 55N 124 38W
a Quiaca, *Argentina* **94 A2** 22 5S 65 35W
a Restinga, *Canary Is.* . . **22 G2** 27 38N 17 59W
a Rioja, *Argentina* **94 B2** 29 20S 67 0W
a Rioja, *Spain* **19 A4** 42 20N 2 20W
a Rioja □, *Spain* **19 A3** 42 50N 5 41W
a Robla, *Spain* **19 A3** 42 50N 5 41W
a Roche-en-Ardenne,
 Belgium **15 D5** 50 11N 5 35 E
a Roche-sur-Yon, *France* . **18 C3** 46 40N 1 25W
a Rochelle, *France* **18 C3** 46 10N 1 9W
a Roda, *Spain* **19 C4** 39 13N 2 15W
a Romana, *Dom. Rep.* . . **89 C6** 18 27N 68 57W
a Ronge, *Canada* **73 B7** 55 5N 105 20W

La Rumorosa, *Mexico* **85 N10** 32 33N 116 4W
La Sabina = Sa Savina,
 Spain **22 C7** 38 44N 1 25 E
La Salle, *U.S.A.* **80 E10** 41 20N 89 6W
La Santa, *Canary Is.* **22 E6** 29 5N 13 40W
La Sarre, *Canada* **70 C4** 48 45N 79 15W
La Scie, *Canada* **71 C8** 49 57N 55 36W
La Selva Beach, *U.S.A.* . . **84 J5** 36 56N 121 51W
La Serena, *Chile* **94 B1** 29 55S 71 10W
La Seu d'Urgell, *Spain* . . **19 A6** 42 22N 1 23 E
La Seyne-sur-Mer, *France* . **18 E6** 43 7N 5 52 E
La Soufrière, *St. Vincent* . **89 D7** 13 20N 61 11W
La Spézia, *Italy* **18 D8** 44 7N 9 50 E
La Tagua, *Colombia* **92 C4** 0 3N 74 40W
La Tortuga, *Venezuela* . . . **89 D6** 11 0N 65 22W
La Tuque, *Canada* **70 C5** 47 30N 72 50W
La Unión, *Chile* **96 E2** 40 10S 73 0W
La Unión, *El Salv.* **88 D2** 13 20N 87 50W
La Unión, *Mexico* **86 D4** 17 58N 101 49W
La Urbana, *Venezuela* . . . **92 B5** 7 8N 66 56W
La Vall d'Uixó, *Spain* **19 C5** 39 49N 0 15W
La Vega, *Dom. Rep.* **89 C5** 19 20N 70 30W
La Vela de Coro, *Venezuela* **92 A5** 11 27N 69 34W
La Venta, *Mexico* **87 D6** 18 8N 94 3W
La Ventura, *Mexico* **86 C4** 24 38N 100 54W
Labe = Elbe →, *Europe* . **16 B5** 53 50N 9 0 E
Labé, *Guinea* **50 F3** 11 24N 12 16W
Laberge, L., *Canada* **72 A1** 61 11N 135 12W
Labinsk, *Russia* **25 F7** 44 40N 40 48 E
Labis, *Malaysia* **39 L4** 2 22N 103 2 E
Laboulaye, *Argentina* **94 C3** 34 10S 63 30W
Labrador, *Canada* **71 B7** 53 20N 61 0W
Labrador City, *Canada* . . . **71 B6** 52 57N 66 55W
Labrador Sea, *Atl. Oc.* . . . **69 C14** 57 0N 54 0W
Lábrea, *Brazil* **92 E6** 7 15S 64 51W
Labuan, *Malaysia* **36 C5** 5 20N 115 14 E
Labuan, Pulau, *Malaysia* . **36 C5** 5 21N 115 13 E
Labuha, *Indonesia* **37 E7** 0 30S 127 30 E
Labuhan, *Indonesia* **37 G11** 6 22S 105 50 E
Labuhanbajo, *Indonesia* . . **37 F6** 8 28S 120 1 E
Labuk, Telok, *Malaysia* . . **36 C5** 6 10N 117 50 E
Labyrinth, L., *Australia* . . . **63 E2** 30 40S 135 11 E
Labytnangi, *Russia* **26 C7** 66 39N 66 21 E
Lac Bouchette, *Canada* . . **71 C5** 48 16N 72 11W
Lac Édouard, *Canada* . . . **70 C5** 47 40N 72 16W
Lac La Biche, *Canada* . . . **72 C6** 54 45N 111 58W
Lac la Martre = Wha Ti,
 Canada **68 B8** 63 8N 117 16W
Lac La Ronge Prov. Park,
 Canada **73 B7** 55 9N 104 41W
Lac-Mégantic, *Canada* . . . **71 C5** 45 35N 70 53W
Lac Seul, Res., *Canada* . . **70 B1** 50 25N 92 30W
Lac Thien, *Vietnam* **38 F7** 12 25N 108 11 E
Lacanau, *France* **18 D3** 44 58N 1 5W
Lacantúm →, *Mexico* . . . **87 D6** 16 36N 90 40W
Laccadive Is. =
 Lakshadweep Is., *Ind. Oc.* **28 H11** 10 0N 72 30 E
Lacepede B., *Australia* . . . **63 F2** 36 40S 139 40 E
Lacepede Is., *Australia* . . . **60 C3** 16 55S 122 0 E
Lacerdónia, *Mozam.* **55 F4** 18 3S 35 35 E
Lacey, *U.S.A.* **84 C4** 47 7N 122 49W
Lachhmangarh, *India* **42 F6** 27 50N 75 4 E
Lachi, *Pakistan* **42 C4** 33 25N 71 20 E
Lachine, *Canada* **79 A11** 45 30N 73 40W
Lachlan →, *Australia* . . . **63 E3** 34 22S 143 55 E
Lachute, *Canada* **70 C5** 45 39N 74 21W
Lackawanna, *U.S.A.* **78 D6** 42 50N 78 50W
Lackawaxen, *U.S.A.* **79 E10** 41 29N 74 59W
Lacolle, *Canada* **79 A11** 45 5N 73 22W
Lacombe, *Canada* **72 C6** 52 30N 113 44W
Lacona, *U.S.A.* **79 C8** 43 39N 76 10W
Laconia, *U.S.A.* **79 C13** 43 32N 71 28W
Ladakh Ra., *India* **43 C8** 34 0N 78 0 E
Ladismith, *S. Africa* **56 E3** 33 28S 21 15 E
Ladnun, *India* **42 F6** 27 38N 74 25 E
Ladoga, L. = Ladozhskoye
 Ozero, *Russia* **24 B5** 61 15N 30 30 E
Ladozhskoye Ozero, *Russia* **24 B5** 61 15N 30 30 E
Lady Elliott I., *Australia* . . **62 C5** 24 7S 152 42 E
Lady Grey, *S. Africa* **56 E4** 30 43S 27 13 E
Ladybrand, *S. Africa* **56 D4** 29 9S 27 29 E
Ladysmith, *Canada* **72 D4** 49 0N 123 49W
Ladysmith, *S. Africa* **57 D4** 28 32S 29 46 E
Ladysmith, *U.S.A.* **80 C9** 45 28N 91 12W
Lae, *Papua N. G.* **64 H6** 6 40S 147 2 E
Laem Ngop, *Thailand* . . . **39 F4** 12 10N 102 26 E
Laem Pho, *Thailand* **39 J3** 6 55N 101 19 E
Læsø, *Denmark* **9 H14** 57 15N 11 5 E
Lafayette, *Colo., U.S.A.* . . **80 F2** 39 58N 105 12W
Lafayette, *Ind., U.S.A.* . . . **76 E2** 40 25N 86 54W
Lafayette, *La., U.S.A.* . . . **81 K9** 30 14N 92 1W
Lafayette, *Tenn., U.S.A.* . . **77 G2** 36 31N 86 2W
Laferte →, *Canada* **72 A5** 61 53N 117 44W
Lafia, *Nigeria* **50 G7** 8 30N 8 34 E
Laflèche, *Canada* **73 D7** 49 45N 106 40W
Lagan →, *U.K.* **13 B6** 54 36N 5 55W
Lagarfljót →, *Iceland* **8 D6** 65 40N 14 18W
Lågen →, *Oppland,*
 Norway **9 F14** 61 8N 10 25 E
Lågen →, *Vestfold,*
 Norway **9 G14** 59 3N 10 3 E
Laghouat, *Algeria* **50 B6** 33 50N 2 59 E
Lagoa Vermelha, *Brazil* . . **95 B5** 28 13S 51 32W
Lagonoy G., *Phil.* **37 B6** 13 50N 123 50 E
Lagos, *Nigeria* **50 G6** 6 25N 3 27 E
Lagos, *Portugal* **19 D1** 37 5N 8 41W
Lagos de Moreno, *Mexico* . **86 C4** 21 21N 101 55W
Lagrange, *Australia* **60 C3** 18 45S 121 43 E
Lagrange B., *Australia* . . . **60 C3** 18 38S 121 42 E
Laguna, *Brazil* **95 B6** 28 30S 48 50W
Laguna, *U.S.A.* **83 J10** 35 2N 107 25W
Laguna Beach, *U.S.A.* . . . **85 M9** 33 33N 117 47W
Laguna Limpia, *Argentina* . **94 B4** 26 32S 59 45W
Laguna Madre, *U.S.A.* . . **87 B5** 27 0N 97 20W
Lagunas, *Chile* **94 A2** 21 0S 69 45W
Lagunas, *Peru* **92 E3** 5 10S 75 35W
Lahad Datu, *Malaysia* . . . **37 D5** 5 0N 118 20 E
Lahad Datu, Teluk, *Malaysia* **37 D5** 4 50N 118 20 E
Lahan Sai, *Thailand* **38 E4** 14 25N 102 52 E
Lahanam, *Laos* **38 D5** 16 16N 105 16 E
Lahar, *India* **43 F8** 26 12N 78 57 E
Laharpur, *India* **43 F9** 27 43N 80 56 E
Lahat, *Indonesia* **36 E2** 3 45S 103 30 E
Lahewa, *Indonesia* **36 D1** 1 22N 97 12 E
Lāhījān, *Iran* **45 B6** 37 10N 50 6 E
Lahn →, *Germany* **16 C4** 50 19N 7 37 E

Laholm, *Sweden* **9 H15** 56 30N 13 2 E
Lahore, *Pakistan* **42 D6** 31 32N 74 22 E
Lahri, *Pakistan* **42 E3** 29 11N 68 13 E
Lahti, *Finland* **9 F21** 60 58N 25 40 E
Lahtis = Lahti, *Finland* . . . **9 F21** 60 58N 25 40 E
Laï, *Chad* **51 G9** 9 25N 16 18 E
Laila = Laylá, *Si. Arabia* . **46 C4** 22 10N 46 40 E
Laingsburg, *S. Africa* **56 E3** 33 9S 20 52 E
Lainio älv →, *Sweden* . . . **8 C20** 67 35N 22 40 E
Lairg, *U.K.* **12 C4** 58 2N 4 24W
Laishui, *China* **34 E8** 39 23N 115 45 E
Laiwu, *China* **35 F9** 36 15N 117 40 E
Laixi, *China* **35 F11** 36 50N 120 31 E
Laiyang, *China* **35 F11** 36 59N 120 45 E
Laiyuan, *China* **34 E8** 39 20N 114 40 E
Laizhou, *China* **35 F10** 37 8N 119 57 E
Laizhou Wan, *China* **35 F10** 37 30N 119 30 E
Laja →, *Mexico* **86 C4** 20 55N 100 46W
Lajes, *Brazil* **95 B5** 27 48S 50 20W
Lak Sao, *Laos* **38 C5** 18 11N 104 59 E
Lakaband, *Pakistan* **42 D3** 31 2N 69 15 E
Lake Alpine, *U.S.A.* **84 G7** 38 29N 120 0W
Lake Andes, *U.S.A.* **80 D5** 43 9N 98 32W
Lake Arthur, *U.S.A.* **81 K8** 30 5N 92 41W
Lake Cargelligo, *Australia* . **63 E4** 33 15S 146 22 E
Lake Charles, *U.S.A.* **81 K8** 30 14N 93 13W
Lake City, *Colo., U.S.A.* . . **83 G10** 38 2N 107 19W
Lake City, *Fla., U.S.A.* . . . **77 K4** 30 11N 82 38W
Lake City, *Mich., U.S.A.* . . **76 C3** 44 20N 85 13W
Lake City, *Minn., U.S.A.* . . **80 C8** 44 27N 92 16W
Lake City, *Pa., U.S.A.* . . . **78 D4** 42 1N 80 21W
Lake City, *S.C., U.S.A.* . . **77 J6** 33 52N 79 45W
Lake Cowichan, *Canada* . . **72 D4** 48 49N 124 3W
Lake District, *U.K.* **10 C4** 54 35N 3 20 E
Lake Elsinore, *U.S.A.* **85 M9** 33 38N 117 20W
Lake George, *U.S.A.* **79 C11** 43 26N 73 43W
Lake Grace, *Australia* . . . **61 F2** 33 7S 118 28 E
Lake Harbour = Kimmirut,
 Canada **69 B13** 62 50N 69 50W
Lake Havasu City, *U.S.A.* . **85 L12** 34 27N 114 22W
Lake Hughes, *U.S.A.* **85 L8** 34 41N 118 26W
Lake Isabella, *U.S.A.* **85 K8** 35 38N 118 28W
Lake Jackson, *U.S.A.* **81 L7** 29 3N 95 27W
Lake Junction, *U.S.A.* . . . **82 D8** 44 35N 110 28W
Lake King, *Australia* **61 F2** 33 5S 119 45 E
Lake Lenore, *Canada* **73 C8** 52 24N 104 59W
Lake Louise, *Canada* **72 C5** 51 30N 116 10W
Lake Mead National
 Recreation Area, *U.S.A.* . **85 K12** 36 15N 114 30W
Lake Mills, *U.S.A.* **80 D8** 43 25N 93 32W
Lake Placid, *U.S.A.* **79 B11** 44 17N 73 59W
Lake Pleasant, *U.S.A.* . . . **79 C10** 43 28N 74 25W
Lake Providence, *U.S.A.* . . **81 J9** 32 48N 91 10W
Lake St. Peter, *Canada* . . **78 A6** 45 18N 78 2W
Lake Superior Prov. Park,
 Canada **70 C3** 47 45N 84 45W
Lake Village, *U.S.A.* **81 J9** 33 20N 91 17W
Lake Wales, *U.S.A.* **77 M5** 27 54N 81 35W
Lake Worth, *U.S.A.* **77 M5** 26 37N 80 3W
Lakefield, *Canada* **78 B6** 44 25N 78 16W
Lakehurst, *U.S.A.* **79 F10** 40 1N 74 19W
Lakeland, *Australia* **62 B3** 15 49S 144 57 E
Lakeland, *U.S.A.* **77 M5** 28 3N 81 57W
Lakemba, *Fiji* **59 D9** 18 13S 178 47W
Lakeport, *Calif., U.S.A.* . . **84 F4** 39 3N 122 55W
Lakeport, *Mich., U.S.A.* . . **78 C2** 43 7N 82 30W
Lakes Entrance, *Australia* . **63 F4** 37 50S 148 0 E
Lakeside, *Ariz., U.S.A.* . . . **83 J9** 34 9N 109 58W
Lakeside, *Calif., U.S.A.* . . **85 N10** 32 52N 116 55W
Lakeside, *Nebr., U.S.A.* . . **80 D3** 42 3N 102 26W
Lakeside, *Ohio, U.S.A.* . . . **78 E2** 41 32N 82 46W
Lakeview, *U.S.A.* **82 E3** 42 11N 120 21W
Lakeville, *U.S.A.* **80 C8** 44 39N 93 14W
Lakewood, *Colo., U.S.A.* . . **80 F2** 39 44N 105 5W
Lakewood, *N.J., U.S.A.* . . **79 F10** 40 6N 74 13W
Lakewood, *N.Y., U.S.A.* . . **78 D5** 42 6N 79 19W
Lakewood, *Ohio, U.S.A.* . . **78 E3** 41 29N 81 48W
Lakewood, *Wash., U.S.A.* . **84 C4** 47 11N 122 32W
Lakha, *India* **42 F4** 26 9N 70 54 E
Lakhania, *Greece* **23 D9** 35 58N 27 54 E
Lakhimpur, *India* **43 F9** 27 57N 80 46 E
Lakhnadon, *India* **43 H8** 22 36N 79 36 E
Lakhonpheng, *Laos* **38 E5** 15 54N 105 34 E
Lakhpat, *India* **42 H3** 23 48N 68 47 E
Lakin, *U.S.A.* **81 G4** 37 57N 101 15W
Lakitusaki →, *Canada* . . . **70 B3** 54 21N 82 25W
Lakki, *Pakistan* **42 C4** 32 36N 70 55 E
Lákkoi, *Greece* **23 D5** 35 24N 23 57 E
Lakonikós Kólpos, *Greece* . **21 F10** 36 40N 22 40 E
Lakor, *Indonesia* **37 F7** 8 15S 128 17 E
Lakota, *Ivory C.* **50 G4** 5 50N 5 30W
Lakota, *U.S.A.* **80 A5** 48 2N 98 21W
Laksar, *India* **42 E8** 29 46N 78 3 E
Laksefjorden, *Norway* . . . **8 A22** 70 45N 26 50 E
Lakselv, *Norway* **8 A21** 70 2N 25 0 E
Lakshadweep Is., *Ind. Oc.* . **28 H11** 10 0N 72 30 E
Lakshmanpur, *India* **43 H10** 22 58N 83 3 E
Lakshmikantapur, *India* . . . **43 H13** 22 5N 88 20 E
Lala Ghat, *India* **41 G18** 24 30N 92 40 E
Lala Musa, *Pakistan* **42 C5** 32 40N 73 57 E
Lalago, *Tanzania* **54 C3** 3 28S 33 58 E
Lalapanzi, *Zimbabwe* **55 F3** 19 20S 30 15 E
Lalgolgi, *India* **43 G13** 24 25N 88 15 E
Lāli, *Iran* **45 C6** 32 21N 49 6 E
Lalibela, *Ethiopia* **46 E2** 12 2N 39 2 E
Lalín, *China* **35 B14** 45 12N 127 0 E
Lalín, *Spain* **19 A1** 42 40N 8 5W
Lalin He →, *China* **35 B13** 45 32N 125 40 E
Lalitapur = Patan, *Nepal* . . **41 F14** 27 40N 85 20 E
Lalitpur, *India* **43 G8** 24 42N 78 28 E
Lalkua, *India* **43 E8** 29 5N 79 31 E
Lalsot, *India* **42 F7** 26 34N 76 20 E
Lam, *Vietnam* **38 B6** 21 21N 106 31 E
Lam Pao Res., *Thailand* . . **38 D4** 16 50N 103 15 E
Lamaing, *Burma* **41 M20** 15 25N 97 53 E
Lamar, *Colo., U.S.A.* **80 F3** 38 5N 102 37W
Lamar, *Mo., U.S.A.* **81 G7** 37 30N 94 16W
Lamas, *Peru* **92 E3** 6 28S 76 31W
Lambaréné, *Gabon* **52 E2** 0 41S 10 12 E
Lambasa, *Fiji* **59 C8** 16 30S 179 10 E
Lambay I., *Ireland* **13 C5** 53 29N 6 1W
Lambert Glacier, *Antarctica* **5 D6** 71 0S 70 0 E
Lamberts Bay, *S. Africa* . . **56 E2** 32 5S 18 17 E
Lambeth, *Canada* **78 D3** 42 54N 81 18W

Lambi Kyun, *Burma* **39 G2** 10 50N 98 20 E
Lame Deer, *U.S.A.* **82 D10** 45 37N 106 40W
Lamego, *Portugal* **19 B2** 41 5N 7 52W
Lamèque, *Canada* **71 C7** 47 45N 64 38W
Lameroo, *Australia* **63 F3** 35 19S 140 33 E
Lamesa, *U.S.A.* **81 J4** 32 44N 101 58W
Lamía, *Greece* **21 E10** 38 55N 22 26 E
Lammermuir Hills, *U.K.* . . . **12 F6** 55 50N 2 40W
Lamoille →, *U.S.A.* **79 B11** 44 38N 73 13W
Lamon B., *Phil.* **37 B6** 14 30N 122 20 E
Lamont, *Canada* **72 C6** 53 46N 112 50W
Lamont, *Calif., U.S.A.* . . . **85 K8** 35 15N 118 55W
Lamont, *Wyo., U.S.A.* . . . **82 E10** 42 13N 107 29W
Lampa, *Peru* **92 G4** 15 22S 70 22W
Lampang, *Thailand* **38 C2** 18 16N 99 32 E
Lampasas, *U.S.A.* **81 K5** 31 4N 98 11W
Lampazos de Naranjo,
 Mexico **86 B4** 27 2N 100 32W
Lampedusa, *Medit. S.* . . . **20 G5** 35 36N 12 40 E
Lampeter, *U.K.* **11 E3** 52 7N 4 4W
Lampione, *Medit. S.* **20 G5** 35 33N 12 20 E
Lampman, *Canada* **73 D8** 49 25N 102 50W
Lampung □, *Indonesia* . . **36 F2** 5 30S 104 30 E
Lamta, *India* **43 H9** 22 8N 80 7 E
Lamu, *Kenya* **54 C5** 2 16S 40 55 E
Lamy, *U.S.A.* **83 J11** 35 29N 105 53W
Lan Xian, *China* **34 E6** 38 15N 111 35 E
Lanai, *U.S.A.* **74 H16** 20 50N 156 55W
Lanak La, *India* **43 B8** 34 27N 79 32 E
Lanak'o Shank'ou = Lanak
 La, *India* **43 B8** 34 27N 79 32 E
Lanark, *Canada* **79 A8** 45 1N 76 22W
Lanark, *U.K.* **12 F5** 55 40N 3 47W
Lancang Jiang →, *China* . **32 D5** 21 40N 101 10 E
Lancashire □, *U.K.* **10 D5** 53 50N 2 48W
Lancaster, *Canada* **79 A10** 45 10N 74 30W
Lancaster, *U.K.* **10 C5** 54 3N 2 48W
Lancaster, *Calif., U.S.A.* . . **85 L8** 34 42N 118 8W
Lancaster, *Ky., U.S.A.* . . . **76 G3** 37 37N 84 35W
Lancaster, *N.H., U.S.A.* . . **79 B13** 44 29N 71 34W
Lancaster, *N.Y., U.S.A.* . . **78 D6** 42 54N 78 40W
Lancaster, *Ohio, U.S.A.* . . **76 F4** 39 43N 82 36W
Lancaster, *Pa., U.S.A.* . . . **79 F8** 40 2N 76 19W
Lancaster, *S.C., U.S.A.* . . **77 H5** 34 43N 80 46W
Lancaster, *Wis., U.S.A.* . . **80 D9** 42 51N 90 43W
Lancaster Sd., *Canada* . . . **69 A11** 74 13N 84 0W
Lancelin, *Australia* **61 F2** 31 0S 115 18 E
Lanchow = Lanzhou, *China* **34 F2** 36 1N 103 52 E
Lanciano, *Italy* **20 C6** 42 14N 14 23 E
Lancun, *China* **35 F11** 36 25N 120 10 E
Landeck, *Austria* **16 E6** 47 9N 10 34 E
Lander, *U.S.A.* **82 E9** 42 50N 108 44W
Lander →, *Australia* **60 D5** 22 0S 132 0 E
Landes, *France* **18 D3** 44 0N 1 0W
Landi Kotal, *Pakistan* **42 B4** 34 7N 71 6 E
Landisburg, *U.S.A.* **78 F7** 40 21N 77 19W
Land's End, *U.K.* **11 G2** 50 4N 5 44W
Landsborough Cr. →,
 Australia **62 C3** 22 28S 144 35 E
Landshut, *Germany* **16 D7** 48 34N 12 8 E
Landskrona, *Sweden* **9 J15** 55 53N 12 50 E
Lanesboro, *U.S.A.* **79 E9** 41 57N 75 34W
Lanett, *U.S.A.* **77 J3** 32 52N 85 12W
Lang Qua, *Vietnam* **38 A5** 22 16N 104 27 E
Lang Shan, *China* **34 D4** 41 0N 106 30 E
Lang Suan, *Thailand* **39 H2** 9 57N 99 4 E
La'nga Co, *China* **41 D12** 30 45N 81 15 E
Langar, *Iran* **45 C9** 35 23N 60 25 E
Langara I., *Canada* **72 C2** 54 14N 133 1W
Langdon, *U.S.A.* **80 A5** 48 45N 98 22W
Langeberg, *S. Africa* **56 E3** 33 55S 21 0 E
Langeberge, *S. Africa* . . . **56 D3** 28 15S 22 33 E
Langeland, *Denmark* **9 J14** 54 56N 10 48 E
Langenburg, *Canada* **73 C8** 50 51N 101 43W
Langholm, *U.K.* **12 F5** 55 9N 3 0W
Langjökull, *Iceland* **8 D3** 64 39N 20 12W
Langkawi, Pulau, *Malaysia* . **39 J2** 6 25N 99 45 E
Langklip, *S. Africa* **56 D3** 28 12S 20 20 E
Langkon, *Malaysia* **36 C5** 6 30N 116 40 E
Langlade, *St- P. & M.* . . . **71 C8** 46 50N 56 20W
Langley, *Canada* **84 A4** 49 7N 122 39W
Langøya, *Norway* **8 B16** 68 45N 14 50 E
Langreo, *Spain* **19 A3** 43 18N 5 40W
Langres, *France* **18 C6** 47 52N 5 20 E
Langres, Plateau de, *France* **18 C6** 47 45N 5 3 E
Langsa, *Indonesia* **36 D1** 4 30N 97 57 E
Langtry, *U.S.A.* **81 L4** 29 49N 101 34W
Langu, *Thailand* **39 J2** 6 53N 99 47 E
Languedoc, *France* **18 E5** 43 58N 3 55 E
Langxiangzhen, *China* . . . **34 E9** 39 43N 116 8 E
Lanigan, *Canada* **73 C7** 51 51N 105 2W
Lankao, *China* **34 G8** 34 48N 114 50 E
Länkäran, *Azerbaijan* **25 G8** 38 48N 48 52 E
Lannion, *France* **18 B2** 48 46N 3 29W
L'Annonciation, *Canada* . . **70 C5** 46 25N 74 55W
Lansdale, *U.S.A.* **79 F9** 40 14N 75 17W
Lansdowne, *Australia* **63 E5** 31 48S 152 30 E
Lansdowne, *Canada* **79 B8** 44 24N 76 1W
Lansdowne, *India* **43 E8** 29 50N 78 41 E
Lansdowne House, *Canada* **70 B2** 52 14N 87 53W
L'Anse, *Mich., U.S.A.* . . . **76 B1** 46 42N 88 25W
L'Anse, *Mich., U.S.A.* . . . **80 B10** 46 45N 88 27W
L'Anse au Loup, *Canada* . **71 B8** 51 32N 56 50W
L'Anse aux Meadows,
 Canada **71 B8** 51 36N 55 32W
Lansford, *U.S.A.* **79 F9** 40 50N 75 53W
Lansing, *U.S.A.* **76 D3** 42 44N 84 33W
Lanta Yai, Ko, *Thailand* . . **39 J2** 7 35N 99 3 E
Lantian, *China* **34 G5** 34 11N 109 20 E
Lanus, *Argentina* **94 C4** 34 44S 58 27W
Lanusei, *Italy* **20 E3** 39 52N 9 34 E
Lanzarote, *Canary Is.* . . . **22 F6** 29 0N 13 40W
Lao Bao, *Laos* **38 D6** 16 35N 106 30 E
Laoag, *Phil.* **37 A6** 18 7N 120 34 E
Laoang, *Phil.* **37 B7** 12 32N 125 8 E
Laoha He →, *China* **35 C11** 43 25N 120 35 E
Laois □, *Ireland* **13 D4** 52 57N 7 36W
Laon, *France* **18 B5** 49 33N 3 35 E
Laona, *U.S.A.* **76 C1** 45 34N 88 40W
Laos ■, *Asia* **38 D5** 17 45N 105 0 E
Lapa, *Brazil* **95 B6** 25 46S 49 44W
Lapeer, *U.S.A.* **76 D4** 43 3N 83 19W
Lapithos, *Cyprus* **23 D12** 35 21N 33 11 E
Lapland = Lappland, *Europe* **8 B21** 68 7N 24 0 E
Laporte, *U.S.A.* **79 E8** 41 25N 76 30W

Lappeenranta

Lappeenranta, *Finland* **9 F23** 61 3N 28 12 E
Lappland, *Europe* **8 B21** 68 7N 24 0 E
Laprida, *Argentina* **94 D3** 37 34S 60 45W
Lapseki, *Turkey* **21 D12** 40 20N 26 41 E
Laptev Sea, *Russia* **27 B13** 76 0N 125 0 E
Lapua, *Finland* **8 E20** 62 58N 23 0 E
L'Aquila, *Italy* **20 C5** 42 22N 13 22 E
Lār, *Āzarbājān-e Sharqi, Iran* **44 B5** 38 30N 47 52 E
Lār, *Fārs, Iran* **45 E7** 27 40N 54 14 E
Laramie, *U.S.A.* **80 E2** 41 19N 105 35W
Laramie →, *U.S.A.* **82 F11** 42 13N 104 33W
Laramie Mts., *U.S.A.* **80 E2** 42 0N 105 30W
Laranjeiras do Sul, *Brazil* **95 B5** 25 23S 52 23W
Larantuka, *Indonesia* **37 F6** 8 21S 122 55 E
Larat, *Indonesia* **37 F8** 7 0S 132 0 E
Larde, *Mozam.* **55 F4** 16 28S 39 43 E
Larder Lake, *Canada* **70 C4** 48 5N 79 40W
Lardhos, Ákra = Líndhos,
 Ákra, *Greece* **23 C10** 36 4N 28 10 E
Lardhos, Órmos, *Greece* .. **23 C10** 36 4N 28 2 E
Laredo, *U.S.A.* **81 M5** 27 30N 99 30W
Laredo Sd., *Canada* **72 C3** 52 30N 128 53W
Largo, *U.S.A.* **77 M4** 27 55N 82 47W
Largs, *U.K.* **12 F4** 55 47N 4 52W
Lariang, *Indonesia* **37 E5** 1 26S 119 17 E
Larimore, *U.S.A.* **80 B6** 47 54N 97 38W
Lārīn, *Iran* **45 C7** 35 55N 52 19 E
Lárisa, *Greece* **21 E10** 39 36N 22 27 E
Larkana, *Pakistan* **42 F3** 27 32N 68 18 E
Larnaca, *Cyprus* **23 E12** 34 55N 33 38 E
Larnaca Bay, *Cyprus* **23 E12** 34 53N 33 45 E
Larne, *U.K.* **13 B6** 54 51N 5 51W
Larned, *U.S.A.* **80 F5** 38 11N 99 6W
Larose, *U.S.A.* **81 L9** 29 34N 90 23W
Larrimah, *Australia* **60 C5** 15 35S 133 12 E
Larsen Ice Shelf, *Antarctica* **5 C17** 67 0S 62 0W
Larvik, *Norway* **9 G14** 59 4N 10 2 E
Las Animas, *U.S.A.* **80 F3** 38 4N 103 13W
Las Anod, *Somali Rep.* ... **46 F4** 8 26N 47 19 E
Las Aves, Is., *W. Indies* .. **89 C7** 15 45N 63 55W
Las Brenãs, *Argentina* ... **94 B3** 27 5S 61 7W
Las Cejas, *Argentina* **94 B2** 26 53S 64 44W
Las Chimeneas, *Mexico* .. **85 N10** 32 8N 116 5W
Las Cruces, *U.S.A.* **83 K10** 32 19N 106 47W
Las Flores, *Argentina* ... **94 D4** 36 10S 59 7W
Las Heras, *Argentina* **94 C2** 32 51S 68 49W
Las Lajas, *Argentina* **96 D2** 38 30S 70 25W
Las Lomitas, *Argentina* .. **94 A3** 24 43S 60 35W
Las Palmas, *Argentina* ... **94 B4** 27 8S 58 45W
Las Palmas, *Canary Is.* ... **22 F4** 28 7N 15 26W
Las Palmas →, *Mexico* .. **85 N10** 32 26N 116 54W
Las Piedras, *Uruguay* **95 C4** 34 44S 56 14W
Las Pipinas, *Argentina* ... **94 D4** 35 30S 57 19W
Las Plumas, *Argentina* ... **96 E3** 43 40S 67 15W
Las Rosas, *Argentina* **94 C3** 32 30S 61 35W
Las Tablas, *Panama* **88 E3** 7 49N 80 14W
Las Termas, *Argentina* ... **94 B3** 27 29S 64 52W
Las Toscas, *Argentina* ... **94 B4** 28 21S 59 18W
Las Truchas, *Mexico* **86 D4** 17 57N 102 13W
Las Varillas, *Argentina* .. **94 C3** 31 50S 62 50W
Las Vegas, *N. Mex., U.S.A.* **83 J11** 35 36N 105 13W
Las Vegas, *Nev., U.S.A.* . **85 J11** 36 10N 115 9W
Lascano, *Uruguay* **95 C5** 33 35S 54 12W
Lashburn, *Canada* **73 C7** 53 10N 109 40W
Lashio, *Burma* **41 H20** 22 56N 97 45 E
Lashkar, *India* **42 F8** 26 10N 78 10 E
Lasíthi, *Greece* **23 D7** 35 11N 25 31 E
Lasíthi □, *Greece* **23 D7** 35 5N 25 50 E
Lāsjerd, *Iran* **45 C7** 35 24N 53 4 E
Lassen Pk., *U.S.A.* **82 F3** 40 29N 121 31W
Lassen Volcanic National
 Park, *U.S.A.* **82 F3** 40 30N 121 20W
Last Mountain L., *Canada* **73 C7** 51 5N 105 14W
Lastchance Cr. →, *U.S.A.* **84 E5** 40 2N 121 15W
Lastoursville, *Gabon* **52 E2** 0 55S 12 38 E
Lastovo, *Croatia* **20 C7** 42 46N 16 55 E
Lat Yao, *Thailand* **38 E2** 15 45N 99 48 E
Latacunga, *Ecuador* **92 D3** 0 50S 78 35W
Latakia = Al Lādhiqīyah,
 Syria **44 C2** 35 30N 35 45 E
Latchford, *Canada* **70 C4** 47 20N 79 50W
Latehar, *India* **43 H11** 23 45N 84 30 E
Latham, *Australia* **61 E2** 29 44S 116 20 E
Lathi, *India* **42 F4** 27 43N 71 23 E
Lathrop Wells, *U.S.A.* ... **85 J10** 36 39N 116 24W
Latina, *Italy* **20 D5** 41 28N 12 52 E
Latium = Lazio □, *Italy* .. **20 C5** 42 10N 12 30 E
Laton, *U.S.A.* **84 J7** 36 26N 119 41W
Latouche Treville, C.,
 Australia **60 C3** 18 27S 121 49 E
Latrobe, *Australia* **62 G4** 41 14S 146 30 E
Latrobe, *U.S.A.* **78 F5** 40 19N 79 23W
Latvia ■, *Europe* **9 H20** 56 50N 24 0 E
Lau Group, *Fiji* **59 C9** 17 0S 178 30W
Lauchhammer, *Germany* . **16 C7** 51 29N 13 47 E
Laughlin, *U.S.A.* **83 J6** 35 8N 114 35W
Laukaa, *Finland* **9 E21** 62 24N 25 56 E
Launceston, *Australia* ... **62 G4** 41 24S 147 8 E
Launceston, *U.K.* **11 G3** 50 38N 4 22W
Laune →, *Ireland* **13 D2** 52 7N 9 47W
Launglon Bok, *Burma* ... **38 F1** 13 50N 97 54 E
Laura, *Australia* **62 B3** 15 32S 144 32 E
Laurel, *Miss., U.S.A.* ... **81 K10** 31 41N 89 8W
Laurel, *Mont., U.S.A.* ... **82 D9** 45 40N 108 46W
Laurencekirk, *U.K.* **12 E6** 56 50N 2 28W
Laurens, *U.S.A.* **77 H4** 34 30N 82 1W
Laurentian Plateau, *Canada* **71 B6** 52 0N 70 0W
Lauria, *Italy* **20 E6** 40 2N 15 50 E
Laurie L., *Canada* **73 B8** 56 35N 101 57W
Laurinburg, *U.S.A.* **77 H6** 34 47N 79 28W
Lausanne, *Switz.* **18 C7** 46 32N 6 38 E
Laut, *Indonesia* **39 K6** 4 45N 108 0 E
Laut, Pulau, *Indonesia* .. **39 E3** 3 40S 116 10 E
Laut Kecil, Kepulauan,
 Indonesia **36 E5** 4 45S 115 40 E
Lautoka, *Fiji* **59 C7** 17 37S 177 27 E
Lavagh More, *Ireland* ... **13 B3** 54 46N 8 6W
Laval, *France* **18 B3** 48 4N 0 48W
Lavalle, *Argentina* **94 B2** 28 15S 65 15W
Lavant Station, *Canada* .. **79 A8** 45 3N 76 42W
Lävar Meydän, *Iran* **45 D7** 30 20N 54 30 E
Laverton, *Australia* **61 E3** 28 44S 122 29 E
Lavras, *Brazil* **95 A7** 21 20S 45 0W
Lávrion, *Greece* **21 F11** 37 40N 24 4 E
Lávris, *Greece* **23 D6** 35 25N 24 40 E

Lavumisa, *Swaziland* **57 D5** 27 20S 31 55 E
Lawas, *Malaysia* **36 D5** 4 55N 115 25 E
Lawele, *Indonesia* **37 F6** 5 16S 123 3 E
Lawng Pit, *Burma* **41 G20** 25 30N 97 25 E
Lawqah, *Si. Arabia* **44 D4** 29 49N 42 45 E
Lawrence, *N.Z.* **59 L2** 45 55S 169 41 E
Lawrence, *Kans., U.S.A.* . **80 F7** 38 58N 95 14W
Lawrence, *Mass., U.S.A.* . **79 D13** 42 43N 71 10W
Lawrenceburg, *Ind., U.S.A.* **76 F3** 39 6N 84 52W
Lawrenceburg, *Tenn., U.S.A.* **77 H2** 35 14N 87 20W
Lawrenceville, *Ga., U.S.A.* **77 J4** 33 57N 83 59W
Lawrenceville, *Pa., U.S.A.* **78 E7** 41 59N 77 8W
Laws, *U.S.A.* **84 H8** 37 24N 118 20W
Lawton, *U.S.A.* **81 H5** 34 37N 98 25W
Lawu, *Indonesia* **37 G14** 7 40S 111 13 E
Laxford, L., *U.K.* **12 C3** 58 24N 5 6W
Laylá, *Si. Arabia* **46 C4** 22 10N 46 40 E
Laylān, *Iraq* **44 C5** 35 18N 44 31 E
Layton, *U.S.A.* **82 F7** 41 4N 111 58W
Laytonville, *U.S.A.* **82 G2** 39 41N 123 29W
Lazio □, *Italy* **20 C5** 42 10N 12 30 E
Lazo, *Russia* **30 C6** 43 25N 133 55 E
Le Creusot, *France* **18 C6** 46 48N 4 24 E
Le François, *Martinique* . **89 D7** 14 38N 60 57W
Le Havre, *France* **18 B4** 49 30N 0 5 E
Le Mans, *France* **18 C4** 48 0N 0 10 E
Le Mars, *U.S.A.* **80 D6** 42 47N 96 10W
Le Mont-St-Michel, *France* **18 B3** 48 40N 1 30W
Le Moule, *Guadeloupe* .. **89 C7** 16 20N 61 22W
Le Puy-en-Velay, *France* . **18 D5** 45 3N 3 52 E
Le Sueur, *U.S.A.* **80 C8** 44 28N 93 55W
Le Thuy, *Vietnam* **38 D6** 17 14N 106 49 E
Le Touquet-Paris-Plage,
 France **18 A4** 50 30N 1 36 E
Le Tréport, *France* **18 A4** 50 3N 1 20 E
Le Verdon-sur-Mer, *France* **18 D3** 45 33N 1 4W
Lea →, *U.K.* **11 F8** 51 31N 0 1 E
Leach, *Cambodia* **39 F4** 12 21N 103 46 E
Lead, *U.S.A.* **80 C3** 44 21N 103 46W
Leader, *Canada* **73 C7** 50 50N 109 30W
Leadville, *U.S.A.* **83 G10** 39 15N 106 18W
Leaf →, *U.S.A.* **81 K10** 30 59N 88 44W
Leaf Rapids, *Canada* ... **73 B9** 56 30N 99 59W
Leamington, *Canada* ... **78 D2** 42 3N 82 36W
Leamington, *U.S.A.* ... **82 G7** 39 32N 112 17W
Leamington Spa = Royal
 Leamington Spa, *U.K.* . **11 E6** 52 18N 1 31W
Leandro Norte Alem,
 Argentina **95 B4** 27 34S 55 15W
Leane, L., *Ireland* **13 D2** 52 2N 9 32W
Learmonth, *Australia* .. **60 D1** 22 13S 114 10 E
Leask, *Canada* **73 C7** 53 5N 106 45W
Leatherhead, *U.K.* **11 F7** 51 18N 0 20W
Leavenworth, *Kans., U.S.A.* **80 F7** 39 19N 94 55W
Leavenworth, *Wash., U.S.A.* **82 C3** 47 36N 120 40W
Lebak, *Phil.* **37 C6** 6 32N 124 5 E
Lebam, *U.S.A.* **84 D3** 46 34N 123 33W
Lebanon, *Ind., U.S.A.* .. **76 E2** 40 3N 86 28W
Lebanon, *Kans., U.S.A.* . **80 F5** 39 49N 98 33W
Lebanon, *Ky., U.S.A.* .. **76 G3** 37 34N 85 15W
Lebanon, *Mo., U.S.A.* .. **81 G8** 37 41N 92 40W
Lebanon, *N.H., U.S.A.* .. **79 C12** 43 39N 72 15W
Lebanon, *Oreg., U.S.A.* . **82 D2** 44 32N 122 55W
Lebanon, *Pa., U.S.A.* ... **79 F8** 40 20N 76 26W
Lebanon, *Tenn., U.S.A.* . **77 G2** 36 12N 86 18W
Lebanon ■, *Asia* **47 B5** 34 0N 36 0 E
Lebec, *U.S.A.* **85 L8** 34 50N 118 52W
Lebel-sur-Quévillon, *Canada* **70 C4** 49 3N 76 59W
Lebomboberge, *S. Africa* **57 C5** 24 30S 32 0 E
Lębork, *Poland* **17 A9** 54 33N 17 46 E
Lebrija, *Spain* **19 D2** 36 53N 6 5W
Lebu, *Chile* **94 D1** 37 40S 73 47W
Lecce, *Italy* **21 D8** 40 23N 18 11 E
Lecco, *Italy* **18 D8** 45 51N 9 23 E
Lech →, *Germany* **16 D6** 48 43N 10 56 E
Lecontes Mills, *U.S.A.* .. **78 E6** 41 5N 78 17W
Łęczyca, *Poland* **17 B10** 52 5N 19 15 E
Ledong, *China* **38 C7** 18 41N 109 5 E
Leduc, *Canada* **72 C6** 53 15N 113 30W
Lee, *U.S.A.* **79 D11** 42 19N 73 15W
Lee →, *Ireland* **13 E3** 51 53N 8 56W
Lee Vining, *U.S.A.* **84 H7** 37 58N 119 7W
Leech L., *U.S.A.* **80 B7** 47 10N 94 24W
Leechburg, *U.S.A.* **78 F5** 40 37N 79 36W
Leeds, *U.K.* **10 D6** 53 48N 1 33W
Leeds, *U.S.A.* **77 J2** 33 33N 86 33W
Leek, *Neths.* **15 A6** 53 10N 6 24 E
Leek, *U.K.* **10 D5** 53 7N 2 1W
Leeman, *Australia* **61 E1** 29 57S 114 58 E
Leeper, *U.S.A.* **78 E5** 41 22N 79 18W
Leer, *Germany* **16 B4** 53 13N 7 26 E
Leesburg, *U.S.A.* **77 L5** 28 49N 81 53W
Leesville, *U.S.A.* **81 K8** 31 9N 93 16W
Leeton, *Australia* **63 E4** 34 33S 146 23 E
Leetonia, *U.S.A.* **78 F4** 40 53N 80 45W
Leeu Gamka, *S. Africa* .. **56 E3** 32 47S 21 59 E
Leeuwarden, *Neths.* ... **15 A5** 53 15N 5 48 E
Leeuwin, C., *Australia* .. **61 F2** 34 20S 115 9 E
Leeward Is., *Atl. Oc.* ... **89 C7** 16 30N 63 30W
Lefka, *Cyprus* **23 D11** 35 6N 32 51 E
Lefkoniko, *Cyprus* **23 D12** 35 18N 33 44 E
Lefroy, *Canada* **78 B5** 44 16N 79 34W
Lefroy, L., *Australia* ... **61 F3** 31 21S 121 40 E
Leganés, *Spain* **19 B4** 40 19N 3 45W
Legazpi, *Phil.* **37 B6** 13 10N 123 45 E
Legendre I., *Australia* .. **60 D2** 20 22S 116 55 E
Leghorn = Livorno, *Italy* **20 C4** 43 33N 10 19 E
Legionowo, *Poland* **17 B11** 52 25N 20 50 E
Legnago, *Italy* **20 B4** 45 11N 11 18 E
Legnica, *Poland* **16 C9** 51 12N 16 10 E
Leh, *India* **43 B7** 34 9N 77 35 E
Lehigh Acres, *U.S.A.* .. **77 M5** 26 36N 81 39W
Lehighton, *U.S.A.* **79 F9** 40 50N 75 43W
Lehututu, *Botswana* ... **56 C3** 23 54S 21 55 E
Leiah, *Pakistan* **42 D4** 30 58N 70 58 E
Leicester, *U.K.* **11 E6** 52 38N 1 8W
Leicester City □, *U.K.* . **11 E6** 52 38N 1 9W
Leicestershire □, *U.K.* .. **11 E6** 52 41N 1 17W
Leichhardt →, *Australia* **62 B2** 17 35S 139 48 E
Leichhardt Ra., *Australia* **62 C4** 20 46S 147 40 E
Leiden, *Neths.* **15 B4** 52 9N 4 30 E
Leie →, *Belgium* **15 C3** 51 2N 3 45 E
Leigh Creek, *Australia* . **63 E2** 30 38S 138 26 E
Leine →, *Germany* ... **16 B5** 52 43N 9 36 E
Leinster, *Australia* **61 E3** 27 51S 120 36 E
Leinster □, *Ireland* **13 C4** 53 3N 7 8W

Leinster, Mt., *Ireland* ... **13 D5** 52 37N 6 46W
Leipzig, *Germany* **16 C7** 51 18N 12 22 E
Leiria, *Portugal* **19 C1** 39 46N 8 53W
Leirvik, *Norway* **9 G11** 59 47N 5 28 E
Leisler, Mt., *Australia* .. **60 D4** 23 23S 129 20 E
Leith, *U.K.* **12 F5** 55 59N 3 11W
Leith Hill, *U.K.* **11 F7** 51 11N 0 22W
Leitrim, *Ireland* **13 B3** 54 0N 8 5W
Leitrim □, *Ireland* **13 B4** 54 8N 8 0W
Leizhou Bandao, *China* . **33 D6** 21 0N 110 0 E
Lek →, *Neths.* **15 C4** 51 54N 4 35 E
Leka, *Norway* **8 D14** 65 5N 11 35 E
Lékva Óros, *Greece* ... **23 D6** 35 18N 24 3 E
Leland, *Mich., U.S.A.* .. **76 C3** 45 1N 85 45W
Leland, *Miss., U.S.A.* .. **81 J9** 33 24N 90 54W
Leleque, *Argentina* **96 E2** 42 28S 71 0W
Lelystad, *Neths.* **15 B5** 52 30N 5 25 E
Léman, L., *Europe* **18 C7** 46 26N 6 30 E
Lemera,
 Dem. Rep. of the Congo **54 C2** 3 0S 28 55 E
Lemhi Ra., *U.S.A.* **82 D7** 44 30N 113 30W
Lemmer, *Neths.* **15 B5** 52 51N 5 43 E
Lemmon, *U.S.A.* **80 C3** 45 57N 102 10W
Lemon Grove, *U.S.A.* .. **85 N9** 32 45N 117 2W
Lemoore, *U.S.A.* **84 J7** 36 18N 119 46W
Lemvig, *Denmark* **9 H13** 56 33N 8 20 E
Lena →, *Russia* **27 B13** 72 52N 126 40 E
Léndas, *Greece* **23 E6** 34 56N 24 56 E
Lendenxa, *India* **45 D6** 30 58N 50 25 E
Lenggong, *Malaysia* ... **39 K3** 5 6N 100 58 E
Lengua de Vaca, Pta., *Chile* **94 C1** 30 14S 71 38W
Leninabad = Khudzhand,
 Tajikistan **26 E7** 40 17N 69 37 E
Leninakan = Gyumri,
 Armenia **25 F7** 40 47N 43 50 E
Leningrad = Sankt-
 Peterburg, *Russia* **24 C5** 59 55N 30 20 E
Leninogorsk, *Kazakstan* . **26 D9** 50 20N 83 30 E
Leninsk, *Russia* **25 E8** 48 40N 45 15 E
Leninsk-Kuznetskiy, *Russia* **26 D9** 54 44N 86 10 E
Lenkoran = Länkäran,
 Azerbaijan **25 G8** 38 48N 48 52 E
Lenmalu, *Indonesia* ... **37 E8** 1 45S 130 15 E
Lennox, *U.S.A.* **80 D6** 43 21N 96 53W
Lennoxville, *Canada* ... **79 A13** 45 22N 71 51W
Lenoir, *U.S.A.* **77 H5** 35 55N 81 32W
Lenoir City, *U.S.A.* ... **77 H3** 35 48N 84 16W
Lenore L., *Canada* **73 C8** 52 30N 104 59W
Lenox, *U.S.A.* **79 D11** 42 22N 73 17W
Lens, *France* **18 A5** 50 26N 2 50 E
Lensk, *Russia* **27 C12** 60 48N 114 55 E
Lentini, *Italy* **21 F6** 37 17N 15 0 E
Lenwood, *U.S.A.* **85 L9** 34 53N 117 7W
Lenya, *Burma* **36 B1** 11 33N 98 57 E
Leoben, *Austria* **16 E8** 47 22N 15 5 E
Leodhas = Lewis, *U.K.* . **12 C2** 58 9N 6 40W
Leola, *U.S.A.* **80 C5** 45 43N 98 56W
Leominster, *U.K.* **11 E5** 52 14N 2 43W
Leominster, *U.S.A.* ... **79 D13** 42 32N 71 46W
León, *Mexico* **86 C4** 21 7N 101 40W
León, *Nic.* **88 D2** 12 20N 86 51W
León, *Spain* **19 A3** 42 38N 5 34W
León □, *Spain* **19 B3** 42 40N 5 55W
Leon →, *U.S.A.* **81 K6** 31 14N 97 28W
León, Montes de, *Spain* . **19 A2** 42 30N 6 18W
Leonardtown, *U.S.A.* .. **76 F7** 38 17N 76 38W
Leongatha, *Australia* .. **63 F4** 38 30S 145 58 E
Leonora, *Australia* **61 E3** 28 49S 121 19 E
Léopold II, Lac = Mai-
 Ndombe, L.,
 Dem. Rep. of the Congo **52 E3** 2 0S 18 20 E
Leopoldina, *Brazil* **95 A7** 21 28S 42 40W
Leopoldsburg, *Belgium* . **15 C5** 51 7N 5 13 E
Léopoldville = Kinshasa,
 Dem. Rep. of the Congo **52 E3** 4 20S 15 15 E
Leoti, *U.S.A.* **80 F4** 38 29N 101 21W
Leova, *Moldova* **17 E15** 46 28N 28 15 E
Leoville, *Canada* **73 C7** 53 39N 107 33W
Lepel = Lyepyel, *Belarus* **24 D4** 54 50N 28 40 E
Lépo, L. do, *Angola* ... **56 B2** 17 0S 19 0 E
Leppävirta, *Finland* ... **9 E22** 62 29N 27 46 E
Lerdo, *Mexico* **86 B4** 25 32N 103 32W
Lérida = Lleida, *Spain* .. **19 B6** 41 37N 0 39 E
Lerwick, *U.K.* **12 A7** 60 9N 1 9W
Les Cayes, *Haiti* **89 C5** 18 15N 73 46W
Les Sables-d'Olonne, *France* **18 C3** 46 30N 1 45W
Lesbos = Lésvos, *Greece* **21 E12** 39 10N 26 20 E
Leshan, *China* **32 D5** 29 33N 103 41 E
Leshukonskoye, *Russia* . **24 B8** 64 54N 45 46 E
Leskov I., *Antarctica* ... **5 B1** 56 0S 28 0W
Leskovac, *Serbia, Yug.* . **21 C9** 43 0N 21 58 E
Lesopilnoye, *Russia* ... **30 A7** 46 44N 134 20 E
Lesotho ■, *Africa* **57 E14** 29 40S 28 0 E
Lesozavodsk, *Russia* ... **27 E14** 45 30N 133 29 E
Lesse →, *Belgium* **15 D4** 50 15N 4 54 E
Lesser Antilles, *W. Indies* **89 D7** 15 0N 61 0W
Lesser Slave L., *Canada* . **72 B5** 55 30N 115 25W
Lesser Sunda Is., *Indonesia* **37 F6** 7 0S 120 0 E
Lessines, *Belgium* **15 D3** 50 42N 3 50 E
Lester, *U.S.A.* **84 C5** 47 12N 121 29W
Lestock, *Canada* **73 C8** 50 40N 103 59W
Lesuer I., *Australia* **60 B4** 13 50S 127 17 E
Lésvos, *Greece* **21 E12** 39 10N 26 20 E
Leszno, *Poland* **17 C9** 51 50N 16 30 E
Letchworth, *U.K.* **11 F7** 51 59N 0 13W
Lethbridge, *Canada* ... **72 D6** 49 45N 112 45W
Lethem, *Guyana* **92 C7** 3 20N 59 50W
Leti, Kepulauan, *Indonesia* **37 F7** 8 10S 128 0 E
Leti Is. = Leti, Kepulauan,
 Indonesia **37 F7** 8 10S 128 0 E
Letiahau →, *Botswana* . **56 C3** 21 16S 24 0 E
Leticia, *Colombia* **92 D5** 4 9S 70 0W
Leting, *China* **35 E10** 39 23N 118 55 E
Letjiesbos, *S. Africa* ... **56 E3** 32 34S 22 16 E
Letlhakeng, *Botswana* .. **56 C3** 24 0S 24 59 E
Letong, *Indonesia* **36 D3** 2 58N 105 42 E
Letpadan, *Burma* **41 L19** 17 45N 95 45 E
Letpan, *Burma* **41 K19** 19 28N 94 10 E
Letsôk-aw Kyun, *Burma* **39 G1** 11 30N 98 25 E
Letterkenny, *Ireland* ... **13 B4** 54 57N 7 45W
Leucadia, *U.S.A.* **85 M9** 33 4N 117 18W
Leuser, G., *Indonesia* .. **36 D1** 3 46N 97 12 E
Leuven, *Belgium* **15 D4** 50 52N 4 42 E
Leuze-en-Hainaut, *Belgium* **15 D3** 50 36N 3 37 E
Levádhia, *Greece* **21 E10** 38 27N 22 54 E

Levanger, *Norway* **8 E14** 63 45N 11 19 E
Levelland, *U.S.A.* **81 J3** 33 35N 102 23W
Leven, *U.K.* **12 E6** 56 12N 3 0W
Leven, L., *U.K.* **12 E5** 56 12N 3 22W
Leven, Toraka, *Madag.* . **57 A8** 12 30S 47 45 E
Leveque C., *Australia* .. **60 C3** 16 20S 123 0 E
Levice, *Slovak Rep.* ... **17 D10** 48 13N 18 35 E
Levin, *N.Z.* **59 J5** 40 37S 175 18 E
Lévis, *Canada* **71 C5** 46 48N 71 9W
Levis, L., *Canada* **72 A5** 62 37N 117 58W
Levittown, *N.Y., U.S.A.* . **79 F11** 40 44N 73 31W
Levittown, *Pa., U.S.A.* . **79 F10** 40 9N 74 51W
Levkás, *Greece* **21 E9** 38 40N 20 43 E
Levkímmi, *Greece* **23 B4** 39 25N 20 3 E
Levkímmi, Ákra, *Greece* **23 B4** 39 29N 20 4 E
Levkôsia = Nicosia, *Cyprus* **23 D12** 35 10N 33 25 E
Levskigrad = Karlovo,
 Bulgaria **21 C11** 42 38N 24 47 E
Lewes, *U.K.* **11 G8** 50 52N 0 1 E
Lewes, *U.S.A.* **76 F8** 38 46N 75 9W
Lewis, *U.K.* **12 C2** 58 9N 6 40W
Lewis →, *U.S.A.* **84 E4** 45 51N 122 48W
Lewis, Butt of, *U.K.* ... **12 C2** 58 31N 6 16W
Lewis Ra., *Australia* ... **60 D4** 20 3S 128 50 E
Lewis Range, *U.S.A.* .. **82 C7** 48 5N 113 5W
Lewis Run, *U.S.A.* **78 E6** 41 52N 78 40W
Lewisburg, *Pa., U.S.A.* . **78 F8** 40 58N 76 54W
Lewisburg, *Tenn., U.S.A.* **77 H2** 35 27N 86 48W
Lewisburg, *W. Va., U.S.A.* **76 G5** 37 48N 80 27W
Lewisporte, *Canada* ... **71 C8** 49 15N 55 3W
Lewiston, *Idaho, U.S.A.* **82 C5** 46 25N 117 1W
Lewiston, *Maine, U.S.A.* **77 C11** 44 6N 70 13W
Lewiston, *N.Y., U.S.A.* . **78 C5** 43 11N 79 3W
Lewistown, *Mont., U.S.A.* **82 C9** 47 4N 109 26W
Lewistown, *Pa., U.S.A.* . **78 F7** 40 36N 77 34W
Lexington, *Ill., U.S.A.* . **80 E10** 40 39N 88 47W
Lexington, *Ky., U.S.A.* . **76 F3** 38 3N 84 30W
Lexington, *Mich., U.S.A.* **78 C2** 43 16N 82 32W
Lexington, *Mo., U.S.A.* . **80 F8** 39 11N 93 52W
Lexington, *N.C., U.S.A.* . **77 H5** 35 49N 80 15W
Lexington, *Nebr., U.S.A.* **80 E5** 40 47N 99 45W
Lexington, *Ohio, U.S.A.* **78 F2** 40 41N 82 35W
Lexington, *Tenn., U.S.A.* **77 H1** 35 39N 88 24W
Lexington, *Va., U.S.A.* . **76 G6** 37 47N 79 27W
Lexington Park, *U.S.A.* . **76 G7** 38 16N 76 27W
Leyburn, *U.K.* **10 C6** 54 19N 1 48W
Leyland, *U.K.* **10 D5** 53 42N 2 43W
Leyte, *Phil.* **37 B7** 11 0N 125 0 E
Lezha, *Albania* **21 D8** 41 47N 19 39 E
Lhasa, *China* **32 D4** 29 25N 90 58 E
Lhazê, *China* **32 D3** 29 5N 87 38 E
Lhokkruet, *Indonesia* .. **36 D1** 4 55N 95 24 E
Lhokseumawe, *Indonesia* **36 C1** 5 10N 97 10 E
L'Hospitalet de Llobregat,
 Spain **19 B7** 41 21N 2 6 E
Lhuntsi Dzong, *India* .. **41 F17** 27 39N 91 10 E
Li, *Thailand* **38 D2** 17 48N 98 57 E
Li Xian, *Gansu, China* . **34 G3** 34 10N 105 5 E
Li Xian, *Hebei, China* .. **34 E8** 38 30N 115 35 E
Lianga, *Phil.* **37 C7** 8 38N 126 6 E
Liangcheng,
 Nei Mongol Zizhiqu, China **34 D7** 40 28N 112 25 E
Liangcheng, *Shandong,
 China* **35 G10** 35 32N 119 37 E
Liangdang, *China* **34 H4** 33 56N 106 18 E
Liangpran, *Indonesia* .. **36 D4** 1 4N 114 23 E
Lianshanguan, *China* .. **35 D12** 40 53N 123 43 E
Lianshui, *China* **35 H10** 33 42N 119 20 E
Lianyungang, *China* ... **35 D11** 41 0N 121 50 E
Liao He →, *China* **35 D11** 41 0N 121 50 E
Liaocheng, *China* **34 F8** 36 28N 115 58 E
Liaodong Bandao, *China* **35 E12** 40 0N 122 30 E
Liaodong Wan, *China* .. **35 D11** 40 20N 121 10 E
Liaoning □, *China* **35 D12** 41 40N 122 30 E
Liaoyang, *China* **35 D12** 41 15N 122 58 E
Liaoyuan, *China* **35 C13** 42 58N 125 2 E
Liaozhong, *China* **35 D12** 41 23N 122 50 E
Liard →, *Canada* **72 A4** 61 51N 121 18W
Liard River, *Canada* ... **72 B3** 59 25N 126 5W
Liari, *Pakistan* **42 G2** 25 37N 66 30 E
Libau = Liepāja, *Latvia* . **9 H19** 56 30N 21 0 E
Libby, *U.S.A.* **82 B6** 48 23N 115 33W
Libenge,
 Dem. Rep. of the Congo **52 D3** 3 40N 18 55 E
Liberal, *U.S.A.* **81 G4** 37 3N 100 55W
Liberec, *Czech Rep.* ... **16 C8** 50 47N 15 7 E
Liberia, *Costa Rica* **88 D2** 10 40N 85 30W
Liberia ■, *W. Afr.* **50 G4** 6 30N 9 30W
Liberty, *Mo., U.S.A.* .. **80 F7** 39 15N 94 25W
Liberty, *N.Y., U.S.A.* .. **79 E10** 41 48N 74 45W
Liberty, *Pa., U.S.A.* ... **78 E7** 41 34N 77 6W
Liberty, *Tex., U.S.A.* .. **81 K7** 30 3N 94 48W
Lībīya, Sahrā', *Africa* .. **51 C10** 25 0N 25 0 E
Libobo, Tanjung, *Indonesia* **37 E7** 0 54S 128 28 E
Libode, *S. Africa* **57 E4** 31 33S 29 2 E
Libourne, *France* **18 D3** 44 55N 0 14W
Libramont, *Belgium* ... **15 E5** 49 55N 5 23 E
Libreville, *Gabon* **52 D1** 0 25N 9 26 E
Libya ■, *N. Afr.* **51 C9** 27 0N 17 0 E
Libyan Desert = Lībīya,
 Sahrā', *Africa* **51 C10** 25 0N 25 0 E
Licantén, *Chile* **94 D1** 35 55S 72 0W
Licata, *Italy* **20 F5** 37 6N 13 56 E
Licheng, *China* **34 F7** 36 28N 113 20 E
Lichfield, *U.K.* **11 E6** 52 41N 1 49W
Lichinga, *Mozam.* **55 E4** 13 13S 35 11 E
Lichtenburg, *S. Africa* .. **56 D4** 26 8S 26 8 E
Lichuan, *China* **32 C6** 30 18N 108 57 E
Lida, *Belarus* **9 K21** 53 53N 25 15 E
Lidköping, *Sweden* **9 G15** 58 31N 13 7 E
Liebig, Mt., *Australia* .. **60 D5** 23 18S 131 22 E
Liechtenstein ■, *Europe* **18 C8** 47 8N 9 35 E
Liège, *Belgium* **15 D5** 50 38N 5 35 E
Liège □, *Belgium* **15 D5** 50 32N 5 35 E
Liegnitz = Legnica, *Poland* **16 C9** 51 12N 16 10 E
Lienart,
 Dem. Rep. of the Congo **54 B2** 3 3N 25 31 E
Lienyünchiangshih =
 Lianyungang, *China* .. **35 G10** 34 40N 119 11 E
Lienz, *Austria* **16 E7** 46 50N 12 46 E
Liepāja, *Latvia* **9 H19** 56 30N 21 0 E
Lier, *Belgium* **15 C4** 51 7N 4 34 E
Liffey →, *Ireland* **13 C5** 53 21N 6 13W
Lifford, *Ireland* **13 B4** 54 51N 7 29W

Lifudzin, Russia	30 B7	44 21N	134 58 E
Lightning Ridge, Australia	63 D4	29 22S	148 0 E
Ligonier, U.S.A.	78 F5	40 15N	79 14W
Liguria □, Italy	18 D8	44 30N	8 50 E
Ligurian Sea, Medit. S.	20 C3	43 20N	9 0 E
Lihou Reefs and Cays, Australia	62 B5	17 25S	151 40 E
Lihue, U.S.A.	74 H15	21 59N	159 23W
Lijiang, China	32 D5	26 55N	100 20 E
Likasi, Dem. Rep. of the Congo	55 E2	10 55S	26 48 E
Likoma I., Malawi	55 E3	12 3S	34 45 E
Likumburu, Tanzania	55 D4	9 43S	35 8 E
Lille, France	18 A5	50 38N	3 3 E
Lille Bælt, Denmark	9 J13	55 20N	9 45 E
Lillehammer, Norway	9 F14	61 8N	10 30 E
Lillesand, Norway	9 G13	58 15N	8 23 E
Lillian Pt., Australia	61 E4	27 40S	126 6 E
Lillooet, Canada	72 C4	50 44N	121 57W
Lillooet →, Canada	72 C4	49 15N	121 57W
Lilongwe, Malawi	55 E3	14 0S	33 48 E
Liloy, Phil.	37 C6	8 4N	122 39 E
Lim →, Bos.-H.	21 C8	43 45N	19 15 E
Lima, Indonesia	37 E7	3 37S	128 4 E
Lima, Peru	92 F3	12 0S	77 0W
Lima, Mont., U.S.A.	82 D7	44 38N	112 36W
Lima, Ohio, U.S.A.	76 E3	40 44N	84 6W
Lima →, Portugal	19 B1	41 41N	8 50W
Liman, Indonesia	37 G14	7 48S	111 45 E
Limassol, Cyprus	23 E12	34 42N	33 1 E
Limavady, U.K.	13 A5	55 3N	6 56W
Limay →, Argentina	96 D3	39 0S	68 0W
Limay Mahuida, Argentina	94 D2	37 10S	66 45W
Limbang, Brunei	36 D5	4 42N	115 6 E
Limbaži, Latvia	9 H21	57 31N	24 42 E
Limbdi, India	42 H4	22 34N	71 51 E
Limbe, Cameroon	52 D1	4 1N	9 10 E
Limburg, Germany	16 C5	50 22N	8 4 E
Limburg □, Belgium	15 C5	51 2N	5 25 E
Limburg □, Neths.	15 C5	51 20N	5 55 E
Limeira, Brazil	95 A6	22 35S	47 28W
Limerick, Ireland	13 D3	52 40N	8 37W
Limerick □, Ireland	13 D3	52 30N	8 50W
Limestone, U.S.A.	78 D6	42 2N	78 38W
Limestone →, Canada	73 B10	56 31N	94 7W
Limfjorden, Denmark	9 H13	56 55N	9 0 E
Limia = Lima →, Portugal	19 B1	41 41N	8 50W
Limingen, Norway	8 D15	64 48N	13 35 E
Limmen Bight, Australia	62 A2	14 40S	135 35 E
Limmen Bight →, Australia	62 B2	15 7S	135 44 E
Límnos, Greece	21 E11	39 50N	25 5 E
Limoges, Canada	79 A9	45 20N	75 16W
Limoges, France	18 D4	45 50N	1 15 E
Limón, Costa Rica	88 E3	10 0N	83 2W
Limon, U.S.A.	80 F3	39 16N	103 41W
Limousin, France	18 D4	45 30N	1 30 E
Limoux, France	18 E5	43 4N	2 12 E
Limpopo →, Africa	57 D5	25 5S	33 30 E
Limuru, Kenya	54 C4	1 2S	36 35 E
Lin Xian, China	34 F6	37 57N	110 58 E
Linares, Chile	94 D1	35 50S	71 40W
Linares, Mexico	87 C5	24 50N	99 40W
Linares, Spain	19 C4	38 10N	3 40W
Lincheng, China	34 F8	37 25N	114 30 E
Lincoln, Argentina	94 C3	34 55S	61 30W
Lincoln, N.Z.	59 K4	43 38S	172 30 E
Lincoln, U.K.	10 D7	53 14N	0 32W
Lincoln, Calif., U.S.A.	84 G5	38 54N	121 17W
Lincoln, Ill., U.S.A.	80 E10	40 9N	89 22W
Lincoln, Kans., U.S.A.	80 F5	39 3N	98 9W
Lincoln, Maine, U.S.A.	77 C11	45 22N	68 30W
Lincoln, N.H., U.S.A.	79 B13	44 3N	71 40W
Lincoln, N. Mex., U.S.A.	83 K11	33 30N	105 23W
Lincoln, Nebr., U.S.A.	80 E6	40 49N	96 41W
Lincoln City, U.S.A.	82 D1	44 57N	124 1W
Lincoln Hav = Lincoln Sea, Arctic	4 A5	84 0N	55 0W
Lincoln Sea, Arctic	4 A5	84 0N	55 0W
Lincolnshire □, U.K.	10 D7	53 14N	0 32W
Lincolnshire Wolds, U.K.	10 D7	53 26N	0 13W
Lincolnton, U.S.A.	77 H5	35 29N	81 16W
Lind, U.S.A.	82 C4	46 58N	118 37W
Linda, U.S.A.	84 F5	39 8N	121 34W
Linden, Guyana	92 B7	6 0N	58 10W
Linden, Ala., U.S.A.	77 J2	32 18N	87 48W
Linden, Calif., U.S.A.	84 G5	38 1N	121 5W
Linden, Tex., U.S.A.	81 J7	33 1N	94 22W
Lindenhurst, U.S.A.	79 F11	40 41N	73 23W
Lindesnes, Norway	9 H12	57 58N	7 3 E
Líndhos, Greece	23 C10	36 6N	28 4 E
Líndhos, Ákra, Greece	23 C10	36 4N	28 10 E
Lindi, Tanzania	55 D4	9 58S	39 38 E
Lindi □, Tanzania	55 D4	9 40S	38 30 E
Lindi →, Dem. Rep. of the Congo	54 B2	0 33N	25 5 E
Lindsay, Canada	78 B6	44 22N	78 43W
Lindsay, Calif., U.S.A.	84 J7	36 12N	119 5W
Lindsay, Okla., U.S.A.	81 H6	34 50N	97 38W
Lindsborg, U.S.A.	80 F6	38 35N	97 40W
Linesville, U.S.A.	78 E4	41 39N	80 26W
Linfen, China	34 F6	36 3N	111 30 E
Ling Xian, China	34 F9	37 22N	116 30 E
Lingao, China	38 C7	19 56N	109 42 E
Lingayen, Phil.	37 A6	16 1N	120 14 E
Lingayen G., Phil.	37 A6	16 10N	120 15 E
Lingbi, China	35 H9	33 33N	117 33 E
Lingchuan, China	34 G7	35 45N	113 12 E
Lingen, Germany	16 B4	52 31N	7 19 E
Lingga, Indonesia	36 E2	0 12S	104 37 E
Lingga, Kepulauan, Indonesia	36 E2	0 10S	104 30 E
Lingga Arch. = Lingga, Kepulauan, Indonesia	36 E2	0 10S	104 30 E
Lingle, U.S.A.	80 D2	42 8N	104 21W
Lingqiu, China	34 E8	39 28N	114 22 E
Lingshi, China	34 F6	36 48N	111 48 E
Lingshou, China	34 E8	38 20N	114 20 E
Lingshui, China	38 C8	18 27N	110 0 E
Lingtai, China	34 G4	35 0N	107 40 E
Linguère, Senegal	50 E2	15 25N	15 5W
Lingyuan, China	35 D10	41 10N	119 15 E
Linhai, China	33 D7	28 50N	121 8 E
Linhares, Brazil	93 G10	19 25S	40 4W
Linhe, China	34 D4	40 48N	107 20 E
Linjiang, China	35 D14	41 50N	127 0 E
Linköping, Sweden	9 G16	58 28N	15 36 E
Linkou, China	35 B16	45 15N	130 18 E
Linnhe, L., U.K.	12 E3	56 36N	5 25W
Linqi, China	34 G7	35 45N	113 52 E
Linqing, China	34 F8	36 50N	115 42 E
Linqu, China	35 F10	36 25N	118 30 E
Linru, China	34 G7	34 11N	112 52 E
Lins, Brazil	95 A6	21 40S	49 44W
Linton, Ind., U.S.A.	76 F2	39 2N	87 10W
Linton, N. Dak., U.S.A.	80 B4	46 16N	100 14W
Lintong, China	34 G5	34 20N	109 10 E
Linwood, Canada	78 C4	43 35N	80 43W
Linxi, China	35 C10	43 36N	118 2 E
Linxia, China	32 C5	35 36N	103 10 E
Linyanti →, Africa	56 B4	17 50S	25 5 E
Linyi, China	35 G10	35 5N	118 21 E
Linz, Austria	16 D8	48 18N	14 18 E
Linzhenzhen, China	34 F5	36 30N	109 59 E
Linzi, China	35 F10	36 50N	118 20 E
Lion, G. du, France	18 E6	43 10N	4 0 E
Lionárisso, Cyprus	23 D13	35 28N	34 8 E
Lions, G. of = Lion, G. du, France	18 E6	43 10N	4 0 E
Lion's Den, Zimbabwe	55 F3	17 15S	30 5 E
Lion's Head, Canada	78 B3	44 58N	81 15W
Lipa, Phil.	37 B6	13 57N	121 10 E
Lipali, Mozam.	55 F4	15 50S	35 50 E
Lípari, Italy	20 E6	38 26N	14 58 E
Lípari, Is. = Éolie, Ís., Italy	20 E6	38 30N	14 57 E
Lipcani, Moldova	17 D14	48 14N	26 48 E
Lipetsk, Russia	24 D6	52 37N	39 35 E
Lipkany = Lipcani, Moldova	17 D14	48 14N	26 48 E
Lipovcy Manzovka, Russia	30 B6	44 12N	132 26 E
Lipovets, Ukraine	17 D15	49 12N	29 1 E
Lippe →, Germany	16 C4	51 39N	6 36 E
Lipscomb, U.S.A.	81 G4	36 14N	100 16W
Liptrap C., Australia	63 F4	38 50S	145 55 E
Lira, Uganda	54 B3	2 17N	32 57 E
Liria = Lliria, Spain	19 C5	39 37N	0 35W
Lisala, Dem. Rep. of the Congo	52 D4	2 12N	21 38 E
Lisboa, Portugal	19 C1	38 42N	9 10W
Lisbon = Lisboa, Portugal	19 C1	38 42N	9 10W
Lisbon, N. Dak., U.S.A.	80 B6	46 27N	97 41W
Lisbon, N.H., U.S.A.	79 B13	44 13N	71 55W
Lisbon, Ohio, U.S.A.	78 F4	40 46N	80 46W
Lisbon Falls, U.S.A.	77 D10	44 0N	70 4W
Lisburn, U.K.	13 B5	54 31N	6 3W
Liscannor B., Ireland	13 D2	52 55N	9 24W
Lishi, China	34 F6	37 31N	111 8 E
Lishu, China	35 C13	43 20N	124 18 E
Lisianski I., Pac. Oc.	64 E10	26 2N	174 0W
Lisichansk = Lysychansk, Ukraine	25 E6	48 55N	38 30 E
Lisieux, France	18 B4	49 10N	0 12 E
Liski, Russia	25 D6	51 3N	39 30 E
Lismore, Australia	63 D5	28 44S	153 21 E
Lismore, Ireland	13 D4	52 8N	7 55W
Lista, Norway	9 G12	58 7N	6 39 E
Lister, Mt., Antarctica	5 D11	78 0S	162 0 E
Liston, Australia	63 D5	28 39S	152 6 E
Listowel, Canada	78 C4	43 44N	80 58W
Listowel, Ireland	13 D2	52 27N	9 29W
Litani →, Lebanon	47 B4	33 20N	35 15 E
Litchfield, Calif., U.S.A.	84 E6	40 24N	120 23W
Litchfield, Conn., U.S.A.	79 E11	41 45N	73 11W
Litchfield, Ill., U.S.A.	80 F10	39 11N	89 39W
Litchfield, Minn., U.S.A.	80 C7	45 8N	94 32W
Lithgow, Australia	63 E5	33 25S	150 8 E
Líthinon, Ákra, Greece	23 E6	34 55N	24 44 E
Lithuania ■, Europe	9 J20	55 30N	24 0 E
Lititz, U.S.A.	79 F8	40 9N	76 18W
Litoměřice, Czech Rep.	16 C8	50 33N	14 10 E
Little Abaco I., Bahamas	88 A4	26 50N	77 30W
Little Barrier I., N.Z.	59 G5	36 12S	175 8 E
Little Belt Mts., U.S.A.	82 C8	46 40N	110 45W
Little Blue →, U.S.A.	80 F6	39 42N	96 41W
Little Buffalo →, Canada	72 A6	61 0N	113 46W
Little Cayman, Cayman Is.	88 C3	19 41N	80 3W
Little Churchill →, Canada	73 B9	57 30N	95 22W
Little Colorado →, U.S.A.	83 H8	36 12N	111 48W
Little Current, Canada	70 C3	45 55N	82 0W
Little Current →, Canada	70 B3	50 57N	84 36W
Little Falls, Minn., U.S.A.	80 C7	45 59N	94 22W
Little Falls, N.Y., U.S.A.	79 C10	43 3N	74 51W
Little Fork →, U.S.A.	80 A8	48 31N	93 35W
Little Grand Rapids, Canada	73 C9	52 0N	95 29W
Little Humboldt →, U.S.A.	82 F5	41 1N	117 43W
Little Inagua I., Bahamas	89 B5	21 40N	73 50W
Little Karoo, S. Africa	56 E3	33 45S	21 0 E
Little Lake, U.S.A.	85 K9	35 56N	117 55W
Little Laut Is. = Laut Kecil, Kepulauan, Indonesia	36 E5	4 45S	115 40 E
Little-Mécatina = Petit-Mécatina →, Canada	71 B8	50 40N	59 30W
Little Minch, U.K.	12 D2	57 35N	6 45W
Little Missouri →, U.S.A.	80 B3	47 36N	102 25W
Little Ouse →, U.K.	11 E9	52 22N	1 12 E
Little Rann, India	42 H4	23 25N	71 25 E
Little Red →, U.S.A.	81 H9	35 11N	91 27W
Little River, N.Z.	59 K4	43 45S	172 49 E
Little Rock, U.S.A.	81 H8	34 45N	92 17W
Little Ruaha →, Tanzania	54 D4	7 57S	37 53 E
Little Sable Pt., U.S.A.	76 D2	43 38N	86 33W
Little Sioux →, U.S.A.	80 E6	41 48N	96 4W
Little Smoky →, Canada	72 C5	54 44N	117 11W
Little Snake →, U.S.A.	82 F9	40 27N	108 26W
Little Valley, U.S.A.	78 D6	42 15N	78 48W
Little Wabash →, U.S.A.	76 G1	37 55N	88 5W
Little White →, U.S.A.	80 D4	43 40N	100 40W
Littlefield, U.S.A.	81 J3	33 55N	102 20W
Littlehampton, U.K.	11 G7	50 49N	0 32W
Littleton, U.S.A.	79 B13	44 18N	71 46W
Liu He →, China	35 D11	40 55N	121 35 E
Liuba, China	34 H4	33 38N	106 55 E
Liugou, China	35 D10	41 0N	118 15 E
Liuhe, China	35 C13	42 17N	125 43 E
Liukang Tenggaja = Sabalana, Kepulauan, Indonesia	37 F5	6 45S	118 50 E
Liuli, Tanzania	55 E3	11 3S	34 38 E
Liuwa Plain, Zambia	53 G4	14 20S	22 30 E
Liuzhou, China	33 D5	24 22N	109 22 E
Liuzhuang, China	35 H11	33 12N	120 18 E
Livadhia, Cyprus	23 E12	34 57N	33 38 E
Live Oak, Calif., U.S.A.	84 F5	39 17N	121 40W
Live Oak, Fla., U.S.A.	77 K4	30 18N	82 59W
Liveras, Cyprus	23 D11	35 23N	32 57 E
Livermore, U.S.A.	84 H5	37 41N	121 47W
Livermore, Mt., U.S.A.	81 K2	30 38N	104 11W
Livermore Falls, U.S.A.	77 C11	44 29N	70 11W
Liverpool, Canada	71 D7	44 5N	64 41W
Liverpool, U.K.	10 D4	53 25N	3 0W
Liverpool, U.S.A.	79 C8	43 6N	76 13W
Liverpool Bay, U.K.	10 D4	53 30N	3 20W
Liverpool Plains, Australia	63 E5	31 15S	150 15 E
Liverpool Ra., Australia	63 E5	31 50S	150 30 E
Livingston, Guatemala	88 C2	15 50N	88 50W
Livingston, U.K.	12 F5	55 54N	3 30W
Livingston, Ala., U.S.A.	77 J1	32 35N	88 11W
Livingston, Calif., U.S.A.	84 H6	37 23N	120 43W
Livingston, Mont., U.S.A.	82 D8	45 40N	110 34W
Livingston, S.C., U.S.A.	77 J5	33 32N	80 53W
Livingston, Tenn., U.S.A.	77 G3	36 23N	85 19W
Livingston, Tex., U.S.A.	81 K7	30 43N	94 56W
Livingston Manor, U.S.A.	79 E10	41 54N	74 50W
Livingstone, Zambia	55 F2	17 46S	25 52 E
Livingstone Mts., Tanzania	55 D3	9 40S	34 20 E
Livingstonia, Malawi	55 E3	10 38S	34 5 E
Livny, Russia	24 D6	52 30N	37 30 E
Livonia, Mich., U.S.A.	76 D4	42 23N	83 23W
Livonia, N.Y., U.S.A.	78 D7	42 49N	77 40W
Livorno, Italy	20 C4	43 33N	10 19 E
Livramento, Brazil	95 C4	30 55S	55 30W
Liwale, Tanzania	55 D4	9 48S	37 58 E
Lizard I., Australia	62 A4	14 42S	145 30 E
Lizard Pt., U.K.	11 H2	49 57N	5 13W
Ljubljana, Slovenia	16 E8	46 4N	14 33 E
Ljungan →, Sweden	9 E17	62 18N	17 23 E
Ljungby, Sweden	9 H15	56 49N	13 55 E
Ljusdal, Sweden	9 F17	61 46N	16 3 E
Ljusnan →, Sweden	9 F17	61 12N	17 8 E
Ljusne, Sweden	9 F17	61 13N	17 7 E
Llancanelo, Salina, Argentina	94 D2	35 40S	69 8W
Llandeilo, U.K.	11 F4	51 53N	3 59W
Llandovery, U.K.	11 F4	51 59N	3 48W
Llandrindod Wells, U.K.	11 E4	52 14N	3 22W
Llandudno, U.K.	10 D4	53 19N	3 50W
Llanelli, U.K.	11 F3	51 41N	4 10W
Llanes, Spain	19 A3	43 25N	4 50W
Llangollen, U.K.	10 E4	52 58N	3 11W
Llanidloes, U.K.	11 E4	52 27N	3 31W
Llano, U.S.A.	81 K5	30 45N	98 41W
Llano →, U.S.A.	81 K5	30 39N	98 26W
Llano Estacado, U.S.A.	81 J3	33 30N	103 0W
Llanos, S. Amer.	92 C4	5 0N	71 35W
Llanquihue, L., Chile	96 E1	41 10S	75 50W
Llanwrtyd Wells, U.K.	11 E4	52 7N	3 38W
Llebeig, C. des, Spain	22 B9	39 33N	2 18 E
Lleida, Spain	19 B6	41 37N	0 39 E
Llentrisca, C., Spain	22 C7	38 52N	1 15 E
Llera, Mexico	87 C5	23 19N	99 1W
Lleyn Peninsula, U.K.	10 E3	52 51N	4 36W
Llico, Chile	94 C1	34 46S	72 5W
Llobregat →, Spain	19 B7	41 19N	2 9 E
Lloret de Mar, Spain	19 B7	41 41N	2 53 E
Lloyd B., Australia	62 A3	12 45S	143 27 E
Lloyd L., Canada	73 B7	57 22N	108 57W
Lloydminster, Canada	73 C7	53 17N	110 0W
Llucmajor, Spain	22 B9	39 29N	2 53 E
Llullaillaco, Volcán, S. Amer.	94 A2	24 43S	68 30W
Lo →, Vietnam	38 B5	21 18N	105 25 E
Loa, U.S.A.	83 G8	38 24N	111 39W
Loa →, Chile	94 A1	21 26S	70 41W
Loaita I., S. China Sea	36 B4	10 41N	114 25 E
Loange →, Dem. Rep. of the Congo	52 E4	4 17S	20 2 E
Lobatse, Botswana	56 D4	25 12S	25 40 E
Loberia, Argentina	94 D4	38 10S	58 40W
Lobito, Angola	53 G2	12 18S	13 35 E
Lobos, Argentina	94 D4	35 10S	59 0W
Lobos, I., Mexico	86 B2	27 15N	110 30W
Lobos, I. de, Canary Is.	22 F6	28 45N	13 50W
Loc Binh, Vietnam	38 B6	21 46N	106 54 E
Loc Ninh, Vietnam	39 G6	11 50N	106 34 E
Locarno, Switz.	18 C8	46 10N	8 47 E
Loch Baghasdail = Lochboisdale, U.K.	12 D1	57 9N	7 20W
Loch Garman = Wexford, Ireland	13 D5	52 20N	6 28W
Loch Nam Madadh = Lochmaddy, U.K.	12 D1	57 36N	7 10W
Lochaber, U.K.	12 E3	56 59N	5 1W
Locharbriggs, U.K.	12 F5	55 7N	3 35W
Lochboisdale, U.K.	12 D1	57 9N	7 20W
Loche, L. La, Canada	73 B7	56 30N	109 30W
Lochem, Neths.	15 B6	52 9N	6 26 E
Loches, France	18 C4	47 7N	1 0 E
Lochgilphead, U.K.	12 E3	56 2N	5 26W
Lochinver, U.K.	12 C3	58 9N	5 14W
Lochmaddy, U.K.	12 D1	57 36N	7 10W
Lochnagar, Australia	62 C4	23 33S	145 38 E
Lochnagar, U.K.	12 E5	56 57N	3 15W
Lochy, L., U.K.	12 E4	57 0N	4 53W
Lock, Australia	63 E2	33 34S	135 46 E
Lock Haven, U.S.A.	78 E7	41 8N	77 28W
Lockeford, U.S.A.	84 G5	38 10N	121 9W
Lockeport, Canada	71 D6	43 47N	65 4W
Lockhart, U.S.A.	81 L6	29 53N	97 40W
Lockhart, Australia	63 F4	35 14S	146 40 E
Lockhart, L., Australia	61 F2	33 15S	119 3 E
Lockhart River, Australia	62 A3	12 58S	143 30 E
Lockney, U.S.A.	81 H4	34 7N	101 27W
Lockport, U.S.A.	78 C6	43 10N	78 42W
Lod, Israel	47 D3	31 57N	34 54 E
Lodeinoye Pole, Russia	24 B5	60 44N	33 33 E
Lodge Bay, Canada	71 B8	52 14N	55 51W
Lodge Grass, U.S.A.	82 D10	45 19N	107 22W
Lodgepole Cr. →, U.S.A.	80 E2	41 20N	104 30W
Lodhran, Pakistan	42 E4	29 32N	71 30 E
Lodi, Italy	18 D8	45 19N	9 30 E
Lodi, Calif., U.S.A.	84 G5	38 8N	121 16W
Lodi, Ohio, U.S.A.	78 E3	41 2N	82 0W
Lodja, Dem. Rep. of the Congo	54 C1	3 30S	23 23 E
Lodwar, Kenya	54 B4	3 10N	35 40 E
Łódź, Poland	17 C10	51 45N	19 27 E
Loei, Thailand	38 D3	17 29N	101 35 E
Loengo, Dem. Rep. of the Congo	54 C2	4 48S	26 30 E
Loeriesfontein, S. Africa	56 E2	31 0S	19 26 E
Lofoten, Norway	8 B15	68 30N	14 0 E
Logan, Iowa, U.S.A.	80 E7	41 39N	95 47W
Logan, Ohio, U.S.A.	76 F4	39 32N	82 25W
Logan, Utah, U.S.A.	82 F8	41 44N	111 50W
Logan, W. Va., U.S.A.	76 G5	37 51N	81 59W
Logan, Mt., Canada	68 B5	60 34N	140 23W
Logandale, U.S.A.	85 J12	36 36N	114 29W
Logansport, Ind., U.S.A.	76 E2	40 45N	86 22W
Logansport, La., U.S.A.	81 K8	31 58N	94 0W
Logone →, Chad	51 F9	12 6N	15 2 E
Logroño, Spain	19 A4	42 28N	2 27W
Lohardaga, India	43 H11	23 27N	84 45 E
Loharia, India	42 H6	23 45N	74 14 E
Loharu, India	42 E6	28 27N	75 49 E
Lohja, Finland	9 F21	60 12N	24 5 E
Lohri Wah →, Pakistan	42 F2	27 27N	67 37 E
Loi-kaw, Burma	41 K20	19 40N	97 17 E
Loimaa, Finland	9 F20	60 50N	23 5 E
Loir →, France	18 C3	47 33N	0 32W
Loire →, France	18 C2	47 16N	2 10W
Loja, Ecuador	92 D3	3 59S	79 16W
Loja, Spain	19 D3	37 10N	4 10W
Loji = Kawasi, Indonesia	37 E7	1 38S	127 28 E
Lokandu, Dem. Rep. of the Congo	54 C2	2 30S	25 45 E
Lokeren, Belgium	15 C3	51 6N	3 59 E
Lokichokio, Kenya	54 B3	4 19N	34 13 E
Lokitaung, Kenya	54 B4	4 12N	35 48 E
Lokkan tekojärvi, Finland	8 C22	67 55N	27 35 E
Lokoja, Nigeria	50 G7	7 47N	6 45 E
Lola, Mt., U.S.A.	84 F6	39 26N	120 22W
Loliondo, Tanzania	54 C4	2 2S	35 39 E
Lolland, Denmark	9 J14	54 45N	11 30 E
Lolo, U.S.A.	82 C6	46 45N	114 5W
Lom, Bulgaria	21 C10	43 48N	23 12 E
Lom Kao, Thailand	38 D3	16 53N	101 14 E
Lom Sak, Thailand	38 D3	16 47N	101 15 E
Loma, U.S.A.	82 C8	47 56N	110 30W
Loma Linda, U.S.A.	85 L9	34 3N	117 16W
Lomami →, Dem. Rep. of the Congo	54 B1	0 46N	24 16 E
Lomas de Zamóra, Argentina	94 C4	34 45S	58 25W
Lombadina, Australia	60 C3	16 31S	122 54 E
Lombárdia □, Italy	18 D8	45 40N	9 30 E
Lombardy = Lombárdia □, Italy	18 D8	45 40N	9 30 E
Lomblen, Indonesia	37 F6	8 30S	123 32 E
Lombok, Indonesia	36 F5	8 45S	116 30 E
Lomé, Togo	50 G6	6 9N	1 20 E
Lomela, Dem. Rep. of the Congo	52 E4	2 19S	23 15 E
Lomela →, Dem. Rep. of the Congo	52 E4	0 15S	20 40 E
Lommel, Belgium	15 C5	51 14N	5 19 E
Lomond, Canada	72 C6	50 24N	112 36W
Lomond, L., U.K.	12 E4	56 8N	4 38W
Lomphat, Cambodia	38 F6	13 30N	106 59 E
Lompobatang, Indonesia	37 F5	5 24S	119 56 E
Lompoc, U.S.A.	85 L6	34 38N	120 28W
Łomza, Poland	17 B12	53 10N	22 2 E
Loncoche, Chile	96 D2	39 20S	72 50W
Londa, India	40 M9	15 30N	74 30 E
Londiani, Kenya	54 C4	0 10S	35 33 E
London, Canada	78 D3	42 59N	81 15W
London, U.K.	11 F7	51 30N	0 3W
London, Ky., U.S.A.	76 G3	37 8N	84 5W
London, Ohio, U.S.A.	76 F4	39 53N	83 27W
London, Greater □, U.K.	11 F7	51 36N	0 5W
Londonderry, U.K.	13 B4	55 0N	7 20W
Londonderry □, U.K.	13 B4	55 0N	7 20W
Londonderry, C., Australia	60 B4	13 45S	126 55 E
Londonderry, I., Chile	96 H2	55 0S	71 0W
Londres, Argentina	96 B3	27 43S	67 7W
Londrina, Brazil	95 A5	23 18S	51 10W
Lone Pine, U.S.A.	84 J8	36 36N	118 4W
Long B., U.S.A.	77 J6	33 35N	78 45W
Long Beach, Calif., U.S.A.	85 M8	33 47N	118 11W
Long Beach, N.Y., U.S.A.	79 F11	40 35N	73 39W
Long Beach, Wash., U.S.A.	84 D2	46 21N	124 3W
Long Branch, U.S.A.	79 F11	40 18N	74 0W
Long Creek, U.S.A.	82 D4	44 43N	119 6W
Long Eaton, U.K.	10 E6	52 53N	1 15W
Long I., Australia	62 C4	22 8S	149 53 E
Long I., Bahamas	89 B4	23 20N	75 10W
Long I., Canada	70 B4	54 50N	79 20W
Long I., Ireland	13 E2	51 30N	9 34W
Long I., U.S.A.	79 F11	40 45N	73 30W
Long Island Sd., U.S.A.	79 E12	41 10N	73 0W
Long L., Canada	70 C2	49 30N	86 50W
Long Lake, U.S.A.	79 C10	43 58N	74 25W
Long Point B., Canada	78 D4	42 40N	80 10W
Long Prairie →, U.S.A.	80 C7	46 20N	94 36W
Long Pt., Canada	78 D4	42 35N	80 2W
Long Range Mts., Canada	71 C8	49 30N	57 30W
Long Reef, Australia	60 B4	14 1S	125 48 E
Long Spruce, Canada	73 B10	56 24N	94 21W
Long Str. = Longa, Proliv, Russia	4 C16	70 0N	175 0 E
Long Thanh, Vietnam	39 G6	10 47N	106 57 E
Long Xian, China	34 G4	34 55N	106 55 E
Long Xuyen, Vietnam	39 G5	10 19N	105 28 E
Longa, Proliv, Russia	4 C16	70 0N	175 0 E
Longbenton, U.K.	10 B6	55 1N	1 31W
Longboat Key, U.S.A.	77 M4	27 23N	82 39W
Longde, China	34 G4	35 30N	106 20 E
Longford, Australia	62 G4	41 32S	147 3 E
Longford, Ireland	13 C4	53 43N	7 49W
Longford □, Ireland	13 C4	53 42N	7 45W
Longguan, China	34 D8	40 45N	115 30 E
Longhua, China	35 D9	41 18N	117 45 E
Longido, Tanzania	54 C4	2 43S	36 42 E
Longiram, Indonesia	36 E5	0 5S	115 45 E
Longkou, China	35 F11	37 40N	120 18 E
Longlac, Canada	70 C2	49 45N	86 25W
Longmeadow, U.S.A.	79 D12	42 3N	72 34W
Longmont, U.S.A.	80 E2	40 10N	105 6W
Longnawan, Indonesia	36 D4	1 51N	114 55 E
Longreach, Australia	62 C3	23 28S	144 14 E
Longueuil, Canada	79 A11	45 32N	73 28W
Longview, Tex., U.S.A.	81 J7	32 30N	94 44W

M

Mallawan

Marmara, Sea of =
Marmara Denizi, Turkey . **21 D13** 40 45N 28 15 E
Marmara Denizi, Turkey . **21 D13** 40 45N 28 15 E
Marmaris, Turkey **21 F13** 36 50N 28 14 E
Marmion, Mt., Australia . . **61 E2** 29 16S 119 50 E
Marmion L., Canada **70 C1** 48 55N 91 20W
Marmolada, Mte., Italy . . . **20 A4** 46 26N 11 51 E
Marmora, Canada **78 B7** 44 28N 77 41W
Marne →, France **18 B5** 48 48N 2 24 E
Maroala, Madag. **57 B8** 15 23S 47 59 E
Maroantsetra, Madag. . . . **57 B8** 15 26S 49 44 E
Maromandia, Madag. **57 A8** 14 13S 48 5 E
Marondera, Zimbabwe . . . **55 F3** 18 5S 31 42 E
Maroni →, Fr. Guiana . . . **93 B8** 5 30N 54 0W
Maroochydore, Australia . . **63 D5** 26 29S 153 5 E
Maroona, Australia **63 F3** 37 27S 142 54 E
Marosakoa, Madag. **57 B8** 15 26S 46 38 E
Maroua, Cameroon **51 F8** 10 40N 14 20 E
Marovoay, Madag. **57 B8** 16 6S 46 39 E
Marquard, S. Africa **56 D4** 28 40S 27 28 E
Marquesas Is. = Marquises,
Is., Pac. Oc. **65 H14** 9 30S 140 0W
Marquette, U.S.A. **76 B2** 46 33N 87 24W
Marquises, Is., Pac. Oc. . . **65 H14** 9 30S 140 0W
Marra, Djebel, Sudan **51 F10** 13 10N 24 22 E
Marracuene, Mozam. **57 D5** 25 45S 32 35 E
Marrakech, Morocco **50 B4** 31 9N 8 0W
Marrawah, Australia **62 G3** 40 55S 144 42 E
Marree, Australia **63 D2** 29 39S 138 1 E
Marrero, U.S.A. **81 L9** 29 54N 90 6W
Marrimane, Mozam. **57 C5** 22 58S 33 34 E
Marromeu, Mozam. **57 B6** 18 15S 36 25 E
Marrowie Cr. →, Australia **63 E4** 33 23S 145 40 E
Marrubane, Mozam. **57 F4** 18 0S 37 0 E
Marrupa, Mozam. **55 E4** 13 8S 37 30 E
Mars Hill, U.S.A. **77 B12** 46 31N 67 52W
Marsá Matrûh, Egypt **51 B11** 31 19N 27 9 E
Marsabit, Kenya **54 B4** 2 18N 38 0 E
Marsala, Italy **20 F5** 37 48N 12 26 E
Marsalforn, Malta **23 C1** 36 4N 14 15 E
Marsden, Australia **63 E4** 33 47S 147 32 E
Marseille, France **18 E6** 43 18N 5 23 E
Marseilles = Marseille,
France **18 E6** 43 18N 5 23 E
Marsh I., U.S.A. **81 L9** 29 34N 91 53W
Marshall, Ark., U.S.A. . . . **81 H8** 35 55N 92 38W
Marshall, Mich., U.S.A. . . **76 D3** 42 16N 84 58W
Marshall, Minn., U.S.A. . . **80 C7** 44 25N 95 45W
Marshall, Mo., U.S.A. . . . **80 F8** 39 7N 93 12W
Marshall, Tex., U.S.A. . . . **81 J7** 32 33N 94 23W
Marshall, →, Australia . . . **62 C2** 22 59S 136 59 E
Marshall Is. ■, Pac. Oc. . . **64 G9** 9 0N 171 0 E
Marshalltown, U.S.A. **80 D8** 42 3N 92 55W
Marshfield, Mo., U.S.A. . . **81 G8** 37 15N 92 54W
Marshfield, Vt., U.S.A. . . . **79 B12** 44 20N 72 20W
Marshfield, Wis., U.S.A. . . **80 C9** 44 40N 90 10W
Marshûn, Iran **45 B6** 36 19N 49 23 E
Märsta, Sweden **9 G17** 59 37N 17 52 E
Mart, U.S.A. **81 K6** 31 33N 96 50W
Martaban, Burma **41 L20** 16 30N 97 35 E
Martaban, G. of, Burma . . **41 L20** 16 5N 96 30 E
Martapura, Kalimantan,
Indonesia **36 E4** 3 22S 114 47 E
Martapura, Sumatera,
Indonesia **36 E2** 4 19S 104 22 E
Martelange, Belgium **15 E5** 49 49N 5 43 E
Martha's Vineyard, U.S.A. **79 E14** 41 25N 70 38W
Martigny, Switz. **18 C7** 46 6N 7 3 E
Martigues, France **18 E6** 43 24N 5 4 E
Martin, Slovak Rep. **17 D10** 49 6N 18 58 E
Martin, S. Dak., U.S.A. . . . **80 D4** 43 11N 101 44W
Martin, Tenn., U.S.A. **81 G10** 36 21N 88 51W
Martin L., U.S.A. **77 J3** 32 41N 85 55W
Martina Franca, Italy **20 D7** 40 42N 17 20 E
Martinborough, N.Z. **59 J5** 41 14S 175 29 E
Martinez, Calif., U.S.A. . . . **84 G4** 38 1N 122 8W
Martinez, Ga., U.S.A. **77 J4** 33 31N 82 4W
Martinique ■, W. Indies . . **89 D7** 14 40N 61 0W
Martinique Passage,
W. Indies **89 C7** 15 15N 61 0W
Martinópolis, Brazil **95 A5** 22 11S 51 12W
Martins Ferry, U.S.A. **78 F4** 40 6N 80 44W
Martinsburg, Pa., U.S.A. . **78 F6** 40 19N 78 20W
Martinsburg, W. Va., U.S.A. **76 F7** 39 27N 77 58W
Martinsville, Ind., U.S.A. . **76 F2** 39 26N 86 25W
Martinsville, Va., U.S.A. . . **77 G6** 36 41N 79 52W
Marton, N.Z. **59 J5** 40 4S 175 23 E
Martos, Spain **19 D4** 37 44N 3 58W
Marudi, Malaysia **36 D4** 4 11N 114 19 E
Ma'ruf, Afghan. **40 D5** 31 30N 67 6 E
Marugame, Japan **31 G6** 34 15N 133 40 E
Marunga, Angola **56 B3** 17 28S 20 2 E
Marungu, Mts.,
Dem. Rep. of the Congo **54 D3** 7 30S 30 0 E
Marv Dasht, Iran **45 D7** 29 50N 52 40 E
Marvast, Iran **45 D7** 30 30N 54 15 E
Marvel Loch, Australia . . . **61 F2** 31 28S 119 29 E
Marwar, India **42 G5** 25 43N 73 45 E
Mary, Turkmenistan **26 F7** 37 40N 61 50 E
Maryborough = Port Laoise,
Ireland **13 C4** 53 2N 7 18W
Maryborough, Queens.,
Australia **63 D5** 25 31S 152 37 E
Maryborough, Vic., Australia **63 F3** 37 0S 143 44 E
Maryfield, Canada **73 D8** 49 50N 101 35W
Maryland □, U.S.A. **76 F7** 39 0N 76 30W
Maryland Junction,
Zimbabwe **55 F3** 17 45S 30 31 E
Maryport, U.K. **10 C4** 54 44N 3 28W
Mary's Harbour, Canada . **71 B8** 52 18N 55 51W
Marystown, Canada **71 C8** 47 10N 55 10W
Marysvale, U.S.A. **72 G8** 38 27N 112 14W
Marysville, Calif., U.S.A. . **84 F5** 39 9N 121 35W
Marysville, Kans., U.S.A. . **80 F6** 39 51N 96 39W
Marysville, Mich., U.S.A. . **78 D2** 42 54N 82 29W
Marysville, Ohio, U.S.A. . . **76 E4** 40 14N 83 22W
Marysville, Wash., U.S.A. . **84 B4** 48 3N 122 11W
Maryville, Mo., U.S.A. . . . **80 E7** 40 21N 94 52W
Maryville, Tenn., U.S.A. . . **77 H4** 35 46N 83 58W
Marzûq, Libya **51 C8** 25 53N 13 57 E
Masahunga, Tanzania . . . **54 C3** 2 6S 33 18 E
Masai Steppe, Tanzania . . **54 C4** 4 30S 36 30 E
Masaka, Uganda **54 C3** 0 21S 31 45 E
Masalembo, Kepulauan,
Indonesia **36 F4** 5 35S 114 30 E
Masalima, Kepulauan,
Indonesia **36 F5** 5 4S 117 5 E

Masamba, Indonesia **37 E6** 2 30S 120 15 E
Masan, S. Korea **35 G15** 35 11N 128 32 E
Masandam, Ra's, Oman . . **45 E8** 26 30N 56 30 E
Masasi, Tanzania **55 E4** 10 45S 38 52 E
Masaya, Nic. **88 D2** 12 0N 86 7W
Masbate, Phil. **37 B6** 12 21N 123 36 E
Mascara, Algeria **50 A6** 35 26N 0 6 E
Mascota, Mexico **86 C4** 20 30N 104 50W
Masela, Indonesia **37 F7** 8 9S 129 51 E
Maseru, Lesotho **56 D4** 29 18S 27 30 E
Mashaba, Zimbabwe **55 G3** 20 2S 30 29 E
Mashābih, Si. Arabia **44 E3** 25 35N 36 30 E
Masherbrum, Pakistan . . . **43 B7** 35 38N 76 18 E
Mashhad, Iran **45 B8** 36 20N 59 35 E
Mashīz, Iran **45 D8** 29 56N 56 37 E
Mashkel, Hamun-i, Pakistan **40 E3** 28 20N 62 56 E
Mashki Chāh, Pakistan . . **40 E3** 29 5N 62 30 E
Mashonaland, Zimbabwe . **53 H6** 16 30S 31 0 E
Mashonaland Central □,
Zimbabwe **57 B5** 17 30S 31 0 E
Mashonaland East □,
Zimbabwe **57 B5** 18 0S 32 0 E
Mashonaland West □,
Zimbabwe **57 B4** 17 30S 29 30 E
Mashrakh, India **43 F11** 26 7N 84 48 E
Masindi, Uganda **54 B3** 1 40N 31 43 E
Masindi Port, Uganda . . . **54 B3** 1 43N 32 2 E
Maşīrah, Oman **46 C6** 21 0N 58 50 E
Maşīrah, Khalīj, Oman . . . **46 C6** 20 10N 58 10 E
Masisi,
Dem. Rep. of the Congo **54 C2** 1 23S 28 49 E
Masjed Soleymān, Iran . . **45 D6** 31 55N 49 18 E
Mask, L., Ireland **13 C2** 53 36N 9 22W
Maskin, Oman **45 F8** 23 30N 56 50 E
Masoala, Tanjon' i, Madag. **57 B9** 15 59S 50 13 E
Masoarivo, Madag. **57 B7** 19 3S 44 19 E
Masohi = Amahai,
Indonesia **37 E7** 3 20S 128 55 E
Masomeloka, Madag. **57 C8** 20 17S 48 37 E
Mason, Nev., U.S.A. **84 G7** 38 56N 119 8W
Mason, Tex., U.S.A. **81 K5** 30 45N 99 14W
Mason City, U.S.A. **80 D8** 43 9N 93 12W
Maspalomas, Canary Is. . . **22 G4** 27 46N 15 35W
Maspalomas, Pta.,
Canary Is. **22 G4** 27 43N 15 36W
Masqat, Oman **46 C6** 23 37N 58 36 E
Massa, Italy **18 D9** 44 1N 10 9 E
Massachusetts □, U.S.A. . **79 D13** 42 30N 72 0W
Massachusetts B., U.S.A. . **79 D14** 42 20N 70 50W
Massakory, Chad **51 F9** 13 0N 15 49 E
Massanella, Spain **22 B9** 39 48N 2 51 E
Massangena, Mozam. . . . **57 C5** 21 34S 33 0 E
Massango, Angola **52 F3** 8 2S 16 21 E
Massawa = Mitsiwa, Eritrea **46 D2** 15 35N 39 25 E
Massena, U.S.A. **79 B10** 44 56N 74 54W
Massénya, Chad **51 F9** 11 21N 16 9 E
Masset, Canada **72 C2** 54 2N 132 10W
Massif Central, France . . . **18 D5** 44 55N 3 0 E
Massillon, U.S.A. **78 F3** 40 48N 81 32W
Massinga, Mozam. **57 C6** 23 15S 35 22 E
Masson, Canada **79 A9** 45 32N 75 25W
Masson I., Antarctica **5 C7** 66 10S 93 20 E
Mastanli = Momchilgrad,
Bulgaria **21 D11** 41 33N 25 23 E
Masterton, N.Z. **59 J5** 40 56S 175 39 E
Mastic, U.S.A. **79 F12** 40 47N 72 54W
Mastuj, Pakistan **43 A5** 36 20N 72 36 E
Mastung, Pakistan **40 E5** 29 50N 66 56 E
Masty, Belarus **17 B13** 53 27N 24 38 E
Masuda, Japan **31 G5** 34 40N 131 51 E
Masvingo, Zimbabwe **55 G3** 20 8S 30 49 E
Masvingo □, Zimbabwe . . **55 G3** 21 0S 31 30 E
Maşyāf, Syria **44 C3** 35 4N 36 20 E
Matabeleland North □,
Zimbabwe **55 F2** 19 0S 28 0 E
Matabeleland South □,
Zimbabwe **55 G2** 21 0S 29 0 E
Matachewan, Canada **70 C3** 47 56N 80 39W
Matadi,
Dem. Rep. of the Congo **52 F2** 5 52S 13 31 E
Matagalpa, Nic. **88 D2** 13 0N 85 58W
Matagami, Canada **70 C4** 49 45N 77 34W
Matagami, L., Canada . . . **70 C4** 49 50N 77 40W
Matagorda B., U.S.A. **81 L6** 28 40N 96 0W
Matagorda I., U.S.A. **81 L6** 28 15N 96 30W
Matak, Indonesia **39 L6** 3 18N 106 16 E
Mátala, Greece **23 E6** 34 59N 24 45 E
Matam, Senegal **50 E3** 15 34N 13 17W
Matamoros, Campeche,
Mexico **87 D6** 18 50N 90 50W
Matamoros, Coahuila,
Mexico **86 B4** 25 33N 103 15W
Matamoros, Tamaulipas,
Mexico **87 B5** 25 50N 97 30W
Ma'tan as Sarra, Libya . . . **51 D10** 21 45N 22 0 E
Matandu →, Tanzania . . . **55 D3** 8 45S 34 19 E
Matane, Canada **71 C6** 48 50N 67 33W
Matanomadh, India **42 H3** 23 33N 68 57 E
Matanzas, Cuba **88 B3** 23 0N 81 40W
Matapan, C. = Taínaron,
Ákra, Greece **21 F10** 36 22N 22 27 E
Matapédia, Canada **71 C6** 48 0N 66 59W
Matara, Sri Lanka **40 S12** 5 58N 80 30 E
Mataram, Indonesia **36 F5** 8 41S 116 10 E
Matarani, Peru **92 G4** 17 0S 72 10W
Mataranka, Australia **60 B5** 14 55S 133 4 E
Matarma, Râs, Egypt **47 E1** 30 27N 32 44 E
Mataró, Spain **19 B7** 41 32N 2 29 E
Matatiele, S. Africa **57 E4** 30 20S 28 49 E
Mataura, N.Z. **59 M2** 46 11S 168 51 E
Matehuala, Mexico **86 C4** 23 40N 100 40W
Mateke Hills, Zimbabwe . . **55 G3** 21 48S 31 0 E
Matera, Italy **20 D7** 40 40N 16 36 E
Matetsi, Zimbabwe **55 F2** 18 12S 26 0 E
Mathis, U.S.A. **81 L6** 28 6N 97 50W
Mathráki, Greece **23 A3** 39 48N 19 31 E
Mathura, India **42 F7** 27 30N 77 40 E
Mati, Phil. **37 C7** 6 55N 126 15 E
Matiali, India **43 F13** 26 56N 88 49 E
Matías Romero, Mexico . . **87 D5** 16 53N 95 2W
Matibane, Mozam. **55 E5** 14 49S 40 45 E
Matima, Botswana **56 C3** 20 15S 24 26 E
Matiri Ra., N.Z. **59 J4** 41 38S 172 20 E
Matla →, India **43 J13** 21 40N 88 40 E
Matli, Pakistan **42 G3** 25 2N 68 39 E

Matlock, U.K. **10 D6** 53 9N 1 33W
Mato Grosso □, Brazil . . . **93 F8** 14 0S 55 0W
Mato Grosso, Planalto do,
Brazil **93 G8** 15 0S 55 0W
Mato Grosso do Sul □,
Brazil **93 G8** 18 0S 55 0W
Matochkin Shar, Russia . . **26 B6** 73 10N 56 40 E
Matopo Hills, Zimbabwe . . **55 G2** 20 36S 28 20 E
Matopos, Zimbabwe **55 G2** 20 20S 28 29 E
Matosinhos, Portugal **19 B1** 41 11N 8 42W
Maţruḥ, Oman **46 C6** 23 37N 58 30 E
Matsue, Japan **31 G6** 35 25N 133 10 E
Matsumae, Japan **30 D10** 41 26N 140 7 E
Matsumoto, Japan **31 F9** 36 15N 138 0 E
Matsusaka, Japan **31 G8** 34 34N 136 32 E
Matsutō, Japan **31 F8** 36 31N 136 34 E
Matsuura, Japan **31 H4** 33 20N 129 49 E
Matsuyama, Japan **31 H6** 33 45N 132 45 E
Mattagami →, Canada . . . **70 B3** 50 43N 81 29W
Mattancheri, India **40 Q10** 9 50N 76 15 E
Mattawa, Canada **70 C4** 46 20N 78 45W
Matterhorn, Switz. **18 D7** 45 58N 7 39 E
Matthew Town, Bahamas . **89 B5** 20 57N 73 40W
Matthew's Ridge, Guyana . **92 B6** 7 37N 60 10W
Mattice, Canada **70 C3** 49 40N 83 20W
Mattituck, U.S.A. **79 F12** 40 59N 72 32W
Mattoon, U.S.A. **76 F1** 39 29N 88 23W
Matuba, Mozam. **57 C5** 24 28S 32 49 E
Matucana, Peru **92 F3** 11 55S 76 25W
Matūn = Khowst, Afghan. . **42 C3** 33 22N 69 58 E
Maturín, Venezuela **92 B6** 9 45N 63 11W
Mau, India **43 G10** 25 56N 83 33 E
Mau, Mad. P., India **43 F8** 26 17N 78 41 E
Mau, Ut. P., India **43 G9** 25 17N 81 23 E
Mau Escarpment, Kenya . . **54 C4** 0 40S 36 0 E
Mau Ranipur, India **43 G8** 25 16N 79 8 E
Maubeuge, France **18 A6** 50 17N 3 57 E
Maud, Pt., Australia **60 D1** 23 6S 113 45 E
Maude, Australia **63 E3** 34 29S 144 18 E
Maudin Sun, Burma **41 M19** 16 0N 94 30 E
Maués, Brazil **92 D7** 3 20S 57 45W
Maughanj, India **43 G12** 24 50N 81 55 E
Maughold Hd., U.K. **10 C3** 54 18N 4 18W
Maui, U.S.A. **74 H16** 20 48N 156 20W
Maulamyaing = Moulmein,
Burma **41 L20** 16 30N 97 40 E
Maule □, Chile **94 D1** 36 5S 72 30W
Maumee, U.S.A. **76 E4** 41 34N 83 39W
Maumee →, U.S.A. **76 E4** 41 42N 83 28W
Maumere, Indonesia **37 F6** 8 38S 122 13 E
Maun, Botswana **56 C3** 20 0S 23 26 E
Mauna Kea, U.S.A. **74 J17** 19 50N 155 28W
Mauna Loa, U.S.A. **74 J17** 19 30N 155 35W
Maungmagan Is., Burma . **38 F1** 14 0N 97 30 E
Maungmagan Kyunzu,
Burma **41 N20** 14 0N 97 48 E
Maupin, U.S.A. **82 D3** 45 11N 121 5W
Maurepas, L., U.S.A. **81 K9** 30 15N 90 30W
Maurice, L., Australia **61 E5** 29 30S 131 0 E
Mauricie, Parc Nat. de la,
Canada **70 C5** 46 45N 73 0W
Mauritania ■, Africa **50 E3** 20 50N 10 0W
Mauritius ■, Ind. Oc. **49 J9** 20 0S 57 0 E
Mauston, U.S.A. **80 D9** 43 48N 90 5W
Mavli, India **42 G5** 24 45N 73 55 E
Mavuradonha Mts.,
Zimbabwe **55 F3** 16 30S 31 30 E
Mawa,
Dem. Rep. of the Congo **54 B2** 2 45N 26 40 E
Mawai, India **43 H9** 22 30N 81 4 E
Mawana, India **42 E7** 29 6N 77 58 E
Mawand, Pakistan **42 E3** 29 33N 68 38 E
Mawk Mai, Burma **41 J20** 20 14N 97 37 E
Mawlaik, Burma **41 H19** 23 40N 94 26 E
Mawqaq, Si. Arabia **44 E4** 27 25N 41 8 E
Mawson Coast, Antarctica **5 C6** 68 30S 63 0 E
Max, U.S.A. **80 B4** 47 49N 101 18W
Maxcanú, Mexico **87 C6** 20 40N 90 10W
Maxesibeni, S. Africa **57 E4** 30 49S 29 23 E
Maxhamish L., Canada . . . **72 B4** 59 50N 123 17W
Maxixe, Mozam. **57 C6** 23 54S 35 17 E
Maxville, Canada **79 A10** 45 17N 74 51W
Maxwell, U.S.A. **84 F4** 39 17N 122 11W
Maxwelton, Australia **62 C3** 20 43S 142 41 E
May, C., U.S.A. **76 F8** 38 56N 74 58W
May Pen, Jamaica **88 C4** 17 58N 77 15W
Maya →, Russia **27 D14** 60 28N 134 28 E
Maya Mts., Belize **87 D7** 16 30N 89 0W
Mayaguana, Bahamas . . . **89 B5** 22 30N 72 44W
Mayagüez, Puerto Rico . . **89 C6** 18 12N 67 9W
Mayāmey, Iran **45 B7** 36 24N 55 42 E
Mayanup, Australia **61 F2** 33 57S 116 27 E
Mayapan, Mexico **87 C7** 20 30N 89 25W
Mayari, Cuba **89 B4** 20 40N 75 41W
Maybell, U.S.A. **82 F9** 40 31N 108 5W
Maybole, U.K. **12 F4** 55 21N 4 42W
Maydān, Iraq **44 C5** 34 55N 45 37 E
Maydena, Australia **62 G4** 42 45S 146 30 E
Mayenne →, France **18 C3** 47 30N 0 32W
Mayer, U.S.A. **83 J7** 34 24N 112 14W
Mayerthorpe, Canada . . . **72 C5** 53 57N 115 8W
Mayfield, Ky., U.S.A. **77 G1** 36 44N 88 38W
Mayfield, N.Y., U.S.A. **79 C10** 43 6N 74 16W
Mayhill, U.S.A. **83 K11** 32 53N 105 29W
Maykop, Russia **25 F7** 44 35N 40 10 E
Maymyo, Burma **38 A1** 22 2N 96 28 E
Maynard, Mass., U.S.A. . . **79 D13** 42 26N 71 27W
Maynard, Wash., U.S.A. . . **84 C4** 47 59N 122 55W
Maynard Hills, Australia . . **61 E2** 28 28S 119 49 E
Mayne →, Australia **62 C3** 23 40S 141 55 E
Maynooth, Ireland **13 C5** 53 23N 6 34W
Mayo, Canada **68 B6** 63 38N 135 57W
Mayo □, Ireland **13 C2** 53 53N 9 3W
Mayon Volcano, Phil. **37 B6** 13 15N 123 41 E
Mayor I., N.Z. **59 G6** 37 16S 176 17 E
Mayotte, I., Mayotte **53 G9** 12 50S 45 10 E
Mayu, Indonesia **37 D7** 1 30N 126 30 E
Mayumba, Gabon **52 E2** 3 25S 10 39 E
Mayville, N. Dak., U.S.A. . **80 B6** 47 30N 97 20W
Mayville, N.Y., U.S.A. **78 D5** 42 15N 79 30W
Mayya, Russia **27 C14** 61 44N 130 18 E
Mazabuka, Zambia **55 F2** 15 52S 27 44 E
Mazagán = El Jadida,
Morocco **50 B4** 33 11N 8 17W
Mazagão, Brazil **93 D8** 0 7S 51 16W

Mazán, Peru **92 D4** 3 30S 73 0W
Māzandarān □, Iran **45 B7** 36 30N 52 0 E
Mazapil, Mexico **86 C4** 24 38N 101 34W
Mazara del Vallo, Italy . . . **20 F5** 37 39N 12 35 E
Mazarrón, Spain **19 D5** 37 38N 1 19W
Mazaruni →, Guyana **92 B7** 6 25N 58 35W
Mazatán, Mexico **86 B2** 29 0N 110 8W
Mazatenango, Guatemala . **88 D1** 14 35N 91 30W
Mazatlán, Mexico **86 C3** 23 13N 106 25W
Mažeikiai, Lithuania **9 H20** 56 20N 22 20 E
Māzhān, Iran **45 C8** 32 30N 59 0 E
Mazīnān, Iran **45 B8** 36 19N 56 56 E
Mazoe, Mozam. **55 F3** 16 42S 33 7 E
Mazoe →, Mozam. **55 F3** 16 20S 33 30 E
Mazowe, Zimbabwe **55 F3** 17 28S 30 58 E
Mazurian Lakes = Mazurski,
Pojezierze, Poland **17 B11** 53 50N 21 0 E
Mazurski, Pojezierze, Poland **17 B11** 53 50N 21 0 E
Mazyr, Belarus **17 B15** 51 59N 29 15 E
Mbabane, Swaziland **57 D5** 26 18S 31 6 E
Mbaïki, C.A.R. **52 D3** 3 53N 18 1 E
Mbala, Zambia **55 D3** 8 46S 31 24 E
Mbale, Uganda **54 B3** 1 8N 34 12 E
Mbalmayo, Cameroon . . . **52 D2** 3 33N 11 33 E
Mbamba Bay, Tanzania . . **55 E3** 11 13S 34 49 E
Mbandaka,
Dem. Rep. of the Congo **52 D3** 0 1N 18 18 E
Mbanza Congo, Angola . . **52 F2** 6 18S 14 16 E
Mbanza Ngungu,
Dem. Rep. of the Congo **52 F2** 5 12S 14 53 E
Mbarara, Uganda **54 C3** 0 35S 30 40 E
Mbashe →, S. Africa **57 E4** 32 15S 28 54 E
Mbenkuru →, Tanzania . . **55 D4** 9 25S 39 50 E
Mberengwa, Zimbabwe . . **55 G2** 20 29S 29 57 E
Mberengwa, Mt., Zimbabwe **55 G2** 20 37S 29 55 E
Mbesuma, Zambia **55 E3** 10 0S 32 2 E
Mbeya, Tanzania **54 D3** 8 54S 33 29 E
Mbeya □, Tanzania **54 D3** 8 15S 33 30 E
Mbinga, Tanzania **55 E4** 10 50S 35 0 E
Mbini □, Eq. Guin. **52 D2** 1 30N 10 0 E
Mbour, Senegal **50 F2** 14 22N 16 54W
Mbuji-Mayi,
Dem. Rep. of the Congo **54 D1** 6 9S 23 40 E
Mbulu, Tanzania **54 C4** 3 45S 35 30 E
Mburucuyá, Argentina . . . **94 B4** 28 1S 58 14W
Mchinja, Tanzania **55 D4** 9 44S 39 45 E
Mchinji, Malawi **55 E3** 13 47S 32 58 E
Mdantsane, S. Africa **53 L5** 32 56S 27 46 E
Mead, L., U.S.A. **85 J12** 36 1N 114 44W
Meade, U.S.A. **81 G4** 37 17N 100 20W
Meadow Lake, Canada . . . **73 C7** 54 10N 108 26W
Meadow Lake Prov. Park,
Canada **73 C7** 54 27N 109 0W
Meadow Valley Wash →,
U.S.A. **85 J12** 36 40N 114 34W
Meadville, U.S.A. **78 E4** 41 39N 80 9W
Meaford, Canada **78 B4** 44 36N 80 35W
Mealy Mts., Canada **71 B8** 53 10N 58 0W
Meander River, Canada . . **72 B5** 59 2N 117 42W
Meares, C., U.S.A. **82 D2** 45 37N 124 0W
Mearim →, Brazil **93 D10** 3 4S 44 35W
Meath □, Ireland **13 C5** 53 40N 6 57W
Meath Park, Canada **73 C7** 53 27N 105 22W
Meaux, France **18 B5** 48 58N 2 50 E
Mebechi-Gawa →, Japan . **30 D10** 40 31N 141 31 E
Mecanhelas, Mozam. **55 F4** 15 12S 35 54 E
Mecca = Makkah, Si. Arabia **46 C2** 21 30N 39 54 E
Mecca, U.S.A. **85 M10** 33 34N 116 5W
Mechanicsburg, U.S.A. . . . **78 F8** 40 13N 77 1W
Mechanicville, U.S.A. **79 D11** 42 54N 73 41W
Mechelen, Belgium **15 C4** 51 2N 4 29 E
Mecheria, Algeria **50 B5** 33 35N 0 18W
Mecklenburg, Germany . . **16 B6** 53 33N 11 40 E
Mecklenburger Bucht,
Germany **16 A6** 54 20N 11 40 E
Meconta, Mozam. **55 E4** 14 59S 39 50 E
Medan, Indonesia **36 D1** 3 40N 98 38 E
Medanosa, Pta., Argentina **96 F3** 48 8S 66 0W
Médéa, Algeria **50 A6** 36 12N 2 50 E
Medellín, Colombia **92 B3** 6 15N 75 35W
Medelpad, Sweden **9 E17** 62 33N 16 30 E
Medemblik, Neths. **15 B5** 52 46N 5 8 E
Medford, Mass., U.S.A. . . **79 D13** 42 25N 71 7W
Medford, Oreg., U.S.A. . . **82 E2** 42 19N 122 52W
Medford, Wis., U.S.A. **80 C9** 45 9N 90 20W
Medgidia, Romania **17 F15** 44 15N 28 19 E
Media Agua, Argentina . . **94 C2** 31 58S 68 25W
Media Luna, Argentina . . . **94 C2** 34 45S 66 44W
Medianeira, Brazil **95 B5** 25 17S 54 5W
Mediaş, Romania **17 E13** 46 9N 24 22 E
Medicine Bow, U.S.A. **82 F10** 41 54N 106 12W
Medicine Bow Pk., U.S.A. . **82 F10** 41 21N 106 19W
Medicine Bow Ra., U.S.A. . **82 F10** 41 10N 106 25W
Medicine Hat, Canada . . . **73 D6** 50 0N 110 45W
Medicine Lake, U.S.A. . . . **80 A2** 48 30N 104 30W
Medicine Lodge, U.S.A. . . **81 G5** 37 17N 98 35W
Medina = Al Madīnah,
Si. Arabia **46 C2** 24 35N 39 52 E
Medina, N. Dak., U.S.A. . . **80 B5** 46 54N 99 18W
Medina, Ohio, U.S.A. **78 E3** 41 8N 81 52W
Medina, N.Y., U.S.A. **78 C6** 43 13N 78 23W
Medina →, U.S.A. **81 L5** 29 16N 98 29W
Medina del Campo, Spain **19 B3** 41 18N 4 55W
Medina L., U.S.A. **81 L5** 29 32N 98 56W
Medina Sidonia, Spain . . . **19 D3** 36 28N 5 57W
Medinipur, India **43 H12** 22 25N 87 21 E
Mediterranean Sea, Europe **6 H7** 35 0N 15 0 E
Médoc, France **18 D3** 45 10N 0 50W
Medveditsa →, Russia . . . **25 E7** 49 35N 42 41 E
Medvezhi, Ostrava, Russia **27 B17** 71 0N 161 0 E
Medvezhyegorsk, Russia . **24 B5** 63 0N 34 25 E
Medway →, U.K. **11 F8** 51 27N 0 46 E
Medway Towns □, U.K. . . . **11 F8** 51 25N 0 32 E
Meekatharra, Australia . . . **61 E2** 26 32S 118 29 E
Meeker, U.S.A. **82 F10** 40 2N 107 55W
Meelpaeg Res., Canada . . **71 C8** 48 15N 56 33W
Meerut, India **42 E7** 29 1N 77 42 E
Meeteetse, U.S.A. **82 D9** 44 9N 108 52W
Mega, Ethiopia **46 H7** 3 57N 38 19 E
Mégara, Greece **21 F10** 37 58N 23 22 E
Megasini, India **43 J12** 21 38N 86 21 E
Meghalaya □, India **41 G17** 25 50N 91 0 E
Mégiscane, L., Canada . . . **70 C4** 48 35N 75 55W
Meharry, Mt., Australia . . . **60 D2** 22 59S 118 35 E
Mehlville, U.S.A. **80 F9** 38 30N 90 19W
Mehndawal, India **43 F10** 26 58N 83 5 E

Mehr Jān, *Iran* 45 C7 33 50N 55 6 E
Mehrābād, *Iran* 44 B5 36 53N 47 55 E
Mehrān, *Iran* 44 C5 33 7N 46 10 E
Mehriz, *Iran* 45 D7 31 35N 54 28 E
Mei Xian, *China* 34 G4 34 18N 107 55 E
Meiktila, *Burma* 41 J19 20 53N 95 54 E
Meissen, *Germany* 16 C7 51 9N 13 29 E
Meizhou, *China* 33 D6 24 16N 116 6 E
Meja, *India* 43 G10 25 9N 82 7 E
Mejillones, *Chile* 94 A1 23 10S 70 30W
Mekele, *Ethiopia* 46 E2 13 33N 39 30 E
Mekhtar, *Pakistan* 40 D6 30 30N 69 15 E
Meknès, *Morocco* 50 B4 33 57N 5 33W
Mekong →, *Asia* 39 H6 9 30N 106 15 E
Mekongga, *Indonesia* 37 E6 3 39S 121 15 E
Mekvari = Kür →, *Azerbaijan* 25 G8 39 29N 49 15 E
Melagiri Hills, *India* 40 N10 12 20N 77 30 E
Melaka, *Malaysia* 39 L4 2 15N 102 15 E
Melalap, *Malaysia* 36 C5 5 10N 116 5 E
Mélambes, *Greece* 23 D6 35 8N 24 40 E
Melanesia, *Pac. Oc.* 64 H7 4 0S 155 0 E
Melbourne, *Australia* 63 F4 37 50S 145 0 E
Melbourne, *U.S.A.* 77 L5 28 5N 80 37W
Melchor Múzquiz, *Mexico* 86 B4 27 50N 101 30W
Melchor Ocampo, *Mexico* . 86 C4 24 52N 101 40W
Mélèzes →, *Canada* 69 C12 57 30N 71 0W
Mélèzes →, *Qué., Canada* 70 A5 57 40N 69 29W
Melfort, *Canada* 73 C8 52 50N 104 37W
Melfort, *Zimbabwe* 55 F3 18 0S 31 25 E
Melhus, *Norway* 8 E14 63 17N 10 18 E
Melilla, *N. Afr.* 19 E4 35 21N 2 57W
Melipilla, *Chile* 94 C1 33 42S 71 15W
Mélissa, Ákra, *Greece* 23 D6 35 6N 24 33 E
Melita, *Canada* 73 D8 49 15N 101 0W
Melitopol, *Ukraine* 25 E6 46 50N 35 22 E
Melk, *Austria* 16 D8 48 13N 15 20 E
Mellansel, *Sweden* 8 E18 63 25N 18 17 E
Mellen, *U.S.A.* 80 B9 46 20N 90 40W
Mellerud, *Sweden* 9 G15 58 41N 12 28 E
Mellette, *U.S.A.* 80 C5 45 9N 98 30W
Mellieha, *Malta* 23 D1 35 57N 14 21 E
Melo, *Uruguay* 95 C5 32 20S 54 10W
Melolo, *Indonesia* 37 F6 9 53S 120 40 E
Melouprey, *Cambodia* 38 F5 13 48N 105 16 E
Melrose, *Australia* 63 E4 32 42S 146 57 E
Melrose, *U.K.* 12 F6 55 36N 2 43W
Melrose, *Minn., U.S.A.* 80 C7 45 40N 94 49W
Melrose, *N. Mex., U.S.A.* 81 H3 34 26N 103 38W
Melstone, *U.S.A.* 82 C10 46 36N 107 52W
Melton Mowbray, *U.K.* 10 E7 52 47N 0 54W
Melun, *France* 18 B5 48 32N 2 39 E
Melville, *Canada* 73 C8 50 55N 102 50W
Melville, C., *Australia* 62 A3 14 11S 144 30 E
Melville, I., *Canada* 71 B8 53 30N 60 0W
Melville, B., *Australia* 62 A2 12 0S 136 45 E
Melville I., *Australia* 60 B5 11 30S 131 0 E
Melville I., *Canada* 4 B2 75 30N 112 0W
Melville Pen., *Canada* 69 B11 68 0N 84 0W
Memba, *Mozam.* 55 E5 14 11S 40 30 E
Memboro, *Indonesia* 37 F5 9 30S 119 30 E
Memel = Klaipėda, *Lithuania* 9 J19 55 43N 21 10 E
Memel, *S. Africa* 57 D4 27 38S 29 36 E
Memmingen, *Germany* 16 E6 47 58N 10 10 E
Mempawah, *Indonesia* 36 D3 0 30N 109 5 E
Memphis, *Mich., U.S.A.* 78 D2 42 54N 82 46W
Memphis, *Tenn., U.S.A.* 81 H10 35 8N 90 3W
Memphis, *Tex., U.S.A.* 81 H4 34 44N 100 33W
Memphrémagog, L., *U.S.A.* 79 B12 45 0N 72 12W
Mena, *U.S.A.* 81 H7 34 35N 94 15W
Menai Strait, *U.K.* 10 D3 53 11N 4 13W
Ménaka, *Mali* 50 E6 15 59N 2 18 E
Menan = Chao Phraya →, *Thailand* 38 F3 13 32N 100 36 E
Menarandra →, *Madag.* 57 D7 25 17S 44 30 E
Menard, *U.S.A.* 81 K5 30 55N 99 47W
Mendawai →, *Indonesia* 36 E4 3 30S 113 0 E
Mende, *France* 18 D5 44 31N 3 30 E
Mendez, *Mexico* 87 B5 25 7N 98 34W
Mendhar, *India* 43 C6 33 35N 74 10 E
Mendip Hills, *U.K.* 11 F5 51 17N 2 40W
Mendocino, *U.S.A.* 82 G2 39 19N 123 48W
Mendocino, C., *U.S.A.* 82 F1 40 26N 124 25W
Mendooran, *Australia* 63 E4 31 50S 149 6 E
Mendota, *Calif., U.S.A.* 84 J6 36 45N 120 23W
Mendota, *Ill., U.S.A.* 80 E10 41 33N 89 7W
Mendoza, *Argentina* 94 C2 32 50S 68 52W
Mendoza □, *Argentina* 94 C2 33 0S 69 0W
Mene Grande, *Venezuela* 92 B4 9 49N 70 56W
Menemen, *Turkey* 21 E12 38 34N 27 3 E
Menen, *Belgium* 15 D3 50 47N 3 7 E
Menggala, *Indonesia* 36 E3 4 30S 105 15 E
Mengjin, *China* 34 G7 34 55N 112 45 E
Mengyin, *China* 35 G9 35 40N 117 58 E
Mengzi, *China* 32 D5 23 20N 103 22 E
Menihek, *Canada* 71 B6 54 28N 56 36W
Menihek L., *Canada* 71 B6 54 0N 67 0W
Menin = Menen, *Belgium* 15 D3 50 47N 3 7 E
Menindee, *Australia* 63 E3 32 20S 142 25 E
Menindee L., *Australia* 63 E3 32 20S 142 25 E
Meningie, *Australia* 63 F2 35 50S 139 18 E
Menlo Park, *U.S.A.* 84 H4 37 27N 122 12W
Menominee, *U.S.A.* 76 C2 45 6N 87 37W
Menominee →, *U.S.A.* 76 C2 45 6N 87 36W
Menomonie, *U.S.A.* 80 C9 44 53N 91 55W
Menongue, *Angola* 53 G3 14 48S 17 52 E
Menorca, *Spain* 22 B11 40 0N 4 0 E
Mentakab, *Malaysia* 39 L4 3 29N 102 21 E
Mentawai, Kepulauan, *Indonesia* 36 E1 2 0S 99 0 E
Menton, *France* 18 E7 43 50N 7 29 E
Mentor, *U.S.A.* 78 E3 41 40N 81 21W
Menzelinsk, *Russia* 24 C9 55 47N 53 11 E
Menzies, *Australia* 61 E3 29 40S 121 2 E
Me'ona, *Israel* 47 B4 33 1N 35 15 E
Meoqui, *Mexico* 86 B3 28 17N 105 29W
Mepaco, *Mozam.* 55 F3 15 57S 30 48 E
Meppel, *Neths.* 15 B6 52 42N 6 12 E
Merabéllou, Kólpos, *Greece* 23 D7 35 10N 25 50 E
Merak, *Indonesia* 37 F12 6 10N 106 26 E
Meramangye, L., *Australia* 61 E5 28 25S 132 13 E
Meran = Merano, *Italy* 20 A4 46 40N 11 9 E
Merano, *Italy* 20 A4 46 40N 11 9 E
Merauke, *Indonesia* 37 F10 8 29S 140 24 E
Merbein, *Australia* 63 E3 34 10S 142 2 E
Merca, *Somali Rep.* 46 G3 1 48N 44 50 E
Merced, *U.S.A.* 84 H6 37 18N 120 29W

Merced →, *U.S.A.* 84 H6 37 21N 120 59W
Merced Pk., *U.S.A.* 84 H7 37 36N 119 24W
Mercedes, *Buenos Aires, Argentina* 94 C4 34 40S 59 30W
Mercedes, *Corrientes, Argentina* 94 B4 29 10S 58 5W
Mercedes, *San Luis, Argentina* 94 C2 33 40S 65 21W
Mercedes, *Uruguay* 94 C4 33 12S 58 0W
Mercedes, *U.S.A.* 81 M6 26 9N 97 55W
Merceditas, *Chile* 94 B1 28 20S 70 35W
Mercer, *N.Z.* 59 G5 37 16S 175 5 E
Mercer, *U.S.A.* 78 E4 41 14N 80 15W
Mercer Island, *U.S.A.* 84 C4 47 35N 122 15W
Mercury, *U.S.A.* 85 J11 36 40N 115 58W
Mercy C., *Canada* 69 B13 65 0N 63 30W
Mere, *U.K.* 11 F5 51 6N 2 16W
Meredith, C., *Falk. Is.* 96 G4 52 15S 60 40W
Meredith, L., *U.S.A.* 81 H4 35 43N 101 33W
Mergui, *Burma* 38 F2 12 26N 98 34 E
Mergui Arch. = Myeik Kyunzu, *Burma* 39 G1 11 30N 97 30 E
Mérida, *Mexico* 87 C7 20 58N 89 37W
Mérida, *Spain* 19 C2 38 55N 6 25W
Mérida, *Venezuela* 92 B4 8 24N 71 8W
Mérida, Cord. de, *Venezuela* 90 C3 9 0N 71 0W
Meriden, *U.K.* 11 E6 52 26N 1 38W
Meriden, *U.S.A.* 79 E12 41 32N 72 48W
Meridian, *Calif., U.S.A.* 84 F5 39 9N 121 55W
Meridian, *Idaho, U.S.A.* 82 E5 43 37N 116 24W
Meridian, *Miss., U.S.A.* 77 J1 32 22N 88 42W
Merimbula, *Australia* 63 F4 36 53S 149 54 E
Merinda, *Australia* 62 C4 20 2S 148 11 E
Meringur, *Australia* 63 E3 34 20S 141 19 E
Merir, *Pac. Oc.* 37 D8 4 10N 132 30 E
Merirumã, *Brazil* 93 C8 1 15N 54 50W
Merkel, *U.S.A.* 81 J5 32 28N 100 1W
Mermaid Reef, *Australia* 60 C2 17 6S 119 36 E
Merredin, *Australia* 61 F2 31 28S 118 18 E
Merrick, *U.K.* 12 F4 55 8N 4 28W
Merrickville, *Canada* 79 B9 44 55N 75 50W
Merrill, *Oreg., U.S.A.* 82 E3 42 1N 121 36W
Merrill, *Wis., U.S.A.* 80 C10 45 11N 89 41W
Merrimack →, *U.S.A.* 79 D14 42 49N 70 49W
Merriman, *U.S.A.* 80 D4 42 55N 101 42W
Merritt, *Canada* 72 C4 50 10N 120 45W
Merritt Island, *U.S.A.* 77 L5 28 21N 80 42W
Merriwa, *Australia* 63 E5 32 6S 150 22 E
Merry I., *Canada* 70 A4 55 29N 77 31W
Merryville, *U.S.A.* 81 K8 30 45N 93 33W
Mersch, *Lux.* 15 E6 49 44N 6 7 E
Mersea I., *U.K.* 11 F8 51 47N 0 58 E
Merseburg, *Germany* 16 C6 51 22N 11 59 E
Mersey →, *U.K.* 10 D4 53 25N 3 1W
Merseyside □, *U.K.* 10 D4 53 31N 3 2W
Mersin, *Turkey* 25 G5 36 51N 34 36 E
Mersing, *Malaysia* 39 L4 2 25N 103 50 E
Merta, *India* 42 F6 26 39N 74 4 E
Merta Road, *India* 42 F5 26 43N 73 55 E
Merthyr Tydfil, *U.K.* 11 F4 51 45N 3 22W
Merthyr Tydfil □, *U.K.* 11 F4 51 46N 3 21W
Mértola, *Portugal* 19 D2 37 40N 7 40W
Mertzon, *U.S.A.* 81 K4 31 16N 100 49W
Meru, *Kenya* 54 B4 0 3N 37 40 E
Meru, *Tanzania* 54 C4 3 15S 36 46 E
Mesa, *U.S.A.* 83 K8 33 25N 111 50W
Mesa Verde National Park, *U.S.A.* 83 H9 37 11N 108 29W
Mesanagrós, *Greece* 23 C9 36 1N 27 49 E
Mesaoría □, *Cyprus* 23 D12 35 12N 33 14 E
Mesarás, Kólpos, *Greece* 23 D6 35 6N 24 47 E
Mesgouez, L., *Canada* 70 B5 51 20N 75 0W
Meshed = Mashhad, *Iran* 45 B8 36 20N 59 35 E
Meshoppen, *U.S.A.* 79 E8 41 36N 76 3W
Mesilinka →, *Canada* 72 B4 56 6N 124 30W
Mesilla, *U.S.A.* 83 K10 32 16N 106 48W
Mesolóngion, *Greece* 21 E9 38 21N 21 28 E
Mesopotamia = Al Jazirah, *Iraq* 44 C5 33 30N 44 0 E
Mesopotamia, *U.S.A.* 78 E4 41 27N 80 57W
Mesquite, *U.S.A.* 83 H6 36 47N 114 6W
Messad, *Algeria* 50 B6 34 8N 3 30 E
Messalo →, *Mozam.* 55 E4 12 25S 39 15 E
Messina, *Italy* 20 E6 38 11N 15 34 E
Messina, *S. Africa* 57 C5 22 20S 30 5 E
Messina, Str. di, *Italy* 20 F6 38 15N 15 35 E
Messíni, *Greece* 21 F10 37 4N 22 1 E
Messiniakós Kólpos, *Greece* 21 F10 36 45N 22 5 E
Messonghi, *Greece* 23 B3 39 29N 19 56 E
Mesta →, *Bulgaria* 21 D11 40 54N 24 49 E
Meta →, *S. Amer.* 92 B5 6 12N 67 28W
Meta Incognita Peninsula, *Canada* 69 B13 62 40N 68 0W
Metabetchouan, *Canada* 71 C5 48 26N 71 52W
Metairie, *U.S.A.* 81 L9 29 58N 90 10W
Metaline Falls, *U.S.A.* 82 B5 48 52N 117 22W
Metán, *Argentina* 94 B3 25 30S 65 0W
Metangula, *Mozam.* 55 E3 12 40S 34 50 E
Metengobalame, *Mozam.* 55 E3 14 49S 34 30 E
Methven, *N.Z.* 59 K3 43 38S 171 40 E
Metil, *Mozam.* 55 F4 16 24S 39 0 E
Metlakatla, *U.S.A.* 68 C6 55 8N 131 35W
Metropolis, *U.S.A.* 81 G10 37 9N 88 44W
Mettur Dam, *India* 40 P10 11 45N 77 45 E
Metu, *Ethiopia* 46 F2 8 18N 35 35 E
Metz, *France* 18 B7 49 8N 6 10 E
Meulaboh, *Indonesia* 36 D1 4 11N 96 3 E
Meureudu, *Indonesia* 36 C1 5 19N 96 10 E
Meuse →, *Europe* 18 A6 50 45N 5 41 E
Mexia, *U.S.A.* 81 K6 31 41N 96 29W
Mexiana, I., *Brazil* 93 D9 0 0 49 30W
Mexicali, *Mexico* 85 N11 32 40N 115 30W
Mexican Plateau, *Mexico* . 66 G9 25 0N 104 0W
Mexican Water, *U.S.A.* 83 H9 36 57N 109 32W
México, *Mexico* 87 D5 19 20N 99 10W
Mexico, *Maine, U.S.A.* 79 B14 44 34N 70 33W
Mexico, *Mo., U.S.A.* 80 F9 39 10N 91 53W
Mexico, *N.Y., U.S.A.* 79 C8 43 28N 76 18W
México □, *Mexico* 87 D5 19 20N 99 10W
Mexico ■, *Cent. Amer.* 86 C4 25 0N 105 0W
Mexico, G. of, *Cent. Amer.* 87 C7 25 0N 90 0W
Meydān-e Naftūn, *Iran* 45 D6 31 56N 49 18 E
Meydani, Ra's-e, *Iran* 45 E8 25 24N 59 6 E
Meymaneh, *Afghan.* 40 B4 35 53N 64 38 E
Mezen, *Russia* 24 A7 65 50N 44 20 E

Mezen →, *Russia* 24 A7 65 44N 44 22 E
Mézenc, Mt., *France* 18 D6 44 54N 4 11 E
Mezhdurechenskiy, *Russia* 26 D7 59 36N 65 56 E
Mezőkövesd, *Hungary* 17 E11 47 49N 20 35 E
Mezőtúr, *Hungary* 17 E11 47 1N 20 41 E
Mezquital, *Mexico* 86 C4 23 29N 104 23W
Mgeta, *Tanzania* 55 D4 8 22S 36 6 E
Mhlaba Hills, *Zimbabwe* 55 F3 18 30S 30 30 E
Mhow, *India* 42 H6 22 33N 75 50 E
Miahuatlán, *Mexico* 87 D5 16 21N 96 36W
Miami, *Fla., U.S.A.* 77 N5 25 47N 80 11W
Miami, *Okla., U.S.A.* 81 G7 36 53N 94 53W
Miami, *Tex., U.S.A.* 81 H4 35 42N 100 38W
Miami Beach, *U.S.A.* 77 N5 25 47N 80 8W
Mian Xian, *China* 34 H4 33 10N 106 32 E
Mianchi, *China* 34 G6 34 48N 111 48 E
Miandarreh, *Iran* 45 C7 35 37N 53 39 E
Miandowāb, *Iran* 44 B5 37 0N 46 5 E
Miandrivazo, *Madag.* 57 B8 19 31S 45 29 E
Mīāneh, *Iran* 44 B5 37 30N 47 40 E
Mianwali, *Pakistan* 42 C4 32 38N 71 28 E
Miarinarivo, *Madag.* 57 B8 18 57S 46 55 E
Miass, *Russia* 24 D11 54 59N 60 6 E
Michalovce, *Slovak Rep.* 17 D11 48 47N 21 58 E
Michigan □, *U.S.A.* 76 C3 44 0N 85 0W
Michigan, L., *U.S.A.* 76 D2 44 0N 87 0W
Michigan City, *U.S.A.* 76 E2 41 43N 86 54W
Michipicoten I., *Canada* 70 C2 47 40N 85 40W
Michoacan □, *Mexico* 86 D4 19 0N 102 0W
Michurin, *Bulgaria* 21 C12 42 9N 27 51 E
Michurinsk, *Russia* 24 D7 52 58N 40 27 E
Mico, Pta., *Nic.* 88 D3 12 0N 83 30W
Micronesia, *Pac. Oc.* 64 G7 11 0N 160 0 E
Micronesia, Federated States of ■, *Pac. Oc.* 64 G7 9 0N 150 0 E
Midai, *Indonesia* 39 L6 3 0N 107 47 E
Midale, *Canada* 73 D8 49 25N 103 20W
Middelburg, *Neths.* 15 C3 51 30N 3 36 E
Middelburg, *Eastern Cape, S. Africa* 56 E4 31 30S 25 0 E
Middelburg, *Mpumalanga, S. Africa* 57 D4 25 49S 29 28 E
Middelwit, *S. Africa* 56 C4 24 51S 27 3 E
Middle Alkali L., *U.S.A.* 82 F3 41 27N 120 5W
Middle Bass I., *U.S.A.* 78 E2 41 41N 82 49W
Middle East, *Asia* 28 F7 38 0N 40 0 E
Middle Fork Feather →, *U.S.A.* 84 F5 38 33N 121 30W
Middle I., *Australia* 61 F3 34 6S 123 11 E
Middle Loup →, *U.S.A.* 80 E5 41 17N 98 24W
Middleboro, *U.S.A.* 79 E14 41 54N 70 55W
Middleburg, *Fla., U.S.A.* 77 K5 30 4N 81 52W
Middleburg, *N.Y., U.S.A.* 79 D10 42 36N 74 20W
Middleburg, *Pa., U.S.A.* 78 F7 40 47N 77 3W
Middlebury, *U.S.A.* 79 B11 44 1N 73 10W
Middlemount, *Australia* 62 C4 22 50S 148 40 E
Middleport, *N.Y., U.S.A.* 78 C6 43 13N 78 29W
Middleport, *Ohio, U.S.A.* 76 F4 39 0N 82 3W
Middlesboro, *U.S.A.* 77 G4 36 36N 83 43W
Middlesbrough, *U.K.* 10 C6 54 35N 1 13W
Middlesbrough □, *U.K.* 10 C6 54 28N 1 13W
Middlesex, *Belize* 88 C2 17 2N 88 31W
Middlesex, *N.J., U.S.A.* 79 F10 40 36N 74 30W
Middlesex, *N.Y., U.S.A.* 78 D7 42 42N 77 16W
Middleton, *Australia* 62 C3 22 22S 141 32 E
Middleton, *Canada* 71 D6 44 57N 65 4W
Middleton Cr. →, *Australia* 62 C3 22 35S 141 51 E
Middletown, *U.K.* 13 B5 54 17N 6 51W
Middletown, *Calif., U.S.A.* 84 G4 38 45N 122 37W
Middletown, *Conn., U.S.A.* 79 E12 41 34N 72 39W
Middletown, *N.Y., U.S.A.* 79 E10 41 27N 74 25W
Middletown, *Ohio, U.S.A.* 76 F3 39 31N 84 24W
Middletown, *Pa., U.S.A.* 79 F8 40 12N 76 44W
Midhurst, *U.K.* 11 G7 50 59N 0 44W
Midi, Canal du →, *France* 18 E4 43 45N 1 21 E
Midland, *Canada* 78 B5 44 45N 79 50W
Midland, *Calif., U.S.A.* 85 M12 33 52N 114 48W
Midland, *Mich., U.S.A.* 76 D3 43 37N 84 14W
Midland, *Pa., U.S.A.* 78 F4 40 39N 80 27W
Midland, *Tex., U.S.A.* 81 K3 32 0N 102 3W
Midlands □, *Zimbabwe* 55 F2 19 40S 29 0 E
Midleton, *Ireland* 13 E3 51 55N 8 10W
Midlothian, *U.S.A.* 81 J6 32 30N 97 0W
Midlothian □, *U.K.* 12 F5 55 51N 3 5W
Midongy, Tangorombohitr'i, *Madag.* 57 C8 23 30S 47 0 E
Midongy Atsimo, *Madag.* 57 C8 23 35S 47 1 E
Midway Is., *Pac. Oc.* 64 E10 28 13N 177 22W
Midway Wells, *U.S.A.* 85 N11 32 41N 115 7W
Midwest, *U.S.A.* 75 B9 42 0N 90 0W
Midwest, *Wyo., U.S.A.* 82 E10 43 25N 106 16W
Midwest City, *U.S.A.* 81 H6 35 27N 97 24W
Midyat, *Turkey* 44 B4 37 25N 41 23 E
Midzŏr, *Bulgaria* 21 C10 43 27N 23 16 E
Mie □, *Japan* 31 G8 34 30N 136 10 E
Międzychód, *Poland* 16 B8 52 35N 15 53 E
Międzyrzec Podlaski, *Poland* 17 C12 51 58N 22 45 E
Mielec, *Poland* 17 C11 50 15N 21 25 E
Mienga, *Angola* 56 B2 17 12S 19 48 E
Miercurea-Ciuc, *Romania* 17 E13 46 21N 25 48 E
Mieres, *Spain* 19 A3 43 18N 5 48W
Mifflintown, *U.S.A.* 78 F7 40 34N 77 24W
Mifraz Ḥefa, *Israel* 47 C4 32 52N 35 0 E
Miguel Alemán, Presa, *Mexico* 87 D5 18 15N 96 40W
Mihara, *Japan* 31 G6 34 24N 133 5 E
Mikese, *Tanzania* 54 D4 6 48S 37 55 E
Mikhaylovgrad = Montana, *Bulgaria* 21 C10 43 27N 23 16 E
Mikhaylovka, *Russia* 25 D7 50 3N 43 5 E
Mikkeli, *Finland* 9 F22 61 43N 27 15 E
Mikkwa →, *Canada* 72 B6 58 25N 114 46W
Míkonos, *Greece* 21 F11 37 30N 25 25 E
Mikumi, *Tanzania* 54 D4 7 26S 37 0 E
Mikun, *Russia* 24 B9 62 20N 50 0 E
Milaca, *U.S.A.* 80 C8 45 45N 93 39W
Milagro, *Ecuador* 92 D3 2 11S 79 36W
Milan = Milano, *Italy* 18 D8 45 28N 9 12 E
Milan, *Mo., U.S.A.* 80 E8 40 12N 93 7W
Milan, *Tenn., U.S.A.* 77 H1 35 55N 88 46W
Milang, *Australia* 63 F2 35 24S 138 58 E
Milange, *Mozam.* 55 F4 16 3S 35 45 E
Milano, *Italy* 18 D8 45 28N 9 12 E
Milâs, *Turkey* 21 F12 37 20N 27 50 E
Milatos, *Greece* 23 D7 35 18N 25 34 E

Milazzo, *Italy* 20 E6 38 13N 15 15 E
Milbank, *U.S.A.* 80 C6 45 13N 96 38W
Milbanke Sd., *Canada* 72 C3 52 15N 128 35W
Milden, *Canada* 73 C7 51 29N 107 32W
Mildenhall, *U.K.* 11 E8 52 21N 0 32 E
Mildmay, *Canada* 78 B3 44 3N 81 7W
Mildura, *Australia* 63 E3 34 13S 142 9 E
Miles, *Australia* 63 D5 26 40S 150 9 E
Miles City, *U.S.A.* 80 B2 46 25N 105 51W
Milestone, *Canada* 73 D8 49 59N 104 31W
Miletus, *Turkey* 21 F12 37 30N 27 18 E
Milford, *Calif., U.S.A.* 84 E6 40 10N 120 22W
Milford, *Conn., U.S.A.* 79 E11 41 14N 73 3W
Milford, *Del., U.S.A.* 76 F8 38 55N 75 26W
Milford, *N.H., U.S.A.* 79 D13 42 50N 71 39W
Milford, *Pa., U.S.A.* 79 E10 41 19N 74 48W
Milford, *Utah, U.S.A.* 83 G7 38 24N 113 1W
Milford Haven, *U.K.* 11 F2 51 42N 5 7W
Milford Sd., *N.Z.* 59 L1 44 41S 167 47 E
Milh, Baḥr al, *Iraq* 44 C4 32 40N 43 35 E
Milikapiti, *Australia* 60 B5 11 26S 130 40 E
Miling, *Australia* 61 F2 30 30S 116 17 E
Milk →, *U.S.A.* 82 B10 48 4N 106 19W
Milk River, *Canada* 72 D6 49 10N 112 5W
Mill I., *Antarctica* 5 C8 66 0S 101 30 E
Mill Valley, *U.S.A.* 84 H4 37 54N 122 32W
Millau, *France* 18 D5 44 8N 3 4 E
Millbridge, *Canada* 78 B7 44 41N 77 36W
Millbrook, *Canada* 78 B6 44 10N 78 29W
Millbrook, *U.S.A.* 79 E11 41 47N 73 42W
Mille Lacs, L. des, *Canada* . 70 C1 48 45N 90 35W
Mille Lacs L., *U.S.A.* 80 B8 46 15N 93 39W
Milledgeville, *U.S.A.* 77 J4 33 5N 83 14W
Millennium I. = Caroline I., *Kiribati* 65 H12 9 15S 150 3W
Miller, *U.S.A.* 80 C5 44 31N 98 59W
Millersburg, *Ohio, U.S.A.* . 78 F3 40 33N 81 55W
Millersburg, *Pa., U.S.A.* 78 F8 40 32N 76 58W
Millerton, *U.S.A.* 79 E11 41 57N 73 31W
Millerton L., *U.S.A.* 84 J7 37 1N 119 41W
Millheim, *U.S.A.* 78 F7 40 54N 77 29W
Millicent, *Australia* 63 F3 37 34S 140 21 E
Millington, *U.S.A.* 81 H10 35 20N 89 53W
Millinocket, *U.S.A.* 77 C11 45 39N 68 43W
Millmerran, *Australia* 63 D5 27 53S 151 16 E
Millom, *U.K.* 10 C4 54 13N 3 16W
Mills L., *Canada* 72 A5 61 30N 118 20W
Millsboro, *U.S.A.* 78 G5 40 0N 80 0W
Milltown Malbay, *Ireland* . 13 D2 52 52N 9 24W
Millville, *N.J., U.S.A.* 76 F8 39 24N 75 2W
Millville, *Pa., U.S.A.* 79 E8 41 7N 76 32W
Millwood L., *U.S.A.* 81 J8 33 42N 93 58W
Milne →, *Australia* 62 C2 21 10S 137 33 E
Mílos, *Greece* 21 F11 36 44N 24 25 E
Milparinka, *Australia* 63 D3 29 46S 141 57 E
Milton, *N.S., Canada* 71 D7 44 4N 64 45W
Milton, *Ont., Canada* 78 C5 43 31N 79 53W
Milton, *N.Z.* 59 M2 46 7S 169 59 E
Milton, *Calif., U.S.A.* 84 G6 38 3N 120 51W
Milton, *Fla., U.S.A.* 77 K2 30 38N 87 3W
Milton, *Pa., U.S.A.* 78 F8 41 1N 76 51W
Milton, *Vt., U.S.A.* 79 B11 44 38N 73 7W
Milton-Freewater, *U.S.A.* .. 82 D4 45 56N 118 23W
Milton Keynes, *U.K.* 11 E7 52 1N 0 44W
Milton Keynes □, *U.K.* 11 E7 52 1N 0 44W
Milverton, *Canada* 78 C4 43 34N 80 55W
Milwaukee, *U.S.A.* 76 D2 43 2N 87 55W
Milwaukee Deep, *Atl. Oc.* .. 89 C6 19 50N 68 0W
Milwaukie, *U.S.A.* 84 E4 45 27N 122 38W
Min Jiang →, *Fujian, China* 33 D6 26 0N 119 35 E
Min Jiang →, *Sichuan, China* 32 D5 28 45N 104 40 E
Min Xian, *China* 34 G3 34 25N 104 5 E
Mina Pirquitas, *Argentina* . 94 A2 22 40S 66 30W
Minā Sa'ud, *Si. Arabia* 45 D6 28 45N 48 28 E
Mīnā'al Aḥmadī, *Kuwait* .. 45 D6 29 5N 48 10 E
Minago →, *Canada* 73 C9 54 33N 98 59W
Minaki, *Canada* 73 D10 49 59N 94 40W
Minamata, *Japan* 31 H5 32 10N 130 30 E
Minami-Tori-Shima, *Pac. Oc.* 64 E7 24 20N 153 58 E
Minas, *Uruguay* 95 C4 34 20S 55 10W
Minas, Sierra de las, *Guatemala* 88 C2 15 9N 89 31W
Minas Basin, *Canada* 71 C7 45 20N 64 12W
Minas Gerais □, *Brazil* 93 G9 18 50S 46 0W
Minatitlán, *Mexico* 87 D6 17 59N 94 31W
Minbu, *Burma* 41 J19 20 10N 94 52 E
Minchinabad, *Pakistan* 42 D5 30 10N 73 34 E
Mindanao, *Phil.* 37 C7 8 0N 125 0 E
Mindanao Sea = Bohol Sea, *Phil.* 37 C6 9 0N 124 0 E
Mindanao Trench, *Pac. Oc.* . 37 B7 12 0N 126 6 E
Minden, *Canada* 78 B6 44 55N 78 43W
Minden, *Germany* 16 B5 52 17N 8 55 E
Minden, *La., U.S.A.* 81 J8 32 37N 93 17W
Minden, *Nev., U.S.A.* 84 G7 38 57N 119 46W
Mindiptana, *Indonesia* 37 F10 5 55S 140 22 E
Mindoro, *Phil.* 37 B6 13 0N 121 0 E
Mindoro Str., *Phil.* 37 B6 12 30N 120 30 E
Mine, *Japan* 31 G5 34 12N 131 7 E
Minehead, *U.K.* 11 F4 51 12N 3 29W
Mineola, *N.Y., U.S.A.* 79 F11 40 45N 73 39W
Mineola, *Tex., U.S.A.* 81 J7 32 40N 95 29W
Mineral King, *U.S.A.* 84 J8 36 27N 118 36W
Mineral Wells, *U.S.A.* 81 J5 32 48N 98 7W
Minersville, *U.S.A.* 79 F8 40 41N 76 16W
Minerva, *U.S.A.* 78 F3 40 44N 81 6W
Minetto, *U.S.A.* 79 C8 43 24N 76 28W
Mingäçevir Su Anbarı, *Azerbaijan* 25 F8 40 57N 46 50 E
Mingan, *Canada* 71 B7 50 20N 64 0W
Mingechaurskoye Vdkhr. = Mingäçevir Su Anbarı, *Azerbaijan* 25 F8 40 57N 46 50 E
Mingela, *Australia* 62 B4 19 52S 146 38 E
Mingenew, *Australia* 61 E2 29 12S 115 21 E
Mingera Cr. →, *Australia* .. 62 C2 20 38S 137 45 E
Mingin, *Burma* 41 H19 22 50N 94 30 E
Mingo Junction, *U.S.A.* 78 F4 40 19N 80 37W
Mingyuegue, *China* 35 C15 43 2N 128 50 E
Minho = Miño →, *Spain* .. 19 A2 41 52N 8 40W
Minho, *Portugal* 19 B1 41 25N 8 20W
Minidoka, *U.S.A.* 82 E7 42 45N 113 29W

Minigwal, L., Australia 61 E3 29 31S 123 14 E
Minilya →, Australia 61 D1 23 45S 114 0 E
Minilya Roadhouse,
 Australia 61 D1 23 55S 114 0 E
Minipi L., Canada 71 B7 52 25N 60 45W
Mink L., Canada 72 A5 61 54N 117 40W
Minna, Nigeria 50 G7 9 37N 6 30 E
Minneapolis, Kans., U.S.A. 80 F6 39 8N 97 42W
Minneapolis, Minn., U.S.A. 80 C8 44 59N 93 16W
Minnedosa, Canada 73 C9 50 14N 99 50W
Minnesota □, U.S.A. 80 B8 46 0N 94 15W
Minnesota →, U.S.A. 80 C8 44 54N 93 9W
Minnewaukan, U.S.A. 80 A5 48 4N 99 15W
Minnipa, Australia 63 E2 32 51S 135 9 E
Minnitaki L., Canada 70 C1 49 57N 92 10W
Mino, Japan 31 G8 35 32N 136 55 E
Miño →, Spain 19 A2 41 52N 8 40W
Minorca = Menorca, Spain 22 B11 40 0N 4 0 E
Minot, U.S.A. 80 A4 48 14N 101 18W
Minqin, China 34 E2 38 38N 103 20 E
Minsk, Belarus 17 B14 53 52N 27 30 E
Mińsk Mazowiecki, Poland . 17 B11 52 10N 21 33 E
Mintabie, Australia 63 D1 27 15S 133 7 E
Mintaka Pass, Pakistan ... 43 A6 37 0N 74 58 E
Minteke Daban = Mintaka
 Pass, Pakistan 43 A6 37 0N 74 58 E
Minto, Canada 71 C6 46 5N 66 5W
Minto, L., Canada 70 A5 57 13N 75 0W
Minturn, U.S.A. 82 G10 39 35N 106 26W
Minusinsk, Russia 27 D10 53 43N 91 20 E
Minutang, India 41 E20 28 15N 96 30 E
Miquelon, Canada 70 C4 49 25N 76 27W
Miquelon, St- P. & M. 71 C8 47 8N 56 22W
Mir Küh, Iran 45 E8 26 22N 58 55 E
Mir Shahdād, Iran 45 E8 26 15N 58 29 E
Mira, Italy 20 B5 45 26N 12 8 E
Mira por vos Cay, Bahamas 89 B5 22 9N 74 30W
Miraj, India 40 L9 16 50N 74 45 E
Miram Shah, Pakistan 42 C4 33 0N 70 2 E
Miramar, Argentina 94 D4 38 15S 57 50W
Miramar, Mozam. 57 C6 23 50S 35 35 E
Miramichi, Canada 71 C6 47 2N 65 28W
Miramichi B., Canada 71 C7 47 15N 65 0W
Miranda, Brazil 93 H7 20 10S 56 15W
Miranda →, Brazil 92 G7 19 25S 57 20W
Miranda de Ebro, Spain .. 19 A4 42 41N 2 57W
Miranda do Douro, Portugal 19 B2 41 30N 6 16W
Mirandópolis, Brazil 95 A5 21 9S 51 6W
Mirango, Malawi 55 E3 13 32S 34 58 E
Mirassol, Brazil 95 A6 20 46S 49 28W
Mirbāṭ, Oman 46 D5 17 0N 54 45 E
Miri, Malaysia 36 D4 4 23N 113 59 E
Miriam Vale, Australia ... 62 C5 24 20S 151 33 E
Mirim, L., S. Amer. 95 C5 32 45S 52 50W
Mirnyy, Russia 27 C12 62 33N 113 53 E
Mirokhan, Pakistan 42 F3 27 46N 68 6 E
Mirond L., Canada 73 B8 55 6N 102 47W
Mirpur, Pakistan 43 C5 33 32N 73 56 E
Mirpur Batoro, Pakistan .. 42 G3 24 44N 68 16 E
Mirpur Bibiwari, Pakistan . 42 E2 28 33N 67 44 E
Mirpur Khas, Pakistan ... 42 G3 25 30N 69 0 E
Mirpur Sakro, Pakistan ... 42 G2 24 33N 67 41 E
Mirtağ, Turkey 44 B4 38 23N 41 56 E
Miryang, S. Korea 35 G15 35 31N 128 44 E
Mirzapur, India 43 G10 25 10N 82 34 E
Mirzapur-cum-Vindhyachal
 = Mirzapur, India 43 G10 25 10N 82 34 E
Misantla, Mexico 87 D5 19 56N 96 50W
Misawa, Japan 30 D10 40 41N 141 24 E
Miscou I., Canada 71 C7 47 57N 64 31W
Mish'āb, Ra's al, Si. Arabia 45 D6 28 15N 48 43 E
Mishan, China 33 B8 45 37N 131 48 E
Mishawaka, U.S.A. 76 E2 41 40N 86 11W
Mishima, Japan 31 G9 35 10N 138 52 E
Misión, Mexico 85 N10 32 6N 116 53W
Misiones □, Argentina ... 95 B5 27 0S 55 0W
Misiones □, Paraguay ... 94 B4 27 0S 56 0W
Miskah, Si. Arabia 44 E4 24 49N 42 56 E
Miskitos, Cayos, Nic. ... 88 D3 14 26N 82 50W
Miskolc, Hungary 17 D11 48 7N 20 50 E
Misool, Indonesia 37 E8 1 52S 130 10 E
Miṣrātah, Libya 51 B9 32 24N 15 3 E
Missanabie, Canada 70 C3 48 20N 84 6W
Missinaibi →, Canada ... 70 B3 50 43N 81 29W
Missinaibi L., Canada ... 70 C3 48 23N 83 40W
Mission, Canada 72 D4 49 10N 122 15W
Mission, S. Dak., U.S.A. . 80 D4 43 18N 100 39W
Mission, Tex., U.S.A. ... 81 M5 26 13N 98 20W
Mission Beach, Australia . 62 B4 17 53S 146 6 E
Mission Viejo, U.S.A. ... 85 M9 33 36N 117 40W
Missisa L., Canada 70 B2 52 20N 85 7W
Missisicabi →, Canada .. 70 B4 51 14N 79 31W
Mississagi →, Canada .. 70 C3 46 15N 83 9W
Mississauga, Canada ... 78 C5 43 32N 79 35W
Mississippi □, U.S.A. ... 81 J10 33 0N 90 0W
Mississippi →, U.S.A. .. 81 L10 29 9N 89 15W
Mississippi L., Canada .. 79 A8 45 5N 76 10W
Mississippi River Delta,
 U.S.A. 81 L9 29 10N 89 15W
Mississippi Sd., U.S.A. .. 81 K10 30 20N 89 0W
Missoula, U.S.A. 82 C7 46 52N 114 1W
Missouri □, U.S.A. 80 F8 38 25N 92 30W
Missouri →, U.S.A. 80 F9 38 49N 90 7W
Missouri City, U.S.A. ... 81 L7 29 37N 95 32W
Missouri Valley, U.S.A. .. 80 E7 41 34N 95 53W
Mist, U.S.A. 84 E3 45 59N 123 15W
Mistassibi →, Canada .. 71 B5 48 53N 72 13W
Mistassini, Canada 71 C5 48 53N 72 12W
Mistassini →, Canada .. 71 C5 48 42N 72 20W
Mistassini, L., Canada .. 70 B5 51 0N 73 30W
Mistastin L., Canada ... 71 A7 55 57N 63 20W
Mistinibi L., Canada ... 71 A7 55 56N 64 17W
Misty L., Canada 73 B8 58 53N 101 40W
Misurata = Miṣrātah, Libya 51 B9 32 24N 15 3 E
Mitchell, Australia 63 D4 26 29S 147 58 E
Mitchell, Canada 78 C3 43 28N 81 12W
Mitchell, Nebr., U.S.A. .. 80 E3 41 57N 103 49W
Mitchell, Oreg., U.S.A. .. 82 D3 44 34N 120 9W
Mitchell, S. Dak., U.S.A. . 80 D5 43 43N 98 2W
Mitchell →, Australia ... 62 B3 15 12S 141 35 E
Mitchell, Mt., U.S.A. ... 77 H4 35 46N 82 16W
Mitchell Ranges, Australia 62 A2 12 49S 135 36 E
Mitchelstown, Ireland ... 13 D3 52 15N 8 16W

Mitha Tiwana, Pakistan .. 42 C5 32 13N 72 6 E
Mithi, Pakistan 42 G3 24 44N 69 48 E
Mithrao, Pakistan 42 F3 27 28N 69 40 E
Mitilíni, Greece 21 E12 39 6N 26 35 E
Mito, Japan 31 F10 36 20N 140 30 E
Mitrovica = Kosovska
 Mitrovica, Serbia, Yug. . 21 C9 42 54N 20 52 E
Mitsinjo, Madag. 57 B8 16 1S 45 52 E
Mitsiwa, Eritrea 46 D2 15 35N 39 25 E
Mitsukaidō, Japan 31 G9 36 1N 139 59 E
Mittagong, Australia ... 63 E5 34 28S 150 29 E
Mitú, Colombia 92 C4 1 15N 70 13W
Mitumba, Tanzania 54 D3 7 8S 31 2 E
Mitumba, Mts.,
 Dem. Rep. of the Congo . 54 D2 7 0S 27 30 E
Mitwaba,
 Dem. Rep. of the Congo . 55 D2 8 2S 27 17 E
Mityana, Uganda 54 B3 0 23N 32 2 E
Mixteco →, Mexico 87 D5 18 11N 98 30W
Miyagi □, Japan 30 E10 38 15N 140 45 E
Miyah, W. el →, Syria .. 44 C3 34 44N 39 57 E
Miyake-Jima, Japan 31 G9 34 5N 139 30 E
Miyako, Japan 30 E10 39 40N 141 59 E
Miyako-Jima, Japan 31 M2 24 45N 125 20 E
Miyako-Rettō, Japan ... 31 M2 24 24N 125 0 E
Miyakonojō, Japan 31 J5 31 40N 131 5 E
Miyani, India 42 J3 21 50N 69 26 E
Miyanoura-Dake, Japan . 31 J5 30 20N 130 31 E
Miyazaki, Japan 31 J5 31 56N 131 30 E
Miyazaki □, Japan 31 H5 32 30N 131 30 E
Miyazu, Japan 31 G7 35 35N 135 10 E
Miyet, Bahr el = Dead Sea,
 Asia 47 D4 31 30N 35 30 E
Miyoshi, Japan 31 G6 34 48N 132 51 E
Miyun, China 34 D9 40 28N 116 50 E
Miyun Shuiku, China ... 35 D9 40 30N 117 0 E
Mizdah, Libya 51 B8 31 30N 13 0 E
Mizen Hd., Cork, Ireland . 13 E2 51 27N 9 50W
Mizen Hd., Wick., Ireland . 13 D5 52 51N 6 4W
Mizhi, China 34 F6 37 47N 110 12 E
Mizoram □, India 41 H18 23 30N 92 40 E
Mizpe Ramon, Israel 47 E3 30 34N 34 49 E
Mizusawa, Japan 30 E10 39 8N 141 8 E
Mjölby, Sweden 9 G16 58 20N 15 10 E
Mjøsa, Norway 9 F14 60 40N 11 0 E
Mkata, Tanzania 54 D4 5 45S 38 20 E
Mkokotoni, Tanzania ... 54 D4 5 55S 39 15 E
Mkomazi, Tanzania 54 C4 4 40S 38 7 E
Mkomazi →, S. Africa .. 57 E5 30 12S 30 50 E
Mkulwe, Tanzania 55 D3 8 37S 32 20 E
Mkumbi, Ras, Tanzania . 54 D4 7 38S 39 55 E
Mkushi, Zambia 55 E2 14 25S 29 15 E
Mkushi River, Zambia ... 55 E2 14 25S 29 45 E
Mkuze, S. Africa 57 D5 27 10S 32 0 E
Mladá Boleslav, Czech Rep. 16 C8 50 27N 14 53 E
Mlala Hills, Tanzania ... 54 D3 6 50S 31 40 E
Mlange = Mulanje, Malawi 55 F4 16 2S 35 33 E
Mlanje, Pic, Malawi 53 H7 15 57S 35 38 E
Mlawa, Poland 17 B11 53 9N 20 25 E
Mljet, Croatia 20 C7 42 43N 17 30 E
Mmabatho, S. Africa ... 56 D4 25 49S 25 30 E
Mo i Rana, Norway 8 C16 66 20N 14 7 E
Moa, Cuba 89 B4 20 40N 74 56W
Moa, Indonesia 37 F7 8 0S 128 0 E
Moab, U.S.A. 83 G9 38 35N 109 33W
Moala, Fiji 59 D8 18 36S 179 53 E
Moama, Australia 63 F3 36 7S 144 46 E
Moapa, U.S.A. 85 J12 36 40N 114 37W
Moate, Ireland 13 C4 53 24N 7 44W
Moba,
 Dem. Rep. of the Congo . 54 D2 7 0S 29 48 E
Mobārakābād, Iran 45 D7 28 24N 53 20 E
Mobaye, C.A.R. 52 D4 4 25N 21 5 E
Mobayi,
 Dem. Rep. of the Congo . 52 D4 4 15N 21 8 E
Moberley Lake, Canada . 72 B4 55 50N 121 44W
Moberly, U.S.A. 80 F8 39 25N 92 26W
Mobile, U.S.A. 77 K1 30 41N 88 3W
Mobile B., U.S.A. 77 K2 30 30N 88 0W
Mobridge, U.S.A. 80 C4 45 32N 100 26W
Mobutu Sese Seko, L. =
 Albert L., Africa 54 B3 1 30N 31 0 E
Moc Chau, Vietnam 38 B5 20 50N 104 38 E
Moc Hoa, Vietnam 39 G5 10 46N 105 56 E
Mocabe Kasari,
 Dem. Rep. of the Congo . 55 D2 9 58S 26 12 E
Moçambique, Mozam. .. 55 F5 15 3S 40 42 E
Moçâmedes = Namibe,
 Angola 53 H2 15 7S 12 11 E
Mocanaqua, U.S.A. 79 E8 41 9N 76 8W
Mochudi, Botswana 56 C4 24 27S 26 7 E
Mocimboa da Praia, Mozam. 55 E5 11 25S 40 20 E
Moclips, U.S.A. 84 C2 47 14N 124 13W
Mocoa, Colombia 92 C3 1 7N 76 35W
Mococa, Brazil 95 A6 21 28S 47 0W
Mocorito, Mexico 86 B3 25 30N 107 53W
Moctezuma, Mexico 86 B3 29 50N 109 0W
Moctezuma →, Mexico . 87 C5 21 59N 98 34W
Mocuba, Mozam. 55 F4 16 54S 36 57 E
Mocúzari, Presa, Mexico . 86 B3 27 10N 109 10W
Modane, France 18 D7 45 12N 6 40 E
Modasa, India 42 H5 23 30N 73 21 E
Modder →, S. Africa ... 56 D3 29 2S 24 37 E
Modderrivier, S. Africa .. 56 D3 29 2S 24 38 E
Módena, Italy 20 B4 44 40N 10 55 E
Modena, U.S.A. 83 H7 37 48N 113 56W
Modesto, U.S.A. 84 H6 37 39N 121 0W
Módica, Italy 20 F6 36 52N 14 46 E
Moe, Australia 63 F4 38 12S 146 19 E
Moebase, Mozam. 55 F4 17 3S 38 41 E
Moengo, Surinam 93 B8 5 45N 54 20W
Moffat, U.K. 12 F5 55 21N 3 27W
Moga, India 42 D6 30 48N 75 8 E
Mogadishu = Muqdisho,
 Somali Rep. 46 G4 2 2N 45 25 E
Mogador = Essaouira,
 Morocco 50 B4 31 32N 9 42W
Mogalakwena →, S. Africa 57 C4 22 38S 28 40 E
Mogami-Gawa →, Japan . 30 E10 38 45N 140 0 E
Mogaung, Burma 41 G20 25 20N 97 0 E
Mogi das Cruzes, Brazil . 95 A6 23 31S 46 11W
Mogi-Guaçu →, Brazil .. 95 A6 20 53S 48 10W
Mogi-Mirim, Brazil 95 A6 22 29S 47 0W
Mogilev = Mahilyow,
 Belarus 17 B16 53 55N 30 18 E

Mogilev-Podolskiy =
 Mohyliv-Podilskyy,
 Ukraine 17 D14 48 26N 27 48 E
Mogincual, Mozam. 55 F5 15 35S 40 25 E
Mogocha, Russia 27 D12 53 40N 119 50 E
Mogok, Burma 41 H20 23 0N 96 40 E
Mogollon Rim, U.S.A. ... 83 J8 34 10N 110 50W
Mogumber, Australia ... 61 F2 31 2S 116 3 E
Mohács, Hungary 17 F10 45 58N 18 41 E
Mohales Hoek, Lesotho . 56 E4 30 7S 27 26 E
Mohall, U.S.A. 80 A4 48 46N 101 31W
Moḥammadābād, Iran .. 45 B8 37 52N 59 5 E
Mohammedia, Morocco . 50 B4 33 44N 7 21W
Mohana →, India 43 G11 24 43N 85 0 E
Mohanlalganj, India 43 F9 26 41N 80 58 E
Mohave, L., U.S.A. 85 K12 35 12N 114 34W
Mohawk →, U.S.A. 79 D11 42 47N 73 41W
Mohenjodaro, Pakistan .. 42 F3 27 19N 68 7 E
Mohicanville Reservoir,
 U.S.A. 78 F3 40 45N 82 0W
Mohoro, Tanzania 54 D4 8 6S 39 8 E
Mohyliv-Podilskyy, Ukraine 17 D14 48 26N 27 48 E
Moidart, L., U.K. 12 E3 56 47N 5 52W
Moira →, Canada 78 B7 44 21N 77 24W
Moires, Greece 23 D6 35 4N 24 56 E
Moisaküla, Estonia 9 G21 58 3N 25 12 E
Moisie, Canada 71 B6 50 12N 66 1W
Moisie →, Canada 71 B6 50 14N 66 5W
Mojave, U.S.A. 85 K8 35 3N 118 10W
Mojave Desert, U.S.A. .. 85 L10 35 0N 116 30W
Mojo, Bolivia 94 A2 21 48S 65 33W
Mojokerto, Indonesia ... 37 G15 7 28S 112 26 E
Mokai, N.Z. 59 H5 38 32S 175 56 E
Mokambo,
 Dem. Rep. of the Congo . 55 E2 12 25S 28 20 E
Mokameh, India 43 G11 25 24N 85 55 E
Mokelumne →, U.S.A. .. 84 G5 38 13N 121 28W
Mokelumne Hill, U.S.A. . 84 G6 38 18N 120 43W
Mokhós, Greece 23 D7 35 16N 25 27 E
Mokhotlong, Lesotho ... 57 D4 29 22S 29 2 E
Mokokchung, India 41 F19 26 15N 94 30 E
Mokp'o, S. Korea 35 G14 34 50N 126 25 E
Mokra Gora, Serbia, Yug. . 21 C9 42 50N 20 30 E
Mol, Belgium 15 C5 51 11N 5 5 E
Molchanovo, Russia 26 D9 57 40N 83 50 E
Mold, U.K. 10 D4 53 9N 3 8W
Moldavia = Moldova ■,
 Europe 17 E15 47 0N 28 0 E
Molde, Norway 8 E12 62 45N 7 9 E
Moldova ■, Europe 17 E15 47 0N 28 0 E
Moldoveana, Vf., Romania 17 F13 45 36N 24 45 E
Mole →, U.K. 11 F7 51 24N 0 21W
Mole Creek, Australia ... 62 G4 41 34S 146 24 E
Molepolole, Botswana .. 56 C4 24 28S 25 28 E
Molfetta, Italy 20 D7 41 12N 16 36 E
Moline, U.S.A. 80 E9 41 30N 90 31W
Molinos, Argentina 94 B2 25 28S 66 15W
Moliro,
 Dem. Rep. of the Congo . 54 D3 8 12S 30 30 E
Mollendo, Peru 92 G4 17 0S 72 0W
Mollerin, L., Australia ... 61 F2 30 30S 117 35 E
Molodechno =
 Maladzyechna, Belarus . 17 A14 54 20N 26 50 E
Molokai, U.S.A. 74 H16 21 8N 157 0W
Molong, Australia 63 E4 33 5S 148 54 E
Molopo →, Africa 56 D3 28 30S 20 13 E
Molotov = Perm, Russia . 24 C10 58 0N 56 10 E
Molson L., Canada 73 C9 54 22N 96 40W
Molteno, S. Africa 56 E4 31 22S 26 22 E
Molu, Indonesia 37 F8 6 45S 131 40 E
Molucca Sea, Indonesia . 37 E6 2 0S 124 0 E
Moluccas = Maluku,
 Indonesia 37 E7 1 0S 127 0 E
Moma,
 Dem. Rep. of the Congo . 54 C1 1 35S 23 52 E
Moma, Mozam. 55 F4 16 47S 39 4 E
Mombasa, Kenya 54 C4 4 2S 39 43 E
Mombetsu, Japan 30 B11 44 21N 143 22 E
Momchilgrad, Bulgaria .. 21 D11 41 33N 25 23 E
Momi,
 Dem. Rep. of the Congo . 54 C2 1 42S 27 0 E
Mompós, Colombia 92 B4 9 14N 74 26W
Møn, Denmark 9 J15 54 57N 12 20 E
Mon →, Burma 41 J19 20 25N 94 30 E
Mona, Canal de la, W. Indies 89 C6 18 30N 67 45W
Mona, Isla, Puerto Rico .. 89 C6 18 5N 67 54W
Mona, Pta., Costa Rica .. 88 E3 9 37N 82 36W
Monaca, U.S.A. 78 F4 40 41N 80 17W
Monaco ■, Europe 18 E7 43 46N 7 23 E
Monadhliath Mts., U.K. . 12 D4 57 10N 4 4W
Monadnock, Mt., U.S.A. . 79 D12 42 52N 72 7W
Monaghan, Ireland 13 B5 54 15N 6 57W
Monaghan □, Ireland .. 13 B5 54 11N 6 56W
Monahans, U.S.A. 81 K3 31 36N 102 54W
Monapo, Mozam. 55 E5 14 56S 40 19 E
Monar, L., U.K. 12 D3 57 26N 5 8W
Monarch Mt., Canada .. 72 C3 51 55N 125 57W
Monashee Mts., Canada . 72 C5 51 0N 118 43W
Monasterevin, Ireland .. 13 C4 53 8N 7 4W
Monastir = Bitola,
 Macedonia 21 D9 41 1N 21 20 E
Moncayo, Sierra del, Spain 19 B5 41 48N 1 50W
Monchegorsk, Russia ... 24 A5 67 54N 32 58 E
Mönchengladbach,
 Germany 16 C4 51 11N 6 27 E
Monchique, Portugal ... 19 D1 37 19N 8 38W
Moncks Corner, U.S.A. .. 77 J5 33 12N 80 1W
Monclova, Mexico 86 B4 26 50N 101 30W
Moncton, Canada 71 C7 46 7N 64 51W
Mondego →, Portugal .. 19 B1 40 9N 8 52W
Mondego, C., Portugal .. 19 B1 40 28N 8 54W
Mondeodo, Indonesia ... 37 E6 3 34S 122 9 E
Mondovì, Italy 18 D7 44 23N 7 49 E
Mondrain I., Australia ... 61 F3 34 9S 122 14 E
Monessen, U.S.A. 78 F5 40 9N 79 54W
Monett, U.S.A. 81 G8 36 55N 93 55W
Moneymore, U.K. 13 B5 54 41N 6 40W
Monforte de Lemos, Spain 19 A2 42 31N 7 33W
Mong Hsu, Burma 41 J21 21 54N 98 30 E
Mong Kung, Burma 41 J20 21 35N 97 35 E
Mong Nai, Burma 41 J20 20 32N 97 46 E
Mong Pawk, Burma 41 H21 22 4N 99 16 E
Mong Ton, Burma 41 J21 20 17N 98 45 E
Mong Wa, Burma 41 J22 21 26N 100 27 E
Mong Yai, Burma 41 H21 22 21N 98 3 E
Mongala, Sudan 51 G12 5 8N 31 42 E
Mongers, L., Australia .. 61 E2 29 25S 117 5 E

Monghyr = Munger, India . 43 G12 25 23N 86 30 E
Mongibello = Etna, Italy . 20 F6 37 50N 14 55 E
Mongo, Chad 51 F9 12 14N 18 43 E
Mongolia ■, Asia 27 E10 47 0N 103 0 E
Mongu, Zambia 53 H4 15 16S 23 12 E
Môngua, Angola 56 B2 16 43S 15 20 E
Monifieth, U.K. 12 E6 56 30N 2 48W
Monkey Bay, Malawi ... 55 E4 14 7S 35 1 E
Monkey Mia, Australia .. 61 E1 25 48S 113 43 E
Monkey River, Belize ... 87 D7 16 22N 88 29W
Monkoto,
 Dem. Rep. of the Congo . 52 E4 1 38S 20 35 E
Monkton, Canada 78 C3 43 35N 81 5W
Monmouth, U.K. 11 F5 51 48N 2 42W
Monmouth, Ill., U.S.A. .. 80 E9 40 55N 90 39W
Monmouth, Oreg., U.S.A. . 82 D2 44 51N 123 14W
Monmouthshire □, U.K. . 11 F5 51 48N 2 54W
Mono, L., U.S.A. 84 H7 38 1N 119 1W
Monolith, U.S.A. 85 K8 35 7N 118 22W
Monólithos, Greece 23 C9 36 7N 27 45 E
Monongahela, U.S.A. ... 78 F5 40 12N 79 56W
Monroe, Ga., U.S.A. 77 J4 33 47N 83 43W
Monroe, La., U.S.A. 81 J8 32 30N 92 7W
Monroe, Mich., U.S.A. .. 76 E4 41 55N 83 24W
Monroe, N.C., U.S.A. ... 77 H5 34 59N 80 33W
Monroe, N.Y., U.S.A. ... 79 E10 41 20N 74 11W
Monroe, Utah, U.S.A. ... 83 G7 38 38N 112 7W
Monroe, Wash., U.S.A. .. 84 C5 47 51N 121 58W
Monroe, Wis., U.S.A. ... 80 D10 42 36N 89 38W
Monroe City, U.S.A. 80 F9 39 39N 91 44W
Monroeton, U.S.A. 79 E8 41 43N 76 29W
Monroeville, Ala., U.S.A. . 77 K2 31 31N 87 20W
Monroeville, Pa., U.S.A. . 78 F5 40 26N 79 45W
Monrovia, Liberia 50 G3 6 18N 10 47W
Mons, Belgium 15 D3 50 27N 3 58 E
Monse, Indonesia 37 E6 4 0S 123 10 E
Mont-de-Marsan, France . 18 E3 43 54N 0 31W
Mont-Joli, Canada 71 C6 48 37N 68 10W
Mont-Laurier, Canada .. 70 C4 46 35N 75 30W
Mont-Louis, Canada ... 71 C6 49 15N 65 44W
Mont-St-Michel, Le = Le
 Mont-St-Michel, France . 18 B3 48 40N 1 30W
Mont Tremblant, Parc Recr.
 du, Canada 70 C5 46 30N 74 30W
Montagu, S. Africa 56 E3 33 45S 20 8 E
Montagu I., Antarctica .. 5 B1 58 25S 26 20W
Montague, Canada 71 C7 46 10N 62 39W
Montague, I., Mexico ... 86 A2 31 40N 114 56W
Montague Ra., Australia . 61 E2 27 15S 119 30 E
Montague Sd., Australia . 60 B4 14 28S 125 20 E
Montalbán, Spain 19 B5 40 50N 0 45W
Montalvo, U.S.A. 85 L7 34 15N 119 12W
Montana, Bulgaria 21 C10 43 27N 23 16 E
Montaña, Peru 92 E4 6 0S 73 0W
Montana □, U.S.A. 82 C9 47 0N 110 0W
Montaña Clara, I., Canary Is. 22 E6 29 17N 13 33W
Montargis, France 18 C5 47 59N 2 43 E
Montauban, France 18 D4 44 2N 1 21 E
Montauk, U.S.A. 79 E13 41 3N 71 57W
Montauk Pt., U.S.A. 79 E13 41 4N 71 52W
Montbéliard, France ... 18 C7 47 31N 6 48 E
Montceau-les-Mines, France 18 C6 46 40N 4 23 E
Montclair, U.S.A. 79 F10 40 49N 74 13W
Monte Albán, Mexico ... 87 D5 17 2N 96 45W
Monte Alegre, Brazil ... 93 D8 2 0S 54 0W
Monte Azul, Brazil 93 G10 15 9S 42 53W
Monte Bello Is., Australia . 60 D2 20 30S 115 45 E
Monte-Carlo, Monaco ... 18 E7 43 46N 7 23 E
Monte Caseros, Argentina 94 C4 30 10S 57 50W
Monte Comán, Argentina 94 C2 34 40S 67 53W
Monte Cristi, Dom. Rep. . 89 C5 19 52N 71 39W
Monte Lindo →, Paraguay 94 A4 23 56S 57 12W
Monte Patria, Chile 94 C1 30 42S 70 58W
Monte Quemado, Argentina 94 B3 25 53S 62 41W
Monte Rio, U.S.A. 84 G4 38 28N 123 0W
Monte Santu, C. di, Italy . 20 D3 40 5N 9 44 E
Monteagudo, Argentina . 95 B5 27 14S 54 8W
Montebello, Canada 70 C5 45 40N 74 55W
Montecito, U.S.A. 85 L7 34 26N 119 40W
Montecristo, Italy 20 C4 42 20N 10 19 E
Montego Bay, Jamaica .. 88 C4 18 30N 78 0W
Montélimar, France 18 D6 44 33N 4 45 E
Montello, U.S.A. 80 D10 43 48N 89 20W
Montemorelos, Mexico .. 87 B5 25 11N 99 42W
Montenegro, Brazil 95 B5 29 39S 51 29W
Montenegro □, Yugoslavia 21 C8 42 40N 19 20 E
Montepuez, Mozam. 55 E4 13 8S 38 59 E
Montepuez →, Mozam. . 55 E5 12 32S 40 27 E
Monterey, U.S.A. 84 J5 36 37N 121 55W
Monterey B., U.S.A. 84 J5 36 45N 122 0W
Montería, Colombia 92 B3 8 46N 75 53W
Monteros, Argentina ... 94 B2 27 11S 65 30W
Monterrey, Mexico 86 B4 25 40N 100 30W
Montes Claros, Brazil ... 93 G10 16 30S 43 50W
Montesano, U.S.A. 84 D3 46 59N 123 36W
Montesilvano, Italy 20 C6 42 29N 14 8 E
Montevideo, Uruguay .. 95 C4 34 50S 56 11W
Montevideo, U.S.A. 80 C7 44 57N 95 43W
Montezuma, U.S.A. 80 E8 41 35N 92 32W
Montgomery = Sahiwal,
 Pakistan 42 D5 30 45N 73 8 E
Montgomery, U.K. 11 E4 52 34N 3 8W
Montgomery, Ala., U.S.A. 77 J2 32 23N 86 19W
Montgomery, Pa., U.S.A. . 78 E8 41 10N 76 53W
Montgomery, W. Va., U.S.A. 76 F5 38 11N 81 19W
Montgomery City, U.S.A. 80 F9 38 59N 91 30W
Monticello, Ark., U.S.A. . 81 J9 33 38N 91 47W
Monticello, Fla., U.S.A. . 77 K4 30 33N 83 52W
Monticello, Ind., U.S.A. . 76 E2 40 45N 86 46W
Monticello, Iowa, U.S.A. . 80 D9 42 15N 91 12W
Monticello, Ky., U.S.A. .. 76 G3 36 50N 84 51W
Monticello, Minn., U.S.A. 80 C8 45 18N 93 48W
Monticello, Miss., U.S.A. . 81 K9 31 33N 90 7W
Monticello, N.Y., U.S.A. . 79 E10 41 39N 74 42W
Monticello, Utah, U.S.A. . 83 H9 37 52N 109 21W
Montijo, Portugal 19 C1 38 41N 8 54W
Montilla, Spain 19 D3 37 36N 4 40W
Montluçon, France 18 C5 46 22N 2 36 E
Montmagny, Canada ... 71 C5 46 58N 70 34W
Montmartre, Canada ... 73 C8 50 14N 103 27W
Montmorillon, France .. 18 C4 46 26N 0 50 E
Monto, Australia 62 C5 24 52S 151 6 E
Montoro, Spain 19 C3 38 1N 4 27W
Montour Falls, U.S.A. ... 78 D8 42 21N 76 51W

Name	Map	Lat	Long
Montoursville, U.S.A.	78 E8	41 15N	76 55W
Montpelier, Idaho, U.S.A.	82 E8	42 19N	111 18W
Montpelier, Vt., U.S.A.	79 B12	44 16N	72 35W
Montpellier, France	18 E5	43 37N	3 52 E
Montréal, Canada	79 A11	45 31N	73 34W
Montreal →, Canada	70 C3	47 14N	84 39W
Montreal L., Canada	73 C7	54 20N	105 45W
Montreal Lake, Canada	73 C7	54 3N	105 46W
Montreux, Switz.	18 C7	46 26N	6 55 E
Montrose, U.K.	12 E6	56 44N	2 27W
Montrose, Colo., U.S.A.	83 G10	38 29N	107 53W
Montrose, Pa., U.S.A.	79 E9	41 50N	75 53W
Monts, Pte. des, Canada	71 C6	49 20N	67 12W
Montserrat ■, W. Indies	88 C7	16 40N	62 10W
Montuiri, Spain	22 B9	39 34N	2 59 E
Monywa, Burma	41 H19	22 7N	95 11 E
Monza, Italy	18 D8	45 35N	9 16 E
Monze, Zambia	55 F2	16 17S	27 29 E
Monze, C., Pakistan	42 G2	24 47N	66 37 E
Monzón, Spain	19 B6	41 52N	0 10 E
Mooers, U.S.A.	79 B11	44 58N	73 35W
Mooi River, S. Africa	57 D4	29 13S	29 50 E
Moonah →, Australia	62 C2	22 3S	138 33 E
Moonda, L., Australia	62 D3	25 52S	140 25 E
Moonie, Australia	63 D5	27 46S	150 20 E
Moonie →, Australia	63 D4	29 19S	148 43 E
Moonta, Australia	63 E2	34 6S	137 32 E
Moora, Australia	61 F2	30 37S	115 58 E
Moorcroft, U.S.A.	80 C2	44 16N	104 57W
Moore →, Australia	61 F2	31 22S	115 30 E
Moore, L., Australia	61 E2	29 50S	117 35 E
Moore Park, Australia	62 C5	24 43S	152 17 E
Moore Reefs, Australia	62 B4	16 0S	149 5 E
Moorefield, U.S.A.	76 F6	39 5N	78 59W
Moores Res., U.S.A.	79 B13	44 45N	71 50W
Moorfoot Hills, U.K.	12 F5	55 44N	3 8W
Moorhead, U.S.A.	80 B6	46 53N	96 45W
Moorpark, U.S.A.	85 L8	34 17N	118 53W
Moorreesburg, S. Africa	56 E2	33 6S	18 38 E
Moose →, Canada	70 B3	51 20N	80 25W
Moose →, U.S.A.	79 C9	43 38N	75 24W
Moose Creek, Canada	79 A10	45 15N	74 58W
Moose Factory, Canada	70 B3	51 16N	80 32W
Moose Jaw, Canada	73 C7	50 24N	105 30W
Moose Jaw →, Canada	73 C7	50 34N	105 18W
Moose Lake, Canada	73 C8	53 43N	100 20W
Moose Lake, U.S.A.	80 B8	46 27N	92 46W
Moose Mountain Prov. Park, Canada	73 D8	49 48N	102 25W
Moosehead L., U.S.A.	77 C11	45 38N	69 40W
Mooselookmeguntic L., U.S.A.	77 C10	44 55N	70 49W
Moosilauke, Mt., U.S.A.	79 B13	44 3N	71 40W
Moosomin, Canada	73 C8	50 9N	101 40W
Moosonee, Canada	70 B3	51 17N	80 39W
Moosup, U.S.A.	79 E13	41 43N	71 53W
Mopeia Velha, Mozam.	55 F4	17 30S	35 40 E
Mopipi, Botswana	56 C3	21 6S	24 55 E
Mopoi, C.A.R.	54 A2	5 6N	26 54 E
Mopti, Mali	50 F5	14 30N	4 0W
Moqor, Afghan.	42 C2	32 50N	67 42 E
Moquegua, Peru	92 G4	17 15S	70 46W
Mora, Sweden	9 F16	61 2N	14 38 E
Mora, Minn., U.S.A.	80 C8	45 53N	93 18W
Mora, N. Mex., U.S.A.	83 J11	35 58N	105 20W
Mora →, U.S.A.	81 H2	35 35N	104 25W
Moradabad, India	43 E8	28 50N	78 50 E
Morafenobe, Madag.	57 B7	17 50S	44 53 E
Moramanga, Madag.	57 B8	18 56S	48 12 E
Moran, Kans., U.S.A.	81 G7	37 55N	95 10W
Moran, Wyo., U.S.A.	82 E8	43 53N	110 37W
Moranbah, Australia	62 C4	22 1S	148 6 E
Morant Cays, Jamaica	88 C4	17 22N	76 0W
Morant Pt., Jamaica	88 C4	17 55N	76 12W
Morar, India	42 F8	26 14N	78 14 E
Morar, L., U.K.	12 E3	56 57N	5 40W
Moratuwa, Sri Lanka	40 R11	6 45N	79 55 E
Morava →, Serbia, Yug.	21 B9	44 36N	21 4 E
Morava →, Slovak Rep.	17 D9	48 10N	16 59 E
Moravia, U.S.A.	79 D8	42 43N	76 25W
Moravian Hts. = Českomoravská Vrchovina, Czech Rep.	16 D8	49 30N	15 40 E
Morawa, Australia	61 E2	29 13S	116 0 E
Morawhanna, Guyana	92 B7	8 30N	59 40W
Moray □, U.K.	12 D5	57 31N	3 18W
Moray Firth, U.K.	12 D5	57 40N	3 52W
Morbi, India	42 H4	22 50N	70 42 E
Morden, Canada	73 D9	49 15N	98 10W
Mordovian Republic = Mordvinia □, Russia	24 D7	54 20N	44 30 E
Mordvinia □, Russia	24 D7	54 20N	44 30 E
Morea, Greece	6 H10	37 45N	22 10 E
Moreau →, U.S.A.	80 C4	45 18N	100 43W
Morecambe, U.K.	10 C5	54 5N	2 52W
Morecambe B., U.K.	10 C5	54 7N	3 0W
Moree, Australia	63 D4	29 28S	149 54 E
Morehead, U.S.A.	76 F4	38 11N	83 26W
Morehead City, U.S.A.	77 H7	34 43N	76 43W
Morel →, India	42 F7	26 13N	76 36 E
Morelia, Mexico	86 D4	19 42N	101 7W
Morella, Australia	62 C3	23 0S	143 52 E
Morella, Spain	19 B5	40 35N	0 5W
Morelos, Mexico	86 B3	26 42N	107 40W
Morelos □, Mexico	87 D5	18 40N	99 10W
Morena, India	42 F8	26 30N	78 4 E
Morena, Sierra, Spain	19 C3	38 20N	4 0W
Moreno Valley, U.S.A.	85 M10	33 56N	117 15W
Moresby I., Canada	72 C2	52 30N	131 40W
Moreton I., Australia	63 D5	27 10S	153 25 E
Morey, Spain	22 B10	39 44N	3 20 E
Morgan, U.S.A.	82 F8	41 2N	111 41W
Morgan City, U.S.A.	81 L9	29 42N	91 12W
Morgan Hill, U.S.A.	84 H5	37 8N	121 39W
Morganfield, U.S.A.	76 G2	37 41N	87 55W
Morganton, U.S.A.	77 H5	35 45N	81 41W
Morgantown, U.S.A.	76 F6	39 38N	79 57W
Morgenzon, S. Africa	57 D4	26 45S	29 36 E
Morghak, Iran	45 D8	29 7N	57 54 E
Morhar →, India	43 G11	25 29N	85 11 E
Moriarty, U.S.A.	83 J10	34 59N	106 3W
Morice L., Canada	72 C3	53 50N	127 40W
Morinville, Canada	72 C6	53 49N	113 41W
Morioka, Japan	30 E10	39 45N	141 8 E
Moris, Mexico	86 B3	28 8N	108 32W
Morlaix, France	18 B2	48 36N	3 52W
Mornington, Australia	63 F4	38 15S	145 5 E
Mornington, I., Chile	96 F1	49 50S	75 30W
Mornington I., Australia	62 B2	16 30S	139 30 E
Moro, Pakistan	42 F2	26 40N	68 0 E
Moro →, Pakistan	42 E2	29 42N	67 22 E
Moro G., Phil.	37 C6	6 30N	123 0 E
Morocco ■, N. Afr.	50 B4	32 0N	5 50W
Morogoro, Tanzania	54 D4	6 50S	37 40 E
Morogoro □, Tanzania	54 D4	8 0S	37 0 E
Moroleón, Mexico	86 C4	20 8N	101 32W
Morombe, Madag.	57 C7	21 45S	43 22 E
Moron, Argentina	94 C4	34 39S	58 37W
Morón, Cuba	88 B4	22 8N	78 39W
Morón de la Frontera, Spain	19 D3	37 6N	5 28W
Morona →, Peru	92 D3	4 40S	77 10W
Morondava, Madag.	57 C7	20 17S	44 17 E
Morongo Valley, U.S.A.	85 L10	34 3N	116 37W
Moroni, Comoros Is.	49 H8	11 40S	43 16 E
Moroni, U.S.A.	82 G8	39 32N	111 35W
Morotai, Indonesia	37 D7	2 10N	128 30 E
Moroto, Uganda	54 B3	2 28N	34 42 E
Moroto Summit, Kenya	54 B3	2 30N	34 43 E
Morpeth, U.K.	10 B6	55 10N	1 41W
Morphou, Cyprus	23 D11	35 12N	32 59 E
Morphou Bay, Cyprus	23 D11	35 12N	32 50 E
Morrilton, U.S.A.	81 H8	35 9N	92 44W
Morrinhos, Brazil	93 G9	17 45S	49 10W
Morrinsville, N.Z.	59 G5	37 40S	175 32 E
Morris, Canada	73 D9	49 25N	97 22W
Morris, Minn., U.S.A.	80 C7	45 35N	95 55W
Morris, N.Y., U.S.A.	79 D9	42 33N	75 15W
Morris, Pa., U.S.A.	78 E7	41 35N	77 17W
Morris, Mt., Australia	61 E5	26 9S	131 4 E
Morrisburg, Canada	79 B9	44 55N	75 7W
Morristown, Ariz., U.S.A.	83 K7	33 51N	112 37W
Morristown, N.J., U.S.A.	79 F10	40 48N	74 29W
Morristown, N.Y., U.S.A.	79 B9	44 35N	75 39W
Morristown, Tenn., U.S.A.	77 G4	36 13N	83 18W
Morrisville, N.Y., U.S.A.	79 D9	42 53N	75 35W
Morrisville, Pa., U.S.A.	79 F10	40 13N	74 47W
Morrisville, Vt., U.S.A.	79 B12	44 34N	72 36W
Morro, Pta., Chile	94 B1	27 6S	71 0W
Morro Bay, U.S.A.	84 K6	35 22N	120 51W
Morro del Jable, Canary Is.	22 F5	28 3N	14 23W
Morro Jable, Pta. de, Canary Is.	22 F5	28 2N	14 20W
Morrosquillo, G. de, Colombia	88 E4	9 35N	75 40W
Morrumbene, Mozam.	57 C6	23 31S	35 16 E
Morshansk, Russia	24 D7	53 28N	41 50 E
Morteros, Argentina	94 C3	30 50S	62 0W
Mortlach, Canada	73 C7	50 27N	106 4W
Mortlake, Australia	63 F3	38 5S	142 50 E
Morton, Tex., U.S.A.	81 J3	33 44N	102 46W
Morton, Wash., U.S.A.	84 D4	46 34N	122 17W
Morundah, Australia	63 E4	34 57S	146 19 E
Moruya, Australia	63 F5	35 58S	150 3 E
Morvan, France	18 C6	47 5N	4 3 E
Morven, Australia	63 D4	26 22S	147 5 E
Morvern, U.K.	12 E3	56 38N	5 44W
Morwell, Australia	63 F4	38 10S	146 22 E
Morzhovets, Ostrov, Russia	24 A7	66 44N	42 35 E
Moscos Is. = Maungmagan Is., Burma	38 F1	14 0N	97 30 E
Moscow = Moskva, Russia	24 C6	55 45N	37 35 E
Moscow, Idaho, U.S.A.	82 C5	46 44N	117 0W
Moscow, Pa., U.S.A.	79 E9	41 20N	75 31W
Mosel →, Europe	18 A7	50 22N	7 36 E
Moselle = Mosel →, Europe	18 A7	50 22N	7 36 E
Moses Lake, U.S.A.	82 C4	47 8N	119 17W
Mosgiel, N.Z.	59 L3	45 53S	170 21 E
Moshi, Tanzania	54 C4	3 22S	37 18 E
Moshupa, Botswana	56 C4	24 46S	25 29 E
Mosjøen, Norway	8 D15	65 51N	13 12 E
Moskenesøya, Norway	8 C15	67 58N	13 0 E
Moskenstraumen, Norway	8 C15	67 47N	12 45 E
Moskva, Russia	24 C6	55 45N	37 35 E
Mosomane, Botswana	56 C4	24 2S	26 19 E
Moson-magyaróvár, Hungary	17 E9	47 52N	17 18 E
Mosquera, Colombia	92 C3	2 35N	78 24W
Mosquero, U.S.A.	81 H3	35 47N	103 58W
Mosquitia, Honduras	88 C3	15 20N	84 10W
Mosquito Coast = Mosquitia, Honduras	88 C3	15 20N	84 10W
Mosquito Creek L., U.S.A.	78 E4	41 18N	80 46W
Mosquito L., Canada	73 A8	62 35N	103 20W
Mosquitos, G. de los, Panama	88 E3	9 15N	81 10W
Moss, Norway	9 G14	59 27N	10 40 E
Moss Vale, Australia	63 E5	34 32S	150 25 E
Mossbank, Canada	73 D7	49 56N	105 56W
Mossburn, N.Z.	59 L2	45 41S	168 15 E
Mosselbaai, S. Africa	56 E3	34 11S	22 8 E
Mossendjo, Congo	52 E2	2 55S	12 42 E
Mossgiel, Australia	63 E3	33 15S	144 5 E
Mossman, Australia	62 B4	16 21S	145 15 E
Mossoró, Brazil	93 E11	5 10S	37 15W
Mossuril, Mozam.	55 E5	14 58S	40 42 E
Most, Czech Rep.	16 C7	50 31N	13 38 E
Mosta, Malta	23 D1	35 54N	14 24 E
Moştafaābād, Iran	45 C7	33 39N	54 53 E
Mostaganem, Algeria	50 A6	35 54N	0 5 E
Mostar, Bos.-H.	21 C7	43 22N	17 50 E
Mostardas, Brazil	95 C5	31 2S	50 51W
Mostiska = Mostyska, Ukraine	17 D12	49 48N	23 4 E
Mosty = Masty, Belarus	17 B13	53 27N	24 38 E
Mostyska, Ukraine	17 D12	49 48N	23 4 E
Mosul = Al Mawşil, Iraq	44 B4	36 15N	43 5 E
Mosúlpo, S. Korea	35 H14	33 20N	126 17 E
Motagua →, Guatemala	88 C2	15 44N	88 14W
Motala, Sweden	9 G16	58 32N	15 1 E
Moth, India	43 G8	25 43N	78 57 E
Motherwell, U.K.	12 F5	55 47N	3 58W
Motihari, India	43 F11	26 30N	84 55 E
Motozintla de Mendoza, Mexico	87 D6	15 21N	92 14W
Motril, Spain	19 D4	36 31N	3 37W
Mott, U.S.A.	80 B3	46 23N	102 20W
Motueka, N.Z.	59 J4	41 7S	173 1 E
Motueka →, N.Z.	59 J4	41 5S	173 1 E
Motul, Mexico	87 C7	21 0N	89 20W
Mouchalagane →, Canada	71 B6	50 56N	68 41W
Moúdhros, Greece	21 E11	39 50N	25 18 E
Mouila, Gabon	52 E2	1 50S	11 0 E
Moulamein, Australia	63 F3	35 3S	144 1 E
Mouliana, Greece	23 D7	35 10N	25 59 E
Moulins, France	18 C5	46 35N	3 19 E
Moulmein, Burma	41 L20	16 30N	97 40 E
Moulouya, O. →, Morocco	50 B5	35 5N	2 25W
Moultrie, U.S.A.	77 K4	31 11N	83 47W
Moultrie, L., U.S.A.	77 J5	33 20N	80 5W
Mound City, Mo., U.S.A.	80 E7	40 7N	95 14W
Mound City, S. Dak., U.S.A.	80 C4	45 44N	100 4W
Moundou, Chad	51 G9	8 40N	16 10 E
Moundsville, U.S.A.	78 G4	39 55N	80 44W
Moung, Cambodia	38 F4	12 46N	103 27 E
Mount Airy, U.S.A.	77 G5	36 31N	80 37W
Mount Albert, Canada	78 B5	44 8N	79 19W
Mount Barker, S. Austral., Australia	63 F2	35 5S	138 52 E
Mount Barker, W. Austral., Australia	61 F2	34 38S	117 40 E
Mount Beauty, Australia	63 F4	36 47S	147 10 E
Mount Brydges, Canada	78 D3	42 54N	81 29W
Mount Burr, Australia	63 F3	37 34S	140 26 E
Mount Carmel, Ill., U.S.A.	76 F2	38 25N	87 46W
Mount Carmel, Pa., U.S.A.	79 F8	40 47N	76 24W
Mount Charleston, U.S.A.	85 J11	36 16N	115 37W
Mount Clemens, U.S.A.	78 D2	42 35N	82 53W
Mount Coolon, Australia	62 C4	21 25S	147 25 E
Mount Darwin, Zimbabwe	55 F3	16 47S	31 38 E
Mount Desert I., U.S.A.	77 C11	44 21N	68 20W
Mount Dora, U.S.A.	77 L5	28 48N	81 38W
Mount Edziza Prov. Park, Canada	72 B2	57 30N	130 45W
Mount Fletcher, S. Africa	57 E4	30 40S	28 30 E
Mount Forest, Canada	78 C4	43 59N	80 43W
Mount Gambier, Australia	63 F3	37 50S	140 46 E
Mount Garnet, Australia	62 B4	17 37S	145 6 E
Mount Holly, U.S.A.	79 G10	39 59N	74 47W
Mount Holly Springs, U.S.A.	78 F7	40 7N	77 12W
Mount Hope, N.S.W., Australia	63 E4	32 51S	145 51 E
Mount Hope, S. Austral., Australia	63 E2	34 7S	135 23 E
Mount Isa, Australia	62 C2	20 42S	139 26 E
Mount Jewett, U.S.A.	78 E6	41 44N	78 39W
Mount Kisco, U.S.A.	79 E11	41 12N	73 44W
Mount Laguna, U.S.A.	85 N10	32 52N	116 25W
Mount Larcom, Australia	62 C5	23 48S	150 59 E
Mount Lofty Ra., Australia	63 E2	34 35S	139 5 E
Mount Magnet, Australia	61 E2	28 2S	117 47 E
Mount Maunganui, N.Z.	59 G6	37 40S	176 14 E
Mount Molloy, Australia	62 B4	16 42S	145 20 E
Mount Morgan, Australia	62 C5	23 40S	150 25 E
Mount Morris, U.S.A.	78 D7	42 44N	77 52W
Mount Pearl, Canada	71 C9	47 31N	52 47W
Mount Penn, U.S.A.	79 F9	40 20N	75 54W
Mount Perry, Australia	63 D5	25 13S	151 42 E
Mount Pleasant, Iowa, U.S.A.	80 E9	40 58N	91 33W
Mount Pleasant, Mich., U.S.A.	76 D3	43 36N	84 46W
Mount Pleasant, Pa., U.S.A.	78 F5	40 9N	79 33W
Mount Pleasant, S.C., U.S.A.	77 J6	32 47N	79 52W
Mount Pleasant, Tenn., U.S.A.	77 H2	35 32N	87 12W
Mount Pleasant, Tex., U.S.A.	81 J7	33 9N	94 58W
Mount Pleasant, Utah, U.S.A.	82 G8	39 33N	111 27W
Mount Pocono, U.S.A.	79 E9	41 7N	75 22W
Mount Rainier Nat. Park, U.S.A.	84 D5	46 55N	121 50W
Mount Revelstoke Nat. Park, Canada	72 C5	51 5N	118 30W
Mount Robson Prov. Park, Canada	72 C5	53 0N	119 0W
Mount Shasta, U.S.A.	82 F2	41 19N	122 19W
Mount Signal, U.S.A.	85 N11	32 39N	115 37W
Mount Sterling, Ill., U.S.A.	80 F9	39 59N	90 45W
Mount Sterling, Ky., U.S.A.	76 F4	38 4N	83 56W
Mount Surprise, Australia	62 B3	18 10S	144 17 E
Mount Union, U.S.A.	78 F7	40 23N	77 53W
Mount Upton, U.S.A.	79 D9	42 26N	75 23W
Mount Vernon, Ill., U.S.A.	76 F1	38 19N	88 55W
Mount Vernon, Ind., U.S.A.	80 F10	38 17N	88 57W
Mount Vernon, N.Y., U.S.A.	79 F11	40 54N	73 50W
Mount Vernon, Ohio, U.S.A.	78 F2	40 23N	82 29W
Mount Vernon, Wash., U.S.A.	84 B4	48 25N	122 20W
Mountain Ash, U.K.	11 F4	51 40N	3 23W
Mountain Center, U.S.A.	85 M10	33 42N	116 44W
Mountain City, Nev., U.S.A.	82 F6	41 50N	115 58W
Mountain City, Tenn., U.S.A.	77 G5	36 29N	81 48W
Mountain Dale, U.S.A.	79 E10	41 41N	74 32W
Mountain Grove, U.S.A.	81 G8	37 8N	92 16W
Mountain Home, Ark., U.S.A.	81 G8	36 20N	92 23W
Mountain Home, Idaho, U.S.A.	82 E6	43 8N	115 41W
Mountain Iron, U.S.A.	80 B8	47 32N	92 37W
Mountain Pass, U.S.A.	85 K11	35 29N	115 35W
Mountain View, Ark., U.S.A.	81 H8	35 52N	92 7W
Mountain View, Calif., U.S.A.	84 H4	37 23N	122 5W
Mountain View, Hawaii, U.S.A.	74 J17	19 33N	155 7W
Mountainair, U.S.A.	83 J10	34 31N	106 15W
Mountlake Terrace, U.S.A.	84 C4	47 47N	122 19W
Mountmellick, Ireland	13 C4	53 7N	7 20W
Mountrath, Ireland	13 D4	53 0N	7 28W
Moura, Australia	62 C4	24 35S	149 58 E
Moura, Brazil	92 D6	1 32S	61 38W
Moura, Portugal	19 C2	38 7N	7 30W
Mourdi, Dépression du, Chad	51 E10	18 10N	23 0 E
Mourilyan, Australia	62 B4	17 35S	146 3 E
Mourne →, U.K.	13 B4	54 52N	7 26W
Mourne Mts., U.K.	13 B5	54 10N	6 0W
Mournies, Greece	23 D6	35 29N	24 1 E
Mournies = Mourniaí, Greece	23 D6	35 29N	24 1 E
Mouscron, Belgium	15 D3	50 45N	3 12 E
Moussoro, Chad	51 F9	13 41N	16 35 E
Moutohara, N.Z.	59 H6	38 27S	177 32 E
Moutong, Indonesia	37 D6	0 28N	121 13 E
Movas, Mexico	86 B3	28 10N	109 25W
Moville, Ireland	13 A4	55 11N	7 3W
Mowandjum, Australia	60 C3	17 22S	123 40 E
Moy →, Ireland	13 B2	54 8N	9 8W
Moyale, Kenya	54 B4	3 30N	39 0 E
Moyen Atlas, Morocco	50 B4	33 0N	5 0W
Moyne, L. le, Canada	71 A6	56 45N	68 47W
Moyo, Indonesia	36 F5	8 10S	117 40 E
Moyobamba, Peru	92 E3	6 0S	77 0W
Moyyero →, Russia	27 C11	68 44N	103 42 E
Moyynty, Kazakhstan	26 E8	47 10N	73 18 E
Mozambique = Moçambique, Mozam.	55 F5	15 3S	40 42 E
Mozambique ■, Africa	55 F4	19 0S	35 0 E
Mozambique Chan., Africa	57 B7	17 30S	42 30 E
Mozdok, Russia	25 F7	43 45N	44 48 E
Mozdūrān, Iran	45 B9	36 9N	60 35 E
Mozhnābād, Iran	45 C9	34 7N	60 6 E
Mozyr = Mazyr, Belarus	17 B15	51 59N	29 15 E
Mpanda, Tanzania	54 D3	6 23S	31 1
Mpika, Zambia	55 E3	11 51S	31 25
Mpulungu, Zambia	55 D3	8 51S	31 5
Mpumalanga, S. Africa	57 D5	29 50S	30 33
Mpumalanga □, S. Africa	57 B5	26 0S	30 0
Mpwapwa, Tanzania	54 D4	6 23S	36 30
Msambansovu, Zimbabwe	55 F3	15 50S	30 3
M'sila →, Algeria	50 A6	35 30N	4 29
Msoro, Zambia	55 E3	13 35S	31 50
Mstislavl = Mstsislaw, Belarus	17 A16	54 0N	31 50
Mstsislaw, Belarus	17 A16	54 0N	31 50
Mtama, Tanzania	55 E4	10 17S	39 21
Mtilikwe →, Zimbabwe	55 G3	21 9S	31 30
Mtubatuba, S. Africa	57 D5	28 30S	32 8
Mtwara-Mikindani, Tanzania	55 E5	10 20S	40 20
Mu Gia, Deo, Vietnam	38 D5	17 40N	105 47
Mu Us Shamo, China	34 E5	39 0N	109 0
Muang Chiang Rai = Chiang Rai, Thailand	38 C2	19 52N	99 50
Muang Khong, Laos	38 E5	14 5S	105 52
Muang Khong, Laos	38 E5	14 7N	105 51
Muang Lamphun, Thailand	38 C2	18 40N	99 2
Muar, Malaysia	39 L4	2 3N	102 34
Muarabungo, Indonesia	36 E2	1 28S	102 52
Muaraenim, Indonesia	36 E2	3 40S	103 50
Muarajuloi, Indonesia	36 E4	0 12S	114 3
Muarakaman, Indonesia	36 E5	0 2S	116 45
Muaratebo, Indonesia	36 E2	1 30S	102 26
Muaratembesi, Indonesia	36 E2	1 42S	103 8
Muaratewe, Indonesia	36 E4	0 58S	114 52
Mubarakpur, India	43 F10	26 6N	83 18
Mubarraz = Al Mubarraz, Si. Arabia	45 E6	25 30N	49 40
Mubende, Uganda	54 B3	0 33N	31 22
Mubi, Nigeria	51 F8	10 18N	13 16
Mubur, Pulau, Indonesia	39 L6	3 20N	106 12
Mucajaí →, Brazil	92 C6	2 25N	60 52W
Muchachos, Roque de los, Canary Is.	22 F2	28 44N	17 52W
Muchinga Mts., Zambia	55 E3	11 30S	31 30
Muck, U.K.	12 E2	56 50N	6 15W
Muckadilla, Australia	63 D4	26 35S	148 23
Mucuri, Brazil	93 G11	18 0S	39 36W
Mucusso, Angola	56 B3	18 1S	21 25
Muda, Canary Is.	22 F6	28 34N	13 57
Mudanjiang, China	35 B15	44 38N	129 30
Mudanya, Turkey	21 D13	40 25N	28 50
Muddy Cr. →, U.S.A.	83 H8	38 24N	110 42
Mudgee, Australia	63 E4	32 32S	149 31
Mudjatik →, Canada	73 B7	56 1N	107 36
Muecate, Mozam.	55 E4	14 55S	39 40
Mueda, Mozam.	55 E4	11 36S	39 28
Mueller Ra., Australia	60 C4	18 18S	126 46
Muende, Mozam.	55 E3	14 28S	33 0
Muerto, Mar, Mexico	87 D6	16 10N	94 10
Mufulira, Zambia	55 E2	12 32S	28 15
Mufumbiro Range, Africa	54 C2	1 25S	29 30
Mughal Sarai, India	43 G10	25 18N	83 7
Mughayrāʾ, Si. Arabia	44 D3	29 17N	37 41
Mugi, Japan	31 H7	33 40N	134 25
Mugila, Mts., Dem. Rep. of the Congo	54 D2	7 0S	28 50
Muğla, Turkey	21 F13	37 15N	28 22
Mugu, Nepal	43 E10	29 45N	82 30
Muhammad, Râs, Egypt	44 E2	27 44N	34 16
Muhammad Qol, Sudan	51 D13	20 53N	37 9
Muhammadi, India	43 F10	26 43N	80 8
Muhesi →, Tanzania	54 D4	7 0S	35 20
Mühlhausen, Germany	16 C6	51 12N	10 27
Mühlig Hofmann fjell, Antarctica	5 D3	72 30S	0 E
Muhos, Finland	8 D22	64 47N	25 59
Muhu, Estonia	9 G20	58 36N	23 11
Muhutwe, Tanzania	54 C3	1 35S	31 45
Muine Bheag, Ireland	13 D5	52 42N	6 58
Muir, L., Australia	61 F2	34 30S	116 40
Mukacheve, Ukraine	17 D12	48 27N	22 45
Mukachevo = Mukacheve, Ukraine	17 D12	48 27N	22 45
Mukah, Malaysia	36 D4	2 55N	112 5
Mukandwara, India	42 G6	24 49N	75 59
Mukdahan, Thailand	38 D5	16 32N	104 43
Mukden = Shenyang, China	35 D12	41 48N	123 27
Mukerian, India	42 D6	31 57N	75 37
Mukhtuya = Lensk, Russia	27 C12	60 48N	114 55
Mukinbudin, Australia	61 F2	30 55S	118 5
Mukishi, Dem. Rep. of the Congo	55 D1	8 30S	24 44
Mukomuko, Indonesia	36 E2	2 30S	101 10
Mukomwenze, Dem. Rep. of the Congo	54 D2	6 49S	27 15
Muktsar, India	42 D6	30 30N	74 30
Mukur = Moqor, Afghan.	42 C2	32 50N	67 42
Mukutawa →, Canada	73 C9	53 10N	97 24
Mukwela, Zambia	55 F2	17 0S	26 40
Mula, Spain	19 C5	38 3N	1 33
Mula →, Pakistan	42 F2	27 57N	67 36
Mulange, Dem. Rep. of the Congo	54 C2	3 40S	27 10
Mulanje, Malawi	55 F4	16 2S	35 33
Mulchén, Chile	94 D1	37 45S	72 20
Mulde →, Germany	16 C7	51 53N	12 15
Mule Creek Junction, U.S.A.	80 D2	43 19N	104 8
Muleba, Tanzania	54 C3	1 50S	31 37
Mulejé, Mexico	86 B2	26 53N	112 1
Muleshoe, U.S.A.	81 H3	34 13N	102 43
Mulgrave, Canada	71 C7	45 38N	61 31
Mulhacén, Spain	19 D4	37 4N	3 20
Mülheim, Germany	16 C4	51 25N	6 54

Mulhouse, France 18 C7 47 40N 7 20 E
Muling, China 35 B16 44 35N 130 10 E
Mull, U.K. 12 E3 56 25N 5 56W
Mull, Sound of, U.K. 12 E3 56 30N 5 50W
Mullaittivu, Sri Lanka 40 Q12 9 15N 80 49 E
Mullen, U.S.A. 80 D4 42 3N 101 1W
Mullens, U.S.A. 76 G5 37 35N 81 23W
Muller, Pegunungan, Indonesia 36 D4 0 30N 113 30 E
Mullet Pen., Ireland 13 B1 54 13N 10 2W
Mullewa, Australia 61 E2 28 29S 115 30 E
Mulligan →, Australia 62 D2 25 0S 139 0 E
Mullingar, Ireland 13 C4 53 31N 7 21W
Mullins, U.S.A. 77 H6 34 12N 79 15W
Mullumbimby, Australia 63 D5 28 30S 153 30 E
Mulobezi, Zambia 55 F2 16 45S 25 7 E
Mulroy B., Ireland 13 A4 55 15N 7 46W
Multan, Pakistan 42 D4 30 15N 71 36 E
Mulumbe, Mts., Dem. Rep. of the Congo 55 D2 8 40S 27 30 E
Mulungushi Dam, Zambia 55 E2 14 48S 28 48 E
Mulvane, U.S.A. 81 G6 37 29N 97 15W
Mumbai, India 40 K8 18 55N 72 50 E
Mumbwa, Zambia 55 F2 15 0S 27 0 E
Mun →, Thailand 38 E5 15 19N 105 30 E
Muna, Indonesia 37 F6 5 0S 122 30 E
Munabao, India 42 G4 25 45N 70 17 E
Munamagi, Estonia 9 H22 57 43N 27 4 E
München, Germany 16 D6 48 8N 11 34 E
München-Gladbach = Mönchengladbach, Germany 16 C4 51 11N 6 27 E
Muncho Lake, Canada 72 B3 59 0N 125 50W
Munch'ŏn, N. Korea 35 E14 39 14N 127 19 E
Muncie, U.S.A. 76 E3 40 12N 85 23W
Muncoonie, L., Australia 62 D2 25 12S 138 40 E
Mundabbera, Australia 63 D5 25 36S 151 18 E
Munday, U.S.A. 81 J5 33 27N 99 38W
Münden, Germany 16 C5 51 25N 9 38 E
Mundiwindi, Australia 60 D3 23 47S 120 9 E
Mundo Novo, Brazil 93 F10 11 50S 40 29W
Mundra, India 42 H3 22 54N 69 48 E
Mundrabilla, Australia 61 F4 31 52S 127 51 E
Mungallala, Australia 63 D4 26 28S 147 34 E
Mungallala Cr. →, Australia 63 D4 28 53S 147 5 E
Mungana, Australia 62 B3 17 8S 144 27 E
Mungaoli, India 42 G8 24 24N 78 7 E
Mungari, Mozam. 55 F3 17 12S 33 30 E
Mungbere, Dem. Rep. of the Congo 54 B2 2 36N 28 28 E
Mungeli, India 43 H9 22 4N 81 41 E
Munger, India 43 G12 25 23N 86 30 E
Munich = München, Germany 16 D6 48 8N 11 34 E
Munising, U.S.A. 76 B2 46 25N 86 40W
Munku-Sardyk, Russia 27 D11 51 45N 100 20 E
Muñoz Gamero, Pen., Chile 96 G2 52 30S 73 5W
Munroe L., Canada 73 B9 59 13N 98 35W
Munsan, S. Korea 35 F14 37 51N 126 48 E
Münster, Germany 16 C4 51 58N 7 37 E
Munster □, Ireland 13 D3 52 18N 8 44W
Muntadgin, Australia 61 F2 31 45S 118 33 E
Muntok, Indonesia 36 E3 2 5S 105 10 E
Munyama, Zambia 55 F2 16 5S 28 31 E
Muong Et, Laos 38 B5 20 49N 104 1 E
Muong Hiem, Laos 38 B4 20 5N 103 22 E
Muong Kau, Laos 38 E5 15 6N 105 47 E
Muong Khao, Laos 38 C4 19 38N 103 32 E
Muong Liep, Laos 38 C3 18 29N 101 40 E
Muong May, Laos 38 E6 14 49N 106 56 E
Muong Nong, Laos 38 D6 16 22N 106 30 E
Muong Oua, Laos 38 C3 18 18N 101 20 E
Muong Phalane, Laos 38 D5 16 39N 105 34 E
Muong Phieng, Laos 38 C3 19 6N 101 32 E
Muong Phine, Laos 38 D6 16 32N 106 2 E
Muong Saiapoun, Laos 38 C3 18 24N 101 31 E
Muong Sen, Vietnam 38 C5 19 24N 104 8 E
Muong Soui, Laos 38 C4 19 33N 102 52 E
Muong Xia, Vietnam 38 B5 20 19N 104 50 E
Muonio, Finland 8 C20 67 57N 23 40 E
Muonionjoki →, Finland 8 C20 67 11N 23 34 E
Muping, China 35 F11 37 22N 121 36 E
Muqdisho, Somali Rep. 46 G4 2 2N 45 25 E
Mur →, Austria 17 E9 46 18N 16 52 E
Murakami, Japan 30 E9 38 14N 139 29 E
Murallón, Cerro, Chile 96 F2 49 48S 73 30W
Muranda, Rwanda 54 C2 1 52S 29 20 E
Murang'a, Kenya 54 C4 0 45S 37 9 E
Murashi, Russia 24 C8 59 30N 49 0 E
Murat, Turkey 25 G7 38 46N 40 0 E
Muratlı, Turkey 21 D12 41 10N 27 29 E
Murayama, Japan 30 E10 38 30N 140 25 E
Murban, U.A.E. 45 F7 23 50N 53 45 E
Murchison →, Australia 61 E1 27 45S 114 0 E
Murchison, Mt., Antarctica 5 D11 73 0S 168 0 E
Murchison Falls, Uganda 54 B3 2 15N 31 30 E
Murchison Ra., Australia 62 C1 20 0S 134 10 E
Murchison Rapids, Malawi 55 F3 15 55S 34 35 E
Murcia, Spain 19 D5 38 5N 1 10W
Murcia □, Spain 19 D5 37 50N 1 30W
Murdo, U.S.A. 80 D4 43 53N 100 43W
Murdoch Pt., Australia 62 A3 14 37S 144 55 E
Mureş →, Romania 17 E11 46 15N 20 13 E
Mureşul = Mureş →, Romania 17 E11 46 15N 20 13 E
Murfreesboro, N.C., U.S.A. 77 G7 36 27N 77 6W
Murfreesboro, Tenn., U.S.A. 77 H2 35 51N 86 24W
Murgab = Murghob, Tajikistan 26 F8 38 10N 74 2 E
Murgab →, Turkmenistan 45 B9 38 18N 61 10 E
Murgenella, Australia 60 B5 11 34S 132 56 E
Murgha Kibzai, Pakistan 42 D3 30 44N 69 25 E
Murghob, Tajikistan 26 F8 38 10N 74 2 E
Murgon, Australia 63 D5 26 15S 151 54 E
Muri, India 43 H11 23 22N 85 52 E
Muria, Indonesia 37 G14 6 36S 110 53 E
Muriaé, Brazil 95 A7 21 8S 42 23W
Muriel Mine, Zimbabwe 55 F3 17 14S 30 40 E
Müritz, Germany 16 B7 53 25N 12 42 E
Murka, Kenya 54 C4 3 27S 38 0 E
Murliganj, India 43 G12 25 54N 86 59 E
Murmansk, Russia 24 A5 68 57N 33 10 E
Muro, Spain 22 B10 39 44N 3 3 E
Murom, Russia 24 C7 55 35N 42 3 E
Muroran, Japan 30 C10 42 25N 141 0 E

Muroto, Japan 31 H7 33 18N 134 9 E
Muroto-Misaki, Japan 31 H7 33 15N 134 10 E
Murphy, U.S.A. 82 E5 43 13N 116 33W
Murphys, U.S.A. 84 G6 38 8N 120 28W
Murray, Ky., U.S.A. 77 G1 36 37N 88 19W
Murray, Utah, U.S.A. 82 F8 40 40N 111 53W
Murray →, Australia 63 F2 35 20S 139 22 E
Murray, L., U.S.A. 77 H5 34 3N 81 13W
Murray Bridge, Australia 63 F2 35 6S 139 14 E
Murray Harbour, Canada 71 C7 46 0N 62 28W
Murraysburg, S. Africa 56 E3 31 58S 23 47 E
Murree, Pakistan 42 C5 33 56N 73 28 E
Murrieta, U.S.A. 85 M9 33 33N 117 13W
Murrumbidgee →, Australia 63 E3 34 43S 143 12 E
Murrumburrah, Australia 63 E4 34 32S 148 22 E
Murrurundi, Australia 63 E5 31 42S 150 51 E
Murshidabad, India 43 G13 24 11N 88 19 E
Murtle L., Canada 72 C5 52 8N 119 38W
Murtoa, Australia 63 F3 36 35S 142 28 E
Murungu, Tanzania 54 C3 4 12S 31 10 E
Mururoa, Pac. Oc. 65 K14 21 52S 138 55W
Murwara, India 43 H9 23 46N 80 28 E
Murwillumbah, Australia 63 D5 28 18S 153 27 E
Mürzzuschlag, Austria 16 E8 47 36N 15 41 E
Muş, Turkey 25 G7 38 45N 41 30 E
Mûsa, Gebel, Egypt 44 D2 28 33N 33 59 E
Musa Khel, Pakistan 42 D3 30 59N 69 52 E
Mûsá Qal'eh, Afghan. 40 C4 32 20N 64 50 E
Musaffargarh, Pakistan 40 D7 30 10N 71 10 E
Musafirkhana, India 43 F9 26 22N 81 48 E
Musala, Bulgaria 21 C10 42 13N 23 37 E
Musala, Indonesia 36 D1 1 41N 98 28 E
Musan, N. Korea 35 C15 42 12N 129 12 E
Musangu, Dem. Rep. of the Congo 55 E1 10 28S 23 55 E
Musasa, Tanzania 54 C3 3 25S 31 30 E
Musay'īd, Qatar 45 E6 25 0N 51 33 E
Muscat = Masqaṭ, Oman 46 C6 23 37N 58 36 E
Muscat & Oman = Oman ■, Asia 46 C6 23 0N 58 0 E
Muscatine, U.S.A. 80 E9 41 25N 91 3W
Musgrave Harbour, Canada 71 C9 49 27N 53 58W
Musgrave Ranges, Australia 61 E5 26 0S 132 0 E
Mushie, Dem. Rep. of the Congo 52 E3 2 56S 16 55 E
Musi →, Indonesia 36 E2 2 20S 104 56 E
Muskeg →, Canada 72 A4 60 20N 123 20W
Muskegon, U.S.A. 76 D2 43 14N 86 16W
Muskegon →, U.S.A. 76 D2 43 14N 86 21W
Muskegon Heights, U.S.A. 76 D2 43 12N 86 16W
Muskogee, U.S.A. 81 H7 35 45N 95 22W
Muskoka, L., Canada 78 B5 45 0N 79 25W
Muskwa →, Canada 72 B4 58 47N 122 48W
Muslimiyah, Syria 44 B3 36 19N 37 12 E
Musofu, Zambia 55 E2 13 30S 29 0 E
Musoma, Tanzania 54 C3 1 30S 33 48 E
Musquaro, L., Canada 71 B7 50 38N 61 5W
Musquodoboit Harbour, Canada 71 D7 44 50N 63 9W
Musselburgh, U.K. 12 F5 55 57N 3 2W
Musselshell →, U.S.A. 82 C10 47 21N 107 57W
Mussoorie, India 42 D8 30 27N 78 6 E
Mussuco, Angola 56 B2 17 2S 19 3 E
Mustafakemalpaşa, Turkey 21 D13 40 2N 28 24 E
Mustang, Nepal 43 E10 29 10N 83 55 E
Musters, L., Argentina 96 F3 45 20S 69 25W
Musudan, N. Korea 35 D15 40 50N 129 43 E
Muswellbrook, Australia 63 E5 32 16S 150 56 E
Mût, Egypt 51 C11 25 28N 28 58 E
Mut, Turkey 44 B2 36 40N 33 28 E
Mutanda, Mozam. 57 C5 21 0S 33 34 E
Mutanda, Zambia 55 E2 12 24S 26 13 E
Mutare, Zimbabwe 55 F3 18 58S 32 38 E
Muting, Indonesia 37 F10 7 23S 140 20 E
Mutoray, Russia 27 C11 60 56N 101 0 E
Mutshatsha, Dem. Rep. of the Congo 55 E1 10 35S 24 20 E
Mutsu, Japan 30 D10 41 5N 140 55 E
Mutsu-Wan, Japan 30 D10 41 5N 140 55 E
Muttaburra, Australia 62 C3 22 38S 144 29 E
Mutton I., Ireland 13 D2 52 49N 9 32W
Mutuáli, Mozam. 55 E4 14 55S 37 0 E
Muweilih, Egypt 47 E3 30 42N 34 19 E
Muy Muy, Nic. 88 D2 12 39N 85 36W
Muyinga, Burundi 54 C3 3 14S 30 33 E
Muynak, Uzbekistan 26 E6 43 44N 59 10 E
Muzaffarabad, Pakistan 43 B5 34 25N 73 30 E
Muzaffargarh, Pakistan 42 D4 30 5N 71 14 E
Muzaffarnagar, India 42 E7 29 26N 77 40 E
Muzaffarpur, India 43 F11 26 7N 85 23 E
Muzhi, Russia 24 A11 65 25N 64 40 E
Mvuma, Zimbabwe 55 F3 19 16S 30 30 E
Mvurwi, Zimbabwe 55 F3 17 0S 30 57 E
Mwadui, Tanzania 54 C3 3 26S 33 32 E
Mwambo, Tanzania 55 E5 10 30S 40 22 E
Mwandi, Zambia 55 F1 17 30S 24 51 E
Mwanza, Dem. Rep. of the Congo 54 D2 7 55S 26 43 E
Mwanza, Tanzania 54 C3 2 30S 32 58 E
Mwanza, Zambia 55 F1 16 58S 24 28 E
Mwanza □, Tanzania 54 C3 2 0S 33 0 E
Mwaya, Tanzania 55 D3 9 32S 33 55 E
Mweelrea, Ireland 13 C2 53 39N 9 49W
Mweka, Dem. Rep. of the Congo 52 E4 4 50S 21 34 E
Mwene-Ditu, Dem. Rep. of the Congo 52 F4 6 35S 22 27 E
Mwenezi, Zimbabwe 55 G3 21 15S 30 48 E
Mwenezi →, Mozam. 55 G3 22 40S 31 50 E
Mwenga, Dem. Rep. of the Congo 54 C2 3 1S 28 28 E
Mweru, L., Zambia 55 D2 9 0S 28 40 E
Mweza Range, Zimbabwe 55 G3 21 0S 30 0 E
Mwilambwe, Dem. Rep. of the Congo 54 D2 8 7S 25 5 E
Mwimbi, Tanzania 55 D3 8 38S 31 39 E
Mwinilunga, Zambia 55 E1 11 43S 24 25 E
My Tho, Vietnam 39 G6 10 29N 106 23 E
Myajlar, India 42 F4 26 15N 70 20 E
Myanaung, Burma 41 K19 18 18N 95 22 E
Myanmar = Burma ■, Asia 41 J20 21 0N 96 30 E
Myaungmya, Burma 41 L19 16 30N 94 40 E
Mycenæ, Greece 21 F10 37 39N 22 52 E
Myeik Kyunzu, Burma 39 G1 11 30N 97 30 E

Myers Chuck, U.S.A. 72 B2 55 44N 132 11W
Myerstown, U.S.A. 79 F8 40 22N 76 19W
Myingyan, Burma 41 J19 21 30N 95 20 E
Myitkyina, Burma 41 G20 25 24N 97 26 E
Mykines, Færoe Is. 8 E9 62 7N 7 35W
Mykolayiv, Ukraine 25 E5 46 58N 32 0 E
Mymensingh, Bangla. 41 G17 24 45N 90 24 E
Mynydd Du, U.K. 11 F4 51 52N 3 50W
Mýrdalsjökull, Iceland 8 E4 63 40N 19 6W
Myrtle Beach, U.S.A. 77 J6 33 42N 78 53W
Myrtle Creek, U.S.A. 82 E2 43 1N 123 17W
Myrtle Point, U.S.A. 82 E1 43 4N 124 8W
Mysia, Turkey 21 E12 39 50N 27 0 E
Mysore = Karnataka □, India 40 N10 13 15N 77 0 E
Mysore, India 40 N10 12 17N 76 41 E
Mystic, U.S.A. 79 E13 41 21N 71 58W
Myszków, Poland 17 C10 50 45N 19 22 E
Mytishchi, Russia 24 C6 55 50N 37 50 E
Mývatn, Iceland 8 D5 65 36N 17 0W
Mzimba, Malawi 55 E3 11 55S 33 39 E
Mzimkulu →, S. Africa 57 E5 30 44S 30 28 E
Mzimvubu →, S. Africa 57 E4 31 38S 29 33 E
Mzuzu, Malawi 55 E3 11 30S 33 55 E

N

Na Hearadh = Harris, U.K. 12 D2 57 50N 6 55W
Na Noi, Thailand 38 C3 18 19N 100 43 E
Na Phao, Laos 38 D5 17 35N 105 44 E
Na San, Vietnam 38 B5 21 12N 104 2 E
Naab →, Germany 16 D6 49 1N 12 2 E
Naantali, Finland 9 F19 60 29N 22 2 E
Naas, Ireland 13 C5 53 12N 6 40W
Nababiep, S. Africa 56 D2 29 36S 17 46 E
Nabadwip = Navadwip, India 43 H13 23 34N 88 20 E
Nabari, Japan 31 G8 34 37N 136 5 E
Nabawa, Australia 61 E1 28 30S 114 48 E
Nabberu, L., Australia 61 E3 25 50S 120 30 E
Naberezhnyye Chelny, Russia 24 C9 55 42N 52 19 E
Nabeul, Tunisia 51 A8 36 30N 10 44 E
Nabha, India 42 D7 30 26N 76 14 E
Nabīd, Iran 45 D8 29 40N 57 38 E
Nabire, Indonesia 37 E9 3 15S 135 26 E
Nabisar, Pakistan 42 G3 25 8N 69 40 E
Nabisipi →, Canada 71 B7 50 14N 62 13W
Nabiswera, Uganda 54 B3 1 27N 32 15 E
Nablus = Nābulus, West Bank 47 C4 32 14N 35 15 E
Naboomspruit, S. Africa 57 C4 24 32S 28 40 E
Nābulus, West Bank 47 C4 32 14N 35 15 E
Nacala, Mozam. 55 E5 14 31S 40 34 E
Nacala-Velha, Mozam. 55 E5 14 32S 40 34 E
Nacaome, Honduras 88 D2 13 31N 87 30W
Nacaroa, Mozam. 55 E4 14 22S 39 56 E
Naches, U.S.A. 82 C3 46 44N 120 42W
Naches →, U.S.A. 84 D6 46 38N 120 31W
Nachicapau, L., Canada 71 A6 56 40N 68 5W
Nachingwea, Tanzania 55 E4 10 23S 38 49 E
Nachna, India 42 F4 27 34N 71 41 E
Nacimiento L., U.S.A. 84 K6 35 46N 120 53W
Naco, Mexico 86 A3 31 20N 109 56W
Nacogdoches, U.S.A. 81 K7 31 36N 94 39W
Nácori Chico, Mexico 86 B3 29 39N 109 1W
Nacozari, Mexico 86 A3 30 24N 109 39W
Nadiad, India 42 H5 22 41N 72 56 E
Nador, Morocco 50 B5 35 14N 2 58W
Nadur, Malta 23 C1 36 2N 14 17 E
Nadūshan, Iran 45 C7 32 2N 53 35 E
Nadvirna, Ukraine 17 D13 48 37N 24 30 E
Nadvoitsy, Russia 24 B5 63 52N 34 14 E
Nadvornaya = Nadvirna, Ukraine 17 D13 48 37N 24 30 E
Nadym, Russia 26 C8 65 35N 72 42 E
Nadym →, Russia 26 C8 66 12N 72 0 E
Nærbø, Norway 9 G11 58 40N 5 39 E
Næstved, Denmark 9 J14 55 13N 11 44 E
Naft-e Safīd, Iran 45 D6 31 40N 49 17 E
Naftshahr, Iran 44 C5 34 0N 45 30 E
Nafud Desert = An Nafūd, Si. Arabia 44 D4 28 15N 41 0 E
Naga, Phil. 37 B6 13 38N 123 15 E
Nagahama, Japan 31 G8 34 37N 136 16 E
Nagai, Japan 30 E10 38 6N 140 2 E
Nagaland □, India 41 G19 26 0N 94 30 E
Nagano, Japan 31 F9 36 40N 138 10 E
Nagano □, Japan 31 F9 36 15N 138 0 E
Nagaoka, Japan 31 F9 37 27N 138 51 E
Nagappattinam, India 40 P11 10 46N 79 51 E
Nagar →, Bangla. 43 G13 24 27N 89 12 E
Nagar Parkar, Pakistan 42 G4 24 28N 70 46 E
Nagasaki, Japan 31 H4 32 47N 129 50 E
Nagasaki □, Japan 31 H4 32 50N 129 40 E
Nagato, Japan 31 G5 34 19N 131 5 E
Nagaur, India 42 F5 27 15N 73 45 E
Nagda, India 42 H6 23 27N 75 25 E
Nagercoil, India 40 Q10 8 12N 77 26 E
Nagina, India 43 E8 29 30N 78 30 E
Nagīneh, India 45 C8 34 20N 57 15 E
Nagir, Pakistan 43 A6 36 12N 74 42 E
Nagod, India 43 G9 24 34N 80 36 E
Nagoorin, Australia 62 C5 24 17S 151 15 E
Nagorno-Karabakh, Azerbaijan 25 F8 39 55N 46 45 E
Nagornyy, Russia 27 D13 55 58N 124 57 E
Nagoya, Japan 31 G8 35 10N 136 50 E
Nagpur, India 40 J11 21 8N 79 10 E
Nagua, Dom. Rep. 89 C6 19 23N 69 50W
Nagykanizsa, Hungary 17 E9 46 28N 17 0 E
Nagykőrös, Hungary 17 E10 47 5N 19 48 E
Naha, Japan 31 L3 26 13N 127 42 E
Nahan, India 42 D7 30 33N 77 18 E
Nahanni Butte, Canada 72 A4 61 2N 123 31W
Nahanni Nat. Park, Canada 72 A4 61 15N 125 0W
Nahargarh, Mad. P., India 42 G6 24 10N 75 14 E
Nahargarh, Raj., India 42 G7 24 55N 76 50 E
Nahariyya, Israel 44 C2 33 1N 35 5 E
Nahāvand, Iran 45 C6 34 10N 48 22 E
Naicá, Mexico 86 B3 27 53N 105 31W
Naicam, Canada 73 C8 52 30N 104 30W

Naikoon Prov. Park, Canada 72 C2 53 55N 131 55W
Naimisharanya, India 43 F9 27 21N 80 30 E
Nain, Canada 71 A7 56 34N 61 40W
Nā'īn, Iran 45 C7 32 54N 53 0 E
Naini Tal, India 43 E8 29 30N 79 30 E
Nainpur, India 40 H12 22 30N 80 10 E
Nainwa, India 42 G6 25 46N 75 51 E
Nairn, U.K. 12 D5 57 35N 3 53W
Nairobi, Kenya 54 C4 1 17S 36 48 E
Naissaar, Estonia 9 G21 59 34N 24 29 E
Naivasha, Kenya 54 C4 0 40S 36 30 E
Naivasha, L., Kenya 54 C4 0 48S 36 20 E
Najafābād, Iran 45 C6 32 40N 51 15 E
Najd, Si. Arabia 46 B3 26 30N 42 0 E
Najibabad, India 42 E8 29 40N 78 20 E
Najin, N. Korea 35 C16 42 12N 130 15 E
Najmah, Si. Arabia 45 E6 26 42N 50 6 E
Naju, S. Korea 35 G14 35 3N 126 43 E
Nakadōri-Shima, Japan 31 H4 32 57N 129 4 E
Nakalagba, Dem. Rep. of the Congo 54 B2 2 50N 27 58 E
Nakaminato, Japan 31 F10 36 21N 140 36 E
Nakamura, Japan 31 H6 32 59N 132 56 E
Nakano, Japan 31 F9 36 45N 138 22 E
Nakano-Shima, Japan 31 K4 29 51N 129 52 E
Nakashibetsu, Japan 30 C12 43 33N 144 59 E
Nakfa, Eritrea 46 D2 16 40N 38 32 E
Nakhfar al Buşayyah, Iraq 44 D5 30 0N 46 10 E
Nakhichevan = Naxçivan, Azerbaijan 25 G8 39 12N 45 15 E
Nakhichevan Republic = Naxçivan □, Azerbaijan 25 G8 39 25N 45 26 E
Nakhl, Egypt 47 F2 29 55N 33 43 E
Nakhl-e Taqī, Iran 45 E7 27 28N 52 36 E
Nakhodka, Russia 27 C14 42 53N 132 54 E
Nakhon Nayok, Thailand 38 E3 14 12N 101 13 E
Nakhon Pathom, Thailand 38 F3 13 49N 100 3 E
Nakhon Phanom, Thailand 38 D5 17 23N 104 43 E
Nakhon Ratchasima, Thailand 38 E4 14 59N 102 12 E
Nakhon Sawan, Thailand 38 E3 15 35N 100 10 E
Nakhon Si Thammarat, Thailand 39 H3 8 29N 100 0 E
Nakhon Thai, Thailand 38 D3 17 5N 100 44 E
Nakhtarana, India 42 H3 23 20N 69 15 E
Nakina, Canada 70 B2 50 10N 86 40W
Nakodar, India 42 D6 31 8N 75 31 E
Nakskov, Denmark 9 J14 54 50N 11 8 E
Naktong →, S. Korea 35 G15 35 7N 128 57 E
Nakuru, Kenya 54 C4 0 15S 36 4 E
Nakuru, L., Kenya 54 C4 0 23S 36 5 E
Nakusp, Canada 72 C5 50 20N 117 45W
Nal →, Pakistan 42 F2 27 40N 66 12 E
Nalchik, Russia 25 F7 43 30N 43 33 E
Nalgonda, India 40 L11 17 6N 79 15 E
Nalhati, India 43 G12 24 17N 87 52 E
Naliya, India 42 H3 23 16N 68 50 E
Nallamalai Hills, India 40 M11 15 30N 78 50 E
Nam Can, Vietnam 39 H5 8 46N 104 59 E
Nam-ch'on, N. Korea 35 E14 38 15N 126 26 E
Nam Co, China 32 C4 30 30N 90 45 E
Nam Du, Hon, Vietnam 39 H5 9 41N 104 21 E
Nam Ngum Dam, Laos 38 C4 18 35N 102 34 E
Nam-Phan = Cochin China, Vietnam 39 G6 10 30N 106 0 E
Nam Phong, Thailand 38 D4 16 42N 102 52 E
Nam Tok, Thailand 38 E2 14 21N 99 4 E
Namacunde, Angola 56 B2 17 18S 15 50 E
Namacurra, Mozam. 57 B6 17 30S 36 50 E
Namak, Daryācheh-ye, Iran 45 C7 34 30N 52 0 E
Namak, Kavir-e, Iran 45 C8 34 30N 57 30 E
Namakzār, Daryācheh-ye, Iran 45 C9 34 0N 60 30 E
Namaland, Namibia 56 C2 26 0S 17 0 E
Namangan, Uzbekistan 26 E8 41 0N 71 40 E
Namapa, Mozam. 55 E4 13 43S 39 50 E
Namaqualand, S. Africa 56 E2 30 0S 17 25 E
Namasagali, Uganda 54 B3 1 2N 33 0 E
Namber, Indonesia 37 E8 1 2S 134 49 E
Nambour, Australia 63 D5 26 32S 152 58 E
Nambucca Heads, Australia 63 E5 30 37S 153 0 E
Namcha Barwa, China 32 D4 29 40N 95 10 E
Namche Bazar, Nepal 43 F12 27 51N 86 47 E
Namchŏnjŏm = Nam-ch'on, N. Korea 35 E14 38 15N 126 26 E
Namecunda, Mozam. 55 E4 14 54S 37 37 E
Nameponda, Mozam. 55 F4 15 50S 39 50 E
Nametil, Mozam. 55 F4 15 40S 39 21 E
Namew L., Canada 73 C8 54 14N 101 56W
Namgia, India 43 D8 31 48N 78 40 E
Namib Desert = Namibwoestyn, Namibia 56 C2 22 30S 15 0 E
Namibe, Angola 53 H2 15 7S 12 11 E
Namibe □, Angola 56 B1 16 35S 12 30 E
Namibia ■, Africa 56 C2 22 0S 18 9 E
Namibwoestyn, Namibia 56 C2 22 30S 15 0 E
Namlea, Indonesia 37 E7 3 18S 127 5 E
Namoi →, Australia 63 E4 30 12S 149 30 E
Nampa, U.S.A. 82 E5 43 34N 116 34W
Nampo, N. Korea 35 E13 38 52N 125 10 E
Nampō-Shotō, Japan 31 J10 32 0N 140 0 E
Nampula, Mozam. 55 F4 15 6S 39 15 E
Namrole, Indonesia 37 E7 3 46S 126 46 E
Namse Shankou, China 41 E13 30 0N 82 25 E
Namsen →, Norway 8 D14 64 28N 11 37 E
Namsos, Norway 8 D14 64 29N 11 30 E
Namtsy, Russia 27 C13 62 43N 129 37 E
Namtu, Burma 41 H20 23 5N 97 28 E
Namtumbo, Tanzania 55 E4 10 30S 36 4 E
Namur, Canada 72 C4 51 52N 121 0W
Namur, Belgium 15 D4 50 27N 4 52 E
Namur □, Belgium 15 D4 50 17N 5 0 E
Namutoni, Namibia 56 B2 18 49S 16 55 E
Namwala, Zambia 55 F2 15 44S 26 30 E
Namwŏn, S. Korea 35 G14 35 23N 127 23 E
Nan, Thailand 38 C3 18 48N 100 46 E
Nan-ch'ang = Nanchang, China 33 D6 28 42N 115 55 E
Nanaimo, Canada 72 D4 49 10N 124 0W
Nanam, N. Korea 35 D15 41 44N 129 40 E
Nanango, Australia 63 D5 26 40S 152 0 E
Nanao, Japan 31 F8 37 0N 137 0 E
Nanchang, China 33 D6 28 42N 115 55 E
Nanching = Nanjing, China 33 C6 32 2N 118 47 E

Nanchong, China	32 C5	30 43N 106 2 E
Nancy, France	18 B7	48 42N 6 12 E
Nanda Devi, India	43 D8	30 23N 79 59 E
Nanda Kot, India	43 D9	30 17N 80 5 E
Nandan, Japan	31 G7	34 10N 134 42 E
Nanded, India	40 K10	19 10N 77 20 E
Nandewar Ra., Australia	63 E5	30 15S 150 35 E
Nandi, Fiji	59 C7	17 42S 177 20 E
Nandigram, India	43 H12	22 1N 87 58 E
Nandurbar, India	40 J9	21 20N 74 15 E
Nandyal, India	40 M11	15 30N 78 30 E
Nanga-Eboko, Cameroon	52 D2	4 41N 12 22 E
Nanga Parbat, Pakistan	43 B6	35 10N 74 35 E
Nangade, Mozam.	55 E4	11 5S 39 36 E
Nangapinoh, Indonesia	36 E4	0 20S 111 44 E
Nangarhār □, Afghan.	40 B7	34 20N 70 0 E
Nangatayap, Indonesia	36 E4	1 32S 110 34 E
Nangeya Mts., Uganda	54 B3	3 30N 33 30 E
Nangong, China	34 F8	37 23N 115 22 E
Nanhuang, China	35 F11	36 58N 121 48 E
Nanjeko, Zambia	55 F1	15 31S 23 30 E
Nanjing, China	33 C6	32 2N 118 47 E
Nanjirinji, Tanzania	55 D4	9 41S 39 5 E
Nankana Sahib, Pakistan	42 D5	31 27N 73 38 E
Nanking = Nanjing, China	33 C6	32 2N 118 47 E
Nankoku, Japan	31 H6	33 39N 133 44 E
Nanning, China	32 D5	22 48N 108 20 E
Nannup, Australia	61 F2	33 59S 115 48 E
Nanpara, India	43 F9	27 52N 81 33 E
Nanpi, China	34 E9	38 2N 116 45 E
Nanping, China	33 D6	26 38N 118 10 E
Nanripe, Mozam.	55 E4	13 52S 38 52 E
Nansei-Shotō = Ryūkyū-rettō, Japan	31 M3	26 0N 126 0 E
Nansen Sd., Canada	4 A3	81 0N 91 0W
Nanshan I., S. China Sea	36 B5	10 45N 115 49 E
Nansio, Tanzania	54 C3	2 3S 33 4 E
Nantes, France	18 C3	47 12N 1 33W
Nanticoke, U.S.A.	79 E8	41 12N 76 0W
Nanton, Canada	72 C6	50 21N 113 46W
Nantong, China	33 C7	32 1N 120 52 E
Nantucket I., U.S.A.	76 E10	41 16N 70 5W
Nantwich, U.K.	10 D5	53 4N 2 31W
Nanty Glo, U.S.A.	78 F6	40 28N 78 50W
Nanuque, Brazil	93 G10	17 50S 40 21W
Nanusa, Kepulauan, Indonesia	37 D7	4 45N 127 1 E
Nanutarra Roadhouse, Australia	60 D2	22 32S 115 30 E
Nanyang, China	34 H7	33 11N 112 30 E
Nanyuan, China	34 E9	39 44N 116 22 E
Nanyuki, Kenya	54 B4	0 2N 37 4 E
Nao, C. de la, Spain	19 C6	38 44N 0 14 E
Naococane, L., Canada	71 B5	52 50N 70 45W
Napa, U.S.A.	84 G4	38 18N 122 17W
Napa →, U.S.A.	84 G4	38 10N 122 19W
Napanee, Canada	78 B8	44 15N 77 0W
Napanoch, U.S.A.	79 E10	41 44N 74 22W
Nape, Laos	38 C5	18 18N 105 6 E
Nape Pass = Keo Neua, Deo, Vietnam	38 C5	18 23N 105 10 E
Napier, N.Z.	59 H6	39 30S 176 56 E
Napier Broome B., Australia	60 B4	14 2S 126 37 E
Napier Pen., Australia	62 A2	12 4S 135 43 E
Napierville, Canada	79 A11	45 11N 73 25W
Naples = Nápoli, Italy	20 D6	40 50N 14 15 E
Naples, U.S.A.	77 M5	26 8N 81 48W
Napo →, Peru	92 D4	3 20S 72 40W
Napoleon, N. Dak., U.S.A.	80 B5	46 30N 99 46W
Napoleon, Ohio, U.S.A.	76 E3	41 23N 84 8W
Nápoli, Italy	20 D6	40 50N 14 15 E
Napopo, Dem. Rep. of the Congo	54 B2	4 15N 28 0 E
Naqqāsh, Iran	45 C6	35 40N 49 6 E
Nara, Japan	31 G7	34 40N 135 49 E
Nara, Mali	50 E4	15 10N 7 20W
Nara □, Japan	31 G8	34 30N 136 0 E
Nara Canal, Pakistan	42 G3	24 30N 69 20 E
Nara Visa, U.S.A.	81 H3	35 37N 103 6W
Naracoorte, Australia	63 F3	36 58S 140 45 E
Naradhan, Australia	63 E4	33 34S 146 17 E
Naraini, India	43 G9	25 11N 80 29 E
Narasapur, India	41 L12	16 26N 81 40 E
Narathiwat, Thailand	39 J3	6 30N 101 48 E
Narayanganj, Bangla.	41 H17	23 40N 90 33 E
Narayanpet, India	40 L10	16 45N 77 30 E
Narbonne, France	18 E5	43 11N 3 0 E
Nardīn, Iran	45 B7	37 3N 55 59 E
Nardò, Italy	21 D8	40 11N 18 2 E
Narembeen, Australia	61 F2	32 7S 118 24 E
Narendranagar, India	42 D8	30 10N 78 18 E
Nares Str., Arctic	66 A13	80 0N 70 0W
Naretha, Australia	61 F3	31 0S 124 45 E
Narew →, Poland	17 B11	52 26N 20 41 E
Nari →, Pakistan	42 F2	29 40N 67 40 E
Narin, Afghan.	40 A6	36 5N 69 0 E
Narindra, Helodranon' i, Madag.	57 A8	14 55S 47 30 E
Narita, Japan	31 G10	35 47N 140 19 E
Narmada →, India	42 J5	21 38N 72 36 E
Narmland, Sweden	9 F15	60 0N 13 30 E
Narnaul, India	42 E7	28 5N 76 11 E
Narodnaya, Russia	24 A10	65 5N 59 58 E
Narok, Kenya	54 C4	1 55S 35 52 E
Narooma, Australia	63 F5	36 14S 150 4 E
Narowal, Pakistan	42 C6	32 6N 74 52 E
Narrabri, Australia	63 E4	30 19S 149 46 E
Narran →, Australia	63 D4	28 37S 148 12 E
Narrandera, Australia	63 E4	34 42S 146 31 E
Narrogin, Australia	61 F2	32 58S 117 14 E
Narromine, Australia	63 E4	32 12S 148 12 E
Narrow Hills Prov. Park, Canada	73 C8	54 0N 104 37W
Narsimhapur, India	43 H8	22 54N 79 10 E
Narsinghgarh, India	42 H7	23 45N 76 40 E
Naruto, Japan	31 G7	34 11N 134 37 E
Narva, Estonia	24 C4	59 23N 28 12 E
Narva →, Russia	9 G22	59 27N 28 2 E
Narvik, Norway	8 B17	68 28N 17 26 E
Narwana, India	42 E7	29 39N 76 6 E
Naryan-Mar, Russia	24 A9	67 42N 53 12 E
Narym, Russia	26 D9	59 0N 81 30 E
Naryn, Kyrgyzstan	26 E8	41 26N 75 58 E
Nasa, Norway	8 C16	66 29N 15 23 E
Naseby, N.Z.	59 L3	45 1S 170 10 E
Naselle, U.S.A.	84 D3	46 22N 123 49W

Naser, Buheirat en, Egypt	51 D12	23 0N 32 30 E
Nashua, Mont., U.S.A.	82 B10	48 8N 106 22W
Nashua, N.H., U.S.A.	79 D13	42 45N 71 28W
Nashville, Ark., U.S.A.	81 J8	33 57N 93 51W
Nashville, Ga., U.S.A.	77 K4	31 12N 83 15W
Nashville, Tenn., U.S.A.	77 G2	36 10N 86 47W
Nasik, India	40 K8	19 58N 73 50 E
Nasirabad, India	42 F6	26 15N 74 45 E
Nasirabad, Pakistan	42 E3	28 23N 68 24 E
Naskaupi →, Canada	71 B7	53 47N 60 51W
Naşrābād, Iran	45 C6	34 8N 51 26 E
Naşrīān-e Pā'īn, Iran	44 C5	32 52N 46 52 E
Nass →, Canada	72 C3	55 0N 129 40W
Nassau, Bahamas	88 A4	25 5N 77 20W
Nassau, U.S.A.	79 D11	42 31N 73 37W
Nassau, B., Chile	96 H3	55 20S 68 0W
Nasser, L. = Naser, Buheirat en, Egypt	51 D12	23 0N 32 30 E
Nasser City = Kôm Ombo, Egypt	51 D12	24 25N 32 52 E
Nässjö, Sweden	9 H16	57 39N 14 42 E
Nastapoka →, Canada	70 A4	56 55N 76 33W
Nastapoka, Is., Canada	70 A4	56 55N 76 50W
Nata, Botswana	56 C4	20 12S 26 12 E
Natal, Brazil	93 E11	5 47S 35 13W
Natal, Indonesia	36 D1	0 35N 99 7 E
Natal □, S. Africa	53 K6	28 30S 30 30 E
Naţanz, Iran	45 C6	33 30N 51 55 E
Natashquan, Canada	71 B7	50 14N 61 46W
Natashquan →, Canada	71 B7	50 7N 61 50W
Natchez, U.S.A.	81 K9	31 34N 91 24W
Natchitoches, U.S.A.	81 K8	31 46N 93 5W
Nathalia, Australia	63 F4	36 1S 145 13 E
Nathdwara, India	42 G5	24 55N 73 50 E
Nati, Pta., Spain	22 A10	40 3N 3 50 E
Natimuk, Australia	63 F3	36 42S 142 0 E
Nation →, Canada	72 B4	55 30N 123 32W
National City, U.S.A.	85 N9	32 41N 117 6W
Natitingou, Benin	50 F6	10 20N 1 26 E
Natividad, I., Mexico	86 B1	27 50N 115 10W
Natkyizin, Burma	38 E1	14 57N 97 59 E
Natron, L., Tanzania	54 C4	2 20S 36 0 E
Natuna Besar, Kepulauan, Indonesia	39 L7	4 0N 108 15 E
Natuna Is. = Natuna Besar, Kepulauan, Indonesia	39 L7	4 0N 108 15 E
Natuna Selatan, Kepulauan, Indonesia	39 L7	2 45N 109 0 E
Natural Bridge, U.S.A.	79 B9	44 5N 75 30W
Naturaliste, C., Australia	62 G4	40 50S 148 15 E
Nau Qala, Afghan.	42 B3	34 5N 68 5 E
Naugatuck, U.S.A.	79 E11	41 30N 73 3W
Naumburg, Germany	16 C6	51 9N 11 47 E
Nā'ūr at Tunayb, Jordan	47 D4	31 48N 35 57 E
Nauru ■, Pac. Oc.	64 H8	1 0S 166 0 E
Naushahra = Nowshera, Pakistan	40 C8	34 0N 72 0 E
Naushahro, Pakistan	42 F3	26 50N 68 7 E
Naushon I., U.S.A.	79 E14	41 29N 70 45W
Nauta, Peru	92 D4	4 31S 73 35W
Nautanwa, India	41 F13	27 20N 83 25 E
Nautla, Mexico	87 C5	20 20N 96 50W
Nava, Mexico	86 B4	28 25N 100 46W
Navadwip, India	43 H13	23 34N 88 20 E
Navahrudak, Belarus	17 B13	53 40N 25 50 E
Navajo Reservoir, U.S.A.	83 H10	36 48N 107 36W
Navalmoral de la Mata, Spain	19 C3	39 52N 5 33W
Navan = An Uaimh, Ireland	13 C5	53 39N 6 41W
Navarino, I., Chile	96 H3	55 0S 67 40W
Navarra □, Spain	19 A5	42 40N 1 40W
Navarre, U.S.A.	78 F3	40 43N 81 31W
Navarro →, U.S.A.	84 F3	39 11N 123 45W
Navasota, U.S.A.	81 K6	30 23N 96 5W
Navassa I., W. Indies	89 C5	18 30N 75 0W
Naver →, U.K.	12 C4	58 32N 4 14W
Navibandar, India	42 J3	21 26N 69 48 E
Navidad, Chile	94 C1	33 57S 71 50W
Naviraí, Brazil	95 A5	23 8S 54 13W
Navlakhi, India	42 H4	22 58N 70 28 E
Năvodari, Romania	17 F15	44 19N 28 36 E
Navoi = Nawoiy, Uzbekistan	26 E7	40 9N 65 22 E
Navojoa, Mexico	86 B3	27 0N 109 30W
Navolato, Mexico	86 C3	24 47N 107 42W
Návpaktos, Greece	21 E9	38 24N 21 50 E
Návplion, Greece	21 F10	37 33N 22 50 E
Navsari, India	40 J8	20 57N 72 59 E
Nawa Kot, Pakistan	42 E4	28 21N 71 24 E
Nawab Khan, Pakistan	42 D3	30 17N 69 12 E
Nawabganj, Ut. P., India	43 F9	26 56N 81 14 E
Nawabganj, Ut. P., India	43 E8	28 32N 79 40 E
Nawabshah, Pakistan	42 F3	26 15N 68 25 E
Nawada, India	43 G11	24 50N 85 33 E
Nawakot, Nepal	43 F11	27 55N 85 10 E
Nawalgarh, India	42 F6	27 50N 75 15 E
Nawanshahr, India	43 C6	32 33N 74 48 E
Nawoiy, Uzbekistan	26 E7	40 9N 65 22 E
Naxçıvan, Azerbaijan	25 G8	39 25N 45 26 E
Naxçıvan □, Azerbaijan	25 G8	39 25N 45 26 E
Náxos, Greece	21 F11	37 8N 25 25 E
Nay, Mui, Vietnam	38 B3	12 55N 109 23 E
Nāy Band, Būshehr, Iran	45 E7	27 20N 52 40 E
Nāy Band, Khorāsān, Iran	45 C8	32 20N 57 34 E
Nayakhan, Russia	27 C16	61 56N 159 0 E
Nayarit □, Mexico	86 C4	22 0N 105 0W
Nayoro, Japan	30 B11	44 21N 142 28 E
Nayyāl, W. →, Si. Arabia	44 D3	28 35N 39 4 E
Nazaré, Brazil	93 F11	13 2S 39 0W
Nazaré, Brazil		
Nazareth = Nazerat, Israel	47 C4	32 42N 35 17 E
Nazas, Mexico	86 B4	25 10N 104 6W
Nazas →, Mexico	86 B4	25 35N 103 25W
Nazca, Peru	92 F4	14 50S 74 57W
Naze, The, U.K.	11 F9	51 53N 1 18 E
Nazerat, Israel	47 C4	32 42N 35 17 E
Nāzik, Iran	44 B5	39 1N 45 4 E
Nazilli, Turkey	21 F13	37 55N 28 15 E
Nazir Hat, Bangla.	41 H17	22 35N 91 49 E
Nazko, Canada	72 C4	53 1N 123 37W
Nazko →, Canada	72 C4	53 7N 123 34W
Nazret, Ethiopia	46 F2	8 32N 39 22 E
Nazwá, Oman	46 C6	22 56N 57 32 E
Nchanga, Zambia	55 E2	12 30S 27 49 E
Ncheu, Malawi	55 E3	14 50S 34 47 E
Ndala, Tanzania	54 C3	4 45S 33 15 E

Ndalatando, Angola	52 F2	9 12S 14 48 E
Ndareda, Tanzania	54 C4	4 12S 35 30 E
Ndélé, C.A.R.	52 C4	8 25N 20 36 E
Ndjamena, Chad	51 F8	12 10N 14 59 E
Ndola, Zambia	55 E2	13 0S 28 34 E
Ndoto Mts., Kenya	54 B4	2 0N 37 0 E
Nduguti, Tanzania	54 C3	4 18S 34 41 E
Neagh, Lough, U.K.	13 B5	54 37N 6 25W
Neah Bay, U.S.A.	84 B2	48 22N 124 37W
Neale, L., Australia	60 D5	24 15S 130 0 E
Neápolis, Greece	23 D7	35 15N 25 37 E
Near Is., U.S.A.	68 C1	52 30N 174 0 E
Neath, U.K.	11 F4	51 39N 3 48W
Neath Port Talbot □, U.K.	11 F4	51 42N 3 45W
Nebine Cr. →, Australia	63 D4	29 27S 146 56 E
Nebitdag, Turkmenistan	25 G9	39 30N 54 22 E
Nebo, Australia	62 C4	21 42S 148 42 E
Nebraska □, U.S.A.	80 E5	41 30N 99 30W
Nebraska City, U.S.A.	80 E7	40 41N 95 52W
Nébrodi, Monti, Italy	20 F6	37 54N 14 35 E
Necedah, U.S.A.	80 C9	44 2N 90 4W
Nechako →, Canada	72 C4	53 30N 122 44W
Neches →, U.S.A.	81 L8	29 58N 93 51W
Neckar →, Germany	16 D5	49 27N 8 29 E
Necochea, Argentina	94 D4	38 30S 58 50W
Needles, Canada	72 D5	49 53N 118 7W
Needles, U.S.A.	85 L12	34 51N 114 37W
Needles, The, U.K.	11 G6	50 39N 1 35W
Neembucú □, Paraguay	94 B4	27 0S 58 0W
Neemuch = Nimach, India	42 G6	24 30N 74 56 E
Neenah, U.S.A.	76 C1	44 11N 88 28W
Neepawa, Canada	73 C9	50 15N 99 30W
Neftçala, Azerbaijan	25 G8	39 19N 49 12 E
Neftekumsk, Russia	25 F7	44 46N 44 50 E
Nefyn, U.K.	10 E3	52 56N 4 31W
Negapatam = Nagappattinam, India	40 P11	10 46N 79 51 E
Negaunee, U.S.A.	76 B2	46 30N 87 36W
Negele, Ethiopia	46 F2	5 20N 39 36 E
Negev Desert = Hanegev, Israel	47 E4	30 50N 35 0 E
Negombo, Sri Lanka	40 R11	7 12N 79 50 E
Negotin, Serbia, Yug.	21 B10	44 16N 22 37 E
Negra, Pta., Peru	92 E2	6 6S 81 10W
Negrais, C. = Maudin Sun, Burma	41 M19	16 0N 94 30 E
Negril, Jamaica	88 C4	18 22N 78 20W
Negro →, Argentina	96 E4	41 2S 62 47W
Negro →, Brazil	92 D7	3 0S 60 0W
Negro →, Uruguay	95 C4	33 24S 58 22W
Negros, Phil.	37 C6	9 30N 122 40 E
Neguac, Canada	71 C6	47 15N 65 5W
Nehalem →, U.S.A.	84 E3	45 40N 123 56W
Nehāvand, Iran	45 C6	35 56N 49 31 E
Nehbandān, Iran	45 D9	31 35N 60 5 E
Nei Monggol Zizhiqu □, China	34 D7	42 0N 112 0 E
Neijiang, China	32 D5	29 35N 104 55 E
Neillsville, U.S.A.	80 C9	44 34N 90 36W
Neilton, U.S.A.	82 C2	47 25N 123 53W
Neiqiu, China	34 F8	37 15N 114 30 E
Neiva, Colombia	92 C3	2 56N 75 18W
Neixiang, China	34 H6	33 10N 111 52 E
Nejanilini L., Canada	73 B9	59 33N 97 48W
Nejd = Najd, Si. Arabia	46 B3	26 30N 42 0 E
Nekā, Iran	45 B7	36 39N 53 19 E
Nekemte, Ethiopia	46 F2	9 4N 36 30 E
Nekso, Denmark	9 J16	55 4N 15 8 E
Nelia, Australia	62 C3	20 39S 142 12 E
Neligh, U.S.A.	80 D5	42 8N 98 2W
Nelkan, Russia	27 D14	57 40N 136 4 E
Nellore, India	40 M11	14 27N 79 59 E
Nelson, Canada	72 D5	49 30N 117 20W
Nelson, N.Z.	59 J4	41 18S 173 16 E
Nelson, U.K.	10 D5	53 50N 2 13W
Nelson, Ariz., U.S.A.	85 K12	35 31N 113 19W
Nelson, Nev., U.S.A.	85 K12	35 42N 114 50W
Nelson →, Canada	73 C9	54 33N 98 2W
Nelson, C., Australia	63 F3	38 26S 141 32 E
Nelson, Estrecho, Chile	96 G2	51 30S 75 0W
Nelson Bay, Australia	63 E5	32 43S 152 9 E
Nelson Forks, Canada	72 B4	59 30N 124 0W
Nelson House, Canada	73 B9	55 47N 98 51W
Nelson L., Canada	73 B8	55 48N 100 7W
Nelspoort, S. Africa	56 E3	32 7S 23 0 E
Nelspruit, S. Africa	57 D5	25 29S 30 59 E
Néma, Mauritania	50 E4	16 40N 7 15W
Neman, Russia	9 J20	55 25N 22 2 E
Neman →, Lithuania	9 J20	55 25N 21 10 E
Nemeiben L., Canada	73 B7	55 20N 105 20W
Nemiscau, Canada	70 B4	51 18N 76 54W
Nemiscau, L., Canada	70 B4	51 25N 76 40W
Nemunas = Neman →, Lithuania	9 J20	55 25N 21 10 E
Nemuro, Japan	30 C12	43 20N 145 35 E
Nemuro-Kaikyō, Japan	30 C12	43 30N 145 30 E
Nen Jiang →, China	35 B13	45 28N 124 30 E
Nenasi, Malaysia	39 L4	3 9N 103 23 E
Nene →, U.K.	10 E8	52 49N 0 11 E
Nenjiang, China	33 B7	49 10N 125 10 E
Neno, Malawi	55 F3	15 25S 34 40 E
Neodesha, U.S.A.	81 G7	37 25N 95 41W
Neosho, U.S.A.	81 G7	36 52N 94 22W
Neosho →, U.S.A.	81 H7	36 48N 95 18W
Nepal ■, Asia	43 F11	28 0N 84 30 E
Nepalganj, Nepal	43 E9	28 5N 81 40 E
Nepalganj Road, India	43 E9	28 1N 81 41 E
Nephi, U.S.A.	82 G8	39 43N 111 50W
Nephin, Ireland	13 B2	54 1N 9 22W
Neptune, U.S.A.	79 F10	40 13N 74 2W
Nerang, Australia	63 D5	27 58S 153 20 E
Nerchinsk, Russia	27 D12	52 0N 116 39 E
Néret, L., Canada	71 B5	54 45N 70 44W
Neretva →, Croatia	21 C7	43 1N 17 27 E
Neringa, Lithuania	9 J19	55 20N 21 5 E
Neryungri, Russia	27 D13	57 38N 124 28 E
Ness, L., U.K.	12 D4	57 15N 4 32W
Nesodden, U.S.A.	78 B5	48 1N 76 12W
Nesodden, Norway		
Nesterov, Poland	17 C12	50 4N 23 58 E
Nesvizh = Nyasvizh, Belarus	17 B14	53 14N 26 38 E
Netanya, Israel	47 C3	32 20N 34 51 E
Netarhat, India	43 H11	23 29N 84 16 E
Nete →, Belgium	15 C4	51 7N 4 14 E
Netherdale, Australia	62 C4	21 10S 148 33 E

Netherlands ■, Europe	15 C5	52 0N 5 30 E
Netherlands Antilles ■, W. Indies	92 A5	12 15N 69 0W
Netrang, India	42 J5	21 39N 73 21 E
Nettilling L., Canada	69 B12	66 30N 71 0W
Netzahualcoyotl, Presa, Mexico	87 D6	17 10N 93 30W
Neubrandenburg, Germany	16 B7	53 33N 13 15 E
Neuchâtel, Switz.	18 C7	47 0N 6 55 E
Neuchâtel, Lac de, Switz.	18 C7	46 53N 6 50 E
Neufchâteau, Belgium	15 E5	49 50N 5 25 E
Neumünster, Germany	16 A5	54 4N 9 58 E
Neunkirchen, Germany	16 D4	49 7N 7 9 E
Neuquén, Argentina	96 D3	38 55S 68 0W
Neuquén □, Argentina	94 D2	38 0S 69 50W
Neuruppin, Germany	16 B7	52 55N 12 48 E
Neuse →, U.S.A.	77 H7	35 6N 76 29W
Neusiedler See, Austria	17 E9	47 50N 16 47 E
Neustrelitz, Germany	16 B7	53 21N 13 4 E
Neva →, Russia	24 C5	59 50N 30 30 E
Nevada, Iowa, U.S.A.	80 D8	42 1N 93 27W
Nevada, Mo., U.S.A.	81 G7	37 51N 94 22W
Nevada □, U.S.A.	82 G5	39 0N 117 0W
Nevada, Sierra, Spain	19 D4	37 3N 3 15W
Nevada, Sierra, U.S.A.	82 G3	39 0N 120 30W
Nevada City, U.S.A.	84 F6	39 16N 121 1W
Nevado, Cerro, Argentina	94 D2	35 30S 68 32W
Nevel, Russia	24 C4	56 0N 29 55 E
Nevers, France	18 C5	47 0N 3 9 E
Nevertire, Australia	63 E4	31 50S 147 44 E
Neville, Canada	73 D7	49 58N 107 39W
Nevinnomyssk, Russia	25 F7	44 40N 42 0 E
Nevis, W. Indies	89 C7	17 0N 62 30W
Nevşehir, Turkey	44 B2	38 33N 34 40 E
Nevyansk, Russia	24 C11	57 30N 60 13 E
New →, U.S.A.	76 F5	38 10N 81 12W
New Aiyansh, Canada	72 B3	55 12N 129 4W
New Albany, Ind., U.S.A.	76 F3	38 18N 85 49W
New Albany, Miss., U.S.A.	81 H10	34 29N 89 0W
New Albany, Pa., U.S.A.	79 E8	41 36N 76 27W
New Amsterdam, Guyana	92 B7	6 15N 57 36W
New Angledool, Australia	63 D4	29 5S 147 55 E
New Baltimore, U.S.A.	78 D2	42 41N 82 44W
New Bedford, U.S.A.	79 E14	41 38N 70 56W
New Berlin, N.Y., U.S.A.	79 D9	42 37N 75 20W
New Berlin, Pa., U.S.A.	78 F8	40 50N 76 57W
New Bern, U.S.A.	77 H7	35 7N 77 3W
New Bethlehem, U.S.A.	78 F5	41 0N 79 20W
New Bloomfield, U.S.A.	78 F7	40 25N 77 11W
New Boston, U.S.A.	81 J7	33 28N 94 25W
New Braunfels, U.S.A.	81 L5	29 42N 98 8W
New Brighton, N.Z.	59 K4	43 29S 172 43 E
New Brighton, U.S.A.	78 F4	40 42N 80 19W
New Britain, Papua N. G.	64 H7	5 0S 150 20 E
New Britain, U.S.A.	79 E12	41 40N 72 47W
New Brunswick, U.S.A.	79 F10	40 30N 74 27W
New Brunswick □, Canada	71 C6	46 50N 66 30W
New Caledonia ■, Pac. Oc.	64 K8	21 0S 165 0 E
New Castile = Castilla-La Mancha □, Spain	19 C4	39 30N 3 30W
New Castle, Ind., U.S.A.	76 F3	39 55N 85 22W
New Castle, Pa., U.S.A.	78 F4	41 0N 80 21W
New City, U.S.A.	79 E11	41 9N 73 59W
New Concord, U.S.A.	78 G3	39 59N 81 54W
New Cumberland, U.S.A.	78 F4	40 30N 80 36W
New Cuyama, U.S.A.	85 L7	34 57N 119 38W
New Delhi, India	42 E7	28 37N 77 13 E
New Denver, Canada	72 D5	50 0N 117 25W
New Don Pedro Reservoir, U.S.A.	84 H6	37 43N 120 24W
New England, U.S.A.	80 B3	46 32N 102 52W
New England Ra., Australia	63 E5	30 20S 151 45 E
New Forest, U.K.	11 G6	50 53N 1 34W
New Galloway, U.K.	12 F4	55 5N 4 9W
New Glasgow, Canada	71 C7	45 35N 62 36W
New Guinea, Oceania	28 K17	4 0S 136 0 E
New Hamburg, Canada	78 C4	43 23N 80 42W
New Hampshire □, U.S.A.	79 C13	44 0N 71 30W
New Hampton, U.S.A.	80 D8	43 3N 92 19W
New Hanover, S. Africa	57 D5	29 22S 30 31 E
New Hartford, U.S.A.	79 C9	43 4N 75 18W
New Haven, Conn., U.S.A.	79 E12	41 18N 72 55W
New Haven, Mich., U.S.A.	78 D2	42 44N 82 48W
New Hazelton, Canada	72 B3	55 20N 127 30W
New Hebrides = Vanuatu ■, Pac. Oc.	64 J8	15 0S 168 0 E
New Holland, U.S.A.	79 F8	40 6N 76 5W
New Iberia, U.S.A.	81 K9	30 1N 91 49W
New Ireland, Papua N. G.	64 H7	3 0S 151 50 E
New Jersey □, U.S.A.	76 E8	40 0N 74 30W
New Kensington, U.S.A.	78 F5	40 34N 79 46W
New Lexington, U.S.A.	76 F4	39 43N 82 13W
New Liskeard, Canada	70 C4	47 31N 79 41W
New London, Conn., U.S.A.	79 E12	41 22N 72 6W
New London, Ohio, U.S.A.	78 E2	41 5N 82 24W
New London, Wis., U.S.A.	80 C10	44 23N 88 45W
New Madrid, U.S.A.	81 G10	36 36N 89 32W
New Martinsville, U.S.A.	76 F5	39 39N 80 52W
New Meadows, U.S.A.	82 D5	44 58N 116 18W
New Melones L., U.S.A.	84 H6	37 57N 120 31W
New Mexico □, U.S.A.	83 J10	34 30N 106 0W
New Milford, Conn., U.S.A.	79 E11	41 35N 73 25W
New Milford, Pa., U.S.A.	79 E9	41 52N 75 44W
New Norcia, Australia	61 F2	30 57S 116 13 E
New Norfolk, Australia	62 G4	42 46S 147 2 E
New Orleans, U.S.A.	81 L9	29 58N 90 4W
New Philadelphia, U.S.A.	78 F3	40 30N 81 27W
New Plymouth, N.Z.	59 H5	39 4S 174 5 E
New Plymouth, U.S.A.	82 E5	43 58N 116 49W
New Port Richey, U.S.A.	77 L4	28 16N 82 43W
New Providence, Bahamas	88 A4	25 25N 78 35W
New Quay, U.K.	11 E3	52 13N 4 21W
New Radnor, U.K.	11 E4	52 15N 3 9W
New Richmond, Canada	71 C6	48 9N 65 52W
New Richmond, U.S.A.	80 C8	45 7N 92 32W
New Roads, U.S.A.	81 K9	30 42N 91 26W
New Rochelle, U.S.A.	79 F11	40 55N 73 47W
New Rockford, U.S.A.	80 B5	47 41N 99 8W
New Romney, U.K.	11 G8	50 59N 0 57 E
New Ross, Ireland	13 D5	52 23N 6 57W
New Salem, U.S.A.	80 B4	46 51N 101 25W
New Scone, U.K.	12 E5	56 25N 3 24W
New Siberian I. = Novaya Sibir, Ostrov, Russia	27 B16	75 10N 150 0 E
New Siberian Is. = Novosibirskiye Ostrova, Russia	27 B15	75 0N 142 0 E

147

North Koel →, India **43 G10** 24 45N 83 50 E
North Korea ■, Asia **35 E14** 40 0N 127 0 E
North Lakhimpur, India ... **41 F19** 27 14N 94 7 E
North Lanarkshire □, U.K. . **12 F5** 55 52N 3 56W
North Las Vegas, U.S.A. .. **85 J11** 36 12N 115 7W
North Lincolnshire □, U.K. . **10 D7** 53 36N 0 30W
North Little Rock, U.S.A. .. **81 H8** 34 45N 92 16W
North Loup →, U.S.A. ... **80 E5** 41 17N 98 24W
North Magnetic Pole, Canada .. **4 B2** 77 58N 102 8W
North Minch, U.K. **12 C3** 58 5N 5 55W
North Moose L., Canada .. **73 C8** 54 11N 100 6W
North Myrtle Beach, U.S.A. **77 J6** 33 48N 78 42W
North Nahanni →, Canada **72 A4** 62 15N 123 20W
North Olmsted, U.S.A. ... **78 E3** 41 25N 81 56W
North Ossetia □, Russia .. **25 F7** 43 30N 44 30 E
North Pagai, I. = Pagai Utara, Pulau, Indonesia . **36 E2** 2 35S 100 0 E
North Palisade, U.S.A. **84 H8** 37 6N 118 31W
North Platte, U.S.A. **80 E4** 41 8N 100 46W
North Platte →, U.S.A. .. **80 E4** 41 7N 100 42W
North Pole, Arctic **4 A** 90 0N 0 0 E
North Portal, Canada **73 D8** 49 0N 102 33W
North Powder, U.S.A. **82 D5** 45 2N 117 55W
North Pt., U.S.A. **78 A1** 45 2N 83 16W
North Rhine Westphalia = Nordrhein-Westfalen □, Germany **16 C4** 51 45N 7 30 E
North River, Canada **71 B8** 53 49N 57 6W
North Ronaldsay, U.K. ... **12 B6** 59 22N 2 26W
North Saskatchewan →, Canada **73 C7** 53 15N 105 5W
North Sea, Europe **6 D6** 56 0N 4 0 E
North Seal →, Canada ... **73 B9** 58 50N 98 7W
North Somerset □, U.K. .. **11 F5** 51 24N 2 45W
North Sporades = Vórai Sporádhes, Greece **21 E10** 39 15N 23 30 E
North Sydney, Canada ... **71 C7** 46 12N 60 15W
North Syracuse, U.S.A. ... **79 C8** 43 8N 76 7W
North Taranaki Bight, N.Z. . **59 H5** 38 50S 174 15 E
North Thompson →, Canada **72 C4** 50 40N 120 20W
North Tonawanda, U.S.A. . **78 C6** 43 2N 78 53W
North Troy, U.S.A. **79 B12** 45 0N 72 24W
North Truchas Pk., U.S.A. . **83 J11** 36 0N 105 30W
North Twin I., Canada **70 B4** 53 20N 80 0W
North Tyne →, U.K. **10 B5** 55 0N 2 8W
North Uist, U.K. **12 D1** 57 40N 7 15W
North Vancouver, Canada . **72 D4** 49 19N 123 4W
North Vernon, U.S.A. **76 F3** 39 0N 85 38W
North Wabasca L., Canada **72 B6** 56 0N 113 55W
North Walsham, U.K. **10 E9** 52 50N 1 22 E
North-West □, S. Africa .. **56 D4** 27 0S 25 0 E
North West C., Australia .. **60 D1** 21 45S 114 9 E
North West Christmas I. Ridge, Pac. Oc. **65 G11** 6 30N 165 0W
North West Frontier □, Pakistan **42 C4** 34 0N 72 0 E
North West Highlands, U.K. **12 D4** 57 33N 4 58W
North West River, Canada . **71 B7** 53 30N 60 10W
North Western □, Zambia . **55 E2** 13 30S 25 30 E
North Wildwood, U.S.A. .. **76 F8** 39 0N 74 48W
North York Moors, U.K. .. **10 C7** 54 23N 0 53W
North Yorkshire □, U.K. .. **10 C6** 54 15N 1 25W
Northallerton, U.K. **10 C6** 54 20N 1 26W
Northam, Australia **61 F2** 31 35S 116 42 E
Northam, S. Africa **56 C4** 24 56S 27 18 E
Northampton, Australia .. **61 E1** 28 27S 114 33 E
Northampton, U.K. **11 E7** 52 15N 0 53W
Northampton, Mass., U.S.A. **79 D12** 42 19N 72 38W
Northampton, Pa., U.S.A. . **79 F9** 40 41N 75 30W
Northamptonshire □, U.K. . **11 E7** 52 16N 0 55W
Northbridge, U.S.A. **79 D13** 42 9N 71 39W
Northcliffe, Australia **61 F2** 34 39S 116 7 E
Northeast Providence Chan., W. Indies **88 A4** 26 0N 76 0W
Northern □, Malawi **55 E3** 11 0S 34 0 E
Northern □, Uganda **54 B3** 3 5N 32 30 E
Northern □, Zambia **55 E3** 10 30S 31 0 E
Northern Cape □, S. Africa **56 D3** 30 0S 20 0 E
Northern Circars, India ... **41 L13** 17 30N 82 30 E
Northern Indian L., Canada **73 B9** 57 20N 97 20W
Northern Ireland □, U.K. . **13 B5** 54 45N 7 0W
Northern Light L., Canada . **70 C1** 48 15N 90 39W
Northern Marianas ■, Pac. Oc. **64 F6** 17 0N 145 0 E
Northern Territory □, Australia **60 D5** 20 0S 133 0 E
Northern Transvaal □, S. Africa **57 C4** 24 0S 29 0 E
Northfield, Minn., U.S.A. .. **80 C8** 44 27N 93 9W
Northfield, Vt., U.S.A. **79 B12** 44 9N 72 40W
Northland □, N.Z. **59 F4** 35 30S 173 30 E
Northome, U.S.A. **80 B7** 47 52N 94 17W
Northport, Ala., U.S.A. ... **77 J2** 33 14N 87 35W
Northport, Wash., U.S.A. . **82 B5** 48 55N 117 48W
Northumberland □, U.K. .. **10 B6** 55 12N 2 0W
Northumberland, C., Australia **63 F3** 38 5S 140 40 E
Northumberland Is., Australia **62 C4** 21 30S 149 50 E
Northumberland Str., Canada **71 C7** 46 20N 64 0W
Northville, U.S.A. **79 C10** 43 13N 74 11W
Northwest Providence Channel, W. Indies **88 A4** 26 0N 78 0W
Northwest Territories □, Canada **68 B9** 67 0N 110 0W
Northwood, Iowa, U.S.A. . **80 D8** 43 27N 93 13W
Northwood, N. Dak., U.S.A. **80 B6** 47 44N 97 34W
Norton, U.S.A. **80 F5** 39 50N 99 53W
Norton, Zimbabwe **55 F3** 17 52S 30 40 E
Norton Sd., U.S.A. **68 B3** 63 50N 164 0W
Norwalk, Calif., U.S.A. ... **85 M8** 33 54N 118 5W
Norwalk, Conn., U.S.A. .. **79 E11** 41 7N 73 22W
Norwalk, Iowa, U.S.A. ... **80 E8** 41 29N 93 41W
Norwalk, Ohio, U.S.A. ... **78 E2** 41 15N 82 37W
Norway, Maine, U.S.A. ... **77 C10** 44 13N 70 32W
Norway, Mich., U.S.A. ... **76 C2** 45 47N 87 55W
Norway ■, Europe **8 E14** 63 0N 11 0 E
Norway House, Canada .. **73 C9** 53 59N 97 50W
Norwegian Sea, Atl. Oc. .. **4 C8** 66 0N 1 0 E
Norwich, Canada **78 D4** 42 59N 80 36W
Norwich, U.K. **11 E9** 52 38N 1 18 E
Norwich, Conn., U.S.A. .. **79 E12** 41 31N 72 5W
Norwich, N.Y., U.S.A. **79 D9** 42 32N 75 32W
Norwood, Canada **78 B7** 44 23N 77 59W

Norwood, U.S.A. **79 B10** 44 45N 75 0W
Noshiro, Japan **30 D10** 40 12N 140 0 E
Noşratābād, Iran **45 D8** 29 55N 60 0 E
Noss Hd., U.K. **12 C5** 58 28N 3 3W
Nossob →, S. Africa **56 D3** 26 55S 20 45 E
Nosy Barren, Madag. ... **53 H8** 18 25S 43 40 E
Nosy Be, Madag. **53 G9** 13 25S 48 15 E
Nosy Boraha, Madag. ... **57 B8** 16 50S 49 55 E
Nosy Varika, Madag. **57 C8** 20 35S 48 32 E
Noteć →, Poland **16 B8** 52 44N 15 26 E
Notikewin →, Canada .. **72 B5** 57 2N 117 38W
Notodden, Norway **9 G13** 59 35N 9 17 E
Notre Dame B., Canada .. **71 C8** 49 45N 55 30W
Notre Dame de Koartac = Quaqtaq, Canada **69 B13** 60 55N 69 40W
Notre-Dame-des-Bois, Canada **79 A13** 45 24N 71 4W
Notre Dame d'Ivugivic = Ivujivik, Canada **69 B12** 62 24N 77 55W
Notre-Dame-du-Nord, Canada **70 C4** 47 36N 79 30W
Nottawasaga B., Canada . **78 B4** 44 35N 80 15W
Nottaway →, Canada ... **70 B4** 51 22N 78 55W
Nottingham, U.K. **10 E6** 52 58N 1 10W
Nottingham, City of □, U.K. **10 E6** 52 58N 1 10W
Nottingham I., Canada ... **69 B12** 63 20N 77 55W
Nottinghamshire □, U.K. . **10 D6** 53 10N 1 3W
Nottoway →, U.S.A. ... **76 G7** 36 33N 76 55W
Notwane →, Botswana .. **56 C4** 23 35S 26 58 E
Nouâdhibou, Mauritania . **50 D2** 20 54N 17 0W
Nouâdhibou, Ras, Mauritania **50 D2** 20 50N 17 0W
Nouakchott, Mauritania .. **50 E2** 18 9N 15 58W
Nouméa, N. Cal. **64 K8** 22 17S 166 30 E
Noupoort, S. Africa **56 E3** 31 10S 24 57 E
Nouveau Comptoir = Wemindji, Canada **70 B4** 53 0N 78 49W
Nouvelle-Calédonie = New Caledonia ■, Pac. Oc. . **64 K8** 21 0S 165 0 E
Nova Casa Nova, Brazil .. **93 E10** 9 25S 41 5W
Nova Esperança, Brazil .. **95 A5** 23 8S 52 24W
Nova Friburgo, Brazil ... **95 A7** 22 16S 42 30W
Nova Gaia = Cambundi-Catembo, Angola **52 G3** 10 10S 17 35 E
Nova Iguaçu, Brazil **95 A7** 22 45S 43 28W
Nova Iorque, Brazil **93 E10** 7 0S 44 5W
Nova Lima, Brazil **95 A7** 19 59S 43 51W
Nova Lisboa = Huambo, Angola **53 G3** 12 42S 15 54 E
Nova Lusitânia, Mozam. .. **55 F3** 19 50S 34 34 E
Nova Mambone, Mozam. . **57 C6** 21 0S 35 3 E
Nova Scotia □, Canada .. **71 C7** 45 10N 63 0W
Nova Sofala, Mozam. **57 C5** 20 7S 34 42 E
Nova Venécia, Brazil **93 G10** 18 45S 40 24W
Nova Zagora, Bulgaria ... **21 C11** 42 32N 26 1 E
Novar, Canada **78 A5** 45 27N 79 15W
Novara, Italy **18 D8** 45 28N 8 38 E
Novato, U.S.A. **84 G4** 38 6N 122 35W
Novaya Ladoga, Russia .. **24 B5** 60 7N 32 16 E
Novaya Lyalya, Russia ... **24 C11** 59 4N 60 45 E
Novaya Sibir, Ostrov, Russia **27 B16** 75 10N 150 0 E
Novaya Zemlya, Russia .. **26 B6** 75 0N 56 0 E
Nové Zámky, Slovak Rep. . **17 D10** 48 2N 18 8 E
Novgorod, Russia **24 C5** 58 30N 31 25 E
Novgorod-Severskiy = Novhorod-Siverskyy, Ukraine **24 D5** 52 2N 33 10 E
Novhorod-Siverskyy, Ukraine **24 D5** 52 2N 33 10 E
Novi Lígure, Italy **18 D8** 44 46N 8 47 E
Novi Pazar, Serbia, Yug. . **21 C9** 43 12N 20 28 E
Novi Sad, Serbia, Yug. ... **21 B8** 45 18N 19 52 E
Nôvo Hamburgo, Brazil .. **95 B5** 29 37S 51 7W
Novo Mesto, Slovenia ... **20 B6** 45 47N 15 12 E
Novo Remanso, Brazil ... **93 E10** 9 41S 42 4W
Novoataysk, Russia **26 D9** 53 30N 84 0 E
Novocherkassk, Russia .. **25 E7** 47 27N 40 15 E
Novogrudok = Navahrudak, Belarus **17 B13** 53 40N 25 50 E
Novohrad-Volynskyy, Ukraine **17 C14** 50 34N 27 35 E
Novokachalinsk, Russia .. **30 B6** 45 5N 132 0 E
Novokazalinsk = Zhangaqazaly, Kazakstan **26 E7** 45 48N 62 6 E
Novokuybyshevsk, Russia . **24 D8** 53 7N 49 58 E
Novokuznetsk, Russia ... **26 D9** 53 45N 87 10 E
Novomoskovsk, Russia .. **24 D6** 54 5N 38 15 E
Novorossiysk, Russia **25 F6** 44 43N 37 46 E
Novorybnoye, Russia ... **27 B11** 72 50N 105 50 E
Novoselytsya, Ukraine ... **17 D14** 48 14N 26 15 E
Novoshakhtinsk, Russia .. **25 E6** 47 46N 39 58 E
Novosibirsk, Russia **26 D9** 55 0N 83 5 E
Novosibirskiye Ostrova, Russia **27 B15** 75 0N 142 0 E
Novotroitsk, Russia **24 D10** 51 10N 58 15 E
Novouzensk, Russia **25 D8** 50 32N 48 17 E
Novovolynsk, Ukraine ... **17 C13** 50 45N 24 4 E
Novska, Croatia **20 B7** 45 19N 17 0 E
Novvy Urengoy, Russia .. **26 C8** 65 48N 76 52 E
Novyy Bor, Russia **24 A9** 66 43N 52 19 E
Novyy Port, Russia **26 C8** 67 40N 72 30 E
Now Shahr, Iran **45 B6** 36 40N 51 30 E
Nowa Sól, Poland **16 C8** 51 48N 15 44 E
Nowata, U.S.A. **81 G7** 36 42N 95 38W
Nowbaran, Iran **45 C6** 35 8N 49 42 E
Nowghab, Iran **45 C8** 33 53N 59 4 E
Nowgong, Assam, India . **41 F18** 26 20N 92 50 E
Nowgong, Mad. P., India **43 G8** 25 4N 79 27 E
Nowra-Bomaderry, Australia **63 E5** 34 53S 150 35 E
Nowshera, Pakistan **40 C8** 34 0N 72 0 E
Nowy Sącz, Poland **17 D11** 49 40N 20 41 E
Nowy Targ, Poland **17 D11** 49 29N 20 2 E
Nowy Tomyśl, Poland ... **16 B9** 52 19N 16 10 E
Noxon, U.S.A. **82 C6** 48 0N 115 43W
Noyabr'sk, Russia **26 C8** 64 34N 76 21 E
Noyon, France **18 B5** 49 34N 2 59 E
Noyon, Mongolia **34 C2** 43 2N 102 4 E
Nsanje, Malawi **55 F4** 16 55S 35 12 E
Nsomba, Zambia **55 E2** 10 45S 29 51 E
Nu Jiang →, China **32 D4** 29 58N 97 25 E
Nu Shan, China **32 D4** 26 0N 99 20 E
Nubian Desert = Nûbîya, Es Sahrâ en, Sudan **51 D12** 21 30N 33 30 E
Nûbîya, Es Sahrâ en, Sudan **51 D12** 21 30N 33 30 E
Nuboai, Indonesia **37 E9** 2 10S 136 30 E

Nubra →, India **43 B7** 34 35N 77 35 E
Nueces →, U.S.A. **81 M6** 27 51N 97 30W
Nueltin L., Canada **73 A9** 60 30N 99 30W
Nueva Asunción □, Paraguay **94 A3** 21 0S 61 0W
Nueva Gerona, Cuba **88 B3** 21 53N 82 49W
Nueva Palmira, Uruguay . **94 C4** 33 52S 58 20W
Nueva Rosita, Mexico ... **86 B4** 28 0N 101 11W
Nueva San Salvador, El Salv. **88 D2** 13 40N 89 18W
Nuéve de Julio, Argentina . **94 D3** 35 30S 61 0W
Nuevitas, Cuba **88 B4** 21 30N 77 20W
Nuevo, G., Argentina ... **96 E4** 43 0S 64 30W
Nuevo Casas Grandes, Mexico **86 A3** 30 22N 108 0W
Nuevo Laredo, Mexico .. **87 B5** 26 34N 99 15W
Nuevo Laredo, Mexico .. **87 B5** 27 30N 99 30W
Nuevo León □, Mexico .. **86 C5** 25 0N 100 0W
Nuevo Rocafuerte, Ecuador **92 D3** 0 55S 75 27W
Nugget Pt., N.Z. **59 M2** 46 27S 169 50 E
Nuhaka, N.Z. **59 H6** 39 3S 177 45 E
Nukey Bluff, Australia ... **63 E2** 32 26S 135 29 E
Nukhuyb, Iraq **44 C4** 32 4N 42 3 E
Nuku'alofa, Tonga **59 E12** 21 10S 174 0W
Nukus, Uzbekistan **26 E6** 42 27N 59 41 E
Nullagine, Australia **60 D3** 21 53S 120 7 E
Nullagine →, Australia .. **60 D3** 21 20S 120 20 E
Nullarbor, Australia **61 F5** 31 28S 130 55 E
Nullarbor Plain, Australia . **61 F4** 31 10S 129 0 E
Numalla, L., Australia ... **63 D3** 28 43S 144 20 E
Numan, Nigeria **51 G8** 9 29N 12 3 E
Numata, Japan **31 F9** 36 45N 139 4 E
Numazu, Japan **31 G9** 35 7N 138 51 E
Numbulwar, Australia ... **62 A2** 14 15S 135 45 E
Numfoor, Indonesia **37 E8** 1 0S 134 50 E
Numurkah, Australia **63 F4** 36 5S 145 26 E
Nunaksaluk I., Canada ... **71 A7** 55 49N 60 20W
Nunavut □, Canada **69 B11** 66 0N 85 0W
Nunda, U.S.A. **78 D7** 42 35N 77 56W
Nungarin, Australia **61 F2** 31 12S 118 6 E
Nungo, Mozam. **55 E4** 13 23S 37 43 E
Nungwe, Tanzania **54 C3** 2 48S 32 2 E
Nunivak I., U.S.A. **68 C3** 60 10N 166 30W
Nunkun, India **43 C7** 33 57N 76 2 E
Núoro, Italy **20 D3** 40 20N 9 20 E
Nûrābād, Iran **45 E8** 27 47N 57 12 E
Nuremberg = Nürnberg, Germany **16 D6** 49 27N 11 3 E
Nuri, Mexico **86 B3** 28 2N 109 22W
Nuriootpa, Australia **63 E2** 34 27S 139 0 E
Nurmes, Finland **8 E23** 63 33N 29 10 E
Nürnberg, Germany **16 D6** 49 27N 11 3 E
Nurpur, Pakistan **42 D4** 31 53N 71 54 E
Nurran, L. = Terewah, L., Australia **63 D4** 29 52S 147 35 E
Nurrari Lakes, Australia .. **61 E5** 29 1S 130 5 E
Nusa Barung, Indonesia .. **37 H15** 8 30S 113 30 E
Nusa Kambangan, Indonesia **37 G13** 7 40S 108 10 E
Nusa Tenggara Barat □, Indonesia **36 F5** 8 50S 117 30 E
Nusa Tenggara Timur □, Indonesia **37 F6** 9 30S 122 0 E
Nusaybin, Turkey **25 G7** 37 3N 41 10 E
Nushki, Pakistan **42 E2** 29 35N 66 0 E
Nuuk, Greenland **69 B14** 64 10N 51 35W
Nuwakot, Nepal **43 E10** 28 10N 83 55 E
Nuweiba', Egypt **44 D2** 28 59N 34 39 E
Nuweveldberge, S. Africa . **56 E3** 32 10S 21 45 E
Nuyts, C., Australia **61 F5** 32 2S 132 21 E
Nuyts, Pt., Australia **61 G2** 35 4S 116 38 E
Nuyts Arch., Australia ... **63 E1** 32 35S 133 20 E
Nxau-Nxau, Botswana ... **56 B3** 18 57S 21 4 E
Nyabing, Australia **61 F2** 33 33S 118 9 E
Nyack, U.S.A. **79 E11** 41 5N 73 55W
Nyagan, Russia **26 C7** 62 30N 65 38 E
Nyahanga, Tanzania **54 C3** 2 20S 33 37 E
Nyahua, Tanzania **54 D3** 5 25S 33 23 E
Nyahururu, Kenya **54 B4** 0 2N 36 27 E
Nyaingentanglha Shan, China **32 D4** 30 0N 90 0 E
Nyakanazi, Tanzania **54 C3** 3 2S 31 10 E
Nyâlâ, Sudan **51 F10** 12 2N 24 58 E
Nyamandhlovu, Zimbabwe **55 F2** 19 55S 28 16 E
Nyambiti, Tanzania **54 C3** 2 48S 33 27 E
Nyamwaga, Tanzania ... **54 C3** 1 27S 34 33 E
Nyandekwa, Tanzania ... **54 C3** 3 57S 32 32 E
Nyandoma, Russia **24 B7** 61 40N 40 12 E
Nyangana, Namibia **56 B3** 18 0S 20 40 E
Nyanguge, Tanzania **54 C3** 2 30S 33 12 E
Nyanza, Rwanda **54 C2** 2 20S 29 42 E
Nyanza □, Kenya **54 C3** 0 10S 34 15 E
Nyanza-Lac, Burundi ... **54 C2** 4 21S 29 36 E
Nyasa, L., Africa **55 E3** 12 30S 34 30 E
Nyasvizh, Belarus **17 B14** 53 14N 26 38 E
Nyazepetrovsk, Russia .. **24 C10** 56 3N 59 36 E
Nyazura, Zimbabwe **55 F3** 18 40S 32 16 E
Nyazwidzi →, Zimbabwe **55 G3** 20 0S 31 17 E
Nybro, Sweden **9 H16** 56 44N 15 55 E
Nyda, Russia **26 C8** 66 40N 72 58 E
Nyeri, Kenya **54 C4** 0 23S 36 56 E
Nyíregyháza, Hungary .. **17 E11** 47 58N 21 47 E
Nykøbing, Storstrøm, Denmark **9 J14** 54 56N 11 52 E
Nykøbing, Vestsjælland, Denmark **9 J14** 55 55N 11 40 E
Nykøbing, Viborg, Denmark **9 H13** 56 48N 8 51 E
Nyköping, Sweden **9 G17** 58 45N 17 1 E
Nylstroom, S. Africa **57 C4** 24 42S 28 22 E
Nymagee, Australia **63 E4** 32 7S 146 20 E
Nynäshamn, Sweden ... **9 G17** 58 54N 17 57 E
Nyoma Rap, India **43 C8** 33 10N 78 40 E
Nyoman = Neman →, Lithuania **9 J20** 55 25N 21 10 E
Nysa, Poland **17 C9** 50 30N 17 22 E
Nysa →, Europe **16 B8** 52 4N 14 46 E
Nyssa, U.S.A. **82 E5** 43 53N 117 0W
Nyunzu, Dem. Rep. of the Congo **54 D2** 5 57S 27 58 E
Nyurba, Russia **27 C12** 63 17N 118 28 E
Nzega, Tanzania **54 C3** 4 10S 33 12 E
N'zérékoré, Guinea **50 G4** 7 49N 8 48W
Nzeto, Angola **52 F2** 7 10S 12 52 E
Nzilo, Chutes de, Dem. Rep. of the Congo **55 E2** 10 18S 25 27 E
Nzubuka, Tanzania **54 C3** 4 45S 32 50 E

O

Ô-Shima, Japan **31 G9** 34 44N 139 24 E
Oa, Mull of, U.K. **12 F2** 55 35N 6 20W
Oacoma, U.S.A. **80 D5** 43 48N 99 24W
Oahe, L., U.S.A. **80 C4** 44 27N 100 24W
Oahe Dam, U.S.A. **80 C4** 44 27N 100 24W
Oahu, U.S.A. **74 H16** 21 28N 157 58W
Oak Harbor, U.S.A. **84 B4** 48 18N 122 39W
Oak Hill, U.S.A. **76 G5** 37 59N 81 9W
Oak Ridge, U.S.A. **77 G3** 36 1N 84 16W
Oak View, U.S.A. **85 L7** 34 24N 119 18W
Oakan-Dake, Japan **30 C12** 43 27N 144 10 E
Oakdale, Calif., U.S.A. .. **84 H6** 37 46N 120 51W
Oakdale, La., U.S.A. **81 K8** 30 49N 92 40W
Oakes, U.S.A. **80 B5** 46 8N 98 6W
Oakesdale, U.S.A. **82 C5** 47 8N 117 15W
Oakey, Australia **63 D5** 27 25S 151 43 E
Oakfield, U.S.A. **78 C6** 43 4N 78 16W
Oakham, U.K. **11 E7** 52 40N 0 43W
Oakhurst, U.S.A. **84 H7** 37 19N 119 40W
Oakland, U.S.A. **84 H4** 37 49N 122 16W
Oakley, Idaho, U.S.A. ... **82 E7** 42 15N 113 53W
Oakley, Kans., U.S.A. ... **80 F4** 39 8N 100 51W
Oakover →, Australia .. **60 D3** 21 0S 120 40 E
Oakridge, U.S.A. **82 E2** 43 45N 122 28W
Oakville, Canada **78 C5** 43 27N 79 41W
Oakville, U.S.A. **84 D3** 46 51N 123 14W
Oamaru, N.Z. **59 L3** 45 5S 170 59 E
Oasis, Calif., U.S.A. **85 M10** 33 28N 116 6W
Oasis, Nev., U.S.A. **84 H9** 37 29N 117 55W
Oates Land, Antarctica .. **5 C11** 69 0S 160 0 E
Oatlands, Australia **62 G4** 42 17S 147 21 E
Oatman, U.S.A. **85 K12** 35 1N 114 19W
Oaxaca, Mexico **87 D5** 17 2N 96 40W
Oaxaca □, Mexico **87 D5** 17 0N 97 0W
Ob →, Russia **26 C7** 66 45N 69 30 E
Oba, Canada **70 C3** 49 4N 84 7W
Obama, Japan **31 G7** 35 30N 135 45 E
Oban, U.K. **12 E3** 56 25N 5 29W
Obbia, Somali Rep. **46 F4** 5 25N 48 30 E
Obera, Argentina **95 B4** 27 21S 55 2W
Oberhausen, Germany .. **16 C4** 51 28N 6 51 E
Oberlin, Kans., U.S.A. ... **80 F4** 39 49N 100 32W
Oberlin, La., U.S.A. **81 K8** 30 37N 92 46W
Oberlin, Ohio, U.S.A. ... **78 E2** 41 18N 82 13W
Oberon, Australia **63 E4** 33 45S 149 52 E
Obi, Kepulauan, Indonesia **37 E7** 1 23S 127 45 E
Obi Is. = Obi, Kepulauan, Indonesia **37 E7** 1 23S 127 45 E
Óbidos, Brazil **93 D7** 1 50S 55 30W
Obihiro, Japan **30 C11** 42 56N 143 12 E
Obilatu, Indonesia **37 E7** 1 25S 127 20 E
Obluchye, Russia **27 E14** 49 1N 131 4 E
Obo, C.A.R. **54 A2** 5 20N 26 32 E
Oboa, Mt., Uganda **54 B3** 1 45N 34 45 E
Oboyan, Russia **26 D4** 51 15N 36 21 E
Obozerskaya = Obozerskiy, Russia **24 B7** 63 34N 40 21 E
Obozerskiy, Russia **24 B7** 63 34N 40 21 E
Observatory Inlet, Canada . **72 B3** 55 10N 129 54W
Obshchi Syrt, Russia **6 E16** 52 0N 53 0 E
Obskaya Guba, Russia ... **26 C8** 69 0N 73 0 E
Obuasi, Ghana **50 G5** 6 17N 1 40W
Ocala, U.S.A. **77 L4** 29 11N 82 8W
Ocampo, Chihuahua, Mexico **86 B3** 28 9N 108 24W
Ocampo, Tamaulipas, Mexico **87 C5** 22 50N 99 20W
Ocaña, Spain **19 C4** 39 55N 3 30W
Ocanomowoc, U.S.A. ... **80 D10** 43 7N 88 30W
Occidental, Cordillera, Colombia **92 C3** 5 0N 76 0W
Ocean City, Md., U.S.A. .. **76 F8** 38 20N 75 5W
Ocean City, N.J., U.S.A. . **76 F8** 39 17N 74 35W
Ocean City, Wash., U.S.A. **84 C2** 47 4N 124 10W
Ocean Falls, Canada **72 C3** 52 18N 127 48W
Ocean I. = Banaba, Kiribati **64 H8** 0 45S 169 50 E
Ocean Park, U.S.A. **84 D2** 46 30N 124 3W
Oceanport, U.S.A. **79 F10** 40 19N 74 3W
Oceanside, U.S.A. **85 M9** 33 12N 117 23W
Ochil Hills, U.K. **12 E5** 56 14N 3 40W
Ocilla, U.S.A. **77 K4** 31 36N 83 15W
Ocnița, Moldova **17 D14** 48 25N 27 30 E
Oconee →, U.S.A. **77 K4** 31 58N 82 33W
Oconto, U.S.A. **76 C2** 44 53N 87 52W
Oconto Falls, U.S.A. **76 C1** 44 52N 88 9W
Ocosingo, Mexico **87 D6** 17 10N 92 15W
Ocotal, Nic. **88 D2** 13 41N 86 31W
Ocotlán, Mexico **86 C4** 20 21N 102 42W
Ocotlán de Morelos, Mexico **87 D5** 16 48N 96 40W
Ōda, Japan **31 G6** 35 11N 132 30 E
Ódáðahraun, Iceland ... **8 D5** 65 5N 17 0W
Odate, Japan **30 D10** 40 16N 140 34 E
Odawara, Japan **31 G9** 35 20N 139 6 E
Odda, Norway **9 F12** 60 3N 6 35 E
Odei →, Canada **73 B9** 56 6N 96 54W
Ödemiş, Turkey **21 E13** 38 15N 28 0 E
Odendaalsrus, S. Africa .. **56 D4** 27 48S 26 45 E
Odense, Denmark **9 J14** 55 22N 10 23 E
Oder →, Europe **16 B8** 53 33N 14 38 E
Odesa, Ukraine **25 E5** 46 30N 30 45 E
Odessa = Odesa, Ukraine . **25 E5** 46 30N 30 45 E
Odessa, Tex., U.S.A. ... **81 K3** 31 52N 102 23W
Odessa, Wash., U.S.A. .. **82 C4** 47 20N 118 41W
Odiakwe, Botswana **56 C4** 20 12S 25 17 E
Odienné, Ivory C. **50 G4** 9 30N 7 34W
Odintsovo, Russia **24 C6** 55 39N 37 15 E
O'Donnell, U.S.A. **81 J4** 32 58N 101 50W
Odorheiu Secuiesc, Romania **17 E13** 46 21N 25 21 E
Odra = Oder →, Europe . **16 B8** 53 33N 14 38 E
Odzi, Zimbabwe **57 B5** 19 0S 32 20 E
Oelrichs, U.S.A. **80 D3** 43 11N 103 14W
Oelwein, U.S.A. **80 D9** 42 41N 91 55W
Oenpelli, Australia **60 B5** 12 20S 133 4 E
Ofanto →, Italy **20 D7** 41 22N 16 13 E
Offa, Nigeria **50 G6** 8 13N 4 42 E
Offaly □, Ireland **13 C4** 53 15N 7 30W
Offenbach, Germany ... **16 C5** 50 6N 8 44 E
Offenburg, Germany ... **16 D4** 48 28N 7 56 E

Ofotfjorden, *Norway*	8 B17	68 27N	17	0 E
Ōfunato, *Japan*	30 E10	39 4N	141	43 E
Oga, *Japan*	30 E9	39 55N	139	50 E
Oga-Hantō, *Japan*	30 E9	39 58N	139	47 E
Ogaden, *Ethiopia*	46 F3	7 30N	45	30 E
Ōgaki, *Japan*	31 G8	35 21N	136	37 E
Ogallala, *U.S.A.*	80 E4	41 8N	101	43W
Ogasawara Gunto, *Pac. Oc.*	28 G18	27 0N	142	0 E
Ogbomosho, *Nigeria*	50 G6	8 1N	4	11 E
Ogden, *U.S.A.*	82 F7	41 13N	111	58W
Ogdensburg, *U.S.A.*	79 B9	44 42N	75	30W
Ogeechee →, *U.S.A.*	77 K5	31 50N	81	3W
Ogilby, *U.S.A.*	85 N12	32 49N	114	50W
Oglio →, *Italy*	20 B4	45 2N	10	39 E
Ogmore, *Australia*	62 C4	22 37S	149	35 E
Ogoki, *Canada*	70 B2	51 38N	85	58W
Ogoki →, *Canada*	70 B2	51 38N	85	57W
Ogoki L., *Canada*	70 B2	50 50N	87	10W
Ogoki Res., *Canada*	70 B2	50 45N	88	15W
Ogooué →, *Gabon*	52 E1	1 0S	9	0 E
Ogowe = Ogooué →, *Gabon*	52 E1	1 0S	9	0 E
Ogre, *Latvia*	9 H21	56 49N	24	36 E
Ogurchinskiy, Ostrov, *Turkmenistan*	45 B7	38 55N	53	2 E
Ohai, *N.Z.*	59 L2	45 55S	168	0 E
Ohakune, *N.Z.*	59 H5	39 24S	175	24 E
Ohata, *Japan*	30 D10	41 24N	141	10 E
Ohau, L., *N.Z.*	59 L2	44 15S	169	53 E
Ohio □, *U.S.A.*	78 F2	40 15N	82	45W
Ohio →, *U.S.A.*	76 G1	36 59N	89	8W
Ohře →, *Czech Rep.*	16 C8	50 30N	14	10 E
Ohrid, *Macedonia*	21 D9	41 8N	20	52 E
Ohridsko Jezero, *Macedonia*	21 D9	41 8N	20	52 E
Ohrigstad, *S. Africa*	57 C5	24 39S	30	36 E
Oiapoque, *Brazil*	93	3 50N	51	50W
Oikou, *China*	35 E9	38 35N	117	42 E
Oil City, *U.S.A.*	78 E5	41 26N	79	42W
Oil Springs, *Canada*	78 D2	42 47N	82	7W
Oildale, *U.S.A.*	85 K7	35 25N	119	1W
Oise □, *France*	18 B5	49 0N	2	4 E
Ōita, *Japan*	31 H5	33 14N	131	36 E
Ōita □, *Japan*	31 H5	33 15N	131	30 E
Oiticica, *Brazil*	93 E10	5 3S	41	5W
Ojacaliente, *Mexico*	86 C4	22 34N	102	15W
Ojai, *U.S.A.*	85 L7	34 27N	119	15W
Ojinaga, *Mexico*	86 B4	29 34N	104	25W
Ojiya, *Japan*	31 F9	37 18N	138	48 E
Ojos del Salado, Cerro, *Argentina*	94 B2	27 0S	68	40W
Oka →, *Russia*	24 C7	56 20N	43	59 E
Okaba, *Indonesia*	37 F9	8 6S	139	42 E
Okahandja, *Namibia*	56 C2	22 0S	16	59 E
Okahukura, *N.Z.*	59 H5	38 48S	175	14 E
Okanagan L., *Canada*	72 D5	50 0N	119	30W
Okanogan, *U.S.A.*	82 B4	48 22N	119	35W
Okanogan →, *U.S.A.*	82 B4	48 6N	119	44W
Okaputa, *Namibia*	56 C2	20 5S	17	0 E
Okara, *Pakistan*	42 D5	30 50N	73	31 E
Okarito, *N.Z.*	59 K3	43 15S	170	9 E
Okaukuejo, *Namibia*	56 B2	19 10S	16	0 E
Okavango Swamps, *Botswana*	56 B3	18 45S	22	45 E
Okaya, *Japan*	31 F9	36 5N	138	10 E
Okayama, *Japan*	31 G6	34 40N	133	54 E
Okayama □, *Japan*	31 G6	35 0N	133	50 E
Okazaki, *Japan*	31 G8	34 57N	137	10 E
Okeechobee, *U.S.A.*	77 M5	27 15N	80	50W
Okeechobee, L., *U.S.A.*	77 M5	27 0N	80	50W
Okefenokee Swamp, *U.S.A.*	77 K4	30 40N	82	20W
Okehampton, *U.K.*	11 G4	50 44N	4	0W
Okha, *India*	42 H3	22 27N	69	4 E
Okha, *Russia*	27 D15	53 40N	143	0 E
Okhotsk, *Russia*	27 D15	59 20N	143	10 E
Okhotsk, Sea of, *Asia*	27 D15	55 0N	145	0 E
Okhotskiy Perevoz, *Russia*	27 C14	61 52N	135	35 E
Okhtyrka, *Ukraine*	25 D5	50 25N	35	0 E
Oki-Shotō, *Japan*	31 F6	36 5N	133	15 E
Okiep, *S. Africa*	56 D2	29 39S	17	53 E
Okinawa □, *Japan*	31 L4	26 40N	128	0 E
Okinawa-Guntō, *Japan*	31 L4	26 40N	128	0 E
Okinawa-Jima, *Japan*	31 L4	26 32N	128	0 E
Okino-erabu-Shima, *Japan*	31 L4	27 21N	128	33 E
Oklahoma □, *U.S.A.*	81 H6	35 20N	97	30W
Oklahoma City, *U.S.A.*	81 H6	35 30N	97	30W
Okmulgee, *U.S.A.*	81 H7	35 37N	95	58W
Oknitsa = Ocniţa, *Moldova*	17 D14	48 25N	27	30 E
Okolo, *Uganda*	54 B3	2 37N	31	8 E
Okolona, *U.S.A.*	81 J10	34 0N	88	45W
Okotoks, *Canada*	72 C6	50 43N	113	58W
Oksibil, *Indonesia*	37 E10	4 59S	140	35 E
Oksovskiy, *Russia*	24 B6	62 33N	39	57 E
Oktabrsk = Oktyabrsk, *Kazakstan*	25 E10	49 28N	57	25 E
Oktyabrsk, *Kazakstan*	25 E10	49 28N	57	25 E
Oktyabrskiy = Aktsyabrski, *Belarus*	17 B15	52 38N	28	53 E
Oktyabrskiy, *Russia*	24 D9	54 28N	53	28 E
Oktyabrskoy Revolyutsii, Ostrov, *Russia*	27 B10	79 30N	97	0 E
Okuru, *N.Z.*	59 K2	43 55S	168	55 E
Okushiri-Tō, *Japan*	30 C9	42 15N	139	30 E
Okwa →, *Botswana*	56 C3	22 30S	23	0 E
Ola, *U.S.A.*	81 H8	35 2N	93	13W
Ólafsfjörður, *Iceland*	8 C4	66 4N	18	39W
Ólafsvík, *Iceland*	8 D2	64 53N	23	43W
Olancha, *U.S.A.*	85 J8	36 17N	118	1W
Olancha Pk., *U.S.A.*	85 J8	36 15N	118	7W
Olanchito, *Honduras*	88 C2	15 30N	86	30W
Öland, *Sweden*	9 H17	56 45N	16	38 E
Olary, *Australia*	63 E3	32 18S	140	19 E
Olascoaga, *Argentina*	94 D3	35 15S	60	39W
Olathe, *U.S.A.*	80 F7	38 53N	94	49W
Olavarría, *Argentina*	94 D3	36 55S	60	20W
Oława, *Poland*	17 C9	50 57N	17	20 E
Olbia, *Italy*	20 D3	40 55N	9	31 E
Olcott, *U.S.A.*	78 C6	43 20N	78	42W
Old Bahama Chan. = Bahama, Canal Viejo de, *W. Indies*	88 B4	22 10N	77	30W
Old Baldy Pk. = San Antonio, Mt., *U.S.A.*	85 L9	34 17N	117	38W
Old Castile = Castilla y León □, *Spain*	19 B3	42 0N	5	0W
Old Crow, *Canada*	68 B6	67 30N	139	55W
Old Dale, *U.S.A.*	85 L11	34 8N	115	47W

Old Forge, *N.Y., U.S.A.*	79 C10	43 43N	74	58W
Old Forge, *Pa., U.S.A.*	79 E9	41 22N	75	45W
Old Perlican, *Canada*	71 C9	48 5N	53	1W
Old Shinyanga, *Tanzania*	54 C3	3 33S	33	27 E
Old Speck Mt., *U.S.A.*	79 B14	44 34N	70	57W
Old Town, *U.S.A.*	77 C11	44 56N	68	39W
Old Washington, *U.S.A.*	78 F3	40 2N	81	27W
Old Wives L., *Canada*	73 C7	50 5N	106	0W
Oldbury, *U.K.*	11 F5	51 38N	2	33W
Oldcastle, *Ireland*	13 C4	53 46N	7	10W
Oldeani, *Tanzania*	54 C4	3 22S	35	35 E
Oldenburg, *Germany*	16 B5	53 9N	8	13 E
Oldenzaal, *Neths.*	15 B6	52 19N	6	53 E
Oldham, *U.K.*	10 D5	53 33N	2	7W
Oldman →, *Canada*	72 D6	49 57N	111	42W
Oldmeldrum, *U.K.*	12 D6	57 20N	2	19W
Olds, *Canada*	72 C6	51 50N	114	10W
Oldziyt, *Mongolia*	34 B5	44 40N	109	1 E
Olean, *U.S.A.*	78 D6	42 5N	78	26W
Olekma →, *Russia*	27 C13	60 22N	120	42 E
Olekminsk, *Russia*	27 C13	60 25N	120	30 E
Oleksandriya, *Ukraine*	17 C14	50 37N	26	19 E
Olema, *U.S.A.*	84 G4	38 3N	122	47W
Olenegorsk, *Russia*	24 A5	68 9N	33	18 E
Olenek, *Russia*	27 C12	68 28N	112	18 E
Olenek →, *Russia*	27 B13	73 0N	120	10 E
Oléron, Î. d', *France*	18 D3	45 55N	1	15W
Oleśnica, *Poland*	17 C9	51 13N	17	22 E
Olevsk, *Ukraine*	17 C14	51 12N	27	39 E
Olga, *Russia*	27 E14	43 50N	135	14 E
Olga, L., *Canada*	70 C4	49 47N	77	15W
Olga, Mt., *Australia*	61 E5	25 20S	130	50 E
Olhão, *Portugal*	19 D2	37 3N	7	48W
Olifants →, *Africa*	57 C5	23 57S	31	58 E
Olifantshoek, *S. Africa*	56 D3	27 57S	22	42 E
Olivenza, *Spain*	19 C2	38 41N	7	9W
Olivehurst, *U.S.A.*	84 F5	39 6N	121	34W
Oliver, *Canada*	72 D5	49 13N	119	37W
Oliver L., *Canada*	73 B8	56 56N	103	22W
Ollagüe, *Chile*	94 A2	21 15S	68	10W
Olney, *Ill., U.S.A.*	76 F1	38 44N	88	5W
Olney, *Tex., U.S.A.*	81 J5	33 22N	98	45W
Olomane →, *Canada*	71 B7	50 14N	60	37W
Olomouc, *Czech Rep.*	17 D9	49 38N	17	12 E
Olonets, *Russia*	24 B5	61 0N	32	54 E
Olongapo, *Phil.*	37 B6	14 50N	120	18 E
Olot, *Spain*	19 A7	42 11N	2	30 E
Olovyannaya, *Russia*	27 D12	50 58N	115	35 E
Oloy →, *Russia*	27 C16	66 29N	159	29 E
Olsztyn, *Poland*	17 B11	53 48N	20	29 E
Olt →, *Romania*	17 G13	43 43N	24	51 E
Olteniţa, *Romania*	17 F14	44 7N	26	42 E
Olton, *U.S.A.*	81 H3	34 11N	102	8W
Olymbos, *Cyprus*	23 D12	35 21N	33	45 E
Olympia, *Greece*	21 F9	37 39N	21	39 E
Olympia, *U.S.A.*	84 D4	47 3N	122	53W
Olympic Dam, *Australia*	63 E2	30 30S	136	55 E
Olympic Mts., *U.S.A.*	84 C3	47 55N	123	45W
Olympic Nat. Park, *U.S.A.*	84 C3	47 48N	123	30W
Olympus, *Cyprus*	23 E11	34 56N	32	52 E
Olympus, Mt. = Ólimbos, Óros, *Greece*	21 D10	40 6N	22	23 E
Olympus, Mt. = Uludağ, *Turkey*	21 D13	40 4N	29	13 E
Olympus, Mt., *U.S.A.*	84 C3	47 48N	123	43W
Olyphant, *U.S.A.*	79 E9	41 27N	75	36W
Om →, *Russia*	26 D8	54 59N	73	22 E
Om Koi, *Thailand*	38 D2	17 48N	98	22 E
Ōma, *Japan*	30 D10	41 45N	141	5 E
Ōmachi, *Japan*	31 F8	36 30N	137	50 E
Omae-Zaki, *Japan*	31 G9	34 36N	138	14 E
Ōmagari, *Japan*	30 E10	39 27N	140	29 E
Omagh, *U.K.*	13 B4	54 36N	7	19W
Omagh □, *U.K.*	13 B4	54 35N	7	15W
Omaha, *U.S.A.*	80 E7	41 17N	95	58W
Omak, *U.S.A.*	82 B4	48 25N	119	31W
Omalos, *Greece*	23 D5	35 19N	23	55 E
Oman ■, *Asia*	46 C6	23 0N	58	0 E
Oman, G. of, *Asia*	45 E8	24 30N	58	30 E
Omaruru, *Namibia*	56 C2	21 26S	16	0 E
Omaruru →, *Namibia*	56 C1	22 7S	14	15 E
Omate, *Peru*	92 G4	16 45S	71	0W
Ombai, Selat, *Indonesia*	37 F6	8 30S	124	50 E
Omboué, *Gabon*	52 E1	1 35S	9	15 E
Ombrone →, *Italy*	20 C4	42 42N	11	5 E
Omdurmân, *Sudan*	51 E12	15 40N	32	28 E
Omemee, *Canada*	78 B6	44 18N	78	33W
Omeo, *Australia*	63 F4	37 6S	147	36 E
Omeonga, *Dem. Rep. of the Congo*	54 C1	3 40S	24	22 E
Ometepe, I. de, *Nic.*	88 D2	11 32N	85	35W
Ometepec, *Mexico*	87 D5	16 39N	98	23W
Ominato, *Japan*	30 D10	41 17N	141	10 E
Omineca →, *Canada*	72 B4	56 3N	124	16W
Omitara, *Namibia*	56 C2	22 16S	18	2 E
Ōmiya, *Japan*	31 G9	35 54N	139	38 E
Ommen, *Neths.*	15 B6	52 31N	6	26 E
Ömnögovi □, *Mongolia*	34 C3	43 15N	104	0 E
Omo →, *Ethiopia*	46 F2	6 25N	36	11 E
Omodhos, *Cyprus*	23 E11	34 51N	32	48 E
Omolon →, *Russia*	27 C16	68 42N	158	36 E
Omono-Gawa →, *Japan*	30 E10	39 46N	140	3 E
Omsk, *Russia*	26 D8	55 0N	73	12 E
Omsukchan, *Russia*	27 C16	62 32N	155	48 E
Ōmu, *Japan*	30 B11	44 34N	142	58 E
Omul, Vf., *Romania*	17 F13	45 27N	25	29 E
Ōmura, *Japan*	31 H4	32 56N	129	57 E
Omuramba Omatako →, *Namibia*	53 H4	17 45S	20	25 E
Ōmuta, *Japan*	31 H5	33 5N	130	26 E
Onaga, *U.S.A.*	80 F6	39 29N	96	10W
Onalaska, *U.S.A.*	80 D9	43 53N	91	14W
Onancock, *U.S.A.*	76 G8	37 43N	75	45W
Onang, *Indonesia*	37 E5	3 2S	118	49 E
Onaping L., *Canada*	70 C3	47 3N	81	30W
Onavas, *Mexico*	86 B3	28 28N	109	30W
Onawa, *U.S.A.*	80 D6	42 2N	96	6W
Oncócua, *Angola*	56 B1	16 30S	13	25 E
Onda, *Spain*	19 C5	39 55N	0	17W
Ondangua, *Namibia*	56 B2	17 57S	16	4 E
Ondarroa, *N. Korea*	35 D15	41 34N	129	40 E
Ondjiva, *Angola*	56 B2	16 48S	15	50 E
Öndörshil, *Mongolia*	34 B5	45 13N	108	5 E

Öndverðarnes, *Iceland*	8 D1	64 52N	24	0W
One Tree, *Australia*	63 E3	34 11S	144	43 E
Onega, *Russia*	24 B6	64 0N	38	10 E
Onega →, *Russia*	24 B6	63 58N	38	2 E
Onega, G. of = Onezhskaya Guba, *Russia*	24 B6	64 24N	36	38 E
Onega, L. = Onezhskoye Ozero, *Russia*	24 B6	61 44N	35	22 E
Onehunga, *N.Z.*	59 G5	36 55S	174	48 E
Oneida, *U.S.A.*	79 C9	43 6N	75	39W
Oneida L., *U.S.A.*	79 C9	43 12N	75	54W
O'Neill, *U.S.A.*	80 D5	42 27N	98	39W
Onekotan, Ostrov, *Russia*	27 E16	49 25N	154	45 E
Onema, Dem. Rep. of the Congo	54 C1	4 35S	24	30 E
Oneonta, *U.S.A.*	79 D9	42 27N	75	4W
Oneşti, *Romania*	17 E14	46 15N	26	45 E
Onezhskaya Guba, *Russia*	24 B6	64 24N	36	38 E
Onezhskoye Ozero, *Russia*	24 B6	61 44N	35	22 E
Ongarue, *N.Z.*	59 H5	38 42S	175	19 E
Ongerup, *Australia*	61 F2	33 58S	118	28 E
Ongjin, *N. Korea*	35 F13	37 56N	125	21 E
Ongkharak, *Thailand*	38 E3	14 8N	101	1 E
Ongniud Qi, *China*	35 C10	43 0N	118	38 E
Ongoka, Dem. Rep. of the Congo	54 C2	1 20S	26	0 E
Ongole, *India*	40 M12	15 33N	80	2 E
Ongon = Havirga, *Mongolia*	34 B7	45 41N	113	5 E
Onida, *U.S.A.*	80 C4	44 42N	100	4W
Onilahy →, *Madag.*	57 C7	23 34S	43	45 E
Onitsha, *Nigeria*	50 G7	6 6N	6	42 E
Onoda, *Japan*	31 G5	34 2N	131	25 E
Onpyŏng-ni, *S. Korea*	35 H14	33 25N	126	55 E
Onslow, *Australia*	60 D2	21 40S	115	12 E
Onslow B., *U.S.A.*	77 H7	34 20N	77	15W
Ontake-San, *Japan*	31 G8	35 53N	137	29 E
Ontario, *Calif., U.S.A.*	85 L9	34 4N	117	39W
Ontario, *Oreg., U.S.A.*	82 D5	44 2N	116	58W
Ontario □, *Canada*	70 B2	48 0N	83	0W
Ontario, L., *N. Amer.*	75 B11	43 20N	78	0W
Ontonagon, *U.S.A.*	80 B10	46 52N	89	19W
Onyx, *U.S.A.*	85 K8	35 41N	118	14W
Oodnadatta, *Australia*	63 D2	27 33S	135	30 E
Ooldea, *Australia*	61 F5	30 27S	131	50 E
Oombulgurri, *Australia*	60 C4	15 15S	127	45 E
Oorindi, *Australia*	62 C3	20 40S	141	1 E
Oost-Vlaanderen □, *Belgium*	15 C3	51 5N	3	50 E
Oostende, *Belgium*	15 C2	51 15N	2	54 E
Oosterhout, *Neths.*	15 C4	51 39N	4	47 E
Oosterschelde →, *Neths.*	15 C4	51 33N	4	0 E
Oosterwolde, *Neths.*	15 B6	53 0N	6	17 E
Ootacamund = Udagamandalam, *India*	40 P10	11 30N	76	44 E
Ootsa L., *Canada*	72 C3	53 50N	126	2W
Opala, Dem. Rep. of the Congo	54 C1	0 40S	24	20 E
Opanake, *Sri Lanka*	40 R12	6 35N	80	40 E
Opasatika, *Canada*	70 C3	49 30N	82	50W
Opasquia Prov. Park, *Canada*	70 B1	53 33N	93	5W
Opava, *Czech Rep.*	17 D9	49 57N	17	58 E
Opelika, *U.S.A.*	77 J3	32 39N	85	23W
Opelousas, *U.S.A.*	81 K8	30 32N	92	5W
Opémisca, L., *Canada*	70 C5	49 56N	74	52W
Opheim, *U.S.A.*	82 B10	48 51N	106	24W
Ophthalmia Ra., *Australia*	60 D2	23 15S	119	30 E
Opinaca →, *Canada*	70 B4	52 15N	78	2W
Opinaca, Rés., *Canada*	70 B4	52 39N	76	20W
Opinnagau →, *Canada*	70 B3	54 12N	82	25W
Opiscoteo, L., *Canada*	71 B6	53 10N	68	10W
Opole, *Poland*	17 C9	50 42N	17	58 E
Oporto = Porto, *Portugal*	19 B1	41 8N	8	40W
Opotiki, *N.Z.*	59 H6	38 1S	177	19 E
Opp, *U.S.A.*	77 K2	31 17N	86	16W
Oppdal, *Norway*	9 E13	62 35N	9	41 E
Opportunity, *U.S.A.*	82 C5	47 39N	117	15W
Opua, *N.Z.*	59 F5	35 19S	174	9 E
Opunake, *N.Z.*	59 H4	39 26S	173	52 E
Ora, *Cyprus*	23 E12	34 51N	33	12 E
Oracle, *U.S.A.*	83 K8	32 37N	110	46W
Oradea, *Romania*	17 E11	47 2N	21	58 E
Orai, *India*	43 G8	25 58N	79	30 E
Öræfajökull, *Iceland*	8 D5	64 2N	16	39W
Oral = Zhayyq →, *Kazakstan*	25 E9	47 0N	51	48 E
Oral, *Kazakstan*	25 D9	51 20N	51	20 E
Oran, *Algeria*	50 A5	35 45N	0	39W
Orange, *Australia*	63 E4	33 15S	149	7 E
Orange, *France*	18 D6	44 8N	4	47 E
Orange, *Mass., U.S.A.*	79 D12	42 35N	72	19W
Orange, *Tex., U.S.A.*	81 K8	30 6N	93	44W
Orange, *Va., U.S.A.*	76 F6	38 15N	78	7W
Orange →, *S. Africa*	56 D2	28 41S	16	28 E
Orange, C., *Brazil*	93 C8	4 20N	51	30W
Orange Cove, *U.S.A.*	84 J7	36 38N	119	19W
Orange Free State = Free State □, *S. Africa*	56 D4	28 30S	27	0 E
Orange Grove, *U.S.A.*	81 M6	27 58N	97	56W
Orange Walk, *Belize*	87 D7	18 6N	88	33W
Orangeburg, *U.S.A.*	77 J5	33 30N	80	52W
Orangeville, *Canada*	78 C4	43 55N	80	5W
Oranienburg, *Germany*	16 B7	52 45N	13	14 E
Oranje = Orange →, *S. Africa*	56 D2	28 41S	16	28 E
Oranje Vrystaat = Free State □, *S. Africa*	56 D4	28 30S	27	0 E
Oranjemund, *Namibia*	56 D2	28 38S	16	29 E
Oranjerivier, *S. Africa*	56 D3	29 40S	24	12 E
Oranjestad, *Aruba*	89 D5	12 32N	70	2W
Orapa, *Botswana*	53 J5	21 15S	25	30 E
Oras, *Phil.*	37 B7	12 9N	125	28 E
Oraşul Stalin = Braşov, *Romania*	17 F13	45 38N	25	35 E
Orbetello, *Italy*	20 C4	42 27N	11	13 E
Orbisonia, *U.S.A.*	78 F7	40 15N	77	54W
Orbost, *Australia*	63 F4	37 40S	148	29 E
Orcas I., *U.S.A.*	84 B4	48 42N	122	56W
Orchard City, *U.S.A.*	83 G10	38 50N	107	58W
Orchila, I., *Venezuela*	89 D6	11 48N	66	10W
Ord, *U.S.A.*	80 E5	41 36N	98	56W
Ord →, *Australia*	60 C4	15 33S	128	15 E
Ord, Mt., *Australia*	60 C4	17 20S	125	34 E
Orderville, *U.S.A.*	83 H7	37 17N	112	38W

Ordos = Mu Us Shamo, *China*	34 E5	39 0N	109	0 E
Ordu, *Turkey*	25 F6	40 55N	37	53 E
Ordway, *U.S.A.*	80 F3	38 13N	103	46W
Ordzhonikidze = Vladikavkaz, *Russia*	25 F7	43 0N	44	35 E
Ore, Dem. Rep. of the Congo	54 B2	3 17N	29	30 E
Ore Mts. = Erzgebirge, *Germany*	16 C7	50 27N	12	55 E
Örebro, *Sweden*	9 G16	59 20N	15	18 E
Oregon, *U.S.A.*	80 D10	42 1N	89	20W
Oregon □, *U.S.A.*	82 E3	44 0N	121	0W
Oregon City, *U.S.A.*	84 E4	45 21N	122	36W
Orekhovo-Zuyevo, *Russia*	24 C6	55 50N	38	55 E
Orel, *Russia*	24 D6	52 57N	36	3 E
Orem, *U.S.A.*	74 B4	40 19N	111	42W
Ören, *Turkey*	21 F12	37 3N	27	57 E
Orenburg, *Russia*	24 D10	51 45N	55	6 E
Orense = Ourense, *Spain*	19 A2	42 19N	7	55W
Orepuki, *N.Z.*	59 M1	46 19S	167	46 E
Orestiás, *Greece*	21 D12	41 30N	26	33 E
Orestos Pereyra, *Mexico*	86 B3	26 31N	105	40W
Orford Ness, *U.K.*	11 E9	52 5N	1	35 E
Organos, Pta. de los, *Canary Is.*	22 F2	28 12N	17	17W
Orgaz, *Spain*	19 C4	39 39N	3	53W
Orgeyev = Orhei, *Moldova*	17 E15	47 24N	28	50 E
Orhaneli, *Turkey*	21 E13	39 54N	28	59 E
Orhangazi, *Turkey*	21 D13	40 29N	29	18 E
Orhei, *Moldova*	17 E15	47 24N	28	50 E
Orhon Gol →, *Mongolia*	32 A5	50 21N	106	0 E
Oriental, Cordillera, *Colombia*	92 B4	6 0N	73	0W
Orientale □, Dem. Rep. of the Congo	54 B2	2 20N	26	0 E
Oriente, *Argentina*	94 D3	38 44S	60	37W
Orihuela, *Spain*	19 C5	38 7N	0	55W
Orillia, *Canada*	78 B5	44 40N	79	24W
Orinoco →, *Venezuela*	92 B6	9 15N	61	30W
Orion, *Canada*	73 D6	49 27N	110	49W
Oriskany, *U.S.A.*	79 C9	43 10N	75	20W
Orissa □, *India*	41 K14	20 0N	84	0 E
Orissaare, *Estonia*	9 G20	58 34N	23	5 E
Oristano, *Italy*	20 E3	39 54N	8	36 E
Oristano, G. di, *Italy*	20 E3	39 50N	8	29 E
Orizaba, *Mexico*	87 D5	18 51N	97	6W
Orkanger, *Norway*	8 E13	63 18N	9	52 E
Orkla →, *Norway*	8 E13	63 18N	9	51 E
Orkney, *S. Africa*	56 D4	26 58S	26	40 E
Orkney □, *U.K.*	12 B5	59 2N	3	13W
Orkney Is., *U.K.*	12 B6	59 0N	3	0W
Orland, *U.S.A.*	84 F4	39 45N	122	12W
Orlando, *U.S.A.*	77 L5	28 33N	81	23W
Orléanais, *France*	18 C5	48 0N	2	0 E
Orléans, *France*	18 C4	47 54N	1	52 E
Orleans, *U.S.A.*	79 B12	44 49N	72	12W
Orléans, I. d', *Canada*	71 C5	46 54N	70	58W
Ormara, *Pakistan*	40 G4	25 16N	64	33 E
Ormoc, *Phil.*	37 B6	11 0N	124	37 E
Ormond, *N.Z.*	59 H6	38 33S	177	56 E
Ormond Beach, *U.S.A.*	77 L5	29 17N	81	3W
Ormskirk, *U.K.*	10 D5	53 35N	2	54W
Ornstown, *Canada*	79 A11	45 8N	74	0W
Örnsköldsvik, *Sweden*	8 E18	63 17N	18	40 E
Oro, *N. Korea*	35 D14	40 1N	127	27 E
Oro →, *Mexico*	86 B3	25 35N	105	2W
Oro Grande, *U.S.A.*	85 L9	34 36N	117	20W
Oro Valley, *U.S.A.*	83 K8	32 26N	110	58W
Orocué, *Colombia*	92 C4	4 48N	71	20W
Orofino, *U.S.A.*	82 C5	46 29N	116	15W
Orol Dengizi = Aral Sea, *Asia*	26 E7	44 30N	60	0 E
Oromocto, *Canada*	71 C6	45 54N	66	29W
Orono, *Canada*	78 C6	43 59N	78	37W
Orono, *U.S.A.*	77 C11	44 53N	68	40W
Oronsay, *U.K.*	12 E2	56 1N	6	15W
Oroqen Zizhiqi, *China*	33 A7	50 34N	123	43 E
Oroquieta, *Phil.*	37 C6	8 32N	123	44 E
Orosháza, *Hungary*	17 E11	46 32N	20	42 E
Orotukan, *Russia*	27 C16	62 16N	151	42 E
Oroville, *Calif., U.S.A.*	84 F5	39 31N	121	33W
Oroville, *Wash., U.S.A.*	82 B4	48 56N	119	26W
Oroville, L., *U.S.A.*	84 F5	39 33N	121	29W
Orroroo, *Australia*	63 E2	32 43S	138	38 E
Orrville, *U.S.A.*	78 F3	40 50N	81	46W
Orsha, *Belarus*	24 D5	54 30N	30	25 E
Orsk, *Russia*	26 D6	51 12N	58	34 E
Orşova, *Romania*	17 F12	44 41N	22	25 E
Ortaca, *Turkey*	21 F13	36 49N	28	45 E
Ortegal, C., *Spain*	19 A2	43 43N	7	52W
Orthez, *France*	18 E3	43 29N	0	48W
Ortigueira, *Spain*	19 A2	43 40N	7	50W
Orting, *U.S.A.*	84 C4	47 6N	122	12W
Ortles, *Italy*	18 C9	46 31N	10	33 E
Ortón →, *Bolivia*	92 F5	10 50S	67	0W
Ortonville, *U.S.A.*	80 C6	45 19N	96	27W
Orūmīyeh, *Iran*	44 B5	37 40N	45	0 E
Orūmīyeh, Daryācheh-ye, *Iran*	44 B5	37 50N	45	30 E
Oruro, *Bolivia*	92 G5	18 0S	67	9W
Orust, *Sweden*	9 G14	58 10N	11	40 E
Oruzgān □, *Afghan.*	40 C5	33 30N	66	0 E
Orvieto, *Italy*	20 C5	42 43N	12	7 E
Orwell, *N.Y., U.S.A.*	79 C9	43 35N	75	50W
Orwell, *Ohio, U.S.A.*	78 E4	41 32N	80	52W
Orwell →, *U.K.*	11 F9	51 59N	1	18 E
Orwigsburg, *U.S.A.*	79 F8	40 38N	76	6W
Oryakhovo, *Bulgaria*	21 C10	43 40N	23	57 E
Osa, *Russia*	24 C10	57 17N	55	26 E
Osa, Pen. de, *Costa Rica*	88 E3	8 0N	84	0W
Osage, *U.S.A.*	80 D8	43 17N	92	49W
Osage →, *U.S.A.*	80 F9	38 35N	91	57W
Osage City, *U.S.A.*	80 F7	38 38N	95	50W
Ōsaka, *Japan*	31 G7	34 40N	135	30 E
Osan, *S. Korea*	35 F14	37 11N	127	4 E
Osawatomie, *U.S.A.*	80 F7	38 31N	94	57W
Osborne, *U.S.A.*	80 F5	39 26N	98	42W
Osceola, *Ark., U.S.A.*	81 H10	35 42N	89	58W
Osceola, *Iowa, U.S.A.*	80 E8	41 2N	93	46W
Oscoda, *U.S.A.*	78 B1	44 26N	83	20W
Ösel = Saaremaa, *Estonia*	9 G20	58 30N	22	30 E
Osgoode, *Canada*	79 A9	45 8N	75	36W
Osh, *Kyrgyzstan*	26 E8	40 37N	72	49 E
Oshakati, *Namibia*	53 H3	17 45S	15	40 E
Oshawa, *Canada*	78 C6	43 50N	78	50W
Oshkosh, *Nebr., U.S.A.*	80 E3	41 24N	102	21W
Oshkosh, *Wis., U.S.A.*	80 C10	44 1N	88	33W

P

Pangkalpinang, Indonesia . 36 E3 2 0S 106 0 E
Pangnirtung, Canada ... 69 B13 66 8N 65 54W
Pangong Tso, India 42 B8 34 40N 78 40 E
Panguitch, U.S.A. 83 H7 37 50N 112 26W
Pangutaran Group, Phil. . 37 C6 6 18N 120 34 E
Panhandle, U.S.A. 81 H4 35 21N 101 23W
Pani Mines, India 42 H5 22 29N 73 50 E
Pania-Mutombo,
 Dem. Rep. of the Congo . 54 D1 5 11S 23 51 E
Panikota I., India 42 J4 20 46N 71 21 E
Panipat, India 42 E7 29 25N 77 2 E
Panjal Range, India 42 C7 32 30N 76 50 E
Panjang, Hon, Vietnam .. 39 H4 9 20N 103 28 E
Panjgur, Pakistan 40 F4 27 0N 64 5 E
Panjim = Panaji, India .. 40 M8 15 25N 73 50 E
Panjin, China 35 D12 41 3N 122 2 E
Panjinad Barrage, Pakistan 40 E7 29 22N 71 15 E
Panjnad →, Pakistan ... 42 E4 28 57N 70 30 E
Panjwai, Afghan. 42 D1 31 26N 65 27 E
Panmunjom, N. Korea ... 35 F14 37 59N 126 38 E
Panna, India 43 G9 24 40N 80 15 E
Panna Hills, India 43 G9 24 40N 81 15 E
Pannawonica, Australia . 60 D2 21 39S 116 19 E
Pano Akil, Pakistan 42 F3 27 51N 69 7 E
Pano Lefkara, Cyprus .. 23 E12 34 53N 33 20 E
Pano Panayia, Cyprus .. 23 E11 34 55N 32 38 E
Panorama, Brazil 95 A5 21 21S 51 51W
Pansemal, India 42 J6 21 39N 74 42 E
Panshan = Panjin, China . 35 D12 41 3N 122 2 E
Panshi, China 35 C14 42 58N 126 5 E
Pantanal, Brazil 92 H7 17 30S 57 40W
Pantar, Indonesia 37 F6 8 28S 124 10 E
Pante Macassar, Indonesia 37 F6 9 30S 123 58 E
Pantelleria, Italy 20 F4 36 50N 11 57 E
Pánuco, Mexico 87 C5 22 0N 98 15W
Paola, Malta 23 D2 35 52N 14 30 E
Paola, U.S.A. 80 F7 38 35N 94 53W
Paonia, U.S.A. 83 G10 38 52N 107 36W
Paoting = Baoding, China . 34 E8 38 50N 115 28 E
Paot'ou = Baotou, China . 34 D6 40 32N 110 2 E
Paoua, C.A.R. 52 C3 7 9N 16 20 E
Pápa, Hungary 17 E9 47 22N 17 30 E
Papa Stour, U.K. 12 A7 60 20N 1 42W
Papa Westray, U.K. 12 B6 59 20N 2 55W
Papagayo →, Mexico .. 87 D5 16 36N 99 43W
Papagayo, G. de, Costa Rica 88 D2 10 30N 85 50W
Papakura, N.Z. 59 G5 37 4S 174 59 E
Papantla, Mexico 87 C5 20 30N 97 30W
Papar, Malaysia 36 C5 5 45N 116 0 E
Papeete, Tahiti 65 J13 17 32S 149 34W
Paphos, Cyprus 23 E11 34 46N 32 25 E
Papigochic →, Mexico . 86 B3 29 9N 109 40W
Paposo, Chile 94 B1 25 0S 70 30W
Papoutsa, Cyprus 23 E12 34 54N 33 4 E
Papua New Guinea ■,
 Oceania 64 H6 8 0S 145 0 E
Papudo, Chile 94 C1 32 29S 71 27W
Papun, Burma 41 K20 18 2N 97 30 E
Papunya, Australia 60 D5 23 15S 131 54 E
Pará = Belém, Brazil .. 93 D9 1 20S 48 30W
Pará □, Brazil 93 D8 3 20S 52 0W
Paraburdoo, Australia .. 60 D2 23 14S 117 32 E
Paracatu, Brazil 93 G9 17 10S 46 50W
Paracel Is., S. China Sea . 36 A4 15 50N 112 0 E
Parachilna, Australia .. 63 E2 31 10S 138 21 E
Parachinar, Pakistan ... 42 C4 33 55N 70 5 E
Paradhísi, Greece 23 C10 36 18N 28 7 E
Paradip, India 41 J15 20 15N 86 35 E
Paradise, Calif., U.S.A. . 84 F5 39 46N 121 37W
Paradise, Nev., U.S.A. . 85 J11 36 9N 115 10W
Paradise →, Canada .. 71 B8 53 27N 57 19W
Paradise Hill, Canada .. 73 C7 53 32N 109 28W
Paradise River, Canada . 71 B8 53 27N 57 17W
Paradise Valley, U.S.A. . 82 F5 41 30N 117 32W
Parado, Indonesia 37 F5 8 42S 118 30 E
Paragould, U.S.A. 81 G9 36 3N 90 29W
Paragua →, Venezuela . 92 B6 6 55N 62 55W
Paraguaçu →, Brazil .. 93 F11 12 45S 38 54W
Paraguaçu Paulista, Brazil 95 A5 22 22S 50 35W
Paraguaná, Pen. de,
 Venezuela 92 A5 12 0N 70 0W
Paraguarí, Paraguay ... 94 B4 25 36S 57 0W
Paraguarí □, Paraguay . 94 B4 26 0S 57 10W
Paraguay ■, S. Amer. .. 94 A4 23 0S 57 0W
Paraguay →, Paraguay . 94 B4 27 18S 58 38W
Paraíba = João Pessoa,
 Brazil 93 E12 7 10S 34 52W
Paraíba □, Brazil 93 E11 7 0S 36 0W
Paraíba do Sul →, Brazil . 95 A7 21 37S 41 3W
Parainen, Finland 9 F20 60 18N 22 18 E
Paraíso, Mexico 87 D6 18 24N 93 14W
Parak, Iran 45 E7 27 38N 52 25 E
Parakou, Benin 50 G6 9 25N 2 40 E
Paralimni, Cyprus 23 D12 35 2N 33 58 E
Paramaribo, Surinam ... 93 B7 5 50N 55 10W
Paramushir, Ostrov, Russia 27 D16 50 24N 156 0 E
Paran →, Israel 47 E4 30 20N 35 10 E
Paraná, Argentina 94 C3 31 45S 60 30W
Paraná, Brazil 93 F9 12 30S 47 48W
Paraná □, Brazil 95 A5 24 30S 51 0W
Paraná →, Argentina .. 94 C4 33 43S 59 15W
Paranaguá, Brazil 95 B6 25 30S 48 30W
Paranaíba, Brazil 93 G8 19 40S 51 11W
Paranaíba →, Brazil ... 93 H8 20 6S 51 4W
Paranapanema →, Brazil . 95 A5 22 40S 53 9W
Paranapiacaba, Serra do,
 Brazil 95 A6 24 31S 48 35W
Paranavaí, Brazil 95 A5 23 4S 52 56W
Parang, Jolo, Phil. 37 C6 5 55N 120 54 E
Parang, Mindanao, Phil. . 37 C6 7 23N 124 16 E
Parângul Mare, Vf., Romania 17 F12 45 20N 23 37 E
Parbati →, India 42 F6 26 54N 77 53 E
Parbati →, India 42 G7 25 50N 76 30 E
Parbhani, India 40 K10 19 8N 76 52 E
Parchim, Germany 16 B6 53 26N 11 52 E
Pardes Hanna-Karkur, Israel 47 C3 32 28N 34 57 E
Pardo →, Bahia, Brazil . 93 G11 15 40S 39 0W
Pardo →, Mato Grosso,
 Brazil 95 A5 21 46S 52 9W
Pardubice, Czech Rep. . 16 C8 50 3N 15 45 E
Pare, Indonesia 37 G15 7 43S 112 12 E
Pare Mts., Tanzania 54 C4 4 0S 37 45 E
Parecis, Serra dos, Brazil . 92 F7 13 0S 60 0W
Paren, Russia 27 C17 62 30N 163 15 E
Parent, Canada 70 C5 47 55N 74 35W

Parent, L., Canada 70 C4 48 31N 77 1W
Parepare, Indonesia 37 E5 4 0S 119 40 E
Párga, Greece 21 E9 39 15N 20 29 E
Pargo, Pta. do, Madeira . 22 D2 32 49N 17 17W
Pariaguán, Venezuela .. 92 B6 8 51N 64 34W
Paricutín, Cerro, Mexico . 86 D4 19 28N 102 15W
Parigi, Indonesia 37 E6 0 50S 120 5 E
Parika, Guyana 92 B7 6 50N 58 20W
Parima, Serra, Brazil ... 92 C6 2 30N 64 0W
Parinari, Peru 92 D4 4 35S 74 25W
Pariñas, Pta., S. Amer. . 90 D2 4 30S 82 0W
Parintins, Brazil 93 D7 2 40S 56 50W
Pariparit Kyun, Burma .. 41 M18 14 55N 93 45 E
Paris, Canada 78 C4 43 12N 80 25W
Paris, France 18 B5 48 50N 2 20 E
Paris, Idaho, U.S.A. 82 E8 42 14N 111 24W
Paris, Ky., U.S.A. 76 F3 38 13N 84 15W
Paris, Tenn., U.S.A. 77 G1 36 18N 88 19W
Paris, Tex., U.S.A. 81 J7 33 40N 95 33W
Parish, U.S.A. 79 C8 43 25N 76 8W
Parishville, U.S.A. 79 B10 44 38N 74 49W
Park, U.S.A. 84 B4 48 45N 122 18W
Park City, U.S.A. 81 G6 37 48N 97 20W
Park Falls, U.S.A. 80 C9 45 56N 90 27W
Park Head, Canada 78 B3 44 36N 81 9W
Park Hills, U.S.A. 81 G9 37 53N 90 28W
Park Range, U.S.A. 82 G10 40 0N 106 30W
Park Rapids, U.S.A. 80 B7 46 55N 95 4W
Park River, U.S.A. 80 A6 48 24N 97 45W
Park Rynie, S. Africa ... 57 E5 30 25S 30 45 E
Parkå Bandar, Iran 45 E8 25 55N 59 35 E
Parkano, Finland 9 E20 62 1N 23 0 E
Parker, Ariz., U.S.A. ... 85 L12 34 9N 114 17W
Parker, Pa., U.S.A. 78 E5 41 5N 79 41W
Parker Dam, U.S.A. 85 L12 34 18N 114 8W
Parkersburg, U.S.A. ... 76 F5 39 16N 81 34W
Parkes, Australia 63 E4 33 9S 148 11 E
Parkfield, U.S.A. 84 K6 35 54N 120 26W
Parkhill, Canada 78 C3 43 15N 81 38W
Parkland, U.S.A. 84 C4 47 9N 122 26W
Parkston, U.S.A. 80 D6 43 24N 97 59W
Parksville, Canada 72 D4 49 20N 124 21W
Parla, Spain 19 B4 40 14N 3 46W
Parma, Italy 18 D9 44 48N 10 20 E
Parma, Idaho, U.S.A. ... 82 E5 43 47N 116 57W
Parma, Ohio, U.S.A. ... 78 E3 41 23N 81 43W
Parnaguá, Brazil 93 F10 10 10S 44 38W
Parnaíba, Brazil 93 D10 2 54S 41 47W
Parnaíba →, Brazil 93 D10 3 0S 41 50W
Parnassós, Greece 21 E10 38 35N 22 30 E
Pärnu, Estonia 9 G21 58 28N 24 33 E
Paroo →, Australia 63 E3 31 28S 143 32 E
Páros, Greece 21 F11 37 5N 25 12 E
Parowan, U.S.A. 83 H7 37 51N 112 50W
Parral, Chile 94 D1 36 10S 71 52W
Parras, Mexico 86 B4 25 30N 102 20W
Parrett →, U.K. 11 F4 51 12N 3 1W
Parris I., U.S.A. 77 J5 32 20N 80 41W
Parrsboro, Canada 71 C7 45 30N 64 25W
Parry I., Canada 78 A4 45 18N 80 10W
Parry Is., Canada 4 B2 77 0N 110 0W
Parry Sound, Canada .. 78 A5 45 20N 80 0W
Parsnip →, Canada ... 72 B4 55 10N 123 2W
Parsons, U.S.A. 81 G7 37 20N 95 16W
Parsons Ra., Australia . 62 A2 13 30S 135 15 E
Partinico, Italy 20 E5 38 3N 13 7 E
Partridge I., Canada ... 70 A2 55 59N 87 37W
Paru →, Brazil 93 D8 1 33S 52 38W
Parvān □, Afghan. 40 B6 35 0N 69 0 E
Parvatipuram, India 41 K13 18 50N 83 25 E
Parvatsar, India 42 F6 26 52N 74 49 E
Parys, S. Africa 56 D4 26 52S 27 29 E
Pas, Pta. des, Spain ... 22 C7 38 46N 1 26 E
Pasadena, Canada 71 C8 49 1N 57 36W
Pasadena, Calif., U.S.A. . 85 L8 34 9N 118 9W
Pasadena, Tex., U.S.A. . 81 L7 29 43N 95 13W
Pasaje →, Argentina .. 94 B3 25 39S 63 56W
Pascagoula, U.S.A. 81 K10 30 21N 88 33W
Pascagoula →, U.S.A. . 81 K10 30 23N 88 37W
Pașcani, Romania 17 E14 47 14N 26 45 E
Pasco, U.S.A. 82 C4 46 14N 119 6W
Pasco, Cerro de, Peru .. 92 F3 10 45S 76 10W
Pasco I., Australia 60 D2 20 57S 115 20 E
Pascoag, U.S.A. 79 E13 41 57N 71 42W
Pascua, I. de, Pac. Oc. . 65 K17 27 0S 109 0W
Pasfield L., Canada 73 B7 58 24N 105 20W
Pashiwari, Pakistan 43 B6 34 40N 75 10 E
Pashmakli = Smolyan,
 Bulgaria 21 D11 41 36N 24 38 E
Pasir Mas, Malaysia 39 J4 6 2N 102 8 E
Pasir Putih, Malaysia ... 39 K4 5 50N 102 24 E
Pasirian, Indonesia 37 H15 8 13S 113 8 E
Pasirkuning, Indonesia . 36 E2 0 30S 104 33 E
Pasküh, Iran 45 E9 27 34N 61 39 E
Pasley, C., Australia ... 61 F3 33 52S 123 35 E
Pašman, Croatia 16 G8 43 58N 15 20 E
Pasni, Pakistan 40 G3 25 15N 63 27 E
Paso Cantinela, Mexico . 85 N11 32 33N 115 47W
Paso de Indios, Argentina . 96 E3 43 55S 69 0W
Paso de los Libres,
 Argentina 94 B4 29 44S 57 10W
Paso de los Toros, Uruguay 94 C4 32 45S 56 30W
Paso Robles, U.S.A. ... 83 J3 35 38N 120 41W
Paspébiac, Canada 71 C6 48 3N 65 17W
Pasrur, Pakistan 42 C6 32 16N 74 43 E
Passage West, Ireland . 13 E3 51 52N 8 21W
Passaic, U.S.A. 79 F10 40 51N 74 7W
Passau, Germany 16 D7 48 34N 13 28 E
Passero, C., Italy 20 F6 36 41N 15 10 E
Passo Fundo, Brazil ... 95 B5 28 10S 52 20W
Passos, Brazil 93 H9 20 45S 46 37W
Pastaza →, Peru 92 D3 4 50S 76 52W
Pasto, Colombia 92 C3 1 13N 77 17W
Pasuruan, Indonesia ... 37 G15 7 40S 112 44 E
Patagonia, Argentina .. 96 F3 45 0S 69 0W
Patagonia, U.S.A. 83 L8 31 33N 110 45W
Patambar, Iran 45 D9 29 45N 60 17 E
Patan, India 40 H8 23 54N 72 14 E
Patan, Maharashtra, India . 42 H5 23 54N 72 14 E
Patani, Indonesia 37 D7 0 20N 128 50 E
Pataudi, India 42 E7 28 18N 76 48 E
Patchewollock, Australia . 63 F3 35 22S 142 12 E
Patchogue, U.S.A. 79 F11 40 46N 73 1W
Patea, N.Z. 59 H5 39 45S 174 30 E

Patensie, S. Africa 56 E3 33 46S 24 49 E
Paternò, Italy 20 F6 37 34N 14 54 E
Pateros, U.S.A. 82 B4 48 3N 119 54W
Paterson, U.S.A. 79 F10 40 56N 74 11W
Paterson Ra., Australia . 60 D3 21 45S 122 10 E
Pathankot, India 42 C6 32 18N 75 45 E
Pathfinder Reservoir, U.S.A. 82 E10 42 28N 106 51W
Pathiu, Thailand 39 G2 10 42N 99 19 E
Pathum Thani, Thailand . 38 E3 14 1N 100 32 E
Pati, Indonesia 37 G14 6 45S 111 1 E
Patía →, Colombia 92 C3 2 13N 78 40W
Patiala, Punjab, India .. 42 D7 30 23N 76 26 E
Patiala, Ut. P., India ... 43 F8 27 43N 79 1 E
Patkai Bum, India 41 F19 27 0N 95 30 E
Pátmos, Greece 21 F12 37 21N 26 36 E
Patna, India 43 G11 25 35N 85 12 E
Pato Branco, Brazil ... 95 B5 26 13S 52 40W
Patonga, Uganda 54 B3 2 45N 33 15 E
Patos, Brazil 93 E11 6 55S 37 16W
Patos, L. dos, Brazil ... 95 C5 31 20S 51 0W
Patos, Río de los →,
 Argentina 94 C2 31 18S 69 25W
Patos de Minas, Brazil . 93 G9 18 35S 46 32W
Patquía, Argentina 94 C2 30 2S 66 55W
Pátrai, Greece 21 E9 38 14N 21 47 E
Pátraikós Kólpos, Greece . 21 E9 38 17N 21 30 E
Patras = Pátrai, Greece . 21 E9 38 14N 21 47 E
Patrocínio, Brazil 93 G9 18 57S 47 0W
Patta, Kenya 54 C5 2 10S 41 0 E
Pattani, Thailand 39 J3 6 48N 101 15 E
Pattaya, Thailand 36 B2 12 52N 100 55 E
Patten, U.S.A. 77 C11 46 0N 68 38W
Patterson, Calif., U.S.A. . 84 H5 37 28N 121 8W
Patterson, La., U.S.A. .. 81 L9 29 42N 91 18W
Patterson, Mt., U.S.A. . 84 G7 38 29N 119 20W
Patti, Punjab, India 42 D6 31 17N 74 54 E
Patti, Ut. P., India 43 G10 25 55N 82 12 E
Pattoki, Pakistan 42 D5 31 5N 73 52 E
Patton, U.S.A. 78 F6 40 38N 78 39W
Patuakhali, Bangla. 41 H17 22 20N 90 25 E
Patuanak, Canada 73 B7 55 55N 107 43W
Patuca →, Honduras .. 88 C3 15 50N 84 18W
Patuca, Punta, Honduras . 88 C3 15 49N 84 14W
Pátzcuaro, Mexico 86 D4 19 30N 101 40W
Pau, France 18 E3 43 19N 0 25W
Pauk, Burma 41 J19 21 27N 94 30 E
Paul I., Canada 71 A7 56 30N 61 20W
Paul Smiths, U.S.A. ... 79 B10 44 26N 74 15W
Paulatuk, Canada 68 B7 69 25N 124 0W
Paulis = Isiro,
 Dem. Rep. of the Congo . 54 B2 2 53N 27 40 E
Paulistana, Brazil 93 E10 8 9S 41 9W
Paulo Afonso, Brazil ... 93 E11 9 21S 38 15W
Paulpietersburg, S. Africa . 57 D5 27 23S 30 50 E
Pauls Valley, U.S.A. ... 81 H6 34 44N 97 13W
Pauma Valley, U.S.A. .. 85 M10 33 16N 116 58W
Pauri, India 43 D8 30 9N 78 47 E
Pāveh, Iran 44 C5 35 3N 46 22 E
Pavia, Italy 18 D8 45 7N 9 8 E
Pavilion, U.S.A. 78 D6 42 52N 78 1W
Pāvilosta, Latvia 9 H19 56 53N 21 14 E
Pavlodar, Kazakstan ... 26 D8 52 33N 77 0 E
Pavlograd = Pavlohrad,
 Ukraine 25 E6 48 30N 35 52 E
Pavlohrad, Ukraine 25 E6 48 30N 35 52 E
Pavlovo, Russia 24 C7 55 58N 43 5 E
Pavlovsk, Russia 25 D7 50 26N 40 5 E
Pavlovskaya, Russia ... 25 E6 46 17N 39 47 E
Pawayan, India 43 E9 28 4N 80 6 E
Pawhuska, U.S.A. 81 G6 36 40N 96 20W
Pawling, U.S.A. 79 E11 41 34N 73 36W
Pawnee, U.S.A. 81 G6 36 20N 96 48W
Pawnee City, U.S.A. ... 80 E6 40 7N 96 9W
Pawtucket, U.S.A. 79 E13 41 53N 71 23W
Paximádhia, Greece ... 23 E6 35 0N 24 35 E
Paxoí, Greece 21 E9 39 14N 20 12 E
Paxton, Ill., U.S.A. 76 E1 40 27N 88 6W
Paxton, Nebr., U.S.A. .. 80 E4 41 7N 101 21W
Payakumbuh, Indonesia . 36 E2 0 20S 100 35 E
Payette, U.S.A. 82 D5 44 5N 116 56W
Payne Bay = Kangirsuk,
 Canada 69 C13 60 0N 70 0W
Payne L., Canada 69 C12 59 30N 74 30W
Paynes Find, Australia . 61 E2 29 15S 117 42 E
Paynesville, U.S.A. ... 80 C7 45 23N 94 43W
Paysandú, Uruguay ... 94 C4 32 19S 58 8W
Payson, Ariz., U.S.A. .. 83 J8 34 14N 111 20W
Payson, Utah, U.S.A. .. 74 B4 40 3N 111 44W
Paz →, Guatemala ... 88 D1 13 44N 90 10W
Paz, B. la, Mexico 86 C2 24 15N 110 25W
Pāzanān, Iran 45 D6 30 35N 49 59 E
Pazardzhik, Bulgaria .. 21 C11 42 12N 24 20 E
Pe Ell, U.S.A. 84 D3 46 34N 123 18W
Peabody, U.S.A. 79 D14 42 31N 70 56W
Peace →, Canada 72 B6 59 0N 111 25W
Peace Point, Canada .. 72 B6 59 7N 112 27W
Peace River, Canada .. 72 B5 56 15N 117 18W
Peach Springs, U.S.A. . 83 J7 35 32N 113 25W
Peachland, Canada 72 D5 49 47N 119 45W
Peachtree City, U.S.A. . 77 J3 33 25N 84 35W
Peak, The = Kinder Scout,
 U.K. 10 D6 53 24N 1 52W
Peak District, U.K. 10 D6 53 10N 1 50W
Peak Hill, N.S.W., Australia . 63 E4 32 47S 148 11 E
Peak Hill, W. Austral.,
 Australia 61 E2 25 35S 118 43 E
Peak Ra., Australia 62 C4 22 50S 148 20 E
Peake Cr. →, Australia . 63 D2 28 2S 136 7 E
Peale, Mt., U.S.A. 83 G9 38 26N 109 14W
Pearblossom, U.S.A. .. 85 L9 34 30N 117 55W
Pearl →, U.S.A. 81 K10 30 11N 89 32W
Pearl City, U.S.A. 74 H16 21 24N 157 59W
Pearl Harbor, U.S.A. .. 74 H16 21 21N 157 57W
Pearl River, U.S.A. ... 79 E10 41 4N 74 2W
Pearsall, U.S.A. 81 L5 28 54N 99 6W
Peary Land, Greenland . 4 A6 82 40N 33 0W
Pease →, U.S.A. 81 H5 34 12N 99 2W
Peawanuck, Canada ... 69 C11 55 15N 85 12W
Pebane, Mozam. 55 F4 17 10S 38 8 E
Pebas, Peru 92 D4 3 10S 71 46W
Pebble Beach, U.S.A. .. 84 J5 36 34N 121 57W
Peć, Yugoslavia 21 C9 42 40N 20 17 E
Pechenga, Russia 24 A5 69 29N 31 4 E
Pechenizhyn, Ukraine . 17 D13 48 30N 24 48 E
Pechiguera, Pta., Canary Is. 22 F6 28 51N 13 53W
Pechora, Russia 24 A10 65 10N 57 11 E

Pechora →, Russia ... 24 A9 68 13N 54 15 E
Pechorskaya Guba, Russia . 24 A9 68 40N 54 0 E
Pečory, Russia 9 H22 57 48N 27 40 E
Pecos, U.S.A. 81 K3 31 26N 103 30W
Pecos →, U.S.A. 81 L3 29 42N 101 22W
Pécs, Hungary 17 E10 46 5N 18 15 E
Pedder, L., Australia ... 62 G4 42 55S 146 10 E
Peddie, S. Africa 57 E4 33 14S 27 7 E
Pédernales, Dom. Rep. . 89 C5 18 2N 71 44W
Pedieos →, Cyprus ... 23 D12 35 10N 33 54 E
Pedirka, Australia 63 D2 26 40S 135 14 E
Pedra Azul, Brazil 93 G10 16 2S 41 17W
Pedreiras, Brazil 93 D10 4 32S 44 40W
Pedro Afonso, Brazil .. 93 E9 9 0S 48 10W
Pedro Cays, Jamaica .. 88 C4 17 5N 77 48W
Pedro de Valdivia, Chile . 94 A2 22 55S 69 38W
Pedro Juan Caballero,
 Paraguay 95 A4 22 30S 55 40W
Pee Dee →, U.S.A. ... 77 J6 33 22N 79 16W
Peebinga, Australia ... 63 E3 34 52S 140 57 E
Peebles, U.K. 12 F5 55 40N 3 11W
Peekskill, U.S.A. 79 E11 41 17N 73 55W
Peel, U.K. 10 C3 54 13N 4 40W
Peel →, Australia 63 E5 30 50S 150 29 E
Peel →, Canada 68 B6 67 0N 135 0W
Peel Sound, Canada ... 68 A10 73 0N 96 0W
Peera Peera Poolanna L.,
 Australia 63 D2 26 30S 138 0 E
Peerless Lake, Canada . 72 B6 56 37N 114 40W
Peers, Canada 72 C5 53 40N 116 0W
Pegasus Bay, N.Z. 59 K4 43 20S 173 10 E
Pegu, Burma 41 L20 17 20N 96 29 E
Pegu Yoma, Burma 41 K20 19 0N 96 0 E
Pehuajó, Argentina ... 94 D3 35 45S 62 0W
Pei Xian = Pizhou, China . 34 G9 34 44N 116 55 E
Peine, Chile 94 A2 23 45S 68 8W
Peine, Germany 16 B6 52 19N 10 14 E
Peip'ing = Beijing, China . 34 E9 39 55N 116 20 E
Peipus, L. = Chudskoye,
 Ozero, Russia 9 G22 58 13N 27 30 E
Peixe, Brazil 93 F9 12 0S 48 40W
Peixe →, Brazil 93 H8 21 31S 51 58W
Pekalongan, Indonesia . 37 G13 6 53S 109 40 E
Pekan, Malaysia 39 L4 3 30N 103 25 E
Pekanbaru, Indonesia . 36 D2 0 30N 101 15 E
Pekin, U.S.A. 80 E10 40 35N 89 40W
Peking = Beijing, China . 34 E9 39 55N 116 20 E
Pelabuhan Kelang, Malaysia 39 L3 3 0N 101 23 E
Pelabuhan Ratu, Teluk,
 Indonesia 37 G12 7 5S 106 30 E
Pelabuhanratu, Indonesia . 37 G12 7 0S 106 32 E
Pelagie, Is., Italy 20 G5 35 39N 12 33 E
Pelaihari, Indonesia ... 36 E4 3 55S 114 45 E
Peleaga, Vf., Romania . 17 F12 45 22N 22 55 E
Pelée, Mt., Martinique . 89 D7 14 48N 61 10W
Pelee, Pt., Canada 70 D3 41 54N 82 31W
Pelee I., Canada 78 E2 41 47N 82 40W
Pelekech, Kenya 54 B4 3 52N 35 8 E
Peleng, Indonesia 37 E6 1 20S 123 30 E
Pelican, U.S.A. 72 B1 57 58N 136 14W
Pelican L., Canada 73 C8 52 28N 100 20W
Pelican Narrows, Canada . 73 B8 55 10N 102 56W
Peljesac, Croatia 20 C7 42 55N 17 25 E
Pelkosenniemi, Finland . 8 C22 67 6N 27 28 E
Pella, S. Africa 56 D2 29 1S 19 6 E
Pella, U.S.A. 80 E8 41 25N 92 55W
Pello, Finland 8 C21 66 47N 23 59 E
Pelly →, Canada 68 B6 62 47N 137 19W
Pelly Bay, Canada 69 B11 68 38N 89 50W
Peloponnese □ =
 Pelopónnisos □, Greece . 21 F10 37 10N 22 0 E
Pelopónnisos □, Greece . 21 F10 37 10N 22 0 E
Pelorus Sd., N.Z. 59 J4 40 59S 173 59 E
Pelotas, Brazil 95 C5 31 42S 52 23W
Pelotas →, Brazil 95 B5 27 28S 51 55W
Pelvoux, Massif du, France . 18 D7 44 52N 6 20 E
Pemalang, Indonesia .. 37 G13 6 53S 109 23 E
Pemanggil, Pulau, Malaysia . 39 L5 2 37N 104 21 E
Pematangsiantar, Indonesia . 36 D1 2 57N 99 5 E
Pemba, Mozam. 55 E5 12 58S 40 30 E
Pemba, Zambia 55 F2 16 30S 27 28 E
Pemba Channel, Tanzania . 54 D4 5 0S 39 37 E
Pemba I., Tanzania 54 D4 5 0S 39 45 E
Pemberton, Australia .. 61 F2 34 30S 116 0 E
Pemberton, Canada ... 72 C4 50 25N 122 50W
Pembina, U.S.A. 80 A6 48 58N 97 15W
Pembroke, Canada 70 C4 45 50N 77 7W
Pembroke, U.K. 11 F3 51 41N 4 55W
Pembrokeshire □, U.K. . 11 F3 51 52N 4 56W
Pen-y-Ghent, U.K. 10 C5 54 10N 2 14W
Penang = Pinang, Malaysia . 39 K3 5 25N 100 15 E
Penápolis, Brazil 95 A6 21 30S 50 0W
Peñarroya-Pueblonuevo,
 Spain 19 C3 38 19N 5 16W
Penarth, U.K. 11 F4 51 26N 3 11W
Peñas, C. de, Spain ... 19 A3 43 42N 5 52W
Penas, G. de, Chile ... 96 F2 47 0S 75 0W
Peñas del Chache,
 Canary Is. 22 E6 29 6N 13 33W
Pench'i = Benxi, China . 35 D12 41 20N 123 48 E
Pend Oreille →, U.S.A. . 82 B5 49 4N 117 37W
Pend Oreille, L., U.S.A. . 82 C5 48 10N 116 21W
Pendembu, S. Leone .. 50 G3 9 7N 11 14W
Pender B., Australia ... 60 C3 16 45S 122 42 E
Pendleton, U.S.A. 82 D4 45 40N 118 47W
Pendra, India 43 H9 22 46N 81 57 E
Penedo, Brazil 93 F11 10 15S 36 36W
Penetanguishene, Canada . 78 B5 44 50N 79 55W
Pengalengan, Indonesia . 37 G12 7 9S 107 30 E
Penge, Kasai-Or.,
 Dem. Rep. of the Congo . 54 D1 5 30S 24 33 E
Penge, Sud-Kivu,
 Dem. Rep. of the Congo . 54 C2 4 27S 28 25 E
Penglai, China 35 F11 37 48N 120 42 E
Penguin, Australia 62 G4 41 8S 146 6 E
Penhalonga, Zimbabwe . 55 F3 18 52S 32 40 E
Peniche, Portugal 19 C1 39 19N 9 22W
Penicuik, U.K. 12 F5 55 50N 3 13W
Penida, Indonesia 36 F5 8 45S 115 30 E
Peninsular Malaysia □,
 Malaysia 39 L4 4 0N 102 0 E
Penitente, Serra do, Brazil . 93 E9 8 45S 46 20W
Penkridge, U.K. 10 E5 52 44N 2 6W
Penmarch, Pte. de, France . 18 C1 47 48N 4 22W
Penn Hills, U.S.A. 78 F5 40 28N 79 52W

Penn Yan, U.S.A. 78 D7 42 40N 77 3W
Pennant, Canada 73 C7 50 32N 108 14W
Penner →, India 40 M12 14 35N 80 10 E
Pennines, U.K. 10 C5 54 45N 2 27W
Pennington, U.S.A. 84 F5 39 15N 121 47W
Pennsburg, U.S.A. 79 F9 40 23N 75 29W
Pennsylvania □, U.S.A. .. 76 E7 40 45N 77 30W
Penny, Canada 72 C4 53 51N 121 20W
Penobscot →, U.S.A. 77 C11 44 30N 68 48W
Penobscot B., U.S.A. 77 C11 44 35N 68 50W
Penola, Australia 63 F3 37 25S 140 48 E
Penong, Australia 61 F5 31 56S 133 1 E
Penonomé, Panama 88 E3 8 31N 80 21W
Penrith, Australia 63 E5 33 43S 150 38 E
Penrith, U.K. 10 C5 54 40N 2 45W
Penryn, U.K. 11 G2 50 9N 5 7W
Pensacola, U.S.A. 77 K2 30 25N 87 13W
Pensacola Mts., Antarctica 5 E1 84 0S 40 0W
Pense, Canada 73 C8 50 25N 104 59W
Penshurst, Australia 63 F3 37 49S 142 20 E
Penticton, Canada 72 D5 49 30N 119 38W
Pentland, Australia 62 C4 20 32S 145 25 E
Pentland Firth, U.K. 12 C5 58 43N 3 10W
Pentland Hills, U.K. 12 F5 55 48N 3 25W
Penza, Russia 24 D8 53 15N 45 5 E
Penzance, U.K. 11 G2 50 7N 5 33W
Penzhino, Russia 27 C17 63 30N 167 55 E
Penzhinskaya Guba, Russia 27 C17 61 30N 163 0 E
Peoria, Ariz., U.S.A. 83 K7 33 35N 112 14W
Peoria, Ill., U.S.A. 80 E10 40 42N 89 36W
Pepacton Reservoir, U.S.A. 79 D10 42 5N 74 58W
Pera Hd., Australia 62 A3 12 55S 141 37 E
Perabumulih, Indonesia . 36 E2 3 27S 104 15 E
Perak →, Malaysia 39 K3 4 0N 100 50 E
Pérama, Kérkira, Greece . 23 A3 39 34N 19 54 E
Pérama, Kríti, Greece ... 23 D6 35 20N 24 40 E
Peräpohjola, Finland 8 C22 66 16N 26 10 E
Percé, Canada 71 C7 48 31N 64 13W
Perche, Collines du, France 18 B4 48 30N 0 40 E
Percival Lakes, Australia . 60 D4 21 25S 125 0 E
Percy Is., Australia 62 C5 21 39S 150 16 E
Perdido, Mte., Spain 19 A6 42 40N 0 5 E
Perdu, Mt. = Perdido, Mte.,
 Spain 19 A6 42 40N 0 5 E
Pereira, Colombia 92 C3 4 49N 75 43W
Perenjori, Australia 61 E2 29 26S 116 16 E
Pereyaslav-Khmelnytskyy,
 Ukraine 25 D5 50 3N 31 28 E
Pérez, I., Mexico 87 C7 22 24N 89 42W
Pergamino, Argentina ... 94 C3 33 52S 60 30W
Pergau →, Malaysia 39 K3 5 23N 102 2 E
Perham, U.S.A. 80 B7 46 36N 95 34W
Perhentian, Kepulauan,
 Malaysia 36 C2 5 54N 102 42 E
Péribonca →, Canada .. 71 C5 48 45N 72 5W
Péribonca, L., Canada ... 71 B5 50 1N 71 10W
Perico, Argentina 94 A2 24 20S 65 5W
Pericos, Mexico 86 B3 25 3N 107 42W
Périgueux, France 18 D4 45 10N 0 42 E
Perijá, Sierra de, Colombia 92 B4 9 30N 73 3W
Peristerona →, Cyprus . 23 D12 35 8N 33 5 E
Perito Moreno, Argentina 96 F2 46 36S 70 56W
Perkasie, U.S.A. 79 F9 40 22N 75 18W
Perlas, Arch. de las,
 Panama 88 E4 8 41N 79 7W
Perlas, Punta de, Nic. ... 88 D3 12 30N 83 30W
Perm, Russia 24 C10 58 0N 56 10 E
Pernambuco = Recife, Brazil 93 E12 8 0S 35 0W
Pernambuco □, Brazil .. 93 E11 8 0S 37 0W
Pernatty Lagoon, Australia 63 E2 31 30S 137 12 E
Pernik, Bulgaria 21 C10 42 35N 23 2 E
Peron Is., Australia 60 B5 13 9S 130 4 E
Peron Pen., Australia ... 61 E1 26 0S 113 10 E
Perow, Canada 72 C3 54 35N 126 10W
Perpendicular Pt., Australia 63 E5 31 37S 152 52 E
Perpignan, France 18 E5 42 42N 2 53 E
Perris, U.S.A. 85 M9 33 47N 117 14W
Perry, Fla., U.S.A. 77 K4 30 7N 83 35W
Perry, Ga., U.S.A. 77 J4 32 28N 83 44W
Perry, Iowa, U.S.A. 80 E7 41 51N 94 6W
Perry, Okla., U.S.A. 81 G6 36 17N 97 14W
Perryton, U.S.A. 81 G4 36 24N 100 48W
Perryville, U.S.A. 81 G10 37 43N 89 52W
Persepolis, Iran 45 D7 29 55N 52 50 E
Pershotravensk, Ukraine . 17 C14 50 13N 27 40 E
Persia = Iran ■, Asia ... 45 C7 33 0N 53 0 E
Persian Gulf = Gulf, The,
 Asia 45 E6 27 0N 50 0 E
Perth, Australia 61 F2 31 57S 115 52 E
Perth, Canada 79 B8 44 55N 76 15W
Perth, U.K. 12 E5 56 24N 3 26W
Perth & Kinross □, U.K. . 12 E5 56 45N 3 55W
Perth Amboy, U.S.A. ... 79 F10 40 31N 74 16W
Perth-Andover, Canada . 71 C6 46 44N 67 42W
Peru, Ind., U.S.A. 76 E2 40 45N 86 4W
Peru, N.Y., U.S.A. 79 B11 44 35N 73 32W
Peru ■, S. Amer. 92 D4 4 0S 75 0W
Peru-Chile Trench, Pac. Oc. 92 G3 20 0S 72 0W
Perúgia, Italy 20 C5 43 7N 12 23 E
Pervomaysk, Ukraine ... 25 E5 48 10N 30 46 E
Pervouralsk, Russia 24 C10 56 59N 59 59 E
Pésaro, Italy 20 C5 43 54N 12 55 E
Pescara, Italy 20 C6 42 28N 14 13 E
Peshawar, Pakistan 42 B4 34 2N 71 37 E
Peshkopi, Albania 21 D9 41 41N 20 25 E
Peshtigo, U.S.A. 76 C2 45 4N 87 46W
Pesqueira, Brazil 93 E11 8 20S 36 42W
Petah Tiqwa, Israel 47 C3 32 6N 34 53 E
Petaling Jaya, Malaysia . 39 L3 3 4N 101 42 E
Petaloudhes, Greece ... 23 C10 36 18N 28 5 E
Petaluma, U.S.A. 84 G4 38 14N 122 39W
Pétange, Lux. 15 E5 49 33N 5 55 E
Petaro, Pakistan 42 G3 25 31N 68 18 E
Petatlán, Mexico 86 D4 17 31N 101 16W
Petauke, Zambia 55 E3 14 14S 31 20 E
Petawawa, Canada 70 C4 45 54N 77 17W
Petén Itzá, L., Guatemala 88 C2 16 58N 89 50W
Peter I. Øy, Antarctica .. 5 C16 69 0S 91 0W
Peter Pond L., Canada .. 73 B7 55 55N 108 44W
Peterbell, Canada 70 C3 48 36N 83 21W
Peterborough, Australia . 63 E2 32 58S 138 51 E
Peterborough, Canada .. 78 B6 44 20N 78 20W
Peterborough, U.K. 11 E7 52 35N 0 15W
Peterborough, U.S.A. ... 79 D13 42 53N 71 57W
Peterborough □, U.K. ... 11 E7 52 35N 0 15W
Peterculter, U.K. 12 D6 57 6N 2 16W

Peterhead, U.K. 12 D7 57 31N 1 48W
Peterlee, U.K. 10 C6 54 47N 1 20W
Petermann Bjerg,
 Greenland 66 B17 73 7N 28 25W
Petermann Ranges,
 Australia 60 E5 26 0S 130 30 E
Petersburg, Alaska, U.S.A. 68 C6 56 48N 132 58W
Petersburg, Pa., U.S.A. . 78 F6 40 34N 78 3W
Petersburg, Va., U.S.A. . 76 G7 37 14N 77 24W
Petersburg, W. Va., U.S.A. 76 F6 39 1N 79 5W
Petersfield, U.K. 11 F7 51 1N 0 56W
Petit Goâve, Haiti 89 C5 18 27N 72 51W
Petit Jardin, Canada 71 C8 48 28N 59 14W
Petit Lac Manicouagan,
 Canada 71 B6 51 25N 67 40W
Petit-Mécatina →, Canada 71 B8 50 40N 59 30W
Petit-Mécatina, Í. du,
 Canada 71 B8 50 30N 59 25W
Petitcodiac, Canada 71 C6 45 57N 65 11W
Petite Baleine →, Canada 70 A4 56 0N 76 45W
Petite Saguenay, Canada . 71 C5 48 15N 70 4W
Petitot →, Canada 72 A4 60 14N 123 29W
Petitsikapau L., Canada . 71 B6 54 37N 66 25W
Petlad, India 42 H5 22 30N 72 45 E
Peto, Mexico 87 C7 20 10N 88 53W
Petone, N.Z. 59 J5 41 13S 174 53 E
Petorca, Chile 94 C1 32 15S 70 56W
Petra, Jordan 47 E4 30 20N 35 22 E
Petra, Spain 22 B10 39 37N 3 6 E
Petra, Ostrova, Russia .. 4 B13 76 15N 118 30 E
Petra Velikogo, Zaliv,
 Russia 30 C6 42 40N 132 0 E
Petrich, Bulgaria 21 D10 41 24N 23 13 E
Petrified Forest National
 Park, U.S.A. 83 J9 35 0N 109 30W
Petrikov = Pyetrikaw,
 Belarus 17 B15 52 11N 28 29 E
Petrograd = Sankt-
 Peterburg, Russia 24 C5 59 55N 30 20 E
Petrolândia, Brazil 93 E11 9 5S 38 20W
Petrolia, Canada 78 D2 42 54N 82 9W
Petrolina, Brazil 93 E10 9 24S 40 30W
Petropavl, Kazakstan ... 26 D7 54 53N 69 13 E
Petropavlovsk = Petropavl,
 Kazakstan 26 D7 54 53N 69 13 E
Petropavlovsk-
 Kamchatskiy, Russia .. 27 D16 53 3N 158 43 E
Petrópolis, Brazil 95 A7 22 33S 43 9W
Petroşani, Romania 17 F12 45 28N 23 20 E
Petrovaradin, Serbia, Yug. 21 B8 45 16N 19 55 E
Petrovsk, Russia 24 D8 52 22N 45 19 E
Petrovsk-Zabaykalskiy,
 Russia 27 D11 51 20N 108 55 E
Petrozavodsk, Russia ... 24 B5 61 41N 34 20 E
Petrus Steyn, S. Africa .. 57 D4 27 38S 28 8 E
Petrusburg, S. Africa ... 56 D4 29 4S 25 26 E
Peumo, Chile 94 C1 34 21S 71 12W
Peureulak, Indonesia ... 36 D1 4 48N 97 45 E
Pevek, Russia 27 C18 69 41N 171 19 E
Pforzheim, Germany ... 16 D5 48 52N 8 41 E
Phagwara, India 40 D9 31 10N 75 40 E
Phaistós, Greece 23 D6 35 2N 24 50 E
Phala, Botswana 56 C4 23 45S 26 50 E
Phalera = Phulera, India . 42 F6 26 52N 75 16 E
Phalodi, India 42 F5 27 12N 72 24 E
Phan, Thailand 38 C2 19 28N 99 43 E
Phan Rang, Vietnam ... 39 G7 11 34N 109 0 E
Phan Ri = Hoa Da, Vietnam 39 G7 11 16N 108 40 E
Phan Thiet, Vietnam ... 39 G7 11 1N 108 9 E
Phanat Nikhom, Thailand . 38 F3 13 27N 101 11 E
Phangan, Ko, Thailand .. 39 H3 9 45N 100 0 E
Phangnga, Thailand ... 39 H2 8 28N 98 30 E
Phanom Sarakham,
 Thailand 38 F3 13 45N 101 21 E
Phaphund, India 43 F8 26 36N 79 28 E
Pharenda, India 43 F10 27 5N 83 17 E
Pharr, U.S.A. 81 M5 26 12N 98 11W
Phatthalung, Thailand .. 39 J3 7 39N 100 6 E
Phayao, Thailand 38 C2 19 11N 99 55 E
Phelps, U.S.A. 78 D7 42 58N 77 3W
Phelps L., Canada 73 B8 59 15N 103 15W
Phenix City, U.S.A. 77 J3 32 28N 85 0W
Phet Buri, Thailand 38 F2 13 1N 99 55 E
Phetchabun, Thailand .. 38 D3 16 25N 101 8 E
Phetchabun, Thiu Khao,
 Thailand 38 E3 16 0N 101 20 E
Phetchaburi = Phet Buri,
 Thailand 38 F2 13 1N 99 55 E
Phi Phi, Ko, Thailand ... 39 J2 7 45N 98 46 E
Phiafay, Laos 38 E6 14 48N 106 0 E
Phibun Mangsahan,
 Thailand 38 E5 15 14N 105 14 E
Phichai, Thailand 38 D3 17 22N 100 10 E
Phichit, Thailand 38 D3 16 26N 100 22 E
Philadelphia, Miss., U.S.A. 81 J10 32 46N 89 7W
Philadelphia, N.Y., U.S.A. 79 B9 44 9N 75 43W
Philadelphia, Pa., U.S.A. 79 G9 39 57N 75 10W
Philip, U.S.A. 80 C4 44 2N 101 40W
Philippeville, Belgium .. 15 D4 50 12N 4 33 E
Philippi, U.S.A. 76 F5 39 9N 80 3W
Philippi L., Australia ... 62 C2 24 20S 138 55 E
Philippines ■, Asia 37 B6 12 0N 123 0 E
Philippolis, S. Africa ... 56 E4 30 15S 25 16 E
Philippopolis = Plovdiv,
 Bulgaria 21 C11 42 8N 24 44 E
Philipsburg, Canada 79 A11 45 2N 73 5W
Philipsburg, Mont., U.S.A. 82 C7 46 20N 113 18W
Philipsburg, Pa., U.S.A. . 78 F6 40 54N 78 13W
Philipstown = Daingean,
 Ireland 13 C4 53 18N 7 17W
Philipstown, S. Africa ... 56 E3 30 28S 24 30 E
Phillips, U.S.A. 63 F4 38 30S 145 12 E
Phillips, U.S.A. 80 C9 45 42N 90 24W
Phillipsburg, Kans., U.S.A. 80 F5 39 45N 99 19W
Phillipsburg, N.J., U.S.A. 79 F9 40 42N 75 12W
Philmont, U.S.A. 79 D11 42 15N 73 39W
Philomath, U.S.A. 82 D2 44 32N 123 22W
Phimai, Thailand 38 E4 15 13N 102 30 E
Phitsanulok, Thailand .. 38 D3 16 50N 100 12 E
Phnom Dangrek, Thailand 36 B2 14 20N 104 0 E
Phnom Penh, Cambodia . 39 G5 11 33N 104 55 E
Phnom Penh = Phnom
 Penh, Cambodia 39 G5 11 33N 104 55 E
Phoenicia, U.S.A. 79 D10 42 5N 74 14W
Phoenix, Ariz., U.S.A. .. 83 K7 33 27N 112 4W
Phoenix, N.Y., U.S.A. .. 79 C8 43 14N 76 18W

Phoenix Is., Kiribati ... 64 H10 3 30S 172 0W
Phoenixville, U.S.A. 79 F9 40 8N 75 31W
Phon, Thailand 38 E4 15 49N 102 36 E
Phon Tiou, Laos 38 D5 17 53N 104 37 E
Phong →, Thailand ... 38 D4 16 23N 102 56 E
Phong Tho, Vietnam ... 38 A4 22 32N 103 21 E
Phonhong, Laos 38 C4 18 30N 102 25 E
Phonum, Thailand 39 H2 8 49N 98 48 E
Phosphate Hill, Australia . 62 C2 21 53S 139 58 E
Photharam, Thailand ... 38 F2 13 41N 99 51 E
Phra Nakhon Si Ayutthaya,
 Thailand 38 E3 14 25N 100 30 E
Phra Thong, Ko, Thailand . 39 H2 9 5N 98 17 E
Phrae, Thailand 38 C3 18 7N 100 9 E
Phrom Phiram, Thailand . 38 D3 17 2N 100 12 E
Phu Dien, Vietnam 38 C5 18 58N 105 31 E
Phu Loi, Laos 38 B4 20 14N 103 14 E
Phu Quoc, Dao, Vietnam . 39 G4 10 20N 104 0 E
Phuket, Thailand 39 J2 7 52N 98 22 E
Phuket, Ko, Thailand ... 39 J2 8 0N 98 22 E
Phul, India 42 D6 30 19N 75 14 E
Phulad, India 42 G5 25 38N 73 49 E
Phulchari, Bangla. 43 G13 25 11N 89 37 E
Phulera, India 42 F6 26 52N 75 16 E
Phulpur, India 43 G10 25 31N 82 49 E
Phun Phin, Thailand ... 39 H2 9 7N 99 12 E
Piacenza, Italy 18 D8 45 1N 9 40 E
Pian Cr. →, Australia .. 63 E4 30 2S 148 12 E
Pianosa, Italy 20 C4 42 35N 10 5 E
Piapot, Canada 73 D7 49 59N 109 8W
Piatra Neamţ, Romania . 17 E14 46 56N 26 21 E
Piauí □, Brazil 93 E10 7 0S 43 0W
Piauí →, Brazil 93 E10 6 38S 42 42W
Piave →, Italy 20 B5 45 32N 12 44 E
Pibor Post, Sudan 51 G12 6 47N 33 3 E
Picardie, France 18 B5 49 50N 3 0 E
Picardy = Picardie, France . 18 B5 49 50N 3 0 E
Picayune, U.S.A. 81 K10 30 32N 89 41W
Pichhor, India 43 G8 25 58N 78 20 E
Pichilemu, Chile 94 C1 34 22S 72 0W
Pichor, India 42 G8 25 11N 78 11 E
Pickerel L., Canada 70 C1 48 40N 91 25W
Pickering, U.K. 10 C7 54 15N 0 46W
Pickering, Vale of, U.K. . 10 C7 54 14N 0 45W
Pickle Lake, Canada ... 70 B1 51 30N 90 12W
Pickwick L., U.S.A. 77 H1 35 4N 88 15W
Pico Truncado, Argentina 96 F3 46 40S 68 0W
Picos, Brazil 93 E10 7 5S 41 28W
Picton, Australia 63 E5 34 12S 150 34 E
Picton, Canada 78 B7 44 1N 77 9W
Picton, N.Z. 59 J5 41 18S 174 3 E
Pictou, Canada 71 C7 45 41N 62 42W
Picture Butte, Canada .. 72 D6 49 55N 112 45W
Picún Leufú, Argentina . 96 D3 39 30S 69 5W
Pidurutalagala, Sri Lanka . 40 R12 7 10N 80 50 E
Piedmont = Piemonte □,
 Italy 18 D7 45 0N 8 0 E
Piedmont, Ala., U.S.A. .. 77 J3 33 55N 85 37W
Piedmont, S.C., U.S.A. . 75 D10 34 0N 81 30W
Piedras Negras, Mexico . 86 B4 28 42N 100 31W
Pieksämäki, Finland ... 9 E22 62 18N 27 10 E
Piemonte □, Italy 18 D7 45 0N 8 0 E
Piercefield, U.S.A. 79 B10 44 13N 74 35W
Pierceland, Canada 73 C7 54 20N 109 46W
Pierpont, U.S.A. 78 E4 41 45N 80 34W
Pierre, U.S.A. 80 C4 44 22N 100 21W
Piet Retief, S. Africa ... 57 D5 27 1S 30 50 E
Pietarsaari, Finland 8 E20 63 40N 22 43 E
Pietermaritzburg, S. Africa 57 D5 29 35S 30 25 E
Pietersburg, S. Africa ... 57 C4 23 54S 29 25 E
Pietrosul, Vf., Maramureș,
 Romania 17 E13 47 35N 24 43 E
Pietrosul, Vf., Suceava,
 Romania 17 E13 47 12N 25 18 E
Pigeon L., Canada 78 B6 44 27N 78 30W
Piggott, U.S.A. 81 G9 36 23N 90 11W
Pigüe, Argentina 94 D3 37 36S 62 25W
Pihani, India 43 F9 27 36N 80 15 E
Pihlajavesi, Finland 9 F23 61 45N 28 45 E
Pijijiapan, Mexico 87 D6 15 42N 93 14W
Pikangikum Berens, Canada 73 C10 51 49N 94 0W
Pikes Peak, U.S.A. 80 F2 38 50N 105 3W
Piketberg, S. Africa 56 E2 32 55S 18 40 E
Pikeville, U.S.A. 76 G4 37 29N 82 31W
Pikou, China 35 E12 39 18N 122 22 E
Pikwitonei, Canada 73 B9 55 35N 97 9W
Piła, Poland 17 B9 53 10N 16 48 E
Pilani, India 42 E6 28 22N 75 33 E
Pilar, Paraguay 94 B4 26 50S 58 20W
Pilaya →, Bolivia 92 H6 20 55S 64 4W
Pilbara, Australia 60 D2 23 35S 117 25 E
Pilcomayo →, Paraguay . 94 B4 25 21S 57 42W
Pilibhit, India 43 E8 28 40N 79 50 E
Pilica →, Poland 17 C11 51 52N 21 17 E
Pilkhawa, India 42 E7 28 43N 77 42 E
Pilliga, Australia 63 E4 30 21S 148 54 E
Pilos, Greece 21 F9 36 55N 21 42 E
Pilot Mound, Canada ... 73 D9 49 15N 98 54W
Pilot Point, U.S.A. 81 J6 33 24N 96 58W
Pilot Rock, U.S.A. 82 D4 45 29N 118 50W
Pilsen = Plzeň, Czech Rep. 16 D7 49 45N 13 22 E
Pima, U.S.A. 83 K9 32 54N 109 50W
Pimba, Australia 63 E2 31 18S 136 46 E
Pimenta Bueno, Brazil . 92 F6 11 35S 61 10W
Pimentel, Peru 92 E3 6 45S 79 55W
Pinang, Malaysia 39 K3 5 25N 100 15 E
Pinar, C. des, Spain ... 22 B10 39 53N 3 12 E
Pinar del Río, Cuba 88 B3 22 26N 83 40W
Pinarhisar, Turkey 21 D12 41 37N 27 30 E
Pinatubo, Phil. 37 A6 15 8N 120 21 E
Pincher Creek, Canada . 72 D6 49 30N 113 57W
Pinchi L., Canada 72 C4 54 38N 124 30W
Pinckneyville, U.S.A. ... 80 F10 38 5N 89 23W
Pińczów, Poland 17 C11 50 32N 20 32 E
Pindar, Australia 61 E2 28 30S 115 47 E
Pindi Gheb, Pakistan ... 42 C5 33 14N 72 21 E
Pindos Óros, Greece ... 21 E9 40 0N 21 0 E
Pindus Mts. = Pindos Óros,
 Greece 21 E9 40 0N 21 0 E
Pine →, B.C., Canada .. 72 B4 56 8N 120 43W
Pine →, Sask., Canada . 73 B7 58 50N 105 38W
Pine, C., Canada 71 C9 46 37N 53 32W
Pine Bluff, U.S.A. 81 H9 34 13N 92 1W
Pine Bluffs, U.S.A. 80 E2 41 11N 104 4W
Pine City, U.S.A. 80 C8 45 50N 92 59W
Pine Cr. →, U.S.A. 78 E7 41 10N 77 16W
Pine Creek, Australia .. 60 B5 13 50S 131 50 E

Pine Falls, Canada 73 C9 50 34N 96 11W
Pine Flat Res., U.S.A. ... 84 J7 36 50N 119 20W
Pine Grove, U.S.A. 79 F8 40 33N 76 23W
Pine Pass, Canada 72 B4 55 25N 122 42W
Pine Point, Canada 72 A6 60 50N 114 28W
Pine Ridge, U.S.A. 80 D3 43 2N 102 33W
Pine River, Canada 73 C8 51 45N 100 30W
Pine River, U.S.A. 80 B7 46 43N 94 24W
Pine Valley, U.S.A. 85 N10 32 50N 116 32W
Pinecrest, U.S.A. 84 G6 38 12N 120 1W
Pinedale, Calif., U.S.A. . 84 J7 36 50N 119 48W
Pinedale, Wyo., U.S.A. . 82 E9 42 52N 109 52W
Pinega →, Russia 24 B8 64 30N 44 19 E
Pinehill, Australia 62 C4 23 38S 146 57 E
Pinehouse L., Canada .. 73 B7 55 32N 106 35W
Pineimuta →, Canada . 70 B1 52 8N 88 33W
Pinerolo, Italy 18 D7 44 53N 7 21 E
Pinetop, U.S.A. 83 J9 34 8N 109 56W
Pinetown, S. Africa 57 D5 29 48S 30 54 E
Pineville, U.S.A. 81 K8 31 19N 92 26W
Ping →, Thailand 38 E3 15 42N 100 9 E
Pingaring, Australia ... 61 F2 32 40S 118 32 E
Pingding, China 34 F7 37 47N 113 38 E
Pingdingshan, China ... 34 H7 33 43N 113 27 E
Pingdong, Taiwan 33 D7 22 39N 120 30 E
Pingdu, China 35 F10 36 42N 119 59 E
Pingelly, Australia 61 F2 32 32S 117 5 E
Pingliang, China 34 G4 35 35N 106 31 E
Pinglu, China 34 E7 39 31N 112 30 E
Pingluo, China 34 E4 38 52N 106 30 E
Pingquan, China 35 D10 41 1N 118 37 E
Pingrup, Australia 61 F2 33 32S 118 29 E
P'ingtung, Taiwan 33 D7 22 38N 120 30 E
Pingwu, China 34 H3 32 25N 104 30 E
Pingxiang, China 32 D5 22 6N 106 46 E
Pingyao, China 34 F7 37 12N 112 10 E
Pingyi, China 35 G9 35 30N 117 35 E
Pingyin, China 34 F9 36 20N 116 25 E
Pingyuan, China 34 F9 37 10N 116 22 E
Pinhal, Brazil 95 A6 22 10S 46 46W
Pinheiro, Brazil 93 D9 2 31S 45 5W
Pinheiro Machado, Brazil 95 C5 31 34S 53 23W
Pinhel, Portugal 19 B2 40 50N 7 1W
Pini, Indonesia 36 D1 0 10N 98 40 E
Piniós →, Greece 21 E10 39 55N 22 41 E
Pinjarra, Australia 61 F2 32 37S 115 52 E
Pink Mountain, Canada . 72 B4 57 3N 122 52W
Pinnacles, U.S.A. 84 J5 36 33N 121 19W
Pinnaroo, Australia 63 F3 35 17S 140 53 E
Pinnes, Ákra, Greece ... 21 D11 40 5N 24 20 E
Pinon Hills, U.S.A. 85 L9 34 26N 117 39W
Pinos, Mexico 86 C4 22 20N 101 40W
Pinos, Mt., U.S.A. 85 L7 34 49N 119 8W
Pinos Pt., U.S.A. 83 H3 36 38N 121 57W
Pinotepa Nacional, Mexico 87 D5 16 19N 98 3W
Pinrang, Indonesia 37 E5 3 46S 119 41 E
Pins, Pte. aux, Canada . 78 D3 42 15N 81 51W
Pinsk, Belarus 17 B14 52 10N 26 1 E
Pintados, Chile 92 H5 20 35S 69 40W
Pinyug, Russia 24 B8 60 5N 48 0 E
Pioche, U.S.A. 83 H6 37 56N 114 27W
Piombino, Italy 20 C4 42 55N 10 32 E
Pioner, Ostrov, Russia .. 27 B10 79 50N 92 0 E
Piorini, L., Brazil 92 D6 3 15S 62 35W
Piotrków Trybunalski,
 Poland 17 C10 51 23N 19 43 E
Pip, Iran 45 E9 26 45N 60 10 E
Pipar, India 42 F5 26 25N 73 31 E
Pipar Road, India 42 F5 26 25N 73 31 E
Piparia, Mad. P., India .. 42 H8 22 45N 78 23 E
Piparia, Mad. P., India .. 42 J7 21 49N 77 37 E
Pipestone, U.S.A. 80 D6 44 0N 96 19W
Pipestone →, Canada . 70 B2 52 53N 89 23W
Pipestone Cr. →, Canada 73 D8 49 38N 100 15W
Piplan, Pakistan 42 C4 32 17N 71 21 E
Piploda, India 42 H6 23 37N 74 56 E
Pipmuacan, Rés., Canada 71 C5 49 45N 70 30W
Pippingarra, Australia .. 60 D2 20 27S 118 42 E
Piqua, U.S.A. 76 E3 40 9N 84 15W
Piquiri →, Brazil 95 A5 24 3S 54 14W
Pir Sohrâb, Iran 45 E9 25 44N 60 54 E
Piracicaba, Brazil 95 A6 22 45S 47 40W
Piracuruca, Brazil 93 D10 3 50S 41 50W
Piræus = Piraiévs, Greece 21 F10 37 57N 23 42 E
Piraiévs, Greece 21 F10 37 57N 23 42 E
Pirajuí, Brazil 95 A6 21 59S 49 29W
Piram I., India 42 J5 21 36N 72 21 E
Pirané, Argentina 94 B4 25 42S 59 6W
Pirapora, Brazil 93 G10 17 20S 44 56W
Pirawa, India 42 G7 24 10N 76 2 E
Pírgos, Greece 21 F9 37 40N 21 27 E
Piribebuy, Paraguay ... 94 B4 25 26S 57 2W
Pirimapun, Indonesia .. 37 F9 6 45S 138 10 E
Pirin Planina, Bulgaria . 21 D10 41 40N 23 30 E
Pírineos = Pyrénées,
 Europe 18 E4 42 45N 0 18 E
Piripiri, Brazil 93 D10 4 15S 41 46W
Pirmasens, Germany ... 16 D4 49 12N 7 36 E
Pirot, Serbia, Yug. 21 C10 43 9N 22 39 E
Piru, Indonesia 37 E7 3 4S 128 12 E
Piru, U.S.A. 85 L8 34 25N 118 48W
Pisa, Italy 20 C4 43 43N 10 23 E
Pisagua, Chile 92 G4 19 40S 70 15W
Pisco, Peru 92 F3 13 50S 76 5W
Písek, Czech Rep. 16 D8 49 19N 14 10 E
Pishan, China 32 C2 37 30N 78 33 E
Pishin, Iran 45 E9 26 6N 61 47 E
Pishin, Pakistan 42 D2 30 35N 67 0 E
Pishin Lora →, Pakistan 42 E1 29 9N 64 5 E
Pising, Indonesia 37 F6 5 8S 121 53 E
Pismo Beach, U.S.A. ... 85 K6 35 9N 120 38W
Pissis, Cerro, Argentina . 94 B2 27 45S 68 48W
Pissouri, Cyprus 23 E11 34 40N 32 42 E
Pístoia, Italy 20 C4 43 55N 10 54 E
Pisuerga →, Spain 19 B3 41 33N 4 52W
Pit →, U.S.A. 82 F2 40 47N 122 6W
Pitarpunga, L., Australia . 63 E3 34 24S 143 30 E
Pitcairn I., Pac. Oc. 65 K14 25 5S 130 5W
Pite älv →, Sweden ... 8 D19 65 20N 21 25 E
Piteå, Sweden 8 D19 65 20N 21 25 E
Piteşti, Romania 17 F13 44 52N 24 54 E
Pithapuram, India 41 L13 17 10N 82 15 E
Pithara, Australia 61 F2 30 20S 116 35 E
Pithoragarh, India 43 E9 29 35N 80 13 E
Pithoro, Pakistan 42 G3 25 31N 69 23 E
Pitlochry, U.K. 12 E5 56 42N 3 44W

Posse

Posse, Brazil 93 F9 14 4S 46 18W
Possession I., Antarctica .. 5 D11 72 4S 172 0 E
Possum Kingdom L., U.S.A. 81 J5 32 52N 98 26W
Post, U.S.A. 81 J4 33 12N 101 23W
Post Falls, U.S.A. 82 C5 47 43N 116 57W
Postavy = Pastavy, Belarus 9 J22 55 4N 26 50 E
Poste-de-la-Baleine =
Kuujjuarapik, Canada ... 70 A4 55 20N 77 35W
Postmasburg, S. Africa ... 56 D3 28 18S 23 5 E
Postojna, Slovenia 16 F8 45 46N 14 12 E
Poston, U.S.A. 85 M12 34 0N 114 24W
Postville, Canada 71 B8 54 54N 59 47W
Potchefstroom, S. Africa .. 56 D4 26 41S 27 7 E
Poteau, U.S.A. 81 H7 35 3N 94 37W
Poteet, U.S.A. 81 L5 29 2N 98 35W
Potenza, Italy 20 D6 40 38N 15 48 E
Poteriteri, L., N.Z. 59 M1 46 5S 167 10 E
Potgietersrus, S. Africa ... 57 C4 24 10S 28 55 E
Poti, Georgia 25 F7 42 10N 41 38 E
Potiskum, Nigeria 51 F8 11 39N 11 2 E
Potomac →, U.S.A. 76 G7 38 0N 76 23W
Potosí, Bolivia 92 G5 19 38S 65 50W
Potosi Mt., U.S.A. 85 K11 35 57N 115 29W
Pototan, Phil. 37 B6 10 54N 122 38 E
Potrerillos, Chile 94 B2 26 30S 69 30W
Potsdam, Germany 16 B7 52 25N 13 4 E
Potsdam, U.S.A. 79 B10 44 40N 74 59W
Pottersville, U.S.A. 79 C11 43 43N 73 50W
Pottstown, U.S.A. 79 F9 40 15N 75 39W
Pottsville, U.S.A. 79 F8 40 41N 76 12W
Pottuvil, Sri Lanka 40 R12 6 55N 81 50 E
Pouce Coupé, Canada 72 B4 55 40N 120 10W
Poughkeepsie, U.S.A. 79 E11 41 42N 73 56W
Poulaphouca Res., Ireland . 13 C5 53 8N 6 30W
Poulsbo, U.S.A. 84 C4 47 44N 122 39W
Poultney, U.S.A. 79 C11 43 31N 73 14W
Poulton-le-Fylde, U.K. ... 10 D5 53 51N 2 58W
Pouso Alegre, Brazil 95 A6 22 14S 45 57W
Pouthisat, Cambodia 38 F4 12 34N 103 50 E
Považská Bystrica,
Slovak Rep. 17 D10 49 8N 18 27 E
Povenets, Russia 24 B5 62 50N 34 50 E
Poverty B., N.Z. 59 H7 38 43S 178 2 E
Póvoa de Varzim, Portugal 19 B1 41 25N 8 46W
Povungnituk = Puvirnituq,
Canada 69 B12 60 2N 77 10W
Powassan, Canada 70 C4 46 5N 79 25W
Poway, U.S.A. 85 N9 32 58N 117 2W
Powder →, U.S.A. 80 B2 46 45N 105 26W
Powder River, U.S.A. 82 E10 43 2N 106 59W
Powell, U.S.A. 82 D9 44 45N 108 46W
Powell, L., U.S.A. 83 H8 36 57N 111 29W
Powell River, Canada 72 D4 49 50N 124 35W
Powers, U.S.A. 76 C2 45 41N 87 32W
Powys □, U.K. 11 E4 52 20N 3 0W
Poyang Hu, China 33 D6 29 5N 116 20 E
Poyarkovo, Russia 27 E13 49 36N 128 41 E
Poza Rica, Mexico 87 C5 20 33N 97 27W
Požarevac, Serbia, Yug. .. 21 B9 44 35N 21 18 E
Poznań, Poland 17 B9 52 25N 16 55 E
Pozo, U.S.A. 85 K6 35 20N 120 24W
Pozo Almonte, Chile 92 H5 20 10S 69 50W
Pozo Colorado, Paraguay . 94 A4 23 30S 58 45W
Pozoblanco, Spain 19 C3 38 23N 4 51W
Pozzuoli, Italy 20 D6 40 49N 14 7 E
Prachin Buri, Thailand ... 38 F3 14 0N 101 25 E
Prachuap Khiri Khan,
Thailand 39 G2 11 49N 99 48 E
Prado, Brazil 93 G11 17 20S 39 13W
Prague = Praha, Czech Rep. 16 C8 50 5N 14 22 E
Praha, Czech Rep. 16 C8 50 5N 14 22 E
Praia, C. Verde Is. 49 E1 14 55N 23 30W
Prainha, Amazonas, Brazil . 92 E6 7 10S 60 30W
Prainha, Pará, Brazil 93 D8 1 45S 53 30W
Prairie, Australia 62 C3 20 50S 144 35 E
Prairie City, U.S.A. 82 D4 44 28N 118 43W
Prairie Dog Town Fork →,
U.S.A. 81 H5 34 30N 99 23W
Prairie du Chien, U.S.A. .. 80 D9 43 3N 91 9W
Prairies, L. of the, Canada . 73 C8 51 16N 101 32W
Pran Buri, Thailand 38 F2 12 23N 99 55 E
Prapat, Indonesia 36 D1 2 41N 98 58 E
Prasonísi, Ákra, Greece ... 23 D9 35 42N 27 46 E
Prata, Brazil 93 G9 19 25S 48 54W
Pratabpur, India 43 H10 23 28N 83 15 E
Pratapgarh, Raj., India ... 42 G6 24 2N 74 40 E
Pratapgarh, Ut. P., India .. 43 G9 25 56N 81 59 E
Prato, Italy 20 C4 43 53N 11 6 E
Pratt, U.S.A. 81 G5 37 39N 98 44W
Prattville, U.S.A. 77 J2 32 28N 86 29W
Pravia, Spain 19 A2 43 30N 6 12W
Praya, Indonesia 36 F5 8 39S 116 17 E
Precordillera, Argentina .. 94 C2 30 0S 69 1W
Preeceville, Canada 73 C8 51 57N 102 40W
Preiļi, Latvia 9 H22 56 18N 26 43 E
Premont, U.S.A. 81 M5 27 22N 98 7W
Prentice, U.S.A. 80 C9 45 33N 90 17W
Preobrazheniye, Russia ... 30 C6 42 54N 133 54 E
Preparis North Channel,
Ind. Oc. 41 M18 15 12N 93 40 E
Preparis South Channel,
Ind. Oc. 41 M18 14 36N 93 40 E
Přerov, Czech Rep. 17 D9 49 28N 17 27 E
Prescott, Canada 79 B9 44 45N 75 30W
Prescott, Ariz., U.S.A. ... 83 J7 34 33N 112 28W
Prescott, Ark., U.S.A. ... 81 J8 33 48N 93 23W
Prescott Valley, U.S.A. ... 83 J7 34 40N 112 18W
Preservation Inlet, N.Z. ... 59 M1 46 8S 166 35 E
Presho, U.S.A. 80 D4 43 54N 100 3W
Presidencia de la Plaza,
Argentina 94 B4 27 0S 59 50W
Presidencia Roque Saenz
Peña, Argentina 94 B3 26 45S 60 30W
Presidente Epitácio, Brazil . 93 H8 21 56S 52 6W
Presidente Hayes □,
Paraguay 94 A4 24 0S 59 0W
Presidente Prudente, Brazil 95 A5 22 5S 51 25W
Presidio, Mexico 86 B4 29 29N 104 23W
Presidio, U.S.A. 81 L2 29 34N 104 22W
Prešov, Slovak Rep. 17 D11 49 0N 21 15 E
Prespa, L. = Prespansko
Jezero, Macedonia 21 D9 40 55N 21 0 E
Prespansko Jezero,
Macedonia 21 D9 40 55N 21 0 E
Presque I., U.S.A. 78 D4 42 9N 80 6W
Presque Isle, U.S.A. 77 B12 46 41N 68 1W

Prestatyn, U.K. 10 D4 53 20N 3 24W
Presteigne, U.K. 11 E5 52 17N 3 0W
Preston, Canada 78 C4 43 23N 80 21W
Preston, U.K. 10 D5 53 46N 2 42W
Preston, Idaho, U.S.A. ... 82 E8 42 6N 111 53W
Preston, Minn., U.S.A. ... 80 D8 43 40N 92 5W
Preston, C., Australia 60 D2 20 51S 116 12 E
Prestonburg, U.S.A. 76 G4 37 39N 82 46W
Prestwick, U.K. 12 F4 55 29N 4 37W
Pretoria, S. Africa 57 D4 25 44S 28 12 E
Préveza, Greece 21 E9 38 57N 20 47 E
Prey Veng, Cambodia ... 39 G5 11 35N 105 29 E
Pribilof Is., U.S.A. 68 C2 57 0N 170 0W
Příbram, Czech Rep. 16 D8 49 41N 14 2 E
Price, U.S.A. 82 G8 39 36N 110 49W
Price I., Canada 72 C3 52 23N 128 41W
Prichard, U.S.A. 77 K1 30 44N 88 5W
Priekule, Latvia 9 H19 56 26N 21 35 E
Prienai, Lithuania 9 J20 54 38N 23 57 E
Prieska, S. Africa 56 D3 29 40S 22 42 E
Priest L., U.S.A. 82 B5 48 35N 116 52W
Priest River, U.S.A. 82 B5 48 10N 116 54W
Priest Valley, U.S.A. 84 J6 36 10N 120 39W
Prievidza, Slovak Rep. ... 17 D10 48 46N 18 36 E
Prikaspiyskaya Nizmennost
= Caspian Depression,
Eurasia 25 E8 47 0N 48 0 E
Prilep, Macedonia 21 D9 41 21N 21 32 E
Priluki = Pryluky, Ukraine . 25 D5 50 30N 32 24 E
Prime Seal I., Australia ... 62 G4 40 3S 147 43 E
Primrose L., Canada 73 C7 54 55N 109 45W
Prince Albert, Canada ... 73 C7 53 15N 105 50W
Prince Albert, S. Africa ... 56 E3 33 12S 22 2 E
Prince Albert Mts.,
Antarctica 5 D11 76 0S 161 30 E
Prince Albert Nat. Park,
Canada 73 C7 54 0N 106 25W
Prince Albert Pen., Canada . 68 A8 72 30N 116 0W
Prince Albert Sd., Canada . 68 A8 70 25N 115 0W
Prince Alfred, C., Canada .. 4 B1 74 20N 124 40W
Prince Charles I., Canada .. 69 B12 67 47N 76 12W
Prince Charles Mts.,
Antarctica 5 D6 72 0S 67 0 E
Prince Edward I. □, Canada 71 C7 46 20N 63 20W
Prince Edward Is., Ind. Oc. . 3 G11 46 35S 38 0 E
Prince Edward Pt., Canada . 78 C8 43 56N 76 52W
Prince George, Canada ... 72 C4 53 55N 122 50W
Prince of Wales, C., U.S.A. . 66 C3 65 36N 168 5W
Prince of Wales I., Australia 62 A3 10 40S 142 10 E
Prince of Wales I., Canada . 68 A10 73 0N 99 0W
Prince of Wales I., U.S.A. . 68 C6 55 47N 132 50W
Prince Patrick I., Canada .. 4 B2 77 0N 120 0W
Prince Regent Inlet, Canada 4 B3 73 0N 90 0W
Prince Rupert, Canada ... 72 C2 54 20N 130 20W
Princess Charlotte B.,
Australia 62 A3 14 25S 144 0 E
Princess May Ranges,
Australia 60 C4 15 30S 125 30 E
Princess Royal I., Canada . 72 C3 53 0N 128 40W
Princeton, Canada 72 D4 49 27N 120 30W
Princeton, Calif., U.S.A. .. 84 F4 39 24N 122 1W
Princeton, Ill., U.S.A. ... 80 E10 41 23N 89 28W
Princeton, Ind., U.S.A. ... 76 F2 38 21N 87 34W
Princeton, Ky., U.S.A. ... 76 G2 37 7N 87 53W
Princeton, Mo., U.S.A. ... 80 E8 40 24N 93 35W
Princeton, N.J., U.S.A. ... 79 F10 40 21N 74 39W
Princeton, W. Va., U.S.A. . 76 G5 37 22N 81 6W
Principe, I. de, Atl. Oc. ... 48 F4 1 37N 7 27 E
Principe da Beira, Brazil .. 92 F6 12 20S 64 30W
Prineville, U.S.A. 82 D3 44 18N 120 51W
Prins Harald Kyst, Antarctica 5 D4 70 0S 35 1 E
Prinsesse Astrid Kyst,
Antarctica 5 D3 70 45S 12 30 E
Prinsesse Ragnhild Kyst,
Antarctica 5 D4 70 15S 27 30 E
Prinzapolca, Nic. 88 D3 13 20N 83 35W
Priozersk, Russia 24 B5 61 2N 30 7 E
Pripet = Prypyat →,
Europe 17 C16 51 20N 30 15 E
Pripet Marshes = Pripyat
Marshes, Europe 17 B15 52 10N 28 10 E
Pripyats = Prypyat →,
Europe 17 C16 51 20N 30 15 E
Priština, Yugoslavia 21 C9 42 40N 21 13 E
Privas, France 18 D6 44 45N 4 37 E
Privolzhskaya
Vozvyshennost, Russia .. 25 D8 51 0N 46 0 E
Prizren, Yugoslavia 21 C9 42 13N 20 45 E
Probolinggo, Indonesia .. 37 G15 7 46S 113 13 E
Proctor, U.S.A. 79 C11 43 40N 73 2W
Proddatur, India 40 M11 14 45N 78 30 E
Prodhromos, Cyprus 23 E11 34 57N 32 50 E
Profítis Ilías, Greece 23 C9 36 17N 27 56 E
Profondeville, Belgium ... 15 D4 50 23N 4 52 E
Progreso, Mexico 87 C7 21 20N 89 40W
Progreso, Yucatán, Mexico 86 B4 21 17N 89 40W
Prokopyevsk, Russia 26 D9 54 0N 86 45 E
Prokuplje, Serbia, Yug. ... 21 C9 43 16N 21 36 E
Prome = Pyè, Burma 41 K19 18 49N 95 13 E
Prophet →, Canada 72 B4 58 48N 122 40W
Prophet River, Canada ... 72 B4 58 6N 122 43W
Propriá, Brazil 93 F11 10 13S 36 51W
Proserpine, Australia 62 C4 20 21S 148 36 E
Prosna →, Poland 17 B9 52 6N 17 44 E
Prospect, U.S.A. 79 C9 43 18N 75 9W
Prosser, U.S.A. 82 C4 46 12N 119 46W
Prostějov, Czech Rep. ... 17 D9 49 30N 17 9 E
Proston, Australia 63 D5 26 8S 151 32 E
Provence, France 18 E6 43 40N 5 46 E
Providence, Ky., U.S.A. .. 76 G2 37 24N 87 46W
Providence, R.I., U.S.A. .. 79 E13 41 49N 71 24W
Providence Bay, Canada .. 70 C3 45 41N 82 15W
Providence Mts., U.S.A. .. 85 K11 35 10N 115 15W
Providencia, I. de, Colombia 88 D3 13 25N 81 26W
Provideniya, Russia 27 C19 64 23N 173 18W
Provins, France 18 B5 48 33N 3 15 E
Provo, U.S.A. 82 F8 40 14N 111 39W
Provost, Canada 73 C6 52 25N 110 20W
Prudhoe Bay, U.S.A. 68 A5 70 18N 148 22W
Prudhoe I., Australia 62 C4 21 19S 149 41 E
Prud'homme, Canada ... 73 C7 52 20N 105 54W
Prut →, Romania 17 F15 45 28N 28 10 E
Pruzhany, Belarus 17 B13 52 33N 24 28 E
Prydz B., Antarctica 5 C6 69 0S 74 0 E

Pryluky, Ukraine 25 D5 50 30N 32 24 E
Pryor, U.S.A. 81 G7 36 19N 95 19W
Prypyat →, Europe 17 C16 51 20N 30 15 E
Przemyśl, Poland 17 D12 49 50N 22 45 E
Przhevalsk, Kyrgyzstan .. 26 E8 42 30N 78 20 E
Psará, Greece 21 E11 38 37N 25 38 E
Psira, Greece 23 D7 35 12N 25 52 E
Pskov, Russia 24 C4 57 50N 28 25 E
Pskovskoye, Ozero, Russia . 9 H22 58 0N 27 58 E
Ptich = Ptsich →, Belarus . 17 B15 52 9N 28 52 E
Ptolemaís, Greece 21 D9 40 30N 21 43 E
Ptsich →, Belarus 17 B15 52 9N 28 52 E
Pu Xian, China 34 F6 36 24N 111 6 E
Pua, Thailand 38 C3 19 11N 100 55 E
Puán, Argentina 94 D3 37 30S 62 45W
Puan, S. Korea 35 G14 35 44N 126 44 E
Pucallpa, Peru 92 E4 8 25S 74 30W
Pudasjärvi, Finland 8 D22 65 23N 26 53 E
Pudozh, Russia 24 B6 61 48N 36 32 E
Pudukkottai, India 40 P11 10 28N 78 47 E
Puebla, Mexico 87 D5 19 3N 98 12W
Puebla □, Mexico 87 D5 18 30N 98 0W
Pueblo, U.S.A. 80 F2 38 16N 104 37W
Pueblo Hundido, Chile ... 94 B1 26 20S 70 5W
Puelches, Argentina 94 D2 38 5S 65 51W
Puelén, Argentina 94 D2 37 32S 67 38W
Puente Alto, Chile 94 C1 33 32S 70 35W
Puente-Genil, Spain 19 D3 37 22N 4 47W
Puerco →, U.S.A. 83 J10 34 22N 107 50W
Puerto, Canary Is. 22 F2 28 5N 17 20W
Puerto Aisén, Chile 96 F2 45 27S 73 0W
Puerto Ángel, Mexico ... 87 D5 15 40N 96 29W
Puerto Arista, Mexico ... 87 D6 15 56N 93 48W
Puerto Armuelles, Panama 88 E3 8 20N 82 51W
Puerto Ayacucho, Venezuela 92 B5 5 40N 67 35W
Puerto Barrios, Guatemala 88 C2 15 40N 88 32W
Puerto Bermejo, Argentina 94 B4 26 55S 58 34W
Puerto Bermúdez, Peru .. 92 F4 10 20S 74 58W
Puerto Bolívar, Ecuador .. 92 D3 3 19S 79 55W
Puerto Cabello, Venezuela . 92 A5 10 28N 68 1W
Puerto Cabezas, Nic. 88 D3 14 0N 83 30W
Puerto Cabo Gracias á Dios,
Nic. 88 D3 15 0N 83 10W
Puerto Carreño, Colombia . 92 B5 6 12N 67 22W
Puerto Castilla, Honduras . 88 C2 16 0N 86 0W
Puerto Chicama, Peru ... 92 E3 7 45S 79 20W
Puerto Coig, Argentina ... 96 G3 50 54S 69 15W
Puerto Cortés, Costa Rica . 88 E3 8 55N 84 0W
Puerto Cortés, Honduras . 88 C2 15 51N 88 0W
Puerto Cumarebo,
Venezuela 92 A5 11 29N 69 30W
Puerto de Alcudia = Port
d'Alcúdia, Spain 22 B10 39 50N 3 7 E
Puerto de Andraitx, Spain . 22 B9 39 32N 2 23 E
Puerto de Cabrera, Spain . 22 B9 39 8N 2 56 E
Puerto de Gran Tarajal,
Canary Is. 22 F5 28 13N 14 1W
Puerto de la Cruz, Canary Is. 22 F3 28 24N 16 32W
Puerto de Pozo Negro,
Canary Is. 22 F6 28 19N 13 55W
Puerto de Sóller = Port de
Sóller, Spain 22 B9 39 48N 2 42 E
Puerto del Carmen,
Canary Is. 22 F6 28 55N 13 38W
Puerto del Rosario,
Canary Is. 22 F6 28 30N 13 52W
Puerto Deseado, Argentina 96 F3 47 55S 66 0W
Puerto Escondido, Mexico . 87 D5 15 50N 97 3W
Puerto Heath, Bolivia ... 92 F5 12 34S 68 39W
Puerto Inírida, Colombia . 92 C5 3 53N 67 52W
Puerto Juárez, Mexico ... 87 C7 21 11N 86 49W
Puerto La Cruz, Venezuela 92 A6 10 13N 64 38W
Puerto Leguízamo,
Colombia 92 D4 0 12S 74 46W
Puerto Limón, Colombia .. 92 C4 3 23N 73 30W
Puerto Lobos, Argentina . 96 E3 42 0S 65 3W
Puerto Madryn, Argentina 96 E3 42 48S 65 4W
Puerto Maldonado, Peru . 92 F5 12 30S 69 10W
Puerto Manotí, Cuba 88 B4 21 22N 76 50W
Puerto Montt, Chile 96 E2 41 28S 73 0W
Puerto Morazán, Nic. ... 88 D2 12 51N 87 11W
Puerto Morelos, Mexico .. 87 C7 20 49N 86 52W
Puerto Natales, Chile 96 G2 51 45S 72 15W
Puerto Padre, Cuba 88 B4 21 13N 76 35W
Puerto Páez, Venezuela .. 92 B5 6 13N 67 28W
Puerto Peñasco, Mexico .. 86 A2 31 20N 113 33W
Puerto Pinasco, Paraguay . 94 A4 22 36S 57 50W
Puerto Plata, Dom. Rep. .. 89 C5 19 48N 70 45W
Puerto Pollensa = Port de
Pollença, Spain 22 B10 39 54N 3 4 E
Puerto Princesa, Phil. 37 C5 9 46N 118 45 E
Puerto Quepos, Costa Rica 88 E3 9 29N 84 6W
Puerto Rico, Canary Is. .. 22 G4 27 47N 15 42W
Puerto Rico ■, W. Indies . 89 C6 18 15N 66 45W
Puerto Rico Trench, Atl. Oc. 89 C6 19 50N 66 0W
Puerto San Julián,
Argentina 96 F3 49 18S 67 43W
Puerto Sastre, Paraguay .. 94 A4 22 2S 57 55W
Puerto Suárez, Bolivia ... 92 G7 18 58S 57 52W
Puerto Vallarta, Mexico .. 86 C3 20 36N 105 15W
Puerto Wilches, Colombia 92 B4 7 21N 73 54W
Puertollano, Spain 19 C3 38 43N 4 7W
Pueyrredón, L., Argentina 96 F2 47 20S 72 0W
Puffin I., Ireland 13 E1 51 50N 10 24W
Pugachev, Russia 24 D8 52 0N 48 49 E
Pugal, India 42 E5 28 30N 72 48 E
Puge, Tanzania 54 C3 4 45S 33 11 E
Puget Sound, U.S.A. 82 C2 47 50N 122 30W
Pugŏdong, N. Korea 35 C16 42 5N 130 0 E
Puig Major, Spain 22 B9 39 48N 2 47 E
Puigcerdà, Spain 19 A6 42 24N 1 50 E
Puigpunyent, Spain 22 B9 39 38N 2 32 E
Pujon-chŏsuji, N. Korea .. 35 D14 40 35N 127 35 E
Pukaki, L., N.Z. 59 L3 44 4S 170 1 E
Pukapuka, Cook Is. 65 J11 10 53S 165 49W
Pukaskwa Nat. Park, Canada 70 C2 48 20N 86 0W
Pukatawagan, Canada ... 73 B8 55 45N 101 20W
Pukchin, N. Korea 35 D13 40 12N 125 45 E
Pukch'ŏng, N. Korea 35 D15 40 14N 128 10 E
Pukekohe, N.Z. 59 G5 37 12S 174 55 E
Pukhrayan, India 43 F8 26 14N 79 51 E
Pula, Croatia 16 F7 44 54N 13 57 E
Pulacayo, Bolivia 92 H5 20 25S 66 41W
Pulandian, China 35 E11 39 25N 121 58 E

Pularumpi, Australia 60 B5 11 24S 130 26 E
Pulaski, N.Y., U.S.A. 79 C8 43 34N 76 8W
Pulaski, Tenn., U.S.A. ... 77 H2 35 12N 87 2W
Pulaski, Va., U.S.A. 76 G5 37 3N 80 47W
Pulau →, Indonesia 37 F9 5 50S 138 15 E
Puławy, Poland 17 C11 51 23N 21 59 E
Pulga, U.S.A. 84 F5 39 48N 121 29W
Pulicat L., India 40 N12 13 40N 80 15 E
Pullman, U.S.A. 82 C5 46 44N 117 10W
Pulo-Anna, Pac. Oc. 37 D8 4 30N 132 5 E
Pulog, Phil. 37 A6 16 40N 120 50 E
Pultusk, Poland 17 B11 52 43N 21 6 E
Pumlumon Fawr, U.K. ... 11 E4 52 28N 3 46W
Puná, I., Ecuador 92 D2 2 55S 80 5W
Punakha, Bhutan 41 F16 27 42N 89 52 E
Punasar, India 42 F5 27 6N 73 6 E
Punata, Bolivia 92 G5 17 32S 65 50W
Punch, India 43 C6 33 48N 74 4 E
Punch →, Pakistan 42 C5 33 12N 73 40 E
Pune, India 40 K8 18 29N 73 57 E
P'ungsan, N. Korea 35 D15 40 50N 128 9 E
Pungue, Ponte de, Mozam. 55 F3 19 0S 34 0 E
Punjab □, India 42 D7 31 0N 76 0 E
Punjab □, Pakistan 42 E6 32 0N 74 30 E
Puno, Peru 92 G4 15 55S 70 3W
Punpun →, India 43 G11 25 31N 85 18 E
Punta Alta, Argentina ... 96 D4 38 53S 62 4W
Punta Arenas, Chile 96 G2 53 0S 71 0W
Punta de Diaz, Chile 94 B1 28 0S 70 45W
Punta Gorda, Belize 87 D7 16 10N 88 45W
Punta Gorda, U.S.A. 77 M5 26 56N 82 3W
Punta Prieta, Mexico ... 86 B2 28 58N 114 17W
Punta Prima, Spain 22 B11 39 48N 4 16 E
Puntarenas, Costa Rica .. 88 E3 10 0N 84 50W
Punto Fijo, Venezuela ... 92 A4 11 50N 70 13W
Punxsatawney, U.S.A. ... 78 F6 40 57N 78 59W
Puquio, Peru 92 F4 14 45S 74 10W
Pur →, Russia 26 C8 67 31N 77 55 E
Purace, Vol., Colombia .. 92 C3 2 21N 76 23W
Puralia = Puruliya, India . 43 H12 23 17N 86 24 E
Puranpur, India 43 E9 28 31N 80 9 E
Purbeck, Isle of, U.K. ... 11 G6 50 39N 1 59W
Purcell, U.S.A. 81 H6 35 1N 97 22W
Purcell Mts., Canada ... 72 C5 49 55N 116 15W
Puri, India 41 K14 19 50N 85 58 E
Purmerend, Neths. 15 B4 52 32N 4 58 E
Purnia, India 43 G12 25 45N 87 31 E
Pursat = Pouthisat,
Cambodia 38 F4 12 34N 103 50 E
Purukcahu, Indonesia ... 36 E4 0 35S 114 35 E
Puruliya, India 43 H12 23 17N 86 24 E
Purus →, Brazil 92 D6 3 42S 61 28W
Purvis, U.S.A. 81 K10 31 9N 89 25W
Purwa, India 43 F9 26 28N 80 47 E
Purwakarta, Indonesia .. 37 G12 6 35S 107 29 E
Purwodadi, Indonesia ... 37 G14 7 7S 110 55 E
Purwokerto, Indonesia .. 37 G13 7 25S 109 14 E
Puryŏng, N. Korea 35 C15 42 5N 129 43 E
Pusan, S. Korea 35 G15 35 5N 129 0 E
Pushkino, Russia 25 D8 51 16N 47 0 E
Putahow L., Canada 73 B8 59 54N 100 40W
Putao, Burma 41 F20 27 28N 97 30 E
Putaruru, N.Z. 59 H5 38 2S 175 50 E
Puthein Myit →, Burma .. 41 M19 15 56N 94 18 E
Putignano, Italy 20 D7 40 51N 17 7 E
Puting, Tanjung, Indonesia 36 E4 3 31S 111 46 E
Putnam, U.S.A. 79 E13 41 55N 71 55W
Putorana, Gory, Russia .. 27 C10 69 0N 95 0 E
Puttalam, Sri Lanka 40 Q11 8 1N 79 55 E
Puttgarden, Germany ... 16 A6 54 30N 11 10 E
Putumayo →, S. Amer. .. 92 D5 3 7S 67 58W
Putussibau, Indonesia ... 36 D4 0 50N 112 56 E
Puvirnituq, Canada 69 B12 60 2N 77 10W
Puy-de-Dôme, France ... 18 D5 45 46N 2 57 E
Puyallup, U.S.A. 84 C4 47 12N 122 18W
Puyang, China 34 G8 35 40N 115 1 E
Pūzeh Rig, Iran 45 E8 27 20N 58 40 E
Pwani □, Tanzania 54 D4 7 0S 39 0 E
Pweto,
Dem. Rep. of the Congo . 55 D2 8 25S 28 51 E
Pwllheli, U.K. 10 E3 52 53N 4 25W
Pya-ozero, Russia 24 A5 66 5N 30 58 E
Pyapon, Burma 41 L19 16 20N 95 40 E
Pyasina →, Russia 27 B9 73 30N 87 0 E
Pyatigorsk, Russia 25 F7 44 2N 43 6 E
Pyè, Burma 41 K19 18 49N 95 13 E
Pyetrikaw, Belarus 17 B15 52 11N 28 29 E
Pyinmana, Burma 41 K20 19 45N 96 12 E
Pyla, C., Cyprus 23 E12 34 56N 33 51 E
Pymatuning Reservoir,
U.S.A. 78 E4 41 30N 80 28W
Pyŏktong, N. Korea 35 D13 40 50N 125 50 E
Pyŏnggang, N. Korea ... 35 E14 38 24N 127 17 E
P'yŏngt'aek, S. Korea ... 35 F14 37 1N 127 4 E
P'yŏngyang, N. Korea ... 35 E13 39 0N 125 30 E
Pyote, U.S.A. 81 K3 31 32N 103 8W
Pyramid L., U.S.A. 82 G4 40 1N 119 35W
Pyramid Pk., U.S.A. 85 J10 36 25N 116 37W
Pyrénées, Europe 18 E4 42 45N 0 18 E
Pyu, Burma 41 K20 18 30N 96 28 E

Q

Qaanaaq = Thule,
Greenland 4 B4 77 40N 69 0W
Qachasnek, S. Africa 57 E4 30 6S 28 42 E
Qa'el Jafr, Jordan 47 E5 30 20N 36 25 E
Qa'emābād, Iran 45 D9 31 44N 60 2 E
Qā'emshahr, Iran 45 B7 36 30N 52 53 E
Qagan Nur, China 34 C8 43 30N 114 55 E
Qahar Youyi Zhongqi, China 34 D7 41 12N 112 40 E
Qahremānshahr =
Bākhtarān, Iran 44 C5 34 23N 47 0 E
Qaidam Pendi, China ... 32 C4 37 0N 95 0 E
Qajarīyeh, Iran 45 D6 31 1N 48 22 E
Qala, Ras il, Malta 23 C1 36 1N 14 20 E
Qala-i-Jadid = Spīn Būldak,
Afghan. 42 D2 31 1N 66 25 E
Qala Viala, Pakistan 42 D2 30 49N 67 17 E
Qala Yangi, Afghan. 42 B2 34 20N 66 30 E

155

Rasca, Pta. de la

Rasca, Pta. de la, Canary Is.	22 G3	27 59N	16 41W
Raseiniai, Lithuania	9 J20	55 25N	23 5 E
Rashmi, India	42 G6	25 4N	74 22 E
Rasht, Iran	45 B6	37 20N	49 40 E
Rasi Salai, Thailand	38 E5	15 20N	104 9 E
Rason L., Australia	61 E3	28 45S	124 25 E
Rasra, India	43 G10	25 50N	83 50 E
Rasul, Pakistan	42 C5	32 42N	73 34 E
Rat Buri, Thailand	38 F2	13 30N	99 54 E
Rat Islands, U.S.A.	68 C1	52 0N	178 0 E
Rat L., Canada	73 B9	56 10N	99 40W
Ratangarh, India	42 E6	28 5N	74 35 E
Raţāwi, Iraq	44 D5	30 38N	47 13 E
Ratcatchers L., Australia	63 E3	32 38S	143 10 E
Rath, India	43 G8	25 36N	79 37 E
Rath Luirc, Ireland	13 D3	52 21N	8 40W
Rathdrum, Ireland	13 D5	52 56N	6 14W
Rathenow, Germany	16 B7	52 37N	12 19 E
Rathkeale, Ireland	13 D3	52 32N	8 56W
Rathlin I., U.K.	13 A5	55 18N	6 14W
Rathmelton, Ireland	13 A4	55 2N	7 38W
Ratibor = Racibórz, Poland	17 C10	50 7N	18 18 E
Ratlam, India	42 H6	23 20N	75 0 E
Ratnagiri, India	40 L8	16 57N	73 18 E
Ratodero, Pakistan	42 F3	27 45N	68 0 E
Raton, U.S.A.	81 G2	36 54N	104 24W
Rattaphum, Thailand	39 J3	7 8N	100 16 E
Rattray Hd., U.K.	12 D7	57 38N	1 50W
Ratz, Mt., Canada	72 B2	57 23N	132 12W
Raub, Malaysia	39 L3	3 47N	101 52 E
Rauch, Argentina	94 D4	36 45S	59 5W
Raudales de Malpaso, Mexico	87 D6	17 30N	23 30W
Raufarhöfn, Iceland	8 C6	66 27N	15 57W
Raufoss, Norway	9 F14	60 44N	10 37 E
Raukumara Ra., N.Z.	59 H6	38 5S	177 55 E
Rauma, Finland	9 F19	61 10N	21 30 E
Raurkela, India	43 H11	22 14N	84 50 E
Rausu-Dake, Japan	30 B12	44 4N	145 7 E
Rava-Ruska, Poland	17 C12	50 15N	23 42 E
Rava Russkaya = Rava-Ruska, Poland	17 C12	50 15N	23 42 E
Ravalli, U.S.A.	82 C6	47 17N	114 11W
Ravānsar, Iran	44 C5	34 43N	46 40 E
Rāvar, Iran	45 D8	31 20N	56 51 E
Ravena, U.S.A.	79 D11	42 28N	73 49W
Ravenna, Italy	20 B5	44 25N	12 12 E
Ravenna, Nebr., U.S.A.	80 E5	41 1N	98 55W
Ravenna, Ohio, U.S.A.	78 E3	41 9N	81 15W
Ravensburg, Germany	16 E5	47 46N	9 36 E
Ravenshoe, Australia	62 B4	17 37S	145 29 E
Ravensthorpe, Australia	61 F3	33 35S	120 2 E
Ravenswood, Australia	62 C4	20 6S	146 54 E
Ravenswood, U.S.A.	76 F5	38 57N	81 46W
Ravi →, Pakistan	42 D4	30 35N	71 49 E
Rawalpindi, Pakistan	42 C5	33 38N	73 8 E
Rawāndūz, Iraq	44 B5	36 40N	44 30 E
Rawang, Malaysia	39 L3	3 20N	101 35 E
Rawene, N.Z.	59 F4	35 25S	173 32 E
Rawlinna, Australia	61 F4	30 58S	125 28 E
Rawlins, U.S.A.	82 F10	41 47N	107 14W
Rawlinson Ra., Australia	61 D4	24 40S	128 30 E
Rawson, Argentina	96 E3	43 15S	65 5W
Raxaul, India	43 F11	26 59N	84 51 E
Ray, U.S.A.	80 A3	48 21N	103 10W
Ray, C., Canada	71 C8	47 33N	59 15W
Rayadurg, India	40 M10	14 40N	76 50 E
Rayagada, India	41 K13	19 15N	83 20 E
Raychikhinsk, Russia	27 E13	49 46N	129 25 E
Rāyen, Iran	45 D8	29 34N	57 26 E
Rayleigh, U.K.	11 F8	51 36N	0 37 E
Raymond, Canada	72 D6	49 30N	112 35W
Raymond, Calif., U.S.A.	84 H7	37 13N	119 54W
Raymond, N.H., U.S.A.	79 C13	43 2N	71 11W
Raymond, Wash., U.S.A.	84 D3	46 41N	123 44W
Raymond Terrace, Australia	63 E5	32 45S	151 44 E
Raymondville, U.S.A.	81 M6	26 29N	97 47W
Raymore, Canada	73 C8	51 25N	104 31W
Rayna, India	43 H12	23 5N	87 52 E
Rayón, Mexico	86 B2	29 43N	110 35W
Rayong, Thailand	38 F3	12 40N	101 20 E
Rayville, U.S.A.	81 J9	32 29N	91 46W
Raz, Pte. du, France	18 C1	48 2N	4 47W
Razan, Iran	45 C6	35 23N	49 2 E
Razdel'naya = Rozdilna, Ukraine	17 E16	46 50N	30 2 E
Razdolnoye, Russia	30 C5	43 30N	131 52 E
Razeh, Iran	45 C6	32 47N	48 9 E
Razgrad, Bulgaria	21 C12	43 33N	26 34 E
Razim, Lacul, Romania	17 F15	44 50N	29 0 E
Razmak, Pakistan	42 C3	32 45N	69 50 E
Ré, Î. de, France	18 C3	46 12N	1 30W
Reading, U.K.	11 F7	51 27N	0 58W
Reading, U.S.A.	79 F9	40 20N	75 56W
Reading □, U.K.	11 F7	51 27N	0 58W
Realicó, Argentina	94 D3	35 0S	64 15W
Ream, Cambodia	39 G4	10 34N	103 39 E
Reata, Mexico	86 B4	26 8N	101 5W
Reay Forest, U.K.	12 C4	58 22N	4 55W
Rebi, Indonesia	37 F8	6 23S	134 7 E
Rebiana, Libya	51 D10	24 12N	22 10 E
Rebun-Tō, Japan	30 B10	45 23N	141 2 E
Recherche, Arch. of the, Australia	61 F3	34 15S	122 50 E
Rechna Doab, Pakistan	42 D5	31 35N	73 30 E
Rechytsa, Belarus	17 B16	52 21N	30 24 E
Recife, Brazil	93 E12	8 0S	35 0W
Recklinghausen, Germany	15 C7	51 37N	7 12 E
Reconquista, Argentina	94 B4	29 10S	59 45W
Recreo, Argentina	94 B2	29 25N	65 10 E
Red →, La., U.S.A.	81 K9	31 1N	91 45W
Red →, N. Dak., U.S.A.	68 C10	49 0N	97 15W
Red Bank, U.S.A.	79 F10	40 21N	74 5W
Red Bay, Canada	71 B8	51 44N	56 25W
Red Bluff, U.S.A.	82 F2	40 11N	122 15W
Red Bluff L., U.S.A.	81 K3	31 54N	103 55W
Red Cliffs, Australia	63 E3	34 19S	142 11 E
Red Cloud, U.S.A.	80 E5	40 5N	98 32W
Red Creek, U.S.A.	79 C8	43 14N	76 45W
Red Deer, Canada	72 C6	52 20N	113 50W
Red Deer →, Alta., Canada	73 C8	50 58N	110 0W
Red Deer →, Man., Canada	73 C8	52 53N	101 1W
Red Deer L., Canada	73 C8	52 55N	101 20W
Red Hook, U.S.A.	79 E11	41 55N	73 53W
Red Indian L., Canada	71 C8	48 35N	57 0W
Red L., Canada	73 C10	51 3N	93 49W
Red Lake, Canada	73 C10	51 3N	93 49W
Red Lake Falls, U.S.A.	80 B6	47 53N	96 16W
Red Lake Road, Canada	73 C10	49 59N	93 25W
Red Lodge, U.S.A.	82 D9	45 11N	109 15W
Red Mountain, U.S.A.	85 K9	35 37N	117 38W
Red Oak, U.S.A.	80 E7	41 1N	95 14W
Red Rock, Canada	70 C2	48 55N	88 15W
Red Rock, L., U.S.A.	80 E8	41 22N	92 59W
Red Rocks Pt., Australia	61 F4	32 13S	127 32 E
Red Sea, Asia	46 C2	25 0N	36 0 E
Red Slate Mt., U.S.A.	84 H8	37 31N	118 52W
Red Sucker L., Canada	70 B1	54 9N	93 40W
Red Tower Pass = Turnu Roşu, P., Romania	17 F13	45 33N	24 17 E
Red Wing, U.S.A.	80 C8	44 34N	92 31W
Redang, Malaysia	36 C2	5 49N	103 2 E
Redange, Lux.	15 E5	49 46N	5 52 E
Redcar, U.K.	10 C6	54 37N	1 4W
Redcar & Cleveland □, U.K.	10 C7	54 29N	1 0W
Redcliff, Canada	73 C6	50 10N	110 50W
Redcliffe, Mt., Australia	61 E3	28 30S	121 30 E
Reddersburg, S. Africa	56 D4	29 41S	26 10 E
Redding, U.S.A.	82 F2	40 35N	122 24W
Redditch, U.K.	11 E6	52 18N	1 55W
Redfield, U.S.A.	80 C5	44 53N	98 31W
Redford, U.S.A.	79 B11	44 38N	73 48W
Redlands, U.S.A.	85 M9	34 4N	117 11W
Redmond, Oreg., U.S.A.	82 D3	44 17N	121 11W
Redmond, Wash., U.S.A.	84 C4	47 41N	122 7W
Redon, France	18 C2	47 40N	2 6W
Redonda, Antigua	89 C7	16 58N	62 19W
Redondela, Spain	19 A1	42 15N	8 38W
Redondo Beach, U.S.A.	85 M8	33 50N	118 23W
Redruth, U.K.	11 G2	50 14N	5 14W
Redvers, Canada	73 D8	49 35N	101 40W
Redwater, Canada	72 C6	53 55N	113 6W
Redwood, U.S.A.	79 B9	44 18N	75 48W
Redwood City, U.S.A.	84 H4	37 30N	122 15W
Redwood Falls, U.S.A.	80 C7	44 32N	95 7W
Redwood National Park, U.S.A.	82 F1	41 40N	124 5W
Ree, L., Ireland	13 C3	53 35N	8 0W
Reed, L., Canada	73 C8	54 38N	100 30W
Reed City, U.S.A.	76 D3	43 53N	85 31W
Reedley, U.S.A.	84 J7	36 36N	119 27W
Reedsburg, U.S.A.	80 D9	43 32N	90 0W
Reedsport, U.S.A.	82 E1	43 42N	124 6W
Reedsville, U.S.A.	78 F7	40 39N	77 35W
Reefton, N.Z.	59 K3	42 6S	171 51 E
Reese →, U.S.A.	82 F5	40 48N	117 4W
Refugio, U.S.A.	81 L6	28 18N	97 17W
Regensburg, Germany	16 D7	49 1N	12 6 E
Réggio di Calábria, Italy	20 E6	38 6N	15 39 E
Réggio nell'Emília, Italy	20 B4	44 43N	10 36 E
Reghin, Romania	17 E13	46 46N	24 42 E
Regina, Canada	73 C8	50 27N	104 35W
Regina Beach, Canada	73 C8	50 47N	105 0W
Registro, Brazil	95 A6	24 29S	47 49W
Rehar →, India	43 H10	23 55N	82 40 E
Rehli, India	43 H8	23 38N	79 5 E
Rehoboth, Namibia	56 C2	23 15S	17 4 E
Rehovot, Israel	47 D3	31 54N	34 48 E
Reichenbach, Germany	16 C7	50 37N	12 17 E
Reid, Australia	61 F4	30 49S	128 26 E
Reidsville, U.S.A.	77 G6	36 21N	79 40W
Reigate, U.K.	11 F7	51 14N	0 12W
Reims, France	18 B6	49 15N	4 1 E
Reina Adelaida, Arch., Chile	96 G2	52 20S	74 0W
Reindeer →, Canada	73 B8	55 36N	103 11W
Reindeer I., Canada	73 C9	52 30N	98 0W
Reindeer L., Canada	73 B8	57 15N	102 15W
Reinga, C., N.Z.	59 F4	34 25S	172 43 E
Reinosa, Spain	19 A3	43 2N	4 15W
Reitz, S. Africa	57 D4	27 48S	28 29 E
Reivilo, S. Africa	56 D3	27 36S	24 8 E
Reliance, Canada	73 A7	63 0N	109 20W
Remarkable, Mt., Australia	63 E2	32 48S	138 10 E
Rembang, Indonesia	37 G14	6 42S	111 21 E
Remedios, Panama	88 E3	8 15N	81 50W
Remeshk, Iran	45 E8	26 55N	58 50 E
Remich, Lux.	15 E6	49 32N	6 22 E
Remscheid, Germany	15 C7	51 11N	7 12 E
Ren Xian, China	34 F8	37 8N	114 40 E
Rendsburg, Germany	16 A5	54 17N	9 39 E
Renfrew, Canada	79 A8	45 30N	76 40W
Renfrewshire □, U.K.	12 F4	55 49N	4 38W
Rengat, Indonesia	36 E2	0 30S	102 45 E
Rengo, Chile	94 C1	34 24S	70 50W
Reni, Ukraine	17 F15	45 28N	28 15 E
Renmark, Australia	63 E3	34 11S	140 43 E
Rennell Sd., Canada	72 C2	53 23N	132 35W
Renner Springs, Australia	62 B1	18 20S	133 47 E
Rennes, France	18 B3	48 7N	1 41W
Rennie L., Canada	73 A7	61 32N	105 35W
Reno, U.S.A.	84 F7	39 31N	119 48W
Reno →, Italy	20 B5	44 38N	12 16 E
Renovo, U.S.A.	78 E7	41 20N	77 45W
Renqiu, China	34 E9	38 43N	116 5 E
Rensselaer, Ind., U.S.A.	76 E2	40 57N	87 9W
Rensselaer, N.Y., U.S.A.	79 D11	42 38N	73 45W
Rentería, Spain	19 A5	43 19N	1 54W
Renton, U.S.A.	84 C4	47 29N	122 12W
Reotipur, India	43 G10	25 33N	83 45 E
Republic, Mo., U.S.A.	81 G8	37 7N	93 29W
Republic, Wash., U.S.A.	82 B4	48 39N	118 44W
Republican →, U.S.A.	80 F6	39 4N	96 48W
Repulse Bay, Canada	69 B11	66 30N	86 30W
Requena, Peru	92 E4	5 5S	73 52W
Requena, Spain	19 C5	39 30N	1 4W
Reşadiye = Datça, Turkey	21 F12	36 46N	27 40 E
Reserve, U.S.A.	83 K9	33 43N	108 45W
Resht = Rasht, Iran	45 B6	37 20N	49 40 E
Resistencia, Argentina	94 B4	27 30S	59 0W
Reşiţa, Romania	17 F11	45 18N	21 53 E
Resolution I., Canada	69 B13	61 30N	65 0W
Resolution I., N.Z.	59 L1	45 40S	166 40 E
Ressano Garcia, Mozam.	57 D5	25 25S	32 0 E
Reston, Canada	73 D8	49 33N	101 6W
Retalhuleu, Guatemala	88 D1	14 33N	91 46W
Retenue, L. de, Dem. Rep. of the Congo	55 E2	11 0S	27 0 E
Retford, U.K.	10 D7	53 19N	0 56W
Réthímnon, Greece	23 D6	35 18N	24 30 E
Réthímnon □, Greece	23 D6	35 23N	24 28 E
Reti, Pakistan	42 E3	28 5N	69 48 E
Réunion ■, Ind. Oc.	49 J9	21 0S	56 0 E
Reus, Spain	19 B6	41 10N	1 5 E
Reutlingen, Germany	16 D5	48 29N	9 12 E
Reval = Tallinn, Estonia	9 G21	59 22N	24 48 E
Revda, Russia	24 C10	56 48N	59 57 E
Revelganj, India	43 G11	25 50N	84 40 E
Revelstoke, Canada	72 C5	51 0N	118 10W
Reventazón, Peru	92 E2	6 10S	80 58W
Revillagigedo, Is. de, Pac. Oc.	86 D2	18 40N	112 0W
Revuè →, Mozam.	55 F3	19 50S	34 0 E
Rewa, India	43 G9	24 33N	81 25 E
Rewari, India	42 E7	28 15N	76 40 E
Rexburg, U.S.A.	82 E8	43 49N	111 47W
Rey, Iran	45 C6	35 35N	51 25 E
Rey, I. del, Panama	88 E4	8 20N	78 30W
Rey Malabo, Eq. Guin.	52 D1	3 45N	8 50 E
Reyðarfjörður, Iceland	8 D6	65 2N	14 13W
Reyes, Pt., U.S.A.	84 H3	38 0N	123 0W
Reykjahlíð, Iceland	8 D5	65 40N	16 55W
Reykjanes, Iceland	8 E2	63 48N	22 40W
Reykjavík, Iceland	8 D3	64 10N	21 57W
Reynolds Ra., Australia	60 D5	22 30S	133 0 E
Reynoldsville, U.S.A.	78 E6	41 5N	78 58W
Reynosa, Mexico	87 B5	26 5N	98 18W
Rēzekne, Latvia	9 H22	56 30N	27 17 E
Rezvān, Iran	45 E8	27 34N	56 6 E
Rhayader, U.K.	11 E4	52 18N	3 29W
Rhein, Canada	73 C8	51 25N	102 15W
Rhein →, Europe	15 C6	51 52N	6 2 E
Rhein-Main-Donau-Kanal, Germany	16 D6	49 15N	11 15 E
Rheine, Germany	16 B4	52 17N	7 26 E
Rheinland-Pfalz □, Germany	16 C4	50 0N	7 0 E
Rhin = Rhein →, Europe	15 C6	51 52N	6 2 E
Rhine = Rhein →, Europe	15 C6	51 52N	6 2 E
Rhinebeck, U.S.A.	79 E11	41 56N	73 55W
Rhineland-Palatinate = Rheinland-Pfalz □, Germany	16 C4	50 0N	7 0 E
Rhinelander, U.S.A.	80 C10	45 38N	89 25W
Rhinns Pt., U.K.	12 F2	55 40N	6 29W
Rhino Camp, Uganda	54 B3	3 0N	31 22 E
Rhir, Cap, Morocco	50 B4	30 38N	9 54W
Rhode Island □, U.S.A.	79 E13	41 40N	71 30W
Rhodes = Ródhos, Greece	23 C10	36 15N	28 10 E
Rhodesia = Zimbabwe ■, Africa	55 F3	19 0S	30 0 E
Rhodope Mts. = Rhodopi Planina, Bulgaria	21 D11	41 40N	24 20 E
Rhodopi Planina, Bulgaria	21 D11	41 40N	24 20 E
Rhön = Rhön, Germany	16 C5	50 24N	9 58 E
Rhön, Germany	16 C5	50 24N	9 58 E
Rhondda, U.K.	11 F4	51 39N	3 31W
Rhondda Cynon Taff □, U.K.	11 F4	51 42N	3 27W
Rhône →, France	18 E6	43 28N	4 42 E
Rhum, U.K.	12 E2	57 0N	6 20W
Rhyl, U.K.	10 D4	53 20N	3 29W
Riachão, Brazil	93 E9	7 20S	46 37W
Riasi, India	43 C6	33 10N	74 50 E
Riau □, Indonesia	36 E2	0 0	102 35 E
Riau, Kepulauan, Indonesia	36 D2	0 30N	104 20 E
Riau Arch. = Riau, Kepulauan, Indonesia	36 D2	0 30N	104 20 E
Ribadeo, Spain	19 A2	43 35N	7 5W
Ribas do Rio Pardo, Brazil	93 H8	20 27S	53 46W
Ribble →, U.K.	10 D5	53 52N	2 25W
Ribe, Denmark	9 J13	55 19N	8 44 E
Ribeira Brava, Madeira	22 D2	32 41N	17 4W
Ribeirão Prêto, Brazil	95 A6	21 10S	47 50W
Riberalta, Bolivia	92 F5	11 0S	66 0W
Riccarton, N.Z.	59 K4	43 32S	172 37 E
Rice, U.S.A.	85 L12	34 5N	114 51W
Rice L., Canada	78 B6	44 12N	78 10W
Rice Lake, U.S.A.	80 C9	45 30N	91 44W
Rich, C., Canada	78 B4	44 43N	80 38W
Richards Bay, S. Africa	57 D5	28 48S	32 6 E
Richardson →, Canada	73 B6	58 25N	111 14W
Richardson Lakes, U.S.A.	76 C10	44 46N	70 58W
Richardson Springs, U.S.A.	84 F5	39 51N	121 46W
Richey, U.S.A.	80 B2	47 39N	105 4W
Richfield, U.S.A.	83 G8	38 46N	112 5W
Richfield Springs, U.S.A.	79 D10	42 51N	74 59W
Richford, U.S.A.	79 B12	45 0N	72 40W
Richibucto, Canada	71 C7	46 42N	64 54W
Richland, Ga., U.S.A.	77 J3	32 5N	84 40W
Richland, Wash., U.S.A.	82 C4	46 17N	119 18W
Richland Center, U.S.A.	80 D9	43 21N	90 23W
Richlands, U.S.A.	76 G5	37 6N	81 48W
Richmond, Australia	62 C3	20 43S	143 8 E
Richmond, N.Z.	59 J4	41 20S	173 12 E
Richmond, U.K.	10 C6	54 25N	1 43W
Richmond, Calif., U.S.A.	84 H4	37 56N	122 21W
Richmond, Ind., U.S.A.	76 F3	39 50N	84 53W
Richmond, Ky., U.S.A.	76 G3	37 45N	84 18W
Richmond, Mich., U.S.A.	78 D2	42 49N	82 45W
Richmond, Mo., U.S.A.	80 F8	39 17N	93 58W
Richmond, Tex., U.S.A.	81 L7	29 35N	95 46W
Richmond, Utah, U.S.A.	82 F8	41 56N	111 48W
Richmond, Vt., U.S.A.	79 B12	44 24N	72 59W
Richmond Hill, Canada	78 C5	43 52N	79 27W
Richmond Ra., Australia	63 D5	29 0S	152 45 E
Richwood, U.S.A.	76 F5	38 14N	80 32W
Ridder = Leninogorsk, Kazakstan	26 D9	50 20N	83 30 E
Riddlesburg, U.S.A.	78 F6	40 9N	78 15W
Ridgecrest, U.S.A.	85 K9	35 38N	117 40W
Ridgefield, Conn., U.S.A.	79 E11	41 17N	73 30W
Ridgefield, Wash., U.S.A.	84 E4	45 49N	122 45W
Ridgeland, U.S.A.	77 J5	32 29N	80 59W
Ridgetown, Canada	78 D3	42 26N	81 52W
Ridgewood, U.S.A.	79 F10	40 59N	74 7W
Ridgway, U.S.A.	78 E6	41 25N	78 44W
Riding Mountain Nat. Park, Canada	73 C9	50 50N	100 0W
Ridley, Mt., Australia	61 F3	33 12S	100 7 E
Riebeek, Austria	16 C7	48 14N	13 30 E
Riesa, Germany	16 C7	51 17N	13 17 E
Riet →, S. Africa	56 D3	29 0S	23 54 E
Rieti, Italy	20 C5	42 24N	12 51 E
Riffe L., U.S.A.	84 D4	46 32N	122 26W
Rift Valley □, Kenya	54 B4	0 20N	36 0 E
Rīga, Latvia	9 H21	56 53N	24 8 E
Riga, G. of, Latvia	9 H20	57 40N	23 45 E
Rīgān, Iran	45 D8	28 37N	58 58 E
Rīgas Jūras Līcis = Riga, G. of, Latvia	9 H20	57 40N	23 45 E
Rigaud, Canada	79 A10	45 29N	74 18W
Rigby, U.S.A.	82 E8	43 40N	111 55W
Rigestān □, Afghan.	40 D4	30 15N	65 0 E
Riggins, U.S.A.	82 D5	45 25N	116 19W
Rigolet, Canada	71 B8	54 10N	58 23W
Rihand Dam, India	43 G10	24 9N	83 2 E
Riihimäki, Finland	9 F21	60 45N	24 48 E
Riiser-Larsen-halvøya, Antarctica	5 C4	68 0S	35 0 E
Rijeka, Croatia	16 F8	45 20N	14 21 E
Rijssen, Neths.	15 B6	52 19N	6 31 E
Rikuzentakada, Japan	30 E10	39 0N	141 40 E
Riley, U.S.A.	82 E4	43 32N	119 28W
Rimah, Wadi ar →, Si. Arabia	44 E4	26 5N	41 30 E
Rimbey, Canada	72 C6	52 35N	114 15W
Rimersburg, U.S.A.	78 E5	41 3N	79 30W
Rímini, Italy	20 B5	44 3N	12 33 E
Rimouski, Canada	71 C6	48 27N	68 30W
Rimrock, U.S.A.	84 D5	46 38N	121 10W
Rinca, Indonesia	37 F5	8 45S	119 35 E
Rincón de Romos, Mexico	86 C4	22 14N	102 18W
Rinconada, Argentina	94 A2	22 26S	66 10W
Rind →, India	43 G9	25 53N	80 33 E
Ringas, India	42 F6	27 21N	75 34 E
Ringkøbing, Denmark	9 H13	56 5N	8 15 E
Ringvassøy, Norway	8 B18	69 56N	19 15 E
Ringwood, U.S.A.	79 E10	41 7N	74 15W
Rinjani, Indonesia	36 F5	8 24S	116 28 E
Rio Branco, Brazil	92 E5	9 58S	67 49W
Rio Branco, Uruguay	95 C5	32 40S	53 40W
Río Bravo del Norte →, Mexico	87 B5	25 57N	97 9W
Rio Brilhante, Brazil	95 A5	21 48S	54 33W
Río Claro, Brazil	95 A6	22 19S	47 35W
Río Claro, Trin. & Tob.	89 D7	10 20N	61 25W
Río Colorado, Argentina	96 D4	39 0S	64 0W
Río Cuarto, Argentina	94 C3	33 10S	64 25W
Rio das Pedras, Mozam.	57 C6	23 8S	35 28 E
Rio de Janeiro, Brazil	95 A7	23 0S	43 12W
Rio de Janeiro □, Brazil	95 A7	22 50S	43 0W
Río do Sul, Brazil	95 B6	27 13S	49 37W
Río Gallegos, Argentina	96 G3	51 35S	69 15W
Río Grande = Grande, Rio →, U.S.A.	81 N6	25 58N	97 9W
Río Grande, Argentina	96 G3	53 50S	67 45W
Rio Grande, Brazil	95 C5	32 0S	52 20W
Río Grande, Mexico	86 C4	23 50N	103 2W
Río Grande, Nic.	88 D3	12 54N	83 33W
Rio Grande City, U.S.A.	81 M5	26 23N	98 49W
Río Grande de Santiago →, Mexico	86 C3	21 36N	105 26W
Río Grande del Norte →, N. Amer.	75 E7	26 0N	97 0W
Rio Grande do Norte □, Brazil	93 E11	5 40S	36 0W
Rio Grande do Sul □, Brazil	95 C5	30 0S	53 0W
Rio Hato, Panama	88 E3	8 22N	80 10W
Río Lagartos, Mexico	87 C7	21 36N	88 10W
Rio Largo, Brazil	93 E11	9 28S	35 50W
Río Mulatos, Bolivia	92 G5	19 40S	66 50W
Río Muni = Mbini □, Eq. Guin.	52 D2	1 30N	10 0 E
Rio Negro, Brazil	95 B6	26 0S	49 55W
Rio Pardo, Brazil	95 C5	30 0S	52 30W
Río Rancho, U.S.A.	83 J10	35 14N	106 38W
Río Segundo, Argentina	94 C3	31 40S	63 59W
Río Tercero, Argentina	94 C3	32 15S	64 8W
Rio Verde, Brazil	93 G8	17 50S	51 0W
Río Verde, Mexico	87 C5	21 56N	99 59W
Rio Vista, U.S.A.	84 G5	38 10N	121 42W
Riobamba, Ecuador	92 D3	1 50S	78 45W
Ríohacha, Colombia	92 A4	11 33N	72 55W
Ríosucio, Colombia	92 B3	7 27N	77 7W
Riou L., Canada	73 B7	59 7N	106 25W
Ripley, Canada	78 B3	44 4N	81 35W
Ripley, Calif., U.S.A.	85 M12	33 32N	114 39W
Ripley, N.Y., U.S.A.	78 D5	42 16N	79 43W
Ripley, Tenn., U.S.A.	81 H10	35 45N	89 32W
Ripley, W. Va., U.S.A.	76 F5	38 49N	81 43W
Ripon, U.K.	10 C6	54 9N	1 31W
Ripon, Calif., U.S.A.	84 H5	37 44N	121 7W
Ripon, Wis., U.S.A.	76 D1	43 51N	88 50W
Rishā', W. ar →, Si. Arabia	44 E5	25 33N	44 5 E
Rishiri-Tō, Japan	30 B10	45 11N	141 15 E
Rishon le Ziyyon, Israel	47 D3	31 58N	34 48 E
Rison, U.S.A.	81 J8	33 58N	92 11W
Risør, Norway	9 G13	58 43N	9 13 E
Rita Blanca Cr. →, U.S.A.	81 H3	35 40N	102 29W
Ritter, Mt., U.S.A.	84 H7	37 41N	119 12W
Rittman, U.S.A.	78 F3	40 58N	81 47W
Ritzville, U.S.A.	82 C4	47 8N	118 23W
Riva del Garda, Italy	20 B4	45 53N	10 50 E
Rivadavia, Buenos Aires, Argentina	94 D3	35 29S	62 59W
Rivadavia, Mendoza, Argentina	94 C2	33 13S	68 30W
Rivadavia, Salta, Argentina	94 A3	24 5S	62 54W
Rivadavia, Chile	94 B1	29 57S	70 35W
Rivas, Nic.	88 D2	11 30N	85 50W
River Cess, Liberia	50 G4	5 30N	9 32W
River Jordan, Canada	84 B2	48 26N	124 3W
Rivera, Argentina	94 D3	37 12S	63 14W
Rivera, Uruguay	95 C4	31 0S	55 50W
Riverbank, U.S.A.	84 H6	37 44N	120 56W
Riverdale, U.S.A.	84 J7	36 26N	119 52W
Riverhead, U.S.A.	79 F12	40 55N	72 40W
Riverhurst, Canada	73 C7	50 55N	106 50W
Rivers, Canada	73 C8	50 2N	100 14W
Rivers Inlet, Canada	72 C3	51 42N	127 15W
Riversdale, S. Africa	56 E3	34 7S	21 15 E
Riverside, U.S.A.	85 M9	33 59N	117 22W
Riverton, Australia	63 E2	34 10S	138 46 E
Riverton, Canada	73 C9	51 1N	97 0W
Riverton, N.Z.	59 M2	46 21S	168 0 E
Riverton, U.S.A.	82 E9	43 2N	108 23W
Riverton Heights, U.S.A.	84 C4	47 28N	122 17W
Riviera, U.S.A.	85 K12	35 4N	114 35W
Riviera di Levante, Italy	18 D8	44 15N	9 30 E
Rivière-au-Renard, Canada	71 C7	48 59N	64 23W
Rivière-du-Loup, Canada	71 C6	47 50N	69 30W
Rivière-Pentecôte, Canada	71 C6	49 57N	67 1W

Rivière-Pilote, Martinique .. 89 D7 14 26N 60 53W
Rivière St. Paul, Canada . 71 B8 51 28N 57 45W
Rivne, Ukraine 17 C14 50 40N 26 10 E
Rivoli, Italy 18 D7 45 3N 7 31 E
Rivoli B., Australia 63 F3 37 32S 140 3 E
Riyadh = Ar Riyāḍ,
 Si. Arabia 46 C4 24 41N 46 42 E
Rize, Turkey 25 F7 41 0N 40 30 E
Rizhao, China 35 G10 35 25N 119 30 E
Rizokarpaso, Cyprus 23 D13 35 36N 34 23 E
Rizzuto, C., Italy 20 E7 38 53N 17 5 E
Rjukan, Norway 9 G13 59 54N 8 33 E
Road Town, Virgin Is. ... 89 C7 18 27N 64 37W
Roan Plateau, U.S.A. 82 G9 39 20N 109 20W
Roanne, France 18 C6 46 3N 4 4 E
Roanoke, Ala., U.S.A. ... 77 J3 33 9N 85 22W
Roanoke, Va., U.S.A. ... 76 G6 37 16N 79 56W
Roanoke →, U.S.A. 77 H7 35 57N 76 42W
Roanoke I., U.S.A. 77 H8 35 55N 75 40W
Roanoke Rapids, U.S.A. . 77 G7 36 28N 77 40W
Roatán, Honduras 88 C2 16 18N 86 35W
Robät Sang, Iran 45 C8 35 35N 59 10 E
Robbins I., Australia ... 62 G4 40 42S 145 0 E
Robe, Australia 63 F2 37 11S 139 45 E
Robe →, Australia 60 D2 21 42S 116 15 E
Robert Lee, U.S.A. 81 K4 31 54N 100 29W
Robertsdale, U.S.A. 78 F6 40 11N 78 6W
Robertsganj, India 43 G10 24 44N 83 4 E
Robertson, S. Africa 56 E2 33 46S 19 50 E
Robertson I., Antarctica . 5 C18 65 15S 59 30W
Robertson Ra., Australia . 60 D3 23 15S 121 0 E
Robertstown, Australia .. 63 E2 33 58S 139 5 E
Roberval, Canada 71 C5 48 32N 72 15W
Robeson Chan., Greenland 4 A4 82 0N 61 30W
Robesonia, U.S.A. 79 F8 40 21N 76 8W
Robinson, U.S.A. 76 F2 39 0N 87 44W
Robinson →, Australia .. 62 B2 16 3S 137 16 E
Robinson Ra., Australia . 61 E2 25 40S 119 0 E
Robinvale, Australia ... 63 E3 34 40S 142 45 E
Roblin, Canada 73 C8 51 14N 101 21W
Roboré, Bolivia 92 G7 18 10S 59 45W
Robson, Mt., Canada ... 72 C5 53 10N 119 10W
Robstown, U.S.A. 81 M6 27 47N 97 40W
Roca, C. da, Portugal ... 19 C1 38 40N 9 31W
Roca Partida, I., Mexico . 86 D2 19 1N 112 2W
Rocas, I., Brazil 93 D12 4 0S 34 1W
Rocha, Uruguay 95 C5 34 30S 54 25W
Rochdale, U.K. 10 D5 53 38N 2 9W
Rochefort, Belgium 15 D5 50 9N 5 12 E
Rochefort, France 18 D3 45 56N 0 57W
Rochelle, U.S.A. 80 E10 41 56N 89 4W
Rocher River, Canada ... 72 A6 61 23N 112 44W
Rochester, U.K. 11 F8 51 23N 0 31 E
Rochester, Ind., U.S.A. . 76 E2 41 4N 86 13W
Rochester, Minn., U.S.A. 80 C8 44 1N 92 28W
Rochester, N.H., U.S.A. . 79 C14 43 18N 70 59W
Rochester, N.Y., U.S.A. . 78 C7 43 10N 77 37W
Rock →, Canada 72 A3 60 7N 127 7W
Rock Creek, U.S.A. 78 E4 41 40N 80 52W
Rock Falls, U.S.A. 80 E10 41 47N 89 41W
Rock Hill, U.S.A. 77 H5 34 56N 81 1W
Rock Island, U.S.A. 80 E9 41 30N 90 34W
Rock Rapids, U.S.A. 80 D6 43 26N 96 10W
Rock Sound, Bahamas .. 88 B4 24 54N 76 12W
Rock Springs, Mont., U.S.A. 82 C10 46 49N 106 15W
Rock Springs, Wyo., U.S.A. 82 F9 41 35N 109 14W
Rock Valley, U.S.A. 80 D6 43 12N 96 18W
Rockall, Atl. Oc. 6 D3 57 37N 13 42W
Rockdale, Tex., U.S.A. .. 81 K6 30 39N 97 0W
Rockdale, Wash., U.S.A. . 84 C5 47 22N 121 28W
Rockefeller Plateau,
 Antarctica 5 E14 80 0S 140 0W
Rockford, U.S.A. 80 D10 42 16N 89 6W
Rockglen, Canada 73 D7 49 11N 105 57W
Rockhampton, Australia . 62 C5 23 22S 150 32 E
Rockhampton Downs, Australia 61 F2 32 15S 115 38 E
Rockingham, U.S.A. 77 H6 34 57N 79 46W
Rockingham B., Australia 62 B4 18 5S 146 10 E
Rocklake, U.S.A. 80 A5 48 47N 99 15W
Rockland, Canada 79 A9 45 33N 75 17W
Rockland, Idaho, U.S.A. . 82 E7 42 34N 112 53W
Rockland, Maine, U.S.A. . 77 C11 44 6N 69 7W
Rockland, Mich., U.S.A. . 80 B10 46 44N 89 11W
Rocklin, U.S.A. 84 G5 38 48N 121 14W
Rockport, Mass., U.S.A. . 79 D14 42 39N 70 37W
Rockport, Mo., U.S.A. .. 80 E7 40 25N 95 31W
Rockport, Tex., U.S.A. .. 81 L6 28 2N 97 3W
Rocksprings, U.S.A. 81 K4 30 1N 100 13W
Rockville, Conn., U.S.A. . 79 E12 41 52N 72 28W
Rockville, Md., U.S.A. .. 76 F7 39 5N 77 9W
Rockwall, U.S.A. 81 J6 32 56N 96 28W
Rockwell City, U.S.A. ... 80 D7 42 24N 94 38W
Rockwood, Canada 78 C4 43 37N 80 8W
Rockwood, Maine, U.S.A. 77 C11 45 41N 69 45W
Rockwood, Tenn., U.S.A. 77 H3 35 52N 84 41W
Rocky Ford, U.S.A. 80 F3 38 3N 103 43W
Rocky Gully, Australia .. 61 F2 34 30S 116 57 E
Rocky Harbour, Canada . 71 C8 49 36N 57 55W
Rocky Island L., Canada . 70 C3 46 55N 83 0W
Rocky Lane, Canada 72 B5 58 31N 116 22W
Rocky Mount, U.S.A. ... 77 H7 35 57N 77 48W
Rocky Mountain House,
 Canada 72 C6 52 22N 114 55W
Rocky Mountain National
 Park, U.S.A. 82 F11 40 25N 105 45W
Rocky Mts., N. Amer. ... 72 C4 49 0N 115 0W
Rod, Pakistan 40 E3 28 10N 63 5 E
Rødbyhavn, Denmark ... 9 J14 54 39N 11 22 E
Roddickton, Canada ... 71 B8 50 51N 56 8W
Rodez, France 18 D5 44 21N 2 33 E
Ródhos, Greece 23 C10 36 15N 28 10 E
Rodney, C., N.Z. 59 G5 36 17S 174 50 E
Rodriguez, Ind. Oc. 3 E13 19 45S 63 20 E
Roe →, U.K. 13 A5 55 6N 6 59W
Roebling, U.S.A. 79 F10 40 7N 74 47W
Roebourne, Australia ... 60 D2 20 44S 117 9 E
Roebuck B., Australia .. 60 C3 18 5S 122 20 E
Roermond, Neths. 15 C6 51 12N 6 0 E
Roes Welcome Sd., Canada 69 B11 65 0N 87 0W
Roeselare, Belgium 15 D3 50 57N 3 7 E
Rogachev = Ragachow,
 Belarus 17 B16 53 8N 30 5 E
Rogaguado, L., Bolivia .. 92 F5 13 43S 66 50W

Rogatyn, Ukraine 17 D13 49 24N 24 36 E
Rogdhia, Greece 23 D7 35 22N 25 1 E
Rogers, U.S.A. 81 G7 36 20N 94 7W
Rogers City, U.S.A. 76 C4 45 25N 83 49W
Rogersville, Canada ... 71 C6 46 44N 65 26W
Roggan →, Canada 70 B4 54 24N 79 25W
Roggan L., Canada 70 B4 54 8N 77 50W
Roggeveldberge, S. Africa 56 E3 32 10S 20 10 E
Rogojampi, L., Bolivia .. 92 F5 13 0S 65 30W
Rogue →, U.S.A. 82 E1 42 26N 124 26W
Róhda, Greece 23 A3 39 48N 19 46 E
Rohnert Park, U.S.A. ... 84 G4 38 16N 122 40W
Rohri, Pakistan 42 F3 27 45N 68 51 E
Rohri Canal, Pakistan .. 42 F3 26 15N 68 27 E
Rohtak, India 42 E7 28 55N 76 43 E
Roi Et, Thailand 38 D4 16 4N 103 40 E
Roja, Latvia 9 H20 57 29N 22 43 E
Rojas, Argentina 94 C3 34 10S 60 45W
Rojo, C., Mexico 87 C5 21 33N 97 20W
Rokan →, Indonesia ... 36 D2 2 0N 100 50 E
Rokiškis, Lithuania 9 J21 55 55N 25 35 E
Rolândia, Brazil 95 A5 23 18S 51 23W
Rolla, U.S.A. 81 G9 37 57N 91 46W
Rolleston, Australia ... 62 C4 24 28S 148 35 E
Rollingstone, Australia . 62 B4 19 2S 146 24 E
Roma, Australia 63 D4 26 32S 148 49 E
Roma, Italy 20 D5 41 54N 12 29 E
Roma, Sweden 9 H18 57 32N 18 26 E
Roma, U.S.A. 81 M5 26 25N 99 1W
Romain C., U.S.A. 77 J6 33 0N 79 22W
Romaine, Canada 71 B7 50 13N 60 40W
Romaine →, Canada ... 71 B7 50 18N 63 47W
Roman, Romania 17 E14 46 57N 26 55 E
Romang, Indonesia 37 F7 7 30S 127 20 E
Români, Egypt 47 E1 30 59N 32 38 E
Romania ■, Europe ... 17 F12 46 0N 25 0 E
Romano, Cayo, Cuba ... 88 B4 22 0N 77 30W
Romanovka =
 Basarabeasca, Moldova 17 E15 46 21N 28 58 E
Romans-sur-Isère, France . 18 D6 45 3N 5 3 E
Romblon, Phil. 37 B6 12 33N 122 17 E
Rome = Roma, Italy ... 20 D5 41 54N 12 29 E
Rome, Ga., U.S.A. 77 H3 34 15N 85 10W
Rome, N.Y., U.S.A. 79 C9 43 13N 75 27W
Rome, Pa., U.S.A. 79 E8 41 51N 76 21W
Romney, U.S.A. 76 F6 39 21N 78 45W
Romney Marsh, U.K. ... 11 F8 51 2N 0 54 E
Rømø, Denmark 9 J13 55 10N 8 30 E
Romorantin-Lanthenay,
 France 18 C4 47 21N 1 45 E
Romsdalen, Norway ... 9 E12 62 25N 7 52 E
Romsey, U.K. 11 G6 51 0N 1 29W
Ron, Vietnam 38 D6 17 53N 106 27 E
Rona, U.K. 12 D3 57 34N 5 59W
Ronan, U.S.A. 82 C6 47 32N 114 6W
Roncador, Cayos, Caribbean 88 D3 13 32N 80 4W
Roncador, Serra do, Brazil 93 F8 12 30S 52 30W
Ronda, Spain 19 D3 36 46N 5 12W
Rondane, Norway 9 F13 61 57N 9 50 E
Rondônia □, Brazil 92 F6 11 0S 63 0W
Rondonópolis, Brazil ... 93 G8 16 28S 54 38W
Rong, Koh, Cambodia .. 39 G4 10 45N 103 15 E
Ronge, L. la, Canada ... 73 B7 55 6N 105 17W
Rønne, Denmark 9 J16 55 6N 14 43 E
Ronne Ice Shelf, Antarctica 5 D18 78 0S 60 0W
Ronsard, C., Australia .. 61 D1 24 46S 113 10 E
Ronse, Belgium 15 D3 50 45N 3 35 E
Roodepoort, S. Africa .. 57 D4 26 11S 27 54 E
Roof Butte, U.S.A. 83 H9 36 28N 109 5W
Roorkee, India 42 E7 29 52N 77 59 E
Roosendaal, Neths. 15 C4 51 32N 4 29 E
Roosevelt, U.S.A. 82 F8 40 18N 109 59W
Roosevelt →, Brazil ... 92 E6 7 35S 60 20W
Roosevelt, Mt., Canada . 72 B3 58 26N 125 20W
Roosevelt I., Antarctica . 5 D12 79 30S 162 0W
Roper →, Australia 62 A2 14 43S 135 27 E
Roper Bar, Australia ... 62 A1 14 44S 134 44 E
Roque Pérez, Argentina . 94 D4 35 25S 59 24W
Roquetas de Mar, Spain . 19 D4 36 46N 2 36W
Roraima □, Brazil 92 C6 2 0N 61 30W
Roraima, Mt., Venezuela . 92 B6 5 10N 60 40W
Røros, Norway 9 E14 62 35N 11 23 E
Rosa, Zambia 55 D3 9 33S 31 15 E
Rosa, L., Bahamas 89 B5 21 0N 73 30W
Rosa, Monte, Europe ... 18 D7 45 57N 7 53 E
Rosalia, U.S.A. 82 C5 47 14N 117 22W
Rosamond, U.S.A. 85 L8 34 52N 118 10W
Rosario, Argentina 94 C3 33 0S 60 40W
Rosário, Brazil 93 D10 3 0S 44 15W
Rosario, Baja Calif., Mexico 86 B1 30 0N 115 50W
Rosario, Sinaloa, Mexico 86 C3 23 0N 105 52W
Rosario de la Frontera,
 Argentina 94 B3 25 50S 65 0W
Rosario de Lerma, Argentina 94 A2 24 59S 65 35W
Rosario del Tala, Argentina 94 C4 32 20S 59 10W
Rosário do Sul, Brazil .. 95 C5 30 15S 54 55W
Rosarito, Mexico 85 N9 32 18N 117 4W
Roscoe, U.S.A. 79 E10 41 56N 74 55W
Roscommon, Ireland ... 13 C3 53 38N 8 11W
Roscommon □, Ireland . 13 C3 53 49N 8 23W
Roscrea, Ireland 13 D4 52 57N 7 49W
Rose →, Australia 62 A2 14 16S 135 45 E
Rose Blanche, Canada .. 71 C8 47 38N 58 45W
Rose Pt., Canada 72 C2 54 11N 131 39W
Rose Valley, Canada ... 73 C8 52 19N 103 49W
Roseau, Domin. 89 C7 15 20N 61 24W
Roseau, U.S.A. 80 A7 48 51N 95 46W
Rosebery, Australia 62 G4 41 46S 145 33 E
Rosebud, S. Dak., U.S.A. 80 D4 43 14N 100 51W
Rosebud, Tex., U.S.A. .. 81 K6 31 4N 96 59W
Roseburg, U.S.A. 82 E2 43 13N 123 20W
Rosedale, U.S.A. 81 J9 33 51N 91 2W
Rosemary, Canada 72 C6 50 46N 112 5W
Rosenberg, U.S.A. 81 L7 29 34N 95 49W
Rosenheim, Germany .. 16 E7 47 51N 12 7 E
Roses, G. de, Spain 19 A7 42 10N 3 15 E
Rosetown, Canada 73 C7 51 35N 107 59W
Roseville, Calif., U.S.A. . 84 G5 38 45N 121 17W
Roseville, Mich., U.S.A. . 78 D2 42 30N 82 56W
Rosewood, Australia ... 63 D5 27 38S 152 36 E
Roshkhvār, Iran 45 C8 34 58N 59 37 E
Rosignano Maríttimo, Italy 20 C4 43 24N 10 28 E
Rosignol, Guyana 92 B7 6 15N 57 30W
Roşiori-de-Vede, Romania 17 F13 44 7N 24 59 E

Roskilde, Denmark 9 J15 55 38N 12 3 E
Roslavl, Russia 24 D5 53 57N 32 55 E
Rosmead, S. Africa 56 E4 31 29S 25 8 E
Ross, Australia 62 G4 42 2S 147 30 E
Ross, N.Z. 59 K3 42 53S 170 49 E
Ross I., Antarctica 5 D11 77 30S 168 0 E
Ross Ice Shelf, Antarctica 5 E12 80 0S 180 0 E
Ross L., U.S.A. 82 B3 48 44N 121 4W
Ross-on-Wye, U.K. 11 F5 51 54N 2 34W
Ross River, Australia ... 62 C1 23 44S 134 30 E
Ross River, Canada 72 A2 62 30N 131 30W
Ross Sea, Antarctica ... 5 D11 74 0S 178 0 E
Rossall Pt., U.K. 10 D4 53 55N 3 3W
Rossan Pt., Ireland 13 B3 54 42N 8 47W
Rossano, Italy 20 E7 39 36N 16 39 E
Rossburn, Canada 73 C8 50 40N 100 49W
Rosseau, Canada 78 A5 45 16N 79 39W
Rosseau L., Canada ... 78 A5 45 10N 79 35W
Rosses, The, Ireland ... 13 A3 55 2N 8 20W
Rossignol, L., Canada .. 70 B5 52 43N 73 39W
Rossignol Res., Canada . 71 D6 44 12N 65 10W
Rossland, Canada 72 D5 49 6N 117 50W
Rosslare, Ireland 13 D5 52 17N 6 24W
Rosso, Mauritania 50 E2 16 40N 15 45W
Rossosh, Russia 25 D6 50 15N 39 28 E
Røssvatnet, Norway ... 8 D16 65 45N 14 5 E
Røst, Norway 8 C15 67 32N 12 0 E
Rosthern, Canada 73 C7 52 40N 106 20W
Rostock, Germany 16 A7 54 5N 12 8 E
Rostov, Don, Russia ... 25 E6 47 15N 39 45 E
Rostov, Yaroslavl, Russia 24 C6 57 14N 39 25 E
Roswell, Ga., U.S.A. ... 77 H3 34 2N 84 22W
Roswell, N. Mex., U.S.A. 81 J2 33 24N 104 32W
Rotan, U.S.A. 81 J4 32 51N 100 28W
Rother →, U.K. 11 G8 50 59N 0 45 E
Rotherham, U.K. 10 D6 53 26N 1 20W
Rothes, U.K. 12 D5 57 32N 3 13W
Rothesay, Canada 71 C6 45 23N 66 0W
Rothesay, U.K. 12 F3 55 50N 5 3W
Roti, Indonesia 37 F6 10 50S 123 0 E
Roto, Australia 63 E4 33 0S 145 30 E
Rotondo Mte., France .. 18 E8 42 14N 9 8 E
Rotoroa, L., N.Z. 59 J4 41 55S 172 39 E
Rotorua, N.Z. 59 H6 38 9S 176 16 E
Rotorua, L., N.Z. 59 H6 38 5S 176 18 E
Rotterdam, Neths. 15 C4 51 55N 4 30 E
Rotterdam, U.S.A. 79 D10 42 48N 74 1W
Rottnest I., Australia ... 61 F2 32 0S 115 27 E
Rottumeroog, Neths. .. 15 A6 53 33N 6 34 E
Rottweil, Germany 16 D5 48 9N 8 37 E
Rotuma, Fiji 64 J9 12 25S 177 5 E
Roubaix, France 18 A5 50 40N 3 10 E
Rouen, France 18 B4 49 27N 1 4 E
Rouleau, Canada 73 C8 50 10N 104 56W
Round Mountain, U.S.A. 82 G5 38 43N 117 4W
Round Mt., Australia ... 63 E5 30 26S 152 16 E
Round Rock, U.S.A. 81 K6 30 31N 97 41W
Roundup, U.S.A. 82 C9 46 27N 108 33W
Rousay, U.K. 12 B5 59 10N 3 2W
Rouses Point, U.S.A. ... 79 B11 44 59N 73 22W
Rouseville, U.S.A. 78 E5 41 28N 79 42W
Roussillon, France 18 E5 42 30N 2 35 E
Rouxville, S. Africa 56 E4 30 25S 26 50 E
Rouyn-Noranda, Canada . 70 C4 48 20N 79 0W
Rovaniemi, Finland 8 C21 66 29N 25 41 E
Rovereto, Italy 20 B4 45 53N 11 3 E
Rovigo, Italy 20 B4 45 4N 11 47 E
Rovinj, Croatia 16 F7 45 5N 13 40 E
Rovno = Rivne, Ukraine 17 C14 50 40N 26 10 E
Rovuma = Ruvuma →,
 Tanzania 55 E5 10 29S 40 28 E
Row'ān, Iran 45 C6 35 8N 48 51 E
Rowena, Australia 63 D4 29 48S 148 55 E
Rowley Shoals, Australia . 60 C2 17 30S 119 0 E
Roxas, Phil. 37 B6 11 36N 122 49 E
Roxboro, U.S.A. 77 G6 36 24N 78 59W
Roxburgh, N.Z. 59 L2 45 33S 169 19 E
Roxbury, U.S.A. 79 F10 40 6N 77 39W
Roy, Mont., U.S.A. 82 C9 47 20N 108 58W
Roy, N. Mex., U.S.A. ... 81 H2 35 57N 104 12W
Roy, Utah, U.S.A. 82 F7 41 10N 112 2W
Royal Canal, Ireland ... 13 C4 53 30N 7 13W
Royal Leamington Spa, U.K. 11 E6 52 18N 1 31W
Royal Tunbridge Wells, U.K. 11 F8 51 7N 0 16 E
Royan, France 18 D3 45 37N 1 2W
Royston, U.K. 11 E7 52 3N 0 0W
Rozdilna, Ukraine 17 E16 46 50N 30 2 E
Rozhyshche, Ukraine .. 17 C13 50 54N 25 15 E
Rtishchevo, Russia 24 C7 52 18N 43 46 E
Ruacaná, Angola 56 B1 17 20S 14 12 E
Ruahine Ra., N.Z. 59 H6 39 55S 176 2 E
Ruapehu, N.Z. 59 H5 39 17S 175 35 E
Ruapuke I., N.Z. 59 M2 46 46S 168 31 E
Ruâq, W. →, Egypt ... 47 F2 30 0N 33 49 E
Rub' al Khālī, Si. Arabia 46 D4 18 0N 48 0 E
Rubeho Mts., Tanzania . 54 D4 6 50S 36 25 E
Rubh a' Mhail, U.K. ... 12 F2 55 56N 6 8W
Rubha Hunish, U.K. ... 12 D2 57 42N 6 20W
Rubha Robhanais = Lewis,
 Butt of, U.K. 12 C2 58 31N 6 16W
Rubicon →, U.S.A. 84 G5 38 53N 121 4W
Rubio, Venezuela 92 B4 7 43N 72 22W
Rubtsovsk, Russia 26 D9 51 30N 81 10 E
Ruby L., U.S.A. 82 F6 40 10N 115 28W
Ruby Mts., U.S.A. 82 F6 40 30N 115 20W
Rubyvale, Australia ... 62 C4 23 25S 147 42 E
Rūd Sar, Iran 45 B6 37 8N 50 18 E
Rudall, Australia 63 E2 33 43S 136 17 E
Rudall →, Australia ... 60 D3 22 34S 122 13 E
Rudewa, Tanzania 55 E3 10 7S 34 40 E
Rudnyy, Kazakstan 26 D7 52 57N 63 7 E
Rudolfa, Ostrov, Russia . 26 A6 81 45N 58 30 E
Rudyard, U.S.A. 76 B3 46 14N 84 36W
Rufiji →, Tanzania 54 D4 7 50S 39 15 E
Rufino, Argentina 94 C3 34 20S 62 50W
Rufunsa, Zambia 55 F2 15 4S 29 34 E
Rugby, U.K. 11 E6 52 23N 1 16W
Rugby, U.S.A. 80 A5 48 22N 100 0W
Rügen, Germany 16 A7 54 22N 13 24 E
Ruhengeri, Rwanda 54 C2 1 30S 29 36 E
Ruhnu, Estonia 9 H20 57 48N 23 15 E
Ruhr →, Germany 16 C4 51 27N 6 43 E
Ruhuhu →, Tanzania .. 55 E3 10 31S 34 34 E
Ruidoso, U.S.A. 83 K11 33 20N 105 41W
Ruivo, Pico, Madeira ... 22 D3 32 45N 16 56W

Rujm Tal'at al Jamā'ah,
 Jordan 47 E4 30 24N 35 30 E
Ruk, Pakistan 42 F3 27 50N 68 42 E
Rukhla, Pakistan 42 C4 32 27N 71 57 E
Ruki →,
 Dem. Rep. of the Congo 52 E3 0 5N 18 17 E
Rukwa □, Tanzania 54 D3 7 0S 31 30 E
Rukwa, L., Tanzania ... 54 D3 8 0S 32 20 E
Rulhieres, C., Australia . 60 B4 13 56S 127 22 E
Rum = Rhum, U.K. 12 E2 57 0N 6 20W
Rum Cay, Bahamas 89 B5 23 40N 74 58W
Rum Jungle, Australia .. 60 B5 13 0S 130 59 E
Rumāḥ, Si. Arabia 44 E5 25 29N 47 10 E
Rumania = Romania ■,
 Europe 17 F12 46 0N 25 0 E
Rumaylah, Iraq 44 D5 30 47N 47 37 E
Rumbêk, Sudan 51 G11 6 54N 29 37 E
Rumford, U.S.A. 77 C10 44 33N 70 33W
Rumia, Poland 17 A10 54 37N 18 25 E
Rumoi, Japan 30 C10 43 56N 141 39 E
Rumonge, Burundi 54 C2 3 59S 29 26 E
Rumson, U.S.A. 79 F11 40 23N 74 0W
Rumuruti, Kenya 54 B4 0 17N 36 32 E
Runan, China 34 H8 33 0N 114 30 E
Runanga, N.Z. 59 K3 42 25S 171 15 E
Runaway, C., N.Z. 59 G6 37 32S 177 59 E
Runcorn, U.K. 10 D5 53 21N 2 44W
Rundu, Namibia 53 H3 17 52S 19 43 E
Rungwa, Tanzania 54 D3 6 55S 33 32 E
Rungwa →, Tanzania .. 54 D3 7 36S 31 50 E
Rungwe, Tanzania 55 D3 9 11S 33 32 E
Rungwe, Mt., Tanzania . 52 F6 9 8S 33 40 E
Runton Ra., Australia .. 60 D3 23 31S 123 6 E
Ruoqiang, China 32 C3 38 55N 88 10 E
Rupa, India 41 F18 27 15N 92 21 E
Rupar, India 42 D7 31 2N 76 38 E
Rupat, Indonesia 36 D2 1 45N 101 40 E
Rupen →, India 42 H4 23 28N 71 31 E
Rupert, U.S.A. 82 E7 42 37N 113 41W
Rupert →, Canada 70 B4 51 29N 78 45W
Rupert B., Canada 70 B4 51 35N 79 0W
Rupert House =
 Waskaganish, Canada . 70 B4 51 30N 78 40W
Rupsa, India 43 J12 21 37N 87 1 E
Rurrenabaque, Bolivia . 92 F5 14 30S 67 32W
Rusambo, Zimbabwe .. 55 F3 16 30S 32 4 E
Rusape, Zimbabwe 55 F3 18 35S 32 8 E
Ruschuk = Ruse, Bulgaria 21 C12 43 48N 25 59 E
Ruse, Bulgaria 21 C12 43 48N 25 59 E
Rush, Ireland 13 C5 53 31N 6 6W
Rushan, China 35 F11 36 56N 121 30 E
Rushden, U.K. 11 E7 52 18N 0 35W
Rushmore, Mt., U.S.A. . 80 D3 43 53N 103 28W
Rushville, Ill., U.S.A. .. 80 E9 40 7N 90 34W
Rushville, Ind., U.S.A. .. 76 F3 39 37N 85 27W
Rushville, Nebr., U.S.A. . 80 D3 42 43N 102 28W
Russas, Brazil 93 D11 4 55S 37 50W
Russell, Canada 73 C8 50 50N 101 20W
Russell, Kans., U.S.A. .. 80 F5 38 54N 98 52W
Russell, N.Y., U.S.A. ... 79 B9 44 27N 75 9W
Russell, Pa., U.S.A. 78 E5 41 56N 79 8W
Russell L., Man., Canada 73 B8 56 15N 101 30W
Russell L., N.W.T., Canada 72 A5 63 5N 115 44W
Russellkonda, India ... 41 K14 19 57N 84 42 E
Russellville, Ala., U.S.A. 77 H2 34 30N 87 44W
Russellville, Ark., U.S.A. 81 H8 35 17N 93 8W
Russellville, Ky., U.S.A. . 77 G2 36 51N 86 53W
Russia ■, Eurasia 27 C11 62 0N 105 0 E
Russian →, U.S.A. 84 G3 38 27N 123 8W
Russkoye Ustie, Russia . 4 B15 71 0N 149 0 E
Rustam, Pakistan 42 B5 34 25N 72 13 E
Rustam Shahr, Pakistan 42 F2 26 58N 66 6 E
Rustavi, Georgia 25 F8 41 30N 45 0 E
Rustenburg, S. Africa .. 56 D4 25 41S 27 14 E
Ruston, U.S.A. 81 J8 32 32N 92 38W
Rutana, Burundi 54 C3 3 55S 30 0 E
Ruteng, Indonesia 37 F6 8 35S 120 30 E
Ruth, U.S.A. 78 C2 43 42N 82 45W
Rutherford, U.S.A. 84 G4 38 26N 122 24W
Rutland, U.S.A. 79 C12 43 37N 72 58W
Rutland □, U.K. 11 E7 52 38N 0 40W
Rutland Water, U.K. ... 11 E7 52 39N 0 38W
Rutledge →, Canada .. 73 A6 61 4N 112 0W
Rutledge L., Canada ... 73 A6 61 33N 110 47W
Rutshuru,
 Dem. Rep. of the Congo 54 C2 1 13S 29 25 E
Ruvu, Tanzania 54 D4 6 49S 38 43 E
Ruvu →, Tanzania 54 D4 6 23S 38 52 E
Ruvuma □, Tanzania .. 55 E4 10 20S 36 0 E
Ruvuma →, Tanzania . 55 E5 10 29S 40 28 E
Ruwais, U.A.E. 45 E7 24 5N 52 50 E
Ruwenzori, Africa 54 B3 0 30N 29 55 E
Ruyigi, Burundi 54 C3 3 29S 30 15 E
Ružomberok, Slovak Rep. 17 D10 49 3N 19 17 E
Rwanda ■, Africa 54 C3 2 0S 30 0 E
Ryan, L., U.K. 12 G3 55 0N 5 2W
Ryazan, Russia 24 D6 54 40N 39 40 E
Ryazhsk, Russia 24 D7 53 45N 40 3 E
Rybache = Rybachye,
 Kazakstan 26 E9 46 40N 81 20 E
Rybachiy Poluostrov, Russia 24 A5 69 43N 32 0 E
Rybachye = Ysyk-Köl,
 Kyrgyzstan 26 E8 42 26N 76 12 E
Rybachye, Kazakstan .. 26 E9 46 40N 81 20 E
Rybinsk, Russia 24 C6 58 5N 38 50 E
Rybinskoye Vdkhr., Russia 24 C6 58 30N 38 25 E
Rybnitsa = Râbniţa,
 Moldova 17 E15 47 45N 29 0 E
Rycroft, Canada 72 B5 55 45N 118 40W
Ryde, U.K. 11 G6 50 43N 1 9W
Ryderwood, U.S.A. 84 D3 46 23N 123 3W
Rye, U.K. 11 G8 50 57N 0 45 E
Rye →, U.K. 10 C7 54 11N 0 44W
Rye Bay, U.K. 11 G8 50 52N 0 49 E
Rye Patch Reservoir, U.S.A. 82 F4 40 28N 118 19W
Ryegate, U.S.A. 82 C9 46 18N 109 15W
Ryley, Canada 72 C6 53 17N 112 26W
Rylstone, Australia 63 E4 32 46S 149 58 E
Rypin, Poland 17 B10 53 3N 19 25 E
Ryōtsu, Japan 30 E9 38 5N 138 26 E
Ryūgasaki, Japan 31 G10 35 54N 140 11 E
Ryukyu Is. = Ryūkyū-rettō,
 Japan 31 M3 26 0N 126 0 E
Ryūkyū-rettō, Japan ... 31 M3 26 0N 126 0 E
Rzeszów, Poland 17 C11 50 5N 21 58 E
Rzhev, Russia 24 C5 56 20N 34 20 E

S

Sánchez

Sánchez, *Dom. Rep.* **89 C6** 19 15N 69 36W
Sanchor, *India* **42 G4** 24 45N 71 55 E
Sancti Spíritus, *Cuba* **88 B4** 21 52N 79 33W
Sancy, Puy de, *France* ... **18 D5** 45 32N 2 50 E
Sand →, *S. Africa* **57 C5** 22 25S 30 5 E
Sand Hills, *U.S.A.* **80 D4** 42 10N 101 30W
Sand Springs, *U.S.A.* **81 G6** 36 9N 96 7W
Sanda, *Japan* **31 G7** 34 53N 135 14 E
Sandakan, *Malaysia* **36 C5** 5 53N 118 4 E
Sandan = Sambor,
 Cambodia **38 F6** 12 46N 106 0 E
Sandanski, *Bulgaria* **21 D10** 41 35N 23 16 E
Sanday, *U.K.* **12 B6** 59 16N 2 31W
Sandefjord, *Norway* **9 G14** 59 10N 10 15 E
Sanders, *U.S.A.* **83 J9** 35 13N 109 20W
Sanderson, *U.S.A.* **81 K3** 30 9N 102 24W
Sandersville, *U.S.A.* **77 J4** 32 59N 82 48W
Sandfire Roadhouse,
 Australia **60 C3** 19 45S 121 15 E
Sandfly L., *Canada* **73 B7** 55 43N 106 6W
Sandía, *Peru* **92 F5** 14 10S 69 30W
Sandila, *India* **43 F9** 27 5N 80 31 E
Sandnes, *Norway* **9 G11** 58 50N 5 45 E
Sandnessjøen, *Norway* ... **8 C15** 66 2N 12 38 E
Sandoa,
 Dem. Rep. of the Congo . **52 F4** 9 41S 23 0 E
Sandomierz, *Poland* **17 C11** 50 40N 21 43 E
Sandover →, *Australia* .. **62 C2** 21 43S 136 32 E
Sandoway, *Burma* **41 K19** 18 20N 94 30 E
Sandpoint, *U.S.A.* **82 B5** 48 17N 116 33W
Sandray, *U.K.* **12 E1** 56 53N 7 31W
Sandringham, *U.K.* **10 E8** 52 51N 0 31 E
Sandstone, *Australia* ... **61 E2** 27 59S 119 16 E
Sandusky, *Mich., U.S.A.* . **78 C2** 43 25N 82 50W
Sandusky, *Ohio, U.S.A.* . **78 E2** 41 27N 82 42W
Sandviken, *Sweden* **9 F17** 60 38N 16 46 E
Sandwich, C., *Australia* . **62 B4** 18 14S 146 18 E
Sandwich B., *Canada* ... **71 B8** 53 40N 57 15W
Sandwich B., *Namibia* .. **56 C1** 23 25S 14 20 E
Sandwip Chan., *Bangla.* . **41 H17** 22 35N 91 35 E
Sandy, *Oreg., U.S.A.* ... **84 E4** 45 24N 122 16W
Sandy, *Pa., U.S.A.* **78 E6** 41 6N 78 46W
Sandy, *Utah, U.S.A.* **82 F8** 40 35N 111 50W
Sandy Bay, *Canada* **73 B8** 55 31N 102 19W
Sandy Bight, *Australia* .. **61 F3** 33 50S 123 20 E
Sandy C., *Queens., Australia* **62 C5** 24 42S 153 15 E
Sandy C., *Tas., Australia* . **62 G3** 41 25S 144 45 E
Sandy Cay, *Bahamas* ... **89 B4** 23 13N 75 18W
Sandy Cr. →, *U.S.A.* ... **82 F9** 41 51N 109 47W
Sandy L., *Canada* **70 B1** 53 2N 93 0W
Sandy Lake, *Canada* ... **70 B1** 53 0N 93 15W
Sandy Valley, *U.S.A.* ... **85 K11** 35 49N 115 36W
Sanford, *Fla., U.S.A.* ... **77 L5** 28 48N 81 16W
Sanford, *Maine, U.S.A.* . **77 D10** 43 27N 70 47W
Sanford, *N.C., U.S.A.* ... **77 H6** 35 29N 79 10W
Sanford →, *Australia* .. **61 E2** 27 22S 115 53 E
Sanford, Mt., *U.S.A.* ... **68 B5** 62 13N 144 8W
Sang-i-Masha, *Afghan.* .. **42 C2** 33 8N 67 27 E
Sanga, *Mozam.* **55 E4** 12 22S 35 21 E
Sanga →, *Congo* **52 E3** 1 5S 17 0 E
Sangamner, *India* **40 K9** 19 37N 74 15 E
Sangar, *Afghan.* **42 C1** 32 56N 65 30 E
Sangar, *Russia* **27 C13** 64 2N 127 31 E
Sangar Sarai, *Afghan.* .. **42 B4** 34 27N 70 35 E
Sangarh →, *Pakistan* .. **42 D4** 30 43N 70 44 E
Sangay, *Ecuador* **92 D3** 2 0S 78 20W
Sange,
 Dem. Rep. of the Congo . **54 D2** 6 58S 28 21 E
Sangeang, *Indonesia* ... **37 F5** 8 12S 119 6 E
Sanger, *U.S.A.* **84 J7** 36 42N 119 33W
Sangerhausen, *Germany* . **16 C6** 51 28N 11 18 E
Sanggan He →, *China* . **34 E9** 38 12N 117 15 E
Sanggau, *Indonesia* ... **36 D4** 0 5N 110 30 E
Sanghar, *Pakistan* **42 F3** 26 2N 68 57 E
Sangihe, Kepulauan,
 Indonesia **37 D7** 3 0N 126 0 E
Sangihe, Pulau, *Indonesia* **37 D7** 3 45N 125 30 E
Sangju, *S. Korea* **35 F15** 36 25N 128 10 E
Sangkapura, *Indonesia* . **36 F4** 5 52S 112 40 E
Sangkhla, *Thailand* **38 E2** 14 57N 98 28 E
Sangkulirang, *Indonesia* **36 D5** 0 59N 117 58 E
Sangla, *Pakistan* **42 D5** 31 43N 73 23 E
Sangli, *India* **40 L9** 16 55N 74 33 E
Sangmélima, *Cameroon* . **52 D2** 2 57N 12 1 E
Sangod, *India* **42 G7** 24 55N 76 17 E
Sangre de Cristo Mts.,
 U.S.A. **81 G2** 37 30N 105 20W
Sangrur, *India* **42 D6** 30 14N 75 50 E
Sangudo, *Canada* **72 C6** 53 50N 114 54W
Sangue →, *Brazil* **92 F7** 11 1S 58 39W
Sanibel, *U.S.A.* **77 M4** 26 26N 82 1W
Sanirajak, *Canada* **69 B11** 68 46N 81 12W
Sanjawi, *Pakistan* **42 D3** 30 17N 68 21 E
Sanje, *Uganda* **54 C3** 0 49S 31 30 E
Sanjo, *Japan* **30 F9** 37 37N 138 57 E
Sankh →, *India* **43 H11** 22 15N 84 48 E
Sankt Gallen, *Switz.* ... **18 C8** 47 26N 9 22 E
Sankt Moritz, *Switz.* ... **18 C8** 46 30N 9 50 E
Sankt-Peterburg, *Russia* . **24 C5** 59 55N 30 20 E
Sankt Pölten, *Austria* .. **16 D8** 48 12N 15 38 E
Sankuru →,
 Dem. Rep. of the Congo . **52 E4** 4 17S 20 25 E
Sanliurfa, *Turkey* **25 G6** 37 12N 38 50 E
Sanlúcar de Barrameda,
 Spain **19 D2** 36 46N 6 21W
Sanmenxia, *China* **34 G6** 34 47N 111 12 E
Sanming, *China* **33 D6** 26 15N 117 40 E
Sannaspos, *S. Africa* ... **56 D4** 29 6S 26 34 E
Sannicandro Gargánico,
 Italy **20 D6** 41 50N 15 34 E
Sânnicolau Mare, *Romania* **17 E11** 46 5N 20 39 E
Sannieshof, *S. Africa* ... **56 D4** 26 30S 25 47 E
Sannin, J., *Lebanon* **47 B4** 33 57N 35 52 E
Sanniquellie, *Liberia* ... **50 G4** 7 19N 8 38W
Sanok, *Poland* **17 D12** 49 35N 22 10 E
Sanquhar, *U.K.* **12 F5** 55 22N 3 54W
Sant Antoni Abat, *Spain* . **22 C7** 38 59N 1 19 E
Sant Carles, *Spain* **22 B8** 39 3N 1 34 E
Sant Feliu de Guíxols, *Spain* **19 B7** 41 45N 3 1 E
Sant Ferran, *Spain* **22 C7** 38 42N 1 28 E
Sant Francesc de
 Formentera, *Spain* **22 C7** 38 42N 1 26 E
Sant Jaume, *Spain* **22 B11** 39 54N 4 4 E
Sant Joan Baptista, *Spain* **22 B8** 39 5N 1 31 E
Sant Jordi, *Spain* **22 B9** 39 33N 2 46 E

Sant Jordi, G. de, *Spain* ... **19 B6** 40 53N 1 2 E
Sant Llorenç des Cardassar,
 Spain **22 B10** 39 37N 3 17 E
Sant Mateu, *Spain* **22 B7** 39 3N 1 23 E
Sant Miquel, *Spain* **22 B7** 39 3N 1 26 E
Sant Telm, *Spain* **22 B9** 39 35N 2 21 E
Santa Agnès, *Spain* **22 B7** 39 3N 1 21 E
Santa Ana, *Bolivia* **92 F5** 13 50S 65 40W
Santa Ana, *El Salv.* **88 D2** 14 0N 89 31W
Santa Ana, *Mexico* **86 A2** 30 31N 111 8W
Santa Ana, *U.S.A.* **85 M9** 33 46N 117 52W
Sant' Antíoco, *Italy* **20 E3** 39 4N 8 27 E
Santa Barbara, *Chile* ... **94 D1** 37 40S 72 1W
Santa Barbara, *Honduras* **88 D2** 14 53N 88 14W
Santa Bárbara, *Mexico* . **86 B3** 26 48N 105 50W
Santa Barbara, *U.S.A.* .. **85 L7** 34 25N 119 42W
Santa Barbara Channel,
 U.S.A. **85 L7** 34 15N 120 0W
Santa Barbara I., *U.S.A.* . **85 M7** 33 29N 119 2W
Santa Catalina, Gulf of,
 U.S.A. **85 N9** 33 10N 117 50W
Santa Catalina, I., *Mexico* **86 B2** 25 40N 110 50W
Santa Catalina, I., *U.S.A.* **85 M8** 33 23N 118 25W
Santa Catarina □, *Brazil* . **95 B6** 27 25S 48 30W
Santa Catarina, I. de, *Brazil* **95 B6** 27 30S 48 40W
Santa Cecília, *Brazil* **95 B5** 26 56S 50 18W
Santa Clara, *Cuba* **88 B4** 22 20N 80 0W
Santa Clara, *Calif., U.S.A.* **84 H5** 37 21N 121 57W
Santa Clara, *Utah, U.S.A.* **83 H7** 37 8N 113 39W
Santa Clara, El Golfo de,
 Mexico **86 A2** 31 42N 114 30W
Santa Clara de Olimar,
 Uruguay **95 C5** 32 50S 54 54W
Santa Clarita, *U.S.A.* ... **85 L8** 34 24N 118 30W
Santa Clotilde, *Peru* **92 D4** 2 33S 73 45W
Santa Coloma de Gramenet,
 Spain **19 B7** 41 27N 2 13 E
Santa Cruz, *Argentina* .. **96 G3** 50 0S 68 32W
Santa Cruz, *Bolivia* **92 G6** 17 43S 63 10W
Santa Cruz, *Chile* **94 C1** 34 38S 71 27W
Santa Cruz, *Costa Rica* . **88 D2** 10 15N 85 35W
Santa Cruz, *Madeira* ... **22 D3** 32 42N 16 46W
Santa Cruz, *Phil.* **37 B6** 14 20N 121 24 E
Santa Cruz, *U.S.A.* **84 J4** 36 58N 122 1W
Santa Cruz →, *Argentina* **96 G3** 50 10S 68 20W
Santa Cruz de la Palma,
 Canary Is. **22 F2** 28 41N 17 46W
Santa Cruz de Tenerife,
 Canary Is. **22 F3** 28 28N 16 15W
Santa Cruz del Norte, *Cuba* **88 B3** 23 9N 81 55W
Santa Cruz del Sur, *Cuba* **88 B4** 20 44N 78 0W
Santa Cruz do Rio Pardo,
 Brazil **95 A6** 22 54S 49 37W
Santa Cruz do Sul, *Brazil* **95 B5** 29 42S 52 25W
Santa Cruz I., *U.S.A.* ... **85 M7** 34 1N 119 43W
Santa Cruz Is., *Solomon Is.* **64 J8** 10 30S 166 0 E
Santa Domingo, Cay,
 Bahamas **88 B4** 21 25N 75 15W
Santa Elena, *Argentina* .. **94 C4** 30 58S 59 47W
Santa Elena, C., *Costa Rica* **88 D2** 10 54N 85 56W
Santa Eulàlia des Riu, *Spain* **22 C8** 38 59N 1 32 E
Santa Fe, *Argentina* **94 C3** 31 35S 60 41W
Santa Fe, *U.S.A.* **83 J11** 35 41N 105 57W
Santa Fé □, *Argentina* .. **94 C3** 31 50S 60 55W
Santa Fé do Sul, *Brazil* . **93 H8** 20 13S 50 56W
Santa Filomena, *Brazil* .. **93 E9** 9 6S 45 50W
Santa Gertrudis, *Spain* .. **22 C7** 39 0N 1 26 E
Santa Inês, *Brazil* **93 F11** 13 17S 39 48W
Santa Inés, I., *Chile* **96 G2** 54 0S 73 0W
Santa Isabel = Rey Malabo,
 Eq. Guin. **52 D1** 3 45N 8 50 E
Santa Isabel, *Argentina* . **94 D2** 36 10S 66 54W
Santa Isabel do Morro,
 Brazil **93 F8** 11 34S 50 40W
Santa Lucía, *Corrientes,*
 Argentina **94 B4** 28 58S 59 5W
Santa Lucía, *San Juan,*
 Argentina **94 C2** 31 30S 68 30W
Santa Lucia, *Uruguay* ... **94 C4** 34 27S 56 24W
Santa Lucia Range, *U.S.A.* **84 K5** 36 0N 121 20W
Santa Magdalena, I., *Mexico* **86 C2** 24 40N 112 15W
Santa Margarita, *Argentina* **94 D3** 38 28S 61 35W
Santa Margarita, *Spain* .. **22 B10** 39 42N 3 6 E
Santa Margarita, *U.S.A.* . **84 K6** 35 23N 120 37W
Santa Margarita →, *U.S.A.* **85 M9** 33 13N 117 23W
Santa Margarita, I., *Mexico* **86 C2** 24 30N 111 50W
Santa María, *Argentina* . **94 B2** 26 40S 66 0W
Santa Maria, *Brazil* **95 B5** 29 40S 53 48W
Santa Maria, *U.S.A.* ... **85 L6** 34 57N 120 26W
Santa María →, *Mexico* . **86 A3** 31 0N 107 14W
Santa María, B. de, *Mexico* **86 B3** 25 10N 108 40W
Santa Maria da Vitória,
 Brazil **93 F10** 13 24S 44 12W
Santa Maria del Camí, *Spain* **22 B9** 39 38N 2 47 E
Santa Maria di Léuca, C.,
 Italy **21 E8** 39 47N 18 22 E
Santa Marta, *Colombia* . **92 A4** 11 15N 74 13W
Santa Marta, Sierra Nevada
 de, *Colombia* **92 A4** 10 55N 73 50W
Santa Marta Grande, C.,
 Brazil **95 B6** 28 43S 48 50W
Santa Maura = Levkás,
 Greece **21 E9** 38 40N 20 43 E
Santa Monica, *U.S.A.* ... **85 M8** 34 1N 118 29W
Santa Paula, *U.S.A.* **85 L7** 34 21N 119 4W
Santa Ponsa, *Spain* **22 B9** 39 30N 2 28 E
Santa Rita, *U.S.A.* **83 K10** 32 48N 108 4W
Santa Rosa, *La Pampa,*
 Argentina **94 D3** 36 40S 64 17W
Santa Rosa, *San Luis,*
 Argentina **94 C2** 32 21S 65 10W
Santa Rosa, *Brazil* **95 B5** 27 52S 54 29W
Santa Rosa, *Calif., U.S.A.* **84 G4** 38 26N 122 43W
Santa Rosa, *N. Mex., U.S.A.* **81 H2** 34 57N 104 41W
Santa Rosa de Copán,
 Honduras **88 D2** 14 47N 88 46W
Santa Rosa de Río Primero,
 Argentina **94 C3** 31 8S 63 20W
Santa Rosa del Sara, *Bolivia* **92 G6** 17 7S 63 35W
Santa Rosa I., *U.S.A.* ... **85 M6** 33 58N 120 6W
Santa Rosa Range, *U.S.A.* **82 F5** 41 45N 117 40W
Santa Rosalía, *Mexico* .. **86 B2** 27 20N 112 20W
Santa Sylvina, *Argentina* **94 B3** 27 50S 61 10W
Santa Tecla = Nueva San
 Salvador, *El Salv.* **88 D2** 13 40N 89 18W
Santa Teresa, *Argentina* ... **94 C3** 33 25S 60 47W

Santa Teresa, *Australia* ... **62 C1** 24 8S 134 22 E
Santa Teresa, *Mexico* ... **87 B5** 25 17N 97 51W
Santa Vitória do Palmar,
 Brazil **95 C5** 33 32S 53 25W
Santa Ynez, *U.S.A.* **85 L6** 34 37N 120 5W
Santa Ynez →, *U.S.A.* . **85 L6** 35 41N 120 36W
Santa Ynez Mts., *U.S.A.* . **85 L6** 34 30N 120 0W
Santa Ysabel, *U.S.A.* ... **85 M10** 33 7N 116 40W
Santai, *China* **32 C5** 31 5N 104 58 E
Santana, *Madeira* **22 D3** 32 48N 16 52W
Santana, Coxilha de, *Brazil* **95 C4** 30 50S 55 35W
Santana do Livramento,
 Brazil **95 C4** 30 55S 55 30W
Santander, *Spain* **19 A4** 43 27N 3 51W
Santander Jiménez, *Mexico* **87 C5** 24 11N 98 29W
Santanyí, *Spain* **22 B10** 39 20N 3 5 E
Santaquin, *U.S.A.* **82 G8** 39 59N 111 47W
Santarém, *Brazil* **93 D8** 2 25S 54 42W
Santarém, *Portugal* **19 C1** 39 12N 8 42W
Santaren Channel, *W. Indies* **88 B4** 24 0N 79 30W
Santee, *U.S.A.* **85 N10** 32 50N 116 58W
Santee →, *U.S.A.* **77 J6** 33 7N 79 17W
Santiago, *Brazil* **95 B5** 29 11S 54 52W
Santiago, *Chile* **94 C1** 33 24S 70 40W
Santiago, *Panama* **88 E3** 8 0N 81 0W
Santiago □, *Chile* **94 C1** 33 30S 70 50W
Santiago →, *Mexico* ... **66 G9** 25 11N 105 26W
Santiago →, *Peru* **92 D3** 4 27S 77 38W
Santiago de Compostela,
 Spain **19 A1** 42 52N 8 37W
Santiago de Cuba, *Cuba* . **88 C4** 20 0N 75 49W
Santiago de los Cabelleros,
 Dom. Rep. **89 C5** 19 30N 70 40W
Santiago del Estero,
 Argentina **94 B3** 27 50S 64 15W
Santiago del Estero □,
 Argentina **94 B3** 27 40S 63 15W
Santiago del Teide,
 Canary Is. **22 F3** 28 17N 16 48W
Santiago Ixcuintla, *Mexico* **86 C3** 21 50N 105 11W
Santiago Papasquiaro,
 Mexico **86 C3** 25 0N 105 20W
Santiaguillo, L. de, *Mexico* **86 C4** 24 50N 104 50W
Santo Amaro, *Brazil* ... **93 F11** 12 30S 38 43W
Santo Anastácio, *Brazil* . **95 A5** 21 58S 51 39W
Santo André, *Brazil* **95 A6** 23 39S 46 29W
Santo Ângelo, *Brazil* ... **95 B5** 28 15S 54 15W
Santo Antônio do Içá, *Brazil* **92 D5** 3 5S 67 57W
Santo Antônio do Leverger,
 Brazil **93 G7** 15 52S 56 5W
Santo Domingo, *Dom. Rep.* **89 C6** 18 30N 69 59W
Santo Domingo, *Baja Calif.,*
 Mexico **86 A1** 30 43N 116 2W
Santo Domingo,
 Baja Calif. S., Mexico . **86 B2** 25 32N 112 2W
Santo Domingo, *Nic.* ... **88 D3** 12 14N 84 59W
Santo Domingo de los
 Colorados, *Ecuador* .. **92 D3** 0 15S 79 9W
Santo Domingo Pueblo,
 U.S.A. **83 J10** 35 31N 106 22W
Santo Tomás, *Mexico* .. **86 A1** 31 33N 116 24W
Santo Tomás, *Peru* **92 F4** 14 26S 72 8W
Santo Tomé, *Argentina* . **95 B4** 28 40S 56 5W
Santo Tomé de Guayana =
 Ciudad Guayana,
 Venezuela **92 B6** 8 0N 62 30W
Santoña, *Spain* **19 A4** 43 29N 3 27W
Santorini = Thira, *Greece* . **21 F11** 36 23N 25 27 E
Santos, *Brazil* **95 A6** 24 0S 46 20W
Santos Dumont, *Brazil* .. **95 A7** 22 55S 43 10W
Sanwer, *India* **42 H6** 22 59N 75 50 E
Sanyuan, *China* **34 G5** 34 35N 108 58 E
São Bernardo do Campo,
 Brazil **95 A6** 23 45S 46 34W
São Borja, *Brazil* **95 B4** 28 39S 56 0W
São Carlos, *Brazil* **95 A6** 22 0S 47 50W
São Cristóvão, *Brazil* ... **93 F11** 11 1S 37 15W
São Domingos, *Brazil* .. **93 F9** 13 25S 46 19W
São Francisco, *Brazil* ... **93 G10** 16 0S 44 50W
São Francisco →, *Brazil* **93 F11** 10 30S 36 24W
São Francisco do Sul, *Brazil* **95 B6** 26 15S 48 36W
São Gabriel, *Brazil* **95 C5** 30 20S 54 20W
São Gonçalo, *Brazil* ... **95 A7** 22 48S 43 5W
Sao Hill, *Tanzania* **55 D4** 8 20S 35 12 E
São João da Boa Vista,
 Brazil **95 A6** 22 0S 46 52W
São João da Madeira,
 Portugal **19 B1** 40 54N 8 30W
São João del Rei, *Brazil* . **95 A7** 21 8S 44 15W
São João do Araguaia,
 Brazil **93 E9** 5 23S 48 46W
São João do Piauí, *Brazil* **93 E10** 8 21S 42 15W
São Joaquim, *Brazil* ... **95 B6** 28 18S 49 56W
São Jorge, Pta. de, *Madeira* **22 D3** 32 50N 16 53W
São José, *Brazil* **95 B5** 27 38S 48 39W
São José do Norte, *Brazil* **95 C5** 32 1S 52 3W
São José do Rio Prêto,
 Brazil **95 A6** 20 50S 49 20W
São José dos Campos,
 Brazil **95 A6** 23 7S 45 52W
São Leopoldo, *Brazil* ... **95 B5** 29 50S 51 10W
São Lourenço, *Brazil* ... **95 A6** 22 7S 45 3W
São Lourenço →, *Brazil* **93 G7** 17 53S 57 27W
São Lourenço, Pta. de,
 Madeira **22 D3** 32 44N 16 39W
São Lourenço do Sul, *Brazil* **95 C5** 31 22S 51 58W
São Luís, *Brazil* **93 D10** 2 39S 44 15W
São Luís Gonzaga, *Brazil* **95 B5** 28 25S 55 0W
São Marcos →, *Brazil* . **93 G9** 18 15S 47 37W
São Marcos, B. de, *Brazil* **93 D10** 2 0S 44 0W
São Mateus, *Brazil* **93 G11** 18 44S 39 50W
São Miguel do Oeste, *Brazil* **95 B5** 26 45S 53 34W
São Paulo, *Brazil* **95 A6** 23 32S 46 37W
São Paulo □, *Brazil* **95 A6** 22 0S 49 0W
São Paulo, I., *Atl. Oc.* .. **2 D8** 0 50N 31 40W
São Paulo de Olivença,
 Brazil **92 D5** 3 27S 68 48W
São Roque, *Madeira* ... **22 D3** 32 46N 16 48W
São Roque, C. de, *Brazil* . **93 E11** 5 30S 35 16W
São Sebastião, I. de, *Brazil* **95 A6** 23 50S 45 18W
São Sebastião do Paraíso,
 Brazil **95 A6** 20 54S 46 59W
São Tomé, *Atl. Oc.* **48 F4** 0 10N 6 39 E
São Tomé, C. de, *Brazil* . **95 A7** 22 0S 40 59W
São Tomé & Príncipe ■,
 Africa **49 F4** 0 12N 6 39 E

São Vicente, *Brazil* **95 A6** 23 57S 46 23W
São Vicente, *Madeira* **22 D2** 32 48N 17 3W
São Vicente, C. de, *Portugal* **19 D1** 37 0N 9 0W
Saona, I., *Dom. Rep.* **89 C6** 18 10N 68 40W
Saône →, *France* **18 D6** 45 44N 4 50 E
Saonek, *Indonesia* **37 E8** 0 22S 130 55 E
Saparua, *Indonesia* **37 E7** 3 33S 128 40 E
Sapele, *Nigeria* **50 G7** 5 50N 5 40 E
Sapelo I., *U.S.A.* **77 K5** 31 25N 81 12W
Saposoa, *Peru* **92 E3** 6 55S 76 45W
Sapphire, *Australia* **62 C4** 23 28S 147 43 E
Sapporo, *Japan* **30 C10** 43 0N 141 21 E
Sapulpa, *U.S.A.* **81 H6** 35 59N 96 5W
Saqqez, *Iran* **44 B5** 36 15N 46 20 E
Sar Dasht, *Iran* **45 C6** 32 32N 48 52 E
Sar Gachineh, *Iran* **45 D6** 30 31N 51 31 E
Sar Planina, *Macedonia* . **21 C9** 42 0N 21 0 E
Sara Buri = Saraburi,
 Thailand **38 E3** 14 30N 100 55 E
Saráb, *Iran* **44 B5** 37 55N 47 40 E
Sarabadi, *Iraq* **44 C5** 33 1N 44 48 E
Saraburi, *Thailand* **38 E3** 14 30N 100 55 E
Sarada →, *India* **41 F12** 27 21N 81 23 E
Saradiya, *India* **42 J4** 21 34N 70 2 E
Saragossa = Zaragoza,
 Spain **19 B5** 41 39N 0 53W
Saraguro, *Ecuador* **92 D3** 3 35S 79 16W
Sarai Naurang, *Pakistan* . **42 C4** 32 50N 70 47 E
Saraikela, *India* **43 H11** 22 42N 85 56 E
Sarajevo, *Bos.-H.* **21 C8** 43 52N 18 26 E
Sarakhs, *Turkmenistan* .. **45 B9** 36 32N 61 13 E
Saran, Gunung, *Indonesia* **36 E4** 0 30S 111 25 E
Saranac L., *U.S.A.* **79 B10** 44 20N 74 10W
Saranac Lake, *U.S.A.* ... **79 B10** 44 20N 74 8W
Saranda, *Tanzania* **54 D3** 5 45S 34 59 E
Sarandí del Yi, *Uruguay* . **95 C4** 33 18S 55 38W
Sarandí Grande, *Uruguay* **94 C4** 33 44S 56 20W
Sarangani B., *Phil.* **37 C7** 6 0N 125 13 E
Sarangani Is., *Phil.* **37 C7** 5 25N 125 25 E
Sarangarh, *India* **41 J13** 21 30N 83 5 E
Saransk, *Russia* **24 D8** 54 10N 45 10 E
Sarapul, *Russia* **24 C9** 56 28N 53 48 E
Sarasota, *U.S.A.* **77 M4** 27 20N 82 32W
Saratoga, *Calif., U.S.A.* . **84 H4** 37 16N 122 2W
Saratoga, *Wyo., U.S.A.* . **82 F10** 41 27N 106 49W
Saratoga Springs, *U.S.A.* **79 C11** 43 5N 73 47W
Saratok, *Malaysia* **36 D4** 1 55N 111 17 E
Saratov, *Russia* **25 D8** 51 30N 46 2 E
Saravane, *Laos* **38 E6** 15 43N 106 25 E
Sarawak □, *Malaysia* .. **36 D4** 2 0N 113 0 E
Saray, *Turkey* **21 D12** 41 26N 27 55 E
Saraykôy, *Turkey* **21 F13** 37 55N 28 54 E
Sarbāz, *Iran* **45 E9** 26 38N 61 19 E
Sarbisheh, *Iran* **45 C8** 32 30N 59 40 E
Sarda = Sarada →, *India* **41 F12** 27 21N 81 23 E
Sardarshahr, *India* **42 E6** 28 30N 74 29 E
Sardhana, *India* **42 E7** 29 9N 77 39 E
Sardina, Pta., *Canary Is.* . **22 F4** 28 9N 15 44W
Sardinia = Sardegna □,
 Italy **20 D3** 40 0N 9 0 E
Sardis, *Turkey* **21 E12** 38 28N 28 2 E
Sârdûiyeh = Dar Mazār, *Iran* **45 D8** 29 14N 57 20 E
S'Arenal, *Spain* **22 B9** 39 30N 2 45 E
Sargasso Sea, *Atl. Oc.* .. **66 G13** 27 0N 72 0W
Sargodha, *Pakistan* **42 C5** 32 10N 72 40 E
Sarh, *Chad* **51 G9** 9 5N 18 23 E
Sārī, *Iran* **45 B7** 36 30N 53 4 E
Saria, *India* **43 J10** 21 38N 83 22 E
Sariab, *Pakistan* **42 D2** 30 6N 66 59 E
Sarikei, *Malaysia* **36 D4** 2 8N 111 30 E
Sarila, *India* **43 G8** 25 46N 79 41 E
Sarina, *Australia* **62 C4** 21 22S 149 13 E
Sarita, *U.S.A.* **81 M6** 27 13N 97 47W
Sariwôn, *N. Korea* **35 E13** 38 31N 125 46 E
Sarju →, *India* **43 F9** 27 21N 81 23 E
Sark, *U.K.* **11 H5** 49 25N 2 22W
Sarkari Tala, *India* **42 F4** 27 39N 70 52 E
Sarköy, *Turkey* **21 D12** 40 36N 27 6 E
Sarlat-la-Canéda, *France* . **18 D4** 44 54N 1 13 E
Sarmi, *Indonesia* **37 E9** 1 49S 138 44 E
Sarmiento, *Argentina* .. **96 F3** 45 35S 69 5W
Särna, *Sweden* **9 F15** 61 41N 13 8 E
Sarnia, *Canada* **78 D2** 42 58N 82 23W
Sarolangun, *Indonesia* .. **36 E2** 2 19S 102 42 E
Saronikós Kólpos, *Greece* . **21 F10** 37 45N 23 45 E
Saros Körfezi, *Turkey* ... **21 D12** 40 30N 26 15 E
Sarpsborg, *Norway* **9 G14** 59 16N 11 7 E
Sarre = Saar →, *Europe* . **18 B7** 49 41N 6 32 E
Sarreguemines, *France* . **18 B7** 49 5N 7 4 E
Sarthe →, *France* **18 C3** 47 33N 0 31W
Saruna →, *Pakistan* ... **42 F2** 26 31N 67 7 E
Sarvar, *India* **42 F6** 26 4N 75 0 E
Sarvestán, *Iran* **45 D7** 29 20N 53 10 E
Sary-Tash, *Kyrgyzstan* .. **26 F8** 39 44N 73 15 E
Saryshagan, *Kazakhstan* **26 E8** 46 12N 73 38 E
Sasan Gir, *India* **42 J4** 21 10N 70 36 E
Sasaram, *India* **43 G11** 24 57N 84 5 E
Sasebo, *Japan* **31 H4** 33 10N 129 43 E
Saser, *India* **43 B7** 34 50N 77 50 E
Saskatchewan □, *Canada* **73 C7** 54 40N 106 0W
Saskatchewan →, *Canada* **73 C8** 53 37N 100 40W
Saskatoon, *Canada* **73 C7** 52 10N 106 38W
Saskylakh, *Russia* **27 B12** 71 55N 114 1 E
Sasolburg, *S. Africa* ... **57 D4** 26 46S 27 49 E
Sasovo, *Russia* **24 D7** 54 25N 41 55 E
Sassandra, *Ivory C.* **50 H4** 4 55N 6 8W
Sassandra →, *Ivory C.* . **50 H4** 4 58N 6 5W
Sássari, *Italy* **20 D3** 40 43N 8 34 E
Sassnitz, *Germany* **16 A7** 54 29N 13 39 E
Sassuolo, *Italy* **20 B4** 44 33N 10 47 E
Sasumua Dam, *Kenya* .. **54 C4** 0 45S 36 40 E
Sasyk, Ozero, *Ukraine* .. **17 F15** 45 45N 29 20 E
Sata-Misaki, *Japan* **31 J5** 31 0N 130 40 E
Satakunta, *Finland* **9 F20** 61 45N 23 0 E
Satara, *India* **40 L8** 17 44N 73 58 E
Satarwa, *India* **43 H11** 23 55N 84 16 E
Satevó, *Mexico* **86 B3** 27 57N 106 7W
Satilla →, *U.S.A.* **77 K5** 30 59N 81 29W
Satka, *Russia* **24 C10** 55 3N 59 1 E
Satmala Hills, *India* **40 J9** 20 15N 74 40 E
Satna, *India* **43 G9** 24 35N 80 50 E
Sátoraljaújhely, *Hungary* **17 D11** 48 25N 21 41 E

Sikinos, Greece 21 F11 36 40N 25 8 E
Sikkani Chief →, Canada . 72 B4 57 47N 122 15W
Sikkim □, India 41 F16 27 50N 88 30 E
Sikotu-Ko, Japan 30 C10 42 45N 141 25 E
Sil →, Spain 19 A2 42 27N 7 43W
Silacayoapan, Mexico 87 D5 17 30N 98 9W
Silawad, India 42 J6 21 54N 74 54 E
Silchar, India 41 G18 24 49N 92 48 E
Siler City, U.S.A. 77 H6 35 44N 79 28W
Silesia = Śląsk, Poland . 16 C9 51 0N 16 30 E
Silgarhi Doti, Nepal 43 E9 29 15N 81 0 E
Silghat, India 41 F18 26 35N 93 0 E
Silifke, Turkey 25 G5 36 22N 33 58 E
Siliguri = Shiliguri, India . 41 F16 26 45N 88 25 E
Siling Co, China 32 C3 31 50N 89 20 E
Silistra, Bulgaria 21 B12 44 6N 27 19 E
Silivri, Turkey 21 D13 41 4N 28 14 E
Siljan, Sweden 9 F16 60 55N 14 45 E
Silkeborg, Denmark 9 H13 56 10N 9 32 E
Silkwood, Australia 62 B4 17 45S 146 2 E
Sillamäe, Estonia 9 G22 59 24N 27 45 E
Silloth, U.K. 10 C4 54 52N 3 23W
Siloam Springs, U.S.A. .. 81 G7 36 11N 94 32W
Silsbee, U.S.A. 81 K7 30 21N 94 11W
Šilute, Lithuania 9 J19 55 21N 21 33 E
Silva Porto = Kuito, Angola 53 G3 12 22S 16 55 E
Silvani, India 43 H8 23 18N 78 25 E
Silver City, U.S.A. 83 K9 32 46N 108 17W
Silver Cr. →, U.S.A. 82 E4 43 16N 119 13W
Silver Creek, U.S.A. 78 D5 42 33N 79 10W
Silver L., U.S.A. 84 G6 38 39N 120 6W
Silver Lake, Calif., U.S.A. 85 K10 35 21N 116 7W
Silver Lake, Oreg., U.S.A. 82 E3 43 8N 121 3W
Silver Streams, S. Africa . 56 D3 28 20S 23 33 E
Silverton, Colo., U.S.A. .. 83 H10 37 49N 107 40W
Silverton, Tex., U.S.A. .. 81 H4 34 28N 101 19W
Silvies →, U.S.A. 82 E4 43 34N 119 2W
Simaltala, India 43 G12 24 43N 86 33 E
Simanggang = Bandar Sri
 Aman, Malaysia 36 D4 1 15N 111 32 E
Simard, L., Canada 70 C4 47 40N 78 40W
Simav, Turkey 21 E13 39 4N 28 58 E
Simba, Tanzania 54 C4 2 10S 37 36 E
Simbirsk, Russia 24 D8 54 20N 48 25 E
Simbo, Tanzania 54 C2 4 51S 29 41 E
Simcoe, Canada 78 D4 42 50N 80 20W
Simcoe, L., Canada 78 B5 44 25N 79 20W
Simdega, India 43 H11 22 37N 84 31 E
Simeria, Romania 17 F12 45 51N 23 1 E
Simeulue, Indonesia 36 D1 2 45N 95 45 E
Simferopol, Ukraine 25 F5 44 55N 34 3 E
Sími, Greece 21 F12 36 35N 27 50 E
Simi Valley, U.S.A. 85 L8 34 16N 118 47W
Simikot, Nepal 43 E9 30 0N 81 50 E
Simla, India 42 D7 31 2N 77 9 E
Simmie, Canada 73 D7 49 56N 108 6W
Simmler, U.S.A. 85 K7 35 21N 119 59W
Simojoki →, Finland ... 8 D21 65 35N 25 1 E
Simojovel, Mexico 87 D6 17 12N 92 38W
Simonette →, Canada . 72 B5 55 9N 118 15W
Simonstown, S. Africa .. 56 E2 34 14S 18 26 E
Simplonpass, Switz. 18 C8 46 15N 8 3 E
Simpson Desert, Australia 62 D2 25 0S 137 0 E
Simpson Pen., Canada .. 69 B11 68 34N 88 45W
Simpungdong, N. Korea . 35 D15 40 56N 129 29 E
Simrishamn, Sweden ... 9 J16 55 33N 14 22 E
Simsbury, U.S.A. 79 E12 41 53N 72 48W
Simushir, Ostrov, Russia . 27 E16 46 50N 152 30 E
Sin Cowe I., S. China Sea 36 C4 9 53N 114 19 E
Sinabang, Indonesia 36 D1 2 30N 96 24 E
Sinadogo, Somali Rep. .. 46 F4 5 50N 47 0 E
Sinai = Es Sînâ', Egypt . 47 F3 29 0N 34 0 E
Sinai, Mt. = Mûsa, Gebel,
 Egypt 44 D2 28 33N 33 59 E
Sinai Peninsula, Egypt .. 47 F3 29 30N 34 0 E
Sinaloa □, Mexico 86 C3 25 0N 107 30W
Sinaloa de Leyva, Mexico . 86 B3 25 50N 108 20W
Sinarádhes, Greece 23 A3 39 34N 19 51 E
Sincelejo, Colombia 92 B3 9 18N 75 24W
Sinch'ang, N. Korea 35 D15 40 7N 128 28 E
Sinchang-ni, N. Korea .. 35 E14 39 24N 126 8 E
Sinclair, U.S.A. 82 F10 41 47N 107 7W
Sinclair Mills, Canada .. 72 C4 54 5N 121 40W
Sinclair's B., U.K. 12 C5 58 31N 3 5W
Sinclairville, U.S.A. 78 D5 42 16N 79 16W
Sincorá, Serra do, Brazil . 93 F10 13 30S 41 0W
Sind, Pakistan 42 G3 26 0N 69 0 E
Sind □, Pakistan 42 G3 26 0N 69 0 E
Sind →, India 43 F8 26 26N 79 13 E
Sind →,
 Jammu & Kashmir, India 43 B6 34 18N 74 45 E
Sind Sagar Doab, Pakistan 42 D4 32 0N 71 30 E
Sindangan, Phil. 37 C6 8 10N 123 5 E
Sindangbarang, Indonesia 37 G12 7 27S 107 1 E
Sinde, Zambia 55 F2 17 28S 25 51 E
Sindri, India 43 H12 23 45N 86 42 E
Sines, Portugal 19 D1 37 56N 8 51W
Sines, C. de, Portugal .. 19 D1 37 58N 8 53W
Sineu, Spain 22 B10 39 38N 3 1 E
Sing Buri, Thailand 38 E3 14 53N 100 25 E
Singa, Sudan 51 F12 13 10N 33 57 E
Singapore ■, Asia 39 M4 1 17N 103 51 E
Singapore, Straits of, Asia . 39 M5 1 15N 104 0 E
Singaraja, Indonesia ... 36 F5 8 6S 115 10 E
Singatoka, Tanzania ... 54 C3 4 49S 34 48 E
Singida □, Tanzania 54 D3 6 0S 34 30 E
Singitikós Kólpos, Greece 21 D11 40 6N 24 0 E
Singkaling Hkamti, Burma . 41 G19 26 0N 95 39 E
Singkang, Indonesia 37 E6 4 8S 120 1 E
Singkawang, Indonesia .. 36 D3 1 0N 108 57 E
Singleton, Australia 63 E5 32 33S 151 0 E
Singleton, Mt., N. Terr.,
 Australia 60 D5 22 0S 130 46 E
Singleton, Mt., W. Austral.,
 Australia 61 E2 29 27S 117 15 E
Singoli, India 42 G6 25 0N 75 22 E
Singora = Songkhla,
 Thailand 39 J3 7 13N 100 37 E
Singosan, N. Korea 35 E14 38 52N 127 25 E
Sinhung, N. Korea 35 D14 40 11N 127 34 E
Sînî, Egypt 47 F3 30 0N 34 0 E
Sinjai, Indonesia 37 F6 5 7S 120 20 E
Sinjār, Iraq 44 B4 36 19N 41 52 E
Sinkat, Sudan 51 E13 18 55N 36 49 E

Sinkiang Uighur = Xinjiang
 Uygur Zizhiqu □, China . 32 C3 42 0N 86 0 E
Sinmak, N. Korea 35 E14 38 25N 126 14 E
Sinnamary, Fr. Guiana .. 93 B8 5 25N 53 0W
Sinni →, Italy 20 D7 40 8N 16 41 E
Sinop, Turkey 25 F6 42 1N 35 11 E
Sinor, India 42 J5 21 55N 73 20 E
Sinp'o, N. Korea 35 E15 40 0N 128 13 E
Sinsk, Russia 27 C13 61 8N 126 48 E
Sintang, Indonesia 36 D4 0 5N 111 35 E
Sinton, U.S.A. 81 L6 28 2N 97 31W
Sintra, Portugal 19 C1 38 47N 9 25W
Sinŭiju, N. Korea 35 D13 40 5N 124 24 E
Siocon, Phil. 37 C6 7 40N 122 10 E
Siófok, Hungary 17 E10 46 54N 18 3 E
Sioma, Zambia 56 B3 16 25S 23 28 E
Sion, Switz. 18 C7 46 14N 7 20 E
Sion Mills, U.K. 13 B4 54 48N 7 29W
Sioux City, U.S.A. 80 D6 42 30N 96 24W
Sioux Falls, U.S.A. 80 D6 43 33N 96 44W
Sioux Lookout, Canada . 70 B1 50 10N 91 50W
Sioux Narrows, Canada . 73 D10 49 25N 94 10W
Siping, China 35 C13 43 8N 124 21 E
Sipiwesk L., Canada ... 73 B9 55 5N 97 35W
Sipra →, India 42 H6 23 55N 75 28 E
Sipura, Indonesia 36 E1 2 18S 99 40 E
Siquia →, Nic. 88 D3 12 10N 84 20W
Siquijor, Phil. 37 C6 9 12N 123 35 E
Siquirres, Costa Rica ... 88 D3 10 6N 83 30W
Şir Banī Yās, U.A.E. ... 45 E7 24 19N 52 37 E
Sir Edward Pellew Group,
 Australia 62 B2 15 40S 137 10 E
Sir Graham Moore Is.,
 Australia 60 B4 13 53S 126 34 E
Sir James MacBrien, Mt.,
 Canada 68 B7 62 8N 127 40W
Sira →, Norway 9 G12 58 23N 6 34 E
Siracusa, Italy 20 F6 37 4N 15 17 E
Sirajganj, Bangla. 43 G13 24 25N 89 47 E
Sirathu, India 43 G9 25 39N 81 19 E
Sirdān, Iran 45 B6 36 39N 49 12 E
Sirdaryo = Syrdarya →,
 Kazakstan 26 E7 46 3N 61 0 E
Siren, U.S.A. 80 C8 45 47N 92 24W
Sirer, Spain 22 C7 38 56N 1 22 E
Siret →, Romania 17 F14 45 24N 28 1 E
Sirghāyā, Syria 47 B5 33 51N 36 8 E
Sirmaur, India 43 G9 24 51N 81 23 E
Sirohi, India 42 G5 24 52N 72 53 E
Sironj, India 42 G7 24 5N 77 39 E
Síros, Greece 21 F11 37 28N 24 57 E
Sirretta Pk., U.S.A. 85 K8 35 56N 118 19W
Sirrī, Iran 45 E7 25 55N 54 32 E
Sirsa, India 42 E6 29 33N 75 4 E
Sirsa →, India 43 F8 26 51N 79 4 E
Sisak, Croatia 16 F9 45 30N 16 21 E
Sisaket, Thailand 38 E5 15 8N 104 23 E
Sishen, S. Africa 56 D3 27 47S 22 59 E
Sishui, Henan, China ... 34 G7 34 48N 113 15 E
Sishui, Shandong, China . 35 G9 35 42N 117 18 E
Sisipuk L., Canada 73 B8 55 45N 101 50W
Sisophon, Cambodia ... 38 F4 13 38N 102 59 E
Sisseton, U.S.A. 80 C6 45 40N 97 3W
Sīstān, Asia 45 D9 30 50N 61 0 E
Sīstān, Daryācheh-ye, Iran . 45 D9 31 0N 61 0 E
Sīstān va Balūchestān □,
 Iran 45 E9 27 0N 62 0 E
Sisters, U.S.A. 82 D3 44 18N 121 33W
Siswa Bazar, India 43 F10 27 9N 83 46 E
Sitamarhi, India 43 F11 26 37N 85 30 E
Sitapur, India 43 F9 27 38N 80 45 E
Siteki, Swaziland 57 D5 26 32S 31 58 E
Sitges, Spain 19 B6 41 17N 1 47 E
Sitía, Greece 23 D8 35 13N 26 6 E
Sitka, U.S.A. 72 B1 57 3N 135 20W
Sitoti, Botswana 56 C3 23 15S 23 40 E
Sittang Myit →, Burma . 41 L20 17 20N 96 45 E
Sittard, Neths. 15 C5 51 0N 5 52 E
Sittingbourne, U.K. 11 F8 51 21N 0 45 E
Sittwe, Burma 41 J18 20 18N 92 45 E
Situbondo, Indonesia ... 37 G16 7 42S 114 0 E
Siuna, Nic. 88 D3 13 37N 84 45W
Siuri, India 43 H12 23 50N 87 34 E
Sīvand, Iran 45 D7 30 5N 52 55 E
Sivas, Turkey 25 G6 39 43N 36 58 E
Siverek, Turkey 44 B3 37 50N 39 19 E
Sivomaskinskiy, Russia . 24 A11 66 40N 62 35 E
Sivrihisar, Turkey 25 G5 39 30N 31 35 E
Sîwa, Egypt 51 C11 29 11N 25 31 E
Sîwa Oasis, Egypt 48 D6 29 10N 25 30 E
Siwalik Range, Nepal ... 43 F10 28 0N 83 0 E
Siwan, India 43 F11 26 13N 84 21 E
Siwana, India 42 G5 25 38N 72 25 E
Sixmilebridge, Ireland .. 13 D3 52 44N 8 46W
Sixth Cataract, Sudan .. 51 E12 16 20N 32 42 E
Siziwang Qi, China 34 D6 41 25N 111 40 E
Sjælland, Denmark 9 J14 55 30N 11 30 E
Sjumen = Shumen, Bulgaria 21 C12 43 18N 26 55 E
Skadarsko Jezero,
 Montenegro, Yug. 21 C8 42 10N 19 20 E
Skaftafell, Iceland 8 D5 64 1N 17 0W
Skagafjörður, Iceland .. 8 D4 65 54N 19 35W
Skagastølstindane, Norway 9 F12 61 28N 7 52 E
Skagaströnd, Iceland ... 8 D3 65 50N 20 19W
Skagen, Denmark 9 H14 57 43N 10 35 E
Skagerrak, Denmark 9 H13 57 30N 9 0 E
Skagit →, U.S.A. 84 B4 48 23N 122 22W
Skagway, U.S.A. 68 C6 59 28N 135 19W
Skala-Podilska, Ukraine . 17 D14 48 50N 26 15 E
Skala Podolskaya = Skala-
 Podilska, Ukraine 17 D14 48 50N 26 15 E
Skåne, Sweden 9 J15 55 59N 13 30 E
Skaneateles, U.S.A. ... 79 D8 42 57N 76 26W
Skaneateles L., U.S.A. . 79 D8 42 51N 76 22W
Skara, Sweden 9 G15 58 25N 13 30 E
Skardu, Pakistan 43 B6 35 20N 75 44 E
Skarżysko-Kamienna, Poland 17 C11 51 7N 20 52 E
Skeena →, Canada 72 C2 54 9N 130 5W
Skeena Mts., Canada ... 72 B3 56 40N 128 30W
Skegness, U.K. 10 D8 53 9N 0 20 E
Skeldon, Guyana 92 B7 5 55N 57 20W
Skellefte älv →, Sweden 8 D19 64 45N 21 10 E
Skellefteå, Sweden 8 D19 64 45N 20 50 E
Skelleftehamn, Sweden . 8 D19 64 40N 21 9 E
Skerries, The, U.K. 10 D3 53 25N 4 36W

Ski, Norway 9 G14 59 43N 10 52 E
Skíathos, Greece 21 E10 39 12N 23 30 E
Skibbereen, Ireland 13 E2 51 33N 9 16W
Skiddaw, U.K. 10 C4 54 39N 3 9W
Skidegate, Canada 72 C2 53 15N 132 1W
Skien, Norway 9 G13 59 12N 9 35 E
Skierniewice, Poland ... 17 C11 51 58N 20 10 E
Skikda, Algeria 50 A7 36 50N 6 58 E
Skilloura, Cyprus 23 D12 35 14N 33 10 E
Skipton, U.K. 10 D5 53 58N 2 3W
Skírmish Pt., Australia .. 62 A1 11 59S 134 17 E
Skiros, Greece 21 E11 38 55N 24 34 E
Skive, Denmark 9 H13 56 33N 9 2 E
Skjálfandafljót →, Iceland 8 D5 65 59N 17 25W
Skjálfandi, Iceland 8 C5 66 5N 17 30W
Skoghall, Sweden 9 G15 59 20N 13 30 E
Skole, Ukraine 17 D12 49 3N 23 30 E
Skópelos, Greece 21 E10 39 9N 23 47 E
Skopí, Greece 23 D8 35 11N 26 2 E
Skopje, Macedonia 21 C9 42 1N 21 26 E
Skövde, Sweden 9 G15 58 24N 13 50 E
Skovorodino, Russia ... 27 D13 54 0N 124 0 E
Skowhegan, U.S.A. 77 C11 44 46N 69 43W
Skull, Ireland 13 E2 51 32N 9 34W
Skunk →, U.S.A. 80 E9 40 42N 91 7W
Skuodas, Lithuania 9 H19 56 16N 21 33 E
Skvyra, Ukraine 17 D15 49 44N 29 40 E
Skye, U.K. 12 D2 57 15N 6 10W
Skykomish, U.S.A. 82 C3 47 42N 121 22W
Skyros = Skiros, Greece . 21 E11 38 55N 24 34 E
Slættaratindur, Færøe Is. . 8 E9 62 18N 7 1W
Slagelse, Denmark 9 J14 55 23N 11 19 E
Slamet, Indonesia 37 G13 7 16S 109 8 E
Slaney →, Ireland 13 D5 52 26N 6 33W
Śląsk, Poland 16 C9 51 0N 16 30 E
Slate Is., Canada 70 C2 48 40N 87 0W
Slatina, Romania 17 F13 44 28N 24 22 E
Slatington, U.S.A. 79 F9 40 45N 75 37W
Slaton, U.S.A. 81 J4 33 26N 101 39W
Slave →, Canada 72 A6 61 18N 113 39W
Slave Coast, W. Afr. 50 G6 6 0N 2 30 E
Slave Lake, Canada 72 B6 55 17N 114 43W
Slave Pt., Canada 72 A5 61 11N 115 56W
Slavgorod, Russia 26 D8 53 1N 78 37 E
Slavonski Brod, Croatia . 21 B8 45 11N 18 1 E
Slavuta, Ukraine 17 C14 50 15N 27 2 E
Slavyanka, Russia 30 C5 42 53N 131 21 E
Slavyansk = Slovyansk,
 Ukraine 25 E6 48 55N 37 36 E
Slawharad, Belarus 17 B16 53 27N 31 0 E
Sleaford, U.K. 10 D7 53 0N 0 24W
Sleaford B., Australia .. 63 E2 34 55S 135 45 E
Sleat, Sd. of, U.K. 12 D3 57 5N 5 47W
Sleeper Is., Canada 69 C11 58 30N 81 0W
Sleepy Eye, U.S.A. 80 C7 44 18N 94 43W
Slemon L., Canada 72 A5 63 13N 116 4W
Slide Mt., U.S.A. 79 E10 42 0N 74 25W
Slidell, U.S.A. 81 K10 30 17N 89 47W
Sliema, Malta 23 D2 35 54N 14 30 E
Slieve Aughty, Ireland .. 13 C3 53 4N 8 30W
Slieve Bloom, Ireland .. 13 C4 53 4N 7 40W
Slieve Donard, U.K. 13 B6 54 11N 5 55W
Slieve Gamph, Ireland .. 13 B3 54 6N 9 0W
Slieve Gullion, Ireland .. 13 B5 54 7N 6 26W
Slieve Mish, Ireland 13 D2 52 12N 9 50W
Slievenamon, Ireland ... 13 D4 52 25N 7 34W
Sligeach = Sligo, Ireland . 13 B3 54 16N 8 28W
Sligo, Ireland 13 B3 54 16N 8 28W
Sligo, U.S.A. 78 E5 41 6N 79 29W
Sligo □, Ireland 13 B3 54 8N 8 42W
Sligo B., Ireland 13 B3 54 18N 8 40W
Slippery Rock, U.S.A. .. 78 E4 41 3N 80 3W
Slite, Sweden 9 H18 57 42N 18 48 E
Sliven, Bulgaria 21 C12 42 42N 26 19 E
Sloan, U.S.A. 85 K11 35 57N 115 13W
Sloansville, U.S.A. 79 D10 42 45N 74 22W
Slobodskoy, Russia 24 C9 58 40N 50 6 E
Slobozia, Romania 17 F14 44 34N 27 23 E
Slocan, Canada 72 D5 49 48N 117 28W
Slonim, Belarus 17 B13 53 4N 25 19 E
Slough, U.K. 11 F7 51 30N 0 36W
Slough □, U.K. 11 F7 51 30N 0 36W
Sloughhouse, U.S.A. ... 84 G5 38 26N 121 12W
Slovak Rep. ■, Europe . 17 D10 48 30N 20 0 E
Slovakia = Slovak Rep. ■,
 Europe 17 D10 48 30N 20 0 E
Slovakian Ore Mts. =
 Slovenské Rudohorie,
 Slovak Rep. 17 D10 48 45N 20 0 E
Slovenia ■, Europe 16 F8 45 58N 14 30 E
Slovenija = Slovenia ■,
 Europe 16 F8 45 58N 14 30 E
Slovenské Rudohorie,
 Slovak Rep. 17 D10 48 45N 20 0 E
Slovyansk, Ukraine 25 E6 48 55N 37 36 E
Sluch →, Ukraine 17 C14 51 37N 26 38 E
Sluis, Neths. 15 C3 51 18N 3 23 E
Słupsk, Poland 17 A9 54 30N 17 3 E
Slurry, S. Africa 56 D4 25 49S 25 42 E
Slutsk, Belarus 17 B14 53 2N 27 31 E
Slyne Hd., Ireland 13 C1 53 25N 10 10W
Slyudyanka, Russia 27 D11 51 40N 103 40 E
Småland, Sweden 9 H16 57 15N 15 25 E
Smalltree L., Canada ... 73 A8 61 0N 105 0W
Smallwood Res., Canada . 71 B7 54 0N 64 0W
Smara, Morocco 50 B4 32 9N 8 16W
Smarhon, Belarus 17 A14 54 20N 26 24 E
Smartt Syndicate Dam,
 S. Africa 56 E3 30 45S 23 10 E
Smartville, U.S.A. 84 F5 39 13N 121 18W
Smeaton, Canada 73 C8 53 30N 104 49W
Smederevo, Serbia, Yug. . 21 B9 44 40N 20 57 E
Smerwick Harbour, Ireland . 13 D1 52 12N 10 23W
Smethport, U.S.A. 78 E6 41 49N 78 27W
Smidovich, Russia 27 E14 48 36N 133 49 E
Smith, Canada 72 B6 55 10N 114 0W
Smith Center, U.S.A. .. 80 F5 39 47N 98 47W
Smith Sund, Greenland . 4 B4 78 30N 74 0W
Smithburne →, Australia . 62 B3 17 3S 140 57 E
Smithers, Canada 72 C3 54 45N 127 10W
Smithfield, S. Africa ... 57 E4 30 9S 26 30 E
Smithfield, N.C., U.S.A. . 77 H6 35 31N 78 21W
Smithfield, Utah, U.S.A. . 82 F8 41 50N 111 50W
Smiths Falls, Canada ... 79 B9 44 55N 76 0W
Smithton, Australia 62 G4 40 53S 145 6 E
Smithville, Canada 78 C5 43 6N 79 33W

Smithville, U.S.A. 81 K6 30 1N 97 10W
Smoky →, Canada 72 B5 56 10N 117 21W
Smoky Bay, Australia ... 63 E1 32 22S 134 13 E
Smoky Hill →, U.S.A. .. 80 F6 39 4N 96 48W
Smoky Hills, U.S.A. 80 F5 39 15N 99 30W
Smoky Lake, Canada ... 72 C6 54 10N 112 30W
Smøla, Norway 8 E13 63 23N 8 3 E
Smolensk, Russia 24 D5 54 45N 32 5 E
Smolikas, Óros, Greece . 21 D9 40 9N 20 58 E
Smolyan, Bulgaria 21 D11 41 36N 24 38 E
Smooth Rock Falls, Canada 70 C3 49 17N 81 37W
Smoothstone L., Canada . 73 C7 54 40N 106 50W
Smorgon = Smarhon,
 Belarus 17 A14 54 20N 26 24 E
Smyrna = İzmir, Turkey . 21 E12 38 25N 27 8 E
Smyrna, U.S.A. 76 F8 39 18N 75 36W
Snæfell, Iceland 8 D6 64 48N 15 34W
Snaefell, U.K. 10 C3 54 16N 4 27W
Snæfellsjökull, Iceland . 8 D2 64 49N 23 46W
Snake →, U.S.A. 82 C4 46 12N 119 2W
Snake I., Australia 63 F4 38 47S 146 33 E
Snake Range, U.S.A. ... 82 G6 39 0N 114 20W
Snake River Plain, U.S.A. 82 E7 42 50N 114 0W
Snåsavatnet, Norway ... 8 D14 64 12N 12 0 E
Sneek, Neths. 15 A5 53 2N 5 40 E
Sneeuberge, S. Africa .. 56 E3 31 46S 24 20 E
Snelling, U.S.A. 84 H6 37 31N 120 26W
Sněžka, Europe 16 C8 50 41N 15 50 E
Snizort, L., U.K. 12 D2 57 33N 6 28W
Snøhetta, Norway 9 E13 62 19N 9 16 E
Snohomish, U.S.A. 84 C4 47 55N 122 6W
Snoul, Cambodia 39 F6 12 4N 106 26 E
Snow Hill, U.S.A. 76 F8 38 11N 75 24W
Snow Lake, Canada 73 C8 54 52N 100 3W
Snow Mt., Calif., U.S.A. . 84 F4 39 23N 122 45W
Snow Mt., Maine, U.S.A. . 79 A14 45 18N 70 48W
Snow Shoe, U.S.A. 78 E7 41 2N 77 57W
Snowbird L., Canada ... 73 A8 60 45N 103 0W
Snowdon, U.K. 10 D3 53 4N 4 5W
Snowdrift →, Canada .. 73 A6 62 24N 110 44W
Snowflake, U.S.A. 83 J8 34 30N 110 5W
Snowshoe Pk., U.S.A. .. 82 B6 48 13N 115 41W
Snowtown, Australia ... 63 E2 33 46S 138 14 E
Snowville, U.S.A. 82 F7 41 58N 112 43W
Snowy →, Australia 63 F4 37 46S 148 30 E
Snowy Mt., U.S.A. 79 C10 43 42N 74 23W
Snowy Mts., Australia .. 63 F4 36 30S 148 20 E
Snug Corner, Bahamas . 89 B5 22 33N 73 52W
Snyatyn, Ukraine 17 D13 48 27N 25 38 E
Snyder, Okla., U.S.A. .. 81 H5 34 40N 98 57W
Snyder, Tex., U.S.A. ... 81 J4 32 44N 100 55W
Soahanina, Madag. 57 B7 18 42S 44 13 E
Soalala, Madag. 57 B8 16 6S 45 20 E
Soan →, Pakistan 42 C4 33 1N 71 44 E
Soanierana-Ivongo, Madag. 57 B8 16 55S 49 35 E
Sobat, Nahr →, Sudan . 51 G12 9 22N 31 33 E
Sobhapur, India 42 H8 22 47N 78 17 E
Sobradinho, Reprêsa de,
 Brazil 93 E10 9 30S 42 0 E
Sobral, Brazil 93 D10 3 50S 40 20W
Soc Trang, Vietnam 39 H5 9 37N 105 50 E
Socastee, U.S.A. 77 J6 33 41N 79 1W
Soch'e = Shache, China . 32 C2 38 20N 77 10 E
Sochi, Russia 25 F6 43 35N 39 40 E
Société, Is. de la, Pac. Oc. 65 J12 17 0S 151 0W
Society Is. = Société, Is. de
 la, Pac. Oc. 65 J12 17 0S 151 0W
Socompa, Portezuelo de,
 Chile 94 A2 24 27S 68 18W
Socorro, N. Mex., U.S.A. . 83 J10 34 4N 106 54W
Socorro, Tex., U.S.A. .. 83 L10 31 39N 106 18W
Socorro, I., Mexico 86 D2 18 45N 110 58W
Socotra, Ind. Oc. 46 E5 12 30N 54 0 E
Soda, L., U.S.A. 83 J5 35 10N 116 4W
Soda Plains, India 43 B8 35 30N 79 0 E
Soda Springs, U.S.A. .. 82 E8 42 39N 111 36W
Sodankylä, Finland 8 C22 67 29N 26 40 E
Soddy-Daisy, U.S.A. ... 77 H3 35 17N 85 10W
Söderhamn, Sweden ... 9 F17 61 18N 17 10 E
Söderköping, Sweden .. 9 G17 58 31N 16 20 E
Södermanland, Sweden . 9 G17 59 10N 16 30 E
Södertälje, Sweden 9 G17 59 12N 17 39 E
Sodiri, Sudan 51 F11 14 27N 29 0 E
Sodus, U.S.A. 78 C7 43 14N 77 4W
Soekmekaar, S. Africa .. 57 C4 23 30S 29 55 E
Soest, Neths. 15 B5 52 9N 5 19 E
Sofia = Sofiya, Bulgaria . 21 C10 42 45N 23 20 E
Sofia →, Madag. 57 B8 15 27S 47 23 E
Sofiya, Bulgaria 21 C10 42 45N 23 20 E
Sōfu-Gan, Japan 31 K10 29 49N 140 21 E
Sogamoso, Colombia ... 92 B4 5 43N 72 56W
Sogār, Iran 45 E8 25 53N 58 6 E
Sogndalsfjøra, Norway . 9 F12 61 14N 7 5 E
Søgne, Norway 9 G12 58 5N 7 48 E
Sognefjorden, Norway .. 9 F11 61 10N 5 50 E
Sŏgwipo, S. Korea 35 H14 33 13N 126 34 E
Soh, Iran 45 C6 33 26N 51 27 E
Sohâg, Egypt 51 C12 26 33N 31 43 E
Sohagpur, India 42 H8 22 42N 78 12 E
Sŏhori, N. Korea 35 D15 40 7N 128 23 E
Soignies, Belgium 15 D4 50 35N 4 5 E
Soissons, France 18 B5 49 25N 3 19 E
Sōja, Japan 31 G6 34 40N 133 45 E
Sojat, India 42 G5 25 55N 73 45 E
Sokal, Ukraine 17 C13 50 31N 24 15 E
Söke, Turkey 21 F12 37 48N 27 28 E
Sokelo,
 Dem. Rep. of the Congo . 55 D1 9 55S 24 36 E
Sokhumi, Georgia 25 F7 43 0N 41 0 E
Sokodé, Togo 50 G6 9 0N 1 11 E
Sokol, Russia 24 C7 59 30N 40 5 E
Sokółka, Poland 17 B12 53 25N 23 30 E
Sokołów Podlaski, Poland 17 B12 52 25N 22 15 E
Sokoto, Nigeria 50 F7 13 2N 5 16 E
Sol Iletsk, Russia 24 D10 51 10N 55 0 E
Solai, Kenya 54 B4 0 2N 36 12 E
Solan, India 42 D7 30 55N 77 7 E
Solano, Phil. 37 A6 16 31N 121 15 E
Solapur, India 40 L9 17 43N 75 56 E
Soldotna, U.S.A. 68 B4 60 29S 151 3 E
Soléá □, Cyprus 23 D12 35 5N 33 4 E
Soledad, Colombia 92 A4 10 55N 74 46W
Soledad, U.S.A. 84 J5 36 26N 121 20W
Soledad, Venezuela 92 B6 8 10N 63 34W
Solent, The, U.K. 11 G6 50 45N 1 25W
Solfonn, Norway 9 F12 60 2N 6 57 E

Tha Song Yang

168

dinarrain, Argentina ... 94 C4 32 37S 58 52W
dzhar, Kazakstan ... 26 E9 47 5N 81 38 E
es ~, U.K. ... 10 C6 54 5N 1 20W
es, Mexico ... 86 B2 29 30N 110 30W
a = Sanlıurfa, Turkey ... 25 G6 37 12N 38 50 E
ganch = Urganch,
gench, Uzbekistan ... 26 E7 41 40N 60 41 E
güp, Turkey ... 44 B2 38 38N 34 56 E
, India ... 43 B6 34 8N 74 2 E
bia, Colombia ... 92 A4 11 43N 72 16W
ondo, Bolivia ... 94 A3 21 41S 64 41W
que, Mexico ... 86 B3 27 13N 107 55W
, Mexico ... 86 B3 26 29N 107 58W
, Neths. ... 15 B5 52 39N 5 36 E
a, Turkey ... 26 D8 41 20N 26 47 E
mia = Orümïyeh, Iran ... 44 B5 37 40N 45 0 E
Daryächeh-ye, Iran,
mia = Orümïyeh, Iran ... 44 B5 37 50N 45 30 E
ševac, Yugoslavia ... 21 C9 42 23N 21 10 E
aaçu, Brazil ... 93 F9 14 30S 49 10W
Japan, Mexico ... 86 D4 19 30N 102 0W
ubamba ~, Peru ... 92 F4 10 43S 73 48W
uçara, Brazil ... 92 D7 2 20S 57 50W
uçui, Brazil ... 93 E10 7 20S 44 28W
uguai ~, Brazil ... 95 B5 26 0S 53 30W
uguaiana, Brazil ... 94 B4 29 50S 57 0W
uguay ■, S. Amer. ... 94 C4 32 30S 56 30W
uguay ~, S. Amer. ... 94 C4 34 12S 58 18W
umchi = Ürümqi, China ... 26 E9 43 45N 87 45 E
ümqi, China ... 26 E9 43 45N 87 45 E
up, Ostrov, Russia ... 27 E16 46 0N 151 0 E
~, Russia ... 24 A10 66 16N 59 49 E
ak, Turkey ... 25 G4 38 43N 29 28 E
oševac, Namibia ... 56 C2 21 54S 15 31 E
edom, Germany ... 16 B8 53 55N 14 2 E
eless Loop, Australia ... 61 E1 26 8S 113 23 E
n-Tobe, Kazakstan ... 26 E8 45 16N 78 0 E
hakova, Ostrov, Russia . 4 A12 82 0N 80 0 E
hant = Ouessant, Î. d',
France ... 18 B1 48 28N 5 6W
nashi, Tanzania ... 54 C3 1 59S 33 57 E
hibuka, Japan ... 31 H5 32 11N 130 1 E
huaia, Argentina ... 96 G3 54 50S 68 23W
humun, Russia ... 27 D13 52 47N 126 32 E
k, Canada ... 72 C3 54 38N 128 26W
~, U.K. ... 11 F5 51 33N 2 58W
ka, India ... 43 F10 27 12N 83 7 E
man, Russia ... 24 D6 52 5N 39 48 E
oke, Tanzania ... 54 D3 5 8S 32 24 E
olye Sibirskoye, Russia . 27 D11 52 48N 103 40 E
pallata, P. de, Argentina 94 C2 32 37S 69 22W
penskiy, Kazakstan ... 26 E8 48 41N 72 43 E
suri ~, Asia ... 30 A7 48 27N 135 0 E
suriysk, Russia ... 27 E14 43 48N 131 59 E
surka, Russia ... 30 B6 45 12N 133 31 E
t-Aldan = Batamay,
Russia ... 27 C13 63 30N 129 15 E
t Amginskoye,
Khandyga, Russia ... 27 C14 62 42N 135 35 E
t-Bolsheretsk, Russia ... 27 D16 52 50N 156 15 E
t-Chaun, Russia ... 27 C18 68 47N 170 30 E
t Ilimpeya = Yukta,
Russia ... 27 C11 63 26N 105 42 E
t-Ilimsk, Russia ... 27 D11 58 3N 102 39 E
t Ishim, Russia ... 26 D8 57 45N 71 10 E
t-Kamchatsk, Russia ... 27 D17 56 10N 162 28 E
t-Kamenogorsk =
Öskemen, Kazakstan ... 26 E9 50 0N 82 36 E
t Khayryuzovo, Russia . 27 D16 57 15N 156 45 E
t-Kut, Russia ... 27 D11 56 50N 105 42 E
t Kuyga, Russia ... 27 B14 70 1N 135 43 E
t Maya, Russia ... 27 C14 60 30N 134 28 E
t-Mil, Russia ... 27 D14 59 40N 133 11 E
t-Nera, Russia ... 27 C15 64 35N 143 15 E
t-Nyukzha, Russia ... 27 D13 56 34N 121 37 E
t Olenek, Russia ... 27 B12 73 0N 120 5 E
t-Omchug, Russia ... 27 C15 61 9N 149 38 E
t Port, Russia ... 27 C9 69 40N 84 26 E
t Tsilma, Russia ... 24 A9 65 28N 52 11 E
t Urt = Ustyurt Plateau,
Asia ... 26 E6 44 0N 55 0 E
t Usa, Russia ... 24 A10 66 2N 56 57 E
t Vorkuta, Russia ... 24 A11 67 24N 64 0 E
í nad Labem, Czech Rep. 16 C8 50 41N 14 3 E
tica, Italy ... 20 E5 38 42N 13 11 E
tinov = Izhevsk, Russia . 24 C9 56 51N 53 14 E
yurt Plateau, Asia ... 26 E6 44 0N 55 0 E
u, China ... 32 B3 44 27N 84 40 E
uki, Japan ... 31 H6 33 8N 131 49 E
ulután, El Salv. ... 88 D2 13 25N 88 28W
umacinta ~, Mexico ... 87 D6 17 0N 91 0W
umbura = Bujumbura,
Burundi ... 54 C2 3 16S 29 18 E
ure, Tanzania ... 54 C3 4 40S 34 22 E
a, Indonesia ... 37 E9 4 33S 136 0 E
U.S.A. ... 82 G8 39 20N 111 30W
ah ☐, U.S.A. ... 82 F8 40 10N 111 58W
arni, India ... 42 D6 24 5N 71 58 E
atlan, Guatemala ... 88 C1 15 2N 91 11W
e Creek ~, U.S.A. ... 81 H3 35 21N 103 50W
ena, Lithuania ... 9 J21 55 27N 25 40 E
hai Thani, Thailand ... 38 E3 15 22N 100 3 E
nal, Pakistan ... 42 G2 25 44N 66 40 E
tara Pradesh ☐, India ... 92 F7 13 0S 58 10W
ica, N.Y., U.S.A. ... 79 C9 43 6N 75 14W
ica, Ohio, U.S.A. ... 78 F2 40 14N 82 27W
tsira, Australia ... 63 B4 17 13S 134 33 E
raula, India ... 43 F10 27 19N 82 25 E
recht, Neths. ... 15 B5 52 5N 5 8 E
recht ☐, Neths. ... 15 B5 52 6N 5 7 E
era, Spain ... 19 D3 37 12N 5 48W
sjoki, Finland ... 8 B22 69 51N 26 59 E
sunomiya, Japan ... 31 F9 36 30N 139 50 E
tar Pradesh ☐, India ... 43 F9 27 0N 80 0 E
taradit, Thailand ... 38 D3 17 36N 100 5 E
toxeter, U.K. ... 10 E6 52 54N 1 52W
mannsuaq = Farvel,
Kap, Greenland ... 4 D5 59 48N 43 55W
usikaarlepyy, Finland ... 8 E20 63 32N 22 31 E
usikaupunki, Finland ... 9 F19 60 47N 21 25 E
a, Russia ... 24 C9 56 59N 52 13 E
ale, U.S.A. ... 81 L5 29 13N 99 47W

Uvat, Russia ... 26 D7 59 5N 68 50 E
Uvinza, Tanzania ... 54 D3 5 5S 30 24 E
Uvira,
Dem. Rep. of the Congo . 54 C2 3 22S 29 3 E
Uvs Nuur, Mongolia ... 32 A4 50 20N 92 30 E
'Uwairidh, Harrat al,
Si. Arabia ... 44 E3 26 50N 38 0 E
Uwajima, Japan ... 31 H6 33 10N 132 35 E
Uweinat, Jebel, Sudan ... 51 D10 21 54N 24 58 E
Uxbridge, Canada ... 78 B5 44 6N 79 7W
Uxin Qi, China ... 34 E5 38 50N 109 5 E
Uxmal, Mexico ... 87 C7 20 22N 89 46W
Üydzin, Mongolia ... 34 B4 44 9N 107 0 E
Uyo, Nigeria ... 50 G7 5 1N 7 53 E
Uyûn Mûsa, Egypt ... 47 F1 29 53N 32 40 E
Uyuni, Bolivia ... 92 H5 20 28S 66 47W
Uzbekistan ■, Asia ... 26 E7 41 30N 65 0 E
Uzen, Kazakstan ... 25 F9 43 29N 52 54 E
Uzen, Mal ~, Kazakstan . 25 E8 49 4N 49 44 E
Uzerche, France ... 18 D4 45 25N 1 34 E
Uzh ~, Ukraine ... 17 C16 51 15N 30 12 E
Uzhgorod = Uzhhorod,
Ukraine ... 17 D12 48 36N 22 18 E
Uzhhorod, Ukraine ... 17 D12 48 36N 22 18 E
Užice, Serbia, Yug. ... 21 C8 43 55N 19 50 E
Uzunköprü, Turkey ... 21 D12 41 16N 26 43 E

V

Vaal ~, S. Africa ... 56 D3 29 4S 23 38 E
Vaal Dam, S. Africa ... 57 D4 27 0S 28 14 E
Vaalwater, S. Africa ... 57 C4 24 15S 28 8 E
Vaasa, Finland ... 8 E19 63 6N 21 38 E
Vác, Hungary ... 17 E10 47 49N 19 10 E
Vacaria, Brazil ... 95 B5 28 31S 50 52W
Vacaville, U.S.A. ... 84 G5 38 21N 121 59W
Vach = Vakh ~, Russia .. 26 C8 60 45N 76 45 E
Vache, Î. à, Haiti ... 89 C5 18 2N 73 35W
Vadnagar, India ... 42 H5 23 47N 72 40 E
Vadodara, India ... 42 H5 22 20N 73 10 E
Vadsø, Norway ... 8 A23 70 3N 29 50 E
Vaduz, Liech. ... 18 C8 47 8N 9 31 E
Værøy, Norway ... 8 C15 67 40N 12 40 E
Vágar, Færoe Is. ... 8 E9 62 5N 7 15W
Vågsfjorden, Norway 8 B17 68 50N 16 50 E
Váh ~, Slovak Rep. ... 17 D9 47 43N 18 7 E
Vahsel B., Antarctica ... 5 D1 75 0S 35 0W
Vái, Greece ... 23 D8 35 15N 26 18 E
Vaigach, Russia ... 26 B6 70 10N 59 0 E
Vail, U.S.A. ... 74 C5 39 40N 106 20W
Vaisali ~, India ... 43 F8 26 28N 78 53 E
Vakh ~, Russia ... 26 C8 60 45N 76 45 E
Val-d'Or, Canada ... 70 C4 48 7N 77 47W
Val Marie, Canada ... 73 D7 49 15N 107 45W
Valahia, Romania ... 17 F13 44 35N 25 0 E
Valandovo, Macedonia ... 21 D10 41 19N 22 34 E
Valcheta, Argentina ... 96 E3 40 40S 66 8W
Valdayskaya Vozvyshennost,
Russia ... 24 C5 57 0N 33 30 E
Valdepeñas, Spain ... 19 C4 38 43N 3 25W
Valdés, Pen., Argentina . 96 E4 42 30S 63 45W
Valdez, U.S.A. ... 68 B5 61 7N 146 16W
Valdivia, Chile ... 96 D2 39 50S 73 14W
Valdosta, U.S.A. ... 77 K4 30 50N 83 17W
Valdres, Norway ... 9 F13 61 5N 9 5 E
Vale, U.S.A. ... 82 E5 43 59N 117 15W
Vale of Glamorgan ☐, U.K. 11 F4 51 28N 3 25W
Valemount, Canada ... 72 C5 52 50N 119 15W
Valença, Brazil ... 93 F11 13 20S 39 5W
Valença do Piauí, Brazil . 93 E10 6 20S 41 45W
Valence, France ... 18 D6 44 57N 4 54 E
Valencia, Spain ... 19 C5 39 27N 0 23W
Valencia, U.S.A. ... 83 J10 34 48N 106 43W
Valencia, Venezuela ... 92 A5 10 11N 68 0W
Valencia ☐, Spain ... 19 C5 39 20N 0 40W
Valencia, G. de, Spain ... 19 C6 39 30N 0 20 E
Valencia de Alcántara, Spain 19 C2 39 25N 7 14W
Valencia I., Ireland ... 13 E1 51 54N 10 22W
Valenciennes, France ... 18 A5 50 20N 3 34 E
Valentim, Sa. do, Brazil . 93 E10 6 0S 43 30W
Valentin, Russia ... 30 C7 43 8N 134 17 E
Valentine, Nebr., U.S.A. . 74 B4 42 52N 100 33W
Valentine, Tex., U.S.A. .. 81 K2 30 35N 104 30W
Valera, Venezuela ... 92 B4 9 19N 70 37W
Valga, Estonia ... 9 H22 57 47N 26 2 E
Valier, U.S.A. ... 82 B7 48 18N 112 16W
Valjevo, Serbia, Yug. ... 21 B8 44 18N 19 53 E
Valka, Latvia ... 9 H21 57 42N 25 57 E
Valkeakoski, Finland ... 9 F20 61 16N 24 2 E
Valkenswaard, Neths. ... 15 C5 51 21N 5 29 E
Vall de Uxó = La Vall
d'Uixó, Spain ... 19 C5 39 49N 0 15W
Valladolid, Mexico ... 87 C7 20 40N 88 11W
Valladolid, Spain ... 19 B3 41 38N 4 43W
Valldemossa, Spain ... 22 B9 39 43N 2 37 E
Valle de la Pascua,
Venezuela ... 92 B5 9 13N 66 0W
Valle de las Palmas, Mexico 85 N10 32 20N 116 43W
Valle de Santiago, Mexico . 86 C4 20 25N 101 15W
Valle de Suchil, Mexico .. 86 C4 23 38N 103 55W
Valle de Zaragoza, Mexico 86 B3 27 28N 105 49W
Valle Fértil, Sierra del,
Argentina ... 94 C2 30 20S 68 0W
Valle Hermoso, Mexico .. 87 B5 25 35N 97 40W
Valledupar, Colombia ... 92 A4 10 29N 73 15W
Vallehermoso, Canary Is. . 22 F2 28 10N 17 15W
Vallejo, U.S.A. ... 84 G4 38 7N 122 14W
Vallenar, Chile ... 94 B1 28 30S 70 50W
Valletta, Malta ... 23 D2 35 54N 14 31 E
Valley Center, U.S.A. ... 85 M9 33 13N 117 2W
Valley City, U.S.A. ... 80 B6 46 55N 98 0W
Valley Falls, Oreg., U.S.A. 82 E3 42 29N 120 17W
Valley Falls, R.I., U.S.A. . 79 E13 41 54N 71 24W
Valley Springs, U.S.A. ... 84 G6 38 12N 120 50W
Valley View, U.S.A. ... 79 F8 40 39N 76 33W
Valley Wells, U.S.A. ... 85 K11 35 27N 115 46W
Valleyview, Canada ... 72 B5 55 5N 117 17W
Vallimanca, Arroyo,
Argentina ... 94 D4 35 40S 59 10W
Valls, Spain ... 19 B6 41 18N 1 15 E
Valmiera, Latvia ... 9 H21 57 37N 25 29 E
Valognes, France ... 18 B3 49 30N 1 28W
Valona = Vlóra, Albania . 21 D8 40 32N 19 28 E

Valozhyn, Belarus ... 17 A14 54 3N 26 30 E
Valparaíso, Chile ... 94 C1 33 2S 71 40W
Valparaiso, Mexico ... 86 C4 22 50N 103 32W
Valparaíso ☐, Chile ... 94 C1 33 2S 71 40W
Valparaiso, U.S.A. ... 76 E2 41 28N 87 4W
Vals ~, S. Africa ... 56 D4 27 23S 26 30 E
Vals, Tanjung, Indonesia . 37 F9 8 26S 137 25 E
Valsad, India ... 40 J8 20 40N 72 58 E
Valverde, Canary Is. ... 22 G2 27 48N 17 55W
Valverde del Camino, Spain 19 D2 37 35N 6 47W
Vammala, Finland ... 9 F20 61 20N 22 54 E
Vámos, Greece ... 23 D6 35 24N 24 13 E
Van, Turkey ... 25 G7 38 30N 43 20 E
Van, L. = Van Gölü, Turkey 25 G7 38 30N 43 0 E
Van Alstyne, U.S.A. ... 81 J6 33 25N 96 35W
Van Blommestein Meer,
Surinam ... 93 C7 4 45N 55 5W
Van Buren, Canada ... 71 C6 47 10N 67 55W
Van Buren, Ark., U.S.A. . 81 H7 35 26N 94 21W
Van Buren, Maine, U.S.A. 77 B11 47 10N 67 58W
Van Buren, Mo., U.S.A. .. 81 G9 37 0N 91 1W
Van Canh, Vietnam ... 38 F7 13 37N 109 0 E
Van Diemen, C., N. Terr.,
Australia ... 60 B5 11 9S 130 24 E
Van Diemen, C., Queens.,
Australia ... 62 B2 16 30S 139 46 E
Van Diemen G., Australia . 60 B5 11 45S 132 0 E
Van Gölü, Turkey ... 25 G7 38 30N 43 0 E
Van Horn, U.S.A. ... 81 K2 31 3N 104 50W
Van Ninh, Vietnam ... 38 F7 12 42N 109 14 E
Van Rees, Pegunungan,
Indonesia ... 37 E9 2 35S 138 15 E
Van Wert, U.S.A. ... 76 E3 40 52N 84 35W
Vanadzor, Armenia ... 25 F7 40 48N 44 30 E
Vanavara, Russia ... 27 C11 60 22N 102 16 E
Vancouver, Canada ... 72 D4 49 15N 123 10W
Vancouver, U.S.A. ... 84 E4 45 38N 122 40W
Vancouver, C., Australia .. 61 G2 35 2S 118 11 E
Vancouver I., Canada ... 72 D3 49 50N 126 0W
Vandalia, Ill., U.S.A. ... 80 F10 38 58N 89 6W
Vandalia, Mo., U.S.A. ... 80 F9 39 19N 91 29W
Vandenburg, U.S.A. ... 85 L6 34 35N 120 33W
Vanderbijlpark, S. Africa . 57 D4 26 42S 27 54 E
Vandergrift, U.S.A. ... 78 F5 40 36N 79 34W
Vanderhoof, Canada ... 72 C4 54 0N 124 0W
Vanderkloof Dam, S. Africa 56 E3 30 4S 24 40 E
Vanderlin I., Australia ... 62 B2 15 44S 137 2 E
Vänern, Sweden ... 9 G15 58 47N 13 30 E
Vänersborg, Sweden ... 9 G15 58 26N 12 19 E
Vang Vieng, Laos ... 38 C4 18 58N 102 32 E
Vanga, Kenya ... 54 C4 4 35S 39 12 E
Vangaindrano, Madag. ... 57 C8 23 21S 47 36 E
Vanguard, Canada ... 73 D7 49 55N 107 20W
Vanino, Russia ... 27 E15 48 50N 140 5 E
Vanna, Norway ... 8 A18 70 6N 19 50 E
Vännäs, Sweden ... 8 E18 63 58N 19 48 E
Vannes, France ... 18 C2 47 40N 2 47W
Vanrhynsdorp, S. Africa .. 56 E2 31 36S 18 44 E
Vansbro, Sweden ... 9 F16 60 32N 14 15 E
Vansittart B., Australia ... 60 B4 14 3S 126 17 E
Vantaa, Finland ... 9 F21 60 18N 24 58 E
Vanua Levu, Fiji ... 59 C8 16 33S 179 15 E
Vanua Mbalavu, Fiji ... 59 C9 17 40S 178 57W
Vanuatu ■, Pac. Oc. ... 64 J8 15 0S 168 0 E
Vanwyksvlei, S. Africa ... 56 E3 30 18S 21 49 E
Vanzylsrus, S. Africa ... 56 D3 26 52S 22 4 E
Vapnyarka, Ukraine ... 17 D15 48 32N 28 45 E
Varanasi, India ... 43 G10 25 22N 83 0 E
Varanger-halvøya, Norway 8 A23 70 25N 29 30 E
Varangerfjorden, Norway . 8 A23 70 3N 29 25 E
Varaždin, Croatia ... 16 E9 46 20N 16 20 E
Varberg, Sweden ... 9 H15 57 6N 12 20 E
Vardak ☐, Afghan. ... 40 B6 34 0N 68 0 E
Vardar = Axiós ~, Greece 21 D10 40 57N 22 35 E
Varde, Denmark ... 9 J13 55 38N 8 29 E
Vardø, Norway ... 8 A24 70 23N 31 5 E
Varella, Mui, Vietnam ... 38 F7 12 54N 109 26 E
Varena, Lithuania ... 9 J21 54 12N 24 30 E
Varese, Italy ... 18 D8 45 48N 8 50 E
Varginha, Brazil ... 95 A6 21 33S 45 25W
Varillas, Chile ... 94 A1 24 0S 70 10W
Varkaus, Finland ... 9 E22 62 19N 27 50 E
Varna, Bulgaria ... 21 C12 43 13N 27 56 E
Värnamo, Sweden ... 9 H16 57 10N 14 3 E
Vars, Canada ... 79 A9 45 21N 75 21W
Varysburg, U.S.A. ... 78 D6 42 46N 78 19W
Varzaneh, Iran ... 45 C7 32 25N 52 40 E
Vasa Barris ~, Brazil ... 93 F11 11 10S 37 10W
Vascongadas = País
Vasco ☐, Spain ... 19 A4 42 50N 2 45W
Vasht = Khäsh, Iran ... 40 E2 28 15N 61 15 E
Vasilevichi, Belarus ... 17 B15 52 15N 29 50 E
Vasilkov = Vasylkiv, Ukraine 17 C16 50 7N 30 15 E
Vaslui, Romania ... 17 E14 46 38N 27 42 E
Vassar, Canada ... 73 D9 49 10N 95 55W
Vassar, U.S.A. ... 76 D4 43 22N 83 35W
Västerås, Sweden ... 9 G17 59 37N 16 38 E
Västerbotten, Sweden ... 8 D18 64 36N 20 4 E
Västerdalälven ~, Sweden 9 F16 60 30N 14 7 E
Västervik, Sweden ... 9 H17 57 43N 16 33 E
Västmanland, Sweden ... 9 G16 59 45N 16 20 E
Vasto, Italy ... 20 C6 42 8N 14 40 E
Vasylkiv, Ukraine ... 17 C16 50 7N 30 15 E
Vatersay, U.K. ... 12 E1 56 55N 7 32W
Vatican City ■, Europe .. 20 D5 41 54N 12 27 E
Vatili, Cyprus ... 23 D12 35 6N 33 40 E
Vatnajökull, Iceland ... 8 D5 64 30N 16 48W
Vatoa, Fiji ... 59 D9 19 50S 178 13W
Vatólakkos, Greece ... 23 D5 35 27N 23 53 E
Vatoloha, Madag. ... 57 B8 17 52S 47 48 E
Vatomandry, Madag. ... 57 B8 19 20S 48 59 E
Vatra-Dornei, Romania ... 17 E13 47 22N 25 22 E
Vatrak ~, India ... 42 H5 23 9N 73 2 E
Vättern, Sweden ... 9 G16 58 25N 14 30 E
Vaughn, Mont., U.S.A. ... 82 C8 47 33N 111 33W
Vaughn, N. Mex., U.S.A. . 83 J11 34 36N 105 13W
Vaujours, Canada ... 70 A5 55 27N 74 15W
Vaupés = Uaupés ~,
Brazil ... 92 C5 0 2N 67 16W
Vaupes ☐, Colombia ... 92 C4 1 0N 71 0W
Vauxhall, Canada ... 72 C6 50 5N 112 9W
Vav, India ... 42 G4 24 22N 71 31 E
Vava'u, Tonga ... 59 D12 18 36S 174 0W
Vawkavysk, Belarus ... 17 B13 53 9N 24 30 E
Växjö, Sweden ... 9 H16 56 52N 14 50 E
Vaygach, Ostrov, Russia . 26 C7 70 0N 60 0 E
Váyia, Ákra, Greece ... 23 C10 36 15N 28 11 E

Vechte ~, Neths. ... 15 B6 52 34N 6 6 E
Vedea ~, Romania ... 17 G13 43 42N 25 41 E
Vedia, Argentina ... 94 C3 34 30S 61 31W
Veendam, Neths. ... 15 A6 53 5N 6 52 E
Veenendaal, Neths. ... 15 B5 52 2N 5 34 E
Vefsna ~, Norway ... 8 D15 65 48N 13 10 E
Vega, Norway ... 8 D14 65 40N 11 55 E
Vega, U.S.A. ... 81 H3 35 15N 102 26W
Vegreville, Canada ... 72 C6 53 30N 112 5W
Vejer de la Frontera, Spain 19 D3 36 15N 5 59W
Vejle, Denmark ... 9 J13 55 43N 9 30 E
Velas, C., Costa Rica ... 88 D2 10 21N 85 52W
Velasco, Sierra de,
Argentina ... 94 B2 29 20S 67 10W
Velddrif, S. Africa ... 56 E2 32 42S 18 11 E
Velebit Planina, Croatia .. 16 F8 44 50N 15 20 E
Veles, Macedonia ... 21 D9 41 46N 21 47 E
Vélez-Málaga, Spain ... 19 D3 36 48N 4 5W
Vélez Rubio, Spain ... 19 D4 37 41N 2 5W
Velhas ~, Brazil ... 93 G10 17 13S 44 49W
Velika Kapela, Croatia ... 16 F8 45 10N 15 5 E
Velikaya ~, Russia ... 24 C4 57 48N 28 10 E
Velikaya Kema, Russia ... 30 B8 45 30N 137 12 E
Veliki Ustyug, Russia ... 24 B8 60 47N 46 20 E
Velikiye Luki, Russia ... 24 C5 56 25N 30 32 E
Veliko Türnovo, Bulgaria . 21 C11 43 5N 25 41 E
Velikonda Range, India ... 40 M11 14 45N 79 10 E
Velletri, Italy ... 20 D5 41 41N 12 47 E
Vellore, India ... 40 N11 12 57N 79 10 E
Velsk, Russia ... 24 B7 61 10N 42 5 E
Velva, U.S.A. ... 80 A4 48 4N 100 56W
Venado Tuerto, Argentina . 94 C3 33 50S 62 0W
Vendée ☐, France ... 18 C3 46 50N 1 35W
Vendôme, France ... 18 C4 47 47N 1 3 E
Venézia, Italy ... 20 B5 45 27N 12 21 E
Venézia, G. di, Italy ... 20 B5 45 15N 13 0 E
Venezuela ■, S. Amer. ... 92 B5 8 0N 66 0W
Venezuela, G. de, Venezuela 92 A4 11 30N 71 0W
Vengurla, India ... 40 M8 15 53N 73 45 E
Venice = Venézia, Italy ... 20 B5 45 27N 12 21 E
Venice, U.S.A. ... 77 M4 27 6N 82 27W
Venkatapuram, India ... 41 K12 18 20N 80 30 E
Venlo, Neths. ... 15 C6 51 22N 6 11 E
Vennesla, Norway ... 9 G12 58 15N 7 59 E
Venray, Neths. ... 15 C6 51 31N 6 0 E
Ventana, Punta de la,
Mexico ... 86 C3 24 4N 109 48W
Ventana, Sa. de la,
Argentina ... 94 D3 38 0S 62 30W
Ventersburg, S. Africa ... 56 D4 28 7S 27 9 E
Venterstad, S. Africa ... 56 E4 30 47S 25 48 E
Ventnor, U.K. ... 11 G6 50 36N 1 12W
Ventotène, Italy ... 20 D5 40 47N 13 25 E
Ventoux, Mt., France ... 18 D6 44 10N 5 17 E
Ventspils, Latvia ... 9 H19 57 25N 21 32 E
Ventuari ~, Venezuela ... 92 C5 3 58N 67 2W
Ventucopa, U.S.A. ... 85 L7 34 50N 119 29W
Ventura, U.S.A. ... 85 L7 34 17N 119 18W
Venus B., Australia ... 63 F4 38 40S 145 42 E
Vera, Argentina ... 94 B3 29 30S 60 20W
Vera, Spain ... 19 D5 37 15N 1 51W
Veracruz, Mexico ... 87 D5 19 10N 96 10W
Veracruz ☐, Mexico ... 87 D5 19 0N 96 15W
Veraval, India ... 42 J4 20 53N 70 27 E
Verbánia, Italy ... 18 D8 45 56N 8 33 E
Vercelli, Italy ... 18 D8 45 19N 8 25 E
Verdalsøra, Norway ... 8 E14 63 48N 11 30 E
Verde ~, Argentina ... 96 E3 41 56S 65 5W
Verde ~, Goiás, Brazil ... 93 G8 1 1S 50 14W
Verde ~,
Mato Grosso do Sul,
Brazil ... 93 H8 21 25S 52 20W
Verde ~, Chihuahua,
Mexico ... 86 B3 26 29N 107 58W
Verde ~, Oaxaca, Mexico . 87 D5 15 59N 97 50W
Verde ~, Veracruz, Mexico 86 C4 21 10N 102 50W
Verde ~, Paraguay ... 94 A4 23 9S 57 37W
Verde ~, U.S.A. ... 74 D4 33 33N 111 40W
Verde, Cay, Bahamas ... 88 B4 23 0N 75 5W
Verden, Germany ... 16 B5 52 55N 9 14 E
Verdi, U.S.A. ... 84 F7 39 31N 119 59W
Verdun, France ... 18 B6 49 9N 5 24 E
Vereeniging, S. Africa ... 57 D4 26 38S 27 57 E
Verga, C., Guinea ... 50 F3 10 30N 14 10W
Vergara, Uruguay ... 95 C5 32 56S 53 57W
Vergemont Cr. ~,
Australia ... 62 C3 24 16S 143 16 E
Vergennes, U.S.A. ... 79 B11 44 10N 73 15W
Verín, Spain ... 19 B2 41 57N 7 27W
Verkhnedvinsk, Russia ... 27 C13 63 27N 120 18 E
Verkhniy Baskunchak,
Russia ... 25 E8 48 14N 46 44 E
Verkhoyansk, Russia ... 27 C14 67 35N 133 25 E
Verkhoyansk Ra. =
Verkhoyanskiy Khrebet,
Russia ... 27 C13 66 0N 129 0 E
Verkhoyanskiy Khrebet,
Russia ... 27 C13 66 0N 129 0 E
Vermilion, Canada ... 73 C6 53 20N 110 50W
Vermilion, U.S.A. ... 78 E2 41 25N 82 22W
Vermilion ~, Alta., Canada 73 C6 53 22N 110 51W
Vermilion ~, Qué., Canada 70 C5 47 38N 72 56W
Vermilion, B., U.S.A. ... 81 L9 29 45N 91 55W
Vermilion Bay, Canada ... 73 D10 49 51N 93 34W
Vermilion L., Canada ... 80 B8 47 53N 92 26W
Vermillion, U.S.A. ... 80 D6 42 47N 96 56W
Vermont ☐, U.S.A. ... 79 C12 44 0N 73 0W
Vernal, U.S.A. ... 82 F9 40 27N 109 32W
Vernalis, U.S.A. ... 84 H5 37 36N 121 17W
Verner, Canada ... 70 C3 46 25N 80 8W
Verneukpan, S. Africa ... 56 E3 30 0S 21 0 E
Vernon, Canada ... 72 C5 50 20N 119 15W
Vernon, U.S.A. ... 81 H5 34 9N 99 17W
Vernonia, U.S.A. ... 84 E3 45 52N 123 11W
Vero Beach, U.S.A. ... 77 M5 27 38N 80 24W
Véroia, Greece ... 21 D10 40 34N 22 12 E
Verona, Canada ... 79 B8 44 29N 76 42W
Verona, Italy ... 18 D9 45 27N 10 59 E
Verona, U.S.A. ... 80 D10 42 59N 89 32W
Versailles, France ... 18 B5 48 48N 2 8 E
Vert, C., Senegal ... 50 F2 14 45N 17 30W
Verulam, S. Africa ... 57 D5 29 38S 31 2 E
Verviers, Belgium ... 15 D5 50 37N 5 52 E
Veselovskoye Vdkhr., Russia 25 E7 46 58N 41 25 E
Vesoul, France ... 18 C7 47 40N 6 11 E
Vesterålen, Norway ... 8 B16 68 45N 15 0 E

Name	Ref	Lat	Long
Vestfjorden, *Norway*	8 C15	67 55N	14 0 E
Vestmannaeyjar, *Iceland*	8 E3	63 27N	20 15W
Vestspitsbergen, *Svalbard*	4 B8	78 40N	17 0 E
Vestvågøy, *Norway*	8 B15	68 18N	13 50 E
Vesuvio, *Italy*	20 D6	40 49N	14 26 E
Vesuvius, Mt. = Vesuvio, *Italy*	20 D6	40 49N	14 26 E
Veszprém, *Hungary*	17 E9	47 8N	17 57 E
Vetlanda, *Sweden*	9 H16	57 24N	15 3 E
Vetlugu →, *Russia*	24 C8	56 36N	46 4 E
Vettore, Mte., *Italy*	20 C5	42 49N	13 16 E
Veurne, *Belgium*	15 C2	51 5N	2 40 E
Veys, *Iran*	45 D6	31 30N	49 0 E
Vezhen, *Bulgaria*	21 C11	42 50N	24 20 E
Vi Thanh, *Vietnam*	39 H5	9 42N	105 26 E
Viacha, *Bolivia*	92 G5	16 39S	68 18W
Viamão, *Brazil*	95 C5	30 5S	51 0W
Viana, *Brazil*	93 D10	3 13S	44 55W
Viana do Alentejo, *Portugal*	19 C2	38 17N	7 59W
Viana do Castelo, *Portugal*	19 B1	41 42N	8 50W
Vianden, *Lux.*	15 E6	49 56N	6 12 E
Vianópolis, *Brazil*	93 G9	16 40S	48 35W
Viaréggio, *Italy*	20 C4	43 52N	10 14 E
Vibo Valéntia, *Italy*	20 E7	38 40N	16 6 E
Viborg, *Denmark*	9 H13	56 27N	9 23 E
Vic, *Spain*	19 B7	41 58N	2 19 E
Vicenza, *Italy*	20 B4	45 33N	11 33 E
Vich = Vic, *Spain*	19 B7	41 58N	2 19 E
Vichada →, *Colombia*	92 C5	4 55N	67 50W
Vichy, *France*	18 C5	46 9N	3 26 E
Vicksburg, Ariz., *U.S.A.*	85 M13	33 45N	113 45W
Vicksburg, Miss., *U.S.A.*	81 J9	32 21N	90 53W
Victor, *India*	42 J4	21 0N	71 30 E
Victor, *U.S.A.*	78 D7	42 58N	77 24W
Victor Harbor, *Australia*	62 F2	35 30S	138 37 E
Victoria = Labuan, *Malaysia*	36 C5	5 20N	115 14 E
Victoria, *Argentina*	94 C3	32 40S	60 10W
Victoria, *Canada*	72 D4	48 30N	123 25W
Victoria, *Chile*	96 D2	38 13S	72 20W
Victoria, *Malta*	23 C1	36 2N	14 14 E
Victoria, Kans., *U.S.A.*	80 F5	38 52N	99 9W
Victoria, Tex., *U.S.A.*	81 L6	28 48N	97 0W
Victoria □, *Australia*	63 F3	37 0S	144 0 E
Victoria →, *Australia*	60 C4	15 10S	129 40 E
Victoria, Grand L., *Canada*	70 C4	47 31N	77 30W
Victoria, L., *Africa*	54 C3	1 0S	33 0 E
Victoria, L., *Australia*	63 E3	33 57S	141 15 E
Victoria Beach, *Canada*	73 C9	50 40N	96 35W
Victoria de Durango = Durango, *Mexico*	86 C4	24 3N	104 39W
Victoria de las Tunas, *Cuba*	88 B4	20 58N	76 59W
Victoria Falls, *Zimbabwe*	55 F2	17 58S	25 52 E
Victoria Harbour, *Canada*	78 B5	44 45N	79 45W
Victoria I., *Canada*	68 A8	71 0N	111 0W
Victoria L., *Canada*	71 C8	48 20N	57 27W
Victoria Ld., *Antarctica*	5 D11	75 0S	160 0 E
Victoria Nile →, *Uganda*	54 B3	2 14N	31 26 E
Victoria River, *Australia*	60 C5	16 25S	131 0 E
Victoria Str., *Canada*	68 B9	69 30N	100 0W
Victoria Taungdeik, *Burma*	41 J18	21 15N	93 55 E
Victoria West, *S. Africa*	56 E3	31 25S	23 4 E
Victoriaville, *Canada*	71 C5	46 4N	71 56W
Victorica, *Argentina*	94 D2	36 20S	65 30W
Victorville, *U.S.A.*	85 L9	34 32N	117 18W
Vicuña, *Chile*	94 C1	30 0S	70 50W
Vicuña Mackenna, *Argentina*	94 C3	33 53S	64 25W
Vidal, *U.S.A.*	85 L12	34 7N	114 31W
Vidal Junction, *U.S.A.*	85 L12	34 11N	114 34W
Vidalia, *U.S.A.*	77 J4	32 13N	82 25W
Vídho, *Greece*	23 A3	39 38N	19 55 E
Vidin, *Bulgaria*	21 C10	43 59N	22 50 E
Vidisha, *India*	42 H7	23 28N	77 53 E
Vidzy, *Belarus*	9 J22	55 23N	26 37 E
Viedma, *Argentina*	96 E4	40 50S	63 0W
Viedma, L., *Argentina*	96 F2	49 30S	72 30W
Vielsalm, *Belgium*	15 D5	50 17N	5 54 E
Vienna = Wien, *Austria*	16 D9	48 12N	16 22 E
Vienna, Ill., *U.S.A.*	81 G10	37 25N	88 54W
Vienna, Mo., *U.S.A.*	80 F9	38 11N	91 57W
Vienne, *France*	18 D6	45 31N	4 53 E
Vienne →, *France*	18 C4	47 13N	0 5 E
Vientiane, *Laos*	38 D4	17 58N	102 36 E
Vientos, Paso de los, *Caribbean*	89 C5	20 0N	74 0W
Vierzon, *France*	18 C5	47 13N	2 5 E
Vietnam ■, *Asia*	38 C6	19 0N	106 0 E
Vigan, *Phil.*	37 A6	17 35N	120 28 E
Vigévano, *Italy*	18 D8	45 19N	8 51 E
Vigia, *Brazil*	93 D9	0 50S	48 5W
Vigia Chico, *Mexico*	87 D7	19 46N	87 35W
Víglas, Ákra, *Greece*	23 D9	35 54N	27 51 E
Vigo, *Spain*	19 A1	42 12N	8 41W
Vihowa, *Pakistan*	42 D4	31 8N	70 30 E
Vihowa →, *Pakistan*	42 D4	31 8N	70 41 E
Vijayawada, *India*	41 L12	16 31N	80 39 E
Vik, *Iceland*	8 E4	63 25N	19 1W
Vikeke, *Indonesia*	37 F7	8 52S	126 23 E
Viking, *Canada*	72 C6	53 7N	111 50W
Vikna, *Norway*	8 D14	64 55N	10 58 E
Vila da Maganja, *Mozam.*	55 F4	17 18S	37 30 E
Vila de João Belo = Xai-Xai, *Mozam.*	57 D5	25 6S	33 31 E
Vila do Bispo, *Portugal*	19 D1	37 5N	8 53W
Vila do Chibuto, *Mozam.*	57 C5	24 40S	33 33 E
Vila Franca de Xira, *Portugal*	19 C1	38 57N	8 59W
Vila Gamito, *Mozam.*	55 E3	14 12S	33 0 E
Vila Gomes da Costa, *Mozam.*	57 C5	24 20S	33 37 E
Vila Machado, *Mozam.*	55 F3	19 15S	34 14 E
Vila Mouzinho, *Mozam.*	55 E3	14 48S	34 25 E
Vila Nova de Gaia, *Portugal*	19 B1	41 8N	8 37W
Vila Real, *Portugal*	19 B2	41 17N	7 48W
Vila-real de los Infantes, *Spain*	19 C5	39 55N	0 3W
Vila Real de Santo António, *Portugal*	19 D2	37 10N	7 28W
Vila Vasco da Gama, *Mozam.*	55 E3	14 54S	32 14 E
Vila Velha, *Brazil*	95 A7	20 20S	40 17W
Vilagarcía de Arousa, *Spain*	19 A1	42 34N	8 46W
Vilaine →, *France*	18 C2	47 30N	2 27W
Vilanandro, Tanjona, *Madag.*	57 B7	16 11S	44 27 E
Vilanculos, *Mozam.*	57 C6	22 1S	35 17 E
Vilanova i la Geltrú, *Spain*	19 B6	41 13N	1 40 E
Vileyka, *Belarus*	17 A14	54 30N	26 53 E

Name	Ref	Lat	Long
Vilhelmina, *Sweden*	8 D17	64 35N	16 39 E
Vilhena, *Brazil*	92 F6	12 40S	60 5W
Viliga, *Russia*	27 C16	61 36N	156 56 E
Viliya →, *Lithuania*	9 J21	55 8N	24 16 E
Viljandi, *Estonia*	9 G21	58 28N	25 30 E
Vilkovo = Vylkove, *Ukraine*	17 F15	45 28N	29 32 E
Villa Abecia, *Bolivia*	94 A2	21 0S	68 18W
Villa Ahumada, *Mexico*	86 A3	30 38N	106 30W
Villa Ana, *Argentina*	94 B4	28 28S	59 40W
Villa Ángela, *Argentina*	94 B3	27 34S	60 45W
Villa Bella, *Bolivia*	92 F5	10 25S	65 22W
Villa Bens = Tarfaya, *Morocco*	50 C3	27 55N	12 55W
Villa Cañás, *Argentina*	94 C3	34 0S	61 35W
Villa Cisneros = Dakhla, *W. Sahara*	50 D2	23 50N	15 53W
Villa Colón, *Argentina*	94 C2	31 38S	68 20W
Villa Constitución, *Argentina*	94 C3	33 15S	60 20W
Villa de María, *Argentina*	94 B3	29 55S	63 43W
Villa Dolores, *Argentina*	94 C2	31 58S	65 15W
Villa Frontera, *Mexico*	86 B4	26 56N	101 27W
Villa Guillermina, *Argentina*	94 B4	28 15S	59 29W
Villa Hayes, *Paraguay*	94 B4	25 5S	57 20W
Villa Iris, *Argentina*	94 D3	38 12S	63 12W
Villa Juárez, *Mexico*	86 B4	27 37N	100 44W
Villa María, *Argentina*	94 C3	32 20S	63 10W
Villa Mazán, *Argentina*	94 B2	28 40S	66 30W
Villa Montes, *Bolivia*	94 A3	21 10S	63 30W
Villa Ocampo, *Argentina*	94 B4	28 30S	59 20W
Villa Ocampo, *Mexico*	86 B3	26 29N	105 30W
Villa Ojo de Agua, *Argentina*	94 B3	29 30S	63 44W
Villa San José, *Argentina*	94 C4	32 12S	58 15W
Villa San Martín, *Argentina*	94 B3	28 15S	64 9W
Villa Unión, *Mexico*	86 C3	23 12N	106 14W
Villacarlos, *Spain*	22 B11	39 53N	4 17 E
Villacarrillo, *Spain*	19 C4	38 7N	3 3W
Villach, *Austria*	16 E7	46 37N	13 51 E
Villafranca de los Caballeros, *Spain*	22 B10	39 34N	3 25 E
Villagrán, *Mexico*	87 C5	24 29N	99 29W
Villaguay, *Argentina*	94 C4	32 0S	59 0W
Villahermosa, *Mexico*	87 D6	17 59N	92 55W
Villajoyosa, *Spain*	19 C5	38 30N	0 12W
Villalba, *Spain*	19 A2	43 26N	7 40W
Villanueva, *U.S.A.*	81 H2	35 16N	105 22W
Villanueva de la Serena, *Spain*	19 C3	38 59N	5 50W
Villanueva y Geltrú = Vilanova i la Geltrú, *Spain*	19 B6	41 13N	1 40 E
Villarreal = Vila-real de los Infantes, *Spain*	19 C5	39 55N	0 3W
Villarrica, *Chile*	96 D2	39 15S	72 15W
Villarrica, *Paraguay*	94 B4	25 40S	56 30W
Villarrobledo, *Spain*	19 C4	39 18N	2 36W
Villavicencio, *Argentina*	94 C2	32 28S	69 0W
Villavicencio, *Colombia*	92 C4	4 9N	73 37W
Villaviciosa, *Spain*	19 A3	43 32N	5 27W
Villazón, *Bolivia*	94 A2	22 0S	65 35W
Ville-Marie, *Canada*	70 C4	47 20N	79 30W
Ville Platte, *U.S.A.*	81 K8	30 41N	92 17W
Villena, *Spain*	19 C5	38 39N	0 52W
Villeneuve-d'Ascq, *France*	18 A5	50 38N	3 9 E
Villeneuve-sur-Lot, *France*	18 D4	44 24N	0 42 E
Villiers, *S. Africa*	57 D4	27 2S	28 36 E
Villingen-Schwenningen, *Germany*	16 D5	48 3N	8 26 E
Vilna, *Canada*	72 C6	54 7N	111 55W
Vilnius, *Lithuania*	9 J21	54 38N	25 19 E
Vilvoorde, *Belgium*	15 D4	50 56N	4 26 E
Vilyuy →, *Russia*	27 C13	64 24N	126 26 E
Vilyuysk, *Russia*	27 C13	63 40N	121 35 E
Viña del Mar, *Chile*	94 C1	33 0S	71 30W
Vinarós, *Spain*	19 B6	40 30N	0 27 E
Vincennes, *U.S.A.*	76 F2	38 41N	87 32W
Vincent, *U.S.A.*	85 L8	34 33N	118 11W
Vinchina, *Argentina*	94 B2	28 45S	68 15W
Vindelälven →, *Sweden*	8 E18	63 55N	19 50 E
Vindeln, *Sweden*	8 D18	64 12N	19 43 E
Vindhya Ra., *India*	42 H7	22 50N	77 0 E
Vineland, *U.S.A.*	76 F8	39 29N	75 2W
Vinh, *Vietnam*	38 C5	18 45N	105 38 E
Vinh Linh, *Vietnam*	38 D6	17 4N	107 2 E
Vinh Long, *Vietnam*	39 G5	10 16N	105 57 E
Vinita, *U.S.A.*	81 G7	36 39N	95 9W
Vinkovci, *Croatia*	21 B8	45 19N	18 48 E
Vinnitsa = Vinnytsya, *Ukraine*	17 D15	49 15N	28 30 E
Vinnytsya, *Ukraine*	17 D15	49 15N	28 30 E
Vinton, Calif., *U.S.A.*	84 F6	39 48N	120 10W
Vinton, Iowa, *U.S.A.*	80 D8	42 10N	92 1W
Vinton, La., *U.S.A.*	81 K8	30 11N	93 35W
Virac, *Phil.*	37 B6	13 30N	124 20 E
Virachei, *Cambodia*	38 F6	13 59N	106 49 E
Virago Sd., *Canada*	72 C2	54 0N	132 30W
Viramgam, *India*	42 H5	23 5N	72 0 E
Viranşehir, *Turkey*	44 B3	37 13N	39 45 E
Virawah, *Pakistan*	42 G4	24 31N	70 46 E
Virden, *Canada*	73 D8	49 50N	100 56W
Vire, *France*	18 B3	48 50N	0 53W
Vírgenes, C., *Argentina*	96 G3	52 19S	68 21W
Virgin →, *U.S.A.*	83 H6	36 28N	114 21W
Virgin Gorda, *Virgin Is.*	89 C7	18 30N	64 26W
Virgin Is. (British) ■, *W. Indies*	89 C7	18 30N	64 30W
Virgin Is. (U.S.) ■, *W. Indies*	89 C7	18 20N	65 0W
Virginia, *S. Africa*	56 D4	28 8S	26 55 E
Virginia, *U.S.A.*	80 B8	47 31N	92 32W
Virginia □, *U.S.A.*	76 G7	37 30N	78 45W
Virginia Beach, *U.S.A.*	76 G8	36 51N	75 59W
Virginia City, Mont., *U.S.A.*	82 D8	45 18N	111 56W
Virginia City, Nev., *U.S.A.*	84 F7	39 19N	119 39W
Virginia Falls, *Canada*	72 A3	61 38N	125 42W
Virginiatown, *Canada*	70 C4	48 9N	79 36W
Viroqua, *U.S.A.*	80 D9	43 34N	90 53W
Virovitica, *Croatia*	20 B7	45 51N	17 21 E
Virpur, *India*	42 J4	21 51N	70 42 E
Virton, *Belgium*	15 E5	49 35N	5 32 E
Virudunagar, *India*	40 Q10	9 30N	77 58 E
Vis, *Croatia*	20 C7	43 4N	16 10 E
Visalia, *U.S.A.*	84 J7	36 20N	119 18W
Visayan Sea, *Phil.*	37 B6	11 30N	123 30 E
Visby, *Sweden*	9 H18	57 37N	18 18 E
Viscount Melville Sd., *Canada*	4 B2	74 10N	108 0W
Visé, *Belgium*	15 D5	50 44N	5 41 E

Name	Ref	Lat	Long
Višegrad, *Bos.-H.*	21 C8	43 47N	19 17 E
Viseu, *Brazil*	93 D9	1 10S	46 5W
Viseu, *Portugal*	19 B2	40 40N	7 55W
Vishakhapatnam, *India*	41 L13	17 45N	83 20 E
Visnagar, *India*	42 H5	23 45N	72 32 E
Viso, Mte., *Italy*	18 D7	44 38N	7 5 E
Visokoi I., *Antarctica*	5 B1	56 43S	27 15W
Vista, *U.S.A.*	85 M9	33 12N	117 14W
Vistula = Wisła →, *Poland*	17 A10	54 22N	18 55 E
Vitebsk = Vitsyebsk, *Belarus*	24 C5	55 10N	30 15 E
Viterbo, *Italy*	20 C5	42 25N	12 6 E
Viti Levu, *Fiji*	59 C7	17 30S	177 30 E
Vitigudino, *Spain*	19 B2	41 1N	6 26W
Vitim, *Russia*	27 D12	59 28N	112 35 E
Vitim →, *Russia*	27 D12	59 26N	112 34 E
Vitória, *Brazil*	93 H10	20 20S	40 22W
Vitória da Conquista, *Brazil*	93 F10	14 51S	40 51W
Vitória de São Antão, *Brazil*	93 E11	8 10S	35 20W
Vitoria-Gasteiz, *Spain*	19 A4	42 50N	2 41W
Vitsyebsk, *Belarus*	24 C5	55 10N	30 15 E
Vittória, *Italy*	20 F6	36 57N	14 32 E
Vittório Véneto, *Italy*	20 B5	45 59N	12 18 E
Viveiro, *Spain*	19 A2	43 39N	7 38W
Vivian, *U.S.A.*	81 J8	32 53N	93 59W
Vizcaíno, Desierto de, *Mexico*	86 B2	27 40N	113 50W
Vizcaíno, Sierra, *Mexico*	86 B2	27 30N	114 0W
Vize, *Turkey*	21 D12	41 34N	27 45 E
Vizianagaram, *India*	41 K13	18 6N	83 30 E
Vjosa →, *Albania*	21 D8	40 37N	19 24 E
Vlaardingen, *Neths.*	15 C4	51 55N	4 21 E
Vladikavkaz, *Russia*	25 F7	43 0N	44 35 E
Vladimir, *Russia*	24 C7	56 15N	40 30 E
Vladimir Volynskiy = Volodymyr-Volynskyy, *Ukraine*	17 C13	50 50N	24 18 E
Vladivostok, *Russia*	27 E14	43 10N	131 53 E
Vlieland, *Neths.*	15 A4	53 16N	4 55 E
Vlissingen, *Neths.*	15 C3	51 26N	3 34 E
Vlóra, *Albania*	21 D8	40 32N	19 28 E
Vltava →, *Czech Rep.*	16 D8	50 21N	14 30 E
Vo Dat, *Vietnam*	39 G6	11 9N	107 31 E
Voe, *U.K.*	12 A7	60 21N	1 16W
Vogelkop = Doberai, Jazirah, *Indonesia*	37 E8	1 25S	133 0 E
Vogelsberg, *Germany*	16 C5	50 31N	9 12 E
Voghera, *Italy*	18 D8	44 59N	9 1 E
Vohibinany, *Madag.*	57 B8	18 49S	49 4 E
Vohimarina = Iharana, *Madag.*	57 A9	13 25S	50 0 E
Vohimena, Tanjon' i, *Madag.*	57 D8	25 36S	45 8 E
Vohipeno, *Madag.*	57 C8	22 22S	47 51 E
Voi, *Kenya*	54 C4	3 25S	38 32 E
Voiron, *France*	18 D6	45 22N	5 35 E
Voisey B., *Canada*	71 A7	56 15N	61 50W
Vojmsjön, *Sweden*	8 D17	64 55N	16 40 E
Vojvodina □, *Serbia, Yug.*	21 B9	45 20N	20 0 E
Volborg, *U.S.A.*	80 C2	45 51N	105 41W
Volcano Is. = Kazan-Rettō, *Pac. Oc.*	64 E6	25 0N	141 0 E
Volda, *Norway*	9 E12	62 9N	6 5 E
Volga →, *Russia*	25 E8	46 0N	48 30 E
Volga Hts. = Privolzhskaya Vozvyshennost, *Russia*	25 D8	51 0N	46 0 E
Volgodonsk, *Russia*	25 E7	47 33N	42 5 E
Volgograd, *Russia*	25 E7	48 40N	44 25 E
Volgogradskoye Vdkhr., *Russia*	25 E8	50 0N	45 20 E
Volkhov →, *Russia*	24 B5	60 8N	32 20 E
Volkovysk = Vawkavysk, *Belarus*	17 B13	53 9N	24 30 E
Volksrust, *S. Africa*	57 D4	27 24S	29 53 E
Volochanka, *Russia*	27 B10	71 0N	94 28 E
Volodymyr-Volynskyy, *Ukraine*	17 C13	50 50N	24 18 E
Vologda, *Russia*	24 C6	59 10N	39 45 E
Vólos, *Greece*	21 E10	39 24N	22 59 E
Volovets, *Ukraine*	17 D12	48 43N	23 11 E
Volozhin = Valozhyn, *Belarus*	17 A14	54 3N	26 30 E
Volsk, *Russia*	24 D8	52 5N	47 22 E
Volta →, *Ghana*	48 F4	5 46N	0 41 E
Volta, L., *Ghana*	50 G6	7 30N	0 0 E
Volta Redonda, *Brazil*	95 A7	22 31S	44 5W
Voltaire, C., *Australia*	60 B4	14 16S	125 35 E
Volterra, *Italy*	20 C4	43 24N	10 51 E
Volturno →, *Italy*	20 D5	41 1N	13 55 E
Volzhskiy, *Russia*	25 E7	48 56N	44 46 E
Vondrozo, *Madag.*	57 C8	22 49S	47 20 E
Vopnafjörður, *Iceland*	8 D6	65 45N	14 50W
Vóriai Sporádhes, *Greece*	21 E10	39 15N	23 30 E
Vorkuta, *Russia*	24 A11	67 48N	64 20 E
Vormsi, *Estonia*	9 G20	59 1N	23 13 E
Voronezh, *Russia*	25 D6	51 40N	39 10 E
Voroshilovgrad = Luhansk, *Ukraine*	25 E6	48 38N	39 15 E
Voroshilovsk = Alchevsk, *Ukraine*	25 E6	48 30N	38 45 E
Võrts Järv, *Estonia*	9 G22	58 16N	26 3 E
Võru, *Estonia*	9 H22	57 48N	26 54 E
Vosges, *France*	18 B7	48 20N	7 10 E
Voss, *Norway*	9 F12	60 38N	6 26 E
Vostok I., *Kiribati*	65 J12	10 5S	152 23W
Votkinsk, *Russia*	24 C9	57 0N	53 55 E
Votkinskoye Vdkhr., *Russia*	24 C10	57 22N	55 12 E
Votsuri-Shima, *Japan*	31 M1	25 45N	123 29 E
Vouga →, *Portugal*	19 B1	40 41N	8 40W
Voúxa, Ákra, *Greece*	23 D5	35 37N	23 32 E
Vozhe, Ozero, *Russia*	24 B6	60 45N	39 0 E
Voznesenye, *Russia*	24 B6	61 0N	35 28 E
Vrangelya, Ostrov, *Russia*	27 B19	71 0N	180 0 E
Vranje, *Serbia, Yug.*	21 C9	42 34N	21 54 E
Vratsa, *Bulgaria*	21 C10	43 15N	23 30 E
Vrbas →, *Bos.-H.*	20 B7	45 8N	17 29 E
Vrede, *S. Africa*	57 D4	27 24S	29 6 E
Vredefort, *S. Africa*	56 D4	27 0S	27 22 E
Vredenburg, *S. Africa*	56 E2	32 56S	18 0 E
Vredendal, *S. Africa*	56 E2	31 41S	18 35 E
Vrindavan, *India*	42 F7	27 37N	77 40 E
Vríses, *Greece*	23 D6	35 23N	24 13 E
Vršac, *Serbia, Yug.*	21 B9	45 8N	21 0 E
Vryburg, *S. Africa*	56 D3	26 55S	24 45 E
Vryheid, *S. Africa*	57 D5	27 45S	30 47 E
Vu Liet, *Vietnam*	38 C5	18 43N	105 23 E

Name	Ref	Lat	Long
Vukovar, *Croatia*	21 B8	45 21N	18 59 E
Vulcan, *Canada*	72 C6	50 25N	113 15W
Vulcan, *Romania*	17 F12	45 23N	23 17 E
Vulcaneşti, *Moldova*	17 F15	45 41N	28 18 E
Vulcano, *Italy*	20 E6	38 24N	14 58 E
Vulkaneshty = Vulcaneşti, *Moldova*	17 F15	45 41N	28 18 E
Vunduzi →, *Mozam.*	55 F3	18 56S	34 1 E
Vung Tau, *Vietnam*	39 G6	10 21N	107 4 E
Vyatka = Kirov, *Russia*	24 C8	58 35N	49 40 E
Vyatka →, *Russia*	24 C9	55 37N	51 28 E
Vyatskiye Polyany, *Russia*	24 C9	56 14N	51 5 E
Vyazemskiy, *Russia*	27 E14	47 32N	134 45 E
Vyazma, *Russia*	24 C5	55 10N	34 15 E
Vyborg, *Russia*	24 B4	60 43N	28 47 E
Vychegda →, *Russia*	24 B8	61 18N	46 36 E
Vychodné Beskydy, *Europe*	17 D11	49 20N	22 0 E
Vyg-ozero, *Russia*	24 B5	63 47N	34 29 E
Vylkove, *Ukraine*	17 F15	45 28N	29 32 E
Vynohradiv, *Ukraine*	17 D12	48 9N	23 2 E
Vyrnwy, L., *U.K.*	10 E4	52 48N	3 31W
Vyshniy Volochek, *Russia*	24 C5	57 30N	34 30 E
Vyškov, *Czech Rep.*	17 D9	49 17N	17 0 E
Vytegra, *Russia*	24 B6	61 0N	36 27 E

W

Name	Ref	Lat	Long
W.A.C. Bennett Dam, *Canada*	72 B4	56 2N	122 6W
Waal →, *Neths.*	15 C5	51 37N	5 0 E
Waalwijk, *Neths.*	15 C5	51 42N	5 4 E
Wabana, *Canada*	71 C9	47 40N	53 0W
Wabasca →, *Canada*	72 B5	58 22N	115 20W
Wabasca-Desmarais, *Canada*	72 B6	55 57N	113 56W
Wabash, *U.S.A.*	76 E3	40 48N	85 49W
Wabash →, *U.S.A.*	76 G1	37 48N	88 2W
Wabigoon L., *Canada*	73 D10	49 44N	92 44W
Wabowden, *Canada*	73 C9	54 55N	98 38W
Wabuk Pt., *Canada*	70 A2	55 20N	85 5W
Wabush, *Canada*	71 B6	52 55N	66 52W
Waco, *U.S.A.*	81 K6	31 33N	97 9W
Waconichi, L., *Canada*	70 B5	50 8N	74 0W
Wad Hamid, *Sudan*	51 E12	16 30N	32 45 E
Wâd Medanî, *Sudan*	51 F12	14 28N	33 30 E
Wad Thana, *Pakistan*	42 F2	27 22N	66 23 E
Wadai, *Africa*	48 E5	12 0N	19 0 E
Wadayama, *Japan*	31 G7	35 19N	134 52 E
Waddeneilanden, *Neths.*	15 A5	53 20N	5 10 E
Waddenzee, *Neths.*	15 A5	53 6N	5 10 E
Waddington, *U.S.A.*	79 B9	44 52N	75 12W
Waddington, Mt., *Canada*	72 C3	51 23N	125 15W
Waddy Pt., *Australia*	63 C5	24 58S	153 21 E
Wadebridge, *U.K.*	11 G3	50 31N	4 51W
Wadena, *Canada*	73 C8	51 57N	103 47W
Wadena, *U.S.A.*	80 B7	46 26N	95 8W
Wadeye, *Australia*	60 B4	14 28S	129 52 E
Wadhams, *Canada*	72 C3	51 30N	127 30W
Wâdi as Sîr, *Jordan*	47 D4	31 56N	35 49 E
Wadi Halfa, *Sudan*	51 D12	21 53N	31 19 E
Wadsworth, Nev., *U.S.A.*	82 G4	39 38N	119 17W
Wadsworth, Ohio, *U.S.A.*	78 E3	41 2N	81 44W
Waegwan, S. Korea	35 G15	35 59N	128 23 E
Wafangdian, *China*	35 E11	39 38N	121 58 E
Wafrah, *Si. Arabia*	44 D5	28 33N	47 56 E
Wageningen, *Neths.*	15 C5	51 58N	5 43 E
Wager B., *Canada*	69 B11	65 26N	88 40W
Wagga Wagga, *Australia*	63 F4	35 7S	147 24 E
Waghete, *Indonesia*	37 E9	4 10S	135 50 E
Wagin, *Australia*	61 F2	33 17S	117 25 E
Wagner, *U.S.A.*	80 D5	43 5N	98 18W
Wagon Mound, *U.S.A.*	81 G2	36 1N	104 42W
Wagoner, *U.S.A.*	81 H7	35 58N	95 22W
Wah, *Pakistan*	42 C5	33 45N	72 40 E
Wahai, *Indonesia*	37 E7	2 48S	129 35 E
Wahiawa, *U.S.A.*	74 H15	21 30N	158 2W
Wâhid, *Egypt*	47 E1	30 48N	32 21 E
Wahnai, *Afghan.*	42 C1	32 40N	65 50 E
Wahoo, *U.S.A.*	80 E6	41 13N	96 37W
Wahpeton, *U.S.A.*	80 B6	46 16N	96 36W
Wai, Koh, *Cambodia*	39 H4	9 55N	102 55 E
Waiau →, *N.Z.*	59 K4	42 47S	173 22 E
Waibeem, *Indonesia*	37 E8	0 30S	132 59 E
Waigeo, *Indonesia*	37 E8	0 20S	130 40 E
Waihi, *N.Z.*	59 G5	37 23S	175 52 E
Waihou →, *N.Z.*	59 G5	37 15S	175 40 E
Waika, *Dem. Rep. of the Congo*	54 C2	2 22S	25 42 E
Waikabubak, *Indonesia*	37 F5	9 45S	119 25 E
Waikari, *N.Z.*	59 K4	42 58S	172 41 E
Waikato →, *N.Z.*	59 G5	37 23S	174 43 E
Waikerie, *Australia*	63 E3	34 9S	140 0 E
Waikokopu, *N.Z.*	59 H6	39 3S	177 52 E
Waikouaiti, *N.Z.*	59 L3	45 36S	170 41 E
Wailuku, *U.S.A.*	74 H16	20 53N	156 30W
Waimakariri →, *N.Z.*	59 K4	43 24S	172 42 E
Waimate, *N.Z.*	59 L3	44 45S	171 3 E
Wainganga →, *India*	40 K11	18 50N	79 55 E
Waingapu, *Indonesia*	37 F6	9 35S	120 11 E
Waini →, *Guyana*	92 B7	8 20N	59 50W
Wainwright, *Canada*	73 C6	52 50N	110 50W
Waiouru, *N.Z.*	59 H5	39 28S	175 41 E
Waipara, *N.Z.*	59 K4	43 3S	172 46 E
Waipawa, *N.Z.*	59 H6	39 56S	176 38 E
Waipiro, *N.Z.*	59 H7	38 2S	178 22 E
Waipu, *N.Z.*	59 F5	35 59S	174 29 E
Waipukurau, *N.Z.*	59 J6	40 1S	176 33 E
Wairakei, *N.Z.*	59 H6	38 37S	176 6 E
Wairarapa, L., *N.Z.*	59 J5	41 14S	175 15 E
Wairoa, *N.Z.*	59 H6	39 3S	177 25 E
Waitaki →, *N.Z.*	59 L3	44 56S	171 7 E
Waitara, *N.Z.*	59 H5	38 59S	174 15 E
Waitsburg, *U.S.A.*	82 C4	46 16N	118 9W
Waiuku, *N.Z.*	59 G5	37 15S	174 45 E
Wajima, *Japan*	31 F8	37 30N	137 0 E
Wajir, *Kenya*	54 B5	1 42N	40 5 E
Wakasa, *Japan*	31 G7	35 20N	134 24 E
Wakasa-Wan, *Japan*	31 G7	35 40N	135 30 E
Wakatipu, L., *N.Z.*	59 L2	45 5S	168 33 E
Wakaw, *Canada*	73 C7	52 39N	105 44W
Wakayama, *Japan*	31 G7	34 15N	135 15 E
Wakayama □, *Japan*	31 H7	33 50N	135 30 E
Wake Forest, *U.S.A.*	77 H6	35 59N	78 30W

West Indies

West Indies, Cent. Amer.. . **89 D7** 15 0N 65 0W
West Jordan, U.S.A. **82 F8** 40 36N 111 56W
West Lorne, Canada **78 D3** 42 36N 81 36W
West Lothian □, U.K. **12 F5** 55 54N 3 36W
West Lunga →, Zambia . . . **55 E1** 13 6S 24 39 E
West Memphis, U.S.A. **81 H9** 35 9N 90 11W
West Midlands □, U.K. **11 E6** 52 26N 2 0W
West Mifflin, U.S.A. **78 F5** 40 22N 79 52W
West Milton, U.S.A. **78 E8** 41 1N 76 50W
West Monroe, U.S.A. **81 J8** 32 31N 92 9W
West Newton, U.S.A. **78 F5** 40 14N 79 46W
West Nicholson, Zimbabwe **55 G2** 21 2S 29 20 E
West Palm Beach, U.S.A. . **77 M5** 26 43N 80 3W
West Plains, U.S.A. **81 G9** 36 44N 91 51W
West Point, N.Y., U.S.A. . . **79 E11** 41 24N 73 58W
West Point, Nebr., U.S.A. . **80 E6** 41 51N 96 43W
West Point, Va., U.S.A. . . . **76 G7** 37 32N 76 48W
West Pt. = Ouest, Pte. de l',
　Canada **71 C7** 49 52N 64 40W
West Pt., Australia **63 F2** 35 1S 135 56 E
West Road →, Canada . . . **72 C4** 53 18N 122 53W
West Rutland, U.S.A. **75 B12** 43 38N 73 5W
West Schelde =
　Westerschelde →,
　Neths. **15 C3** 51 25N 3 25 E
West Seneca, U.S.A. **78 D6** 42 51N 78 48W
West Siberian Plain, Russia **28 C11** 62 0N 75 0 E
West Sussex □, U.K. **11 G7** 50 55N 0 30W
West-Terschelling, Neths. . **15 A5** 53 22N 5 13 E
West Valley City, U.S.A. . . **82 F8** 40 42N 111 57W
West Virginia □, U.S.A. . . . **76 F5** 38 45N 80 30W
West-Vlaanderen □,
　Belgium **15 D2** 51 0N 3 0 E
West Walker →, U.S.A. . . . **84 G7** 38 54N 119 9W
West Wyalong, Australia . . **63 E4** 33 56S 147 10 E
West Yellowstone, U.S.A. . **82 D8** 44 40N 111 6W
West Yorkshire □, U.K. . . . **10 D6** 53 45N 1 40W
Westall Pt., Australia **63 E1** 32 55S 134 4 E
Westbrook, U.S.A. **77 D10** 43 41N 70 22W
Westbury, Australia **62 G4** 41 30S 146 51 E
Westby, U.S.A. **80 A2** 48 52N 104 3W
Westend, U.S.A. **85 K9** 35 42N 117 24W
Westerland, Germany **9 J13** 54 54N 8 17 E
Westerly, U.S.A. **79 E13** 41 22N 71 50W
Western □, Kenya **54 B3** 0 30N 34 30 E
Western □, Uganda **54 B3** 1 45N 31 30 E
Western □, Zambia **55 F1** 15 15S 24 30 E
Western Australia □,
　Australia **61 E2** 25 0S 118 0 E
Western Cape □, S. Africa **56 E3** 34 0S 20 0 E
Western Dvina =
　Daugava →, Latvia **9 H21** 57 4N 24 3 E
Western Ghats, India **40 N9** 14 0N 75 0 E
Western Isles □, U.K. **12 D1** 57 30N 7 10W
Western Sahara ■, Africa . **50 D3** 25 0N 13 0W
Western Samoa ■ =
　Samoa ■, Pac. Oc. **59 B13** 14 0S 172 0W
Westerport, U.S.A. **76 F6** 39 29N 79 3W
Westerschelde →, Neths. . **15 C3** 51 25N 3 25 E
Westerwald, Germany **16 C4** 50 38N 7 56 E
Westfield, Mass., U.S.A. . . **79 D12** 42 7N 72 45W
Westfield, N.Y., U.S.A. . . . **78 D5** 42 20N 79 35W
Westfield, Pa., U.S.A. **78 E7** 41 55N 77 32W
Westhill, U.K. **12 D6** 57 9N 2 19W
Westhope, U.S.A. **80 A4** 48 55N 101 1W
Westland Bight, N.Z. **59 K3** 42 55S 170 5 E
Westlock, Canada **72 C6** 54 9N 113 55W
Westmar, Australia **63 D4** 27 55S 149 44 E
Westmeath □, Ireland . . . **13 C4** 53 33N 7 34W
Westminster, Canada **76 F7** 39 34N 76 59W
Westmont, U.S.A. **78 F6** 40 19N 78 58W
Westmorland, U.S.A. **85 M11** 33 2N 115 37W
Weston, Oreg., U.S.A. **82 D4** 45 49N 118 26W
Weston, W. Va., U.S.A. . . . **76 F5** 39 2N 80 28W
Weston I., Canada **70 B4** 52 33N 79 36W
Weston-super-Mare, U.K. . **11 F5** 51 21N 2 58W
Westover, U.S.A. **78 F6** 40 45N 78 40W
Westport, Canada **79 B8** 44 40N 76 25W
Westport, Ireland **13 C2** 53 48N 9 31W
Westport, N.Z. **59 J3** 41 46S 171 37 E
Westport, N.Y., U.S.A. . . . **79 B11** 44 11N 73 26W
Westport, Oreg., U.S.A. . . **84 D3** 46 8N 123 23W
Westport, Wash., U.S.A. . . **84 D2** 46 53N 124 6W
Westray, Canada **73 C8** 53 36N 101 24W
Westray, U.K. **12 B5** 59 18N 3 0W
Westree, Canada **70 C3** 47 26N 81 34W
Westville, U.S.A. **84 F6** 39 8N 120 42W
Westwood, U.S.A. **82 F3** 40 18N 121 0W
Wetar, Indonesia **37 F7** 7 30S 126 30 E
Wetaskiwin, Canada **72 C6** 52 55N 113 24W
Wete, Tanzania **52 F7** 5 4S 39 43 E
Wetherby, U.K. **10 D6** 53 56N 1 23W
Wethersfield, U.S.A. **79 E12** 41 42N 72 40W
Wetteren, Belgium **15 D3** 51 0N 3 53 E
Wetzlar, Germany **16 C5** 50 32N 8 31 E
Wewoka, U.S.A. **81 H6** 35 9N 96 30W
Wexford, Ireland **13 D5** 52 20N 6 28W
Wexford □, Ireland **13 D5** 52 20N 6 25W
Wexford Harbour, Ireland . **13 D5** 52 20N 6 25W
Weyburn, Canada **73 D8** 49 40N 103 50W
Weymouth, Canada **71 D6** 44 30N 66 1W
Weymouth, U.K. **11 G5** 50 37N 2 28W
Weymouth, U.S.A. **79 D14** 42 13N 70 58W
Weymouth, C., Australia . . **62 A3** 12 37S 143 27 E
Wha Ti, Canada **68 B8** 63 8N 117 16W
Whakatane, N.Z. **59 G6** 37 57S 177 1 E
Whale →, Canada **71 A6** 58 15N 67 40W
Whale Cove, Canada **73 A10** 62 11N 92 36W
Whales, B. of, Antarctica . **5 D12** 78 0S 165 0W
Whalsay, U.K. **12 A8** 60 22N 0 59W
Whangamomona, N.Z. . . . **59 H5** 39 8S 174 44 E
Whangarei, N.Z. **59 F5** 35 43S 174 21 E
Whangarei Harb., N.Z. . . . **59 F5** 35 45S 174 28 E
Wharfe →, U.K. **10 D6** 53 51N 1 9W
Wharfedale, U.K. **10 C5** 54 6N 2 1W
Wharton, N.J., U.S.A. **79 F10** 40 54N 74 35W
Wharton, Pa., U.S.A. **78 E6** 41 31N 78 1W
Wharton, Tex., U.S.A. **81 L6** 29 19N 96 6W
Wheatland, Calif., U.S.A. . **84 F5** 39 1N 121 25W
Wheatland, Wyo., U.S.A. . **80 D2** 42 3N 104 58W
Wheatley, Ont., Canada . . **78 D2** 42 6N 82 27W
Wheatley, Canada **78 D2** 42 6N 82 27W
Wheaton, Md., U.S.A. **76 F7** 39 3N 77 3W
Wheaton, Minn., U.S.A. . . **80 C6** 45 48N 96 30W
Wheelbarrow Pk., U.S.A. . . **84 H10** 37 26N 116 5W
Wheeler, Oreg., U.S.A. . . . **82 D2** 45 41N 123 53W
Wheeler, Tex., U.S.A. **81 H4** 35 27N 100 16W

Wheeler →, Canada **71 A6** 57 2N 67 13W
Wheeler L., U.S.A. **77 H2** 34 48N 87 23W
Wheeler Pk., N. Mex.,
　U.S.A. **83 H11** 36 34N 105 25W
Wheeler Pk., Nev., U.S.A. . **83 G6** 38 57N 114 15W
Wheeler Ridge, U.S.A. . . . **85 L8** 35 0N 118 57W
Wheeling, U.S.A. **78 F4** 40 4N 80 43W
Whernside, U.K. **10 C5** 54 14N 2 24W
Whiskey Jack L., Canada . **73 B8** 58 23N 101 55W
Whistleduck Cr. →,
　Australia **62 C2** 20 15S 135 18 E
Whistler, Canada **72 C4** 50 7N 122 58W
Whitby, Canada **78 C6** 43 52N 78 56W
Whitby, U.K. **10 C7** 54 29N 0 37W
White →, Ark., U.S.A. . . . **81 J9** 33 57N 91 5W
White →, Ind., U.S.A. **76 F2** 38 25N 87 45W
White →, S. Dak., U.S.A. . **80 D5** 43 42N 99 27W
White →, Tex., U.S.A. **81 J4** 33 14N 100 56W
White →, Utah, U.S.A. . . . **82 F9** 40 4N 109 41W
White →, Vt., U.S.A. **79 C12** 43 37N 72 20W
White →, Wash., U.S.A. . . **84 C4** 47 12N 122 15W
White, L., Australia **60 D4** 21 9S 128 56 E
White B., Canada **82 D5** 45 46N 116 18W
White Butte, U.S.A. **80 B3** 46 23N 103 18W
White City, U.S.A. **82 E2** 42 26N 122 51W
White Cliffs, Australia **63 E3** 30 50S 143 10 E
White Hall, U.S.A. **80 F9** 39 26N 90 24W
White Haven, U.S.A. **79 E9** 41 4N 75 47W
White I., N.Z. **59 G6** 37 30S 177 13 E
White L., Canada **79 A8** 45 18N 76 31W
White L., U.S.A. **81 L8** 29 44N 92 30W
White Mountain Peak,
　U.S.A. **83 G4** 37 38N 118 15W
White Mts., Calif., U.S.A. . **84 H8** 37 30N 118 15W
White Mts., N.H., U.S.A. . . **75 B12** 44 15N 71 15W
White Mts., N.H., U.S.A. . . **76 C10** 44 10N 71 20W
White Nile = Nîl el
　Abyad →, Sudan **51 E12** 15 38N 32 31 E
White Otter L., Canada . . . **70 C1** 49 5N 91 55W
White Pass, Canada **84 D5** 46 38N 121 24W
White Plains, U.S.A. **79 E11** 41 2N 73 46W
White River, Canada **70 C2** 48 35N 85 20W
White River, S. Africa **57 D5** 25 20S 31 0 E
White River, U.S.A. **80 D4** 43 34N 100 45W
White Rock, Canada **84 A4** 49 2N 122 48W
White Russia = Belarus ■,
　Europe **17 B14** 53 30N 27 0 E
White Sea = Beloye More,
　Russia **24 A6** 66 30N 38 0 E
White Sulphur Springs,
　Mont., U.S.A. **82 C8** 46 33N 110 54W
White Sulphur Springs,
　W. Va., U.S.A. **76 G5** 37 48N 80 18W
White Swan, U.S.A. **84 D6** 46 23N 120 44W
Whitecliffs, N.Z. **59 K3** 43 26S 171 55 E
Whitecourt, Canada **72 C5** 54 10N 115 45W
Whiteface Mt., U.S.A. **79 B11** 44 22N 73 54W
Whitefield, U.S.A. **79 B13** 44 23N 71 37W
Whitefish, U.S.A. **82 B6** 48 25N 114 20W
Whitefish L., Canada **73 A7** 62 41N 106 48W
Whitefish Point, U.S.A. . . . **76 B3** 46 45N 84 59W
Whitegull, L., Canada **71 A7** 55 27N 64 17W
Whitehall, Mich., U.S.A. . . **76 D2** 43 24N 86 21W
Whitehall, Mont., U.S.A. . . **82 D7** 45 52N 112 6W
Whitehall, N.Y., U.S.A. . . . **79 C11** 43 33N 73 24W
Whitehall, Wis., U.S.A. . . . **80 C9** 44 22N 91 19W
Whitehaven, U.K. **10 C4** 54 33N 3 35W
Whitehorse, Canada **72 A1** 60 43N 135 3W
Whitemark, Australia **62 G4** 40 7S 148 3 E
Whiteriver, U.S.A. **83 K9** 33 50N 109 58W
Whitesand →, Canada . . **72 A5** 60 9N 115 45W
Whitesboro, N.Y., U.S.A. . . **79 C9** 43 7N 75 18W
Whitesboro, Tex., U.S.A. . . **81 J6** 33 39N 96 54W
Whiteshell Prov. Park,
　Canada **73 D9** 50 0N 95 40W
Whitesville, U.S.A. **78 D7** 42 2N 77 46W
Whiteville, U.S.A. **77 H6** 34 20N 78 42W
Whitewater, U.S.A. **76 D1** 42 50N 88 44W
Whitewater Baldy, U.S.A. . **83 K9** 33 20N 108 39W
Whitewater L., Canada . . . **70 B2** 50 50N 89 10W
Whitewood, Australia **62 C3** 21 28S 143 30 E
Whitewood, Canada **73 C8** 50 20N 102 20W
Whithorn, U.K. **12 G4** 54 44N 4 26W
Whitianga, N.Z. **59 G5** 36 47S 175 41 E
Whitman, U.S.A. **79 D14** 42 5N 70 56W
Whitney, Canada **78 A6** 45 31N 78 14W
Whitney, Mt., U.S.A. **84 J8** 36 35N 118 18W
Whitney Point, U.S.A. . . . **79 D9** 42 20N 75 58W
Whitstable, U.K. **11 F9** 51 21N 1 3 E
Whitsunday I., Australia . . **62 C4** 20 15S 149 4 E
Whittier, U.S.A. **85 M8** 33 58N 118 3W
Whittlesea, Australia **63 F4** 37 27S 145 9 E
Wholdaia L., Canada **73 A8** 60 43N 104 20W
Whyalla, Australia **63 E2** 33 2S 137 30 E
Wiarton, Canada **78 B3** 44 40N 81 10W
Wiay, U.K. **12 D1** 57 24N 7 13W
Wibaux, U.S.A. **80 B2** 46 59N 104 11W
Wichian Buri, Thailand . . . **38 E3** 15 39N 101 7 E
Wichita, U.S.A. **81 G6** 37 42N 97 20W
Wichita Falls, U.S.A. **81 J5** 33 54N 98 30W
Wick, U.K. **12 C5** 58 26N 3 5W
Wicked Pt., Canada **78 C7** 43 52N 77 15W
Wickenburg, U.S.A. **83 K7** 33 58N 112 44W
Wickepin, Australia **61 F2** 32 50S 117 30 E
Wickham, Australia **60 D2** 20 42S 117 11 E
Wickham, C., Australia . . . **62 F3** 39 35S 143 57 E
Wickliffe, U.S.A. **78 E3** 41 36N 81 28W
Wicklow, Ireland **13 D5** 52 59N 6 3W
Wicklow □, Ireland **13 D5** 52 57N 6 25W
Wicklow Hd., Ireland **13 D5** 52 58N 6 0W
Wicklow Mts., Ireland . . . **13 C5** 52 58N 6 26W
Widgeegoara Cr. →,
　Australia **63 D4** 28 51S 146 34 E
Widgiemooltha, Australia . **61 F3** 31 30S 121 34 E
Widnes, U.K. **10 D5** 53 23N 2 45W
Wieluń, Poland **17 C10** 51 15N 18 34 E
Wien, Austria **16 D9** 48 12N 16 22 E
Wiener Neustadt, Austria . **16 E9** 47 49N 16 16 E
Wiesbaden, Germany **16 C5** 50 4N 8 14 E
Wigan, U.K. **10 D5** 53 33N 2 38W
Wiggins, Colo., U.S.A. . . . **80 E2** 40 14N 104 4W
Wiggins, Miss., U.S.A. . . . **81 K10** 30 51N 89 8W
Wight, I. of □, U.K. **11 G6** 50 40N 1 20W
Wigston, U.K. **11 E6** 52 35N 1 6W
Wigton, U.K. **10 C4** 54 50N 3 10W

Wigtown, U.K. **12 G4** 54 53N 4 27W
Wigtown B., U.K. **12 G4** 54 46N 4 15W
Wilber, U.S.A. **80 E6** 40 29N 96 58W
Wilberforce, Canada **78 A6** 45 2N 78 13W
Wilberforce, C., Australia . **62 A2** 11 54S 136 35 E
Wilburton, U.S.A. **81 H7** 34 55N 95 19W
Wilcannia, Australia **63 E3** 31 30S 143 26 E
Wilcox, U.S.A. **78 E6** 41 35N 78 41W
Wildrose, U.S.A. **85 J9** 36 14N 117 11W
Wildspitze, Austria **16 E6** 46 53N 10 53 E
Wilge →, S. Africa **57 D4** 27 3S 28 20 E
Wilhelm II Coast, Antarctica **5 C7** 68 0S 90 0 E
Wilhelmshaven, Germany . **16 B5** 53 31N 8 7 E
Wilhelmstal, Namibia **56 C2** 21 58S 16 21 E
Wilkes-Barre, U.S.A. **79 E9** 41 15N 75 53W
Wilkie, Canada **73 C7** 52 27N 108 42W
Wilkinsburg, U.S.A. **78 F5** 40 26N 79 53W
Wilkinson Lakes, Australia **61 E5** 29 40S 132 39 E
Willandra Creek →,
　Australia **63 E4** 33 22S 145 52 E
Willapa B., U.S.A. **82 C2** 46 40N 124 0W
Willapa Hills, U.S.A. **84 D3** 46 35N 123 25W
Willard, N.Y., U.S.A. **78 D8** 42 40N 76 50W
Willard, Ohio, U.S.A. **78 E2** 41 3N 82 44W
Willcox, U.S.A. **83 K9** 32 15N 109 50W
Willemstad, Neth. Ant. . . . **89 D6** 12 5N 69 0W
Willet, U.S.A. **79 D9** 42 28N 75 55W
William →, Canada **73 B7** 59 8N 109 19W
William 'Bill' Dannely Res.,
　U.S.A. **77 J2** 32 10N 87 10W
William Creek, Australia . . **63 D2** 28 58S 136 22 E
Williams, Australia **61 F2** 33 2S 116 52 E
Williams, Ariz., U.S.A. . . . **83 J7** 35 15N 112 11W
Williams, Calif., U.S.A. . . . **84 F4** 39 9N 122 9W
Williams Harbour, Canada **71 B8** 52 33N 55 47W
Williams Lake, Canada . . . **72 C4** 52 10N 122 10W
Williamsburg, Ky., U.S.A. . **77 G3** 36 44N 84 10W
Williamsburg, Pa., U.S.A. . **78 F6** 40 28N 78 12W
Williamsburg, Va., U.S.A. . **76 G7** 37 17N 76 44W
Williamson, N.Y., U.S.A. . . **78 C7** 43 14N 77 11W
Williamson, W. Va., U.S.A. **76 G4** 37 41N 82 17W
Williamsport, U.S.A. **78 E7** 41 15N 77 0W
Williamston, U.S.A. **77 H7** 35 51N 77 4W
Williamstown, Australia . . **63 F3** 37 51S 144 52 E
Williamstown, Ky., U.S.A. . **76 F3** 38 38N 84 34W
Williamstown, Mass.,
　U.S.A. **79 D11** 42 41N 73 12W
Williamstown, N.Y., U.S.A. **79 C9** 43 26N 75 53W
Willimantic, U.S.A. **79 E12** 41 43N 72 13W
Willingboro, U.S.A. **76 F8** 40 3N 74 54W
Willis Group, Australia . . . **62 B5** 16 18S 150 0 E
Williston, S. Africa **56 E3** 31 20S 20 53 E
Williston, Fla., U.S.A. **77 L4** 29 23N 82 27W
Williston, N. Dak., U.S.A. . **80 A3** 48 9N 103 37W
Williston L., Canada **72 B4** 56 0N 124 0W
Willits, U.S.A. **82 G2** 39 25N 123 21W
Willmar, U.S.A. **80 C7** 45 7N 95 3W
Willoughby, U.S.A. **78 E3** 41 39N 81 24W
Willow Bunch, Canada . . . **73 D7** 49 20N 105 35W
Willow L. →, Canada . . . **72 A5** 62 10N 119 8W
Willow Wall, The, China . . **35 C12** 42 10N 122 0 E
Willowick, U.S.A. **78 E3** 41 38N 81 28W
Willowlake →, Canada . . **72 A4** 62 42N 123 8W
Willowmore, S. Africa . . . **56 E3** 33 15S 23 30 E
Willows, U.S.A. **84 F4** 39 31N 122 12W
Willowvale = Gatyana,
　S. Africa **57 E4** 32 16S 28 31 E
Wills, L., Australia **60 D4** 21 25S 128 51 E
Wills Cr. →, Australia **62 C3** 22 43S 140 2 E
Willsboro, U.S.A. **79 B11** 44 21N 73 24W
Willunga, Australia **63 F2** 35 15S 138 30 E
Wilmette, U.S.A. **76 D2** 42 5N 87 42W
Wilmington, Australia . . . **63 E2** 32 39S 138 7 E
Wilmington, Del., U.S.A. . . **76 F8** 39 45N 75 33W
Wilmington, N.C., U.S.A. . **77 H7** 34 14N 77 55W
Wilmington, Ohio, U.S.A. . **76 F4** 39 27N 83 50W
Wilmington, Vt., U.S.A. . . **79 D12** 42 52N 72 52W
Wilmslow, U.K. **10 D5** 53 19N 2 13W
Wilpena →, Australia **63 E2** 31 25S 139 29 E
Wilsall, U.S.A. **82 D8** 45 59N 110 38W
Wilson, N.C., U.S.A. **77 H7** 35 44N 77 55W
Wilson, N.Y., U.S.A. **78 C6** 43 19N 78 50W
Wilson, Pa., U.S.A. **79 F9** 40 41N 75 15W
Wilson →, Australia **62 C3** 21 18S 128 16 E
Wilson Bluff, Australia . . . **61 F4** 31 41S 129 0 E
Wilson Inlet, Australia . . . **61 G2** 35 0S 117 22 E
Wilsons Promontory,
　Australia **63 F4** 38 55S 146 25 E
Wilton, U.S.A. **80 B4** 47 10N 100 47W
Wilton →, Australia **62 A1** 14 45S 134 33 E
Wiltshire □, U.K. **11 F6** 51 18N 1 53W
Wiltz, Lux. **15 E5** 49 57N 5 55 E
Wiluna, Australia **61 E3** 26 36S 120 14 E
Wimborne Minster, U.K. . . **11 G6** 50 48N 1 59W
Wimmera →, Australia . . . **63 F3** 36 8S 141 56 E
Winam G., Kenya **54 C3** 0 20S 34 15 E
Winburg, S. Africa **56 D4** 28 30S 27 2 E
Winchendon, U.S.A. **79 D12** 42 41N 72 3W
Winchester, U.K. **11 F6** 51 4N 1 18W
Winchester, Conn., U.S.A. **79 E11** 41 53N 73 9W
Winchester, Idaho, U.S.A. . **82 C5** 46 14N 116 38W
Winchester, Ind., U.S.A. . . **76 E3** 40 10N 84 59W
Winchester, Ky., U.S.A. . . **76 G3** 38 0N 84 11W
Winchester, N.H., U.S.A. . . **79 D12** 42 46N 72 23W
Winchester, Nev., U.S.A. . . **85 J11** 36 6N 115 10W
Winchester, Tenn., U.S.A. . **77 H2** 35 11N 86 7W
Winchester, Va., U.S.A. . . **76 F6** 39 11N 78 10W
Wind →, U.S.A. **82 E9** 43 12N 108 12W
Wind River Range, U.S.A. . **82 E9** 43 0N 109 30W
Windau = Ventspils, Latvia **9 H19** 57 25N 21 32 E
Windber, U.S.A. **78 F6** 40 14N 78 50W
Windermere, Cumb., U.K. . **10 C5** 54 23N 2 55W
Windermere, Cumb., U.K. . **10 C5** 54 22N 2 56W
Windhoek, Namibia **56 C2** 22 35S 17 4 E
Windorah, Australia **62 D3** 25 24S 142 36 E
Window Rock, U.S.A. **83 J9** 35 41N 109 3W
Windrush →, U.K. **11 F6** 51 43N 1 24W
Windsor, Australia **63 E5** 33 37S 150 50 E
Windsor, N.S., Canada . . . **71 D7** 44 59N 64 5W
Windsor, Ont., Canada . . . **78 D2** 42 18N 83 0W
Windsor, U.K. **11 F7** 51 29N 0 36W
Windsor, Colo., U.S.A. . . . **80 E2** 40 29N 104 54W
Windsor, Mo., U.S.A. **80 F8** 38 32N 93 31W
Windsor, N.Y., U.S.A. **79 D9** 42 5N 75 37W

Windsor, Vt., U.S.A. **79 C12** 43 29N 72 24W
Windsor & Maidenhead □,
　U.K. **11 F7** 51 29N 0 40W
Windsorton, S. Africa **56 D3** 28 16S 24 44 E
Windward Is., W. Indies . . **89 D7** 13 0N 61 0W
Windward Passage =
　Vientos, Paso de los,
　Caribbean **89 C5** 20 0N 74 0W
Winefred L., Canada **73 B6** 55 30N 110 30W
Winfield, U.S.A. **81 G6** 37 15N 96 59W
Wingate Mts., Australia . . **60 B5** 14 25S 130 40 E
Wingham, Australia **63 E5** 31 48S 152 22 E
Wingham, Canada **78 C3** 43 55N 81 20W
Winisk, Canada **70 A2** 55 20N 85 15W
Winisk →, Canada **70 A2** 55 17N 85 5W
Winisk L., Canada **70 B2** 52 55N 87 22W
Wink, U.S.A. **81 K3** 31 45N 103 9W
Winkler, Canada **73 D9** 49 10N 97 56W
Winlock, U.S.A. **84 D4** 46 30N 122 56W
Winnebago, L., U.S.A. . . . **76 D1** 44 0N 88 26W
Winnecke Cr. →, Australia **60 C5** 18 35S 131 34 E
Winnemucca, U.S.A. **82 F5** 40 58N 117 44W
Winnemucca L., U.S.A. . . . **82 F4** 40 7N 119 21W
Winnett, U.S.A. **82 C9** 47 0N 108 21W
Winnfield, U.S.A. **81 K8** 31 56N 92 38W
Winnibigoshish, L., U.S.A. **80 B7** 47 27N 94 13W
Winnipeg, Canada **73 D9** 49 54N 97 9W
Winnipeg →, Canada . . . **73 C9** 50 38N 96 19W
Winnipeg, L., Canada . . . **73 C9** 52 0N 97 0W
Winnipeg Beach, Canada . **73 C9** 50 30N 96 58W
Winnipegosis, Canada . . . **73 C9** 51 39N 99 55W
Winnipegosis L., Canada . **73 C9** 52 30N 100 0W
Winnipesaukee, L., U.S.A. **79 C13** 43 38N 71 21W
Winnisquam L., U.S.A. . . . **79 C13** 43 33N 71 31W
Winnsboro, La., U.S.A. . . . **81 J9** 32 10N 91 43W
Winnsboro, S.C., U.S.A. . . **77 H5** 34 23N 81 5W
Winnsboro, Tex., U.S.A. . . **81 J7** 32 58N 95 17W
Winokapau, L., Canada . . **71 B7** 53 15N 62 50W
Winona, Minn., U.S.A. . . . **80 C9** 44 3N 91 39W
Winona, Miss., U.S.A. . . . **81 J10** 33 29N 89 44W
Winooski, U.S.A. **79 B11** 44 29N 73 11W
Winooski →, U.S.A. **79 B11** 44 32N 73 17W
Winschoten, Neths. **15 A7** 53 9N 7 3 E
Winsford, U.K. **10 D5** 53°12N 2 31W
Winslow, Ariz., U.S.A. . . . **83 J8** 35 2N 110 42W
Winslow, Wash., U.S.A. . . **84 C4** 47 38N 122 31W
Winsted, U.S.A. **79 E11** 41 55N 73 4W
Winston-Salem, U.S.A. . . . **77 G5** 36 6N 80 15W
Winter Garden, U.S.A. . . . **77 L5** 28 34N 81 35W
Winter Haven, U.S.A. **77 M5** 28 1N 81 44W
Winter Park, U.S.A. **77 L5** 28 36N 81 20W
Winterhaven, U.S.A. **85 N12** 32 47N 114 39W
Winters, U.S.A. **84 G5** 38 32N 121 58W
Wintersville, U.S.A. **78 F4** 40 23N 80 42W
Winterswijk, Neths. **15 C6** 51 58N 6 43 E
Winterthur, Switz. **18 C8** 47 30N 8 44 E
Winthrop, U.S.A. **82 B3** 48 28N 120 10W
Winton, Australia **62 C3** 22 24S 143 3 E
Winton, N.Z. **59 M2** 46 8S 168 20 E
Wirrulla, Australia **63 E1** 32 24S 134 31 E
Wisbech, U.K. **11 E8** 52 41N 0 9 E
Wisconsin □, U.S.A. **80 C10** 44 45N 89 30W
Wisconsin →, U.S.A. **80 D9** 43 0N 91 15W
Wisconsin Rapids, U.S.A. . **80 C10** 44 23N 89 49W
Wisdom, U.S.A. **82 D7** 45 37N 113 27W
Wishaw, U.K. **12 F5** 55 46N 3 54W
Wishek, U.S.A. **80 B5** 46 16N 99 33W
Wisła →, Poland **17 A10** 54 22N 18 55 E
Wismar, Germany **16 B6** 53 54N 11 29 E
Wisner, U.S.A. **80 E6** 41 59N 96 55W
Witbank, S. Africa **57 D4** 25 51S 29 14 E
Witdraai, S. Africa **56 D3** 26 58S 20 48 E
Witham, U.K. **11 F8** 51 48N 0 40 E
Witham →, U.K. **10 E7** 52 59N 0 2W
Withernsea, U.K. **10 D8** 53 44N 0 1 E
Witney, U.K. **11 F6** 51 48N 1 28W
Witnossob →, Namibia . . **56 D3** 26 55S 20 37 E
Wittenberge, Germany . . . **16 B6** 53 0N 11 45 E
Wittenoom, Australia **60 D2** 22 15S 118 20 E
Wkra →, Poland **17 B11** 52 27N 20 44 E
Wlingi, Indonesia **37 H15** 8 5S 112 25 E
Włocławek, Poland **17 B10** 52 40N 19 3 E
Włodawa, Poland **17 C12** 51 33N 23 31 E
Woburn, U.S.A. **79 D13** 42 29N 71 9W
Wodian, China **34 H7** 32 50N 112 35 E
Wokam, Indonesia **37 F8** 5 45S 134 28 E
Woking, U.K. **11 F7** 51 19N 0 34W
Wokingham □, U.K. **11 F7** 51 25N 0 51W
Wolf →, Canada **72 A2** 60 17N 132 33W
Wolf Creek, U.S.A. **82 C7** 47 0N 112 4W
Wolf L., Canada **72 A2** 60 24N 131 40W
Wolf Point, U.S.A. **80 A2** 48 5N 105 39W
Wolfe I., Canada **79 B8** 44 7N 76 20W
Wolfeboro, U.S.A. **79 C13** 43 35N 71 13W
Wolfsberg, Austria **16 E8** 46 50N 14 52 E
Wolfsburg, Germany **16 B6** 52 25N 10 48 E
Wolin, Poland **16 B8** 53 50N 14 37 E
Wollaston, Is., Chile **96 H3** 55 40S 67 30W
Wollaston L., Canada **73 B8** 58 7N 103 10W
Wollaston Lake, Canada . . **73 B8** 58 3N 103 33W
Wollaston Pen., Canada . . **68 B8** 69 30N 115 0W
Wollongong, Australia . . . **63 E5** 34 25S 150 54 E
Wolmaransstad, S. Africa . **56 D4** 27 12S 25 59 E
Wolsey, U.S.A. **80 C5** 44 24N 98 28W
Wolstenholme, C., Canada **66 C12** 62 35N 77 30W
Wolvega, Neths. **15 B6** 52 52N 6 0 E
Wolverhampton, U.K. . . . **11 E5** 52 35N 2 7W
Wondai, Australia **63 D5** 26 20S 151 49 E
Wongalarroo L., Australia . **63 E3** 31 32S 144 0 E
Wongan Hills, Australia . . **61 F2** 30 51S 116 37 E
Wŏnju, S. Korea **35 F14** 37 22N 127 58 E
Wonosari, Indonesia **37 G14** 7 58S 110 36 E
Wonosobo, Indonesia . . . **37 G13** 7 22S 109 54 E
Wonowon, Canada **72 B4** 56 44N 121 48W
Wŏnsan, N. Korea **35 E14** 39 11N 127 27 E
Wonthaggi, Australia **63 F4** 38 37S 145 37 E
Wood Buffalo Nat. Park,
　Canada **72 B6** 59 0N 113 41W
Wood Is., Australia **60 C3** 16 24S 123 19 E
Wood L., Canada **73 B8** 55 17N 103 17W
Woodah I., Australia **62 A2** 13 27S 136 10 E
Woodbridge, Canada **78 C5** 43 47N 79 36W
Woodbridge, U.K. **11 E9** 52 6N 1 20 E
Woodburn, U.S.A. **82 D2** 45 9N 122 51W
Woodenbong, Australia . . **63 D5** 28 24S 152 39 E

Yezd = Yazd, *Iran* 45 D7 31 55N 54 27 E
Yhati, *Paraguay* 94 B4 25 45S 56 35W
Yhú, *Paraguay* 95 B4 25 0S 56 0W
Yi →, *Uruguay* 94 C4 33 7S 57 8W
Yi 'Allaq, G., *Egypt* 47 E2 30 22N 33 32 E
Yi He →, *China* 35 G10 34 10N 118 8 E
Yi Xian, *Hebei, China* 34 E8 39 20N 115 30 E
Yi Xian, *Liaoning, China* .. 35 D11 41 30N 121 22 E
Yialiás →, *Cyprus* 23 D12 35 9N 33 44 E
Yialousa, *Cyprus* 23 D13 35 32N 34 10 E
Yianisádhes, *Greece* 23 D8 35 20N 26 10 E
Yiannitsa, *Greece* 21 D10 40 46N 22 24 E
Yibin, *China* 32 D5 28 45N 104 32 E
Yichang, *China* 33 C6 30 40N 111 20 E
Yicheng, *China* 34 G6 35 42N 111 40 E
Yichuan, *China* 34 F6 36 2N 110 10 E
Yichun, *China* 33 B7 47 44N 128 52 E
Yidu, *China* 35 F10 36 43N 118 28 E
Yijun, *China* 34 G5 35 28N 109 8 E
Yildiz Dağlari, *Turkey* 21 D12 41 48N 27 36 E
Yilehuli Shan, *China* 33 A7 51 20N 124 20 E
Yimianpo, *China* 35 B15 45 7N 128 2 E
Yinchuan, *China* 34 E4 38 30N 106 15 E
Yindarlgooda, L., *Australia* 61 F3 30 40S 121 52 E
Ying He →, *China* 34 H9 32 30N 116 30 E
Ying Xian, *China* 34 E7 39 32N 113 10 E
Yingkou, *China* 35 D12 40 37N 122 18 E
Yining, *China* 26 E9 43 58N 81 10 E
Yinmabin, *Burma* 41 H19 22 10N 94 55 E
Yiofiros →, *Greece* 23 D7 35 20N 25 6 E
Yirga Alem, *Ethiopia* 46 F2 6 48N 38 22 E
Yirrkala, *Australia* 62 A2 12 14S 136 56 E
Yishan, *China* 32 D5 24 28N 108 38 E
Yishui, *China* 35 G10 35 47N 118 30 E
Yithion, *Greece* 21 F10 36 46N 22 34 E
Yitiaoshan, *China* 34 F3 37 5N 104 2 E
Yitong, *China* 35 C13 43 13N 125 20 E
Yiyang, *Henan, China* 34 G7 34 27N 112 10 E
Yiyang, *Hunan, China* 33 D6 28 35N 112 18 E
Yli-Kitka, *Finland* 8 C23 66 8N 28 30 E
Ylitornio, *Finland* 8 C20 66 19N 23 39 E
Ylivieska, *Finland* 8 D21 64 4N 24 28 E
Yoakum, *U.S.A.* 81 L6 29 17N 97 9W
Yog Pt., *Phil.* 37 B6 14 6N 124 12 E
Yogyakarta, *Indonesia* 37 G14 7 49S 110 22 E
Yoho Nat. Park, *Canada* ... 72 C5 51 25N 116 30W
Yojoa, L. de, *Honduras* ... 88 D2 14 53N 88 0W
Yōju, *S. Korea* 35 F14 37 20N 127 35 E
Yokadouma, *Cameroon* ... 52 D2 3 26N 14 55 E
Yokkaichi, *Japan* 31 G8 34 55N 136 38 E
Yoko, *Cameroon* 52 C2 5 32N 12 20 E
Yokohama, *Japan* 31 G9 35 27N 139 28 E
Yokosuka, *Japan* 31 G9 35 20N 139 40 E
Yokote, *Japan* 30 E10 39 20N 140 30 E
Yola, *Nigeria* 51 G8 9 10N 12 29 E
Yolaina, Cordillera de, *Nic.* 88 D3 11 30N 84 0W
Yoloten, *Turkmenistan* 45 B9 37 18N 62 21 E
Yom →, *Thailand* 36 A2 15 35N 100 1 E
Yonago, *Japan* 31 G6 35 25N 133 19 E
Yonaguni-Jima, *Japan* 31 M1 24 27N 123 0 E
Yōnan, *N. Korea* 35 F14 37 55N 126 11 E
Yonezawa, *Japan* 30 F10 37 57N 140 4 E
Yong Peng, *Malaysia* 39 M4 2 0N 103 3 E
Yong Sata, *Thailand* 39 J2 7 8N 99 41 E
Yongam'po, *N. Korea* 35 E13 39 56N 124 23 E
Yongcheng, *China* 34 H9 33 55N 116 20 E
Yŏngch'ŏn, *S. Korea* 35 G15 35 58N 128 56 E
Yongdeng, *China* 34 F2 36 38N 103 25 E
Yŏngdŏk, *S. Korea* 35 F15 36 24N 129 22 E
Yŏngdŭngpo, *S. Korea* ... 35 F14 37 31N 126 54 E
Yonghe, *China* 34 F6 36 46N 110 38 E
Yŏnghŭng, *N. Korea* 35 E14 39 31N 127 18 E
Yongji, *China* 34 G6 34 52N 110 28 E
Yŏngju, *S. Korea* 35 F15 36 50N 128 40 E
Yongnian, *China* 34 F8 36 47N 114 29 E
Yongning, *China* 34 E4 38 15N 106 14 E
Yongqing, *China* 34 E9 39 25N 116 28 E
Yŏngwŏl, *S. Korea* 35 F15 37 11N 128 28 E
Yonibana, *S. Leone* 50 G3 8 30N 12 19W
Yonkers, *U.S.A.* 79 F11 40 56N 73 54W
Yonne →, *France* 18 B5 48 23N 2 58 E
York, *Australia* 61 F2 31 52S 116 47 E
York, *U.K.* 10 D6 53 58N 1 6W
York, *Nebr., U.S.A.* 80 E6 40 52N 97 36W
York, *Pa., U.S.A.* 76 F7 39 58N 76 44W
York, C., *Australia* 62 A3 10 42S 142 31 E
York, City of □, *U.K.* 10 D6 53 58N 1 6W
York, Kap, *Greenland* 4 B4 75 55N 66 25W
York, Vale of, *U.K.* 10 C6 54 15N 1 25W
York Haven, *U.S.A.* 78 F8 40 7N 76 46W
York Sd., *Australia* 60 C4 15 0S 125 5 E
Yorke Pen., *Australia* 63 E2 34 50S 137 40 E
Yorketown, *Australia* 63 E2 35 0S 137 33 E
Yorkshire Wolds, *U.K.* 10 C7 54 8N 0 31W
Yorkton, *Canada* 73 C8 51 11N 102 28W
Yorkville, *U.S.A.* 84 G3 38 52N 123 13W
Yoro, *Honduras* 88 C2 15 9N 87 7W
Yoron-Jima, *Japan* 31 L4 27 2N 128 26 E
Yos Sudarso, Pulau =
 Dolak, Pulau, *Indonesia* . 37 F9 8 0S 138 30 E
Yosemite National Park,
 U.S.A. 84 H7 37 45N 119 40W
Yosemite Village, *U.S.A.* .. 84 H7 37 45N 119 35W
Yoshkar Ola, *Russia* 24 C8 56 38N 47 55 E
Yŏsu, *S. Korea* 35 G14 34 47N 127 45 E
Yotvata, *Israel* 47 F4 29 55N 35 2 E
Youbou, *Canada* 84 B2 48 53N 124 13W
Youghal, *Ireland* 13 E4 51 56N 7 52W
Youghal B., *Ireland* 13 E4 51 55N 7 49W
Young, *Australia* 63 E4 34 19S 148 18 E
Young, *Canada* 73 C7 51 47N 105 45W
Young, *Uruguay* 94 C4 32 44S 57 36W
Younghusband, L., *Australia* 63 E2 30 50S 136 5 E
Younghusband Pen.,
 Australia 63 F2 36 0S 139 25 E
Youngstown, *Canada* 73 C6 51 35N 111 10W
Youngstown, *N.Y., U.S.A.* . 78 C5 43 15N 79 3W
Youngstown, *Ohio, U.S.A.* . 78 E4 41 6N 80 39W
Youngsville, *U.S.A.* 78 E5 41 51N 79 19W
Youngwood, *U.S.A.* 78 F5 40 14N 79 34W
Youyu, *China* 34 D7 40 10N 112 20 E
Yozgat, *Turkey* 25 G5 39 51N 34 47 E
Ypané →, *Paraguay* 94 A4 23 29S 57 19W
Ypres = Ieper, *Belgium* ... 15 D2 50 51N 2 53 E
Yreka, *U.S.A.* 82 F2 41 44N 122 38W
Ystad, *Sweden* 9 J15 55 26N 13 50 E
Ysyk-Köl, *Kyrgyzstan* 28 E11 42 26N 76 12 E

Ysyk-Köl, Ozero, *Kyrgyzstan* 26 E8 42 25N 77 15 E
Ythan →, *U.K.* 12 D7 57 19N 1 59W
Ytyk Kyuyel, *Russia* 27 C14 62 30N 133 45 E
Yu Jiang →, *China* 33 D6 23 22N 110 3 E
Yu Xian = Yuzhou, *China* . 34 G7 34 10N 113 28 E
Yu Xian, *Hebei, China* 34 E8 39 50N 114 35 E
Yu Xian, *Shanxi, China* ... 34 E7 38 5N 113 20 E
Yuan Jiang →, *China* 33 D6 28 55N 111 50 E
Yuanqu, *China* 34 G6 35 18N 111 40 E
Yuanyang, *China* 34 G7 35 3N 113 58 E
Yuba →, *U.S.A.* 84 F5 39 8N 121 36W
Yuba City, *U.S.A.* 84 F5 39 8N 121 37W
Yūbari, *Japan* 30 C10 43 4N 141 59 E
Yūbetsu, *Japan* 30 B11 44 13N 143 50 E
Yucatán □, *Mexico* 87 C7 21 30N 86 30W
Yucatán, Canal de,
 Caribbean 88 B2 22 0N 86 30W
Yucatán, Península de,
 Mexico 66 H11 19 30N 89 0W
Yucatan Str. = Yucatán,
 Canal de, *Caribbean* ... 88 B2 22 0N 86 30W
Yucca, *U.S.A.* 85 L12 34 52N 114 9W
Yucca Valley, *U.S.A.* 85 L10 34 8N 116 27W
Yucheng, *China* 34 F9 36 55N 116 32 E
Yuci, *China* 34 F7 37 42N 112 46 E
Yuendumu, *Australia* 60 D5 22 16S 131 49 E
Yugoslavia ■, *Europe* 21 B9 43 20N 20 0 E
Yukon →, *U.S.A.* 68 B3 62 32N 163 54W
Yukon Territory □, *Canada* 68 B6 63 0N 135 0W
Yukta, *Russia* 27 C11 63 26N 105 42 E
Yukuhashi, *Japan* 31 H5 33 44N 130 59 E
Yulara, *Australia* 61 E5 25 10S 130 55 E
Yule →, *Australia* 60 D2 20 41S 118 17 E
Yuleba, *Australia* 63 D4 26 37S 149 24 E
Yulin, *Shaanxi, China* 34 E5 38 20N 109 30 E
Yulin, *Shensi, China* 38 C7 38 15N 109 30 E
Yuma, *Ariz., U.S.A.* 85 N12 32 43N 114 37W
Yuma, *Colo., U.S.A.* 80 E3 40 8N 102 43W
Yuma, B. de, *Dom. Rep.* ... 89 C6 18 20N 68 35W
Yumbe, *Uganda* 54 B3 3 28N 31 15 E
Yumbi,
 Dem. Rep. of the Congo 54 C2 1 12S 26 15 E
Yumen, *China* 32 C4 39 50N 97 30 E
Yun Ho →, *China* 35 E9 39 10N 117 10 E
Yuna, *Australia* 61 E2 28 20S 115 0 E
Yuncheng, *Henan, China* . 34 G8 35 36N 115 57 E
Yuncheng, *Shanxi, China* . 34 G6 35 2N 111 0 E
Yungas, *Bolivia* 92 G5 17 0S 66 0W
Yungay, *Chile* 94 D1 37 10S 72 5W
Yunnan □, *China* 32 D5 25 0N 102 0 E
Yunta, *Australia* 63 E2 32 34S 139 36 E
Yunxi, *China* 34 H6 33 0N 110 22 E
Yupyongdong, *N. Korea* .. 35 D15 41 49N 128 53 E
Yurga, *Russia* 26 D9 55 42N 84 51 E
Yurimaguas, *Peru* 92 E3 5 55S 76 7W
Yuryung Kaya, *Russia* 27 B12 72 48N 113 23 E
Yuscarán, *Honduras* 88 D2 13 58N 86 45W
Yushe, *China* 34 F7 37 4N 112 58 E
Yushu, *Jilin, China* 35 B14 44 43N 126 38 E
Yushu, *Qinghai, China* ... 32 C4 33 5N 96 55 E
Yutai, *China* 34 G9 35 0N 116 45 E
Yutian, *China* 35 E9 39 53N 117 45 E
Yuxan Qarabağ = Nagorno-
 Karabakh, *Azerbaijan* .. 25 F8 39 55N 46 45 E
Yuxi, *China* 32 D5 24 30N 102 35 E
Yuzawa, *Japan* 30 E10 39 10N 140 30 E
Yuzhno-Sakhalinsk, *Russia* 27 E15 46 58N 142 45 E
Yuzhou, *China* 34 G7 34 10N 113 28 E
Yvetot, *France* 18 B4 49 37N 0 44 E

Z

Zaanstad, *Neths.* 15 B4 52 27N 4 50 E
Zāb al Kabīr →, *Iraq* 44 C4 36 1N 43 24 E
Zāb aş Şaghīr →, *Iraq* ... 44 C4 35 17N 43 29 E
Zabaykalsk, *Russia* 27 E12 49 40N 117 25 E
Zābol, *Iran* 45 D9 31 0N 61 32 E
Zābolī, *Iran* 45 E9 27 10N 61 35 E
Zabrze, *Poland* 17 C10 50 18N 18 50 E
Zacapa, *Guatemala* 88 D2 14 59N 89 31W
Zacapu, *Mexico* 86 D4 19 50N 101 43W
Zacatecas, *Mexico* 86 C4 22 49N 102 34W
Zacatecas □, *Mexico* 86 C4 23 30N 103 0W
Zacatecoluca, *El Salv.* 88 D2 13 29N 88 51W
Zachary, *U.S.A.* 81 K9 30 39N 91 9W
Zacoalco, *Mexico* 86 C4 20 14N 103 33W
Zacualtipán, *Mexico* 87 C5 20 39N 98 36W
Zadar, *Croatia* 16 F8 44 8N 15 14 E
Zadetkyi Kyun, *Burma* ... 39 H2 10 0N 98 25 E
Zafarqand, *Iran* 45 C7 33 11N 52 29 E
Zafra, *Spain* 19 C2 38 26N 6 30W
Żagań, *Poland* 16 C8 51 39N 15 22 E
Zagaoua, *Chad* 51 E10 15 30N 22 24 E
Zagazig, *Egypt* 51 B12 30 40N 31 30 E
Zagnanado, *Benin* 45 C6 33 30N 48 42 E
Zagorsk = Sergiyev Posad,
 Russia 24 C6 56 20N 38 10 E
Zagreb, *Croatia* 16 F9 45 50N 15 58 E
Zāgros, Kūhhā-ye, *Iran* .. 45 C6 33 45N 48 5 E
Zagros Mts. = Zāgros,
 Kūhhā-ye, *Iran* 45 C6 33 45N 48 5 E
Zāhedān, *Fārs, Iran* 45 D7 28 46N 53 52 E
Zāhedān,
 *Sīstān va Balūchestān,
 Iran* 45 D9 29 30N 60 50 E
Zahlah, *Lebanon* 47 B4 33 52N 35 50 E
Zaïre = Congo →, *Africa* . 52 F2 6 4S 12 24 E
Zaječar, *Serbia, Yug.* 21 C10 43 53N 22 18 E
Zakamensk, *Russia* 27 D11 50 23N 103 17 E
Zakhodnya Dzvina =
 Daugava →, *Latvia* 9 H21 57 4N 24 3 E
Zākhū, *Iraq* 44 B4 37 10N 42 50 E
Zákinthos, *Greece* 21 F9 37 47N 20 57 E
Zakopane, *Poland* 17 D10 49 18N 19 57 E
Zakros, *Greece* 23 D8 35 6N 26 10 E
Zalaegerszeg, *Hungary* ... 17 E9 46 53N 16 47 E
Zalău, *Romania* 17 E12 47 12N 23 3 E
Zaleshchiki = Zalishchyky,
 Ukraine 17 D13 48 45N 25 45 E
Zalew Wiślany, *Poland* ... 17 A10 54 20N 19 50 E
Zalingei, *Sudan* 51 F10 12 51N 23 29 E
Zalishchyky, *Ukraine* 17 D13 48 45N 25 45 E
Zama L., *Canada* 72 B5 58 45N 119 5W

Zambeke,
 Dem. Rep. of the Congo 54 B2 2 8N 25 17 E
Zambeze →, *Africa* 55 F4 18 35S 36 20 E
Zambezi = Zambeze →,
 Africa 55 F4 18 35S 36 20 E
Zambezi, *Zambia* 53 G4 13 30S 23 15 E
Zambezia □, *Mozam.* 55 F4 16 15S 37 30 E
Zambia ■, *Africa* 55 F2 15 0S 28 0 E
Zamboanga, *Phil.* 37 C6 6 59N 122 3 E
Zamora, *Mexico* 86 D4 20 0N 102 21W
Zamora, *Spain* 19 B3 41 30N 5 45W
Zamość, *Poland* 17 C12 50 43N 23 15 E
Zandvoort, *Neths.* 15 B4 52 22N 4 32 E
Zangue →, *Mozam.* 55 F4 17 50S 35 21 E
Zangābād, *Iran* 44 B5 38 26N 46 44 E
Zanjān, *Iran* 45 B6 36 40N 48 35 E
Zanjān □, *Iran* 45 B6 37 20N 49 30 E
Zanjān →, *Iran* 45 B6 37 8N 47 47 E
Zante = Zákinthos, *Greece* 21 F9 37 47N 20 57 E
Zanthus, *Australia* 61 F3 31 2S 123 34 E
Zanzibar, *Tanzania* 54 D4 6 12S 39 12 E
Zaouiet El-Kala = Bordj
 Omar Driss, *Algeria* ... 50 C7 28 10N 6 40 E
Zaouiet Reggane, *Algeria* . 50 C6 26 32N 0 3 E
Zaozhuang, *China* 35 G9 34 50N 117 35 E
Zap Suyu = Zāb al
 Kabīr →, *Iraq* 44 C4 36 1N 43 24 E
Zapadnaya Dvina =
 Daugava →, *Latvia* 9 H21 57 4N 24 3 E
Západné Beskydy, *Europe* . 17 D10 49 30N 19 0 E
Zapala, *Argentina* 96 D2 39 0S 70 5W
Zapaleri, Cerro, *Bolivia* ... 94 A2 22 49S 67 11W
Zapata, *U.S.A.* 81 M5 26 55N 99 16W
Zapolyarnyy, *Russia* 24 A5 69 26N 30 51 E
Zaporizhzhya, *Ukraine* ... 25 E6 47 50N 35 10 E
Zaporozhye = Zaporizhzhya,
 Ukraine 25 E6 47 50N 35 10 E
Zara, *Turkey* 44 B3 39 58N 37 43 E
Zaragoza, Coahuila, *Mexico* 86 B4 28 30N 101 0W
Zaragoza, Nuevo León,
 Mexico 87 C5 24 0N 99 46W
Zaragoza, *Spain* 19 B5 41 39N 0 53W
Zarand, *Kermān, Iran* 45 D8 30 46N 56 34 E
Zarand, *Markazī, Iran* 45 C6 35 18N 50 25 E
Zaranj, *Afghan.* 40 D2 30 55N 61 55 E
Zarasai, *Lithuania* 9 J22 55 40N 26 20 E
Zárate, *Argentina* 94 C4 34 7S 59 0W
Zard, Kūh-e, *Iran* 45 C6 32 22N 50 4 E
Zāreh, *Iran* 45 C6 35 7N 49 9 E
Zaria, *Nigeria* 50 F7 11 0N 7 40 E
Zarneh, *Iran* 44 C5 33 55N 46 10 E
Zarós, *Greece* 23 D6 35 8N 24 54 E
Zarqā', Nahr az →, *Jordan* 47 C4 32 10N 35 37 E
Zarrīn, *Iran* 45 C7 32 46N 54 37 E
Zaruma, *Ecuador* 92 D3 3 40S 79 38W
Żary, *Poland* 16 C8 51 37N 15 10 E
Zarzis, *Tunisia* 51 B8 33 31N 11 2 E
Zaskar →, *India* 43 B7 34 13N 77 20 E
Zaskar Mts., *India* 43 C7 33 15N 77 30 E
Zastron, *S. Africa* 56 E4 30 18S 27 7 E
Zāvareh, *Iran* 45 C7 33 29N 52 28 E
Zavitinsk, *Russia* 27 D13 50 10N 129 20 E
Zavodovski, I., *Antarctica* . 5 B1 56 0S 27 45W
Zawiercie, *Poland* 17 C10 50 30N 19 24 E
Zāwiyat al Bayḍā = Al
 Bayḍā, *Libya* 51 B10 32 50N 21 44 E
Zāyā, *Iraq* 44 C5 33 33N 44 13 E
Zāyandeh →, *Iran* 45 C7 32 35N 52 0 E
Zaysan, *Kazakstan* 26 E9 47 28N 84 52 E
Zaysan, Oz., *Kazakstan* ... 26 E9 48 0N 83 0 E
Zayü, *China* 32 D4 28 48N 97 27 E
Zbarazh, *Ukraine* 17 D13 49 43N 25 44 E
Zdolbuniv, *Ukraine* 17 C14 50 30N 26 15 E
Zduńska Wola, *Poland* ... 17 C10 51 37N 18 59 E
Zeballos, *Canada* 72 D3 49 59N 126 50W
Zebediela, *S. Africa* 57 C4 24 20S 29 17 E
Zeebrugge, *Belgium* 15 C3 51 19N 3 12 E
Zeehan, *Australia* 62 G4 41 52S 145 25 E
Zeeland □, *Neths.* 15 C3 51 30N 3 50 E
Zeerust, *S. Africa* 56 D4 25 31S 26 4 E
Zefat, *Israel* 47 C4 32 58N 35 29 E
Zeila = Saylac, *Somali Rep.* 46 E3 11 21N 43 30 E
Zeist, *Neths.* 15 B5 52 5N 5 15 E
Zeitz, *Germany* 16 C7 51 2N 12 7 E
Zelenograd, *Russia* 24 C6 56 1N 37 12 E
Zelenogradsk, *Russia* 9 J19 54 53N 20 29 E
Zelienople, *U.S.A.* 78 F4 40 48N 80 8W
Zémio, *C.A.R.* 54 A2 5 2N 25 5 E
Zemun, *Serbia, Yug.* 21 B9 44 51N 20 25 E
Zenica, *Bos.-H.* 21 B7 44 10N 17 57 E
Žepče, *Bos.-H.* 21 B8 44 28N 18 2 E
Zevenaar, *Neths.* 15 C6 51 56N 6 5 E
Zeya, *Russia* 27 D13 53 48N 127 14 E
Zeya →, *Russia* 27 D13 51 42N 128 53 E
Zêzere →, *Portugal* 19 C1 39 28N 8 20W
Zghartā, *Lebanon* 47 A4 34 21N 35 53 E
Zgorzelec, *Poland* 16 C8 51 10N 15 0 E
Zhabinka, *Belarus* 17 B13 52 13N 24 2 E
Zhailma, *Kazakstan* 26 D7 51 37N 61 33 E
Zhambyl, *Kazakstan* 26 E8 42 54N 71 22 E
Zhangaqazaly, *Kazakstan* . 26 E7 45 48N 62 25 E
Zhangbei, *China* 34 D8 41 10N 114 45 E
Zhangguangcai Ling, *China* 35 B15 45 0N 129 0 E
Zhangjiakou, *China* 34 D8 40 48N 114 55 E
Zhangwu, *China* 35 C12 42 43N 123 52 E
Zhangye, *China* 32 C5 38 50N 100 23 E
Zhangzhou, *China* 33 D6 24 30N 117 35 E
Zhanhua, *China* 35 F10 37 40N 118 8 E
Zhanjiang, *China* 33 D6 21 15N 110 20 E
Zhannetty, Ostrov, *Russia* . 27 B16 76 43N 158 0 E
Zhanyi, *China* 32 D5 25 38N 103 48 E
Zhao Xian, *China* 34 F8 37 43N 114 45 E
Zhaocheng, *China* 34 F6 36 22N 111 38 E
Zhaotong, *China* 32 D5 27 20N 103 44 E
Zhaoyuan, *Heilongjiang,
 China* 35 B13 45 27N 125 0 E
Zhaoyuan, *Shandong, China* 35 F11 37 20N 120 23 E
Zhashkiv, *Ukraine* 17 D16 49 15N 30 5 E
Zhashui, *China* 34 H5 33 40N 109 8 E
Zhayylma, *Kazakstan* 25 E9 50 51N 48 E

Zheleznodorozhnyy, *Russia* 24 B9 62 35N 50 55
Zheleznogorsk-Ilimskiy,
 Russia 27 D11 56 34N 104 8
Zhen'an, *China* 34 H5 33 27N 109 9
Zhengding, *China* 34 E8 38 8N 114 32
Zhengzhou, *China* 34 G7 34 45N 113 34
Zhenlai, *China* 35 B12 45 50N 123 5
Zhenping, *China* 34 H7 33 10N 112 16
Zhenyuan, *China* 34 G4 35 6N 107 30
Zhetiqara, *Kazakstan* 26 D7 52 11N 61 12
Zhezqazghan, *Kazakstan* . 26 E7 47 44N 67 40
Zhidan, *China* 34 F5 36 48N 108 48
Zhigansk, *Russia* 27 C13 66 48N 123 27
Zhilinda, *Russia* 27 C12 70 0N 114 20
Zhitomir = Zhytomyr,
 Ukraine 17 C15 50 20N 28 40
Zhlobin, *Belarus* 17 B16 52 55N 30 0
Zhmerinka = Zhmerynka,
 Ukraine 17 D15 49 2N 28 2
Zhmerynka, *Ukraine* 17 D15 49 2N 28 2
Zhob, *Pakistan* 42 D3 31 20N 69 31
Zhob →, *Pakistan* 42 C3 32 4N 69 50
Zhodino = Zhodzina,
 Belarus 17 A15 54 5N 28 17
Zhodzina, *Belarus* 17 A15 54 5N 28 17
Zhokhova, Ostrov, *Russia* . 27 B16 76 4N 152 40
Zhongdian, *China* 32 D4 27 48N 99 42
Zhongning, *China* 34 F3 37 29N 105 40
Zhongtiao Shan, *China* ... 34 G6 35 0N 111 10
Zhongwei, *China* 34 F3 37 30N 105 12
Zhongyang, *China* 34 F6 37 20N 111 11
Zhoucun, *China* 35 F9 36 47N 117 48
Zhouzhi, *China* 34 G5 34 10N 108 12
Zhuanghe, *China* 35 E12 39 40N 123 0
Zhucheng, *China* 35 G10 36 0N 119 27
Zhugqu, *China* 34 H3 33 40N 104 30
Zhumadian, *China* 34 H8 32 59N 114 2
Zhuo Xian = Zhuozhou,
 China 34 E8 39 28N 115 58
Zhuolu, *China* 34 D8 40 20N 115 12
Zhuozhou, *China* 34 E8 39 28N 115 58
Zhuozi, *China* 34 D7 41 0N 112 25
Zhytomyr, *Ukraine* 17 C15 50 20N 28 40
Ziārān, *Iran* 45 B6 36 7N 50 32
Ziarat, *Pakistan* 42 D2 30 25N 67 49
Zibo, *China* 35 F10 36 47N 118 3
Zichang, *China* 34 F5 37 18N 109 40
Zielona Góra, *Poland* 16 C8 51 57N 15 31
Zierikzee, *Neths.* 15 C3 51 40N 3 55
Zigey, *Chad* 51 F9 14 43N 15 50
Zigong, *China* 32 D5 29 15N 104 48
Ziguinchor, *Senegal* 50 F2 12 35N 16 20
Zihuatanejo, *Mexico* 86 D4 17 38N 101 33
Žilina, *Slovak Rep.* 17 D10 49 12N 18 42
Zillah, *Libya* 51 C9 28 30N 17 33
Zima, *Russia* 27 D11 54 0N 102 5
Zimapán, *Mexico* 87 C5 20 54N 99 20
Zimba, *Zambia* 55 F2 17 20S 26 11
Zimbabwe, *Zimbabwe* ... 55 G3 20 16S 30 54
Zimbabwe ■, *Africa* 55 F3 19 0S 30 0
Zimnicea, *Romania* 17 G13 43 40N 25 22
Zinder, *Niger* 50 F7 13 48N 9 0
Zinga, *Tanzania* 54 D4 9 16S 38 49
Zion National Park, *U.S.A.* . 83 H7 37 15N 113 5
Ziros, *Greece* 23 D8 35 5N 26 8
Zitácuaro, *Mexico* 86 D4 19 28N 100 21
Zitundo, *Mozam.* 57 D5 26 48S 32 47
Ziway, L., *Ethiopia* 46 F2 8 0N 38 50
Ziyang, *China* 34 H5 32 32N 108 31
Zlatograd, *Bulgaria* 21 D11 41 22N 25 7
Zlatoust, *Russia* 24 C10 55 10N 59 40
Zlín, *Czech Rep.* 17 D9 49 14N 17 40
Zmeinogorsk, *Kazakstan* . 26 D9 51 10N 82 13
Znojmo, *Czech Rep.* 16 D9 48 50N 16 2
Zobeyrī, *Iran* 44 C5 34 10N 46 40
Zobia,
 Dem. Rep. of the Congo 54 B2 3 0N 25 59
Zoetermeer, *Neths.* 15 B4 52 3N 4 30
Zolochev = Zolochiv,
 Ukraine 17 D13 49 45N 24 51
Zolochiv, *Ukraine* 17 D13 49 45N 24 51
Zomba, *Malawi* 55 F4 15 22S 35 19
Zongo,
 Dem. Rep. of the Congo 54 B3 4 20N 18 35
Zonguldak, *Turkey* 25 F5 41 28N 31 50
Zonqor Pt., *Malta* 23 D2 35 57N 14 34
Zorritos, *Peru* 92 D2 3 43S 80 40
Zou Xiang, *China* 34 G9 35 30N 116 58
Zouar, *Chad* 51 D9 20 30N 16 32
Zouérate = Zouîrât,
 Mauritania 50 D3 22 44N 12 21
Zouîrât, *Mauritania* 50 D3 22 44N 12 21
Zoutkamp, *Neths.* 15 A6 53 20N 6 18
Zrenjanin, *Serbia, Yug.* ... 21 B9 45 22N 20 23
Zufär, *Oman* 46 D5 17 40N 54 0
Zug, *Switz.* 18 C8 47 10N 8 31
Zugspitze, *Germany* 16 E6 47 25N 10 59
Zuid-Holland □, *Neths.* .. 15 C4 52 0N 4 35
Zuidbeveland, *Neths.* 15 C3 51 30N 3 50
Zuidhorn, *Neths.* 15 A6 53 15N 6 23
Zula, *Eritrea* 46 D2 15 17N 39 40
Zumbo, *Mozam.* 55 F3 15 35S 30 26
Zumpango, *Mexico* 87 D5 19 48N 99 6
Zunhua, *China* 35 D9 40 18N 117 58
Zuni, *U.S.A.* 83 J9 35 4N 108 51
Zunyi, *China* 32 D5 27 42N 106 53
Zuoquan, *China* 34 F7 37 5N 113 22
Zurbātiyah, *Iraq* 44 C5 33 9N 46 3
Zürich, *Switz.* 18 C8 47 22N 8 32
Zutphen, *Neths.* 15 B6 52 9N 6 12
Zuwārah, *Libya* 51 B8 32 58N 12 1
Zūzan, *Iran* 45 C8 34 22N 59 53
Zverinogolovskoye, *Russia* 26 D7 54 26N 64 50
Zvishavane, *Zimbabwe* ... 55 G3 20 17S 30 2
Zvolen, *Slovak Rep.* 17 D10 48 33N 19 10
Zwelitsha, *S. Africa* 53 L5 32 55S 27 22
Zwettl, *Austria* 16 D8 48 35N 15 9
Zwickau, *Germany* 16 C7 50 44N 12 30
Zwolle, *Neths.* 15 B6 52 31N 6 6
Zwolle, *U.S.A.* 81 K8 31 38N 93 39
Żyrardów, *Poland* 17 B11 52 3N 20 28
Zyryan, *Kazakstan* 26 E9 49 43N 84 20
Zyryanka, *Russia* 27 C16 65 45N 150 51
Zyryanovsk = Zyryan,
 Kazakstan 26 E9 49 43N 84 20
Żywiec, *Poland* 17 D10 49 42N 19 10
Zyyi, *Cyprus* 23 E12 34 43N 33 20